Contemporary Business Law

Contemporary Business Law

Second Edition

C. Kerry Fields
Professor of Clinical Finance and Business Economics
Marshall School of Business
University of Southern California

Kevin C. Fields
Professor of Clinical Finance and Business Economics
Marshall School of Business
University of Southern California

ASPEN PUBLISHING

Cover image: iStock.com/Sean Pavone

To contact Customer Service, e-mail customer.service@aspenpublishing.com,
call 1-800-950-5259, or mail correspondence to:

Aspen Publishing
Attn: Order Department
1 Wall Street
Burlington, MA 01803

Printed in the United States of America.

1 2 3 4 5 6 7 8 9 0

ISBN 979-8-8890-6630-9

Library of Congress Cataloging-in-Publication Data
Names: Fields, C. Kerry, author. | Fields, Kevin C., author.
Title: Contemporary Business Law / C. Kerry Fields, Professor of Clinical Finance and Business Economics, Marshall School of Business, University of Southern California, Kevin C. Fields, Professor of Clinical Finance and Business Economics, Marshall School of Business, University of Southern California.
Description: Second edition. | Burlington: Aspen Publishing, 2025. | Includes bibliographical references and index. | Summary: "Introductory text for undergraduate business law courses" — Provided by publisher.
Identifiers: LCCN 2024043100 | ISBN 9798889066309 (paperback) | ISBN 9798889066323 (ebook)
Subjects: LCSH: Commercial law — United States — Textbooks. | Business enterprises--Law and legislation — United States — Textbooks. | LCGFT: Textbooks
Classification: LCC KF889.F54 2025 | DDC 346.7307 — dc23/eng/20240913
LC record available at https://lccn.loc.gov/2024043100

About Aspen Publishing

Aspen Publishing is a leading provider of legal educational content and digital learning solutions in the U.S. and around the world. Aspen provides best-in-class solutions through authoritative textbooks, written by renowned authors, and breakthrough products such as Connected eBooks, Connected Quizzing, PracticePerfect, and JD-Next.

The Aspen Casebook Series (famously known among law faculty and students as the "red and black" casebooks) encompasses hundreds of highly regarded textbooks in more than eighty disciplines, from large enrollment courses, such as Torts and Contracts, to emerging electives, like Sustainability and the Law of Policing. Study aids such as *Examples & Explanations* help law students master complex subject matter. Aspen's Paralegal, Criminal Justice, and Business Law series bring our hallmark publishing standards to undergraduate students. JD-Next is an innovative online law school prep course and admissions test that offers a realistic preview of law school, teaches underlying skills for academic success, and assesses applicants' academic readiness for law school.

Aspen Publishing is proud to be a UWorld company

Since 2003, UWorld has been a global leader in developing high-quality learning tools for students preparing for high-stakes exams. With a commitment to excellence, UWorld has helped millions of students in undergraduate, graduate, and professional programs in fields such as medicine, nursing, finance, and law achieve their academic and career goals.

Founded by Chandra S. Pemmasani, M.D., during his medical residency, UWorld began focusing on medical education and has since expanded into various academic fields, including law. In 2020, UWorld launched its Legal vertical, starting with its comprehensive Multistate Bar Exam (MBE®) Question Bank, followed by the acquisition of Themis Bar Review, which integrated resources to provide a complete bar exam preparation experience. In 2024, UWorld expanded its offerings by acquiring Aspen Publishing, enhancing its suite of legal education products.

Today, UWorld offers an unparalleled range of study materials that blend active learning methods with expert content, ensuring students and educators can access the most effective resources. From bar preparation to law school success, UWorld is committed to supporting the next generation of legal professionals. Learn more at uworld.com.

Summary of Contents

Contents

Chapter 2: Business Ethics 17

Chapter 3: Courts, Litigation, and Alternative Dispute Resolution 39

Chapter 4: Constitutional Law for Businesses 71

Chapter 5: Torts 93

Chapter 7: Intellectual Property 143

Chapter 8: Criminal Law 177

Part II: Contract Law Fundamentals

Chapter 9: Nature and Formation of Contracts 209

Chapter 10: Consideration and Promissory Estoppel 239

Chapter 11: Capacity and Legality of Subject Matter 255

Chapter 12: Defenses to Formation: Mistake, Fraudulent Misrepresentation, Undue Influence, and Duress 275

Chapter 14: Performance, Discharge, Breach, and Remedies 319

Part III: Agency and Employment Law

Chapter 15: Agency Relationships 347

Chapter 16: Employment, Immigration, and Labor Law 377

Chapter 17: Employment Discrimination 403

Part IV: Business Organizations

Chapter 19: Forming the Small Business and Operating Franchises 453

Chapter 20: Partnerships 477

Chapter 25: Securities Laws and Investor Protection 617

Chapter 30: Banking 753

Chapter 31: Creditors' Rights and Secured Transactions 777

Chapter 32: Financing, Defaults, and Foreclosures of Real Property 809

Chapter 33: Bankruptcy 829

Part VI: Government Regulation

Chapter 34: Administrative Law 855

Chapter 35: Antitrust and Unfair Competition 879

Chapter 36: Consumer Laws and Regulations 907

Chapter 37: Environmental Law 933

Part VII: Property

Chapter 38: Personal Property Law and Bailments 953

Chapter 39: Real Property and Landlord-Tenant Law 977

Chapter 40: Wills, Intestacy, Probate, and Trusts 1009

Part VIII: Special Topics

Chapter 41: Insurance 1033

Chapter 42: Liabilities of Accountants and Other Licensed Professionals 1059

Chapter 43: International Business Transactions 1083

About the Authors

C. Kerry Fields

C. Kerry Fields is a Professor of Clinical Finance and Business Economics at the University of Southern California, Marshall School of Business, where he teaches courses in the undergraduate and MBA programs. He is also a practicing attorney who has represented clients in business and real estate–related transactional and litigation matters for many years.

He has received several teaching awards and is a frequent media commentator on issues pertaining to business ethics and corporate governance. He is an author or co-author of four other Aspen Publishing texts: *Contemporary Employment Law*, Fifth Edition; *Contemporary Real Estate Law*, Third Edition; *Essentials of Real Estate Law*; and *The Legal Environment of Business*. Professor Fields received his bachelor's degree in business administration from the University of Southern California and his Juris Doctor from Santa Clara University School of Law.

Kevin C. Fields

Kevin C. Fields is a Professor of Clinical Finance and Business Economics at the University of Southern California, Marshall School of Business, where he teaches undergraduate and graduate school courses on business and real estate law. He is also the academic director for the Master of Business for Veterans (MBV) program at the university.

When not teaching, he is a practicing attorney specializing in business and construction-related disputes. Through his practice, he has tried many cases in state and federal courts and implemented all forms of alternative dispute resolution techniques to resolve cases. He is a California licensed real estate broker. He has received many teaching awards at the University of Southern California. In addition to co-authoring the second edition of this text, he is a co-author of three other Aspen Publishing texts: *Contemporary Real Estate Law*, Third Edition; *Essentials of Real Estate Law*; and *The Legal Environment of Business*. Professor Fields received his bachelor's degree in business administration from the University of Southern California and his Juris Doctor from Chapman University School of Law. He has received a certificate in mediation from Harvard University.

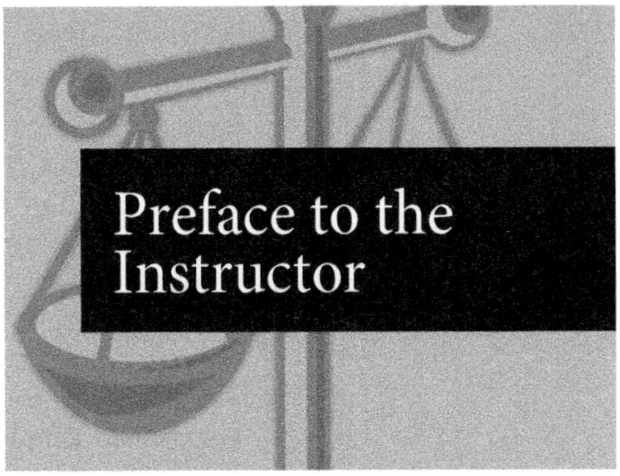

Preface to the Instructor

Remarkable changes have taken place within the American legal landscape since the publication of the last edition. As the American government has responded to repeated national and international crises, expanding responsibilities have been imposed upon businesses. As a result, managers and executives must be aware of and be able to timely respond to these developments. As the legal environment evolves, texts such as this one must identify and explain those responsibilities.

The Second Edition of *Contemporary Business Law* provides the information your students need in both a practical and contemporary way. This newest edition of this text continues its tradition of being the most up-to-date text on the market.

To ensure engagement of your students and their proficiency in difficult legal concepts, this edition features the best ancillary teaching tools at CasebookConnect.com. This product is an all-in-one online learning solution of Aspen Publishing.

What Is Special About This Text

Our goal is to explain legal concepts in a straightforward, student-friendly manner; however, definitions and references alone would not distinguish our efforts from our worthy competitors. We bring the rich context of many years of practicing and teaching business law to our work. Abundant website references and statistics are woven into the text to keep the material relevant. Complex concepts are broken down into a series of easy-to-follow explanations. Typically, after a substantive point is introduced, an actual summarized case example follows. They give context to those legal principles under discussion.

Thorough coverage of all major aspects of business law is included. We took to heart the advice of reviewers. As a result, we rewrote, edited, and added topics for our text. They allowed us to appreciate what and why certain topics were important in their classrooms. They were generous with their commentary, and we thank them.

The text's rich pedagogical design includes:

- Learning objectives
- Clear introductions at the outset of each chapter
- Landmark as well as current cases, edited to give attention to the key points while using the actual language of the court in its decision
- Every briefed case includes thought provoking *Focus on Ethics* questions
- Management applications which encourage students to research or apply a relevant topic to the context of contemporary business.
- A new addition to our topical coverage is the AI Feature at the end of each chapter. Following internet research or application of chapter material, students

have the opportunity to draft documents applying what they have learned to a business issue. The product of an AI query should prompt an engaging class discussion led by the instructor.
- Key terms and concepts are defined in the margins
- A robust glossary
- Related governmental websites are identified to allow the student to explore a topic from the point of view of the regulatory agency.
- Ten cases are provided at the end of each chapter to engage students in the research and application of the law on the chapter topics.

Updated Forms

As a learning tool, current forms used in a business law practice are included. Sample forms are placed throughout the text. They enable students to appreciate how a concept is applied in the real world.

Management Applications

It is one thing to tell a student something is important, but to have the student apply the material in response to a prompt fully engages the student in active learning. Based upon our years of applying the law to business disputes and shaping strategies for clients to execute their plans, we have included many practical management applications for students to apply the material. We include them often throughout the chapters to continue to demonstrate the practicality of the material and allow students to analyze, evaluate, and create material from the management applications. Our AI Feature at the end of each chapter offers a similar learning experience.

AI Feature in Every Chapter

At the end of each chapter, we offer a chapter-related prompt, leading to a query of an artificial intelligence program. This novel approach allows the student to appreciate the significance of the substantive rules presented in the chapter. More importantly, they can use the results of a query to succinctly summarize the application of those rules. Additionally, they can identify the shortcomings of such searches, spot issues, and critically think of how to improve their draft documents.

New Examples and End of Chapter Problems

For the Second Edition of *Contemporary Business Law* examples and case problems have been carefully chosen. Examples are integrated into the text following a legal term or concept while case problems are meant to serve as learning tools at the end of each chapter.

Instructors will find these examples and case problems helpful in illustrating legal concepts, and students will enjoy reading these cases because they involve interesting facts.

PowerPoint Slides

Supplementing the Contemporary Business Law are PowerPoint slides to accompany each chapter. The slides provide instructors and students with a summary of the main topics in each chapter and serve as a tool for studying and note taking.

Acknowledgements

The authors thank Joe Terry, Publisher, and Denise Clinton, Managing Editor, of Aspen Publishing. A special acknowledgement is due our long-time developmental editor Betsy Kenny of The Froebe Group. She has offered many useful suggestions, coordinated reviews, and advocated for us. Their continuing interest, enthusiasm, and support is greatly appreciated.

We are indebted to Lisa Connery, our Project Editor, whose tireless work in polishing our work cannot be appreciated enough.

The improvements made in this edition are due in part to the reviewers who contributed much time and direction to making this text a worthy reflection of their efforts. They alerted us to topics of interest, made thoughtful suggestions, and were supportive of our efforts.

We thank Kaitlyn Arias and Melanie Wu, law students at Chapman University School of Law, Izabelle Khanzetyan, a student at Southwestern Law School, and Dylan Sartor, a law student at Quinnipiac University School of Law. We appreciate their research efforts and many suggestions to us. We know that they will be well prepared for their professional responsibilities. We wish them well on their journey to becoming attorneys.

Finally, we want to express our appreciation for the valuable contributions of Kaitlyn Fields. Her research for our AI features was insightful, offering helpful suggestions from the student's perspective and exploring additional ideas that enriched our approach.

Personal Acknowledgments

I offer a special thanks and dedicate this book to my best friend and wife, Patricia. Who would have predicted that a friendship begun in high school would grow to produce a wonderful family and volumes of love, memories, and support? You are my rock!

As to other members of the family, thanks to our son, law partner, and colleague at the USC Marshall School of Business, Kevin. Our son Brian and his wife Leigh helped manage so many things connected with this project for which I am grateful. I recognize the special love and support of our daughter, Megan. She is my personal hero. I also thank Devon, Kaitlyn, and Ryan Fields for allowing this project to take me away from family events. To my brother, Patrick, and his family, thank you.

To the thousands of students I have taught over the years, thank you all. To those whom I have not mentioned by name, the error is mine and unintended.

Fight On!

—C. Kerry Fields

I thank my wife, Devon, and children, Kaitlyn and Ryan, for supporting me and allowing me the time to write and edit this textbook. Your smiles and laughter helped me finish this endeavor.

A special thanks to my co-author and father. Our personal and business relationship working on this project has been one of the most rewarding experiences I have had. You have always been a wonderful mentor and friend. I cannot think of a better person with whom I would have wanted to write this book.

Lastly, to the students at the University of Southern California, you motivate me by your spirit and inquisitiveness. Our classroom experiences have helped guide and shape the material of this text. I hope you enjoy the product of our efforts.

Fight On!

—Kevin C. Fields

PART I: INTRODUCTION TO LAW

The Legal Environment in Business: Laws and Regulations

1

No man is above the law, and no man is below it; nor do we ask any man's permission when we require him to obey it. — Theodore Roosevelt, Twenty-sixth President of the United States (1858-1919)

Chapter Outline

- Introduction
- What Is the Law?
- The Law as Rights and Duties
- Sources of Business Law
- The Role of Government
- Common Law
- Classifications of Law
- Briefing a Case
- AI Feature: The Attributes of the Civil and Criminal Law Systems

Learning Objectives

After studying this chapter, you should be able to:

1. Define the law.
2. Distinguish between a legal right and a legal duty.
3. Identify the primary sources of law in the United States.
4. Explain precedence and its application to *stare decisis.*
5. Describe how to brief a case using the IRAC method.

Introduction

The chapter epigraph is from President Roosevelt's 1903 State of the Union address to Congress. Roosevelt continued by stating, "Obedience to the law is demanded as a right; not asked as a favor." The law is at the heart of every society. We form communities by common agreement and maintain them by requiring everyone to obey recognized standards of behavior. The law defines these relationships, the duties that exist, and what remedies can be pursued when those duties are breached. The law is dynamic and evolves to changing societal values and circumstances. Collectively, these understandings and standards become sanctioned by the society and are known as the law.

The law has a broad reach and affects almost every aspect of our personal and professional lives. In this text, we will primarily review laws as they apply to the business context. Businesses are subject to the laws of the countries in which they operate. Further, states, local governments, and administrative agencies can enact laws governing a business's conduct. These laws and government regulations have a profound impact on all business activities — they affect employment decisions (such as the ability to fire someone), financing (such as securities regulations), and conduct (such as antitrust regulations), to name a few, plus many more that will be addressed throughout this text. Businesspersons must have a basic understanding of the laws and regulations governing these business decisions in order to make the most effective decisions for their businesses.

Throughout this text, our study of law will encompass a survey of the most important legal relationships that affect business operations. It is our goal to equip readers with the knowledge to identify potential legal issues before they develop into larger, unmanageable problems.

In this chapter, we begin with recognizing that the law is comprised of legal rights with corresponding legal duties. We then discuss the sources from which we derive our laws in the United States and the role the government plays in shaping these laws. Then we will conclude the chapter with a discussion of the classifications of laws and how students can analyze case law using the IRAC (Issue, Rules, Analysis, Conclusion) method.

What Is the Law?

Law
A set of enforceable rules governing the conduct of persons in society.

Because of the breadth and complexity of numerous laws governing persons and businesses, there are various definitions of "the law." Generally, the "**law**" is considered a set of enforceable rules governing the conduct of persons in society. Persons include both natural persons and artificial persons, such as corporations. The law gives power to government to act and to classify right behavior from wrong behavior. Laws govern the social and economic order among individuals and their relationships with society. Further, the law acts as a common bond and promoter of civil behavior among us. Throughout this book, we consider the law as arising from those laws enacted by legislatures, rules and regulations issued by administrative agencies, and judicial decisions issued by courts.

The Law as Rights and Duties

Legal right
The ability to have an individual interest respected by others and enforced through a legal procedure.

Legal rights and legal duties have been recognized as two components of what we mean by "the law." Each must coexist with the other. A **legal right** is a claim that must be respected by others and is enforced through legal procedure (such as the court system).

A legal right can arise from a constitution, statute, or contract and be enforced by the government or a private party.

To respect the legal rights of others, the law recognizes a corresponding obligation of a **legal duty**. Legal duties are the standard of care that society demands from us in our interactions with government and other individuals. Owners and employees must be aware of legal duties to operate businesses lawfully. These may be negative duties (such as an obligation not to engage in fraudulent behavior) or may be affirmative duties (such as a business's obligation to conform to the Americans with Disabilities Act requirements for employee accommodations).

Legal duty
A requirement not to interfere with the legal rights of another.

Sources of Business Law

Business law is a broad subject and often encompasses a number of legal subject areas. As a result, there are a variety of sources that define the rights and duties that apply to businesses. The sources of law include:

- Constitutions (the United States Constitution and the state constitutions)
- Treaties
- Executive orders
- Statutory law (laws passed by Congress, states, and local legislatures)
- Administrative agency rules, regulations, and orders
- Judicial decisions
- Contractual agreements

Constitutions

Both the federal government and the states have enacted their own constitutions. The United States Constitution and its amendments are the supreme law of the land. Any law that contradicts the U.S. Constitution is unconstitutional and thereby unenforceable. The U.S. Constitution created three branches of government and bestowed upon each branch certain powers. While most business law is enacted at the state level, several provisions of the Constitution affect business, such as the Commerce Clause and the Equal Protection Clauses. The Constitution will be discussed further in Chapter 4.

State constitutions can vary in the length and scope of protections granted to their citizens. Typically, state constitutions are more expansive and detailed than the U.S. Constitution. Further, these state constitutions allow for each state's own diverse constituency, traditions, and political cultures to be reflected therein. State constitutions are amended more often than the U.S. Constitution and are able to provide additional protections and rights to their citizens not found in the U.S. Constitution. However, state constitutions are limited and cannot deprive state citizens of their federal constitutional rights. As long as the state constitution does not conflict with the U.S. Constitution or federal law, its provisions are valid within that state's borders.

Example: While Congress has enacted laws to protect an individual's privacy in some specific areas, some states have expanded the scope of the privacy protections. Hawaii's state constitution provides, "The right of the people to privacy is recognized and shall not be infringed without the showing of a compelling state interest. The legislature shall take affirmative steps to implement this right."[1]

Treaties

Treaty
A formal agreement between two or more countries.

Treaties are created when two or more countries enter into a formal agreement. In the United States, the President is authorized to negotiate and commit the United States to a treaty, but only upon the advice and consent of two-thirds of the Senate.

> **Example:** The United States has entered into the United States-Mexico-Canada Agreement (USMCA) updating provisions to promote trade and investment between the North American countries.

Executive Orders

Executive order
Directives by the President or a state governor to promote or prohibit policy decisions.

Executive orders are orders issued by the President or a state governor to promote or prohibit policy decisions.

> **Example:** Presidential Executive Order 13859 was issued to drive technological breakthroughs in artificial intelligence across the federal government, industry, and academia in order to promote scientific discovery, economic competitiveness, and national security.

Statutory Law

Statutory law
A system of laws comprised of laws and ordinances enacted by federal, state, and local legislatures and governing bodies.

Statutes
Laws created by the legislative branch to promote or prohibit conduct.

Statutory law is comprised of laws and ordinances enacted by federal, state, and local governments. If a state adopts a set of uniform laws, those laws will be considered part of the state's statutory law.

Statutes are one of the primary sources of law in the United States. The legislative branch, of both federal and state governments, enacts **statutes** that promote or prohibit certain conduct. Legislative bodies can enact statutes that cover business issues such as business formation, securities regulation, or insurance.

Statutory law is distinct from case law, which is decided by the courts, and regulations, which are issued by government agencies. Unlike common law (discussed below), statutes are more strictly construed, so there is often less for the court to interpret. Therefore, the court is generally bound by the express terms of the statute. Statutes may not violate the U.S. Constitution or any state constitution and will be overturned if they are found to be unconstitutional or are overruled by a later statute.

FEDERAL STATUTES. Federal statutes are contained in the United States Code. These statutes establish laws carrying out the U.S. Constitution and operations of the federal government. Federal statutes are enacted by Congress and then approved by the President. These statutes then apply to all states.

> **Example:** Federal statutes that apply to bankruptcy are found in Title 11 of the United States Code.

---

1. Haw. Const. art. I, § 6.

STATE STATUTES. Like the federal government, each state's legislature can enact laws promoting or prohibiting conduct. State statutes only apply within the state and may vary from state to state. State statutes may not violate the U.S. Constitution or their state's constitution.

Uniform Laws

With each state having the power to adopt its own statutes, the differences in state laws may create conflicts and difficulties for businesses that conduct business in several states. A company doing business nationally is subject to the laws of every state in which it conducts business. To address this problem, legal scholars and lawyers formed organizations to draft **uniform laws** that a state can then decide to adopt or reject. Once a state legislature decides to adopt the uniform law, that law becomes a part of the state's statute. The state legislature has the discretion to adopt all or only part of the uniform law.

Most states have adopted the **Uniform Commercial Code (UCC)**. Article 2 of the UCC establishes a uniform set of laws related to the sale of goods. Article 2 has been adopted by every state except Louisiana, plus the District of Columbia. The UCC primarily deals with transactions involving movable "goods" (personal property).

MUNICIPAL ORDINANCES. State governments may grant some power to the local governments. Once power is granted from the state, counties, cities, and municipalities can enact their own **ordinances** promoting or prohibiting conduct. Typically, these local laws regulate matters that affect the local community, such as rent, zoning, and local safety.

Uniform law
A model law created by an organization for the state to either adopt or reject. Once a state adopts the law, it then becomes a part of the state's statutory law.

> **Example:** Rent control ordinances are adopted most often at the municipal level of government.

Uniform Commercial Code (UCC)
A uniform set of laws that are related to the sale of goods.

Administrative Agencies

When the government enacts a new statute, an administrative agency will often administer and enforce the statute. The administrative agency creates rules, enforces the laws, and can adjudicate those who have violated administrative laws. Administrative agencies are discussed in more detail in Chapter 34.

Ordinance
A law created by a town or city council, county board, or other form of municipal government.

FEDERAL ADMINISTRATIVE REGULATIONS. As a general principle, federal administrative agencies direct, supervise, and implement important legislative acts passed by Congress. Because Congress does not have unlimited resources, it delegates some of its authority to administrative agencies. These administrative agencies have

Regulation
A rule adopted by an administrative agency on how to follow laws passed by the legislature.

Administrative law
The body of rules, orders, and decisions issued by administrative agencies in order to regulate industries and businesses.

the power to enact **regulations** to implement particular legislative acts that create new laws. Additionally, certain agencies are granted the right to enforce those regulations. **Administrative law** is the body of rules, orders, and decisions issued by administrative agencies to regulate industries and businesses.

STATE ADMINISTRATIVE REGULATIONS. Similar to federal administrative agencies, states have created administrative agencies to regulate business matters. The state's constitution generally gives the state the power to establish a state-level administrative agency. Like federal agencies, state agencies work with the state's governor and legislature to administer and enforce state statutes. Common state agencies that may affect business include those that control transportation, public health, education, and law enforcement.

> **Example:** Individual states have the authority to issue drivers' licenses. Most states have a Department of Motor Vehicles (DMV), a state level government agency, to administer driver licensing.

Judicial Decisions

Lawsuits in federal and state courts may result in the issuance of judicial decisions by the court. Judicial decisions interpret the meaning of statutes, ordinances, and regulations to shape what is known as common law.

> **Example:** One appellate court stated: "The judiciary's responsibility to interpret statutes often places courts in the position of trying to decide how the Legislature would have resolved an issue we strongly suspect it never actually considered. We endeavor, as best we can, to be prognosticators. Sometimes, however, our role in statutory interpretation is more that of a detective. The Legislature included a provision or used a particular term in a statute, and it is our job to uncover what it had in mind when it employed those words. In this case we function largely as detectives, hopefully more like Sherlock Holmes than Inspector Clouseau." *Wood v. Kaiser Foundation Hospitals*, 88 Cal. App. 5th 742, 748 (Cal. App. 2023)

International law
A body of rules that has been established through customs and treaties.

International Law

With the increasing number of business transactions that occur internationally, business owners must consider these different laws. **International law** is a body of rules established through customs and treaties that have been recognized as binding between nations and that govern their relations with one another. The United States has recognized international law as part of our laws with several judicial decisions. International law will be discussed in further detail in Chapter 43.

> **Example:** The Supreme Court in 1900 recognized international law as part of U.S. law. The Court stated, "International law

is part of our law, and must be ascertained and administered by the courts of justice of appropriate jurisdiction as often as questions of right depending upon it are duly presented for their determination. For this purpose, where there is no treaty and no controlling executive or legislative act or judicial decision, resort must be had to the customs and usages of civilized nations." *The Paquete Habana*, 175 U.S. 677,700 (1900)

Contractual Agreements

Contracts between two or more parties can have a major effect on business and professional relationships. These agreements can establish rights and duties between parties. That is, contracts can affect the manner in which the parties will conduct business.

Example: An employment contract between an employer and its employees will dictate the employee's duties.

The Role of Government

Each of the three branches of government created by the federal or state constitution is equal to the other branches. The **legislative branch** enacts laws that govern the rights and responsibilities of persons and businesses. The **executive branch** enforces the laws. To assist the executive branch, many administrative agencies have been created. Most administrative agencies are within the executive branch of government; they possess the legal authority to affect the rights of private persons through their rules, regulations, and orders.

The **judicial branch** is known as the court system, and its responsibility is to interpret and apply the laws, rules, and regulations created by the legislative and executive branches of government and to determine private disputes. The consequence of establishing separately instituted forces to exercise governmental power is known as the American system of checks and balances.

Legislative branch
The branch of government that enacts the laws that govern the rights and responsibilities of citizens.

Executive branch
The branch of government that enforces the laws, with the assistance of various administrative agencies.

Judicial branch
The branch of government that interprets and applies the laws, rules, and regulations created by the legislative and executive branches.

Common Law

American law traces its development to the laws of England. The Norman Conquest of 1066 brought to England a court system that sought the common application of uniform rules over the entire country. Prior to that time, each region of the country could dispense its own justice according to local customs and community practices. The implementation of the uniform laws across England became known as the "**common law.**" Over time, these rules became **precedent** that judges used to decide future cases. Common law began to be utilized across the British colonies, which is where the origins of the U.S. common law began. In the U.S, common law is the primary source of law for contracts and torts.

Common law
Law created and developed primarily by courts.

Precedent
The rule of law established by a court decision that can be used to decide future similar cases.

Stare decisis
Latin for "to stand by the decision." A legal principle that requires a court to apply prior appellate case holdings as precedent binding upon the court once certain facts have been established.

As the body of court decisions grew, American courts adopted a practice known as ***stare decisis***. Under this doctrine, lower courts, in considering similar cases, apply the precedent of the highest court in a jurisdiction on the subject at issue. Lower trial courts in both federal and state venues are required to follow *stare decisis* until the higher court reverses or amends its prior decision. Until then, the decision of the higher court is followed as binding precedent by all lower courts in that jurisdiction. The U.S. Constitution establishes precedent for all federal, state, and local laws and ordinances. Federal statutes establish precedent for all state constitutions and state statutes. *Stare decisis* does not require courts to follow decisions of equal status (such as by courts from two different states) or of two courts in the same state court (such as two different county courts).

If the Supreme Court issues a decision interpreting a federal statute, then *stare decisis* would compel all inferior federal courts to apply that interpretation in future cases involving similar facts.

Following *Stare Decisis*

Another application of the *stare decisis* doctrine is that a court will usually follow its own precedent and defer to its previous decisions on a subject. However, the doctrine is not rigidly enforced. A court may revisit its earlier precedents if good reasons exist to change them or if permanent shifts in public policies or norms require them. As the U.S. Supreme Court has stated, "What we can decide, we can undecide. But *stare decisis* teaches that we should exercise that authority sparingly."[2]

Example: The Supreme Court in *Janus v. American Federation of State, County, and Municipal Employees* overturned precedent followed for over 40 years by holding that the application of public-sector union fees to non-members is a violation of the non-members' First Amendment rights. Previously, unions were able to collect fees from non-members and use the funds for political campaign donations.

As the Supreme Court noted, departing from precedent should be done sparingly. There are several benefits that society and businesses obtain when courts follow *stare decisis*, including:

- Predictability and stability of the application of laws
- Judicial efficiency, as courts do not have to repeatedly retry the same disputes
- Uniform application of the law in the jurisdiction

To explore *stare decisis* and the relevance of legal precedents, see, *https://www.americanbar.org/groups/public_education/publications/preview_home/understand-stare-decisis/*.

2. *Kimble v. Marvel Entm't, LLC*, 576 U.S. 446, 485 (2015).

FIGURE 1.1: Hierarchy of Laws

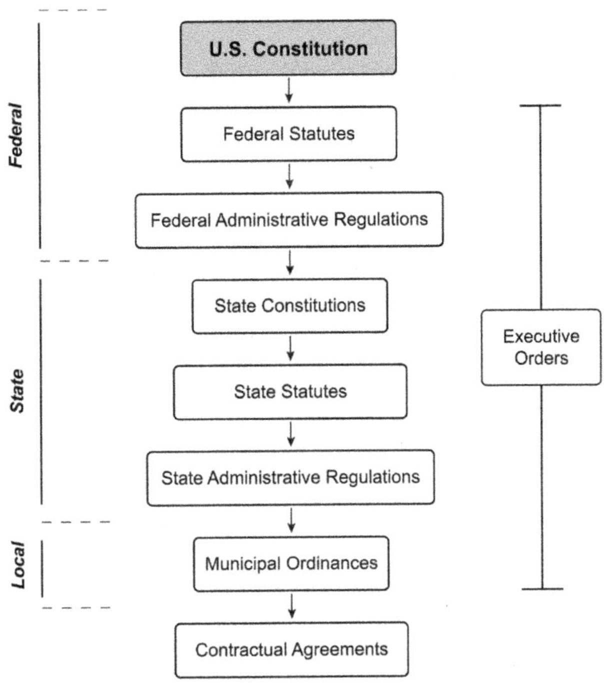

Cases of First Impression

When there is no precedent for a court to follow in a jurisdiction, known as a case of first impression, the court may look to cases outside its jurisdiction for guidance. The precedent used in other jurisdictions is **persuasive authority**. Persuasive authority is not binding on the court but can be used to guide and inform a jurisdiction as to how other jurisdictions have resolved the matter. Because there is no precedent to follow in the jurisdiction, the court can decide the case by following persuasive authority or by establishing its own precedent.

Persuasive authority A source of law which carries some authoritative weight but does not bind a court.

> **Example:** A state, when dealing with a case of first impression, can review precedent followed by other states or decide to establish its own precedent on the subject matter.

Classifications of Law

The law can be organized into various classifications. For example, the law may be divided into substantive law and procedural law or civil law and public law. In the substantive and procedural law classification, **substantive law** is comprised of the laws that define one's legal rights. **Procedural law** is comprised of the laws that enforce legal rights or provide a remedy for the injured party.

Substantive law The part of the law that defines legal rights.

Procedural law The part of the law that enforces legal rights or provides a remedy for an injured party.

> **Example:** A public university's right to search a student's backpack is subject to the Fourth Amendment's substantive law protections. If the university were to

seek to enforce a violation against the student, it would have to follow procedural law to provide due process to the student.

Civil law
A system of law that deals with the private relations between persons in a community.

Public law
A system of law that governs an individual's personal rights and obligations in relation to the government.

Civil law involves private disputes while **public law** governs an individual's personal rights and obligations in relation to government. Civil and public laws can be created by either statutory law or common law. Our study of contract law (including its application to covenants not to compete and nondisclosure of trade secrets) and tort law (which addresses wrongful conduct within the employment relationship) involve the civil law branch. Other features of civil law include property law, inheritance, family law, and the law relating to business entities. The public law branch of our law tree includes criminal law (relating to offenses against society), constitutional law (relating to individuals' rights and relationships to their local, state, and federal governments), administrative law (which focuses on the powers of executive branch administrative agencies), and international law (which involves the legal relationships among nations).

Civil Law

Purpose	The purpose of civil law is to deal with disputes between individuals, businesses, or between the two.
Case Filed By	Private parties.
Standard of Proof	Preponderance of evidence.
Jury Verdict	Laws will vary by state and country, but the verdict of the jury does not have to be unanimous.
Examples	Contract disputes, divorce proceedings, and/or personal injury cases.

Briefing a Case

Implementing the IRAC method to brief a case is not as interesting as reading the latest novel. Unfamiliar words and principles are often used. Judges, lawyers, and others assume that the reader knows the law. Further, the facts may dictate a result that you may not view as reasonable today.

IRAC is an acronym for the terms Issue, Rule, Analysis, Conclusion (however, the information is commonly presented as Facts, Issue, Rule, Analysis, Conclusion).

It is one of the most popular methods of organizing and structuring legal related essay answers. The IRAC method is a useful tool for organizing legal thinking and writing. For those new to legal thinking and writing, it provides a framework for weaving together the threads of a legal argument and helps provide direction to the conclusion.

IRACs are presented in the form of a memorandum, the focus of which is to distill the important aspects of a court opinion into a clear presentation of why and how the court reached its decision.

The first step in briefing a case is to read the original case in the textbook or on an online source. In this textbook, case facts and the language of the court are summarized; the original case text is often quite long and denser.

Understanding Case Citations

A case citation is the common identifier for the decision across research platforms. It begins with the title of the case followed by its references. For example, the case citation for a landmark Supreme Court decision is *Brown v. Board of Education*, 347 U.S. 483 (1954).

The first number of the citation shows the volume of the reporter (that is, a collection of cases from a given region of the United States or court system). In this citation, the decision is found in the 347th volume of the United States Reports (U.S.). There may be alternative ("parallel") reporter references, such as in the 74th volume of the Supreme Court Reports (S. Ct.) in this case.

Next comes the page number of the decision within that reporter (483), followed by the year of the decision in parentheses (1954). Because they may not be from the authorized publisher, internet addresses from which the decision can be downloaded are not used.

Framing the Opinion

The next step is to frame the opinion using the following components.

- *State the names of the parties:* Name and describe the plaintiff(s) and defendant(s). Use the names of the parties throughout the IRAC.
- *State the facts of the case:* Present a summary of the facts so the reader will understand the context in which the dispute arose. Recognize that the heart of an IRAC lies not in the statement of the facts but in the material following the factual recounting.

  Briefly describe the nature of the dispute; for example, is it one of contract, personal injury, employment discrimination, or the interpretation of a regulation? Keep this section brief, not a full recounting of all that occurred at the trial court level. Unless necessary, summarize and do not detail the procedural history of how the case came before the appellate court.

Example: The ABC Bank foreclosed upon the residence of Eric and Tanya Smith. The Smiths alleged in their defense to the bank's foreclosure lawsuit that the bank had failed to give proper notice under a state real estate foreclosure statute. The trial court held that the notice was not needed because the Smiths waived that requirement in the loan documents they executed in favor of the bank. The trial court granted the bank's motion for summary judgment, which the Smiths have now appealed.

- *State the **Issue** of the case:* Issue spotting is an important skill. Articulate the issue by creating the legal question presented by the facts. The legal rules you learned in class will guide you to the issues. You should only discuss legal rules that can be applied to the facts. Frequently, your instructor will ask that the issue be stated in the form of the essential questions that, when answered, supply the basis for the conclusion the court reached in its decision. A well-stated issue could be in the form of a question that could be answered by a "yes" or "no" response.

Example: In the *Brown* decision, the Supreme Court stated the issue as: "*Does segregation of children in public schools solely on the basis of race, even though the physical facilities and other 'tangible' factors may be equal, deprive the children of the minority group of equal educational opportunities?*"

The issue in the same case may be stated as: "*In deciding whether the Equal Protection Clause bars segregation in public education, should the Supreme Court apply* stare decisis *or interpret the Equal Protection Clause in light of the importance of providing equal education in a modern context?*"

In the above bank foreclosure example, the issue might be stated as: "*Does due process require that a written notice be timely given to defaulting borrowers prior to the lender instituting a mortgage foreclosure action if such notice is waived in writing by the borrowers in their loan documents?*"

In another dispute, the issue might be stated as: "*Does a corporate officer violate their fiduciary duties if they influence the corporation's banking relationship to issue them a personal loan when they are otherwise not qualified for such a loan?*"

Other instructors may prefer that the issue be in the form of a statement and not a question.

Examples: The stare decisis doctrine does not prevent the Court from reconsidering its prior approval of segregated physical facilities in public schools based upon race.

Due process requires proper and prompt notice before governmental taking of a person's personal property.

An example of what not to do is to simply state that the defendant prevailed. Such a statement tells the reader nothing about the case or the issue. State the issue in terms of the facts unique to the case and the law.

- *State the **Rule** of law:* In the second section, the rules or legal principles involved in applying the facts are stated. They are the rules and principles that are necessary to reach a resolution of the parties' dispute. Concisely state the legal rule the court used to reach its holding. Avoid long insertions of the applicable language from the statute, regulation, or case law involved. You will want to identify the following, if relevant to your facts: (1) definition of the law; (2) the elements of the law; (3) exceptions or limitations relevant to the general rule; and (4) applicable defenses to the rule.

Example: Illinois state law provides that corporate officers may not seek personal gain from the corporation's banking relationships without the consent of the board of directors.

- ***Analyze** the facts to the law:* The analysis or application is the heart of the discussion and where you will apply the specific fact pattern to the rules you have introduced above. The evidence relied upon by the court is reviewed. You can match each element you have identified in the applicable rule to the facts presented. State the reasons or justification for the court's holding and include the arguments of both sides. Reference relevant precedents and public policies when necessary. It is often helpful to use the words "in this case," "since," or "because," as this will force you to explain your reasoning and apply the facts to the rule.

Example: In this proceeding, the bank officer argued that she was entitled to coax the corporation's bank to extend a favorable loan to her because all managers were personally aware of what she was doing. She urges that there is no harm to the corporation or its shareholders if all managers are aware and tacitly approve of her actions.

- *State a **Conclusion**:* In this section, the court's "holding," which is the court's application of the governing rule(s) to the facts, is stated. Sometimes courts will state the holding explicitly; in other opinions, the holding must be inferred from the result reached and the court's reasoning. The holding is that part of the opinion which may be cited as precedent in a later case involving a similar issue. The holding is different from the court's factual "findings" on factual issues. The holding follows the application of the relevant rules to the facts before the court. Sometimes, the court will summarize the conclusion for you.

Example: In the *Brown* decision, the Court stated: "*We conclude that in the field of public education the doctrine of 'separate but equal' has no place. Separate educational facilities are inherently unequal. Therefore, we hold that the plaintiffs and others similarly situated for whom the actions have been brought are, by reason of the segregation complained of, deprived of the equal protection of the laws guaranteed by the Fourteenth Amendment.*"

In a legal memorandum, most often the conclusion is placed at the end. However, depending upon the instructor's preference, a summary of the conclusion may be stated at the start of the memorandum. Such summaries can be titled "Executive Summary" or use similar title language.

AI Feature: The Attributes of the Civil and Criminal Law Systems

Using an AI program, create a summary to distinguish between civil and criminal law systems. Include the parties to each proceeding, the procedures unique to each system, the differing burdens of proof, as well as the right to appeal from a trial court judgment.

Key Terms

- Administrative law, 6
- Civil law, 10
- Common law, 7
- Executive branch, 7
- Executive order, 4
- International law, 6
- Judicial branch, 7
- Law, 2
- Legal duty, 3
- Legal right, 2
- Legislative branch, 7
- Ordinance, 5
- Persuasive authority, 9
- Precedent, 7
- Procedural law, 9
- Public law, 10
- Regulation, 6
- *Stare decisis, 8*
- Statutes, 4
- Statutory law, 4
- Substantive law, 9
- Treaty, 4
- Uniform Commercial Code (UCC), 5
- Uniform law, 5

Applying the Law

1.1 Research the Law. Using an internet search engine, review a recent decision of the United States Supreme Court. Analyze how the Court presented the facts, stated the issue(s) to be decided, and applied precedent to reach its decision. How would you have stated the issue if you were to prepare an IRAC of the decision? Among the many websites to review such case law is the Court's official website at *https://www.supremecourt.gov/.*

1.2 Research the Law. Using an internet search engine, review the website of the state supreme court of your home state. What cases of interest have been decided in its last term? What important cases remain to be decided as listed on the court's docket? Are there more particular types of cases that predominate on the court's calendar, such as criminal search and seizure or administrative law cases?

1.3 Research the Law. Review your state's constitution. Does it provide for a right to privacy? Who is protected, and from what forms of invasions of personal privacy are they protected? If not, then review the law of another state such as New York, which has enacted a privacy law.

1.4 Substantive or Procedural Law. Patrick sues Darlene for damages resulting from a breach of an employment contract. The court found that Patrick waited for three years to file the lawsuit, which meant that the statute of limitations (the period of time in which one can bring a lawsuit) had lapsed. As a result, the court dismissed Patrick's lawsuit against Darlene. In the court's decision, was substantive law or procedural law applied?

1.5 Sources of Law. Suppose you wish to form and operate a business. What levels of government are most often the source of law that applies to these issues:

- **a.** Business formation
- **b.** Zoning
- **c.** Income taxes
- **d.** Employment

1.6 *Stare Decisis.* Ten-year-old Levi Rutherford was a member of the Summit Ski Team and was an advanced skier. Levi's father signed him up for the team and signed an "Assumption of Risk and Release of Liability" on Levi's behalf. This release allegedly waived Levi's right to sue the ski team and any ski area operator for an injury due to any reason, including negligence. During ski team practice, Levi sustained a brain injury after crashing into machine-made snow. The Rutherfords filed suit on Levi's behalf against the ski team and ski area operator. If pre-injury releases are governed by contract law and generally allowed, should a court follow this precedent? Are there any facts that may suggest otherwise? *Rutherford v. Talisker Canyons Finance Co., LLC*, 445 P.3d 474 (Utah 2019)

1.7 Sources of Law. Recent U.S. presidents have acted often unilaterally without a bill having been approved by Congress. Using an internet search engine, review the executive orders issued by Presidents Trump and Biden. One president attempts to roll back executive orders of their predecessor by executive order. Review those executive orders of President Biden following his inauguration. Do executive orders have an oversized role in governing America within its political divide? When should a president issue an executive order, and when should they engage Congress to act to pass legislation? What are the limits of presidents to act unilaterally by executive order?

1.8 International Law. Eight residents of Peru sued a Delaware corporation that was conducting mining operations in Peru. The plaintiffs claimed that they suffered from asthma and lung disease as a result of the miner's environmental pollution. The Delaware corporation had its principal place of business in Peru but was owned in majority by a company headquartered in Arizona, which was wholly owned by a Mexican corporation. The Peruvians asserted that the local operations violated international law and that they could sue for damages in U.S. federal court under a U.S. law passed in 1789. How should a federal court apply such old law within a modern context? Is it reasonable to continue to apply a statute in this manner if there is no precedent to do so? Review the decision and analyze the merits of the arguments made by both sides. *Flores v. Southern Peru Copper Corp.*, 253 F. Supp. 2d 510 (S.D.N.Y. 2002)

1.9 IRAC. Brief a case you have found online, or one provided by your instructor, using the IRAC method.

1.10 Sources of Law. The state of Texas Supreme Court is deciding a case of first impression on a student privacy issue. The Oklahoma Supreme Court, one year prior, decided a student privacy issue that had very similar facts. Is the Texas Supreme Court obligated to follow the Oklahoma Supreme Court's decision? Discuss your rationale.

Business Ethics

2

Virtue is not meant to stand alone. He who practices it shall have neighbors. — Confucius (aka Kong Qiu), *The Analects* (551-479 B.C.)

Chapter Outline

- Introduction
- The Origins of Ethical Theory
- Ethical Frameworks

Case 2.1: *Hinojos v. Kohl's Corporation*
Case 2.2: *MG Altus Apache Co. v. United States*

  - *Management Application: An Early View of the Purpose of a Corporation*
- The Process of Reaching an Ethical Decision
  - *Management Application: Dealing with a Business Crisis*
  - *Management Application: Special Purpose Corporations*
- Developing an Ethical Business Culture
- AI Feature: Which Industrial Plant to Close?

Learning Objectives

After studying this chapter, you should be able to:

1. Define the meaning of business ethics.
2. Describe values-based ethics and its origins.
3. Explain how culture and ethical behavior are related.
4. Distinguish among common ethical theories.
5. Explain how ethics assists in decision making.

Introduction

Business enterprises are diverse in purpose and activity. They encounter ethical challenges in their efforts to operate lawfully while balancing the many demands made upon them. In this chapter, we review ethical theories that can assist decision makers

Ethics
The values and principles guiding one's actions and decisions.

in making better choices. **Ethics** refers to the values and principles that guide the actions and decisions of individuals, organizations, and governments. Ethics is a process of analyzing choices. Ethics requires that we consider fundamental and important questions, such as "*How should we behave?*" and "*What should we do in this situation?*"

Ethical decisions are those grounded in the values that the decision maker considers important. In making an ethically sound decision, we review the facts and identify the stakeholders and the available alternatives. Ultimately, we must consider our values to make an ethically sound decision.

The misdeeds of prominent officials, business leaders, and celebrities rivet our attention. Society is fascinated by the innuendo and intrigue of a precipitous fall from grace. The human experience tells us scandals will never cease, thereby necessitating a continued need to study ethics. Ethical decision making means doing something more than avoiding selfishness. Ultimately, we must ask ourselves, "*Are we doing the right thing?*" Ignoring that nagging question reminds us that every wrongdoing begins with an ethical breach. It is the dualism of good and evil within all of us that provides the opportunity to make wrong choices; however, it is our informed reason that helps us to avoid them.

We do not live in a vacuum; our individual acts and omissions are judged by the systems and structures to which we must respond. We know our communities are served best by those policies and institutions that promote the collective good, but merely complying with the law is not enough to avoid ethical conflicts. Law is about what one *has a right to do*, while ethics is about what one *should do*. The law often sets low thresholds for behavior, while business ethics rely upon adopted values to distinguish right from wrong. In this chapter, we review the origins of ethics, compare ethical theories (known as *normative ethics*), and apply those theories to current issues (known as *applied ethics*). Our study should assist us in making ethical decisions despite the unpredictable challenges we will encounter in our business careers.

The Origins of Ethical Theory

Since the beginning of recorded history, the philosophical roots of ethics, or moral philosophy, have presented *ethics* as knowledge that focuses upon the big questions, such as the following:

- What *ought* we to do?
- Can we reach common acceptance of moral values (duties and obligations)?
- Are there absolute moral values?
- How should our values evolve to account for changes in knowledge, culture, and circumstances?

Evidence from the earliest historical records of Assyrian governments shows that they were concerned with codifying rules; for example, proper weights and measures were adopted to protect consumers from dishonest food selling practices. Such traditions continue today in the form of consumer protection statutes. We must acknowledge the contributions of the ancient Greeks from whom we learn what it means to act ethically. This chapter also reviews selected schools of ethical thought as part of our journey to become ethical business leaders.

In *The Republic*, Plato, a disciple of Socrates, introduced the concept that individuals owed respect for the interests of others. The community's interests must be considered and balanced against individual self-interests. This concept is comparable to what we would define as *morality*—roughly equivalent to the language of that time for the word "*justice*." *The Republic* posed the question, "*Why should I be just?*" Today, businesses and society may frame that question as, "*Why should I act in a moral manner?*" The dialogue in the first chapter of *The Republic* includes the statement, "Justice is the advantage of the stronger." Framed differently, justice is defined as a system that rewards its powerful institutions. This statement is demonstrated today through the frequent reporting on how politicians, business insiders, and influencers subvert the public interest.

Consider further, most foolish Socrates, that the just is always a loser in comparison with the unjust. [A] just man comes off worse than an unjust man everywhere. First of all, in contracts with one another wherever two are in partnership, and the partnership is dissolved, you would never find the just man getting the better of the unjust, but he always gets the worst of it. Secondly, in public matters, when there are taxes, the just man pays more and the unjust less from an equal estate; when there are distributions the one gains nothing and the other much. . . .—(Plato, *The Republic*, Book I)

Great wealth is often obtained by those who act unjustly. Socrates concludes later in this text that moral behavior follows only because we fear the consequences of not acting morally. A companion of Socrates offers the observation that ethics involves compromises; namely, that we cannot escape injustice in society, so we agree to neither do, nor suffer, injustice. Plato, as a student of Socrates, urges that rational justifications for good behavior will not sway the many; only when the laws are enforced by government will ethics be realized in society. Even today, laws are most often written to deter harmful behaviors and actions rather than promote positive behaviors and actions.

Later in time, Aristotle, an ancient Greek philosopher, offered insights upon which authors of business management texts have long relied. His approach to business ethics addresses how we *should* act. High moral standards (individual virtue and integrity) promote personal *and* societal well-being. Today, we call this approach normative ethics. Aristotle argued that virtues are individual habits exhibiting what is right for one to do. The act of making a choice requires the application of reason to achieve the ends we seek. He stated that among the highest states for human behavior is the habit of acting honorably. In a similar vein, he concluded that the role of a leader was to create an environment in which all members could realize their individual potential. In its modern application, his ethics of leadership would include these questions:

- Am I acting virtuously?
- To what extent can my workers develop their talents?
- May they participate in decision making?
- How do they benefit from my decisions?

Happiness is the "complete and fulfilling good."—Aristotle, *The Nicomachean Ethics* (385-323 B.C.)

Ethical Frameworks

Having reviewed ethics' origins, we consider ethical frameworks to answer two important questions: "*What does it mean to act ethically?*" and "*How do we measure ethics?*" In other words, who decides what behavior is acceptable, and how do they decide if something is ethical? As a result of differing cultural, religious, and life experiences, it is not surprising that certain actions will be considered ethical by some and unethical by others. The ethical traditions we discuss have been influential in establishing ethical frameworks for answering these questions. At its heart, deciding what is ethical is a process by which we determine what we *ought* to do.

In practice, ethical decision making involves a series of steps, presented below. This activity is the process of trying to reach an informed decision consistent with our values; doing so is our obligation in acting as ethical business leaders. When the process is completed, these alternative theories often point to the same decision being made.

There are several major philosophical theories to employ in ethical decision making:

1. Virtue-Based Ethics
2. Ethical Fundamentalism
3. Utilitarianism
4. Kantian Ethics
5. Rawls's Social Justice Theory
6. Ethical Relativism
7. Moral Minimum
8. Maximizing Profits
9. Corporate Social Responsibility
10. Stakeholder Theory

Character is destiny. — Heraclitus, Greek philosopher (c. 535-475 B.C.)

Virtue-Based Ethics — The Common Ground for Decision Making

Building upon Plato's foundation discussed above, principle-based compliance systems focus on promoting an ethical corporate culture. According to the Greek philosophers, a person should seek a balance among the primary four cardinal virtues of wisdom (observation and reflection); temperance (self-control); courage; and justice (which results when the first three are in balance). Through reason and habit, each person can live a life that we would recognize as virtuous. The importance placed upon virtues in the development of our characters is reflected in the decisions we make.

Virtue-based ethics Decisions involve consideration of the moral character of individuals; how character traits can contribute to, or impair, a good life.

Virtue-based ethics arise from the social contract model; that is, individuals have consented to surrender some of their personal freedoms and submit to the authority of government in exchange for the protection of their remaining reserved rights. Many famous philosophers have rested their theories upon the nature of that social contract. It has been applied from the time of its ancient origins through to the Framers of the Declaration of Independence (as in, certain rights are inalienable) and is part of utilitarianism and the development of the social justice theory, both of which are discussed below.

Nevertheless, it is unclear what decision should be made when only one choice can be made. Sometimes, a decision requires a choice between advancing one's interest (like that of a shareholder) or those of others (such as the promotion of sustainable practices). How a company balances these interests may be found within an organization's culture. **Organizational culture** is the shared pattern of beliefs, meanings, and intentions that influence and guide the behaviors of the organization's members. Most often, employees within the same level of responsibility have the most impact upon an individual's ethical choices in the workplace.

Organizational culture Shared beliefs and values established by the organization's leaders shaping the behaviors of employees and agents.

Without a healthy corporate culture, corruption and malaise can take root in an organization. Unless senior managers insist upon ethical practices in the actions of their employees, scandals will inevitably result.

> **Example:** The failings of senior management teams to maintain an ethical culture led to the scandals involving Wells Fargo Bank® (opening unauthorized consumer accounts to generate bank fees) and Volkswagen® (falsifying air pollution control testing in diesel engine products).

Management theory holds that if virtue-based ethics are ingrained within company culture, fewer severe problems will arise. Ethical practices are fostered, and clear statements of the values to be practiced influence ethical decision making. Those personal, lived values help us decide what we should do.

> **Example:** The Johnson & Johnson® Credo. Review the business conduct standards of this company. These statements alone do not insulate the corporation from class action products liability lawsuits when managers fail to meet its aspirational goals. For example, J&J paid billions of dollars to resolve hip implant lawsuits brought against the company for alleged defects in the product. Such lapses can harm a company's reputation. Was the company living up to the values stated in its credo? Such contrasts between intent and practice can illuminate the failures of a company to act ethically.

Ethical Fundamentalism

Ethical fundamentalism involves making a decision based upon an outside source of rules or commands. It does not permit a person to determine what is right or wrong for themselves — they must use that outside source to govern their actions. Some people may relate to it as a theory invoking religious dogma or tradition to resolve an issue. However, it may just as easily apply from the historical practices and procedures of an organization, such as not permitting any variance with prior employment practices.

Ethical fundamentalism
Persons look to outside sources to decide what action is ethical or unethical.

> **Example:** Suppose a middle-aged employee wishes to adjust their work schedule to allow the employee to act as a part-time caretaker for others. If the company is averse to implementing flexible work schedules because its employment practices and policies do not provide for them, ethical fundamentalism may be at work. The company's inflexible response may result in that employee quitting their position.

In the following case, a federal court of appeals found that consumers suffered economic injury when they were induced to purchase allegedly discounted merchandise via false advertisements. Marketeers must be cautious about asserting that an advertised sale price is substantially reduced from their regular price, when it was not.

CASE 2.1

FALSE AND MISLEADING ADVERTISING IS AN UNFAIR BUSINESS PRACTICE

HINOJOS v. KOHL'S CORPORATION

718 F.3d 1098 (2013)

United States Court of Appeals for the Ninth Circuit

Kohl's Corporation and its wholly owned subsidiary Kohl's Department Stores, Inc., are retailers that operate a chain of general department stores selling clothing, footwear, home products, and accessories. Antonio Hinojos purchased several items of apparel and luggage at a Kohl's department store. Hinojos alleged in his class action lawsuit for unfair business practices that he and other class members relied upon deceptive advertisements in deciding to purchase these items from Kohl's. He alleged that he purchased several items that were advertised as substantially reduced from their "original" or "regular" prices but that were, in reality, routinely sold by Kohl's at the advertised "sale" prices rather than the purported "original" or "regular" prices. Hinojos further alleged that he "would not have purchased [these] products at Kohl's in the absence of Kohl's misrepresentations."

The federal district court interpreted California law, which applied because the court was exercising diversity jurisdiction, as holding that when a merchant misrepresents the "regular" price of its wares, it does not misrepresent the innate value of those wares, so the misled consumer has suffered no economic injury; he gets the product he expected at the price he expected. Hinojo appealed from that decision.

Language of the Court. *Most consumers have, at some point, purchased merchandise that was marketed as being "on sale" because the proffered discount seemed too good to pass up. Retailers, well aware of consumers' susceptibility to a bargain, therefore have an incentive to lie to their customers by falsely claiming that their products have previously sold at a far higher "original" price in order to induce customers to purchase merchandise at a purportedly marked-down "sale" price. Antonio Hinojos, alleges that he was a victim of such a practice and bought merchandise from a Kohl's Department Store that he would not have purchased had he not been misled by advertisements stating that the merchandise was marked down from a fictitious "original" or "regular" price.*

By creating an impression of savings, the presence of a higher reference price enhances subjects' perceived value and willingness to buy the product. Empirical studies indicate that as discount size increases, consumers' perceptions of value and their willingness to buy the product increase, while their intention to search for a lower price decreases. Misinformation about a product's "normal" price is, therefore, significant to many consumers in the same way as a false product label would be. Caselaw recognizes that falsely labeling a watch as a Rolex would be an actionable misrepresentation even if the watch was a functional equivalent of a Rolex. That, of course, is why retailers like Kohl's have an incentive to advertise false "sales." It is also why the California legislature has prohibited them from doing so. In fact, the deceived bargain hunter suffers a more obvious economic injury as a result of false advertising than the Kwikset consumer who was duped into buying foreign-made goods, because the bargain hunter's expectations about the product he just purchased is precisely that it has a higher perceived value and therefore has a higher resale value.

Hinojos specifically and plausibly alleges that Kohl's falsely markets its products at reduced prices precisely because consumers such as himself reasonably regard price reductions as material information when making purchasing decisions. Furthermore, both state and federal law specifically prohibit retailers from advertising false "sales." In sum, price advertisements matter. We hold that when a consumer purchases merchandise on the basis of false price information, and when the consumer alleges that he would not have made the purchase but for the misrepresentation, he has standing to sue under the UCL and FAL because he has suffered an economic injury.

Decision. The federal court of appeals reversed the decision of the district court.

Focus on Ethics

Consider the question: What is "truth" in advertising? Should the law define "truth" more precisely or is it context based for which only general guidance may be given? When does it become misleading? How might such practices affect fair competition?

Live your life so that there is standing room only at your funeral.
—Anonymous, as it is attributed to many

Utilitarianism

Utilitarianism Ethical theory endorsing actions producing the greatest good to society.

The **utilitarianism** theory has evolved to the view that one should promote actions that produce *the greatest good to society*. Inherent in this view is that absolute moral rules are rejected. It is not a theory advocating that the decision of the majority (that is, the greatest number of people) should prevail, it is one of producing the *greatest good* to society. Its supporters argue that the consequences of the actions should determine the choice to be made, and that the consequences of actions can be measured.

Critics argue that common moral standards bind society; that is, society is served by deeply held moral beliefs. Moreover, it is difficult to measure the *good* resulting from different actions. Using a *cost-benefit analysis* may be unfair, discriminatory, or too simplistic to aid a decision maker looking to consequences as the tool to use. Critics argue utilitarianism may entail approval of actions that most people view as morally wrong, for example, executing an innocent man if it would avoid widespread civil unrest. Moreover, they argue that the decision maker's judgment does not always result in a fair and just result.

Example: If a doctor had a choice of saving the lives of three convicted serial killers versus saving the life of the President of the United States and chose to save the President's life because it provided the greatest good to society, the doctor made the decision using a utilitarianism theory.

Kantian Ethics—Duty-Based Ethics

Kantian ethics Rules of behavior apply universally to everyone. People are not to be treated as a means to an end but as an end in themselves.

Immanuel Kant argued that moral action is determined by reason and demands obedience to universal rules because they arise from reason. One should act as if one is willing to have everyone else act in the same manner. His theory of ethical action requires asking the question, "*What if everyone acted this way?*" A Kantian would argue that a rational person will act as all others do in common situations. A person acts in a certain way because all other rational people *ought* to behave in the same way, despite our inclinations to do otherwise. Such moral actions must be followed, because if they are not, humanity is harmed.

Kant argued that rational people use reasoning and common sense to reach ethical decisions; they do so through free will. These rules are rational conclusions made after observation of and reflection on human behaviors. These conclusions are deemed universal rules governing human actions. They are based upon two important principles, namely, *consistency* (all problems are decided alike without exception) and *reversibility* (the actor must follow the rules imposed upon others to judge the morality of their acts).

Kant believed that humans were of unique dignity and that all persons are to be considered equals, regardless of their station in life, and therefore the law should treat all persons in the same manner. He argued that rational humans should be treated as an end in themselves and not as a means to something. Thus, respect for human life has value.

Kant defined the ideals of moral law through his "categorical imperative." The categorical imperative is an absolute nonnegotiable universal moral law that is applied regardless of the outcomes. It is imperative because it is something a person must do. It is categorical because it applies always and in all circumstances. The categorical imperative provides that the right moral choice is the one that could become a universal law without creating a logical fallacy. For example, we obey the law because it is universal and necessary to govern society.

Kantian ethics holds that we are not responsible for the outcomes (or consequences) of our acts because it is the intention of our actions that defines the moral action to undertake. To give an example, saving another's life is morally correct even when the life saved is that of a heinous criminal.

> **Example:** A familiar framing of this theory is the trolley problem. Suppose a runaway trolley is approaching five people tied up on the railway tracks. There is also a separate track where one person is tied up on the railway tracks. You have the choice to move a lever to divert the trolley to the other track, but if you do so, the one person on that other track will be killed as a result. Kantian ethics would forbid taking control of the lever to divert the trolley to the other track. Respect for life requires that one should not take the life of one person to save the lives of five others. A Kantian would argue the decision to kill another human being is always immoral.

Critics of this theory argue that it lacks context. Context defeats the universality of rules. They argue that sometimes bad behavior should be condoned for the benefits achieved. For example, it is acceptable for some lives to be lost during clinical research trials if the results of the trials save the lives of many others. Sometimes, the ends do matter to us. Despite its critics, Kantian ethics remains an influential force among contemporary thinkers.

Rawls's social justice theory
As rational, equal, and free persons we begin from an original position of equality and ignorance. Such ignorance motivates us to choose to act fairly.

Rawls's Social Justice Theory

John Rawls was a philosopher and proponent of what became known as **Rawls's social justice theory**. Influenced by Kant's theories, Rawls argued that a just society was one of fairness. In his view, we should enact rules that would apply prior to the formation of a society; that is, what society would we construct if we all faced a *veil of ignorance*? This veil would shield us from knowing our attributes and our place in society, and, thus, everyone would begin from a position of equality. This veil should protect the most vulnerable in our society because in the beginning, we do not know if we are within the vulnerable group. We would not know who we would become, as we would remain in ignorance of our status.

This conception of "justice as fairness" recognizes equality of rights and opportunity and promotion of the less advantaged members of society. Each person is presumed to have entered into a social contract with the others in society. This social contract demands that individuals follow moral rules and act in a way that is necessary to promote peace and harmony. We are motivated to help society's disadvantaged because we might find ourselves in that position. Utilitarian views of maximizing utility (wealth, for example) have no place within Rawls's philosophy because justice is the criterion by which goods and services are to be distributed.

Rawls's theory provides that those who are the least advantaged can set the standard for justice. Each person should be treated as having worth and importance, and it is immoral to consider them otherwise. Ideally, attainment of equality in our liberties should be sought, followed by equal opportunity so far as is practical. Rawls would then apply a *difference principle* that permits diverging from strict equality so long as the inequalities would make the least advantaged persons in society materially better off than they would be under strict equality, for example where a wealthy person gifts their wealth to disadvantaged populations. The theory of justice requires fairness in decision making and the consequences of that process.

> **Example:** The COVID-19 pandemic greatly impacted employees. Businesses that made downsizing decisions could have been aided by using this theory of justice. If downsizing was necessary, who should be terminated and when were questions to be answered from a veil of ignorance. That means the decision maker should decide what's fair to all those impacted because the decision maker does not know if they, themselves, might be retained, terminated, or demoted. Fairness is paramount.

Critics of this theory insist that it is not possible to be blind to our station in life. It is inherently wrong to redistribute goods within a legal system based upon property rights. This theory ignores the reality of how wealth is created, and under it the products of personal industry are replaced by the coercive effects of mandated fairness. It is not the province of government to grant everyone a right of entitlement to the distribution of goods and services. Nevertheless, Rawls's social justice theory has remained an important component of ethical leadership in establishing inclusion and protecting and promoting the least advantaged within our institutions.

Ethics is "a conception of the person, the relations among persons, and the general goals and ends of social cooperation."—John Rawls, Harvard ethicist, *A Theory of Justice* (1921-2002)

Ethical Relativism

Relativism is generally defined as decision making independent of any framework of absolute rights and wrongs. Individuals decide what is "ethical" based on their own beliefs and norms. As such, relativism lacks an agreed-on core philosophy. If differences of opinion cannot be reconciled, each side has an equal claim to truth and should be recognized as right, each according to their own point of view. Respect for views alien to our own beliefs ought to be recognized. In practice, relativism accepts a wide spectrum of choices and practices.

Relativism
Individuals may decide what is ethical based on their own beliefs about right and wrong.

The weakness of relativism is that nothing is necessarily right or wrong. Its critics argue that it is a theory of no ethics. Relativism would embrace every point of view over time as circumstances changed. It is for this reason that very few philosophers endorse this type of theory as acceptable.

> **Example:** A foreign government official's receipt of a bribe, while not legal, might be a customary practice. Bribes could be ethical under relativism. However, other countries might prosecute that behavior as a crime.

Moral Minimum

Moral minimum A business should pursue profits while avoiding intentional harm.

Another ethical theory is known as the **moral minimum**. Under it, a business should strive to make a profit while avoiding harm to others. Thus, if businesses avoid or correct any injury they cause, the moral minimum has been met.

The law reflects ethics in an imperfect way. The tradition of the law is to react to tragedy and consequence as it does not lead behaviors but responds to them. Moreover, human inventiveness and free choice compound and frustrate the reach and application of the law. Conduct can be illegal only if the prohibited behavior is declared and published in advance of that conduct. Stated differently, the unscrupulous will create schemes and adopt behaviors that evade the reach of the law. The moral minimum theory does not prevent harm, it reacts to it.

> **Example:** A fracking operation that is contaminating local water supplies maintains insurance coverage to pay for any claims made against it arising from its operations for the harm it causes. The operation has met its burden of responding to the harm under the moral minimum theory. What happens when the insurance proceeds are inadequate to remedy the contamination?

Critics of the moral minimum theory argue that if mere avoidance or the correcting of unethical behavior is enough, businesses have no incentive to promote ethical behavior. For example, administrative agencies are empowered to issue rules and regulations governing the operation of businesses. It is within the public interest to ensure that minimal standards are observed by regulated companies. However, if the regulators are unaware of a company's detrimental practices that cause environmental damage, the regulators are blind to the harms that should be prevented. Unless compelled by law to follow stringent standards, competition alone will not cause the businesses to adopt better practices.

Lex iniusta non est lex (An unjust law is not law at all). — St. Augustine (354-430 A.D.)

Maximizing Profits

Maximizing profits The traditional view of corporate social responsibility that the business should strive to maximize profits for a business's shareholders.

Maximizing profits while operating lawfully is what Milton Friedman, a Nobel laureate in economics, argued was a corporation's primary responsibility to its shareholders. He argued that it is the duty of a business to use its resources to increase profits and operate without deception and fraud. One of the unfortunate consequences of doing so is that profit-maximizing practices may replace the promotion of other values. All too often, the over-zealous pursuit of profits has been at the heart of corporate wrongdoing.

Example: Volkswagen® knowingly violated U.S. air-pollution standards despite the risks to which it was exposing its reputation and balance sheet. The justification was that the costs of compliance with the law were too high, so managers chose to develop a software solution to defeat the pollution control systems. VW suffered public embarrassment, a change in management, heavy European and U.S. fines, class action lawsuits, and a loss of its moral leadership in engineering.

Today, executive compensation plans are heavily weighted to provide compensation in the form of stock incentives. This form of executive pay focuses on slashing costs and increasing profitability, which improves the company's public stock price. Corporate boards of directors retain outside compensation consultants who provide opinions justifying the pay demands of the executives. For the most part, there is little accountability in executive compensation.

The following decision of the United States Court of Federal Claims involved a determination that a bidder lacked the requisite integrity and business ethics to be awarded a federal contract. The federal government requires that federal contracts must be awarded to the lowest responsive and responsible bidder. Responsibility involves, among other things, a consideration of "integrity and business ethics." A contractor who is nonresponsible is debarred, meaning it cannot enter into such a contract.

CASE 2.2

FEDERAL CONTRACTORS MUST DEMONSTRATE BUSINESS INTEGRITY

MG ALTUS APACHE CO. v. UNITED STATES

111 Fed. Cl. 425 (2013)

United States Court of Federal Claims

The U.S. Army solicited bids on a federal contract for national trucking services in Afghanistan. MG Altus Apache Company (MG AA) submitted a bid to the U.S. Army. The bid solicitation required that a bidder have a satisfactory record of integrity and business ethics. The Army found that MG AA was nonresponsible due to its prior membership in a joint venture known as MG ALTUS, which had failed to faithfully perform a government contract. MG AA was then informed that it had been eliminated from the bidding competition because it had been determined to be nonresponsible. MG AA then filed a bid protest challenging the U.S. Army's nonresponsibility determination. Following the Army's determination, MG AA appealed to the Court of Federal Claims in Washington, D.C.

Language of the Court. *MG AA alleges that the contracting officer's nonresponsibility determination was unreasonable. MG AA contends that the contracting officer improperly considered the performance occurring in prior contract to evaluate MG AA's integrity qualifications. It was reasonable for the contracting officer to consider performance of a related company on a past contract because that company and the protester shared a common joint venture member with managerial* *responsibilities and the related company's performance, cited as a reference in the protester's proposal, reasonably predicted protester's ability to perform the contract at issue. As the Comptroller General has recognized, the adverse past performance of a prior joint venture may be attributed to a member of the joint venture in a nonresponsibility determination.*

The contracting officer found that MG AA did not satisfy the requirement for a satisfactory record of integrity and business ethics. The contracting officer cited several incidents, which she found showed "a systemic pattern of fraudulent behavior and activity." First, [with reference to the prior joint venture contract], MG AA failed to establish proper internal controls to prevent [contract performance breaches]. Second, she found that with the earlier contract many millions of dollars had been withheld from payment because of performance failures. Third, as to that contract, the contracting officer referred to the submission of false transportation documents. Fourth, the contracting officer noted that MG AA had been referred for proposed debarment based on numerous alleged acts of criminal misconduct such as forgery and false claims, and violations of federal law further substantiating MG AA's integrity issues and lack of business ethics. Fifth, a report prepared by a U.S. military intelligence unit concluded it lacked business ethics. Sixth, she referenced intelligence reports indicating that an employee of the prior joint venture attempted to access a military facility with false identification provided by it. The employee reported that the manager of the prior joint venture had a "standard practice" of providing false identification badges to circumvent base access issues and allow employees to assist in moving cargo quickly.

The contracting officer reasonably determined that performance under the prior contract as a whole raised serious doubts about MG AA's ability to perform the subject contract. These findings were sufficient to justify the contracting officer's conclusion that MG AA was nonresponsible. MG AA's arguments that it subsequently improved its nonperformance do not alter the evidence that such misconduct occurred. Federal regulations do not require that each of the contracting officer's conclusions be independently sufficient on its own to support a finding of nonresponsibility. Rather, the contracting officer's nonresponsibility determination as a whole must be rational. Even acknowledging those instances where the contracting officer was imprecise in her assessment of prior performance, the cumulative failures on the prior contract provided a reasonable basis for the contracting officer's business judgment that MG AA lacked the requisite business integrity, ethics, and perseverance to perform the subject contract.

Decision. The court found that the contracting officer's reliance upon the facts in the record was rational and that MG AA had been afforded due process. The award to another contractor was recognized.

Focus on Ethics

Why is it ethical for the government to consider past performance as a predictor of a bidder's future performance under a proposed contract?

Corporate Social Responsibility

Corporate social responsibility (CSR) is a broadly defined concept that measures the impact a business has upon society. The term corporate citizenship is often used interchangeably with CSR; however, corporate citizenship is used in reference to the company's legal responsibilities.

Corporate social responsibility (CSR) Corporations should act ethically and be accountable to their communities for their actions.

CSR is an ethical and operating model promoting the achievement of a social benefit in addition to making a profit while following the law. CSR proposes that businesses have a responsibility to act as good citizens and do good by the community. While CSR is not required of corporations, proponents of this theory argue that businesses should do their best to help solve social problems, even if they did not contribute to such problems.

CSR recognizes that corporations have significant influence within our society. Businesses are an important social organization providing benefits to the members of our society; these include personal employment, financial support and fringe benefits, public revenues through taxation of their revenues, and the creation of wealth for their owners, the shareholders. Corporate social responsibility urges that the corporation be operated to produce higher standards of living and improve the quality of life for the communities in which they operate.

Stakeholder Those who are immediately affected by the decisions that a business makes.

> **Example:** Lyft, Inc. incorporates corporate social responsibility in its business purpose. It acknowledges that individuals, millennials in particular, gravitate towards brands that value community engagement and embrace social and environmental responsibility. Further, Lyft Inc registration statements state "88% of millennials expect companies to produce and communicate the results of corporate social responsibility efforts, and 89% of consumers are likely to switch brands to one that is associated with a good cause, given similar price and quality." *In re Lyft Inc. Securities. Litigation*, 2020 U.S. Dist. LEXIS 163601

Stakeholder theory Another view of Corporate Social Responsibility. Provides that businesses must consider the effects the decision will have upon the stakeholders and should provide the stakeholders the opportunity to participate in managing those decisions.

Stakeholder Theory

Another view of CSR is the **stakeholder theory**. Stakeholders are the people who will be affected by the company's actions. The stakeholder theory provides that businesses must consider the effects the decision will have upon the stakeholders (employees, customers, suppliers, creditors, and the community) and should provide them the opportunity to participate in managing those decisions. In some circumstances, the stakeholders may be more greatly impacted by a corporation's decision making than the company's shareholders. The biggest criticism of this theory is that all businesses deal with limited funding, and it is difficult to balance the interests of conflicting stakeholders. The corporation must be selective in its outreach activities due to its limitations of capital.

Take care of your employees and they will take care of your business. It's as simple as that. —Richard Branson, entrepreneur, investor, and philanthropist (1950-)

Ethical Theories

Virtue-based ethics	Focusing on character habits that contribute to a good human life.
Ethical fundamentalism	Decisions should be made according to sources such as religious traditions and prior company policies and procedures.
Utilitarianism	Decisions should be made based upon their social consequences—maximizing utility.
Kantian ethics	Principles and rights must be applied. Consequences are ignored.
Rawls's social justice theory	Fairness is the essence of justice. What is just should be chosen by persons who do not yet know their station in society—they are behind a veil of ignorance. Also, the least advantaged must receive special assistance to allow them to realize their equal opportunity.
Ethical relativism	Individuals may decide what is ethical based on their own beliefs about right and wrong.
Moral minimum	At the very least, corporations should avoid causing harm. If they do cause harm, the moral minimum requires them to compensate for any harm caused.
Maximizing profits	Businesses should focus their efforts upon maximizing profits while operating legally.
Corporate social responsibility	Corporations have the moral and legal responsibility to do well by using their resources to alleviate social problems.
Stakeholder theory	Stakeholders should be able to influence business decisions.

Management Application An Early View of the Purpose of a Corporation

An early view of the purpose of the corporation was expressed in the 1919 *Dodge v. Ford* decision of the Michigan Supreme Court. In this case, the court considered the claim of John and Horace Dodge, who later founded the Dodge automobile business. As Ford shareholders, they sued Ford to continue to pay dividends to the shareholders, which Henry Ford had stopped. It was Ford's view that the available cash generated from operations should be used instead to build more plants to increase production, increase employee compensation, and reduce the consumer price of Ford vehicles. The court allowed Ford's expansion plans to proceed but ordered the release of millions of dollars to be paid to the shareholders. Otherwise, the failure to declare and pay a shareholder dividend would constitute fraud upon the shareholders.

The court stated: "A business corporation is organized and carried on primarily for the profit of the stockholders. The powers of the directors are to be employed for that end. . . . [T]he directors have discretion 'to be used in good faith' in the exercise of their best judgment in deciding on 'the infinite details of business, including the wages which shall be paid to employees, the number of hours they shall work, the conditions under which the labor shall be carried on, and the prices for which products shall be offered to the public.'"

The Process of Reaching an Ethical Decision

The approaches discussed below will provide a reasoned decision of *why* we should act ethically.

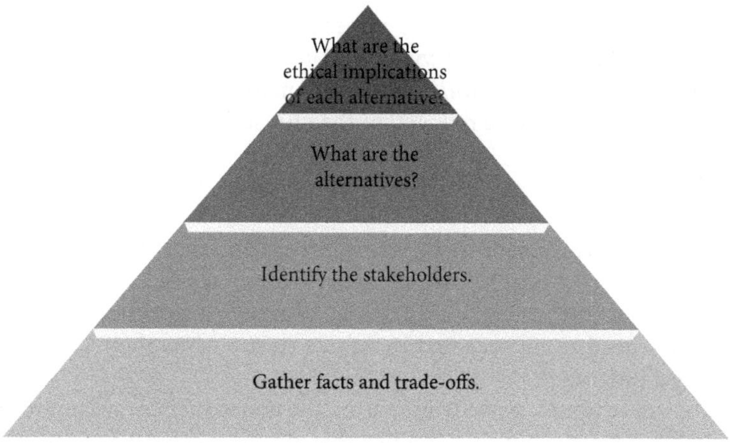

First, recognize that an ethical issue exists.

- *Gather the relevant facts.* Investigate to obtain and confirm the relevant facts. Not doing so may oversimplify the problem to be solved.
- *Identify the stakeholders.* They are those people immediately impacted by the proposed decision. Are some of their concerns more important than others?
- *What are the alternatives and their consequences?* In considering the alternatives, the attributes of each and their outcomes are identified. What values are involved?

- *What are the ethical implications of each alternative?* While identifying alternative actions, many businesses should simultaneously consider the ethical implications of each alternative.

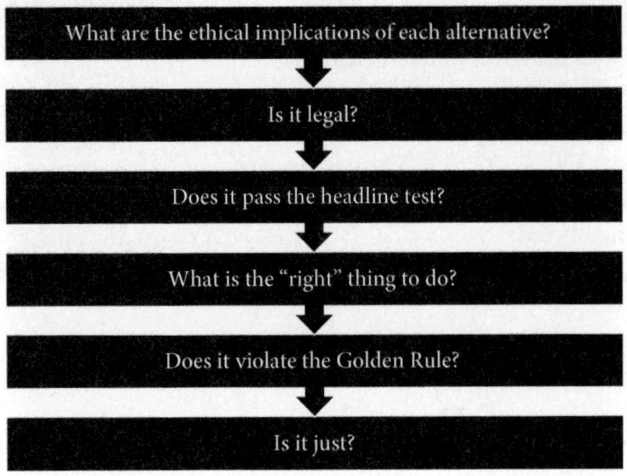

We do not err because truth is difficult to see. It is visible at a glance. We err because this is more comfortable. — Alexander Solzhenitsyn, Russian novelist, philosopher, and political prisoner (1918-2008)

- *Determine the legality of the proposed alternatives.* Generally, it is ethical to do what is legally permitted, but that alone may not be what we *should* do.
- *Does the action pass the headline test?* If we could reduce the proposed action to a few words, *is this an honorable act*?
- *Is it the "right" thing to do?* This is a question reflective of personal experiences and a consideration of others' views.
- *Does it violate the Golden Rule?* The three major religions embrace an ethic of reciprocity, which may be reduced to the phrase "*treat others as you want to be treated.*"
- *Is it just?*

When a difficult decision must be made, an organized approach, one applying ethical principles, is preferred. Otherwise, the following may occur:

- A person's need to be accepted by others overwhelms their independence in reaching a judgment.
- Euphemisms disguise painful outcomes (the consequences are not recognized).
- Reliance is placed upon generalities that do not account for the details of a situation.
- Arrogant ignorance may exist. Some people may lack the humility to consider the circumstances of others. They may be blinded by their relative positions of power, their age, or even their wealth. They may demand a quick solution because they simply "know more."
- Financial considerations push ethics aside; however, an ethics-based decision may offer a more effective and efficient outcome.

Sometimes, relational comparisons will be made when ethics is broached in a business meeting. Attendees will use similes that are logically unsound. In other forums, the impact upon stakeholders will be mischaracterized. There can be many causes for such results, which may be attributable to time constraints, implicit biases, or a lack of information.

Corporate Compliance and Culture The Use of Nudges

Nudges are positive reinforcements and indirect suggestions to influence desirable behavior and decision making. Corporations are liable for the acts of their agents under the theory of *respondeat superior*, so they are eager to deter their agents from wrongdoing. To promote good choices, nudges can come in the form of reminders, training, issue framing, and policy enforcement.

Management Application Dealing with a Business Crisis

When dealing with a business crisis, here are some tips that a business can follow to minimize the negative impacts.

- Show genuine concern for the crisis.
- Be honest and upfront with consumers and the government.
- Be prepared for public outrage.

Management Application Special Purpose Corporations

Most states have enacted laws that permit and promote the use of special corporate forms. One form, known as a benefit corporation, has an expanded purpose beyond maximizing shareholder value — to consider general and specific public benefits. One of the important features of such an organization is that the directors and officers are allowed to consider the interests of stakeholders in their operational decision making. Benefit corporations can only be for-profit organizations.

Example: King Arthur Flour®, Patagonia®, and Kickstarter® are examples of benefit corporations.

A similar organization, the certified B corporation, is an entity holding a certificate from a third party, which audits the entity's social and environmental performance against a third-party standard.

Example: Ben & Jerry's®, New Belgium Brewing®, and Allbirds, Inc.® are examples of certified B corporations.

Another similar organization is the social purpose corporation, which has been recognized in a few states. Typically, this form of corporation would allow its shareholders and directors to put a social purpose (such as promoting environmental causes) above the purpose of making a profit. That is, it can pursue social purposes along with maximizing profits. It is a for-profit organization that does not qualify for tax-exempt status as a nonprofit corporation.

Example: HydroBee SPC® is a company engaged in creating new renewable energy platforms and product lines in the State of Washington.

A related entity is the public benefit corporation. It must be formed for public or charitable purposes and may not be organized for the private gain of any person. A public benefit corporation cannot distribute profits, gains, or dividends to any person. Public benefit corporations often qualify for exemption from income tax.

Example: Amtrak®, the United States Postal Service®, and the Corporation for Public Broadcasting® are public benefit corporations created by the federal government.

Conduct an internet search to evaluate how well these initiatives are fulfilling their purpose. Is there less enthusiasm to form and operate such entities, if so, why?

Developing an Ethical Business Culture

Mission statement
A formal summary of the aims and values of a company, organization, or individual.

Companies seeking to develop an ethical business culture may create and follow a mission statement. A company's **mission statement** communicates to employees and third persons in a concise manner the company's purpose and goals. Well-written mission statements should explain what your company does for its customers, employees, and owners. Some companies may include in their mission statement what the company does for the community (local, regional, national) and, if applicable, the world.

Example: The Walt Disney Company's mission statement provides: "The mission of The Walt Disney Company is to entertain, inform and inspire people around the globe through the power of unparalleled storytelling, reflecting the iconic brands, creative minds and innovative technologies that make ours the world's premier entertainment company."

Associated with mission statements are a company's core values. **Core values** are the values through which the business pursues its mission. These core values apply to all the company's business transactions with its stakeholders.

Core values
The fundamental beliefs of a person or organization that dictate behavior and can help people understand the difference between right and wrong.

Example: Google's values are expressed in the following philosophies: (1) Focus on the user and all else will follow; (2) It's best to do one thing really, really well; (3) Fast is better than slow; (4) Democracy on the web works; (5) You don't need to be at your desk to need an answer; (6) You can make money without doing evil; (7) There's always more information out there; (8) The need for information crosses all borders; (9) You can be serious without a suit; and (10) Great just isn't good enough.

Once a business has a mission statement and core values, it is the responsibility of both the management and employees of the organization to strive to uphold those values in their interactions with their various stakeholders, including customers, competitors, and shareholders.

Company's Code of Conduct (Ethics)

An effective way for companies to promote and develop an ethical business culture is to create and abide by a code of conduct (also known as a code of ethics). A company's **code of conduct** is a written document describing the company's core values and the ethical behavior in which the company expects its managers, employees, suppliers, and customers to engage. Effective codes of conduct reiterate the company's commitment to ethical behavior.

Code of conduct
A written set of guidelines describing the company's core values and the manner in which the company expects its managers, employees, suppliers, and customers to act.

Some types of companies are nudged to have a code of conduct. To reduce corporate fraud, Congress enacted the Sarbanes-Oxley Act of 2002. The Act requires publicly held companies to disclose whether they have adopted a code of ethics for senior financial officers. Companies that have not adopted a code of ethics are required to explain why they have not done so.[1] The Act defines a code of ethics to mean standards necessary to promote "honest and ethical conduct, including the ethical handling of actual or apparent conflicts of interest between personal and professional relationships."

Further, publicly held companies that are listed on the New York Stock Exchange and the Nasdaq Stock Market are required to have codes of ethics governing the conduct of all their directors, officers, and employees, and to disclose any waivers granted to directors and executive officers.

For a code of conduct to be effective, the company must adequately train employees on ethics, and management must buy into, abide by, and be held accountable to the standards set forth in a code of conduct. Companies can create incentives to motivate employees to live up to the core values and follow the code of ethics. To reinforce a code of ethics, companies should reward employees for ethical behavior and have a reporting mechanism whereby employees and third parties (such as suppliers and customers) can report unethical conduct. In many companies, implementation of and compliance with a company's code of ethics is the responsibility of the chief compliance officer.

1. Sarbanes-Oxley Act § 406.

AI Feature: Which Industrial Plant to Close?

Using an AI program, use ethical principles to determine which one of two industrial plants you will recommend to the Chief Executive Officer (CEO) of your United States based company to close. One is in the United States with higher labor costs than a second plant located in India. Assume all other considerations are equal between the two locations. Did the program weigh the ethical considerations as you would have done without its assistance? To what extent does ethical theory lend itself to such decision making? Explain your answer and alternatives to consider other than a cost-benefit analysis.

Key Terms

- Code of conduct (ethics), 35
- Core values, 35
- Corporate social responsibility (CSR), 29
- Ethical fundamentalism, 21
- Ethics, 18
- Kantian ethics, 23
- Maximizing profits, 26
- Mission statement, 34
- Moral minimum, 26
- Organizational culture, 20
- Rawls's social justice theory, 24
- Relativism, 25
- Stakeholder, 29
- Stakeholder theory, 29
- Utilitarianism, 23
- Virtue-based ethics, 20

Applying Ethics to the Law

2.1 When and What Material Information to Disclose? Since the 1930s, public companies have operated under the materiality standard. It is a foundational premise in U.S. corporate and securities laws that public companies have an obligation to publicly disclose to prospective investors and existing shareholders information important to making an informed investment or stock vote decision. Is it ethical that this duty applies only to publicly traded companies? Conduct research using an internet search engine to identify and describe recent corporate ethical breaches that led to securities law violations.

2.2 Corporate Vision and Mission Statements. Since the adoption of websites by U.S. businesses, American companies have been engaged in marketing their commitment to ethical values. Conduct a review of five publicly traded companies across industries. What do these statements have in common? Is there one that suggests that the company has a deep commitment to acting ethically? Being aware that mistakes are inevitable in the operation of businesses, are there any businesses that you have identified which have "repurposed" their mission statements in response to recent crises they have encountered?

2.3 Focusing on Shareholder Value. Proponents of maximizing shareholder value argue that doing so maximizes organizational efficiency. Using an internet search engine, research the concept that a business exists to promote the creation of shareholder wealth. Then, survey the corporate scandals of the last few decades. It has been observed that the intense focus on short-term earnings, among other things, neglects capital investment, fails to mitigate environmental issues, and promotes the exploitation of workers, all to permit corporate profits to soar. Provide a written statement reflecting your thoughts on the role shareholder value has played in the societal and economic problems we currently face.

2.4 The Role of CSR and ESG. Corporate social responsibility (CSR) is the business effort to improve through its operations the conditions of its employees, its customers, the environment, and the community at large. Environmental, social, and governance (ESG) criteria are the tools to measure the results of the company's actions. They present a set of practices and metrics that are used to evaluate their impact on the environment, social, and governance bodies, while maintaining financial performance. The goal of ESG is to identify a company's non-financial risks and opportunities. Using an internet search engine, identify some for-profit corporations that prominently incorporate these matters into their statements of business purpose.

2.5 Presidential Persuasion. In response to the short-term focus upon earnings, corporations have transferred the production of goods to overseas suppliers. Increased operating efficiencies through well-managed supply chains have contributed to the strength of the American economy. However, doing so has come at many societal costs, including affordable housing for workers, factory closings, and the loss of employment in domestic industries. Using an internet search engine, identify corporate initiatives to correct these imbalances. Additionally, are there any lasting successes following the efforts of American Presidents to persuade domestic industries to keep their U.S.-based factories open?

2.6 Tax System. Tax law can both promote and discourage behaviors. If you were to revise American tax law to promote ethical behavior, what one issue would you suggest to improve the ethical behavior of American businesses? How would your suggestion encourage accountability in executive decision making?

2.7 The Decline in Moral Leadership. Through an internet search, review the sordid history of Purdue Pharma L.P. Consider the role of others within the health care system who contributed to America's opioid epidemic. Did these other actors abandon ethics in exchange for compensation from drug companies? See, for example, *https://www.ncbi.nlm.nih.gov/pmc/articles/PMC6139931/*.

2.8 Coronavirus Business Impact. Conduct an internet search for well-balanced discussions about how COVID-19 impacted American and international businesses. What operational and human resource issues continue to challenge businesses in its aftermath? To what degree does business ethics play a role in providing solutions or pathways to engagement with stakeholders?

2.9 The #MeToo Movement. Using an internet search engine, identify the reasons for the long history of sexual abuse, harassment, and lack of respect for women in the entertainment industry. Describe the culture that perpetuated these practices.

2.10 DEI. Conduct internet research as to the emphasis publicly held companies are placing upon diversity, equity, and inclusion initiatives. Are they being implemented? What arguments are being made on both sides for their adoption (or lack of inclusion)? Using an AI program, prepare a draft policy for adoption by a public corporate board of directors in the context of the current political climate.

Courts, Litigation, and Alternative Dispute Resolution

3

A long dispute means that both parties are wrong. — Voltaire, French author (1694-1778)

Chapter Outline

- Introduction
- Standing
- Jurisdiction

Case 3.1: *Ford Motor Co. v. Montana Eighth Judicial District*

- *Management Application: Personal Jurisdiction Factors*

Case 3.2: *Coinbase, Inc., Petitioner v. David Suski, et al.*

- *Management Application: Choice of Law Rules*

- Venue
- The State and Federal Court Systems
  - *Management Application: Specialized U.S. Courts*
- Civil Litigation and Procedure
- Alternative Dispute Resolution
  - *Management Application: Other Forms of ADR*
- AI Feature: Drafting an Arbitration Provision

Learning Objectives

After studying this chapter, you should be able to:

1. Explain the concept of personal jurisdiction.
2. State when a federal court has subject matter jurisdiction.
3. Distinguish between federal and state court systems.
4. Describe the litigation process.
5. Identify the requirements for a class action.
6. Describe the types of alternative dispute resolution.

Introduction

Disputes among individuals and businesses arise constantly. Negligent and intentional acts, breaches of contract, and disputes over property and individual rights arise every day. The court

Judiciary system
The system of courts that interpret and apply the laws and provide a forum for dispute resolution.

or **judiciary system** exist to provide a forum for interpretation and application of the law, resolving the present disputes that are left for determination. In this chapter, we review how the judiciary system operates on the federal and state levels, the procedures adopted by these tribunals to effectively manage the resolution of these disputes, and what rights to appeal may exist from an adverse determination at the trial court level of the court system. Finally, we will discuss the nonjudicial process of alternative dispute resolution.

Standing

Standing
A legal requirement that a party must have a sufficient stake in the outcome of the controversy to seek relief from a court.

Before a claimant may file a case in a court, that person must have **standing**; that is, the party must have a sufficient stake in the outcome of an actual controversy to be permitted to file the lawsuit. The **plaintiff** (the party who files a lawsuit) must have suffered or be threatened with an injury, damage, or loss. Without standing to seek relief from the court, the case is dismissed.

Plaintiff
The party who files a lawsuit.

Jurisdiction

Jurisdiction
The authority of a court or agency to make a legal determination regarding a person or the property of another person.

In addition to having standing, the plaintiff must file the lawsuit with a court that has jurisdiction. **Jurisdiction** is the power of a court to receive evidence relating to the dispute and render a final judgment that binds the parties to the proceeding. To have jurisdiction, a court must have:

- Subject matter jurisdiction, *and*
- Jurisdiction over the parties by either:
  - Personal jurisdiction over the parties to the suit, or
  - *In rem* jurisdiction.

Subject Matter Jurisdiction

Subject matter jurisdiction
The authority of a court to hear a type of dispute.

Subject matter jurisdiction is the power of a court to hear a particular type of dispute. The scope of this power may be limited or general. General subject matter jurisdiction allows courts to decide all other types of disputes. For example, contract and real property disputes are decided in trial courts with general subject matter jurisdiction. In contrast, if a court has limited subject matter jurisdiction, it may only decide specific types of cases. For example, criminal courts can only decide matters involving offenses committed against society. Family law courts may address matters relating to adoption, divorce, and child and spousal support. Later in this chapter we discuss the differences between the subject matter jurisdiction of federal and state courts.

Jurisdiction over the Parties

A court may have jurisdiction over the parties (plaintiff and defendant) through either personal jurisdiction (jurisdiction over a person) or through *in rem* jurisdiction (jurisdiction over the "thing").

PERSONAL JURISDICTION. A court must have **personal** (or *in personam*) **jurisdiction** over both the plaintiff and defendant. The court obtains jurisdiction over a plaintiff when the plaintiff files a complaint or petition with the court clerk to commence the legal proceedings.

Personal (*in personam*) jurisdiction Personal jurisdiction exists when the court has power over the person(s) participating in the action.

However, jurisdiction over the **defendant** (the party who has been served with a complaint and must respond to the complaint) occurs differently. The court has jurisdiction over a defendant who (1) lives in the state, (2) is present in the state when served, or (3) consents to service in the state. The jurisdiction rules for business entities, as well as limits to personal jurisdiction over nonstate defendants, are discussed below.

Defendant The party who has been served with a complaint and must respond to the complaint.

Business Entity Jurisdiction. A court can exercise personal jurisdiction over business entities (such as corporations and limited liability companies). Business entities are subject to jurisdiction; that is, they can be sued) in a state in which the business entity was incorporated (or organized), has its principal office, or in states in which it conducts business (subject to the minimum contacts test discussed below).

Jurisdiction over Nonresidents. A state court may exercise personal jurisdiction over out-of-state defendants under the state's **long-arm statute**. The long-arm statutes require that the defendant had sufficient *minimum contacts* with the state so that exercising jurisdiction over the nonresident person would not offend traditional notions of fair play and substantial justice (that is, it would be fair to subject the person to jurisdiction in the state). The court will review if the defendant *purposefully availed* itself of the privilege of conducting activities within the state where the court is located. While the minimum contact doctrine depends on the facts of each case, minimum contacts are usually met if the corporation sells (or advertises for sale) products in a state or places its goods into the stream of commerce with the intent that they be sold in the state.

Long-arm statute State statutes that enable state courts to exercise personal jurisdiction over nonresidents, within the bounds of the Constitution.

> **Example:** A business that is incorporated in Delaware and breached a contract in Texas can be subject to personal jurisdiction in Texas because it has sufficient minimum contacts to be sued in Texas since it *purposefully availed* itself of the privilege of conducting activities within that state.

In the following decision, the Supreme Court clarified when a state court may exercise personal jurisdiction over a nonresident defendant when none of the defendant's contacts with that state were the cause of the plaintiff's claims. The Court analyzed how a defendant's activities in a forum state may be exposed to suit in that state.

CASE 3.1

A STATE COURT MAY EXERCISE JURISDICTION WHEN THE SUIT ARISES OUT OF THE DEFENDANT'S CONTACTS WITH THE FORUM

FORD MOTOR CO. v. MONTANA EIGHTH JUDICIAL DISTRICT

592 U.S. 351 (2021)

Supreme Court of the United States

In 2015, Markkaya Jean Gullett, a Montana resident, was driving a Ford Explorer on a Montana highway when the tread on one of her tires separated. She lost control of the vehicle and died because the vehicle rolled into a ditch.

The personal representative of Gullett's estate sued Ford Motor Co.® in Montana state court, alleging design defect, failure-to-warn as a product defect claim, and negligence claims. Ford moved to dismiss the claims for lack of personal jurisdiction. The case was consolidated for hearing before the Supreme Court with a Ford case involving a 1994 Crown Victoria, pending in Minnesota. In these state actions, Ford argued that prior Supreme Court decisional law provided that each state court would have jurisdiction over it only if Ford's conduct in the state gave rise to the plaintiff's claims. It claimed that a causal link to Ford's activities would occur only if the company had designed, manufactured, or sold in the state the particular vehicles involved in the accidents. Ford asserted that the vehicles were designed and manufactured elsewhere and that the company had originally sold the cars outside the forum states. Only later resales and consumer relocations brought the vehicles to Montana and Minnesota.

The supreme courts of the two states rejected Ford's argument. Ford appealed to the Supreme Court on the grounds that such holdings violated the Due Process Clause. The Court granted *certiorari.*

Language of the Court. *Ford is a global auto company. It is incorporated in Delaware and headquartered in Michigan. But its business is everywhere. Ford markets, sells, and services its products across the United States and overseas. In this country alone, the company annually distributes over 2.5 million new cars, trucks, and SUVs to over 3,200 licensed dealerships. Ford also encourages a resale market for its products: Almost all its dealerships buy and sell used Fords, as well as selling new ones. To enhance its brand and increase its sales, Ford engages in wide-ranging promotional activities, including television, print, online, and direct-mail advertisements. No matter where you live, you've seen them: "Have you driven a Ford lately?" or "Built Ford Tough." Ford also ensures that consumers can keep their vehicles running long past the date of sale. The company provides original parts to auto supply stores and repair shops across the country. (Goes another slogan: "Keep your Ford a Ford.") And Ford's own network of dealers offers an array of maintenance and repair services, thus fostering an ongoing relationship between Ford and its customers.*

The Fourteenth Amendment's Due Process Clause limits a state court's power to exercise jurisdiction over a defendant. The canonical decision in this area remains International Shoe Co. v. Washington, *326 U.S. 310 (1945). There, the Court held that a tribunal's authority depends on the defendant's having such "contacts" with the forum State that "the maintenance of the suit" is "reasonable, in the context of our federal system of government," and "does not offend traditional notions of fair play and substantial justice." In giving content to that formulation, the Court has long focused on the nature and extent of the defendant's relationship to the forum State. That focus led to our recognizing two kinds of personal jurisdiction: general (sometimes called all-purpose) jurisdiction and specific (sometimes called case-linked) jurisdiction.*

A state court may exercise general jurisdiction only when a defendant is "essentially at home" in the State. General jurisdiction, as its name implies, extends to "any and all claims" brought against a defendant. Those claims need not relate to the forum State or the defendant's activity there; they may concern events and conduct anywhere in the world. But that breadth imposes a correlative limit: Only a select "set of affiliations with a forum" will expose a defendant to such sweeping jurisdiction.

In what we have called the "paradigm" case, an individual is subject to general jurisdiction in her place of domicile. And the "equivalent" forums for a corporation are its place of incorporation and principal place of business. Leaving open the possibility that, in an exceptional case, a corporation might also be "at home" elsewhere. So general jurisdiction over Ford (as all parties agree) attaches in Delaware and Michigan — not in Montana and Minnesota.

Specific jurisdiction is different: It covers defendants less intimately connected with a State, but only as to a narrower class of claims. The contacts needed for this kind of jurisdiction often go by the name "purposeful availment." The defendant must take some act by which [it] purposefully avails itself of the privilege of conducting activities within the forum State. The contacts must be the defendant's own choice and not random, isolated, or fortuitous. They must show that the defendant deliberately "reached out beyond" its home — by, for example, "exploi[ting] a market" in the forum State or entering a contractual relationship centered there. Yet even then — because the defendant is not "at home" — the forum State may exercise jurisdiction in only certain cases. The plaintiff's claims, we have often stated, must arise out of or relate to the defendant's contacts with the forum. Or put just a bit differently, "there must be 'an affiliation between the forum and the underlying controversy, principally, an activity or an occurrence that takes place in the forum State and is therefore subject to the State's regulation.' "

Ford's claim is instead that those activities do not sufficiently connect to the suits, even though the resident-plaintiffs allege that Ford cars malfunctioned in the forum States. In Ford's view, the needed link must be causal in nature: Jurisdiction attaches "only if the defendant's forum conduct gave rise to the plaintiff's claims." And that rule reduces, Ford thinks, to locating specific jurisdiction in the State where Ford sold the car in question, or else the States where Ford designed and manufactured the vehicle. On that view, the place of accident and injury is immaterial. So (Ford says) Montana's and Minnesota's courts have no power over these cases.

But Ford's causation-only approach finds no support in this Court's requirement of a "connection" between a plaintiff's suit and a defendant's activities. That rule indeed serves to narrow the class of claims over which a state court may exercise specific jurisdiction. But not quite so far as Ford wants. None of our precedents has suggested that only a strict causal relationship between the defendant's in-state activity and the litigation will do. As just noted, our most common formulation of the rule demands that the suit "arise out of or relate to the defendant's contacts with the forum." The first half of that standard asks about causation; but the back half, after the "or," contemplates that some relationships will support jurisdiction without a causal showing. That does not mean anything goes. In the sphere of specific jurisdiction, the phrase "relate to" incorporates real limits, as it must to adequately protect defendants foreign to a forum. But again, we have never framed the specific jurisdiction inquiry as always requiring proof of causation—i.e., proof that the plaintiff's claim came about because of the defendant's in-state conduct.

Allowing jurisdiction in these cases treats Ford fairly, as this Court's precedents explain. In conducting so much business in Montana and Minnesota, Ford enjoys the benefits and protection of [their] laws—the enforcement of contracts, the defense of property, the resulting formation of effective markets. All that assistance to Ford's in-state business creates reciprocal obligations—most relevant here, that the car models Ford so extensively markets in Montana and Minnesota be safe for their citizens to use there.

Here, resident-plaintiffs allege that they suffered in-state injury because of defective products that Ford extensively promoted, sold, and serviced in Montana and Minnesota. For all the reasons we have given, the connection between the plaintiffs' claims and Ford's activities in those States—or otherwise said, the "relationship among the defendant, the forum[s], and the litigation"—is close enough to support specific jurisdiction. The judgments of the Montana and Minnesota Supreme Courts are therefore affirmed.

Decision. In its decision, the Court held the state courts properly exercised personal jurisdiction over Ford because of the connection between the plaintiffs' product-liability claims arising from car accidents occurring in each plaintiff's state of residence and Ford's activities in those states.

Focus on Ethics

In concurring opinions, three justices argued against the majority's focus on the phrase "relate to" the defendant's activities because it may lead to "needless complications." Is the "relating to a defendant's activities" standard too broad to give fair notice to businesses considering whether to do business in another jurisdiction?

Jurisdiction over Online Businesses. The Supreme Court established the **sliding scale standard** to determine when it is appropriate to exercise personal jurisdiction over an out-of-state defendant that operates online. The sliding scale standard divides defendants into three categories:

Sliding scale standard
The test courts use to determine when it is appropriate to exercise personal jurisdiction over online businesses.

1. When the defendant *primarily* does its business over the internet, including things like executing contracts and conducting sales online. In this category, it is proper to assert *personal jurisdiction* over the out-of-state online business.
2. When the defendant operates an *interactive* website where a user can exchange information with the host but does not conduct its primary business online. For example, the website permits the user to insert personal data from which other features may be explored. An example might be a financial institution website, which might screen applicants for credit cards. In this category, *personal jurisdiction* may be proper if the contact with the state is directly related to the lawsuit.
3. When the defendant operates a *passive* website that only shows information to consumers. In this category, *personal jurisdiction* is never proper.

Example: A manufacturer of lighters located in Pennsylvania brought a claim against a company located in California for trademark infringement. The manufacturer filed the suit in Pennsylvania. The court found that the California company was subject to personal jurisdiction in Pennsylvania because it used a website to actively sell subscriptions to customers in Pennsylvania. *Zippo Mfg. Co. v. Zippo Dot Com, Inc.*, 952 F. Supp. 1119 (W.D. Pa. 1997)

***IN REM* JURISDICTION (JURISDICTION OVER PROPERTY)** ***In rem* jurisdiction** refers to the court's jurisdiction over a piece of property or "thing." A court has *in rem* jurisdiction to determine title to personal or real property. To exercise such jurisdiction the following requirements must be met:

***In rem* jurisdiction**
Refers to the court's jurisdiction over a piece of property or "thing."

- The property must be valuable,
- The property must be located within the court's jurisdiction,
- The court must have control over the property,
- The parties to the proceeding must have sufficient notice of the action and the opportunity to be heard, and
- The state must have an interest in the proceeding.

Example: Two people have a dispute over the title to real property. A court located in the state where the real property is situated could exercise *in rem* jurisdiction.

Forum Selection Clauses

Forum selection clause
A contract provision by which the parties have agreed to the jurisdiction in which a claim may be arbitrated or litigated.

A **forum selection clause** is a provision in a contract by which the parties have agreed in advance to the jurisdiction in which a claim may be litigated or arbitrated. This clause alleviates some of the uncertainty that is present when parties from different jurisdictions execute a contract. By using a forum selection clause, the parties essentially have consented in advance to the jurisdiction where a dispute will be resolved.

In *Bremen v. Zapata Off-Shore Co.*,[1] the Supreme Court indicated that a forum selection clause should be enforced unless enforcement would result in an unreasonable and unjust result. As a result, forum selection clauses are enforceable *unless* the party wishing to move the case to another jurisdiction can show that one or more of the following exceptions exists:

1. The inclusion of the clause in the agreement was the product of fraud or overreaching.
2. The party wishing to set aside the clause would effectively be deprived of their day in court if the clause is enforced.
3. The enforcement of the clause would be contrary to a strong public policy of the forum in which the lawsuit is filed.

Arbitration agreements often include a delegation clause providing that an arbitrator, not a court, should decide threshold questions about the agreement's scope, applicability, and validity. But problems will arise if parties have agreed to two contracts—one sending arbitrability disputes to arbitration, and the other either explicitly or implicitly sending arbitrability disputes to the courts. Such a dispute was the subject of the following case.

CASE 3.2

A PARTY MUST DEMONSTRATE EXCEPTIONAL CIRCUMSTANCES TO JUSTIFY DISREGARDING A FORUM SELECTION CLAUSE

COINBASE, INC. v. SUSKI

602 U.S. _____, 144 S. Ct. 1186 (2024)

Supreme Court of the United States

Coinbase, an online cryptocurrency exchange, launched a sweepstakes that required participants to opt into "Official Rules" with a forum selection clause stipulating exclusive jurisdiction of California courts for related disputes. David Suski and three other users, who had agreed to the "Coinbase User Agreement" containing an arbitration provision when they created their accounts, entered the sweepstakes. Subsequently, they filed a lawsuit against Coinbase alleging violations of California's consumer protection laws. Coinbase sought to compel arbitration based on the User Agreement, but the district court denied Coinbase's motion, interpreting the contractual documents to conclude that the Sweepstakes' Official Rules, with their forum selection clause, took precedence over the User Agreement's arbitration clause. On appeal, the U.S. Court of Appeals for the Ninth Circuit affirmed, concluding that the dispute should be

1. 407 U.S. 1 (1972).

resolved within the California court system as through the Official Rules of the Sweepstakes, not through arbitration as Coinbase had sought. The Court granted *certiorari* to decide which contract dispute resolution term should govern.

Language of the Court. *The parties in this case executed two contracts. The first contained an arbitration provision with a delegation clause; per that provision, an arbitrator must decide all disputes under the contract, including whether a given disagreement is arbitrable. The second contract contained a forum selection clause, providing that all disputes related to that contract must be decided in California courts. Once the sweepstakes concluded, the conflict between these contracts came to a head.*

Coinbase insists that the first contract's delegation clause established the terms by which all subsequent disputes were to be resolved, so the arbitrability of a contract-related dispute between these parties is a matter for the arbitrator to decide. But Coinbase maintains—and the Ninth Circuit held—that the second contract's forum selection clause superseded that prior agreement. This case thus presents the following question: When two such contracts exist, who decides the arbitrability of a contract-related dispute between the parties—an arbitrator or the court?

The Federal Arbitration Act (FAA) reflects the fundamental principle that arbitration is a matter of contract. As a result, arbitration agreements are valid, irrevocable, and enforceable, save upon such grounds as exist at law or in equity for the revocation of any contract. If a court is satisfied that the making of the agreement for arbitration . . . is not in issue, it must send the dispute to an arbitrator. The FAA thereby places arbitration agreements on an equal footing with other contracts.

Given that arbitration agreements are simply contracts, the first principle that underscores all of our arbitration decisions is that arbitration is strictly a matter of consent. Arbitration is "a way to resolve those disputes—but only those disputes—that the parties have agreed to submit to arbitration. Consequently, the first question in any arbitration dispute must be: What have these parties agreed to? Suski and the others each agreed to the User Agreement, complete with the above-quoted arbitration language. If that were the only contract at issue, we would not be deciding this case, since the Arbitration Agreement quite clearly sends to arbitration disputes between Coinbase and its users, including disputes about arbitrability.

In prior cases, we have addressed three layers of arbitration disputes: (1) merits, (2) arbitrability, and (3) who decides arbitrability. This case involves a fourth: What happens if parties have multiple agreements that conflict as to the third-order question of who decides arbitrability?

Thus, the question whether these parties agreed to arbitrate arbitrability can be answered only by determining which contract applies. When we home in on the conflict between the delegation clause in the first contract and forum selection clause in the second, the question is whether the parties agreed to send the given dispute to arbitration—and, per usual, that question must be answered by a court. Under the severability principle, an arbitration [or delegation] provision is severable from the remainder of the contract, and unless the challenge is to the arbitration [or delegation] clause itself, the issue of the contract's validity is considered by the arbitrator in the first instance.

In cases where parties have agreed to only one contract, and that contract contains an arbitration clause with a delegation provision, then, absent a successful challenge to the delegation provision, courts must send all arbitrability disputes to arbitration. But, where, as here, parties have agreed to two contracts — one sending arbitrability disputes to arbitration, and the other either explicitly or implicitly sending arbitrability disputes to the courts — a court must decide which contract governs. To hold otherwise would be to impermissibly "'elevate [a delegation provision] over other forms of contract.'"

Decision. The Supreme Court held where parties have agreed to two contracts — one sending arbitrability disputes to arbitration, and the other either explicitly or implicitly sending arbitrability disputes to the courts — a court must decide which contract governs.

Focus on Ethics

If this dispute involved a forum selection clause in a retail consumer contract, would such a clause be fair to the consumer?

Read Sections 1 and 2 of Article III of the Constitution to review what power is given to the federal courts in the Constitution. https://www.senate.gov/civics/constitution_item/constitution.htm.

Federal Court Subject Matter Jurisdiction

The federal courts have limited jurisdiction because the federal government has limited powers, as will be discussed in Chapter 4. Therefore, a case may be filed in federal court only if the court has *subject matter jurisdiction*. Federal courts have *subject matter jurisdiction* when:

- The case is a *federal question*, or
- There is *diversity of citizenship* among the parties.

Federal question jurisdiction
A case arising under the Constitution, treaties, or federal statutes and regulations.

Diversity of citizenship jurisdiction
A case in which the amount in controversy exceeds $75,000 and all parties to the litigation are citizens of different states, or a citizen of a state and a citizen or a subject of a foreign country.

FEDERAL QUESTION. Federal question jurisdiction (also known as a federal claim) exists when the issue of the case is based substantially on the United States Constitution, a treaty, or federal law. When there is *federal question jurisdiction*, a federal trial court (known as a district court) can hear the case *and the court will apply the relevant federal law, rule, or regulation*. No minimum amount in dispute or controversy is required in a federal question case.

DIVERSITY OF CITIZENSHIP JURISDICTION. A frequent method to obtain federal court jurisdiction is through diversity of citizenship jurisdiction. It arises where the matter in controversy exceeds the sum or value of $75,000, exclusive of costs and interest, and the plaintiff and defendants have complete diversity of citizenship. Diversity of citizenship is commonly met when the plaintiff and defendant are:

- Citizens of different U.S. states; or
- Citizens of a U.S. state and citizens or subjects of a foreign nation.[2]

Example: Fernando, a Texas resident, wants to file a lawsuit against Caleb and Krista, both residents of California, for $100,000 due to damages from a significant automobile accident. Fernando meets the requirements to file in federal court under diversity of citizenship.

As noted above, business entities are residents of the state where they are incorporated (or organized) and where their principal place of business is located. It is possible for a business entity to be a citizen of two states under this test. Because diversity of citizenship jurisdiction requires *complete diversity* among the parties, it is important to determine the citizenship status of a corporation at the time the action is filed against that party.

*In diversity of citizenship jurisdiction cases, f*ederal law applies to procedural issues (processes and procedures), and state law applies to substantive matters (legal rights and duties). Therefore, *the court will apply the relevant state law to the facts.* Generally, the law to be applied by the trial court is the law of the state where the court sits, including its choice of law rules. These rules determine which jurisdiction's laws apply in a case with connections to more than one jurisdiction.

Example: The parties may be from one state, whose laws are directly applicable to the harm suffered, yet the injury took place in another state that is also the location of where the complaint was filed. In such a case, the district court could decide to apply the laws of the nonforum state.

Some jurisdictions analyze different areas of the law, such as torts, real property, and contracts, with specific choice of law rules.

Example: In the area of tort law, subject to exceptions, the traditional rule is that the case will be governed by the specific laws of the particular jurisdiction where the injury to the plaintiff occurred. In another area, such as contracts, in the absence of a choice of law clause agreed upon in a contract, a state court must consider several factors in determining which jurisdiction's laws should apply to a contract dispute. These factors include the residence of all parties involved, the place where the contract was negotiated, the place where the contract was executed, and the place where the contract was to be performed.

---

2. Diversity of citizenship can also be met between (1) citizens of different U.S. states and in cases in which citizens or subjects of a foreign state are additional parties; or (2) a foreign state as plaintiff and citizens of a U.S. state or of different states (e.g., Mexico seeks the return of archeological artifacts unlawfully removed from a national historical site and transported to the United States by an American tourist).

Management Application
Choice of Law Rules

- Sometimes, if a business is sued in a state court and can claim diversity of citizenship jurisdiction, the business may remove the lawsuit to a federal court. Removal transfers the case from state court to the federal court.
- When a federal court is exercising diversity of citizenship jurisdiction, the question of which state's law to apply to the case can arise.
- Depending on the primary issues of the case, the courts weigh several factors to determine which law is the proper one to apply. Those factors include the location of the court, the citizenship of the parties, the location of the injury, or the location where the contract or instrument was signed or was to be performed.
- Known as choice of law rules, these rules minimize the efforts of a plaintiff seeking to file their lawsuit in a state whose law favors its positions. This effort is known as forum shopping.
- A significant problem with choice of law rules is that each state maintains its own rules which, among the states, vary and are not uniformly applied.

Does this rule encourage a party to be the first to file in a jurisdiction with favorable choice of law rules? How can unfairness be prevented?

Exclusive and Concurrent Jurisdiction

Concurrent jurisdiction
When both the federal and state courts have authority over a particular dispute.

Exclusive jurisdiction
When one court system has the only authority to hear a particular dispute.

Concurrent jurisdiction exists when a lawsuit can be brought in either federal or state court. For example, a breach of contract might arise under state law, but if diversity of jurisdiction exists, the case could also be brought in federal court.

Exclusive jurisdiction arises if a case can only be heard in federal court. Cases "arising under" federal law that are within the exclusive jurisdiction of the federal courts include bankruptcy proceedings, patent and copyright disputes, suits against the United States (provided the government has agreed to be a party), federal crimes, and federal antitrust, admiralty, internal revenue, and federal securities issues.

Example: Petitions for relief under the bankruptcy laws are heard only in a federal court.

Concept Summary
Concurrent and Exclusive Jurisdiction

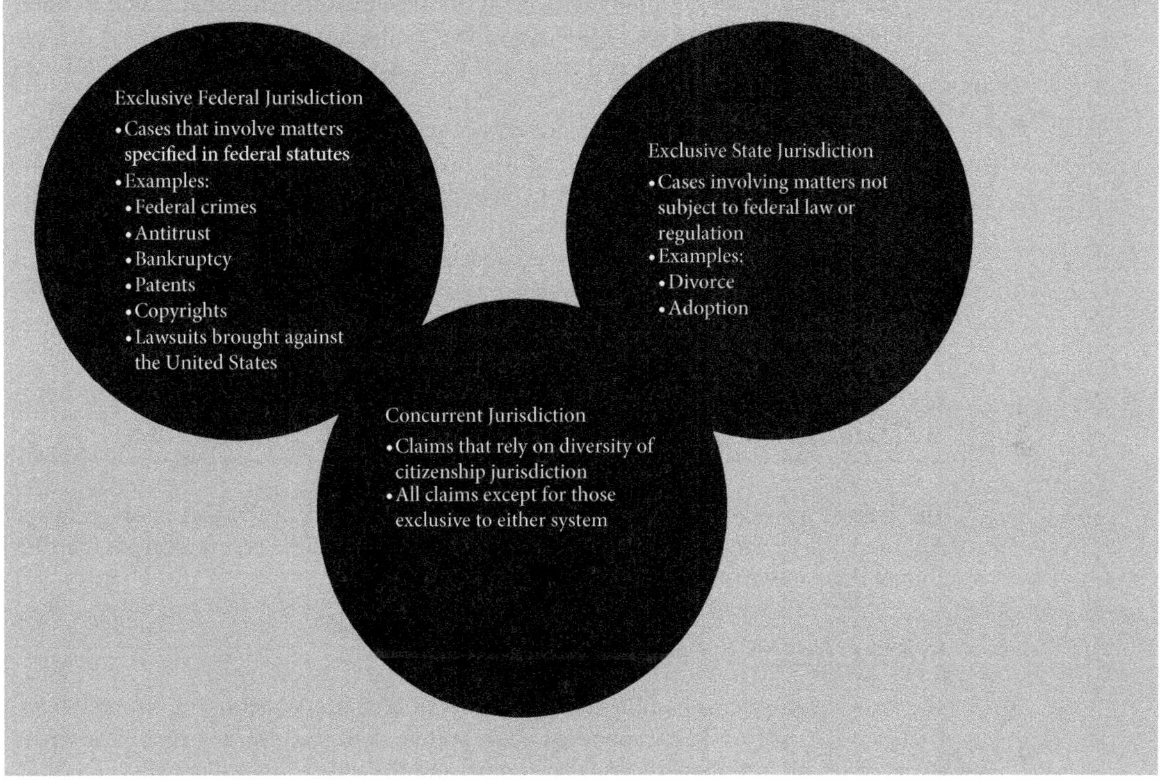

Venue

While jurisdiction is concerned with the authority of a court to hear a case, the concept of **venue** addresses the proper location for a lawsuit to proceed. Venue permits the lawsuit to be transferred to another court having jurisdiction. Generally, in a civil case, this location will be the county in which the defendant resides or the county in which the tort or breach of contract occurred. In a criminal case, venue is proper in the county where the crime occurred. Federal rules exist to determine venue in federal claim and diversity cases.

Venue
A legal requirement that the court most connected to the event in dispute, if it also has jurisdiction, must decide the dispute.

If the venue is improper, the court can dismiss the case or, in the case of federal courts, transfer the case to any district court in which the matter could have been brought. In some circumstances, even if the plaintiff's venue choice is proper, the case may be transferred to another more convenient court or forum under the doctrine of *forum non conveniens*. Such circumstances may be that the plaintiff's choice of forum is inconvenient or that the evidence and witnesses are located elsewhere. Note that a forum selection clause can supersede this doctrine.

> **Example:** Natasha and Scott Mueller purchased an all-inclusive trip to a Dominican Republic resort for their honeymoon from Apple Leisure Corp. They booked their trip through a travel agent located in Fond Du Lac, Wisconsin. Their contract with Apple included a forum selection clause that stated in boldface type that "[t]he exclusive forum for the litigation of any claim or dispute arising out of . . . [this] trip shall be the Court of Common Pleas of Delaware County, Pennsylvania."
>
> During their vacation, Natasha became ill from eating contaminated fish served to her by the resort. The Muellers filed suit seeking damages against Apple Leisure in federal court in Wisconsin. Apple Leisure moved to dismiss the complaint for lack of personal jurisdiction and improper venue. It prevailed, and the case was dismissed because they did not sue in the agreed-upon Pennsylvania state court. *Mueller v. Apple Leisure Corp.*, 800 F.3d 890 (7th Cir. 2018)

The State and Federal Court Systems

The federal government and each of the states maintain individual court systems. Although there are differences between the systems, there are several similarities among them as well.

State Court System

The state court systems handle most civil and criminal cases filed in the United States. Each state maintains an independent court system, and the typical structure involves a trial court, an intermediate appellate court, and the state's highest appellate court.

STATE TRIAL COURTS. State trial courts are divided into two categories—those with *general jurisdiction* and those with *limited subject matter jurisdiction*. Courts with general subject matter jurisdiction handle all other disputes that the state allows them to hear.

A limited jurisdiction trial court has the authority to decide only specific Issues brought before it. These courts can be limited by the subject of the dispute, by the value in dispute, or by the seriousness of the criminal charge.

> **Example:** Courts that are limited in jurisdiction by the value of the dispute are state small claims courts, which hear civil claims under a certain dollar amount. The amount can vary depending on the state, ranging from a high of $25,000 in Tennessee to a low of $2,500 in Rhode Island and Kentucky.
>
> Many of these trial courts specialize in cases of a specific subject matter. Some of the most common specialized state trial courts of limited jurisdiction include small claims courts, probate courts, traffic courts, and family courts.

STATE APPELLATE COURTS. All states have **appellate courts**, which review the decisions of the trial courts. Some states only have one level of appellate courts, which would be the state's highest appellate court. Other states have *intermediate appellate courts*, which exist between the trial court and the highest appellate court. Generally, appellate courts review the record of the trial court for any errors of law. No new evidence or testimony is admitted at the appellate level. Appellate courts will typically defer to the trial court ruling unless there was a clear error in the application of the law; moreover, in rare circumstances, an appeals court can overturn fact-finding by a judge or jury if the underlying evidence was clearly inadmissible—resulting in an erroneous result.

Appellate courts
Courts that have the authority to hear appeals from lower courts.

STATE HIGHEST APPELLATE COURT. All states have a highest-level appellate court; typically referred to as state supreme courts. Through the doctrine of *stare decisis* (discussed in Chapter 1), these decisions serve as binding precedent for all state appellate and trial courts to follow in similar cases. Review of their decisions by the United States Supreme Court is limited to instances where a question of federal law is involved.

Federal Court System

The federal court system is comprised of trial courts of general jurisdiction, known as district courts, and courts of limited jurisdiction (such as the U.S. Bankruptcy Court and U.S. Tax Court), intermediate appellate courts (federal courts of appeal), and the United States Supreme Court.

Federal court judges are nominated by the President, confirmed by the Senate, and granted a lifetime appointment.

UNITED STATES DISTRICT COURTS. The federal district courts are the primary trial courts of the federal court system. Like the state trial courts, these courts decide disputes by hearing the evidence submitted by the parties and issuing a final judgment. U.S. district courts have jurisdiction in cases arising from federal law and may decide cases based upon diversity of citizenship.

UNITED STATES COURTS OF APPEALS. The decision of a district court may be appealed to a United States court of appeal, also known as the **circuit courts of appeal**. Twelve of these courts are located in the nation's specific geographic regions (circuits). The thirteenth appellate court, known as the United States Court of Appeals for the Federal Circuit, is not limited by geography, but rather by the types of cases assigned to it, such as those involving patent laws and cases appealed from the United States Court of International Trade and the United States Court of Federal Claims.

Circuit courts
The alternative name for the United States courts of appeals. They are the intermediate appellate courts in the federal system.

Management Application
Specialized U.S. Courts

The specialized federal courts are federal courts of limited jurisdiction. Examples of such federal courts include:

- U.S. bankruptcy courts, which hear cases involving bankruptcy.
- U.S. Court of Federal Claims, which hears cases involving monetary claims against the federal government.
- U.S. Court of International Trade, which hears cases involving international trade disputes.
- U.S. Tax Court, which hears cases involving disputes over federal taxes.

Can you think of other subjects which should be reserved to courts with special expertise? For example, those involving the complexity of patent and copyright disputes.

FIGURE 3.1: The Federal and State Court Systems

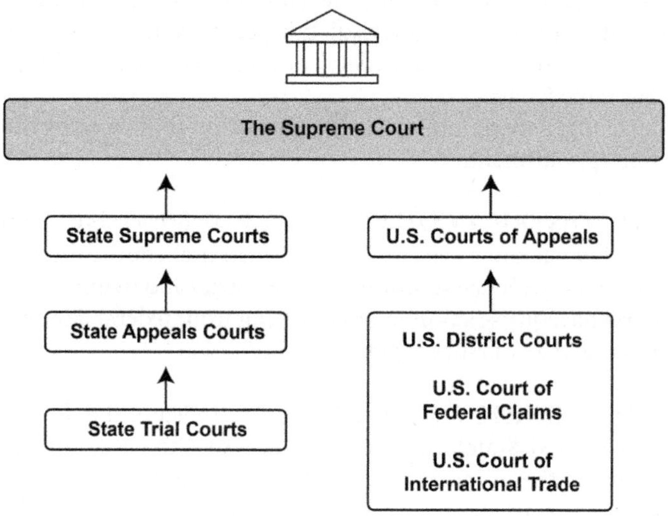

SUPREME COURT OF THE UNITED STATES. The Supreme Court of the United States is the highest appellate court in the federal system. In all but a narrow set of cases that it alone may decide, the Supreme Court has appellate jurisdictions over all federal and state court cases that involve a matter of federal law. It has the power to invalidate a state or federal law or regulation for violating the Constitution, as well as presidential directives that violate either the Constitution or federal statutory law.

Writ of certiorari The order of the Supreme Court granting a case an appellate review before the Court.

In most cases, there is no automatic right of appeal to the Supreme Court. Rather, a party formally petitions the Supreme Court through a petition for ***writ of certiorari***. A minimum of four of the nine Justices must agree to review the case. If this occurs, the Court issues a *writ of certiorari* and hears the case. If the Supreme Court denies a *writ*

FIGURE 3.2: Geographic Boundaries

Geographic Boundaries

of United States Courts of Appeals and United States District Courts

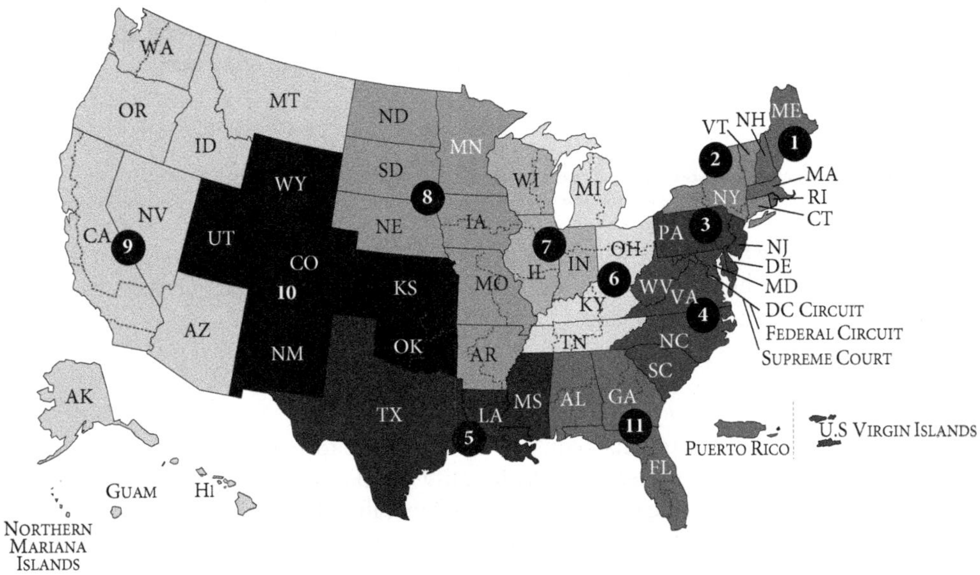

of certiorari, the decision of the lower court remains unaffected. Denial of *certiorari* does not indicate that the Supreme Court agreed with the outcome, only that fewer than the required four Justices felt the case required review. Recently, only 80 or so cases are granted a *writ of certiorari* each year.

Makeup of the Court. The Supreme Court is made up of nine Justices, who are nominated by the President and appointed subject to the consent of the Senate. They are granted a lifetime appointment upon confirmation.

Decisions of the Court. As a result of the makeup of the Court, there are a variety of decisions that the Court can issue:

- *Unanimous.* When all nine Justices vote for an outcome with the same reasoning. This result is precedent and is binding on all lower courts.
- *Majority.* When a majority of the nine Justices vote for an outcome with the same reasoning. This result is precedent and binding on all lower courts.
- *Plurality.* When a majority of the Justices agree to the outcome of the case, but for different reasons. The result is binding on the parties to the case but cannot be used as precedent.
- *Tie.* The Court does not always have nine Justices and can sit with an even number. If the Court splits in a tie, the lower court's decision is affirmed, but only for that jurisdiction. The decision cannot be used as precedent elsewhere.

To review the workload of the federal judiciary, see https://www.supremecourt.gov/publicinfo/year-end/year-endreports.aspx.

The Justices can write different types of opinions based on the decision the Court has made. When writing for the majority, a Justice will write a *majority opinion*—this is

Litigation
The process of resolving a dispute through the court system.

Pleadings
The documents required by the court to commence the judicial process. They serve to outline the factual and legal issues, identify the parties, and provide notice to the defendant parties that litigation has started.

Complaint
The pleading the plaintiff files with the court, which sets forth alleged facts, breaches of duty, and the relief sought against the defendant(s).

Remedy
The relief the plaintiff seeks to cure the injury caused by the defendant, usually monetary damages.

Summons
The court's written notice that a lawsuit has been filed against a defendant and that orders the defendant to respond to the complaint in a timely manner.

Service of process
Where the summons and complaint are served on the defendant, usually by a private process server or a sheriff.

Answer
The pleading that a defendant files admitting or denying the allegations made in the plaintiff's complaint.

Default judgment
When the court enters judgment in favor of the plaintiff, after the defendant was properly served but failed to answer the complaint.

the opinion of the Court that is binding on all lower courts. If a Justice agrees with the outcome, but for a different reason, they can write a *concurring opinion*. These are not mandatory precedents but can be persuasive in cases pending before other courts. If a Justice disagrees with the outcome, he or she can write a *dissenting opinion*. The prior Supreme Court decisions are used as binding precedent for lower federal appellate and district courts to follow in similar cases under the doctrine of *stare decisis*.

Civil Litigation and Procedure

Litigation is the process by which the court system resolves legal disputes. In this section, we review the procedures adopted by the judicial and legislative systems to process disputes in the court system.

Pleadings

Pleadings are the documents required by the court to begin litigation. They serve to outline the factual and legal issues, identify the parties, and provide notice to the defendant parties that litigation has started. Generally, they consist of a complaint, an answer to the complaint, and, sometimes, a counterclaim or cross-claim by the defendant against the plaintiff or a third party.

COMPLAINT. To begin a lawsuit, the plaintiff files a **complaint**. The complaint states:

- The facts upon which the plaintiff relies to show that the plaintiff is entitled to recover from the defendant;
- The legal theory (or cause of action) that entitles the plaintiff to that relief; and
- The **remedy** the plaintiff seeks, which most often is in the form of monetary damages.

After the plaintiff has filed the complaint with the court, the court issues a **summons**. The summons is a written notice that a lawsuit has been filed against the defendant. It informs the defendant that a response in proper form must be filed with the court within a specified time. **Service of process** occurs when the summons and complaint are personally served on the defendant. This service of process informs the defendant that they have been sued. Usually, a private process server or a sheriff serves the summons and complaint on a defendant.

Once served, the defendant has a period of 20-30 days to **answer** the complaint. The answer is the defendant's response, which admits or denies the plaintiff's allegations in the complaint. The disputed issues are what will be resolved in the court proceedings.

If the defendant fails to file an answer, the plaintiff will seek a **default judgment**. In such situations, the court accepts the allegations of the complaint as true and renders a judgment in favor of the plaintiff without the necessity of a trial. Defendants may seek to vacate a default judgment, but they must do so upon legitimate grounds and within statutory periods.

CROSS-COMPLAINT AND REPLY. A defendant may wish to assert their own claims against the plaintiff or other persons. These are known as **cross-complaints** or counterclaims. If the defendant has filed a cross-complaint against the plaintiff, the response to it will be in the form of a **reply**. A reply will admit or deny the allegations contained in the cross-complaint.

Cross-complaint
A legal claim made by the defendant against the plaintiff or other persons seeking legal relief against them.

Reply
The plaintiff's response to the cross-complaint.

Pretrial Motions

Motions are requests made to the court by the attorneys for each party. Often, early in the litigation process through a **motion to dismiss**, a defendant will request that the court dismiss the case for reasons such as lack of personal or subject matter jurisdiction, improper service, improper venue, and/or failure to state a claim for which relief can be granted.

Once parties have filed their pleadings, either party may make a **motion for judgment on the pleadings**. The judge will grant the motion only if there are no facts in dispute and the disputed issue is a question of law. For example, the defendant can show by the plaintiff's complaint that the court lacks jurisdiction over the dispute.

A **motion for summary judgment** is like a motion for judgment on the pleadings; however, ruling on this motion requires the judge to consider evidence beyond that contained in the pleadings. The evidence can be an affidavit, or the recorded testimony of witnesses from depositions, or other forms of admissible evidence. If the weight of the evidence is so clear that a trial is unnecessary, the court may rule on the motion and issue a judgment. If the judge determines there are genuine issues of fact in dispute, the motion will be denied, and the case will continue to trial.

Motion to dismiss
When a party makes a formal request to dismiss a case based upon the pleadings.

Motion for judgment on the pleadings
A request for the court to decide the case based upon the complaint and answer.

Motion for summary judgment
A motion for judgment on any claim or issue will be granted where there is no genuine dispute of material fact. The court may consider evidence beyond that contained in the pleadings.

Discovery

Discovery is a process by which parties to a lawsuit gather information about the case from each other and from associated third parties. Discovery also serves to promote settlement between the parties by allowing them to fully assess their respective positions. The discovery devices explained below require that their responses be made under penalty of perjury or under oath. It is a written response including a statement that everything set forth within it is true.

Discovery
Pretrial process for obtaining information relating to a dispute.

> **Example:** In responding to discovery, a party might state: "I certify (or declare) under penalty of perjury that the foregoing is true and correct."

Discovery allows parties to access the other parties' documents, records, and witnesses as long as the information is not **privileged**. For example, communications between an attorney and a client are generally protected from disclosure.

Privileged
Information that is protected from discovery as provided by statute or legal precedent.

INTERROGATORIES. Interrogatories are sets of written questions sent by one party to an opposing party. The recipient must respond with written answers and verify the accuracy of the answers provided, all within the period established by law.

> **Example:** INTERROGATORY NO. 1: Do you attribute any loss of income or earning capacity to the alleged accident in your complaint? If so, please state with particularity each item comprising your claim of loss and the amount of such loss.

Interrogatories
Written questions submitted by one party to an opposing party.

Request for the production of documents
Within pretrial discovery a party may request documents relevant to the dispute.

REQUEST FOR THE PRODUCTION OF DOCUMENTS. A **request for the production of documents** allows a party to request documents from the other party. Within pretrial discovery, a party may request another party from the litigation to produce documents relevant to the dispute. The request may extend to all tangible items or electronically stored information (emails, computer files) that are in the custody or control of the other party. The request must describe each item or category of information requested.

> **Example:** REQUEST FOR PRODUCTION NO. 1: PRODUCE ALL DOCUMENTS, as defined herein, that support your contention that the injuries or the extent of the injuries claimed by you were due to the accident for which you seek damages in this proceeding.

Request for admission
A written request from one party to the opposing party, but the questions can only request the party to admit or deny the genuineness of a writing or truth of an assertion of fact.

REQUEST FOR ADMISSION. **Requests for admission** are like interrogatories, in that they are written requests from one party to the opposing party, but the questions can only request the party to admit or deny the truth of the assertion. Like interrogatories, they assist the parties in narrowing the issues in dispute so that the parties agree upon the genuineness of documents or material facts, thus eliminating issues for resolution before a court.

> **Example:** REQUEST FOR ADMISSION NO. 1: Admit that at the time of the automobile accident alleged in your complaint, you were using your cellphone to respond to a text message.

REQUEST FOR PHYSICAL OR MENTAL EXAMINATION. When a party asserts a physical or emotional injury, the opposing party can request the court to order the party to submit to a physical or mental examination. In the request, the party must specify the location, the time, the medical professional conducting the examination, and what is to be examined. The medical professional will generate a report of their findings, which is sent to all parties to the lawsuit.

Deposition
When one party to an action formally interviews either a party or nonparty who is under oath, and the answers are transcribed for the record.

Subpoena
A court order requiring an individual to appear as part of a legal proceeding, usually to give evidence in the form of testimony.

DEPOSITIONS. A **deposition** is a pretrial procedure by which a witness's testimony is recorded under oath. It is used to gather information and sometimes may be used at trial. The deposition takes place in an informal location, such as a lawyer's office or that of the court reporter who transcribes the testimony. Parties to a lawsuit must submit a request for a deposition. Witnesses can voluntarily appear or may be compelled to appear by service of a **subpoena** upon them, requiring them to appear and give testimony and to produce documents in their possession.

The individuals present at a deposition are the deponent, attorneys for all the parties to the lawsuit, and a stenographer, who will administer an oath to the witness, and/or a video recorder.

E-Discovery

Discovery is not limited to tangible items. Discovery also applies to any relevant electronically stored items. For example, any of the following may be relevant to a party's case: word-processing documents, graphics, email messages and drafts, databases, computer-usage and operations information, calendaring and scheduling, and financial records. A computer forensics expert can help identify what is retrievable and how to do so.

> **Example:** REQUEST FOR PRODUCTION NO. 1: Produce for inspection, impounding, and cloning your computer servers, hard drives, and individual workstation PC(s), laptops, and other items containing digital or electronic data concerning the contract in dispute in this litigation.

Pretrial Conference

The rules of federal and state courts require that the parties discuss, at the conclusion of discovery, the possibility of settling the dispute. If this does not happen, the court will outline the issues to be tried in a pretrial order. At that time, the parties will exchange witness and document lists to be used at trial. Additionally, the judge will make rulings regarding trial procedures and the admission of evidence to be introduced at trial.

Voir dire
The examination of potential jurors by the court and attorneys for the parties.

Challenge for cause
During *voir dire* an attorney can request that the court dismiss a potential juror for a particular reason, usually bias against their client.

Peremptory challenge
During *voir dire* an attorney can automatically dismiss a potential juror with no reason required. These are limited in number.

Jury Selection

The jury selection process is known as ***voir dire***. Rules vary on the *voir dire* procedure, but generally, attorneys for the parties ask questions of prospective jurors. These questions are designed to detect any bias the potential juror may have. With a **challenge for cause** a party may seek to disqualify a potential juror for nondiscriminatory reasons. For example, a proposed juror works for one of the parties to the lawsuit. A party may also exercise a limited number of **peremptory challenges**, allowing prospective jurors to be dismissed for no given reason. For example, a party may use a peremptory challenge and remove a proposed juror who appeared hostile toward the questions asked during *voir dire*. The court may also appoint a few alternate jurors who will serve on the jury if needed, especially in lengthy trials.

Trial

Burden of proof
The duty of a party to prove the truth of their assertions.

Standard of proof
The minimum amount of evidence required to prove the assertion.

Direct examination
The first examination of a witness on a matter that is related to the trial.

Cross-examination
The examination of a witness by an opposing party to check or discredit the witness's testimony, knowledge, or credibility.

OPENING ARGUMENT. Each party may make an opening argument to the judge or jury. These statements summarize the story of the case as viewed by that party and the evidence that will be presented to support that position. Having the burden to prove the case, the prosecution (criminal cases) or plaintiff (civil cases) proceeds first, followed by the defendant, who may postpone the opening argument until the prosecution or plaintiff has finished presenting the case.

PLAINTIFF 'S CASE. The plaintiff bears the **burden of proof** of proving their claims by a preponderance of the evidence. A preponderance of the evidence means that, in consideration of all the evidence, one outcome is more likely than another. Sometimes, this is referred to as at least 51 percent likely; that amount is known as the **standard of proof**. This is the standard of proof in business law cases.

To meet its burden of proof, the plaintiff will introduce evidence in the form of documents and testimony of witnesses. When the plaintiff calls a witness to the stand, the attorney will ask the witness questions called **direct examination**. The opposing attorney may ask questions of the witness as part of **cross-examination** but is not required to do so. During the trial, either attorney may object to evidence, or the questions being asked of witnesses; the judge will either sustain or overrule the objection.

FIGURE 3.3: Subpoena to Testify at a Deposition

AO 88A (Rev. 12/20) Subpoena to Testify at a Deposition in a Civil Action

UNITED STATES DISTRICT COURT
for the

_____________________ Plaintiff
v.
_____________________ Defendant

Civil Action No.

SUBPOENA TO TESTIFY AT A DEPOSITION IN A CIVIL ACTION

To:
____
(Name of person to whom this subpoena is directed)

❐ Testimony: YOU ARE COMMANDED to appear at the time, date, and place set forth below to testify at a deposition to be taken in this civil action. If you are an organization, you must promptly confer in good faith with the party serving this subpoena about the following matters, or those set forth in an attachment, and you must designate one or more officers, directors, or managing agents, or designate other persons who consent to testify on your behalf about these matters:

Place:	Date and Time:

The deposition will be recorded by this method: _____________________

❐ *Production:* You, or your representatives, must also bring with you to the deposition the following documents, electronically stored information, or objects, and must permit inspection, copying, testing, or sampling of the material:

The following provisions of Fed. R. Civ. P. 45 are attached – Rule 45(c), relating to the place of compliance; Rule 45(d), relating to your protection as a person subject to a subpoena; and Rule 45(e) and (g), relating to your duty to respond to this subpoena and the potential consequences of not doing so.

Date: ___________

CLERK OF COURT

OR

_____________________ *Signature of Clerk or Deputy Clerk*

_____________________ *Attorney's signature*

The name, address, e-mail address, and telephone number of the attorney representing *(name of party)* ___________ _____________________, who issues or requests this subpoena, are:

Notice to the person who issues or requests this subpoena

If this subpoena commands the production of documents, electronically stored information, or tangible things before trial, a notice and a copy of the subpoena must be served on each party in this case before it is served on the person to whom it is directed. Fed. R. Civ. P. 45(a)(4).

These objections often control the evidentiary record of the trial court proceedings that an appellate court may review if an appeal is taken.

DEFENDANT'S CASE. Once the plaintiff has finished presenting evidence, the attorney for the defendant will often make a *motion for a directed verdict*. A defendant may argue that the plaintiff has failed to meet its burden of proof; namely, it failed to produce evidence to persuade by a preponderance of the evidence that the plaintiff should prevail. Generally, such a motion is denied. The defendant then presents its evidence to support its defense of the case. Each party may examine and cross-examine witnesses presented by the defense.

CLOSING ARGUMENT. At the conclusion of the presentation of evidence, each party will make a closing argument. The plaintiff proceeds first, followed by the defendant, and, finally, the plaintiff may offer a rebuttal argument to the defendant's argument.

JURY INSTRUCTIONS AND DELIBERATION. After the conclusion of the closing arguments, if it is a jury trial, the judge will provide the jury with instructions needed to guide the jury in the application of the law. Thereafter, the jury retires to consider the evidence and apply the law to reach a verdict. In civil cases, typically, the jury must reach a verdict representing a vote of 9 out of 12 jurors. A verdict in a criminal case must be made by the unanimous vote of the jury. If a jury in a criminal case cannot agree on a verdict, a hung jury results, leading to a mistrial. The case is not decided, and it may be tried again before a new jury.

Motions After Verdict

Once a verdict is reached in a civil jury trial, either party can make a **motion for judgment notwithstanding the verdict** (also known as a "JNOV"). In a civil suit, the judge may set aside the jury verdict, increase or decrease the amount of damages awarded by the jury, or make modifications to its findings. In criminal cases, the judge generally has no authority to modify the jury verdict.

Motion for judgment notwithstanding the verdict
The trial judge may overrule the decision of a jury and set aside or amend the jury verdict.

> **Example:** A jury trial awarded a plaintiff $635,000 on defamation claims. The court affirmed the granting of a judgment notwithstanding the verdict and vacated the jury's verdict after concluding the plaintiff was a public figure and an actual malice standard should have been applied to the defamation claims, the statements made by the defendants were opinion, and there was no evidence of actual malice. *Cottrell v. Smith*, 788 S.E. 2d 772 (Ga. 2016)

A party may also make a **motion for a new trial** based on errors committed by the judge during the trial or irregularities regarding the evidence introduced at trial. In some states, the losing party must make a motion for a new trial before filing an appeal.

Motion for a new trial
A request by a party, after a judgment is entered in a case, that the judge vacate that judgment and order a new trial because of legal errors or problems with the evidence.

> **Example:** A defendant was prosecuted for forging money orders. Following the trial, the defense counsel discovered evidence that the assistant U.S. Attorney promised the co-conspirator that he would not be prosecuted if he testified for the government. The government's case depended significantly on the co-conspirator's testimony, and the government falsely represented that such promise was made to the witness. The court held the nondisclosure affected the co-conspirator's credibility, violated due process, and justified a new trial. *Giglio v. United States*, 405 U.S. 150 (1972)

The decision (or verdict) of the jury is not effective until the judge enters a **judgment** on the decision, which is an order that it be filed in the public court records.

Judgment
The final ruling of the court from which an appeal may be taken.

Appeal

While most cases are not appealed, after entry of judgment a party may appeal to a higher court. There must be a legal basis for the appeal, such as a material error of law that occurred during the trial. Appeals cannot be filed just because a losing party did not like the result. The party appealing is called the **appellant**, or sometimes the petitioner. The other party is the **appellee**, or the respondent. In a civil case, either party may appeal to a higher court. In a criminal case, only the defendant has a right to an appeal in most states, although prosecutors may have a limited right to appeal regarding points of law.

Appellant
Party seeking to reverse the trial court decision.

Appellee
Party responding to the appellant's appeal.

An appeal is *not* a retrial of the case. Appellate courts in civil matters rarely, if ever, consider new witnesses or new evidence. The same holds true in criminal appeals. Appeals are based on arguments that material errors occurred in the trial procedures or the court's application of the law.

Brief
Written legal argument summarizing the facts, relevant law, and the basis for seeking a reversal of the trial court decision.

There are set periods within which the appellant must file a **brief**, a written argument containing that side's view of the facts and the legal arguments upon which they rely in seeking a reversal of the trial court. The appellee then has a specified time to file an answering brief. The appellant may then file a second brief answering the appellee's brief.

Class action
A lawsuit in which individuals with the same or similar claims are grouped together into a single action against the same defendant.

After reviewing the record of the evidence adduced at trial and the briefs filed, the appellate court will issue a decision. The court may:

- *Affirm* the trial court decision
- *Reverse* the trial court decision because of an error of law
- *Remand* the case to the trial court for further action (such as recalculating damages)
- *Modify* the decision reached in the trial court

Concept Summary
Civil Case Flowchart

Injury to a Party	May start the litigation process. Examples: ■ Breach of contract ■ Personal injury ■ Real property disputes

Stage of Litigation	Description
Pleadings	The documents required by the court to begin litigation. Filed by plaintiff: ■ Complaint ■ Summons Filed by defendant: ■ Answer with affirmative defenses alleged ■ Cross-complaint ■ Reply filed to the cross-complaint by the plaintiff or a third party
Pretrial Motions	Motions by each party. Examples: ■ Motion to dismiss ■ Motion for judgment on the pleadings ■ Motion for summary judgment
Discovery	The process by which parties in a lawsuit gather information about the case from each other and from third parties. Examples: ■ Interrogatories ■ Requests for the production of documents ■ Requests for admission ■ Requests for physical or mental examinations ■ Depositions
Pretrial Conference	The Federal Rules of Civil Procedure, and most state rules, require the parties and their attorneys to narrow the issues in dispute and discuss: ■ An exchange of evidence to be introduced at trial ■ An exchange of witness lists, including expert witnesses ■ The court will issue rulings on trial procedures ■ Define the issues to be determined at trial
Jury Selection	■ *Voir dire* Juror interrogation ■ Challenges Dismiss potential jurors
Trial	During trial, the order of proof proceeds as follows: ■ Opening arguments followed by the plaintiff's presentation of evidence, that of the defense, and rebuttal evidence introduced by the plaintiff ■ Closing arguments ■ Verdict, whether by the court or a jury ■ Judgment
Appeal	■ Reversal of the judgment of the trial court is sought based upon an error occurring in the trial procedures or the court's application of law ■ Not a retrial of the case

Class Actions

A **class action** is a lawsuit in which individuals with the same or similar claims group together to file a single action against the same defendant. Typically, a class action arises when the individual harm is marginal, but that same harm occurred to a large *class* of people and was caused by the same defendant and in the same manner.

The requirements for a class to be certified are:

1. Numerosity
   - There must be a significant number of individuals with the same claim; generally, courts require more than 50 claimants. The larger the group, the more likely the class will be certified.
2. Commonality
   - The key questions of law and fact need to be common among the class. The more common, the more likely the class will be certified.
3. Typicality
   - The claims or defenses of the represented parties are typical of the larger class. The more representative, the more likely the class will be certified.
4. Adequacy of Representation
   - The representative parties will adequately represent the absent members of the class. The courts will require a minimum level of adequacy to certify the class.

Once the class is certified, the lawsuit will progress in substantially the same manner as any other lawsuit. If a judgment is entered, notification is made to the class members of the result, and if a party did not opt out of the class, the judgment is binding upon them.

Alternative dispute resolution
A nonjudicial process that seeks to resolve disputes between parties, typically through mediation and arbitration.

Alternative Dispute Resolution

Due to the cost and time commitment of litigation, parties may pursue methods of **alternative dispute resolution** (ADR). Most frequently, these are mediation and arbitration.

Mediation
A form of alternative dispute resolution in which a neutral third party assists the parties in a dispute to reach a settlement.

Mediation

Mediation is a voluntary, nonbinding form of alternative dispute resolution. A mediator, an impartial third party, assists the parties to reach a settlement of their dispute. The parties select the mediator in advance and pay the mediator's fees. The parties may proceed to litigate or arbitrate their dispute if the mediation is unsuccessful.

Arbitration
A legal proceeding in which disputes are resolved by a neutral third party appointed by the parties to make a binding and final determination.

Arbitration

Arbitration is the process by which parties to a dispute submit their differences to an impartial person or panel of persons appointed by the parties' mutual consent or statute to decide their dispute. Unlike mediation, both sides present their evidence to the arbitrator, and after hearing all the evidence, the arbitrator issues an award (the decision of the arbitrator). Awards may be binding or nonbinding. The most common is binding arbitration where the decision of the arbitrator is final and can only be appealed on limited grounds. In nonbinding arbitration, the decision cannot be enforced against either party.

Arbitration is more formal than mediation but less formal than court. Arbitration can take place anywhere, such as an office as opposed to a courtroom. Generally, the arbitrator is selected because of their experience in resolving the type of dispute at issue. Contracting parties often agree in their original contract to resolve disputes through arbitration and can limit the scope of discovery each can undertake before the arbitration hearing date.

An arbitration award can be converted into an enforceable court judgment by a party's application to a court to confirm the arbitration award. At that point, the court processes of enforcing judgments can be pursued.

STATE AND FEDERAL ARBITRATION STATUTES. Most states have enacted the *Uniform Arbitration Act*, which establishes a default set of rules by which arbitration is conducted.

The *Federal Arbitration Act* governs the arbitration of claims that arise from interstate business transactions. It is frequently used to resolve contractual and employment law disputes. Any award provided under the Act must be confirmed by a court of law; once confirmed, the award will be entered as a judgment, enforceable as any other judgment would be. The Supreme Court has consistently upheld the enforceability of agreements to arbitrate.

Concept Summary
Types of ADR

ADR	Description	Neutral Third Party?	Who Resolves the Dispute?
Mediation	A form of alternative dispute resolution in which a neutral third party assists the parties in a dispute to reach a settlement.	Yes	All parties must mutually agree on a resolution. However, a mediator may suggest one as well.
Arbitration	A legal proceeding in which disputes are resolved by a neutral third party appointed by the parties to make a final determination of their disputes.	Yes	In binding arbitration, the arbitrator's decision is final. In nonbinding arbitration, the arbitrator's decision is subject to agreement by the parties.

Management Application
Other Forms of ADR

If a dispute cannot be resolved through negotiation between the parties, mediation, and arbitration, other forms of ADR include:

1. **Early Neutral Case Evaluation**

   The parties select a neutral third party who hears both sides of the case; and assesses each side's strengths and weaknesses.

2. **Mini-trial**

   The parties briefly argue their case in front of each other, with a panel of representatives from each party, in front of a neutral third party (advisor). If the parties fail to settle, the advisor informs the parties how a court would most likely resolve their case.

3. **Summary Jury Trial**

   The parties present their cases in front of a jury, and the jury issues a verdict. The verdict is nonbinding but acts as a standard so that the parties understand their positions.

Considering that the court system is subsidized by the government, do these alternative dispute resolution methods deny a litigant their right to a judicial proceeding? Is it fair that ADR is imposed upon consumers by multinational enterprises? What results follow from having only an ADR remedy and not the right to present a dispute for resolution by a jury?

AI Feature: Drafting an Arbitration Provision

You are working as a manager of a company and have been requested to include an arbitration agreement to be executed by your employer and employees within the organization. After conducting an internet search on the following topics, use an AI program to draft the arbitration agreement. The agreement should address material concerns of the employer including:

- What claims are and are not subject to mandatory arbitration;
- Which arbitration service is to be used;
- Who will pay for the costs of arbitration;
- What are the qualifications of the arbitrator(s);
- Whether the arbitrator(s) decide what claims are subject to arbitration;
- Whether there are rights to conduct discovery from the other side;
- Whether the law must be applied by the arbitrator(s);
- Whether the parties have the right to cross-examine witnesses; and,
- Whether there is a right to appeal and on what grounds.

Key Terms

- Alternative dispute resolution, 64
- Answer, 56
- Appellant, 62
- Appellate courts, 53
- Appellee, 62
- Arbitration, 64
- Brief, 62
- Burden of proof, 59
- Challenge for cause, 59
- Circuit courts, 53
- Class action, 62
- Complaint, 56
- Concurrent jurisdiction, 50
- Cross-complaint, 57
- Cross-examination, 59
- Default judgment, 56
- Defendant, 41
- Deposition, 58
- Direct examination, 59
- Discovery, 57
- Diversity of citizenship jurisdiction, 48
- Exclusive jurisdiction, 50
- Federal question jurisdiction, 48
- Forum selection clause, 45
- *In rem* jurisdiction, 45
- Interrogatories, 57
- Judgment, 61
- Judiciary system, 40
- Jurisdiction, 40
- Litigation, 56
- Long-arm statute, 41
- Mediation, 64
- Motion for a new trial, 61
- Motion for judgment notwithstanding the verdict, 61
- Motion for judgment on the pleadings, 57
- Motion for summary judgment, 57
- Motion to dismiss, 57
- Peremptory challenge, 59
- Personal (*in personam*) jurisdiction, 41
- Plaintiff, 40
- Pleadings, 56
- Privileged, 57
- Remedy, 56
- Reply, 57
- Request for admission, 58
- Request for production of documents, 58
- Service of process, 56
- Sliding scale standard, 45
- Standard of proof, 59
- Standing, 40
- Subject matter jurisdiction, 40
- Subpoena, 58
- Summons, 56
- Venue, 51
- *Voir dire*, 59
- *Writ of certiorari*, 54

Applying the Law

3.1 Forum Selection Clauses. In a dispute among parties to an investment contract, a federal court of appeals weighed the factors to decide if a forum selection clause in their contract should be enforced. What factors would you consider in addition to those identified by the court? *Sun v. Advanced China Healthcare, Inc.* 901 F.3d 1081 (9th Cir. 2018)

3.2 Jurisdiction over Nonresidents. Baskin-Robbin®, a well-known ice cream franchise, entered into a franchise agreement with Alpenrose Dairy Inc. The agreement allowed Alpenrose the right to renew every six years by sending notice to Baskin-Robbins headquarters. Alpenrose operated its stores in Washington, Oregon, Montana, and parts of Idaho, and was headquartered and incorporated in Oregon. Baskin-Robbins was incorporated in Delaware and headquartered in Massachusetts. In 2014, a dispute arose regarding the renewal of the contract, and Baskin-Robbins sued Alpenrose in federal court in Massachusetts. Alpenrose moved to dismiss for lack of personal jurisdiction, arguing that it lacked sufficient minimum contacts with the forum state. The trial court granted the motion, which was appealed. What do you think the court of appeals will hold? Does sending notice to renew a contract to a company's headquarters justify courts in that state exercising power over the company? See, *Baskin-Robbins Franchising LLC v. Alpenrose Dairy, Inc.*, 825 F.3d 28 (1st Cir. 2016)

3.3 Personal Jurisdiction and the Internet. Matthew Pavlovich, a Texas resident, created a website in Indiana on which he posted information instructing users on how to circumvent encryptions of DVDs. Pavlovich's website provided information and did not solicit or transact any business. Additionally, Pavlovich did not reside or work in California, nor did he have any business contacts in the state. The DVD Copy Control Association (CCA), a nonprofit trade association organized under Delaware law with its principal place of business in California, filed for an injunction in a California state court against Pavlovich for misappropriation of trade secrets for posting information regarding the decryption program on his website. Is it appropriate for this court to exercise personal jurisdiction over Pavlovich? If not, what facts would be necessary for this court to have personal jurisdiction? *Pavlovich v. Superior Court*, 29 Cal. 4th 262 (2002)

3.4 Jurisdiction over Corporations. Hertz employees in California sued Hertz for failure to follow California's wage and hours laws. Hertz sought to remove to federal court by claiming diversity jurisdiction. The employees disagreed, claiming Hertz was a California citizen. The employees argued that California was Hertz's principal place of business because it earned more revenue in California than in other states and a large amount of Hertz's business activities took place in California. Have the employees provided sufficient evidence to show diversity jurisdiction is lacking? Why or why not? *Hertz Corp. v. Friend*, 559 U.S. 77 (2010)

3.5 Diversity of Citizenship Jurisdiction. Redner asserted federal jurisdiction based on diversity of citizenship. Redner's complaint alleged that he is a citizen of the United States residing in France and the two defendants are residents of New York. Would a court find there is diversity of citizenship jurisdiction? Why or why not? *Redner v. Sanders*, 2000 U.S. Dist. LEXIS 11877 (S.D.N.Y. 2000)

3.6 Venue. Fontaine filed a complaint against Florida Gamco, alleging breaches of fiduciary duty due to misappropriation of corporate funds, and asserted that the officers breached their duty by exploiting the corporation's assets for their own gain. Where is venue proper if the action is against the corporation's officers? What about the corporation? *Florida Gamco, Inc. v. Fontaine*, 68 So. 3d 923 (Fla. Dist. Ct. App. 2011)

3.7 Pleadings. Dr. Stradford was a dentist with an office insured by Zurich. During the term of the insurance policy, Stradford failed to pay the required insurance premium and his policy was cancelled between October and December. In December, Stradford submitted a "no claims" letter certifying that he had no losses during that time. Stradford's insurance was then reinstated in January. A few days later, Stradford filed a claim on the policy, claiming excessive water damage to the dental office. Following a rejection of the claim, the dentist sued for benefits under the policy. The insurer sought to counterclaim, alleging Stradford had attempted to defraud the insurer and obtain money by false pretenses. In the insurer's counterclaim, the insurance company alleged that Stradford "knowingly and willfully devised a scheme and artifice . . . to defraud defendants and obtain money by false pretenses and representations." Would a court find these pleadings sufficient? Why or why not? How would you write the pleadings for the insurance company? *Stradford v. Zurich Insurance Co.*, 2002 U.S. Dist. LEXIS 16993 (S.D.N.Y. 2002)

3.8 Motion for Summary Judgment. Nathan Smith believed that he had discovered the location of a lost nineteenth-century Spanish treasure ship in a lake in Refugio County, Texas. Morgan O'Connor owned the land surrounding the lake, and the State of Texas owned the land underneath. To access the supposed treasure ship, Smith trespassed on O'Connor's property. Both the State of Texas and O'Connor sued Smith, seeking a court order preventing him from trespassing on and damaging the land, and moved for summary judgment. Together, the plaintiffs asserted with evidence that Smith's plan to salvage the ship would cause irreparable harm to the land. Smith relied only on his lawyer's assertions that he had "investors" involved in the salvage project and would be harmed by a court order stopping his project. Has Smith created a genuine issue of material fact, or is summary judgment proper? See *O'Connor v. Smith*, 427 F. App'x 359 (5th Cir. 2011)

3.9 Class Action. Adrianna Ault filed a complaint against J.M. Smucker Co.®, alleging a breach of an express warranty for labeling certain cooking oils as "All Natural." Ault claimed this was misleading because the oils were made using genetically modified organism crops. In seeking class certification, Ault's proposed class included "consumers who purchased one or more of the following products in New York: Crisco Pure Vegetable Oil and/or Crisco Pure Corn Oil between February 15, 2009, and June 1, 2014; and/or Crisco Pure Canola Oil and/or Crisco Natural Blend Oil between June 1, 2010, and June 1, 2014." Would a court certify Ault's class? Make the argument for or against certification. *Ault v. J.M. Smucker Co.*, 310 F.R.D. 59 (S.D.N.Y. 2015)

3.10 Research the Law. Some state rules require parties to utilize ADR as part of the litigation process. Using an internet search engine, research whether your home state requires parties involved in civil litigation to attempt to resolve their disputes pursuant to ADR before trial. Which type of ADR is commonly used?

Constitutional Law for Businesses

4

The problem is whether the American people have honesty enough, loyalty enough, honor enough, patriotism enough to live up to their own Constitution. — Frederick Douglass, speech given at the 1893 Chicago World's Fair (1818-1895)

Chapter Outline

- Introduction to Constitutional Law for Businesses
- Commerce Clause

Case 4.1: *United States v. Lopez*
Case 4.2: *Producers Council v. Ross*

- Supremacy Clause
- Necessary and Proper Clause
- Taxing and Spending Clause
- Privileges and Immunities Clause
  - *Management Application: Is Higher Tuition for Out-of-State Residents Unconstitutional?*
- Full Faith and Credit Clause
- Bill of Rights
- Due Process and Equal Protection Clauses
- AI Feature: Government's Right to Regulate Industries

Learning Objectives

After studying this chapter, you should be able to:

1. Explain the system of federalism.
2. Identify the branches of government and explain their areas of responsibility.
3. Describe the extent of the federal government's power under the Commerce Clause.
4. Explain the role of the Supremacy Clause in the Constitution.
5. Describe the purpose of the Privileges and Immunities Clause.
6. Distinguish between procedural due process and substantive due process.
7. Identify the three standards of review the courts apply under the Equal Protection Clause.
8. Identify the Bill of Rights.
9. Explain the types of protected speech.

Introduction

In this chapter, we will introduce constitutional concepts and clauses and their impact upon businesses. The chapter then discusses (1) the Commerce Clause, which provides Congress expansive powers to regulate businesses and their operations; (2) the Due Process and Equal Protection Clauses, which together establish a limit on the powers of government and the businesses they regulate; and (3) the Bill of Rights and two provisions related to freedom of speech and freedom of religion as they relate to businesses.

Federalism

Federalism
The balance of power shared between the federal government and state governments.

Federalism is the balance of powers between the federal government and the powers of the states. The United States is composed of two sovereigns, the federal government and the state governments. The Constitution sets out specific powers that the federal government can use to govern, but also reserves many powers to the states. Since the creation of the Constitution, courts have been left to determine how the federal government and the state governments share their power.

Separation of Powers

Separation of powers
The division of legislative, executive, and judicial power between three co-equal branches of government.

To prevent a concentration of power, the Framers of the Constitution divided the powers granted to the federal government. Through the **separation of powers**, the Constitution established three branches of government, each with separate powers and duties. These three branches are the legislative branch, the executive branch, and the judicial branch.

1. *The legislative branch.* The legislative branch is comprised of the House of Representatives and the Senate, collectively known as the Congress. Together, the two houses of Congress write bills that become national laws.
2. *The executive branch.* The executive branch is responsible for enforcing the laws Congress enacts. This branch consists of the President and their advisors, as well as various departments and agencies. As head of this branch, the President has the power to veto laws and has broad power in foreign affairs as the commander in chief of the armed forces. The President also appoints officers throughout the federal government, with some officer appointments needing the approval of the Senate.
3. *The judicial branch.* The Constitution established a Supreme Court and gives the power to Congress to establish all other federal courts. Federal courts interpret the laws passed by Congress and have the ability to declare an act of government unconstitutional.

Checks and balances
The system of shared power under which each branch of government can ensure that no one branch controls the others.

Checks and Balances

By separating the branches of the federal government, the framers of the Constitution developed a system of shared power, known as **checks and balances**, under which each branch of government has certain powers over the other to ensure that no one branch controls the others.

Example: The President has the power to appoint Justices to the Supreme Court with the advice and consent of the Senate.

Example: The judicial branch can review actions taken by the other branches and can declare them unconstitutional.

Commerce Clause

The Commerce Clause, which grants Congress the authority to regulate commerce, has had a large impact on business. The lack of federal commerce power under the Articles of Confederation permitted states to pass discriminatory legislation in an effort to favor their own economies. In response to the states' economic protections, the Founders delegated the power to regulate commerce to Congress. Found in Article I, Section 8, Clause 3 of the Constitution, the **Commerce Clause** provides "Congress shall have power to regulate Commerce with foreign Nations, and among the several States, and with the Indian Tribes."

Commerce Clause
An enumerated power under the Constitution that grants Congress the authority to regulate commerce.

The scope of the Commerce Clause has evolved over time through the Supreme Court's interpretation of the word "commerce." Initially, the Commerce Clause only applied to foreign trade (trade with other nations) and interstate trade (trade between and among the states). Today, courts understand the Commerce Clause to also apply to wholly intrastate commerce (trade within a state) due to its effects on or relation to interstate commerce. This broad interpretation of the Commerce Clause allows Congress to regulate an expansive range of activities, affecting nearly all businesses in the United States today.

Review the Constitution and its amendments at https://www.senate.gov/civics/constitution_item/constitution.htm.

Foreign Commerce

The Commerce Clause delegates exclusive authority to the federal government to regulate all commerce between the United States and foreign nations. This prevents individual states from passing laws that interfere with foreign trade or commerce.

Example: Kraft General Foods, Inc.® (Kraft) challenged an Iowa statute that imposed a business tax that did not allow a credit for taxes paid to foreign countries. The Supreme Court held that the statute facially discriminated against foreign commerce and violated the Commerce Clause. *Kraft General Foods, Inc. v. Iowa Dep't of Revenue and Finance*, 505 U.S. 71 (1992)

Interstate Commerce

Originally, interstate commerce was understood as commerce that physically moved across state borders — that is, the government could only regulate businesses engaged in transporting items across state lines, and through the channels (such as highways, waterways, or the internet) or instrumentalities of interstate commerce (such as trains, cars, and ships). However, this limited definition has been expanded to include all commerce that *substantially affects* interstate commerce. The expansion allows the federal government to regulate intrastate commercial activity, activity that occurs entirely within a single state, so long as the regulated activity substantially affects interstate commerce.

Example: In response to the Great Depression, Congress passed the New Deal to improve the economy. One part of the legislation sought to regulate the price of wheat nationwide by limiting production through the use of penalties. Filburn, a farmer who was growing wheat to be used only for his family's consumption, challenged this law, arguing that the production was for his sole consumption, the wheat was never bought, never sold, and would never enter the stream of commerce. The Supreme Court rejected his argument and held that Congress did not exceed its authority under the Commerce Clause. The Court reasoned that allowing farmers to grow excess wheat for personal consumption would reduce demand and, thus, prices for wheat in the aggregate. The production of excess wheat would create a *substantial effect* on interstate commerce. *Wickard v. Filburn*, 317 U.S. 111 (1942)

Following *Wickard*, courts will uphold an intrastate regulation if the court can conceive a rational basis for the regulation affecting interstate commerce. With the expansion of the Commerce Clause to include intrastate commerce under the *substantial effects* test, congressional authority seems potentially unlimited in scope. The Supreme Court infrequently places limits on Congress's power. The following case outlines one such limitation of the Commerce Clause's power where the Supreme Court placed limits on Congress, only allowing it to regulate economic activity that has a direct effect on commerce.

CASE 4.1

FEDERAL LAW THAT DOES NOT SUBSTANTIALLY AFFECT INTERSTATE COMMERCE MAY BE HELD UNCONSTITUTIONAL

UNITED STATES v. LOPEZ

514 U.S. 549 (1995)

Supreme Court of the United States

On March 10, 1992, Alfonzo Lopez, a twelfth-grade student, carried a concealed handgun and five bullets into his high school. School authorities, acting on an anonymous tip, confronted Lopez, who admitted that he was carrying a firearm. Lopez was arrested and charged under Texas law with firearm possession on school premises. The following day, the state charges were dismissed, and federal agents charged Lopez with a violation of the federal Gun-Free School Zones Act of 1990. Under this Act, Congress made it a federal offense "for any individual knowingly to possess a firearm at a place that the individual knows is a school zone."

After being found guilty under the act, Lopez challenged his conviction based on his claim that Congress had exceeded its power to legislate under the Commerce Clause. In reversing, the United States Court of Appeals for the Fifth Circuit held that the Act was invalid as beyond Congress's power under the Commerce Clause. The United States appealed to the Supreme Court.

Language of the Court. *We have identified three broad categories of activity that Congress may regulate under its commerce power. First, Congress may regulate the use of the channels of interstate commerce. Second, Congress is empowered to regulate and protect the instrumentalities of interstate commerce, or persons or things in interstate commerce, even though the threat may come only from intrastate activities. Finally, Congress' commerce authority includes the power to regulate those activities having a substantial relation to interstate commerce, i.e., those activities that substantially affect interstate commerce.*

Within this final category, admittedly, our case law has not been clear whether an activity must "affect" or "substantially affect" interstate commerce in order to be within Congress' power to regulate it under the Commerce Clause. We conclude, consistent with the great weight of our case law, that the proper test requires an analysis of whether the regulated activity "substantially affects" interstate commerce.

We have upheld a wide variety of congressional Acts regulating intrastate economic activity where we have concluded that the activity substantially affected interstate commerce. Where economic activity substantially affects interstate commerce, legislation regulating that activity will be sustained. The Gun-Free School Zones Act is a criminal statute that has nothing to do with commerce nor is it an essential part of a larger regulation of economic activity, in which the regulatory scheme could be undercut unless the intrastate activity were regulated.

The possession of a gun in a local school zone is in no sense an economic activity that might, through repetition elsewhere, substantially affect any sort of interstate commerce. Respondent was a local student at a local school; there is no indication that he had recently moved in interstate commerce, and there is no requirement that his possession of the firearm have any concrete tie to interstate commerce.

Decision. The Court found in favor of Lopez, as it concluded that the Act had "nothing to do with commerce" and therefore exceeded Congress's Commerce Clause authority. The Act did not regulate economic activity nor did the activity of carrying guns to school have a substantial effect on interstate commerce. Rather, the activity in question was more about school safety than commerce.

Focus on Ethics

Do you think Congress should be granted the authority to regulate guns nationwide? Do you think the regulation of controlled substances should be treated differently?

Landmark Case
Heart of Atlanta Motel v. United States, 379 U.S. 241 (1964)

Congress passed the Civil Rights Act in 1964 (CRA) in response to the Civil Rights Movement of the 1950s and 1960s. The CRA prohibited racial discrimination by places of public accommodation, such as hotels, motels, and restaurants. The owner of the Heart of Atlanta Motel refused to rent rooms to African Americans, in violation of the CRA. The owner of the motel brought suit against the United States, challenging the CRA and claiming that the Act was an unconstitutional extension of Congress's Commerce Clause authority. The trial court held that the Act did not violate the Constitution, and the court of appeals affirmed the decision. Heart of Atlanta appealed to the Supreme Court.

The Supreme Court held that the Act was constitutional. The Court reasoned that "the transportation of passengers in interstate commerce, is within the regulatory power of Congress, under the Commerce Clause of the Constitution, and the authority of Congress to keep the channels of interstate commerce free from immoral and injurious uses has been frequently sustained and is no longer open to question." In so doing, the Court found that the operation of a motel, despite its seemingly local character, *affected* interstate commerce such that the Congress had the authority to regulate it. In upholding the CRA, the Court empowered Congress to remedy moral wrongs through the use of the Commerce Clause.

Concept Summary
Commerce Clause

The Commerce Clause allows the *federal government* to regulate:

1. The *channels* (e.g., highways, roads, rivers, lakes, etc.) of interstate commerce;
2. The *instrumentalities* (e.g., buses, cars, trucks, boats, etc.) of interstate commerce; and,
3. Activities that have a *substantial effect* on interstate commerce.

It is every American's right and obligation to read and interpret the Constitution for himself. — Thomas Jefferson, President of the United States (1743-1826)

Dormant Commerce Clause

While the Commerce Clause grants exclusive authority to Congress to regulate commerce, Congress may decline to legislate in a particular area. States may be compelled to enact state and local legislation to regulate commerce in the absence of congressional action. However, the **Dormant Commerce Clause** prohibits states from passing legislation that would unduly burden interstate commerce by preventing states from passing state policies that would favor in-state citizens or businesses at the expense of nonresidents conducting business within the state. The Dormant Commerce Clause is not actually a clause, but an interpretation of the Commerce Clause.

Dormant Commerce Clause In the absence of congressional regulation, states are prohibited from passing legislation that discriminates against or creates an undue burden on interstate commerce.

> **Example:** Arizona law prohibited a cantaloupe grower from transporting uncrated cantaloupes from its Arizona ranch to a nearby California city for packing and processing. The grower filed an action against Arizona to enjoin this prohibition. The Supreme Court held that this constituted an unlawful burden upon interstate commerce, thus violating the Dormant Commerce Clause. *Pike v. Bruce Church*, 397 U.S. 137 (1970)

In the following case, the Court considered whether a California law that prohibited the in-state sale of pork from animals confined in a manner inconsistent with California standards violated the Dormant Commerce Clause. Its decision reduced the application of the dormant Commerce Clause.

CASE 4.2

LAWS WHICH APPLY EQUALLY TO IN- AND OUT-OF-STATE INTERESTS DO NOT POSE A DISCRIMINATORY EFFECT ON INTERSTATE COMMERCE

NATIONAL PORK PRODUCERS' COUNCIL v. ROSS

598 U.S. 356 (2023)

Supreme Court of the United States

California's voters approved a state proposition that sought to better the treatment of pigs kept for livestock by barring the sale of pork produced in conditions that were common in the industry. Much of the pork consumed in the state was imported from other parts of the United States, so the proposition affected the national pork industry as a whole. A group of farmers and corporations in the pork industry, led by the National Pork Producers Council (NPPC), sued the California Department of Food and Agriculture, led by Karen Ross. They asserted that the proposition violated the dormant Commerce Clause, which prohibits laws that substantially burden interstate commerce.

The district court dismissed the lawsuit, holding that the proposition did not attempt to fully regulate the pork industry in other states. The ruling was upheld by the Court of Appeals for the Ninth Circuit. The White House asked the Court to overturn the law in order to protect the country's pork industry. The Court granted a *writ of certiorari*.

Language of the Court. *What goods belong in our stores? Usually, consumer demand and local laws supply some of the answers. California adopted just such a law banning the in-state sale of certain pork products derived from breeding pigs confined in stalls so small they cannot lie down, stand up, or turn around. In response, two groups of out-of-state pork producers filed this lawsuit, arguing that the law unconstitutionally interferes with their preferred way of doing business in violation of this Court's dormant Commerce Clause precedents.*

We affirm. Companies that choose to sell products in various States must normally comply with the laws of those various States. Assuredly, under this Court's dormant Commerce Clause decisions, no State may use its laws to discriminate purposefully against out-of-state economic interests. But the pork producers do not suggest that California's law offends this principle. Instead, they invite us to fashion two new and more aggressive constitutional restrictions on the ability of States to regulate goods sold within their borders. We decline that invitation. While the Constitution addresses many weighty issues, the type of pork chops California merchants may sell is not on that list.

That has led petitioners to resort to litigation, pinning their hopes on what has come to be called the dormant Commerce Clause. Reading between the Constitution's lines, this Court has held that the Commerce Clause not only vests Congress with the power to regulate interstate trade; the Clause also "contain[s] a further, negative command," one effectively forbidding the enforcement of "certain state [economic regulations] even when Congress has failed to legislate on the subject." The Court has held that state laws offend the Commerce Clause when they seek to "build up . . . domestic commerce" through "burdens upon the industry and business of other States," regardless of whether Congress has spoken. At the same time, though, the Court reiterated that, absent discrimination, "a State may exclude from its territory, or prohibit the sale therein of any articles which, in its judgment, fairly exercised, are prejudicial to" the interests of its citizens.

In its "modern" cases, this Court has said that the Commerce Clause prohibits the enforcement of state laws driven by economic protectionism—that is, regulatory measures designed to benefit in-state economic interests by burdening out-of-state competitors. A state law that does have extraterritorial effects but does not purposefully discriminate does not necessarily violate the dormant Commerce Clause. Under the balancing test established in Pike v. Bruce Church, Inc., *a court must assess "the burden imposed on interstate commerce" by the state law and prevent its enforcement if the law's burdens are "clearly excessive in relation to the putative local benefits."*

Decision. In this case, the parties agreed that California's law was not discriminatory as it applied equally to in-state producers of pork, and it therefore did not violate the dormant Commerce Clause. The Court rejected what it called the pork producers' more "ambitious theories," including the "extraterritoriality doctrine," which would invalidate laws regardless of any discriminatory purpose or effect on interstate commerce.

Focus on Ethics

Does this decision open the door for the largest states to dictate the laws and regulations for consumers and businesses to the rest of America? Does it promote a state-by-state patchwork of ever-changing and costly requirements that will increase the cost of production and drive higher costs for food and other consumer products? What are the ethical implications of allowing one jurisdiction to effect dramatic changes upon small businesses in other jurisdictions?

Comparing the Federal and State Government Economic Regulatory Powers

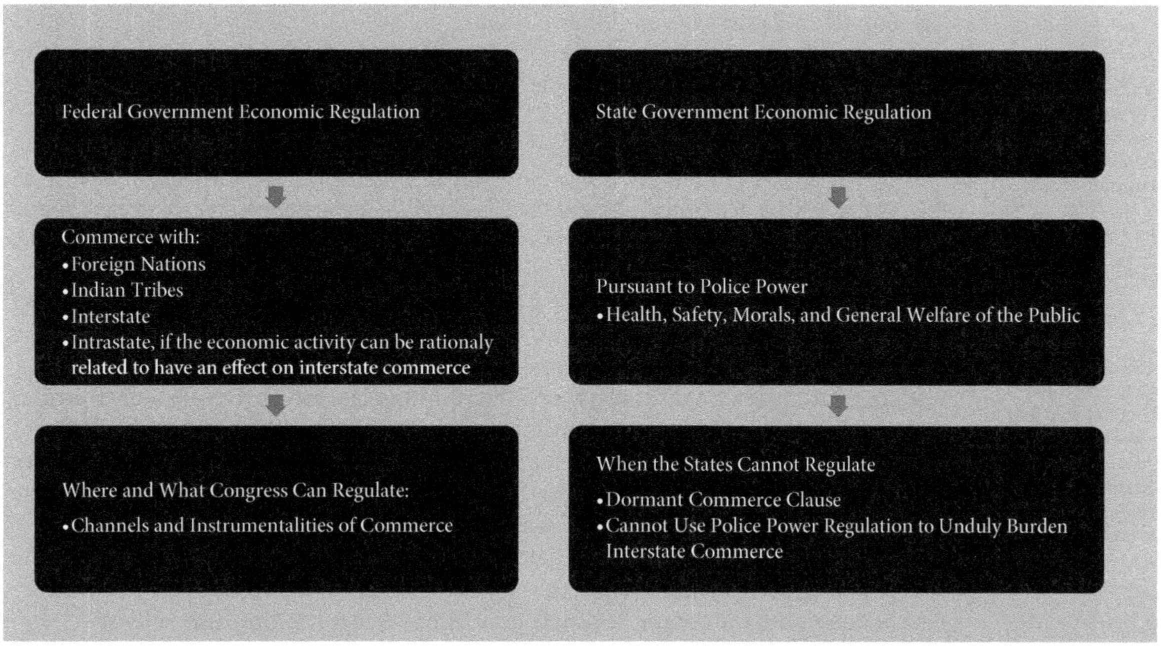

State Police Power

Although the federal government has the exclusive authority to regulate commerce, the states, through the Tenth Amendment to the Constitution, have the power to regulate the health, safety, morals, and general welfare of the public. This combination of powers is known as the **police power**. These types of laws will often regulate businesses and the products they sell.

Police power
The power of the states to regulate the health, safety, morals, and general welfare of the public.

Example: The City of New Orleans passed a local ordinance prohibiting street food vendors from using pushcarts in the French Quarter but exempted pushcart vendors who had operated in the French Quarter for 8 years prior to the ordinance. The city regulated the businesses to preserve the French Quarter's values as a tourist attraction but allowed vendors to continue who had become part of the distinctive charm of the French Quarter. A vendor in operation for only 2 years sued the city, challenging the law as unconstitutional. The Supreme Court held that the law was valid under the state's police power. *City of New Orleans v. Dukes*, 427 U.S. 297 (1976)

Often when a state attempts to regulate an activity using the police power, the regulation will burden businesses from other states, which those businesses may see as a violation of the Commerce Clause. These types of state regulations may trigger Dormant Commerce Clause analysis.

Supremacy Clause

Supremacy Clause
Provision of the Constitution establishing the Constitution and federal laws, treaties, and regulations as the supreme law of the land.

Preemption
A legal doctrine providing that federal law will prevail in the event of conflict with state laws or local ordinances on the same subject.

The Founding Fathers ensured that the supreme law of the land would be the United States Constitution, and that all federal laws, treaties, and regulations be enacted in accordance with its provisions. Article VI sets out the **Supremacy Clause**:

> This Constitution, and the Laws of the United States which shall be made in Pursuance thereof; and all Treaties made, or which shall be made, under the Authority of the United States, shall be the supreme Law of the Land; and the Judges in every State shall be bound thereby, any Thing in the Constitution or Laws of any State to the Contrary notwithstanding.

It is often the case that federal law and state or local law regulate the same subject matter. In the event that state law or local law is in conflict with the applicable federal law, the federal law prevails. This legal doctrine is known as **preemption**. Whenever Congress enacts laws within its power, the resulting legislation *preempts* or overrides any conflicting state law or local ordinance. In an 1819 decision of the United States Supreme Court, *McCulloch v. Maryland*,[1] Chief Justice John Marshall wrote, "In every such case, the act of Congress, or the treaty, is the supreme; and the law of the State, though enacted in the exercise of powers not controverted, must yield to it."

In addition, Congress may legislate in a given area, but not intend to preempt the states from also legislating in such an area; this is called *concurrent power*. It is concurrent because both the federal and state governments regulate the same activity.

> **Example:** California law provides that before a nuclear power plant may be built, the state must determine on a case-by-case basis that there is "adequate capacity" for the plant's interim storage of spent fuel. Pacific Gas and Electric sued the state regulatory agency alleging this provision was invalid under the Supremacy Clause because it was preempted by the Atomic Energy Act. The Supreme Court found that California's law was not invalid under the Supremacy Clause because the California law regulated activity outside the occupied field of nuclear safety regulation. *Pacific Gas and Elec. Co. v. State Energy Resources Conservation & Development Comm'n*, 461 U.S. 190 (1983)

> **Example:** Congress may also choose to exclusively regulate a specific area or activity through a federal statute. In such cases, no state or local law regulating the activity is valid.

> **Example:** The federal retirement statute commonly known as ERISA preempts all state laws, court decisions, and administrative regulations relating to retirement plans.

1. 17 U.S. 316 (1819).

Necessary and Proper Clause

Necessary and Proper Clause
Congress has the authority to enact laws deemed necessary and proper for carrying out its enumerated powers.

Within Article I, Section 8 of the Constitution is the statement that Congress may make laws *necessary and proper* for carrying out its enumerated powers (that is, those that are expressly stated in the Constitution). As such, Congress can enact any law that advances a goal or purpose within the scope of the Constitution.

> **Example:** The Necessary and Proper Clause allows Congress to legislate as to how any judgment issued in federal courts can be collected.

Taxing and Spending Clause

Taxing and Spending Clause
Congress has the authority to tax and spend for the general welfare.

Article I, Section 8 of the Constitution provides that "the Congress shall have power to lay and collect taxes, duties, Imposts and Excises, to pay the Debts and provide for the common defense and general welfare of the United States." Contained within this Clause is the grant of power to the federal government to raise taxes, but it also includes the implicit power to spend those raised taxes for the *general welfare.*

Taxation

The power to tax is recognized as a broad power of the federal government because a government that cannot tax is difficult to sustain. The power to tax is expansive, in that it reaches into all segments of life—personal and business. The power is limited by the requirement that the taxes be used to provide for the *common defense* and *general welfare* of the nation. The Constitution also expressly requires that taxes be imposed *uniformly*, or evenly, across the nation.

Spending

As part of the power to tax, the federal government has the power to spend the money that it has raised. The spending power is also limited by the requirements of common defense, general welfare, and uniformity. Further, Congress must spend in pursuit of one of its granted (enumerated) powers. The prevailing view is that tax revenues raised may be spent for lawful purposes if the spending would benefit the general welfare.

Privileges and Immunities Clause

Article IV, Section 2 of the Constitution provides that "Citizens of each State shall be entitled to all Privileges and Immunities of Citizens in the several States." This Clause prevents individual states from imposing unreasonable burdens on citizens of another state. A state must have a substantial reason for treating a nonresident differently from its own residents. The discrimination must be substantially related to the state's purpose in adopting the law or regulation.

Privileges and Immunities Clause
This Clause prevents states from unfairly discriminating against citizens of another state.

The **Privileges and Immunities Clause** is related to the Dormant Commerce Clause and is frequently an issue when a Dormant Commerce Clause violation is alleged. However, unlike the Dormant Commerce Clause, the Privileges and Immunities Clause does not apply to corporations or businesses since corporations or businesses (in the eyes of the courts) are not "citizens." This Clause is only triggered when a state places a burden on a *fundamental right* of a citizen of another state. Perhaps the most commonly cited fundamental right is the right to earn a living.

Although the Privileges and Immunities Clause does not directly apply to corporations, in certain circumstances they may still find themselves subject to review under it.

Example: Alaska passed a law that required all companies extracting oil from the state to prefer hiring Alaska residents over nonresidents. A group of nonresidents challenged the law as a violation of the Privileges and Immunities Clause. The Supreme Court held that the law violated the Privileges and Immunities Clause, reasoning that the law unfairly discriminated against nonresidents' rights to earn a living. *Hicklin v. Orbeck*, 437 U.S. 518 (1978)

Management Application
Is Higher Tuition for Out-of-State Residents Unconstitutional?

State universities may charge higher tuition for out-of-state residents than they charge in-state residents. This practice does not violate the Privileges and Immunities Clause, which is involved when a state burdens a *fundamental right* of a citizen from another state. Unfortunately for those students currently paying more for out-of-state tuition, there is no fundamental right to higher education. Therefore, states are free to place a higher burden on those out-of-state individuals.

Should states cooperate to remove out-of-state barriers with respect to tuition pricing? How would such a process work?

Full Faith and Credit Clause

Full Faith and Credit Clause
State courts must respect the judgments of courts from other states.

The **Full Faith and Credit Clause** requires the states to respect the "public acts, records, and judicial proceedings of every other state." This Clause ensures that judicial determinations made in one state have the same force and effect in a different state. This prevents parties from moving from one state to another to avoid the enforcement of a judgment against them or requesting that a new lawsuit be brought in another state to obtain a better outcome than that received in the first state. However, there are some limitations upon the extent to which the Full Faith and Credit Clause may require a state to enforce the law or judgment of the other state even if it be in contravention of its own statutes or policy.

As one court has explained, "The very purpose of the full-faith and credit clause was to alter the status of the several states as independent foreign sovereignties, each free to ignore obligations created under the laws or by the judicial proceedings of the others, and to make them integral parts of a single nation throughout which a remedy upon a just obligation might be demanded as of right, irrespective of the state of its origin. That purpose ought not lightly to be set aside out of deference to a local policy which, if it exists, would seem to be too trivial to merit serious consideration when weighed against the policy of the constitutional provision and the interest of the state whose judgment is challenged." *City of Jacksonville, Florida v. Municipal Electric Authority of Georgia*. 608 F. Supp. 3d 1262 (N.D.Ga. 2020)

Bill of Rights

Bill of Rights The first ten amendments to the U.S. Constitution.

The **Bill of Rights** is comprised of the first ten amendments to the United States Constitution. These amendments serve to establish fundamental rights and protect them from violation by the government.

While the protections of the Bill of Rights apply to all individuals, some of the protections apply to businesses as well. Corporations are considered distinct legal entities under the law, and they are granted some of the protections of the Bill of Rights. Following is a summary of the Bill of Rights:

1. The First Amendment contains the rights of freedom of religion, freedom of speech, freedom of the press, freedom to assemble, and freedom to petition the government.
2. The Second Amendment protects the right of the people to keep and bear arms.
3. The Third Amendment prevents the government from forcing homeowners to house soldiers during times of peace.
4. The Fourth Amendment protects against unreasonable searches and seizures of both people and private property and requires the use of warrants.
5. The Fifth Amendment requires the government to use a grand jury for criminal charges, mandates due process of law, prohibits double jeopardy, and includes the privilege against self-incrimination.
6. The Sixth Amendment contains a number of rights for criminal defendants, such as the right to a speedy, public jury trial, the right to confront witnesses, and the right to counsel.
7. The Seventh Amendment establishes the right to a jury trial in civil cases, as long as they involve a dispute of at least $20.
8. The Eighth Amendment prevents the government from employing cruel and unusual punishments.
9. The Ninth Amendment provides that there are additional rights beyond those listed in the Constitution.
10. The Tenth Amendment asserts that all powers not expressly given to the federal government are retained by the states or the people.

Beyond the first ten amendments, the Constitution has been amended an additional 17 times, for a total of 27 amendments. A few highlights from the remaining amendments include the abolition of slavery, the prohibition of voting discrimination based on race or sex, and establishing the voting age of 18, as well as providing for the direct election of senators, prohibiting poll taxes, and establishing term limits for the presidency.

When the Bill of Rights was first written and adopted, the restrictions applied only to the federal government. It was not until the adoption of the Fourteenth Amendment, after the Civil War, that the protections contained in the Bill of Rights began to apply to the states through the **incorporation doctrine**. The incorporation doctrine is the method by which courts have applied the rights contained in the Bill of Rights to the state governments. The courts have moved slowly over time, but currently nearly all of the protections granted by the Bill of Rights apply to state and local governments.

Incorporation doctrine
The process by which provisions of the Bill of Rights are made applicable to the states through the Due Process Clause of the Fourteenth Amendment.

Freedom of Speech

The primary purpose of the guarantee of freedom of speech is to allow engagement in the political process, and this right to **political speech** is granted the highest level of protection by the courts. The freedom of speech also includes the freedom not to speak (such as not saluting the flag) and the freedom to speak anonymously.

Political speech
Speech that comments on or about political subject matter.

> **Example:** The distribution of anonymous leaflets regarding a proposed school tax levy is constitutional. The Supreme Court held, "anonymous pamphleteering is not a pernicious, fraudulent practice, but an honorable tradition of advocacy and of dissent. Anonymity is a shield from the tyranny of the majority. *McIntyre v. Ohio Elections Comm'n*, 514 U.S. 334 (1995)

In addition to traditional verbal (that is, oral) or written speech, the First Amendment also protects **symbolic speech**. Symbolic speech is any form of expressive conduct that aims to communicate a message. Some examples of *symbolic speech* are body gestures, body movements, hand signs, paintings, clothing, jewelry, or any item or movement that expresses an idea.

Symbolic speech
Speech that is nonverbal but expresses an idea to an observer.

> **Example:** Paul Cohen was convicted under state law of disturbing the peace by wearing a jacket bearing the words "F*** the Draft." The Supreme Court reversed the conviction holding that prohibiting the display of an offensive word was unconstitutional, in violation of free speech as a form of symbolic speech. *Cohen v. California*, 403 U.S. 15 (1971)

Consider the following types of speech and their corresponding level of protection.

FULLY PROTECTED SPEECH. Speech that is granted this level of protection can never be infringed upon by the government. The most common type of fully protected speech is *political speech*, which is speech that comments on or about the political process. Political speech can be verbal or nonverbal.

> **Example:** Gregory Johnson burned an American flag in protest while standing outside the site of the Republican National Convention. Texas law prohibited flag burning, and he was convicted of the crime. The Supreme Court reversed and held that flag burning is symbolic political speech and thus granted full protection under the First Amendment. *Texas v. Johnson*, 491 U.S. 397 (1989)

LIMITED PROTECTED SPEECH. Certain types of speech can be limited by the government without violating the First Amendment, for example, commercial speech.

Time, Place, and Manner Restrictions. While the government cannot forbid limited protected speech, the government can pass **content-neutral** laws that regulate the **time, place, and manner** of speech. Laws that restrict expression by time, place, and manner are called *content-neutral* laws because the substance of the speech does not matter. Courts allow for these content-neutral restrictions in an effort to balance the rights of individuals to engage in free speech, against protecting the general welfare of society. To qualify as a reasonable time, place and manner restriction, the law must (1) be content neutral, (2) be narrowly tailored to advance a substantial government interest, and (3) leave open alternative channels of communication.

Content-neutral laws
Laws that do not discriminate based on the substance of the speech.

Time, place, and manner laws
Laws that restrict speech based only on the time, location, or method of speaking.

> **Example:** A group of protesters were granted a permit to protest for 24 hours in Lafayette Park in Washington, D.C. The protesters wished to sleep overnight in the park. The National Park Service prohibited sleeping as part of the no-camping regulation in place for the park. The protesters challenged the law as a violation of free speech. The Court found that the law was valid, and the protesters were not allowed to sleep in the park, because it was content neutral. *Clark v. Community for Creative Non-Violence*, 468 U.S. 288 (1984)

Commercial Speech. This is speech that consists primarily of advertising and marketing, across all media, which relates to the commercial interests of the business or individual making the speech. Commercial speech is not granted unlimited protection, like political speech, but is granted limited protection. To be protected as commercial speech, the speech must be truthful and not misleading.

> **Example:** Rhode Island enacted a law banning the advertisement of retail liquor prices except inside the stores themselves. Liquormart, a Rhode Island liquor retailer, challenged the law as an unconstitutional restriction on commercial speech. The Court held that the law was an unconstitutional restriction on commercial speech. In so deciding, the Court stated that Rhode Island failed to prove the law would reduce alcohol consumption, and the law was too expansive in comparison to that goal. *44 Liquormart, Inc. v. Rhode Island*, 517 U.S. 484 (1996)

UNPROTECTED SPEECH. The courts have found that not all speech is protected by the First Amendment. Some types of speech are granted no protection at all, and the government is able to regulate those types of speech freely. The following categories of speech are unprotected:

- Obscene Speech. The Supreme Court, in *Miller v. California*, created a test for legal obscenity. The court held that speech is obscene when: (1) the average person in the community (local or statewide) would find that the work appeals to the prurient interest (unwholesome or arousing interest), (2) the work depicts or describes in a patently offensive way sexual conduct, and (3) taken as a whole the work lacks serious literary, artistic, political or scientific value.

Because community standards vary widely, one Supreme Court Justice has stated, "I know it when I see it."[2]

- Fighting Words
- Defamation
- Perjury
- Threats
- Attempting to Convince Others to Commit Crimes
- Speech that Incites Violent Action

Example: Minnesota law made it a crime to stalk and harass an individual by making repeated calls intending to intimidate them. The defendant was convicted under the law of making repeated calls and leaving threatening voicemails. He challenged the law as a violation of free speech. The court of appeals for Minnesota held that the threats were fighting words and thus not protected speech. *State v. Hall*, 887 N.W.2d 847 (Minn. Ct. App. 2016)

CORPORATE POLITICAL SPEECH. Corporate political speech was not always considered to be within the protection of the First Amendment. However, after a series of cases starting in the 1970s, the Supreme Court greatly expanded the protections given to corporate political speech. Corporations capitalized on these protections by spending money in support of their preferred political candidates. Congress then responded by limiting the amount corporations can spend on elections.

Example: Citizens United, a nonprofit corporation, released a critical documentary about Hillary Clinton before the 2008 election. Federal law prohibited corporations from using their general treasury funds to engage in corporate political speech that directly supports or opposes a candidate within 30 days of an election. Citizens United challenged the law as an unconstitutional violation of its freedom of speech. The Supreme Court found in favor of Citizens United and overturned the law that limited the amount of money a corporation can spend engaging in political speech. *Citizens United v. F.E.C.*, 558 U.S. 310 (2010)

Establishment Clause Under the First Amendment, the government is prohibited from establishing, advancing, or promoting a state-sponsored religion.

Free Exercise Clause Under the First Amendment, American citizens are protected from government interference with the exercise of their religion.

Freedom of Religion

The free practice of religion is another bedrock principle of the United States. The Founders sought to protect that right through two clauses in the First Amendment, the **Establishment Clause** and the **Free Exercise Clause**. The First Amendment states that "Congress shall make no law respecting an establishment of religion or prohibiting the free exercise thereof."

ESTABLISHMENT CLAUSE. The Establishment Clause prohibits the government from *establishing* a state-sponsored religion, but it also means that the government cannot seek to advance or promote a single religion above all others, or any religion above none at all. This Clause ensures that neither the states nor the federal government sponsor a specific religion.

2. *Jacobellis v. Ohio*, 84 S. Ct. 1676 (1964).

Example: As part of a public high school graduation ceremony, the school invited a local rabbi to give an invocation. The rabbi was provided a pamphlet that recommended that prayers be inclusive and sensitive. A student at the school challenged the school practice of offering prayers at the graduation as a violation of the Establishment Clause. The Supreme Court held that it was a violation of the Establishment Clause to have clergy speak at a public high school graduation. *Lee v. Weisman*, 505 U.S. 577 (1992)

FREE EXERCISE CLAUSE. The Free Exercise Clause expressly prohibits the government from interfering with the free exercise of one's religion (freedom to believe and freedom to act). However, that does not mean that the government can never interfere with a religious exercise, but when doing so the government must meet strict scrutiny. Strict scrutiny requires the government to prove a compelling state interest, and that the law is narrowly tailored to meet that interest. This usually requires the government to prove that the current law is the only way to achieve the compelling interest, which is a heavy burden.

If the law is neutral toward religion, and applies equally to all, courts will review the law under rational basis review, which requires only a legitimate purpose and that the law can reasonably further that purpose.

Example: A Washington state law required that all pharmacies deliver and dispense drugs as prescribed, with a few secular exceptions but none that were religious. A collection of pharmacies and pharmacists who had religious objections to dispensing emergency contraceptives challenged the law as a violation of their free exercise of religion. The court found in favor of the state and upheld the law. The court reasoned that the law was neutral and generally applicable, and therefore subject to a rational basis review. Washington's legitimate interest in ensuring people quick and safe access to their medicine satisfied that review. *Stormans, Inc. v. Wiesman*, 794 F.3d 1064 (9th Cir. 2015)

Example: Trinity Lutheran Church operated a nonprofit preschool and daycare, which included a playground for the children. Trinity Lutheran sought to participate in Missouri's scrap tire recycling program to upgrade their playground surface. The state denied the application because Trinity is a church. Trinity challenged the law as a violation of its free exercise right. The Supreme Court held that denying the benefit to Trinity was a violation of the Free Exercise Clause. *Trinity Lutheran Church of Columbia, Inc. v. Comer*, 582 U.S. 449 (2017)

Due Process and Equal Protection Clauses

The Due Process Clause of the Fifth and Fourteenth Amendments, in conjunction with the Equal Protection Clause of the Fourteenth Amendment, serve to enhance the rights and protections contained in the Constitution.

Due Process

Contained in the Due Process Clauses of the Fifth and Fourteenth Amendments are the protections that no "life, liberty, or property" shall be deprived from any person without "due process of law." These Clauses prohibit federal and state governments from infringing on the life, liberty, or property of an individual without a just and fair legal process. There are two types of due process: **procedural due process** and **substantive due process.**

Procedural due process
Laws that burden life, liberty, or property must provide notice, a meaningful hearing, and an impartial decision maker.

Substantive due process
Requires that a law be fair and reasonable and have an adequate justification.

PROCEDURAL DUE PROCESS. Procedural due process requires when an individual is to be deprived of a protected interest (life, liberty, property), the government must give the individual notice and a reasonable opportunity to be heard by an impartial decision maker. That is, a court will find that a law that may be otherwise valid, but is enforced or applied unfairly, is unconstitutional as a violation of procedural due process.

The courts use a balancing test to determine when a hearing must occur and how complete it must be. The test has three factors:

- The significance of the private interest that will be affected by the governmental action;
- The extent to which additional procedural safeguards would reduce the risk of error; and
- The public interest in resolving the matter quickly and efficiently.

The test is a cost-benefit analysis in which the court evaluates the need for a particular procedure by balancing these factors.

> **Example:** New York offered need-based aid to families with dependent children. Recipients of the aid alleged that state officials terminated their aid without prior notice and hearing in violation of their procedural due process rights. The Court held that the interest of the recipients in receiving uninterrupted payments from the state outweighed the state's interest in reducing fiscal and administrative burdens. Thus, the state violated procedural due process, and the recipients were granted a pretermination hearing. *Goldberg v. Kelly*, 397 U.S. 254 (1970)

SUBSTANTIVE DUE PROCESS. Governmental legislative or regulatory action may be subject to a substantive due process challenge. The objection asserts that a law is invalid because the government lacks sufficient reason to warrant interfering with an individual's protected interest. These claims challenge the power of the government to pass a law in a particular area by asserting that the government has no legitimate purpose to pass the law, and that the law does little, if anything, to advance that purpose.

> **Example:** Texas law required that estheticians have a license to do business in the state. A group of businesses engaged in "threading," a specialty eyebrow treatment, challenged the law as a violation of their right to earn a living. The court overturned the law, and held in favor of the "threaders," reasoning that the law violated their substantive due process right to earn a living. *Patel v. Texas Dep't of Licensing & Regulation*, 469 S.W.3d 69 (Tex. 2015)

In cases where the government has passed a law that infringes on a *fundamental right*, the courts require the government to prove that there is a compelling interest and that the law is the only way to further that interest.

Equal Protection

The **Equal Protection Clause** states, "No State shall . . . deny to any person within its jurisdiction the equal protection of the laws." The Clause does not prohibit all forms of discrimination, as almost every law is somewhat discriminatory. Instead, courts have developed appropriate *standards of review* to evaluate laws challenged under this doctrine. When determining whether a law complies with the Equal Protection Clause, the courts employ three standards of review: *strict scrutiny*, *intermediate scrutiny*, and *rational basis review*.

Equal Protection Clause
The Clause contained in the Fourteenth Amendment that prohibits the state from unfairly discriminating.

STRICT SCRUTINY. Strict scrutiny reviews the lawfulness of any government regulation that classifies persons based on a suspect classification, which includes race, national origin, citizenship, or involves fundamental rights (such as domestic travel or voting). Under strict scrutiny, the law will be upheld only if it is *necessary to achieve a compelling government purpose*. Laws reviewed under this standard are almost always struck down.

> **Example:** Edward Daly suffered from a medical disorder that caused seizures. The Motor Vehicle Commissioner for the State of Connecticut suspended Mr. Daly's driver's license unless he agreed to report to the state regular medical checkups. Mr. Daly challenged the law. The court reviewed under strict scrutiny, finding that the law violated equal protection because it was not narrowly tailored. *Daly v. DelPonte*, 624 A.2d 876 (1993)

INTERMEDIATE SCRUTINY. Under intermediate scrutiny, a law is upheld only if it is *substantially related to an important government purpose*. Intermediate scrutiny is involved where there is a classification based on a protected class, such as gender. This standard requires that the classification must have an exceedingly persuasive justification. Some First Amendment cases can fall into this category, such as *time, place, and manner* restrictions. Laws that fall into this category can survive but are overturned more often than under rational basis review.

> **Example:** Oklahoma law set different drinking ages for men and women. Craig Boren challenged the law as a violation of equal protection. Oklahoma argued that the objective was to reduce drunk driving and provided statistical evidence in support of its classification. However, the Court found the law was not sufficiently related to meeting that objective. Thus, the law was overturned. *Craig v. Boren*, 429 U.S. 190 (1976)

RATIONAL BASIS REVIEW. This test reviews the lawfulness of all other government classifications not involving a suspect or protected class. Under rational basis review, the courts will uphold a government regulation so long as it is *rationally related to a legitimate government purpose*. This standard permits much government business regulation.

> **Example:** Palm Beach County, Florida, entered into an agreement with Uber®, a ride service provider, which allowed it to operate without a taxi license. A taxi company challenged the agreement as a violation of equal protection because the taxi company was subject to stricter regulation. The court held that the agreement was valid and did not violate equal protection because the county had a legitimate interest, and the law was rationally related to it. *VTS Transportation, Inc. v. Palm Beach Cnty.*, 239 F. Supp. 3d 1350 (S.D. Fla. Mar. 9, 2017)

Concept Summary The Standards of Review

	Strict Scrutiny	Intermediate Scrutiny	Rational Basis
Test	The regulation must be necessary to achieve a compelling governmental purpose.	The regulation must be substantially related to an important governmental purpose.	The regulation must be rationally related to a legitimate government purpose.
Examples of Classifications That Trigger Test	Race, national origin, citizenship, domestic travel, voting	Gender	Age, wealth, occupation, disability

AI Feature: Government's Right to Regulate Industries

Use an internet search engine to research the Dormant Commerce Clause. Assume your nonprofit health organization wishes to propose state legislation. Your organization is lobbying for a law setting the minimum number of green energy vehicles that must be available for sale by each automobile manufacturer within your state in the next four years. What constitutional challenges, including extraterritoriality, do you expect to receive based upon the Dormant Commerce Clause? Then, using an AI program, draft a memorandum supporting the law's adoption; include arguments supporting its constitutionality. What data, including health research studies, should be introduced in support of the law's adoption? Explain how they may impact the constitutionality of the law.

Key Terms

- Bill of Rights, 83
- Checks and balances, 72
- Commerce Clause, 73
- Content-neutral laws, 85
- Dormant Commerce Clause, 77
- Equal Protection Clause, 89
- Establishment Clause, 86
- Federalism, 72
- Free Exercise Clause, 86
- Full Faith and Credit Clause, 82

- Incorporation doctrine, 84
- Necessary and Proper Clause, 81
- Police power, 79
- Political speech, 84
- Preemption, 80
- Privileges and Immunities Clause, 82
- Procedural due process, 88
- Separation of powers, 72
- Substantive due process, 88
- Supremacy Clause, 80
- Symbolic speech, 84
- Taxing and Spending Clause, 81
- Time, place, and manner laws, 85

Applying the Law

4.1 Taxation to Promote Compliance. As part of the Affordable Care Act (ACA), Congress included a provision that required all Americans to purchase health insurance. If they failed to purchase health insurance, they were charged a tax by the IRS. The provision that required individuals to purchase the insurance was called the individual mandate. Congress passed this law in part under its Commerce Clause authority. A coalition of businesses challenged the individual mandate as unconstitutional and in violation of the Commerce Clause. They argued that while Congress does have the power to regulate existing economic activity, it does not have the power to force individuals to participate unwillingly. Their argument rested on the distinction between voluntary activity and inactivity, claiming that Congress can only regulate the former and not the latter. Is their argument correct? *NFIB v. Sebelius*, 567 U.S. 519 (2012)

4.2 Dormant Commerce Clause. South Dakota passed a law allowing it to collect sales tax from out-of-state online sellers. Overturning two of its prior decisions, the Supreme Court held that physical presence in a state is not needed for a seller to be subject to the state's sales tax requirements. Although the Commerce Clause is written as an affirmative grant of authority to Congress, the Court held that in some instances it imposes limitations on the states absent congressional action. What made the Court change its position and what are these limitations? *South Dakota v. Wayfair, Inc.* 585 U.S. 162 (2018)

4.3 Equal Protection. A banking law enacted by the state of New York held that any savings bank subject to its law was entitled to sell life insurance, but the law prohibited the sale of such policies to any person who neither resided nor worked regularly in New York state. Edwin Gorin, a resident of New Jersey and regularly employed in that state, and others sued to overturn this prohibition, asserting that they violated the federal and state equal protection laws. How should the federal court rule and why? *Consumers Union of United States, Inc. v. Albright*, 427 F. Supp. 840 (S.D.N.Y. 1977)

4.4 Privileges and Immunities. Kathryn Piper, a Vermont resident, was allowed to take and passed the New Hampshire bar examination. However, the New Hampshire Supreme Court limited bar admission to state residents. Piper requested an exception to the residency requirement, which was denied. Does the bar admission limitation violate the Privileges and Immunities Clause? Would the state have legitimate reasons to require residency? *Supreme Court of New Hampshire v. Piper*, 470 U.S. 274 (1985)

4.5 Police Power. David Lucas paid $975,000 for two residential lots on the Isle of Palms, in South Carolina, on which he intended to build single family homes. However, the state legislature had enacted a law which had the direct effect of barring him from building habitable structures on his two parcels. The law had the intent of preserving the coastline. He claimed that the actions made his property valueless and, essentially, was a taking of private property under the Fifth and Fourth Amendments requiring the payment of just compensation. Was this a lawful exercise of the state's police power or an unlawful taking of private property by the government? *Lucas v. South Carolina Coastal Council*, 505 U.S. 1003 (1992)

4.6 Checks and Balances. An investment company and its owner, Raymond Lucia, petitioned for a review of an order by the SEC that imposed sanctions for a violation of antifraud regulations. The SEC delegated the review to an administrative law judge (ALJ) selected by staff members. Lucia argued that SEC ALJs were "Officers of the United States" and were subject to the Constitution's Appointments Clause. The SEC and the Court of Appeals for the D.C. Circuit rejected Lucia's argument and held that SEC ALJs are not "Officers of the United States" and are mere employees. Should judges deciding regulatory matters be subject to appointment by the president and confirmation by the Senate? Why or why not? *Lucia v. SEC*, 138 S. Ct. 2044 (2018)

4.7 Commerce Clause. The Professional and Amateur Sports Protection Act (PASPA) makes it unlawful for a state or its subdivisions to "sponsor, operate, advertise, promote, license, or authorize by law or compact . . . a lottery, sweepstakes, or other betting, gambling . . . on" competitive sporting events. PASPA does not make sports gambling a federal crime; instead, the Attorney General and professional and amateur sports organizations bring civil actions to enjoin violations. New Jersey enacted a law to repeal state law provisions that prohibited such schemes. Professional and amateur sports leagues brought this action to enjoin New Jersey from passing the new law. Does the Constitution prevent states from enacting laws pertaining to the same legislative area as Congress? *Murphy v. National Collegiate Athletic Association*, 584 U.S. 453 (2018)

4.8 Time and Place Laws. Freeman, a treasurer for a political campaign in Tennessee, filed an action. Her complaint alleged that a law that prohibits the solicitation of votes and the display and distribution of campaign materials within 100 feet of a polling place violates the First and Fourteenth Amendments. What standard of review should be applied? Is there a compelling governmental interest at issue? Why or why not? *Burson v. Freeman*, 504 U.S. 191 (1992)

4.9 Commerce Clause. Complete Auto Transit, which transported motor vehicles from train stops in Mississippi-to-Mississippi car dealers, was assessed back taxes for the sales of transportation services. The taxes were imposed pursuant to Miss. Code Ann. § 10105 (1972), which imposed a "privilege of doing business" tax within the state upon activity in interstate commerce. Was this tax constitutional when it was applied to this interstate commerce activity? Explain your answer. *Complete Auto Transit, Inc. v. Brady*, 430 U.S. 274 (1977)

4.10 Commercial Speech. New York state law prevented sellers in any sales transaction from imposing a surcharge on a holder who uses a credit card instead of cash payments. Five New York businesses and their owners challenged this law and filed suit against state officials arguing that the law violated the First Amendment by regulating how they communicate their prices. Does this statute violate the First Amendment? Why or why not? *Expressions Hair Design v. Schneiderman*, 581 U.S. 37 (2017)

Torts

5

You have to accept whatever comes, and the only important thing is that you meet it with the best you have to give. — Eleanor Roosevelt, political figure, diplomat, and activist (1884-1962)

Chapter Outline

Learning Objectives

After studying this chapter, you should be able to:

1. Define the boundaries of tort law.
2. Define what constitutes an intentional tort.
3. Identify the legal duties owed by tortfeasors.
4. Explain the elements of negligence.
5. Discuss the common defenses to negligence claims.

Introduction

Tort
A civil wrong, whether intentional or accidental, for which a claim for damages may be sought.

Tortfeasor
A person who commits a tort.

A **tort** is any civil wrong for which the law provides an injured party some remedy against the wrongdoer, who is known as a **tortfeasor**. Through tort law, people are responsible not only for the results of their willful acts, but also for injuries caused to another by their lack of ordinary care or skill in managing their person or property. Occasionally, the injured party can sue for strict liability, a form of tort liability discussed in the next chapter. This chapter discusses intentional torts and negligence.

Tort law concerns whether an individual's harmful conduct to another makes that individual liable for damages for the harm suffered. Many of the torts we will study have their beginnings in the English common law. Modern courts and legislatures have expanded tort law to adjust to society's needs. For example, the courts have extended tort law to cover the harm caused due to defamatory social media postings about a person's character or a business's reputation.

Classification of Torts

Intentional torts
Torts that are committed through the tortfeasor's deliberate effort.

Negligence
Torts that are unintentional, but still impose liability due to the defendant's conduct.

Tortious intent
Tortfeasor desired or believed the consequences of their act were likely to occur.

There are two categories of torts: (1) intentional torts, and (2) the unintentional tort of negligence. **Intentional torts** are torts that cause harm to another because of the tortfeasor's deliberate effort. **Negligence** does not require intent but imposes liability because of the circumstances of the defendant's conduct.

To commit an intentional tort, the wrongdoer must demonstrate the intent to perform the wrongful conduct. **Tortious intent** means either (1) the tortfeasor desired the consequences of the act, or (2) that the tortfeasor believed the consequences were substantially likely to occur. An intentional motive is not required.

Transferred Intent

Transferred intent
The defendant's intent will be transferred when the defendant intended to commit a tort against one party, but the tort caused harm to another party. Intent is also transferred when the defendant intends to commit one tort against a party but actually commits a different tort against that party.

A tortfeasor can also be liable for a tort where transferred intent exists. **Transferred intent** applies when a defendant intended a tort against one party, but the tort caused harm to another party.

Example: Miguel intended to throw a baseball at Josef, but Josef avoided the throw and the ball hit Kari. In this instance, Miguel's intent transfers from the intended party (Josef) to the party actually harmed (Kari). Miguel is liable in tort for Kari's injuries.

Transferred intent also arises when a tortfeasor intends to commit a certain tort against a party, but actually commits a different tort against that same party.

Example: Miguel had intended to scare Josef (assault) by pretending to throw a baseball at him, but instead, he lost control of the ball and struck Josef in the face (battery). The intent of committing one tort transfers to the tort actually committed in this case.

The doctrine of transferred intent applies to the following torts: assault, battery, false imprisonment, and trespass. Generally, minors and those lacking mental capacity are held responsible for intentional torts they commit, despite lacking the knowledge of the wrongfulness of their acts or the ability to foresee the consequences of their acts.

For an overview of the tort litigation handled by the U.S. Department of Justice, see https://www.justice.gov/jm/jm-4-5000-tort-litigation.

Intentional Torts Against Persons

Assault

An **assault** is an act that leads another person to believe that they are about to suffer imminent bodily harm or offensive (non-permitted) contact. *It does not require actual contact with the person.* Assault may occur with words, gestures, or threatening actions.

Assault
An act that leads another person to believe they are about to suffer imminent bodily harm or offensive contact.

> **Example:** A person who is fearful of having water thrown in their face by an irate patron at a restaurant who has picked up the drink container and appears ready to throw it can sue the irate person for assault.

The law requires apprehension by the plaintiff in order to find assault. Unlike in battery, the plaintiff must be aware or have knowledge of the defendant's act. The law only requires reasonable apprehension of someone's apparent ability to impose harm.

> **Example:** A threat made while pointing an unloaded gun at another would be an assault if the person believes the gun is loaded. However, this same action done to a sleeping person would not be an assault.

Threats of future harm, those lacking immediacy, are insufficient for an act of assault. For example, if Alex threatened Adrian that he would intentionally throw a fast pitch at Adrian's head in a *future* softball game, there is no apprehension of immediate harm.

Battery

Battery is the intentional harmful or offensive (non-permitted) contact to another person. Battery occurs if the act that created the apprehension of contact occurs, and results in harm to the plaintiff. For offensive contact, it is the intentional, unprivileged, and unwanted contact of another person that causes battery. The intent to injure is immaterial; the defendant is liable for all of the consequences that directly and naturally result, even if they were unintended. As noted above, if the defendant attempts to hit one person and actually hits another, the defendant is liable to the second person under the theory of transferred intent.

Battery
A tort that arises through the intentional, unprivileged, and unwanted contact of another person.

> **Example:** Amy decided to play a practical joke on Chris during a business presentation. After Chris stood up to applaud a speaker and just as he was about to sit down in his chair, Amy pulled Chris's chair out from behind him. As a result, Chris fell hard to the floor. In addition to suffering embarrassment, he reinjured a prior back injury in the incident. Amy is subject to liability for committing a battery against Chris.

No liability for battery arises unless the defendant acted negligently, or with reckless or willful intent.

> **Example:** If Heather innocently tripped while jogging and knocked over a fellow jogger there is no battery.

False Imprisonment

False imprisonment The intentional confinement or restraint of another person without legal authority, justification, or consent.

False imprisonment is the intentional confinement or restraint of another person without legal authority, justification, or consent. A person must be aware of the confinement or be otherwise harmed by the confinement. False imprisonment violates the personal liberty of another by confining the person against their will. A person may be restrained through physical force, barriers, restraint, or threats of physical force. Moral pressure or threats of future harm to an individual do not constitute false imprisonment.

False imprisonment also requires there must be no reasonable or safe means of escape known to the plaintiff.

> **Example:** Irwin, a collection agent for the finance division of a furniture company, went to the home of the plaintiff to repossess furniture for delinquent payments. For several hours, he blocked her driveway to prevent her from driving off, ordered her to stay until the repossession truck arrived, and refused to allow her to get food. Upon arrival, the truck removed the furniture from the plaintiff's home and left. False imprisonment occurred in this instance because Irwin's conduct effectively prevented the plaintiff from leaving, and her car was her only means of transportation.

Shoplifting is a problem for some businesses, and most states have enacted statutes to protect merchants from suspected shoplifters. The *shopkeeper's privilege* allows merchants to detain persons reasonably suspected of shoplifting to investigate the situation without fear of liability for false imprisonment. To qualify for this protection, merchants must have a reasonable suspicion of shoplifting, conduct the investigation in a reasonable manner, and detain the person for a reasonable amount of time.

> **Example:** A retail store employee suspected a customer of shoplifting. The employee briefly detained the customer and performed a search of the customer's bag. Because this detention was not for an unreasonable period of time, there was no false imprisonment. *Gordon v. May Dep't Stores Co.*, 254 A.D.2d 327 (1998)

Intentional Infliction of Emotional Distress

Intentional infliction of emotional distress Viewed by a reasonable person, the intentional, extreme, and outrageous conduct of another person certain or substantially certain to cause emotional distress to the victim.

The tort of **intentional infliction of emotional distress** involves *extreme and outrageous* conduct that results in a person suffering severe emotional distress. It can occur without physical injury or contact between the parties. The conduct must be so extreme and outrageous that it exceeds all bounds of decency. Repeated harassment or conduct directed at a fragile class of persons (such as children or the elderly) can constitute extreme and outrageous conduct. The mental distress suffered must be severe, such that its intensity, duration, and mental and physical distress interfere with normal life activities.

The workplace is often the setting for this tort. While courts hold that termination of employment alone does not support an emotional distress claim, along with a request for punitive damages, the circumstances might invite such an award.

Example: Suppose a business continued to allow vulgar and sexually harassing comments to be directed to a single mother who was the sole support of her family. In addition to a claim for sexual harassment, the former employee may recover additional damages for intentional infliction of emotional distress to the extent that the conduct was extreme and outrageous.

Courts will consider on a case-by-case basis whether the conduct is extreme and outrageous.

Example: Michael Jarrard sued his employer, UPS®, for intentional infliction of emotional distress after he received a scathing evaluation of his job performance at UPS after returning from 6 weeks of medical leave for extended psychiatric care. In a twenty-page evaluation form covering numerous topics, Jarrard received grades of two or three on a scale of 0 to 6, whereas his prior evaluations were primarily ranks of 5 or 6. Jarrard disagreed with the rankings given to him, but the harsh evaluation was apparently in retaliation for past conflicts between Jarrard and management. As a result of the evaluation, Jarrard experienced a complete mental breakdown. The state appellate court held that a single brutal employment evaluation did not rise to the level of outrageousness required to be actionable for intentional infliction of emotional distress. *Jarrard v. United Parcel Service, Inc.*, 529 S.E.2d 144 (Ga. Ct. App. 2000)

Management Application Who Can Be Sued?

Plaintiffs often name many parties as defendants in addition to the original wrongdoer. The defendants in a tort lawsuit might include:

1. *The tortfeasor.* The general rule is that every person is liable for their own torts.
2. *Multiple tortfeasors.* When people act in concert with each other or pursuant to a common plan, the concerted action can result in each of them being liable to the injured person. Under what is known as joint and several liability, each defendant who acted in concert with the other is liable for the entire amount of the plaintiff's damages.
3. *An employer.* A private employer is ordinarily liable under the doctrine of *respondeat superior* for torts of its agents and employees committed while they are acting within the course and scope of their employment. It is immaterial that the business neither authorized nor ratified the tort. This concept extends liability to the employer, who presumably can more easily pay damages. When someone is not an employee but is instead an independent contractor, the doctrine does not apply.
4. *Those who have a duty to protect or control others.* This class of persons would include those who have a special relationship with the plaintiff, such as a duty to aid or protect the plaintiff. Examples include trained emergency personnel, innkeepers, possessors of land who hold the land open to the public, and parents to their minor children.

Defamation

Defamation
A factually false statement communicated to a third person regarding a person or business that causes injury to reputation or character.

Defamation refers to false statements causing injury to a person's reputation or exposing the person to public hatred, contempt, or ridicule. A defamation plaintiff might contend that the publication tended to prevent third parties from dealing or associating with them. The elements of a cause of action for defamation are:

1. The defendant made a false statement of material fact about the plaintiff;
2. The statement was published or communicated to a third party; and
3. The plaintiff suffered an injury due to their reputation being damaged.

The defamatory statement does not include a mere opinion — it is an unprivileged publication of a false statement to a third person that injures the plaintiff. Speech protected by the First Amendment may still create liability for defamation.

Libel
A form of defamation through use of written false statements.

Slander
A form of defamation through use of spoken false statements.

Defamatory statements come in two forms: **libel**, which is defamation arising from a written or other permanent form of publication (such as a podcast), and **slander**, which arises from an oral utterance. The law treats defamatory remarks made through an internet communication as libelous.

> **Example:** Defamatory material that is published and disseminated to company employees through a company intranet, wiki, or even an emailed cartoon can result in the author being sued for defamation. An employer may be liable as a publisher of defamatory statements if the company knew or reasonably should have known the publication was untrue.

THE PUBLICATION REQUIREMENT. The essence of the tort addresses the harm caused by the publication or communication of defamatory information to persons other than the defamed party. The publication to persons other than the target of the defamatory remarks can occur intentionally or accidentally. Statements made to others in casual environments, such as at a party or through social media or messaging applications, can lead to liability for defamation.

> **Example:** If an Instagram® subscriber created an account and disseminated false and defamatory allegations against another person, they could be sued for defamation.

DEFAMATION DAMAGES. There is a presumption of damages when the defamation is libelous. Therefore, in libel cases, the plaintiff need not prove that they were injured or harmed because of the libelous statement to recover damages.

> **Example:** If an automobile repair facility falsely claimed on a social media site that a competitor secretly repaired vehicles with used and not new parts, damages to the affected business are presumed. The targeted business does not have to show actual loss of business due to the false accusation.

A person suing for slander, on the other hand, must show actual monetary losses (that is, *special damages*) to prevail. The underlying policy for this requirement is that continuing and residual harm is unlikely to be suffered because oral statements are temporary; however, a victim of libel may be affected for many years because of the permanency of the publication.

In special types of slander lawsuits known as **slander *per se*** cases, the plaintiff does not need to prove special damages if the defendant's statement accuses the plaintiff of any of the following:

Slander *per se*
Statements that are so inherently defamatory on their face that damage to the plaintiff's reputation is presumed.

1. Having committed a serious, morally reprehensible criminal offense;
2. A loathsome disease (such as allegations that another has an STD or leprosy);
3. Matters incompatible with one's business, trade, profession, or office (for example, alleging that an attorney bribes the local judges); or
4. Unchastity of a woman.

Special damages are those that are quantifiable and were actually suffered by the plaintiff. Aside from these four categories of slander *per se*, the law generally requires proof of special damages in slander actions.

DEFAMATION OF PUBLIC OFFICIALS OR PUBLIC FIGURES. Where the plaintiff is a public official or public figure (one who has achieved fame or notoriety), there is an additional requirement that must be proved when alleging defamation: The defamatory statement must be made by the defendant with **actual malice**. Actual malice occurs if the person who made the statement either knew the statement was false or acted with reckless disregard as to its truth or falsity.

Actual malice
The defendant made the statement with actual knowledge of its falsity or with reckless disregard as to its truth or falsity.

The actual malice standard provides defendants with wide latitude in exercising their First Amendment rights of free speech, association, and press with respect to matters of public interest. There is a reasonable expectation that public figures should withstand some criticisms or unflattering statements that are published about them.

Example: A former assistant football coach at the University of Alabama was alleged by the NCAA after an investigation to have arranged at least one fraudulent American College Test ("ACT") score for a prospective student-athlete and had stolen videotapes from the university's athletic department. The NCAA published these statements on its website and the former assistant football coach sued for defamation. The court ruled that the former assistant football coach was a public figure, had failed to prove that the NCAA acted with actual malice in publishing the statements on its website and entered judgment for the NCAA. *Cottrell v. NCAA*, 975 So.2d 306 (2007)

Why, if thou never wast at court, thou never sawest good manners; if thou never sawest good manners, then thy manners must be wicked; and wickedness is sin, and sin is damnation.— Shakespeare, *As You Like it, 3.2.30*

Concept Summary Defamation

- Defamatory statements involve language that holds the plaintiff up to scorn or ridicule in the eyes of people within the community.
- Libel consists of publication of defamatory material in a written medium. Damages are presumed.
- Slander consists of the publication of defamatory matter by spoken words or gestures. The law requires proof of special damages unless it is a slander *per se* case.

Absolute privilege
A person making a statement has the absolute right to make the statement without fear of liability for defamation.

Qualified privilege
A person making a statement may have the right to make the statement without fear of liability for defamation.

DEFENSES TO DEFAMATION CLAIMS. Sometimes, defamatory statements are protected from liability by either an absolute privilege or a qualified privilege. An **absolute privilege** is one that completely insulates the defendant from liability. Statements made in certain governmental proceedings, such as from the floor of a legislature or in a judicial proceeding, are entitled to an absolute privilege. A **qualified privilege** is one that protects someone from being liable for defamation if the statements were made without malice. Defenses to defamation claims include the following:

- *Truth.* Generally, a person does not need to prove the literal truth of every detail, but the communication must be *substantially* true for the absolute privilege or defense of truth to apply. Since defamation is an untrue statement of fact, truth is an absolute defense if all of the statement is accurate.

Example: Phoenix Newspapers, Inc., published a statement that a candidate for Congress "was sentenced to 24 hours in jail on a misdemeanor charge for firing a gun after a motorist accidentally leaned on a car horn." The candidate demanded the newspaper retract the statement as untrue and sued for libel when the newspaper refused. The candidate was not convicted of firing a weapon but instead convicted of displaying a weapon and he was not sentenced to 24 hours in jail but was sentenced to one day in jail. The court held that the slight inaccuracies did not prevent the statement from being true in substance and held for the newspaper. *Read v. Phoenix Newspapers*, 819 P.2d 939 (Ariz. 1991)

- *Opinion.* Another absolute privilege is a communication based on opinion. Statements of opinion are protected speech under the First Amendment. The publication of an assertion of a fact, however, can subject a person to liability for defamation.

Example: The publication of a statement that the chief financial officer of BigMart lies to her shareholders is a statement of fact that could subject the publisher of the statement to defamation. However, publishing a statement stating the chief financial officer of BigMart is "too inexperienced" is a statement of opinion. This opinion would not subject the publisher of the statement to liability for defamation.

Example: A statement by an attorney to a polygraph operator saying, "You are simply a con artist," was an opinion and not defamatory. *Niotti-Soltesz v. Piotrowski*, 86 N.E.3d 1 (Ohio Ct. App. 2017)

- *Job references.* Most jurisdictions recognize a qualified privilege for former employers to respond to job reference inquiries from subsequent prospective employers if the communications are limited to factual, truthful statements about performance where the employer communicates reasons for terminating employees within the company on a "need-to-know" basis.

Example: Janet Olsson was an education major at Indiana University. As part of her training, Olsson was assigned to a supervising teacher, Janice Stockton, and her university supervisor was Linda Null. At the end of the semester, Stockton submitted a final evaluation of Olsson's teaching abilities and issued her a passing grade in student teaching. After Olsson applied for a full-time teaching position at the school, Null wrote a letter that described Olsson as a marginal student teacher and did not recommend Olsson for a full-time teaching position.

After not receiving an interview or a job at the school and seeking an explanation for her nonhire from the school district, Olsson was shown a copy of the letter written by Null. Olsson sued Indiana University, alleging defamation. The court held that the university had a qualified privilege to write the letter. It had a defense to the defamation claim. *Olsson v. Indiana Univ. Bd. of Trustees*, 571 N.E.2d 585 (Ind. Ct. App. 1991)

- *Parody.* When a public figure from politics or entertainment or a media personality is parodied, the First Amendment has protected such artistic expressions from civil liability.

In the following case, the court considered whether a network's news reports intentionally inflicted emotional distress upon family members. The network defended on the basis that knowledge of emotional fragility is not sufficient for proving intentional infliction of emotional distress.

CASE 5.1

KNOWLEDGE OF SUSCEPTIBILITY IS RELEVANT TO PROVE INTENTIONAL INFLICTION OF EMOTIONAL DISTRESS

RICH v. FOX NEWS NETWORK, LLC

939 F.3d 112 (2nd Cir. 2019)

United States Court of Appeals for the Second Circuit

Seth Rich was murdered during a botched robbery. He was a 27-year-old staffer for the Democratic National Committee ("DNC"). Soon after Seth's murder, uncorroborated theories—contradicted by official U.S. intelligence reports—surfaced on the internet. Seth had leaked thousands of DNC emails to WikiLeaks, the theories asserted, and that is why he had been assassinated. Seth's parents, the Riches, objected to this theory and issued a statement asking the public to "refrain from pushing unproven and harmful theories about Seth's murder."

Malia Zimmerman (a Fox News reporter) and Ed Butowsky (a Fox News commentator) recruited a Fox News contributor, Rod Wheeler, to help them infiltrate the Rich family. They convinced the plaintiffs, Seth's parents, to hire him as a private investigator to look into the circumstances of Seth's death. And they then exploited Wheeler's connection to the Riches to give credence to what Zimmerman and Butowsky knew were false accusations against Seth—which Zimmerman and Butowsky widely disseminated through Fox News. They did this, it was claimed, with full knowledge of the harm it would do to Seth's parents.

As a result of two articles the Fox employees published, Joel and Mary Rich were harassed and experienced symptoms of post-traumatic stress disorder and social anxiety disorder, leading to their claim for intentional infliction of emotional distress. The defendants were granted a dismissal of the case on the grounds that the defendants' conduct was not extreme or outrageous. The Riches appealed, arguing that Butowsky, Zimmerman, and Fox News engaged in an intentional harassment campaign against them and knew that they were vulnerable to emotional distress.

Language of the Court. *Under New York law a claim for IIED requires a showing of: (i) extreme and outrageous conduct; (ii) intent to cause, or disregard of a substantial probability of causing, severe emotional distress; (iii) a causal connection between the conduct and injury; and (iv) severe emotional distress. Where severe mental pain or anguish is inflicted through a deliberate and malicious campaign of harassment or intimidation IIED provides a remedy. In other words, the proper inquiry is not merely whether each individual act might be outrageous. Rather, the question is whether those actions—under the totality of the circumstances—amounted to a deliberate and malicious campaign.*

We have no trouble concluding that—taking their allegations as true—the Riches plausibly alleged what amounted to a campaign of emotional torture. In order to publish a knowingly false article accusing Seth of leaking the DNC emails, Butowsky and Zimmerman needed a reliable source. They settled on a purportedly independent investigator, hired by the Riches. But they had to fabricate that source. So Butowsky—through lies, religious appeals, and financial support—convinced the Riches to hire Wheeler, a Fox News contributor, as their private investigator. Eventually, Butowsky and Zimmerman told Wheeler that an anonymous FBI investigator had seen emails between Seth and WikiLeaks. Wheeler then regurgitated that unsubstantiated information back to Zimmerman, giving her a named source (himself) for her Fox News article. The article emphasized Wheeler's connection to the Riches, thus lending credibility to his statements.

Zimmerman and Butowsky had enough specific knowledge of the family and the circumstances surrounding Seth's murder to be keenly aware of the Riches' susceptibility to emotional distress in this regard. Zimmerman personally spoke with Joel Rich on at least three occasions in the process of deceiving the Riches into hiring Wheeler, Butowsky falsely assured Joel that he only wanted to help them "get closure, as a family." Butowsky acknowledged to Joel that "'I know what you've been through.'" The fact that the defendants proceeded with their plan in the face of this knowledge of the grieving family's susceptibility makes Zimmerman and Butowsky's conduct plausibly extreme and outrageous.

Decision. The district court erred in dismissing the case, since plaintiffs plausibly alleged the defendants' intent to inflict emotional distress.

Focus on Ethics

What role does ethics play when determining the severity of emotional distress?

Tort of Stalking

Sadly, each year thousands of persons are the targets of hurtful, cruel, or harsh speech on social media sites. People use technology to repeat health-harming statements about an individual, and they can also make threatening, humiliating, or intimidating comments about an individual. While it can occur unintentionally because the recipient does not appreciate the sender's tone or intent, most often such online postings are not accidental. Bullying can have serious effects on its targets, including severe depression, sleep issues, loss of self-esteem, and post-traumatic stress (PTS). Victims often do not know the perpetrator's identity, but the poster usually knows the victim. Within the workplace, bullying can negatively impact the work environment, leading to low employee morale, high turnover and absenteeism, and litigation.

In response to this problem, federal and state laws have been enacted to make persons liable for the tort of stalking when they engage in a pattern of conduct with the intent to follow, alarm, or harass a plaintiff. When the plaintiff reasonably fears for their safety or for those within their immediate family, the plaintiff may recover general damages, special damages, and punitive damages from the defendant. Additionally, the defendant may face criminal cyberstalking charges for the same conduct.

Misuse of Legal Proceedings

Parties are prohibited from using the legal system as a means of harassing a person. A party can be sued for **malicious prosecution** when they (1) sue for an improper purpose (that is, with malice); and (2) lose the lawsuit. In a claim for malicious prosecution, the original defendant sues the original plaintiff.

Malicious prosecution
A tort in which the defendant is alleged to have used the legal system as a means of harassing a person, group of people, or entity.

If a person uses the legal process against another in an improper, unjustified manner or to achieve a result for which it was not intended, they may be liable for **abuse of process**. This may arise in either civil or criminal proceedings. This tort does not require the plaintiff to show the defendant acted with malice or lost in a prior legal proceeding.

Abuse of process
Using the legal process against another in an improper, unjustified manner or to achieve a result for which it was not intended to be used.

Fraud

One who willfully deceives another with the intent to induce that person to alter their position and causes injury is liable for any damage resulting from such deception. **Fraud**, also known as *intentional misrepresentation*, is the assertion or suggestion of untrue facts by a person who does not believe the facts to be true. In order to establish a case of fraud, intentional misrepresentation, or deceit, the plaintiff must prove the following:

Fraud
An intentional misstatement or omission of material fact upon which another party reasonably relies to their detriment.

1. The defendant made a *false representation of material fact*;
2. The defendant *knew* the representation was false (that is, the defendant had *scienter*);
3. The defendant *acted to induce* the plaintiff to rely upon the false representation;
4. The plaintiff *justifiably relied* upon the misrepresentation;
5. The plaintiff *suffered damage* as a result of the reliance upon the statement; and
6. The defendant's misrepresentation *caused* the damages.

Business transactions often involve efforts to persuade customers to purchase a product or service. For fraud to occur in this context, more than statements of opinion or puffery must be involved. When someone recklessly disregards the truth of a statement, intent to defraud may be inferred.

NONDISCLOSURE LIABILITY. Generally, there is no duty to disclose a material fact or opinion to another person. Consequently, the failure to disclose material facts or information will typically not satisfy the first element of fraud. However, there are four exceptions under which liability may be imposed for failing to disclose information:

1. *Fiduciary's statements.* If a person is in a fiduciary or confidential relationship with another person, there is a duty to disclose all material facts to the principal.
2. *Concealment.* When a person actively conceals a material fact, they must disclose that fact (for example, if an automobile dealership turns back the mileage odometer on its used automobiles).
3. *Incomplete statements.* If a person does speak, they must disclose enough information to prevent their words from being misleading.
4. *New information.* If a person makes a statement and subsequently learns new information that makes the earlier statement untrue or misleading, they must disclose such information to anyone whom the person knows may still be relying on the original statement.

Negligent Misrepresentation

In addition to intentional misrepresentations, a tort can arise when a representation is made negligently. This tort occurs when the defendant carelessly makes a representation while believing it to be true but has no reasonable basis to believe its truth. Where the representation is made both honestly and reasonably, there is no tort liability because it is an innocent misrepresentation.

Example: An interested buyer asks a real estate broker about the market value of a property in a nearby county. The broker provides a statement of value without inspection or conducting a market analysis. He does so believing the nearby county property values are the same as the properties he routinely values in his county. The broker has made a negligent misrepresentation and may be liable for harm he causes a buyer who relies on his statement of value and overpays for a property.

Trespass to real property
The act of entering or remaining on the land of another or causing someone or something else to enter or remain on the land of another.

Torts Involving Real Property

Trespass to Real Property

Entering the land of another without permission or privilege can result in liability for trespass. **Trespass to real property** occurs if someone intentionally:

1. Enters another's land or causes a thing or a third person to do so;
2. Remains on the land; or
3. Fails to remove something that he is under duty to remove from another's land.

The law does not require that the real property suffer damage to find liability for trespass. Posting a "No Trespassing" sign can help establish that the entry was unauthorized, but it is not required. Trespass claims can arise in a number of situations, including using a neighbor's land for recreation or parking, constructing an improvement upon it, releasing airborne particles from an industrial plant, and intruding into the protected airspace of another.

PRIVILEGE. In situations involving entering land for a private or public necessity, a party is privileged to trespass if it is a true emergency and not just for a person's convenience. When a party enters land for a private necessity (to protect someone's own interest), they are liable for any harm caused because of their trespass. Where a person enters land for a public necessity (to protect the community), that person is not liable for trespassing.

> **Example:** Entering another's land to suppress a fire racing down a hillside toward many homes is privileged as a public necessity. The trespasser is not liable for the harm caused because of the trespass.

CONSENT. Entry onto another's land is lawful if consent is given. Once consent is given, a person may become a trespasser if they exceed the scope of the consent given. For example, trespassing occurs when a landowner's consent was withdrawn, and the person remains on the land.

Trespass to Personal Property

When a person intentionally takes or harms the personal property of another or interferes with the owner's possession of personal property, they may be liable for **trespass to personal property**. Damages are measured by the amount of harm caused or by the loss of use of the object.

Trespass to personal property
When a person intentionally takes, harms, or interferes with the personal property of another.

> **Example:** If a vacationer were to use a watercraft without paying for its rental, they could be sued for the lost rental value of the property.

Conversion

When someone intentionally takes or retains possession of another's personal property, the tort of **conversion** occurs. Wrongful acts that deny the true owner's use of their property may begin as a trespass to personal property, but the wrongful retention of that property is considered conversion. The difference between the two torts concerns the degree of possession. The more serious the interference, the more likely the conduct is conversion, which is the civil version of larceny (that is, theft).

Conversion
The act of intentionally taking or retaining possession of another's personal property.

> **Example:** A person who seized the opportunity to drive a vehicle when keys were left in the ignition might be considered a trespasser to personal property. If the person never intended to return the car, they are liable for conversion.

Damages for conversion are measured by the value of the personal property at the time of the wrongful retention of the property. Many states also permit the recovery of punitive damages against the wrongdoer.

Concept Summary
Comparing Trespass and Conversion

Tort	Trespass to Personal Property	Conversion
Conduct	Intentionally removes possession or meddles with another's possession of their personal property	Intentionally exercises control over the personal property and thus seriously interferes with the rights of the true owner
Liability	Defendant liable for damage to property or loss of use	Defendant liable for the value of the personal property

Duty of Landowners to Third Persons

A landowner's right to use and enjoy their property is not absolute. Public policy concerns over public safety have created specific duties that a landowner owes to others based on the status or category of persons entering the land. These categories include (1) trespassers, (2) licensees, and (3) invitees.

Trespasser
A person who enters another's land without permission.

TRESPASSERS. Under common law, trespassers could not hold the owner liable for harm the trespasser suffered on the premises. In many states, the rule is modified to impose upon the owner a reasonable duty of care and that the landowner may not intentionally injure them. This will include the duty to warn of any man-made concealed dangers, but, not as to open and obvious conditions or those that occur naturally on the property (e.g., waterfalls, deep ravines).

Attractive Nuisance Doctrine
Landowners will be liable for injuries caused to trespassing children if the injury is caused by a hazardous object or condition on the property and the child was on the property because of an object or condition likely to attract children.

The common law rule has also been amended by many states to protect children who trespass onto property. The **attractive nuisance doctrine** provides that a landowner will be liable for injuries caused to trespassing children if the injury is caused by a hazardous object or condition on the property and the child was on the property because of an object or condition likely to attract children.

Licensee
A person who enters land with permission of the owner.

LICENSEES. Licensees are persons who enter land with permission of the owner. The majority of licensees involve social guests and relatives on property. The landowner's duties to a licensee are greater than the common law rule for trespassers and similar to those owed to a known trespasser. The landowner must not intentionally injure the licensee and must either warn about or make safe any known dangers on the property. Common examples of things a landowner must provide a warning for include uneven or slick surfaces; dangerous animals or devices; and any defects in construction that may cause injury, such as cracked or missing railings, flooring, and steps.

INVITEES. Invitees are people who enter land that is generally open to the public or enter land for a business purpose. Most often they are customers visiting retail premises, but invitees can also be businesses that are called or invited by a homeowner to perform a service. For example, service repair persons are invitees.

Invitee
Persons who enter land that is generally open to the public or who enter land for a business purpose.

Landowners owe the highest duty of care to invitees. They must not intentionally injure them and must warn or make safe known dangers, as required for trespassers and licensees. In addition, they owe invitees a duty to reasonably inspect and discover non-obvious or hidden dangerous conditions and warn against or make safe those conditions.

Concept Summary
Landowner's duties

	Duty
Trespassers	1. Not to intentionally injure
Trespassers (known or anticipated)	1. Not to intentionally injure 2. Warn of any man-made concealed dangers
Child Trespassers	1. Not to intentionally injure 2. Must reasonably protect children from dangers
Licensees	1. Not to intentionally injure 2. Must either warn against or make safe any known dangers on the property
Invitees	1. Not to intentionally injure 2. Must either warn against or make safe any known dangers on the property 3. Must reasonably inspect and discover non-obvious or hidden dangerous conditions and warn against or make safe those conditions

Interference with Business Relations

Competing fiercely within the free enterprise system has legal limits. A tort may occur when a business exceeds the boundaries of fair competition. Some of these business torts are discussed in this section.

Disparagement

Disparagement
False statements of fact that are made about the products, services, character, or ownership rights of another's business.

Defamation-like harm is not limited to the harm caused by individuals. **Disparagement** (also known as *trade libel*, *product disparagement*, or *slander of title*) occurs when false statements of fact are made about the products, services, character, or ownership rights of another's business. To prevail, the plaintiff must prove they suffered actual economic damages (such as lost profits), and that the defendant acted with an intent to injure the plaintiff (malice).

Example: If one retailer made an unsubstantiated, and ultimately false, claim that a family of four would save hundreds of dollars a month by shopping at its stores in comparison to shopping at a competitor's store, executives of the affected store might assert trade libel claims.

Interference with Contractual Relations

Interference with contractual relations Tortious conduct involving actions that intentionally and inexcusably interfere with the contractual benefits of another person.

Interference with contractual relations is a tort that imposes liability on a company because it has induced the breach of or interfered with an existing third-party contract. The facts and circumstances are unique to each case but acts beyond those of mere competition may give rise to a cause of action. Merely persuading a person to break a contract is generally not improper, but if the persuasion to breach the contract was done with the purpose of injuring the plaintiff, or if it benefited the defendant at the expense of the plaintiff, that act is generally improper. The tort occurs when a defendant:

1. Is aware a contract between two or more parties exists;
2. Intentionally and improperly interferes with the performance or induces a party to breach the contract; and
3. As a result of interference, a party suffers monetary loss.

Example: BigMart Produce and Meats has a longstanding contract with the Acme Market chain to supply Acme with all the produce Acme needs. FLG Farms and Produce is a direct competitor of BigMart and is aware of the unexpired contract between the parties. If FLG improperly induces Acme to terminate its contract with BigMart, BigMart can sue FLG for the lost profits arising from interference with its contractual relationship with Acme Markets.

Defenses to Intentional Torts

In addition to those defenses relating to the specific torts discussed above, other defenses to a defendant's intentional tort that reduce or eliminate liability include the following:

1. *Consent.* A plaintiff may have expressly or impliedly (such as failing to timely object) expressed a willingness to accept that a tort may occur to them. Often, implied consent to a possible injury is given by those who attend sporting events because they sit within a field of danger of an object or player injuring them. If the defendant exceeds the scope of the consent given, the defendant may be liable.

Example: During an operation in which the patient is under anesthesia, a doctor who elects to perform a different surgery would be going beyond the scope of the original consent. However, in a surgical emergency, going beyond the scope of the consent may be justified.

2. *Privilege.* A privilege defense arises when conduct that under ordinary circumstances might result in tort liability does not result in liability under the specific circumstances. The law entitles a person to use reasonable force to prevent any threatened, harmful, or offensive bodily contact and any threatened confinement or imprisonment.
3. *Self-defense or defense of others.* People also have the privilege to use reasonable force to defend themselves against unprivileged harmful or offensive conduct that they or another person might suffer. However, this force must be reasonable under the circumstances. Where people believe their lives or the lives of others may be in peril, they may use deadly force.

Example: Pushing the person away may be an appropriate use of reasonable force as opposed to striking the person with a fist.

The self-defense argument applies only when defendants use the force necessary to protect themselves and their families against immediate harm. It does not permit any force to be used in retaliation for a tort already committed.

4. *Defense of property.* People may only use reasonable force to defend their real and personal property. Generally, the owner must first make a demand that the intruder stop and then allow the intruder time to comply, unless it reasonably appears that violence or serious harm will occur immediately or that the request to stop will be useless. The law does not permit deadly force in the defense of property.

Negligence — The Unintentional Tort

The tort of negligence occurs when a defendant causes injury to another by failing to abide by a standard of care. Although not intentional, a court may find a negligent defendant liable for failing to provide care.

To prevail in a tort action for negligence, the plaintiff must prove four things:

1. The defendant owed a *duty* of care to the person;
2. The defendant *breached* the duty of care owed to the person;
3. The defendant's conduct is the *cause* of the harm; and
4. The plaintiff suffered *harm.*

Duty of Care

The standard of care owed to a person is what a reasonable and prudent person acting with ordinary care and skill would provide in the situation. This is known as the *reasonable person* standard of care.

Who Is a Reasonable Person?

A reasonable person is someone of average intelligence, temperament, and training. Each negligence claim presents its own set of special circumstances. The question of whether a defendant behaved reasonably will depend upon factors such as the following:

- The defendant's physical and mental capacities factor in whether they can provide reasonable care. Note that intoxication is never a defense.
- Children are held to the level of care of a person of the same age, intelligence, and experience.
  Some jurisdictions hold children under 7 as being incapable of negligence; children aged 7-14 are held to the same level of care of a similarly aged person but this can be rebutted by evidence of the child's understanding of the negligent act; and children over 14 are considered capable of negligence. Persons with disabilities are held to the standard of a reasonable person with the same disability.
- Emergency situations require the defendant to behave as a reasonable person would if confronted with the same situation.
- A defendant should anticipate the negligence of third persons. For example, a roadway designer might anticipate that motorists may drive at excessive speeds and the roadway should be constructed to take into consideration such excessive rates of speed.

For purposes of determining whether a defendant's conduct involves a risk, the defendant is deemed to know:

- The obvious habits of human beings and animals; the qualities, characteristics, and capacities of things and forces in nature; and things common within the community (such as the necessity of properly stopping an automobile); and
- The common law, the laws of that state, and the general customs as they may relate to how an individual should act toward others.

DUTY OF PROFESSIONALS. Those who are highly educated or skilled in an occupation or profession, such as accountants, lawyers, physicians, and architects, are held to a higher standard equal to the knowledge, ability, and skill expected of their fellow professionals. Thus, instead of applying a reasonable standard to determine whether or not there was a duty, this heightened standard of a professional's duty is applied.

Breach

If there is a duty owed, a breach of the duty of care arises when a person fails to act as a reasonable person would act under similar circumstances. Failing to act can arise when a person acts improperly or fails to act.

> **Example:** A driver of an automobile breaches their duty of care when they look down at their phone and text while driving.

NEGLIGENCE *PER SE*. A breach of a duty of care occurs when a defendant violates a statute intended to protect a certain class of persons of which the plaintiff is a member.

The violation of the statute is deemed negligence *per se*, which means that there is a presumption of a duty owed and a breach of that duty. In such a case, the plaintiff need only prove causation and damages.

> **Example:** To save on costs, a building contractor deliberately ignored building code requirements relating to the framing of a building. Later, an occupant became seriously injured when the building collapsed because of the code violations. The injured person can assert this doctrine against the builder.

RES IPSA LOQUITUR. The Latin translation is "the thing speaks for itself." This doctrine shifts the burden of explaining the harm that occurred from the plaintiff to the defendant. Under this special theory of liability, the harm suffered by the plaintiff is inferred to have been caused by the negligence of the defendant. *Res ipsa loquitur* is used when the occurrence of an act suggests negligence, but the plaintiff is unable to identify what the defendant(s) did wrong. *Res ipsa loquitur* is recognized when:

- The accident or event is a kind that ordinarily does not occur in the absence of negligence; and
- The defendant had exclusive control of the instrument causing the injury.

> **Example:** An escalator malfunctioned in a department store, causing injury. The court held that application of *res ipsa loquitur* was warranted, since an injury from an escalator normally does not happen in the absence of negligence and the store had exclusive control of the escalator, since it was located inside the store. *Lopez ex rel. Lopez v. Sears, Roebuck and Co.*, 187 Misc. 2d 165 (N.Y. Sup. Ct. 2001)

Causation

The next step is to apply two tests to determine whether the defendant's wrongful conduct caused the injury to the plaintiff. To be liable for negligence both of the following tests must be met: (1) actual cause, and (2) proximate cause.

ACTUAL CAUSE (CAUSATION IN FACT). Actual cause is a test to determine if the defendant's conduct actually caused the harm to the plaintiff. In most cases, to determine if the element is met, the law applies a "but for" test. The plaintiff must show the harm would not have occurred "but for" the defendant's act or omission. If the defendant's conduct caused the harm, the proximate cause test can also be applied.

Actual cause
The plaintiff's injury would not have occurred "but for" the defendant's tortious conduct.

> **Example:** A plaintiff was injured because of a car accident. The actual causation of the plaintiff's injuries would not exist but for the defendant's conduct of driving through an intersection with a red light, the pedestrian walking in the intersection would not have been hit by the vehicle.

When multiple people cause the harm, a different test is applied. This is known as the "substantial factor" test. In this test, if the defendant's conduct was a substantial factor in causing the plaintiff's injury, the defendant will be liable even though other people also contributed to the result.

Example: A plaintiff was injured because of a multi-car accident. The actual causation of the plaintiff's injuries would exist if the actions of the multiple defendants, taken together, were a substantial factor in causing the plaintiff's injuries.

Proximate cause
The defendant's tortious conduct was a substantial factor in causing the plaintiff's injury and it was foreseeable that the conduct would result in a risk of unreasonable harm to the plaintiff.

PROXIMATE CAUSE. In addition to the actual cause test, the next step is to apply the **proximate cause** test to establish whether the defendant's tortious conduct bears a reasonable relationship to the plaintiff's injury. Determining the appropriate scope of liability for the defendant's conduct requires asking whether it was foreseeable to the defendant that their conduct would result in a risk of unreasonable harm to the plaintiff. The defendant can be liable even though others also contributed to the result.

Landmark Case
Palsgraf v. Long Island R.R. Company, 162 N.E. 99 (N.Y. 1928)

In this famous case, a man was carrying a package about 15 inches long and wrapped in newspaper. The package did not give anyone concern about its contents. However, it contained fireworks. The man rushed aboard an already moving train. Two railroad employees helped him get aboard, and as he did, the man dropped his package onto the rails. The package then exploded. The shockwaves caused scales at the other end of the platform to fall onto Mrs. Palsgraf, who was standing some distance away from the three men and the exploding package.

A divided court of appeal held that Mrs. Palsgraf was not a foreseeable plaintiff. Without perceiving that the employees' actions with respect to another passenger could harm Mrs. Palsgraf, no duty was owed to her. Thus, if injury to her could not be reasonably foreseen, the railroad company could not be held liable. This landmark case helped establish the concept of foreseeability as the test for proximate cause, an element limiting liability for negligence.

Additional Negligence Theories

The law recognizes other circumstances where negligence may occur. Some of these theories include:

1. *"Danger invites rescue" doctrine.* Under this theory, a person who is trying to rescue another or trying to avoid harm (such as swerving to avoid a collision with another car that has been suddenly involved in an accident) has a defense against those whom they cause harm (such as hitting an unrelated third party). The tortfeasor who caused the original accident is liable to anyone injured—even if the injury occurred during someone's attempt to avoid harm.
2. *Dram shop acts.* At common law, dram shops (that is, bars or similar commercial establishments selling alcoholic beverages) were not subject to liability when their intoxicated patrons caused injury to third parties. However, many states have since enacted dram shop acts to deter these establishments from serving alcohol to obviously intoxicated individuals who risk inflicting serious

injury on themselves or on the general public. A plaintiff alleging a violation of a dram shop act must meet a high burden of proof to hold the dram shop liable for damages proximately caused by its employees or patrons.

In the following case, the court considered whether it was foreseeable that a person could be held liable for another person's misconduct by preventing the escape of a victim.

CASE 5.2

THE DUTY OF CARE CAN EXTEND TO THIRD PARTIES UNDER CERTAIN CIRCUMSTANCES

DORSEY v. REIDER

139 So. 3d 860 (Fla. 2014)

Supreme Court of Florida

Dennis J. Dorsey was drinking with Robert J. Reider and Reider's friend, Russell Noordhoek, at a neighborhood bar. All three men were over the legal limit of intoxication. While in the bar, Reider became boisterous and belligerent, saying he wanted to fight everyone. Exasperated with his behavior, Dorsey used a vulgar term to describe Reider. Dorsey walked out of the bar. Reider and Noordhoek followed, with Reider demanding to know why Dorsey called him that name. Dorsey ignored Reider and kept walking.

Reider continued to accost Dorsey over the derogatory term. Several minutes into the altercation, Dorsey heard a truck's door open behind him, turned, and saw Noordhoek reach into Reider's truck and retrieve a tomahawk. Dorsey then grabbed Reider and attempted to push him to one side in order to escape. Dorsey testified the two men grappled for about 15 seconds when, suddenly, Noordhoek struck Dorsey in the head with the tomahawk, rendering him temporarily unconscious. Noordhoek and Reider fled the scene. Dorsey regained consciousness and drove himself to the hospital. Reider could recall nothing about the tomahawk or Noordhoek's actions. A jury awarded Dorsey substantial damages.

The court of appeal reversed the jury verdict because it held that Reider did not owe a relevant duty of care to Dorsey when Dorsey was attacked by Noordhoek and could not be held liable for Dorsey's injuries as there was no evidence Reider colluded with Noordhoek or knew that Noordhoek had the tomahawk and would strike Dorsey. Dorsey appealed to the state supreme court.

Language of the Court. *The duty element of negligence focuses on whether the defendant's conduct foreseeably created a broader 'zone of risk' that poses a general threat of harm to others. This requirement is a "minimal threshold legal requirement for opening the courthouse doors." Once the courthouse doors are opened based on the existence of a legal duty, the proximate cause element still remains and "is concerned with whether and to what extent the defendant's conduct foreseeably and substantially caused the specific injury that actually occurred."*

Establishing proximate cause requires a factual showing that the dangerous activity foreseeably caused the specific harm suffered by those claiming injury. We conclude that the facts establish a legal duty on the part of Reider. His conduct in blocking Dorsey's ability to escape from the escalating situation created a foreseeable zone of risk posing a general threat of harm to others.

We turn next to the question of whether Reider's duty to Dorsey extended to injuries caused by the misconduct of a third person, Noordhoek. Generally, a party has no legal duty to prevent the misconduct of third persons. The courts have carved out exceptions where such a duty might arise: where the defendant is in actual or constructive control of: (1) the instrumentality; (2) the premises on which the tort was committed; or (3) the tortfeasor. Reider's conduct created a broader zone of foreseeable risk to Dorsey.

The inquiry then turns to whether the duty of care created by this conduct extends to the misconduct of Noordhoek, a third party. Reider was present and had the ability to control access to his truck in which the tomahawk was located. Moreover, Reider did not "merely provide access" to the tomahawk, he blocked Dorsey's escape and was present when the instrument was used to injure Dorsey. In addition, Reider was in a position to retake control of the tomahawk and prevent the injury. The totality of the circumstances takes this case out of the "general rule" that one is not liable for injuries caused by a third party. Under the specific facts of this case, Reider's duty of care extended to the misconduct of a third party, Noordhoek.

Decision. The duty of care extended to the misconduct of a third party.

Focus on Ethics

Is this an ethical result? Why party be held liable for foreseeable misconduct of another?

Defenses to Negligence

Defendants who are sued for damages arising from their negligence may assert defenses for their actions. These can reduce and may eliminate the defendant's liability.

Comparative negligence Doctrine that apportions damages based on the plaintiff's and defendant's respective degrees of fault.

Comparative Negligence

The doctrine of **comparative negligence** applies when the negligence of both the plaintiff and the defendant concurrently cause the plaintiff's injuries. Any damages awarded to the plaintiff are reduced by an amount proportionate to the degree of the plaintiff's fault. There are several variations of this defense. The majority of states adopting the comparative negligence doctrine do not allow recovery if the plaintiff's own negligence contributed 50 percent or more to the injury.

> **Example:** California has adopted the comparative negligence defense. A San Francisco Giants® fan named Bryan Stow filed a negligence lawsuit for injuries he suffered after attending an opening day game at Dodgers Stadium. He sued the Los Angeles Dodgers®, the then-owner of the team, Frank McCourt, and the two men who beat him and left him with grievous, life-altering injuries. He claimed the team and its former owner failed to provide adequate security at the stadium. The defense argued that security was stronger than ever that day, and that Stow was partially at fault because he was intoxicated. Stow's blood alcohol content was more than twice the legal limit in California for driving a motor vehicle. The jury awarded Stow damages of almost $18 million, but allocated fault to the Dodgers for only a quarter of that sum and allocated the rest to the two men and Stow himself. Note, California has a special state statute that shifted responsibility for Stow's medical damages to the Dodgers.

Some states provide for a "pure" comparative negligence theory, which allows the plaintiff to recover regardless of the percentage of harm they caused to themselves.

> **Example:** If, because of an injury, a jury found that the plaintiff caused 90 percent of the harm, the plaintiff could still recover 10 percent against the defendant.

Contributory Negligence

The defense of **contributory negligence** may apply when the plaintiff's own conduct falls below the standard to which the plaintiff should conform for their own protection. A minority of states apply this defense. Under the contributory negligence theory, if the plaintiff was negligent and that negligence contributed to their injuries, the defendant is relieved from all liability, even if the defendant's negligence was much greater than that of the plaintiff. Due to the perceived unfairness of this standard, the majority of states have adopted the comparative negligence standard.

Contributory negligence
Where a plaintiff's negligent conduct contributes to their harm, contributory negligence prevents the plaintiff from recovering damages.

> **Example:** A driver fails to check the weather and road conditions before undertaking a highway trip during the winter. Meanwhile, the defendant transportation agency negligently failed to warn drivers of icy road conditions or act to remove the snow and ice. In a contributory negligence jurisdiction, the driver's failure to exercise reasonable care to discover the treacherous conditions would bar his recovery following an accident caused by the road conditions.

Assumption of risk
Where a plaintiff has knowingly and voluntarily faced a dangerous or harmful situation, assumption of risk absolves the defendant from all liability.

Assumption of Risk

When a plaintiff has knowingly and voluntarily faced a dangerous or harmful situation, the law absolves the defendant from all liability. The key elements of **assumption of risk** are:

Volenti non fit injuria (Damage suffered by consent gives no cause of action)—Latin expression of the rule that if one puts themself in a position of harm, that may not bring a complaint against the other party.

- Knowledge of the risk using the standard of an objective, reasonable person who would appreciate the particular risk; and

- Voluntary assumption involving consent to relieve the defendant of their duty of reasonable care.

> **Example:** A hockey player who is injured during a routine play of a game has assumed the risk of injury and cannot recover damages for the injury under a negligence cause of action.

Superseding or Intervening Cause

A superseding cause is an unforeseeable intervening cause that breaks the chain of causation between the initial wrongful act and the ultimate injury. A person is liable for the intervening acts that are foreseeable. Types of superseding causes include acts of God, criminal acts of a third person, and the intentional torts of third persons.

> **Example:** After a car accident a person is transported by ambulance to a hospital. On the way to the hospital, the ambulance is involved in an accident causing additional injuries to the victim. The ambulance accident is a superseding cause and the defendants' actions in causing the first accident were not the proximate cause of the second accident.

Last Clear Chance Doctrine

In those cases where the plaintiff has been negligent, this defense applies if injury could have been avoided had the defendant acted with reasonable care to avoid harm.

> **Example:** If a delivery truck saw another vehicle stopped within a traffic lane, despite operating the truck at a safe speed when he saw the stopped vehicle, the truck driver would be liable because the driver had the "last clear chance" to avoid a collision with the stopped vehicle.

Good Samaritan Statutes

Some states have passed laws protecting those who voluntarily come to the aid of others. Under these laws, a volunteer who aids another is not liable for negligence to the injured victim. Some states limit the protection under these statutes only to medical personnel and others render emergency medical aid to the injured.

Tort Remedies

Once a tort has occurred, tort law provides a compensation system for those who have suffered a loss or injury due to another's wrongful act. The tortfeasor's wrongful act may be the intentional or negligent conduct. The three types of remedies that a plaintiff may seek are compensatory damages, punitive damages, or equitable relief.

Compensatory damages
Damages awarded to compensate for the actual loss or harm suffered, such as for personal property loss or pain and suffering.

Compensatory Damages

Generally, an injured plaintiff in a tort case will seek **compensatory damages**. Compensatory damages are monetary damages awarded to compensate the plaintiff for all the damages suffered.

Typically, an individual plaintiff will receive a *general damage* award to compensate them for the nonmonetary aspects of a harm suffered, such as for the pain and suffering suffered in an automobile accident. A business entity is not entitled to compensation. Compensatory damages are those that would naturally result from the wrong. In addition, *special damages* may be assessed for losses or expenses that are unique or special to the injured plaintiff. These would include such things as wage losses following a physical injury, medical expenses incurred in rehabilitation, the loss of irreplaceable or unique property, and the costs of repairing or replacing damaged property, such as an automobile. General damages are not subject to precise calculation, while special damages may be quantified.

> **Example:** A plaintiff injured in a car accident could seek to collect damages for the pain and suffering the plaintiff incurs, the cost to repair the vehicle, past and future wages lost while the plaintiff was unable to work, and the present and future medical costs that the plaintiff will incur.

Punitive Damages

In certain cases, punitive damages are available in tort cases when the wrongdoer has acted maliciously or willfully in causing the harm. **Punitive damages** are monetary damages designed to punish the tortfeasor and set an example for others, and they are available in addition to compensatory damages. They are appropriate when the defendant has acted so reprehensively that it should be assessed additional damages for the purpose of punishing its wrongdoing. This remedy is available in cases of intentional torts, and in negligence actions only in instances of gross negligence (such as an employer's reckless disregard for workplace safety regulations). Most state laws do not have a fixed standard for measuring punitive damages in tort cases. The Supreme Court has held that the amount of punitive damages must bear some reasonable relationship to the amount of compensatory damages recoverable by the plaintiff. Since the objective of punitive damages is to deter wrongdoing, insurance companies may not indemnify a wrongdoer for punitive damages.

Punitive damages Damages beyond those necessary to compensate for losses suffered awarded to an injured party for intentional or egregious conduct, assessed with the intention of punishing the wrongdoer or setting an example.

> **Example:** A jury found Norcon, Inc. liable for sexual harassment, intentional infliction of emotional distress, and negligent infliction of emotional distress and awarded plaintiff \$8,494.40 for lost earnings, \$1,850 for emotional distress and \$3,770,260.63 for punitive damages. The court of appeals held the punitive damage award excessive and concluded that the maximum allowable punitive damage award is the case was \$500,000. *Norcon v. Kotowski*, 917 P. 2d 158 (Alaska 1999)

Equitable Relief

In some circumstances, the injured party may seek **equitable relief** instead of monetary damages. Such a remedy might include an injunction to stop or prevent the continued harm suffered by the plaintiff. When a court orders equitable relief, it is because the award of monetary damages will not be sufficient to compensate the plaintiff for the harm. Equitable remedies are specific and direct orders to personally perform some action or refrain from taking some action or to remedy a harm suffered.

Equitable relief Court orders providing nonmonetary relief, such as injunctions.

For example, an injunction may be appropriate to stop a neighbor from playing loud music during normal sleeping hours. By its equitable order, a court coerces a person to either continue or refrain from some action, as opposed to ordering the defendant to pay a monetary damage claim to the plaintiff. If the wrongdoer fails to comply, the court can hold the defendant in civil contempt. Equitable orders bind only the parties to the particular civil lawsuit.

Online Torts

The law adjusts to societal needs. The expansion of tort liability to the online environment is not an exception. Leaving matters of e-commerce agreements to our study of contracts, we turn our attention to the issues arising from torts committed using the internet.

Recently, the attention of the courts and legislatures to online torts has been focused primarily upon online defamation and cyberbullying. Since postings of hateful and malicious speech can occur while using a pseudonym, it is often a challenge to identify the anonymous online authors. Federal court decisions make it clear that the Internet Service Providers (ISPs) will not provide the identity of those posters without a court order directing them to do so. Considering all of the public interests involved, Congress enacted the Communications Decency Act, which provides immunity for ISPs from claims of defamation. When contacted over a defamatory or trade libel claim, the ISP promptly removes the offending communication from its system. Thus, unlike a print publisher, the ISP can quickly limit the republication of the defamatory statement.

The text of the Communications Decency Act may be found at https://www.congress.gov/bill/104th-congress/senate-bill/314.

Some professionals and small business owners have been victimized by vicious marketing campaigns conducted by competitors, subjecting them to unsubstantiated assertions such as they are incompetent, render poor quality services, overcharge for their goods and services, and maintain rude staffing. It is often an expensive and almost impossible undertaking to identify the authors of such trade libel.

AI Feature: Dealing with Social Media Defamation

Social media defamation is a growing issue that affects individuals and organizations. Reputations both personal and professional may be damaged when someone posts or shares false statements online about a person. Conduct internet research on the liability of social media platforms for defamation. Persuasion does not always convince the webhost/ISP/website to redact some or all the content. This is particularly true if it is not clear that the posting violates any of the site's terms or is objectionable. After conducting such internet research, assume you have been victimized by online defamation. Then, using an AI program, create a memorandum as to what legal options you could pursue. Your memorandum should address what to do if, after you sue, a court considers the subject statement to be of public interest and not actually defamatory. Explain the application of SLAPP and anti-SLAPP lawsuits in the context of your action plan. The acronym "SLAPP" stands for Strategic Lawsuit Against Public Participation, which is a lawsuit filed against a defendant in retaliation for speaking out on a public issue or controversy on an online site. However, more than half of the states have enacted anti-SLAPP legislation that helps defendants obtain an early dismissal of SLAPP lawsuits.

Key Terms

- Absolute privilege, 100
- Abuse of process, 103
- Actual cause, 111
- Actual malice, 99
- Assault, 95
- Assumption of risk, 115
- Attractive Nuisance Doctrine, 106
- Battery, 95
- Comparative negligence, 114
- Compensatory damages, 116
- Contributory negligence, 115
- Conversion, 105
- Defamation, 98
- Disparagement, 107
- Equitable relief, 117
- False imprisonment, 96
- Fraud, 103
- Intentional infliction of emotional distress, 96
- Intentional torts, 94
- Interference with contractual relations, 108
- Invitee, 107
- Libel, 98
- Licensee, 106
- Malicious prosecution, 103
- Negligence, 94
- Proximate cause, 112
- Punitive damages, 117
- Qualified privilege, 100
- Slander, 98
- Slander per se, 99
- Tort, 94
- Tortfeasor, 94
- Tortious intent, 94
- Transferred intent, 94
- Trespasser, 106
- Trespass to personal property, 105
- Trespass to real property, 104

Applying the Law

5.1 False Imprisonment. Brianna Sharp was a registered nurse who worked at the Cleveland Clinic®. On several occasions, Sharp was counseled by supervisors regarding documentation errors for narcotic medications. Due to these errors, some narcotic medications went unaccounted for. Sharp met with the nurse manager and a representative of the Employee Assistance Program. They informed Sharp that there were suspicions that she possessed and used controlled substances. Sharp denied any drug use and consented to a drug test. After the test was conducted, Sharp asked if she could go home. The nurses allowed her to leave, but she was not allowed to drive her car. Following her discharge for poor performance, Sharp sued for false imprisonment. Is she likely to succeed? Why or why not? *Sharp v. Cleveland Clinic*, 891 N.E.2d 809 (Ohio Ct. App. 2008)

5.2 Public Figures. An allegedly defamatory statement in an online article published by Buzzfeed implicated Aleksej Gubarev, the CEO of XBT Holdings, in the Russian hacking of Democratic Party computers and interference in the 2016 U.S. presidential election. When Gubarev and XBT brought a defamation action against Buzzfeed, the news website presented the affirmative defense that the publication was protected by the First Amendment since the statement concerned a public figure. Gubarev and his company hired public relations firms to promote their brands and enjoyed more media attention than regular private citizens. However, Gubarev's only public statement related to Russian interference in the election was a technical opinion about logs of a campaign server that may have been tied to servers at a Russian bank.

Should Gubarev be considered a public figure in light of the foregoing? What is the appropriate standard that the plaintiff must meet to establish defamation in this instance? *Gubarev v. BuzzFeed, Inc.*, 354 F. Supp. 3d 1317 (S.D. Fla. 2018)

5.3 Defenses for Defamation. Rick Gonzales and Silvia Trevino were opposing candidates in the general election for the position of Harris County Constable. Trevino's cousin and her sons published negative statements about Gonzales on their social media accounts regarding his past relationships. Gonzales sued them for defamation. What are possible defenses against this claim of defamation? *Rodriguez v. Gonzales*, 566 S.W.3d 844 (Tex. App. 2018)

5.4 Misappropriation or Parody? Busch, a bodybuilder, brought an action against Viacom® and Jon Stewart for defamation and misappropriation of image. Stewart, the anchor of *The Daily Show*, created a satiric segment that involved a "fake endorsement" of a dietary shake that included Busch's image. What must Busch prove to succeed on his claims of defamation and misappropriation of image? *Busch v. Viacom Int'l, Inc.*, 477 F. Supp. 2d 764 (N.D. Tex. 2007)

5.5 Intentional Misrepresentation. The National Association of Home Builders of the United States® (NAHB) collaborated with North Star Finance LLC to offer a loan program to its members. Under the program, NAHB members working on development projects were to be given non-recourse debt financing at below-market interest rates and with other favorable terms. The financing never materialized, and the program was revealed to be a fraudulent investment scheme conducted by North Star. Applicants to the loan program paid substantial application fees to North Star and were not repaid after the financing fell through. What must investors in the loan program establish to state a claim for fraud against NAHB? *Boomer Development, LLC v. National Association of Home Builders of the United States*, 258 F. Supp. 3d 1 (D.D.C. 2017)

5.6 Negligence. A roller coaster rider filed suit against Fun-Tastic Rides Co., the roller coaster operator and manufacturer, after sustaining a subdural hematoma from hitting her head on the safety harness of a roller coaster during a ride at the Washington State Fair. Under what theory of negligence is the plaintiff most likely to succeed? *Brugh v. Fun-Tastic Rides Co.*, 437 P.3d 751 (Wash. Ct. App. 2019)

5.7 Trespass. Goldingay and Otis purchased real property and hired Evergreen Environmental to perform an environmental assessment. Evergreen identified the presence of petroleum contamination on the property. Goldingay and Otis sued Chevron, an operator of a petroleum plant on a nearby property now owned by Progressive Casualty. They sought to recover the costs they incurred for the environmental assessment. Goldingay and Otis then filed an action for trespass against Progressive. What do they need to prove to succeed under this tort theory? *Goldingay v. Progressive Casualty Insurance Co.*, 306 F. Supp. 3d 1259 (D. Or. 2018)

5.8 Interference with Contractual Relations. A surgeon who performed facial plastic surgery on Kelly Turkoly received a negative review from her on a website used to review doctors. Turkoly wrote: "This surgeon is not a Board Certified Plastic Surgeon" and warned others to "stay away from this unscrupulous doctor." The surgeon sued Turkoly, alleging interference with contractual relations on the grounds that the review induced patients to cancel scheduled surgeries. Will the surgeon succeed? *Gentile v. Turkoly*, 86 N.E.3d 991 (Ohio Ct. App. 2017)

5.9 Defenses. Darren Clayton is the father of two children, Kinser and Kyra. Clayton worked from home in his garage and usually had Kinser secured in a play area in the garage while he worked. One afternoon, Clayton was working from home and decided to move Kinser from the garage and into the house to be watched by Kyra. He left the house and garage doors open so that he could monitor the children, and physically checked on them every ten minutes. At some point later that evening, Clayton went to check on Kinser and Kyra. After searching through the house, he found Kinser floating in the family's swimming pool, unresponsive. Clayton removed his son from the pool and called 911, requesting guidance for providing CPR. However, the CPR instructions were not given until nearly three minutes into the call. Firefighters and paramedics arrived on the scene and transported Kinser to the hospital, where he was later pronounced dead. The Claytons filed a complaint against the fire department and the sheriff's department alleging that they failed to adequately train their emergency operators. Discuss any possible defenses the defendants might have against the Claytons' suit and their likelihood of success. *Clayton v. Morgan County Sheriff's Dep't*, 95 N.E.3d 189 (Ind. Ct. App. 2018)

5.10 Defamation, Tyrone Clark and his company, Brokers' Choice of America (BCA), sued NBC Universal for defamation in response to a *Dateline* segment entitled "Tricks of the Trade." The aired segment featured snippets of Clark's statements taken from filming one of his seminars for insurance brokers. With the assistance of Alabama officials in obtaining false insurance identification, the *Dateline* crew had access to a BCA closed seminar and filmed the seminar with hidden cameras. The aired program depicted Clark as someone who taught insurance agents how to employ misrepresentations and other questionable tactics in order to dupe senior citizens into purchasing inappropriate annuity products. Clark claimed NBC Universal victimized him through selective editing and commenting. He asserted his statements were taken out of context in order to create a false impression, thereby defaming him and BCA. Does context matter in a defamation lawsuit? What ethical concerns arise in these circumstances? *Brokers' Choice of America, Inc. v. NBC Universal, Inc.*, 757 F.3d 1125 (10th Cir. 2014)

Strict and Products Liability

6

The Congressional charge to the Consumer Safety Product Commission is to *"protect the public against unreasonable risks of injuries and deaths associated with consumer products."*

Chapter Outline

- Introduction
- Strict Liability
- The Evolution of Products Liability
- Products Liability

Case 6.1: *Palermo v. LifeLink Foundation, Inc.*

- *Management Application: Avoiding Product Liability Claims*

- Negligence
- Misrepresentation
- Defenses to Products Liability Claims

Case 6.2: *Lindholm v. BMW of North America, LLC*

Case 6.3: *Mutual Pharmaceutical Co. v. Bartlett*

- AI Feature: Gathering the Facts and Alleging Fault for a Defective Product

Learning Objectives

After reading this chapter, you should be able to:

1. Distinguish strict liability from other theories of recovery for product liability.
2. Define when a product is considered defective.
3. Explain who may be held liable for harm caused by a defective product.
4. Describe the defenses to a products liability claim.

Introduction

Strict liability
Torts which result in liability to the defendant without finding the defendant was at fault.

Occasionally, an injured party can sue for strict liability. Under the doctrine of **strict liability**, liability is imposed without finding the defendant was at fault. A subset of this legal theory is that of products liability. We will address who can pursue such claims and what damages may be awarded as a result. Originally, the law limited a party's remedies for a defective product to those arising from negligence, fraud (misrepresentation), and express warranties by a seller. The law developed to hold the many parties involved in the manufacture, distribution, and sale of goods accountable for the harm caused by defects. Over time, the concept of products liability would encompass legal protections arising from several legal theories, which are discussed in this chapter. Each legal theory seeks to address the harm caused by a defective product in a manner unique to itself.

The frequency with which products liability cases are filed in state courts may be reviewed at the National Center for State Courts, Caseload Digest. A recent report may be found at https://www.ncsc.org/services-and-experts/areas-of-expertise/court-statistics.

We begin our study with strict liability. We proceed with the application of negligence and misrepresentation, torts which are familiar from our study in Chapter 5. The law discussed in this chapter applies only to harm caused by products (and not by the performance of services). For example, a service provider does not provide a product to the consumer. While the services rendered may cause harm, the usual remedy is an action in negligence to recover damages.

Strict Liability

Under the doctrine of strict liability, a person is liable for injuries despite the absence of negligence or intentional acts. As explained below, strict liability can be imposed on defective products. An additional application of strict liability relates to inherently or imminently dangerous activities. Certain abnormally dangerous activities pose a risk of serious harm that cannot be eliminated regardless of how much care is used.

> **Example:** Inherently dangerous activities include blasting (used in connection with building implosions), transportation of hazardous chemicals, crop dusting, and the keeping of wild animals.

Persons who keep wild animals are liable because of the dangerous habits that are characteristic of wild animals. Keeping a domestic animal as a pet does not involve strict liability unless the pet owner has knowledge of a particular animal's dangerous tendencies.

> **Example:** An owner of a Shetland Sheepdog became aware of the dog's dangerous tendency to bite if petted near its side. The dog had previously been bitten by a coyote in that area and after recovery would bite even the owner if petted near the area. Because the owner is aware of the animal's dangerous tendency, they can be held strictly liable for harm caused.

Products Liability and Its Evolution

Almost 200 years ago, the general rule was that a manufacturer or seller of a product was liable for injuries or damages only to those with whom they were in contract (that is, in privity with). However, the defense of privity eroded, and liabilities were first imposed upon remote sellers through the theory of negligence (that is, a duty of care was owed to non-purchasers) and, later, through breach of warranties claims (discussed in Chapter 28). These traditional theories of consumer protection of negligence and breach of warranty began to show their inadequacies. In a negligence action, an injured party must show that a specific manufacturer or seller failed to exercise proper care in making or marketing the allegedly defective product, an often difficult task. To prove breach of warranty, the plaintiff must prove several contract elements, including privity, reliance, and notice. The courts took notice of these high barriers. The earliest of the developments of products liability occurred in the New York state courts. Justice Cardozo's decision in *MacPherson v. Buick Motor Co.* is recognized as the most influential and best known of all products liability decisions.

The privity requirement has been abandoned, and the law extended its protections to liability to cover the warranties implied in the sale of a product. Finally, in the mid 1960s the widespread acceptance of strict liability in tort occurred. Over the following decades, the extension of liability in tort would become available to injured third parties, bystanders, and others who were not purchasers or users of the product. Most states have adopted strict liability either by case law or by statute in products cases. As courts were broadening the reach of products liability, they were also increasingly more receptive to exercising jurisdiction in cases involving minimum contacts with a forum state, a theory discussed in Chapter 3. The result is that those involved in the production, distribution, and sale of goods must respond now to an expanding number of products liability claims filed in dispersed jurisdictions.

Landmark Case
MacPherson v. Buick Motor Co., 217 N.Y. 382 (1916)

MacPherson is a landmark case in products liability. In this case, New York's highest court, the Court of Appeals, eliminated the requirement of privity of contract for duty in negligence cases.

Donald MacPherson owned a car manufactured by Buick Motor Company which he had purchased from a retail dealer. While in the car, it collapsed suddenly. He was thrown out and injured. One of the wheels was made of defective wood, and its spokes crumbled into fragments. The wheel was not made by Buick Motor Company; it was bought from another manufacturer. There was evidence, however, that its defects could have been discovered by reasonable inspection, and that inspection was omitted. Although MacPherson purchased his Buick from a dealer, he sued Buick, the manufacturer of the vehicle. Buick Motor Company denied liability because it had not manufactured the defective wheel.

The Court held "We are dealing now with the liability of the manufacturer of the finished product, who puts it on the market to be used without inspection by his customers. If he is negligent, where danger is to be foreseen, a liability will follow ... The obligation to inspect must vary with the nature of the thing to be inspected. The more probable the danger, the greater the need of caution." The Court held for MacPherson because if the manufacturer of the finished product placed it within marketplace to be used without inspection, then, it could be held liable to him.

If a product is reasonably expected to be dangerous if negligently made and the product is known to be used by those other than the original purchaser, a duty of care extends to such third persons.

Products Liability

Products liability
Liability imposed by law regardless of fault upon a manufacturer, assembler, distributor, retailer, and others within the stream of commerce for harm caused by a defective product.

Products liability imposes liability on the seller of a defective product without the requirement that the injured party prove fault. That liability has been extended to parties other than the seller.

Strict liability imposes liability without fault even when reasonable care has been exercised in the preparation and sale of the product. A party may be held liable even if the party did not intend to cause harm or took all possible care to mitigate the harm that might arise from the use of its product. The doctrine applies to sellers, those in the chain of distribution, and lessors of products who are engaged in the sale and leasing of products. Strict liability does not apply to casual sales and transactions by nonmerchants. The sale of the product must be made in the regular course of the defendant's business. For example, a homeowner conducting a garage sale is not liable for a product defect. However, that same person who conducts a home-based business and sells those products in the regular course of their business could be liable for a product defect.

Before we analyze the elements of this tort, recognize that strict liability should not be regarded as absolute liability. The presence of injury alone is insufficient. Proof of defectiveness and causation between the defect and the injury must be established by the plaintiff. Moreover, as will be discussed, legislatures and courts have recognized defenses to products liability claims.

All in the Chain of Distribution Are Liable

Chain of distribution
All manufacturers, assemblers, distributors, wholesalers, retailers, and lessors involved in the sale or use of a product.

Those in the **chain of distribution** of a defective product are strictly liable in tort for the harm caused by that product. These parties are:

- Manufacturers of the product;
- Subcomponent manufacturers;
- Product assemblers or installers;
- Distributors of the product;
- Wholesalers of the product;
- Retailers who sell the product to the consumer; and
- Lessors of the product.

Holding these parties liable without fault fosters protection of the consumer. These parties may insure against the risks of a product defect. The imposition of liability encourages best practices in the design, manufacturing, and labeling of products. They may also include the costs of mitigating the risks of handling a defective product in their product pricing and seek contractual protection from others within this chain of distribution.

Example: A state supreme court held that a manufacturer of windows installed during construction in a mass-produced housing tract could be held strictly liable in tort for the harm resulting from defects in those windows. *Jimenez v. Superior Court*, 29 Cal. 4th 473 (2002)

Indemnity
A rule that permits an innocent defendant to sue other parties for the total amount of damages sought by plaintiff.

A product liability defendant can seek to be indemnified or receive contribution from other parties. **Indemnity** allows a defendant to sue other parties for the entire amount of the plaintiff's damages because that defendant is without fault. While remaining liable to the plaintiff, it shifts the obligation of the defendant to compensate the plaintiff to the indemnifying party. For example, an innocent retailer could seek indemnification from the manufacturer of a defective component which harmed the plaintiff. In contrast, **contribution** allows that defendant to sue other parties for only a portion of the plaintiff's damages. This usually occurs when the defendant is partially at fault and desires other parties to assume their share of the damages.

Contribution
Rule that permits a defendant to sue other parties for only a portion of the plaintiff's damages. Typically applies when the defendant is partially at fault and desires other parties to assume their share of the damages.

Products Liability Claim Requirements

Under products liability, the plaintiff must prove:

1. The defendant was *in the business of* manufacturing, distributing, or otherwise selling products (that is, a merchant);
2. The defendant *manufactured or sold either a defective product* or *one that was in an unreasonably dangerous condition*;
3. The defendant expected and intended that the product would reach the consumer *without substantial changes* to the product; and
4. Either the plaintiff was *physically injured* or the plaintiff's property was *physically damaged* by the defective product.

MERCHANT. The defendant must be one who is normally engaged in the business of selling, distributing, or manufacturing the product.

> **Example:** Joyce and Michael Ferrucci were hotel guests at the Showboat Hotel & Casino in Atlantic City. During their stay, Joyce's foot became stuck on a corner of the bed in the hotel room, causing her to fall and sustain injuries. At issue was whether the hotel was a "product seller." The court held that the hotel owner and operator was not a seller or manufacturer of the defective bed and was not liable for a product defect. *Ferrucci v. Atlantic City Showboat, Inc.*, 51 F. Supp. 2d 129 (D. Conn. 1999)

MANUFACTURED OR SOLD A DEFECTIVE PRODUCT. The plaintiff must also show that the defendant either manufactured or sold a defective product. To understand what a defective product is, it is important to first understand how a defective product differs from a "safe" product.

A "safe" product is not a perfect product that cannot possibly cause injury. Almost any product, regardless of how well it is made, has the potential to be harmful. Thus, a product is "safe" if (1) the product is as safe as a reasonable consumer would expect the product to be when it is used for its intended purpose or used in a way that is a reasonably foreseeable for use or misuse; and (2) the benefits of the product outweigh the risks of the product.

The fact that a product has caused an injury does not automatically make the product "unsafe." Products like pharmaceutical drugs have been considered on occasion as "unavoidably unsafe" by courts. Strict liability applies to an unsafe product when it is defective.

There are four types of defects that give rise to products liability:

1. Manufacturing defects;
2. Design defects;

3. Inadequate warnings (also known as *failure to warn* or *informational defects*); and
4. Defects in packaging.

Manufacturing defect
A defect in which a product departs from its intended design during the manufacturing process.

Manufacturing Defect. A **manufacturing defect** occurs when there is a mistake or lapse of process in the manufacture of the product such that it deviates from its intended design. The product must differ from the other products produced. If all products share similar problems, it may be a defective design.

> **Example:** Charles Allen removed a bottle of Coca-Cola® from the refrigerator. He opened the bottle by unscrewing the cap, noting at the time that it made the normal "whoosh" sound when the seal was broken. Both he and his grandmother Ellie Mae Parker drank several swallows from the bottle. Later, she felt something in her throat and expectorated blood. He felt something going down his throat and found a small piece of glass lying on his tongue. Upon peeling the wrapper from the bottle, he saw particles of glass in the bottle. To prove Coca-Cola's liability, the plaintiffs presented extensive evidence as to the company's failure, prior to this incident, to provide appropriate quality control measures for the detection of foreign objects in bottles. The court of appeal upheld their products liability jury verdict arising from a manufacturing defect. *Coca-Cola Bottling Co. v. Parker*, 451 So. 2d 786 (Ala. 1984)

Design defect
A defect resulting from a faulty design that stems across the entire product line.

Design Defect. A **design defect** is one that results from faulty design. A design defect arises when an alternative design exists which is safer and economically feasible. Consider the following example, where the court held that there was no design defect without evidence of feasible alternative designs.

> **Example:** Laura Hollister was severely burned when the rayon shirt that she was wearing ignited upon contact with a hot electric burner on her apartment stove. She sued Dayton Hudson Corporation, the owner of the department store where her shirt was purchased, alleging that the shirt was defective because of its susceptibility to extreme flammability. The court held in favor of Dayton Hudson Corporation, stating that Ms. Hollister failed to establish a design defect since she could not offer any evidence of feasible alternative designs that would have reduced the risk of accident. *Hollister v. Dayton Hudson Corp.*, 201 F.3d 731 (6th Cir. 2000)

In determining whether there is a design defect, a court may consider a range of factors, including things such as the gravity of the harm, the advantages or disadvantages of the product, and any available feasible alternative designs.

Courts also engage in either a risk-utility analysis or a consumer-expectation test. A risk-utility analysis is one in which the court decides whether the risk of harm from the product as designed outweighs its utility to the user and to the public. Under the consumer-expectation test, the court determines if a product is defective based upon whether the product fails to perform in a manner that an ordinary consumer would reasonably expect.

Example: "A risk-utility test is used in design defect cases. The applicable test is whether an ordinarily prudent company being fully aware of the risk would not have put the product on the market. To establish liability in a design defect claim, there must be proof of a safer and feasible alternative design. *Owens v. Ethicon, Inc.*, 2020 U.S. Dist. LEXIS 72587 (E.D. Ky. 2020)

Inadequate Warning. An **inadequate warning**, also known as a failure to warn or informational defect, can be categorized as a type of product defect, and occurs when the business fails to instruct the consumer in the effective use of the product or fails to warn of the dangers involved in the ordinary use or misuse of the product. The content of a warning that would relieve a seller of responsibility to the user is one that, if followed, would render the product safe for users. Factors that must be considered by a jury include consumer expectations as to how the product operates, how complicated the product is, the severity and likelihood of harm to which the user will be subject if the product is not properly used, and if a warning is likely to prevent injury (such as warning is conspicuous).

Inadequate warning A defect in which the business fails to instruct the consumer in the effective use of the product or fails to warn of the dangers involved in the ordinary use or misuse of a product.

Example: A one-year-old boy sustained severe, disabling burns when he was left alone in a room where a Rival Company® electric potpourri pot was operating on the floor. After the pot had been on the market for a short time, Rival began to receive reports of young children who were burned by accidental contact with the heated potpourri mixture but failed to make any modification to the design or warn users of such reports. In this case, the court found that after Rival learned of the dangers associated with the reasonably foreseeable use of its product after distribution, Rival failed to warn reasonably foreseeable users about the dangers. Therefore, Rival was found strictly liable. *Moulton v. Rival Co.*, 116 F.3d 22 (1st Cir. 1997)

Defect in packaging A defect arising when a product has been placed in packaging that lacks protection from tampering.

Defect in Packaging. A **defect in packaging** may arise from a manufacturer's failure to design and distribute safe packages for their products. For example, prescriptive medicines and over-the-counter remedies should be made safe from tampering or the acts of curious children.

PRODUCT IS SUBSTANTIALLY UNCHANGED. The plaintiff must prove that the product was defective at the time it left the seller's or manufacturer's possession. If the product was delivered in a non-defective, safe condition but was subsequently altered in a way that became dangerous to the user, the seller or manufacturer usually will not be held strictly liable.

The Consumer Products Safety Commission seeks to promote the safety of consumer products by addressing unreasonable risks of injury; developing uniform safety standards; and conducting research into product-related illness and injury. See https://www.cpsc.gov.

INJURY. The defective product must cause either personal injury or property damage to the plaintiff.

If the plaintiff can prove these elements, the defendant may be held strictly liable for a product defect.

Concept Summary
Types of Product Defects

One of the requirements in establishing a products defect claim is that the product itself must be defective.

There are four types of product defects:

1. Manufacturing Defects;
2. Design Defects;
3. Inadequate Warnings; and
4. Defect in Packaging.

The scope of the term "product" for purposes of the imposition of products liability has greatly expanded over the years. While doing so, courts have distinguished between those transactions that involve the sale of a product and are subject to strict liability and those transactions that are primarily services only incidentally involving the sale of a product, to which strict liability does not apply. If the primary object of a transaction is the provision of a service, generally strict liability will not be applied. Consider the following case which addressed this issue.

CASE 6.1

A SERVICE PROVIDER IS NOT A "MANUFACTURER" AND IS NOT LIABLE FOR A DEFECTIVE PRODUCT

PALERMO v. LIFELINK FOUNDATION, INC.

152 So. 3d 1099 (2014)

Supreme Court of Mississippi

Richard Palermo injured his right knee while working and, as a result, sought treatment from an orthopedic surgeon. The surgeon recommended surgery described as "anterior cruciate ligament construction and medical meniscus repair and the use of an allograft." In preparation for the surgery, LifeLink, a nonprofit tissue bank, filled an order placed by NuTech for an allograft. LifeLink shipped the allograft to NuTech, which then shipped the allograft to the surgeon.

After surgery, Palermo's knee began to exhibit signs of infection. After the surgeon removed the allograft, the infection subsided. Palermo sued the hospital, the surgeon, NuTech, and LifeLink on the grounds that the allograft was a defective product and that LifeLink was a "manufacturer" of the product.

The court found that human tissue provided to others in medical procedures is not a product subject to products liability law, and that the distribution of human tissue, including reasonable payments for related services, does not constitute a "sale" for purposes of strict liability.

Language of the Court. *The crux of Palermo's argument is that he has a viable products liability claim with regard to human tissue. However, under Mississippi law, liability exists due to the relationship arising from the purchase of a product. Also under Mississippi law, there is a blood banking statute that provides: "the procurement, processing, storage, distribution and/or use of whole blood, plasma, blood products, and blood derivatives for the purpose of injecting or transfusing, transplanting the same or any of them into the human body for all purposes whatsoever is the rendering of a service by every person participating therein, and does not constitute a sale."*

Given the historical context and the fact that the common law and Restatement (Second) of Torts predicated products liability in tort on the existence of a sale, the logical conclusion is that the Legislature intended to exempt blood from products liability law. In its present form, the Mississippi law has statutorily defined products liability and noted that people involved in the procurement, processing, storage, distribution and/or use of human tissue were statutory defined as service providers.

This Court has defined "manufacturer" for strict liability purposes as "a person or company who regularly and in the course of their principal business creates, assembles, and/or prepares goods for sale to the consuming public. A "service" is the "act of doing something useful for a person or company," "a person or company whose business is to do useful things for others," and "an intangible commodity in the form of human effort, such as labor, skill, or advice."

A service provider does not "produce" a good for sale. "Produce" means "to bring into existence" or "to create." Thus, the manufacturer of a good is the person or company who brings the good into its tangible form. In this circumstance, LifeLink is statutorily defined as a service provider. Thus, the trial court did not err by granting LifeLink's motion for summary judgment on the Palermos' product liability claim, nor did the Court of Appeals err by affirming the trial court's judgment.

Decision. The court held that LifeLink was not a manufacturer, and the human tissue was not a "product" for purposes of products liability.

Focus on Ethics

The court cites the Mississippi statute and states that to "produce" means to "bring into existence" or "to create." Allografts are tissue grafts from a donor of the same species as the recipient but not genetically identical. Is there an argument to be made that grafts are actually "created," and therefore a product, notwithstanding the statute? With respect to this plaintiff, was this decision fairly decided or should there be a change in the law?

The product must be leased or sold for strict liability to apply. Strict liability has been extended beyond manufacturers who sell their products to others in the chain of distribution to lessors. Under both a sale or a lease the seller and lessor have placed a product in the stream of commerce and are in a better position to exercise more control over a product than the consumer.

Negligence

If a manufacturer fails to exercise reasonable care to make a product safe, a person who is injured by the product can sue the manufacturer under the theory of negligence. Negligence involves the breach of a duty of care that is owed to others. Where the breach causes harm to others, the manufacturer may be held liable for negligence.

Duty

A duty of care is a legal obligation that requires an individual or entity to act as a reasonably prudent person would under similar circumstances. Such duty is owed to foreseeable plaintiffs, which includes *any person* who is a foreseeable user, consumer, or bystander of the product. More specifically, a manufacturer has a duty to exercise due care in:

- Designing the product;
- Manufacturing the product;
- Inspecting and testing the product; and
- Furnishing consumers with all necessary information about the product, including instructions on the product's effective and safe use, as well as warning against dangers that are either known or should be known by the manufacturer.

Breach

A breach of duty occurs when an individual or business owes a duty of care toward another individual but fails to live up to that standard.

Causation

The plaintiff must show that the defective product caused the plaintiff's harm. This element is that of proximate cause which involves foreseeability. In negligence and in the context of strict tort liability for defective design and failure to warn, a manufacturer must have been able to know the risk to be liable for failing to take steps to avoid that risk.

Damages

Damages are a measure of harm; thus, the plaintiff must show that they suffered either a personal injury or property damage.

Notice that the number of parties who might be liable to a plaintiff in a product liability action may be more numerous than those in a negligence action. Moreover, some jurisdictions allow recovery of punitive damages in products liability actions. Punitive damages are *not* awarded in negligence actions because the negligent acts are not intentional in nature.

Management Application
Avoiding Product Liability Claims

Management should consider whether the products they produce will lead to a product liability lawsuit in the future. The best method of avoiding products liability lawsuits is to correctly design and manufacture products and provide adequate warnings on products. When seeking to avoid litigation, management should:

1. Review the product to:
   a. Determine if the product is dangerous in its intended use or performance.
   b. Determine whether the physical condition of the product causes harm (such as sharp edges, parts can be easily separated, and so on).
   c. Analyze whether the product has been misused or if misuse of the product is foreseeable.
2. Review the dangers of using the product.
   a. Identify the probability of the occurrence of the danger.
   b. Identify the severity of the harm from the occurrence of the danger.
3. Analyze whether any dangers of use can be eliminated.
   a. Review the product design to determine if the product can be made safer in an economically feasible manner.
   b. Determine if the product warnings are appropriate and conspicuous or adequate instructions for the product's use/assembly are provided.

Misrepresentation

If a user or consumer of a product is injured as result of a manufacturer's or seller's false statements about a product the defrauded person will be able to sue on the basis of fraud. The misrepresentation must concern a material fact (that is, a fact related to the quality, nature, or proper use of the product on which a reasonable purchaser may be expected to rely). Mere sales puffery or statements of opinion are not considered statements of material fact.

A plaintiff can show that the defendant intended to induce reliance by the public by providing evidence of the product's advertisements or labels. Liability will only be found if there is justifiable reliance by the buyer, which can be established if the representation was a substantial factor in deciding to buy the product.

Example: Christopher Meta filed suit against Target Corporation® and Nice-Pak based on his purchase of flushable wipes from Target. According to Target's website and the product packaging, the wipes at issue were "flushable" and safe for septic and sewer systems. However, Meta encountered plumbing issues in his home allegedly caused by the buildup of the flushable wipes in his pipes and septic system. On his misrepresentation claim against the manufacturer and seller of the products, he alleged that the defendants knew that the wipes were not flushable or septic or sewer system safe. Meta properly stated an action for fraud. *Meta v. Target Corp.*, 74 F. Supp. 3d 858 (N.D. Ohio 2015)

Defenses to Products Liability Claims

Among the most common defenses to a products liability claim are the following: open and obvious danger, alteration or modification of the product, contributory negligence, comparative negligence, assumption of risk, product misuse, federal preemption, and statutes of limitations and repose.

Open and Obvious Danger

If the danger presented by a product is open and obvious, and the product is not defectively designed or manufactured, the manufacturer or supplier has no duty to warn the consumer. The policy behind this rule is that a warning would not prevent an injury from occurring.

> **Example**: Josephine Wiley tripped over a twelve-inch-tall orange warning cone on the floor at Sam's Club®. She blamed the store for her resulting injuries and sued for negligence. The federal district court granted Sam's Club's motion for summary judgment, finding that the orange cone was an open and obvious condition that did not pose an unreasonable risk of harm. *Wiley v. Sam's Club, Inc.*, 2015 U.S. Dist. LEXIS 76305 (W.D. Ky. 2015)

Alteration or Modification of the Product

A manufacturer may raise an affirmative defense that the allegedly defective product was substantially altered after the sale and that this condition was the proximate cause of the injury sustained. This defense has been incorporated by statute in an increasing number of states and may be raised by the manufacturer when the injury was proximately caused by the alteration. This action is considered as an intervening or superseding cause of the harm.

> **Example**: Neither the manufacturer nor seller of a seat belt assembly were liable for the death of a dune buggy passenger who was thrown from the vehicle when the seat belt failed to hold him. The seat belt assembly had been removed by the vehicle's owner from another vehicle he owned and installed in the dune buggy. Reinstallation of a seat belt was an alteration in the product amounting to an intervening or superseding cause. *Trotter v. Hamill Mfg. Co.*, 372 N.W. 2d 622 (Mich. 1985)

Contributory Negligence

Contributory negligence
Where a plaintiff's negligent conduct contributes to their harm, contributory negligence prevents the plaintiff from recovering damages.

Contributory negligence is traditionally a complete bar to recovery. As applied to products liability, contributory negligence is generally not a defense to strict liability but can be an appropriate defense in jurisdictions that adopt such a defense. For states that permit a form of the defense of contributory negligence, a plaintiff may be barred from recovery if it is determined that they were also negligent. However, in the case of intentional misrepresentation, contributory negligence is not a defense.

> **Example:** Orville Williams, a St. Louis dentist, was playing racquetball with a friend and was wearing a lens-less eye guard manufactured by Pro-Tec. During

a match a return shot struck Williams's right eye, injuring it severely and subsequently resulting in a 20 percent loss of Williams's peripheral vision and complete loss of his depth perception. Prior to purchasing the eye guard, Williams had read in a racquetball magazine that the eye guard was made from a "tough, virtually indestructible polycarbonate" and will "stop a lot of accidents." There was no claim, however, that the eye guard would prevent all accidents. At trial, Williams testified he was proficient in the game of racquetball and understood its hazards. As a result, the jury denied him any recovery because he assumed the risk. Thus, the court believed that the jury could properly infer that Williams must have known of the hazards that existed notwithstanding his use of the eye guard. As a result, the court believed that there was sufficient evidence to support a finding of contributory negligence. *Williams v. Pro-Tec, Inc.*, 908 F.2d 345 (8th Cir. 1990)

Comparative Negligence

In **comparative negligence** states, the plaintiff's recovery is reduced according to the percentage of fault due to contributory negligence. This defense applies to products liability claims based on negligence.

Comparative negligence Doctrine that apportions damages based on the plaintiff's and defendant's respective degrees of fault.

Example: Jeanette Delery, a paralegal, was seated at her desk in a chair manufactured by Steelcase®. The chair had a plexiglass mat underneath it. She backed her chair away from the desk to get up and turned the chair while getting up. The chair then flipped, hit her in the back of the neck, and caused her to fall to the floor. The chair contained a warning advising that use on hard surfaces like plexiglass would make the chair less stable. The manufacturer asserted as a defense that Ms. Delery was comparatively negligent. The court held that there was sufficient evidence to support the finding that Ms. Delery was 30 percent negligent for failing to read the warning on the underside of the chair, even though Steelcase had failed to provide an adequate warning. *Delery v. Prudential Insurance Co.*, 643 So. 2d 807 (La. Ct. App. 1994)

Assumption of Risk

Assumption of risk is another defense in a products liability action. To establish such a defense, the defendant must show the following:

Assumption of risk Where a plaintiff has knowingly and voluntarily faced a dangerous or harmful situation, assumption of risk absolves the defendant from all liability.

1. The plaintiff knew and appreciated the risk created by the product defect; and
2. Despite knowing and appreciating the risk, the plaintiff still voluntarily assumed the risk even though it was unreasonable to do so.

However, just like contributory negligence, some states do not recognize assumption of risk as a defense to strict liability in products liability cases.

Example: Karl-Heinz Dullmaier was killed when he fell off his horse during a horseback riding trip through Yellowstone National Park. When his heirs sued, on appeal the federal appellate court followed a Wyoming statute that stated, "[a]ny person who takes part in any sport or recreational opportunity assumes the inherent risks in that sport or recreational opportunity." The court held the horseback riding company was entitled to summary judgment because Karl-Heinz knew the risks of horseback riding and still voluntarily chose to engage. *Dullmaier v. Xanterra Parks & Resorts*, 883 F.3d 1278 (10th Cir. 2018)

Product Misuse

Product misuse
A defense to a products liability claim allowed when a consumer does not use a product as it was intended to be used, and such misuse was not reasonably foreseeable.

Product misuse is another defense to products liability. Generally, it is important to remember that *foreseeable misuse* is not a defense to products liability. However, *unforeseeable misuse* is taken into consideration and is relevant as to whether there is liability. To establish this defense, the manufacturer, distributor, or retailer must show the following:

1. The product was not used as it was intended to be used; and
2. The injury caused by such misuse was not reasonably foreseeable.

The following case explores the defenses of both product misuse and contributory negligence, involving a jack stand, which is used to lift a vehicle for repairs.

CASE 6.2

UNFORESEEABLE PRODUCT MISUSE IS A DEFENSE TO PRODUCTS LIABILITY

LINDHOLM v. BMW OF NORTH AMERICA, LLC

862 F.3d 648 (8th Cir. 2017)

United States Court of Appeals for the Eighth Circuit

Alex Lindholm was repairing his car when, tragically, he was killed when the car fell on him. Lindholm was working on the car's exhaust system located near the center of the car's undercarriage the day before the accident. Lindholm continued working on the job the next day, and the car was lifted in the back passenger area with the manufacturer's (BMW's) jack. Using that jack, Alex Lindholm was repairing his car when, tragically, it fell and killed him. Relying on federal courts' diversity jurisdiction, Alex's father sued BMW of North America, LLC, the car's American distributor, on behalf of Alex's estate, and both of Alex's parents sued in their individual capacities. They laid claims for strict liability based on defective design, negligent design, breach of implied warranties, and wrongful death. The district court granted BMW's motion for summary judgment on each of the Lindholms' claims, and they appealed.

Language of the Court. The district court concluded that *BMW was not liable because Alex had misused the jack on the day of the accident. Misuse can involve using a product for an unintended function or using the product for its intended function but in an improper manner. Though a product manufacturer can be liable for a customer's reasonably foreseeable misuse, a manufacturer cannot be liable for a misuse that it cannot reasonably anticipate.*

The parties dispute whether Alex misused the jack. The Lindholms argue that Alex used the jack in exactly the way it was intended to be used — to lift a car. They also maintain that, should we nonetheless conclude that Alex misused the jack, BMW should be liable because his misuse was reasonably foreseeable. BMW emphasizes the warnings that Alex disregarded: The car's owner's manual said that the jack "is designed for changing tires only" and that one should "[n]ever lie beneath the vehicle or start the engine while the car is supported by the jack - risk of fatal injury!" And a picture on the jack itself warned against lying under the car while using the jack. BMW argues that Alex's disregard for these warnings resulted in misuse.

We agree with BMW and the district court that a reasonable jury would have to conclude that Alex misused the jack. Though it could be said that Alex used the jack for its intended purpose — to lift a car — he did so in an improper manner. The warnings in the owner's manual and on the jack made it clear that Alex should not have used the jack while doing something other than changing a tire or while lying under the car. Alex could have used other available jacks or jack stands to support the car; in fact, the evidence showed that he had done so the day before the fatal accident. The manufacturer's warnings make it clear that Alex used the jack for a purpose for which it was not intended.

Alex's misuse of the jack was not foreseeable as a matter of law, given the warnings that accompanied it. Here, a seller may reasonably assume that a warning will be read and heeded; and a product bearing such a warning, which is safe for use if it is followed, is not in defective condition, nor is it unreasonably dangerous. As for the negligent design claims, we think that Alex's misuse of the jack also constitutes contributory negligence, which bars the Lindholms from recovering. Even assuming that BMW was somehow negligent, we think that a reasonable factfinder would have to conclude that Alex's contributory negligence was anything but slight; it was quite clearly the primary cause of the accident. We therefore have no trouble concluding as a matter of law that Alex's contributory negligence defeats the Lindholms' negligence and negligent-design claims.

Decision. BMW was not liable because of the decedent's unforeseen product misuse.

Focus on Ethics

Do you think the way Alex used the jack that ultimately led to his death was an unforeseeable misuse? Why or why not?

Federal Preemption

The Supremacy Clause of Article VI of the United States Constitution states that when a federal law and a state law conflict, federal law will prevail. If Congress intended to occupy a particular field through regulations that are comprehensive in scope, a plaintiff may not be able to sue a manufacturer of defective products if the regulations preempt claims for products liability.

For an in-depth illustration of how federal preemption works, consider the next case, which deals with two sets of laws; namely, New Hampshire products liability law and the Federal Food, Drug, and Cosmetic Act (FDCA).

CASE 6.3

A STATE STATUTE IS PREEMPTED BY FEDERAL LAW IF IT IS IMPOSSIBLE FOR A DEFENDANT TO COMPLY WITH BOTH LAWS

MUTUAL PHARMACEUTICAL CO. v. BARTLETT

570 U.S. 472 (2013)

Supreme Court of the United States

In 2004, Karen Bartlett was prescribed Clinoril, the brand-name version of the anti-inflammatory drug sulindac, for shoulder pain. Her pharmacist dispensed a generic form of sulindac manufactured by Mutual Pharmaceutical. Soon after taking the medication, Ms. Bartlett developed an acute case of toxic epidermal necrolysis. Approximately 65 percent of the surface of her body deteriorated, was burned off, or turned into an open wound. This resulted in Ms. Bartlett having to spend months in a medically induced coma, undergo 12 eye surgeries, and be on a feeding tube for a year. The conditions ultimately led Ms. Bartlett to be severely disfigured, physically disabled, and nearly blind.

Ms. Bartlett sued, asserting both failure to warn and design defect claims. For a multiplicity of reasons, redesigning sulindac was impossible. Under New Hampshire state law, there was a duty imposed on manufacturers to strengthen the warning labels on their drugs. However, under federal law, manufacturers were not allowed to alter the warning labels of drugs after they had been approved—which sulindac had been. Thus, there was a conflict between the state law and the federal law, which meant that federal law prohibited Mutual from taking the remedial action required to avoid liability under New Hampshire law. At issue was whether federal law preempted the New Hampshire design defect claim. Upon the grant of a *writ of certiorari*, the manufacturer appealed the judgment of the U.S. Court of Appeals for the First Circuit which affirmed a federal district court judgment in favor of the patient.

Language of the Court. *Under the Federal Food, Drug, and Cosmetic Act (FDCA), drug manufacturers must gain approval from the United States Food and Drug Administration (FDA) before marketing any drug in interstate commerce. Once a drug is approved, the manufacturer is prohibited from making any major changes to the formulation of the drug product. Generic manufacturers are also prohibited from making any unilateral changes to a drug's label.*

At the time Karen Bartlett was prescribed sulindac, the drug's label did not specifically refer to Stevens-Johnson Syndrome or toxic epidermal necrolysis, but did warn that the drug could cause "severe skin reactions" and "[f]atalities." However, Stevens-Johnson Syndrome and toxic epidermal necrolysis were listed as potential adverse reactions on the drug's package. Once she was already suffering from toxic epidermal necrolysis—the FDA completed a comprehensive review of the risks and benefits, [including the risk of toxic epidermal necrolysis], of all approved NSAID products. As a result of that review, the FDA recommended changes to the labeling of all NSAIDs, including sulindac, to more explicitly warn against toxic epidermal necrolysis.

New Hampshire tort law requires manufacturers to ensure that the products they design, manufacture, and sell are not "unreasonably dangerous." This duty can be satisfied either by changing a drug's design or by changing its labeling. Thus, under New Hampshire law, Mutual was required to change sunlidac's labeling. Because it was impossible to redesign sunlindac, the only way for Mutual to escape liability under New Hampshire law was to strengthen the warning label.

However, federal law prevents generic drug manufacturers from changing their labels. Federal drug regulations, as interpreted by the FDA, prevented manufacturers from independently changing their generic drugs' safety labels. Thus, federal law prohibited Mutual from taking the remedial action required to avoid liability under New Hampshire law. When a federal law forbids an action that state law requires, the state law is "without effect." Because it is impossible for Mutual and other similarly situated manufacturers to comply with both state and federal law, New Hampshire's warning-based design-defect cause of action is pre-empted with respect to FDA-approved drugs sold in interstate commerce.

The dreadful injuries from . . . products liabilities cases often engender passionate responses. Today is no exception, but sympathy for Ms. Bartlett does not relieve us of the responsibility of following the law.

Decision. The Court held that New Hampshire tort law was preempted by federal law and that was a valid defense for the drug manufacturer.

Focus on Ethics

The dissent argued that "federal law gives pharmaceutical companies a right to sell a federally approved drug free from common law liability," while the majority opinion argues that sympathy for the victim does not relieve the court of the responsibility of following the law. Is this a fair outcome? Would a consumer have been protected by a stronger product label?

Statutes of Limitations and Repose

There are two types of limitation defenses available to a defendant: statutes of limitations and statutes of repose.

Statute of limitations A specified time within which a lawsuit must be filed.

STATUTE OF LIMITATIONS. A **statute of limitations** is a specified period within which a cause of action must be brought. Typically, it begins to run when the injury giving rise to the cause of action occurs. At that point, the plaintiff may sue. A plaintiff's failure to file an action within the specified statutory time would bar the plaintiff's right to sue.

Statute of repose
A limit on the length of time that can elapse from the date of the first sale of the defective product to the filing of a products liability lawsuit.

STATUTE OF REPOSE. Much like a statute of limitations, a **statute of repose** places a limit on the amount of time that can pass between the date of the first sale of the defective product and the filing of a products liability claim. A statute of repose limits the obligation of a manufacturer, distributor, or retailer to an injured product user, whereas the statute of limitations places a time limit on the plaintiff's right to seek recovery. Accordingly, after the statute of repose runs, there is no longer any legal obligation on behalf of the seller or manufacturer, so no remedy can be sought.

AI Feature: Gathering the Facts and Alleging Fault for a Defective Product

Identify the prospective product defects and responsible parties in the following set of facts.

Marc, an enthusiastic first-time new homeowner, was unaware of the risks of shallow depths posed by an installed above-ground swimming pool. The pool had been installed by the person who sold the home to Marc. After topping off the pool's waterline, he dove headfirst into it. But, as a result of hitting the pool bottom, he suffered a severe spine injury. He sues the seller from whom he purchased his home, the pool designer, the manufacturer (Above Ground Pools), and the swimming pool installation company (Cheap Pools) for the physical injuries he suffered. During discovery, it is revealed that there was a 4-inch warning label on the bottom of the pool that read "Caution: Shallow Water May Cause Serious Injury or Death." Marc never saw the warning label before he was injured.

Consider who might be a responsible party to Marc and under what theories of liability. Then, using an AI program state the allegations of liability Marc would assert in his lawsuit. Your allegations should include the tort theories discussed in this and the last chapter. Separately, set forth the allegations of the defenses the defendants would assert in response to his complaint for damages

Key Terms

- Assumption of risk, 135
- Chain of distribution, 126
- Comparative negligence, 135
- Contribution, 127
- Contributory negligence, 134
- Defect in packaging, 129
- Design defect, 128
- Inadequate warning, 129
- Indemnity, 126
- Manufacturing defect, 128
- Product misuse, 136
- Products liability, 126
- Statute of limitations, 139
- Statute of repose, 140
- Strict liability, 123

Applying the Law

6.1 Failure to Warn. David Livingston ate some vegetable soup produced by Marie Callender's restaurant chain and suffered a severe adverse reaction to the monosodium glutamate (MSG) in the soup. Mr. Livingston sued for products liability based on the restaurant's failure to warn of an ingredient to which a substantial number of the population were allegedly allergic. Can Marie Callender's potentially be held liable? What defenses can the company reasonably assert? *Livingston v. Marie Callender's, Inc.*, 72 Cal. App. 4th 830 (1999)

6.2 Foreseeability. Steven Iliades sustained serious injuries after reaching inside a 500-ton press machine to retrieve molded rubber parts. Iliades then brought a products liability action against the manufacturer, alleging negligence and breach of warranty. To prevail, Iliades must show that the particular misuse was reasonably foreseeable by the manufacturer. Make arguments for and against a finding that the misuse was foreseeable. *Iliades v. Dieffenbacher North America Inc.*, 915 N.W.2d 338 (Mich. 2018)

6.3 Products Liability Defenses. Brad Westlye injured himself while skiing, allegedly due to defective ski equipment rented from Klein's Ski Shop and distributed by Look Sports, Inc. The rental contract contained a written release acknowledging that Brad had assumed the risk of injury. Brad signed the release. Nonetheless, Brad sued for products liability, negligence, and breach of warranty. For which claims is the release an applicable defense? *Westlye v. Look Sports, Inc.*, 17 Cal. App. 4th 1715 (1993)

6.4 Assumption of Risk. Candice Wimberley was injured while using an inverted leg press machine manufactured by Bodymasters Sports Industries, Inc. The machine contained a sticker warning that handles were required to be in a locked position while doing certain types of exercises. The machine had no safety mechanism to stop the descent of the weights while certain exercises were being performed. Candice was aware of this and was injured when the weight was too much for her to bear and her legs were forced down toward her chest, resulting in a knee fracture and hyperflexation. Did Candice assume the risk of injury? Why or why not? *Bodymasters Sports Industries, Inc. v. Wimberley*, 501 S.E.2d 556 (Ga. Ct. App. 1998)

6.5 Products Liability. Robert Houston, a garbage truck worker, died during an accident because of a dangerous condition existing on the leased premises of Clarence Coffee. Robert's estate brought a negligence action against both Clarence Coffee and H Leasing, which owned the truck and leased it to another defendant that was H Leasing's corporate sibling. The court held that products liability did not apply to H Leasing because it was simply a finance lessor. Under New York law, finance lessors who merely offer the use of money to acquire goods but otherwise neither market a product nor place it in the stream of commerce are not liable under products liability. Instead, the court held that products liability actions against lessors involve leasing entities that either take possession of the equipment at issue and lease it to the public or are financing arms of the manufacturer. As a matter of policy, does it make sense for the New York law to draw the line between different types of lessors? Why or why not? *Houston v. McNeilus Truck and Mfg., Inc.*, 124 A.D.3d 1205 (N.Y. App. Div. 2015)

6.6 Product Misuse. Paul Johnson purchased a mini air die grinder (a tool that can be used for grinding and shaping metal, plastic, and wood). The grinder came with various warnings and instructions, stating that the failure to comply with instructions could result in personal injury. The instructions advised users to use "safety glasses and ear protection" during operation. The packaging also warned against using attachments rated for a minimum of 25,000 RPM and advised using a safety guard. Johnson attached a cut-off disc with a lower RPM rating and believed his prescription glasses were sufficient to serve as safety glasses. While using the grinder, the disc came apart and a piece hit Johnson on the left side of his face. As a result, his eyeglasses were broken, and Johnson sustained serious injuries to his cheek and eye. Johnson sued, claiming there was a failure to warn. What defenses may Campbell assert? How should the court rule? *Campbell Hausfeld/Scott Fetzer Company v. Johnson*, 109 N.E.3d 953 (Ind. 2018)

6.7 Failure to Warn. Kathleen Sollami was injured while jumping on a large recreational trampoline. She was injured attempting to perform a "rocket jump," where other jumpers cause one jumper to be propelled higher than the others. Her father sued on her behalf, bringing a products liability claim against the manufacturer. Her father claimed that the manufacturer had failed in its duty to warn. Should Sollami's claim prevail? Why or why not? *Sollami v. Eaton*, 772 N.E.2d 215 (Ill. 2002)

6.8 Risk-Utility. Constantine Varazo injured his finger while moving an exercise bike manufactured by Keiser Corporation. Varazo sued Keiser, alleging that Kaiser failed to warn that picking up the bike could cause injury. Did the duty to exercise reasonable care in manufacturing its products require a warning? Was the danger open and obvious? *Varazo v. Keiser Corporation*, 754 F. App'x 918 (11th Cir. 2018)

6.9 Comparative Negligence. Daly was driving his Opel® at a speed of 50 to 70 miles per hour and collided with a metal divider. After the impact, Daly's door was thrown open and he was forcibly ejected from the car. Daly sustained fatal head injuries. His widow and surviving minor children brought a products liability action against the automobile manufacturer alleging the door latch was improperly designed. General Motors argued that the car was equipped with a seat belt harness system and a door lock that, if used, would have prevented Daly's ejection. Should this reduce the plaintiff's recovery? Make arguments for and against such a finding. *Daly v. General Motors Corp.*, 575 P.2d 1162 (Cal. 1978)

6.10 Retailer Liability. Eileen Oser sued Wal-Mart Stores® for strict liability and negligence. A jar of juice purchased by Oser fell through a plastic bag at the checkout counter and shattered, causing Oser to slip on the juice and injure herself on the glass-strewn floor. Wal-Mart asserted that it was not liable because it used the bag only as it was instructed to by the bag manufacturer. Further, it argued that it did not contribute to bag's defective manufacture or design. Should the retailer be held liable for Oser's injuries? *Oser v. Wal-Mart Stores*, 951 F. Supp. 115 (S.D. Tex. 1996)

Intellectual Property

7

Intellectual property is the oil of the 21st century. — Mark Getty, founder of Getty Images and billionaire philanthropist (1960-)

Chapter Outline

- Introduction
- Trademarks

Case 7.1: *Matal v. Tam*

Case 7.2: *Iancu v. Brunetti*

  - *Management Application: Challenges to Ownership of Intellectual Property*
- Trade Secrets
  - *Management Application: Trade Secret Agreement*
- Copyrights
  - *Management Application: Artist Disputes*

Case 7.3: *Authors Guild v. Google*

- Patents

Case 7.4: *TC Heartland LLC v. Kraft Foods LLC*

- Licensing
  - *Management Application: Excerpts from Licensing Agreement for Use of Software*
- International Intellectual Property
- Internet Law
- AI Feature: Protecting IP Rights Domestically and Internationally

Learning Objectives

After studying this chapter, you should be able to:

1. Describe the different types of marks.
2. Distinguish between trademark infringement and trademark dilution.
3. Explain what qualifies for trade secret protection, and how to maintain it.
4. Describe the requirements for copyright protection.
5. Describe what can be patented and the requirements of a patentable invention.
6. Describe the scope of international protection for intellectual property.
7. Explain the concept of cybersquatting.

Introduction

Intellectual property
The general term for the fields of trademarks, trade secrets, copyrights, and patents.

Intellectual property is a broad term that refers to creations of the mind. In contrast to real property, intellectual property is intangible, which means the creation cannot be touched or held in one's hands. However, despite the abstract nature of intellectual property, it has come to dominate many areas of everyday life. Businesses can differentiate their services and products through the creation of intellectual property and the applications range from the world of Silicon Valley (Apple®, Google®, Facebook®) to Detroit (Ford®, GM®) to Hollywood (Disney®, Universal®, Sony®), and extend to every business operating in the United States today. Many of these businesses spend billions of dollars a year on the creation of intellectual property.

The importance of intellectual property is reinforced by the inclusion of the Patent and Copyright Clause in the Constitution. This clause conveys authority to the federal government to regulate both patents and copyrights, to "promote the progress of science and useful arts." Other areas of intellectual property are also governed by federal law, including trade secrets and trademarks. Collectively, these four areas of law converge under the umbrella of intellectual property to promote development of science, business, art, and culture.

This chapter covers trademarks, trade secrets, copyrights, and patents. The requirements of each concept and the protections granted are identified, and the best strategies for protecting one's intellectual property from both a business and legal perspective are examined. This chapter also evaluates the current state of intellectual property and provides insight into future challenges the law will face as technology develops. In addition, this chapter surveys the state of internet law as it currently exists—including domain name registration and squatting, and copyright and trademark infringement online.

Trademarks

Trademark
Symbols and designs that organizations use to mark their products.

A **trademark** can be any name, symbol, word, design, or any combination thereof that identifies the source of the goods or services and distinguishes the good or service from other providers. The policy of trademark protection is to prevent consumer confusion in the marketplace, and to encourage companies to compete on the quality of their products. While trademarks are not required to be registered to be valid, the federal government provides a database for trademark registration under the Lanham Act. Both state and federal law govern trademarks.

Example: Just Do It®, Nike®, In-N-Out Burger®, and the Levi "V" shaped stitching design on the back of Levi's blue jeans are all examples of trademarks.

The Lanham Act: Federal Registration of Trademarks

Lanham Act
Federal law that governs trademarks.

The **Lanham Act** provides for the federal registration and protection of trademarks. The Act protects trademarks to prevent consumer confusion as to the source of goods. The law encourages companies to compete over the quality of their products, because companies will be rewarded for the investment they make in their brands.

The federal government maintains a directory of registered marks with the United States Patent and Trademark Office (USPTO). To successfully register a mark, a party must file an application with the USPTO and pay a fee at the time of publication. To qualify for registration, a mark must either already be in use in commerce or intended to be used in commerce within six months. Once registered, the owner of the mark must periodically file maintenance documents with the USPTO to continue use of the mark. Trademarks are protected for 10 years, but there is no limitation on the number of times the mark may be renewed.

The Act encourages registration of *marks* by granting nationwide protection to the mark. Registered marks are also allowed to use the ® symbol, which provides notice of their federal registration. The ™ symbol is used for unregistered marks.

Types of Marks

A mark is the name for the actual symbol, design, or other identifying aspect that is used in connection with the product. Not all marks are trademarks. Certain marks can be classified into the following categories:

- A *trademark* is a mark that is used in connection with a good. The symbol ™ can be used if the goods are not registered with the USPTO, or ® if it is registered.
  - **Example:** iPhone® is a registered trademark of Apple® used in connection with its smartphones.
- A *service mark* is a mark that is used in connection with a service. The symbol ℠ can be used if the service is not registered with the USPTO, or ® can be used if it is registered.
  - **Example:** AT&T® is both the name for the company and a registered service mark.
- A *certification mark* is a mark that is owned by an entity other than the producer of the good or service, which is used to certify that the good or service has a specific quality, such as the way it was manufactured or the geographic region that the good is from.
  - **Example:** Underwriters Laboratories® offers to certify goods as "UL Listed," which informs consumers that the product meets UL standards.
- A *collective mark* is a mark that is owned by an association, collective, or other organization, which is used to certify that a good or service is being offered in accordance with the standards of the organization.
  - **Example:** The Motion Pictures Association of America® (MPAA) issues ratings for movies that are released. Each rating, such as PG-13, is a collective mark that the movie contains content consistent with that rating's standards.
- *Trade dress* is a type of trademark that refers to the design or presentation of a product. Trade dress is a diverse category that encompasses things such as the decoration of a restaurant, colors, smells, or sounds a product is marked with. Trade dress must be nonfunctional to be eligible for protection. Once registered, trade dress is subject to the same protections as all other marks.
  - **Example:** The Coca-Cola® bottle, with its hourglass shape and clear glass, is a registered trade dress of the Coca-Cola Company.

Distinctiveness

Inherently distinct
Marks that bear no obvious connection to the good or service, such that the association is unique.

Secondary meaning
A mark that has acquired a connection with a specific product in the minds of consumers.

To qualify as a valid trademark, the mark must identify the source of goods or services clearly enough to be considered *distinct.* A mark is distinct when (1) the mark is **inherently distinct**, which is when a mark has no obvious connection to the good or service (such as Nike®), or (2) the mark has acquired a **secondary meaning**, which is when consumers have come to associate the mark with a particular seller over time (such as Just Do It® from Nike).

The protection against trademark infringement depends on the distinctiveness of the mark. The distinctiveness of the mark depends on which category the mark is classified into. Trademarks are classified, from strongest to weakest, as follows:

1. *Fanciful.* A mark that is a wholly new word that did not exist prior to the application for trademark protection. The mark is automatically eligible for trademark protection.

Example: The "Wii®" video game console by Nintendo® because, prior to trademark registration, the word did not exist.

2. *Arbitrary.* A mark that is an existing word in the English language, but totally arbitrary as applied to the good or service. The mark is automatically eligible for trademark protection.

Example: "Apple®" as applied to computers, because it is an English word but bears no relation to computing.

3. *Suggestive.* A mark that suggests the category of the product it is associated with. The mark must require the consumer to use their imagination, thoughts, and perceptions to discern the nature of the product or service. Suggestive marks are automatically eligible for trademark protection.

Example: "Netflix®," because the mark suggests the combination of internet and "flix," shorthand for movies.

4. *Descriptive.* A mark that describes the product. Descriptive marks can obtain trademark protection only when they acquire *secondary meaning.*

Example: "Fast" when used in connection with a delivery service. "Delicious" when used in connection with food and restaurants.

5. *Generic.* A term that has a standard meaning. You cannot obtain a trademark in a generic term, nor can it ever gain secondary meaning. Typically, these are common words that are required to describe the product, or it may be a former trademark that has become common to all similar products.

Example: The word "apple" is a generic term. Also, the term "escalator" refers to a moving staircase. The latter is an example of a trademark that lost its meaning and became generic.

In the following case, the U.S. Supreme Court considered whether preventing registration of potentially offensive marks violated free speech rights.

CASE 7.1

IT IS A VIOLATION OF FREE SPEECH TO PROHIBIT THE REGISTRATION OF DISPARAGING MARKS

MATAL v. TAM

582 U.S. 218 (2017)

Supreme Court of the United States

Simon Tam, an Asian-American musician and lead singer of the group "The Slants," filed for trademark registration for the band name. He sought to adopt the denigrating term as the band's name to "reclaim" it, and to reduce the derogatory force of the term. The USPTO, under a section of the Lanham Act that prohibited registration of disparaging marks, denied the application. Tam challenged the law as a violation of the Free Speech Clause. After Tam lost an administrative appeal with the USPTO, the U.S. Court of Appeals for the Federal Circuit agreed with Tam that the anti-disparagement provision was a violation of the Free Speech Clause. The Supreme Court granted review.

Language of the Court. *The disparagement clause cannot be sustained under the Government's proposed "government-program" doctrine, so we must confront a dispute between the parties on the question whether trademarks are commercial speech and are subject to relaxed scrutiny. However, a restriction of speech must serve "a substantial interest," and it must be "narrowly drawn." It is claimed that the disparagement clause serves two interests: (1) preventing underrepresented groups from being bombarded with demeaning messages in commercial advertising; and (2) protecting the orderly flow of commerce.*

It is far-fetched to suggest that the content of a registered mark is government speech. If the federal registration of a trademark makes the mark government speech, the Federal Government is babbling prodigiously and incoherently. It is saying many unseemly things. It is expressing contradictory views. It is unashamedly endorsing a vast array of commercial products and services. And it is providing Delphic advice to the consuming public. For example, if trademarks represent government speech, what does the Government have in mind when it advises Americans to "make.believe" (Sony), "Think different" (Apple), "Just do it" (Nike), or "Have it your way" (Burger King)? Was the Government warning about a coming disaster when it registered the mark "Endtime Ministries"?

Companies spend huge amounts to create and publicize trademarks that convey a message. It is true that the necessary brevity of trademarks limits what they can say. But powerful messages can sometimes be conveyed in just a few words. Trademarks are private, not government, speech.

Speech that demeans on the basis of race, ethnicity, gender, religion, age, disability, or any other similar ground is hateful; but the proudest boast of our free speech jurisprudence is that we protect the freedom to express "the thought that we hate."

Additionally, the disparagement clause is not "narrowly drawn" to drive out trademarks that support invidious discrimination. The clause reaches any trademark that disparages any person, group, or institution. It applies to trademarks like the following: "Down with racists," "Down with sexists," "Down with homophobes." It is not an anti-discrimination clause; it is a happy-talk clause. In this way, it goes much further than is necessary to serve the interest asserted.

Decision. The Court found in favor of Tam. Specifically, the Court held that the anti-disparagement provision of the Act was a violation of the Free Speech Clause because it was overly restrictive toward private speech.

Focus on Ethics

Do you think that trademark protection should be granted to marks that are patently offensive? Is this an ethical approach to managing free speech?

In *Iancu v. Brunetti*, the Supreme Court invalidated another provision of the Lanham Act as unconstitutional. All nine Justices agreed that the USPTO did not have the authority to determine what words or images were immoral and thus ineligible to benefit from federal trademark registration. However, three Justices dissented, finding that the ban on immoral or scandalous trademarks could be narrowly read to serve a legitimate purpose in prohibiting vulgarity and profanity. After reading the following case, consider whether the "viewpoint bias" standard as articulated by the Court adequately balances the compelling government interest in protecting our sensibilities with the constitutional right to free expression.

CASE 7.2

IF A TRADEMARK REGISTRATION BAR IS VIEWPOINT-BASED, IT IS UNCONSTITUTIONAL

IANCU v. BRUNETTI

588 U.S. 388 (2019)

Supreme Court of the United States

Erik Brunetti is an artist who founded a clothing line that uses the trademark FUCT. The Patent and Trademark Office (PTO) denied his application for a federal trademark under a provision of the Lanham Act prohibiting registration of trademarks that "consist of or comprise immoral or scandalous matter." Brunetti brought a First Amendment challenge to the "immoral or scandalous" bar in the Federal Circuit, which invalidated the provision. The Supreme Court granted *certiorari.*

Language of the Court. *In* Matal v. Tam, *this Court declared unconstitutional the Lanham Act's ban on registering marks that "disparage any person, living or dead." A divided Court agreed on two propositions. First, if a trademark registration bar is viewpoint based, it is unconstitutional. And second, the disparagement bar was viewpoint based. The Justices thus found common ground in a core postulate of free speech law: The government may not discriminate against speech based on the ideas or opinions it conveys.*

The "immoral or scandalous" bar similarly discriminates on the basis of viewpoint and so collides with this Court's First Amendment doctrine. Expressive material is "immoral" when it is "inconsistent with rectitude, purity, or good morals"; "wicked"; or "vicious." So the Lanham Act permits registration of marks that champion society's sense of rectitude and morality, but not marks that denigrate those concepts. And material is "scandalous" when it "gives offense to the conscience or moral feelings"; "excites reprobation"; or "calls out condemnation." So the Lanham Act allows registration of marks when their messages accord with, but not when their messages defy, society's sense of decency or propriety. The statute, on its face, distinguishes between two opposed sets of ideas: those aligned with conventional moral standards and those hostile to them; those inducing societal nods of approval and those provoking offense and condemnation.

This facial viewpoint bias in the law results in viewpoint-discriminatory application. The PTO has refused to register marks communicating "immoral" or "scandalous" views about (among other things) drug use, religion, and terrorism. But all the while, it has approved registration of marks expressing more accepted views on the same topics.

Here are some samples. The PTO rejected marks conveying approval of drug use (YOU CAN'T SPELL HEALTHCARE WITHOUT THC for pain-relief medication, MARIJUANA COLA and KO KANE for beverages) because it is scandalous to "inappropriately glamorize drug abuse." But at the same time, the PTO registered marks with such sayings as D.A.R.E. TO RESIST DRUGS AND VIOLENCE and SAY NO TO DRUGS—REALITY IS THE BEST TRIP IN LIFE. Similarly, the PTO disapproved registration for the mark BONG HITS 4 JESUS because it "suggests that people should engage in an illegal activity in connection with worship" and because "Christians would be morally outraged by a statement that connects Jesus Christ with illegal drug use." And the PTO refused to register trademarks associating religious references with products (AGNUS DEI for safes and MADONNA for wine) because they would be "offensive to most individuals of the Christian faith" and "shocking to the sense of propriety." But once again, the PTO approved marks—PRAISE THE LORD for a game and JESUS DIED FOR YOU on clothing—whose message suggested religious faith rather than blasphemy or irreverence. Of course, all these decisions are understandable. The rejected marks express opinions that are, at the least, offensive to many Americans. But as the Court made clear in Tam, *a law disfavoring "ideas that offend" discriminates based on viewpoint, in violation of the First Amendment.*

The Government says the statute is susceptible of a limiting construction that would remove its viewpoint bias. The Government's idea is to narrow the statutory bar to "marks that are offensive or shocking because of their mode of expression, independent of any views that they may express," which would mostly restrict the PTO to refusing marks that are lewd, sexually explicit, or profane. But this Court cannot accept the Government's proposal, because the statute says something markedly different. The "immoral or scandalous" bar does not draw the line at lewd, sexually explicit, or profane marks. Nor does it refer only to marks whose "mode of expression," independent of viewpoint, is particularly offensive. To cut the statute off where the Government urges is not to interpret the statute Congress enacted, but to fashion a new one.

And once the "immoral or scandalous" bar is interpreted fairly, it must be invalidated. The Government just barely argues otherwise. In the last paragraph of its brief, the Government gestures toward the idea that the provision is salvageable by virtue of its constitutionally permissible applications (in the Government's view, its applications to lewd, sexually explicit, or profane marks). In other words, the Government invokes our First Amendment overbreadth doctrine, and asks us to uphold the statute against facial attack because its unconstitutional applications are not "substantial" relative to "the statute's plainly legitimate sweep." But to begin with, this Court has never applied that kind of analysis to a viewpoint-discriminatory law.

In Tam, *for example, we did not pause to consider whether the disparagement clause might admit some permissible applications (say, to certain libelous speech) before striking it down. The Court's finding of viewpoint bias ended the matter. And similarly, it seems unlikely we would compare permissible and impermissible applications if Congress outright banned "offensive" (or to use some other examples, "divisive" or "subversive") speech. Once we have found that a law "aims at the suppression of" views, why would it matter that Congress could have captured some of the same speech through a viewpoint-neutral statute? But in any event, the "immoral or scandalous" bar is substantially overbroad. There are a great many immoral and scandalous ideas in the world (even more than there are swearwords), and the Lanham Act covers them all. It therefore violates the First Amendment.*

Decision. The Supreme Court ruled that the Lanham Act's bar on registration of "immoral" or "scandalous" trademarks discriminates because of viewpoint and thus violates the First Amendment.

Focus on Ethics

If the "immoral or scandalous" provision of the Lanham Act instead prohibited federal registration of obscene, vulgar, or profane trademarks, would the statute still violate the First Amendment? Why or why not? Is it ethical to protect such trademarks?

The Supreme Court has also held that the Trademark Office was authorized under the Lanham Act to refuse to register a trademark using a person's name without the person's consent.

Example: Steve Elster sought to trademark "TRUMP TOO SMALL." In his application he stated he intended to use the mark on shirts that he planned to sell. The government's examiner rejected the application stating that the use of the word "TRUMP" in the mark would likely be construed by the public as a reference to Donald Trump and that, without the then-President's written consent, the registration had to be refused. The Supreme Court decided the provision did not violate Elster's free speech rights. *Vidal v. Elster*, 602 U.S. 286 (2024)

Trademark Infringement

A party with a valid trademark may enforce their rights by bringing a lawsuit for **trademark infringement** against parties that used the mark (1) without authorization and (2) in a way that would lead to a likelihood of consumer confusion. When determining if the use of the mark caused consumer confusion, courts will consider the strength and distinctiveness of the mark, the similarities between the marks, the similarities of the products, and any other evidence of consumer confusion.

Trademark infringement Unauthorized use of a trademark that is likely to lead to consumer confusion.

Example: Virgin Enterprises® (VE) owns the world-famous mark "Virgin" and applies it in a variety of business ventures, such as stores and airlines. VE decided to offer wireless telecommunication services under its mark "Virgin Mobile." At the same time, an independent company (Cel-Net) started to offer wireless communications under "Virgin Wireless." VE sued Cel-Net for trademark infringement. The court found in favor of VE, reasoning that Cel-Net's use of "Virgin Wireless" would cause consumer confusion. *Virgin Enters. Ltd. v. Nawab*, 335 F.3d 141 (2d Cir. 2003)

Trademark Dilution

Trademark dilution is a legal concept that grants additional trademark protections to owners of **famous marks.** It is different from trademark infringement because the owner of the famous mark does not have to prove that there is a likelihood of consumer confusion. Instead, the owner must prove that its mark is *famous* and that the other mark dilutes the value of the famous mark by *blurring* the difference between the marks or *tarnishing* the reputation of the mark.

Trademark dilution The unauthorized use of a famous mark that tends to dilute the value of the mark.

Famous marks Trademarks that have acquired special protections due to their widespread recognition.

Example: Nike® is the owner of the trademark "swoosh" logo. Nike became aware of T-shirts and socks bearing the swoosh logo that were manufactured by Variety Inc., without a license to do so. Nike brought both trademark infringement and dilution claims against Variety. The court found that Variety infringed on Nike's mark because consumers were confused as to the source of the product. It also found that Variety diluted Nike's mark because it was a famous mark. *Nike Inc. v. Variety Wholesalers, Inc.*, 274 F. Supp. 2d 1352 (S.D. Ga. 2003)

Example: Ate My Heart, Inc., the company that does business for Lady Gaga, owns the mark LADY GAGA® for clothing. Ga Ga Jeans wanted to apply to register the mark GA GA JEANS; however, Ate My Heart contended that this registration would violate and dilute its current trademark. Yet, the Trademark Board found that the LADY GAGA® mark was not famous enough strictly in terms of clothing and, as such, could not stop Ga Ga Jeans from registering its mark. *Ate My Heart,*

Inc. v. Ga Ga Jeans Limited, Opposition No. 91205110 to Application Serial No. 85456166 (2016)

Scope of Protection and Loss of Rights

SCOPE OF PROTECTION. When a mark is registered with the USPTO, the mark receives nationwide protection. But registration is not mandatory to have a valid trademark. A trademark can be obtained and maintained through use in a geographic location. An unregistered trademark is protected in the geographically limited area in which they have historically conducted business and are known. Two or more parties are permitted to have the same unregistered trademark for the same product in different geographic regions. If two trademarks begin to overlap in geographic locations (such as expansion of one of the trademarks into a new area), the party with the older mark (used first in commerce) will have priority. Additionally, an unregistered trademark may have priority in a specific region over a nationally registered trademark, if it was used first in commerce.

When Burger King Corporation®, the multinational chain of hamburger restaurants, first sought to expand operations into the state of Illinois, it encountered the Hoots, who operated a restaurant already using the name Burger King. Burger King Corporation had registered the mark through the USPTO; however, the Hoots had previously registered the mark under Illinois' trademark act and were using the mark in Mattoon, Illinois, without notice of Burger King Corporation's use of the same trademark. When the Hoots sought to expand to Charleston, Illinois, and use the Burger King mark, the parties sued each other for trademark infringement. The court held that Burger King Corporation can use the mark in any part of Illinois except Mattoon, Illinois, and the Hoots are restricted to using the mark only in Mattoon, Illinois. *Burger King of Fla., Inc. v. Hoots*, 403 F.2d 904 (7th Cir. 1968)

LOSS OF RIGHTS. While trademarks may be used continually without expiring, it is possible for a trademark to be abandoned. Under federal law, a mark is presumed to be abandoned when it has not been used in commerce for three years, or where the owner of the mark has failed to prevent the mark from becoming *generic*.

Counterfeiting

As the number of goods imported into the United States continues to grow, so does the number of counterfeit goods entering the market. Counterfeiting is the act of copying or duplicating a trademarked good. To address this issue, Congress passed the Stop Counterfeiting in Manufactured Goods Act (SCMGA) in 2006. SCMGA criminalized the act of intentionally importing, or attempting to import, counterfeit goods (which includes labels, patches, stickers, or packaging of any type with a counterfeit mark applied), into the United States. It also criminalized the act of knowingly using a counterfeit mark.

ENFORCEMENT. Under SCMGA, those found guilty may face fines of up to $2 million. Additionally, a party may be imprisoned for up to ten years, with the sentence being increased if they have previously been found guilty of violating SCMGA. When a court determines SCMGA has been violated, it will order the counterfeit goods to be seized and destroyed. The court will also require the defendant to repay the trademark holder for any actual losses suffered because of the counterfeit activity.

Comparison of Intellectual Property Types

Type of IP	Subject Matter	Requirements	Scope of Protection	Duration	Infringement Remedy
Trademark	Any symbol, design, or other identifying aspect used in connection with a product or service.	Must be either inherently distinct or have secondary meaning.	Prevents other brands from creating a likelihood of confusion among consumers.	Indefinite, but must be renewed every ten years.	Monetary damages for lost profits. An injunction preventing use of the mark.
Trade Secret	Confidential information, including any formula, pattern, compilation, program, device, method, technique, or process.	Must be valuable due to its secrecy and is subject to reasonable efforts to remain secret.	Prevents others from stealing the information and using it, but not from reverse engineering it.	Indefinite.	Misappropriation of trade secrets tort. Monetary damages.
Copyright	Literary, musical, dramatic, pantomimes, choreographic, pictorial, graphic, sculptural, film, sound recordings, and architectural works.	Originality and authorship, fixation, and expression.	Prevents the copying, displaying, or performing of the protected material.	Life of the author plus 70 years. If company is author, 95 years from publication, or 120 years from creation.	Monetary damages may be set by statute. Can include all profits earned by unauthorized copy.
Patent	New and useful processes, machine, manufacture, composition of matter. Except cannot be product of nature, abstract idea, or physical phenomenon.	Must be novel, useful, and nonobvious.	Exclusive right to make, sell, manufacture, license, and in any way distribute.	Generally, 20 years from date of application. However, design patent term is 15 years.	An injunction preventing infringing party from continuing. Monetary damages, such as royalties.

Management Application Challenges to Ownership of Intellectual Property

The failure to protect one's intellectual property can result in a large loss when it occurs throughout the domestic or international markets. The following are recent examples of intellectual property challenges that have been publicized:

- McDonald's® Corp. no longer holds a trademark for the Big Mac in the European Union because the European Union Intellectual Property Office believed that McDonald's had not provided adequate evidence of genuine use over the past five years.
- Various celebrities have brought legal challenges to Epic Games® over their video game *Fortnite*®. They claim copyright infringement for various dance moves allegedly taken without permission or compensation.

Trade Secrets

Trade secret
Information that has either actual or potential independent economic value by virtue of not being generally known, has values to others who cannot legitimately obtain the information, and is subject to reasonable efforts to maintain its secret.

Misappropriation of trade secrets
A legal action in tort law that accuses a party of illegally acquiring a trade secret.

Uniform Trade Secrets Act
A model act adopted by the majority of states that sets out trade secret protections.

A **trade secret** can be any information that is valuable to a company because it is confidential. Trade secret law protects certain business information against unauthorized acquisition or disclosure by a person who has obtained it through improper means, or in breach of a confidentiality agreement. Trade secret law is primarily concerned with encouraging ethical commercial behavior and permitting companies to keep confidential or sensitive information secret without having to expend considerable resources to do so. While a trade secret might also qualify for protection through a patent or copyright, the holder of the trade secret may prefer to protect it through trade secret protections. Unlike patents or copyrights, trade secret protection can last indefinitely. Information that is kept as a trade secret is not registered with any government agency; rather, the tort of **misappropriation of trade secrets** is used to protect trade secrets.

Requirements for a Trade Secret

Both federal and state law protect trade secrets. Most states created their trade secret laws through the adoption of the **Uniform Trade Secrets Act** (UTSA). The UTSA provides a uniform definition of a trade secret and establishes frameworks and governing rules for approaching trade secret violations. In the states that have not adopted the UTSA, trade secret law originates from the state common law. The UTSA defines trade secrets as:

> Information, including a formula, pattern, compilation, program, device, method, technique, or process, that:
>
> 1. Derives independent economic value, actual or potential, from not being generally known to, and not being readily ascertainable by proper means by, other persons who obtain economic value from its disclosure or use; and
> 2. Is the subject of efforts that are reasonable under the circumstances to maintain its secrecy.

Management Application Trade Secret Agreement

Many business relationships require the use of a trade secret agreement. One such relationship is that of an employer with employees. Where an employee will have access to or utilize confidential or sensitive company information, an employer should always have employees execute a confidentiality and trade secrets agreement. The following is a sample of such an agreement:

TRADE SECRET AGREEMENT

The Company ("COMPANY") has disclosed or may disclose to [Name] ("EMPLOYEE") business information, technical information, and/or proprietary and confidential information COMPANY wishes to protect from public disclosure ("Proprietary Information") in connection with a proposed employment of EMPLOYEE.

Confidential Proprietary Information, as used in this Agreement, is all information or material that gives COMPANY some competitive business advantage, or the opportunity to obtain that advantage, or the disclosure of which could be detrimental to COMPANY's interests, is owned by COMPANY or in which COMPANY has an interest and is marked either "Confidential Information" or "Proprietary Information."

Proprietary Information includes but is not limited to: inventions; drawings; file data; documentation; diagrams; specifications; know-how; processes; formulas; models; flow charts; research and development procedures and test results; marketing techniques, materials, and plans; price lists; pricing policies; business plans; information relating to the identities, characteristics, and agreements of customers and/or suppliers; financial information and projections; and employee files. Proprietary Information also includes any information described above that the COMPANY obtains from another party and treats as Proprietary Information and designates as confidential. Notwithstanding the above, no information is Proprietary Information if it is generic information or general knowledge that any person could have learned in the ordinary course of business or is otherwise publicly known and in the public domain.

In consideration of any disclosure of Proprietary Information and any negotiations concerning the proposed employment EMPLOYEE agrees that:

1. EMPLOYEE will hold in confidence and not detrimentally possess or use or disclose any Proprietary Information except information EMPLOYEE can document (a) is in the public domain through no fault of EMPLOYEE, (b) was properly known to EMPLOYEE, without restriction, before disclosure by COMPANY, or (c) was properly disclosed by EMPLOYEE to another person without restriction, and will not reverse engineer or attempt to derive the composition or underlying information, structure, or ideas of any Proprietary Information. The foregoing does not grant EMPLOYEE a license in or to any of the Proprietary Information.
2. During and after the term of this Agreement, EMPLOYEE will not intentionally disclose and will use EMPLOYEE'S best efforts to prohibit the unintentional disclosure, to any third party of any Proprietary Information concerning COMPANY, unless COMPANY expressly agrees in advance in writing to such disclosure. This obligation applies not only to technical information, but also to any business information that the COMPANY treats as confidential. Any information of COMPANY that is not readily or publicly available will be considered Proprietary Information unless COMPANY advises to the contrary.

3. EMPLOYEE will not make any unauthorized copy of any Proprietary Information disclosed or otherwise reduced to written form, including without limitation any sales literature, business forms, policy directives, commission schedules, and customer lists.
4. EMPLOYEE will immediately notify COMPANY if Proprietary Information is disclosed.
5. If EMPLOYEE breaches, or threatens to commit a breach of, EMPLOYEE'S duty to maintain the confidentiality of the Proprietary Information, COMPANY will have the following rights and remedies, each of which will be in addition to, and not in lieu of, any other rights and remedies available to COMPANY at law or in equity:
   a. *Specific Performance*: The right and remedy to have the duty of confidentiality specifically enforced by any court having equity jurisdiction, all without the need to post a bond or any other security, or to prove any amount of actual damage, or that money damages would not provide an adequate remedy, it being acknowledged and agreed that any such breach or threatened breach will cause irreparable injury to COMPANY and that monetary damages will not provide an adequate remedy.
   b. *Accounting and Indemnification*: The right and remedy to require (i) to account for and pay over to COMPANY all compensation, profits, monies, accruals, increments, or other benefits derived or received by EMPLOYEE or by any associated party deriving such benefits as a result of any breach of the duty of confidentiality; and (ii) to indemnify COMPANY against any other losses, damages (including special and consequential damages), costs and expenses, including actual attorney's fees and court costs, which may be incurred by COMPANY and which result from, or arise out of, any breach or threatened breach of the duty of confidentiality.
6. The terms of this Agreement remain in effect with respect to any Proprietary Information until COMPANY can document that the information has become generic information or general knowledge that any person could have learned in the ordinary course of business or is otherwise publicly known and in the public domain.
7. This Agreement is governed by the laws of the State of [State] and may be modified or waived only in writing. If any provision is found to be unenforceable, such provision will be limited or deleted to the minimum extent necessary so that the remaining terms remain in full force and effect. The prevailing party in any dispute or legal action regarding the subject matter of this agreement shall be entitled to recover attorney's fees and costs.

Dated: ______________

Company:

By: ________________

Title: Director of Human Resources

____

[Name] Employee

Famous examples of trade secrets include the Coca-Cola® recipe, or KFC's® combination of herbs and spices; however, protectable information can also include customer lists, internal processes, or manufacturing procedures, as long as they are valuable to the company due to their secrecy.

The owner of a trade secret must take all reasonable precautions to maintain the information's secrecy depending on the information sought to be protected. Generally, companies that have trade secrets require their employees, and independent contractors, to sign confidentiality or nondisclosure agreements or covenants not to compete. Further efforts, such as limiting the way employees can access the information with passwords or with physical barriers like safes, also bolster a company's claim of trade secret protection.

> **Example:** A toy designer sought to contract with a toy manufacturer. The parties orally agreed to keep the negotiations confidential. While negotiating the deal, the manufacturer disclosed its new "clickety-clack" track to the designer. The negotiations failed. Subsequently, the designer started to sell the same "clickety-clack" track. The manufacturer sued for trade secret misappropriation. The court found in favor of the manufacturer, holding that the track was a trade secret because the track had independent economic value and was the subject of reasonable efforts to maintain its secrecy. *See Learning Curve Toys, Inc. v. PlayWood Toys, Inc.*, 342 F.3d 714 (7th Cir. 2003)

Misappropriation of Trade Secrets

Misappropriation of a trade secret occurs when the trade secret is (1) disclosed without authorization; (2) used by someone who acquired it by improper means; or (3) used by someone who reasonably should have known the information was a trade secret and yet acquired it by improper means from a third party. Merely possessing another's trade secret information is not actionable. It is the improper use of trade secret information that creates the liability for misappropriation.

STATE LAW OF TRADE SECRETS. Under the UTSA and the laws of many states, a court may issue an injunction to stop the actual or threatened disclosure and/or use of the trade secret. The parties may dispute the existence of a trade secret and what relief, if any, should be afforded to the injured party. The wrongdoer may be liable for damages that may include lost profits and unjust enrichment damages. Punitive damages may also be awarded in cases of willful or intentional theft of trade secrets.

> **Example:** Stephen Jarrells worked for Applied Medical Distribution Corporation (Applied) from 2011. In 2018, he took a job at Bruin Biometrics, LLC (Bruin) as vice president of sales, but only left Applied in 2019. While at Applied, he was not allowed to share any confidential information. However, he copied trade secrets onto a thumb drive and gave them to Bruin. The court ruled that this violated the California Uniform Trade Secrets Act and awarded Applied injunctive relief, attorney's fees, and costs. *Applied Med. Distribution Corp. v. Jarrells*, 100 Cal. App. 5th 556 (2024)

Economic Espionage Act
Federal law that criminalizes trade secret theft that benefits a foreign government, business, or agent.

FEDERAL LAW OF TRADE SECRETS. The **Economic Espionage Act** of 1996 makes the theft or misappropriation of a trade secret a federal crime. The law criminalizes any trade secret theft that benefits a foreign government, business, or agent.

Defend Trade Secrets Act
The federal law that establishes a federal cause of action for trade secret protection.

The **Defend Trade Secrets Act** of 2016 (DTSA) is a federal law that amended the Economic Espionage Act and supplements, rather than preempts, state trade secret law. The law allows civil lawsuits to be filed in federal court for a cause of action for the misappropriation of trade secrets. The DTSA definition for a trade secret is substantially the same as the UTSA, aligning both state and federal law, and it also establishes a three-year statute of limitations.

The DTSA provides for a number of remedies available to the injured party, including the following:

1. Ability to obtain an *ex parte* (Latin for "by or for one party") court order seizing a defendant's property at the request of plaintiffs without any notice to the adverse party. To discourage potential abuse, the plaintiff must meet an extremely high standard of proof before the court will order such a seizure. The seizure is of property "necessary to prevent the propagation or dissemination of the trade secret."
2. Damages for actual loss and damages for unjust enrichment. Instead of damages, a plaintiff may also obtain a reasonable royalty for the unauthorized use or disclosure of the trade secret.

Example: The Court of Appeals for the Fifth Circuit has stated, "If the defendant enjoyed actual profits, a type of restitutionary remedy can be afforded the plaintiff— either recovering the full total of defendant's profits or some apportioned amount designed to correspond to the actual contribution the plaintiff 's trade secret made to the defendant's commercial success. Because the primary concern in most cases is to measure the value to the defendant of what he actually obtained from the plaintiff, the proper measure is to calculate what the parties would have agreed to as a fair price for licensing the defendant to put the trade secret to the use the defendant intended at the time the misappropriation took place. *University Computing v. Lykes-Youngstown Corp.*, 504 F.2d 518 (5th Cir. 1974)

3. Punitive damages for willful or malicious misappropriation.
4. Attorney's fees and injunctive relief, or where an injunctive would be inequitable, payment of a reasonable royalty.

Reverse Engineering of Trade Secrets

Reverse engineering The process in which a competitor dissembles, recreates, or otherwise works to discover the trade secret.

Competitors may lawfully reverse engineer a trade secret. **Reverse engineering** is the process in which a competitor dissembles, recreates, or otherwise works to discover the trade secret. As long as the reverse engineering was done through fair and honest means, the competitor can use the trade secret; however, they still would be subject to other intellectual property restrictions such as trademarks.

Example: A microprocessor chip manufacturer can purchase a competitor's newest microprocessor and dissemble the product to discover how the microprocessor was engineered. The chip manufacturer can then utilize that information in upcoming microprocessor designs

Trade Secrets or Patents — Which Is Better?

Information that is considered a trade secret may also be subject to other intellectual property protections, but this is not always the case. If a company has a piece of intellectual property that can be both patented and kept as a trade secret, it is up to the owner of the information to decide which protection to obtain. A benefit of trade secret protection is that it is unlimited in time, as long as the information is kept secret. However, other parties can either reverse engineer or independently develop the information and not be held liable as they would be under patent law.

Example: Consider the Rubik's Cube®. What protection should the inventor seek to gain the most profit from his invention? A trade secret would not be appropriate because the inventor wants to sell his product, and, as soon as he does so, a competitor could easily reverse engineer it and sell it at a lower price. However, if the cube receives patent protection, the inventor will have a 20-year monopoly to make a profit from it.

Example: In contrast, consider the Google® search algorithm. What protection is better suited for this invention? A patent would require full disclosure of the algorithm, and, after 20 years, competitors could legally copy it. However, because its algorithm is difficult to reverse engineer, keeping it as a trade secret grants it a potentially unlimited time of protection.

Copyrights

Copyright
A protected intellectual property interest that is granted to original works of authorship that are fixed in a tangible medium of expression.

A **copyright** is a protected intellectual property interest that is granted to original works of authorship that are fixed in a tangible medium of expression. Copyright law is conceptually distinct from patent and trade secret law because instead of protecting the *idea*, copyright protects the *expression* of an idea. Federal law sets out what can and cannot be copyrighted. There is no state law that governs copyrights — it is *exclusive* to the federal government.

Congress enacted the Copyright Act of 1976, which currently governs copyright law in the United States. As a result of the Act, copyright protection vests automatically in the author at the time of creation. Although a party may register their copyright with the U.S. Copyright Office, registration is not mandatory. In addition, the Act does not require a party to affix a logo indicating that the material is copyrighted, such as the ubiquitous ©.

The author of a copyright may not be the author of the work under the work-for-hire doctrine. In a work made for hire, the employer or other person for whom the work was prepared is considered the author for copyright purposes. This can arise when (1) an employee prepares work within the scope of their employment (in such case the employer is the author of the work), or (2) the work is specially ordered or commissioned for certain purposes specified in the Copyright Act and the parties expressly agree in writing that the work shall be considered a work made for hire (the person ordering or commissioning the work is the author).

Copyright protection does not last indefinitely. The length of time a copyright is protected is based on who holds the copyright, an individual person or a business. If the copyright is held by an individual person, the copyright lasts for the life of the author plus 70 years. If the author is a business or company, the term is either 95 years from date of publication or 120 years from date of creation, whichever comes first.

Public domain
The term for all works that no longer have copyright protection.

The **public domain** comprises all works that are either no longer protected by copyright or never were. As a result of the copyright periods, each year thousands of copyrighted works enter the public domain. All materials created since March 1, 1989, except for those of the U.S. government, are presumed automatically protected by copyright protection. Works prior to March 1, 1989, required formal notice in order to be protected by the Copyright Act.

> **Example:** Google Books® (*https://books.google.com/*) provides more than 10 million free books to read. These books have either entered the public domain or were made free on request of the copyright owner. One such book, *The Great Gatsby* by F. Scott Fitzgerald is available to read or download because the book entered the public domain in 2021.

Requirements for Copyright Protection

For a work to be granted copyright protection, it must be an original work of authorship and be fixed in a tangible medium of expression. These requirements are known as *originality and authorship, fixation,* and *expression.*

Originality
A copyright requirement that a work be independently created and be at least minimally creative.

ORIGINALITY AND AUTHORSHIP. The courts define **originality** as a work that is *independently created* and that contains a *minimal degree of creativity.* The work cannot be the result of merely copying someone else's work. Courts are reluctant to withhold copyright protection from a work based on their artistic opinions, and thus require only minimal creativity.

Authorship
The maker, originator, or creator of the expression contained by a work.

Authorship is defined as the maker, originator, or creator of the expression contained in the work. It may be a party who merely recorded an idea and who gave it expression, or it may be a party who had an idea and expressed it in a creative fashion. Authorship in copyright is not constrained to mean a person who writes a book, but can also apply to a photographer or musician, among many others.

> **Example:** Rural Telephone Co. provided a telephone directory as required by Kansas state law, the "white pages." A competitor, Feist Publications, produced a similar directory for a much larger region. To complete its directory, Feist copied the Rural directory without consent. Rural then sued Feist for copyright infringement. The Supreme Court found for Feist, holding that the mere listing of facts (the directory listings) in alphabetical order had no *minimal degree of creativity*

and thus was not *original*. Therefore, there was no copyright infringement. *Feist Publications, Inc. v. Rural Tel. Serv. Co.*, 499 U.S. 340 (1991)

FIXATION. A work is *fixed* in a tangible medium of expression when it is sufficiently permanent or stable to be perceived over time. The fixation requirement is satisfied not only with traditional media like books and photographs, but also with video games and movies because they are *fixed* to computer chips, or film respectively.

EXPRESSION. Copyright protection extends only to the *expression* contained by the work. Federal law states that in no case does copyright protection for an original work of authorship extend to any idea, procedure, process, system, method of operation, concept, principle, or discovery, regardless of the form in which it is described, explained, illustrated, or embodied in such work.

Example: Pieter Folkens, the copyright owner of a pen and ink illustration entitled "Two Dolphins," filed suit against Robert Wyland, a muralist best known for his depictions of aquatic life. Folken's "Two Dolphins" illustration depicted two dolphins crossing each other underwater as they swam. Folkens sued Wyland claiming copyright infringement based on Wyland's depiction of an underwater scene that contained the similar element of two dolphins crossing underwater. The court found that two dolphins crossing underwater is an idea that is first found in nature and is therefore not a protectable element of a copyright. The court further explained that the only commonalities between the two works were elements that occur in nature and therefore have already been expressed for all. *Folkens v. Wyland Worldwide, LLC*, 882 F.3d 768 (9th Cir. 2018)

Subject Matter of Copyrights

Beyond the above requirements, to qualify for copyright protection, a work must fit into one of the following categories:

1. Literary works;
2. Musical works, including any accompanying words;
3. Dramatic works, including any accompanying music;
4. Pantomimes and choreographic works;
5. Pictorial, graphic, and sculptural works;
6. Motion pictures and other audiovisual works;
7. Sound recordings; and
8. Architectural works.

Copyright Infringement

The owner of a copyright may enforce their rights by bringing an action for **copyright infringement**. This requires that the copyright holder prove:

Copyright infringement The unauthorized reproduction of a copyrighted work.

1. The ownership of a valid copyright; and that
2. The accused work copied the expressive elements of the copyrighted work.

Management Application
Artist Disputes

Use an internet search engine to research and review the following copyright infringement disputes. Were there any similarities among the claims?

- The settlement reached by Queen and David Bowie with Vanilla Ice over music sampling of an iconic baseline from Under Pressure©.
- The federal appeals court decision holding that the song "Blurred Lines©" by Pharrell Williams, Robin Thicke, and Clifford Harris infringed upon the copyright of the Marvin Gaye estate for Gaye's 1977 song "Got to Give It Up©."
- George Harrison's "My Sweet Lord©" song on his *All Things Must Pass*© album—the plagiarism lawsuit brought by Bright Tunes Music Corporation relative to the Chiffons' 1963 hit "He's So Fine©." The court found Harrison liable for subconscious plagiarism. Review the allegations of breach of fiduciary duties by Harrison's former manager.

In other cases, songs that were not popular become worth more if they are infringed. In the context of copyright infringement, should the law be changed?

PENALTIES FOR COPYRIGHT INFRINGEMENT. An infringer may be sued for reproducing the publication or redistributing the work of a copyright holder without permission. If the copyright holder has registered the work with the U.S. Copyright Office prior to the infringement, the copyright holder may sue for statutory damages in a sum of not less than $750 or more than $30,000 per work. These damages can include lost profits from the infringing activity, plus attorney's fees. Even higher damages may be awarded if the trier of fact (judge or jury, for example) determines the defendant committed the infringement "willfully." There is also criminal liability for the willful copying of work for profit or financial gain if the copied work has a value of $1,000 or more.

Fair use
An exception to copyright infringement that allows for certain uses of the work, without the consent of the rights holder.

Fair Use

Unlike patents, copyright protection is subject to a number of exceptions. The two most important of these are *fair use* and *limited copying by libraries and archives.*

FAIR USE. Fair use allows the limited use of copyrighted material without consent of the copyright holder. This exception includes, among other things, limited reproduction for scholarly, classroom, and review purposes as well as parody. The defense is codified in the Copyright Act. To determine whether the use is fair, four factors are considered:

1. The purpose and character of the use (such as nonprofit versus commercial use).
2. The nature of the copyrighted work.

3. The proportionate importance of the part used in comparison to the work as a whole.
4. The use's effect on the potential market for or value of the copyrighted work.

Example: The Supreme Court held that portraits of the musician Prince by Andy Warhol do not constitute fair use under copyright law. The Court decided against Warhol's foundation, which produced silkscreen portraits of Prince derived from an original photograph of Prince taken by photographer Lynn Goldsmith. The Court held that the silkscreens had the same commercial purpose as the original photograph that was infringed upon by the foundation. A "somewhat different" portrayal of Prince did not suffice to be protected by the fair use doctrine. *Andy Warhol Foundation for Visual Arts, Inc. v. Goldsmith*, 598 U.S. 508 (2023)

Parody of a work can be a fair use. That is why comedic skits and routines are non-infringing parodies. A parody should use no more of the original work than is needed to make it recognizable. Fair use also allows libraries limited copying of portions of work to replace part of a damaged copy. In addition, professors, teachers, and students are allowed to reproduce a small part of a copyrighted work to demonstrate an example or lesson. These persons are allowed limited reproduction for noncommercial purposes.

In the following case, the court considered whether a searchable database of copyrighted material was justifiable fair use.

CASE 7.3

GOOGLE'S DIGITAL LIBRARY THAT ALLOWED USERS TO SEARCH FOR SPECIFIC TEXT WAS A FAIR USE OF COPYRIGHTED MATERIAL

AUTHORS GUILD v. GOOGLE, INC.

804 F.3d 202 (2d Cir. 2015)

United States Court of Appeals for the Second Circuit

Google initiated a project to make digital copies of books held by libraries and allowed the general public to search the database by returning small "snippets" of text from the books. A collection of authors (the Authors Guild) who owned copyrighted works included in the database sued Google for copyright infringement. Google defended under the fair use exception. The trial court ruled in favor of Google, and the Authors Guild appealed.

Language of the Court. *The ultimate goal of copyright is to expand public knowledge and understanding, which copyright achieves by giving potential creators exclusive control over copying of their works. While authors are intended beneficiaries of copyright, the ultimate, primary intended beneficiary is the public. The fair use doctrine provides that "for the purposes of criticism, comment, news reporting, teaching, scholarship, or research, is not an infringement of copyright." The following factors are used to determine whether fair use is present: (1)*

the purpose and character of the use, including whether such use is a commercial or nonprofit educational purpose; (2) the nature of the copyrighted work; (3) the amount and substantiality of the portion used in relation to the copyrighted work as a whole; and (4) the effect of the use upon the potential market for or the value of the copyrighted work.

The purpose of Google's copying of the original copyrighted books is to make available significant information about those books, permitting a searcher to identify those that contain a word or term of interest, as well as those that do not include reference to it. In addition, Google allows readers to learn the frequency of usage of selected words in the aggregate corpus of published books in different historical periods. We have no doubt that the purpose of this copying is the sort of transformative purpose that strongly favors a finding of fair use.

While Google makes an unauthorized digital copy of the entire book, it does not reveal that digital copy to the public. The copy is made to enable the search functions to reveal limited, important information about the books. What matters in such cases is not "the amount and substantiality of the portion used" but rather the amount and substantiality of what is made accessible to the public.

We recognize that the search function can cause some loss of sales. But the possibility of some loss of sales does not suffice to make the copy an effectively competing substitute that would tilt the result in favor of the rights holder in the original. The normal purchase price of a book is relatively low in relation to the cost of manpower needed to secure an arbitrary assortment of randomly scattered snippets, and we conclude that the snippet function does not give searchers access to effectively competing substitutes. Considering the four fair use factors in light of the goals of copyright, we conclude that Google's making of a complete digital copy of Plaintiffs' works for the purpose of providing the public with its search function is a fair use and does not infringe Plaintiffs' copyrights in their books.

Decision. The appellate court held in favor of Google. The court reasoned that even though Google created exact copies, it did not reveal them to the public, but rather provided a new database that did not compete with the original books.

Focus on Ethics

If Google allowed the public to see copies of the entire books would this be ethical treatment to the texts' authors?

First Sale Doctrine

One of the rights of a copyright holder is the right to sell, display, or otherwise dispose of a copy of the work. Once the sale has been made, the right to restrict the distribution of that single copy is extinguished. Therefore, once the sale has been made, the party who purchased the copy may resell it without violating copyright law.

However, the **first sale doctrine** does not apply to products that are acquired via a rental, lease, or a licensing agreement. For example, most computer software is distributed via licensing agreements; this allows the company to retain its copyright in the software and prevent the user from legally reselling its copy. Savvy business owners may seek to distribute their products under a licensing model to protect their copyrights and limit the resale market for their goods.

First sale doctrine
The concept that copyright protection on a work expires once it has been sold or distributed.

Digital Millennium Copyright Act (DMCA)
A congressional act enacted to enhance the protections granted to copyright owners by imposing civil and criminal penalties for online copyright infringement.

> **Example:** Included with each copy of Apple's iTunes® software is a Software License Agreement (SLA). The agreement contains, in part, language that informs the user that it is granted a "limited non-exclusive license" to use the software. The agreement also provides for restrictions on transfer by prohibiting "rent, lease, lend, redistribute or sublicense" of the program by the user.

The Digital Millennium Copyright Act

In response to the ease of potential and actual copyright infringement in the digital age, Congress enacted the **Digital Millennium Copyright Act (DMCA)**. The primary purpose of the law is to enhance the protections granted to copyright owners by imposing civil and criminal penalties for online copyright infringement.

In order to protect their copyrighted material, companies and individuals install digital rights management (DRM) software on their copyrighted materials. DRM software encompasses a variety of schemes designed to prevent the unauthorized copying of copyrighted material. The DMCA supports copyright owners by making it illegal to tamper with, or circumvent, DRM software to illegally copy the protected material. In addition, the DMCA limits liability for "intermediary" internet service providers as long as they comply with certain provisions. Violations of the DMCA can result in both criminal and civil penalties.

> **Example:** Adobe Systems Inc.® designs and develops a suite of popular software programs, such as Adobe Photoshop CS3. Michael Feather owned and operated a website through which he distributed unauthorized copies of Adobe's software, and also distributed "access keys" to the software. The access keys were designed with the intent to circumvent Adobe's DRM software. Adobe sued Mr. Feather under the DMCA. The court found in favor of Adobe, holding the access keys illegally circumvented Adobe's DRM software. The court awarded Adobe $2,520,000 in damages. *Adobe Sys. Inc. v. Feather*, 895 F. Supp. 2d 297 (D. Conn. 2012)

Patents

Patent
A protected intellectual property interest establishing that the holder has the sole authority to produce, use, sell, license, or distribute their invention.

Patents provide legal protections for certain types of inventions. When a patent is granted, the owner of the patent is entitled to a legal monopoly over the specific invention for a specified term of 20 years. During the patent period, patent holders may produce, use, sell, license, distribute, or even withhold their inventions as they desire. The rights granted by patents are exclusive to the patent holders, and patent holders can prevent all other parties from copying, selling, or otherwise distributing their inventions for the term of the patent, absent a license (contractual grant of permission) to do so. The monopoly period provided by a patent is designed to provide an adequate incentive for inventors to spend time and resources to innovate. Once the patent period expires, any party can copy, make, use, or sell the invention.

The Constitution vests in Congress the authority to issue patents to inventors. The process by which patents are issued is governed by the U.S. Patent and Trademark Office (USPTO).

Patent Protection Period

The priority of the invention is given to the party who *filed* an application with the USPTO first. The period of patent protections begins on the date in which the patent application is filed, not when the patent is issued by the USPTO.

Patent Application Process

The USPTO receives all patent applications and is based in Washington, D.C. The office receives both paper and electronic applications. After an inventor files an application, the USPTO must issue a decision within three years from the file date. For an additional fee, the applicant can request a prioritized examination. The prioritized examination fee ranges from $1,050 to $4,200 and the office will issue a decision within one year. The patent application process can be costly, as there are a variety of fees associated with each step. Thus, it is a good idea to retain a patent attorney to assist throughout the process.

During the application process, a patent examiner will determine the validity of the patent and may request additional information from the applicant. If the patent is rejected, an applicant may appeal to the Patent Trial and Appeal Board, an internal administrative appeal body.

Provisional application
An application that allows a party to establish an earlier filing date and allows "patent pending" to be placed on a product.

Parties may elect to file a **provisional application**, which is a quicker and cheaper way to establish an earlier filing date and allows a party to print the phrase "patent pending" on its products. Upon submitting a provisional application, a party has 12 months to file a full patent application. The application is not available for public inspection. During this period inventors can try to attract investors.

Patentable Subject Matter

The Patent Act states that "whoever invents or discovers any new and useful *process*, *machine*, *manufacture*, or *composition of matter*, or any new and useful *improvement* thereof, may obtain a patent therefor, subject to the conditions and requirements of this title"[1] (emphasis added). Despite this broad language, the United States Supreme Court has defined three areas that are *not* to be considered patentable subject matter:

1. Products of nature (such as plants found in nature);
2. Abstract ideas; and
3. Physical phenomena or laws of nature (such as the law of gravity).

In delineating these limitations, the Court reasoned that these categories are the building blocks of invention, and allowing parties to patent them would stifle the overall goal of increasing innovation. For example, plants that reproduce asexually are patentable given that they are genetically modified and not the sole product of nature.

> **Example:** Sir Isaac Newton, upon his discovery of the theory of gravity, would be barred from patenting an invention that claimed gravity because it is a *physical phenomenon.*
>
> **Example:** A biologist discovers a new flower that can cure a certain disease and wants to patent it. The biologist would be barred from patenting the flower because it is a *product of nature*. However, if the biologist uses that flower to develop a stronger and more effective vaccine for a disease, the resulting compound is patentable.

Patent Requirements

There are three requirements for an invention to be patentable. It must be:

1. *Novel.* A novel invention is one that is new and not anticipated by the prior art. A patent can be invalided by evidence that the invention was known prior to the file date.
2. *Useful.* A useful invention is one that has a real and practical use. An invention with no defined use or a theoretical benefit is not patentable.
3. *Nonobvious.* A nonobvious invention is one that, when collectively considering the prior art, would have been nonobvious to a person having ordinary skill in the art to make the invention. An obvious invention does not qualify for a patent.

> **Example:** Qualcomm® was awarded a patent for wireless charging of electric vehicles parked above an induction coil. The invention was *novel* because no prior art properly disclosed the invention, it was *useful* because it assisted the charging of electric cars, and it was *nonobvious* because of the complexity of the invention considering the prior art. U.S. Patent No. 9130602.

Public Use Doctrine

An invention that has been in public use or is publicly accessible must be timely filed with the USPTO. Under the public use doctrine (also known as the one-year-on-sale

---

1. 35 U.S.C. § 101.

doctrine), a patent will not be granted if the invention was used publicly or was accessible to the public for more than one year prior to the filing of a patent application. Public use does not necessarily mean widespread use; even use by a single individual qualifies.

Patent Infringement

Patent holders have a legal monopoly over their inventions and can exclude all potential competitors from using the patented inventions during the patent period. If an unauthorized party "makes, uses, offers to sell, or sells" a patented invention, or imports to the United States a patented invention, that party has committed **patent infringement**.

Patent infringement When a party makes, sells, imports, or otherwise distributes a patented product without authorization.

It is not a defense to patent infringement for a party to claim that they reverse engineered the invention, nor is it a defense to claim independent discovery of the invention. As long as a valid patent covers the invention, no unauthorized copies can be produced.

PATENT INFRINGEMENT REMEDIES. If a patent holder can prove infringement, they can seek both monetary damages and an injunction. An injunction is a legal order that stops the infringing party from continuing their illegal actions. A patent holder may seek a permanent injunction to prevent the infringer from ever selling their product again. Additionally, if the infringing party sold large quantities of the product, monetary damages could add up to substantial amounts. A court may also require the infringer to pay a **royalty** to the patent holder.

Royalty A set fee paid by one party to another. The fee is typically set at a fixed price per unit sold, or as a percentage of revenues.

The following case was monumental in deciding venue in patent cases. Patent venue is limited to the defendant's state of incorporation or any district where the defendant has a "regular and established place of business."

CASE 7.4

PATENT LAWSUITS AGAINST CORPORATIONS MUST BE FILED IN THEIR STATE OF INCORPORATION

TC HEARTLAND LLC v. KRAFT FOODS GRP. BRANDS LLC

581 U.S. 258 (2017)

Supreme Court of the United States

Under existing patent law, a patent holder could bring an action for infringement against a defendant corporation "where the defendant resides." The federal courts have come to define where a corporation "resides" as wherever it is subject to *personal jurisdiction*, which can amount to a number of locations for a large corporation. Under this doctrine, Kraft Foods LLC (Kraft) filed a patent infringement suit against a competitor, TC Heartland LLC (TC). The lawsuit was filed in Delaware, and Kraft asserted the court had personal jurisdiction over TC. Kraft asserted that while TC was organized under Indiana law and headquartered in Indiana, TC shipped the allegedly infringing products into Delaware. TC argued that the proper definition for "resides" should be the state of incorporation for the entity, which for it would be Indiana. TC argued to transfer venue to Indiana, claiming it did not reside in Delaware and had no "regular and established place of business" in Delaware. The trial and appellate courts agreed with Kraft's definition. The Supreme Court granted *certiorari* to resolve conflicting federal decisions on proper venue in patent lawsuits.

Language of the Court. *The question presented in this case is where proper venue lies for patent infringement lawsuits brought against domestic corporations. Congress has not amended the patent act but has amended the general venue statute twice. The current venue statute provides that "for all venue purposes," a corporation "shall be deemed to reside, if a defendant, in any judicial district in which such defendant is subject to the court's personal jurisdiction with respect to the civil action in question." Courts have reached differing conclusions regarding whether the patent act's use of the word "resides" incorporates the general venue statute's definition of "residence." The Supreme Court has rejected the interpretation that defined residence in the patent act incorporates sections of the general venue statute. Instead, the Supreme Court has previously held that the patent act "is the sole and exclusive provision controlling venue in patent infringement actions, and . . . is not to be supplemented by the general venue statute." The Supreme Court understood that Congress enacted the patent act as a standalone venue statue and nothing in the previous recodification evidenced an intent to change that status.*

We reverse the Federal Circuit. This Court definitively and unambiguously held that the word "residence" in the patent act has a particular meaning as applied to domestic corporations: It refers only to the State of incorporation. Accordingly, the only question we must answer is whether Congress changed the meaning of "residence" when it amended the general venue statute. When Congress intends to effect a change of that kind, it ordinarily provides a relatively clear indication of its intent in the text of the amended provision.

The current version of the law does not contain any indication that Congress intended to alter the meaning of the patent venue statue. As applied to domestic corporations, "residence" in the patent act refers only to the State of incorporation.

Decision. The Court held that no longer would a patent owner be able to sue an infringing defendant in a district court where the defendant is subject to personal jurisdiction. Instead, patent infringement lawsuits could only be filed in districts within states where the infringing defendant is incorporated, or in districts where there has been an act of infringement and the defendant has a regular and established place of business.

Focus on Ethics

As the explosion of new patent infringement cases in the patent-holder friendly United States District Court for the Western District of Texas shows, differing procedural rules, judicial tendencies, and potential jury pools often give litigants strong preferences on the favorability of different forums for litigating patent disputes. Is this an ethical result?

Licensing

License
Legal permission to use a party's intellectual property.

Licensing permits third parties to use another's intellectual property. Licenses are commonly used for trademarks as a license can allow manufacturers to sell goods with the licensed trademark (such as a logo on clothing). An intellectual property license is usually in the form of a contract between the parties. The parties to the agreement will outline in detail the scope of the license, including the length of time, the geographic scope, the limitations on other uses, and the *royalties* to which the owner of the intellectual property will be entitled. Licensing agreements that involve intellectual property are complex and often result in disputes.

> **Example:** As a result of a patent dispute between Apple® and Nokia® the parties agreed to settle their dispute in the form of a patent license. The specific details of the agreement remain confidential, but the companies reported that Apple would pay Nokia a sum of cash up front, and a royalty for use going forward. In turn, Nokia would license its patents to Apple.

Management Application
Excerpts from Licensing Agreement for Use of Software

3.1 License Grant. Subject to the provisions of this Agreement as well as the payment of all applicable license fees for the term of such license, Licensor grants Customer and Customer accepts a limited, personal, nonexclusive, nontransferable, non-assignable Object Code license to use the Standard Software for Customer's internal use only in the United States.

3.4 Reverse Engineering. Customer shall not and shall not permit its affiliate or any third party to translate, reverse engineer, decompile, recompile, update, or modify all or any part of the Software or merge the Software into any other software.

International Intellectual Property

The United States has become a party to a number of international treaties, conventions, and agreements in order to enhance the protections granted to holders of intellectual property. Although the international agreements may extend intellectual property rights to certain countries, often enforcement of those rights is cost-prohibitive or otherwise difficult to do.

The Berne Convention

There is no such thing as an international copyright, that is, one that automatically protects a work throughout the world. However, through the **Berne Convention**, a copyright treaty, protection branded in one of the convention member countries is protected by copyright in all of them. There are approximately 179 countries, including the United States, that have become signatories to the Berne Convention. While the Berne Convention may extend protection of a copyright throughout the world, enforcing copyrights through infringement actions would be impractical in many parts of the world.

Berne Convention
An international agreement on the enforcement of copyright protections.

Note that while U.S. copyrights are valid in other countries due to the Berne Convention, other forms of intellectual property, such as trade secrets, patents, and trademarks, which might be protected under U.S. law usually enjoy no such protection elsewhere unless they are also in compliance with the local country's laws.

The TRIPS Agreement

The **TRIPS Agreement** is a more expansive intellectual property agreement between all the **World Trade Organization (WTO)** members. The Agreement established international standards of protection for copyrights, patents, and trademarks. Because the Agreement is enacted by members of the WTO, enforcement of intellectual property rights is done through the WTO instead of through each nation's legal system. This can provide a benefit in countries with lax enforcement, but it can also be a long and costly process. The general provisions of the TRIPS Agreement obligate the signing members to protect the rights of intellectual property holders in their country as outlined by the Agreement. The Agreement also prohibits nations from preferring their own citizens' rights over the rights of citizens of a foreign nation when adjudicating a dispute.

TRIPS Agreement
An agreement among WTO members to enforce agreed-upon standards for all intellectual property.

World Trade Organization (WTO)
An international organization comprised of member nations who agree to abide by certain terms.

The Madrid Protocol

The **Madrid Protocol** provides for a cost-effective trademark registration and enforcement mechanism on the international scale. Prior to the adoption of the Madrid Protocol, trademark owners were required to register and enforce their marks across each nation individually. This led to high costs for businesses and consumers.

Madrid Protocol
An agreement among nations to provide for international trademark protection and registration.

The Madrid Protocol provides for an international registration database for trademarks. As of the date of publication of this book, approximately 124 countries, including the United States, are signatories to the Madrid Protocol. The Madrid Protocol is administered by the World Intellectual Property Organization (WIPO).

The Anti-Counterfeiting Trade Agreement

In an additional step to prevent international trademark infringement, and online copyright infringement, the United States, along with Australia, Canada, Japan, Morocco, New Zealand, Singapore, South Korea, Mexico, and the European Union all signed the **Anti-Counterfeiting Trade Agreement** (ACTA). Although the Agreement has been *signed* by the member nations, only Japan has ratified the Agreement as of the date of publication of this book. The Agreement is not binding on the signatories until six members have ratified it.

Anti-Counterfeiting Trade Agreement
An agreement designed to limit international trademark and copyright infringement.

The Agreement provides that rights holders will have access to civil and administrative procedures in each country to enforce their rights. It also establishes stronger border measures that allow border agents to seize products that may be counterfeit. This seizure can be initiated by a border agent, or at the request of a rights holder who suspects their rights are infringed by the imported products. The Agreement also establishes criminal penalties for certain willful violations of the Agreement.

Concept Summary International Intellectual Property Agreements

Name	Year of Creation	Description	Types of IP Protected
The Berne Convention	1886	Requires a copyright obtained in a member country to be recognized by all member countries. Established a minimum copyright 50 years after author's death (excluding photographic and cinematographic works).	Copyrights
TRIPS	1994	Established standards of protection and enforcement procedures for member countries. Also prohibits the preferential treatment of domestic IP rights.	Patents, trademarks, and copyrights
The Madrid Protocol	2003	Created an international registration database in order to reduce the cost and time spent obtaining international protection.	Trademarks
Anti-Counterfeiting Trade Agreement (ACTA)	2011	Creation of civil and administrative enforcement mechanisms in member countries to deter counterfeiting. Provides for criminal penalties in limited circumstances.	Trademarks and copyrights

Calculating IP Damages and the *Panduit* Test

Broadly speaking, U.S. law recognizes three major theories for recovering IP damages:

1. Damages resulting from the IP owner's loss, which is intended to compensate the owner for actual harm caused by the wrongful use and disclosure of the IP.
2. Damages in the amount of the wrongdoer's gain, since this amount is how much the IP owner was deprived of. This amount usually is calculated by looking at the gain from profits.
3. Damages based on reasonable royalties. This method is used if any of the two methods above would be unlikely to adequately compensate the IP owner.

For patents, the *Panduit* test is usually the starting point for determining whether profits have been lost due to infringement. In order to obtain lost profit damages, the patent owner must establish the following:

1. There is *demand* for the patented product;
2. There are no acceptable substitutes in the marketplace that are also non-infringing;
3. The wrongdoer had both the manufacturing and marketing capability to exploit the demand; and
4. The amount of profit that the wrongdoer would have made or made.

Internet Law

The convergence of the internet and the law is complex and ongoing. As business and personal transactions are now conducted universally on the internet, the law has struggled to keep up with the challenges presented by technological change. Both federal and state legislatures have difficulty in writing laws that apply equally well across the physical and digital domains, and courts strain to apply old doctrines to modern problems. The application of the law to the internet is an evolving process, but one to which the law is beginning to adapt.

Domain Names and Registration

A **domain name** is the internet address of a website, typically typed into an address bar in a web browser. For example, the domain name for Google is "google.com." Because these domains are both addresses and brand identifiers, their use can raise issues of trademark infringement and dilution.

Domain name
The internet address of a website.

Cybersquatting When a party registers a domain for an established trademark with the intent of profiting from that mark.

CYBERSQUATTING. The practice of **cybersquatting** occurs when a party registers an unclaimed domain name that includes or is very similar to the name of an established brand. The party usually tries to profit from this by selling similar goods or services from the website or offers to sell the domain name to the company for a large sum of money. In response, rights holders are forced to file trademark infringement and dilution lawsuits in order to recover their trademarks.

Anticybersquatting Consumer Protection Act Federal law designed to prevent cybersquatting.

In response, Congress enacted the **Anticybersquatting Consumer Protection Act** in 1999. The Act aims to limit cybersquatting by providing a cause of action to a rights holder when the squatter (1) has a bad faith intent to profit from the trademark, and (2) registers a domain that is either identical or confusingly similar to the trademark.

AI Feature: Protecting IP Rights Domestically and Internationally

Assume that your family-owned restaurant chain has decided to expand its domestic operations while opening three franchises in Europe. The recipes are not protectable as lists of ingredients. However, your family has specific instructional notes and methods for assembling and cooking the ingredients that are known to only a few senior managers and trusted family members in the business. You are now confronted with competitors who are beginning to copy the names and ingredients of your most popular dishes. Using an AI program, develop a legal strategy to protect your recipes, as well as the names of the dishes from being copied in the United States and Europe. Include a discussion of obtaining trademark and copyright protection as needed. What additional content or action should be undertaken to protect your intellectual property interests domestically and in Europe?

Key Terms

- Anti-Counterfeiting Trade Agreement, 171
- Anti-cybersquatting Consumer Protection Act, 174
- Authorship, 160
- Berne Convention, 171
- Copyright, 159
- Copyright infringement, 161
- Cybersquatting, 174
- Defend Trade Secrets Act, 157
- Digital Millennium Copyright Act (DMCA), 165
- Domain name 173
- Economic Espionage Act, 157
- Fair use, 162
- Famous marks, 151
- First sale doctrine, 165
- Inherently distinct, 146
- Intellectual property, 144
- Lanham Act, 144

- License, 170
- Madrid Protocol, 171
- Misappropriation of trade secrets, 154
- Originality, 160
- Patent, 166
- Patent infringement, 168
- Provisional application, 166
- Public domain, 160
- Reverse engineering, 158
- Royalty, 168
- Secondary meaning, 146
- Trade secret, 154
- Trademark, 144
- Trademark dilution, 151
- Trademark infringement, 151
- TRIPS Agreement, 171
- Uniform Trade Secrets Act, 154
- World Trade Organization (WTO), 171

Applying the Law

7.1 Research the Law. Ringing the bell over "Taco Tuesday." Taco Bell®, owned by Yum Brands, has filed petitions with the U.S. Patent and Trademark Office seeking to cancel Taco Tuesday trademarks held by a chain called Taco John's and a New Jersey restaurant. Taco Bell argues the term is generic and any restaurant that makes tacos should be able to use the name. Using an internet search engine, report what has happened in the litigation. Also, there are some colors that identify certain brands. What are some examples of these colors and what companies come to mind? Do you think a business can trademark a color? *Qualitex Co. v. Jacobson Products Co.*, 514 U.S. 159 (1995)

7.2 Patent of a Process Performed on a Computer. Alice Corp. owned patents relating to the computerized transaction of escrow. CLS Bank® filed a lawsuit challenging Alice's patents as unpatentable subject matter. CLS argued that the escrow process is an abstract idea that is not sufficiently different when performed on a computer. Alice argues that its process is a patentable method. Which argument prevails? *Alice Corp. Pty. v. CLS Bank Int'l*, 573 U.S. 208 (2014)

7.3 Does Applying for a Patent Destroy Trade Secret Protection? Tweari Systems® claims to own trade secrets that allow it to create low-oxygen storage containers for meat products. The CEO of Tweari® visited and showed MTSR LLC its process, but only after having MTSR sign a confidentiality agreement. Later, Tewari® accused MTSR of stealing trade secrets disclosed as part of the confidentiality agreement. MTSR defended by showing that Tewari applied for a patent for the process. Does disclosing the process in the patent application destroy the trade secret protection? *Tewari De-Ox Sys., Inc. v. Mountain States/Rosen, L.L.C.*, 637 F.3d 604 (5th Cir. 2011)

7.4 Copyright. Hoopla Sports Inc. hosted a basketball game that was sponsored by Nike®. The next year Nike® hosted an identical event called the "Nike Hoops Summit." Subsequently, Hoopla sued Nike® for copyright infringement, asserting that Hoopla owned a copyright to the international tournament idea. Does Hoopla's tournament qualify for copyright protection? *Hoopla Sports & Entm't, Inc. v. Nike, Inc.*, 947 F. Supp. 347 (N.D. Ill. 1996)

7.5 Generic Trademarks. Abercrombie & Fitch (AF)® owns a variety of registered trademarks with the word "Safari." Hunting World (HW)® produced a few clothing items with the name Safari. AF sued HW for trademark infringement. HW argued that as applied to items like shoes and hats, the term had become *generic* and not subject to trademark protections. AF argued that applied to their unique items the terms were *descriptive* and deserving of copyright protection. Is the term "Safari" generic or descriptive? *Abercrombie & Fitch Co. v. Hunting World, Inc.*, 537 F.2d 4 (2d Cir. 1976)

7.6 Works Made for Hire. In 1985, the Community for Creative Non-Violence (CCNV), a D.C.-based organization, entered into an oral agreement with Reid, a sculptor, to produce a statue. Reid worked on the statue in his studio in Baltimore, and CCNV members would visit on occasion to check on the progress. Neither party discussed copyright, and both filed competing copyright registrations. Is the sculptor's work a work made for hire? Make arguments for or against such a finding. *Community for Creative Non-Violence v. Reid*, 490 U.S. 730 (1989)

7.7 Fair Use. Campbell, a member of 2 Live Crew®, had written a parody of "Oh, Pretty Woman©," and sent a letter to Acuff-Rose saying that he would afford credit for ownership and authorship of the original song to Acuff-Rose. However, Acuff-Rose refused permission. Nevertheless, 2 Live Crew released records, cassette tapes, and compact discs of "Pretty Woman." A year later, Acuff-Rose sued 2 Live Crew for copyright infringement. Does the commercial character of a song parody create a presumption that defeats the fair use doctrine? *Campbell v. Acuff Rose*, 510 U.S. 569 (1994)

7.8 Secondary Meaning. Zatarain's® is the manufacturer and distributor of "Fish-Fri," a coating or batter mix used to fry foods. Zatarain's® packages their "Fish-Fri" with a prominent display on their front panel, and the term has been used since 1950 and has been registered as a trademark since 1962. Oak Grove Smokehouse, Inc. began marketing a "fish fry" in March 1979. Oak Grove packages its product in clear glassine packets labelled with Oak Grove's name along with the word "Fish Fry." Zatarain's® has argued that "Fish-Fri" is a suggestive mark, while Oak Grove asserts it is a generic term. Has the "Fish-Fri" acquired secondary meaning that allows it to be protected under trademark law? *Zatarain's v. Oak Grove Smokehouse, Inc.*, 698 F.2d 786 (5th Cir. 1983)

7.9 Fair Use in the Generative AI Era. A copyright holder has the exclusive right to reproduce copyrighted content, create derivative works from it, and distribute copies of it. But what happens if an AI user asks a program for drawings related to a movie character? Is that fair use of a derivative work for which permission or a license to copy the work should be obtained? An AI model is a program that uses algorithms to analyze data and make decisions or predictions. Conduct both a search on the internet and employ an AI program to discuss if it is fair use to build an AI model that relies upon copyrighted material.

7.10 Consumer Confusion. Customers go online to Amazon.com® and search for a "MTM Special Ops®" wristwatch, manufactured and marketed by Multi Time Machine, Inc. However, Amazon® does not sell MTM Special Ops watches—instead the search produces a list, with photographs, of several military style watches that Amazon® does carry. MTM sued Amazon®, alleging the response to a search on its website is a trademark infringement in violation of the Lanham Act. Is there a substantial likelihood of consumer confusion? Why or why not? *Multi Time Machine, Inc. v. Amazon .com, Inc.*, 804 F.3d 930 (9th Cir. 2015)

Criminal Law

8

Laws too gentle are seldom obeyed; too severe, seldom executed. —Benjamin Franklin, a Founding Father of the United States (1706-1790)

Chapter Outline

- Introduction
- Differences Between Civil Law and Criminal Law
- General Principles of Criminal Liability
- The Penal Code
- Types of Crimes

Case 8.1: *United States v. Weaver*
Case 8.2: *United States v. Philip Morris USA Inc.*

- Defenses to Criminal Charges
- Constitutional Rights and Protections

Case 8.3: *Gamble v. United States*

- Criminal Procedure
- AI Feature: Draft a Deferred Prosecution Agreement

Learning Objectives

After studying this chapter, you should be able to:

1. Describe the differences between criminal law and civil law.
2. Identify the elements of a crime and classify several types of crimes.
3. State common crimes encountered in business.
4. Explain how a business entity may commit a crime.
5. Define defenses available to the accused.
6. Describe significant stages of criminal procedure.

Introduction

Criminal law is an organized system of imposing punishment for actions that are harmful to society. Although criminal law is derived from the English common law, the constitutional and criminal laws of the United States, both at the federal and state levels, require a crime to be defined by statute. As a result, governments have enacted criminal laws, which are designed to protect society from those who violate the criminal codes. Criminal law extends to businesses, as they can be both the victims and perpetrators of criminal acts.

This chapter begins with a discussion of the differences between civil and criminal law. While civil law provides remedies for tortious acts and breaches of contract, criminal statutes impose harsh consequences for their violation. We will identify activity society views as criminal and the criminal state of mind required to commit a particular crime. We will also review criminal defenses, rights, and limitations the Constitution grants to criminal defendants, and criminal procedure from arrest to sentencing.

Differences Between Civil Law and Criminal Law

Parties Involved

In criminal law, the party enforcing the statutes is the government. The government is represented by an attorney who, on behalf of the people, prosecutes individuals for violations of specific laws. The party who is accused of a violation is the defendant. Typically, the defendant is represented by a defense attorney. That defense attorney may be a private defense attorney or a public defender if the defendant cannot afford private representation.

Burden of Proof

In the United States, those accused of committing a crime are entitled to exercise several protections in their defense. For example, criminal defendants are presumed innocent until proven guilty beyond a reasonable doubt. This presumption requires the criminal defendant to be treated as innocent of committing the crime and ensures none of their rights are deprived.

Burden of proof
In criminal law, the prosecution has the duty to prove each element of the crime.

The **burden of proof** required for conviction under a criminal statute is placed on the prosecution. The government is required to offer sufficient evidence to prove each element of the charged crime to persuade the jury that the defendant committed the crime of which they have been charged. It is a degree of proof greater than that required in civil court proceedings.

Beyond a reasonable doubt
To convict a defendant, the prosecution must establish the essential elements as to the criminal defendant's guilt to each juror without reasonable doubt.

The burden of proof the government must meet is **beyond a reasonable doubt**, the highest burden of proof under the law. Under this standard the prosecution is required to prove to the trier of fact, which is usually a jury, that there is no reasonable doubt as to the criminal defendant's guilt of the crime charged. To convict the defendant, the jury must render a unanimous, guilty verdict. That is, all jurors must agree to find the criminal defendant guilty of the alleged crime without reasonable doubt. If convicted, the individual is subject to punishment such as fines, imprisonment, or under federal law and that of some states depending upon the crime, death.

Burden of Proof

The burden of proof used depends on the type of case and the severity of the consequences. While there are some other burdens of proof used by judges during pretrial hearings, the following chart contains the most common burdens of proof used in civil and criminal cases during trial.

Burden of Proof	Description
Beyond a Reasonable Doubt	Beyond a reasonable doubt is the highest legal standard. This burden of proof is used to prove a defendant guilty in criminal cases. Beyond a reasonable doubt requires the prosecution to prove to a reasonable juror the guilt of the defendant. Beyond a reasonable doubt does not require absolute certainty.
Clear and Convincing Evidence	In certain civil cases, a higher burden of proof called "clear and convincing evidence" is used. Clear and convincing evidence requires evidence that is highly and substantially more likely to be true than not.
Preponderance of the Evidence	The default standard for most civil cases. Preponderance of the evidence is met if the jury believes the evidence shows a defendant is more likely than not (> 50%) responsible.
Substantial Evidence	This burden of proof is used most often at an administrative hearing. Substantial evidence requires a plaintiff to provide enough evidence that a reasonable mind could accept as adequate proof for a particular conclusion.

Ranked from Highest to Lowest

Concept Summary
Selected Differences Between Criminal Law and Civil Law

Concept	Civil Law	Criminal Law
Party Who Brings Action	The injured party	The government
Cause of Action	Causing harm to an individual or corporation	Violation of a criminal statute

Concept	Civil Law	Criminal Law
Burden of Proof	By a preponderance of the evidence	Beyond a reasonable doubt
Verdict	Generally, three-quarters of the jury	Unanimous jury
Remedy	Generally, monetary damages. In other situations, the court may order equitable remedies such as an injunction.	Can range from fines to imprisonment or death, depending on the specific statute

General Principles of Criminal Liability

Typically, crimes have two elements: (1) an illegal action, and (2) a "guilty" state of mind. A criminal statute identifies the prohibited activity as well as the required state of mind of the actor *at the time the act is committed.*

The Criminal Act

Actus reus
A voluntary action prohibited by law. The act is defined as a crime.

COMMISSION OR OMISSION. Criminal law targets specific behavior. It seeks to prevent harm by prohibiting certain actions. A party must engage in an **actus reus**, or guilty act, to be guilty of a crime.

The guilty act can be one of three things: (1) specific *conduct*, such as theft of property; (2) specific *circumstance*, such as committing a crime while possessing a deadly weapon; or (3) specific *result*, such as causing the death of a person.

Criminal conduct also includes acts of *omission*, which are failures to act when there is a legal duty to act.

> **Example:** The Steeds formed several Utah corporations and hired an accountant, Oliphant, to help them file tax returns. Oliphant was unable to file the Steeds' tax returns for certain years because the Steeds had failed to provide all the necessary information. The Steeds were each convicted of three counts of failure to file a proper tax return. *State v. Steed*, 325 P.3d 87 (Utah 2014)

Accessory

Accessory
An individual who assists in the commission of the crime but does not directly participate in the criminal act with the principal actor.

In criminal law, a person may be liable for a crime committed by another. An **accessory** is an individual who assists in the commission of the crime but does not directly participate in the criminal act with the person primarily responsible for the crime. An accessory *aids or abets* the criminal actor without directly committing the criminal act. The following must occur for a person to be charged as an accessory: (1) another individual committed a crime; (2) the accessory assisted that person with the commission of the crime; and (3) the accessory had knowledge of the individual's criminal intent.

ACCESSORY BEFORE THE FACT. An individual who has knowledge of the criminal act prior to the commission is an accessory before the fact. They may aid or abet the criminal actor by performing an overt act, by giving advice, or providing encouragement to commit the crime. An accessory before the fact is punished to the same degree as the actor for all crimes committed within the scope of the crime the actor intended to commit, even if the accessory is not present at the scene.

> **Example:** Aware of Dante's malevolent intentions, Alex purchases several firearms for Dante. Dante uses the firearms during an armed robbery. Alex's purchase of the firearms is an overt act, and he is considered an accessory before the fact.

ACCESSORY AFTER THE FACT. Anyone who aids a criminal after the commission of a criminal act is an accessory after the fact. This includes assisting a felon, hindering their apprehension, or impeding their conviction or punishment, all with knowledge of the crime. Often, this occurs when there is a failure to report the commission of a felony or when an individual actively assists in the cover-up of another's unlawful act.

> **Example:** Constance assisted her co-workers with covering up their misappropriation of client funds. Constance is considered an accessory after the fact.

The Criminal State of Mind

Criminal statutes establish the mental state necessary for a finding of guilt—that is, ***mens rea***. Under the statutes, a criminal defendant must have the mental state required for the crime to be found guilty. Crimes requiring *mens rea* may be identified as either *general* or *specific intent* crimes. The *mens rea* for a particular crime is defined in either the criminal statute or case law.

Mens rea
The mental state required to be convicted of a crime.

GENERAL INTENT. General intent refers to crimes committed without a specific *mens rea*. These crimes only require a criminal defendant to have intended to perform the criminal act. Under general intent, either *negligence* or *recklessness* may be sufficient for a finding of a criminal state of mind, because the actor should have been aware or was aware of a risk that a crime could occur.

General intent
The intent to commit the criminal act.

> **Example:** Arson is a general intent crime. The required state of mind is the *general intent* to damage property with the use of fire.

SPECIFIC INTENT. Specific intent crimes require the criminal defendant to have the intent to commit the criminal act *and* cause the specific result. The criminal statute will establish the required mental state. As such, those statutes requiring specific intent for a conviction may define the required mental state as *knowingly*.

Specific intent
The intent to commit the criminal act and cause a specific result.

> **Example:** Forgery is a specific intent crime. The guilty act could require the creation of false documents, and the required guilty state of mind *to use* the false documents for financial gain. It is the intent to use the false documents for financial gain that make this a specific intent crime.

Concept Summary
Common *Mens Rea* Terms

Acting Negligently	A person is criminally negligent when they *should be aware of a substantial and unjustifiable risk that results in harm.*
Acting Recklessly	A person is criminally reckless when they *consciously disregard a substantial and unjustifiable risk that results in harm.*
Acting Knowingly	A person commits a criminal act knowingly when they are *aware that their conduct is of that nature or that such circumstances exist.*

The Penal Code

Penal code
A written collection of criminal offenses recognized in a particular jurisdiction.

A written collection of criminal offenses recognized in a jurisdiction is traditionally referred to as the **penal code**, or the *criminal code*. The criminal code of the federal government is set forth within Title 18 of the United States Code. States have enacted penal codes, which define what constitutes a crime under state law. Recognize that a criminal act or omission may be concurrently charged under both federal and state law.

To standardize the penal codes in the United States, independent legal organizations have developed the Model Penal Code (MPC). While the MPC is not binding law, many states have enacted their penal codes based on the MPC.

Language from Title 18 of the U.S. Code

The following language is excerpted from 18 U.S.C. § 2113, dealing with bank robbery and incidental crimes:

> (a) Whoever, by force and violence, or by intimidation, takes, or attempts to take, from the person or presence of another, or obtains or attempts to obtain by extortion any property or money or any other thing of value belonging to, or in the care, custody, control, management, or possession of, any bank, credit union, or any savings and loan association; or Whoever enters or attempts to enter any bank, credit union, or any savings and loan association, or any building used in whole or in part as a bank, credit union, or as a savings and loan association, with intent to commit in such bank, credit union, or in such savings and loan association, or building, or part thereof, so used, any felony affecting such bank, credit union, or such savings and loan association and in violation of any statute of the United States, or any larceny—Shall be fined under this title or imprisoned not more than twenty years, or both.

Classification of Crimes

Crimes are classified according to the severity of their consequences. The three broad categories of crime from least to most severe are:

- *Infractions.* Minor offenses are usually punishable by a fine. Typically, due to their limited punishments, violators are not required to be tried in front of a jury and judge, although the punishment can be appealed.

Example: Parking tickets are infractions.

- *Misdemeanors.* Misdemeanors are crimes that are punishable by imprisonment but only up to one year in duration. Other punishments for misdemeanors include fines, mandatory community service, and probation. Typically, a right to a jury trial in misdemeanor cases applies only when a "serious" offense is at issue. This is often described as an offense with a potential sentence of more than six months.

Example: Petty theft, such as shoplifting, can be classified as a misdemeanor.

- *Felonies.* Felonies are punishable by more than one year of imprisonment. Punishment can also include fines and probation. Felonies are the most serious crimes and carry the heaviest sentences. Due to their severity, the accused have a right to a jury trial and legal representation.

Example: Fraud, hate crimes, and domestic violence are examples of behaviors that can be charged as a felony.

Types of Crimes

Property Crimes

Property crimes are commonly perpetrated upon commercial businesses. Property crimes involve the illegal removal or damage of property. The elements of proof are the same for misdemeanor and felony larceny, the only difference being the value or nature of the property stolen. The common types of property crimes are:

LARCENY. Larceny is the unlawful taking and carrying away of the personal property of another with the intent to permanently deprive the owner of the property. Statutes have expanded the definition of personal property to include the theft of data stored in the cloud.

Often, larceny is synonymous with theft; they are considered the same crime. Larceny may sometimes be confused with **robbery**, the unlawful taking of the property of another by force or threat of force. The important distinction is that robbery requires the use of or the threat of force in the taking of the property, while this is not required for larceny.

Larceny
The unlawful taking of the property of another with the intent to permanently deprive the owner of the property.

Robbery
The unlawful taking of the property of another by force or threat of force.

Example: Nancy Fluker entered a Durham, North Carolina, JCPenney® store wherein she removed dolls from a shelf and walked out of the store with them in her possession. She was convicted of misdemeanor larceny of property. *State v. Fluker*, 139 N.C. App. 768 (2000)

Obtaining goods by false pretenses
The unlawful act of making a false statement with the intent to defraud and obtain title to another's personal property.

OBTAINING GOODS BY FALSE PRETENSES. **Obtaining goods by false pretenses** is the act of making a false statement with the intent to defraud and obtain title of another's personal property. This form of theft requires fraud or deceit (that is, trickery). While the name suggests the crime covers only goods or property illegally acquired, a person may also obtain services by false pretenses. Statutes regulating the crime of obtaining goods by false pretenses vary by state.

> **Example:** Nelson Bell opened an account at a savings and loan institution using his own name, but giving a false address, birth date, and Social Security number. Later that day, at another branch, he deposited into his account a third party's $10,000 check on which the endorsement had been altered to show Bell's account number. Subsequently, Bell closed his account and was paid the total balance in cash. His conviction for obtaining money under false pretenses was upheld by the Supreme Court. *Bell v. United States*, 462 U.S. 356 (1983)

Receiving stolen property
The unlawful receipt of property with the knowledge that the property is stolen.

RECEIVING STOLEN PROPERTY. A person **receiving stolen property** that they know or should have known is stolen is criminally liable. To be convicted, the recipient of the stolen goods does not need to know the identity of either the owner or thief, nor does the recipient need to have paid for the goods. It is only required that at the time of receipt of the goods, the recipient knows or should have known the goods were stolen.

Burglary
The act of entering the building of another with the intent to commit a felony while inside.

BURGLARY. Under common law, burglary was defined as the breaking and entering of a dwelling of another a night with the intent to commit a felony. The original intention behind this definition was to protect the home. In modern times, state statutes have changed the elements of the crime of burglary. Now, the definition of **burglary** has been expanded to include the act of entering the building of another with the intent to commit a felony while inside, such as larceny.

Arson
The willful act of setting fire to a building, car, or property.

ARSON. Under common law, arson was defined as the intentional burning of another person's house. The original intention behind criminalizing arson was to protect the occupants of the home. Like burglary, the criminal statutes defining arson have expanded from the common law to protect more than a person's home. Now, **arson** is the willful act of setting fire to a building, car, or property.

Concept Summary
Selected Property Crimes

Type of Property Crime	Prohibited Act
Larceny	The unlawful taking of the property of another with the intent to permanently deprive the owner of the property.
Robbery	The unlawful taking of the property of another by force or threat of force.

Type of Property Crime	Prohibited Act
Obtaining Goods by False Pretenses	The unlawful act of making a false statement with the intent to defraud and obtain title of another's personal property.
Receiving Stolen Property	The unlawful receipt of property with the knowledge that the property is stolen.
Burglary	The act of entering the building of another with the intent to commit a felony while inside.
Arson	The willful act of setting fire to a building, car, or property.

Business Crimes

Business crimes occur in a passive setting and are nonviolent. Also known as *white collar crimes*, all follow the same basic premise, often involving an individual or a company engaging in illegal activity for profit.

Business crimes
Nonviolent crime typically committed by individuals or organizations for financial gain.

EMBEZZLEMENT. Embezzlement is the fraudulent appropriation of property by a person entrusted with its care. Embezzlement is most often committed by an agent or employee of a company with access to the property, such as bookkeepers, accountants, financial officers and advisors, wealth managers, and attorneys. Embezzlement is distinguishable from larceny and robbery in that to embezzle property, the criminal actor must have been in a position of trust—that is, have *lawful possession* of the property.

Embezzlement
The fraudulent appropriation of property by a party entrusted with its care.

Embezzlement is a crime of opportunity. A person entrusted with corporate funds takes for personal use the employer's cash or property. Frequently, the perpetrator will alter the financial records to disguise their acts.

> **Example:** William Bailey was the closing attorney on several federally funded real estate loan transactions. Bailey acted as a fiduciary because he acted as the escrow agent for the disbursement of the loan funds. He unlawfully retained funds from these transactions. After the federal lender discovered irregularities, it was revealed that Bailey converted loan funds to his own use. He was tried in federal court and convicted of embezzlement. *United States v. Bailey*, 734 F.2d 296 (7th Cir. 1984)

FORGERY. Forgery is the fraudulent creation or alteration of any written document that alters the legal rights of a party. The common understanding of forgery is that it involves a party signing another's name on a legal document, but forgery can also include changing or falsifying a legal document, such as a will or trust, or altering a document that relates to finances, such as a check. Possession of forged documents is illegal in many jurisdictions.

Forgery
The fraudulent creation or alteration of any written document of apparent legal status with the intent to defraud.

> **Example:** As part of a criminal investigation, a complainant identified Isidro Rodriguez as a possible suspect. New York City Police Detective Steven Goetz arrested Rodriguez and during a search incident to the arrest, Goetz found false identification documents on Rodriguez. Following a jury trial, Rodriguez was convicted of criminal possession of a forged document with the intent to defraud, deceive, or injury another person. *People v. Rodriguez*, 17 N.Y.3d 486 (2011)

Bribery
The offering of anything of value to a recipient to obtain a personal benefit.

BRIBERY. **Bribery** is the offering of anything of value to the recipient to obtain a personal benefit from that person. After receiving the bribe, the recipient is guilty of a separate bribery crime, accepting a bribe. A bribe can include anything the recipient considers of value.

There are two general types of bribery, which depend on the recipient and the benefit sought:

Kickback
A general term for a benefit received from a party who assisted in the execution of a bribery scheme.

- *Commercial bribery.* When a party offers a bribe to a businessperson, such as an executive, to obtain business from the company. As part of these agreements, the recipient will often ask for a **kickback**.
- *Bribery of a public official.* The corrupt promise or the transfer of anything of value to influence an official act of a governmental employee or office holder. It is extended by statute to jury tampering, which is the attempt to influence the decision of a jury during a trial.

> **Example:** The Supreme Court has decided that bribery before a governmental official act is a crime. However, if given as a token of appreciation after the official act, it is not. "Gratuities after the official act are not the same as bribes before the official act. After all, unlike gratuities, bribes can corrupt the official act—meaning that the official takes the act for private gain, not for the public good. That said, gratuities can sometimes also raise ethical and appearance concerns. For that reason, Congress, States, and local governments have long regulated gratuities to public officials." *Snyder v. United States*, 603 U.S. ____, 144 S. Ct. 1947 (2024)

The Foreign Corrupt Practices Act of 1977 (FCPA) was enacted to prohibit the bribery of foreign officials to obtain or retain businesses. Violations of the FCPA can lead to both civil and criminal penalties. The FCPA is explained in more detail in Chapter 43.

Mail and wire fraud
The use of mail service or the telecommunications networks to commit fraud.

MAIL AND WIRE FRAUD. The use of either a domestic or express mail service (USPS®, UPS®, or FedEx®), or a telecommunication network (telephone, email, text messaging, or television) to commit fraud is prohibited by federal law. **Mail and wire fraud** is the intentional participation in a fraudulent scheme conducted over wire or by mail. These crimes are often charged in connection with other criminal behavior, as almost all criminal actions involve the use of mail or telecommunication facilities.

> **Example:** Justice Department prosecutors use the federal mail and wire fraud statutes to prosecute health care fraud and abuse. These crimes encompass a wide range of practices including overcharging for services, billing for services not rendered, and rendering services that are unnecessary or inappropriate. Paying kickbacks to physicians for referring patients and routinely waiving copayments or deductibles from patients are also considered fraudulent activities by the Medicare and Medicaid programs.

In the following case, the court considered how contract law intersects with criminal mail and wire fraud.

CASE 8.1

CONTRACTUAL DISCLAIMERS CANNOT DEFEAT LIABILITY FOR FRAUD

UNITED STATES v. WEAVER

860 F.3d 90 (2017)

United States Court of Appeals for the Second Circuit

Edward Weaver was the CEO of Vendstar, a corporation that sold candy vending machines to thousands of customers who spent nearly $62 million on the investments. As part of its operation, Vendstar marketed its machines to start a successful home business that would earn the customer profits of up to $800 a day. Although Vendstar's promotional materials and salespeople represented that the investment opportunities would be profitable, the customers earned almost no money. Many customers lost virtually all their investments in Vendstar machines.

Potential customers responded to Internet or newspaper advertisements for vending machine opportunities. After the initial inquiry, Vendstar mailed customers a brochure, order form, and certain disclosure documents. The company claimed that there was "little risk" and promised unrealistic potential earnings to customers over the phone. The salespeople also falsely claimed they owned the machines themselves. Once a customer decided to purchase a machine, they were required to sign a contract. The contract stated, in part, that customers should not rely on any of the statements made by the salespeople. If customers expressed concern about the contract's language, salespeople would misleadingly dismiss the provisions as unimportant "legalese" or "mumbo-jumbo." Weaver was charged and convicted with mail and wire fraud. On appeal, he argued that he should be found not guilty due to the language contained in the contracts informing the customers of the disclaimer.

Language of the Court. *The essential elements of mail and wire fraud are (1) a scheme to defraud, (2) money or property as the object of the scheme, and (3) use of the mails or wires to further the scheme. The gravamen of the offense is the scheme to defraud. In order to prove the existence of a scheme to defraud, the government must also prove that the misrepresentations were material, and that the defendant acted with fraudulent intent. A statement is material if the "misinformation or omission would naturally tend to lead or is capable of leading a reasonable [person] to change [his] conduct." (citation omitted) In other words, a "lie can support a fraud conviction only if it is material, that is, if it would affect a reasonable person's evaluation of a proposal." (citation omitted). A "false statement is material if it has a natural tendency to influence, or is capable of influencing, the decision of the [decision maker] to which it was addressed." (citation omitted). Recently, the Supreme Court explained that, "[u]nder any understanding of the concept, materiality looks to the effect on the likely or actual behavior of the recipient of the alleged misrepresentation.*

We agree with our sister circuits and hold that contractual disclaimers of reliance on prior misrepresentations do not render those misrepresentations immaterial under the criminal mail and wire fraud statutes. The Vendstar purchase agreements included several prominent disclaimers of reliance on prior oral representations. While such disclaimers may in some circumstances defeat a civil claim for damages based on fraud, they do not bear on the defendant's criminal liability. We conclude that they had the natural tendency to influence the decision makers to whom they were addressed—potential Vendstar customers.

Fraudsters may not escape criminal liability for lies told to induce gullible victims to make worthless investments by inducing them to sign a contract containing disclaimers of reliance. Thus, they did not render extra-contract misrepresentations immaterial as a matter of law.

Decision. The court found Weaver guilty of mail and wire fraud. The court held that liability disclaimers will not insulate defendants from criminal fraud.

Focus on Ethics

Weaver claimed he was not guilty of fraud or conspiracy because Vendstar customers executed purchase agreements in which they disclaimed reliance on extra-contract (that is, the salespersons oral) representations. If he were sued for civil fraud these disclaimers may have provided a defense, but why should he be liable under a criminal statute in this situation?

Insider trading
The purchase or sale of securities on a stock exchange by individuals who have access to material, nonpublic information that provides an unfair advantage to those traders.

INSIDER TRADING. Insider trading refers to the purchase or sale of a security on a stock exchange by an individual having access to material and nonpublic information about the security. Such information is that which could substantially impact an investor's decision to purchase or sell the security. Federal law prohibits trading on such information because of the unfair advantage it gives the individual who trades on that information. Insider trading is discussed in greater detail in Chapter 25.

Conspiracy

Conspiracy
Conspiracy is the combination of two or more persons, by concerted action, to accomplish criminal or unlawful purpose, or some purpose not in itself criminal or unlawful, by criminal or unlawful means. The statute may require that at least one of those in agreement to have acted in furtherance of the crime.

Conspiracy is the combination of two or more persons, acting in concert, to accomplish criminal or unlawful purpose, or some purpose not in itself criminal or unlawful, by criminal or unlawful means. In most cases, the federal criminal conspiracy statute, and some state statutes, require that at least one party to the agreement take an overt act in furtherance of the conspiracy to establish liability. An overt act is any step taken by one conspirator toward completing the criminal purpose. A person may be guilty of conspiracy even if the agreed-upon crime is not completed. Additionally, criminal defendants can be charged with both the conspiracy to commit a crime and the crime itself, if completed. Unlike an attempt to commit a crime (which merges into the crime once it is committed), conspiracy is a separate and distinct offense. As stated, some criminal offenses set forth in a statute do not require the overt act. For example, under the federal money laundering statute, proof of an overt act in furtherance of the conspiracy is not required.[1]

Extortion

Extortion is the use of force or the threat of force, to obtain something of value or elicit action. The force or threat of force must be one of future harm, not present or imminent harm. State statutes have expanded the element of threat to include not only physical harm, but financial harm or the destruction of property. Sometimes synonymous with *blackmail,* extortion can also involve the use of damaging information instead of force.

Extortion
The use of force or threat of force to obtain something of value from another or provoke action.

> **Example:** McClure and Williams entered into an agreement in which McClure would reside in Williams's double wide trailer without rent for a year in exchange for performing repairs on the trailer. After the year was up, Williams asked McClure to pay rent or he would evict him. McClure responded with partial destruction of the trailer and threats to destroy the trailer unless Williams would forgo filing a police report for the damages he caused to the trailer. McClure was convicted of extortion. *State v. McClure,* 200 Wash. App. 231 (2017)

Liability of Corporate Officers and Directors

Corporations are separate entities created under the laws of various states and are treated as *legal persons.* Corporations have similar rights and responsibilities to obey the law as do humans. Under the common law, corporations were not held responsible for criminal acts because they lacked the required *intent* to commit the crimes. Under current law, the United States Supreme Court has held that criminal liability can be imputed to corporations through the actions of their agents and employees acting within the scope of their employment. Although corporations cannot serve time in prison, they are subject to fines and revocation of licenses necessary to do business. The prosecutor must establish that the corporation had an opportunity to prevent the act or that proper supervision would have prevented the act from occurring.

Agents and employees of a corporation can be *individually* liable for the crimes they commit within the scope of their employment. In addition, managers and directors can be criminally liable for the actions of their employees if they fail to exercise adequate supervision. In the following case, the court considered whether a corporation could be guilty of crimes that require specific intent.

1. *Whitfield v. United States,* 543 U.S. 209 (2005).

CASE 8.2

CORPORATIONS CAN BE GUILTY OF SPECIFIC INTENT CRIMES SUCH AS FRAUD

UNITED STATES v. PHILIP MORRIS USA INC.

566 F.3d 1095 (2009)

United States Court of Appeals for the D.C. Circuit

Philip Morris USA is a large cigarette manufacturer that marketed its products as "light" and "low tar." The federal government claimed that Philip Morris engaged in a violation of RICO by conducting a conspiracy to deceive the consuming public as to the harmful effects of smoking, addictiveness of nicotine, and health benefits from low tar "light" cigarettes, and for purposely designing the composition of the cigarettes to sustain nicotine addiction. Specifically, the federal government alleged that Philip Morris fraudulently denied that smoking causes cancer and emphysema, that secondhand smoke causes lung cancer and negatively affects children's respiratory systems, that nicotine is an addictive drug, that light and low tar cigarettes are not less harmful, and that Philip Morris intentionally marketed to young people.

The trial court found in favor of the government, concluding that Philip Morris, as a corporation, showed the specific intent necessary to be guilty of fraud. Philip Morris appealed to the D.C. Circuit Court.

Language of the Court. *Corporations may be held liable for specific intent offenses based on the "knowledge and intent" of their employees. Because a corporation only acts and wills by virtue of its employees, the proscribed corporate intent depends on the wrongful intent of specific employees. Thus, to determine whether a corporation made a false or misleading statement with specific intent to defraud, we look to the state of mind of the individual corporate officers and employees who made, ordered, or approved the statement. The state of mind is rarely proved by direct evidence, so specific intent to defraud may be inferred from the totality of the circumstances, including indirect and circumstantial evidence.*

Here, the district court concluded that the chief executive officers and other highly placed officials in the Defendant corporations made or approved statements they knew to be false or misleading, evincing their specific intent to defraud consumers. In some instances, the court found by direct evidence that representatives of the Defendant companies "willfully stated something which they knew to be untrue." For example, the court found that, in a televised interview in 1971, Philip Morris President Joseph Cullman III denied that cigarettes posed a health hazard to pregnant women or their infants, "contradicting the information Helmut Wakeham, Philip Morris's Vice President for Corporate Research and Development, had given him two years earlier." In the main, however, the district court relied on indirect and circumstantial evidence indicating that the senior corporate officials knew that their public statements, and those that they approved for their corporations, were false or misleading.

Decision. The court found in favor of the government and against Philip Morris, holding that corporations can be guilty of specific intent crimes when their high-level employees evidence behavior consistent with the charged crime of fraud.

Focus on Ethics

How senior does an employee have to be within an organization to cause it to be liable for the criminal activity of the employee?

Cybercrime

As legitimate businesses continue to adapt to the expansion of use of the internet, so have criminal organizations. The general term for criminal activity that occurs on computers and online is **cybercrime**. Cybercrimes can be unique to the online environment, but many are merely traditional crimes that involve the use of a computer or the internet.

Cybercrime
Criminal activity conducted with the use of the internet.

IDENTITY THEFT. Identity theft is the unauthorized use of personal information (such as names, dates of birth, addresses, Social Security numbers, or account numbers) to profit financially. Most commonly, an identity thief uses the personal information to open credit accounts or to access existing bank accounts for their financial gain. While identity theft existed before the internet, the increased disclosure of sensitive information online has increased the risk. Today, criminals can access websites and databases that house thousands or millions of identifying pieces of information and use that information to engage in identity theft.

> **Example:** Damien Hernandez Cortez was stopped for a traffic violation. An officer found Cortez's fingerprints on the following: (1) a canceled check with a stranger's name, driver's license number, bank account number, and mailing address; (2) a Visa credit card, which bore another person's name and address; and (3) a Texas Medicaid form with a third person's name, date of birth, driver's license number, and Social Security number. A grand jury indicted Cortez for fraudulent possession of items of identifying information. *Cortez v. State*, 469 S.W.3d 593 (Tex. Crim. App. 2015)

PHISHING. Phishing is a type of identity theft whereby users are tricked into disclosing their identifying personal information online. Phishing is accomplished when criminals alter a website to resemble a bank portal, social media site, or other trusted source, thus prompting the user to enter the information the criminal requests. Phishing scams are frequently conducted through emails, in which a recipient is asked to enter or confirm sensitive information. The emails will attempt to copy the look and feel of a standard email from a trusted source, such as a bank or credit card company. When a user enters the information, the "phisher" can then use it to engage in identity theft or sell the information on the black market.

CREDIT CARD THEFT. One of the most popular targets for criminals are online databases that store credit card numbers. Most online transactions require the use of a credit card or other bank card. Online retailers who fail to adequately protect the information using encryption or other methods risk being infiltrated by wrongdoers. Credit card theft is a greater issue for banks and retailers than for cardholders because cardholders are not held responsible for fraudulent charges made on their accounts.

HACKING. Hacking is the act of gaining unauthorized access into a computer or network using a computer or other smart device. While some hackers are nonthreatening, others can cause serious damage to property and disrupt essential societal services, such as financial institutions. Hackers can covertly install malware onto targeted computer systems, thereby giving themselves access to an individual's personal information or allowing them to take control of the computer. Once they have entered a network, hackers steal valuable information from a company and completely delete it or hold it for a ransom.

MALWARE. Malware is a term for computer programs that damage, disable, or otherwise compromise computers on which they have been installed. Types of malware include botnets, worms, viruses, Trojan horses, ransomware, and spyware, among others. The type of malware depends on the purpose of the program, but it is essentially designed to be easily spread and undetectable to benefit the malware designer.

CYBERTERRORISM. Traditional terrorism is the use of violence or the threat of violence to achieve a political gain. Cyberterrorism is nearly the same, except that violence or threat of violence is conducted online. While hackers may attempt to steal information from a company for financial gain, cyberterrorists seek to destroy the company as a threat to a specific group of people. Cyberterrorists may also employ hacking techniques and malware to harm hostile governments or groups that they consider adverse to their cause. Certain high-value targets, such as the energy infrastructure, banking and securities institutions, and transportation networks, are highly susceptible to a disruptive cyberterrorist attack. These industries work closely with the federal government to shield themselves from terrorist threats.

COMPUTER FRAUD AND ABUSE ACT. The Computer Fraud and Abuse Act (CFAA) is a federal law prohibiting an individual from gaining *unauthorized access* to an internet-connected computer to obtain information stored on the computer system. Violations of the CFAA are punishable by fines and imprisonment, and civil damages are available to plaintiffs who bring private actions.

> **Example:** Christopher Phillips entered the University of Texas at Austin and was admitted to the Department of Computer Sciences in 2003. Upon admission, Phillips signed UT's "acceptable use" computer policy. After a few weeks, Phillips began using various programs to steal encrypted data and passwords. Phillips was indicted and convicted after a jury trial on a count of computer fraud pursuant to CFAA. *United States v. Phillips*, 477 F.3d 215 (5th Cir. 2007)

Organized Crime

Organized crime
Organizations with an identified hierarchy used to engage in a variety of criminal activity.

Organized crime, also known as a *criminal enterprise*, refers to organizations that structure their criminal activity in a centralized manner. These organizations typically have an identified hierarchy or structure within which they engage in a variety of criminal endeavors. While organized crime and criminal enterprise may be used synonymously, federal criminal statutes that target organized crime specifically define a criminal enterprise. One such statute is the Racketeer Influenced and Corrupt Organizations Act (RICO), which is discussed below.

MONEY LAUNDERING. Criminal organizations are unable to spend or invest the money earned from illegal ventures because the size of these transactions could reveal their illegal activity to the government. To avoid detection, criminal organizations engage in **money laundering**, a financial transaction scheme that conceals the origin of the illegally obtained money. Money laundering is accomplished by engaging in financial transactions that make the money appear legitimate to financial institutions and governmental agencies.

Money laundering
A series of financial transactions used by criminal organizations to conceal the origin of money derived from criminal activity.

RACKETEER INFLUENCED AND CORRUPT ORGANIZATIONS ACT (RICO). To eradicate organized crime in the United States, Congress enacted the Racketeer Influenced and Corrupt Organizations Act (RICO). RICO is one of the most powerful tools deployed against organized crime and businesses engaged in illegal activities. Some states have adopted similar laws that are known as Little RICO Acts.

RICO prohibits the use of income from racketeering to purchase, maintain, invest, or participate in an enterprise. *Enterprise* is defined by statute to include any individual, partnership, corporation, association, or other legal entity, or any group associated in a non-legal entity.

A *racketeering activity* is any criminal act defined in the statute, such as mail and wire fraud, kidnapping, gambling, arson, robbery, bribery, embezzlement, and extortion, among others. A pattern of racketeering activity involves committing two or more of the listed crimes within a ten-year period. While targeted to eliminate organized crime, it has most often been applied to illicit business transactions, including kickback schemes. RICO also permits private parties whose business or property has been damaged by a "racketeer" to file a civil suit against the wrongdoer.

The severe penalties associated with RICO violations include imprisonment for up to 20 years and payment of large fines. RICO includes a forfeiture provision that allows the government to seize any property or business interest involved in or gained because of a RICO violation. The government can seize legitimate businesses if they are part of a criminal organization or were funded with money from racketeering activities. The government can also seek civil remedies against RICO violators, such as injunctions or monetary damages to the victims.

> **Example:** As part of a conspiracy, David Morris planned and participated in multiple rigged card games in Las Vegas, Nevada. Illegal gambling is a prohibited racketeering activity under RICO. At trial, he was convicted of participating in a pattern of racketeering in violation of RICO. *United States v. Morris*, 532 F.2d 436 (5th Cir. 1976)

Defenses to Criminal Charges

Affirmative defense
A legal defense that negates or reduces liability, even if the allegations against the defendant are true.

Criminal defendants have several defenses they can assert. An **affirmative defense** is a legal defense that, if proved by the criminal defendant, will negate, or reduce liability for the commission of a crime. For example, an individual who commits a felony while acting under the immediate threat of serious harm to a family member would likely assert an affirmative defense of duress.

Justification

Justification
A defense that negates criminal liability because the defendant's actions were justified.

Under the defense of **justification**, the defendant's actions are justified and exempt from criminal liability. Typically, a court will find that a defendant could not have acted differently in the given circumstance. This defense is an encompassing term and includes a variety of defenses, such as defense of property, defense of others, and self-defense.

> **Example:** Dennis Haugen was charged with carrying a loaded firearm in a vehicle. Haugen said he received a phone call from an angry neighbor who wanted money. After the interaction, Haugen began carrying a loaded gun. At his jury trial, Haugen requested jury instructions on justification. The court disallowed the instruction because it was not applicable to the strict liability offense of carrying a loaded firearm in a vehicle. *State v. Haugen*, 742 N.W.2d 796 (N.D. 2007)

Self-defense
A justification defense in which the defendant claims to have acted to protect themself from bodily harm or death and that they therefore should be found not guilty.

Self-defense is the use of force to protect oneself from an attempted bodily harm or death by another individual. Self-defense is a type of justification defense that, if proven, can be used as a defense to criminal liability. Generally, self-defense statutes provide that a defendant is permitted to use the *proportional* amount of force required to defend against an attack that posed a threat of bodily harm or death to the defendant. A person cannot use self-defense as justification to attack a party who is no longer a threat.

In cases of self-defense with deadly force, victims must *reasonably believe* they are about to die or be seriously injured by an attack from a person using unlawful force.

Mistake

Mistake of fact
A defense that undermines the intent element of the crime because the defendant claims they made a reasonable mistake as to the facts of the situation.

In criminal law, **mistake of fact** is defense that negates the intent requirement of the charged crime. Recall that to be guilty of a crime, one must satisfy both the criminal act and the criminal intent elements. If a defendant made a reasonable mistake and committed a criminal act, they may present a defense to the intent requirement. In essence, the defendant is asserting that they did not have the criminal state of mind to be guilty.

Insanity

Criminal law recognizes that in some instances, a person's mental state is so degraded that the person is not responsible for their actions. This results in the person being classified as legally insane, and, therefore, unable to satisfy the *intent* element of crime because the person's state of mind is impaired by a disease or defect. Because state of mind is difficult, if not impossible, to prove, the law excuses the legally insane from traditional modes of punishment such as prison. Instead, legally insane criminals are confined to mental hospitals or institutions.

While most states and the federal government agree that there should be an excuse for legal insanity, they do not agree on what the test for legal insanity should be. Most states use the *M'Naghten* test, while the federal government and a minority of states use the Model Penal Code insanity test, or a slightly modified version of it.

THE *M'NAGHTEN* TEST. The defendant must prove that they were incapable of:

- Knowing or understanding the nature and quality of their act; or
- Distinguishing between right and wrong at the time of the act.

THE MODEL PENAL CODE INSANITY TEST. The defendant must prove that at the time of the criminal act, and because of mental disease or defect, they lacked *substantial capacity* either to:

- Appreciate the criminality of their conduct; or
- Conform their conduct to the requirements of the law.

Duress

A defendant is under **duress** when they commit a criminal act under an *immediate threat of coercion*, and the defendant acted reasonably given the threat. The defense of duress operates similarly to the other affirmative defenses because the law assumes a person operating under duress did not have the required state of mind to be guilty of the crime. The availability of the duress defense for certain violent crimes varies depending on the jurisdiction. For example, most states do not allow duress as a defense to murder, while others will allow it as a mitigating factor, reducing the defendant's criminal liability.

Duress
A defense available to a defendant when they commit a criminal act under a threat of coercion, and that the action was reasonable given the threat.

> **Example:** Matt Heath was arrested and found in possession of jewelry and coins taken from a nearby residence. He admitted to committing the burglary but defended his actions under the defense of duress. Heath claimed a Mr. Sodersten threatened to kill him if he did not steal the valuables to repay his debt. The defense was insufficient, and he was convicted. The court found that Heath was not under an *immediate* threat while he committed the crime. *People v. Heath*, 207 Cal. App. 3d 892 (Ct. App. 1989)

Entrapment

Entrapment is an affirmative defense by which the defendant proves they were induced by the government to commit a crime that they were not predisposed to commit. There are two elements to an entrapment defense: (1) the government improperly *induced* the crime, and (2) the defendant *lacked a predisposition* to engage in the criminal act. To satisfy the first element, a government agent must do more than merely suggest a criminal opportunity—there must be conduct that induces a person who would not otherwise commit the crime. For the second element, the court will determine whether the defendant had the predisposition to commit the crime before the government's inducement, and will consider several factors, such as the defendant's character or reluctance.

Entrapment
A defense available to the defendant if it is proved that the defendant was induced by the government to commit a crime that the defendant was not predisposed to commit.

> **Example:** Arnold Hollingsworth and a business partner started an international banking enterprise, even though they had no prior expertise in doing so. The business lost money rapidly. An undercover federal agent contacted them and solicited their services to launder money. After weeks of pressure, and with no other business income available, Hollingsworth agreed to the agent's terms. He was arrested

and convicted of money laundering under federal law. The appellate court overturned his conviction, finding as a matter of law that he was entrapped. *United States v. Hollingsworth*, 27 F.3d 1196 (7th Cir. 1994)

Statutes of Limitations

Statute of limitations (criminal) A specified period within which a criminal charge can be prosecuted against an accused.

Statutes of limitations are laws that establish a period for a charge to be brought against a criminal defendant. State and federal statutes dictate different time periods depending on the crime. For certain crimes punishable by death or life imprisonment, there is typically no statute of limitations, whereas for misdemeanors, charges must be brought within one year from the commission of the offense. In addition, state and federal laws pause the elapse of statutes of limitations from continuing to run in instances when a defendant is a fugitive from the law.

Immunity from Prosecution

Immunity from prosecution Exemption in full or in part from legal punishment.

Immunity from prosecution arises from an agreement whereby the government may grant use or transaction immunity from prosecution. Immunity may be granted arising from statute, prosecutorial discretion, or international agreement. For example, a prosecutor may offer immunity to not prosecute an accused in exchange for valuable information or testimony on a related matter. Transactional immunity is a broad exception from liability for the crime. Use immunity means that the evidence obtained by the witness's testimony cannot be used against the witness.

Another type of immunity available to public officials, such as police officers, is qualified immunity against certain claims brought against them. Diplomats who operate in the United States are often granted diplomatic immunity.

Constitutional Rights and Protections

The United States Constitution recognizes several rights granted to criminal defendants and places limits upon the government's unrestricted ability to use evidence regardless of its source or reliability. These rights and limitations are designed to act as a balance between the parties.

Fourth Amendment Rights

The Fourth Amendment prohibits the government from conducting unreasonable searches and seizures of property or people while making arrests. The Amendment states that "the right of the people to be secure in their persons, houses, papers and effects" shall not be violated without a warrant obtained with probable cause. The warrant issued must specifically describe the place to be searched and the items or persons to be seized.

When the government decides to search a property, it must obtain the signature of a judge on a search and seizure warrant. That is, the judge must be persuaded there is *probable cause* for the issuance of the search and seizure warrant.

Courts recognize that search warrants cannot always be easily obtained, so they allow law enforcement officers to conduct *warrantless searches* immediately following an arrest if the evidence is in plain view of the officer or if the evidence would otherwise be destroyed.

EXPECTATION OF PRIVACY. Courts have struggled to define what qualifies a search within the meaning of the Constitution. The Supreme Court has ruled that a search occurs when the government invades a citizen's *reasonable expectation of privacy*. A reasonable expectation of privacy is found if (1) the individual displayed behavior showing a subjective belief of privacy, and (2) society recognizes that belief as reasonable.

EXCLUSIONARY RULE. The **exclusionary rule** prohibits the government from presenting evidence at trial that was obtained in violation of the Fourth Amendment. The rule also applies to evidence that was subsequently discovered using information wrongly obtained by the government. By barring admittance of the evidence, the rule aims to ensure government compliance with the requirements of the Fourth Amendment.

Exclusionary rule The rule that bars evidence being used against a criminal defendant if it was acquired in violation of a constitutional requirement, such as under the Fourth Amendment.

Example: Dollree Mapp was convicted of possession of prohibited obscene materials. The police obtained the materials by forcing open a door and gaining access into Mapp's house, despite her refusing the police entry and demanding to see a search warrant. The Supreme Court overturned her conviction because the evidence was obtained in violation of the Fourth Amendment. *Mapp v. Ohio*, 367 U.S. 643 (1961)

Fifth Amendment Rights

The Fifth Amendment includes several protections related to criminal proceedings. Three of them include the requirement of due process of law, the prohibition on double jeopardy, and the privilege against self-incrimination.

DUE PROCESS. Due process of law requires the government to conduct criminal prosecutions in a "fair" manner. As explained in Chapter 4, due process has both *substantive* and *procedural* aspects. In a criminal law proceeding, *procedural due process* requires supplying the defendant notice of the charges (that is, an arraignment) and providing a fair hearing (that is, a trial).

DOUBLE JEOPARDY. The prohibition on **double jeopardy** is a complete bar on the government's attempt to try to convict the same criminal for the same crime, on more than one occasion. Once a defendant has been acquitted (that is, found not guilty), the government is prohibited from trying that same case in the future. The acquitted defendant cannot be tried for a lesser crime if prosecutors could have originally charged the lesser crime from the same set of facts. However, double jeopardy does not extend to civil trials. A defendant may be found not guilty of a crime, but nonetheless remain liable for damages to the victim in a civil case.

Double jeopardy The government is prohibited from prosecuting a defendant twice for substantially the same crime.

In the following case, the Supreme Court considered if the Double Jeopardy Clause limits successive prosecutions by separate sovereigns (such as the federal and state governments).

CASE 8.3

DOUBLE JEOPARDY CLAUSE ALLOWS SUCCESSIVE PROSECUTION BY SEPARATE SOVEREIGNS

GAMBLE v. UNITED STATES

587 U.S. 678 (2019)

Supreme Court of the United States

In November 2015, local police in Mobile, Alabama, pulled Gamble over for a damaged headlight. Smelling marijuana, an officer searched Gamble's car, where he discovered a loaded handgun. Gamble had been convicted of second-degree robbery in the past, so his possession of the handgun violated Alabama law, which prohibited a convicted felon of possessing a firearm. Gamble pleaded guilty to the charge of violating Alabama's statute. Federal prosecutors then indicted Gamble for the same instance of firearm possession under federal law, which prohibits convicted felons from possessing any firearm.

Gamble moved to dismiss the federal charge, claiming that the federal indictment was for "the same offence" as what was at issue in the State of Alabama case and that he was exposed to double jeopardy. The federal district court denied Gamble's motion to dismiss. Gamble pleaded guilty to the federal offense but preserved his right to challenge the denial of his motion to dismiss on the grounds of double jeopardy. On appeal, the federal court of appeals affirmed. The Supreme Court granted *certiorari* to determine whether to overturn that doctrine.

Language of the Court. *Gamble argues the Double Jeopardy Clause forbids successive prosecutions by different sovereigns because of common-law. However, the language of the Clause protects individuals from being twice put in jeopardy "for the same offence," not for the same conducts or actions. The original understanding of "offence" was defined by a law, and each law is defined by a sovereign. As such, where there are two sovereigns, there are two laws, and two "offences."*

Past cases reflect the same understanding of the substantive differences between the interests that two sovereigns can have in punishing the same act. Gamble claims the Court's precedent contradicts common-law rights that the Double Jeopardy Clause was originally understood to protect. However, a departure from precedent requires special justification which Gamble lacks. The Court finds English cases and treatises to offer little support for Gamble's arguments.

Gamble contends that the recognition of the Double Jeopardy Clause's incorporation against the States breaks the theoretical foundation for the dual-sovereignty rule. However, this rule rests on the fact that only same-sovereign prosecutions can involve the "same offence." Incorporation meant that the States were now required to abide by this Court's interpretation of the Double Jeopardy Clause, which has long included the dual-sovereignty doctrine. Gamble further argues the increase of federal criminal laws has increased the risk of successive prosecutions under state and federal law for the same criminal conduct. However, this argument assumes that precedent was legal error from the start. Eliminating the dual-sovereignty rule would do little to trim the reach of federal criminal law, and it would not even prevent many successive state and federal prosecutions for the same criminal conduct unless we also overruled the long-settled rule that an "offence" for double jeopardy purposes is defined by statutory elements, not by what might be described in a looser sense as a unit of criminal conduct.

Decision. The Supreme Court affirmed the district court decision. It held that under the dual-sovereignty doctrine, the Double Jeopardy Clause does allow for successive prosecutions by separate sovereigns for the same offense.

Focus on Ethics

Does this decision make convictions under federal and state laws more likely to occur? Is this an ethical position to take relative to an accused person?

PRIVILEGE AGAINST SELF-INCRIMINATION. The Fifth Amendment also contains the privilege against self-incrimination, providing that no person "shall be compelled in any *criminal* case to be a witness against himself." This privilege grants individuals the right to remain silent in a criminal interrogation. Importantly, this *right does not extend to organizations, but only to natural persons.* If an individual is potentially subject to criminal charges because of disclosure of corporate documents, neither the corporation (nor the individual) can claim the privilege to prevent the government from accessing them.

The Fifth Amendment's protection against self-incrimination does not extend to nontestimonial evidence (such as fingerprints or bodily fluids). These may be obtained without violation of the Fifth Amendment.

***MIRANDA* WARNING.** In *Miranda v. Arizona*, 384 U.S. 436 (1966), the Supreme Court held that all persons subject to an arrest must be informed of their *right to remain silent* and their *right to an attorney*. The typical *Miranda* warning given is as follows:

> You have the right to remain silent. Anything you say may be used against you in a court of law. You have the right to consult an attorney before speaking to the police and to have an attorney present during questioning now or in the future. If you cannot afford an attorney, one will be appointed for you before any questioning if you wish. If you decide to answer questions now without an attorney present, you will still have the right to stop answering at any time until you talk to an attorney. Knowing and understanding your rights as I have explained them to you, are you willing to answer my questions without an attorney present?

If an individual is arrested (that is, taken into custody whereby their freedom of movement is restrained such as being handcuffed or put into a police car), and interrogated (asked questions designed to elicit an incriminating response), and is not informed of their *Miranda* rights, any part of the information gathered from the arrested person is barred from use at trial under the *Miranda* exclusionary rule. If, during police questioning, the arrested person does not affirmatively assert their desire for an attorney, the police are free to continue questioning. Passive statements by the individual arrested do not trigger the protection.

There are a few exceptions to the *Miranda* rule, such as the *public safety exception*. Under this exception, when the questioning was designed to limit an immediate threat to public safety, statements from arrested individuals made prior to *Miranda* warnings can be admissible, with limitations.

> **Example:** Jasmine Eskew was a 21-year-old new mother of a six-month-old daughter. When paramedics were called to Eskew's home, they found her baby unresponsive and to have suffered head trauma. Police arrested Eskew and advised her of her *Miranda* rights. During interrogation, the officers promised Eskew that the information was for her daughter's medical care, and she would see her daughter as soon as she confessed. Eskew confessed to shaking her child and was convicted for felony assault on a minor. The Supreme Court of Montana overturned her conviction because her confession was involuntary. *State v. Eskew*, 390 P.3d 129 (Mont. 2017)

Privileges Granted to Criminal Defendants

The Fifth Amendment has recognized a variety of privileges that a criminal defendant may claim to protect communications and prevent other individuals from being used as witnesses against the accused. Among them are the following:

- *Attorney-client privilege.* The attorney-client privilege is recognized by the Fifth Amendment and protects disclosures between the accused and their lawyer. This encourages the accused to tell the attorney the truth so the attorney can prepare a proper defense. This privilege is held by the client, and only the client may waive this privilege.
- *Spousal privilege and parent-child privilege.* Courts have given recognition to Fifth Amendment privileges to protect the family. However, a spouse or child may waive this privilege and testify against the accused.
- *Psychiatrist/psychologist-patient privilege.* This privilege is related to confidentiality in the medical profession and protects communication between patients and their mental health providers. This encourages the accused to tell the truth to seek help for their condition.
- *Clergy-penitent privilege.* The clergy-penitent privilege is an evidentiary rule that protects communications between members of the clergy and members of their congregation.

Sixth Amendment Rights

The Sixth Amendment also contains several important rights for criminal defendants, such as the right to a *speedy trial*, the right to a *public trial*, and the right to a *jury trial*, as well as the right to *confront adverse witnesses* and *obtain counsel* for the duration of the proceedings.

RIGHT TO TRIAL. The Sixth Amendment's *Speedy Trial Clause* protects criminal defendants from delay between their arrest and trial, as well as from convictions by biased jurors. The Clause provides that "the accused shall enjoy the right to a speedy and public trial, by an impartial jury of the state and district." The appropriate length of time constituting a speedy trial varies depending on the jurisdiction. Under federal law, most crimes must come to trial within 70 days of indictment. However, trials are often postponed with the defendant's consent.

A *public trial* is one where members of the public may come and observe the proceedings. The purpose of a public trial was to prevent corrupt courts from abusing their power during secret proceedings. However, in some high-profile cases, the court will limit public access to maintain courtroom order.

A *trial by jury* is guaranteed by the Sixth Amendment, but only for serious criminal offenses. Generally, the punishment for serious crimes amounts to at least one year of imprisonment, or a fine exceeding $1,000. However, in a *bench trial*, a criminal defendant can choose to waive this right and instead have only a judge determine the outcome.

CONFRONTATION CLAUSE. Criminal defendants also have a constitutional right under the Sixth Amendment to *confront* the witnesses against them. This right allows defendants to engage in an effective cross-examination of witnesses and allows the jury to reliably assess the truthfulness of the accusations.

RIGHT TO COUNSEL. All criminal defendants have the right to an attorney under the Sixth Amendment. In cases where a criminal defendant is unable to afford an attorney, one must be appointed by the government.

> **Example:** The Supreme Court found that the Sixth Amendment provides a constitutional guarantee to the defendant to choose the objective of their defense. The Court reasoned that even when the counsel's experience-based view was that confessing guilt would remove the possibility of the death penalty for the defendant, the lawyer must abide by the defendant's wishes to maintain his innocence in relation to the charged criminal acts. The lawyer must follow the defendant's wishes by seeking acquittal rather than conceding guilt. *McCoy v. Louisiana*, 584 U.S. 414 (2018)

Eighth Amendment Prohibitions

CRUEL AND UNUSUAL PUNISHMENT. Another constitutional protection for criminal defendants and convicted criminals is the prohibition on cruel and unusual punishment. The Supreme Court has defined *cruel and unusual punishment* as punishment so severe it is (1) degrading to human dignity, (2) arbitrary, (3) rejected by society, and (4) patently unnecessary.

> **Example:** The Maryland Court of Appeals has held that the Eighth Amendment's proscription against cruel and unusual punishments prohibits the imposition of the death penalty against a defendant who committed the offense as a

juvenile—that is, when the defendant was less than 18 years old. *Carter v. State*, 192 A.3d 695 (Md. 2018)

CAPITAL PUNISHMENT. Capital punishment, also known as the *death penalty*, remains a complex and controversial issue in many areas. Under current law, capital punishment does not violate the Eighth Amendment, but application of the death penalty must not violate evolving standards of decency. The court considers the same factors for evolving standards of decency as for cruel and unusual punishment.

Criminal Procedure

The process involved in a criminal prosecution differs in many respects from the process for civil lawsuits. The balance between protecting the public from harm and protecting criminal defendants' rights combined with other constitutional considerations influence this detailed procedure.

Arrest

To arrest an individual, courts must issue an arrest warrant to an officer. The legal standard officers must meet to obtain an arrest warrant is probable cause that the individual has committed, or is about to commit, a crime. An officer can also conduct an arrest without a warrant if the officer has probable cause to do so.

BOOKING. Once a party has been arrested, the arrest is processed through booking, usually at the police station. Booking involves recording the details of the arrest and includes photographing the arrestee, taking fingerprints, and noting other identifying information.

Indictment and Information

All parties who have been arrested must be formally charged with a crime before trial. There are two ways charges can be issued: either by a *grand jury* in the form of an *indictment*, or by a *prosecutor* in the form of an *information*.

Grand jury
A panel of individuals assigned the duty of investigating and issuing criminal charges (indictments).

Indictment
Formal criminal charges issued by a grand jury.

Information
A list of formal charges against the defendant and the factual basis for them. Begins a criminal proceeding.

Grand juries issue criminal **indictments**, and usually consist of between 16 and 23 people. The federal government is required to use grand juries for all felonies, though not misdemeanors, by the Fifth Amendment. Not all states require grand juries. Once empaneled, the grand jury is tasked with assessing the evidence offered by the government against the accused. If the grand jury believes there is probable cause to indict the accused, it will issue a formal indictment.

In the majority of state criminal proceedings, and primarily for less serious crimes, a prosecutor can bring an **information** to the court if the prosecutor believes there is sufficient evidence to support the charge. An information is a formal charging document that describes the criminal charges against a person and the factual basis for those charges. Unlike an indictment, an information does not require the vote of a grand jury. The information is presented to a judicial officer, usually a magistrate judge, who reviews the information and decides if there is probable cause that a crime occurred.

Arraignment

After the defendant is formally charged, they must be *arraigned.* An **arraignment** is a proceeding in front of a judge in which defendants are informed of the charges being issued and of their right to counsel and are asked to enter a plea. Defendants can enter a plea of *guilty* or *not guilty* to each of the charges.

Arraignment
A proceeding in front of a judge in which the defendant is informed of the charges issued against them.

BAIL. The judge will consider the charges, the plea, and the defendant's status before setting a bail amount. A defendant posts bail by depositing cash or bonds of a set amount with the court to be released from jail until the trial date. The bail is forfeited if the defendant fails to appear. A judge can decline to set bail and jail the defendant until the conclusion of the trial. This is most common for defendants who are considered flight risks or who face serious charges.

NOLO CONTENDERE. A defendant may enter a plea of *nolo contendere*—that is, the defendant agrees to the punishment but does not admit guilt. This is distinguishable from a *guilty plea* in that a *nolo contendere* plea cannot be used against the defendant in a subsequent civil action against the accused. When the *nolo contendere* plea is entered, the government has the option of accepting it or requiring the defendant to either plead guilty or not guilty.

PLEA BARGAIN. A defendant, with assistance from their attorney, may agree to a *plea bargain* with the prosecutor. A plea bargain can be agreed to at any point pretrial or during trial but is often first discussed after the arraignment. A plea bargain often results in the defendant pleading guilty to a lesser charge. The government benefits from the plea bargain by reducing its overall enforcement costs and ensuring a conviction. The accused may agree to a plea bargain to avoid the risk of greater penalty if found guilty at trial.

Trial

The Sixth Amendment requires those charged with serious offenses to be afforded a jury trial unless the defendant waives it. A serious offense is one that carries a potential sentence of a term of more than six months' imprisonment. Procedurally, once a jury is empaneled, the prosecution will present all its evidence. In a criminal trial, the burden of proof lies with the government. If the government fails to establish any element of the crime, the defendant can be found not guilty without presenting a defense.

Recall that to find a defendant guilty, the jury must conclude unanimously that the defendant was guilty of the charges *beyond a reasonable doubt.* Alternatively, the jury could acquit the defendant of the charges. If the jury cannot agree on a unanimous verdict, the defendant is not convicted—a situation known as a hung jury. The government may choose to retry the case with a new jury. The Double Jeopardy Clause does not bar retrial following a hung jury.

> **Example:** The Supreme Court has held that the Sixth Amendment's right to trial by jury requires a unanimous jury verdict to convict a defendant of a serious offense. *Ramos v. Louisiana*, 590 U.S. 83 (2020)

Sentencing

During sentencing, a judge will issue a punishment to the convicted individual. Sentences can include death, imprisonment, fines, probation, community service, and mandatory drug and alcohol rehabilitation. Often, judges are required to follow sentencing guidelines adopted by either the state or federal systems in which they serve.

Appeal

If the defendant is found guilty of a crime, or believes the sentence was too harsh, they may file an appeal. If the defendant is found not guilty, no appeal may be filed by either party.

Concept Summary
Criminal Procedure

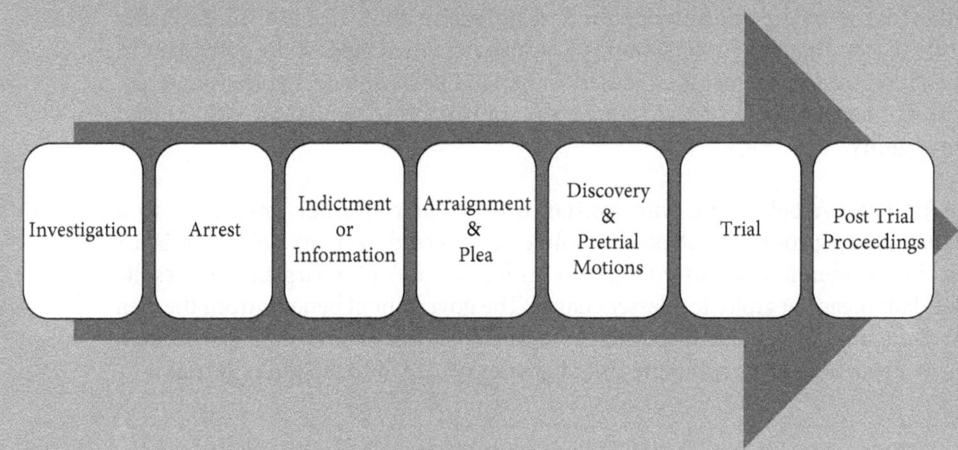

AI Feature: Draft a Deferred Prosecution Agreement

Using an internet search engine, research prior deferred prosecution agreements involving corporate fraud. Consider the United States Department of Justice guidelines on the prosecution of business organizations. What are plea agreements for corporate wrongdoers and how do they relate to a deferred prosecution agreement? Employ an AI program to provide the outline of a deferred prosecution agreement. Use the facts, terms, and conditions in the actual the actual Boeing 737 Max aircraft case as a guide to create a similar one involving a hospital chain that has pled guilty to fraud for overbilling Medicare for procedures never rendered. Would there be a need for a monitor of the hospital chain's remediation efforts? What would be the consequences if the fraud were to continue unabated? What corporate personnel could be charged as well?

Key Terms

- Accessory, 180
- *Actus reus*, 180
- Affirmative defense, 193
- Arraignment, 203
- Arson, 184
- Beyond a reasonable doubt, 178
- Bribery, 186
- Burden of proof, 178
- Burglary, 184
- Business crimes, 185
- Conspiracy, 188
- Cybercrime, 191
- Double jeopardy, 197
- Duress, 195
- Embezzlement, 185
- Entrapment, 195
- Exclusionary rule, 197
- Extortion, 189
- Forgery, 185
- General intent, 181
- Grand jury, 202
- Immunity from prosecution, 196
- Indictment, 202
- Information, 202
- Insider trading, 188
- Justification, 194
- Kickback, 186
- Larceny, 183
- Mail and wire fraud, 186
- *Mens rea*, 181
- Mistake of fact, 194
- Money laundering, 193
- Obtaining goods by false pretenses, 184
- Organized crime, 192
- Penal code, 182
- Receiving stolen property, 184
- Robbery, 183
- Self-defense, 194
- Specific intent, 181
- Statutes of limitations (criminal), 196

Applying the Law

8.1 Extortion. The general counsel for the employee pension fund of the State of New York recommended against investing in a fund managed by FA Technology Ventures. Thereafter, the lawyer received anonymous emails demanding that he recommend the investment and threatening, if he did not, to expose his extramarital affair to his wife, government officials, and the media. Some of the emails were traced to Mr. Sekhar, a managing partner of the fund manager. He was convicted of attempted extortion. In his defense, Mr. Sekhar argued that extortion required the obtaining of *property* of another, and that a *recommendation* is not property. Do the facts support a finding of extortion? Why or why not? *Sekhar v. United States*, 570 U.S. 729 (2013)

8.2 Embezzlement. Eugene Selivanov and Tatyana Berkovich founded a charter school. The school district that issued the charter conducted a random audit of the school's finances. The audit showed several irregularities, which prompted further investigation. Large sums of money were spent at bowling alleys and restaurants for "teacher appreciation" events and on charging meals for "business meetings" that occurred late at night and on weekend afternoons. Would these facts be enough to convict Selivanov and Berkovich of embezzlement of public funds? What if they asserted that they had the mistaken belief that they had the right to spend funds in this manner? *People v. Selivanov*, 5 Cal. App. 5th 726 (2016)

8.3 When Does Authority Become Theft? Dennis Kozlowski was the CEO of Tyco, a multi-billion-dollar company. While he was CEO, he received millions in salary and bonuses. He used corporate funds to purchase items such as paintings and paid $2 million for his wife's birthday party. Mr. Kozlowski was accused of theft of approximately $150 million in his role as CEO. In his defense, he asserted that he had authority to spend up to $200 million without approval of the board of directors and that the expenditures were appropriate. The prosecution argued that he engaged in grand larceny and exceeded his authority. Did he take property from Tyco with the intent to deprive it of its property? *People v. Kozlowski*, 47 A.D.3d 111 (N.Y. App. Div. 2007)

8.4 False Credit Application. Thomas Everrette applied for a collateralized loan from Weyco Community Credit Union. As part of the loan application, he completed a verification of employment form, his home address and telephone number. He listed Bail American Surety, LLC as his employer. When the credit union loan for the purchase of a motorcycle and a credit card issued by the credit union went into default, the loan officer discovered that Everrette was not employed by Bail American Surety. What criminal charges could be filed against Everrette? *State v. Everrette*, 807 S.E.2d 168 (N.C. Ct. App. 2017)

8.5 Conspiracy. Chinasa and Chambliss used Cisco's warranty program to obtain replacement parts for the purpose of reselling them. They obtained replacement parts by exchanging them for nonconforming parts they sent to Cisco. Suppose you are charging Chinasa with conspiracy. What facts (evidence) would you need to produce to prove he committed a conspiracy? *United States v. Chinasa*, 789 F. Supp. 2d 691 (E.D. Va. 2011)

8.6 Criminal Liability of Officers. Kennie Childers was the president of Olde Fern, Inc., which operated a coal mine and preparation plant. After meeting with a compliance officer for the West Virginia Department of Labor, Childers was informed that the company would be required to post a wage bond to comply with the law or cease operations. Childers did not do so, although he received several cease-and-desist orders from the state to stop the coal mine operations. Childers was indicted for failure to secure the wage bond. Childers argued that he should not have been indicted because the liability rested with the corporation. Was he criminally liable if he caused the corporation to violate the law? *State v. Childers*, 415 S.E.2d 460 (W. Va. 1992)

8.7 Corporate Criminal Liability. Mary McGahagin suffered brain damage from a surgery and sued the hospital and the doctors and nurses involved in the surgery. During the malpractice trial, the nurse anesthetist and surgeon testified that McGahagin had suffered a slowed heart rate for approximately three to five minutes during the surgery. Later, the nurse anesthetist testified that McGahagin had a slowed heart rate for over ten minutes. The nurse stated that false testimony had been given in the first trial at the direction of his lawyer and an employee of the malpractice insurance carrier. Based on this testimony, the state indicted the nurse anesthetist and St. Paul, the hospital's insurance carrier, for perjury. St. Paul asserted that a corporation could not be charged with perjury because Alabama law did not expressly provide that a corporation could be found guilty of perjury. The indictment against the carrier was dismissed. What arguments can be made for and against this result? *State v. St. Paul Fire & Marine Ins. Co.*, 835 So. 2d 230 (Ala. Crim. App. 2000)

8.8 Cell Phone Searches. Kanton Thomas was arrested for possession of a small amount of marijuana. After his arrest, police officers searched Thomas's cell phone without his permission. The officers saw pictures of Thomas holding firearms, cash, and drugs. The officers used the information from those pictures to obtain a search warrant for the contents of the phone. The pictures were then used for an additional charge of illegal possession of firearms after a former felony conviction. Was the act of examining the phone a lawful search? Make arguments for and against such a finding. *State v. Thomas*, 334 P.3d 941 (Okla. Crim. App. 2014)

8.9 Reasonable Expectation of Privacy. The police in Kent County, Michigan, had an arrest warrant for Mr. Riley for armed robbery. While a fugitive from police, the police tracked Riley's movement through the GPS coordinates of his cell phone. After seven hours of continuous tracking, they apprehended him at a motel and found a gun in his possession. He was charged with multiple crimes. Riley moved to suppress the gun possession evidence because of an unlawful search in violation of the Fourth Amendment. The prosecution argued that there was no reasonable expectation of privacy in tracking public movements, and because of that there was no search within the meaning of the Amendment. When a fugitive subject to an arrest warrant for armed robbery hides in a motel, may the government track his cell phone's GPS coordinates to locate and arrest him? *United States v. Riley*, 858 F.3d 1012 (6th Cir. 2017)

8.10 Privilege. The IRS was investigating a taxpayer for potential tax law violations. The IRS sought the appearance of the taxpayer's accountant to provide testimony and to produce records for examination relating to the taxpayer personally and to two corporate entities owned by the taxpayer and his father-in-law. The accountant asserted his Fifth Amendment privilege against self-incrimination. Is the accountant able to assert this privilege, or is it unavailable to him? Why would he want to assert this privilege? *United States v. Marra*, 2005 U.S. Dist. LEXIS 23411 (2005)

PART II: CONTRACT LAW FUNDAMENTALS

Nature and Formation of Contracts

9

When a law is in its nature a contract, when absolute rights have vested under that contract, a repeal of the law cannot divest those rights. — John Marshall, Founding Father and Fourth Chief Justice of the United States (1755-1835)

Chapter Outline

- Introduction
- Requirements of a Valid Contract
- Classification of Contracts
  - *Management Application: Unilateral and Bilateral Contracts: What is the Significance?*

Case 9.1: *Boswell v. Panera Bread Co.*
Case 9.2: *Hickey v. University of Pittsburgh*

- Agreement
- The Offer
  - *Management Application: Making a Clear Offer*
- Acceptance of the Offer
- AI Feature: Enforcing a Contract

Learning Objectives

After studying this chapter, you should be able to:

1. Identify the elements of a contract.
2. Describe what is needed for mutual consent.
3. Explain what is needed for an effective offer.
4. Recognize how an offer may be accepted.
5. Explain how offers may terminate.

Introduction

A **contract** is a legally enforceable agreement. Although a contract often refers to a written agreement, a writing need not be a physical paper copy. Today, many enforceable contracts are made online. A contract may be made through oral or written promises stated expressly or implied through actions or conduct.

Contract
A legally enforceable agreement.

In this part of the text, the general rules of contract formation are introduced. References to "party" or "person" may include not only individuals but also businesses and governmental entities. The nature of contract law is best understood within its historical rules, legal theories, public policies, and the legal processes in which the laws are applied. When an organization enters into a contract, it does so through an authorized agent. The subject of our discussion in Chapter 15 will concern the law of agency, where the rules pertaining to the liability of a principal for contracts entered into by its agent will be discussed.

Sources of Contract Law

The law of contract is based upon a combination of judge-created law (case law) and statutory law. Lower courts in the same jurisdiction are bound to the decisions of their corresponding appellate courts under the principal of *stare decisis*, a concept presented in Chapter 1.

American contract law could become overly complicated to enforce due to the interplay of laws and regulations at the state, municipal, and federal levels, as well as court decisions across various jurisdictions, across all 50 states. Businesses would not be able to predict how a contract might be enforced in another state. As a result, when considering contract law, although each state is independent of each other, the legislatures and court systems try to develop common legal principles to ensure uniformity and promote predictability of the law. This is particularly true in commercial law, the subject of our study in Chapters 26 through 33.

The National Conference of Commissioners on Uniform State Laws (NCCUSL) is another source when it comes to proposing adoption of uniform laws by the state legislatures. Experts in specialized fields of law, those in government, and those in the legal industry are engaged to draft and reach a common proposal on a subject for adoption by the states. The goal of these proposals is to promote uniform treatment of a subject throughout the United States. One example that seeks to promote uniformity is the Uniform Commercial Code (UCC). The UCC has been adopted in 49 states and partially in the State of Louisiana. The UCC covers a variety of commercially related subjects, such as: contracts between merchants, negotiable instruments, bank collection procedures, letters of credit, documents of title, investment securities, and secured transactions. Although the UCC contained a fairly complete set of rules when it was proposed for its adoption by states, different states have modified the proposed law once adopted by their legislatures or have varied interpretations of the rules as a result of state court decisions interpreting the UCC. Where the UCC is silent, courts turn to the common law to fill in the gaps.

The American Law Institute (ALI) is a group of recognized experts in the law. The ALI consists of experienced lawyers, judges, and academics who study developing legal issues, produce reports, and propose Restatements of Law for consideration by legislatures and courts. A Restatement of Law is mentioned often in our study of business law. For example, it was discussed in our review of the law of products liability. A Restatement of Law is a proposal for consideration and guidance to legislatures and courts. Restatements will present a legal concept for general adoption or application throughout the United States. They often will state new developments in the law and provide related legal and public policy arguments. They allow for the continual development of legal theory as it is actually applied in state statutes and court decisions.

Finally, Congress and state legislatures have adopted statutes requiring some contracts to follow certain statutory requirements. Most often, these statutes are consumer protection statutes, such as statutes that require the full disclosure of the cost of financing consumer goods or real estate. If a statute does not require a specific form of the contract, common law will apply. In most business applications, the common law of contracts will be used.

Requirements of a Valid Contract

The four essentials of a contract are:

1. *Agreement.* A contract requires mutual agreement between the parties. Mutual agreement requires an offer by one party and an acceptance by the party who received the offer.
2. *Consideration.* Any promise must be supported by lawful bargained-for consideration. Consideration requires both parties to exchange something of legal value, such as money, property, services, or the forbearance of a legal right.
3. *Capacity.* Both parties to the contract must have contractual capacity to enter into a contract. The law recognizes certain persons as lacking contractual capacity.
4. *Legality of the subject matter.* The purpose of the contract must be lawful and comply with legal requirements.

TABLE 9.1: Introduction to Contract Formation

<table>
<tr><th colspan="2">Contract Formation</th></tr>
<tr><th colspan="2">Agreement</th></tr>
<tr><th>Offer</th><th>Acceptance</th></tr>
<tr><td>Check for:
▪ An express intent to make a contract;
▪ Definite terms; and
▪ Communication of the offer to the offeree</td><td>Be certain there has not been a:
▪ Revocation;
▪ Rejection;
▪ Counteroffer; or
▪ Termination by operation of law</td></tr>
<tr><th>Consideration</th><th>Capacity</th></tr>
<tr><td>There must be:
▪ Legal value and
▪ Bargained-for exchange
Check for:
▪ Gift promises;
▪ Illusory promises;
▪ Preexisting duties; and
▪ Past consideration</td><td>Be sure the parties are:
▪ 18 or older and
▪ Competent</td></tr>
<tr><th colspan="2">Legality</th></tr>
<tr><td colspan="2">Check for contracts that:
▪ Violate statutes and
▪ Violate public policy</td></tr>
</table>

Classification of Contracts

Contracts may be classified in several ways, notably the forms discussed below.

Bilateral and Unilateral Contracts

Bilateral contract
A contract where both the offeror and offeree exchange promises.

Contracts are classified as either bilateral or unilateral based upon the type of performance required of the offeree to accept the offer. A **bilateral contract** arises when the offeree may accept by promising to perform. In a bilateral contract, *both* the offeror and the offeree make *promises* to each other—that is, a "promise for a promise." If all other requirements of contract formation are met, a contract is formed upon the mutual exchange of promises.

Example: Rafael offers to sell his laptop for $100 to Xavier, who orally accepts Rafael's offer. Rafael and Xavier have formed a bilateral contract with the mutual exchange of promises (Rafael promised to sell his laptop for $100 and Xavier promised to pay the $100).

Unilateral contract
A contract where the offeree must perform an act to create a contract.

In contrast, a **unilateral contract** arises when an offer expressly requires performance as the only means for accepting the offer; therefore, unilateral contracts are a promise for the performance of an act. A unilateral contract is formed upon the completion of the act. Unilateral contracts are not as common as bilateral contracts and often arise in the following circumstances: (1) where the offeror expressly requires performance as the only means of acceptance, (2) rewards, and (3) contests or prize situations.

Example: If a dog goes missing and the dog owner puts up lost dog posters promising $500 for the safe return of their beloved dog, this is a unilateral contract because people can only accept the offer by completing the act; performance is not promised nor required.

Difficulties may arise when an offeree begins to perform the required act and then the offeror tries to revoke their offer before the offeree is able to complete the required act. Today, the offer cannot be revoked once performance has started, if the performance is substantial (a clear commitment to completing the performance required by the offer).

Example: Olivia tells Jesse she will pay him $7,500 if he will paint her house by Saturday. Jesse begins to immediately paint the house. Normally Olivia is prohibited from revoking the offer. Jesse may complete the painting by Saturday and is entitled to the $7,500.

Management Application Unilateral and Bilateral Contracts: What Is the Significance?

A unilateral contract is not formed until the offeree performs the requested act. It may not be enforced until the offeree communicates acceptance through their performance. A bilateral contract may be enforced if the offeree does not perform.

Why is this difference significant in the operation of a business? The answer lies in how the offer is framed. If someone is obligated to purchase and pay for goods in a bilateral contract, the contract is enforceable. However, if the offer is framed as a unilateral contract, the offeror can revoke or cancel their offer to contract prior to the offeree's performance. What tactical advantage might a unilateral contract bring to the offeror business owner? Why should an offeree of a unilateral offer confirm acceptance to the offeror?

In the following case, the federal court applied the law of Missouri, the state where the lawsuit was filed, to determine if the employer could revoke a unilateral compensation offer.

CASE 9.1

UNILATERAL CONTRACTS ARE NOT REVOCABLE ONCE PERFORMANCE HAS BEGUN OR HAS BEEN SUBSTANTIALLY PERFORMED

BOSWELL v. PANERA BREAD CO.

879 F.3d 296 (2018)

United States Court of Appeals for the Eighth Circuit

To recruit and retain general managers for its restaurants, Panera created a program under which qualifying managers were eligible to receive a relatively large one-time bonus. The amount of the bonus depended heavily on the profitability of the manager's restaurant over the final two years of the five-year period. Panera decided in 2010 that it would set a $100,000 cap on the amount of the bonus, to be effective starting January of 2012.

Boswell and two other managers sued Panera for breach of contract on behalf of themselves and a class of similarly situated managers, maintaining that Panera had violated the agreements by imposing the cap. Panera responded that the parties had orally terminated and replaced—or, in legal parlance, novated—the agreement because the managers, by their words and actions, assented to a new agreement containing the cap. Panera also asserted that the managers had waived any claims they had regarding the cap by continuing to work without complaint or were estopped from raising any claims about it because it was too late. It argued as well that an economic downturn allowed it to impose the cap because the purpose of the contract had been commercially frustrated. The federal district court granted summary judgment to the at-will employees, allowing them to enforce the employer's promise to pay them a bonus. Panera appealed the judgment.

Language of the Court. *As the district court correctly pointed out, an employer's promise to pay a bonus in return for an at-will employee's continued employment is an offer for a unilateral contract. An offeror in a unilateral contract receives performance, rather than a promise, as consideration in return for the offeror's promise.*

The question that arises at this point is whether Panera could modify or terminate the terms of its offer to pay the one-time bonus by imposing a cap on it. Generally, an offeror can withdraw an offer at any time before the offeree accepts it. But the Missouri Court of Appeals has said several times that a party may not revoke an offer to make a unilateral contract after the offeree has substantially performed it because the offeree, at that point, has supplied consideration to make the contract enforceable against the offeror to the extent it has been performed, Panera takes issue with the district court's conclusion that all the managers in the class had substantially performed under the offer as a matter of law so as to render the offer irrevocable.

We do not think, though, that the Supreme Court of Missouri, if confronted with the issue, would conclude that the offeree of a unilateral-contract offer must render a substantial part of the requested performance to make the offer irrevocable. We think it would conclude instead that an offeree must merely begin performance, and since each of the managers in the class here had at least begun performing under the offer, we conclude that Panera could not modify the offer terms as to any manager.

We reject Panera's contention that it reserved the power to modify or terminate its bonus offer before the managers began performing in accordance with that offer. We disagree with Panera that, under unilateral contract principles, a court would have to determine on a case-by-case basis whether each manager had worked enough to render the offer irrevocable. By working for more than a year in accordance with the unilateral contract offer, each class member had necessarily begun performance, so no individual analysis is needed.

Decision. The court held that the managers at Panera Bread were found to have begun performance before Panera implemented the $100,000 bonus cap. Therefore, the bonus cap was unenforceable because Panera cannot revoke its offer.

Focus on Ethics

In considering whether this decision was fair, consider Panera's commercial frustration defense, a defense available if the happening of an event not foreseen by the parties and not caused by or under the control of a party destroys or nearly destroys either the value of the performance or the object or purpose of the contract. If the event is foreseeable, though, the parties should provide for its occurrence in the contract, and when they do not, the risk falls on the promisor. Panera imposed the cap essentially because a change in general business conditions made the bonus payments too expensive. Indeed, everyone knows that business is risky and markets are undependable. Panera could have accounted for lower-than-anticipated profits when it devised the program and changed the formula for the bonus program, but it did not. So, it bears the risk of changing market conditions.

Executed and Executory Contracts

Contracts can be classified as executory or executed. An **executory contract** means that one or more parties has an obligation remaining to be performed to fulfill the terms of the contract. An **executed contract** is one that has been fully performed by all parties to the contract.

Executory contract A contract in which one or more parties have obligations to perform.

Executed contract A contract that has been fully performed by both parties.

Example: A car dealership offers generous warranty plans for the cars sold to their customers. Until the warranty expires, these warranty plans remain executory contracts because the dealership's obligations are continuing. *McCarty v. E.J. Korvette, Inc.*, 347 A.2d 253 (Md. Ct. Spec. App. 1975)

Formal and Informal Contracts

Contracts may be classified as either formal or informal. **Formal contracts** require a special format or method of creation to be enforceable. Examples of formal contracts include negotiable instruments, such as checks and promissory notes, which are discussed in Chapter 29, and letters of credit, which are discussed in Chapter 30.

Formal contract A contract requiring a special format or method of creation to be enforceable.

Contracts not requiring a special form or method of creation to be enforceable are known as **informal contracts** (or simple contracts). The majority of contracts formed are informal contracts.

Informal contract (simple contract) A contract not requiring a special form or method of creation to be enforceable.

Express and Implied Contracts

Whether by words, actions, or a combination thereof, the parties to a contract form an agreement by consenting to the same terms at the same time. An **express contract** is created if the agreement is stated by words, either oral or written. If the agreement is established by conduct, rather than by words, the result is an **implied-in-fact contract**. It is the conduct of the parties that creates the implied-in-fact contract. In determining a dispute, the trier of fact will ask: "Would a reasonable person, aware of the circumstances, including the words and actions of the parties, find that a contract was created?"

Express contract A contract clearly stated in written or spoken words or partly oral and partly written.

Implied-in-fact contract A contract manifested by conduct, rather than words.

Example: While at an auction, a prospective purchaser raises her paddle to bid on an item for sale. During the auction for the item, she continues to bid and secures the highest bid for that item when the auction ends. Her conduct of raising her paddle is an objective manifestation that she is agreeing to be bound to the bid price. Her conduct creates an implied-in-fact contract.

Implied-in-law contract (quasi-contract) A contract created to avoid unjust enrichment of one party at the expense of the other.

Both express and implied-in-fact contracts are contracts that exhibit some form of mutual assent to be bound by the parties' agreement. In contrast, an **implied-in-law contract** is a legal fiction. Also known as a **quasi-contract**, it is not an actual contract. Rather, a contractual duty between the parties is created by operation of law. A court implies the existence of a contract to avoid one party unfairly benefiting at the expense of the other party. Otherwise, one party would be unjustly enriched at the expense of the other party. Ultimately, it is the court's attempt to make an exchange fair between two parties when agreement is lacking but performance has been rendered.

Implied-in-law contracts arise where (1) a benefit has been conferred to another party; (2) the benefit was conferred with the reasonable expectation of compensation (that is, the party receiving the benefit knew or should have known that it was not done as a gift); and (3) it would be unjust if the person providing the benefit was not compensated.

> **Example:** Even without an express contract, an implied contract can be created as a result of the parties' actions. "The difference between an express contract and an implied contract is that in the former the parties arrive at an agreement by words, either oral or written, while in the latter the agreement is arrived at by a consideration of their acts and conduct." *Johnson v. Amerbank, LLC (In re Miles)*, 652 B.R. 512 (2023)

This rule implies a promise of one party to pay the reasonable value of what was received. The measure of recovery is often referred to in its Latin form of *quantum meruit* (Latin for "the reasonable value of what one merits").

> **Example:** An attorney failed to secure the client's consent to a written contingency fee agreement before rendering services on behalf of the client as required by state law. The attorney was not permitted to recover under an oral contract but was granted *quantum meruit* for the reasonable worth of legal services provided. *Mullens v. Hansel-Henderson*, 65 P.3d 992 (Colo. 2002)

A party receiving a benefit is not always responsible for paying the reasonable value of what they received. If a party confers the benefit on someone else unnecessarily or because of misconduct or negligence, they are not entitled to recovery under an implied-in-law contract. It would not be unjust to require the person who received the benefit to pay in those situations. For example, if the person receiving the benefit was unaware of the actions of the other party during that party's performance, they may not be responsible.

> **Example:** Aggravated that his neighbor has an unkempt-looking front yard, Harvey spent many hours performing gardening work at his neighbor's home while the neighbor was at work. Feeling entitled to payment of a reasonable sum for his services, Harvey demanded payment from his neighbor. Harvey is not entitled to such payment because Harvey conferred those services unnecessarily and the neighbor was unaware of the rendering of the services until after they were completed.

For use in exceptional situations, some states have adopted a rule permitting a mistaken improver of real estate to recover in *quantum meruit* for the improvement of land owned by another. Known as a good faith improver, the person acts under an erroneous belief, because of a mistake of law or fact, that he is the owner of the land. For example, someone may build a permanent improvement, such as a wall, on real property in the honest but erroneous belief that he is the owner of the land. In such cases, the court may award compensation to the improver

The following case illustrates how conduct may manifest the intention to agree to an implied-in-fact contract.

CASE 9.2

SURROUNDING CIRCUMSTANCES MAY DEMONSTRATE AN IMPLIED-IN-FACT CONTRACT

HICKEY v. UNIVERSITY OF PITTSBURGH

81 F.4th 301 (2023)

United States Court of Appeals for the Third Circuit

The University of Pittsburgh (Pitt) and Temple University, situated in Pittsburgh and Philadelphia respectively, responded to the COVID-19 pandemic by closing their campuses the day the World Health Organization declared COVID-19 a global pandemic. Classes were moved online, on-campus events were canceled, and students were advised not to return to campus housing. Despite these changes, both universities maintained their tuition and fees at existing levels, prompting students to file lawsuits alleging breach of contract or unjust enrichment. The students argued that they paid for a high-quality educational experience and campus facilities, which they did not receive due to the shift to online learning.

They sought prorated refunds for the difference in value between in-person and online instruction, as well as disgorgement of any profits retained by the universities. Additionally, Pitt students requested reimbursement for unused housing and dining fees for those who did not receive prorated refunds. Two district courts considered the Financial Responsibility Agreement (FRA) that students were required to sign upon enrollment.

Pitt's FRA stated: "I understand that when I register for any class at the University of Pittsburgh, or receive any service from the University of Pittsburgh, I accept full responsibility to pay all tuition, fees and other associated costs assessed as a result of my registration and/or receipt of services,"

Temple's FRA stated: "[B]y registering for classes at Temple University, I agree to pay all assessed tuition and fees that result from my initial registration and/or future drop/add activity. I understand that I am responsible to pay for all classes in which I am registered after the final day of the term's drop/add period."

The district courts dismissed the students' claims based on these FRAs. The two cases were consolidated when the students appealed the dismissals.

Language of the Court. *The Universities closed campus buildings, canceled all on-campus student events, announced that classes would be conducted online for the remainder of the semester, and urged students not to return to campus housing. Neither university offered any reduction in tuition or mandatory fees. Temple issued pro-rata housing and dining refunds for all students, while Pitt did so only for students who moved out by a certain date. The students argued that an implied contract existed through the Universities websites, academic catalogs, student handbooks, marketing materials and other circulars, bulletins, and publications," which described the benefits of campus life. As additional evidence of this implied promise, they pointed to the Universities' pre-pandemic practices of holding in-person classes and the reduced pricing for online courses.*

By way of remedy, the Students sought pro-rated tuition and fees reflecting the difference in value between what they purportedly bargained and paid for—in-person classes and services—and what they received—a fully remote experience. They sought disgorgement of any profits that the Universities retained by moving online. The Pitt Students (only) also sought reimbursement for unused housing and dining fees for those who did not move out by the deadline and thus did not receive prorated refunds.

Pennsylvania law permits implied-in-fact contracts that may arise from "surrounding circumstances." And here, the Students' Complaints highlight three university practices that could plausibly support an implied-in-fact contract: (1) the Universities' publications touting the benefits of the "on-campus experience"; (2) their longstanding pre-pandemic tradition of in-person education; and (3) the separate marketing and pricing of online and in-person programs. This history, custom, and course of dealing, along with the school's statements, plausibly created an implied promise of in-person classes. Recognizing the university's "historic practice" of on-campus education as supporting plausible allegation of implied contract for in-person instruction.

In sum, the Students have adequately pleaded their implied contract claims as to tuition in exchange for in-person education, Pitt's mandatory fees, and Temple's University Services fee—but not as to Pitt's housing and dining fees. For the foregoing reasons, we will affirm the dismissal of the Pitt Students' housing and dining fee claims [because the students did not allege that they had paid Pitt such fees], reverse the dismissal of all other claims, and remand for further proceedings.

Decision. The court of appeals held that the students sufficiently pleaded their implied contract claims with regard to tuition in exchange for in-person education amidst the COVID-19 global pandemic.

Focus on Ethics

In considering whether this decision was fair, note that the students argued that several university publications were replete with references to in-person, on-campus instruction, as well as to the "campus experience." The universities responded that these representations were only "generalized, aspirational statements." Moreover, the universities argued that "[n]o objective methodology could reasonably calculate the difference in value between in-person and online instruction" and inherently speculative damages are not recognized under Pennsylvania law. The appellate court disagreed with these arguments. Thus, what is a fair methodology to use in remedying these alleged wrongs?

Concept Summary Classifications of Contracts

Performance Required by the Offeree	• Unilateral: Offer requires performance of an act to create a contract. • Bilateral: Both parties exchange promises to create a contract.
Obligations by Parties	• Executory: One or more parties have obligations to perform the contract. • Executed: The contract has been fully performed by both the parties.
Formalities Required for Enforcement	• Formal: To be enforceable, contract requires a special method of creation. • Informal: The contract does not require a special format of creation to be enforceable.
Words of Agreement	• Express: Contract clearly states the agreement in written or spoken words. • Implied-in-fact: The parties' conduct creates a contract.

Valid, Void, Voidable, and Unenforceable Contracts

Contracts can also be classified by their enforceability. The terms we use are valid and unenforceable contracts, and void and voidable contracts.

Valid contract (enforceable contract)
A contract that is legally enforceable.

A **valid contract** (also known as an enforceable contract) is an agreement that is legally enforceable because it contains all the elements necessary to create a contract.

Void contract
A contract that has no validity. Unenforceable by either party.

A contradiction in terms, a **void contract** has no legal validity and cannot be enforced by either party. The performance of the contract violates public policy. Examples of void contracts include contracts in violation of the law, such as agreements that restrain trade, create monopolies, or require the commission of a crime.

Voidable contract A contract that may be affirmed or rejected by one of the parties.

A **voidable contract** is one that one party may, at their option, either enforce or not enforce. If the contract is voided, both parties are released from liability under the contract. If the party with the option decides to ratify (make valid) the contract, both parties must perform the contract. Examples of voidable contracts include contracts made by minors and contracts made under extreme duress.

Unenforceable contract A contract that will not be enforced by the courts but may be voluntarily performed by the parties.

An **unenforceable contract** is an otherwise valid contract that cannot be enforced because there is a legal defense to its enforcement. The difference between an unenforceable contract and a void contract is that the unenforceable contract may be converted into an enforceable contract by the act of one of the parties, while a void contract may not. If the parties perform an unenforceable contract, it will be valid, but a court will not compel them to perform it if they do not.

> **Example:** An oral agreement for the sale of real property is unenforceable until it is reduced to a writing and executed (signed) by the parties.

FIGURE 9.1: Distinguishing Void and Valid Contracts

Agreement

A contract begins with the free, mutual consent of the parties communicated by each party to the other. Consent means agreement to the terms made by one party ("the offeror" or "promisor") to the other party (the "offeree" or "promisee"). The consent between the offeror and offeree to the terms of their agreement is known as a *meeting of the minds*.

The Offer

The **offer** empowers the offeree to bring the contract into existence by accepting the promise. A contract offer arises from the words or conduct of the offeree. The offer embodies a promise to complete or refrain from doing an act. If the offeree rejects the offer, either through express statements or by conduct such as not accepting the offer within the required time, the offer lapses and a contract does not come into existence.

Offer
An expression of intent to enter into a binding and enforceable contract that may be oral, written, or arising from a party's conduct.

Every offer that forms the basis of a contract must contain the following elements in order to constitute an effective offer:

1. An express or clear intent (desire) to make an enforceable agreement.
2. Sufficiently definite terms so that the content of the offer is understood.
3. The offer must be communicated to the offeree. It may or may not state how and by what time the acceptance is to be communicated to the offeror.

Intent

Since courts are not mind readers, an objective theory of contracts is applied to determine whether the parties intended to enter a contract. Subjective intentions are irrelevant. Courts consider the parties' intentions by determining what a reasonable person in the position of the other party would have thought was intended by the first party based on the first party's words or actions and the circumstances surrounding the agreement. This is known as the **objective theory of contracts**.

Objective theory of contracts
Determining a party's intention to enter into a contract or the meaning of a term by what a reasonable person in the position of the other party would conclude from the first party's objective manifestations (displays of intent).

Business transactions are normally presumed to be enforceable. This presumption decreases the cost of doing business, as it would be costly for business owners to allocate time and resources to determine the other party's intention to enter into a contract.

When applying the objective theory of contracts to determine intent, the law finds a lack of intent to enter into an agreement in the following circumstances:

SECRET INTENTIONS. A court does not consider the unexpressed, secret intentions of a party when determining the intent to enter into a contract. If one party manifests to the other that they intend to be bound by the contract, but actually have no intention of doing so, it would be unfair to set the agreement aside, because the party has actually expressed the intention. A party will be held accountable for inducing another to rely upon their words or conduct at the time of entering into their agreement.

> **Example:** Blake, a restaurateur, orders ten cases of cupcakes at a cost of $25 per case from Mollie, a local baker. Mollie agrees and tells him they will be ready the following day and he can pay for them when he picks them up. Blake confirms these terms during the call. If Blake at the time of the cupcake delivery offered Mollie a lesser sum of money because he never intended to pay $25 a case, his secret intention to not be bound to the terms of the sale is irrelevant. He is bound to the terms expressed during the call.

JEST, ANGER, OR UNDUE EXCITEMENT. Contracts made in obvious jest, anger, or undue excitement, where no reasonable person would conclude a serious offer was being made, are not enforceable.

Example: A purchaser of a new car suffers buyer's remorse because of the high price he paid for the car. Venting his angry feelings, he states he will sell the car for one dollar to anyone who will purchase it. Though a neighbor hands him the dollar, the circumstances suggest the car owner lacked the intent to contract, and no contract would result from this exchange.

EXPRESSIONS OF OPINION. If the statements are expressions of opinion, this is not an offer. An offer will indicate a clear expression of an intention to enter into a binding agreement.

Example: A vanilla latte with these premium ingredients *should* sell for 6 dollars.

STATEMENTS OF FUTURE INTENT. Statements of future intent to enter into a contract are not offers.

Example: Emilio tells Angelica, "I plan to enter into a partnership with you next year and capitalize the business with $10,000 of my savings." This is not an offer because the statement only indicates that a future action may occur.

PRELIMINARY NEGOTIATIONS. Preliminary negotiations or invitations to negotiate (such as "will you sell your vehicle?") are not offers. Statements such as this are not considered offers because they lack a present intent to form an agreement — they are simply an inquiry into the other party's willingness to engage in discussion.

Example: Edward Spigler was advised that his employment would be terminated unless he resigned from his position and assisted his employer in sales efforts. Spigler was provided with a draft of a "Resignation, Release, and Sales Commission Agreement" by his employer. Spigler did not sign the agreement. His employment was then terminated, but his employer informed him the proposed agreement could be discussed for the next two weeks. Spigler signed the agreement but it was never executed by the employer. When Spigler sued to enforce the agreement, the court found the parties did not enter into a contract; there were simply preliminary negotiations designed to lead to an agreement that did not by themselves constitute an agreement. *Spigler v. Southeastern Public Service Co.*, 610 So. 2d 521 (Fla. Dist. Ct. App. 1992)

AGREEMENTS TO NEGOTIATE. At the contract formation stage, leaving key issues for future negotiation can result in only an agreement to agree rather than an enforceable agreement. However, when parties have simply agreed to core terms of the agreement and decide to leave the rest of the terms to be negotiated by the parties at a later date, the agreement is only binding in the sense that it requires the parties to negotiate the remaining terms in good faith.

Example: Kevin Copeland negotiated with Baskin Robbins® to buy an ice cream manufacturing plant. The purchase transaction was contingent on Baskin Robbins' agreeing to a co-packing agreement to buy the ice cream that Copeland manufactured at the plant. After several months of negotiations, Baskin Robbins offered to sell the plant to Copeland for $1.3 million and buy the ice cream manufactured at the plant for three years, "subject to a separate co-packing agreement and negotiated pricing." Copeland agreed and the parties continued negotiating over the terms of the co-packing agreement. Two months later, Baskin Robbins ceased negotiating due to a change in its overall business strategy. Copeland sued for breach of contract, but the court held that so long as the parties negotiated in good faith, the failure to reach an agreement was not a breach of the agreement to negotiate. *Copeland v. Baskin Robbins*, 96 Cal. App. 4th 1251 (2002)

The art of negotiation lies in understanding the perspective of the counterpart and guiding the dialogue towards a mutually beneficial outcome. — Nasir al-Din al-Tusi, Persian polymath, *The Nasirean Ethics* (1201-1274)

OFFER SUBJECT TO FURTHER APPROVAL. An offer subject to further approval is not an offer. By its terms, it is made clear that additional information or verification is required before the offer can actually be made. Until the requisite information is received or verified, no offer will exist.

Example: "All accepted offers are subject to OAC" (that is, on the approved credit of the buyer) would require approved credit in order for there to be a valid offer.

CONTRACTS OF DOMESTIC AND SOCIAL CIRCUMSTANCES. When the subject matter of the offer involves commitments made in the context of family or social situations, the law considers the matter too unimportant to be enforced as a contract.

Example: A business law student invites her brilliant instructor to an extravagant dinner the student will host. The instructor accepts the invitation. Following a no-show by the instructor, the student sues the instructor for the hundreds of dollars spent in preparing the special meal. Absent an agreement between them that the instructor would contribute to the cost of the meal, the agreement is presumed unenforceable.

De minimis non curat lex (the law does not concern itself with minimal (trifling) matters).

GENERAL ADVERTISEMENTS. Typically, advertisements do not contain sufficient words of commitment to be offers. They are instead invitations to make offers. Businesses must comply with consumer protection laws protecting the consumer from unfair business practices. As such, businesses should be careful in the phrasing of the advertisements they issue.

Example: A new car deal advertises: "We offer top dollar on all trade-ins."

Landmark Case
Lucy v. Zehmer, 84 S.E.2d 516 (Va. 1954)

The following landmark case from Virginia is remembered well by many legal professionals. In a business context, where one party makes an offer *in jest*, but the other party reasonably believes that he is serious in making the offer, and freely accepts the offer, a binding enforceable contract can result. The contract in this case was made under unusual circumstances while the parties sat drinking one evening in Zehmer's restaurant. Zehmer had known Lucy for many years and Lucy had expressed interest in purchasing Zehmer's farm. Zehmer had previously offered to sell, but rescinded that prior offer. One night, Lucy entered the restaurant with a bottle of whiskey, of which both Lucy and Zehmer consumed a considerable amount. Zehmer testified that, "I was already high as a Georgia pine, and didn't have any better sense than to pour another great big slug [of whiskey] out and gulp it down, and [Lucy] took one too." They eventually discussed the sale of the farm. Zehmer asked Lucy if he would give $50,000 and Lucy said yes. Zehmer replied, "You haven't got $50,000 in cash." Lucy said he did and Zehmer replied that he did not believe it. They argued "pro and con for a long time," mainly about "whether he had $50,000 in cash that he could put up right then and buy that farm." Finally, said Zehmer, Lucy told him if he didn't believe he had $50,000, "you sign that piece of paper here and say you will take $50,000.00 for the farm." Zehmer wrote on the back of the restaurant's receipt stating, "We hereby agree to sell to W.O. Lucy the Ferguson Farm complete for $50,000, title satisfactory to buyer." The note was signed by both Zehmer and his wife, who later testified that she did so only because her husband assured her that his intent to sell the farm was merely in jest. The next day, Lucy spoke to his brother about the property and received assurances from a title attorney that clear title to the farm could be obtained. He wrote and delivered a written acceptance to Zehmer. Zehmer refused to sell and at trial argued he was too drunk to agree to the sale and prevailed. However, upon appeal, the appellate court unanimously held that the pretrial discovery showed that Zehmer was not intoxicated to the point of being unable to comprehend the nature and consequences of what he was signing. The Chief Justice of the Supreme Court of Virginia stated: "*The mental assent of the parties is not requisite for the formation of a contract. If the words or other acts of one of the parties have but one reasonable meaning, his undisclosed intention is immaterial except when an unreasonable meaning which he attaches to his manifestations is known to the other party.*" The state supreme court ordered the Zehmers to sell the farm to Lucy.

Concept Summary
When an Offer Is Not an Offer

The intent to enter into a contract is absent in the following situations:

- Secret intentions not to enter in contract
- Statements made in jest, anger, or undue excitement
- Expressions of opinion
- Statements of future intent
- Preliminary negotiations
- Agreements to negotiate for a separate agreement
- Offers subject to further approval
- Contracts of domestic and social circumstances
- Advertisements (nonspecific)

Special Situations

General Advertisements That Are Clear, Definite, and Explicit. If the content of an advertisement is specific enough to identify the subject matter, the pricing, and the person or a group to whom the advertisement should apply, contractual intent may be inferred and the advertisement will be considered an offer.

> **Example:** A fur store advertised the sale of a fur stole worth $139 for $1. The advertisement said, "first come, first serve." The male plaintiff arrived first at the store and offered to buy the goods. The store refused, saying that it was a house rule that the sale was only for women. The appellate court found that the subject matter was sufficiently described, the price stated, and the persons who could accept the offer were stated. The court held that the store had made a binding offer. *Lefkowitz v. Great Minneapolis Surplus Store, Inc.*, 86 N.W.2d 689 (Minn. 1957)

Auctions. Under current case law and the Uniform Commercial Code, an auctioneer's opening remarks do not make an offer on the item that is up for sale.

- *With reserve.* Auction sales with a reserve means that even after the bidding starts, the auctioneer may withdraw the goods from the sale any time before the auctioneer closes the auction. A reserve is the minimum price that the seller must obtain at the auction. Auctions are presumed to be auctions with reserve unless explicitly announced to be without reserve.
- *Without reserve.* Auction sales without reserve means that the auctioneer has made an irrevocable offer to sell the goods to the highest bidder. Once the bidding starts, the auctioneer cannot withdraw the bids because the bids are too low.

Terms

An offer must contain definite terms. The purpose of having definite terms is that they allow a court to determine if a breach of the contract has occurred and, if applicable, to issue the appropriate remedy. The terms that are required to be definite will vary depending upon the subject matter of the agreement. However, a contract must usually include the following terms:

1. Identification of the parties
2. Identification of the subject matter (and quantities, when appropriate)
3. The consideration to be paid or exchanged (that is, money, property, the rendering of a service or the forbearance of an act (such as agreeing not to sue))
4. Time of performance

Although an offer must state the essential terms of the proposed contract, the modern trend of the law assumes that many unstated terms may be understood by the parties from their prior dealings, or are implied, or arise from trade usages.

> **Example:** Stu owns a seafood restaurant in a coastal city and needs a fresh supply of fish for his evening seafood entrees. He agrees with Andrew, a local fisherman, that at 11:30 every morning Andrew will bring Stu all the fish he caught that morning. Stu agrees to pay Andrew $2 per pound above the market price for each specific type of fish. Although the exact price and quantity of fish is not stated, the parties have a clear understanding of the intent of the essential terms, and the agreement would be enforceable.

Sometimes, the court only needs to be able to imply or reasonably infer terms of a contract. Two examples of this type of situation occur in the context of consideration and the time for performance.

- *Consideration.* In many cases, the consideration (or price) does not need to be stated. A court can imply a reasonable price based upon the parties' prior course of conduct or the industry practices, or it can set a reasonable term.
- *Time for performance.* If the details of time for performance are left open, a court can imply that the parties agreed to reasonable or commercially reasonable time standards.

Communication of the Offer

An offer must also be communicated by the offeror to the offeree in order to be effective. If the offer is not communicated to the offeree in the manner selected by the offeror, an offer is not made.

> **Example:** A business owner prepares a formal offer to acquire a competitor. The offer is composed and saved on the desktop computer of the owner. While the owner is at lunch, an assistant, knowing of the owner's desire to proceed with an offer as quickly as possible, calls her friend who works for the competitor. In that call, she reads the terms of the offer to her friend, who, in turn, informs her employer of all of the details of the transaction. Before sending the offer by email, the competitor calls the owner to accept the offer. No contract results. Until the offer is communicated in the manner intended by the offeror, no communication of the offer has occurred.

Termination of the Offer

After an offer is communicated, an offer may be terminated either by actions of the parties or by operation of law.

The following actions of the parties can terminate the offer:

1. Revocation (withdrawing) the offer by offeror before acceptance
2. Rejection by the offeree
3. Counteroffer by the offeree

Offers are terminated upon the occurrence of certain events, such as the following:

1. Destruction of the subject matter
2. Death or incompetency of the offeror or offeree
3. Supervening illegality
4. Lapse of time

ACTIONS OF THE PARTIES

Revocation
The act of withdrawing an offer.

Revocation. The act of withdrawing an offer is known as **revocation**. It can occur as follows:

- *Revocation by the offeror prior to acceptance.* An offer may be withdrawn at any time before it is accepted. There are four exceptions to this rule:
  - *Options.* In an option contract, the offeror agrees to keep the offer open for a period of time in return for the receipt of consideration, such as the payment of money. For example, a contractor is given an option to purchase a backhoe for $15,000 for a period of 45 days upon giving the proposed seller $100.

- *Unilateral contracts.* Most courts consider that when the offeree has clearly commenced to perform, the commencement is treated as acceptance and the offeree must be allowed to complete the performance.
- *Firm offers under the Uniform Commercial Code.* The law of the commercial sale of goods is discussed in Chapter 26. A merchant's firm written offer to buy or sell goods cannot be revoked during the time stated in the offer.
- *Promissory estoppel.* A doctrine that provides that an offer is deemed irrevocable if, under the circumstances, the offeree reasonably relies on the offer being held open and will suffer harm if it is revoked. This concept is discussed in the next chapter.

- *Inconsistent acts (indirect revocation).* Performance of acts inconsistent with the offer that has already been made would terminate an offer. For example, if an offeror made an offer to sell a property to the offeree but instead sold it to a third party, there would be a revocation.

A revocation is effective when it is known to the offeree — when the revocation is delivered to the offeree or when the offeree has learned from other reliable sources the offer has been withdrawn.

Landmark Case
Dickinson v. Dodds, 2 Ch. Div. 463 (1876) (England)

A landmark common law case recognizing indirect revocation is found in the 1876 decision of an English court of appeal. In this decision, Dodds made an offer to sell real property to Dickinson. The offer stated that it expired on Friday at 9 A.M. On Thursday, Dickinson heard from a third party that Dodds had been "offering or agreeing to sell" the property to a third person. Immediately after hearing this, and before the deadline, Dickinson communicated his acceptance to Dodds. Dodds refused and told Dickinson that he had sold the property. The court found that although Dodds had not communicated his revocation, Dickinson was made aware that Dodds no longer intended to sell the property to him. The court held that since Dodds had changed his mind before Dickinson accepted, there was no mutual consent or meeting of the minds.

How can this case holding be reconciled with the objective theory of contracts?

Rejection. The offeree can also terminate the offer by words or conduct, otherwise known as a **rejection**. If, after rejecting the offer, the offeree makes any subsequent attempts to accept it, these attempts will be construed as a new offer. This would result in the original offeree becoming the offeror and the original offeror becoming the offeree. Like a revocation, a rejection of an offer is effective only when the offeror or its agent receives it. However, minor inquiries requiring a firm offer or requesting clarifications are not rejections.

Rejection
The termination of an offer by words or conduct.

Example: Marie Guzman was laid off by Visalia Community Bank as part of a "reduction in force." Later, she filed a complaint alleging Visalia's president and CEO had engaged in sexual discrimination and had created a hostile work environment. The parties were in the process of settling when Visalia offered $60,000. Guzman's attorney responded that the offer was "insulting and demeaning." The next day, Guzman accepted the $60,000 offer, but Visalia argued that when Guzman's attorney criticized the settlement offer, that constituted a rejection. The court held that criticism was not a rejection. In its reasoning, the court said that one would expect that criticism of the offer is merely a normal part of the negotiating strategy, which can be viewed as an indirect inquiry for a better offer. *Guzman v. Visalia Community Bank*, 71 Cal. App. 4th 1370 (1999)

Counteroffer
A rejection of the original offer and the simultaneous making of a new offer by the offeree to the offeror.

Counteroffer. A **counteroffer** is a rejection of the original offer and the simultaneous making of a new offer by the offeree to the offeror. Under common law, the *mirror image rule* requires that an offeree's acceptance match the offeree's offer exactly. Any change in or addition to the terms of the original offer automatically terminates that offer and substitutes that counteroffer back to the original offeror. If the original offeror accepts the terms of the counteroffer, an enforceable contract will be created based on the terms of the counteroffer.

Example: Andrew and Joyce Pride retained a real estate broker to sell their home. Larry Lewis made an offer to purchase the house for $55,000, with financing to be provided by the sellers, which Andrew and Joyce rejected. Lewis made a second offer for the same purchase price but with bank financing, which constituted a counteroffer. The Prides accepted this counteroffer but changed the closing date for the transaction—a change that Lewis did not agree to in writing. When the Prides later sought to enforce the contract against Lewis, Lewis prevailed because Lewis had not accepted the Prides' counteroffer (that is, the change to the closing date). *Pride v. Lewis*, 179 S.W.3d 375 (Mo. Ct. App. 2005)

TERMINATION BY OPERATION OF LAW An offer may also be terminated by operation of law. This occurs upon any of the following events:

Destruction of the Subject Matter. The subject matter of the contract is the purpose for entering into the contract. It can take many forms, such as the purchase of tangible objects. When the subject matter is destroyed before the offer is accepted, the offer will be automatically terminated because the party can no longer perform under the contract. This is also known as the doctrine of legal impossibility, which excuses performance of a contract only when performance is rendered objectively impossible. Therefore, even if the offeree attempted to accept the offer, not knowing that the subject matter was destroyed, there would be no contract because the offer terminated at the time the subject matter was destroyed.

Example: Tiffany seeks to secure the use of a conference center for her company's event, and the conference center provides an offer to Tiffany. Prior to Tiffany's accepting the offer, if the conference center is destroyed by a fire, the offer is automatically terminated due to the destruction of the subject matter.

Death or Incompetence of a Party. If a party to the offer dies or becomes incompetent, the offer is terminated. When the offeror is the party who dies or becomes incapacitated, the offer is considered terminated at the time of death or incapacity. When the offeree is the party who dies or becomes incapacitated, the offer is considered to be rejected at the time of death or incapacity.

> **Example:** Russell and Mary Keen owed a large parcel of land in Indiana. In 1972, the Keens sold a part of that property (a 6.56-acre parcel) to Richard and Elizabeth Ryan, while retaining the remaining part of the property. In the purchase agreement, the Ryans were given a right of first refusal if the Keens ever elected to sell the remaining part of the property. Mary Keen died before the Ryans ever exercised the right of first refusal, and Russell had predeceased Mary. The court held that the right of first refusal terminated upon Mary Keen's death because she was the last surviving grantor of the right. The court reasoned that the purchase agreement expressly provided that the right of first refusal was not to be construed to be available if the Keens' heirs, assigns, or personal representatives offered the property for sale. *Ryan v. Lawyers Title Ins. Corp.*, 959 N.E.2d 870 (Ind. Ct. App. 2011)

A Supervening Illegality with Respect to the Subject Matter of the Offer. If parties agree to perform a specific task but that task is later deemed to be illegal (commonly by a statute or an administrative or judicial order), the offer is terminated.

> **Example:** A farmer offers to purchase 1,000 pounds of pesticide from a farm supplier. If the sale of that pesticide is made illegal due to environmental concerns prior to acceptance, the offer is terminated by operation of law.

Lapse of Time. Offers cannot last forever—they lapse if not timely accepted. The offeror may specify the date the offer will expire. If no express expiration date is provided, the law implies that an offer must be accepted within a reasonable time. What is "reasonable" is troublesome, because a trier of fact may need expert testimony to determine what amount of time would be needed to receive, consider, and reply to the offer under all the circumstances.

> **Example:** Following an automobile accident between Wilkins and Butler, Wilkins, as the plaintiff, was willing to settle for $4,500. Wilkins communicated the settlement offer in a letter to Butler. Butler sought time to verify that his insurance company would pay that amount. A few months elapsed, and Butler accepted the offer. The trial court held the lapse of time terminated the power to accept since the offer was not accepted within a reasonable time under the circumstances. *Wilkins v. Butler*, 369 S.E.2d 267 (Ga. Ct. App. 1988)

It may appear that a late acceptance is no acceptance of the offer. History provides too many examples of why this may not be a fair rule to apply in every case. For example, if the offeree sends a late acceptance, the trier of fact might reach a reasonable conclusion that the offeree was submitting a counteroffer to the offeror, permitting the offeror the power to accept. How might this confusing situation arise? Imprecise wording in our communications is often to blame.

> **Example:** Suppose Owner had many prior real estate transactions with several investors regarding property sales. If prior offers were vaguely stated as to acceptance deadlines, but Owner never objected previously to a late acceptance of their offer, Owner's acts may suggest that no matter when it arrived, the acceptance was never considered late and the parties proceeded to close the prior transactions.

FIGURE 9.2: Termination Concept Summary

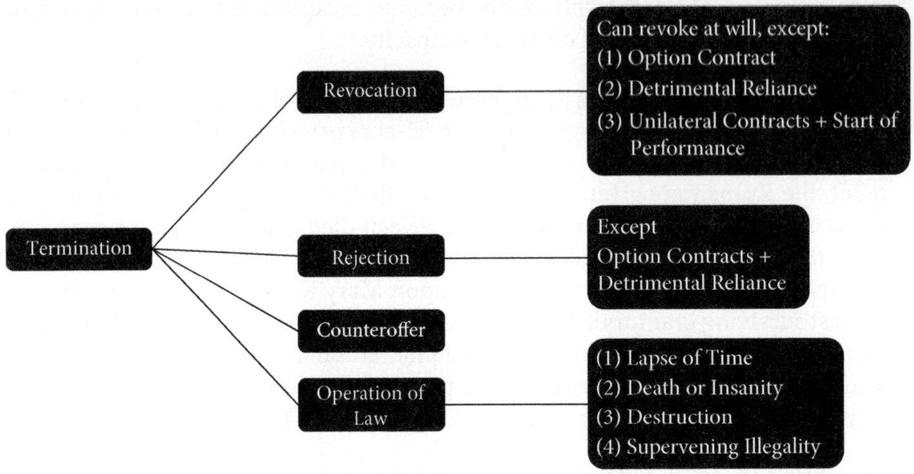

Management Application
Making a Clear Offer

Assume that ABC Company submits an offer to acquire the assets of a competitor. The offer is written informally and attempts to eliminate ambiguity in the acceptance of the offer. Suppose the offer requires acceptance within three working days. This offer is ambiguous because it does not state if the three "working" days are business or calendar days, or if the period runs from the date the offer is sent or when it is received. Moreover, could the offeree have until midnight of that final day to accept? Which time zone applies to the acceptance period? When planning what must be stated in a contract, clarity is paramount. What can go wrong often does, because of ambiguous or incomplete drafting. How should this offer be phrased?

Concept Summary
Offers

- An offer must (1) be communicated, (2) express a clear intent to make a contract, and (3) be sufficiently definite that it could be enforced.
- Some terms may be implied or understood by the parties arising from their prior course of conduct or industry practices.

- If the content of an advertisement is specific enough to identify the subject matter, the pricing, and identification of the person or a group to whom it should apply, contractual intent may be inferred.
- An offer lasts for the period stated or, if none is stated, for a reasonable period of time.
- An offer may lapse because of (1) revocation (withdrawing) the offer by offeror before acceptance, (2) rejection by the offeree, (3) counteroffer by the offeree, (4) destruction of the subject matter, (5) death or incompetency of the offeror or offeree, (6) supervening illegality, and (7) lapse of time.

Acceptance of the Offer

An **acceptance** of an offer consists of an expression of present, unequivocal, unconditional assent by the offeree to the entirety of the offer. The consent of the parties to a contract must be mutual. Consent is not mutual unless all the parties to a contract agree on the same thing in the same sense. Mutual consent generally takes the form of an acceptance following an offer. The courts also apply the objective theory of contracts to determine if the offeree intended to accept the offer.

Acceptance
The offeree's manifestation of assent to the terms of the offer, made in a manner requested or required by the offer.

Who May Accept

Once an offer is made, only the person to whom the offer is made can accept. Moreover, in order to accept, the offeree must *know of the offer* at the time he accepts. If not, the rule is that the offer has not been validly communicated by the offeror.

Form of the Acceptance

If the offer involves a bilateral contract, the acceptance will usually occur using words at the time of contract formation. Acceptance may also be in the form of actions, if the actions make clear that the offeree intends to accept. Acceptance of a unilateral contract occurs by performance of the requested act.

Unqualified Acceptance and the Mirror Image Rule

An acceptance must be absolute and unqualified. The **mirror image rule** provides that the offeree must accept the terms stated by the offeror. There can be no changes or alterations to the offer by the offeree. Any changes to the offer by the offeree would constitute a counteroffer.

Mirror image rule
An offer must be accepted without modifications by the offeree.

Example: Calvin and Cheryl Hotzler owned commercial property that they listed for sale. Michael Gresser, a real estate investor, began negotiating with the Hotzlers to purchase the property. Gresser submitted to the Hotzlers an unsigned, proposed purchase agreement that, among other items, required the Hotzlers to deliver a survey of the property a month later and set forth a closing date for a

> month after that. The Hotzlers changed several terms, initialed the changes, signed the purchase agreement, and returned it to Gresser. The court held the Hotzlers had not accepted Gresser's offer under the mirror image rule. An acceptance must mirror the offer and may not introduce additional terms or conditions. *Gresser v. Hotzler*, 604 N.W.2d 379 (Minn. Ct. App. 2000)

In practice, many jurisdictions have adopted a more liberal interpretation of this rule. As a result, minor differences in the response will not disqualify it as an acceptance. However, all jurisdictions continue to hold that changes to material terms in the contract will constitute a counteroffer.

Communication of the Acceptance

If the offer does not state the means of acceptance, any reasonable and ordinary mode of communication may be used. What is considered reasonable will vary under the circumstances. At common law, the courts held that the form of acceptance should be in the form that the offer was made. Thus, if the offer was mailed, the acceptance should be mailed.

Mailbox rule
The offeree's acceptance was effective upon mailing the offeree's acceptance.

In the past, the rule for acceptance by the offeree was known as the **mailbox rule**, because the alternatives for acceptance were hand delivery or the use of the postal system. The offeree's acceptance was effective upon mailing the offeree's acceptance — that is, upon dispatch of the acceptance.

An offeror may specify the way acceptance is to be communicated, in which case no other method will suffice. The terms of a mirror image acceptance may be limited to the authorized channel of communication specified by the offeror (such as by express mail delivery). The acceptance has to be properly addressed with all delivery fees prepaid.

If the offeree did not use an authorized channel of communication for acceptance (such as the offeror requirement that acceptance must be made by express mail), a contract might still be formed. However, acceptance (and, thus formation) is delayed until the offeror receives the acceptance. Until acceptance is received, the offer remains revocable.

The modern trend is to be more adaptable in recognizing that acceptance has occurred. The law now favors the use of any reasonable channel for communicating an acceptance of the offer. As before, acceptance is effective upon dispatch.

> **Example:** PCGH made a written offer of employment to Keck on November 30. Keck signed the offer, and on December 1 sent PCGH's CEO an email informing him that he had signed the agreement. The CEO responded by sending Keck an email that stated, "Great." PCGH argued that the November 30 offer letter expressly required that Keck sign and return the offer letter, and that both Keck and the CEO testified that they understood that an exchange of signatures was required to establish a binding agreement. PCGH further contended that the undisputed evidence established that Keck never "signed *and* returned" the offer letter. The appellate court found that an email response was an acceptable form

of acceptance. *Pacific Company Group Holdings, LLC v. Keck*, 232 Cal. App. 4th 294 (2014)

Cross Talk Communications

Under the law of most jurisdictions, a revocation is only effective upon receipt by the offeree. If an offeree dispatches an acceptance concurrent with the offeror's revocation, a contract is formed depending upon which communication — the revocation or the acceptance — is first received.

If the offeree's first reaction is to communicate a rejection, there has been no acceptance, but if the offeree changes her mind and communicates acceptance of the offer before the rejection is received by the offeror, a contract is formed. However, if the rejection arrives first, the later acceptance is too late to form a contract. The offer has been terminated by the received rejection.

If the offeree's first reaction is to communicate an acceptance, then, under the mailbox rule, this acceptance has formed a contract. It is too late for either party to retract an offer or recall the acceptance.

Silence as Acceptance

Generally, silence does not constitute acceptance of an offer to enter into a bilateral contract. For example, if a neighbor began parking cars on the neighbor's property and sent an email offering to pay for that use, the burdened neighbor has not accepted the neighbor's actions or offer of payment. Remember, a unilateral contract is accepted by the performance of an act or occurrence of an event.

Silence *can* constitute acceptance of a bilateral contract if any one of the following occurs:

- The offeror, observing the offeree acting in response to the offer, says nothing;
- The parties agree that silence means acceptance; or
- In prior dealings, the parties have considered silence to be acceptance.

It is important to note that the offeror cannot require a specific method of rejecting an offer. For example, the offeror cannot tell the offeree, "If you do not wish to accept this offer, you must come to my office and deliver the rejection. If you do not, you have accepted the offer."

FIGURE 9.3: Traditional Offer and Acceptance Model

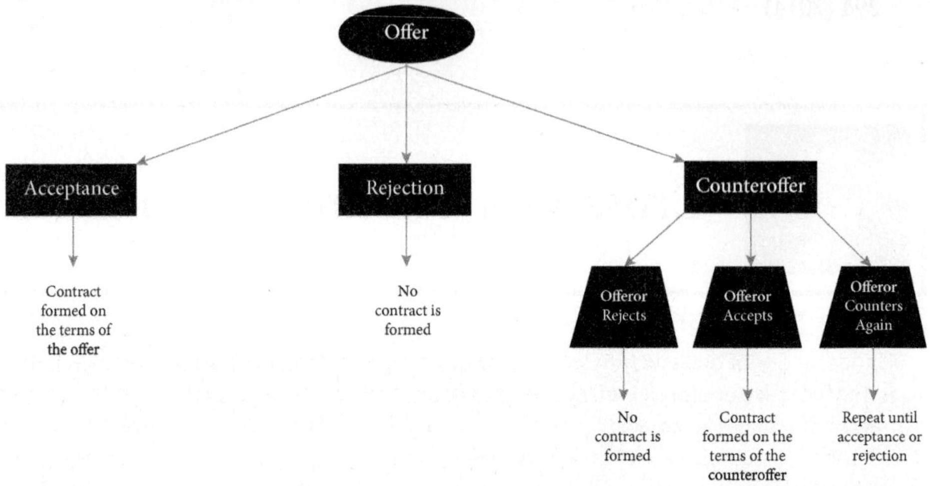

Concept Summary Acceptance

- The acceptance of the offer must be definite.
- The acceptance must be unconditional (otherwise, it is a counteroffer).
    - ☐ A counteroffer is both a rejection of the offer and a new offer.
- The acceptance must be communicated to the offeror.
- Unilateral offers are accepted by a clear commencement of the act to be performed.
- Silence to an offer is not acceptance unless (1) the offeror, observing the offeree acting in response to the offer, says nothing; (2) the parties agree that silence means acceptance; or (3) in prior dealings, the parties have considered silence to be acceptance.

AI Feature: Enforcing a Contract

Use an AI program to analyze the following dispute: A homeowner is frustrated with his gardener and fires the gardener. He decides to post a sign on his front lawn that reads "Mow this lawn for $40.00!" Kelvin, a neighbor, mows the lawn without any contact or discussion with the homeowner. Quickly, Kelvin finishes the lawn work and proceeds to knock on the door to collect the money. The homeowner answers the door and, although silently impressed with the quality of the service rendered, refuses to pay Kelvin. He states he "didn't authorize Kelvin to mow the lawn and did not know he was out there."

Did a valid contract exist for Kelvin to enforce? If so, what facts would support the claim for compensation. Because he views the services rendered as having a reasonable value of more than 40 dollars, is Kelvin entitled to more than that sum? Assume Kelvin is paid, and the homeowner does not remove his sign. Another person spends a few minutes clipping grass that Kelvin missed. Is this second person entitled to 40 dollars as well? If not, why not?

Key Terms

- Acceptance, 231
- Bilateral contract, 212
- Contract, 209
- Counteroffer, 228
- Executed contract, 215
- Executory contract, 215
- Express contract, 215
- Formal contract, 215
- Implied-in-fact contract, 215
- Implied-in-law contract (quasi-contract), 216
- Informal contract (simple contract), 215
- Mailbox rule, 232
- Mirror image rule, 231
- Objective theory of contracts, 221
- Offer, 221
- Rejection, 227
- Revocation, 226
- Unenforceable contract, 220
- Unilateral contract, 212
- Valid contract (enforceable contract), 219
- Void contract, 219
- Voidable contract, 220

Applying the Law

9.1 Intention to be Bound. Tony Maroni's, Inc., signed a written commercial lease for Seattle retail space. Anthony Riviera, Tony Maroni's president, signed the lease. Contemporaneously with the execution of the lease, Riviera executed a guaranty agreement, which was incorporated by reference in the lease. Riviera wrote the description "President" by hand after his name on the signature line of the guaranty. Tony Maroni's filed for bankruptcy shortly after the execution of the lease. The lessor sought to enforce the lease guarantee against Riviera. Was he personally liable for the lease obligations of the corporation? *Wilson Court v. Tony Maroni's, Inc.*, 952 P.2d 590 (Wash 2d. 1998)

9.2 Letters of Intent. Dennis Block and Mark Magura executed a letter of intent that Magura would purchase Block's interest in a partnership for $600,000. Magura did not complete the purchase, Block filed suit, and the trial court granted summary judgment to Magura and denied summary judgment to Block on the issue of whether the parties' letter of intent created an enforceable contract. Under what circumstances may a letter of intent be an enforceable agreement? *Block v. Magura*, 949 N.E.2d 1261 (Ind. App. 2011)

9.3 Agreements to Agree. Walker entered into a ten-year lease agreement with Keith. The lease provided the opportunity to renew the lease for an additional ten-year term, under the same terms and conditions, except for the rent to be paid. Regarding the future rent to be paid, the contract provided: "[R]ental will be fixed in such amount as shall actually be agreed upon by the lessors and the lessee . . . with rental values at this time reflected by the comparative business conditions of the two periods." Walker notified Keith of his intent to renew the lease, but the parties could not agree upon the rent. Does Keith have an argument that this contract is unenforceable because the terms are uncertain? *Walker v. Keith*, 382 S.W.2d 198 (Ky. Ct. App. 1964)

9.4 Definiteness. Robert Gutkowski sued George Steinbrenner for failing to honor a promise. He claimed that after presenting Steinbrenner with the idea of creating what ultimately became the Yankees Entertainment and SportsNetwork®, Steinbrenner failed to abide by the terms of an oral agreement under which Gutkowski would "have a role in the network as long as it existed, or otherwise be compensated for his efforts and contributions." Was the contract definite in its terms to allow recovery? Explain your answer. *Gutkowski v. Steinbrenner*, 680 F. Supp. 2d 602 (S.D.N.Y. 2010)

9.5 Unilateral Contract. Amos Cobaugh was playing in the East End Open Golf Tournament on the Fairview Golf Course in Cornwall, Pennsylvania. When he arrived at the ninth tee, he found a new Chevrolet Beretta, together with signs which proclaimed: "HOLE-IN-ONE Wins this 1988 Chevrolet Beretta GT Courtesy of KLICK-LEWIS Buick Chevy Pontiac $49.00 OVER FACTORY INVOICE in Palmyra." Cobaugh aced the ninth hole and attempted to claim his prize. Klick-Lewis refused to deliver the car. It had offered the car as a prize for a charity golf tournament sponsored by a service club two days earlier and had neglected to remove the car and posted signs prior to Cobaugh's hole-in-one. Cobaugh sued to compel delivery of the car, which the dealership had refused to do. What result and why? *Cobaugh v. Klick-Lewis, Inc.*, 561 A.2d 1248 (Pa. Super 1989)

9.6 Timeliness of Acceptance. Irwin Schiff was a self-styled "tax rebel," who has made a career and substantial profits out of his tax protest activities. Schiff's basic contention was that the federal income tax is a voluntary tax which no one is required to pay. During a live television interview he said, "If anybody calls this show—I have the Code—and cites any section of this Code that says an individual is required to file a tax return, I will pay them $100,000." He did, however, see a two-minute taped segment of the original interview that was rebroadcast several hours later on the CBS Morning News®. The CBS Morning News rebroadcast included Schiff's reward proposal. John Newman, a practicing attorney, claimed that he accepted the public offer and sued when he was not paid. Who wins and why? *Newman v. Schiff*, 778 F.2d 460 (8th Cir. 1985)

9.7 Meeting of the Minds. Morales was a Spanish-speaking employee who was required to attend an employee orientation at the time he was hired. At the orientation, he executed a standard employment agreement containing an arbitration clause. The orientation was conducted in English and the employment agreement was also in English, which Morales did not understand. A bilingual applicant who knew the employee was asked to help him complete the documents. However, Morales did not ask the applicant-translator what he was signing including the requirement to arbitrate all disputes. After Morales was fired, he tried to sue the employer for wrongful termination and claimed that he was not bound to the arbitration clause because he never agreed to it. What are the arguments to be made for each party? *Morales v. Sun Constructors, Inc.*, 541 F.3d 218 (3d Cir. 2008)

9.8 Lapse of Time. A dog bite victim sued the dog's owners, seeking damages. The owners proposed a settlement offer of $32,843. The victim waited a year to accept because she wanted to see what award an arbitrator would give her. When she submitted her dispute to be resolved by arbitration, an arbitrator awarded her $25,069. Disappointed, she then sought to accept the offer. Had the offer lapsed? *Sherrod ex rel. Cantone v. Kidd*, 155 P.3d 976 (Wash. Ct. App. 2007)

9.9 Express and Implied Contracts. Michael Johnson and Robert Larson entered into an oral contract whereby Johnson agreed to remove rock from Larson's farmland in exchange for Johnson receiving the value of the rock removed. Johnson removed rock from Larson's land. He also installed drain tile. Johnson claimed that he extracted approximately 1,100 tons of rock. Of that amount, Johnson only removed between three to five semi-truck loads from Larson's land. The rest Johnson stored on Larson's land to the west of Larson's home, for removal later. According to Johnson, Larson permitted him to store the rocks on his land until Johnson needed them. Larson tried several times to get Johnson to remove the rock, but ultimately gave Joel Penny permission to remove the rock, which he did. When Johnson learned that his rock piles were no longer on Larson's land, he invoiced him for his unpaid work. Johnson sued Larson and Penny for breach of implied-in-law contract (*quantum meruit*). Explain Johnson's rights to recover, if at all, against the defendants. *Johnson v. Larson*, 779 N.W.2d 412 (S.D. 2010)

9.10 Offer and Counteroffers. Robert and Margo Rebar entered into a one-year renewable "Termite Control Agreement." Under the agreement, Cook's Pest Control was obligated to continue treating and inspecting the Rebars' home for termites during the term of the agreement, which, with certain limited exceptions, continued so long as the Rebars continued to pay the annual renewal fee. The agreement contained a mandatory, binding arbitration provision. When the initial term of the agreement was about to expire, Cook's Pest Control notified the Rebars and requested that they renew the agreement for another year by paying the renewal fee. Margo Rebar submitted a payment to Cook's Pest Control; with the payment she included an insert entitled "Addendum to Customer Agreement" which required the Rebars prior consent to arbitrate. The addendum clearly stated that negotiating the renewal check or continuing to provide services would make the company subject to the addendum. The company did both things; soon, the Rebars sued the company for the failure to treat and control a termite infestation in the Rebars' home and to repair the damage to the home caused by the termites. The company sought to compel arbitration. Whose contract language prevails? *Cook's Pest Control, Inc. v. Rebar*, 852 So. 2d 730 (Ala. 2002)

Consideration and Promissory Estoppel

10

The whole duty of government is to prevent crime and to preserve contracts. —William Lamb, British politician (1779-1848)

Chapter Outline

- Introduction
- The Requirements of Consideration
- Adequacy of the Consideration
- Contracts Lacking Consideration

Case 10.1: *Gross v. Diehl Specialties International, Inc.*

- *Management Application: Best Efforts Clause as Consideration*

- Settlement of Claims
- Promises Binding Without Consideration

Case 10.2: *Brueck v. John Maneely Co.*

- AI Feature: Promissory Estoppel and Compensation

Learning Objectives

After studying this chapter, you should be able to:

1. Identify the elements of consideration.
2. Describe the contracts that lack consideration.
3. Discuss how claims may be settled through an accord and satisfaction.
4. Define promissory estoppel.

Introduction

To be enforceable, a contract must provide consideration. Consideration is the bargained-for exchange of legal value between the parties. Both parties to a contract must provide consideration for a contract to be valid. Where consideration is lacking in a contract, the contract is usually unenforceable. While a court will usually not enforce a contract lacking consideration, the parties may agree to mutually perform the contract. If such a contract is performed, the parties cannot thereafter assert that the contract lacked consideration to rescind the contract. Where only one party provides consideration to another, there is not a contract, but there may be a gift.

Courts will enforce a contract that lacks consideration when promissory estoppel is present. Promissory estoppel arises when a person provides a promise, and the other party relies on the promise to their detriment. The elements of both consideration and promissory estoppel are discussed in this chapter.

The Requirements of Consideration

Consideration The bargained-for exchange of legal value.

Consideration is the bargained-for exchange of legal value given in return for a promise (in a bilateral contract) or in return for performance or non-performance of an act (in a unilateral contract). Consideration for a legally enforceable contract requires the presence of two elements:

1. Legal value; and,
2. Bargained-for exchange.

Legal Value

Consideration must have legal value. Legal value is outlined in the listed items below:

1. Refraining from an act that one has a legal right to perform (known as **forbearance**).

Forbearance Refraining from an act that one has a legal right to perform.

Example: An uncle promised his nephew, William, $5,000 (~$93,000 today) if William would stop drinking alcohol, using tobacco, swearing, and gambling for money until he reached the age of 21 (note that at that time, it was legal in the state to drink and gamble before the age of 21). William accepted the promise and did refrain from the prohibited acts until he turned the agreed-upon age of 21. After celebrating his 21st birthday, William wrote to his uncle and requested payment, which his uncle refused to provide. The court held that there was consideration because William suffered a detriment in forbearing his legal rights to drink, use tobacco, swear, and gamble, while the uncle enjoyed a benefit of a better family reputation. *Hamer v. Sidway*, 27 N.E. 256 (N.Y. 1891)

When a person refrains from doing an illegal act, the law does not recognize such forbearance as consideration.

Example: A middle school–aged child who agrees to quit smoking cigarettes in exchange for $500 does not provide legal consideration because this child is not old enough to legally smoke cigarettes.

2. Promising to refrain from an act that one has a legal right to perform.
3. Performing an act that the promisee does not already have a legal duty to perform.

Example: The police department offered a reward for a wanted criminal. Gore, a police officer, captured the wanted criminal and demanded his reward. Consideration was lacking because the police officer was merely doing his duty, for which he was already being paid. *Ex parte Gore*, 57 Miss. 251 (1879)

4. Promising to perform an act that the promisee does not already have a legal duty to perform.
5. The promisor receives money or property.

Example: A homeowner contracts with a painter to paint her house for $3,000. The painter has provided consideration by promising to paint the house and the homeowner has provided consideration by promising to pay $3,000.

Bargained-for Exchange

To be enforceable, there must be *mutuality of consideration*, which requires *each party* to furnish consideration to the other. The consideration provided by both parties must be bargained for between them. That is, the parties must agree to what each of them will provide as consideration for the contract. A party cannot force consideration to be accepted on the other side.

Example: Olivia offers to sell her car to Jarvis for $7,500. Jarvis only wants to pay $5,000 for the car. Olivia is not required to accept the $5,000 as consideration that Jarvis is offering.

Adequacy of the Consideration

Usually, a court will not review the fairness of the amount or value of the consideration provided by the parties. Courts are not referees for the deals struck between the parties. Under the doctrine of freedom to contract, "adequacy" is left to the parties to negotiate. Otherwise, parties would sue to rescind a contract when it became apparent that they did not receive as great a benefit as did the other side.

If the purported consideration is deemed to be a sham, a court may find that there was no consideration provided. While adequacy is irrelevant, when there is a substantial difference in the amount or value of the consideration exchanged, the court may choose to examine the bargain more closely. Inadequate consideration that "shocks the conscience" may indicate that the bargained-for exchange element was missing (such as cases where there is fraud, duress, or undue influence).

Example: McKeague owned a large parcel of land for many years on which he operated a sugar plantation. However, over time, McKeague's physical and mental condition deteriorated. McKeague wanted to sell the land, since his condition made him unable to tend to the land. As a result, the land became unprofitable. Dr. Kennedy, a friend and physician who was aware of McKeague's condition, made an offer and purchased the land for a nominal sum of $15,000, even though the parcel of land was worth over $1 million. The court held that there was no consideration, given the high likelihood of undue influence. *McKeague v. Kennedy*, 5 Haw. 347 (1885)

Contracts Lacking Consideration

Sometimes, the parties to a contract may believe that they have provided consideration; however, under some circumstances no consideration actually has been provided. Under such circumstances, the contracts are unenforceable. Consideration is lacking if the exchange involves any of the following: (1) gift promises, (2) illusory promises, (3) preexisting duties, or (4) past consideration.

Gift Promises

A promise to make a gift is unenforceable for lack of consideration. In a gift, only one party has offered consideration (the one offering the gift). Once the promisor completes the gift, he cannot rescind the completed gift for lack of consideration.

> **Example:** Ira promises to gift his car to his nephew. If Ira never gifts his car to his nephew, his nephew cannot sue to enforce the gift.

To make a gift enforceable, the promisee must provide consideration (such as a detriment). Instead of being treated as a gift, here the parties have both provided consideration and the gift becomes an enforceable promise.

> **Example:** Ira promises to gift his golf clubs to his nephew if his nephew mows Ira's lawn for the summer. If the nephew does so and Ira does not deliver the clubs, Ira's nephew can sue to receive the clubs.

Illusory Promises

Illusory promise
A promise in which one or more of the parties has not bound itself to do anything.

An **illusory promise** is one in which one or more of the parties has not bound itself to do anything (that is, a party has not promised to do anything). Illusory promises are words of promise upon which performance is entirely optional on the part of one or both parties. Illusory promises often arise when the promisor reserves the right to change his mind about his promise.

> **Example:** Aiden promises to sell his house to Caitlyn. Caitlyn agrees to purchase the home unless she changes her mind. Caitlyn has provided an illusory promise.

> **Example:** The president of a corporation informs her employees, "You have all worked very hard so far this year, and if profits are still strong at the end of the year, everyone gets a 20 percent bonus—if management thinks a bonus is in order." This is an illusory promise because payment of the bonus is in management's sole discretion. There was no bargained-for exchange. Management may or may not pay the bonus at its discretion.

OPTION TO CANCEL. If a promisor has a right to cancel a contract, there may be consideration depending upon whether the right to cancel is somehow restricted. Where a party has the option to cancel a contract and there is no restriction on the right to cancel, the promisor has not bound themself to anything and the promise is illusory. Such situations arise when the promisor has a right to cancel without providing any notice and prior to the start of performance.

> **Example:** Landlord agrees to rent a space to tenant beginning July 1. The landlord contracts that it shall have the right to terminate the lease any time prior to July 1. The landlord's promise is illusory. It has not bound itself to the lease because the lease contract is entirely optional on the part of the landlord.

Where a promisor has a right to cancel a contract, but that right is somehow restricted (such as by providing a certain number of days' notice prior to terminating), the right to cancel is enforceable.

> **Example:** Landlord shall have the right to cancel this lease upon thirty (30) days' written notice. The cancellation right is enforceable as the landlord must provide thirty (30) days' written notice prior to termination.

REQUIREMENTS AND OUTPUT CONTRACTS. Where a buyer agrees to buy all its requirements for a particular good from the seller at an agreed price, this is known as a **requirements contract**. Similarly, if the seller agrees to sell all its output of a good to the buyer, this is known as an **output contract**.

Requirements contract
A contract in which one party agrees to supply as much of a good or service as is required by the other party, and in exchange the other party expressly or implicitly promises that it will obtain its goods or services exclusively from the first party.

Output contract
An output contract is an agreement in which a producer agrees to sell its entire production to the buyer, who, in turn, agrees to purchase the entire output.

> **Example:** McDonald's® sells hamburgers throughout the world. If McDonald's contracts with a large meat supplier to have the meat supplier sell all the meat it produces, this would be an example of a valid output contract.

Under modern contract law, these contracts are upheld so long as both parties act in good faith. However, where a party can choose how much it wants to buy or sell, the promise is illusory and held unenforceable. It is important to analyze the wording of the contract terms because the language determines whether the requirements or output contract is illusory. Where the terms provide "I want" or "all you will sell me," the contract terms are illusory because the parties have not agreed to bind themselves to anything.

> **Example:** In the above example, if the McDonald's contract allowed it to buy all the meat it wanted, the contract with the meat supplier would be illusory.

Past Consideration

Past consideration is something that was performed without any expectation of obtaining something in return from the other party. If one party later promises to compensate the other party for the benefit already received, this promise would not be enforceable because it was not concurrently bargained for in the transaction.

Past consideration
Unenforceable consideration based on past activities.

> **Example:** A woman and her three adult children lived together. The wife of one of the children, Marjorie McArdle, performed some decorating and repairs inside the house. After she had finished her remodeling work, the children promised to pay her $500 and signed a document stating they would pay her. However, the

promise to pay was unenforceable because all the work was completed before the promise to pay was made. *In re McArdle*, Ch. 669 (1951) (UK)

Example: One day after promising to grant bonuses to all employees for past services, the employer changes her mind and terminates the payment of any bonuses. The prior services would not be sufficient consideration to bind the company to pay the bonuses.

Moral Obligation

A moral obligation is not measurable and has no commercial effect. As a rule, a moral obligation, even if it is the subject of a promise, is not binding.

Example: Levi returned from a voyage at sea and suddenly became ill. He was taken in by the Mills family, who nursed him back to health. After Levi returned home, Levi's father thanked the Mills and said that he would cover any expenses incurred in nursing his son back to health. The court found that this was a promise based on a moral obligation and was unenforceable since Levi's father made the promise only after Levi had been nursed back to health, at which point Levi's father may have felt he was morally obliged to pay. *Mills v. Wyman*, 20 Mass. 207 (1825)

Preexisting Duty

Usually, an agreement to do what one is already under an obligation or a duty to do is not consideration. If a person already has a contract to perform, an additional agreement to perform the same duties lacks consideration under the **preexisting duty** doctrine.

Preexisting duty
A duty that someone is already obligated to perform.

Example: A little-known band contracts to sing at a wedding for $5,000. Two weeks before the wedding, the band's single became popular and the band is now in high demand. The band now demands additional compensation of $10,000 to sing at the wedding. The engaged couple agrees to the additional compensation, feeling that they have no choice. But the couple is not obligated to pay the additional compensation, due to the band's preexisting duty.

UNFORESEEN DIFFICULTIES. The preexisting duty rule does not apply when a party to the contract runs into an unforeseen difficulty. An unforeseen difficulty must be one that is not the type of risk that would ordinarily be assumed at the time the contract was formed.

Example: In the wedding example above, if the band had contracted to play with amplified sound but it was later discovered that the building lacked electrical power, this would be an unforeseen difficulty, and the band could seek additional compensation for having to play acoustically.

Concept Summary
Common Consideration Issues

Common Consideration Issues

Illusory Promise

- When one of the parties does not actually bind themselves to do anything

Moral Obligation

- Commonly occurs when someone has already performed a benefit for another out of a sense of moral duty

Past Consideration

- Occurs when one of the parties performs before there is any expectation for the other party to do anything in return

Gift Promise

- Occurs when only one party has offered consideration

Preexisting Duty

- Occurs when one of the parties already has a duty to perform

In the following decision, consideration for the modification of an existing employment agreement was lacking.

CASE 10.1

A CONTRACT MODIFICATION TO A PREEXISTING DUTY REQUIRES NEW OR ADDITIONAL CONSIDERATION

GROSS v. DIEHL SPECIALTIES INTERNATIONAL, INC.

776 S.W.2d 879 (1989)

Court of Appeals of Missouri

Under a 1977 employment contract, George Gross had a 15-year employment contract with Dairy Specialties, Inc., a company in the business of formulating ingredients to produce non-dairy products for use by customers allergic to cow's milk. It provided him a base salary of $14,400 plus cost-of-living adjustments; he would receive additional profit bonuses and would equally own an invention and would receive a royalty even after the term of the agreement. Prior to his employer selling the business to Diehl Specialties International in 1982, Diehl insisted that a new contract between the Gross and Diehl be executed. The new owner reset the base pay back to $14,400, ignored the cost-of-living increases, and continued the gross profit provision, but eliminated ownership of the invention and royalty payments would not extend beyond the ten-year term of the new contract. Gross received no compensation for executing the new contract. After the sale, Diehl assigned Gross additional duties not required by the original agreement. Gross sued when he was terminated after the business revenue severely declined. Gross appealed a jury verdict for the employer in his breach of employment contract case.

Language of the Court. *Plaintiff contends this holding is erroneous because there existed no consideration for the 1982 agreement. We agree. A modification of a contract constitutes the making of a new contract and such new contract must be supported by consideration. While consideration may consist of either a detriment to the promisee or a benefit to the promisor, a promise to carry out an already existing contractual duty does not constitute consideration.*

Under the 1982 contract defendant Diehl assumed no detriment it did not already have. The term of the contract expired on the same date under both contracts. Defendant Diehl undertook no greater obligations than it already had. Gross on the other hand received less than he had under the original contract. His base pay was reduced back to its amount in 1977 despite the provision in the 1977 contract for cost of living adjustments. He lost his equal ownership in his formula during the term of the agreement and his exclusive ownership after the termination of the agreement. He lost all royalties after termination of the agreement and the right to use and license the formulae subject to defendant's right to non-exclusive use upon payment of royalties. In exchange for nothing, defendant acquired exclusive ownership of the formulae during and after the agreement, eliminated royalties after the agreement terminated, turned its non-exclusive use after termination into exclusive use and control, and achieved a reduction in plaintiff's base salary. Defendant did no more than promise to carry out an already existing contractual duty. There was no consideration for the 1982 agreement.

Diehl asserts that consideration flowed to plaintiff because the purchase of Gross's former employer by the Diehls might not have occurred without the agreement and the purchase provided plaintiff with continued employment and a financially viable employer. There is no evidence to support this contention. Plaintiff had continued employment with the same employer under the 1977 agreement. Nothing in the 1982 agreement provided for any additional financial protection to plaintiff. The essence of defendant's position is that the seller received more from his sale of the company because of the new agreement than he would have without it. We have difficulty converting seller's windfall into a benefit to plaintiff.

Decision. The trial court erred when it determined that the 1982 contract was the operative contract. The 1982 contract was void for lack of consideration. The appellate court remanded the case to determine the amount of compensation to which Gross was entitled.

Focus on Ethics

If consideration was missing in the new agreement, suggest the forms of new consideration that should have been offered to Gross to ensure that the agreement was fair and enforceable.

Concept Summary
Modifying a Preexisting Contract

When parties to the contract mutually agree to change one or more of its terms, the parties modify a preexisting contract. Under common law, this modification must be supported by new consideration to be enforceable.

Management Application
Best Efforts Clause as Consideration

A promise made to exercise one's best efforts to achieve the objectives of a contract may be recognized as consideration. However, jurisdictions differ as to the meaning of best efforts; some equate it to reasonable efforts, while other states, such as Delaware, hold that the term requires something more. In many states, courts will refuse to enforce a best efforts promise unless either objective criteria is stated against which the efforts can be measured or there are industry standards to which reference can be made. In the absence of such guidance, the phrase may be too vague to be enforced. If the objection can be overcome by concrete, measurable standards, it is more likely that the clause will be enforced. Consider the case of a manufacturer who has developed a greatly improved version of 4K television sets. The manufacturer has contracted with an American retailer to deliver the television sets in time for the holiday season at locations across the United States. If a dock strike occurs, which is an event excluded from the clause allowing permissible delays (known as the *force majeure* clause), take one side of the transaction and present how such best efforts should be measured in these circumstances.

Settlement of Claims

Accord
A subsequent agreement between parties to resolve a disputed debt.

Satisfaction
The performance of an accord.

Parties to a contract do not always perform as they are supposed to. The parties may then attempt to settle the claims among themselves. When they do so, they enter into an accord and satisfaction. An accord and satisfaction may only occur when the amount of debt is in dispute. An **accord** is an agreement wherein the parties agree to accept something that is different than originally contracted. **Satisfaction** arises when the performance of the accord has been completed.

> **Example:** A contractor is hired to design and install a pool at a homeowner's property. The contractor designs and installs the pool; however, the homeowner alleges that the pool design and construction are inferior and not built according to the plans created. If the contractor agrees to accept a lessor sum due to the dispute, there is an accord. Once the homeowner pays the accord, there is satisfaction of the debt.

When satisfaction of the accord is completed, the original debt is discharged. However, if the accord is not satisfied, the non-breaching party can sue to enforce either the accord or the original contract.

Promises Binding Without Consideration

There are several situations in which a promise, made without consideration, is still enforceable. Among the common types are a revival of discharged debts and promissory estoppel.

Revival of Discharged Debts

Most states will enforce a written promise to pay a past debt even though no consideration for the promise is given. For example, debts that may not be collected because of the elapse of the statute of limitations or that have been discharged in bankruptcy are enforceable in most states. The new promise revives the discharged obligation. The obligation due is on the terms of the new promise and needs no consideration to be enforceable.

> **Example:** A owed B $5,000 for a business debt that was later discharged in bankruptcy. The post-bankruptcy written promise is enforceable but only to the extent stated in the agreement. If A agreed to pay B $2,000 of that discharged debt, only that amount would be due.

Promissory Estoppel

Considering the situations described in which consideration is lacking, there is one notable exception to the rule that consideration is required for an enforceable contract. It is a concept known as promissory estoppel. When a person has reasonably and substantially relied on the promise of another, they may be able to obtain the rights to enforce a contract. **Promissory estoppel** arises from the legal fiction that the conduct of one party has so caused the detrimental reliance of another party that it is only fair to enforce said promise. It applies in a variety of contexts, and it is applied in those situations when a promise is made without consideration. The court seeks to enforce the promise to avoid the inevitable injustice.

Promissory estoppel
A doctrine used to prevent unjust enrichment where a party makes a promise and the promisee reasonably, detrimentally, and foreseeably relies on the promise to their detriment.

For promissory estoppel to apply, the following elements are *required*:

- A clear and definite promise was given.
- The promisor should have reasonably expected that the promisee would rely on the promise.
- The promisee did reasonably rely on the promise.
- The promisee's reliance was definite and resulted in substantial detriment or harm to the promisee.
- Enforcement of the promise is necessary to avoid injustice.

When promissory estoppel applies, the promisor may not argue the lack of consideration as a defense.

Example: Walter Fields and Marjorie Conrad were friends. Walter started his own business and became a financially successful businessman. Walter also was known for his philanthropic work, having sometimes paid education costs for others. In 2000, Walter suggested to Marjorie that she should attend law school and he offered to pay for her education. Marjorie, who had recently paid off a $11,000 medical bill and still owed $5,000 for undergraduate student loans, did not feel capable of paying for law school on her own. Walter promised that he would pay tuition and other expenses associated with law school as they became due. Acting on these promises, Marjorie quit her job at Qwest, where she had been earning $45,000 per year, to attend law school. Walter made one payment for tuition but ceased making payments afterwards. As a result, Marjorie incurred more debt, at which point Walter said, "I will pay your tuition once you graduate law school and pass the bar exam."

Marjorie sued under the doctrine of promissory estoppel to recover the costs of tuition as they became due. The court held that Marjorie had proved the elements of a promissory estoppel claim. *Conrad v. Fields*, 2007 WL 2106302 (Minn. 2007)

Concept Summary
How to Apply Promissory Estoppel: Look for Consideration First

Before applying the doctrine of promissory estoppel to enforce a contract, it is important to first determine if there is consideration.

Promissory estoppel is only relevant to an analysis of contractual enforcement if consideration is not present.

The following case illustrates how promissory estoppel can be applied in an employment context.

CASE 10.2

PROMISSORY ESTOPPEL MAY SUPPORT ENFORCEMENT OF AN OFFER OF EMPLOYMENT

BRUECK v. JOHN MANEELY CO.

131 F. Supp. 3d 774 (2015)

United States District Court for the Northern District of Indiana

Kelly Brueck had accepted an offer of employment with JMC Steel Group, Inc., signing an offer letter for at-will employment that stated the offer was contingent upon successfully completing a background check. Glen Belk, who would have been her supervisor at JMC Steel, had sent several emails and correspondences to Ms. Brueck encouraging her to quit her current job as well as welcome emails to Ms. Brueck as a new employee. She was even given a start date for her new job. Ms. Brueck then notified her existing employer (a competitor to JMG Steel) that she had accepted a new job and that she was resigning from her position. Three days before her start date, JMC Steel retracted its offer, citing a background check that revealed falsehoods in Ms. Brueck's job application. Ms. Brueck did admit later that her application falsely listed her educational credentials. Ms. Brueck then sued, alleging a claim for promissory estoppel.

Language of the Court. *Promissory estoppel may be found in claims for damages resulting from a plaintiff's detrimental reliance on a defendant's promise of employment. A claim of promissory estoppel requires the following elements: (1) a promise by the promisor; (2) made with the expectation that the promisee will rely thereon; (3) which induces reasonable reliance by the promisee; (4) of a definite and substantial nature; and (5) injustice can be avoided only by enforcement of the promise. In the context of a retracted offer for at-will employment, a plaintiff who establishes those elements can recover any reliance damages sustained because of the promise, but they cannot recover any wages they might have earned through that employment. These reliance damages can include moving expenses and foregone wages, but not prospective wages that might have been earned at the new job.*

Ms. Brueck alleges that JMC offered her a job and that she quit her existing job in reliance on JMC's promise of employment. She further alleges that JMC broke that promise when it retracted its offer, and that fairness thus requires that JMC be held accountable for damages she sustained in reliance on that promise. That contingency and the falsehood on Ms. Brueck's job application are undoubtedly problematic. However, the offer letter is not the only promise Ms. Brueck alleges she relied on. She also alleges that Glen Belk, who would have been her supervisor at JMC Steel sent several emails and correspondences to her encouraging her to quit her current job and welcomed her as a new employee. She was even given a new start date for her job. Depending on the content and context of communications between the prospective employer and employee, encouraging someone to quit their job, welcoming them as a new employee, and giving them a start date could imply that any contingency to the job offer had either been satisfied or waived, and could be interpreted as a definite promise of employment. As to Ms. Brueck's reliance, quitting her job could constitute reliance of a definite and substantial nature. Ms. Brueck alleged that she quit her existing job to accept the new position in reliance on JMC Steel's offer, so it is plausible that she could still recover any expenses she incurred or any foregone wages.

Decision. The court held that promissory estoppel applied, and Ms. Brueck was entitled to damages incurred for reliance, but not for lost wages.

Focus on Ethics

Do you think it is fair for a prospective employee to lie on their application and still be entitled to damages from the prospective employer? If you were the employer, what would you have done differently?

AI Feature: Promissory Estoppel and Compensation

Use an AI program to answer the questions presented in the following prompt. Assume Good Doctors Surgical Center (Good Doctors) has contracted with Healthco, a health insurance company. Good Doctors sued Healthco, seeking payment for surgical procedures it performed on Healthco's insureds. Further, Good Doctor claims that Healthco had promised to pay Good Doctors the "usual and customary" rate—a rate determined by the amounts charged by other healthcare providers in the geographic area—when, in actuality, it paid Good Doctors at the rates Medicare providers charged, which were much lower. Healthco denies that it agreed to pay the usual and customary rate. What are the essential elements of promissory estoppel that Good Doctors must prove? What evidence should Good Doctors seek to obtain in discovery to prove additional compensation is due based upon promissory estoppel? Do these alleged promises need to be explicitly stated or can they be something less, such as unambiguously communicating by conduct that the higher rates would be paid? For promissory estoppel to apply, does a promise have to be capable of only one reasonable interpretation?

Key Terms

- Accord, 248
- Consideration, 240
- Forbearance, 240
- Illusory promise, 242
- Output contract, 243
- Past consideration, 243
- Preexisting duty, 244
- Promissory estoppel, 249
- Requirements contract, 243
- Satisfaction, 248

Applying the Law

10.1 Substitute Consideration. Charles Wilkins loaned $110,000 to J.R. Owen for use in operating his business. Mildred Owen, his wife, executed along with her husband a promissory note in favor of Wilkins. Then, when the borrowers were in default and, in exchange for not seeking to recover funds in the debtor's business account, Wilkins received a second note to replace the unpaid balance of the first note. The second note was executed in the amount of money then due Wilkins in the sum of $90,875. This second note was secured by a deed of trust on the Owens' residence, although the wife was the sole owner of the property, both husband and wife executed the deed of trust. When the note was unpaid, Wilkins foreclosed on the deed of trust. The trial court found that the second note was a valid indebtedness to Wilkins. They argued that no benefit accrued to Mildred Owen as a borrower, and that the note was invalid because she did not operate the business. What result? *In re Owen*, 303 S.E.2d 351 (N.C. 1983)

10.2 Bargained for Consideration. After working three years as a sales representative of GAC, a dental supply company, Timothy Thiesing was told to execute an employment agreement as a condition of continued employment with GAC. He executed it at a GAC conference in Texas. The agreement contained a post-employment restrictive covenant prohibiting him from working for a competitor for two years after termination of his employment. Five years later, he was hired by a direct competitor to GAC to service his old GAC sales territory. Thiesing and his new employer stated that the employment agreement with GAC lacked consideration. The agreement required that Minnesota law apply, a state whose laws favor enforcing such agreements against employees. Was there bargained-for consideration or was this a coercive agreement? *Thiesing v. Dentsply Int'l, Inc.*, 748 F. Supp. 2d 932 (E.D. Wis. 2010)

10.3 Forbearance. Four months after buying a home, Ozma Tabassum learned that her husband, Javed Younis, was having an extramarital affair with a co-worker. However, they negotiated the terms of a postmarital agreement that designated the marital home as Tabassum's nonmarital property in the event of a divorce. She filed for divorce five months later. Younis argued that they had negotiated the agreement while Tabassum was out of the country and had taken their daughter to visit relatives. He claimed that, at the time that he signed the agreement, he was still concerned that she would "take off" with their daughter, and he was feeling very vulnerable. The trial court found the agreement lacked consideration. What factors would compel the appellate court to reverse the trial court's decision? *In re Marriage of Tabassum*, 881 N.E.2d 396 (Ill. App. 2007)

10.4 Benefits and Detriments. Mary Iacono had been friends with Carolyn Lyons for almost 35 years when Lyons invited Iacono to join her on a trip to Las Vegas, Nevada. Lyons paid all the expenses for the trip, including providing money for gambling.

Sometime before the trip, Iacono had a dream about winning on a Las Vegas slot machine. It convinced her to go to Las Vegas and she accepted Lyons's offer to split "50-50 any gambling winnings." Lyons hit it big at Caesar's Palace® with an almost $2,000,000 payout on a slot machine, but Lyons refused to share the winnings. Iacono sued Lyons for breach of contract. The trial court held there was a lack of consideration for the promise, but the court of appeal reversed. What analysis of consideration rules would compel that result? *Iacono v. Lyons*, 16 S.W.3d 92 (Tex. App. 2000)

10.5 The Timing of Giving Consideration. Take It Away, Inc., was organized to function as a broker in a contemplated business of supplying dumpsters that do-it-yourselfers could rent from The Home Depot, Inc.®, and other retailers. Information was disclosed to Home Depot in a proposal that the association, Take It Away, would supply dumpsters that Home Depot would rent directly to its customers, pocketing 10 percent of the charge and remitting the balance to Take It Away. After solicitation from Take It Away disclosed the concept in sufficient detail, Home Depot signed a confidentiality agreement with Take It Away. Following several years in which Home Depot was not interested in becoming a dumpster lessor, it eventually signed agreements allowing four suppliers to use space in Home Depot stores to offer dumpster rentals directly as lessors to Home Depot customers. Take It Away sued Home Depot for violating the non-disclosure agreement and theft of trade secrets. Was there consideration for the confidentiality agreement? *Take It Away, Inc. v. Home Depot, Inc.*, 374 Fed. Appx. 47 (1st Cir. 2010)

10.6 Mutuality of Consideration. American Airlines® sued Frequent Flyer Depot, Inc., a broker for the purchase and sale of its airline frequent flyer miles and awards. It sought an injunction to prohibit the broker from doing so. The defendant broker asserted, among other things, that American did not have a binding contract with its program members that prohibited them from buying and selling program points. While prohibiting such sales, American reserved to itself the right to change the program rules at any time with or without notice to the members. The broker asserted that the provision in the members' User Agreement lacked mutuality and made the agreement unenforceable. Who should prevail and why? *Frequent Flyer Depot, Inc. v. Am. Airlines, Inc.*, 281 S.W.3d 215 (Tex. App. 2009)

10.7 Exclusivity. At a meeting, Mid-South Packers, Inc., presented Shoney's, Inc.®, a restaurant chain, a proposal letter to supply meat to the restaurant. The letter also stated that Shoney's would be informed 45 days prior to any adjustment in price. The letter contained neither quantity nor durational terms. Shoney's expressed neither assent to nor rejection of the prices outlined in the letter. Shoney's claimed that they had a valid requirements contract and, ultimately, offset from an amount due the supplier the increased costs it paid more than those quoted in the proposal letter. The supplier claimed that there was no continuing contract between them. Each purchase order from Shoney's constituted a separate contract for the amount stated by the supplier. Read the decision and determine why this was not held to be a requirements contract. *Mid-South Packers, Inc. v. Shoney's, Inc.*, 761 F.2d 1117 (5th Cir. 1985)

10.8 Binding Consideration. Approximately one week before his actual retirement from 25 years of service, Edward Hayes spoke with an officer of his employer who stated that the employee would be taken care of after retirement. There was no mention of the sum of money and no formal authorization for payments by the shareholders. He chose to retire from his job. For four years, the employee received an annual sum from the employer, then the payments stopped. Hayes sued for their continuance. Who prevails and why? *Hayes v. Plantations Steel Co.*, 438 A.2d 1091 (R.I. 1982)

10.9 Illusory Promises. Neil Stokes and Craig Felzien, DISH® long-time subscribers, filed a class action lawsuit seeking damages following interruptions in the availability of FOX® network programming. In the subscription agreement, DISH had reserved to itself the right to change prices, packages, and programming at any time during the term of the agreement. It also had a limitation of liability clause. Was this an illusory contract as the trial court had held? *Stokes v. DISH Network, L.L.C.*, 838 F.3d 948 (8th Cir. 2016)

10.10 Promissory Estoppel. Robb and Craig Knauf and Knauf Realty, LLC (Knauf) brought a lawsuit against Prudential Real Estate Affiliates, Inc. (Prudential). Knauf alleged that Prudential made promises of a real estate franchise to Knauf and that Knauf reasonably relied on the promises to its detriment by signing a lease for office space and paying for office improvements that proved unusable after the franchise negotiations failed. For Knauf to prevail on a claim of promissory estoppel, what other facts do you think would be helpful to Knauf? *Knauf Realty, LLC v. Prudential Real Estate Affiliates, Inc.*, 486 F. Supp. 2d 855 (W.D. Wis. 2007)

Capacity and Legality of Subject Matter

11

Perhaps no branch of jurisprudence is more elusive than that dealing with one's mental capacity to contract. — *Waggoner v. Atkins*, 204 Ark. 264 (1942)

Chapter Outline

- Introduction
- Capacity of the Parties

Case 11.1: *Berg v. Traylor*
Case 11.2: *Oak Crest Manor Nursing Home, LLC v. Barba*

- Legality of the Subject Matter
- Effect of Illegality
  - *Management Application: Severability Clause*
- AI Feature: Disaffirmance and Capacity

Learning Objectives

After studying this chapter, you should be able to:

1. Explain how capacity affects the enforceability of contracts.
2. Define and explain minors' contracts.
3. Describe how mental competency may affect contractual capacity.
4. Define an illegal contract.
5. Explain when a contract violates public policy.

Introduction

The preceding contract law chapters dealt with agreement and consideration for a contract. In this chapter, we address the last two elements required for contract formation. Parties must have the capacity to contract, and the contract cannot involve an illegal subject matter.

The requirement of capacity arises out of our common sense and desire for fairness. The effect of a lack of capacity to contract affects the parties' agreement in dramatic ways. Depending upon the circumstances, the agreement may be void or voidable. In other cases, where capacity may be lacking, the law may impose a binding contract because it is fair to do so. Such statutory commands include the obligation of a minor or his or her parents to pay for the necessities of life, such as food, shelter, clothing, and medical care.

When the subject of the contract involves illegality, it may arise from unlawful consideration given in exchange for a promise or may arise from a purpose that promotes immoral or unlawful conduct. This prohibition is rooted in strong public policy considerations, which are addressed in this chapter.

Our study involves contracts that have been formed but, because of the circumstances relating either to the parties' capacity to contract or the subject matter of the agreement, may or may not be enforced.

Capacity of the Parties

Capacity
A legally recognized level of mental ability to understand the nature of an agreement.

One of the goals of our legal system is to promote fairness. Inherently, this goal requires that all parties to a contract have the capacity to enter into a valid agreement. The general rule is that all persons are capable of contracting. Those who lack capacity include minors, intoxicated persons, the mentally incompetent, and, in some jurisdictions, persons who have been deprived of their civil rights.

When a person is unable to understand the nature and consequences of an agreement, the agreement will be either void or voidable by the party lacking capacity. A void contract is unenforceable by either party. Voiding a contract allows a party to avoid liability and not have the contract enforced.

Minors

In most states, the age of majority for a person to have capacity to enter into a contract is at least 18 years of age. Once reaching the age of 18, the person is treated as an adult. **Minors** are believed to lack the mental capacity to understand what a contract entails. However, by state law, some contracts, such as the purchase of intoxicating beverages, require the person to be at least 21 years of age.

Minor
A person who is under the age of majority.

Emancipation
The right of a minor to be freed from parental control.

An emancipated minor may be treated differently. **Emancipation** is the right of a minor to be free from parental control. State laws vary as to the conditions required to reach emancipation, but, generally, they involve the granting of permission by one or both parents, and, sometimes, the approval of a court. Once a minor is emancipated, the parents no longer have custody or control over the minor. Emancipated minors enjoy certain rights, including the right to contract for medical care and enroll in school or college. In some jurisdictions, they remain subject to juvenile court proceedings if they break the law before reaching the age of majority. For commercial purposes, a minor may petition a court to be treated as an adult to enter into contracts.

DISAFFIRMANCE. To protect minors, the law provides a minor who enters into a contract with the right to reject the entire contract or to perform it. This principle is also known as the infancy doctrine. The act of cancelling or rejecting the contract due to age of minority is known as **disaffirmance**. There are some exceptions to this right to disaffirm, which are discussed below.

Disaffirmance
The act of rejecting or avoiding a contract by reason of the infancy doctrine.

To disaffirm, the minor must express an intention by words or actions not to be bound to the contract. The disaffirmance can be made at any time during the age of minority or, in some states, within a reasonable time after reaching the age of majority, such as six months. What is a reasonable period is decided on the facts of each case. Only the minor may disaffirm the contract. The adult assumes the risk that the minor may later disaffirm the contract, and the adult has no right to disaffirm. When a minor disaffirms, the disaffirmance is to the entirety of the contract; the minor may not retain the benefits of part of the contract and disaffirm the balance.

DUTIES FOLLOWING DISAFFIRMANCE. If the contract is executory (a contract where one or more parties has an obligation remaining to be performed to fulfil the terms of the contract), nothing needs to be done by either party upon disaffirmance by the minor. The contract is nullified and treated as if it never came into existence. If the contract is executed, several general rules apply.

Duty of Restoration. Subject to some exceptions, most states require that a minor need *only* return the property received from the adult in the condition it was in at the time of disaffirmance. Once disaffirmance occurs, the minor (but not the adult) must be restored to the same position the minor was in prior to entering into the contract. Subject to a few exceptions discussed below, the amount owed to the minor is not reduced if the item has been consumed, damaged, depreciated, or has otherwise lost value. A minor who has used services received is not liable for anything upon disaffirmance.

> **Example:** Jaime, a 17-year-old, buys a new laptop. After six months of use, Jaime accidentally spills a soft drink on the laptop, causing it to not operate. If Jaime disaffirms the contract, his obligation is to return the damaged laptop, and he is entitled to be paid the original purchase price.

However, a few states require full restitution. Minors in those states must take whatever additional steps are necessary to restore the adult to the position the adult was in prior to entering into the contract with the minor.

If the minor has transferred the property to an innocent third party, that party will acquire good title with respect to the goods, but the minor still has the right to disaffirm the contract and recover the property.

> **Example:** Mia, a 17-year-old, buys a motorcycle from a relative. Mia sells the bike to an innocent third party. Mia retains the right to disaffirm the contract before majority and can compel the third party to restore ownership and possession of the bike to her.

EXCEPTIONS TO A MINOR'S RIGHT TO DISAFFIRM. While a minor can disaffirm most contracts, most states have created the following exceptions where a minor cannot disaffirm a contract. These include (1) necessaries of life; (2) where a minor's intentional, reckless, or grossly negligent conduct caused the loss of value; (3) where a minor misrepresents his or her age; and (4) certain types of contracts a minor executes.

Necessities of Life. A minor who enters into a contract to purchase necessities of life is liable for the reasonable value of those goods and services *even if the minor disaffirms the contract.* While there is no standard definition for a necessary of life, necessaries of life include food, shelter, clothing, medical attention, and/or other goods or services necessary to maintain the minor's well-being and standard of living. That is, necessaries may be subjective depending on the individual. The provider of the necessaries of life may recover the reasonable value of the necessaries from the minor under the theory of quasi-contract.

> **Example:** A university freshman, aged 17, enters into an apartment lease at above-market rates. While she is still a minor, she disaffirms the contract because she wants to move to a less expensive location. She must pay the reasonable rental rate during her time of occupancy because the apartment is a necessity of life.

Intentional, Reckless, or Grossly Negligent Conduct. If the minor's intentional, reckless, or grossly negligent conduct caused the loss of value to the adult's property, most states require that the loss of value of the adult's property be restored to the adult. This is the duty of restitution.

> **Example:** As a minor, Caleb purchases and recklessly rides a motorcycle, causing extensive damage to its frame and motor. If Caleb disaffirms the motorcycle purchase, Caleb would be responsible for the cost of restoring the bike to its pre-sale condition when returning the motorcycle because of the damage caused by his reckless conduct.

Misrepresentation of Age. While most states will permit disaffirmance *even if the minor misrepresented his or her age* when entering into the agreement, some state laws prohibit disaffirmance if the minor induced reliance by the adult. Merely consenting to age of majority through a preprinted form contract is not enough. Other states permit disaffirmance only upon the condition that all the property received by the minor is restored to the adult.

> **Example:** In the example above, suppose Caleb used false identification when purchasing a new motorcycle from a retailer. Most states will permit Caleb to disaffirm the contract, but some states would prohibit Caleb from disaffirming.

Binding Contracts of Minors. State legislatures have recognized that some contracts should be binding upon minors and not subject to disaffirmance. These include the following:

- Contracts involving necessaries
  - **Example:** Hospitals are relieved of potential tort liability for failing to obtain parental consent to treat a minor in the event of an emergency
- Marital agreements (applicable in those states where a minor may lawfully marry)
- Child support agreements of the minor
- Transactions with financial institutions

- Educational loan agreements
  - **Example:** Financing a college education through loans
- Enlistment in active-duty military service (with permission received from a parent)
- Contracts of a creative artist, entertainer, or athlete subject to court approval

Concept Summary Disaffirmance

These are the conditions under which a minor may "avoid" a contract:

- He or she need only express an intention by words or actions not to be bound.
- He or she may disaffirm the entire contract at any time during minority or for a reasonable time after reaching the age of majority.
- Upon disaffirmance, most states require that the minor return any goods or other consideration in his or her possession. But the modern trend of disaffirmance law requires the minor to restore the adult to the position the adult was in prior to entering the contract with the minor.

Only the minor has the option of disaffirming his or her contractual obligations; any adult party to the contract remains bound by it unless released by the minor's words or conduct.

RATIFICATION. If the minor has failed to disaffirm during minority or within a reasonable time after reaching the age of majority, the individual is bound to the contract. That is, the failure to timely disaffirm the contract is deemed to be a ratification. **Ratification** is the acceptance or confirmation of a contract once the minor has reached the age of majority. A minor cannot ratify a contract while still being under the age of majority.

Ratification
The acceptance or confirmation of a contract once the minor has reached the age of majority.

The ratification may be either *express* or *implied.* Express ratification arises when the new adult either orally or in writing ratifies the contract. Implied ratification arises from the conduct of the party that would be inconsistent with someone who was disaffirming a contract. If a minor takes no action within a reasonable time after reaching the age of majority and remains silent, the inaction of the new adult causes the contract to be ratified. In this case, silence constitutes acceptance.

Example: As a minor, Aaron purchases an automobile. After reaching the age of majority, Aaron continues to drive the vehicle. Courts may hold that Aaron's action of continuing to use the vehicle for a reasonable time after reaching the age of majority has ratified the contract.

Attaining or Regaining Contractual Capacity

Express Ratification

A person lacking contractual capacity at the inception of the contract may, upon attaining or regaining the capacity to do so, expressly ratify (or consent to) the contract by stating, orally or in writing, that the person intends to be bound by the contract.

Implied Ratification

Similarly, a person lacking contractual capacity at the inception of the contract may, upon attaining or regaining the capacity to do so, impliedly ratify the contract (1) by acting in a manner that is clearly inconsistent with disaffirmance or avoidance; or (2) in the case of a minor, by failing to disaffirm within a reasonable time after reaching the age of majority.

Concept Summary Ratification and Timing

Incapacity	Incapacity Terminates	Capacity
• Age of minority: • contract may not be ratified • contract may be disaffirmed	• Reaches the age of majority	• Contract may be ratified: • expressly or through implication • Contract may be disaffirmed within a reasonable time • If a contract is not disaffirmed within a reasonable time, the contract is ratified

PARENTAL LIABILITY. The general rule is that parents are not liable for the contracts made by their minor children, with the following exceptions:

1. One or more of the parents co-signs the contract. When they do so, the parents are responsible for its performance, even if the minor child later disaffirms the contract.

2. The minor commits a tort associated with the contract at the direction of a parent. For example, a parent would be liable to the third party if the parent assisted the minor in obtaining false identification to misstate the minor's age to later exercise the right of disaffirmance.
3. The minor enters into a contract for necessaries of life, since parents are obligated to provide for necessaries of life to their minor children.

In the following case, a Hollywood television talent that was a minor, disaffirmed a talent management contract. As you read the case, note that the conflict of interest between the young actor's mother and the actor extended the time for him to disaffirm the contract.

CASE 11.1

A PARENT CAN BE LIABLE FOR DAMAGES FOLLOWING THE CHILD'S DISAFFIRMANCE OF THE CONTRACT

BERG v. TRAYLOR

148 Cal. App. 4th 809 (2007)

Court of Appeal of California

Meshiel Traylor and Craig Traylor, mother and son, entered into a two-page, three-year contract with Sharyn Berg to retain Berg as the film industry manager of Craig, who was ten years old at the time. The contract contained an arbitration agreement and expressly stated that Craig's disaffirmance would not release his mother from the contract's terms.

Berg was to receive a 15 percent commission on Craig's industry income during the three-year period, including income from employment offers received during that period, even if the money was earned after the three years ended. During the term of the contract, Craig received a recurring television role on *Malcolm in the Middle.* Four months prior to the expiration of the agreement, Meshiel sent a letter to Berg terminating the agreement and stating that the Traylors would no longer be paying Berg. Berg sued the Traylors for breach of contract. The case went to arbitration, and the Traylors lost, with Berg awarded approximately $580,000 in damages, including syndication earnings. At the arbitration hearing, the Traylors did not have an attorney representing them nor was a separate guardian appointed for Craig. Berg filed a petition to confirm the arbitration award, and the Traylors responded with Craig's disaffirmance of the contract and a petition to vacate the arbitration award. The trial court ruled for Berg, finding that the Traylors' petition was untimely. The Traylors appealed.

Language of the Court. *We find that Craig was entitled to and did disaffirm the arbitration award because he was never represented by an appointed guardian. The right of disaffirmance by a minor of a judgment rendered voidable by the fact that he was not represented by a guardian in the action is absolute, and such right continues throughout his minority.*

Such an appointment was required here due to the inherent conflict of interest between Craig and Meshiel. The agreement expressly provided that even if Craig disaffirmed, Meshiel would remain liable for commissions due Berg. It was therefore not in Meshiel's interest to have Craig disaffirm the agreement because Berg would look to her, personally, for satisfaction of Craig's obligations under the agreement. As such, Meshiel's interests in the lawsuit were in direct conflict with those of her son. It is clear that Meshiel, as Craig's guardian, could not adequately represent his interests. It was necessary for Craig to have a guardian appointed to separately represent his interest with respect to Berg's claims. Because no guardian was appointed for Craig, we conclude that he was entitled to disaffirm the arbitration award, the stipulated orders pertaining to the arbitration award and the subsequent judgment rendered against him.

The Traylors do not generally distinguish their arguments between mother and son, apparently assuming that if Craig disaffirms the agreement and judgment, Meshiel would be permitted to escape liability as well. But a disaffirmance of an agreement by a minor does not operate to terminate the contractual obligations of the parent who signed the agreement. The agreement Meshiel signed provided that Craig's disaffirmance would not serve to void or avoid Meshiel's obligations under the agreement and that Meshiel remained liable for commissions due Berg regardless of Craig's disaffirmance. Accordingly, we find no basis for Meshiel to avoid her independent obligations under the agreement.

Decision. The appellate court reversed the judgment as to the child actor but affirmed it as to the mother.

Focus on Ethics

Does it seem fair that the mother is responsible for the more than half-million-dollar award? Was it unfair for the talent agent to draft a contract with these terms at a point in time when a parent might be unfamiliar with entertainment contracts?

Contracts Made by Intoxicated Persons

Persons who are under the influence of drugs or alcohol at the time of entering into a contract may be entitled to have the contract set aside by a court. Where the person is intoxicated to a degree that they lack an understanding of the nature and consequences of an agreement, the other party may not take advantage of the situation. In such case, a contract would be voidable by the intoxicated person when returning to sobriety. Most states allow for the avoidance of the contract even when the intoxication was voluntary. However, if a person while under the influence of drugs or alcohol can still understand the nature and consequences of an agreement, the agreement will be valid and enforceable against that person.

Courts objectively review the circumstances to determine whether the person likely was intoxicated to the extent necessary to avoid the contract and can consider the physical characteristics of the individual and previous experiences with drugs or alcohol.

Where a contract is rescinded due to intoxication, the intoxicated person must be returned to status quo. The person claiming intoxication must return all consideration received and return the other party to the status quo.

> **Example:** The degree of intoxication is subject to the facts of each case. If a person is in a state of intoxication resulting in slightly impaired judgment, a contract may be enforced against them even if they did not negotiate its terms well.

> **Example:** If that same person lapses into states of unconsciousness (blackout drunk), a third party cannot take advantage of the circumstance. Any resulting contract is voidable by the intoxicated person once they regain capacity.

Landmark Case
Thackrah v. Haas, 119 U.S. 499 (1866)

Thackrah was the owner of 80,000 shares of the capital stock of a Utah mining company. He was in a continuous state of alcohol intoxication for three months. During that period, a local bank hired Haas to contract with the inebriated Thackrah to accept the grossly inadequate sum of $1,200 for his mining stock. When Thackrah sobered, he filed suit against Hass and the bank. Eventually the case was appealed to the United States Supreme Court. The Court ruled that the contract with the bank was void because the bank and Haas knew that Thackrah lacked the capacity to enter into the contract. The bank was ordered to return the shares to Thackrah, less the $1,200 previously paid to him.

Contracts Made by Mentally Incompetent Persons

Some persons lack the mental competency to enter into a contract. A person is legally incompetent if they are incapable of understanding or comprehending the nature of the transaction. This impairment may be temporary or permanent in nature. Common examples of people who may lack mental capacity are those suffering from mental illness, brain damage, and brain deterioration due to old age.

The mere presence of a disability, however, does not itself impair the capacity to contract. As the Supreme Court of Arkansas stated, "[T]he fact that the [person] was . . . filthy, believed in witchcraft, and had dogs eat at the same table with him or . . . would lie in bed with his clothes on for two weeks at a time, or that he would leave his home only at night. . . does not establish lack of capacity."[1] Contracts made with

1. *Simmons First National Bank, Administrator v. Luzader*, 438 S.W.2d 25 (Ark. 1969), citing *Harwell v. Garrett*, 239 Ark. 551 (1965).

mentally incompetent persons will be treated as void, voidable, or valid depending on the circumstances.

VOID CONTRACTS. Where a person has been adjudged mentally incompetent, the contract is void. Void contracts are considered as having no legal effect and cannot be enforced. A person who has been declared incompetent by a court is **adjudged mentally incompetent** and may not make a valid contract. Similarly, if a person is subject to a court-approved conservatorship or guardianship, they lack the ability to contract; however, a conservator or guardian can enter into binding contracts on the mentally incompetent person's behalf.

Adjudged mentally incompetent
A person who has been declared incompetent by a court and cannot make valid contracts.

VOIDABLE CONTRACTS. Where a person has not been adjudged mentally incompetent, but they lack mental capacity because they are incapable of understanding or comprehending the nature of the transaction, the contracts entered into by such person are voidable. The mentally competent person does not have an option to make the contract void. Such circumstances are encountered by many families whose members act as caretakers for the elderly members of their family.

> **Example:** If an elderly person has dementia, affecting their ability to understand or comprehend that they are selling their home or the value of that property, a purchase and sale contract executed by that person will be voidable.

VALID CONTRACTS. Some people as they age may experience alternating periods of mental capacity and incapacity. Contracts entered into while such a person is mentally competent are enforceable. When made during a period of mental incompetency, the person may disaffirm contracts when they recover their mental competency. If they never return to competency, a conservator may be appointed to set the contract aside.

Not reading a contract, being illiterate, or not understanding complex terms in an agreement is not grounds to be declared legally incompetent. Further, circumstances such as a lack of business experience, poor education, or a lack of judgment in financial decision making are insufficient grounds to rescind (that is, set aside) a contract.

> **Example:** If a person suffers from a lower-than-average mental capacity but is not without the ability to understand the nature of the agreement, the resulting contract would be valid and binding.

In the following case, the plaintiff sued a nursing home for negligently allowing a patient with mental disorders to leave the facility. The issue to be determined was whether the patient had the mental capacity to execute an admissions agreement excusing the facility from liability for harm suffered following the admission to the facility. The nursing home contended that the patient had exhibited periods of lucidity and that the agreement to arbitrate claims against it should be enforced.

CASE 11.2

MEDICAL ARBITRATION CLAUSES MAY BE VOIDED FOR LACK OF MENTAL CAPACITY

OAK CREST MANOR NURSING HOME, LLC v. BARBA

2016 Tex. App. LEXIS 12710 (Tex. App.-Austin, 2016)

Barba sued on behalf of her 40-year-old son Frank, who was injured when attempting to flee from a nursing home where he was being treated for depression, schizophrenia, and bipolar disorder. After escaping, Frank jumped off a freeway overpass in a suicide attempt. Barba sued the nursing home for negligence in failing to properly administer a care plan for such a gravely ill patient. She further alleged that Frank transferred to Oak Crest because it held itself out as being able to care for patients with risks of flight and elopement. Barba also alleged that the nursing home was aware of Frank's "tendencies, proclivities, and risks" because a care plan was developed at the time of his admission due to his multiple psychiatric conditions, history, and prior suicide attempts.

Two days before Frank sustained his injuries, Barba had been appointed his guardian by a probate court. Seeking to avoid the risk of a jury trial, the nursing home defendants filed a motion to compel arbitration and stay the court proceedings. They argued that Frank "voluntarily admitted himself into Oakcrest Manor" and understood the terms of a standard "Facility Admission Agreement." The agreement provided that any dispute between the patient and the facility would be resolved by binding arbitration. In response, Barba contended that due to Frank's psychological and mental disorders (evidenced by the probate court's adjudication of him as "totally incapacitated," and other documents), he lacked capacity to enter into an enforceable contract and that the contract was void. Seeking to enforce the arbitration provision, the nursing home appealed to the Texas court of appeals.

Language of the Court. *While a trial court's determination of the formation, validity, and enforcement of an arbitration agreement is ordinarily a question of law, the extent to which a person knows or understands the nature and consequences of executing a contract (and therefore has contractual capacity) is a question of fact. Accordingly, we will review the record to determine whether there was legally sufficient evidence to support the implied factual finding that Frank did not have sufficient capacity to enter into the Agreement.*

While the time of execution of a contract is indeed the relevant time for ascertaining competency to contract, evidence of competency from other periods is probative to establish competency at the time of execution if there is evidence that the later mental condition had some probability of being the same condition at the time of execution. Dr. McRoberts's report, issued only 49 days after the Agreement's execution, is probative of Frank's mental condition on the date of execution considering the other evidence in the record indicating that Frank's psychiatric diagnoses were already present and were the same as when Dr. McRoberts examined him. Further, Oak Crest's own records (created either at the precise date and time of his admission or only days later), demonstrate that upon admission Frank had already been long suffering from the precise mental conditions that were the basis of the probate court's determination just a few months later that he was incapacitated as a matter of law. Because Frank's alleged incapacity implicates the issue of contract formation, the contract is void by virtue of the probate court's implied finding that Frank was incapacitated when he signed the Agreement and that there was, accordingly, no contract and no agreement to arbitrate. We conclude that the record contains legally sufficient evidence to support the probate court's implied determination that Frank did not possess the requisite capacity to contract when he signed the Agreement, and the probate court did not abuse its discretion in refusing to compel arbitration on this basis.

Decision. The court denied the motion to compel arbitration of the guardian's claims for injuries to the patient.

Focus on Ethics

Does this decision raise concerns for institutions who deal with elderly clients or others who present some mental disability? What steps should be undertaken to protect both the provider and the patient?

Persons Deprived of Civil Rights

In a few jurisdictions, those who have been convicted of certain felonies are deemed to permanently lack the capacity to enter into binding agreements. In most states, this harsh rule of permanent incapacity after release from confinement has been relaxed. The prior approach would permanently bar a felon from entering into contracts. In most jurisdictions, the felon, upon release, may petition for a restoration of civil rights. Moreover, in many states the felon's civil rights are suspended only during the period of confinement and only as to rights that are reasonably related to legitimate correctional interests.

When such a prohibition applies, the contract rights otherwise enjoyed by a felon are unavailable. As noted, the relaxed and more modern trend is to permit such individuals personal liberties and commercial opportunities. Such restrictions can be made part of the sentencing of the individual following conviction.

Example: David Berkowitz was a serial killer who committed murders during the mid-1970s in New York. In response to the fear that he might sell his story to a filmmaker or publisher, the New York legislature swiftly passed a law preempting his right to do so. This law was quickly copied throughout the United States and other nations. Commonly known as a "Son of Sam" law, the law deprives a convicted felon from financially benefiting from the sale of their life story or selling items relating to their crimes. The law has also been extended to apply to friends, family, and others closely associated with the felon. These laws have been subject to many revisions, including granting the right to victims to sue the accused for civil damages if the convicted person did obtain financial gain.

Concept Summary Capacity to Contract

Some persons are not competent to understand the nature and consequences of a contract. The law presumes certain classes of persons to be incompetent:

- Minors (under the age of majority—18 years, unless legally emancipated or married)
- Persons under a conservatorship or guardianship
- Persons declared by a court to be adjudged mentally incompetent
- Persons who are deprived of their civil rights (in some jurisdictions)

Legality of the Subject Matter

Enforceable contracts must have a lawful purpose. If the subject matter is not recognized as lawful, i.e. it violates federal or state law, the resulting agreement is void. The law does not recognize contracts that violate a statute or are contrary to public policy. Public policy is the government response to a perceived problem. But what would happen if the parties to an illegal contract have partially or fully performed their agreement? The law will leave the parties in their positions and will refuse to enforce their agreement.

Example: If a business conspired with a competitor to restrain trade, that contract would be unlawful because it would violate federal and state antitrust laws. While still subject to potential criminal prosecution and the claims of other competitors, the two competitors could not seek court intervention in a dispute between them related to this illegal contract.

Contracts That Violate Statutes

Our government on all levels enacts statutes, ordinances, and rules and regulations prohibiting certain conduct. These prohibitions are enacted to promote the public's health, safety, and welfare. If conduct is prohibited by a statute, ordinance, or rule or regulation, an agreement that promotes that conduct is illegal or not permissible. In such a case, if either the subject of the contract or the participation of one or both parties is defined as an "illegal" activity, the entire contract is void. Following are examples of contracts that violate statutes and are, therefore, illegal.

CONTRACTS TO COMMIT A CRIME. Any contract to commit a criminal act is void and unenforceable. If the object or performance of the contract becomes illegal *after* the contract has been formed, such as when a statute now makes the object or performance illegal, the contract is discharged by law. If the parties continue to perform the contract after it becomes an illegal one, neither party can enforce the contract.

> **Example:** A company that sells firewood sells American chestnut firewood. If a statute makes selling American chestnut firewood illegal because the tree has become threatened or endangered, any contract entered into to purchase the American chestnut wood is now void, and the parties are discharged from the performance of the contract.

Usury
The interest in excess of the maximum interest rate permissible by law.

USURY. State usury laws establish the maximum interest rate that can be charged for certain types of loans. Interest is a charge for the use of money by another and does not include finance charges relating to the sale of goods. **Usury** is charging an unlawful rate of interest. Usury laws are enacted to protect unsophisticated borrowers from paying excessive rates of interest. Most states provide both criminal and civil penalties for creating a usurious contract. While the penalties vary by statute, most states provide that the lender is limited to the maximum interest rate allowed by law and must repay the borrower for any interest charged over the usury rate. Other states may also penalize the lender by allowing the borrower to recover the amount of interest or principal paid to the borrower.

The usury rates vary widely by state, and state laws exempt certain types of lenders and loan transactions from usury law application. In addition, the federal government does not have a usury law. and many federally chartered financial institutions are exempt from state usury limits.

> **Example:** States often exempt corporate loans from usury laws. In contrast, payday loans for small sums are often accompanied by high interest rates. The borrower usually repays these loans the next payday. States, such as New York, have usury laws setting a limit on the highest lawful annual interest rate. Under New York usury law, loan contracts exceeding an interest rate of 16 percent are unenforceable, irrespective of the lender's mental state. *United States v. Grote*, 961 F.3d 105 (2d Cir. 2020)

GAMBLING STATUTES. Any contract under which one pays consideration that involves a game of skill or chance that one might win or lose is considered gambling. State statutes will prohibit or regulate gambling. Except as permitted by law, contracts promoting prohibited forms of gambling are void. States typically exempt certain forms of gambling from the gambling statutes, such as bingo games, lotteries, and horse racing. As the U.S. Supreme Court has eliminated barriers to sports betting, an increasing number of states are adopting statutes permitting forms of sports betting.

> **Example:** The Indian Gaming Regulatory Act permits and regulates Native American gaming casinos. Federal law authorizes operation of gaming casinos by Native American tribes where state laws permit such gambling.

LICENSING STATUTES. All states require licensure by the state for certain professionals or tradespeople to practice. States will require an applicant for a license to demonstrate their competency through examination, prior experience, and declarations of moral character. Among the occupations so affected are health professionals, attorneys, certified public accountants, insurance agents, contractors, and real estate brokers.

Whether an unlicensed person can be compensated for services performed in licensed occupations depends upon the purpose of the licensing statute. When a licensing statute's purpose is to protect the public from unauthorized activities, a court will regard such regulatory purpose as sufficiently strong to make the contract illegal and unenforceable. In such cases, unlicensed persons may not collect compensation for their services. However, licensing statutes whose purposes are primarily revenue-based (those intended to tax license holders and not govern their activities) do not bar unlicensed persons from collecting compensation.

> **Example:** The failure to obtain a local business license will not bar a physician from collecting compensation for services rendered to a patient.

INTRINSICALLY EVIL OR WRONGFUL CONDUCT. If the contract involves intrinsically evil or wrongful conduct, known as ***malum in se***, a court will not involve itself in any aspect of its enforcement. The test to determine whether the contract is absolutely prohibited is to consider if an informed conscience would so object.

Malum in se Conduct constituting an inherent evil or wrong.

Some matters are regulated for the promotion of public welfare, health, and safety. Such conduct still makes the attempted contract void, but the law permits the person for whose protection the government acted to recover in quasi-contract. Illegal contracts in this form are known as merely ***malum prohibitum***. In these cases, an informed conscience would not suggest to the parties that the conduct was banned. However, if both parties knew that the subject matter was *malum prohibitum* and they consciously defied the law, they are ***in pari delicto*** (meaning they are equally at fault). Quasi-contractual relief will be denied to both parties. If one of the parties was innocent of such knowledge, he or she may recover in quasi-contract for the value of the consideration bestowed upon the other party.

Malum prohibitum Conduct constituting an unlawful act by statute and not inherently evil conduct.

In pari delicto Parties will be denied quasi-contractual relief because they are mutually or equally at fault in violating a statute governing their contract.

> **Example:** Contracts requiring the contamination of food ingredients to increase profits are *malum in se.*

> **Example:** The contract of an employer and employee could be *malum prohibitum* if they mutually but unknowingly agree that the employee will be paid less compensation than the employee would be entitled to under applicable wage and hour laws. Here the employee would still be allowed to recover the correct pay amounts.

BLUE LAWS. Also known as Sunday closing laws, **blue laws** enforce religious standards. Many states, or counties within a state (such as in Florida), prohibit selling alcoholic beverages for consumption on and off premises on Sundays at some restricted time. Others will require that car dealerships must be closed, or that hunting activities be limited.

Blue laws Laws prohibiting certain activities, on a Sunday, for religious or secular reasons.

Contracts to Commit an Act That Violates Public Policy

Courts provide broad powers to persons to contract; however, there are times when a court will not enforce the terms of a contract because of public policy concerns. Courts have sought to void contracts as violative of public policy when the negative impact on society or on the public's safety and welfare exceeds the benefits of the contract. The following types of contracts are contrary to public policy and thus are void:

- Contracts to commit immoral acts

Example: Creating a contract restraining someone's ability to marry is void as violative of public policy.

- Agreements to delay or obstruct justice

Example: Compensating a witness to purposefully be unavailable to testify in a criminal proceeding.

- Agreements involving public corruption (such as bribery).
- Contracts promoting unlawful restraints of trade (anticompetitive agreements) or unfair business practices.

Example: An agreement between competitors to unlawfully divide and allocate the markets in which they will operate.

Example: In some states, covenants not to compete (agreements restricting a person's ability to make a livelihood) are void. In other jurisdictions, such agreements are enforceable if they are reasonable in terms of duration and scope.

- Contracts written with unconscionable terms.

  Generally, courts do not look at the fairness of a contract and presume a person can protect their own interests, some contracts may be deemed unconscionable and not enforceable. Unconscionable contracts arise when the contract is so oppressive or unfair as to be unjust. In such circumstances, courts can enforce some or none of the contractual provisions. We will further discuss unconscionability in Chapter 12.

Example: The use of dense, legalistic contractual language such that understanding of its terms by a reasonable person is not possible. This is also known as a contract of adhesion.

Example: A contract whose terms shock the conscience of the court, such as lengthy automatic renewal terms.

- Unfair exculpatory clauses

  An **exculpatory clause** is a clause that releases one (or both) of the parties to a contract from liability. While not absolutely against public policy, the terms of these contracts are scrutinized by courts to evaluate the relative bargaining positions of the parties. Exculpatory clauses are found in many different agreements, including leases, event tickets, and parking lot tickets. Businesses use the clauses to limit their liability in the event a guest is injured.

Exculpatory clause
A contract clause that releases one (or both) of the parties to a contract from liability.

Example: A tourist attraction relies upon a release of liability excusing any form of harm or injury arising from any cause while at the park. This release is printed on the back of the patron's ticket.

- Contracts that violate constitutional rights.

Example: Property management contracts that violate fair housing laws in the selection of tenants.

Effect of Illegality

In general, contracts with illegal subject matters are considered void. In most situations, both parties to an illegal contract are considered to be equally at fault—*in pari delicto.* As such, a court will not resolve a dispute between the parties. If the contract has not yet been fulfilled, neither party can enforce it. If the contract has been executed, generally neither party can recover damages.

With illegal contracts, courts are generally not involved due to the belief that this may deter parties from entering into illegal contracts. However, there are some exceptions where courts do get involved and a party can either sue for a breach or recover under an illegal contract.

JUSTIFIABLE IGNORANCE. A party may recover if they can show that they were relatively innocent—that is, they had no reason to know the contract was illegal. Here, the court does not enforce the contract. Rather, the parties are allowed to return to their original positions prior to the execution of the illegal contract.

WITHDRAWAL FROM ILLEGAL AGREEMENT. If the illegal act has not yet been performed, the party that is performing can withdraw from the contract. Once the party has withdrawn, they may recover damages, or the consideration paid.

FRAUD, DURESS, OR UNDUE INFLUENCE. Sometimes there are facts to show that a party was induced to enter into an illegal contract through fraud, duress, or undue influence by the other party. In such cases, the first party is allowed to recover damages, or the consideration paid. Fraud, duress, and undue influence are discussed in further detail in Chapter 12.

Management Application
Severability Clause

An invalid or illegal provision may potentially void an entire contract. This could pose significant consequences for businesses, especially if the voided contract followed several months of negotiations. A severability clause in a contract provides that if a term or provision is found to be invalid, illegal, or unenforceable, only that term is void. A severability clause allows the remaining contract terms to be intact and enforceable.

Example: Severability. If any provision of this Agreement is unenforceable or unlawful under any applicable law of any jurisdiction, in such jurisdiction the remainder of this Agreement's provisions shall be deemed to be fully enforceable in accordance with their terms.

AI Feature: Disaffirmance and Capacity

Use an AI program to answer the questions presented in the prompt below.

Marcus (age 82) sells his used car to Matthew (age 17) for $2,000. They execute a bill of sale for the vehicle. Marcus has not been adjudged mentally incompetent, but he has had occasional periods of forgetfulness. A year passes, and Matthew, now age 18 years and 7 months, is responsible for an accident while driving a car he purchased from Marcus. While the vehicle suffers mild damage, Matthew does not have the vehicle repaired. Nevertheless, Matthew decides to disaffirm the contract with Marcus and sends a text message to Marcus, which Marcus does not read. Marcus does not remember now the purchase and sale agreement with Matthew. He says he "can't remember what he signed and when." Marcus refuses to accept the car and return Matthew's purchase money. May Matthew disaffirm the contract? What are Matthew's options to pursue recovery? Can Matthew reasonably claim disaffirmance at his age? Does the mental acuity of Marcus both at the time of contracting and the attempted disaffirmance having any impact upon your analysis.

Key Terms

- Adjudged mentally incompetent, 264
- Blue laws, 269
- Capacity, 256
- Disaffirmance, 257
- Emancipation, 256
- Exculpatory clause, 270
- *In pari delicto*, 269
- *Malum in se*, 269
- *Malum prohibitum*, 269
- Minor, 256
- Ratification, 259
- Usury, 268

Applying the Law

11.1 Minors and Agreements to Arbitrate. S.L. was a minor when she worked at and was injured at a KFC® franchised restaurant operated by PAK Foods Houston, LLC. S.L. filed a personal injury suit alleging she was injured while at work. In response, PAK Foods filed a motion to compel arbitration of her claims. She was a minor when she executed a document in which she agreed to arbitrate all work-related claims against PAK. Is this a void or voidable contract? How should the court rule on the minor's right to disaffirm the arbitration agreement? If S.L.'s mother, Marissa Garcia, brought separate claims against her daughter's employer arising from her daughter's injuries, would she be required to arbitrate under the agreement? *PAK Foods Houston, LLC v. Garcia*, 433 S.W.3d 171 (Tex. App. 2014)

11.2 Excusable Ignorance of Licensing Statute. H. Lee Farthing sued Coco Beach Resort Management, LLC, for breach of employment contract. He sued to recover unpaid base salary and anticipated commissions on real estate sales that Farthing alleged were imminent when Coco Beach fired him. Farthing had been licensed as a real estate broker in South Carolina in the past, but was not licensed as one in Puerto Rico, where the Coco Beach's properties were located. Relying upon Puerto Rico law, the district court held that the agreement was void because Farthing lacked the necessary professional license. But on appeal, the court stated if Farthing were "excusably ignorant" of the fact that his employment agreement may have violated Puerto Rico's public policy and if Coco Beach were not excusably ignorant, Farthing would have a claim for damages for the agreement's breach. What arguments could be made on Farthing's behalf that he should not be completely barred from recovering damages? *Farthing v. Coco Beach Resort Mgmt., LLC*, 864 F.3d 39 (1st Cir. 2017)

11.3 Minor Liability for Necessities. Harun Fountain was shot by a playmate, following which he suffered grievous injuries. A medical provider assisted in extensive lifesaving medical services provided to the minor. The mother refused to pay the bill and a collection judgment against her by the medical provider was discharged in bankruptcy. Neither Fountain nor his guardianship estate was involved in the bankruptcy. Prior to the bankruptcy, the mother obtained a settlement against the playmate in a tort action, as a result of which settlement funds were placed in the estate established on Fountain's behalf. The probate court denied the provider's action to recover against the funds from the tort settlement holding that parents were liable for medical necessities. The provider appealed. Is there an implied contract between the medical service provider and the minor who received those services? *Yale Diagnostic Radiology v. Estate of Fountain*, 838 A.2d 179 (Conn. 2004)

11.4 Disaffirmance. A few months before his 21st birthday, Steven purchased a vehicle from Fred Howe Motors, Inc. At the time, Steven was a working father and husband, and the legal age of majority was 21. Upon having problems with the car, Steven attempted to return the car and be repaid the sales price. The dealership refused. What arguments can be made on behalf of each side as to the enforceability of the contract of sale? *Kiefer v. Fred Howe Motors, Inc.*, 158 N.W.2d 288 (Wis. 1968)

11.5 Disaffirmance. The Basketball Marketing Co. (BMC) entered into an endorsement agreement with Darko Milicic, a 16-year-old Serbian basketball player. Four days after his 18th birthday, Milicic offered to buy out his agreement, and BMC refused. Eleven days after his 18th birthday, Milicic sent a letter to MBC withdrawing from the endorsement agreement. BMC refused to accept Milicic's letter. BMC then wrote to Adidas® and Reebok®, informing them that it had a valid and enforceable endorsement agreement with Milicic. As a result, Adidas stopped negotiating an endorsement agreement with Milicic. Does Milicic have a cause of action against BMC? *Milicic v. The Basketball Marketing Co.*, 857 A.2d 689 (Pa. Super. Ct. 2004)

11.6 Defenses to Illegal Contracts. Despite knowing that it was illegal to participate in a pyramid scheme, Judy Cochran agreed to take part in the "airplane game" at the urging of Michael Dellfava. She gave Dellfava $2,200, which he passed along to the "pilot" of the game. Participants in the scheme solicited "passengers" and gradually moved up the pyramid to become "flight attendants," "co-pilots," and eventually "pilots." When the status of pilot was reached, that person received $17,200. After providing the money, Cochran was dissatisfied with her level within the pyramid. She fruitlessly sought a return of her money from Dellfava. Eventually her plane "crashed," and she lost her entire investment. Will the court uphold this contract? What defense could Dellfava assert to bar enforcement? *Cochran v. Dellfava*, 517 N.Y.S.2d 854 (1987)

11.7 Consumer Protection. Mr. Brooks had his vehicle towed to R. A. Clark's Garage. He requested an estimate on certain repairs and orally authorized them. But the garage never issued a written estimate for them to Brooks nor did Brooks waive such an estimate. Brooks did not pay for the repairs and his vehicle was sold at auction by the garage. Brooks sued for the value of his vehicle. Who will prevail and why? *Brooks v. R. A. Clark's Garage*, 378 A.2d 1144 (N.H. 1977)

11.8 Mental Incapacity. In September, Farber entered into a contract to purchase a plot of land from Sweet Style Manufacturing Corp. Plaintiff had been diagnosed with bipolar disorder and was in a manic phase from August to October. On October 8, Farber was hospitalized in a mental institution. Before this time period, Farber was generally frugal and cautious, but after he signed the contract for the plot of land, he hired a title abstract company to perform a search on the plot of land, hired an employee to head the building project, had a sign built on the land stating that a drug company was coming soon, hired an architect, filed a mortgage application, hired laborers, and filed plans with city officials, among other things. Despite all this activity, closing was not scheduled to occur until October 20. Farber's pretrial examination revealed that he understood the contract but did not explain the reasoning for his sudden change of behavior. His doctor testified that on September 23, he was "incapable of reasoned judgment." Is this contract void or voidable? Would Farber have entered into the contract if he were not under the compulsion of a mental disorder? Does the fact that Farber understood the contract prevent him from asserting mental incapacity as a defense? *Farber v. Sweet Style Mfg. Corp.*, 242 N.Y.S.2d 763 (1963)

11.9 Public Policy. Frederick Richmond was a member of Congress. He agreed to plead guilty to income tax evasion, supplementing the salary of a federal employee, and possession of marijuana. He entered a plea agreement with the government whereby he would resign from Congress and withdraw as a candidate for reelection, and, in return, the government would not prosecute him. Is a plea bargaining agreement that includes a forced resignation void, as it would be against public policy? *United States v. Richmond*, 550 F. Supp. 605 (E.D.N.Y. 1982)

11.10 Intoxication. Carolyn Williamson executed a contract for the sale of her home for $1,800 plus the unpaid balance on the mortgage with Bobby Matthews. Immediately after the sale the seller became concerned that she did not receive full consideration because she had expected to be paid about $17,000 for the home. She sought to set the sale aside for, among other reasons, that she had a mental incapacity because she was a heavy drinker of alcohol. Would this history support a claim of gross inadequacy of consideration for the sale? *Williamson v. Matthews*, 379 So. 2d 1245 (Ala. 1980)

Defenses to Formation: Mistake, Fraudulent Misrepresentation, Undue Influence, and Duress

12

When a man understands the injustice of a contract, that man will always break it. — Victor Hugo, French Senator and Writer (1802-1885)

Chapter Outline

- Introduction
- Mistake
- Fraudulent Misrepresentation
- Undue Influence

Case 12.1: *Vokes v. Arthur Murray, Inc.*

- Duress

Case 12.2: *McDonald v. Whitewater Challengers, Inc.*

- Unconscionability

Case 12.3: *Marquez v. Amazon.com, Inc.*

- AI Feature: Economic Duress

Learning Objectives

After studying this chapter, you should be able to:

1. Explain the circumstances under which a contract may be rescinded because of a mistake.
2. Describe the elements necessary for misrepresentation.
3. Identify the forms of misrepresentation that may allow the rescission of a contract.
4. Identify those confidential relationships that can support a claim of undue influence.
5. Differentiate between undue influence and duress.
6. State the forms of unconscionable contracts that give rise to the remedy of a rescission.

Introduction

As explained in Chapter 9, a contract is a legally enforceable meeting of the minds — a mental state in which the parties have consistent understandings of what is to occur. The mental state is manifested or demonstrated by words or actions of the parties or by both actions and words. This chapter addresses the situations where mutual assent is lacking, even though it may outwardly appear that a meeting of the minds took place. Without a meeting of the minds, a mutual understanding or agreement does not occur, and the formation of that contract is set aside—a procedure known as rescission. In such a case, the contract will be either voidable or void.

There are several reasons why mutual assent may be lacking at the time of contract formation. They are discussed in this chapter and include:

- Mistake
- Fraudulent misrepresentations
- Undue influence
- Duress
- Unconscionability

Mistake

Mistake
An error arising when the parties to a contract differ on their beliefs about the subject matter, value, or other aspect of the contract.

Unilateral mistake
When only one party is mistaken about a fact regarding the contract.

Mutual mistake
When both parties are mistaken about the same fact regarding the contract.

A **mistake** arises when the parties to a contract differ in their beliefs about the subject matter, value, or another aspect of the contract. Many mistakes do not give rise to a defense of the enforcement of a contract, but some do. Mistakes are classified as either unilateral or mutual. A **unilateral mistake** arises when only one party is mistaken about a fact regarding the contract. A **mutual mistake** arises when both parties are mistaken about the *same* fact regarding the contract. If both parties are mistaken about two different facts, each party is treated as having made a unilateral mistake. In order to cause the contract to be rescinded, the mistake must be made at the time the contract is formed.

Only certain types of mistakes entitle a party to rescind a transaction. Courts distinguish between mistakes made as to material facts and mistakes relating to value or quality. Only mistakes as to a material fact at the time of the contract formation may cause the contract to be rescinded. If the mistake involves an incidental or trivial term, the mistake will not set aside the agreement.

> **Example:** Theodore Sherwood contracted with Hiram Walker, a breeder and distiller, to purchase a cow that was infertile. Sherwood and Walker agreed upon a price much less than the value of a fertile cow. After the sale, Walker discovered that the cow was fertile and wanted to cancel the agreement because the cow was worth much more than the price agreed upon. He refused to accept Sherwood's offer of payment or to deliver the cow. Sherwood sued to enforce the agreement. The Michigan Supreme Court held that there was a mutual mistake of material fact because the parties did not know the cow was fertile at the time they made their bargain. The contract was voidable. *Sherwood v. Walker*, 66 Mich. 568 (1887)

Material fact
A fact that is important to the contract's subject matter.

A **material fact** is one that is important to the contract's subject matter. If a party is mistaken as to a transaction's value or quality, no rescission is allowed.

> **Example:** If the buyer purchases a suburban tract home for $300,000 and discovers that a house across the street with the identical floor plan and more amenities sold for $250,000 just a week prior, the buyer cannot rescind the transaction because of a mistake in value.

Unilateral Mistakes

If one party enters into a contract under a mistaken belief regarding some material fact (a unilateral mistake), generally no grounds exist for rescission; the party must continue in its contractual duties. The rationale for this rule is that upon discovering that a person has made a mistake, the person should not be able to claim a lack of mutual assent to reject a contract the person does not choose to perform. For example, if after entering into a contract, a party realized that it was an unprofitable bargain, that party could not claim they were so mistaken that the agreement must be set aside.

There are two exceptions to this rule that allow the mistaken party to rescind the transaction: where (1) the other party (the non-mistaken party) knew or should have known of the mistake of material fact (an obvious mistake); or (2) the material fact mistake was due to an error in arithmetic and was made inadvertently and without gross negligence. In such situations, it would be unfair and unjust to affirm the contract.

> **Example:** If the buyer and seller had orally negotiated a contract to purchase a home for the sum of $257,000, but the buyer wrote $275,000 instead of $257,000 in the written purchase contract, the buyer's unilateral mistake, which was known to the seller, could be corrected. It would be unfair and unjust to affirm the contract at $275,000 under these facts.

> **Example:** A contractor is submitting a bid to an owner for a small commercial construction project. The contractor uses an Excel formula to add up the cost of materials needed for the project from two vendors but fails to add the third vendor. The bid submitted is $75,000 less than it should be, but not too low for the owner to notice any error. The owner accepts the bid. When the contractor discovers the error, it wants to rescind the contract. While this involves a mathematical mistake, the contractor's unilateral mistake will not give rise to the ability to rescind the contract because the mistake of missing one of three vendors was grossly negligent.

Mutual Mistakes

Where both parties to the contract are mistaken as to the same material fact (a mutual mistake), the general rule is that either party can elect to rescind the contract. In such cases, the parties are restored to their pre-contract positions and all consideration paid or received is returned to the original party. With mutual mistakes, the parties have not formed a contract. This is because the agreement requirement (that is, mutual consent) has not been met, as both parties are uncertain regarding the material terms of the contract.

> **Example:** Buyer and Seller enter into a contract for a residential property. Seller believes Buyer is attempting to purchase property "A" for the sum of $100,000, but Buyer believes she is purchasing property "B" for the sum of $100,000. Because both parties are mistaken as to which property is being sold, a mutual mistake exists, allowing either party to rescind the contract.

Be aware that the mistake permitting rescission is one of material fact and not one of value or opinion. Mistakes of this nature are *not* considered factual because they arise from personal assessments of the subject matter. There are several reasons for this rule. Among them is that a party could always cancel a contract after the fact, destroying the very purpose for exchanging enforceable promises; another is that on a practical level, the courts would be overwhelmed with rescission requests.

> **Example:** If the parties mistakenly agree upon the terms for the sale of an antique desk but realize after performance that the desk was actually worth much more than the price paid, the contract is enforced and is not voidable.

FIGURE 12.1: Material Mistakes of Fact

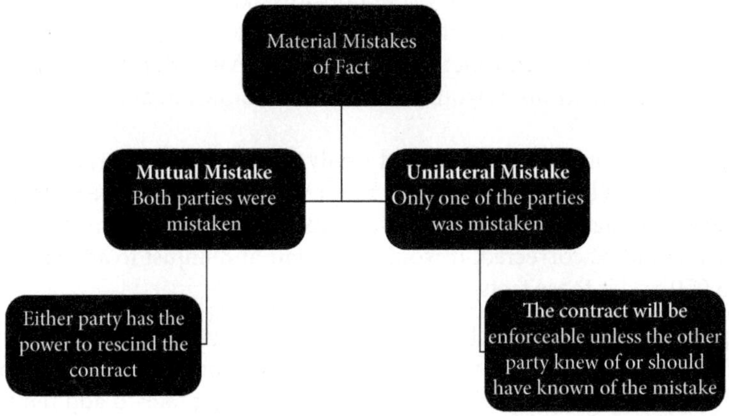

Landmark Case
Raffles v. Wichelhaus, 159 Eng. Rep. 375 (1864) (the "Peerless" case)

Raffles agreed to sell Wichelhaus 125 bales of cotton, to be delivered from Bombay (now Mumbai), India, on a ship called the Peerless to Liverpool, England. Unbeknownst to either party, there were two ships named Peerless, one departing from Bombay in October and one departing from Bombay in December. Wichelhaus believed the Peerless ship would be the one that had departed in October; however, Raffles intended for the cotton to arrive on the Peerless ship that had departed in December. When the cotton arrived from the December Peerless ship, Wichelhaus refused delivery, alleging that the cotton shipment was to be shipped in October. Raffles sued for breach of contract, and the British court held for Wichelhaus. The question of which Peerless ship was to transport the goods was a mutual mistake regarding a material fact to the contract. As there was no agreement as to which Peerless would be transporting the goods, there was no contract between the parties.

In order to reduce the risk that the other party could assert that it did not understand the terms of the executed contract, those drafting a contract might insert the following language in the contract:

> *Advice of Counsel.* The advice of legal counsel has been obtained by the parties to this Agreement prior to its execution. All parties hereby execute this Agreement voluntarily with full knowledge of its significance, and with the express intention of affirming their respective rights, duties, claims, and obligations and claims arising out of or connected with the subject matter of this Agreement.

Fraudulent Misrepresentation

Fraudulent misrepresentation arises when a party intentionally misleads another party into entering into a contract. There is no meeting of the minds when a contract arises from fraud. The innocent party usually has the option to rescind the contract, as no agreement has been knowingly reached, or to enforce the contract and sue for any damages resulting from the fraud. Fraud is commonly known as intentional misrepresentation or fraudulent misrepresentation or referred to simply as fraud. Fraud requires the following elements:

Fraudulent misrepresentation
An intentionally false representation of a material fact to another person upon which reasonable reliance is placed, to that other party's detriment.

1. There is a misrepresentation of a *material* fact (one that is important to the reasons for entering into a contract).
2. The misrepresentation was made with an *intent to deceive.*
3. The innocent party *reasonably* and *justifiably relied* upon the misrepresentation.
4. The misrepresentation *caused injury* to the other party.

Example: Randi Fleischman made arrangements with a friend to dispose of her 2000 Chrysler Sebring automobile. Afterwards, Fleischman contacted the police department to report that her car had been stolen. Fleischman also had an existing contractual relationship with Liberty Mutual Insurance Company, in which Fleischman's insurance policy with Liberty Mutual allowed for payouts in the case of theft. Fleischman filed an insurance claim with Liberty Mutual, which relied on Fleischman's representations. Liberty Mutual paid Fleischman an amount equal to the fair market value of her automobile at the time of the alleged loss. Fleischman was later found to have committed insurance fraud. *State v. Fleischman*, 917 A.2d 722 (N.J. 2007)

Misrepresentation of a Material Fact

The first element to prove fraud requires a misrepresentation of a material fact. The misrepresentation can occur by words (oral or written) or by the conduct of the parties. A party can commit misrepresentation by conduct when a party takes a specific action to conceal a material fact from the other party. This is known as fraud by concealment.

Example: Alex, when listing a car for sale, shows a prospective purchaser the maintenance and repair records for the vehicle. Alex shows all of the records except for the repair record after an accident in which Alex was involved. The accident caused damage to the structural frame of the vehicle, and Alex did not want to disclose that information to the prospective buyer. Alex has committed fraud by concealing a material fact.

The misrepresentation must be one of a material fact to be actionable as fraud. Material facts are those considered significant by a reasonable person in inducing a party to enter into a contract. Further, statements of opinion or predictions about the future do not generally create fraud.

Example: When selling a home, a broker states that the home is the best one on the block. The broker's opinion is not actionable as fraud.

Evaluating a Statement as Fact versus Opinion

Students may struggle with the difference between a statement that is a fact and can be subject to a fraud claim compared to a statement of opinion that is not subject to a fraud claim. Put simply, a fact is a statement that can be proven true or false. "The world is flat" is a statement of fact. It is an incorrect statement of fact, but still a stated fact.

An opinion is an expression of a person's belief, idea, feeling, view, or judgment about something or someone that is not provable. "This house is perfect for young families" is a statement of opinion and not actionable as fraud.

Intent to Deceive

Scienter
Knowledge that a representation was false, or the representation was made without sufficient knowledge of the truth in a fraudulent misrepresentation.

The second element required to prove fraud is that the misrepresentation of a material fact was made with an intent to deceive. This element is often called scienter. **Scienter** (or guilty knowledge) is a mental state required to hold a person accountable for their acts. In fraudulent misrepresentations, scienter requirements are met where the person making the misrepresentation knew that the statement was false. It can also be met where the person making the misrepresentation did so recklessly and without sufficient knowledge of its truth or falsity. In addition, based on the circumstances, scienter can be inferred.

Example: A prospective homeowner at an open house asks the real estate agent whether the home is located in the Princeton Public School District (a prestigious school district located in Princeton, New Jersey). The real estate agent knows that the house is located in the city of Princeton and assumes that the home must also be in the Princeton Public School District. If the home does not fall within the Princeton Public School District's boundaries, the real estate agent may be liable for fraud. Scienter is met as the real estate agent made a statement recklessly and without sufficient knowledge of its truth.

MISREPRESENTATION BY SILENCE. A party is not required to disclose everything the party knows about a transaction to the other party. However, there are situations in which the law considers silence to be concealment. Such cases include the following: (1) a fiduciary relationship exists between the parties (that is, a relationship of trust and confidence, such as partners, members of the same family, attorney and clients, and so on); (2) there is a need to correct a previous assertion made (such as later discovering that the previous assertion made is false or no longer true); and (3) a federal or state statute requires disclosure. In addition, even when there is no duty to disclose, if the other party asks a specific question, the other party cannot lie or misrepresent the facts — that would be actionable as fraud.

Example: Jess is selling his car. His vehicle was involved in an accident that caused structural damage to the vehicle. Jess did not have the money to adequately repair the vehicle, and the vehicle, if involved in another accident, could cause serious injury. Jess is under an obligation to disclose this fact, regardless of whether a prospective buyer asks.

Innocent Party Reasonably and Justifiably Relied on the Misrepresentation

The third element of fraud requires the party to justifiably rely on the misrepresentation. A court will look to the totality of the facts in determining reasonableness and generally hold that the person justifiably relied on the misrepresentation unless (1) the innocent party knew the misrepresentation was false, (2) the misrepresentation was obviously false, or (3) the misrepresentation could not be expected to be taken seriously.

In addition, the misrepresentation must have substantially contributed to the party's decision to enter into the contract (that is, it must be a material fact to the contract). It need not be the sole or even the predominant reason for entering into the contract.

Example: Alan is an inventor who is soliciting prospective investors. He fraudulently alleges that he has created batteries that will be of great use in spacecraft, satellites, and submarines. The investors who invest in this new invention will be able to sue for fraud as they innocently and justifiably relied on the inventor's assertion.

MISREPRESENTATIONS OF LAW. Usually a misrepresentation of the law is not considered fraud. Since Roman times, ignorance of the law or misapplication of the law by a party has not been considered a mistake permitting rescission of the contract. There is one exception to this general rule. If the misrepresentation is made by a party to the contract who is a professional and the professional intentionally misrepresents the law to a less sophisticated party, rescission may be permitted.

Example: A CPA's deliberate misrepresentations of the tax benefit an inexperienced buyer will receive from the purchase of the accountant's office building is fraud.

The Misrepresentation Caused Injury to the Other Party

The last requirement is that the misrepresentation caused injury to the other party. The amount of damages awarded is usually equal to the difference between the value of the property as represented and the actual price paid for the property. A party can also seek to rescind the transaction and obtain the amount paid. In addition, with a fraud claim, a court may award punitive damages against the wrongdoer. These damages will be awarded to punish the wrongdoer for their actions, and would be in addition to the compensatory damages awarded for fraud.

Sample Form Jury Instructions

A jury instruction for a contractual fraud claim might look like the following:

Instruction No. ___ Fraud

Fraud relieves a party of the duty to perform a contract. Fraud includes any statement or act that is intended to deceive another party in order to influence them to enter into the contract. In addition, the party must have relied on the fraudulent statement or act in entering the contract. Fraud consists of:

1. A suggestion, as a fact, of something that is not true, when the person making the suggestion does not believe it to be the truth; or
2. A positive statement of something that is not true, when the person making it had no reasonable basis for the statement; or
3. A person's concealing something that they know is the truth; or
4. A promise made without any intention of performing it; or
5. A person's remaining silent when they had a duty to speak. Plaintiff had a duty to tell Defendant about [INSERT INFORMATION THAT WAS NOT DISCLOSED] because [GIVE SPECIFIC REASON FOR DUTY OF DISCLOSURE]; or
6. Any other statement or act intended to deceive.

Fraud must be proven by clear and convincing evidence. This means you must be persuaded, considering all the evidence in the case, it is highly probable and free from serious doubt that the contract was obtained through fraud.

Common Forms of Fraud

1. *Fraud in the factum (also known as actual fraud).* In such circumstances, a party employs a deceptive strategy to prevent the victim from realizing the entirety of the transaction that forms the contract. Such contracts are void.

Example: A hands B, a famous athlete, a blank piece of paper to sign and asks for an autograph. Later, A transforms the signed paper to a contract requiring B to sell B's sports paraphernalia to A at below-market prices. In such circumstances, B would be unaware that a contract was being considered.

2. *Fraud in the inducement.* In this situation, the victim is aware that a contract is being contemplated, but the victim's consent is induced by material misrepresentations. Many fraud cases fall under fraud by the inducement. The alleged contract is voidable at the election of the victim.

   Example: Following the start of trial relating to the purchase, repair, and sale of large trucks and heavy equipment, Kent Tilley entered into a settlement agreement with Budget Truck Sales. During the negotiations, Tilley proposed to convey certain property to Budget, including title to a CAT 950 front loader, in exchange for $100,000. The $100,000 was to be paid the day after delivery. Tilley misrepresented the condition of the front loader during the negotiations leading to the settlement. The court held that false representations made during negotiations concerning the condition of the subject of a contract can support a finding of fraud in the inducement. *Budget Truck Sales, LLC v. Tilley*, 2018 Idaho LEXIS 93 (Idaho 2018)

3. *Fraud in the execution.* In this case, the victim is aware that a contract is being formed and the consent given is not the result of misrepresentation. The problem arises from the victim's reliance upon the wrongdoer's representations that they have carefully written the contract to reflect their agreement. The victim relies on those assurances and executes the contract without reading it. Later the writing is found to not agree with those representations. Some jurisdictions will hold the negligent party responsible because they did not read the contract before signing. In other cases, the courts would overlook the negligence of the party in signing the contract, if the fraud arose from the wrongdoer's dishonest behavior or practices.

   Example: Following the lengthy negotiation of terms, if a creditor tells a borrower that a promissory note was merely a restatement of an existing outstanding debt, fraud in the execution can be alleged when, in fact, the note that is executed without review fails to include all of the material terms of the agreement.

Innocent Misrepresentations

Innocent misrepresentation is also commonly known as non-fraudulent misrepresentation. It is a concept that is related to fraud; however, unlike fraud, the innocent misrepresentation was made *unknowingly* and/or was made *without an intent to defraud* (that is, scienter is missing). If an innocent misrepresentation is made, the victim may rescind the contract but may not enforce the contract by suing for damages. Some courts may treat innocent misrepresentations forming the basis of a contract as mutual mistake.

Innocent misrepresentation Known as non-fraudulent misrepresentation. Misrepresentation made unknowingly or without an intent to defraud.

Undue Influence

Undue influence occurs when one person takes advantage of another's mental, emotional, or physical condition to unfairly persuade the person to enter into a contract. A contract that is entered into because of undue influence is voidable by the victim. It is set aside because the free will of the victim is lacking.

Undue influence A defense asserted to the enforcement of a contract arising from the misuse of a fiduciary relationship.

The elements that must be proven to show undue influence are:

1. A relationship of trust or confidence existed (such as a financial advisor to a client, a lawyer to a client, a doctor or therapist to a patient);
2. The dominant party abused their position by persuading the victim to contract against the victim's interests.

Consider the following case, which illustrates how inducement by overreaching flattery may lead to a showing of undue influence.

CASE 12.1

INDUCEMENT BY OVERREACHING FLATTERY AND CAJOLERY MAY INDICATE UNDUE INFLUENCE

VOKES v. ARTHUR MURRAY, INC.

212 So. 2d 906 (1968)

District Court of Appeal of Florida

Audrey Vokes, a widow of 51 years and without family, always wanted to be an accomplished dancer. With the hopes of pursuing this interest, she decided to take dance lessons at a franchise of Arthur Murray, Inc., a dance studio owned by Davenport. She was incessantly subjected to overreaching flattery and cajolery. She was assured she had "grace and poise" and was "rapidly improving and developing her dancing skill" as a way to convince her to purchase additional lessons. At one point, she was sold 545 additional hours of dancing lessons to be entitled to a "Bronze Medal" designation. Then she was told that if she wanted to reach the "Silver Medal" designation, she would have to purchase an additional 926 hours, which she did. Later on, she was induced to purchase an additional 151 hours to go on a "student trip to Trinidad" even though she still had over 1,000 unused hours of instruction. Finally, she was influenced to buy an additional 481 hours of instruction in order to be classified as a "Gold Bar" member, the ultimate achievement of the dancing studio. She was sold 14 dance courses totaling 2,302 hours for the sum of $31,090. She filed suit for fraud and sought to recover the portion of the $31,090 not charged against specific hours of instruction given to her. The trial court dismissed her complaint and she appealed.

Language of the Court. *All the foregoing sales promotions, illustrative of the entire fourteen separate contracts, were procured by defendant Davenport and Arthur Murray, Inc., by false representations to Vokes that she was improving in her dancing ability, that she had excellent potential, that she was responding to instructions in dancing grace, and that they were developing her into a beautiful dancer, whereas in truth and in fact she did not develop in her dancing ability, she had no "dance aptitude," and in fact had difficulty in "hearing that musical beat." The complaint alleged that such representations to her "were in fact false and known by the defendant to be false and contrary to Vokes' true ability, the truth of Vokes' ability being fully known to the defendants, but withheld from Vokes for the sole and specific intent to deceive* *and defraud Vokes and to induce her in the purchasing of additional hours of dance lessons." It was averred that the lessons were sold to her "in total disregard to the true physical, rhythm, and mental ability of Vokes." In other words, while she first exulted that she was entering the "spring of her life," she finally was awakened to the fact there was "spring" neither in her life nor in her feet.*

These dance lesson contracts and the money consideration therefore of over $31,000 were procured from her by means and methods which went beyond the unsavory, yet legally permissible, perimeter of "sales puffing" and intruded well into the forbidden area of undue influence, the suggestion of falsehood, the suppression of truth, and the free exercise of rational judgment. From the time of her first contact with the dancing school, she was influenced unwittingly by a constant and continuous barrage of flattery, false praise, excessive compliments, and panegyric encomiums, to such extent that it would be not only inequitable, but unconscionable.

A statement of a party having superior knowledge may be regarded as a statement of fact although it would be considered as opinion if the parties were dealing on equal terms. Even in contractual situations where a party to a transaction owes no duty to disclose facts within his knowledge or to answer inquiries respecting such facts, the law is if he undertakes to do so he must disclose the whole truth. It could be reasonably supposed here that defendants had superior knowledge as to whether Vokes had dance potential and as to whether she was noticeably improving in the art of dance. And it would be a reasonable inference from the undenied averments of the complaint that the flowery eulogiums heaped upon her by Arthur Murray as a prelude to her contracting for 1944 additional hours of instruction in order to attain the rank of the Bronze Standard, thence to the bracket of the Silver Standard, thence to the class of the Gold Bar Standard, and finally to the crowning plateau of a Life Member of the Studio, proceeded as much or more from the urge to ring the cash register as from any honest or realistic appraisal of her dancing ability.

Decision. The appellate court reversed the dismissal of Vokes's complaint to rescind the contract for undue influence and misrepresentation.

Focus on Ethics

To what degree did Vokes's advanced age affect the court's decision? Does the fact that a significant portion of the Florida population is comprised of retirees have any effect in deciding if this was an ethical business practice?

Duress

Duress
A defense asserted to the enforcement of a contract because a party was subjected to unlawful pressure or coercion to enter into the contract.

A contract that may appear to have all the necessary components to an agreement may still be voided if there was duress. **Duress** is a defense asserted to the enforcement of a contract because a party was subjected to unlawful pressure or coercion to enter into the contract. Duress can arise in several forms: physical duress, mental duress, and economic duress. The contract is voidable by the person subjected to the duress.

Physical duress arises when someone is forced to act against their will due to the threat of physical harm. Mental duress (also known as emotional duress) arises when someone's decision making is compromised due to psychological pressure such as fear, guilt, or mental strain that compels the person to act against their better judgment.

Example: Under duress, a celebrity pays a media firm to not run a story about the celebrity's inappropriate behavior.

Economic duress arises upon the doing of a wrongful act that is sufficiently coercive to cause a reasonably prudent person faced with no reasonable alternative to succumb to the perpetrator's pressure. Whether the party asserting economic duress had a reasonable alternative is determined by examining whether a reasonably prudent person would follow the alternative course, or whether a reasonably prudent person might submit. A reasonably prudent person may have no reasonable alternative but to succumb when the only other alternative is bankruptcy, financial ruin, or a real threat of homelessness.

Example: The city of Scottsbluff disposed of 40 tons of solid waste each day and had a contractual relationship with Waste Connections of Nebraska, Inc. There were no other waste disposal services in the city. Nonetheless, the rate charged was about $40/ton for the city and for other customers. Then, one day, Waste Connections increased the rate it charged the city to $60/ton, even though the other customers did not have the increased rate. The court held there to be sufficient evidence of economic duress since the city disposed of so much waste daily and had no reasonable alternative to switch to within a reasonable time. *City of Scottsbluff v. Waste Connections of Nebraska, Inc.*, 809 N.W.2d 725 (Neb. 2011)

Duress does not include hard bargaining, but it can include circumstances in which the stronger party exploits the other's vulnerability in a manner that becomes unreasonable. So long as the stronger party is not responsible for the other's vulnerability, driving a hard bargain does not constitute duress. Further, the threat to bring a valid civil lawsuit (not a criminal lawsuit) does not by itself constitute duress.

In the following case, the court considered whether duress existed if the plaintiff might suffer economic loss in the future.

CASE 12.2

A SHOWING OF DIRECT ECONOMIC LOSS MUST SUPPORT A CLAIM OF DURESS

McDONALD v. WHITEWATER CHALLENGERS, INC.

116 A.3d 99 (2015)

Superior Court of Pennsylvania

Erin McDonald was a schoolteacher employed by the School of the Holy Child in Rye, New York. On May 17, 2006, the Headmaster of the School handed a release form to McDonald, while she was between classes and walking through the school hallway. The release form related to a whitewater rafting field trip down a portion of the Lehigh River in Pennsylvania conducted by Whitewater Challengers, Inc., for which McDonald functioned as a chaperone to seventh and eighth graders who went on the whitewater rafting trip. The release was required by Whitewater prior to participation.

During the field trip, McDonald's raft struck a large rock situated in the riverbed, ejecting her from the raft onto the rock, causing injury. McDonald brought suit, arguing that the exculpatory clause stated in the release should be held unenforceable because she was economically compelled to sign the release by her employer. McDonald argued that she suffered economic loss following her injury because she worked fewer hours resulting in a smaller raise than she had received in the past. The trial court denied motions for summary judgment based upon the release of liability stated in the release. Both parties appealed.

Language of the Court. *Economic duress is a form of duress. To constitute duress there must be more than a mere threat which might possibly result in injury at some future time, such as a threat of injury to credit in the indefinite future. It must be such a threat that, in conjunction with other circumstances and business necessity, the party so coerced fears a loss of business unless he does so enter into the contract as demanded.*

Duress is not established merely by proof that consent was secured by the pressure of financial circumstances, but a threat of serious financial loss may be sufficient to constitute duress and to be ground for relief where an ordinary suit at law or equity might not be an adequate remedy.

It is apparent that the release here is valid. First, the release cannot be said to contravene any policy of the law. Furthermore, McDonald has not alleged that Whitewater—a contracting party—maneuvered her into economic distress and compelled her to sign the contract. Whitewater, which provided recreational services, did not compel McDonald to participate, much less sign the exculpatory agreement. Nor did McDonald allege that she would have violated her contract with the school if she did not sign the Whitewater release.

McDonald's suggestion that unless she signed the release, she could potentially not receive such a raise is, on this record, too conjectural. A minimal raise, after the fact, does not alone demonstrate that when McDonald signed the release in May 2006, she did so because she feared economic injury, that is, not receiving a raise greater than 1%. Thus, economic compulsion is not available to McDonald.

Decision. The Superior Court of Pennsylvania found that there was no economic duress, and that the exculpatory clause was valid and enforceable.

Focus on Ethics

Releases from liability are commonly used by businesses offering recreational services and activities. Because the employer was not a contracting party to the release, McDonald could not show that she suffered economic harm caused by her employer. Although she was injured, does the court's decision seem fair to her?

Unconscionability

Unconscionable contract Contracts set aside because terms are extremely unjust or one-sided.

Closely related to the concepts of consideration and illegality, which were discussed in Chapters 10 and 11, is unconscionability. Under freedom of contract, the law will enforce a contract rooted in poor business judgment; however, where the contract is considered unconscionable, the innocent party may be excused from performing the contract because no reasonable person would otherwise agree to it. An **unconscionable contract** exists where contract terms are so unfair and grossly one-sided that it threatens important public policies or social norms. Unconscionability is determined by examining the circumstances of the bargaining process. Courts will consider a party's bargaining power, age, experience, and mental capacity. In addition, the lack of alternative choices and superior knowledge affecting the terms of the contract will be considered.

Examples of terms likely to be held unconscionable are those that:

- Impose a penalty to punish a party in breach rather than make that party liable for compensatory damages to the non-breaching party
- Attempt to disclaim or limit rights provided by statute, such as consumer protection statutes involving sales warranties and consumer lending (mortgages and credit cards)

Courts have developed two grounds for contracts to be considered unconscionable. The first is procedural unconscionability, which focuses on an absence of meaningful choice; the second is substantive unconscionability, which focuses on unreasonably favorable terms to one of the parties.

Procedural Unconscionability

Procedural unconscionability The disadvantage suffered by a weaker party at the time of entering into the contract.

Contracts of adhesion Contracts that leave the weaker party with no choice but to adhere to the terms of the contract.

Procedural unconscionability is seen as the disadvantage suffered by a weaker party at the time of entering into the contract. The court asks whether there was a severe imbalance in the bargaining strength or sophistication of the parties *and* whether the resulting contract terms were oppressive. Contracts that exhibit procedural unconscionability are also known as **contracts of adhesion**. They are so named because they leave the weaker party with no choice but to adhere to the terms of the contract. This is common in many standardized agreements that are given in a "take it or leave it" manner and do not allow for the weaker party to obtain goods or services without modification of a pre-printed form written with convoluted language or "legalese."

Example: A Washington, D.C., furniture store extended credit to a buyer for a series of furniture purchase installment contracts. The contract provided that if the buyer defaulted upon a payment due for a later purchase, the retailer could repossess each item sold, regardless of whether it had been paid in full. After defaulting on a later contract, the seller tried to repossess all the furniture sold since the first sale. The federal court of appeals held that the contract was unconscionable and refused to enforce it.

Unconscionability has generally been recognized to include an absence of meaningful choice on the part of one of the parties together with contract terms which are unreasonably favorable to the other party. — *Williams v. Walker-Thomas Furniture Co.*, 350 F.2d 445 (D.C. Cir. 1965)

Substantive Unconscionability

Substantive unconscionability *refers to the fairness of the contract terms*, such as an unjustified allocation of risks or costs or a great disparity in the contract price from fair market value.

Substantive unconscionability Refers to the fairness of the contract terms such as an unjustified allocation of risks or costs or a great disparity in the contract price from fair market value.

Example: Comdata, an electronic payment-processing company offering MasterCard services, entered into an agreement with Communs to implement a fuel-card program for assigning its employees fuel cards. After the account was opened, Communs discovered an employee card made fuel purchases totaling $100 a week, despite the card being set to a $25 limit. The agreement provided a liability provision that Comdata's sole responsibility, and Communs sole remedy, for damages for "error, delay, or any action or failure to act" shall be limited to "direct money damages in an amount not to exceed the total amount paid by [Communs] with respect to the defective service causing the damage during the twelve months immediately preceding the loss." The court held that the limitation of liability provision was not unconscionable, as nothing in the agreement was so unequal or oppressive as to shock the judgment of a person of common sense. *Communs. Unlimited Contr. Servs. v. Comdata, Inc.*, 611 F. Supp. 3d 483 (M.D. Tenn. 2020)

The existence of procedural unconscionability without substantive unconscionability may be sufficient to rescind a contract, but substantive unconscionability without procedural unconscionability may not. Like the element of consideration, the court's role is not to determine whether a party made a fair bargain, but merely whether that party had the opportunity to evaluate the opportunity to enter into the contract.

In the following case, a borrower argued that a pandemic-related suspension of rapid delivery service to Amazon Prime customers was a breach of contract, which included a choice-of-law clause requiring the application of Washington law.

CASE 12.3

PROCEDURAL AND SUBSTANTIVE UNCONSCIONABILITY HAVE A HIGH BURDEN OF PROOF

MARQUEZ v. AMAZON.COM, INC.

69 F.4th 1262 (2023)

United States Court of Appeals for the Eleventh Circuit

At the start of the COVID-19 pandemic, Amazon.com, Inc. stopped providing "Rapid Delivery" to Amazon Prime subscribers. Because Prime subscribers were not notified of the suspension and continued to pay full price for their memberships, Andrez Marquez and others brought a class action against Amazon alleging breach of contract and that the contract was both procedurally and substantively unconscionable. The federal district court dismissed all claims with prejudice, but plaintiffs appealed.

Language of the Court. *Prime is a fee-based subscription service. Prime subscribers receive several benefits not available to other Amazon customers, including Rapid Delivery, which is two-hour, same-day, one-day, or two-day shipping at no additional cost for certain Prime-eligible items purchased from Amazon's online marketplace. We find that plaintiffs have not stated a claim for breach of contract because Amazon had the right to limit Rapid Delivery. We also hold that Amazon's significant discretionary authority over Rapid Delivery does not render the contract unconscionable.*

Plaintiffs allege that the contract is procedurally unconscionable because it was part of an adhesion contract, was buried in a maze of fine print, and plaintiffs lacked a reasonable opportunity to understand the provisions. Procedural unconscionability is the lack of a meaningful choice, considering all the circumstances surrounding the transaction. But, the fact that adhesion or the unequal bargaining power exists will not, standing alone, justify a finding of procedural unconscionability. As to the second element of procedural unconscionability (reasonable opportunity to understand the terms) plaintiffs offer no explanation as to how their opportunity to understand the contract was inhibited. On the third element (hidden terms), despite plaintiffs' claim that the terms were buried in a maze of fine print, the evidence again favors Amazon. While there were several hyperlinks between different documents, the pertinent provisions were often in prominent places under clearly labeled subheadings, written in clear language, and/or emphasized in all caps.

Plaintiffs also allege that the contract is substantively unconscionable because it purported to confer on Amazon unfettered discretion to unilaterally modify the contract. Substantive unconscionability involves those cases where a clause or term in the contract is alleged to be one-sided or overly harsh. The terms sometimes used to define "substantive unconscionability" include shocking to the conscience, monstrously harsh, and exceedingly calloused. Unilateral change-in-terms provisions do not render a contract substantively unconscionable. Under the contract, Amazon had authority to suspend certain Prime benefits, but the terms were far from monstrously harsh or shocking to the conscience. Instead, the terms provided the benefits of Prime, described Amazon's authority to alter those benefits, and gave plaintiffs the option to cancel their Prime membership at any time. In the end, Amazon's contractual discretion was substantial, but the contract was not procedurally or substantively unconscionable under Washington law.

Decision. The appellate court affirmed the dismissal of all claims against Amazon, Inc.

Focus on Ethics

What ethical concerns are raised when determining the burden of proof for substantive and procedural unconscionability, especially when one party holds significantly more bargaining power than the other?

FIGURE 12.2: Defenses to Enforcement

AI Feature: Economic Duress

Steve Babich and his wife rented an apartment from Williams. The lease was renewed annually until the end of the fifth year. Williams refused to renew the lease. Babich and Williams signed a release agreement, under which Babich agreed to return the keys to Williams and Williams agreed to pay Babich $500. According to the release, Williams would release all claims against the tenants, and, in turn, they would release Williams from all claims related to the rented apartment. Thereafter, Babich sued Williams, alleging that Williams refused to renew the lease in retaliation against Babich for publishing embarrassing news stories about the condominium association where Williams owned the leased apartment. Williams filed a motion to dismiss the complaint as barred by the release. The facts also show that: (1) Williams angrily served in person a 60-day notice of nonrenewal and threatened to come back and "burn the place down," (2) when told the Babiches would file a police report for the terroristic threat he made while serving the 60-day notice, Williams contacted Babich's wife and made her feel so threatened that she implored Steve Babich not to contact the police for fear of further retribution from Williams, and (3) the Babiches were afraid Williams would slander them to other rental properties and prospective landlords. Use an AI program to assist you in answering the following questions to this prompt. Did Williams interfere with any First Amendment rights of the Babiches? Does economic distress apply to a degree sufficient to justify voiding the release? What damages would the Babiches be entitled to seek in their lawsuit?

Key Terms

- Contracts of adhesion, 288
- Duress, 285
- Fraudulent misrepresentation, 279
- Innocent misrepresentation, 283
- Material fact, 276
- Mistake, 276
- Mutual mistake, 276
- Procedural unconscionability, 288
- Scienter, 280
- Substantive unconscionability, 289
- Unconscionable contract, 288
- Undue influence, 283
- Unilateral mistake, 276

Applying the Law

12.1 Mistake. Monarch Marking System Company (Monarch) sued Reed's Photo Mart, Inc. (Reed's) to recover the price of four million adhesive pricing labels which Monarch furnished Reed's pursuant to a written purchase order. The purchase order required delivery "At Once." Reed's received four million labels and refused shipment. Reed's defenses were that it mistakenly ordered four million instead of four thousand labels. Reed's evidence was that "MM" meant either two thousand in Roman numerals or millimeter. Monarch's evidence showed that "MM," by custom and usage in the label trade, meant one million. Who prevails and why? *Monarch Marking System Co. v. Reed's Photo Mart, Inc.*, 485 S.W.2d 905 (Tex. 1972)

12.2 Mistake. Horst Grasz reached an agreement to buy a truck from a dealership. The sales manager at Bert Allen Toyota entered the agreed numbers into a computer, which displayed a final price of $15,017.50. If the computer had made the computations correctly, the price would have been $17,017.50. Grasz attempted to write a check for $15,017.50 immediately, but the sales manager requested only a $500 deposit because the truck would have to be specially manufactured. The sales manager manually wrote on the sales agreement, "$14,517.50 due at delivery." At the time of delivery of the truck, the sales manager insisted an additional $2,000 be paid. Grasz refused and sued. Who should win and why? *Bert Allen Toyota, Inc. v. Grasz*, 909 So. 2d 763 (Miss. Ct. App. 2005)

12.3 Mistake. Michael A. Moonves and Josephine Moonves purchased property from William Hill. The deed described the land as 60 acres more or less. A subsequent survey revealed that the actual area conveyed was 41.7 acres. The Moonves sued Hill for damages as to the discrepancy as to acreage. How should the court rule? *Moonves v. Hill*, 360 A.2d 59 (Vt. 1976)

12.4 Contractual Fraud. AMF® entered into a lease agreement with Classic Bowl under which AMF leased to Classic and installed in its premises 38 AMF pieces of bowling equipment. Pursuant to the lease, AMF allowed Classic to purchase the leased equipment. Before purchasing the equipment, Classic's president specifically asked AMF's regional vice president and another representative if AMF was in the process of coming out with new equipment, and they denied that they knew of testing and plans for new equipment. This denial caused Classic to purchase equipment. When new equipment was introduced to the market, Classic's equipment dropped in value. What remedies could Classic pursue upon learning that its equipment was worth much less than the purchase price? *Classic Bowl, Inc. v. AMF Pinspotters, Inc.*, 403 F.2d 463 (7th Cir. 1968)

12.5 Misrepresentation. A medical center recruited Dr. Robert Halterman to work as a full-time physician at one of its facilities. Halterman received a signing advance subject to a promissory note, where the monthly note payments would be forgiven incrementally if he remained employed. Halterman resigned after five months. The center demanded repayment of the remaining balance on the note, and Halterman asserted he had been fraudulently induced to execute an employment contract at the same time he executed the note. Is the doctor discharged from the duty to repay the remaining portion of the note? *Johnson Reg'l Med. Ctr. v. Halterman*, 867 F.3d 1013 (8th Cir. 2017)

12.6 Misrepresentation. Jeffrey M. Stambovsky purchased a home from Helen Ackley. After closing, he learned the house had a reputation as being possessed by ghosts. Stambovsky sued to rescind the contract. Should the doctrine of caveat emptor compel a purchaser to assess the fitness and value of the real estate purchase prior to closing? Would it make a difference if the seller, Ackley, was aware of the reputation of the house? *Stambovsky v. Ackley*, 169 A.D.2d 254 (N.Y. App. Div. 1991)

12.7 Undue Influence. Mary Lee Rogers died at the age of 75 years. Willie McCollough was engaged to work for her by the State of Alabama. She cooked, cleaned, chauffeured, and did other chores for Ms. Rogers. Prior to her death, she opened a joint savings account with right of survivorship with Ms. McCollough and funded it with monies from Ms. Rogers's other savings account. Almost immediately Ms. McCollough began withdrawing funds from the account including after Ms. Rogers's death. Does a presumption of undue influence apply under these facts? Explain. *McCollough v. Rogers*, 431 So. 2d 1246 (Ala. 1983)

12.8 Undue Influence. Before she died, Olivia McWilliams, an 83-year-old widow with a fourth-grade education and no business experience, sold her home to owners of a small neighborhood grocery store, who befriended her. The purchase price was low with payments to be made at an interest rate of 1 percent. After her death, the administrator of her estate sued to have the deed set aside. What factors should the court consider in making its ruling on a request for rescission? *Kase v. French*, 325 N.W.2d 678 (S.D. 1982)

12.9 Duress. Victor Kiam and his related corporations sued the NFL® and its member teams for a violation of the anti-trust laws. He alleged that defendants engaged in a conspiracy that prevented the plaintiffs from relocating the New England Patriots® professional football club, of which the plaintiffs were majority owners, to an area of the country in which it would be more profitable. Due to financial problems, the plaintiffs sold their team. As a condition of granting its permission to sell, the NFL required plaintiffs to release all claims against the league. Thirty months later, plaintiffs sued the defendants, alleging antitrust violations. How should the court rule? *VKK Corp. v. NFL*, 244 F.3d 114 (2d. 2001)

12.10 Unconscionability. At the height of a housing crisis, Phillip McFarland entered into a loan agreement with Wells Fargo Bank for a refinanced mortgage because the value of his house had nearly doubled. The court found that a mortgage agreement that provides a borrower with more money than his home is worth is not substantively unconscionable. However, it found that contracts "induced by unconscionable conduct" would not require a finding of substantive unconscionability, and procedural unconscionability would suffice. Is it fair for unsophisticated buyers to be held to such contracts? *McFarland v. Wells Fargo Bank, N.A.*, 810 F.3d 273 (4th Cir. 2016)

13

Writings, Parol Evidence Rule, and Third-Party Rights and Duties

The palest ink is better than the most capricious memory—Chinese Proverb, Qing Dynasty (1644-1911)

Chapter Outline

- Introduction
- Statute of Frauds for Non-Commercial Contracts

Case 13.1: *Browning v. Poirier*

- Parol Evidence Rule
- Third-Party Rights

Case 13.2: *Pennaco Energy, Inc. v. Sorenson*

- AI Feature: Contract Construction and Parol Evidence

Learning Objectives

After studying this chapter, you should be able to:

1. Identify what contracts must be in writing to be enforceable under the Statute of Frauds.
2. Describe the exceptions to the Statute of Frauds.
3. Define the parol evidence rule and its exceptions.
4. Explain the differences between an assignment and a delegation.
5. Define the rights of intended and incidental beneficiaries to enforce contracts.

Introduction

There are two additional defenses to the enforcement of an agreement discussed in Chapter 12: (1) the Statute of Frauds and (2) the parol evidence rule.

The Statute of Frauds requires that certain types of agreements must be evidenced by a writing stating the essential terms signed by the defendant. This requirement of written evidence is called a **memorandum**. In the absence of that writing, the agreement may be unenforceable.

Memorandum The requirement under the Statute of Frauds that there must be evidence of a writing stating the essential terms of the contract.

When an agreement is in writing, the parol evidence rule excludes from admissibility certain evidence that would vary, add to, or contradict the terms of that writing. In this chapter, we discuss these two important concepts and their application to common law (that is, non-commercial contracts). We will explore how the Statute of Frauds applies in the context of commercial contracts and sales in Chapters 27 to 30.

In addition, sometimes parties to an agreement desire to transfer their rights or duties in a contract to third parties. Contracts may also be designed to benefit a third party. The collection of these rights involves the subjects of assignment, delegation, and third-party beneficiaries. We will conclude our chapter discussion with a review of these topics.

Statute of Frauds for Non-Commercial Contracts

Oral contracts may give rise to difficulties in enforcement in the event of a dispute between the parties to the contracts. To ensure that the terms of certain types of contracts are reliable, the **Statute of Frauds**, a rule of law traceable to an English statute enacted by Parliament in 1677, provides that certain contracts may not be enforced unless the party to be held responsible signs a written memorandum of its essential terms. The party to be charged is the defendant, who is resisting the enforcement of the contract in a lawsuit by the other party.

Statute of Frauds A rule of contract law requiring certain contracts to be in writing to be enforceable.

The Statute of Frauds was intended to eliminate uncertainty, prevent fraud, and prevent continuing disputes involving alleged oral agreements over important matters. Each state has adopted a form of the Statute of Frauds.

Both parties may agree to voluntarily perform an oral contract, but certain promises must be in writing under the Statute of Frauds to be enforceable. If the contract is executory (not fully performed), a party cannot be compelled to perform the oral contract because it is unenforceable. However, once the contract is fully performed (that is, an executed contract), neither party can use the Statute of Frauds as a defense to try to rescind the contract because there is no prejudice to either party, as both have performed their apparent agreement.

In addition, if the defendant admits to the terms of the contract in a legal proceeding, the Statute of Frauds has been satisfied because no harm accrues to the defendant. In these cases, neither party to the contract can rescind it for noncompliance with the Statute of Frauds.

Who Must Execute the Writing?

Only the party to be charged must execute (sign) the agreement. If the party against whom a person seeks to enforce the writing has not signed the agreement, the agreement cannot be enforced against that party. However, both parties *do not* have to sign the writing.

Example: Sarah orally agrees to sell Braxton a commercial property. Braxton drafts a written contract and signs his name. Sarah never signs the contract. The contract cannot be enforced against Sarah because she has not signed the contract. However, if Sarah wanted to proceed with the transaction, she could enforce the contract against Braxton because he executed (signed) it.

What Must Be Included in the Writing?

The Statute of Frauds does not require the entire contract to be written. A contract may be recognized by piecing together several agreements that, when construed together, are considered to constitute a contract. These agreements may be assembled from faxes, emails, and written correspondence between the parties. This writing or memorandum satisfies the Statute of Frauds if it identifies the subject of the parties' agreement, shows that they made a contract, and states the essential contract terms with reasonable certainty. Only the essential terms must be stated; details or particulars are not required.

The essential terms of a contract were introduced earlier in our study of contracts. They are the identification of the parties, the subject matter, the time for performance, and the price to be paid. To satisfy the Statute of Frauds, most jurisdictions do not focus on the time of performance. If no time is specified for the performance of an act required to be performed, a reasonable time is allowed. What is "essential" to a transaction will depend on the nature of the agreement and its context, as well as the parties' subsequent conduct.

Example: A contract for the purchase of hops (which is used for flavoring beer) satisfied the Statute of Frauds when it was memorialized by two telegrams employing a form of shorthand notation so arcane that if there were nothing to look to but the telegrams, the court might find it difficult, if not impossible, to determine the nature of the contract, or that any contract was entered into between the parties. Nonetheless, the court found that a court is permitted to interpret the memorandum in light of all the circumstances under which it was made. If when the court is put into possession of all the knowledge that the parties to the transaction had at the time, it can be plainly seen from the memorandum who the parties to the contract were, what the subject of the contract was, and what were its terms, the memorandum is sufficient. *Brewer v. Horst-Lachmund Co.*, 127 Cal. 643 (1900)

Contracts Within the Scope of the Statute of Frauds

Only those subjects within the scope of the Statute of Frauds must have the required signed memorandum of the essential contract terms. While state laws may have additional applications, most commonly, the following subjects are within its scope:

1. *Contracts involving a transfer or conveyance of an interest in land, including any fixture permanently attached to the land.* Oral contracts to sell land are unenforceable unless the part performance exception discussed below applies. An interest in land includes the land itself, as well as buildings, crops, minerals, trees, timber, vegetation, and anything permanently affixed to the land or the building. A real property lease is not considered a contract that involves a transfer or conveyance of an interest in land.

Example: Deeds, mortgages, easements, liens, or agreements affecting the use of real property.

2. *Contracts for the sale of goods for $500 or more.* The Uniform Commercial Code (UCC), which is discussed in more detail in Chapter 22, provides that contracts for the sale of goods priced at $500 or more must be in writing to be enforceable. Contracts for the sale of goods priced at less than $500 do not have to be in writing to be enforceable. If the original contract price was less than $500, but the parties agree to modify the contract and that modification increases the total sales price to $500 or more, the modification must be in writing to be enforceable.

Example: George sees an online advertisement for used dining room furniture for $550. He contacts the seller and they orally agree to a contract at that price. George never arrives when it is time to pay and pick up the furniture. The seller is unable to enforce the contract against George as the contract was required to be in writing to be enforceable under the Statute of Frauds.

3. *Contracts for the lease of goods with payments totaling $1,000 or more.* The UCC Statute of Frauds provision also governs the leasing of goods. Lease contracts where the total payments to be made under the lease are $1,000 or more must be in writing to be enforceable. Like the sale of goods discussed above, contracts for the leasing of goods with total payments to be made under the lease of $1,000 or less do not need to be in writing to be enforceable. Further, suppose the original lease had total payments of less than $1,000 but the parties agree to modify the lease term or payment amounts so that the total payments exceed $1,000. In that case, the modification must be in writing to be enforceable.

Example: Sasha orally contracts to lease a computer server for her office for six months. The monthly lease price for the equipment is $100. The oral contract is enforceable. If, after a few days of using the server, Sasha modifies the contract to increase the memory and computer power, which increases the monthly cost to $200, the modification to the contract needs to be in writing to be enforceable.

4. *Contracts that, by their terms, cannot possibly be performed within one year.* Known as the one-year provision, this rule applies regardless of the subject matter (goods, services, land, and so on). Therefore, while a lease of goods may have total payments of less than $1,000, if the lease term is one year or longer, the agreement must be in writing under the Statute of Frauds. The one-year period commences when the agreement is made, not when the performance begins.

Example: On March 1, an entertainer entered into a contract to perform at a venue on June 1 of the following year. While the contract performance is only one day, the agreement must be in writing to be enforceable, because by its terms, the agreement cannot be completed within one year from the date of the agreement.

The rule applies when a contract cannot *possibly* be performed within one year. It does not matter if the contracting party will not be able to perform the contract within one year. It must be objectively impossible to perform the contract within a year for the Statute of Frauds to apply, requiring the contract to be in writing.

Example: An oral contract for the "construction of twenty industrial buildings, a 280-room hotel and convention center, and housing for 592 graduate students and professors" at a cost of $120 million did not have to be in writing to be enforceable as the contract did not explicitly negate the possibility of performance within one year. *C.R. Klewin, Inc. v. Flagship Properties*, 220 Conn. 569 (1991)

Example: The University hires a highly regarded professor away from another university and offers a lifetime employment contract. The lifetime contract does not have to be in writing to be enforceable because it can be completed within one year (the professor could die the next day, thereby completing a lifetime employment contract within one year).

5. *Promises to act as a surety*. A person who guarantees the performance of another is known as a **surety**. Where the surety promises to perform the obligations of another (the debtor), such as the payment of debt, *if the debtor fails to perform*, the surety's promise to perform must be in writing to be enforceable under the Statute of Frauds. In a surety agreement, both the debtor and the surety can be held liable if the debtor fails to perform.

Surety
A person who guarantees to perform the obligations of another.

Example: A student enters into a lease with an off-campus landlord. The landlord is concerned about the student's creditworthiness and requires a surety. If the student's mother agrees to pay the student's debt if the student is unable to pay, this would be a surety agreement that must be in writing to be enforceable against the mother.

The **main purpose rule** is an exception where a surety's oral promise to perform will be enforceable if the surety's actual or apparent main purpose in making the promise to perform is to provide a financial or personal benefit to the surety.

Main purpose rule
An exception to the Statute of Frauds allowing for an oral guarantee to be enforceable if the main purpose of a transaction is to provide a benefit to the guarantor.

Example: A supplier threatens to cease delivery of supplies unless a corporation pays its outstanding bill. Suppose a majority shareholder orally promises to guarantee the debt of the corporation so that the corporation would have necessary supplies to continue business. In that case, the oral guarantee is enforceable under the main purpose rule as the majority shareholder had a personal financial interest in keeping the corporation's business in operations.

6. *A promise made in consideration of marriage*. This category does not apply to the promise to marry (such as announcing an engagement); however, prenuptial and antenuptial (postnuptial) agreements are covered by this category. These agreements are made either before or after marriage regarding the division of property upon death, divorce, or separation. Because they are made in consideration of marriage, they must be in writing to be enforceable under the Statute of Frauds. (See the Uniform Premarital and Marital Agreements Act.)

In the following case, a lottery winnings agreement was entered into, in 1993, between a boyfriend and girlfriend. In 2007, the girlfriend won the lottery. The boyfriend demanded half the winnings, and the girlfriend refused. This case offers an interesting perspective on the one-year provision.

CASE 13.1

ABSENT A CONTRARY AGREEMENT, A CONTRACT WITH AN INDEFINITE DURATION IS OUTSIDE THE STATUTE OF FRAUDS

BROWNING v. POIRIER

165 So. 3d 663 (2015)

Supreme Court of Florida

Howard Browning and Lynn Anne Poirier lived together in a romantic relationship beginning in 1991. In approximately 1993, the parties entered into an oral agreement in which they each agreed to purchase lottery tickets and to equally share in the proceeds of any winning lottery tickets if they were together. On June 2, 2007, Poirier purchased a winning ticket and collected $1 million dollars. When Browning requested half of the proceeds, Poirier refused, and Browning filed suit for breach of an oral contract and unjust enrichment. Poirier denied the existence of any oral agreement to split lottery proceeds and raised the defense of the Statute of Frauds. The trial court held that the Statute of Frauds barred the action. The trial court's decision was upheld appeal on the grounds that Browning and Poirier intended the oral contract to last as long as they were in a romantic relationship, and the parties contemplated that the relationship would last more than one year. Eventually, the case was appealed to the Florida Supreme Court.

Language of the Court. *Browning argues that his oral agreement with Poirier to equally share in the proceeds of any winning lottery tickets they purchased falls outside the Statute of Frauds. We agree. The issue here focuses on interpreting the one year performance provision of the Statute of Frauds for oral agreements of indefinite duration, where no time is fixed by the parties for the performance of their agreement.*

It is well settled that the oral contracts made unenforceable by the statute because they are not to be performed within a year include only those which cannot be performed within that period. A promise is not within the statute if at the time the contract is made there is a possibility in law and in fact that full performance such as the parties intended may be completed before the expiration of a year.

Stated otherwise, judging from the time the oral contract of indefinite duration is made, if the contract's full performance is possible within one year from the inception of the contract, then it falls outside the Statute of Frauds. In this case, the oral agreement between Browning and Poirier is one of indefinite duration because, as the general rule states, no definite time was fixed by the parties for the performance of their agreement. Additionally, at the time the contract was made there is a possibility in law and in fact that full performance of the agreement between Browning and Poirier could have been completed before the expiration of a year. For example, if Browning or Poirier purchased a winning lottery ticket and they split the proceeds before the expiration of one year, the agreement would have been fully performed before the expiration of one year. Accordingly, nothing in the terms of their contract demonstrates that it could not be performed within one year.

Decision. Because the oral agreement between Browning and Poirier could have possibly been performed within one year, the court held it fell outside the Statute of Frauds.

Focus on Ethics

What decision would you have made if you were in Poirier's position at the time of the lottery winning?

Equal Dignity Rule

A rule related to the Statute of Frauds is the **equal dignity rule,** which requires that if a contract must be in writing to be enforceable, the appointment of an agent with regard to that agreement must also be in writing.

Equal dignity rule
If a contract must be in writing to be enforceable, the appointment of an agent with regard to that agreement must also be in writing.

Example: An agreement to retain a real estate broker or salesperson to sell a commercial property must be in writing to be enforceable.

Part Performance Exception

While full performance satisfies the Statute of Frauds, in real estate transactions, courts have also created a part performance exception for oral contracts that would otherwise violate the Statute of Frauds. While states may have unique requirements, generally, the **part performance exception** allows oral real estate contracts to be enforceable if any two of the following three elements are met: (1) the purchase price has been fully or partially paid, (2) the party has received possession of the property, and (3) valuable improvements have been made to the property. In a few states, however, part performance of an oral contract is not recognized.

Part performance exception
An exception to the Statute of Frauds. This allows oral real estate contracts to be enforceable if any two of the following three elements are met: (1) the purchase price has been fully or partially paid, (2) the party has received possession of the property, and (3) valuable improvements have been made to the property.

Example: Jacob enters into an oral agreement to sell his home to Jennifer. Jennifer pays Jacob $150,000 as a down payment toward the purchase price of $500,000 for the property. Before closing, Jacob gives Jennifer the keys to the property and allows her to take possession of it. This oral contract satisfies the part performance exception to the Statute of Frauds.

Some states require that a party's change in position have been induced by the other party to the oral contract such that it would be unconscionable not to enforce it.

Digital Forms of Contracting Under UETA and ESIGN

The Statute of Frauds requires the actual signature of the party to be bound to a memorandum. As technology evolved, the law responded to needed changes in contract law.

The Uniform Law Commission proposed the Uniform Electronic Transactions Act (UETA), which has been adopted at least in part by 49 states (all but New York), the District of Columbia, and the U.S. Virgin Islands. It was the first comprehensive proposal to promote electronic commerce among the states. Its primary purpose is to establish that "electronic records and electronic signatures relating to a transaction" are the equivalent of paper writings and manually signed contracts. In addition, UETA permits notaries public to act electronically, eliminating the need for a notary stamp or seal on a paper notary acknowledgment to a transaction.

The Electronic Signatures in Global and National Commerce Act (ESIGN) is a federal law passed to facilitate the use of electronic records and electronic signatures in interstate and foreign commerce. The general intent of the ESIGN Act is that a contract or signature "may not be denied legal effect, validity, or enforceability solely because it is in electronic form." The result is that electronic signatures and records are as valid as ones in paper form.

UETA and ESIGN do not require the use of electronic records or signatures. The parties must agree to conduct their transaction by electronic means. However, the intent of these acts is to encourage the use of electronic contracting. UETA provides that evidence of an electronic record or signature may not be excluded in a legal proceeding because it is in electronic and not written in a paper form.

There are some instances where the use of electronic contracting is not permitted. These instances include writing requirements for documents controlled by the UCC and in the creation of estate planning documents, such as wills and testamentary trusts.

Parol Evidence Rule

Parol evidence rule A contract rule prohibiting prior or contemporaneous promises, agreements, or understandings if they would vary, add to, or conflict with the terms of a written contract.

A related concept to the Statute of Frauds is the **parol evidence rule**. If the parties to a contract have reduced their understandings and intentions to a writing that was intended to be the full and final expression of their agreement, any evidence — whether written or oral — of prior or contemporaneous promises, agreements, or understandings is disregarded if they would *vary*, *add to*, or *conflict* with the terms of the writing. The parol evidence rule is a rule of evidence used in interpreting written contracts.

The parol evidence rule applies to evidence of promises and understandings given or discussed *prior to or contemporaneous with* the formation of the written contract. The parol evidence rule does not, by itself, prohibit consideration of matters external to the parties' written agreement. Instead, the rule prohibits the use of external evidence to add to or otherwise modify the terms of a written agreement that has been adopted by the parties as a final expression of their understanding.

Evidence of subsequent promises and understandings is *not* affected by the rule. That means a trial court may consider post-agreement evidence of communications and behavior.

Exceptions to the parol evidence rule exist. Where an exception exists, the evidence is admissible to add to, vary, or modify the contract. The exceptions typically apply in circumstances in which it would be unfair to exclude such evidence, including the following:

- Establishing that a contract was void or voidable (such as through fraud, misrepresentation, duress, undue influence, or mutual mistake);
- Establishing illegality;
- Clarifying an ambiguity in the contract;

Example: In a contract related to the sale of a photography studio, the seller agreed to a covenant not to compete with the buyer for school photograph work in any "school" in the country (with the exception of two high schools). The court allowed parol evidence to show that the parties intended to limit the term "schools" to local schools below a college or university level. *Lawrence v. Cain*, 245 N.E.2d 663 (Ind. Ct. App. 1969)

- Clarifying a term not defined in the agreement. If the parties have defined a term within the agreement, parol evidence to separately define it will be excluded;

Example: For purposes of this Agreement, the word "day" shall mean a business and not a calendar day.

- Correcting an obvious clerical error;

Example: If a deed to a piece of real property identified the property address street number as "11542" instead of "1542," but contained the correct legal description and assessor parcel numbers, parol evidence would allow for the correction.

- Proving trade customs or course of dealings between the parties; and

Example: REA Construction Company submitted a bid to Piland Corporation for stone and asphalt work at the Operational Training Facility of the United States Navy at Dam Neck in Virginia Beach. Piland was awarded the contract by the Navy, but did not timely notify REA. REA assumed the bid was unsuccessful and moved on. Piland sought to force REA to perform the contract. Parol evidence was allowed to show that customs in the trade require a successful prime contractor (Piland) to notify a subcontractor (REA) within a period of 30 days after the prime contractor has been advised of the acceptance of his bid. *Piland Corp. v. REA Constr. Co.*, 672 F. Supp. 244 (E.D. Va. 1987)

- Establishing that the *entire contract* was subject to an oral or written condition precedent that needed to be satisfied before the agreement rose to the level of an enforceable contract. However, proof that a promise within an existing contract was subject to some condition not expressed in the integrated writing would not be permitted.

Concept Summary Parol Evidence Rule

Parol evidence is precluded only if it would add to, vary, or contradict the content of the integrated writing. It may be used to clarify an ambiguity or illegality, prove trade customs or course of dealings between the parties, clarify a term not defined in the agreement, or establish partial integration or proof of fraud.

Merger Clause (Integration Clause)

Parol evidence is used to exclude evidence when parties to a contract intended the writing to represent the full and final expression of their agreement. Therefore, a merger clause (or integration clause) is commonly inserted into contracts. A merger clause stipulates that the agreement represents the full and final agreement between the parties. In effect, the merger clause expressly reiterates the parol evidence rule.

> **Example:** A merger clause may state: "This Agreement constitutes and embodies the full and final agreement and understanding between the parties hereto, and supersedes all prior agreements, understandings, negotiations, representations, and discussions. The parties acknowledge that there are no representations, promises, warranties, conditions, or obligations of the parties hereto concerning the subject matter of this Agreement not stated herein. They have not executed this Agreement in reliance upon any representation, promise, warranty, condition, or obligation not stated herein."

Third-Party Rights

The parties to a contract owe each other rights and duties. For example, in a residential lease, the landlord owes duties to provide safe, fit, and habitable housing, and is entitled to a right of payment. The tenant owes the landlord the duty to pay rent and has a right to be provided safe, fit, and habitable housing.

Privity
The common law rules that in order to have a legal interest in a contract, one must be party to the contract.

A fundamental principle of contract law is the concept of **privity**. It requires a party to have a legal interest or right under the contract to enforce it. In most cases, a person who is *not* a party to a contract enjoys no rights under the contract and cannot be compelled to perform any duties required under the contract. However, a party may want to transfer a right or a duty to a third party or provide benefits to a third party. As the law has developed, courts have recognized two exceptions to the rule of privity, namely, assignment and delegation, and third-party beneficiaries.

Assignment of Rights

An **assignment** is the transfer of a contractual right to a third person. The **assignor** is the party assigning rights to a third-party. The **assignee** is the third party, assigned rights from the assignor. In addition to the assignor and assignee, another party to the agreement is the **obligor,** who owes a duty of performance under the contract. The obligor owes a duty of performance to the **obligee.**

Assignment
A transfer of the rights arising under a contract to a third person.

Assignor
The party who transfers their contract rights to a third person (assignee).

Assignee
The party to whom contract rights have been transferred from the assignor.

Obligee
The party to whom a duty of obligation is owed by the obligor.

Obligor
The party who owes a duty of performance under the contract.

FIGURE 13.1: Assignment

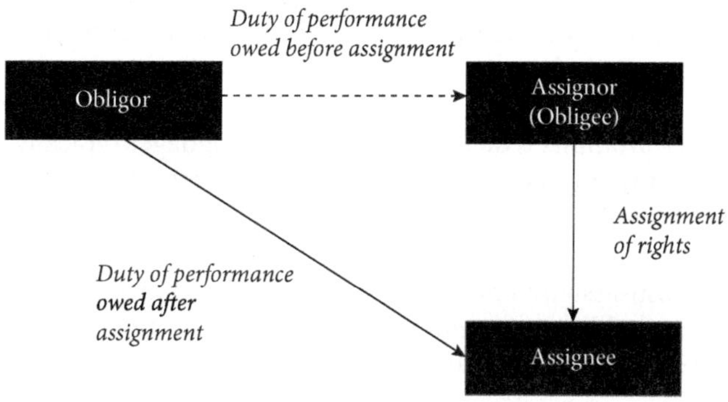

Example: BigMart owes money to its supplier, Supplies Tividad. Supplies Tividad decides to sell its rights to the account receivable to a collection agency, Collect & Sue. BigMart is the obligor (it owes a duty of performance to the obligee). Supplies Tividad is the assignor/obligee. It is owed a duty of performance and has assigned that right to Collect & Sue. Collect & Sue is the assignee and has been assigned the rights under the contract from the assignor, Supplies Tividad.

In general, any act or statement is sufficient to assign rights; however, other rules apply regarding securities, security agreements, and sales of goods. Assignments are extensively used in financing, insurance, real estate leasing, and securities. The following rules only apply to personal property. A contract for the sale of real property interests is subject to different assignment rules.

EFFECT OF THE ASSIGNMENT. When an assignor assigns their rights in a contract to the assignee, the assignee takes only those rights that the assignor had; rights are not expanded because of the assignment. The rights of the assignor are extinguished. The assignee is said to "stand in the shoes of the assignor." If the obligor fails to perform the contract, the assignee can sue the obligor to enforce the agreement.

Example: In the BigMart example above, Supplies Tividad cannot seek to obtain payment from BigMart after the assignment. If BigMart does not pay its debts, Collect & Sue is entitled to enforce the agreement.

While the assignee takes over the rights of the contract from the assignor, an obligor can assert any defense the obligor had against the assignor or the assignee (such as to the formation of the contract, mistake, illegality, or public policy reasons).

Example: In the sale of a business, the accounts receivable of the seller are usually assigned to the buyer. Since the buyer is at risk for paying for the full value of the receivables, the seller will provide post-closing written warranties to the buyer relating to the collectability of the receivables. These warranties act in addition to the implied warranties made by the seller to the buyer discussed above.

RESTRAINTS ON ASSIGNMENTS. Generally, under the freedom to contract, all contract rights are assignable. However, there are some exceptions to this right to assign contracts. They include:

1. *The contract prohibits assignment.* Contract language, typically referred to as an anti-assignment clause, can prohibit (and "void") any assignments. Any attempted assignment without consent is not effective.

Example: An anti-assignment clause may provide, "No party shall assign their rights, duties, and obligations under this agreement, or any interest therein, either voluntarily or by operation of law, without prior written consent of the other party."

However, the following are assignable despite an anti-assignment clause or agreement not to assign: (1) a right to receive money, (2) negotiable instruments (discussed in Chapter 29), and (3) the right to receive damages for breach of contract or proceeds from an account owed for the sale of goods. The rationale for these exceptions is that the free transferability of these rights promotes commerce.

2. *The assignment is prohibited by law.* Some states prohibit the assignment of future wages by an employee, and several statutes prohibit the assignment of certain claims against the federal government. Further, a court may prohibit an assignment as a violation of public policy.

Example: Applied Materials ("Applied") required employees to execute an employment agreement that contained an intellectual property assignment clause. The clause provided that any invention described in a patent application or disclosed to third parties for one year after termination of employment with Applied was to be assigned to Applied. The district court held that the assignment clause was an overly broad restraint on trade and prohibited by law. *Applied Materials v. Advanced Micro-Fabrication Equip. Inc.*, 630 F. Supp. 2d 1084 (N.D. Cal. 2009)

3. *The assignment materially, significantly changes the risk or duties of the obligor.*

Example: When a borrower is pre-approved to obtain a business loan, the borrower may not assign the right to obtain the loan to another. The risk to the bank would significantly change as it has not pre-approved the new borrower and may not have pre-approved a loan with that borrower.

4. *The contract is for personal services.* Contracts for personal services — where the contract calls for skill, credit, or other personal qualities — cannot usually be assigned. However, the parties can agree to assign a personal services contract.

Example: Hector contracts with a renowned artist to sculpt a unique sculpture of his family. As this is a contract for personal services, the contract is not assignable.

Example: Members in the National Football League® agree in their contracts with teams that their contracts may be assigned to another team.

5. *The assignment of a future right.* This involves a right that does not currently exist.

Example: A person cannot assign an interest in a lottery winning before the person wins the lottery.

6. *Rights based upon a legal action.* This involves wrongs of a purely personal nature, such as defamation and personal injuries.

NOTICE OF ASSIGNMENT. When an assignor makes an assignment of a contract right, the assignee is under a duty to notify the obligor that the assignment has been made and that performance must be rendered to the assignee. When the assignee fails to notify the obligor, the assignment is still effective between the assignor and the assignee; however, without such a notice, the obligor may continue to render performance to the assignor since the obligor was not aware of the assignment. The assignee cannot pursue the obligor to recover payment because the obligor has performed the original promise made to pay the original party to the contract (the assignor).

If the assignor fails to provide a notice of assignment to the obligor. In that case, the obligor may continue to render performance to the assignor — even though the assignor has no right to the performance following the assignment. In such cases, until the notice of assignment is given, the assignee's remedies are not against the obligor but against the assignor.

Example: A college graduate's student loan is assigned to a new lender, who gives notice of the assignment to the graduate. The graduate must make payments to the assignee. If the student pays the original lender (the assignor) following receipt of such notice, the graduate will be at risk of having also to pay the assignee lender.

Example: On July 1, Acme assigns its accounts receivable to Baker Finance in exchange for partial payment of the balances due (this is known as factoring). On July 5, one of Acme's customers made a payment of $10,000 to Acme, which it retains. On July 10, Baker Finance notifies Acme's customers that payment is to be made to Baker Finance and not Acme. Baker Finance is entitled to collect $10,000 from Acme.

May Assignments Be Revoked?

An assignment given for consideration is irrevocable; once the assignment is made, the rights assigned belong to the assignee. However, a gratuitous assignment (for example, one made as a gift) is usually revocable by the assignor.

PRIORITIES AMONG SUCCESSIVE ASSIGNEES. Where there are successive assignments by an assignor, it is sometimes necessary to determine which assignee has priority. For example, suppose the Debtor owes money to the Creditor. The Creditor assigns the claim for payment to A1, the first assignee. Later, the Creditor makes a second assignment of the same debt to A2, the second assignee. A2 then notifies the Debtor of the assignment. Which assignee is entitled to the money? The same rights could be assigned to different parties by intent or mistake. Two conflicting rules have been developed to solve this problem.

1. *Assignee first in time.* The American rule gives priority to the assignee first in time. The theory is that legal title has passed from the assignor after the first assignment; after that, nothing further exists to assign.
2. *First assignee to give notice.* The other rule prefers that the first assignee give notice, on the theory that the assignment dispute is to be resolved equitably. Giving notice is effectively the equivalent of possession of the claim. If the subsequent assignee gives the notice, they will prevail over a prior assignee, provided that the subsequent assignee had no notice of the first assignment.

Delegation of Duties

Delegation
A transfer of the contractual duties arising under a contract to a third person.

Delegator
The party who transfers their contract duties to a third person (delegatee).

Delegatee
The party to whom contract duties have been transferred from the delegator.

Similar to how an assignment can transfer rights in a contract to a third person, a **delegation** is the transfer of a contractual duty to another who is then obligated to perform that duty. A person who delegates her contractual duty is the obligor under the contract and is then the **delegator** of the duty. The person who assumes the duty is called the **delegatee**. The other party to the contract, whose right to performance has been delegated, is called the obligee. In general, any act or statement is sufficient to delegate duties.

> **Example:** Big Contractor enters into a contract to paint Jesse's house. Big Contractor delegates its duties to Paint King. Jesse is the obligee, and Big Contractor is the obligor who owed the duty of performance to Jesse. Big Contractor is the delegator, and Paint King is the delegate.

EFFECT OF THE DELEGATION. When the delegator delegates duties in a contract, the delegatee is obligated to perform only those duties that were delegated. The

FIGURE 13.2: Delegation

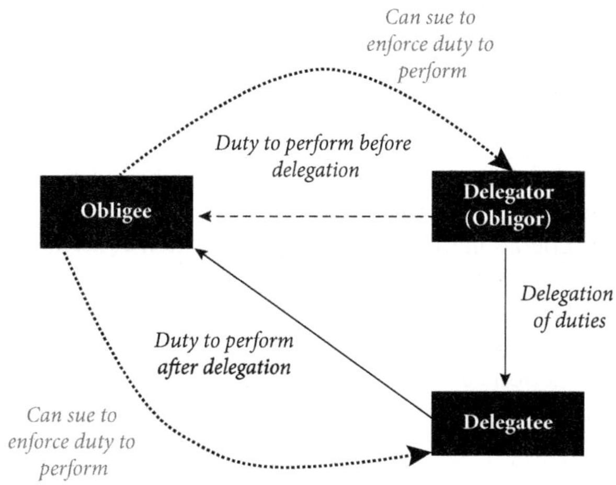

obligee must accept the performance of the duty owed it by the delegatee. While there are exceptions, where the delegatee fails to perform the duties delegated, the obligee can choose to sue either the delegator or the delegatee.

> **Example:** In the Big Contractor example above, after the delegation, Jesse can seek to require the performance of the contract from either Big Contractor or Paint King.

RESTRAINTS ON DELEGATIONS. Generally, all contractual duties may be delegated, with a few exceptions. A determination as to whether a duty can be delegated needs to be examined on a case-by-case basis. Some exceptions to the right to delegate contracts include the following:

1. *The contract is for personal services.* Contracts for personal services—the contract calls for the skill, credit, or other personal qualities of the obligor—cannot be delegated. Contracts that are not for personal duties may be delegated.

> **Example:** A Major League Baseball team hires a person as a scout. The scout's job is to find talent to play in the big leagues. The person was hired because they possessed superior judgment in determining the players' skill level and potential talent. Because this position is one that requires personal judgment, it cannot be delegated.

2. *Special recognized relationships or special trust in the obligor.* There is a limitation upon the right to delegate when a specially recognized relationship exists.

> **Example:** A patient who seeks treatment by a specific physician does so because the doctor possesses a certain level of trust and other factors such as qualifications, certifications, good reputation, etc. Once this trust arises, the service provider, the doctor, cannot delegate their duties.

3. *Delegations of duty are not permitted if the contract expressly prohibits it.* Contract language, typically referred to as an anti-delegation clause, can prohibit (and "void") any delegation. Any attempted delegation without consent is not effective. Often, when there is an anti-assignment clause, there will also be an anti-delegation clause.

Example: An anti-delegation clause may provide, "No party shall delegate their rights, duties and obligations under this agreement, or any interest therein, either voluntarily or by operation of law, without prior written consent of the other party."

Contract terms may allow for delegation of duties.

Example: Construction contracts between an owner and a general contractor will contain provisions that portions of the scope of work may be delegated to specialty subcontractors.

4. *The delegation would materially vary the performance owed to the obligee if the obligor's duties were delegated.*

Example: A corporation hires the local police department to provide security for a high-ranking ambassador who will be visiting the corporation. The local police department cannot delegate its duties to provide security to a third party (such as a private security detail).

Sometimes, contracts are entered into with corporations, rather than individuals. A corporation is entitled to designate performance to a person capable and qualified to carry out the duties of the contract.

In the following case, the court addressed the issue of what happens to the duties owed in a contract when a party assigns their interest to a third person who later assigns the interest again.

CASE 13.2

ABSENT A RELEASE OR NOVATION, THE DELEGATOR REMAINS LIABLE AFTER DELEGATION AND ASSIGNMENT

PENNACO ENERGY, INC. v. SORENSON

371 P.3d 120 (2016)

Supreme Court of Wyoming

Sorenson owned a ranch in Wyoming, in which the surface area was retained by Sorenson, and the subsurface mineral estate was used for mineral development. Nine different parties owned the mineral rights and, as a way of generating income, leased out these rights to various companies as a way of generating income. In the 1990s, Pennaco Energy, Inc. acquired interests in the oil and gas leases underlying Sorenson's ranch. Pennaco and Sorenson entered into a surface damage and use agreement, to give the parties a firm understanding as to what damages would be payable in the event of development of the lands.

The contract gave Pennaco the right to enter upon and use Sorenson's lands for drilling operations. In exchange, Pennaco agreed to restore and reseed well sites, to remove all above-ground equipment, and to restore the land to its original state when mineral production ended. In 2010, Pennaco was sold to CEP-M. As part of the sale, Pennaco assigned its interest in the lease as well as the agreement to restore the land to CEP-M. CEP-M then assigned its interests to High Plains Gas.

After the assignment in 2010, Pennaco did not make annual payments or restore Sorenson's land as required by the agreement. High Plains Gas did not do so either. Sorenson then sued Pennaco and High Plains Gas to collect the annual payments and to enforce the obligations owed under the restoration agreement. A jury awarded Sorenson damages against Pennaco, and Pennaco appealed.

Language of the Court. *We began our analysis by examining well-established principles of contract law concerning assignment and delegation. Rights under a contract are assigned and contractual duties are delegated. The assignor of a right usually has no interest in the contractual rights after assignment. However, and importantly here, when a duty is delegated, the delegant remains liable. If this were not so, every solvent person could obtain freedom from debts by delegating them to an insolvent. While the delegant can appoint another to render performance on the obligor's behalf, such a delegation of a duty does not free the obligor-delegant from the duty to see to it that performance is rendered, unless there is a novation.*

The contract contains nothing indicating that the parties intended Pennaco would be able to relieve itself of its obligations merely by assigning them to a third party. The obligations to reclaim the surface estate and to pay until reclamation is complete presume an ability and willingness to perform after production ends. These obligations were not the kind that the parties would expect to be performed only by the last assignee of Pennaco. The trial court found that the obligations were logically connected to Pennaco, its financial ability, and its initial creation of the gas operation, rather than to whatever the last assignee may have done.

Based on the plain language in the agreement, we hold that the parties intended for Pennaco to remain responsible for obligations in the agreement until Sorenson's land was restored. If Pennaco intended to be released from liability for a breach occurring after assignment, it could have negotiated an exculpatory clause in the contract. Absent such a clause, Pennaco could have tried to obtain a novation from Sorenson at the time of assignment. It did neither.

To find that the assignment released Pennaco from its obligations would require us to read an exculpatory clause that expressly terminated Pennaco's obligations upon assignment into the contract. There is no such clause, and we are not at liberty to rewrite the agreement. We conclude that Pennaco remained liable under the agreement after assignment.

Decision. Pennaco remained liable under the surface damage and use agreement after assignment.

Focus on Ethics

If, following the assignment, Pennaco was financially unable to reclaim (restore) the surface estate, would this decision still have been a fair result?

Third-Party Beneficiaries

Promisee
A party to a contract who directs that a benefit be conferred to another person (the third-party beneficiary).

Promisor
A party to a contract who agrees to confer performance to another person (the third-party beneficiary).

Third-party beneficiary
A party identified in the contract who receives a benefit of the contract but is not one of the contracting parties.

Like the doctrines of assignment and delegation, the rules regarding third-party beneficiaries also involve the introduction of a third party into the contract. However, the difference between a third-party beneficiary and a third party in an assignment or delegation involves the timing of the third-party rights. A third-party beneficiary is a party that is identified *at the time of contracting*. On the other hand, in assignment and delegation, a decision is made by one of the parties to transfer their rights, duties, or both to a third party *after* a contract has been made and after those rights and obligations have existed.

In a third-party beneficiary contract, the parties intend to confer a contract benefit to an identified third party at the time of contract formation. This person is known as an *intended third-party beneficiary*. They are intended third-party beneficiaries because of their identification at the time of contract formation. As an intended beneficiary, the third party has legal rights and can sue the promisor to enforce the contract in the event of a breach.

In a third-party beneficiary contract, there are three parties. The promisee and the promisor enter into a contract. The **promisee** is the party that directs that a benefit be conferred to another person (known as the third-party beneficiary). The **promisor** is the party who agrees to confer the performance to another person. The **third-party beneficiary** is the party identified in the contract who receives a benefit without being one of the contracting parties.

FIGURE 13.3: Third-Party Beneficiary

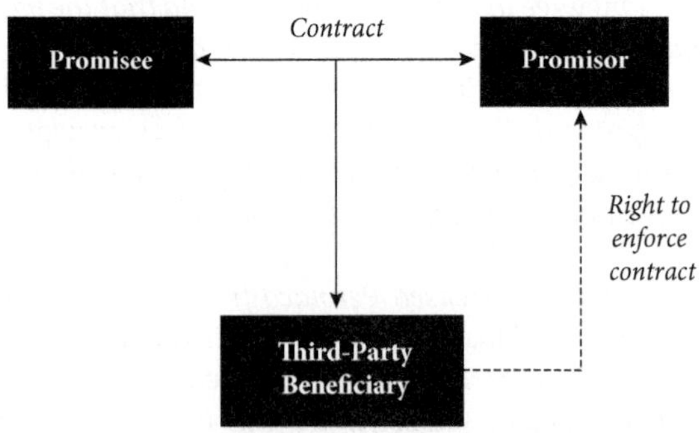

Example: Adoree obtains a life insurance contract with Insurance Co. Adoree directs Insurance Co. to pay the life insurance benefits to Devon. Adoree is the promisee, Insurance Co. is the promisor, and Devon is the third-party beneficiary.

WHEN CAN A THIRD-PARTY BENEFICIARY ENFORCE A CONTRACT? A third party cannot enforce a contract against the original parties (promisor and promise) until the third party's rights have vested. The rights **vest** when they move from a contingent status to fixed, accrued, or absolute status. The rights cannot be taken away from the third-party beneficiary when vested. While courts differ on when vesting occurs, generally, any of the following is present:

Vesting
When a third-party beneficiary is entitled to enforce a contract.

- The third-party expressly consents to receive the performance of the promisor;

Example: Bella contracts with a painter to paint the house of Cheryl (a relative of Bella). Cheryl notifies Bella and the painter that Cheryl will accept the services. The third-party beneficiary is vested.

- The third-party materially and detrimentally changes their position in justifiable reliance on the promises made by the original parties; or
- The conditions for vesting are satisfied.

Example: When a person obtains a life insurance policy that names a third person as an intended third-party beneficiary, the third-party beneficiary is vested when the person who obtained the life insurance policy dies.

Until the rights vest, the original parties may modify or rescind (cancel) the contract without the consent of the proposed intended third-party beneficiary.

INCIDENTAL THIRD-PARTY BENEFICIARY. An **incidental third-party beneficiary** is a nonparty to the contract who is not identified in the contract. This person might derive a benefit if the contract is performed, but the parties to the contract did not intend to benefit that person directly. Since the incidental beneficiary is not an intended beneficiary of the contract, he or she may not sue to enforce the contract. The person's receipt of any benefits following the performance of the contract is purely incidental to the contract.

Incidental third-party beneficiary
A nonparty to contract who is not identified in the contract. This person might derive a benefit if the contract is performed, but the parties to the contract did not intend to benefit that person directly.

Example: Caretta contracted with Colonial to purchase a yacht. Colonial placed the order with a shipyard. The naval architect specified a paint made by U.S. Paint for application on the yacht. When the paint failed after delivery of the yacht, Caretta sued U.S. Paint as an intended third-party beneficiary of the shipyard-U.S. Paint contract. Examining the contracts and the pre-contract dealings between the shipyard and the paint manufacturer, the trial court found that Caretta was never intended to be directly benefitted from the contract. Caretta was only an incidental beneficiary and could not sue the paint manufacturer. *Caretta Trucking, Inc. v. Cheoy Lee Shipyards, Ltd.*, 647 So. 2d 1028 (Fla. Dist. Ct. App. 1994)

Old Terminology

The modern trend is to avoid the use of the terms "creditor beneficiary" and "donee beneficiary." Instead, the terms "intended third-party beneficiary" and "incidental third-party beneficiary" are preferred. However, because the student may encounter the former terms, the following definitions are provided.

If the main purpose of the contract is to discharge a debt the promisor owes to a third party, the third party is a **creditor beneficiary**, who is the person owed the performance of the contract.

> **Example:** A owes B $1,000. Instead of paying the debt directly to B, A contracts with a third party, C, to deliver services that B desires. A contracts with C to pave B's driveway. If the paving contract is breached, the creditor beneficiary (C) may sue the promisor (B) as a third-party beneficiary.

In the above example, the creditor (C) may also sue the original debtor (A).

If the promisee's main purpose is to confer a benefit on a third party as a gift, the third party is a **donee beneficiary**.

> **Example:** A contracts with B, a life insurer, to insure A's life. A designates C as the beneficiary of the life insurance. C is a donee beneficiary.

As noted above, the modern approach is to characterize the donee beneficiary as an incidental beneficiary, which means that the person does not have a legally protected interest in the performance of the contract. For example, in the life insurance example, C is vulnerable to A's later changes in designating a beneficiary to the life insurance policy.

AI Feature: Contract Construction and Parol Evidence

Use an internet search engine to research the law in relation to both the parol evidence rule and the rules of contract construction to resolve an ambiguity in a contract. Then, use an AI program to help you analyze the following facts.

Suppose an owner of a hotel sued its commercial property insurer over whether the full limit of a commercial property insurance policy covered the damage to the hotel caused by a hurricane. While seeking a renewal of its existing policy, it received a policy that stated there would be a lower coverage limit (called a sublimit) for wind-driven rain damage, but the actual sublimit language of $250,000 was accidentally left out of the policy. Before the insurer could correct the policy by adding the sublimit, Hurricane Florence caused catastrophic damage to the hotel. In construing an insurance policy, does the construction favor an insured or the insurance company? If the parties agreed that a sublimit would be applicable, but the dollar limit was never stated, does this make the policy incomplete and require the use of parol evidence? Can such evidence be used when the terms of a contract are vague and indefinite as this one was? Could the remedy of reformation apply? Summarize your legal arguments produced by your AI program and then compare them to the holding in *Ironshore Specialty Ins. Co. v. RPG Hospitality, LLC*, 889 S.E.2d 394 (Ga. App. 2023).

Key Terms

- Assignee, 305
- Assignment, 305
- Assignor, 305
- Delegatee, 308
- Delegation, 308
- Delegator, 308
- Equal dignity rule, 301
- Incidental third-party beneficiary, 313
- Main purpose rule, 299
- Memorandum, 296
- Obligee, 305
- Obligor, 305
- Parol evidence rule, 302
- Part performance exception, 301
- Privity, 304
- Promisee, 312
- Promisor, 312
- Statute of Frauds, 296
- Surety, 299
- Third-party beneficiary, 312
- Vesting, 313

Applying the Law

13.1 Statute of Frauds. Classic Cheesecake was a bakery company. To expand its market to Las Vegas hotels, its executives visited a local branch office of JPMorgan Chase Bank™. After receiving business records verifying the company's finances, a vice president of the bank orally assured Classic's principals (according to Classic) that the loan was a "go." Those within the bank's credit department expressed grave concerns over the loan and had decided to decline the loan, but the officer continued to make oral assurances that the loan would be approved. Some months later, the bank notified Classic in writing that the loan was being denied. Classic sued the bank for breach of contract. How would the statute of frauds and promissory estoppel apply to these facts? *Classic Cheesecake Company, Inc. v. JPMorgan Chase Bank, N.A.*, 546 F.3d 839 (7th Cir. 2008)

13.2 Parol Evidence Rule. An option agreement to purchase a limited liability company stated that it was entered into upon "the mutual covenants and agreements hereinafter set forth, and other good and valuable consideration (the receipt and adequacy of which is hereby acknowledged by the Parties)." It also contained a merger clause, which stated: "This Agreement contains the entire agreement and understanding of the Parties . . . and supersedes and completely replaces all prior and other representations, warranties, promises, assurances and other agreements and understandings (whether written, oral, express, implied or otherwise) among the Parties with respect to the matters contained in this Agreement." The parties entered into a separate agreement at the same time by which the seller would lend $100 million dollars to the purchaser to fund the purchase. Eventually the seller declined to do so, and the purchaser sought specific performance of the agreements. Would the parol evidence rule permit the introduction of evidence that the parties had also agreed to the $100 million dollar loan so that the loan would be the "other good and valuable consideration" mentioned in the purchase agreement? *Rubin Schron v. Troutman Sanders LLP*, 986 N.E.2d 430 (N.Y. 2013)

13.3 Integration Clause. Jason Price advertised a 1994 van for sale. John Baker orally agreed to buy the van for $15,000. They then executed a deposit agreement which stated that Baker would pay a deposit of $2,000. It also stated a few days later, Price would deliver clean title to the van. The deposit agreement did not contain an integration clause. When the title was transferred, it stated that the van was a 1993 model. John refused to accept the title, and Price refused to return the deposit. Baker sued Price for breach of contract. Should the parol evidence rule be applied? Explain. *Barker v. Price*, 48 N.E.3d 367 (Ind. 2015)

13.4 Time for Performance. Klewin Inc. entered into an oral agreement with Flagship Properties to function as its construction manager on a major project in Mansfield, Connecticut. The oral contract failed to specific explicitly the time for performance when performance of that contract within one year of its making was exceedingly unlikely. Flagship later replaced Klewin with another construction manager, and Klewin sued for breach of contract. Is this contract enforceable? What arguments would both sides make? *C.R. Klewin, Inc. v. Flagship Properties, Inc.*, 220 Conn. 569 (Conn. 1991)

13.5 Ambiguity and Mutual Mistake. Patrick Panos sold Olsen and Associates Construction a vacant lot adjacent to his own home. In the real estate contract, a provision prohibited building on the vacant lot any building higher than thirty-two feet when measured "from the road." Panos asserted that the purpose of the height restriction was to preserve his unobstructed view from his property. Olsen constructed a home that was 34.91 feet high from the spot from which the Seller measured. When Olson measured from a different spot on the street, the home was only 31.96 feet high, in compliance with the height restriction. Panos argues that this provision was ambiguous because it could be any spot on the street. Under the merger doctrine, a deed is the final, integrated agreement of the parties. Ambiguity and mutual mistake are exceptions to that doctrine. How should the court rule? *Panos v. Olsen and Associates Const., Inc.*, 123 P.3d 816 (Utah 2005)

13.6 Memorandum. Ellis Canning entered into an oral contract with Arthur Bernstein and other stockholders of a food packaging plant, which Ellis intended to acquire. The original oral agreement between them was tape recorded and involved Ellis's advance of certain sums of money and a schedule of payments involving Ellis's acquisition of the shares of stock. Between the original tape-recorded oral agreement and its reduction to writing, certain terms of the agreement had to be modified due to the financial circumstances of the sellers' corporation. The stockholders then received another more favorable offer for the business and sold it to a third party. At this point, Ellis demanded return of the sums advanced and sued for breach of contract. The stockholders claimed that no contract existed due to a lack of a meeting of the minds between the parties as to the terms and a violation of the Statute of Frauds. Who prevails and why? *Ellis Canning Co. v. Bernstein*, 348 F. Supp. 1212 (D. Colo. 1972)

13.7 Vesting of Third-Party Beneficiaries' Rights. In 1964, Chicago Flame Hardening Co. adopted a corporate resolution to pay a monthly stipend to the widow of an owner upon his death. Mrs. Scott was the wife of owner Marvin Scott. She knew of this resolution but did not act upon it or keep it in mind. When Mr. Keele died, his widow received a monthly stipend. Mrs. Scott was aware that Mrs. Keele was receiving these benefits. In 1971, Chicago Flame adopted another corporate resolution rescinding future widow benefits. Mrs. Scott did not learn of the rescission of her benefits until after her husband died later that year. Mrs. Scott sued Chicago Flame to enforce the 1964 resolution. Is Mrs. Scott a third-party beneficiary who can enforce the benefits of the original corporate resolution? Explain your answer. Discuss. *Detroit Bank and Trust Co. v. Chicago Flame Hardening Co.*, 541 F. Supp. 1278 (N.D. Ind. 1982)

13.8 Assignments. The Rosenbergs sold a Dairy Queen® to Mary Pratt. Pratt then executed an assignment agreement that assigned her rights and delegated her duties under the sales contract to Son, Inc. The Rosenbergs executed the assignment agreement. Son then assigned the sales contract to Merit Co. Merit filed for bankruptcy and failed to make payments under the sales contract. Who may the Rosenbergs sue to enforce the contract? Were Pratt and Son released from liability because of the assignment? *Rosenberg v. Son, Inc.*, 491 N.W.2d 71 (N.D. 1992)

13.9 Assignment of Bilateral Contract. Contemporary Mission, Inc., and Famous Music Corporation®

had multiple contracts, granting Famous exclusive rights to manufacture and sell Contemporary's records, paying Contemporary royalties. All the agreements required Famous to use reasonable efforts to promote and distribute the records. Famous later sold its records division to ABC Records, Inc.® ABC repudiated the agreement and refused to have a relationship with Contemporary. What rights and duties remain between and among the parties? Who can Contemporary sue to enforce the contracts? *Contemporary Mission, Inc. v. Famous Music Corp.*, 557 F.2d 918 (2d Cir. 1977)

13.10 Third-Party Beneficiary. John Gillispie operated a novelty shop specializing in University of Iowa sports memorabilia. Gillispie had no affiliation with the university or any of its sports teams. John Bain was a referee for a basketball game between the University of Iowa and Purdue University. Bain made a call that Iowa fans asserted was clearly in error and allowed Purdue a last-minute victory. Many University of Iowa fans, including Gillispie, blamed Bain for the loss. Gillispie then started to market a T-shirt showing a caricature of Bain hanging from a noose. Bain sued Gillispie seeking damages. Gillispie countersued on the grounds that Bain negligently breached the standard of competence required of a collegiate referee, and that Gillispie was entitled to damages as a third-party beneficiary of Bain's employment contract with the Big Ten Athletic Conference. Iowa's loss of the game to Purdue eliminated Iowa from the championship of the Big Ten Basketball Conference. According to Bain, this, in turn, destroyed a potential market for Gillispie's memorabilia, touting Iowa as a Big Ten champion. Does Gillispie have standing to sue under Bain's employment agreement? *Bain v. Gillispie*, 357 N.W.2d 47 (Iowa Ct. App. 1984)

Performance, Discharge, Breach, and Remedies

14

Breach of promise is a base surrender of truth. — Gandhi (1869-1948)

Chapter Outline

- Introduction
- Rules Governing Performance
- Discharge
- Breach of Contract
- Comparing Material and Minor Breaches of Contract
- Damages
  - *Management Application: Compensatory Damages by Subject Matter*

Case 14.1: *Lava Trading Inc. v. Hartford Fire Ins. Co.*
  - *Management Application: Consequential Damages Disclaimer*
  - *Management Application: Liquidated Damages Clause*

Case 14.2: *Uzan v. 845 UN Limited Partnership*
- Equitable Remedies

Case 14.3: *Oliver v. Ball*
- Defenses to Breach of Contract
- AI Feature: *Force Majeure* Clauses

Learning Objectives

After studying this chapter, you should be able to:

1. Explain the rules governing contract performance.
2. Describe the discharge of a contract by performance, agreement, and operation of law.
3. Distinguish between a material and minor breach of contract.
4. Explain what may be recovered as compensatory damages.
5. Explain when an equitable remedy is applicable to a contract breach.
6. Describe the defenses to a breach of contract.

Introduction

The assessment of damages for a breach of a promise, sometimes in the form of retaliatory justice, is traceable to our oldest records. The Code of Hammurabi, a Babylonian code of law of Mesopotamia, dates to 1754 B.C. The Code addressed a wide breadth of subjects, including the following:

- *If a shipbuilder builds a boat of sixty gur (a unit of measurement) for a man, he shall pay him a fee of two shekels in money.*
- *If a shipbuilder builds a boat for someone, and does not make it tight, if during that same year that boat is sent away and suffers injury, the shipbuilder shall take the boat apart and put it together tight at his own expense. The tight boat he shall be given to the boat owner.*
- *If a man rents his boat to a sailor, and the sailor is careless, and the boat is wrecked or goes aground, the sailor shall give the owner of the boat another boat as compensation.*

By the sixth century B.C., during the reign of King Croesus, in what is now, in part, modern-day Turkey, the use of coinage became a medium of exchange. The payment of money damages as a means of redressing harm became accepted.

Fortunately, the law of contracts has evolved to provide more remedies for breaches of contract. These remedies are divided into two main categories; namely, monetary damages and equitable (non-monetary) remedies, such as reformation, restitution, rescission, specific performance, and injunctive relief. Recognizing the consequences of what may follow from a breach of contract is the subject of our study in this chapter.

Rules Governing Performance

In many contracts, the parties may make promises and conditions to each other governing the performance of the contract. Courts have adopted general rules to assist in the interpretation of contract performance, including the following:

1. Time of Performance
2. Application of Payments
3. Conditions
4. Covenants

Time of Performance

If a contract specifies the time of performance, that is the time required to perform. If a contract does not specify the time of performance, a reasonable time to perform is allowed. There is an exception to this rule when the act required is capable of being done immediately, such as the payment of money. If the amount due is ascertained and clear, the contract requires immediate payment.

Application of Payments

When a debtor owes several debts to a creditor and makes a payment, they may specify the debt obligation to which the payment is to be applied. If the debtor does not specify the obligation to which a payment is to be applied, the creditor can apply it to any obligation the debtor owes. If neither specifies the application of a payment, the law will generally apply the payment in the following order: interest due, principal due, the next obligation due to be paid, unsecured obligations, and, finally, secured obligations.

Conditions

A **condition** is a fact, the occurrence or nonoccurrence of which creates (a condition precedent) or extinguishes (a condition subsequent) a duty on the part of the promisor. There are three types of conditions: (1) a condition precedent, (2) a concurrent condition, and (3) a condition subsequent.

Condition
A fact, the occurrence or nonoccurrence of which creates or extinguishes a duty on the part of the promisor.

CONDITION PRECEDENT. A **condition precedent** is one that requires the occurrence or nonoccurrence of an act or event that must occur before the promisor's duty of performance arises.

Condition precedent
A condition that requires the occurrence or nonoccurrence of an act or event that must occur before the promisor's duty of performance arises.

> **Example:** A parent agrees to reimburse the costs of a child's graduate school tuition upon graduation.

Conditions Based on Satisfaction. One form of condition precedent is a contract requiring performance meeting a party's personal satisfaction (or the satisfaction of a third party). To address the potential issue of whether personal satisfaction creates a condition precedent to payment, the courts have adopted two tests based on the type of contract performed.

Personal Satisfaction Test. Where the contract is personal, that is, the performance involves personal tastes, the performance must meet the actual personal satisfaction. The personal satisfaction is treated as a condition precedent. This type of contract has been upheld despite claims that it is subjective. Courts typically require that the party act in good faith when rejecting a contract based on their own personal satisfaction. However, courts have been inconsistent in adopting standards to determine if the contract is discharged.

> **Example:** A mother contracts for an artist to paint a family portrait. The contract provides that the artist is to render a portrait to the mother's personal satisfaction. The mother's satisfaction with the portrait is a condition precedent to her obligation to pay the artist.

Reasonable Person Test. Unless the contract states otherwise, contracts need to be performed to the satisfaction level of a reasonable person. Where a third person must approve to their satisfaction is specifically identified in the contract, most courts hold that the satisfaction still must be based on a reasonable third person's satisfaction (that is, it is not based on the personal satisfaction of the identified third person).

> **Example:** A homeowner contracts for the repair of a home with a contractor. The contract requires that Kevin Smith, the city's building department supervisor, approve the repair as satisfactory before final payment is due to the contractor. In this case, the reasonable satisfaction of a third party is necessary to meet the condition precedent for final payment.

Concurrent conditions
Conditions that are to be performed at the same time.

CONCURRENT CONDITIONS. These are conditions that are to be performed at the same time.

> **Example:** A parent agrees to pay for university tuition for their child so long as the child is achieving high grades while enrolled.

Condition subsequent
A condition referring to a future event, upon the happening of which the obligation of the other party ceases.

CONDITION SUBSEQUENT. A **condition subsequent** is one that refers to a future event, upon the happening of which the obligation of the other party ceases.

> **Example:** In a child support order, one parent agrees to pay for the support and care of a child until the child reaches the age of majority. Once that age is reached, the support obligation ceases.

Covenant
An unconditional promise to render some performance to another.

I think it is an immutable law in business that words are words, explanations are explanations, promises are promises, but only performance is reality. — Harold Geneen, American businessman (1910-1997)

Covenants

A **covenant** is an unconditional promise to render some performance to another. Failing to perform the covenant entitles the other party to sue for a breach of the covenant. One regularly employed covenant is the covenant of good faith and fair dealing. This covenant imposes upon each party the duty to refrain from doing anything that would render performance of the contract impossible, and also the duty to do everything that is necessary to accomplish the purpose of the contract. This covenant is limited to assuring compliance with the terms of the contract and not to those unstated in the contract. For example, in the absence of an agreement, a party is not under the obligation to negotiate in good faith.

Discharge

Discharge
The release of a debtor from personal liability for certain debts. A discharge prevents creditors owed those debts from taking any action against the debtor to collect them.

Discharge is the termination or completion of a contract. This term is broader than "performance," which is only one of the ways a contract is completed. A contract may be terminated or completed by (1) discharge by performance, (2) discharge by agreement, or (3) discharge by operation of law.

Discharge by Performance

Discharged by performance
Contract is fully executed as both parties have fully performed their contractual promises to the other party.

In most cases, when a contract is performed by both parties, the contract is **discharged by performance**. That means the contract is executed as both parties have fully kept their contractual promises to one another.

> **Example:** After agreeing to purchase Samir's car for $7,500, Taylor tenders that sum to Samir, who transfers title to and possession of the vehicle to Taylor. The contract is discharged.

Sometimes, a party does not render full performance, but substantially performs the contract. When that occurs, a minor breach of contract has occurred (minor breaches of contract are discussed below). If the breaching party does not timely correct the breach, the non-breaching party may recover damages by either deducting the cost of repairing the breach and remitting the balance to the other party or suing to recover the cost to repair the breach if the breaching party has already paid the other party.

Discharge by Agreement

The parties may agree to terminate a contract through discharge by agreement. This can occur in several ways:

- *Mutual rescission.* Since a contract arises from mutual consent of the parties, it can be terminated by mutual agreement of the parties as well. Mutual rescission is a contract to discharge a contract and requires the formalities necessity to create a contract (agreement, consideration, and capacity). Rescission occurs through mutual agreement of the parties. A party lacks the power to unilaterally rescind a contract.
- *Accord and satisfaction.* As discussed in Chapter 10, the parties may agree to substitute a new performance in place of, and in satisfaction of, an existing obligation. The accord is the agreement to accept the substitution, the performance of the accord is the satisfaction.
- *Novation.* A novation is an agreement that substitutes a third party for one of the original contracting parties. The two contracting parties and a third party agree that the third party shall perform the duties of one of the original parties to the contract. For example, a landlord may agree to a novation by agreeing to excuse a tenant from a lease when a third party replaces the tenant for the balance of the lease term.
- *Substituted contract.* The parties may enter into a new contract that revokes and discharges their existing contract. The new contract is a substituted contract. Only that latter contract and not the earlier one is enforceable. For example, a construction firm may agree to deliver a project to an owner for a lump sum price; however, the parties may later agree to a new contract under which the firm is to be paid for its actual costs plus a markup for profit and overhead.

Discharge by Operation of Law

In a few situations, performance of a contract may be discharged by operation of law. This can occur in the following ways:

- *Impossibility.* If the contract cannot possibly be performed, performance is discharged. Impossibility is measured objectively (it cannot be done) and not subjectively (I cannot do it). Such circumstances include the death or disability of a performer in a personal services contract prior to performance (such as an actor); the destruction of the subject matter of the contract; a change in the law making the performance illegal; or an act of God (natural forces that render performance impossible, such as that resulting from a hurricane).

Some courts narrowly apply this principle by excusing performance only when it cannot be performed at any cost by any person. Others follow a rule of commercial impracticability, under which a contract can be performed only at an excessive or unreasonable cost not reasonably foreseen in advance.

Example: A contractor installing a sewer line encounters excessively rocky soil, which was not disclosed in owner-supplied soil reports. The condition exposes the contractor to ruinous cost overruns. The contractor's performance is excused due to impossibility of performance.

Acts of God are often addressed in contract provisions known as *force majeure* clauses. These clauses excuse nonperformance or permit delayed performance because of the events stated. *Force majeure* clauses should be broadly written so that protection is best afforded to a party at risk.

Example: Seller shall not be liable for any delay or failure to deliver any or all of the goods if the cause for such delay or failure arises from labor disputes, strikes, war, riots, insurrection, terrorism, civil commotion, fire, flood, accident, storm, or any act of God, pandemics, cyberattacks, failure or interruption in supplies or utility services supplying Seller's premises, or other causes beyond Seller's reasonable control.

- *Bankruptcy.* Federal law provides that certain contracts are discharged by compliance with the Bankruptcy Act. After discharge in bankruptcy, the debtor is released from liability under the contracts discharged.
- *Statute of limitations.* Liability under a contract can be discharged by the lapse of time. While states can vary on the statute of limitations period for contracts, typically oral contracts have a statute of limitations of two to three years and written contracts have a statute of limitations period of four to five years. However, if a promise to perform is provided after the statute of limitations has lapsed, the obligation to perform is revived and starts anew from the date of the written promise to perform.

Example: In order to maintain a business relationship with a needed vendor, a debtor may agree to revive obligations that would otherwise be barred under the statute of limitations.

Breach of Contract

Breach
A failure to fully perform a contract.

A **breach** occurs when a contract is not fully performed. When a party has not fully performed their obligations, the innocent or non-breaching party is entitled to relief from the other party's breach of contract. The typical remedies available when a party has breached a contract include (1) monetary damages, (2) liquidated damages, (3) rescission of the contract, or (4) specific performance.

Comparing Material and Minor Breaches of Contract

Some breaches are material, while others are minor. The difference between material and minor breaches can yield significant results. The parties' remedies depend upon which type of breach occurred.

Material Breach

A **material breach** of contract occurs when the breaching party fails to substantially perform pursuant to the contract terms. In a material breach, the reasonable expectations of the non-breaching party regarding the performance of the contract have been significantly impaired. With a material breach, the non-breaching party is excused from further contractual performance and can sue the breaching party for damages attributable to the breach.

Material breach
A breach of contract whereby the party renders inferior performance of their duties and fails to substantially perform the contract terms.

Example: A person buys custom-made blouses online for $750. The retailer fails to deliver the blouses, and states that it cannot deliver them due to supplier problems. If the retailer fails to refund the monies paid, the buyer may sue for the amount paid, which will compensate her. A material breach of performance has occurred.

Whether a breach of promise is material is a question of fact determined on a case-by-case basis. A material breach typically occurs when the missing performance by the breaching party seriously disappoints the reasonable expectations of the aggrieved (non-breaching) party. When determining whether a breach is material or minor, the courts consider several factors, including (1) the extent of performance by the breaching party, and (2) whether the breach substantially impairs the results reasonably expected by the non-breaching party.

Minor Breach

A **minor breach** of contract occurs when substantial performance has occurred and the breaching party's performance deviates only slightly from the contract. In a minor breach, unlike a material breach, the reasonable expectations of the non-breaching party are not seriously impaired. Minor breaches of contract do not excuse the breaching party from performance under the contract. The breaching party is still obligated to continue to perform the contract, and the non-breaching party is entitled to damages for the deficiency in the performance.

Minor breach
A non-material breach of contract by which complete performance is not rendered. The breaching party has substantially performed, and the breaching party's performance deviates only slightly from the contract.

Example: A residential purchase and sale contract required that escrow close on June 1. If the closing of escrow was not completed until June 2 due to a delay in the buyer sending a final payment toward the purchase price, a minor breach has occurred. The seller would be entitled to damages.

Divisible contract
A contract in which the performance of the contract can be divided into equal portions.

DIVISIBLE CONTRACTS. A **divisible contract** is a contract in which the performance of the contract can be divided into matching equal portions. With a divisible contract, once a party has performed one of the equal portions of the contract, a breach as to the other portions is considered a minor breach of contract, even if a substantial portion of the contract remains. The breaching party is entitled to the value of the work performed.

> **Example:** A contractor is hired to paint ten houses in a newly built subdivision. All of the houses are identical except for minor deviations in their exteriors. The contractor has agreed to paint the ten houses for $30,000. If the contractor paints nine of the houses and then stops, a minor breach of contract has occurred, and the painter is entitled to $27,000 (nine completed houses at $3,000 each).

A contract does not become divisible simply because it may be completed in parts or stages. The parts and stages must be in equal portions. In the above example, if the 10 houses that the painter agreed to paint differed by size and exterior details, such that each house would not be equal, the contract would not be divisible and painting 5 of the ten houses would be a material breach of the contract.

Anticipatory Breach of Contract

Anticipatory breach Informing the other party to a contract that a party will not be able to perform the contract when performance is due.

An **anticipatory breach** (or anticipatory repudiation) occurs if one of the parties informs the other party before their contractual performance is due that they will not perform the contractual duties. The repudiation language and conduct are such that a reasonable person would interpret it to mean that the other party will not perform the contract. An anticipatory breach is treated as a material breach of contract, allowing the non-breaching party to be excused from performance and to sue immediately for damages (instead of having to wait until performance is due to sue for a breach).

> **Example:** James Decker and Wholesale Sand & Gravel, Inc. entered into a contract whereby Wholesale agreed to install a gravel driveway on Decker's property. The contract contained no provision stating a completion date for the work. Wholesale believed it had 90 days to complete the work but told Decker the driveway would be completed within one week. Wholesale attempted to complete the driveway, but experienced difficulty because the ground was wet. Decker contacted Wholesale three times expressing urgency for the completion of the driveway. Wholesale continued to tell Decker it would "get right on it," but no one showed up or completed the driveway. Decker believed the contract to be repudiated and hired another contractor to finish the job. Wholesale sued Decker for breach of contract. The court held that Wholesale committed anticipatory repudiation by removing its equipment from Decker's property and failing to continue work three times despite its promise to Decker to do so. Decker was relieved of any duty to further perform under the contract. *Wholesale Sand & Gravel, Inc. v. Decker*, 630 A.2d 710 (Me. 1993)

A party who anticipatorily breached the contract can prevent the non-breaching party from treating the contract as terminated by retracting the repudiation before the injured party has acted in response to the repudiation. Once the non-breaching party has relied on the repudiation, it is too late to retract the repudiation.

> **Example:** On the tenth of the month, a contractor informs a homeowner that it will not be able to paint the homeowner's house by the end of the month as agreed,

due to scheduling problems. This statement is an anticipatory repudiation of the contract. If the homeowner does not act, and on the twelfth of the month the contractor informs the homeowner that the scheduling conflict was resolved and that it can perform the contract, the contractor has retracted the repudiation and may perform the contract.

Damages

Damages compensate a person for harm caused. In contract law, damages compensate the injured party as nearly as possible to the equivalent of the benefits of complete performance of the contract. The word **damages** (Latin word *damnum*, meaning loss suffered) refers to the compensation due to the non-breaching party to recover loss or harm foreseeably flowing from a breach of contract. Some general rules apply to contract damages:

Damages
A sum of money claimed or awarded in compensation for a loss or an injury.

1. The injured party must prove causation between the breach and the damages sought;
2. The damages must be clear and measurable;
3. The damages must not be punitive (that is, they must be reasonable and not grossly oppressive);
4. The injured party cannot recover more in damages than they would have received if the contract had been fully performed. This prevents overcompensation; and,
5. The injured party has a duty to mitigate (or reduce) their damages. Any damages that could have been reasonably avoided cannot be claimed.

Several forms of damages are available for a contract breach. These are:

1. Compensatory Damages
2. Consequential Damages
3. Liquidated Damages
4. Nominal Damages

Compensatory Damages

Compensatory damages are the amount of damages awarded that would put the plaintiff in the same position as they would have been if the contract had not been breached. These damages are also known as general or expectation damages.

Compensatory damages
The sum of money awarded sufficient to compensate the plaintiff for the loss or harm incurred.

Example: A homeowner contracts with a contractor to install a concrete patio at his home. Following the contractor's use of inferior materials and poor installation methods, the concrete patio deteriorates within months. The homeowner did not receive the value of what they were promised. The award of compensatory damages would include the cost of removing the defective concrete and replacing it with that which conforms to ordinary standards of workmanship and materials.

Landmark Case *Hawkins v. McGee*, 146 A. 641 (N.H. 1929) (The "Hairy Hand" Case)

Hawkins severely burned his hand on an electric wire. As a result, Hawkins saw Dr. McGee, a surgeon, who suggested a rather novel surgical procedure. When asked about the procedure, Dr. McGee told Hawkins that he guaranteed to make a 100 percent good hand. As a result, Hawkins underwent an operation that consisted of the removal of a considerable quantity of scar tissue from the palm of his right hand and the grafting of skin taken from his chest in its place. Following the procedure, the chest hairs continued growing, creating a hairy hand. Hawkins sued Dr. McGee. After an appeal, the Supreme Court of New Hampshire held that the proper measure of damages was the difference between the value of a perfect hand and value of the hand in its post-operative condition.

COMPONENTS OF COMPENSATORY DAMAGES. Calculating the amount of compensatory damages needed to restore a plaintiff to the position they would have been in if the contract had been fully performed will depend on the type of contract at issue.

Example: A merchant agrees to deliver 100 pallets of widgets for $200,000 on March 1. The merchant is unable to deliver any of the widgets by that date. The buyer secures the widgets from another source one month later for $210,000. The seller-merchant is exposed to a damage claim for $10,000 (the difference between the sales price ($200,000) and the increased market price paid for the goods a month later ($210,000)).

When calculating compensatory damages, an injured party's compensatory damages include:

1. *Incremental costs.* Incremental costs are the additional costs incurred that have been suffered because of the breach. They can be measured by the difference between the contract price and the market price when the seller was to provide the goods or services. These costs include increases in material costs, labor costs, tax or tariff rates, and the like.

Example: A union contractor agrees to construct a five-story apartment for $1 million. The project is delayed by the owner's failure to timely obtain financing. As a result, the union labor rates have increased by a total of $40,000. The contractor is entitled to $40,000 in incremental costs.

2. *Incidental costs.* Incidental costs are those costs directly incurred from the breach that were incidental to the breach. They are often minor costs, when compared to compensatory or consequential damages, and include costs for

materials purchased that cannot be returned, restocking fees, storage fees, and additional inspection fees.

Example: Assume a merchant takes delivery of a shipment of parts, some of which are defective, and that there is insufficient time to obtain replacements from the seller. The merchant's incidental costs for inspection, and those related to securing replacement parts from other sources, are compensable as incidental damages.

3. *Lost profits.* A plaintiff is entitled to the value of lost profits that would have been earned if the contract had been fully performed.

Example: A contractor agrees to paint a home for $2,500. The contractor anticipated making a profit of $500 on the project. One day before it is to start, the homeowner cancels the contract, and the contractor is unable to find replacement work. The contractor is entitled to the $500 as lost profits on the project.

Management Application Compensatory Damages by Subject Matter

How a loss or injury is measured in compensatory damages varies by the subject matter of the contract. The unique nature of the subject matter of a contract often dictates how a breach is calculated.

- *Sale of goods.* While there are many variations, generally, the measure of compensatory damages is the difference between the contract price and the market price paid to replace the goods. However, if the buyer is the breaching party and the seller has not yet produced the goods, the seller may be entitled to compensatory damages equal to the seller's lost profits, instead of the difference between contract and market price.

  Example: A local cafe contracts to buy five artisanal coffee roasters from Coffee Supply for $500 each. Coffee Supply fails to deliver the coffee roasters. The local café has to purchase the roasters from another retailer at the market price of $750 each. The cafe's measure of damages is equal to $1,250 (5 × $250).

- *Sale of land.* Generally, compensatory damages are not used for a breach of this kind of contract. However, if the property has been sold or the buyer is the breaching party, compensatory damages are measured as the difference between the contract price and the market price of the land.

  Example: Develop Co. entered into a contract to purchase agricultural land from Farmer Abe for $1 million. Develop Co. breaches the contract. The market price of the Farmer Abe's land is $1.5 million. Farmer Abe is entitled to $500,000 in compensatory damages.

- *Construction contract.* In a construction contract, the measure of damages is dependent on the identity of the breaching party and the time of the breach. The following table illustrates how compensatory damages can be calculated.

	Breaching Party	
Timing of Breach	**Owner**	**Contractor**
Before construction begins	The contract price less the cost of materials and labor (profits)	The cost in excess of the contract price to complete the work
During construction	Profits, plus costs incurred up to the time of the breach	The costs incurred by owner to complete work
After construction is completed	The full contract price, plus any interest (if applicable)	Not applicable

Consequential Damages

Consequential damages
Foreseeable damages that flow indirectly from a breach of contract.

Consequential damages are foreseeable damages that flow indirectly from the breach. These are also called special damages. They cover losses other than losses in value to which compensatory damages would apply. To recover consequential damages, the breaching party must know or have reason to know that a failure to perform the contract may result in additional loss to the non-breaching party. While lacking a uniform definition of this type of damage claim, generally consequential damages are recognized as arising from the familiarity of what the non-breaching party has at risk in the contract, and knowledge of what additional damages the non-breaching party will suffer in the event of breach.

> **Example:** A furniture retailer promises to deliver and install office furniture on or before a date certain. The retailer knew that the buyer needed the furniture because the buyer intended to move into newly constructed office space and required the new furnishings for its staff. In this case, the consequential damages could include damages such as the company's expense in renting furniture until the promised furniture arrived.

Landmark Case
Hadley v. Baxendale, 156 Eng. Rep. 145 (1854)

During the operation of Hadley's mill in Gloucester, England, a crank shaft on its steam engine milling equipment broke. Not having a spare replacement, Hadley retained Baxendale to transport the shaft to the manufacturer for repair. Before the new crankshaft could be made, the manufacturer required that the broken crankshaft be sent to it in order to ensure that the new crankshaft would properly fit for Hadley's use. Hadley paid in full for the transport, informed Baxendale's clerk that it must be delivered by a certain date, and, in reply, was told the shaft would be delivered the following day. Baxendale delayed the delivery of the shaft. Baxendale failed to deliver on the date required. Hadley sued for the profits lost due to the late delivery. Baxendale argued that Hadley's lost profits were not foreseeable. The court agreed. The mere fact that a party is sending something to be repaired does not indicate that the party would lose profits if it were not delivered on time. It reasoned that Hadley could have a spare shaft for use in such cases, or that the machinery could have been defective for other reasons besides the broken shaft. The special circumstances of the potential for lost profits was never communicated to the Baxendale. The court held the lost profits "cannot reasonably be considered a consequence of the breach of contract as could have been fairly and reasonably contemplated by both parties when they made this contract." Baxendale prevailed.

This rule has the effect of reducing the risk of consequential damages in a transaction. To be recoverable they must be foreseeable and contemplated by the parties at the time the contract was formed.

In the following case, a federal district court considered whether consequential damages were a foreseeable and assumed risk of an insurance carrier when issuing a policy of business insurance to its insured.

CASE 14.1

TO DETERMINE CONSEQUENTIAL DAMAGES, CONSIDER WHAT THE PARTIES WOULD HAVE CONCLUDED HAD THEY CONSIDERED THE SUBJECT

LAVA TRADING INC. v. HARTFORD FIRE INSURANCE CO.

326 F. Supp. 2d 434 (S.D.N.Y. 2004)

United States District Court for the Southern District of New York

Prior to 9/11, Lava had a 75,000-square-foot facility in the World Trade Center. The facility was destroyed in the terrorist attack of 9/11. However, Lava had a back-up location that consisted of 3,000 square feet of office space. After the attack, Lava partially resumed its operations in its back-up location while trying to recover insurance proceeds from its insurer, Hartford. Lava's policy of business insurance provided coverage for physical loss or damage to Lava's property, the loss of business income caused by a suspension of operations in the wake of physical loss or damage, and extra expenses incurred because of such suspension. Hartford did not pay these claims and, in response,

Lava sued to recover consequential damages for Hartford's breach of the policy. Lava claimed compensatory damages for a loss of earnings of approximately $60 million because of the terrorist attack. It also sued Hartford for consequential damages for the insurer's failure to comply with its obligations under the policy, which caused Lava to incur certain other costs, including financing costs for alternate funding that would not have been necessary if Hartford had not breached its contract. Hartford sought to dismiss the claim for consequential damages.

Language of the Court. *It is well established that in actions for breach of contract, the non-breaching party may recover such unusual or extraordinary damages as have been brought within the contemplation of the parties as the probable result of a breach at the time or prior to contracting. In order to determine what damages are reasonably contemplated by the parties, the nature, purpose and particular circumstances of the contract known by the parties should be considered as well as what liability the defendant fairly may be supposed to have assumed consciously, or to have warranted the plaintiff reasonably to suppose that it assumed, when the contract was made. In the absence of an express contractual provision with respect to the consequential damages sought, the common sense rule to apply is to consider what the parties would have concluded had they considered the subject.*

The Policy at issue in this case does expressly exclude "any other consequential loss" from its coverage. However, a policy exclusion speaks only to what constitutes a covered loss under a policy of insurance, and not to what remedies are available for breach of a policy. The scope of a policy's coverage and the damages that are recoverable if the insurer breaches the policy are, of course, distinct concepts. The policy language may have a direct bearing, but will not always be controlling, on the damages that were within the contemplation of the parties at the time of a contract.

Whether consequential damages are available in a given case depends, in part, on whether such damages were foreseeable at the time of contracting. The ultimate question remains: what damages were in the reasonable contemplation of the parties in the event of breach by the insurer at the time they entered into the contract of insurance?

In this case, it remains to be proven whether the parties contemplated that the type of consequential damages alleged to be available here would be the likely result of a breach by Hartford, as well as whether Lava even suffered any losses attributable to Hartford's alleged breach.

Decision. The federal district court declined to dismiss Lava's claim for consequential damages.

Focus on Ethics

In this case, the court extended the analysis to include what the parties to an insurance contract might have contemplated had they considered consequential damages. The case was appealed multiple times, but the court repeatedly declined to dismiss Lava's claim for consequential damages. Does it seem fair to you to consider what the parties *might have* concluded had they considered the subject of consequential damages while negotiating terms of the contract?

Why Classifying Damages Matters

Classifying damages as either direct (compensatory) or consequential is important because consequential damages often involve large damage awards—awards that attract the attention of the media. Often, contracts will waive claims for consequential damages. Then, the argument changes to whether a claim fits within the definition of compensatory damages or consequential damages. That means the parties are disputing whether, at the time of contract formation, the circumstances were such that the breaching party could reasonably have accepted the risk of consequential damages. Frequently, they include these types of damages as consequential:

- Lost profits on *other* contracts that might otherwise have been performed
- Loss of favorable financing
- Costs related to maintaining a workforce and related costs longer than planned
- Loss of use (such as the inability to use equipment allocated for use on this contract on other projects)
- Lost sales contracts or work not undertaken because of delays or interruptions
- Reduced value due to defects in the product (such as a residence plagued by construction defects)

> **Example:** A contractor delays in the completion of a retail store. The retailer is unable to open its location on time and claims damages for the profits it would have realized during the time between when it should have opened and when it did open for business.

The process of assessing compensatory damages is relatively straightforward. There is no need to prove what a breaching party contemplated damages at the time of contracting. Rarely will compensatory damages be waived in a contract, although the parties may adopt a liquidated damages clause, which is discussed below.

In comparison, the award of consequential damages requires that the parties contemplate the possibility of damages at the time of contract formation. The risk of an award of consequential damages that are in a substantial sum often persuades the contract drafter to waive them in the contract.

Management Application
Consequential Damages Disclaimer

To limit exposure to consequential damages, contracts may provide a disclaimer waiving any liability for consequential damages.

> Neither Party shall be liable to the other Party for any special, consequential, indirect, or similar damages (including, without limitation, lost profits, loss of business, loss of business value, or loss of goodwill) suffered or incurred by such Party arising from or relating to a breach of this agreement. This waiver applies, however caused and to all theories of liability, and whether such Party knew or should have reasonably known of the possibility of such damages.

Liquidated Damages

Liquidated damages A contract provision whereby the parties agree at the time of entering into the contract what the amount of damages will be in the event of a breach of contract.

With **liquidated damages**, the parties agree at the time of the contract's formation what the damages will be in the event of a breach. The amount of the liquidated damages reflects the parties' best estimate at the time of contract formation of the damages that a breach would cause. Where a liquidated damages clause exists, it is the exclusive remedy for damages. For the liquidated damages clause to be enforceable, the damages must have been difficult to determine at the time of entering into the contract, and the amount identified as liquidated damages must have been reasonable at the time of entering into the contract.

> **Example:** A municipality contracts with a construction company to complete a new public building by a certain date and inserts a liquidated damages clause into the contract. If the contractor fails to timely complete the project, the lack of use of the building will result in damages to the public; however, calculating for the loss of use would be difficult to determine at the time of contracting.

Liquidated damages may not be used as a penalty. Where damages are punitive or the amount of damages is unconscionable, the liquidated damages will be considered a penalty and unenforceable. Courts are more likely to enforce a liquidated damages clause if:

- Damages that will be incurred because of a breach would be difficult to estimate at the time of contract formation.
- The amount is reasonable and *not a penalty*. For example, if the amount of damages is grossly disproportionate to the actual harm suffered, courts will refuse to enforce the provision, claiming it is a penalty instead of an estimate of actual damages.

> **Example:** Since the damages were not disproportionate nor were they triggered by non-substantial breaches, a court found the following liquidated damages clause in a termination agreement to be enforceable: "Termination Fee Deposit as Liquidated Damages. If the transaction contemplated in this agreement is not consummated due to a default by landlord, tenant may immediately terminate this agreement by written notice to landlord *and without further obligation to landlord under this agreement, tenant shall retain the termination fee deposit as liquidated damages, and the lease (including the extension options) shall remain in full force and effect.* The parties agree that tenant's actual damages as a result of landlord's default would be difficult or impossible to determine, and the termination fee deposit is the best estimate of the amount of damages tenant would suffer as a result of landlord's default. The payment of the termination as liquidated damages is not intended as a forfeiture or penalty, but is intended to constitute liquidated damages to tenant. The parties witness their agreement to this liquidated damages provision by initialing this section." *McKinley Associates, LLC v. McKesson HBOC, Inc.*, 110 F. Supp. 2d 169, 174 (W.D.N.Y. 2000)

Management Application Sample Liquidated Damages Clause

The following is a sample liquidated damages clause provision between a contractor and an owner for a construction contract of significant size:

> In the event the contractor does not achieve completion within the specified contract time, including approved time extensions, the contractor shall pay the owner, as liquidated damages and not as a penalty, the sum of Ten Thousand Dollars ($10,000) for each day the actual time performance exceeds the authorized contract time.

In this example, the liquidated damages must be a reasonable approximation of the actual damages the owner would suffer if the contractor caused project delay. Without a liquidated damages provision, the contractor would be exposed to any damages the owner could prove were caused by an unexcused contractor delay.

The following case discusses the enforceability of a liquidated damages clause involving millions of dollars that pertained to a high-rise building in New York City.

CASE 14.2

A LIQUIDATED DAMAGES CLAUSE IS ENFORCEABLE EVEN IF THE AMOUNT SEEMS EXCESSIVE AT THE TIME OF THE BREACH

UZAN v. 845 UN LIMITED PARTNERSHIP

778 N.Y.S.2d 171 (2004)

New York Supreme Court of New York

In October 1998, 845 UN Limited Partnership ("845 UN") began to sell apartments at the Trump World Tower, a luxury condominium building to be constructed at 845 United Nations Plaza. Donald Trump was the managing general partner of 845 UN. Cem Uzan and Hakan Uzan, two Turkish billionaire brothers, sought to purchase multiple units in the building. The Uzan brothers entered into contracts to purchase seven apartments at Trump World Tower. Two penthouse units on the ninetieth floor and two penthouse units on the eighty-ninth floor were subject to this litigation. The contract provided that, in the event of default not cured within 30 days, 845 UN was entitled to keep as liquidated damages the down payment and any interest earned on the down payment at the time of the default.

On September 11, 2001, terrorists attacked New York City by flying two planes into the World Trade Center, the city's two tallest buildings, killing thousands of people. The Uzan brothers, concerned about future terrorist attacks, defaulted in closing on the penthouse units. 845 UN sent a notice to the brothers to cure the default, which they failed to do. Thereafter, 845 UN kept the 25 percent down payment, totaling $8 million, in an escrow account. The Uzan brothers filed suit, alleging that the 25 percent down payment of $8 million was an unenforceable penalty.

Language of the Court. *Donald Trump stated that he sought 25% down payments from preconstruction purchasers at the Trump World Tower because of the substantial length of time between contract signing and closing, during which period 845 UN had to keep the units off the market. Trump also stated that down payments in the range of 20 to 25 percent are standard practice in the new-construction luxury-condominium submarket in New York City.*

Marilyn Weitzman, president of a nationwide real estate consulting firm headquartered in New York City, echoed Trump's opinion that 20 to 25 percent down payments are customary in New York City for new-construction condominium apartments because of the volatility of the market. Weitzman also noted that the demographic profile for potential purchasers in the luxury-condominium submarket includes many foreign nationals, who are inherently high-risk purchasers because their incomes and assets are often difficult both to measure and to reach.

Real estate down payments have been subject to limited supervision. They have only been refunded upon a showing of disparity of bargaining power between the parties, duress, fraud, illegality, or mutual mistake. It is clear that the Uzan brothers are not entitled to a return of any portion of their down payment. Here the 25% down payment was a specifically negotiated element of the contracts. There is no question that this was an arm's-length transaction. The parties were sophisticated businesspeople, represented by counsel, who spent two months at the bargaining table before executing the amended purchase agreements. Further, the record evidences that it is customary in the preconstruction luxury condominium industry for parties to price the risk of default at 25% of the purchase price. Finally, there was no evidence of a disparity of bargaining power, or of duress, fraud, illegality, or mutual mistake by the parties in drafting the down payment clause of the purchase agreements.

Decision. The court dismissed the complaint. 845 UN was entitled to retain the $8 million as liquidated damages.

Focus on Ethics

Does the retention of a 25 percent down payment seem like an excessive penalty? What percentage of a sales price should be considered a penalty?

Nominal damages
Damages awarded when there are no actual damages or losses from a breach of contract.

Nominal Damages

When no actual damages or loss results from a breach of contract, a non-breaching party can sue for **nominal damages** for the breach of the contract. The court can award in such cases a nominal sum, such as $1, for the technical breach of the agreement, thereby establishing that the defendant acted wrongly. Lawsuits for nominal damages are often brought on principle. Courts tend to disfavor cases for nominal damages due to the inefficient use of judicial resources to resolve them.

> **Example:** A consumer enters into a contract to purchase a television from a retailer for $1,500. The retailer is unable to fill the contract and the consumer purchases the same television from another retailer for $1,450. While the consumer can sue the original retailer for a breach of contract in not fulfilling the order, the court would award nominal damages as the consumer did not incur any monetary loss.

Punitive Damages

Generally, contract law does not provide for the recovery of punitive or exemplary damages. As previously discussed in Chapter 5, punitive damages are monetary damages designed to punish the wrongdoer. The limited circumstances in which they are awarded for contract claims are in claims involving insurance bad faith and cases which involved both tort and contract claims. In addition, claims for breach of contract may not include losses suffered from emotional distress.

> **Example:** While a breach of contract resulting in the closure of a business may result in foreseeable emotional distress, the law does not permit such recovery. Intentional and negligent inflictions of emotional distress may be compensable under tort law, but damages for emotional harm following a breach of contract are not. The focus of contract law is to enforce the promises made.

Mitigation of Damages

Every plaintiff must minimize or mitigate the damages resulting from the breach of contract. The concept of mitigation requires the plaintiff to use reasonable efforts to avoid or minimize losses suffered. If a plaintiff fails to mitigate, such failure may operate as a complete or partial bar to recover damages for the breach of contract. The burden is on the defendant to prove how the damages could have been avoided or minimized.

> **Example:** Landlord rents an apartment to student for the upcoming academic year. The lease is for ten months at $750 a month. The student does not move into the apartment and breaches the contract, failing to pay the landlord any money. The landlord must mitigate its damages against the student by trying to find a replacement tenant.

Equitable Remedies

Some breaches of contract cannot be adequately compensated by monetary damages. Where monetary damages are inadequate, the non-breaching party may seek to sue under several alternative remedies that may be available under principles of equity. Known as **equitable remedies**, they arise from the exercise of the court's equitable

Equitable remedies Actions ordered by a court to resolve a breach or dispute.

powers and are traceable to the common law of England. These remedies are granted only by a court (that is, a bench trial) and not a jury. Equitable remedies include:

- Rescission and Restitution
- Reformation
- Specific Performance
- Injunctions

Rescission and Restitution

Rescission
The cancellation of a contract.

Rescission is used to undo a contract. When invoked, the parties are returned as closely as possible to their pre-contract positions. When that occurs, the party is not entitled to recover damages because the contract is rescinded or canceled. The rescinding party must give adequate notice to the breaching party. For rescission to apply, the grounds for rescinding a contract must be present at the time of formation of the contract. Common grounds for rescinding a contract include fraud, duress, undue influence, lack of capacity, and mistake, which were discussed previously in Chapter 12. In addition, as the example below illustrates, rescission is also appropriate where there is a breach of a material warranty.

> **Example:** Thomas and Pam Marlow purchased a Crystal Valley manufactured home from Van Bibber Home Sales. Numerous problems developed in the home after its installation. The home had settled and was no longer square, leading to more defects such as plumbing system failures. Also, there were leaks, cracks, and water damage in various rooms in the house due to improper installation and location of skylights and ceiling fans. The floors started cracking and installed doors would not close. The Marlows sued for rescission due to Van Bibber's material misrepresentations regarding the components of the home and the way they would be installed. The Indiana Court of Appeals affirmed the trial court's decision that they were entitled to rescission of the contract. *Van Bibber Homes Sales v. Marlow*, 778 N.E.2d 852 (Ind. Ct. App. 2002)

Restitution
A remedy restoring to the plaintiff a benefit wrongfully gained from the defendant's misconduct.

When a contract is rescinded, both parties typically provide restitution to each other. **Restitution** provides recovery of a monetary sum, goods, or property received by the other party. When a good or property has been consumed, an equivalent monetary value must be provided. Restitutionary remedies can provide recovery of the precise thing that was wrongfully obtained by the defendant from the plaintiff. For example, a plaintiff might seek restitution for property stolen from the plaintiff.

Reformation

Reformation
Judicial correction of a change to an existing document to express the parties' true intentions at the time of formation of the contract.

Occasionally, when a contract is written it contains errors that do not accurately express the agreement between the parties. In such an instance, the court may use its equitable powers of reformation. **Reformation** is a remedy permitting a court to rewrite a contract to express the parties' true intentions. Reformation is restricted in application and is usually limited to correcting clerical errors made during the contract's preparation.

> **Example:** Reformation was an appropriate remedy in a contract for the sale of real estate where the agreement incorrectly credited the plaintiff as having made a

payment of principal toward a promissory note issued on its behalf. The incorrect credit was due to a scrivener's error. *Pacwest, Ltd. v. Resolution Trust Corp.*, 108 F.3d 1370 (2d Cir. 1997)

Reformation is rarely invoked, and in the absence of a clerical error it will be permitted only in instances of mutual mistake on a material term of a contract. Alternatively, reformation is *not* appropriate in cases of a unilateral mistake or a mistake of fact.

Example: The McDonnell Douglas Corporation (MCD) agreed to settle multiple separate lawsuits and five class actions relating to alleged violations of the federal securities laws. The settlement agreement required MCD to set aside $5 million to be allocated among the claimants and that no portion of the settlement fund would revert to MCD. It later became apparent that the size of each class was much smaller than forecast. As a result, MCD wanted to reform the settlement agreement to reclaim the amount of the settlement in excess of $1 million. A federal court of appeals denied MCD's request to reform the agreement, holding that "a mistake which leads either one or both of the parties to enter into a contract which they would not have entered into had they been apprised of the actual facts, will not justify reformation." *Beecher v. Able*, 575 F.2d 1010 (2d Cir. 1978)

Specific Performance

In a few circumstances, the court will order a party to perform the act promised in the contract under an equitable remedy known as **specific performance**. Specific performance requires the party in breach to completely perform their obligations under the contract. This can require the breaching party to deliver unique goods or to render specialized services.

Specific performance A court order requiring a party to perform a specific act required by a lawful contract.

Typically, specific performance cases involving breaches of contract arise in contracts where monetary damages are an inadequate remedy. This often arises in contracts related to the sale of land, or unique personal property such as art and rare books.

Example: Henry purchased a property in Ladera Ranch from Lavar for $600,000. The close of escrow for the transaction was scheduled for June 1. On June 1, Henry was ready, willing, and able to close the transaction, but Lavar had second thoughts and did not want to sell the property due to sentimental reasons. Henry could obtain specific performance to force Lavar to sell the property because real property is considered unique.

Specific performance is usually not granted for contracts related to the performance of personal services from a particular person. An exception to this general rule is a contract requiring unique personal services, such as those provided by actors or athletes.

The following case discusses the application of this remedy to the breach of an agreement to sell land.

CASE 14.3

WHEN NO ADEQUATE LEGAL REMEDY IS AVAILABLE A PURCHASER OF LAND IS ENTITLED TO SPECIFIC PERFORMANCE

OLIVER v. BALL

136 A.3d 162 (Pa. 2016)

Superior Court of Pennsylvania

Jerome Oliver entered into a sale of real estate contract with members of the Ball family ("Balls"). The real estate consisted of two tracts of land containing approximately 71.5 acres. Oliver was a real estate investor who saw the opportunity to subdivide the land for future development and develop the included mineral rights. Oliver was also in the timber business, and there was timber on the property that he thought could be harvested. Moreover, the property was located within a reasonable distance from Oliver's home, which was a characteristic shared by Oliver's other investments. When the Balls failed to convey the property, Oliver sued for specific performance of the contract. Oliver claimed that the property was unique and, therefore, his remedy of specific performance was appropriate. The trial court disagreed and denied Oliver's request for specific performance. Oliver appealed.

Language of the Court. *A request for specific performance is an appeal to the court's equitable powers. Specific performance generally is described as the surrender of a thing in itself, because that thing is unique and thus incapable—by its nature—of duplication. Such a decree will be granted only if a plaintiff clearly is entitled to such relief, there is no adequate remedy at law, and the trial court believes that justice requires such a decree. Inequity or hardship may be a valid defense in an action for specific performance and such decree refused if in the exercise of a sound discretion it is determined that, under the facts, specific performance would be contrary to equity or justice. Mere inadequacy of price, however, will not defeat specific performance, unless grossly disproportionate.*

Courts in this Commonwealth consistently have determined that specific performance is an appropriate remedy to compel the conveyance of real estate where a seller violates a realty contract and specific enforcement of the contract would not be contrary to justice.

Contracts for the sale of land have traditionally been accorded a special place in the law of specific performance. A specific tract of land has long been regarded as unique and impossible of duplication by the use of any amount of money.

From the moment an agreement of sale of real estate is executed and delivered, it vests in the purchaser what is known as an equitable title to the real estate. Thereupon the seller is considered as a trustee of the real estate. Hence, if the terms of the agreement are violated by the seller, the purchaser may go into a court of equity seeking to enforce the contract and to compel specific performance.

There is no requirement that specific performance be only available if some characteristic of or structure on the land, or the location of the land itself, is of such importance to a buyer that no other property can duplicate its value. To the contrary, our law makes clear that the remedy of specific performance in realty contracts derives from the proposition that all land is unique.

As is obvious, specific performance for the sale of land is available because no two parcels of land are identical. An award of damages will not suffice to allow a plaintiff to acquire the same parcel of land anywhere else. Thus, in the context of realty agreements breached by a seller, we can assume that a buyer has no adequate remedy at law. In sum, we conclude that the trial court erred when Oliver had clearly established that his remedy at law was inadequate.

Decision. The trial court's decision was reversed. Specific performance was an appropriate remedy, and the Balls were ordered to sell the property to Oliver.

Focus on Ethics

If the property had been a tract home with many adequate substitutes in the same neighborhood (such as the same floor plan, square footage, and upgrades), do you think Oliver would have an adequate remedy at law? Discuss whether it is reasonable for the courts to continue to enforce specific performance in such circumstances.

Injunctions

Another equitable remedy the court may issue is an injunction. An **injunction** prohibits a person from performing a specific act. On rare occasions, the court's injunction can compel a person to do a specific act.

Injunction
A court order requiring a party to continue or cease particular actions.

Generally, injunctions are classified by how long they are enforceable. A temporary injunction, known as a temporary restraining order (TRO), addresses a problem for a brief time, such as ten days. The preliminary injunction is issued after an evidentiary hearing and preserves the status quo until the final decision in the case. For example, a professional athlete may seek a preliminary injunction to stop a suspension from a team during the pendency of their lawsuit disputing a testing protocol.

A permanent injunction is issued as a final judgment in a case. For example, a permanent injunction can be issued to prevent a defendant company from infringing on the patent rights of the plaintiff. The court may hold the target of the injunction in contempt for the willful violation of a lawfully issued injunction.

While the requirements may vary depending upon the jurisdiction, generally courts consider the following four factors before issuing an injunction:

1. Irreparable harm posed by a threat to the requesting party if an injunction is not issued;
2. The effects upon both parties of issuing and not issuing the injunction;

3. The likelihood of success that the party requesting the injunction will prevail; and
4. The injunction's possible effect upon the public interest.

Injunctions are common in the arena of employment, particularly when the disclosure of the former employer's trade secrets by a former employee is occurring. They may also be issued as authorized by statute, such as an injunction to prevent police officers from striking.

Concept Summary
Choosing a Remedy

There are two types of remedies: legal remedies and equitable remedies. A legal remedy seeks an award of damages. An equitable remedy seeks non-monetary relief, such as the examples discussed in this chapter.

In deciding whether an equitable remedy should be granted, the court will consider if monetary compensation (the legal remedy) would afford adequate relief. If monetary damages afford adequate relief and are not difficult to ascertain, the court will deny a request for equitable relief. In some circumstances, a plaintiff may seek legal and equitable remedies if together they would offer complete relief to the plaintiff. For example, Apple® sought both damages and an injunction against Samsung® on the basis that the latter had violated Apple's patents.

FIGURE 14.1: Remedies Overview

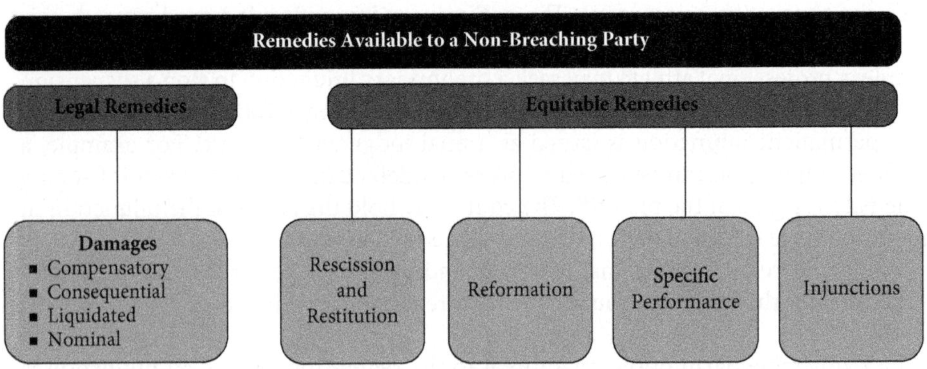

Defenses to Breaches of Contract

Recall from prior chapters the most common defenses to enforcement of a contract or liability for all damages:

- The contract lacks consideration (Chapter 10).
- A party lacked the capacity to contract (Chapter 11).
- The subject matter is illegal or violates public policy (Chapter 11).
- The parties were mutually mistaken as to a material fact (Chapter 12).
- The contract was obtained by undue means, such as undue influence, duress, or fraud (Chapter 12).
- The performance has been discharged (Chapter 14).
- The contract has been terminated by discharge, condition or covenant, rescission, or impossibility (Chapter 14).
- The parties have accepted the contract performance, or a substitution for the performance, is adequate (such as accord and satisfaction) (Chapter 14).

Defenses to Equitable Remedies

With equitable remedies, there are other common defenses that may be asserted. Among the most common are the following:

- *Laches*: When the defense of **laches** is involved, the non-breaching party intentionally delayed in filing a lawsuit for the breach of contract. The resulting delay prejudiced the breaching party.
- *Unclean hands*: When the defense of **unclean hands** is involved, the non-breaching party committed the same type of breach that the breaching party committed. Under equitable principles, the party claiming relief should not violate the contract terms.
- *Hardship*: Equitable remedies are not issued if they would result in undue hardship to the breaching party.
- *Grounds relating to the formation or enforcement of the contract*: These grounds include lack of capacity, illegality, unconscionability, mistake, misrepresentation, undue influence, and duress.

Laches
The prejudice suffered by a defendant from plaintiff's delay in filing a breach of contract case.

Unclean hands
A legal doctrine allowing a defendant to defeat a plaintiff's claim for equitable relief because the plaintiff was involved in some wrongdoing in the underlying dispute.

AI Feature: *Force Majeure* Clauses

Conduct research using an internet search engine on recent *force majeure* cases from around the country. Describe your findings. Then, using an AI program, create a *force majeure* clause for a major construction project. Many courts require specificity of the included events rather than generally described events. Address related issues such as: What should be included as a force majeure event (be specific)? What is an act of God? When does a party have the right to suspend performance and collect increased costs of performance at a later time? When does a contract become impossible to perform at all? When does the right to terminate the contract after a period of contract suspension take effect? And, how will pricing changes occurring in the interim be addressed?

Key Terms

- Anticipatory breach, 326
- Breach, 324
- Compensatory damages, 327
- Concurrent conditions, 322
- Condition, 321
- Condition precedent, 321
- Condition subsequent, 322
- Consequential damages, 330
- Covenant, 322
- Damages, 327
- Discharge, 322
- Discharged by performance, 322
- Divisible contract, 325
- Equitable remedies, 337
- Injunction, 341
- Laches, 343
- Liquidated damages, 334
- Material breach, 325
- Minor breach, 325
- Nominal damages, 336
- Reformation, 338
- Rescission, 338
- Restitution, 338
- Specific performance, 339
- Unclean hands, 343

Applying the Law

14.1 Remedies. The owner of a building leased space on the building's exterior wall to an advertising agency for a term of several years. The wall faced an exit ramp of a tunnel and was visible to drivers using the ramp. The owner of the building breached the contract by terminating the lease, and the advertising agency sued. Would specific performance be the appropriate remedy? *Van Wagner Advertising Corp. v. S&M Enters.*, 492 N.E.2d 756 (N.Y. 1986)

14.2 Certainty. Blinds To Go was not a completely new business. It was a chain with four existing stores in New York City that sold custom window blinds. It planned to open a fifth store in Brooklyn and entered into a lease of retail premises. Before it opened the store, the landlord breached the lease by terminating it without justification. Blinds To Go sued the landlord for damages, including lost profits. Are lost profits for a retailer without an operating history at a new location permitted? If so, how would the damages be calculated? *Blinds To Go, Inc. v. Times Plaza Dev., L.P.*, 931 N.Y.S.2d 105 (App. Div. 2011)

14.3 Allocation of Loss. Severn Peanut Co. alleged breach of contract and negligence claims against Industrial Fumigant Co. According to Severn, IFC improperly applied a dangerous pesticide while fumigating Severn's peanut processing facility, resulting in fire, an explosion, loss of approximately 20 million pounds of peanuts, loss of business, and various cleanup costs. The contract between the parties specified that the contract price of $8,604 was not "sufficient to warrant IFC assuming any risk of incidental or consequential damages" to Severn's "property, product, equipment, downtime, or loss of business." Severn argued that the consequential damages exclusion did not bar its breach of contract claim for damage to its facility and peanuts and its associated remediation and lost business costs. What arguments can be made for and against contractual limitations on consequential damages? *Severn Peanut Co. v. Meherrin Agriculture & Chem. Co.*, 807 F.3d 88 (4th Cir. 2015)

14.4 Calculating Damages. Nationwide Tractor Trailer Training and Placement Corp. contracted to have Aiello Construction, Inc. level a gravel yard for Nationwide's business. Under the contract, Nationwide would pay $33,000 in five monthly installments of $6,600 each. Nationwide made the first payment, and several partial payments, totaling $10,500. Aiello had already spent $21,500 on materials and labor to perform under the contract. If the contract had been fully performed, Aiello would have earned $3,000. How much could Aiello recover in damages? What consequential damages, if any, may Aiello seek? *Aiello Const., Inc. v. Nationwide Tractor Trailer Training & Placement Corp.*, 413 A.2d 85 (R.I. 1980)

14.5 Excuse from Performance. Americold Corp.® owned and operated an underground warehouse facility. A fire broke out in the warehouse, damaging goods of Safeway®, which had leased space in the warehouse. Safeway failed to make subsequent lease payments after the fire. Can Americold sue to enforce the contract against Safeway? What defenses may be asserted? *Butler Mfg. Co. v. Americold Corp.*, 850 F. Supp. 952 (D. Kan. 1994)

14.6 Liquidated Damages. A car rental company installed a global positioning system (GPS) device in its vehicles to track its vehicles' speed and location. It assessed a $150 speeding fee each time the customer's rental vehicle exceeded seventy-nine miles per hour continuously for two minutes. This policy was stated in the rental agreement. Each time the vehicle decelerated below the threshold speed, any subsequent acceleration above that speed detected by the GPS device for two minutes or more was another "occurrence." The customers' credit or debit cards were immediately charged upon each such event. Was the speeding fee a valid liquidated damages charge? Explain. *Am. Car Rental, Inc. v. Comm'r of Consumer Prot.*, 869 A.2d 1198 (Conn. 2005)

14.7 Personal Services. Incomm, Inc., an advertising agency, contracted with Thermo-Spa, Inc., a spa manufacturer, to produce a brochure for Thermo-Spa. The contract terms were for a brochure including the concept, copyedit, contract layout, and all typesetting and materials. When the brochure was almost completed, Thermo-Spa told Incomm that it was dissatisfied with the brochure, and that Thermo-Spa would complete it in-house. Incomm sent a bill to Thermo-Spa, covering the labor, purchased materials, and sales tax for the work done to that date. Incomm refused to pay, stating it was not satisfied with the product. Does Thermo-Spa have a right to cancel the contract based on satisfaction? *Incomm, Inc. v. Thermo-Spa, Inc.*, 595 A.2d 954 (Conn. Super. Ct. 1991)

14.8 Adequacy of Legal Remedy. Aero Micronesia, Inc. (AMI) rented a Boeing 727-200 cargo jet from Trans Pacific Leasing Corporation (TPL). The contract required that the aircraft be operated by a third party. AMI discovered that TPL had applied to the Department of Transportation for certificates necessary to operate the aircraft. AMI sued to prevent TPL from flying the aircraft in breach of the agreement. What remedy should AMI pursue against TPL? *Trans Pacific Leasing Corp. v. Aero Micronesia, Inc.*, 26 F. Supp. 2d 698 (S.D.N.Y. 1998)

14.9 Specific Performance. Holding agreed to purchase Medcom, a Baxter subsidiary. Although Medcom no longer owned or had any investment in Entertainment Partners, Inc., it continued to carry EPI on its list of assets throughout the negotiations with Holding for the sale of Medcom to Holding. At the closing, Baxter did not convey any EPI stock to Holding. Baxter urges that the listing of EPI was a mistake, and that specific performance is not warranted when a contract is entered into mistakenly. Baxter also argues that specific performance is inappropriate because the result would give Holding a windfall. Is Holding entitled to specific performance? *Medcom Holding Co. v. Baxter Travenol Lab.*, 984 F.2d 223 (7th Cir. 1993)

14.10 Injunction. Ruston Zumwalt was employed as a salesman for a subsidiary of Fruit of the Loom®. He executed a confidential information agreement by which he promised that for 12 months after his employment he would not solicit customers of the subsidiary or Fruit of the Loom. The agreement provided the laws of Kentucky would apply. He quit and went to work for a company located in Oklahoma. His former employer sued Zumwalt to enforce the covenant not to compete. What are the arguments to be made for each party as to the enforceability of such a covenant? *Fruit of the Loom, Inc. v. Zumwalt*, 2015 U.S. Dist. LEXIS 161491 (W.D. Ky. 2015)

PART III: AGENCY AND EMPLOYMENT LAW

Agency Relationships

15

Go wisely and slowly. Those who rush, stumble and fall. — Shakespeare, Romeo and Juliet, act 2, sc. 3

Chapter Outline

- Introduction
- The Definition of Agency
- How Agency Relationships Are Formed
- Distinguishing Agency from Other Types of Relationships
- Duties of Agents and Principals

Case 15.1: *Zang v. NRT New England Inc.*

- Liability Arising from Agency

Case 15.2: *Koricic v. Beverly Enters.*

- Independent Contractor Liability
- Termination of the Agency Relationship

Case 15.3: *Parlato v. Equitable Life Assur. Soc'y of the United States*

- AI Feature: Draft a Manufacturer's Representation Agreement

Learning Objectives

After studying this chapter, you should be able to:

1. Define agency and how an agency relationship is created.
2. Explain the fiduciary duties of principals and agents.
3. Describe when an agent may be liable in contract to third parties.
4. Recognize when an agent creates tort liability for the principal.
5. State how an agency relationship is terminated.

Introduction

Agency relationships allow businesses to operate more efficiently and profitably. A company, acting as a principal, can retain many persons as its agents to perform services and can delegate decision-making authority to them. Often, these relationships may be seen between the shareholders of a corporation and executives of the corporation, or between members of a limited liability company and its manager. Agency affords the business the ability to expand its operations by instructing agents to conduct its business affairs. An agent can be an individual or an organization, such as a partnership or corporation. Agency relationships are common among professionals, such as those in insurance, financial management, law, accounting, and real estate.

At its essence, an agency is a relationship of trust and confidence. Because agency relationships are inherent within partnerships, LLCs, and corporations, fiduciary duties are also discussed in Chapters 20 through 23 as well.

The Definition of Agency

Agency
A type of law concerned with any principal-agent relationship, in which one person has legal authority to act for another.

Agent
A person who may act for another, a principal, in dealings with third parties.

Principal
A person who authorizes another, an agent, to act on behalf of the principal.

Agency is the name the law applies to a relationship in which:

- By mutual consent (formal or informal, express or implied)
- One person or entity (called the "**agent**") undertakes to act on behalf of another person or entity (called the "**principal**")
- Subject to the principal's control.

Each of these elements must be present for agency to exist. An agency relationship binds the principal in contract with third parties and protects the agent, who is acting on behalf of the principal, from personal liability to third persons. Thus, agency law really has two components. The first is the creation of the agency itself and the second is the power given to the agent to bind the principal to third parties.

Types of Agents

Agents are classified by the scope of their authority:

1. **General agents.** General agents are authorized to conduct a series of transactions involving one or more goals or activities.
2. **Special agents.** Special agents are retained for a specific transaction and are authorized to perform activities relating to only that transaction.
3. **Universal agents.** Universal agents are authorized to conduct all the principal's affairs that may be legally delegated to an agent. Universal agents can be created only by clear and unequivocal language.

How Agency Relationships Are Formed

Agency law is based on the model of a **principal-agent relationship**. It arises when a principal and agent express assent to one another that the agent shall act on the principal's behalf. The basic premise is that an agent is empowered to act on behalf of (that is, to legally bind) a principal. The scope of the agent's authority to contract will be expressly stated or implied from the circumstances.

Principal-agent relationship
A relationship formed when a party is retained and given authority to act on behalf of and bind a principal.

The principal must have legal capacity to create a principal-agent relationship; however, any person able to act has the capacity to act as an agent. An incompetent agent can bind a competent principal. The agent's capacity is irrelevant because the acts of the agent are deemed to be the acts of the principal.

The resulting agency relationships *arise from the consent given* by a principal to another (so that agency is created). Agency relationships can be created by the following five ways: (1) express agency, (2) implied agency, (3) ratification, (4) apparent agency, and (5) operation of law.

1. *Express agency* is the usual form of creating an agency. **Express agency** occurs when the agent is expressly given the authority to contract or act on the principal's behalf. Express agencies can be created orally or in writing. Express agency arises from a contract and includes all the elements of a contract. In many states, if the contract must be in writing to be enforceable under the Statute of Frauds, the agency appointment must be in writing. This requirement is known as the **equal dignity rule**. Failure to comply with this rule makes the contract (and any resulting commission payable to the agent) voidable at the option of the principal.

Express agency
Agency occurs when principal and an agent expressly agree to enter into an agency relationship.

Equal dignity rule
If a contract must be in writing to be enforceable, the appointment of an agent with regard to that agreement must also be in writing.

Example: A real estate listing agreement between a seller, as a principal, and a real estate broker, as an agent of the seller, expressly grants the broker authority to act on the principal's behalf. The listing agreement must be in writing.

A **power of attorney** is an example of express agency. A principal gives a power of attorney to an agent to authorize the agent to act on the principal's behalf for all or specified purposes as stated in the document. The appointed agent is an **attorney-in-fact**, who does not need to be a licensed attorney (attorney-at-law). The principal can revoke the power of attorney at any time.

Power of attorney
A writing executed by a principal authorizing an agent to act on behalf of principal.

Under the common law, the power of attorney is revoked upon the death or incapacity of the principal, unless the principal expressly granted such continued power of attorney at the time of creation. Where the principal allows a power of attorney to continue upon the principal's incapacity, the power of attorney is a durable power of attorney.

Attorney-in-fact
The agent appointed by the principal through a power of attorney.

A power of attorney is characterized as being general or special. A general power of attorney authorizes the agent to do all that is required to transact the principal's legal affairs. A special power of attorney, also referred to as a limited power of attorney, grants an agent permission to represent the principal regarding specific acts or for a specific period of time (such as during a two-week vacation).

Example: Two partners conducted a business known as The River Edge Company, which owned and managed an apartment complex in New York. One of the partners retired from the business and moved to Florida. He executed a power of attorney designating his son as his attorney-in-fact. The document stated: "The application of this Power of Attorney is limited to affairs, broadly construed, of The River Edge Company, its real and personal property, and other dealings." The son sued in the name of his father to dissolve the company. The other partner moved to dismiss the complaint on the basis that the power did not provide for the right to sue to dissolve a company. The court of appeals held that an attorney-in-fact is essentially an alter ego of the principal and thus the son could take any lawful act on behalf of his father relating to the business. The son held a general power of attorney. *Zaubler v. Picone*, 100 A.D.2d 620 (N.Y. App. Div. 1984)

Implied agency
Agency occurs when a principal and agent create an agency inferred from the parties' conduct and without express agreement.

2. *Implied agency.* A principal and an agent may not have expressly created an agency. Instead, the law implies agency from their conduct—known as **implied agency**. The extent of the implied agent's authority is discussed later in this chapter.

Example: An owner of a retail establishment hires a store manager to run the daily operations. The store manager works under an express agency agreement; however, not all the store manager's daily conduct will be covered by such an agreement. The ability of the store manager to act in the best interests of the retail establishment (such as by providing a discount for an item that has an imperfection even if the express agreement did not mention any discounts) would be within the store manager's implied authority.

Agency by ratification
When a principal knowingly approves an agent's actions after the fact and, in doing so, creates or expands the agency relationship.

Apparent agency
Agency arising from the words or conduct of a principal.

Agency by operation of law
Agency implied in law without a reference to any agreement between a principal and agent.

3. *Agency by ratification.* **Agency by ratification** occurs when a principal approves unauthorized acts committed by the agent, as when the agent acts either without authority or beyond the scope of the authority given by the principal.
4. *Apparent agency.* Words or conduct alone can create an agency relationship. **Apparent agency** arises when a principal creates the appearance of an agency when, in fact, the agency does not exist. Apparent agency is also known as agency by estoppel. It continues to exist until the third party, relying upon the words or conduct of the principal to reasonably believe the agency exists, receives notice of the termination of the agency. The importance of this form of agency lies in whether the principal and agent are liable on contracts with third parties, a matter discussed later in this chapter.
5. *Agency by operation of law.* In a few situations, an agency may be created by law. For example, a spouse may purchase necessities, such as food, and use a joint credit card. The law will impose upon the other spouse the duty to pay for the necessities. Agency by operation of law will also be recognized in cases of emergency response, such as a supervisor contracting with a private ambulance company on behalf of her employer to rush an injured worker to the hospital.

Subagents
An individual to whom the agent delegates as his agent with the principal's authorization.

SUBAGENTS. Typically, an agent does not have the authority to delegate their responsibilities or appoint a subagent. However, a subagency may be created under certain conditions: if the principal explicitly permits it; if it is customary in the nature of the business or trade, or; if it is consistent with the prior conduct of the principal and agent. Subagents act as agents for *both* the principal and the original agent, owing a fiduciary duty to both. They have the authority to bind the principal in the same manner as the original agent.

THE IMPORTANCE OF CONTROL. In addition to the consent of principal and agent, an understanding must exist so that the *principal is in control of the relationship* between the two parties. The agent's consent to act for the principal is subject to the principal's right to control the goals of the relationship. The purpose of the relationship is to serve the principal's interests, not the agent's individual interests. Courts review the parties' words and conduct.

> **Example:** The estates of persons who died in a fire at a Comfort Inn® in Greenville, South Carolina, sued the franchisee and the franchisor. The court granted summary judgment to the franchisor because it did not have a duty to require the franchisees to retrofit the hotel with a sprinkler system before opening under the franchise name. Merely guarding its trademark, the franchisor did not exert enough control over the hotel's daily operations and its security and life safety systems to establish an actual agency. *Allen v. Greenville Hotel Partners, Inc.*, 409 F. Supp. 2d 672 (D.S.C. 2006)

There is a special kind of agency known as an **agency coupled with an interest**. It involves a full or partial transfer of ownership to the agent in order to secure a loan made to the principal or sale on credit to the principal. This type of agency is created for the benefit of the agent; it is one in which the agent is given title or an interest in property. An agency coupled with an interest is irrevocable by the principal. It cannot be terminated by the death or incapacity of either the principal or the agent. It terminates only when the agent's obligations are completed. For example, a literary agent represents a writer who desires to sell a manuscript. The agent will be paid a commission upon the sale of the manuscript, and the agency may not be revoked by the writer.

Agency coupled with an interest
Agency irrevocable by the principal that is created for the benefit of the agent.

Concept Summary
Formation of the Agency Relationship

Express Agency	• Principal and agent agree to enter into agency relationship.
Implied Agency	• Agency is inferred from the parties' conduct and without express agreement.
Agency by Ratification	• Principal knowingly approves an agent's actions after the fact and creates or expands the agency relationship.
Apparent Agency	• Principal's conduct creates the appearance of an agency.
Agency by Operation of Law	• Law creates agency relationship.

Distinguishing Agency from Other Types of Relationships

Other relationships must be distinguished from that of agency. These include the following:

Employer-Employee Relationship

Employer-employee relationship
A relationship formed when an employer retains another while controlling the means and methods of how the work is performed.

Employee
Person who acts under a contract in the service of another, the employer, who can control and direct the means and methods of how the work is to be performed.

An **employer-employee relationship** is formed when an employer hires a person (an employee) to perform services for the employer. An **employee** is a person who acts under a contract in service of another, the employer, who can control and direct the means and methods of how the work is to be performed. Where the employee is given authority to act and enter into contracts on the employer's behalf, there is an agency relationship for the authority given to the employee. That authority is often broad. If the employer hires an employee to perform a task or a service, the agency relationship exists only for those acts that the employee is specifically empowered to perform. This authority is more limited.

> **Example:** A car salesperson assists a customer with purchasing a vehicle. The salesperson is an employee of the car dealership and an agency relationship exists, as the salesperson was performing the service they were hired to perform.

> **Example:** The president of a company seeks to expand its operations into a new territory and enters into a commercial lease in the new territory. The president has authority to act on behalf of the company and the agency relationship exists for all of the power given to the president.

Employer-Independent Contractor Relationship

Principal-independent contractor
A contractual relationship in which a person provides services or a product arising from the performance of the contract.

Independent contractor
Nonemployee worker exercising independent judgment in the manner and means of performing work for a principal.

In the **employer-independent contractor** relationship, a person provides services or a product arising from the performance of a contract. An **independent contractor** is defined as a person who exercises independent judgment in the manner and means of performing work for another. The independent contractor is compensated by the employer, but their working conditions and means and methods of work are not controlled by the employer. The independent contractor is not generally an agent of the employer.

> **Example:** A homeowner employs a contractor to renovate a bathroom. The contractor is an independent contractor of the homeowner and not an agent to the homeowner.

Classifying the Worker

Courts are often used to determine whether a person is an employee or an independent contractor. Courts rarely accept, without further inquiry, an employer's classification of its workers as definitive. States can vary on the criteria used for defining a worker's status, which can be a troublesome issue for employers, workers, governmental agencies, the courts, and students. The Internal Revenue Service uses a set of three factors to determine whether a person is an employee or an independent contractor: (1) behavioral control, (2) financial control, and (3) the relationship between the parties.

BEHAVIOR CONTROL. This factor category examines whether the business directs and controls how the work is performed. The IRS reviews the type and degree of instructions provided to the worker. It reviews whether the company has a right to control what and how the worker performs their job. The IRS reviews the amount of supervision and training provided to the worker. The higher the amount of behavior control, the more it suggests the worker is an employee.

FINANCIAL CONTROL. This factor category examines the extent of the economic control the company has over the worker. The IRS reviews who supplies the tools and equipment the worker uses and whether the company reimburses any of the worker's expenses incurred performing the work. The method of payment is also reviewed. Employees are generally paid weekly or monthly for their work, while independent contractors are paid less frequently and the pay is often tied to the completion of the work or a schedule of the completion of the work. The higher the amount of financial control, the more it suggests that the worker is an employee.

RELATIONSHIP OF THE PARTIES. This factor category examines the extent of the relationship between the parties. The IRS reviews whether there is a written contract between the parties stating that the worker is an independent contractor or an employee. It reviews whether the company provides any fringe benefits such as insurance, retirement contributions, paid vacations, or sick days. The payment of fringe benefits indicates an employee relationship. The IRS also reviews how long the relationship has lasted. Continuous or long-lasting relationships suggest an employment relationship.

Not only can proper classification of workers be difficult but improperly classifying a worker's status presents serious consequences for the business owner. With the application of respondeat superior (vicarious liability imposed on an employer), an employer is liable to third parties for the foreseeable negligent acts and omissions committed by an employee in the course and scope of employment

Latin maxim
Qui facit per alium facit per se. He who acts through another acts for himself.

Duties of Agents and Principals

The status of the agent is a factual determination based upon the factual circumstances, including the agreement of the parties as to the control to be exercised by the principal. The law requires additional duties to be observed by both the agent and the principal.

Fiduciary duty
A standard of care imposed by law based on a relationship of trust and confidence between parties. The fiduciary is required to show loyalty toward the person or entity to which the duty is owed.

Agent's Duties to the Principal

The agent owes the principal two forms of duties: the ones agreed to by the agent within the agency contract, and fiduciary duties imposed upon the agent by law. A **fiduciary duty** is a duty to act in the best interests of the other and not advance personal interests. These fiduciary duties generally begin at the time of retention by the principal. They exist even in the absence of a written agreement with the principal. As a fiduciary of the principal, the agent stands in a special position of trust and confidence. Most states recognize the following fiduciary duties owed by the agent to the principal:

1. Duty of Loyalty
2. Duty of Reasonable Care
3. Duty to Obey the Principal's Instructions
4. Duty of Notification (that is, to inform the principal)
5. Duty to Account

These fiduciary duties are the substance of what every agency encompasses.

Duty of loyalty A fiduciary duty that requires an agent to act solely for the benefit of the principal.

DUTY OF LOYALTY. Perhaps the most important duty that an agent owes to the principal is the **duty of loyalty**. When the agent acts, the agent is doing so in a way meant to achieve the principal's objectives and goals; the agent is important only because this person is the means of accomplishing them. Except when the principal has knowingly agreed to the contrary or when extraordinary circumstances exist, the agent is obliged to prefer the principal's interests over the agent's own and to act solely for the benefit of the principal in all matters relating to the agency. Similarly, the agent must not represent the principal if the agent has a conflict of interest unless the principal consents after receiving full information of all material facts.

The duty of loyalty imposes four restrictions upon the agent:

1. **Self-Dealing**. An agent may not benefit from acts done on behalf of the principal. This does not mean that the agent cannot be compensated for their efforts. Rather, what an agent cannot do is to secretly profit without the principal's knowledge. This is also known as self-dealing by the agent, and all such profits must be paid to the principal. Additionally, the agent may not usurp an opportunity offered to the agent on behalf of the principal. The principal must have the opportunity to become fully informed of the opportunity and accept or reject the offer. If the offer is rejected, the agent may pursue the opportunity personally, provided the other fiduciary duties are observed.
2. **Confidential Information**. An agent has the duty to protect confidential information of the principal and not use that information either for the agent's own benefit or for the benefit of third parties. Examples of confidential information include customer lists, trade secrets, secret formulas, and proprietary information prepared by the principal.
3. **Competing with the Principal**. An agent may not *compete* with the principal in a matter that is within the scope of the principal-agent relationship. This means that an agent cannot use the principal's resources to pursue a business opportunity or use the agent's own free time to pursue a business opportunity.

Example: An LLC was entitled to damages from its founding member and manager for breach of duty of loyalty after the member left the LLC and opened a competing business. The member engaged in pre-departure preparations to compete by soliciting the LLC's employees and patients prior to leaving the LLC, and copying and taking confidential information from the company's computer systems. *Advanced Arm Dynamics of New England, LLC v. Comprehensive Prosthetic Servs., LLC*, 2011 Conn. Super. LEXIS 444 (Conn. Super. Ct. 2011)

Example: Commercial real estate investors were awarded damages against a real estate broker for breach of fiduciary duty when the broker purchased a property for himself in which the investors had made an offer to purchase the same property through that same broker. *Cousins v. Realty Ventures, Inc.*, 844 So. 2d 860 (La. Ct. App. 2003)

4. **Dual Agent.** The agent cannot be a *dual agent*. Absent a waiver of conflict of interest, an agent may not act for another person who has interests conflicting with that of the principal.

Example: The Montana Supreme Court decided a real estate agent breached a duty of loyalty when the agent simultaneously represented more than one buyer competing for the same property. *Zuazua v. Tibbles*, 150 P.3d 361 (Mont. 2006)

DUTY OF REASONABLE CARE. An agent owes a **duty of reasonable care** to the principal. This duty requires a broker to act with the *care*, *competence*, and *diligence* normally (that is, ordinarily) exercised by agents that is standard for the kind of work for which the agent was retained. The modern trend is not to restrict the standard of care to that practiced within the agent's locality but rather to that practiced by agents nationally.

Duty of reasonable care
The duty to render services that others in the same occupation would render under the same circumstances.

Example: Molly Maurer purchased a college student tour from a travel company, acting as an agent for Molly in booking the tour. The tour package included an eighteen-hour "party train" ride from Nogales to Mazatlán, Mexico. During the trip, Molly tragically fell to her death while trying to walk into a forward train car. Molly was the fourth student to die by falling from a moving train on a student tour to Mazatlan organized by the travel agency. The students on Molly's tour were not informed of these prior incidents even though the travel company and its agents knew of other deaths on Mexican trains. Molly's parents argued that the travel company was negligent for failing to warn about prior deaths on the train. In response it argued that it had no duty or control over train safety. The court held that: the client was owed a fiduciary duty by the travel company; and the company had a duty to disclose all information that was material to the object of the transaction. *Maurer v. Cerkvenik-Anderson Travel*, 890 P.2d 69 (Ariz. Ct. App. 1994)

While older case law may not hold gratuitous agents liable for ordinary negligence but only for gross negligence, more recent decisions suggest that the ordinary negligence standard is the same for gratuitous agents as it is for paid agents.

Special skills or knowledge possessed by an agent are considered in determining if an agent acted with due care and diligence. If an agent claims to possess special skills or knowledge, the agent has a duty to the principal to act with the care, competence, and diligence normally exercised by agents with such skills or knowledge.

Example: Trust fund beneficiaries sued BNY Mellon® for a violation of its fiduciary duties by not investing the assets of the trust in well-managed funds of the type invested by better-performing management firms. A federal district court held that BNY Mellon did not exercise such care, skill, caution, and diligence in investing and managing the assets of the trust as would customarily be exercised

> by prudent investors of discretion and intelligence having special investment skills. *Bernard v. BNY Mellon N.A.*, 2019 U.S. Dist. LEXIS 70907 (W.D. Pa. 2019)

Because there is freedom of contract, the principal and agent can agree to change the level of care used by the agent or the consequences of the agent's failure to meet the standard of care. For example, they may agree that the agent is liable for gross negligence and not mere ordinary negligence.

Duty to obey instructions
The agent has a duty to follow lawful instructions provided by the principal.

DUTY TO OBEY PRINCIPAL'S INSTRUCTIONS. The agent must obey lawful instructions provided to it by the principal. This duty is consistent with the duty of loyalty, since the agent must act in a way that is consistent with what the principal wants and cannot act in a way that is contrary to the principal's interests.

Duty to inform the principal
The agent has a duty to inform principal of information principal should know.

DUTY TO INFORM THE PRINCIPAL. If, during the scope and course of performing agency duties, the agent acquires information and has reason to know that the principal should be made aware of this information, there is a duty to provide such information to the principal.

> **Example:** A real estate broker has a duty to communicate to his principal all offers received and may be liable in damages for failure to do so. *Leggio v. Realty Mart, Inc.*, 303 So. 2d 920 (La. App. 1st Cir. 1974)

Information given to the agent is deemed *attributed or imputed* to the principal. If the principal suffers harm for the lack of such information, the principal can sue the agent for breaching this fiduciary duty.

Duty to account
The agent has a duty to render a complete and proper account of all property and funds received and paid on behalf of the principal.

DUTY TO ACCOUNT. The agent must render a complete and proper account of all property and funds received and paid on behalf of the principal. The agent must not commingle the agent's money or property with that received for the benefit of the principal. For example, attorneys, real estate brokers, and escrows must keep the funds of their clients separate and apart from the general funds of their businesses.

The duty to follow instructions was the subject of the following decision.

CASE 15.1

AN AGENT BREACHES ITS FIDUCIARY DUTY IF IT DOES NOT FOLLOW THE PRINCIPAL'S INSTRUCTIONS

ZANG v. NRT NEW ENGLAND INC.

77 Mass. App. Ct. 665 (2010)

Appeals Court of Massachusetts

On January 4, 2006, Neil Bradford and Coldwell Banker executed a listing agreement to sell Bradford's condominium in Beacon Hill. The agreement required the seller to pay Coldwell Banker a fee for professional services of 5 percent of the gross sales price, and authorized Coldwell Banker to pay all commissions payable no later than the closing date and retain any deposits held in escrow and apply said deposits against commission due.

On January 25, 2006, Jonathan Zang entered an offer to buy the Beacon Hill property, providing a $1,000 check to Coldwell Banker to hold the offer. Zang then retained his own escrow agent, Real Estate Café, to represent his interests in the purchase price negotiations. Eventually the parties agreed to a sales price of $1,225,000 and executed a purchase and sale agreement on February 6, 2006. Coldwell Banker did not sign the purchase agreement, which stated that the broker's fee of 5 percent of the purchase price would be split evenly between Coldwell Banker as the seller's agent and Real Estate Café as the buyer's agent at closing. Coldwell Banker deposited the initial $1,000 deposit check as well as Zang's deposit of $122,500, 10 percent of the total purchase price, to be held in escrow until closing. On March 31, 2006, the sale closed. The buyer and seller mutually instructed Coldwell Banker to disburse a portion of the seller's sale proceeds to the buyer's agent. Instead, Coldwell Banker disbursed to the seller 50 percent of the deposit, retaining the other 50 percent and refusing to pay half of the broker's fee to Real Estate Café.

Zang sued Coldwell Banker for breach of fiduciary duty for violating its duties as an escrow agent by refusing to disburse a portion of the deposit to the buyer's agent and instead paying itself money in contravention of the principals' explicit written instructions in the agreement creating the escrows. The trial court granted summary judgment in favor of Coldwell Banker. Zang appealed.

Language of the Court. *After the execution of the contract of sale, a broker's role often involves holding the down payment or deposit made by the purchaser. Sometimes a broker seeks to hold the deposit as assurance that it can be used as a fund from which a commission can be paid. This case represents such a situation. Coldwell Banker played a dual role in this transaction—as seller's agent and as escrow holder.*

An escrow agreement consists of the delivery of money by one party and a promise by the other to hold it until the performance of a condition or the happening of a certain event. The escrow agent need not sign an escrow agreement in order to be bound by the instructions of the principals to the transaction. An escrow agent owes a fiduciary duty to both parties to the escrow agreement. The escrow agent's duty is to "keep the deposit; he could not dispose of it without the express or implied authority of the depositor." The escrow agent, therefore, must strictly follow the instructions of the parties to the transaction.

Here, when Coldwell Banker accepted the $122,500 from Zang and deposited that sum in its escrow account, it assumed the fiduciary duties of an escrow agent. Coldwell Banker was required to act in accordance with the parties' unambiguous instructions. The purchase and sale agreement between the buyer and seller provided unambiguous instructions to Coldwell Banker that it must pay two and one-half percent of the purchase price to the buyer's agent. Although Coldwell Banker did not sign the purchase and sale agreement, it did accept and hold the deposit made to it by the buyer pursuant to the purchase and sale agreement with *knowledge of the dispute. Therefore, the terms of the purchase and sale agreement applied to Coldwell Banker as escrow agent.*

If Coldwell Banker disputed the terms under which it held the escrow, it should have negotiated different terms in the purchase and sale agreement and expressly made its escrow obligations subject to the terms of the listing agreement. If Coldwell Banker did not think that it could respect the parties' instructions for the escrow, it should have declined to hold the funds in the first place. In any event, once it assumed its fiduciary responsibility with respect to the funds, if it believed that moneys should not be split with the buyer's agent, it should have pursued a corrective avenue rather than engaging in self-help and disbursing the disputed funds to itself. Coldwell Banker breached its duty in deciding unilaterally how escrowed funds would be allocated.

Decision. The appellate court held that the agent violated its fiduciary duty by failing to follow the escrow instructions issued by the principals at the time of closing.

Focus on Ethics

Beyond the duty to follow the principals' instructions, what other fiduciary duties were violated by Coldwell Banker in refusing to disburse the money held in escrow as instructed?

Principal's Duties to the Agent

The duties imposed upon the principal do not include a fiduciary duty, but include several contractually related obligations to the agent, including the following:

1. Duty to Compensate
2. Duty to Respect Contractual Terms
3. Duty to Cooperate
4. Duty to Reimburse and Indemnify

Duty to compensate The duty to pay the agreed-on value for the agent's services.

DUTY TO COMPENSATE. The principal owes a duty to reasonably and timely compensate the agent. If the compensation has been agreed upon, it is that amount that must be paid. If it has not been set, the principal must pay the agent the reasonable value of the services rendered. Typically, this would be the ordinary and reasonable fee paid to others within the agent's industry or profession. A principal has no obligation to compensate a gratuitous agent. Some agents are compensated on a contingency fee basis when the agency is completed. Examples of those who work on such a basis include real estate brokers, attorneys, and investment bankers.

Duty to respect contractual terms The duty to honor the agreed-on terms of the agent's services.

DUTY TO RESPECT CONTRACTUAL TERMS. The principal has a duty to honor contractual terms upon which the principal and agent have agreed.

DUTY TO COOPERATE. The principal owes the agent the duty to cooperate in the carrying out of tasks designed to achieve the principal's goals. This means that the principal must act reasonably in ensuring that the principal is not an obstacle to the agent's actions, especially if the agent is acting in a way that is benefiting the principal.

Duty to cooperate
The duty to cooperate with the agent during the course of the agent's services.

DUTY TO REIMBURSE AND INDEMNIFY. As part of the agency relationship, the agent may incur expenses or make payments on the principal's behalf. The principal owes a duty to its agent to reimburse its agent for any payments made or expenses incurred for tasks performed within the scope of the agency relationship. Agents may not recover expenses incurred resulting from their own misconduct or negligence.

The principal must indemnify the agent against liabilities incurred by the agent in the ordinary course of performing duties on behalf of the principal. For example, if a customer sues both an independent sales agent acting for the principal as well as the principal for products liability, the agent is entitled to be held harmless (that is, to be indemnified) by the principal from such claims. Agents must act within the scope of the lawful authority given to them by their principals.

Duty to reimburse and indemnify
The duty to reimburse the agent for funds disbursed at the request of the principal and to indemnify the agent against liabilities incurred by the agent in the ordinary course of performing duties on behalf of the principal.

Concept Summary
Duties Between the Parties

Agent's Fiduciary Duties Owed to Principal	Principal's Contractual Duties Owed to Agent
Duty of Loyalty	Duty to Compensate
Duty of Due Care	Duty to Respect Contractual Terms
Duty to Obey Principal's Instructions	Duty to Cooperate
Duty of Notification	Duty to Reimburse and Indemnify
Duty to Account	

Liability Arising from Agency

Our legal system defines a party's role, authority, and consequences for the party's acts and omissions. For example, if a party is not an agent, that party does not owe fiduciary duties to the other party. When the non-agent party is not authorized to act on behalf of the other party, contractual liability to third parties is not created. However, if the party is an authorized agent, the principal is obligated to perform the contracts that the agent has contracted on behalf of the principal. Similarly, if the agent commits a tort within the scope of the authority given to the agent, the principal may be liable to a third party. We will discuss these rules in more detail in the following sections.

Liability of a Principal to Third Parties for the Agent's Acts

Authority
The legal right to bind another.

Express authority
An agent's power to act on behalf of the principal, explicitly granted by an agreement.

Implied authority
An agent's power to act on behalf of the principal, without express agreement.

Apparent authority
An agent's power to act on behalf of the principal, which arises if a third party reasonably infers authority from the principal's conduct.

For the agent to act, the agent must be given **authority** to act. Authority is the agent's ability to affect the principal's relations with third parties.

The liability of a principal to third parties for the acts of its agent can be established by (1) **express authority** (that is, actual authority); (2) **implied authority**, to do all that is proper, usual, and necessary to the exercise of the authority actually granted *(implied authority is incidental to express authority and only arises when express authority has been given)*; (3) **apparent authority,** and (4) **ratification**. Where a purported agent lacks express authority to act on another's behalf, it may still bind a principal based upon the manifestations of that authority by the principal.

EXPRESS (OR ACTUAL) AUTHORITY. Express (or Actual) authority exists whenever the principal directly states that its agent has the authority to perform an act on the principal's behalf. It grants the agent the right and power to bind the principal to third parties. Actual authority is that authority necessary to carry out the purposes for which the agency was established. Thus, actual authority may arise from express or implied acts and conduct of the principal. For example, a homeowner grants a real estate broker authority to market the home for sale.

IMPLIED AUTHORITY. With implied authority, the principal has not expressly given authority, but the agent believes that the principal has given the agent authority through the principal's actions or conduct. This authority is implied by the conduct of the parties, customs between them, and acts natural and ordinary to carrying out the agent's duties. Express authority given to an agent will control over any implied authority.

> **Example:** Given the nature of the principal's business, the job title, and scope of responsibilities exercised by a company's vice president of administration and purchasing, a third party could rely upon these facts to enter into a contract with the company by dealing with that person.

APPARENT AUTHORITY. Apparent authority is granted by the principal's words or conduct that reasonably induces the third party to rely upon the agent's authority. Apparent authority requires an indication from the principal to the third party—it cannot be based upon the words or the actions of the agent alone. As a result, it can be reasonably implied that the agent does have such authority. The basis for apparent authority lies in the *justifiable reliance* on the words or conduct of the principal. The principal is held liable for the agent's acts within the scope of the agent's apparent authority. The principal will be estopped (that is, prohibited) from claiming that the agent lacked authority to act on his behalf.

This doctrine may not be invoked by one who knows, or has good reason for knowing, the limits and extent of the agent's authority. Any apparent authority that might otherwise exist vanishes in the presence of the third person's knowledge, actual or constructive, of the scope of the agent's authority.

Example: A dispute arose over which party, Sullivan or TOG Properties, owned certain timbered property at the time it was damaged by a fire allegedly set by Pugh. Whichever party owned the property at the time of the fire would hold any insurance claims against Pugh resulting from the damages to the property as a result of the fire. TOG's evidence showed that TOG's president had been terminated before he transferred such claims from TOG to Sullivan. The North Carolina Court of Appeals held the former president did not have actual authority to so act, and that Sullivan knew, or had good reason for knowing, that the former president had no authority to bind TOG. *Sullivan v. Pugh*, 814 S.E.2d 117 (N.C. Ct. App. 2018)

Several forms of agency authority may exist under the circumstances. Apparent authority can coexist and be coextensive with actual authority.

Example: At the end of a long day of attempting to settle his employment claims against a state employer in mediation, the client told his attorney, "I'm leaving, Jim, you handle it." Following the client's departure, the parties, through their legal counsel, settled the client's claims. Later, the client rejected the terms of the settlement and demanded to proceed to trial on his claims, but the state sought to enforce the terms of the settlement agreement. Upon appeal, the Idaho Supreme Court held the representations of the agent alone, who was the client's lawyer, were insufficient to prove the client had given the lawyer actual authority to act on the client's behalf. However, the representations made by the client *and* his lawyer, in combination with inferences "from dealings, circumstances, acts and conduct," constituted substantial, competent evidence supporting a finding of express actual authority given to the lawyer by the client. *Caballero v. Wikse*, 92 P.3d 1076 (Idaho 2004)

CASE 15.2

APPARENT AUTHORITY EXISTS WHEN THE THIRD PARTY'S BELIEF IS BASED UPON THE PRINCIPAL'S WORDS OR ACTIONS

KORICIC v. BEVERLY ENTERS.

773 N.W.2d 145 (2009)

Supreme Court of Nebraska

Frank Koricic resided with his elderly mother, Manda Baker, and managed her daily affairs. When her condition deteriorated, Manda was admitted to Beverly Hallmark, a nursing home in Omaha, Nebraska. At Manda's admission, Frank signed several documents on her behalf. One of the documents was an optional arbitration agreement, which provided that "any and all claims, disputes, and controversies . . . arising out of, or in connection with, or relating in any way to the Admission Agreement or any service or health care provided by the Facility to the Resident shall be resolved exclusively by binding arbitration. . . ."

Before Manda died, she allegedly incurred pain, suffering, and injuries due to Beverly Hallmark's negligence. As Manda's next of kin and trustee of her estate, Frank filed suit against Beverly Hallmark alleging negligence, breach of contract, and breach of fiduciary duty. Beverly Hallmark moved to dismiss the case and to compel arbitration under the arbitration agreement. Frank claimed that Beverly Hallmark could not enforce the arbitration agreement against Manda's estate because Frank, not Manda, had signed the arbitration agreement.

The district court held that the arbitration agreement was valid and enforceable against Manda's estate. Manda had allowed Frank to sign medical authorizations for her as early as 1998. Frank was found to have actual authority to sign the arbitration agreement. Frank appealed the district court's judgment.

Language of the Court. *Because Manda did not sign the arbitration agreement, we focus on whether Frank acted as Manda's agent with authority to enter into the arbitration agreement. Beverly Hallmark claims that Frank, as an agent, had actual authority to bind Manda to the arbitration agreement or, in the alternative, that he had apparent authority.*

Actual authority is authority that the principal expressly grants to the agent or authority to which the principal consents. Frank signed medical documents for Manda under her instructions for 10 years. Based on Frank's testimony, Manda authorized Frank to sign the paperwork required for her admission to Beverly Hallmark.

But the arbitration agreement is another matter—Beverly Hallmark did not require it as a condition of Manda's admission. We agree with the district court's finding that an agency relationship existed between Manda and Frank. We also agree that as Manda's agent, Manda authorized Frank to sign the required admission papers. But we conclude that his actual authority did not extend to signing an arbitration agreement that would waive Manda's right of access to the courts and to trial by jury.

Beverly Hallmark claims that because Manda allowed Frank to leave her room with an employee of Beverly Hallmark to sign the required admission papers, it reasonably believed that Frank had authority to sign the arbitration agreement. Here, no evidence suggests that (1) Manda knew Frank would be asked to sign an arbitration agreement, (2) Manda represented to a Beverly Hallmark employee that she authorized Frank to sign the arbitration agreement, or (3) she later ratified the agreement.

We do not believe that the Beverly Hallmark employee could reasonably believe that Frank had authority to sign the arbitration agreement under these circumstances. Nothing in the record suggests that a reasonable person should have expected an arbitration agreement to be included with admission documents for a nursing home. Beverly Hallmark was not justified in relying solely on Manda's authorization of Frank to sign admission papers as apparent authority to bind her to an arbitration agreement.

Decision. The Supreme Court of Nebraska reversed the trial court's order and held that Beverly Hallmark could not rely on Frank's actual or apparent authority to sign the arbitration agreement.

Focus on Ethics

Is it fair for Frank to have signed the arbitration agreement on his mother's behalf and then receive the benefit of having the agreement declared invalid? Why or why not?

RATIFICATION. Ratification is when a principal approves an unauthorized act committed by the agent. Generally, any words or conduct by the principal showing an intention to adopt the agent's act ratifies the contract. Ratification requires that the principal have knowledge of all the material facts, the agent's actions are ratified in their entirety, and the principal had legal capacity when the agent engaged in the act and when the principal ratified the act. When the principal ratifies the agent's conduct the principal is held liable for the agent's acts that were ratified.

> **Example:** A business agent is given authority to purchase inventory for \$2.5 million. The agent locates the inventory, but the market price had increased to \$2.6 million. The agent submits an offer on the principal's behalf at the increased price. The principal may ratify the \$2.6 million offer made by the agent. Once ratification occurs, the principal will become bound to the terms of the contract (if the seller accepts the offer).

Contract Liability

A principal and agent's contractual liability for contracts entered by the agent on behalf of the principal will largely depend upon two factors: (a) whether the agent's actions were authorized or not, and (b) how the principal is classified. In agency-related contracts, principals can be fully disclosed, partially disclosed, or undisclosed.

AUTHORIZATION OF ACTS

Authorized Acts. If the agent's actions are authorized and the agent acts within the scope of their agency, the principal will be bound to the contract regardless of how the principal is classified (fully disclosed, partially disclosed, or undisclosed).

Unauthorized Acts. If the agent contracts with a third party but has no authority to do so, the principal is not liable on the contract, despite any disclosure of the principal's identity. An unauthorized act makes the agent liable on the contract. The principal may elect to ratify the unauthorized contract. Ratification allows a principal to be bound by an agent's unauthorized contract in circumstances where the principal becomes aware of the contract and retains benefits under it.

CLASSIFYING THE TYPE OF PRINCIPAL. The classification of the principal can affect whether the agent has any liability for an authorized contract.

Fully disclosed principal
A principal whose existence and identity are known to the third party.

Partially disclosed principal
A principal whose existence is known to the third party, but whose identity is not known.

Fully Disclosed or Partially Disclosed Principals. A **fully disclosed principal** is a principal whose existence and identity are known to a third party. A **partially disclosed principal** is one whose existence is known to the third party, but whose identity is unknown. Whether the principal is fully disclosed or partially disclosed, the principal will be liable on a contract entered into on its behalf by an agent. When a third party knows the identity of a principal (fully disclosed principal), the agent does not incur contractual liability because the third party knows the person is acting as an agent for a principal when entering into a contract.

> **Example:** An advertising service sued Margie Beifeld to hold her personally liable for services rendered to her corporate employer. She executed the agreement in her own name, without a reference to being a corporate office holder. The New York court held that it did not matter because the advertising firm knew of a disclosed principal-agent relationship. The court dismissed CBS's claim against Beifeld. CBS® had notice of her status and she could not be held personally liable for the obligations of her employer. *CBS Outdoor Group Inc. v. Beifeld*, 20 Misc. 3d 61 (N.Y. App. Term 2008)

Joint and several
Liability imposed upon each defendant for the payment of the entire obligation owed to the plaintiff.

However, with a partially disclosed principal, the agent is liable to the third party. The liability is known as **joint and several**, and the third party may sue either or both and collect from either of them until the obligation to the third party is satisfied. The concept of joint and several liability is intended to ensure that the plaintiff is made whole where one or more defendants cannot pay the obligation due in full.

Undisclosed principal
A principal whose existence or identity is unknown to the third party.

Undisclosed Principals. Sometimes, neither the existence nor the identity of the principal is disclosed, but the agent is still acting within the scope of their authority. The third party understands that the agent is acting on the agent's own behalf. The third party is unaware of the **undisclosed principal**. Apparent authority to act on behalf of a principal does not apply because the principal's existence is undisclosed to the third party.

An agent who makes a contract without identifying the principal becomes personally liable on the contract. Under general contract law, the third party can sue the agent of the undisclosed principal personally, and the agent can sue the third party. To avoid personal liability, an agent is under a duty to disclose the fact of his agency and the specific identity of the principal, and one who deals with an agent who fails to disclose his principal may, at their election, recover from either the agent or the principal.

> **Example:** Benjamin Yim ordered goods from J's Fashion Accessories but used his own fictitious business (trade) name Ho Tae when he ordered the goods. Yim was actually acting as an agent for the ultimate corporate buyer, Hosung Enterprise, Inc. Following delivery and invoicing to Yim, Fashion sued Yim d/b/a Ho Tae for nonpayment. He was found personally liable because he entered into the sales contract without identifying his principal. *Yim v. J's Fashion Accessories, Inc.*, 680 S.E.2d 466 (Ga. Ct. App. 2009)

Concept Summary Contractual Liability

	Is the principal liable?	Is the agent liable?
Unauthorized acts	No, unless ratified and regardless of whether the principal was disclosed, partially disclosed, or undisclosed	Yes
Fully disclosed principal	Yes, if agent's actions are authorized or ratified	No, unless agent's actions are unauthorized
Partially disclosed principal	Yes, if agent's actions are authorized or ratified	Yes
Undisclosed principal	Yes, if agent's actions are authorized or ratified	Yes

Tort Liability

Most business transactions are conducted through agents, who can commit a tort during the period of the agency. A principal and an agent are individually liable for their own torts. A principal is liable for the conduct of an agent acting within the scope of the agent's authority. In contrast, the agent is liable for the principal's torts only if the agent directly or indirectly participates in or aids in the principal's conduct.

TORTS OF THE AGENT. When conducting business through an agent, a principal may be held liable for the agent's negligent or reckless conduct. For example, a principal can be liable for giving improper instructions or authorizing improper conduct that resulted in the agent committing a tort.

PRINCIPAL AUTHORIZES THE AGENT'S TORT. A principal will be liable when it authorized an agent's tort, since such an action is deemed to be that of the principal. For example, such liability may arise in cases of securities fraud and employment harassment and discrimination.

VICARIOUS LIABILITY. A principal may be vicariously liable to a third party for harm inflicted by their agent even though the principal did not participate in the agent's act or omission. **Vicarious liability** is indirect responsibility imposed by operation of law. The doctrine of vicarious liability rests upon three public policies:

Vicarious liability Indirect liability that is imposed by operation of law to a principal for the conduct of an agent.

- Holding a principal liable because the principal stands to benefit from the agent's acts;
- Risk avoidance through the principal's control of the agent; and

- Risk spreading as the principal is in the best position to insure against foreseeable risks and liabilities that may be created by the agent.

Vicarious Liability and Contracts. If an agent makes a misstatement within the scope of the agent's actual authority, apparent authority, or inherent power, the misstatement itself is attributable to the principal for contract law purposes. In such circumstances, the innocent third party may rescind the contract and recover what consideration was paid or, alternatively, affirm the contract and recover damages.

> **Example:** An insurance company was estopped from rescinding a life insurance policy. The company's agent did not write a false answer on the insurance application but made fraudulent misrepresentations that led an applicant to sign an application without knowing that the signature represented there he had no disqualifying health conditions. *Chism v. Protective Life Ins. Co.*, 234 P.3d 780 (Kan. 2010)

Vicarious Liability for Agent's Negligence— The Agent Acts within the Scope of Their Duties. Courts impose responsibility on the principal for their agent's torts as a matter of public policy. It is the principal's authority to control the agent that justifies the imposition of vicarious liability. Control is essential to the existence of an agency relationship. The principal, having committed no tortious act, is not a "tortfeasor" because liability is imputed by law. The agent is also individually liable for the agent's own torts even where their employer is vicariously liable.

A plaintiff does not have to prove that the principal acted negligently. Rather, to succeed on a vicarious liability claim, a plaintiff need only prove that an agent acted negligently within the scope of the agent's authority. In the context of employment, to determine if a particular act occurred within the **course and scope of employment**, courts look to determine if the harm to third parties was foreseeable from the employee's acts or omissions. In that analysis, courts consider the following factors:

1. Was the act requested, authorized, or ratified by the principal?
2. Was the act commonly performed by employees such that the harm to a third party was a foreseeable event.
3. Whether the act occurred during the workday or on the principal's premises
4. Was the activity advancing the principal's interest or the agent's private interests.
5. Whether the principal furnished the means or instrumentality (such as workplace tools or automobiles) by which the injury occurred.

Frolic and Detour
An employee's frolic is conduct that is not within the course and scope of employment. The conduct does not advance the employer's interests and relieves the employer of vicarious liability. An employee's detour is a minor departure from acting in the course and scope of employment and does not relieve the employer of vicarious liability

Some commentators prefer to refer to these activities as the **Frolic and Detour** doctrine. A frolic is an employee's material departure from the scope of employment, undertaken for the employee's own benefit. The employer would not be liable for any incidents that occur during that time. A detour is an employee's minor departure from their duties, but is still considered acting within the scope of employment. For example, if an employee mails a package on the way to meeting a client. The employer would still be liable for any accidents that occur during that time.

NO LIABILITY FOR INTENTIONAL TORTS OF AN AGENT. Generally, a principal will not be held liable for an agent's intentional torts, since most intentional torts are considered to be outside the scope of the agency; that is, the principal did not promote the intentional tort or receive the benefits of it. The principal has no duty to indemnify the agent.

NO LIABILITY FOR CRIMES OF AN AGENT. As a general rule, a principal will not be liable for the crimes of its agent, even if the crime was committed within the scope of the agency, unless the principal was a co-conspirator or aided and abetted the crime. However, some states impose liability on principals when an agent, during the course and scope of the agency, violates a rule or regulation that carries criminal penalties.

> **Example:** If a law prohibits the sale of alcohol to minors and the agent does, in fact, sell alcohol to minors, some states may impose liability on the principal as well. The consequence is a fine or a suspension of a license to sell alcohol.

Remedies for an Agent's Breach

DAMAGES. If an agent breaches their duty owed to the principal, and such a breach causes damages to the principal, the principal can recover those damages from an agent.

DISGORGEMENT OF PROFITS. As mentioned above, one type of prohibited activity as a result of the duty of loyalty is that an agent may not secretly profit when acting for the principal. If there are such secret profits, the principal is also entitled to disgorgement of any secret profits derived by the agent in addition to damages.

Similarly, a **constructive trust** in favor of the principal will be imposed on property obtained by the agent because of breach of the agent's fiduciary duty. This remedy is granted by a court to transfer to the principal property of the agent that more properly belongs to the principal. The retention of the property by the defendant agent would result in the agent's unjust enrichment. For example, if an agent embezzles funds from the principal and purchases a boat with the funds. The principal may sue for a constructive trust so that the court will transfer title to the boat to the principal.

Constructive trust A court order transferring property held in the name of the debtor to the creditor.

If the principal is sued for the agent's sole negligence, or the agent violates the principal's instructions, the principal has the right to indemnification from the agent for damages incurred.

Remedies for Principal's Breach

DAMAGES. When a principal breaches a duty owed to the agent or wrongfully terminates the agency, the agent is generally entitled to damages from the principal.

INDEMNIFICATION. If the agent suffered losses or expenses while acting as instructed or in a transaction the agent did not know to be unlawful, the principal must indemnify (or compensate for the loss of) the agent.

DEMAND FOR AN ACCOUNTING. If the agent and the principal disagree as to compensation, such as the amount of a commission, the agent can make a demand for an accounting to permit a court to order an accounting and take it into consideration in rendering its decision.

Independent Contractor Liability

As discussed above, independent contractors operate differently from employees. This distinction becomes particularly important when considering the liability to a principal for torts and contracts committed by an independent contractor.

Tort Liability

Like the rule of agency, a principal and an independent contractor are individually liable for their own torts. However, unlike agency, a principal is generally not liable for the torts of the independent contractor. A principal can be held liable for the torts committed by an independent contractor where (1) the work involved inherently dangerous activities, (2) the principal negligently hired, trained, or directed the independent contractor, or (3) the task performed by the independent contractor was one for which responsibility was so important that a statute defined the liability to an independent contractor as non-delegable. In such cases, the principal will be held liable for the acts of the independent contractor.

Contract Liability

The rules for contract liability with an independent contractor mirror those of agency. If the independent contractor's actions are authorized and the independent contractor acts within the scope of their contract, the principal will be bound to the contract regardless of how the principal is classified (fully disclosed, partially disclosed, or undisclosed). If the independent contractor contracts with a third party but has no authority to do so, the principal is not liable on the contract.

The liability of a contractor for an authorized contract will depend on how the principal is classified. The same rules noted above for agency apply when the principals are fully disclosed, partially disclosed, or undisclosed.

Termination of the Agency Relationship

An agency relationship can be terminated either by (1) actions of the principal and agent, or (2) by operation of law. Once the agency relationship is terminated, the agent can no longer bind the principal under actual authority. However, if the agent had apparent authority, it is a best practice that the principal notify third persons who dealt with the agent that the agency relationship has been terminated.

Termination by Actions of the Parties

The principal and the agent may mutually agree to end the agency relationship. Other ways for agency to terminate include the following:

1. *Lapse of time.* The parties may have agreed to the duration of the agency relationship. Upon the lapse of the designated time, the agency terminates

automatically. For example, it is customary practice to retain a real estate broker to represent a seller to market the seller's property. After the elapse of the term, the agency ends. In other cases, a reasonable lapse of time could end the agency relationship as well.

2. *Purpose achieved.* Agency relationships are formed to achieve a purpose, such as the negotiation of a purchase, completion of a transaction, or the execution of a contract. Once this purpose has been achieved, the agency relationship automatically ends.
3. *Occurrence of event.* At the onset, the parties can state that the agency terminates when a specified event occurs.
4. *Unilateral action.* Normally, either party has the right to terminate the agency relationship. However, prior to doing so, the parties should ensure that unilateral termination will not lead to the breach of fiduciary duties.

GIVING NOTICE OF TERMINATION. Once the agency relationship has terminated, the principal should inform third parties who were aware of the relationship of its termination. While the actual authority of an agent ends with the termination, the apparent authority of an agent will continue until the third party receives notice that such authority has been terminated. Otherwise, the principal remains liable for the agent's actions.

The principal can give actual notice of termination directly to third persons with whom the agent has dealt. Unless required by their agreement or by law to be in writing, the notice may be given orally. Alternatively, the principal can give constructive notice of the termination through publication of the termination in a newspaper of general circulation in the locale of the parties. Constructive notice is valid against strangers who may claim the agent continued to possess apparent authority.

In the following case, the issue was when a principal's liability for apparent authority given to an agent ends.

CASE 15.3

AN AGENT'S AUTHORITY CONTINUES UNTIL THE THIRD PARTY RECEIVES NOTICE THAT THE PRINCIPAL HAS REVOKED THE AGENT'S AUTHORITY

PARLATO v. EQUITABLE LIFE ASSUR. SOC'Y OF THE UNITED STATES

299 A.D.2d 108 (2002)

Supreme Court of New York

In April 1990, Equitable Life Assurance Society of the United States (Equitable) hired Kenneth Soule as an agent authorized to sell Equitable financial products, including insurance policies and annuities, to the public. Before he served as Equitable's agent, Soule had been plaintiff Parlato's accountant and financial advisor. Parlato began investing in Equitable financial products through Soule in May 1990. In the spring of 1992, Soule began criminally defrauding Parlato, converting funds generated from her investments for personal use. In 1991, Soule began soliciting plaintiff Perry, Parlato's sister, to invest in Equitable products. Although Perry had entrusted funds to Soule to be used to open Equitable investment accounts, Soule never opened any such accounts. Thus, Perry's existence was unknown to Equitable.

Equitable terminated Soule's contract in July 1992. Although Parlato still had an account with Equitable at that time, Equitable did not notify her of the termination. For four years after his termination, Soule continued to represent himself to plaintiffs as an Equitable agent and to solicit their further investment in purported Equitable financial products. In August 1996, plaintiffs contacted Equitable to verify the status of their investments, at which time Equitable informed them that Soule had been terminated in July 1992.

Parlato and Perry filed suit against Equitable, alleging fraud due to Soule's appearance of authority to act for Equitable. The Supreme Court of New York granted Equitable's motion to dismiss for failure to state a cause of action. Plaintiffs appealed.

Language of the Court. *Equitable argues that it cannot be held liable for any of the frauds Soule committed against either plaintiff, on the ground that Soule was not acting in furtherance of Equitable's business when he stole plaintiffs' money. Contrary to Equitable's position, it is well established that a principal may be held liable in tort for the misuse by its agent of his apparent authority to defraud a third party who reasonably relies on the appearance of authority, even if the agent commits the fraud solely for his personal benefit, and to the detriment of the principal. The reason for this rule is that the principal, by virtue of its ability to select its agents and to exercise control over them, is in a better position than third parties to prevent the perpetration of fraud by such agents through the misuse of their positions.*

The question before us is whether Equitable's termination of Soule's employment in July 1992 had the effect of immediately cutting off his apparent authority to act for Equitable vis-a-vis the two plaintiffs. The Court of Appeals has held that a third party who, like Parlato, is known by a principal to have previously dealt with the principal through the principal's authorized agent, is entitled to assume that the agent's authority continues until the third party receives notice that the principal has revoked the agent's authority.

In this case, Parlato alleges that Soule opened actual Equitable investment accounts for her while he was still an authorized agent of Equitable. If this is proven to be so, Parlato will be entitled to the benefit of the above-described rule permitting her, as a person known to have done business with Equitable through Soule in the past, to presume that Soule remained authorized to act for Equitable in the absence of either (1) notice that his authority had been revoked or (2) other circumstances that would have rendered it unreasonable to believe that Soule had authority to act for Equitable in the transactions he proposed.

As to the viability of Perry's claim against Equitable, Perry's own allegations establish that Equitable had no way of notifying her of Soule's termination in July 1992.

Under these circumstances, any apparent authority Soule may have had vis-a-vis Perry terminated along with his actual authority when his employment by Equitable came to an end.

Decision. The trial court's judgment was modified to vacate the dismissal of the claims of Parlato, who was known to have an account with Equitable.

Focus on Ethics

Should Equitable be held liable to Perry for failing to notify her sister, Parlato, that Soule had been terminated? Why or why not?

Termination by Operation of Law

An agency relationship can also be terminated by operation of law. Unlike terminating an agency by the actions of either party, termination by operation of law typically does not require the principal to notify third parties of the termination.

The following circumstances terminate an agency by operation of law:

1. **Death or incapacity**. Death or mental incapacity of either party after the formation of the agency automatically terminates an agency relationship. The power constituting an agency is founded upon the right of the principal to do the business individually. When that right ceases, the continuing appointment of an agent to undertake that business must also cease. Some states have enacted statutes that change these rules and require the agent to have knowledge of the principal's death or insanity before the agency relationship terminates. The agent continues to have actual authority until such knowledge and apparent authority continues until third parties have knowledge of the principal's death or insanity.
2. **Impossibility of performance**. If the agency becomes impossible to carry out because the purpose or the subject matter is no longer realistically attainable, the agency terminates.
3. **Changed circumstances**. If circumstances change that adversely affect the subject matter of the agency in a way that the principal would not want the relationship to continue, the agency terminates.

Example: Stanhope and Dorn entered into a principal-agent relationship in which Dorn was retained to promote the sale of Stanhope Steel's products diligently and aggressively by calling on customers and prospective customers. When Stanhope voluntarily discontinued operations by selling all of its assets, that action constituted an external change in the relationship, terminating the agency relationship. Dorn v. Stanhope Steel, Inc., 534 A.2d 798 (Pa. 1987)

4. **Bankruptcy of either party**. The bankruptcy of the principal or the agent automatically terminates an agency relationship.

Concept Summary
Termination of Agency Relationship

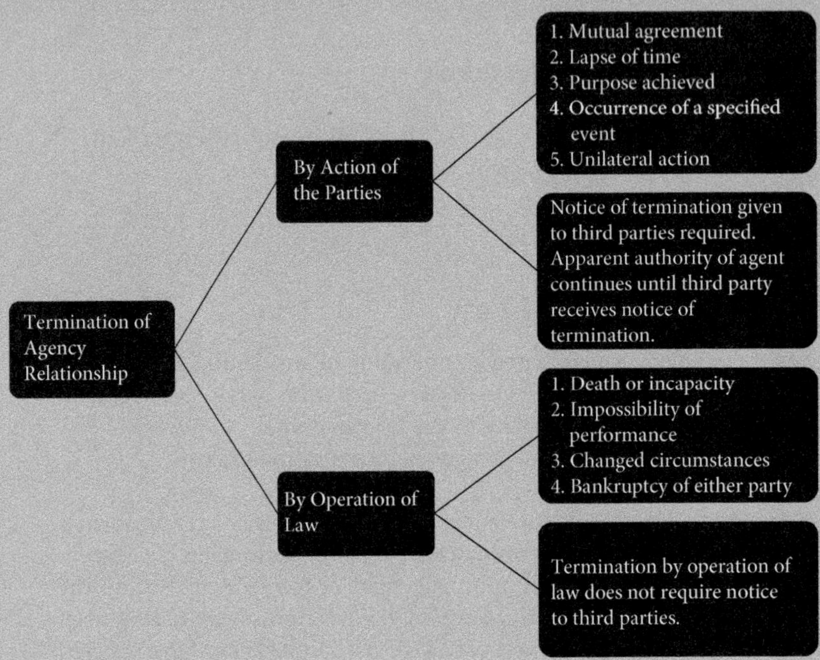

AI Feature: Draft a Manufacturer's Representation Agreement

Using an internet search engine, conduct a review of applicable terms and conditions for an independent company to represent a third-party manufacturer. Then, using an AI program, draft such an agreement. Among other things, your agreement should address the following matters:

- Scope of the representation;
- Duties of the agent and the principal;
- Exclusive representation or agent may represent similar product lines;
- Basis for agent's compensation and when it is to be paid by the principal;
- How to handle returns, claims for defective products by purchasers;
- Managing credit risk presented by purchasers;
- Provisions for nondisclosure of principal's trade secrets by agent;
- Indemnification provisions;
- Term of the agreement and termination provisions;
- Choice-of-law and venue considerations; and,
- Dispute resolution provisions.

Key Terms

- Agency, 348
- Agency by operation of law, 350
- Agency by ratification, 350
- Agency coupled with an interest, 351
- Agent, 348
- Apparent agency, 350
- Apparent authority, 360
- Attorney-in-fact, 349
- Authority, 360
- Constructive trust, 367
- Duty of loyalty, 354
- Duty of reasonable care, 355
- Duty to account, 356
- Duty to compensate, 358
- Duty to cooperate, 359
- Duty to inform the principal, 356
- Duty to obey instructions, 356
- Duty to respect contractual terms, 358
- Duty to reimburse and indemnify, 359
- Employee, 352
- Employer-employee relationship, 352
- Equal dignity rule, 349
- Express agency, 349
- Express authority, 360
- Fiduciary duty, 353
- Frolic and Detour, 366
- Fully disclosed principal, 364
- Implied agency, 350
- Implied authority, 360
- Independent contractor, 352
- Joint and several, 364
- Partially disclosed principal, 364
- Power of attorney, 349
- Principal, 348
- Principal-agent relationship, 349
- Principal-independent contractor, 352
- Subagents, 350
- Undisclosed principal, 364
- Vicarious liability, 365

Applying the Law

15.1 Agency Disclosure. After purchasing a New York City apartment, Sara Tecchia met Bartolomeo Bellati in his New York showroom. He represented that he was the owner of Minimal USA, that he was affiliated with Minimal Cucine, an Italian kitchen designer, and that he could perform the construction improvements that Tecchia sought. The resulting contract was on letterhead of Minimal USA and listed Minimal USA as the "Seller" and Sara Tecchia as the "Customer." When the project did not proceed as planned, Tecchia sued Bellati dba Minimal USA. He defended the case asserting that he was not personally a party to the contract. Instead, he argued that another corporation, Canova, Inc. d/b/a Minimal USA was responsible for the damages. Who wins and why? *Tecchia v. Bellati*, 2016 N.Y. Misc. LEXIS 2608 (2016)

15.2 Scope of Authority. A lessor filed a suit against a radio station in which it claimed that a lease agreement existed between it and the radio station, and that the lease had been breached by the radio station. The radio station argued that the lease agreement was not signed by anyone representing or acting for the radio station's or with its consent or authority. The lessor countered that the program director for the radio station had implied authority to execute the lease on behalf of the radio station. Who should prevail and why? *Mark Century Corp. v. Tiger Broadcasting Co.*, 509 S.W.2d 737 (Mo. App. 1974)

15.3 Who Is the Employer? Sherrie Ann Adcok sued Chrysler Corporation for employment discrimination, alleging that the company's refusal to award her a dealership was the result of sex discrimination. Under the dealership appointment agreement, the dealer (not Chrysler) controls the dealership and the day-to-day vehicle-selling operations. The dealer maintains discretion over dealership employment decisions and over the means and manner of advertising. The dealer (not Chrysler) owns the dealership, premises, equipment, and vehicles sold by the dealership. Adcok argued that it was an employment relationship because Chrysler controlled the decisions about what cars could be purchased, the appearance of the dealership, the dealer location, and certain financial requirements. Chrysler had easy access to and use of the dealer's accounting information. In considering all of the factors that weigh both for and against an employment relationship, how should the court rule? *Adcok v. Chrysler Corp.*, 166 F.3d 1290 (9th Cir. 1999)

15.4 Apparent Authority. Loncarevic and Associates, Inc., a furniture company, received an unsolicited one-page fax advertisement at its office promoting the upholstery services of Stanley Foam Corporation. Loncarevic brought a class action suit against Stanley Foam. It alleged the fax advertisements violated the federal Telephone Consumer Protection Act (TCPA) and that Stanley Foam gave its employees broad authority to make decisions regarding the fax campaign. Stanley Foam argued that the faxes were prepared at the direction of an independent contractor and it was not liable because it had never authorized sending faxes to Loncarevic's area. Can Stanley Foam be liable under the theory of apparent authority for a violation of such a statute? Why or why not? *Loncarevic and Associates, Inc. v. Stanley Foam Corp.*, 72 N.E.3d 798 (Ill. App. Ct. 2017)

15.5 Agency Relationship. Following earlier surgeries at Robert Wood Johnson Hospital, on February 12, 2010, Lakeysha Walton was transferred to Kindred Hospital Philadelphia, where she remained until April 20, 2010. Walton was 36 years old at the time. She was in a coma at the time of her admission to Kindred Hospital. On March 1, 2010, halfway through Lakeysha Walton's stay at the hospital, her mother, Nancy Walton, signed a voluntary alternative dispute resolution agreement as Lakeysha Walton's "Legal Agent." Did Nancy have the authority to execute the agreement, even though Lakeysha never gave her mother a power of attorney and never authorized her mother to make decisions on her behalf? *Walton v. Johnson*, 66 A.3d 782 (Pa. Super. Ct. 2013)

15.6 Misrepresentations. A law school graduate who could not take the bar examination because his school was unaccredited sued the law school, its dean, and others for fraudulent misrepresentation. The graduate alleged he had relied on the dean's recruitment letter, which stated that the American Bar Association's accreditation committee had voted to recommend the school for provisional accreditation and that the dean was highly confident of receiving ratification. The graduate also alleged that, after negative ABA action after his enrollment, he decided not to transfer from the law school because the school's acting dean assured him that there was no cause for pessimism about accreditation. Why should the law school be held liable for the misrepresentations of its dean? *Rodi v. Southern New England School of Law*, 389 F.3d 5 (1st Cir. 2004)

15.7 Duty of Loyalty. The defendants sold a company to the plaintiff and agreed not to compete "as owners" and to act as the company's managing agents. The defendants allegedly stole the company's customer list and used the list to solicit business for a competing enterprise, which they did not own. The trial court granted a temporary injunction against the defendants. The court of appeals affirmed due to the defendants' duty of loyalty as managing agents. What duties have been violated by the agents? *Huong Que, Inc. v. Luu*, 150 Cal. App. 4th 400 (2007)

15.8 Authority. Abdul Mohammed, formerly a driver for Uber Technologies®, sued Uber and a subsidiary over violations of state and federal laws. The defendants moved to compel arbitration of Mohammed's claims because of a compulsory arbitration clause in the smartphone application he downloaded to pair him with those seeking transportation from Uber drivers. Mohammed argued that he was not so bound because the app had been downloaded to his phone not by him but at his request by a representative at Uber's local office; Mohammed had given the representative his username and password to do so. Uber argued that the representative was acting as Mohammed's agent, whether through implied actual authority, apparent authority, or ratification of his acts. Was the Uber representative Mohammed's agent and did he have authority to bind him to arbitrate his claims? *Abdul Mohammed v. Uber Techs., Inc.*, 237 F. Supp. 3d 719 (N.D. Ill. 2017)

15.9 Authority of Real Estate Brokers. To what extent do real estate brokers have authority to bind principals in a real estate transaction? *Leggio v. Realty Mart, Inc.*, 303 So. 2d 920, 923 (La. App. 1st Cir. 1974), *aff'd*, 307 So. 2d 629 (LA. App. 4th Cir. 1975)

15.10 Authority of an Agent. Dayna Samra sued Khaled Shaheen and his corporation for the enforcement of an oral settlement agreement arising out of allegations of sexual harassment by Shaheen. Shaheen requested Hani Ayoub to contact Samra and settle the case. Ayoub telephoned her and she demanded $250,000 in settlement; at the direction of Shaheen, Ayoub counteroffered at $50,000, which Samra rejected. Thereafter, Samra sought to enforce a settlement in which she had agreed to a settlement offer of $150,000, made by Ayoub to her on behalf of Shaheen. In response, Shaheen denied he appointed Ayoub to be his agent or authorized Ayoub to take any action on his or his corporation's behalf. Could Ayoub be an agent of Shaheen and, if so, how would the agency be established? For example, what facts could Samra rely upon to hold Shaheen liable under apparent authority? *Samra v. Shaheen Bus. & Inv. Group, Inc.*, 355 F. Supp. 2d 483 (D.D.C. 2005)

Employment, Immigration, and Labor Law

16

No one gains from fair employment law and legislation if there is no employment to be had. — John F. Kennedy, Thirty-fifth President of the United States (1917-1963)

Chapter Outline

Learning Objectives

After studying this chapter, you should be able to:

1. Define at-will employment.
2. State the exceptions to at-will employment status.
3. Explain the application of the FLSA and its exemptions to overtime pay.
4. Recognize when employees are entitled to the protections of the FMLA.
5. Understand the application of workers' compensation laws to the workplace.
6. Describe the of the immigration and federal labor laws.

Introduction

The broad scope of employment law reaches every aspect of the business-worker relationship. Court decisions, administrative regulations, public policies, and evolving social standards constantly challenge managers and business owners with respect to their workers. As a result, they are compelled to stay informed about both general employment laws and employment discrimination laws. This chapter will provide an overview of employment law, followed by discussions on important federal immigration and labor laws commonly encountered in the workplace.

At-Will Employment

Employment at-will A common law doctrine that states either party may terminate an employment relationship at any time for any reason, absent an agreement to the contrary.

The relationship between an employer and an employee is usually known as **employment at-will**. Employment at-will is a common law doctrine by which either party may terminate an employment relationship at any time for any reason, absent an agreement to the contrary. In studying the laws that apply to this relationship, note that they do not apply to agents or independent contractors.

Exceptions to Employment At-Will

Wrongful discharge Termination of employment involving an exception to the employer's right to terminate an at-will employee.

Even though most employer-employee relationships are characterized as at-will, there are three commonly recognized exceptions to at-will employment. If they apply, the employer may be liable to the job applicant or employee for damages, reinstatement, costs, and attorneys' fees. Such liability arises from an act of **wrongful discharge**. The three exceptions are:

1. Violating an express or implied contract between the employer and employee;
2. Violations of statutory and public policy protections; and
3. In some states, violating an implied covenant of good faith and fair dealing within every employment relationship.

EXPRESS AND IMPLIED CONTRACT EXCEPTIONS. Unlike at-will employment, express contracts are either permanent in duration or terminable only upon certain conditions. The contract would allow the employee to quit but impair the employer's right to terminate the employee. For example, some contracts might require prior notice to the employee of potential grounds to terminate the employee and allow a period for the employee to cure the issue. In other cases, the contract might provide that an employee might be discharged only for good cause.

Implied contractual liability may be created by an employer's employment policies, practices, manuals, and handbooks. The law recognizes an implied employment contract when the parties' words or conduct reasonably imply agreement to certain terms. If the language is specific enough to assure the employee that termination will occur only upon certain conditions, the presumption of at-will status will be overcome.

Example: Nora Duldulao was terminated from St. Mary Nazareth Hospital Center after 11 years of employment. She was terminated without notice for unsatisfactory performance. The hospital's handbook provided that an employee could only be terminated for specific reasons following "proper notice and investigation." The Supreme Court of Illinois held that such a provision created a contract, which barred termination without the safeguards of notice or an investigation. *Duldulao v. St. Mary of Nazareth Hosp. Ctr.*, 505 N.E.2d 314 (Ill. 1987)

STATUTORY AND PUBLIC POLICY EXCEPTIONS. Laws, regulations, and judicially created public policies provide certain exceptions for terminations of at-will employees. Generally, these exceptions fall within these categories:

- *Anti-discrimination statutes*: Refusing to hire, promote, or train; or unfairly discharging or disciplining employees based on their race, color, national origin or ancestry, sex (including pregnancy, childbirth, gender identity, sexual orientation, and transgender status), age, physical or mental disability, religion, and genetic information.
- *Leave of absence statutes*: Covered employers may not discipline or discharge eligible employees for exercising a statutory right to leave, including those for pregnancy, disability, the "serious health condition" of the employee or of a family member, jury duty, and voting (under some state laws), and military service, as well as work-related leaves.
- *Whistleblowing statutes*: **Whistleblowing** statutes protect employees from being discharged, disciplined, or retaliated against by their employer. It can arise in situations when the employee has reported to superiors the employer's violation of a statute; the employer's submission to the government of a false or fraudulent claim for payment; and unsafe work conditions.
- *Public policy considerations* prohibit an employer from coercing employees to commit or conceal unlawful activity. This limitation to at-will employment requires that a fundamental public policy be expressed in a statute or that a constitutional provision must support the claim that the termination violated a law. Usually, retaliatory terminations that violate public policy are based on terminations that occur because of the following: the employee refused to violate the law (such as by refusing to commit perjury); the employee was performing a statutory obligation (as when the employee was subpoenaed to testify or is going to testify in court); or the employee opposed or reported the employer's unlawful conduct (as in the case of reporting the employer's discriminatory acts).

Whistleblowing
Protection from loss of employment involving an exception to the right of an employer to terminate an at-will employee.

IMPLIED COVENANT OF GOOD FAITH AND FAIR DEALING EXCEPTION. Some states recognize an implied covenant of good faith and fair dealing exception with regard to employment relationships. However, courts have varied in their adoption of this exception. They will engage in intensive fact-finding to determine if the covenant was breached.

Example: An employer fires an employee to avoid paying a longevity bonus to them.

Management Application
Documenting At-Will Status

Employers should adopt the following language in employment applications and manuals:

In Applications

If I am hired, I agree to conform to all rules, practices, and standards of the ____ ("Corporation"). I further agree that my employment and all benefits can be terminated at will, with or without cause, and with or without notice to me, at any time, either at my election or that of the Corporation. I understand that no employee or agent of the Corporation, except for the President or the Vice President of Human Resources, has the authority to enter into any agreement for employment for any specified time. If an agreement is made that my employment is to be other than at will, a written agreement specifying the intent to do so must be signed by me and the President of the Corporation for it to be enforceable.

In Written Acknowledgments Executed by New Employees

I have received and read a copy of the Corporation's Employee Handbook. I understand that the policies, rules, and benefits described in it are subject to change at the sole discretion of management at any time. I further understand that my employment is terminable at will, by either myself or the Corporation, regardless of the length of my employment or the granting of benefits of any kind.

I understand that no contract of employment other than "at-will" has been expressed or implied, and that no circumstances arising out of my employment will alter my "at-will" employment relationship unless expressed in writing, with the understanding specifically set forth and signed by the President of the Corporation and myself. I understand that my signature below indicates that I have read and understand the above statements and have read and received a copy of the Corporation Employee Handbook.

In the Employment Manual

At-Will Employment at Our Company. You are free to terminate your employment with the Corporation at any time, with or without a reason, and the Corporation has the right to terminate your employment at any time, with or without a reason. Although the Corporation may choose to terminate employment for cause, cause is not required. This is called "at-will" employment. No one other than the President can enter into an agreement for employment for a specified period or make any agreement or representations contrary to this policy. If an agreement is made that your employment is to be other than at will, a written agreement specifying the intent to do so must be signed by the President of the Corporation and by you for it to be enforceable.

Fair Labor Standards Act (FLSA)
Federal law applicable to employees engaged in interstate commerce or employed by an enterprise engaged in interstate commerce. Sets minimum wages and overtime and regulates youth employment.

Wage and Hour Laws

The most widely applied federal wage-hour legislation regarding employees is the **Fair Labor Standards Act (FLSA)**. It requires payment of a minimum wage and premium pay for overtime hours, and it restricts child labor. State and local laws may impose more stringent rules upon employers, such as requiring the employer to pay overtime when federal law would not require it to be paid. The employer is required to comply with the more generous standard.

The Wage and Hour Division of the U.S. Department of Labor enforces the FLSA. The law provides for both civil and criminal penalties for violating the FLSA. The law also provides that the Secretary of Labor may bring a lawsuit to recover unpaid minimum wages and overtime pay against an offending employer or seek an injunction against prohibited employer acts. In addition, workers have the right to sue for violations of the FLSA and for retaliatory discharge or discrimination relating to wage and hour matters.

Review the Department of Labor website: http://www.dol.gov

The FLSA applies to all employers engaged in interstate commerce who have at least $500,000 in revenue and employees who are engaged in interstate commerce.

Minimum Wage and Overtime Pay Requirements

An employer and employee are free to contract for the wages, hours, and benefits to be paid to the employee. However, the terms must, at minimum, comply with the FLSA's wage and hour requirements. Contracts that violate the FLSA's provisions are void.

FEDERAL MINIMUM WAGE. The FLSA generally requires covered employers to pay their employees at least the federal minimum wage, which is $7.25 per hour for all hours worked, and overtime premium pay of one and one-half times the employee's regular rate of pay for all hours worked over 40 in a workweek.

CALCULATION OF HOURS WORKED. All time that an employer requests an employee to spend on its business is compensable; this is also known as work time not requested, but work suffered or permitted.[1] The work is compensable if the employer knows or has reason to believe that an employee is working. If such work is unauthorized, the employer has a duty to see that work is not performed. For example, the employer cannot allow employees to work at home for their convenience after hours to catch up on projects and not count the work time as hours worked.

SALARIED EMPLOYEES. A salaried employee must receive at least the statutory minimum hourly rate of pay. The regular hourly rate is determined by dividing the employee's total remuneration for the workweek by the total number of hours the employee actually worked during that workweek.

Overtime
Subject to certain industry-specific exemptions, the hourly rate of one and one-half times their normal pay rate due to nonexempt employees for each hour of work beyond 40 in a workweek.

ON-CALL TIME. On-call time poses a special problem for employers. Employers often arrange with employees to be on call. If the employee is required to remain on call on the employer's premises or so close to the premises that the employee cannot use the time effectively for his or her own purposes, the employee is working while on call. These hours are compensable work hours.

Exempt employee
Employees exempt from minimum wage and overtime pay provisions or from the child labor provisions of the FLSA.

OVERTIME COMPENSATION. The FLSA entitles all employees to **overtime** payment unless they are considered an **exempt employee**. Those who are not exempt and are covered by the FLSA must be paid overtime after 40 hours worked per workweek at a rate of at least one and one-half times the employees' regular hourly (or hourly equivalent) rate of pay.

1. 29 U.S.C. §§ 201-219.

Exemptions from Minimum Wage and Overtime

The overtime exemptions of the FLSA are premised on the belief that certain workers often earn compensation well above the minimum wage. Workers who do not earn at least $58,656 a year (as of 2025) must be paid overtime, even if they are classified as managers or professionals. Among the most common exemptions are the following:

- Executive exemption
  - Exemption from overtime pay covering employees whose duties and responsibilities involve managing an enterprise, who customarily and regularly direct two or more employees, who have authority to hire and fire or whose recommendations as to staffing are given particular weight, and who customarily and regularly exercise discretionary powers.
- Administrative employee exemption
  - Primary duty is the performance of office or non-manual work directly related to management or the general business operations of the employer or its customers, and whose work includes exercise of discretion and independent judgment.
- Highly compensated employee exemption (HCE)
  - An exemption is offered if the employee earns more than $151,164 (adjusted periodically). To qualify for the HCE exemption, at least $1,128 per week ($58,656 per year) of the compensation must be paid on a salary or fee basis. Any non-salary or fee-basis compensation must also be non-discretionary. and their primary duty includes performing office or non-manual work. Additionally, the employee customarily and regularly performs at least one of the exempt duties or responsibilities of an exempt executive, administrative, or professional employee.
- Learned professional exemption
  - Primary work requires advanced knowledge in a field of science or learning the mastery of, which is acquired through specialized instruction. Often involves individuals who have been granted professional licensure by a state licensing authority.
- Computer professional exemption
  - Primary duty is the applications of computer system analysis, including consulting with users of computer systems and the design, development, creation, testing, or modification of such systems.
- Retail and service business employees who are paid by commission exemption
  - If more than half of earnings are derived from commission, such employees may be exempt.
- Outside sales representative exemption
  - If the employee's primary duty is to make sales and the employee must be customarily and regularly engaged away from the employer's place of business, the person may be exempt.

For more information on federal overtime rules, see https://www.dol.gov/agencies/whd/overtime.

The people of this country by an overwhelming vote are in favor of having Congress—this Congress—put a floor below which individual wages shall not fall, and a ceiling beyond which the hours of individual labor shall not rise.—Franklin D. Roosevelt, Thirty-second President of the United States, State of the Union Address, January 1938

Youth Employment

The FLSA places restrictions on employment to protect youth from the abusive employment practices of the past. The FLSA prohibits employment for children under age 14 in many non-agricultural occupations. Young people between 14 and 15 years of age are limited to employment outside school hours in non-manufacturing and non-hazardous jobs for limited periods of time under specified conditions. Those 16 and 17 years of age are not subject to limitations to working times and hours, with the exception of those times and hours the Secretary of Labor declares to be hazardous. Employers should be aware that state legislation regarding youth employment may be more restrictive than that permitted by the FLSA. Specific regulations also require an accurate account of the hours worked by youths during each workweek.

Review the Department of Labor website for more information on the FLSA at https://www.dol.gov/agencies/whd/flsa.

Student Unpaid Internships and the FLSA

The student internship has many appealing qualities, except when the work that is performed is unpaid. The answer to the question of whether a student must be paid while they are acquiring on-the-job experience is set forth under the FLSA. The Department of Labor (DOL) has six criteria for differentiating between an employee entitled to minimum wage or above and a learner/trainee who may be unpaid. The criteria are as follows:

1. The training, even though it includes actual operations of the employer's facilities, is similar to that which would be given in a vocational school.
2. The training is for the student's benefit.
3. The student does not displace a regular employee but works under the close observation of a regular employee or supervisor.
4. The employer provides the training and derives no immediate advantage from the activities of the student; and on occasion, the training may actually impede the operations.
5. The student is not necessarily entitled to a job at the conclusion of the training period.
6. The employer and the student understand that the student is not entitled to wages for the time spent training.

No federal statute or regulation clearly applies to the exemption of interns from the minimum wage and overtime requirements, and all six factors do not have to be present for the individual to be considered a trainee. The experience, however, should look more like a training/learning experience than a job. Thus, employers often question the fourth criterion—that the employer derives no immediate benefit from the student's activities.

The Portal-to-Portal Act

Portal-to-Portal Act Federal law specifying the types of work-related time spent that are compensable. Generally, such time includes all activity of benefit to the employer. Time for travel to and from the workplace is not compensable.

The **Portal-to-Portal Act** amended the FLSA to clarify the type of employee activities for which employees should be paid. Generally, the Act does not require compensation for the time an employee spends traveling to and from the place of employment and during preliminary or concluding activities related to the work. The Act requires employers to compensate workers for time spent on job-related activities. Work-related travel during the workday is compensable.

Example: The Supreme Court held that time spent by employees waiting for and undergoing security screenings before leaving the workplace was not compensable under FLSA. The security screenings were not "integral and indispensable" to the employees' duties as warehouse workers. *Integrity Staffing Solutions, Inc. v. Busk*, 574 U.S. 27 (2014)

Concept Summary
Wage and Hour Claims

Fair Labor Standards Act (FLSA) Violations (29 U.S.C. §§ 201 *et seq.*)

Violations could include failure to pay minimum wage or overtime wages due to nonexempt employees. Rest, recovery, and meal periods are not counted if the employee is completely relieved from duty. All waiting time is compensable if the employee is on duty.

- Wage discrimination based on gender is a violation of the Equal Pay Act (which is part of the FLSA).
- Wage or benefit discrimination based upon protected class status may violate any of the grounds for employment discrimination claims.

Portal-to-Portal Act (29 U.S.C. §§ 251-262)

Generally, employers are not liable under FLSA for hours spent:

- walking, riding, or traveling to and from the actual place of performance of the principal activities the employee is to perform; and
- in preliminary and concluding activities.

Layoffs and Leaves of Absence

Layoffs

Congress enacted the Worker Adjustment and Retraining Notification (WARN) Act, which prohibits employers from ordering a plant closing or mass layoff until the end of a 60-day period after the employer serves written notice of such an order. The Act applies to employers of more than 100 full-time employees. Employers who violate the federal WARN Act are liable to each discharged employee affected by a plant closing or a mass layoff for back pay for each day of the violation.

Family and Medical Leave Act (FMLA) A federal act requiring covered employers to provide eligible employees job protections for unpaid leave due to the serious health conditions of the employee or a family member or to care for a new child.

Family and Medical Leave Act

The **Family and Medical Leave Act (FMLA)** entitles employees, both male and female, to take an unpaid leave of absence because of:

- The birth and care of the employee's newborn child;
- The placement with an employee of a child for adoption or foster care;

- The employee's caring for an immediate family member (spouse, child, or parent) with a serious health condition;
- The employee's medical leave because of their own serious health condition;
- The employee's caring for a service member who has experienced a serious injury or illness while on active duty; or
- Any "qualifying exigency" arising because the employee is in the National Guard or Reserves and is or soon will be placed on active duty.

Federal law does not provide time off for parent-teacher conferences or personal counseling. However, many state laws do provide such protections, and employers must comply with more than federal law in operating their businesses. The parental leave period ends 12 months from the date of the birth, adoption, or foster care placement of the child. If an expectant mother's medical condition requires FMLA leave before the birth of the child, that leave is a qualifying event. Note that under the FMLA, an absence by an employee for a pregnancy-related condition could constitute a serious health condition.

COVERED EMPLOYERS. The FMLA applies to:

- Employees who work for a public employer of any size, including state, local, and federal governments;
- Employees of a private company with 50 or more employees; and
- Employees who work for a company with fewer than 50 employees at one worksite may be covered if the employer has at least 50 employees within 75 miles of that worksite.

COVERED EMPLOYEES. The FMLA covers employees who:

- Worked for that employer for at least 12 months before taking leave;
- Worked at least 1,250 hours within the 12 months prior to taking the leave; and
- Experience a qualifying event and give timely notice to the employer of the need for the leave.

CONSEQUENCES OF FMLA LEAVE. Once the employee returns from an FMLA leave, the employer must restore the employee to the same position the employee held before the leave began or to an equivalent position with equivalent benefits, pay, and other terms and conditions of employment.

For more information on the FMLA, see https://www.dol.gov/agencies/whd/fmla.

REMEDIES. Federal law expressly prohibits employers from discriminating against or discharging any employee who exercises or attempts to exercise any rights provided by the FMLA. The consequences for wrongfully denying rights protected under the Act include the following:

1. The right of employees to sue their employer in a private lawsuit or file a claim for administrative enforcement with the U.S. Department of Labor;
2. Lost or denied wages to be paid to the employee;
3. Equitable relief; or,
4. Employer liability for damages and liquidated damages.

Occupational Safety and Health Act

Occupational Safety and Health Act (OSH Act)
Legislation that sets a national standard for workplace safety. Designed to protect workers from danger but not intended to eliminate all dangers from the workplace.

Review the procedures by which a person may file a complaint with this agency at https://www.osha.gov/.

Workers are protected by the federal **Occupational Safety and Health Act (OSH Act)**, which sets national standards for workplace safety. Congress designed it to protect workers from dangers, but it was not intended to eliminate all dangers from the workplace. Employers have both a general and a specific duty to provide their employees with safe workplaces, free from recognized, serious hazards. The recognized hazard must be one "likely" to cause "death or serious physical harm." The OSH Act does not require proof of the probability of harm. Rather, it requires the existence of a hazard to the degree that few people would doubt that it should be abated. Courts liberally construe the Act and its regulations to afford the broadest protection to workers. The Occupational Safety and Health Administration (OSHA) is the federal agency tasked with administering the OSH Act.

Other Employee Rights

Employees have the right to file a complaint with OSHA, the federal agency that enforces safety and health conditions at workplaces. Such complaints may be filed confidentially, and they may contest the amount of time OSHA gives an employer to correct a workplace condition. The Act protects private-sector employees who exercise these OSHA-protected rights against retaliation.

> **Example:** David Shack, a teacher's aide, was concerned about student and staff safety. Shack recommended the school upgrade the electrical systems in its theaters. The school declined to fund the upgrades and ignored Shack's written complaint. Shack filed an anonymous online complaint with OSHA. When OSHA informed the school of the anonymous complaint, the school notified Shack that he was terminated for lacking the required academic credentials. The court found that the school acted in retaliation for Shack's OSHA complaint. *Perez v. Renaissance Arts and Educ., Inc.*, 2013 WL 5487097 (M.D. Fla. 2013)

Concept Summary
An Employer's Duties Under the OSH Act

An employer is obligated to:

- Observe the general duty standard of providing safe work and working conditions for all employees;
- Observe the general industry regulations pertaining to the workplace;
- Observe all OSHA specific duty standards and regulations that apply to the specific job and workplace in which its employees are working; and
- Maintain and observe all requirements relating to recordkeeping, reporting, providing notices, and posting information posters.

A violation of an OSHA standard occurs when:

- An applicable standard, which was violated by a hazard, exists;
- One or more employees were exposed or had access to the hazard; and
- The employer knew or reasonably should have known of the hazard.

According to OSHA guidelines, an effective occupational safety and health program has four parts:

- Management commitment and employee involvement;
- Worksite analysis;
- Hazard prevention and control; and
- Safety and health training.

Reporting Requirements

OSH Act regulations require employers to post required safety and reporting notices at a workplace. Employers with eleven or more employees must maintain a log and summary of all recordable occupational injuries and illnesses and compile an annual summary. Such recordable events include: any work-related fatality, any work-related injury or illness that results in loss of consciousness, days away from work, restricted work, or transfer to another job, and any work-related injury or illness requiring medical treatment beyond first aid. Those records must be made available for inspection when requested by an OSHA compliance official. When a work-related fatality or serious injury requires hospitalization, employers must report the event to OSHA. The notification must occur within 8 hours if an employee dies and file a report within 24 hours for an inpatient hospitalization, amputation, or loss of an eye.

Review OSHA's Form 301 at https://www.osha.gov/recordkeeping/forms.

Inspections

The OSH Act authorizes OSHA to conduct workplace inspections and investigations to determine whether employers are complying with the general duty clause and the standards issued by the agency. Inspections can cover the entire workplace or just a few operations.

The laws we have studied so far have allowed injured parties to file suit or pursue administrative claims for compensatory damages or seek injunctive relief against discriminatory practices. However, unlike statutes such as Title VII or the FLSA, the OSH Act does *not* authorize private-party enforcement. Enforcement lies with OSHA itself.

Workers' Compensation

Workers' compensation is a *no-fault* system of laws and regulations that often provides the only means for an injured worker to recover compensation for medical expenses and lost wages arising from work-related injuries. Primarily governed by state law, the workers' compensation system provides compensation to employees for injuries that occur on the job.

Workers' compensation
A no-fault system of laws and regulations that often provides the only means for an injured worker to recover compensation for medical expenses and lost wages arising from work-related injuries.

Workers' compensation is a system under which employees with workplace injuries are paid monies for their injuries; they may not then sue their employer in court for damages. By providing a speedier resolution and usually finding employer liability, the system prevents the employer from having to defend itself in court. Unfortunately, a claimant's award is often insufficient to restore the person to their prior standard of living. In some states, the employer has committed gross negligence related to the injury or sickness suffered or its intentional conduct, the employee may sue the employer for additional damages on those grounds.

All states have workers' compensation laws that provide for payments to workers for injuries suffered on the job. Most states have enacted laws that provide employees with an exclusive remedy for work-related injury.

> **Example:** Anne Eckis was a full-time secretary for the director of the animal training department at SeaWorld®. Eckis was asked if she would like to ride Shamu, the killer whale, for some publicity pictures for SeaWorld. Eckis trained for the ride during her normal working hours. Her boss knew that Shamu had attacked persons wearing ordinary bathing suits when attempting to ride Shamu and had been behaving erratically. In response to Eckis's apprehension, her boss assured her the ride was "as safe as could be" but did not inform her about the earlier problems with the animal. After her third ride, Eckis was attacked and severely injured. After filing a workers' compensation claim and a personal injury suit against her employer, the California Court of Appeal limited her recovery to the workers' compensation benefits and struck the jury award for damages. *Eckis v. SeaWorld Corp.*, 64 Cal. App. 3d 1 (1976)

REQUIREMENTS TO RECOVER WORKERS' COMPENSATION BENEFITS. The injury or illness in question must arise out of the course and scope of employment. If the injury occurs during the employee's personal time, the injury is not covered. Another basis for making a compensable workers' compensation claim exists if the employee can establish that the personal injury arose out of the employment. This means that the injuries must have a causal connection with the risks that are incident to employment.

The following case presents an interesting example of an employee's contention that her injuries did not arise out of the course and scope of her employment.

CASE 16.1

WHEN INJURED AT WORK ON A DAY OFF, EMPLOYEE'S REMEDY IS LIMITED TO WORKERS' COMPENSATION

BEASLEY v. NEZI, LLC

227 So. 3d 308 (2017)

Court of Appeal of Louisiana

Jocelyn Beasley (Beasley) worked as the manager of a Subway owned by Nezi, LLC (Nezi) and located in Baker, Louisiana. On Beasley's day off, she received a phone call from an employee at the Subway store stating that the ice machine was not working, resulting in no ice for the lunchtime orders. She called the store supervisor, who could not help with the problem. Beasley decided to bring ice to the store. Upon her arrival, she walked toward the ice machine and slipped in a puddle of water, sustaining personal injuries. As a result, Beasley sued Nezi in tort and argued her co-workers had created an unreasonable risk of harm by allowing water to pool on the floor. Further, she argued that her remedy was not limited to workers' compensation as it was her day off and she was delivering the ice without receiving compensation and not under the control of Nezi. Her employer argued that the accident had occurred in the scope of Beasley's employment and that her remedies were limited to a workers' compensation claim. The district court granted this motion and dismissed the case. Beasley appealed.

Language of the Court. *The principal criteria for determining "course of employment" are time, place, and employment activity. An accident occurs in the course of employment when the employee sustains an injury while actively engaged in the performance of her duties during work hours, either on the employer's premises or at other places where employment activities take the employee. An accident arises out of employment if the employee was engaged about her employer's business and the conditions or obligations of the employment cause the employee in the course of employment to be at the place of the accident at the time the accident occurred.*

Beasley maintains her injury did not arise out of or occur in the course of her employment because (1) the accident occurred when she was not scheduled to work, (2) she was not obligated by her employment to take any of the actions she took, and (3) she was not being paid at the time of the accident. However, these factors alone are not necessarily determinative.

The allegations of the petition establish that Beasley is employed as a manager for the defendant, went to her place of employment to assist with an employment-related issue (a broken ice machine), and, while there, was injured when she slipped and fell walking to the ice machine. The origin of her injury is employment rooted, regardless of whether she was being directly compensated at the time for her efforts. The allegedly "gratuitous" nature of her efforts does not change the fact that the reason she was called to respond to the ice machine problem was because she was a manager at the restaurant. Her responsive acts of calling the supervisor, obtaining and delivering ice to the restaurant, agreeing to look at the ice machine, and traversing the area where her accident occurred, are inextricably linked to her employment as a Subway manager. Beasley's accident was directly related, by time and place, to her employment.

Decision. The Court of Appeal of Louisiana affirmed the district court's decision, finding that Beasley's injury occurred in the scope of her employment despite the fact that she was not scheduled to work that day.

Focus on Ethics

Beasley would have recovered more compensation for her injuries if she had been able to prove that the accident occurred outside the course and scope of her employment. She would have sued in tort in that case, but instead she was limited to recovering only what workers' compensation paid her. Under these facts, was she fairly treated under the law?

Similarly, when state workers' compensation law provides that when travel is an essential part of employment, the risks associated with the necessity of eating, sleeping, and ministering to personal needs away from home are an incident of the employment, even though the employee is not actually working at the time of injury. *Providence Corp. Dev. v. Buma*, 531 P.3d 1263 (Nev. 2023)

Medicare and Social Security

Both federal and state governments participate in insurance programs that are aimed at protecting employees' income after retirement, disability, death, hospitalization, or unemployment. These programs are commonly known as Medicare and Social Security.

Medicare

Medicare is a health insurance program provided by the federal government for the benefit of those over age 65, as well as those below age 65 and disabled. People with Medicare insurance can use the insurance to cover hospital costs and non-hospital medical costs.

Social Security

Under the Social Security program, retired workers are eligible to receive monthly payments. These payments are made possible because under the Federal Insurance Contributions Act (FICA), both employers and employees must make contributions to Social Security.

Employee Benefit Plans

Employee Retirement Income Security Act (ERISA) Federal law setting minimum standards for protection of private employee-benefit plan participants and beneficiaries. Law requires disclosure and reporting of information and sets standards of conduct, duties, and obligations for plan fiduciaries, and remedies.

The **Employee Retirement Income Security Act (ERISA)** is the major federal act regulating employee retirement plans. Retirement plans may be characterized as either a defined benefit pension plan or a defined contribution plan according to how the benefits are determined. In the first type, employers guarantee a certain payout or monthly stipend at retirement. This is usually calculated based on the employee's salary and the number of years of participation in the plan. The second type, the defined contribution plan, will provide a payout at retirement that will vary among participants based on the amount of money each contributed (or that was contributed by employers on employees' behalf, as through matching programs) and the performance of the investments made with these contributions.

Welfare benefit plans are any other type of benefit plan covered by ERISA that is not a retirement plan. These include plans, funds, and programs providing medical, surgical, or hospital care; vision or dental benefits; benefits in the event of sickness, accidental disability, unemployment, or death; as well as day care and educational assistance programs. For these types of plans, states may enact supplementary laws that do not conflict with federal law.

Overview of ERISA

ERISA attempts to create a uniform federal system for regulating employee benefit plans, and to prevent conflicting state and local laws and regulations. While pension law has been federally preempted, they have been able to retain jurisdiction in important welfare benefits arenas such as health insurance.

- Title I of ERISA provides for protection of employee benefit rights. Specifically, Title I regulates reporting and disclosure, participation requirements, minimum vesting standards, benefit protections for spouses, fiduciary responsibilities, administration and enforcement, and preemption of state laws.
- Title II covers Internal Revenue Code provisions that relate to ERISA. Title II outlines the requirements for a retirement plan to receive tax-favored or qualified treatment.
- Title III details the jurisdiction, administration, and enforcement of ERISA, providing that the Departments of Labor and Treasury will coordinate efforts to enforce ERISA requirements.
- Title IV creates the Pension Benefit Guaranty Corporation (PBGC). The PBGC provides for federally insured benefits when plans are terminated with insufficient resources to meet future plan obligations to participants.

COBRA and HIPAA

Congress passed the **Consolidated Omnibus Budget Reconciliation Act of 1986 (COBRA)** to address the problem arising when a private-sector employee loses health insurance following termination of employment. COBRA allows employees to continue health benefits at their individual expense. This Act gives workers and their families who lose their health benefits because of separation from their employment the right to choose to continue the group health benefits provided by the group health plan for a limited period.

Consolidated Omnibus Budget Reconciliation Act (COBRA)
Federal law providing some employees with the ability to continue health insurance coverage for a limited time after leaving employment.

To become eligible for COBRA continuation coverage, the individual must have been enrolled in the employer's health plan when the covered employee was working, and the health plan must continue to be in effect for active employees.

The Department of Labor provides information relating to COBRA at https://www.dol.gov/general/topic/health-plans/cobra.

The **Health Insurance Portability and Accountability Act (HIPAA)** protects health insurance coverage for workers and their families who experience a change or loss of employment. Also, HIPAA requires that healthcare providers, health insurance plans, and employers follow specific requirements regarding the security and privacy of health data. HIPAA amended ERISA.

Health Insurance Portability and Accountability Act (HIPAA)
Federal law that provides protections from disclosures of personal health information.

Immigration Law in the Workplace

Undocumented aliens are non-U.S. citizens who enter the United States without permission, overstay their visa, or whose immigration status does not permit employment in the United States. The employer of such persons faces civil and criminal penalties for hiring and continuing to employ unauthorized aliens.

For more information on HIPAA, see https://www.hhs.gov/hipaa/index.html.

Immigration Reform and Control Act (IRCA)

Immigration Reform and Control Act (IRCA) Federal law prohibiting discrimination against applicants and employees based upon their citizenship or national origin.

Intending to control illegal immigration by sanctioning those who employ undocumented immigrants in the United States, Congress enacted the **Immigration Reform and Control Act (IRCA)** in 1986. The Act attempts to control immigration by prohibiting the knowing employment of undocumented aliens by requiring employers to verify the eligibility for employment of prospective workers. The Illegal Immigration Reform and Immigration Responsibility Act (IIRIRA) amended IRCA and clarified the acceptable documentation to be submitted to an employer.

EMPLOYMENT RECRUITMENT AND RETENTION. IRCA makes it unlawful for employers, or those who recruit or refer potential workers to employers for a fee, to knowingly hire, recruit, or refer unauthorized aliens for employment in the United States. It also makes it unlawful for an employer to continue to employ an alien knowing that they are, or have become, an unauthorized alien with respect to such employment.

To review the I-9 form: https://www.uscis.gov/sites/default/files/document/forms/i-9.pdf.

EMPLOYMENT VERIFICATION. IRCA requires employers to examine specified documents of new employees to ensure the employees are authorized to work in the United States. This examination occurs *after* the employee's acceptance of an offer of employment conditioned upon his or her eligibility to be employed in the United States.

For a review of the applicable penalties, see https://www.uscis.gov/i-9-central.

Bureau of Immigration and Customs Enforcement (ICE) Federal investigation and enforcement agency within the Department of Homeland Security that enforces federal statutes relating to national security and public safety, including immigration enforcement, visa fraud, and counterterrorism.

IRCA requires employers to complete Form I-9 for each employee. This form is the employer's verification that, under penalty of perjury, all its employees are U.S. citizens or aliens authorized to work in the United States. In addition, the hired individuals must attest to their own eligibility. The Act requires employers to keep records for each employee showing their eligibility to work in the United States. Employers must make these records available for inspection upon reasonable notice by the **Bureau of Immigration and Customs Enforcement (ICE)**, a division of the United States Citizenship and Immigration Services (USCIS). ICE may compel uncooperative employers to produce the records by serving subpoenas upon the employer.

EMPLOYER PENALTIES. IRCA is violated if the employer has knowledge of an employee's unauthorized work status or if the employer deliberately fails to investigate suspicious circumstances. While there are many levels of fines for various violations, a Form I-9 paperwork violation will result in fines per violation and depending upon the employer's history of compliance with the statute. If an employer has a pattern or practice of immigration employment violations, the employer's principals may be subject to criminal prosecution.

Everywhere immigrants have enriched and strengthened the fabric of American life. —John F. Kennedy, Thirty-fifth President of the United States (1917-1963)

E-Verify Program

For more information, review the following federal website: https://www.e-verify.gov/.

The E-Verify program arose from a presidential executive order requiring federal contractors and subcontractors to verify employee eligibility to work in the United States. The federal government will award contracts only to those firms that enroll in the E-Verify system. This online program uses federal databases to confirm if a worker is authorized to work in the country.

Management Application
U.S. Employment of Foreign Nationals

The Immigration and Naturalization Act of 1965 abolished an earlier quota system based on national origin. It established a new immigration policy based on reuniting immigrant families and attracting skilled labor to the United States. The visas most often encountered include the following:

- **H-1B:** Persons in "specialty occupations" requiring a bachelor's degree or higher (limited to six years of employment) may be accorded an H-1B visa. The visa is reserved for those in positions requiring both theoretical and practical application of highly specialized knowledge. The spouse and children of a person in H-1B status may apply to reside in the United States during the same period.
  - Unlike other classifications of nonimmigrant visa applicants, the H-1B applicant does not have to prove a negative, namely, that they do not intend to immigrate to the United States.
  - An H-1B applicant can intend to work in the country temporarily in H-1B status and to immigrate permanently at a later point in time.
  - The law requires employers to pay H-1B employees at least the prevailing wage in the area where the work will be performed or the actual wage paid other employees with the same job description and qualifications, whichever wage rate is higher. This requirement protects American workers from an influx of foreign workers seeking to work for lower wages. These classifications are granted on the basis that these people are priority workers entitled to special preferences.
- **E5, L, and O:**
  - E5 visas are issued to investors (and their spouses and unmarried children under 21) if they: make the necessary investment in a commercial enterprise in the United States and plan to create or preserve 10 permanent full-time jobs for qualified U.S. workers.
  - L visas are issued to temporary high-level employees in intracompany transfers from a foreign subsidiary to a U.S. operation (limited to seven years of employment for executives and senior managers and five years for those with "specialized knowledge").
  - O visas are issued to persons with "extraordinary ability in the sciences, arts, education, business or athletics," as demonstrated by evidence of national or international recognition.

Labor Law in the Workplace

The desire of workers to organize and fully enjoy the benefits of their labor has a storied past within American history. In this section, we will study one of the exceptions to the at-will rule of employment. An employer's right to discharge an employee can be modified by a **collective bargaining agreement**.

Collective bargaining agreement
A negotiated agreement between a labor union and an employer.

Labor union
Organization or association of individuals formed for the purpose of negotiating with employers on behalf of employees regarding rates of pay, wages, hours of employment, or other conditions of employment.

A **labor union** is an organization or association of individuals formed for the purpose of negotiating with employers on behalf of employees with regard to the terms and conditions of employment.

Before the enactment of the Norris-LaGuardia Act in 1932, a federal court could issue injunctions prohibiting a union's threatened or actual strike, picketing, or boycotting of a company. The Act removed legal and judicial impediments to organizing unions. It declared that union members would have the freedom of association guaranteed to them under the First Amendment. It also barred federal courts from issuing injunctions to prevent lawful strikes, picketing, or boycotts.

National Labor Relations Act (NLRA)

In 1935, Congress enacted the National Labor Relations Act (NLRA), which radically changed federal policy toward the rights of workers to organize and bargain collectively. This legislation substantially preempts the ability of states to enact legislation involving union activities. Also known as the Wagner Act, the NLRA accomplished the following:

Unfair labor practice
Conduct and practices by either employers or unions determined under the NLRA or by the NLRB to be unlawful.

- Recognized the right of employees to organize and join a labor union
- Encouraged collective bargaining agreements (an agreement between the employer and organized workers over wages, hours, rules, and working conditions)
- Created the National Labor Relations Board (NLRB), empowered to supervise union elections, conduct administrative law hearings on **unlawful labor practice** charges, and take appropriate legal action to secure a remedy against such practices
- Outlawed company unions

Example: The NLRB has held that the company's action committees were established in a nonunion company to assist in improving quality-assurance programs. These committees were established to deal with morale problems, resulting in a change in the attendance bonus policies. Participation on committees was voluntary, and the committees discussed wages, bonuses, incentive pay, attendance programs, and leave policy. The administrative law judge found that they were unlawful. The Board held that the action committees were labor organizations and that the company's conduct toward them constituted unlawful domination and interference. *Electromation, Inc. v. NLRB*, 35 F.3d 1148 (7th Cir. 1994)

Concerted protected activities
Right of a worker to address work-related issues with an employer, government agency, or the media.

- Identified unfair labor practices of both employers and unions (that is, unlawful practices)
- Established the procedures by which union organization would occur
- Forbade employer interference with respect to organizing, bargaining, or engaging in **concerted protected activities** by workers (defined by the NLRB as any activity of two or more employees who attempt to improve their working conditions, such as wages and benefits)

Example: Two or more employees request an employer to improve fringe benefit packages offered to employees. The NLRA also covers a single worker speaking on behalf of one or more co-workers about protected subjects. These employees do not have to be members of a union to be protected under the NLRA.

- Recognized the use of lawful strikes
- Protected union members from discrimination by their unions
- Made it unlawful for an employer to refuse to bargain in good faith with a union or nonunion employee engaged in concerted action concerning wages, hours, and other terms and conditions of employment.

Example: Section 7 of the NLRA protects non-supervisory employees from employer retaliation when they discuss their wages or working conditions with their colleagues as part of a concerted activity to improve them, even if there is no union or other formal organization involved in the effort. The NLRB enforces these employee rights. Nevertheless, the NLRA does not address all situations where employers prohibit or discourage employees from discussing their pay with their colleagues.

- Provides that if the union wins a representation election, the union is the exclusive representative of the employees. The union has this position until the employees choose to decertify the union as their bargaining representative. (Unions lose more elections than they win.) The employer may not act unilaterally in any matter within that category of bargaining. The employer may not deal directly with individual employees or groups of employees on such issues.

For more information, visit the NLRB website at https://nlrb.gov/.

Taft-Hartley Act

The Taft-Hartley Act, more formally known as the Labor-Management Relations Act (LMRA), amended the NLRA in 1947. The Act restricted the activities and power of unions in the following ways:

- Outlawed "closed shops" (that is, places in which employees are required to maintain union membership as a condition of employment)
- Required unions to file financial reports with the U.S. Department of Labor
- Stopped the practice of employers' payments to union officials

In response to U.S. Senate hearings on the influence of communism and organized crime in the major unions and employers, Congress enacted the Labor-Management Reporting and Disclosure Act in 1959. The Act promotes enhanced governmental regulation of internal union members, such as union elections.

In the following case, the NLRB considered if an employer violated federal labor law by barring pay discussions and enforcing an overly broad confidentiality policy.

CASE 16.2

CONCERTED ACTIVITY IS THE INTENT TO INDUCE GROUP ACTION

MCPc, INC. v. NLRB

813 F.3d 475 (2016)

United States Court of Appeals for the Third Circuit

During an employee team-building meeting, Jason Galanter, a senior solutions architect based in Pittsburgh, discussed how busy everyone was because of an engineer shortage. He told the director of engineering that he was working many hours a week and urged him to hire additional engineers to alleviate the employees' unduly heavy workloads. Galanter stated that MCPc could afford several additional engineers with the $400,000 salary it was paying a recently hired executive.

A couple of co-workers expressed agreement with Galanter. When the company's CEO learned about the comment about the executive's salary, he investigated how Galanter learned the confidential salary information. The employer asserted that Galanter lied to the company officials during the investigation. The NLRB concluded that the employer's policy barring discussion of salary information was overbroad. It would not support a valid ground for terminating Galanter. The NRLB held such complaints were protected concerted activity under the NLRA. The company appealed.

Language of the Court. *The Board has the authority to broadly construe "concerted activity" and has interpreted the term to cover not only the union and pre-union efforts of groups of employees seeking to protect their rights, but also certain actions undertaken by individuals in the unionized and non-unionized workplace. Furthermore, the Board has stated it recognizes individual conduct as concerted both where the individual employees seek to initiate or to induce or to prepare for group action and where individual employees bring truly group complaints to the attention of management.*

Galanter appears to have complained to management to improve his working position without the imprimatur of other employees, but arguably also to induce group action in the interest of those employees. Moreover, we conclude that Galanter engaged in concerted activity when he communicated his dissatisfaction about shared working conditions to a member of MCPc's management during the February 24th lunch. Although the lunch was not organized for the express purpose of discussing any particular policy, it nonetheless was a team building lunch that provided a group forum within which Galanter could relay to management complaints shared by other employees about workplace conditions they wished to see improved. In addition, any doubt as to whether Galanter's statements qualify as concerted activity is dispelled by the fact that two other employees expressed their agreement when Galanter urged MCPc to hire more engineers and contended that the company had the financial ability to do so.

Moreover, that an employee expresses grievances that are well-known or widely held does not undermine the concerted nature of his activity. MCPc argues that, when considered in conjunction with his failure to organize other employees before or after the lunch, the fact that the engineer shortage was a problem already acknowledged and in the process of being addressed by management is fatal to Galanter's contention that his complaints constituted concerted activity. We disagree. That the engineer shortage was a subject of general concern within the company, if anything, supports rather than undercuts the conclusion that Galanter voiced his grievances for the benefit of others as well as himself.

In short, MCPc's arguments fail because they espouse an unduly cramped interpretation of concerted activity, one that assesses concerted activity in terms of isolated points of conduct rather than the totality of the circumstances.

We conclude Galanter engaged in concerted activity when he communicated his dissatisfaction about shared working conditions to a member of MCPc's management during the lunch. Where the Board found that Galanter's complaints about excessive workloads at the February 24th team building lunch related to improving working conditions for not only himself but also his coworkers and evinced an intent to galvanize his fellow employees into action, the complaints cannot be dismissed as "mere griping" about a condition of employment, except in the absence of substantial supporting evidence. We therefore agree with the Board that those complaints constituted concerted activity.

Decision. The court held that Galanter's complaints about excessive workloads at a team-building lunch related to improving working conditions for not only himself but also his co-workers. As such, these were protected activities. However, the court remanded the case to the Board to determine if the evidence would support terminating Galanter because of his improper access to confidential information.

Focus on Ethics

Federal regulators are intent on protecting the right of employees to complain about their work conditions. What ethical practices may employers adopt to limit disparaging employee comments about pay or working conditions?

Lawful Strikes and Picketing

RIGHT TO STRIKE. Strikes and picketing are included among the concerted activities protected by the NLRA. Strikes and the threat of strikes are important tools for organized labor. In a strike, employees withhold their labor; they refuse to return to work until the employer agrees to changes in the terms of the labor-management agreement. Whether a strike is lawful is not easy to determine; the NLRB often makes this decision.

TYPES OF STRIKERS. Employees who strike for a lawful object fall into two classes: "economic strikers" and "unfair labor practice strikers." Both classes continue as employees, but unfair labor practice strikers have greater rights of reinstatement to their jobs. Employees who participate in an unlawful strike may be discharged and are not entitled to reinstatement.

If the object of a strike is to obtain economic concessions such as higher wages, shorter hours, or better working conditions from the employer. In that case, the striking employees are called **economic strikers**. They retain their status as employees and cannot be discharged, but their employer can replace them.

Economic strikers Workers who strike to obtain an economic concession from the employer, such as better pay, benefits, or working conditions.

Employees who strike to protest an unfair labor practice committed by their employer are **unfair labor practice strikers**. The employer may neither discharge nor permanently replace them. When the strike ends, unfair labor practice strikers, absent serious misconduct on their part, are entitled to have their jobs back, even if replacement employees must be discharged.

Unfair labor practice strikers Workers who strike to protest conduct and practices by either employers or unions determined to be unlawful.

BACK PAY. If the NLRB finds that economic strikers or unfair labor practice strikers who have made an unconditional request for reinstatement have been unlawfully denied reinstatement by their employer. In that case, the NLRB may award such strikers back pay starting from the time they should have been reinstated.

RIGHT TO PICKET. Picketing is the lawful gathering of persons outside an employer's place of business. It is lawful conduct if it is done by persons in furtherance of a trade dispute at or near the place of work. It can only involve the peaceful communication of information or the persuasion of another person to abstain from working. While there are many types of picketing, its legality depends on the circumstances. As with the right to strike, picketing can be prohibited because of its object or its timing or due to misconduct on the picket line. Examples of unlawful activities relating to picketing include:

- Mass picketing in such numbers that non-striking employees are physically barred from entering the employer's facility
- Threats of force or violence on the picket line
- Fining or expelling members for crossing an unlawful picket line or one that is in violation of a collective bargaining agreement

Impasse The stage of not reaching an agreement, where both parties believe further negotiations would be fruitless.

IMPASSE. When no agreement is reached, an **impasse** occurs. Both parties believe that further negotiation would be fruitless. It will last for as long as the parties remain deadlocked in their views on one or more of the mandatory topics of negotiations. If both sides have made substantive proposals, provided relevant information, and continue negotiating, the parties can avoid being charged with a failure to bargain in good faith — an unfair labor practice.

Lockouts

Lockout When an employer refuses to allow employees to return to work without a signed contract.

A **lockout** occurs when an employer refuses to allow employees to return to work without a signed contract. A lockout may occur for several reasons. Following the expiration of a labor agreement, the employer might choose to keep the employees from working despite the employees' interest in continuing to work. The employer might do so because it fears that the union might strike in the future at a more inopportune time for the employer and might also do so when it senses that only part of a union will vote to strike. In that case, the lockout may put pressure on the union and its membership by reducing the number of members who are able to sustain themselves when not working.

An employer may also impose a lockout if the anticipated strike would severely hamper the work of non-striking workers or if violence or damage to the plant and equipment occurs or is threatened. An employer may hire temporary replacement workers following a lockout. Quite often, lockouts are used when union membership decides to reject the company's last, best offer at negotiations and offers to return to work under the same conditions of employment as existed under the expired contract. While employers attempt to provoke a strike, unions counter with work slowdowns.

AI Feature: Collegiate Athletes as Employees

Using an internet search engine, research the court decisions that have supported treating college athletes as employees. The history of their classification as student-athletes is rooted in a 1950's effort to avoid workers' compensation claims posed by injured athletes. Recent case law reflects a changing societal attitude to their entitlement. Using an AI program prepare a memorandum on their current status as employees and their entitlement to compensation. Should they be eligible for overtime? If so, how would the time spent as an employee be captured and verified?

Key Terms

- Bureau of Immigration and Customs Enforcement (ICE), 392
- Collective bargaining agreement, 393
- Concerted protected activities, 394
- Consolidated Omnibus Budget Reconciliation Act (COBRA), 391
- Economic strikers, 397
- Employee Retirement Income Security Act (ERISA), 390
- Employment at-will, 378
- Exempt employee, 381
- Fair Labor Standards Act (FLSA), 380
- Family and Medical Leave Act (FMLA), 384
- Health Insurance Portability and Accountability Act (HIPAA), 391
- Immigration Reform and Control Act (IRCA), 392
- Impasse, 398
- Labor union, 394
- Lockout, 398
- Occupational Safety and Health Act (OSH Act), 386
- Overtime, 381
- Portal-to-Portal Act, 383
- Unfair labor practice, 394
- Unfair labor practice strikers, 398
- Whistleblowing, 379
- Workers' compensation, 387
- Wrongful discharge, 378

Applying the Law

16.1 Handbook Liability. Anthony Nicosia was hired by Wakefern Food Corporation and terminated after 18 years of service. Wakefern claimed that Nicosia had stolen merchandise from the company. Nicosia contends that he was terminated without receiving the benefit of the progressive discipline steps outlined in an 11-page section of the employee manual distributed to all employees. The 11-page section did not contain a disclaimer that immediate termination could occur in the event of serious offenses. Nicosia claimed that the manual created an implied employment contract and that Wakefern breached it by terminating him without following the manual's procedural protections. How should the court rule on Nicosia's claim? *Nicosia v. Wakefern Food Corp.*, 643 A.2d 554 (N.J. Super. Ct. 1994)

16.2 On-Call Time. ITT-Rayonier, a pulp mill operation in Hoquiam, Washington, operated 24 hours a day, seven days a week. Rather than establishing a separate maintenance department for night shifts, the employer's regular policy was to telephone its regular daytime mechanics at home after hours to return to the plant and fix the equipment. The calls could occur at any time of night. After formalizing the policy, employees were required to accept a "fair share" of these call-ins. The employees filed suit under the FLSA seeking overtime compensation for the hours they were required to be available for on-call requests. What factors would you think are important in deciding whether the on-call time was compensable? How should the court rule? *Owens v. Local 169, Ass'n of W. Pulp & Paper Workers*, 971 F.2d 347 (9th Cir. 1992)

16.3 Overtime. Stefani Germanotta, also known as "Lady Gaga," employed Jennifer O'Neill as a personal assistant for two years. O'Neill always traveled with Lady Gaga on tour and agreed to $75,000 per year as her total compensation. O'Neill was never off work and alleged that she worked 24/7. Allegedly, there were times when Lady Gaga would wake O'Neill up in the middle of the night to take care of administrative tasks. Additionally, O'Neill oversaw Lady Gaga's entire schedule—including time for hair, makeup, rehearsal, and press dates. She also handled all her luggage—generally 20 bags including clothing, accessories, makeup, and toiletries. She was responsible for ensuring that the singer received her "special food" at every location. Even when O'Neill was on vacation, she had her phone on her 24/7 and would have to vary her schedule based on Lady Gaga's needs. When reading this chapter, consider if O'Neill would be classified as an exempt employee and not entitled to overtime. Would her on-call time constitute compensable work hours? Should New York law apply because O'Neill was domiciled in New York and her travel throughout the country involved only temporary assignments? *O'Neill v. Mermaid Touring Inc.*, 968 F. Supp. 2d 572 (S.D.N.Y. 2013)

16.4 Failure to Pay Overtime and Minimum Wages. DIRECTV®, through its provider agreements, required technicians to receive their work assignments through a centralized system operated by DIRECTV. DIRECTV also mandated that technicians check in with DIRECTV before and after completing each assigned job, conduct installations and repairs strictly according to DIRECTV's standardized policies and procedures, and interact with DIRECTV employees to activate satellite television service during each installation. The provider agreements also authorized DIRECTV employees to exercise quality control oversight over technicians, categorizing technicians' work as either compensable or non-compensable and imposing various compensation-related penalties for unsatisfactory service. Finally, the provider agreements allowed DIRECTV to effectively terminate technicians by ceasing to assign them work orders through the company's centralized work-assignment system. Claiming that they each regularly worked in excess of 40 hours per week without receiving overtime pay while serving as DIRECTV technicians. The technicians sued DIRECTV, for whom they worked, and DirectSat, which served as a middle manager between DIRECTV and individual technicians. They alleged that both companies qualified as their joint employers, and both were liable for a failure to pay overtime and minimum wages. How should the court rule? *Hall v. DIRECTV, LLC*, 846 F.3d 757 (4th Cir. 2017)

16.5 Workers Compensation. Brian Clodgo was working as a manager of Rentavision's store in Brattleboro. During a lull between customers, Clodgo began firing staples with a staple gun at a coworker who was sitting on a couch watching television. The coworker first protested, but after Clodgo had fired 20 or 30 staples at him, the coworker fired 3 staples back at Clodgo. As Clodgo ducked, the third staple hit him in the eye. Clodgo eventually reported the injury and filed a claim for worker's compensation benefits. What results? *Clodgo v. Rentavision, Inc.*, 166 Vt. 548 (1997)

16.6 Workplace Safety. Jesus Martinez was working on a pump jack—machinery that extracts oil or gas from an underground well site—when the sleeve of his sweatshirt became caught. As a result, Martinez was pulled into the moving belts and his right thumb was severed. Safety guarding did not protect the machinery even though federal regulations and industry standards required it. In his lawsuit, Martinez claimed the company was negligent in its failure to maintain its premises in a reasonably safe condition and, alternatively, that it intentionally created a condition certain to cause harm. Can the employer be held negligent for injuries that could have easily been discovered because they were an open and obvious hazard? *Martinez v. Angel Exploration, LLC*, 798 F.3d 968 (10th Cir. 2015)

16.7 Workers' Compensation. Wood worked for Centers for Youth & Families as a part-time receptionist. The atmosphere at the job was relaxed and Wood did not always stay at the front desk. Occasionally, she would check on things in the kitchen or step away to speak with members. Since she worked full-time, she had no scheduled breaks. One morning after clocking in, Wood walked to the vending machine, where she slipped on water and broke her pelvis. Do you think Wood could recover workers' compensation? More specifically, was she performing employment services when she went to the vending machine? *Centers for Youth & Families v. Wood*, 446 S.W.3d 422 (Ark. 2015)

16.8 Retaliation Claim. Pamela Blackmore-Jenkins was terminated from her employment as a Security Engineer. According to her, after she complained about sexual harassment, Security Engineers reduced her pay and opportunities to earn overtime. In addition, she filed a complaint with the Occupational Safety and Health Administration (OSHA) in which she voiced safety concerns regarding patrol vehicles, general safety concerns, reporting a female (co-worker) that created a hostile work environment, and reporting an employee for operating a vehicle under the influence of alcohol/illegal drug use. She also complained about operating vehicles without proper maintenance which caused several accidents injuring employees. After Ms. Blackmore-Jenkins filed complaints with OSHA, she claimed that Security Engineers demoted her from dispatcher to security officer and then terminated her employment with the company. Are these allegations sufficient to support a claim of OSHA retaliation? *Jenkins v. Sec. Engineers, Inc.*, 2018 U.S. Dist. LEXIS 107120 (N.D. Ala. 2018), *dismissed on other grounds*, 798 F. App'x 362 (11th Cir. 2019)

16.9 Unfair Labor Practice. When Charter Communications reassigned employees who were suspected of union organizing to rural areas it committed an unfair labor practice. The company had closely monitored union sympathizers and transferred employees to rural areas. Review the decision in *Charter Communications, Inc. v. NLRB*, 939 F.3d 798 (6th Cir. 2019), to identify what the employer had done to interfere with protected activities. If you were to counsel management about what it should have done, what advice would you have given?

16.10 Discrimination as an Unfair Labor Practice. Briscoe was a general contractor employing dozens of ironworkers on a project suffering from numerous production problems. When the entire project was shut down because of poor weather conditions, there was a general layoff. Following the layoff, five Black ironworkers filed racial discrimination charges against Briscoe with the Equal Employment Opportunity Commission. After the layoff, each of them requested to be recalled to the project, but Briscoe's job superintendent stated that Briscoe did not intend to hire the men back as long as the discrimination charges were pending. The Black ironworkers filed an unfair labor practice suit against the company because it failed to recall them to work. If racial discrimination is not an unfair labor practice under the NLRB, what argument could you make for the five ironworkers that the employer's actions constituted an unfair labor practice? *Frank Briscoe, Inc. v. NLRB*, 637 F.2d 946 (3d Cir. 1981)

Employment Discrimination

17

The promise of America is a simple promise: Every person shall share in the blessings of this land. And they shall share on the basis of their merits as a person. They shall not be judged by their color or by their beliefs, or by their religion, or by where they were born, or the neighborhood in which they live. —Lyndon B. Johnson, Thirty-sixth President of the United States (1908-1973)

Chapter Outline

- Introduction
- Title VII of the Civil Rights Act of 1964
- Defining Employment Discrimination and Harassment
- Types of Employment Discrimination

Case 17.1: *Griggs v. Duke Power Co.*
Case 17.2: *Burlington Northern & Santa Fe Ry. Co. v. White*

- Prohibited Forms of Discrimination

Case 17.4: *Bostock v. Clayton County, Georgia*

- The Equal Employment Opportunity Commission
- Management's Affirmative Defenses
- Affirmative Action
- AI Feature: Drafting an Anti-Harassment Policy

Learning Objectives

After studying this chapter, you should be able to:

1. Describe the coverage of the Civil Rights Act of 1964.
2. Define the two common forms of workplace discrimination.
3. Explain how gender discrimination may occur.
4. Identify common defenses to employment discrimination claims.

Introduction

Employment discrimination occurred for a long time in the United States before any legislative responses were enacted to prevent its occurrence. Employers could rely upon the legal recognition of "at-will" employment, which allowed them to terminate workers immediately and without cause. However, discrimination in the workplace against women, persons of color, the disabled, older workers, and others continued. Since common law remedies such as breach of contract afforded the workers no relief against the injustices perpetrated upon them by employers, legislation created the opportunity for all to enjoy fair and safe workplaces.

While reading this chapter, keep in mind that federal antidiscrimination laws are broadly supplemented by state and local legislation to combat such discrimination.

Title VII of the Civil Rights Act of 1964

Title VII
Section of the Civil Rights Act of 1964 that pertains to discrimination in employment based upon race, color, national origin, sex, and religion. This federal law prohibits most workplace discrimination and harassment. It covers employers, state and local governments, and educational institutions with 15 or more employees.

Title VII of the Civil Rights Act of 1964 made it unlawful for any business to discriminate in employment because of race, color, religion, sex, or national origin. This law also prohibits retaliation against employees who oppose such unlawful discrimination in the workplace or who testify, assist, or participate in workplace investigations. The Act applies to hiring, terms and conditions of employment, union membership and representation of union members, and employment referral services. Title VII applies only to employers who employ or employed 15 or more persons. Title VII has become the most well-known federal civil rights law. It paved the way for later legislation, that was not limited to civil rights, including the Americans with Disabilities Act of 1990, which is discussed in this chapter.

Recognize that the law in this chapter applies only to employees and not independent contractors.

Amendments to Title VII

Congress has amended Title VII four times:

1. The 1972 amendment expanded the Act's coverage and increased the powers of the Equal Employment Opportunity Commission (EEOC).
2. The Pregnancy Discrimination Act of 1978 included discrimination based on "pregnancy, childbirth, and related medical conditions." This Act has been supplemented by the Pregnant Workers Fairness Act discussed below.
3. The Civil Rights Act of 1991 legislatively reversed several Supreme Court cases relating to the burden of proof. This amendment granted the right to a jury trial and allowed plaintiffs to recover compensatory and punitive damages.
4. The Lilly Ledbetter Fair Pay Act of 2009 clarified the law relating to gender wage disparity claims.

Defining Employment Discrimination and Harassment

The meaning of the term "**employment discrimination**" is subtle. It occurs when an employer distinguishes between two individuals relative to a term or condition of employment because they belong to different protected groups. Making distinctions based on group or individual characteristics invites special scrutiny of the employer's practices. Federal law prohibits discrimination with respect to:

Employment discrimination An employer's unlawful distinction between two individuals relative to a term or condition of employment because they belong to different protected groups.

- Hiring or refusals to hire
- Promotions and discharges
- Classifications of employees
- Referrals of workers
- Acts that tend to limit, segregate, or classify employees and applicants for employment in a way that deprives them of employment opportunities or adversely affects their status

United States discrimination laws seek to eliminate workplace injustice due to characteristics over which the individual has no control. Known as **immutable characteristics**, these include individual attributes that are not subject to change, such as race, gender, national origin, and ancestry. In addition to the federal law protections, state law and local ordinances may offer broader protections. Protected characteristics of individuals under these state laws include marital status, sexual orientation, tobacco and alcohol use, pregnancy, childbirth or related medical conditions, mental disability, HIV/AIDS, arrest and criminal history records, and weight and personal appearance.

Immutable characteristics Unalterable physical traits, including skin color, hair texture, or certain facial features associated with persons of a particular race, color, sex, or national origin, even though not all members of that group necessarily share the trait.

> **Example:** The D.C. Office of Human Rights enforces the D.C. Human Rights Act, which makes discrimination illegal based on 21 protected traits for people who live, visit, or work in the District of Columbia. Review the scope of these protections at *https://ohr.dc.gov/protectedtraits.*

Dimensions of Equal Employment Opportunity

Workplace discrimination may take many forms. Those protected classifications offered by Title VII specifically extend to the individuals in the following circumstances:

Race or color: Persons of all races are included within this category. American case law has defined this term to include Blacks, Whites, persons of Latinx or Asian origin or descent, and Indigenous Americans (including Eskimos, Native Hawaiians, and Native Americans).

Ancestry and national origin: The Supreme Court has interpreted national origin as "the country where a person was born, or, more broadly, the country from which their ancestors came." It does not include discrimination based solely on citizenship.

Sex: Title VII prohibits discrimination based on gender and applies to both men and women.

Equal pay: Protections afforded each gender for differences relating to disparity in pay.

Pregnancy: Protection from discrimination of women who are pregnant or have pregnancy-related disabilities. See discussion of the Pregnant Workers Fairness Act below.

Sexual harassment: Although racial, religious, ethnic, and sexual harassment are all forms of disparate treatment, sexual harassment is treated differently. Two types are recognized:

1. *Quid pro quo* harassment (that is, unwelcome sexual advances, requests for sexual favors, and other verbal or physical conduct of a sexual nature) constitutes sexual harassment when:
   a. submission to such conduct is made either explicitly or implicitly a term or condition of employment; or
   b. submission to or rejection of such conduct by an individual is used as a basis for employment decisions affecting such individual.
2. *Hostile work environment* (that is, unwelcome sexual advances, requests for sexual favors, and other verbal or physical conduct of a sexual nature) constitutes sexual harassment having the purpose or effect of unreasonably interfering with an individual's work performance or creating an intimidating, hostile, or offensive working environment.

Sexual orientation, and gender identity, and status as transgender: The Supreme Court has stated, "Title VII prohibits all forms of discrimination because of sex; however, they may manifest themselves or whatever other labels might attach to them." *Bostock v. Clayton County, Georgia*, 590 U.S. 644 (2020)

Religion: The term "religion" includes "all aspects of religious observance and practice, as well as belief." EEOC guidelines state that protected religious practices "include moral or ethical beliefs as to what is right and wrong which are sincerely held with the strength of traditional religious views."

Disability: Legislative changes have greatly expanded the reach of the Americans with Disabilities Act (ADA). The law now defines a disability as (1) a physical or mental impairment that substantially limits a major life activity; or (2) a record of a physical or mental impairment that substantially limited a major life activity; or (3) when an entity (an employer) takes an action prohibited by the ADA based on an actual or perceived impairment.

Age: All persons 40 years of age and older are protected from discrimination because of age in hiring, promotion, discharge, compensation or terms, and conditions or privileges of employment (the Age Discrimination Act of 1975).

Other protections: Federal law also protects immigrants, members of the armed forces, and the unauthorized disclosure of genetic information.

Types of Employment Discrimination

In the final analysis, the last thing that we can take away from a person is his dignity. We will continue to preserve ourselves with dignity even if we have to suffer in silence. —Cesar Chavez, American Labor and Civil Rights Leader (1927-1993)

To demonstrate unlawful discrimination, a claimant must establish a connection between the employment condition and a prohibited act or practice of discrimination under which they suffered damages.

Federal and state laws prohibit two types of employment discrimination:

1. Intentional discrimination, otherwise known as disparate treatment; and
2. Disparate impact.

A failure to accommodate an applicant or employee in cases involving religion or disability or a retaliation claim against an individual might be considered as other types of discrimination. However, they are considered as forms of harm arising from these two types of discrimination.

Harassment is a subset of workplace discrimination. Prohibited workplace harassment has two forms. It may involve ***quid pro quo*** (Latin for "this for that") harassment, which occurs when employment decisions or treatment are based on submission to or rejection of unwelcome conduct, typically instances of a sexual nature. The second type is a **hostile work environment**. Workplace harassment may also consist of offensive conduct suffered by a person within a protected group that is so severe or pervasive that it creates a hostile or offensive work environment or an adverse employment decision (such as being fired or demoted). The recognized forms of harassment are the same as those for prohibited acts of employment discrimination because of one's race, color, national origin, sex, religion, disability, and age discrimination. An employer's careless or intentional tolerance of an ongoing pattern of offensive or derogatory comments because of protected characteristics can lead to employer liability.

Employers are liable for the acts and omissions of their employees when the employees acted within the course and scope of their employment.

Disparate Treatment

Disparate treatment focuses upon the employer's discriminatory intent and requires proof that the employer *intended* to discriminate. A *prima facie* case of employment discrimination in the form of disparate treatment discrimination requires proof that:

1. The plaintiff belongs to a protected class;
2. The plaintiff applied and was qualified for a job for which the employer was seeking applications;
3. Despite plaintiff's qualifications, plaintiff was rejected; and
4. After the rejection, the position remained open, and the employer continued to seek applicants from persons of plaintiff's qualifications.

Disparate Impact

Proof of discriminatory intent is not required in this type of discrimination. **Disparate impact** claims arise from a neutral employment practice that does not appear discriminatory on its face but is discriminatory in its *application* or *effect* upon a protected class. The employer will then attempt to prove that the challenged employment practice is a business necessity for the operation of its business. This type of discrimination is often proved by statistical data regarding the employer's practices. The employee must show a causal link between the neutral practice and the negative statistical disparity on protected class members.

In the following case, the Supreme Court interpreted the Civil Rights Act of 1964 as including disparate impact, although Congress did not expressly define it in the Act.

Harassment
Persistent, frequent, or severe, offensive, and unwanted behavior in the workplace and arises because of treating individuals unfavorably due to their protected classification. Many forms include intimidation, bullying, stalking, abusive comments, actions or gestures, or hazing.

***Quid pro quo* sexual harassment**
Unlawful conduct in which the harasser uses submission to or rejection of sexual requests as a basis for employment decisions, such as hiring, firing, compensation, and promotion. The Latin phrase translates as "this for that."

Hostile work environment
Workplace activity that is offensive, intimidating, or oppressive. Usually involves a pattern of exposure that is intentional, severe, or pervasive; affects the individual regarding the terms, conditions, or privileges of employment; and constitutes conduct that would offend a reasonable person. Management must have either known about the conduct or should have known and did nothing to stop it.

Disparate treatment
Discrimination that occurs when an individual is intentionally treated less favorably than another because of their race, color, sex, religion, national origin, age, or disability.

Disparate impact Discrimination that occurs when a neutral selection standard, unjustified by a business necessity, disqualifies particular races or groups at a significantly higher rate than it does other races or groups.

CASE 17.1

THE BUSINESS NECESSITY OF HIRING CRITERIA IS NARROWLY TAILORED TO THE POSITION

GRIGGS v. DUKE POWER CO.

401 U.S. 424 (1971)

Supreme Court of the United States

Willie Griggs, a Black employee, filed a class action lawsuit against his employer, Duke Power Company, on behalf of himself and similarly situated Black employees. He challenged the "inside" transfer policy that required employees who wanted to work in all but the lowest-paying jobs to obtain a minimum score on two separate aptitude tests and possess a high school diploma. He contended that Duke's practices unlawfully discriminated against Black employees in violation of Title VII. Duke Power defended the practice as being a business necessity for the safety of employees and the public since the work was conducted at a power plant. The district court dismissed the plaintiffs' claims. The court of appeals reversed that decision to the extent it held that residual discrimination from past employment practices was insulated from remedial action, but it affirmed the lower court's holding that absent a discriminatory purpose, the diploma and test requirements were proper. Griggs appealed to the Supreme Court.

Language of the Court. *In this case, the Court decides whether the Civil Rights Act of 1964, Title VII, prohibits an employer from requiring a high school education or the passing of a standardized general intelligence test as a condition of employment when (a) neither standard is shown to be significantly related to successful job performance, (b) both requirements operate to disqualify Black applicants at a substantially higher rate than White applicants, and (c) the jobs in question formerly had been filled only by White employees as part of a longstanding practice of giving preference to Whites. On the record before us, neither the high school completion requirement nor the general intelligence test is shown to bear a demonstrable relationship to successful performance of the jobs for which it was used. Both were adopted, as the Court of Appeals noted, without meaningful study of their relationship to job-performance ability. Rather, a vice president of the Company testified, the requirements were instituted on the Company's judgment that they generally would improve the overall quality of the work force.*

The evidence, however, shows that employees who have not completed high school or taken the tests have continued to perform satisfactorily and make progress in departments for which the high school and test criteria are now used. The promotion record of present employees who would not be able to meet the new criteria thus suggests the possibility that the requirements may not be needed even for the limited purpose of preserving the avowed policy of advancement within the Company.

Congress did not intend by Title VII, however, to guarantee a job to every person regardless of qualifications. In short, the Act does not command that any person be hired simply because he was formerly the subject of discrimination, or because he is a member of a minority group. Discriminatory preference for any group, minority or majority, is precisely and only what Congress has proscribed. What is required by Congress is the removal of artificial, arbitrary, and unnecessary barriers to employment when the barriers operate invidiously to discriminate on the basis of racial or other impermissible classification.

The Company's lack of discriminatory intent is suggested by special efforts to help the undereducated employees through Company financing of two-thirds the cost of tuition for high school training. But Congress directed the thrust of the Act to the consequences of employment practices, not simply the motivation. More than that, Congress has placed on the employer the burden of showing that any given requirement must have a manifest relationship to the employment in question. The facts of this case demonstrate the inadequacy of broad and general testing devices as well as the infirmity of using diplomas or degrees as fixed measures of capability. Diplomas and tests are useful servants, but Congress has mandated the commonsense proposition that they are not to become determinants of reality.

Nothing in the Act precludes the use of testing or measuring procedures; obviously they are useful. What Congress has forbidden is giving these devices and mechanisms controlling force unless they are demonstrably a reasonable measure of job performance. Congress has not commanded that the less qualified be preferred over the better qualified simply because of minority origins. Far from disparaging job qualifications as such, Congress has made such qualifications the controlling factor, so that race, religion, nationality, and sex become irrelevant. What Congress has commanded is that any tests used must measure the person for the job and not the person in the abstract. The judgment of the Court of Appeals is reversed.

Decision. The Supreme Court decided that the company's employment requirements were not related to applicants' ability to perform the job and were not a business necessity. They were unlawful because a facially neutral practice had discriminatory effects upon Black employees.

Focus on Ethics

Consider the inadequacy of using screening criteria such as requiring a specific undergraduate major or graduate degree or selecting candidates only from certain academic institutions in hiring decisions. What other broad screening methods have you encountered when applying for a position? Were they fair?

The business necessity defense found its origins in the *Griggs* decision, but Congress eventually codified it as part of the Civil Rights Act of 1991.[1] Under the business

1. 42 U.S.C. § 2000e-2(a)-(c).

necessity test, when the plaintiff has proved that they were subjected to the disparate impact of an employment practice, the burden shifts to the employer to clearly demonstrate that the standard at issue is "job-related." The Supreme Court has held that the employment criteria must have a "manifest relationship" to the position. The Court held that if an employment-related test has a disproportionate negative effect on a minority group, the test is permissible only if professionally accepted methods verify the test's ability to predict the essential functions of the job.

EEOC's Four-Fifths Rule

The EEOC and other federal agencies have adopted a set of guidelines entitled the Uniform Guidelines on Employee Selection Procedures. These Guidelines apply to all selection procedures "used as a basis for making employment decisions."

The Guidelines provide that decisions should be based upon meaningful differences in qualifications among candidates. Their primary focus is the effect that selection standards have on disparate impact cases. The Guidelines define the "**four-fifths**" or "**80-percent rule**" as

Four-fifths rule
An EEOC guideline that holds that a selection rate for any race, sex, or ethnic group that is less than four-fifths the selection rate of the most frequently selected group will generally be regarded as evidence of adverse impact.

> *a selection rate for any race, sex, or ethnic group that is less than four-fifths (or eighty percent) of the rate for the group with the highest rate will generally be regarded by the federal enforcement agencies as evidence of adverse impact, while a greater than four-fifths rate will generally not be regarded by federal enforcement agencies as evidence of adverse impact.*

> **Example:** If 100 Black applicants applied for positions as firefighters and 30 were hired, the selection rate would be .30 or 30 percent. If 200 White people were applicants for the same position and 100 were hired, the selection rate for White applicants would be .50 or 50 percent. A 30 percent hiring rate for Black applicants is less than the 80 percent White applicant selection rate; therefore, the selection process has a presumptive disparate impact (.30 is less than the product of .8 times .50).

Business necessity
A requirement that bears a substantial relationship to job performance.

The 80-percent rule is more of a rule of thumb for the convenience of the parties and has been subject to judicial criticism. The defendant can then rebut the plaintiff's *prima facie* case by showing that the selection method is consistent with a **business necessity**.

Retaliation
Adverse action taken against an applicant or employee by an employer because the person alleged, participated in, or pursued a claim of employment discrimination or other violation of the law.

Retaliation

Employers may not engage in **retaliation** against an employee for filing discrimination charges or participating in an employment discrimination proceeding. Claimants do not need to suffer damages to make the claim; merely that they suffered an adverse employment action. This may follow from an employee's opposition to an employer's prohibited practice or participation in a Title VII proceeding or investigation.

CASE 17.2

ANTI-RETALIATION PROVISIONS OF TITLE VII ARE TO BE BROADLY APPLIED

BURLINGTON NORTHERN & SANTA FE RY. CO. v. WHITE

548 U.S. 53 (2006)

Supreme Court of the United States

Sheila White, the only female maintenance employee in the Burlington Northern Santa Fe Railway yard in Memphis, Tennessee, complained of sexual harassment by her supervisor. In response, the employer disciplined her supervisor, but removed Sheila from her forklift duty to standard track laborer tasks. That position involved dirtier and more physically demanding effort on her part. White filed a complaint with the EEOC claiming unlawful gender discrimination and retaliation for her complaint. Burlington suspended her without pay for insubordination; however, after determining that White had not been insubordinate, the company reinstated her and gave her back pay for the days she had been suspended. At trial, a jury awarded damages to her, and the Court of Appeals for the Sixth Circuit affirmed. The employer appealed to the Supreme Court because White had not suffered any "adverse employment action." Given the conflicting decisions of the federal courts of appeal, the Supreme Court granted *certiorari.*

Language of the Court. *A section of the Civil Rights Act—its anti-retaliation provision—forbids an employer from discriminating against an employee or job applicant because that individual opposed any practice made unlawful by Title VII or made a charge, testified, assisted, or participated in a Title VII proceeding or investigation.*

The anti-retaliation provision does not confine the actions and harms it forbids to those that are related to employment or occur at the workplace. The provision covers those (and only those) employer actions that would have been materially adverse to a reasonable employee or job applicant. In the present context that means that the employer's actions must be harmful to the point that they could well dissuade a reasonable worker from making or supporting a charge of discrimination.

Applying this standard to the facts of this case, we believe that there was a sufficient evidentiary basis to support the jury's verdict on White's retaliation claim. The jury found that two of Burlington's actions amounted to retaliation: the reassignment of White from forklift duty to standard track laborer tasks and the 37-day suspension without pay. Burlington does not question the jury's determination that the motivation for these acts was retaliatory.

A reasonable employee facing the choice between retaining her job (and paycheck) and filing a discrimination complaint might well choose the former. For these reasons, the Supreme Court affirms the judgment of the Court of Appeals.

Decision. The Court established a new standard for defining the scope and materiality of actions that could be considered retaliatory under Title VII. The anti-retaliation provision is not confined to actions that are related to employment or occur at the workplace. The actions must be "harmful to the point that they could well dissuade a reasonable worker from making or supporting a charge of discrimination."

Focus on Ethics

Do you think it was ethical for the employer to claim that a retroactive payment of wages to White defeated her claim for damages?

Mixed Motive Discrimination

Mixed motive evidence An employer's evidence showing that the same adverse decision would have been made against an employee even in the absence of the impermissible motivating factor.

A **mixed motive** case is one in which the claim involves both legitimate and unlawful reasons for the adverse employment decision. In mixed motive evidence cases, an unlawful employment practice is established when the plaintiff demonstrates that discrimination because of a protected classification was a motivating factor for the employer's actions, even though other factors also motivated the practice. An employer's evidence must prove that the same adverse decision would have been made even in the absence of the impermissible motivating factor.

Example: Catharina Costa had been fired from her job at a Las Vegas casino. She sued for gender discrimination. The district court instructed the jury to determine that if gender discrimination was a motivating factor in the firing she could prevail, even if other lawful reasons for her termination existed. The Supreme Court held that in order to obtain a mixed motive jury instruction, a plaintiff needs only to present enough evidence for a reasonable jury to conclude by a preponderance of the evidence that a protected characteristic was a *motivating factor* for any employment practice. *Desert Palace v. Costa*, 539 U.S. 90 (2003).

Constructive Discharge

Constructive discharge Employee resigns their job because of intolerable, extraordinary, and egregious workplace conditions.

If the employee resigns because working conditions are so intolerable that any reasonable person in that employee's position would resign, the employer can be liable for **constructive discharge** of the employee. Constructive discharge is neither a tort nor a breach of contract, but a rule that transforms a resignation into a wrongful discharge. Constructive discharge occurs when the *conditions causing the employee to resign* are *extraordinary and egregious* as to go beyond any that might ordinarily lead someone to quit a displeasing job.

- Single, isolated acts of misconduct or personal irritation are insufficient to constitute constructive discharge.

- The conditions must be such that a reasonable employee would not be able to tolerate them.
- The worker must have given the employer actual notice of those conditions.

Example: Repeated instances of sexually harassing behavior by supervisors caused an employee to quit their job. The employee left the company because prior complaints to senior managers about their behavior were ignored. In this situation, the employer may be found liable for constructive discharge.

Prohibited Forms of Discrimination

Race and Color Discrimination

Section 1981 was enacted as the Civil Rights Act of 1866. The Supreme Court has held that although Section 1981 does not itself use the word "**race**," the statute forbids all "racial" discrimination in the making of both private and public contracts. It has recognized that Section 1981 prohibited discrimination in private-sector employment.

Under Title VII, **racial discrimination** involves treating an applicant or an employee unfavorably because they are of a certain race or because of personal characteristics associated with a certain race (such as hair texture, skin color, or facial features).

Example: Racial discrimination includes discrimination based on ancestry or ethnic characteristics. For example, Mamdouh El-Hakem, who was of Arabic heritage, sued his former employer and the company's chief executive officer (CEO), for employment discrimination claiming that the CEO had created a racially hostile work environment. The CEO repeatedly referred to El-Hakem as "Manny" despite El-Hakem's objection to using the non-Arabic name instead of his own. The CEO insisted on using this "more Western" name. The federal appellate court held that the CEO's "intentional conduct created a hostile work environment because his conduct was sufficiently pervasive to create a work environment racially hostile to a reasonable Arab." *El-Hakem v. BJY Inc.*, 415 F.3d 1068 (9th Cir. 2005)

Color discrimination involves treating someone unfavorably in the workplace because of skin color complexion. Discrimination can occur regardless of whether the actor and victim are of the same race or **color**.

National Origin Discrimination

National origin discrimination involves the unfavorable treatment of applicants or employees because they are from a particular country or part of the world; of a particular ethnicity or have an accent; or appear to be of a certain ethnic background, even if they are not.

Religious Discrimination

Employees may also be victims of **religious discrimination**. Courts find beliefs to be a religion if they "occupy the same place in the life of the worker as an orthodox belief in

Section 1981
A federal law protecting individuals from intentional racial or national origin discrimination in employment and housing.

Race
A term not defined in Title VII, but usually interpreted, in the context of discrimination, in terms of ancestry or the physical or cultural characteristics associated with a certain race.

Racial discrimination
Unequal treatment in the workplace based on the race or perceived racial characteristics of a person.

Color discrimination
Discrimination based on skin color, complexion, shade, or tone, which may occur between persons of different races or between persons of the same race or ethnicity.

National origin discrimination
Treating applicants or employees unfavorably because they are from a particular country or part of the world, exhibit a certain ethnicity or accent, or appear to be of certain ethnicity even if they are not.

Religious discrimination
An employer's failure to ensure that the conditions of employment allow for an applicant's or worker's sincerely held religious, ethical, or moral beliefs and practices, unless doing so creates an undue hardship.

God holds in the life of one clearly qualified." The employee must show that the belief is "sincerely held" and "religious" in their own view of behavior, and courts must give "great weight" to the plaintiff's own characterization of their beliefs as a religion. Thus, a belief system need not have a concept of a God, a Supreme Being, or an afterlife. However, the beliefs must be more than "secular" ones.

An employer must make a reasonable accommodation for the employee's practices unless it creates **undue hardship** for the employer.

Undue hardship (religious discrimination) The employer must show that granting an accommodation would result in substantial increased costs for its particular business.

> **Example:** In *Groff v. DeJoy* 600 U.S. 447 (2023), the Supreme Court held that under Title VII, the employer must show that granting an accommodation would result in substantial increased costs for its particular business. The case is important because it departed from prior cases allowing employers to deny accommodations that imposed more than a "*de minimus*" or minimal cost on the employer. Thus, employees have greater rights to religious accommodations.

***De minimis* cost for accommodation** Insubstantial expense to the employer to provide a religious accommodation to an applicant or employee.

Gender Discrimination and Harassment

Federal law prohibits employment discrimination based upon gender, pregnancy, gender identity, gender stereotyping (that is, an individual's failure to conform to stereotypical assumptions relating to gender), and sexual orientation.

GENDER HARASSMENT. Gender harassment is a form of discrimination because it adversely affects the work environment and is based on the victim's protected characteristic (that is, one's gender).

SEXUAL HARASSMENT BY CO-WORKERS AND NONEMPLOYEES. Courts have extended the employer's liability for sexual harassment to actions by co-workers and nonemployees.

> **Example:** A blackjack dealer at a Las Vegas casino alleged she was fired in violation of Title VII in retaliation for reporting sexually charged remarks made by the casino's customers. The employer argued that it could not be held liable for the sexual harassment of its employees by their customers. The court disagreed and found the employer liable when it failed to remedy or prevent a hostile or offensive work environment of which management-level employees were aware. *Powell v. Las Vegas Hilton Corp.*, 841 F. Supp. 1024 (D. Nev. 1992)

Pregnancy Discrimination Act

Title VII prohibits employment discrimination because of pregnancy, childbirth, or related medical conditions. This act has been supplemented by the Pregnant Workers Fairness Act, which expanded protections for pregnancy discrimination by requiring covered employers to provide qualified employees reasonable accommodations to a worker's known limitations related to pregnancy, childbirth, or related medical conditions, unless the accommodation would cause the employer an undue hardship.

Equal Pay Act of 1963 (EPA) A federal law prohibiting wage differentials based on gender for positions requiring equal skill, effort, and responsibility and that are performed under similar working conditions.

Pay Disparity

The **Equal Pay Act of 1963 (EPA)** requires that male and female employees performing the same work for the same employer receive the same pay. The law requires that both sexes must be paid equal rates of pay for employees who perform equal work on jobs requiring substantially similar skill, effort, and responsibilities, and for work performed under similar working conditions. No proof of discriminatory intent is required.

> **Example:** Five standout players from the U.S. women's national soccer team filed an equal pay complaint demanding to be paid the same amount as players on the men's national team. The women's team won the Women's World Cup in 2019. In the past, the team had won three other World Cup titles, while the men's team had not won any. The women claimed that they received 28 to 62 percent less in wages than the members of the men's team. The court dismissed the equal pay claim, finding that the women rejected a pay-to-play structure like the one in the men's collective bargaining agreement and instead chose to accept greater base salaries and benefits. The U.S. Soccer Federation reached a settlement with the women's team regarding their remaining claims of unequal travel, personnel support, and accommodations.[2]

The law permits differences in compensation only if there are bona fide reasons based upon legitimate seniority systems, merit systems, and differences in productivity.

LILLY LEDBETTER ACT OF 2009. Congress enacted the Lilly Ledbetter Act of 2009. Under the Act, employees can sue at any time after the alleged discrimination occurred, as long as they received inadequate compensation in the preceding 180 days. That is, the Act made pay disparity unlawful under federal law regardless of when the disparity began. In effect, each time a person is paid a discriminatory wage, benefit, or other compensation, the person has a new 180-day period to file a charge with the EEOC.

Sexual Orientation Discrimination and Harassment

The Supreme Court has recognized sexual orientation, gender identity, and status as transgender as protected statuses. It did what Congress had not done since the enactment of the Civil Rights Act of 1964.

CASE 17.3

EMPLOYERS WHO DISCRIMINATE AGAINST APPLICANTS OR EMPLOYEES FOR BEING GAY OR TRANSGENDER VIOLATE TITLE VII

BOSTOCK v. CLAYTON COUNTY, GEORGIA

590 U.S. 644 (2020)

Supreme Court of the United States

In each of the following three cases, an employer fired a long-time employee not long after the employee's status as gay or transgender was revealed.

2. "Women's Team, US Soccer Settle Part of Their Lawsuit," *https://apnews.com/article/international-soccer-soccer-womens-soccer-lawsuits-courts-19b5599494006be69d6162ecd35058a3* (last accessed November 27, 2024).

Gerald Bostock worked as a child welfare advocate for Clayton County, Georgia. After ten years of service for the county, Bostock joined a gay recreational softball league. Soon after, prominent members of the community spoke out against Bostock's sexual orientation and participation in the softball league. Bostock was later fired for conduct "unbecoming" a county employee.

Donald Zarda worked for Altitude Express on Long Island, New York, for several seasons as a skydiving instructor. After revealing his sexual orientation to a customer at the skydiving business, Zarda was fired by the company.

When Aimee Stephens began working at R.G. & G.R. Harris Funeral Homes in Garden City, Michigan, she presented herself as male. Two years later, clinicians diagnosed Stephens with gender dysphoria and advised her to start living as a woman. After working for the funeral home for six years, Stephens wrote a letter to her employer stating that she intended to "live and work full-time as a woman." In response, the funeral home fired Stephens.

Each employee filed suit against their respective employers under Title VII for unlawful discrimination because of sex. The Court of Appeals for the Eleventh Circuit dismissed Bostock's case, finding that Title VII does not prohibit employers from firing employees for being gay. The Court of Appeals for the Second Circuit came to a different conclusion in Zarda's case, holding that sexual orientation discrimination does violate the federal law. In Stephens's case, the Court of Appeals for the Sixth Circuit ruled similarly to the Second Circuit and held that employers who fire employees because of their transgender status violate Title VII. The Supreme Court granted *certiorari* to determine if Title VII protects gay and transgender persons.

Language of the Court. *From the ordinary public meaning of the statute's language at the time of the law's adoption, a straightforward rule emerges: An employer violates Title VII when it intentionally fires an individual employee based in part on sex. It doesn't matter if other factors besides the plaintiff 's sex contributed to the decision. And it doesn't matter if the employer treated women as a group the same when compared to men as a group. If the employer intentionally relies in part on an individual employee's sex when deciding to discharge the employee—put differently, if changing the employee's sex would have yielded a different choice by the employer—a statutory violation has occurred. Title VII's message is "simple but momentous": An individual employee's sex is "not relevant to the selection, evaluation, or compensation of employees."*

The statute's message for our cases is equally simple and momentous: An individual's homosexuality or transgender status is not relevant to employment decisions. That's because it is impossible to discriminate against a person for being homosexual or transgender without discriminating against that individual based on sex. Consider, for example, an employer with two employees, both of whom are attracted to men. The two individuals are, to the employer's mind, materially identical in all respects, except that one is a man and the other a woman. If the employer fires the male employee for no reason other than the fact he is attracted to men, the employer discriminates against him for traits or actions it tolerates in his female colleague. Put differently, the employer intentionally singles out an employee to fire based in part on the employee's sex, and the affected employee's sex is a but-for cause of his discharge. Or take an employer who fires a transgender person who was identified as a male at birth but who now identifies as a female. If the employer retains an otherwise identical employee who was identified as female at birth, the employer intentionally penalizes a person identified as male at birth for traits or actions that it tolerates in an employee identified as female at birth. Again, the individual employee's sex plays an unmistakable and impermissible role in the discharge decision.

That distinguishes these cases from countless others where Title VII has nothing to say. Take an employer who fires a female employee for tardiness or incompetence or simply supporting the wrong sports team. Assuming the employer would not have tolerated the same trait in a man, Title VII stands silent. But unlike any of these other traits or actions, homosexuality and transgender status are inextricably bound up with sex. Not because homosexuality or transgender status are related to sex in some vague sense or because discrimination on these bases has some disparate impact on one sex or another, but because to discriminate on these grounds requires an employer to intentionally treat individual employees differently because of their sex.

When an employer fires an employee because she is homosexual or transgender, two causal factors may be in play—both the individual's sex and something else (the sex to which the individual is attracted or with which the individual identifies). But Title VII doesn't care. If an employer would not have discharged an employee but for that individual's sex, the statute's causation standard is met, and liability may attach.

At bottom, these cases involve no more than the straightforward application of legal terms with plain and settled meanings. For an employer to discriminate against employees for being homosexual or transgender, the employer must intentionally discriminate against individual men and women in part because of sex. That has always been prohibited by Title VII's plain terms—and that "should be the end of the analysis."

Ours is a society of written laws. Judges are not free to overlook plain statutory commands on the strength of nothing more than suppositions about intentions or guesswork about expectations. In Title VII, Congress adopted broad language making it illegal for an employer to rely on an employee's sex when deciding to fire that employee. We do not hesitate to recognize today a necessary consequence of that legislative choice: An employer who fires an individual merely for being gay or transgender defies the law.

Decision. The Supreme Court reversed the judgment of the Court of Appeals for the Eleventh Circuit and affirmed the judgments of the Second and Sixth

Circuits, holding that an employer who fires someone simply for being gay or transgender has discriminated against that individual "because of such individual's sex."

Focus on Ethics

The employers in *Bostock* argued that there would be unintended sweeping consequences following the Supreme Court's decision to extend sex discrimination under Title VII to include discrimination based on sexual orientation and transgender status. Do you agree with their claim that sex-segregated bathrooms, locker rooms, and dress codes will no longer be sustainable after *Bostock*? Would the outcome of this case be different if compliance with Title VII required any of the employers to violate their religious beliefs?

Same-Sex Harassment

Same-sex harassment is unlawful under Title VII, as long as the plaintiff can establish the alleged harassment occurred *because of* their sex (that is, it would not have happened to a member of the opposite sex). The Supreme Court has considered one case involving sexual harassment of a male employee by other male employees on an oil-drilling platform, *Oncale v. Sundowner Offshore Services, Inc.*[3] In that decision, the Supreme Court held that Title VII's protection against workplace discrimination "because of sex" applied to harassment between members of the same sex in the workplace. The harassing conduct need not be motivated by sexual desire.

Workplace Bullying

When repeated, health-harming mistreatment of an individual occurs, this is considered workplace bullying. The forms may include verbal abuse and offensive conduct/behaviors (including nonverbal), which are threatening, humiliating, or intimidating. Bullying can have serious effects on its targets, including depression, sleep issues, and post-traumatic stress disorder. It can also wreck the work environment, leading to low employee morale, high turnover and absenteeism, and litigation.

> **Example:** Although there is no universally accepted definition of "bullying," one court has recognized it as a cause of action. Daniel Raess was a heart surgeon and Joseph Doescher operated the heart-lung machine during open-heart surgeries. After Raess became angry because Doescher had complained to the hospital administration about Raess's treatment of co-workers, Doescher testified that

3. *Oncale v. Sundowner Offshore Services, Inc.*, 523 U.S. 75 (1998).

Raess lost control of his temper. Doescher sued the surgeon for workplace bullying. The Supreme Court of Indiana held that workplace bullying could "be considered a form of intentional infliction of emotional distress." *Raess v. Doescher,* 883 N.E.2d 790 (Ind. 2008)

Review the laws of your state and internet sites regarding workplace bullying. Review this website regarding such abuse in the case of children: https://www.stopbullying.gov.

Current discrimination and harassment laws rarely address workplace bullying. Its occurrence is considered far more prevalent than other forms of discrimination. The law is developing to recognize workplace bullying as a cause of action. Plaintiffs can include this claim under either a claim for discrimination or for hostile work environment.

Age Discrimination

The **Age Discrimination in Employment Act of 1967 (ADEA)** protects applicants and employees who are 40 years of age or older from employment discrimination because of age. The Act applies to employers with at least 20 employees in an industry affecting interstate commerce.

Age discrimination Employment discrimination against persons age 40 or older. The ADEA does not protect workers under the age of 40, although some states have laws that protect younger workers from age discrimination.

Age Discrimination in Employment Act of 1967 (ADEA) Federal act applying to employers with 20 or more workers that are engaged in interstate commerce. Prohibits employment discrimination against persons aged 40 and older.

WHAT IS PROHIBITED? Under the ADEA, an employer may not discriminate based on age with respect to any term, condition, or privilege of employment. To succeed on an ADEA claim, the plaintiff must prove that they would not have suffered the harm "but for" the employer's intentional age-based discrimination. The Act also prohibits harassment of older workers (that is, those 40 years and older). However, the ADEA permits employers to favor older workers based on age, even when doing so affects a younger worker. Older workers can prevail in their age discrimination claims when they prove that their employer deliberately retained younger workers and offered untrue reasons for discharging older workers. Circumstantial evidence may be enough to prove age discrimination.

Example: Richard Miller worked in the supply chain management division of Raytheon© for almost three decades. Raytheon initiated a reduction in force (RIF). Management placed the then-53-year-old Miller and four other employees (ages 24, 49, 54, and 55) in a pool of people considered for termination. Miller was terminated and then subsequently applied for new jobs within Raytheon. Human Resources told Miller that he would not be hired in the supply management division and simply stated that the reason was "because you [Miller] wouldn't be considered." The court held that he was a victim of age discrimination. *Miller v. Raytheon Co.*, 716 F.3d (5th Cir. 2013)

Reasonable Factor Other than Age (RFOA) Employers may take an adverse action against an applicant or employee over age 40 if the basis of the decision is reasonable and other than one based upon the person's age.

Two significant defenses may be asserted to this form of discrimination. The employer may assert a bona fide occupational qualification (BFOQ) for the position or a defense involving public safety. For example, airlines may require a pilot to retire upon reaching 60 years of age. The employer may also assert a defense known as any **Reasonable Factor Other than Age**. The defense applies if the adverse employment decision is based upon a reasonable factor other than the person's age. This defense is unique to ADEA cases and does not apply to Title VII cases.

Disability discrimination
The less favorable treatment by a covered employer or entity of an applicant or employee because the person has a history of a disability or is believed to have a physical or mental impairment expected to last six months or longer.

Americans with Disabilities Act of 1990 (ADA)
Federal law imposing obligations upon employers and providers of public transportation, telecommunications, and public accommodations to accommodate individuals with disabilities.

Americans with Disabilities Act Amendments Act of 2008 (ADAAA)
Federal law amending the Americans with Disabilities Act of 1990 by expanding the definition of disability, requiring that the definition be broadly construed, and requiring common-sense, non-technical assessments in applying provisions of the ADA.

Review the statistics for ADA charges filed with the EEOC at https://www.eeoc.gov/data/enforcement-and-litigation-statistics-0.

Disability
A recognized physical or mental impairment that substantially limits one or more of the major life activities of the affected individual.

Disability Discrimination

Disability discrimination in employment is prohibited by the **Americans with Disabilities Act of 1990 (ADA)**, as amended by the **Americans with Disabilities Act Amendments Act of 2008 (ADAAA)**. It requires an employer to provide a reasonable accommodation to both job applicants and employees with a disability, unless doing so would cause significant difficulty or expense for the employer. The amendment requires courts to interpret the term "disability" expansively. The Act covers employers of 15 or more workers.

DISABILITY DEFINED. The term "**disability**" means a qualified individual who meets any one of the following criteria:

- Having a *physical or mental impairment that substantially limits one or more of the major life activities* of the individual;
- Having a *record of such an impairment* that substantially limited a major life activity (such as cancer that is in remission); or
- Being *regarded as having such an impairment* that is not expected to be lasting and is minor.

INDIVIDUAL WITH A DISABILITY WHO IS QUALIFIED. An **individual with a disability who is qualified** for a position is someone who, *with or without* reasonable accommodation, *can perform* the **essential functions of the job**. The employer determines what functions of a job are essential. The following questions help define the essential functions of a job:

- Does the position exist to perform a particular function?
- Are only a few employees available to perform the job function compared to the overall volume of work to be done?
- Does the work require specialized tasks?
- How much time is spent performing the particular function?

Example: The Ford Motor Company® prevailed when the EEOC sued the company under the ADA because it alleged that Ford had failed to reasonably accommodate an employee's telecommuting request. Quoting the EEOC's own guidelines, the court observed, "An employer may refuse a telecommuting request when, among other things, the job requires 'face-to-face interaction and coordination of work with other employees,' 'in-person interaction with outside colleagues, clients, or customers,' and 'immediate access to documents or other information located only in the workplace.' " *EEOC v. Ford Motor Co.*, 782 F.3d 753 (6th Cir. 2015)

PHYSICAL OR MENTAL IMPAIRMENT. The ADA has not defined "**physical or mental impairment**" due to the term's broad scope. An **impairment** is recognized as something affecting a major body system or mental or psychological state. The regulations of the ADA and court opinions require that assessments be made on a case-by-case basis to determine the presence and consequence of such impairments. The impairment will substantially limit Congress, which has mandated that disability law be broadly interpreted and applied. The term has been interpreted to mean:

- Any physiological disorder or condition, cosmetic disfigurement, or anatomical loss affecting a major body system; or
- Any mental or psychological disorder.

Example: An employee who suffered from a temporary dehydration episode was not disabled under the ADA. *Willis v. Noble Environmental Power, LLC*, 143 F. Supp. 3d 475 (N.D. Tex. 2015)

REASONABLE ACCOMMODATION. A **reasonable accommodation** is any change in the work environment (or how things are usually done) to help a disabled person apply for a job, perform the essential functions of a job, or simply enjoy the benefits and privileges of being employed.

Undue hardship to an employer means that the accommodation would be too difficult or expensive for the employer to provide upon consideration of the employer's size, financial resources, and business needs. There is no requirement under the ADA to provide the exact accommodation the employee or job applicant desires. If there is an alternative suitable accommodation, the employer may decide what accommodation to offer.

Associational Discrimination

Except for a provision within the ADA, our antidiscrimination laws do not directly address **associational discrimination**. This form arises from discrimination or retaliation against employees based on their association with members of protected classes under Title VII.

Genetic Information Protection

The **Genetic Information Nondiscrimination Act of 2008 (GINA)** makes it illegal to discriminate against employees or applicants because of their genetic information. Title II of the Act prohibits employers from using genetic information in making employment decisions and restricts employers and other covered entities from requesting, requiring, or purchasing genetic information, and strictly limits the disclosure of genetic information.

CONFIDENTIALITY OF GENETIC INFORMATION. A covered entity must keep genetic information about an applicant or employee in a separate medical file. This information could, however, be kept in the same file as other medical information in compliance with the ADA.

The Equal Employment Opportunity Commission

Title VII established the United States Equal Employment Opportunity Commission (EEOC) to enforce its provisions. A Title VII plaintiff must first file a charge of employment discrimination with the EEOC before filing a suit in federal court against the employer. The plaintiff must do so within 180 days of the alleged violation.

Individual with a disability who is qualified
A person with a disability who meets the legitimate level of skills, experience, education, or other requirements for a position and who can perform the essential functions of the job, with or without reasonable accommodation.

Essential functions of a job
The functions that an individual must be able to perform unaided or with the assistance of a reasonable accommodation.

Physical or mental impairment
Any disorder, condition, disfigurement, or anatomical loss that affects a major body system or mental or psychological state.

Impairment
Condition substantially limiting a person in the performance of one or more life activities as compared to an average person in the general population.

Major life activity
An expansive definition used in disability cases for the variety of tasks important in most people's daily lives.

The moral test of government is how it treats those who are in the dawn of life . . . the children; those who are in the twilight of life . . . the elderly; and those who are in the shadow of life . . . the sick . . . the needy . . . and the disabled. — Hubert H. Humphrey, U.S. Senator and Thirty-eighth Vice President of the United States (1911-1978)

Reasonable accommodation Modification or adjustment to a job or work environment enabling a qualified applicant or employee with a recognized disability to pursue employment or perform the essential job functions.

Undue hardship (disability) The determination that accommodation of a person's disability would be too difficult or expensive to provide, considering the employer's size, financial resources, and the needs of the business.

Associational discrimination Discrimination or retaliation against employees based on their association with members of classes protected under Title VII.

Genetic Information Nondiscrimination Act (GINA) A federal law that prohibits discrimination against applicants or employees because of genetic information.

706 agencies A state agency that contracts with EEOC to assist in the investigation of employment discrimination claims.

Exhausting administrative remedies A litigant is precluded from seeking a remedy in the court until the agency's own procedures are concluded.

The EEOC investigates the claim and, if appropriate, attempts to reach a voluntary settlement between the employer and employee. If that does not occur, the EEOC may then file a suit against the employer. It does so only in exceptional cases due to its limited resources. If the EEOC does not sue, the plaintiff may file a suit. The requirement to file a charge before a suit is known as *exhausting administrative remedies.*

An extended filing period of 300 days may be available to employment discrimination plaintiffs if they file their claims with a state employment discrimination agency. These agencies, which contract with the EEOC, are called **706 agencies** after § 706 of the Civil Rights Act of 1964. One of the purposes of 706 agencies is to help filter and screen the more serious cases requiring EEOC investigation. A state-specific 706 agency handles those cases not requiring an EEOC investigation. Known as **exhausting administrative remedies**, this process is a work-sharing arrangement between the EEOC and the state 706 agencies.

If the EEOC decides not to file a suit, a **right-to-sue letter** is issued to the claimant. That letter allows the employee to file a private lawsuit against the employer in federal court. The EEOC may dismiss a pending charge at any time if it decides in its best judgment to do so. Private litigants file most employment discrimination cases in federal court. A party who has exhausted their administrative remedies has a limited statute of limitations to file suit. The filing with the Equal Employment Opportunity Commission (EEOC) is a prerequisite to filing a suit; otherwise, the federal court lacks subject matter jurisdiction, and the case must be dismissed. For most employment discrimination claims, the claimant must file a lawsuit in federal court within 90 days after the EEOC issues the right-to-sue letter.

Management's Affirmative Defenses

An **affirmative defense** is a response by a defendant to the allegations of the plaintiff, which, if proved, either defeats or mitigates the consequences of the defendant's acts or omissions. The law recognizes that a fair legal system should permit the defendant the opportunity to either excuse or lessen the consequences of its acts and omissions. The defendant attempts to prove the alleged affirmative defenses to the plaintiff's complaint after the plaintiff has offered enough evidence to prove a *prima facie* case. A dozen or more affirmative defenses are available to employers to defend such claims. The five most frequently applied affirmative defenses are: business necessity; bona fide occupational qualification (BFOQ); seniority systems; *Faragher/Ellerth* defense; and after-acquired evidence.

Business Necessity

In a disparate impact case, if the employee proves the employer discriminated against the employee in violation of an antidiscrimination statute, the employer may then show that the requirement(s) were job-related and a business necessity. Following the defendant's proof of the defense, the worker may offer rebuttal evidence to show the employer is relying upon a **pretext**—that is, a false reason given by the employer for its decision. For example, the employer may use selection criteria that, although neutral in application, exclude members of one or more protected classes of persons at a higher rate than other groups. The plaintiff may prevail unless the employer can establish that the hiring standard is job-related and a business necessity.

> **Example:** An applicant for a warehouse labor position is required to take tests requiring intermediate knowledge of Microsoft Excel®. The essential functions of the job are inconsistent with that requirement, unless the employer can establish such skills are necessary for performing the work.

The plaintiff may still prevail on a disparate impact claim if the plaintiff can show that an alternative and effective business practice with a less discriminatory effect might have been used, and the employer refused to adopt it.

Bona Fide Occupational Qualification

An employer seeking to establish a **bona fide occupational qualification (BFOQ)** must prove that a practice that, on its face, excludes an entire protected class is justified because all or substantially all of the members are unable to perform the job requirements safely and efficiently. *The BFOQ defense is only available to disparate treatment cases and not to disparate impact cases. The BFOQ defense applies only when the criterion is essential to perform the job.* The BFOQ defense is an extremely narrow exception and is *never* a defense against race discrimination. In contrast, the business necessity defense applies to disparate impact against all protected groups. For example, having a computer science degree may be a business necessity to secure a job as a software engineer. That requirement may have a disparate impact, but it is a business necessity in order to effectively perform the position.

Seniority Systems

Seniority is the length of time the employer has employed an employee. Seniority may be used to defend a disparate impact case, but seniority may never be used in cases of intentional discrimination.

Supervisors and the *Ellerth/Faragher* Defense

An employer is liable for a supervisor's sexual harassment. The Supreme Court created an affirmative defense arising from its *Ellerth* and *Faragher* decisions.[4] The Court held that the employer was liable for sexual harassment even though the employer was unaware of the behavior. However, an employer is not strictly liable for sexual harassment if it can show the following:

1. It attempted to prevent and promptly correct sexual harassment in the workplace; and
2. The victim unreasonably failed to take advantage of the employer's preventive or corrective measures.

The employer's failure to adopt, enforce, and educate employees about sexual harassment can deny it a defense to a sexual harassment claim.

Right-to-sue letter
Notice issued by the EEOC or 706 agency to a complainant at the time it dismisses the charge(s) of discrimination filed by a claimant against an employer. Starts the 90-day statute of limitations to file a federal employment discrimination lawsuit.

Review the EEOC website for information for the applicable law, filing claims, and its litigation statistics at https://www.eeoc.gov.

Affirmative defense
A legal rule that limits or excuses a defendant's liability because of superseding facts or a strong public policy favoring the defendant.

Pretext
An excuse created to conceal the facts.

Bona fide occupational qualification (BFOQ)
Necessary quality or attribute that employers may consider in the selection, retention, promotion, and termination of employees.

4. *Burlington Indus. v. Ellerth*, 524 U.S. 742 (1998) and *Faragher v. City of Boca Raton*, 524 U.S. 775 (1998).

After-Acquired Evidence

After-acquired evidence Evidence provided by an employer after terminating or taking other adverse employment action against an employee used as evidence to justify the employer's decision and possibly reduce its back-pay liability.

After-acquired evidence is evidence provided by an employer *after* terminating or taking other adverse employment actions against an employee, which is used as evidence to justify the employer's decision and possibly reduce its back-pay liability.

This defense allows the employer to use information gathered after termination to establish it had legitimate grounds for the termination. For example, if the employer is able to discover evidence that would constitute a reasonable ground for refusing to hire or for discharging the plaintiff, the employer can assert that, had it known of the wrongdoing at the time of termination, it would have undertaken the same action based on that after-acquired knowledge.

Affirmative Action

Affirmative action Public policies that consider an individual's protected characteristic in employment, public contracting, and other public programs.

The law of **affirmative action** does not require preferences in the workplace. Title VII prohibits such preferential treatment.

The Supreme Court has interpreted Title VII as not requiring an employer to undertake affirmative action in employment-related decisions. If adopted, these affirmative action programs must comply with the Equal Protection Clause of the Fourteenth Amendment to the Constitution.

For an affirmative action program to be constitutional, it must be crafted in a way that attempts to remedy past discrimination and does not set any quotas or preferential treatment. Once the past discrimination has been remedied, the program must either be altered or abandoned entirely.

Remedies

Employer liability under the statutes discussed in this chapter can be extensive. A successful plaintiff may be entitled to a combination of the following: an injunction against the employer prohibiting the continuance of past conduct; the award of back pay, front pay (pay missing because of missed promotional opportunities), and compensatory and punitive damages; reinstatement, if applicable; and attorney's fees and court costs. Compensatory damage and punitive damages are limited to ceilings under Title VII, Section 1981, and the ADA.

AI Feature: Drafting an Anti-Harassment Policy

Using an AI program, draft an anti-harassment policy suitable for use in the workplace. Ensure that all forms of harassment are addressed under both federal laws and your home state's laws.

How do these policies afford protection to harassment victims? Of what benefit are such policies if the prohibited conduct continues within American workplaces?

Key Terms

- 706 agencies, 422
- Affirmative action, 424
- Affirmative defense, 423
- After-acquired evidence, 424
- Age discrimination, 419
- Age Discrimination in Employment Act of 1967 (ADEA), 419
- Americans with Disabilities Act of 1990 (ADA), 420
- Americans with Disabilities Act Amendments Act of 2008 (ADAAA), 420
- Associational discrimination, 422
- Bona fide occupational qualification (BFOQ), 423
- Business necessity, 410
- Color discrimination, 413
- Constructive discharge, 412
- *De minimis* cost for accommodation, 414
- Disability, 420
- Disability discrimination, 420
- Disparate impact, 408
- Disparate treatment, 407
- Employment discrimination, 405
- Equal Pay Act of 1963 (EPA), 414
- Essential functions of a job, 421
- Exhausting administrative remedies, 422
- Four-fifths rule, 410
- Genetic Information Nondiscrimination Act (GINA), 422
- Harassment, 407
- Hostile work environment, 407
- Immutable characteristics, 405
- Impairment, 421
- Individual with a disability who is qualified, 421
- Major life activity, 421
- Mixed motive evidence, 412
- National origin discrimination, 413
- Physical or mental impairment, 421
- Pretext, 423
- *Quid pro quo* sexual harassment, 407
- Race, 413
- Racial discrimination, 413
- Reasonable accommodation, 422
- Reasonable Factor Other than Age (RFOA), 419
- Religious discrimination, 413
- Retaliation, 410
- Right-to-sue letter, 423
- Section 1981, 413
- Title VII, 404
- Undue hardship (disability), 422
- Undue hardship (religious discrimination), 414

Applying the Law

17.1 Research the Law. Review the EEOC website for employment discrimination charge statistics (*https://www.eeoc.gov/statistics*). Identify the most common types of charges filed in your state. Compare the results to those of other states. What conclusions did you reach based upon your research?

17.2 Research the Law. As noted in this chapter, state laws and local ordinances will provide broader and deeper protections in this area of the law. Using an internet search engine, identify additional protected classifications available under the laws of your state (or another state) that are not yet recognized by federal law.

17.3 Disparate Treatment. Forty-nine persons applied for a compliance officer position. Peters, who was Black, was among the nine candidates selected to be interviewed by the search committee. After interviewing these candidates, each member of the search committee submitted a list of their top five candidates. A White woman was ultimately hired for the position. What would Peters need to prove to establish a *prima facie* case for disparate treatment? *Peters v. Lieuallen*, 568 F. Supp. 261 (D. Or. 1983)

17.4 Accents and National Origin Discrimination. Fragante was a Filipino immigrant who applied for a clerk's job at the Honolulu Division of Motor Vehicles and Licensing. The job involved orally providing information to the public. He had the highest score on the written test given to applicants, and the agency chose to interview him. The interviewers had difficulty understanding Fragante because of his pronounced accent. They determined he would have difficulties communicating with the public. After the agency hired two other applicants who had scored lower, Fragante sued for national origin discrimination. May an employment decision be predicated on someone's accent? *Fragante v. City & County of Honolulu*, 888 F.2d 591 (9th Cir. 1989)

17.5 Severe or Pervasive. Kerry Ellison and Sterling Gray were one-time friends and co-workers at the San Mateo, California, office of the IRS. He wrote her a note, followed by a typed, single-spaced, three-page letter, that Ellison considered weird. She reported the incident to her supervisor and demanded that she or Gray be transferred. After an investigation, the IRS rejected Ellison's complaints of sexual harassment. Ellison sued for sexual harassment due to a hostile working environment. Gray was temporarily transferred to another office but returned after four months. Was the IRS decision to transfer him back to San Mateo after a six-month cooling-off period a sufficient response? Could Gray's mere presence create a hostile work environment? *Ellison v. Brady*, 924 F.2d 872 (9th Cir. 1991)

17.6 Pregnancy-Related Discrimination. Does a person have to be pregnant to sue for pregnancy discrimination? Due to pregnancy complications, Suzanne Kocak resigned as an obstetric nurse at a community hospital. After delivering her child, she applied for, but did not get, a part-time position. She claimed that the personnel manager at the time of her part-time application asked whether she was pregnant or intended to have more children. Kocak asserted that the manager later told her the decision was based on the complications caused by the past pregnancy. The defendant produced evidence that Kocak was not rehired because she was an unreliable employee who was disliked by her peers. How should the federal district court rule on the defendant's motion for summary judgment on Kocak's claim? *Kocak v. Community Health Partners of Ohio, Inc.*, 400 F.3d 466 (6th Cir. 2005)

17.7 Religious Discrimination. Officer Philip Tridico, a Roman Catholic, served in the United States Marine Corps from 1992 until 1999, when he was honorably discharged. He was then employed by the Metropolitan Police Department in 2006. After Tridico arrived in the narcotics division, he approached his lieutenant about his concern with other officers, who had called him "White boy." There was also an incident during lunch in which he crossed himself before eating his lunch. One of the fellow officers repeatedly called him "weirdo," remarked "Church! That is a waste of time," and even said "he believes in that weirdo Jesus ****." Tridico sued, claiming that he was harassed and fired due to his religious beliefs after he reported these incidents. Does he have a plausible case for religious harassment? Is the employer's discharge of Tridico proper? *Tridico v. District of Columbia*, 130 F. Supp. 3d 17 (D.C. Cir. 2015)

17.8 Age Discrimination. An employer terminated Love, age 54. Four months later, the employer terminated Stewart, age 63, and Siler, age 60. Love, Stewart, and Siler were the oldest employees. However, none of the employees were replaced. What would Love, Stewart, and Siler need to prove to establish a *prima facie* case for age discrimination? *Love v. Hajoca Corp.*, 2013 U.S. Dist. LEXIS 129304 (S.D. Tex. 2013)

17.9 Major Life Activities Under the ADA. Deciding what activities constitute a "major life activity" for purposes of complying with the ADA can be a challenging task for employers. Glacier Northwest, Inc. terminated Matthew Head after he negligently caused a piece of heavy construction equipment to become stuck in the mud. In terminating him, Glacier cited damage to the loader as a violation of an equipment abuse policy. Before his termination, Head was diagnosed with bipolar disorder, a severe form of depression. Head had informed Glacier of this diagnosis. Sleeping, interacting with others, reading, and thinking were deemed major life activities by the court. If you were representing Head, how would you argue that the employer's decision was motivated by factors protected within the ADA context? *Head v. Glacier Northwest, Inc.*, 413 F.3d 1053 (9th Cir. 2005)

17.10 Affirmative Action. The Court of Appeals for the Ninth Circuit was required to review a four-month disciplinary suspension as to whether it constituted illegal retaliation. The case involved discipline imposed on several employees who publicly protested an "affirmative action award" given by a local school board, a major customer of their employer. How would the court rule as to the appropriateness of the discipline? When should the employer's economic interests prevail or control employee disciplinary matters? *EEOC v. Crown Zellerbach Corp.*, 720 F.2d 1008 (9th Cir. 1983)

Privacy in the Workplace

18

"The right to be let alone is indeed the beginning of all freedom." Public Utilities Commission v. Pollak, 343 U.S. 451, 467 (1952)—William O. Douglas, Associate Supreme Court Justice (1898–1980)

Chapter Outline

- Introduction
- What Is Workplace Privacy?
- Constitutionally Protected Rights and Rights Under Tort Law

Case 18.1: *Thomas v. University of Pittsburgh*

  - *Management Application: Federal Right to Privacy Laws*

- Collecting and Handling Employee Information
  - *Management Application: What Information Must Be Specially Protected from Disclosure?*
- Pre-Hiring Screenings
- Employee Searches and Investigations

Case 18.2: *Lunsford v. Sterilite of Ohio, L.L.C.*

Case 18.3: *Reed v. Toyota Motor Credit Corp.*

- Controlling the Employee's Lifestyle
- AI Feature: Draft an Employee Privacy Waiver

Learning Objectives

After studying this chapter, you should be able to:

1. Distinguish between constitutionally protected and common law expectations of privacy.
2. State the most common forms of tortious invasions of privacy.
3. Explain the privacy rights of private-sector employees.
4. Describe the types of protections offered by federal privacy statutes.
5. Recognize the kinds of surveillance and monitoring an employer may conduct.

Introduction

This chapter addresses the privacy practices and issues that arise *before* and *after* the worker has been hired. Individuals have the right to keep others from learning information about them. This interest is balanced against the employer's right to manage its business safely and legally. Federal legislation offers limited protection to federal employees, and the law of privacy has remained confused and uneven in the private sector. Moreover, rapid changes within technology and communication have created new legal issues surrounding privacy expectations in the workplace. These opposing interests are the subject of this chapter.

What Is Workplace Privacy?

Privacy
The desire or right to be left alone or the right to restrict public access to personal information, history, and affairs.

Restatement
A treatise by legal scholars addressing uncertainties as to the state of the law and indicating the common trend in understanding or the legal interpretation of an issue.

Many laws relate to workplace privacy and can be found in constitutions, statutes, regulations, and local ordinances. Despite the many sources, employee rights in the workplace are not broad. What complicates our discussion is that the word "**privacy**" is often used without common agreement as to what it encompasses. At its heart, privacy rights recognize a measure of personal control over an individual's autonomy, dignity, and serenity. The essence of an invasion of that right is the mental anguish sustained when it is invaded. Many have sought to define privacy, but its interpretation must rest ultimately on rules individual rights. The **Restatement (Second) of Torts, § 205A** provides:

> One who invades the right to privacy of another is subject to liability for the resulting harm to the interest of the other. The right to privacy is invaded by the unreasonable intrusion upon seclusion of another.

The law struggles to balance the employer's need to know about employee behaviors with the right of the individual employee to be left alone. At the same time, ever-expanding employment-related laws and regulations require employers to collect and retain increasing amounts of information to respond to regulatory oversight and compliance demands.

Constitutionally Protected Rights and Rights Under Tort Law

Although the U.S. Constitution does not expressly state the right to privacy, the Supreme Court in several constitutional rights cases has determined a federal constitutional right to privacy. Beginning with its 1965 decision in *Griswold v. Connecticut*,[1] the Supreme Court has held that various guarantees of liberty stated in the Bill of Rights create privacy zones. These constitutional guarantees prohibit intrusion into

1. 381 U.S. 479 (1965).

these areas of personal freedom. In his concurring opinion in the *Griswold* case, Justice Goldberg, borrowing from Justice Brandeis, stated:

> The protection guaranteed by the [Fourth and Fifth] Amendments is much broader in scope. The makers of our Constitution undertook to secure conditions favorable to the pursuit of happiness. They recognized the significance of man's spiritual nature, of his feelings and of his intellect. They knew that only a part of the pain, pleasure and satisfactions of life are to be found in material things. They sought to protect Americans in their beliefs, their thoughts, their emotions and their sensations. They conferred, as against the Government, the right to be let alone—the most comprehensive of rights and the right most valued by civilized men.

As a result, federal courts have recognized personal privacy rights in a variety of contexts. These rights are among those that the law protects as **fundamental rights**, which are guaranteed to each person even if they are not expressly stated in the Constitution.

Fundamental rights
Court recognition of individual freedoms so essential to liberty that government may not intrude on them.

The Supreme Court infers a federal constitutional right to privacy from Bill of Rights protections and those of the Constitution's Fourth and Fourteenth Amendments. These two Amendments provide, in part, that persons are to be free from unreasonable searches and seizures and from the taking of life, liberty, or property without due process, and that they are to be awarded equal protection of the law. Under the Fourth Amendment, privacy rights apply only to the federal government and its employees and contractors.

Federally recognized privacy protections apply *only* when government action affects an individual's right to privacy. Known as "**state action**," these federal privacy laws *do not apply* to non-governmental intrusions. For example, they do not apply to intrusions by private employers. However, it is a general proposition that public-sector employees have greater rights to privacy in the workplace than private-sector employees will. This follows from the fact that the governmental employer is bound by the constraints of the Constitution in dealing with employees.

State action
Action by or on behalf of a governmental body that violates the civil rights or legal interests of a person.

Fourth Amendment
Relative to employment, this Amendment protects a person's "reasonable expectation of privacy," including the right to be free from unreasonable searches and seizures by the government.

DIFFERENCES IN PRIVACY RIGHTS. Federal and state employers must be aware that these constitutional protections afford the public employee expansive privacy rights. What is reasonable in one context may be found unreasonable and an invasion of privacy in another context. Privacy rights protected by the Constitution differ from the privacy rights protected under state tort law. State laws offer more expansive privacy protections to employees.

Tort Law and the Right to Privacy

Lacking specific state privacy laws to apply, state courts developed a tort theory of recovery for invasion of privacy. Under the heading "invasion of privacy," four distinct causes of action exist. Common to all four causes of action is the idea that an individual has a right to be left alone. These theories allow victims to sue for invasions of their right to privacy:

1. Appropriating the name or likeness of another for one's own commercial use or benefit.

   Example: Advertising copy requiring waivers and releases for the commercial use of photographs or images of a person. An employer may use an employee's likeness in its advertising only if it is incidental and not essential to the content.

2. Unreasonable intrusion into a person's private affairs or right to be left alone, known as the **tort of intrusion**. A privacy violation based on the common law tort of intrusion has two elements: (1) the defendant must intentionally intrude into a place, conversation, or matter as to which the plaintiff has a reasonable expectation of privacy; and (2) the intrusion must occur in a manner highly offensive to a reasonable person. In the typical case, the circumstances are viewed as an affront to one's dignity.

Tort of intrusion
One who intentionally intrudes, physically or otherwise, upon the solitude or seclusion of another or their private affairs or concerns, is subject to liability to the other for invasion of their privacy, if the intrusion would be highly offensive to a reasonable person.

Example: A public employer alleged that its employee was falsifying her timesheet. To investigate further, the employer assigned two employees to conduct surveillance on the employee, which included peering into the windows of the employee's private residence. The court found that this behavior was "highly offensive" and was an unreasonable intrusion. *Vegas v. Chicago Park Dist.*, 958 F. Supp. 2d 943 (N.D. Ill. 2013).

3. Public disclosure of private facts about an individual. This invasion involves the publication of information that would be highly offensive to a reasonable person and is not of legitimate public interest.

Example: A former employee could sue a former employer who posted an interoffice memo about the employee's termination on a bulletin board, which was visible to dozens of employees. *Payton v. City of Santa Clara*, 132 Cal. App. 3d 152 (1982)

4. Placing a person in a **false light** by unreasonable and highly objectionable publicity. This tort requires that the wrongdoer had prior knowledge of its falsity or acted in reckless disregard as to the falsity of the matter and the false light in which the victim would be placed. This form of the tort closely relates to defamation. The employer has placed an employee in a false light by attributing to their conduct or characteristics that are false and offensive to a reasonable person. The usual case involves an invasion of privacy claim, which is defended by asserting the privilege of newsworthy publication.

False light
Liability that may arise from the public publication of information portraying the plaintiff in a false or misleading light. The information is highly offensive or embarrassing and is published with reckless disregard.

To survey state laws protecting an individual's privacy rights, see https://www.ncsl.org/research/telecommunications-and-information-technology/privacy-protections-in-state-constitutions.aspx.

Example: Daryoush Taha was charged with a criminal offense and accepted a plea deal to ensure that the arrest and charge would be expunged. Several years later, the court and jail system created a public website that included Taha's mugshot and arrest records. Taha's false claim lawsuit was able to proceed because the court found that "despite the accuracy of the facts disseminated, discrete presentation of information in a fashion which renders the publication susceptible to inferences casting one in a false light entitles the grievant to recompense." *Taha v. Bucks County*, 9 F. Supp. 3d (E.D. Pa. 2014)

Contractual Protections for the Right of Privacy

An invasion of privacy situation might arise within a contractual context. For example, employee handbooks and manuals become either express or implied contracts between the employer and the employee. Representations made that certain information respecting an employee will be held in confidence may result in a breach of contract action against the employer if that information is improperly disclosed.

Similarly, the employer may rely upon such procedures to defend itself. An employee may have a more difficult time asserting a right to privacy invasion if the employer has reserved the right to conduct reasonable monitoring, surveillance, or searches.

> **Example:** If the search is conducted in a reasonable manner, an employer that has announced a policy of random bag inspections as employees leave the premises can take disciplinary action against an employee who refused to open his lunch box. *Simpson v. Unemployment Corp. Bd. of Review*, 450 A.2d 305 (Pa. Commw. 1982)

However, courts may set such policies aside when the employer has acted unreasonably. If the employer's intrusion is not supported by legitimate business justifications or is beyond that which is justified under the circumstances, the employer may be liable.

> **Example:** After a burglary at its liquor package store, the former employer of Sibbie Deal installed a taping device on a workplace telephone that recorded all conversations made or received on the phone. The employer believed the burglary was an inside job, suspected that Deal was involved, and did not inform her that they were monitoring the phone. They only told her they might do so to reduce time spent on personal calls. Deal was terminated when it was learned she had sold a beer keg at cost. The court held that the monitoring was unnecessary and abusive. The owners were held liable for damages and attorney's fees, despite giving notice to its employees. *Deal v. Spears*, 980 F.2d 1153 (8th Cir. 1992)

If employees are permitted to treat office furniture such as desks and lockers as personal space, the employer may have a difficult time arguing that the employees have no expectation of privacy in such areas. If the employer is diligent in reducing the expectation of privacy in the workplace, policies such as the one in the following case will assist the employer in defending the search against any claimed invasion of privacy.

In the following case, a student athlete sued following her dismissal from a collegiate team and the loss of a scholarship.

CASE 18.1

THE CIRCUMSTANCES OF THE DISMISSAL OF A STUDENT ATHLETE MAY PRODUCE A FALSE LIGHT CLAIM

THOMAS v. UNIVERSITY OF PITTSBURGH

2014 U.S. Dist. LEXIS 90699

United States District Court for the Western District of Pennsylvania

Brittaney Thomas transferred from the University of Florida to the University of Pittsburgh, under a scholarship agreement. After an incident following a basketball game, Thomas alleged another player approached her in a threatening manner. The player argued with Thomas, pushed her, and "sucker punched" her with a closed fist, causing multiple injuries. The coaching staff in the locker room did not try to make the other player stay away from Thomas. Thomas claimed she tried to stop the assault, causing both players to fall to the ground.

When the head coach, Agnus Berenato, returned to the locker room, Thomas informed her of what had happened. She did not reprimand the other player. When Thomas informed Berenato that she would call her father and inform him of the incident, Berenato grabbed Thomas's cellphone and instructed her not to call anyone or go anywhere. When Thomas tried to leave the locker room, Berenato pushed her into the lockers. Thomas was then kept isolated from the team. Later, Berenato confiscated Thomas's second cellphone when she tried to respond to a text from her mother. Later, once the team boarded their bus, Berenato returned Thomas's cellphones.

Thereafter, Berenato contacted Thomas to meet and talk with the coaching staff. At the meeting, Thomas was blamed for the incident. The following day, Thomas met with the coaching staff and the senior associate athletic director. During this meeting, Thomas was indefinitely suspended from the team. Her dismissal was then reported to the *Pittsburgh Post-Gazette* and the *Pittsburgh Tribune Review*, stating that Thomas was dismissed from the basketball team for "violating team rules." Thomas sued the University of Pittsburgh, Berenato and other related University of Pittsburgh employees (collectively "University") for, among other things, false light, alleging that these statements were made without regard to falsity and with malice, to preserve the coaching staff 's reputation and to cover up Thomas's departure.

Language of the Court. *The United States Court of Appeals for the Third Circuit explained the contours of a false light claim in Pennsylvania law as follows:*

> *Pennsylvania has adopted the definition of false light invasion of privacy from the Restatement (Second) of Torts, which imposes liability on a person who publishes material that "is not true, is highly offensive to a reasonable person, and is publicized with knowledge or in reckless disregard of its falsity ..." Although to the best of our knowledge the Pennsylvania Supreme Court has not addressed the contours of falsity in the false-light-invasion-of-privacy context, the Superior Court has defined falsity broadly in that context. A plaintiff can establish falsity by showing that a defendant "selectively printed or broadcast true statements or pictures in a manner which created a false impression." Thus, even where a publication is literally true, "discrete presentation of information in a fashion which renders the publication susceptible to inference casting one in a false light entitles the grievant to recompense for the wrong committed." The Superior Court has drawn this broad definition from defamation law, which permits recovery where a publication was true, but implied falsehoods.*

The University Defendants contend that statements regarding Thomas' dismissal for "violating team rules" are not sufficiently offensive to state a claim for false light. The University counters that she was a "stellar athlete with impeccable credentials both on and off the field of play," and that to be subject to dismissal for an undisclosed "rules violation" "implies conduct by Thomas of the most horrendous nature." At this stage of the litigation, accepting Thomas' allegations as true, the Court is inclined to agree with Thomas. The statements issued by the University and Berenato, in the context of the intended audience of fans, competing teams, and potential recruiters, and given the consequences to Thomas, including dismissal and the loss of a scholarship, are susceptible to inferences that Thomas committed a grievous violation, on par with actional inferences. At this early juncture, Thomas has alleged a plausible claim for false light.

Decision. The University's motion to dismiss was denied and Thomas's false claim lawsuit could proceed to trial. She also was allowed to proceed with her claims of defamation and allegations of disparate treatment based on gender because the university had disciplined female athletes much more harshly than male athletes.

Focus on Ethics

What are actions an employer can take to carefully disclose needed personnel information but also protect its employee's privacy rights? In this case, what should university officials have stated publicly regarding this situation?

Management Application
Federal Right to Privacy Laws

Law	Coverage
Driver's Privacy Protection Act of 1994, 18 U.S.C. § 2721	Confidential driver's license information may not be disclosed to an employer except in limited circumstances.
Fair Credit Reporting Act, 14 U.S.C. §§ 1681 *et seq.*	Job applicants and employees are permitted to know of the existence and content of any personal credit files on them maintained by the employer. If the employer compiles an investigative consumer report, the employee must be informed and given the right to inspect it.
Family Education Rights and Privacy Act — the Buckley Amendment, 20 U.S.C. §§ 1232 *et seq.*	Student records and personal information are protected from disclosure.
Federal Privacy Act of 1974, 5 U.S.C. § 552a	Federal agencies and those contracting with the federal government must provide employees with the opportunity to determine the scope of the information being kept on them by their employers, to review that information, to correct erroneous information, and to prevent the information from being used for a purpose other than that for which it was collected. The Act covers public-sector employees only and allows them to sue for violations.

Law	Coverage
Safe Streets Act, 18 U.S.C. §§ 2510 *et seq.*	It is a crime to intentionally intercept any wire, oral, or electronic communication, including electronic mail or video teleconference. This includes recording conversations when there is a reasonable expectation of privacy, which may be waived by one party's consent. Employers may potentially listen in on an employee's conversation on an extension telephone used in the ordinary course of business if there is a legitimate business reason to do so.
Electronic Communications Privacy Act of 1986 (Electronic Communications Privacy Act or Wiretap Act)	Enacted to address the inadequacies of the federal wiretap law to protect computer transmission technologies, this Act prohibits the interception, recording, or disclosure of wire, electronic, and audio communications, including email and voicemail. Employers may monitor these communications for legitimate business reasons, but they must immediately stop monitoring them if they prove to be or become personal. Interception is permissible if conducted by law enforcement personnel with a warrant in the conduct of a criminal investigation.
Stored Communications Act (part of the **Electronic Communications Privacy Act (ECPA)**)	Providers of communications services may not divulge private communications. The Act covers ECS and RCS entities. An ECS is any service that provides users with the ability to send or receive wire or electronic communications. An ECS may *not* divulge communications without the consent of the addressee or intended recipient of such communication. An RCS provides computer storage or processing services for an electronic communications system. An RCS *may* divulge the contents of a communication with the consent of the customer-subscriber.
Privacy for Consumers and Workers Act of 1993	Employer monitoring of an employee's communications is not prohibited, but the Act requires the employer to give notice to employees when their workplace communications are being monitored or recorded electronically.

Electronic Communications Privacy Act (ECPA) Federal act enacted to prohibit the interception, recording, or disclosure of wire, oral, and electronic communications, including email and voicemail.

Collecting and Handling Employee Information

Federal Employees

The Privacy Act regulates how federal government agencies maintain personnel records. Records are defined under that Act to include "any item, collection, or grouping of information about an individual that is maintained by an agency." Employees of federal agencies must be given copies of their personnel records and may make copies of them.

They are entitled to contest the accuracy of the records by making a written statement to be included in the official records and in the disclosure of those records to other parties.

Federal agencies must obtain the employees' consent before disclosing any information from their personnel records to outside persons. The Act limits the types of information that may be kept about employees and requires agencies to keep accurate personnel records on their employees.

Private-Sector Employees

To ensure employer compliance with statutes that have widespread public policy implications, many laws and regulations that exist on the federal, state, and local level require employers to maintain business records substantiating compliance with those laws and regulations. Like medical records, these required disclosure records should be maintained separate from employees' individual personnel files. Such recordkeeping includes the following:

- Information on the profiles of applicants and employees regarding applications, hires, promotions and demotions, layoffs, and dismissal;
- Work authorization records;
- Payroll records to ensure proper tax reporting compliance; and
- Workplace safety and health records for reportable personal injuries and deaths.

Management Application
What Information Must Be Specially Protected from Disclosure?

Applicable federal and state laws require that the following be kept specially protected because of privacy requirements:

- Verification of the right to work in the United States (Form I-9)
- EEOC charges of discrimination and investigation reports
- "Medical condition" information or any other medical history information obtained under the Americans with Disabilities Act (ADA)
- Employee medical records received by the employer under the Family and Medical Leave Act of 1993
- Medical and hazardous material exposure records created in compliance with the Occupational Safety and Health (OSH) Act
- Workplace investigation reports that may contain sensitive, potentially embarrassing, or humiliating personal information
- Workers' compensation and disability claims

Are there other items of information that should be protected?

Pre-Hiring Screenings

Although thorough screening is essential for avoiding liability for negligent hiring, employers must ensure that their pre-hire screenings are job-related and a business necessity. The following is a general summary of the applicable laws. Many states have enacted legislation specifically applicable to these topics.

PSYCHOLOGICAL TESTS. While allowed, psychological tests should contain only questions that are job-related and a business necessity.

> **Example:** Target® required job applicants for store security officers as a condition of employment to pass a psychological test known as the Psychscreen, which was supposed to evaluate such traits as emotional stability, reliability, and the tendency to follow the rules. A number of the test questions dealt with an applicant's religious attitudes and sexual orientation. Several applicants sued, claiming such questions violated their right of privacy. The applicants contended that the employer could show no compelling interest to justify the use of the test, and a psychologist testified that the test had not been shown to be reliable or valid as a means of evaluating candidates for employment. The employer conceded that the test constituted an invasion of privacy but stressed that the intrusion was limited, justified by its reasonable interest in screening applicants for security positions. The court of appeal disagreed, and Target lost the case. *Soroka v. Dayton Hudson Corp.*, 235 Cal. App. 3d 654 (1991)

INTERVIEWS AND JOB APPLICATIONS. Pre-hire answer gathering should include only job-related questions. Questions on personal history such as neighborhoods, social organization memberships, arrest records, or family status could be considered discriminatory and invasive of privacy.

CREDIT HISTORIES. The Fair Credit Reporting Act imposes duties upon employers when requesting any credit information on an applicant or employee. This Act requires employers to disclose that consumer reports may be used for employment decisions and to secure consent from employees or applicants to obtain such reports. If such reports provide information that results in an adverse employment action, the employer must provide the person with a copy of the report and a written statement of their rights under the Act.

WORKERS' COMPENSATION FILINGS. Under the Americans with Disabilities Act, employers are prohibited from asking questions that are likely to reveal the existence of a disability before making a job offer. For example, employers may not ask applicants whether they have filed for workers' compensation in the past.

CONVICTION RECORDS. An applicant's conviction record must be carefully handled. If the position is related to vulnerable populations (children, abused spouses, or the elderly) or valuable assets, it is more likely that the records may be reviewed. Acting on the conviction in reference to an employment decision must be job-related. Thirty-six states and over 150 cities and counties have adopted what is widely known as "ban the box," requiring employers to consider a job candidate's qualifications first—without the stigma of a conviction or arrest record. These laws require removing the conviction history question from job applications and delaying background checks until later in the hiring process.

The EEOC's position on criminal record investigation is as follows:

> No Federal law clearly prohibits an employer from asking about arrest and conviction records. Since an arrest alone does not necessarily mean that an applicant has committed a crime, the employer should not assume that the applicant committed the offense. Instead, the employer should allow them an opportunity to explain the circumstances of the arrest(s) and should make a reasonable effort to determine the explanation's reliability.[2]

State laws regulate the criminal record investigations of applicants and employees. They vary as to the rights of an employer to request or use arrest, conviction, or sealed or expunged criminal or juvenile records. Other states require a "compelling need" for the information. In those states, an employer must have a compelling need to conduct a background check for prior incidents involving sexual misconduct, controlled substances, or crimes involving weapons or violence. For example, the courts would endorse criminal background checks on potential employees who would be working with children, the disabled, or the elderly.

Review EEOC/FTC, Background Checks: What Employers Need to Know, at http://www1.eeoc.gov//eeoc/publications/background_checks_employers.cfm.

Medical and Physical Exams

PRE-HIRE DRUG TESTING. Some employers—federal agencies, the defense industry, federal contractors, and the transportation industry—are required to test individuals for drug use. However, there are no national regulations governing drug testing by private employers outside of these industries. State laws often regulate drug testing, including how the testing must be conducted. Testing could be challenged under the state constitution's privacy clause or under state common law.

Pre-hire drug tests may be less susceptible to challenge if applicants are informed that it is part of the application process, if the testing itself is done discreetly, and if test results are kept confidential.

POST-HIRE DRUG TESTING. Drug testing after hiring is usually allowed if it falls into one of four categories:

1. Random testing for safety reasons;
2. Testing based on reasonable suspicion of intoxication;
3. Testing related to off-duty activities; and
4. Fitness for duty.

An employer may require a medical examination or undertake reasonable medical inquiries if they are job-related and consistent with a business necessity. The law permits fitness-for-duty medical examinations if an employee's job performance has

2. *https://www.eeoc.gov/laws/guidance/what-you-should-know-eeoc-and-arrest-and-conviction-records* (accessed June 20, 2021).

seriously declined or if there is a risk that the worker may harm themself or others. All persons in similar circumstances should be treated in the same manner.

Mandatory testing of employees, without the presence of other circumstances, has been held as a violation of an employee's right to privacy. Current employees may be subject to random drug testing if they hold safety- or security-sensitive positions. Employees in workplaces where toxic or other hazardous materials or conditions are found may be compelled to undergo periodic drug testing.

> **Example:** A bus driver who transported students to and from school worked for a company with a random, periodic drug testing policy for those in "safety-sensitive positions." The bus driver failed to report to a drug test and was terminated. He sued, alleging wrongful termination and that the drug test violated his workplace privacy. The court rejected this argument and said that there was a compelling reason for testing employees that operate school buses. *Perkins v. Nat'l Express Corp.*, 105 F. Supp. 3d 970 (N.D. Cal. 2015)

An employer may discipline an addict or alcoholic if the use of the substances or alcohol affects job performance. An employer can also prohibit the use of alcohol or drugs altogether in the workplace and can require that employees not be under the influence of alcohol or drugs in the workplace.

Random Drug Testing of Government Employees (Non-Safety Related). Random drug testing of all government employees has been found to be a violation of the Fourth Amendment protections against unreasonable searches and seizures.

State Law Drug Testing and Protections. Some states have enacted legislation governing testing employees for alcohol or drug abuse. The coverage of these statutes varies greatly. These states also have specific requirements regarding confirmatory testing, the use of certified laboratories, the confidentiality of test results, and other privacy safeguards. In other states without specific laws court challenges to private employer drug testing programs often occur. Generally, these suits are based on state law rather than federal constitutional law. They are also based on common law actions that allege specific intentional tort injuries and, occasionally, breach of contract claims. In most states, private-sector employers have been given broad discretion to test their employees provided the invasion of privacy is not too intrusive.

Employee Polygraphs

Employee Polygraph Protection Act of 1988 (EPPA)
A federal law generally preventing employers from requiring lie detector tests from applicants or employees.

The **Employee Polygraph Protection Act (EPPA)** is a federal statute that greatly limits an employer's right to polygraph employees. The use of polygraphs as a screening device for job applicants is generally banned for private employers in all but a few industries. This Act does not apply to federal, state, or local government employees or employees of federal government contractors who deal with defense and intelligence agencies.

A limited exception exists under the EPPA to permit private-sector employers to polygraph current employees. For this exception to apply, four requirements must be met:

1. There must be an *ongoing investigation* of economic loss or injury;
2. The employee must have had *access* to the property that is the subject of the investigation;

3. The employer must have a *reasonable suspicion* based on facts in addition to access that the employee is involved; and
4. The employer must provide the employee with *written notification* before the administration of the test, which must include a wide array of statutorily required information, including:
   a. The specific loss or injury, the fact that the employee had access to what was lost or injured, and the reason the employee is under suspicion;
   b. The time and place of the examination, the nature of instruments to be used, the fact that the examination will be conducted by a licensed examiner (the EPPA requires that the polygraph examiner be licensed, maintain a minimum bond of $50,000, and administer no more than five exams in one day), the duration of the examination, the employee's right to consult with counsel, the employee's right to tape the proceedings, and the employee's right to terminate the examination at any time;
   c. The fact that no degrading or intrusive questions or questions regarding religion, politics, race, sex, or attitudes toward labor unions will be asked;
   d. The fact that the examination is not required as a condition of employment; and
   e. The fact that statements made may be used against the employee.

The employee has the right to review all test questions in writing before the test. The examination may not occur if written evidence shows that the employee suffers from conditions that could cause positive results (that is, the conditions could make responses appear untruthful even if they were not). The employer must discuss the test results with the employee before taking any adverse employment action. No adverse action may be taken solely because of polygraph test results. The employer can disclose the results of the test only to the examinee, in litigation proceedings, or to a governmental agency for criminal prosecution.

Violations of the Act are punishable by fines of up to $10,000. An employee or prospective employee whose rights have been violated may file a civil action in federal or state court within three years and seek reinstatement, promotion, and back pay. The court, in its discretion, may also grant the prevailing party its costs and attorney's fees.

Employee Searches and Investigations

In its plurality decision in *O'Connor v. Ortega*,[3] the Supreme Court decided that:

1. Employees do not lose their protections under the Fourth Amendment because they work for a public employer; and
2. The reasonableness of an employee's expectation of privacy must be considered within the specific facts presented in a case.

PRIVATE EMPLOYER PROPERTY SEARCHES. Little statutory or case authority exists for private-sector employers seeking to search the employees' work areas and

3. 480 U.S. 709 (1987).

property. Quite often, court decisions turn on whether the conduct was inadvertent or intentional concerning the alleged invasion of privacy.

UNAUTHORIZED CREDIT CHECKING. Such action is prohibited unless there is a legitimate reason for doing so.

> **Example:** A disgruntled employer may not obtain, without the targeted employee's consent, the credit card records of a fellow employee suspected of taking unauthorized sick days, nor may such ill-obtained information be shared with management. The employer had no legitimate interest in receiving confidential credit information. *Pulla v. Amoco Oil Co.*, 34 F. Supp. 2d 1299 (N.D. Okla. 1999)

In the following case, employees' expectations of privacy were considered.

CASE 18.2

CONSIDERATIONS OF EMPLOYEES' EXPECTATION OF PRIVACY

LUNSFORD v. STERILITE OF OHIO, L.L.C.

165 N.E.3d 245 (Ohio 2020)

Supreme Court of Ohio

Both former and current at-will employees of Sterilite of Ohio, L.L.C. sued for invasion of privacy. The basis of the lawsuit was that Sterilite, as a private employer, should not have implemented a workplace substance-abuse policy that required the employees to submit a urine sample for drug testing under the "direct-observation method." Under that method, a same-sex monitor was required to accompany the employee to the restroom to visually observe the employee produce the urine sample.

Compliance with the policy was a condition of employment. The policy aimed to "promote a healthy, safe and productive workplace for all employees." Sterilite required drug testing under three circumstances: (1) while investigating a workplace accident or incident, (2) when there was reasonable suspicion that an employee was impaired by drugs or alcohol, and (3) randomly. Under the policy, an employee was informed by their supervisor when and where to report for testing. Disciplinary action could be enforced on employees whose urine samples tested positive for illegal drugs or improper use of unauthorized prescriptions or over-the-counter drugs.

At the beginning of the testing process, each employee executed a statement titled "Consent and Release." When they executed the consent form, they did not know that their urine samples would be collected under the direct-observation method, as previous urine samples that were provided did not require the direct-observation method. They argued that under Ohio law an individual has a right to privacy and freedom. Sterlite argued that absent allegations that the testing was not job-related and consistent with business necessity, an at-will employee could not maintain an action against their employer for invasion of privacy. Eventually, the case was appealed to the Supreme Court of Ohio.

Language of the Court: *This case places two common-law principles—the doctrine of employment at will and the tort of invasion of privacy—in competition with each other. The fundamental principle of the employee's argument is that the employment-at-will doctrine must yield to an employee's right to privacy. Therefore, in their view, the common-law right to privacy enhances their rights under the employment-at-will doctrine and diminishes their employer's rights under the doctrine.*

It is the manner in which the policy was carried out—the use of the direct-observation method during the collection of the urine sample—that is the core of this controversy. Therefore, we turn to the common-law tort of invasion of privacy.

The heart of the employees' argument is that absent just cause—which could include an employee's past positive drug test or evidence or reasonable suspicion of urine-sample tampering or adulteration, or the employee's express consent—an at-will employer may not use what appellees call the "highly offensive" direct-observation method to administer a workplace substance-abuse policy. To say it another way, an employer that without just cause uses the "highly offensive" direct-observation method for collecting a urine sample creates an actionable invasion-of-privacy claim by the employee.

While we recognize that workplace drug-testing policies implicate employees' privacy interests, we find as a matter of law that the facts alleged in the employees' complaint cannot sustain their common-law invasion-of-privacy claim. Despite their assertions that they did not consent to drug testing using the direct-observation method, the facts in the complaint demonstrate they did consent to the use of the direct-observation method.

Sterilite is a private company and is not a state actor. There is no Fourth Amendment challenge before us here, no provision of the Ohio Constitution has been implicated, and there is no Ohio statute underpinning appellees' invasion-of-privacy claim. Our review of their invasion-of-privacy claim is limited to their arguments based on the common-law right to privacy.

Decision. A consenting at-will employee that submits a urine sample, at the request of their employer, under the direct-observation method, does not have sufficient grounds for claiming invasion of privacy.

Focus on Ethics

The dissent argued that collecting the employee's urine samples under the direct-observation method is highly intrusive. Does that perspective affect your opinion regarding the employer's right to request their employees to submit urine samples for drug testing?

Surveillance and Monitoring

It is settled law that an employer has the right to intercept employee email and telephone communications with respect to employer-owned equipment.

The Electronic Communications Privacy Act of 1986 (ECPA) permits employers to intercept the employees' electronic communications under certain conditions. Employers can intercept employee communications:

1. When the employee consents in writing to allow the employer to do so;
2. If, during the ordinary course of business, the employer intercepts such communications because it fits within the business-related exception to the ECPA; or
3. When the business entity provides the email service for use by employees.

SURVEILLANCE RIGHTS. Employers may photograph, surveil, or closely observe employees within their work areas for a legitimate business reason without risk of invading their employees' privacy. When observations are made from public places, employees are unlikely to have any expectation of privacy. Trespassing into private areas will almost surely result in an invasion of privacy claim. The lawful boundary of employer surveillance of employees is uncharted and constantly changing. Balancing the employer's interest and the employee's rights to privacy will be a continuing challenge for employers.

Using a private investigator to surveil an employee outside of the workplace can lead to employer liability. Investigation of employees who have presented suspect workers' compensation or medical claims may lead to employer liability for invasion of privacy. The trier of fact must determine if in the circumstances, the investigator, and eventually, the employer, had a legitimate interest in the surveillance and whether the subject's conduct was unreasonably intrusive or offensive to a reasonable person.

Reasonableness of surveillance is the subject of the next case.

CASE 18.3

INTRUSIONS INTO EMPLOYEE'S PRIVACY ARE ONLY PERMITTED DURING THE EMPLOYMENT RELATIONSHIP

REED v. TOYOTA MOTOR CREDIT CORP.

459 P.3d 253 (2020)

Court of Appeals of Oregon

A Toyota Financial Services employee reported that a fellow employee Erik Reed was wearing a "large dagger-style blade" and informed human resources (HR) that he was concerned for his safety. Toyota has a policy that expressly prohibits its employees from possessing weapons, including knives and daggers, on its property.

Based on employee concerns and a sense of "increasing hostility" from Reed during performance reviews, TFS decided to place Reed on an administrative leave to investigate the safety concerns.

As part of an eventual employment separation agreement, TFS agreed to lease Reed the Toyota Tundra that he had used during his employment under certain conditions. One of the conditions required Reed to take the Tundra to a specific Toyota dealership for maintenance and safety inspection. Despite this condition, Reed had taken the Tundra to a different Toyota dealership. When TFS informed him that they would not honor the settlement unless the truck was taken to Capitol Toyota, Reed then brought the truck to Capitol and left it there for two days.

While the truck was at Capitol, Toyota's corporate security office installed a GPS device on the Tundra without Reed's permission or knowledge. The security office also placed geo-fences across the public roadways to locations TFS considered to be at risk. Reed was not informed about the installation of the GPS device or the geo-fences when the truck was returned.

A month later, Reed discovered the GPS device when he noticed wires behind the gas and brake pedals of the truck. When Reed discovered the GPS device on the truck, he sued for invasion of privacy.

Language of the Court. *This invasion of privacy case relies upon the "intrusion upon seclusion" theory. To prevail at trial, the plaintiff must prove three elements: (1) an intentional intrusion, physical or otherwise, (2) upon the plaintiff's solitude or seclusion or private affairs or concerns, (3) which would be highly offensive to a reasonable person.*

TFS disputes plaintiff's allegation that it intruded upon his privacy by entering the truck for the purpose of secretly installing the tracking device and by monitoring plaintiff's location with the GPS device. First, TFS argues that entry into the truck to install the GPS device was not an intrusion because the truck belonged to TFS and that plaintiff "merely had the right to free use of it under the Separation Agreement." Second, TFS contends that the GPS system did not intrude on plaintiff's privacy because it was a "passive system" that was not monitored and did not alarm. Third, TFS contends that it did not intrude on a "private place" or "area of seclusion." And fourth, TFS contends that its actions would not be highly offensive to a reasonable person—a necessary element for the tort.

Oregon courts follow the Restatement (Second) of Torts approach to evaluation the tort of invasion of privacy. Commentary to the Restatement (Second) of Torts provides that an invasion or intrusion may occur with "the use of the defendant's senses, with or without mechanical aids, to oversee or overhear the plaintiff's private affairs."

TFS disputes that its actions would be highly offensive to a reasonable person, a critical element of the tort. "In determining whether the defendant's conduct was tortious, the fact that it constituted an unlawful trespass is only one factor to be considered." A jury may find other factors relevant to whether the defendant's conduct was "highly offensive," such as "the extent of the intrusion, the context, conduct and circumstances surrounding the intrusion, the defendant's motives, the setting into which defendant intruded and the plaintiff's expectation of privacy."

TFS argues that the context and circumstances of this case include the complaints and concerns of plaintiff's coworkers, and the then-recent shootings at the Clackamas Town Center and Sandy Hook Elementary School. TFS argues that its "only motive was to protect its workforce" and that it took a "narrowly tailored approach" to carry out that "obligation."

But the device in this case was installed after the employment relationship ended. The case before us is not about the reasonableness of an employer's HR process designed to protect its workforce from internal safety threats. This case is about the steps TFS took after it identified safety concerns involving plaintiff and terminated him from employment. Had TFS reported its ongoing safety concerns to the police at that point, a warrant would have been necessary before officers could place any sort of tracking device on plaintiff's truck. A jury might reasonably conclude that TFS's covert placement of the GPS device was highly offensive.

Decision. The court found the trial court erred in granting summary judgment to TFS.

Focus on Ethics

What steps should a company undertake to balance the safety concerns of current employees and the privacy rights of a former employee?

Rights of privacy are not absolute. Occasionally, greater public policy interests may require a minor intrusion into the individual's sense of privacy.

Example: Abigail Hernandez and Maria-Jose Lopez worked at the Hillsides Children Center, Inc., a residential home for abused and neglected children. Their office had a locking door and shades that could be drawn for privacy. After a supervisor learned that someone was using one of the office computers to view pornographic websites, he set up a hidden video camera in the office. The camera could be controlled remotely and could provide a live video feed. The camera was not operated during business hours, and the women were never seen on the video at any time. After discovering the camera, the women sued for the tort of intrusion against Hillsides. The court found the surveillance was narrowly tailored in place, time, and scope, and was prompted by legitimate business concerns. *Hernandez v. Hillsides, Inc.*, 47 Cal. 4th 272 (2009)

Concept Summary Proving a Privacy Invasion

To prevail, the plaintiff must prove:

- A legally protected privacy interest is involved such that society would recognize the information or activity as private;
- There was an objectively reasonable expectation of privacy under the circumstances (circumstances may include whether the employer gave advance notice of the intrusion, the opportunity for the employee to voluntarily consent to the invasion, and the occupation of the plaintiff and the surrounding circumstances); and
- A serious invasion of privacy is involved.

Once the claimant meets the burden of proof on the issue, the defendant employer can establish that its actions were justified by some competing, legally authorized, or socially beneficial interest. If the employer can show that its conduct was reasonably calculated to further that interest, the court gives the plaintiff an opportunity to rebut that defense by showing that a less intrusive alternative was available to further the employer's interest.

EAVESDROPPING AS AN INVASION OF PRIVACY. The overhearing of another's private words, either by ear or through some artificial assistance, such as a mechanical or electronic device, is deemed eavesdropping. Eavesdropping includes the recording of words as well. An eavesdropping episode can involve both criminal and civil proceedings.

PRIVACY OUTSIDE THE WORKPLACE. What should an employer do with respect to retaining an employee if the employer reads in the newspaper that the employee has been released pending trial following the employee's arrest for a crime? The prevailing legal view is that, absent special circumstances, employees' off-duty behavior is not subject to the disciplinary action of an employer. For the employer to act against the employee, the employer must establish a clear relationship between the alleged misconduct and the negative effect on the business or others in the company.

To review resources on the developing field of cybersecurity and privacy rights, see https://www.ncsl.org/in-dc/task-forces/task-force-on-artificial-intelligence-cybersecurity-and-privacy.

Controlling the Employee's Lifestyle

Regulation at the workplace may take the following forms:

1. Off-hours use of tobacco and alcohol
2. Mandated dress and grooming standards
3. Prohibiting outside employment

4. Interfering with social relationships, such as dating or sexual relationships, which the employer perceives to conflict with its business

Only when they directly relate to the employer's business activities and only to the extent reasonably necessary to advance those interests may an employer monitor its employees' private activities, both inside and outside the workplace. The constitutionally and common law protected rights of the employee relating to free speech, association, equal protection, and privacy often collide with the interests of the employer to operate its business in a reasonable manner.

LIFESTYLE. The right of an employer to regulate after-hours lifestyle choices of its employees often creates conflicts. Sometimes, employers seek to justify business codes of conduct upon the grounds that they are justified by business necessity.

> **Example:** After Crystal Chambers, a single, Black woman, became pregnant, the Omaha Girls Club, Inc. fired her from her position as an arts and crafts instructor because she violated the Club's "role model rule." The club was a private, nonprofit corporation that offered programs designed to assist young girls between the ages of 8 and 18 to maximize their life opportunities. Among the Club's many activities are programs directed at pregnancy prevention. Staff members are trained and expected to act as role models for the girls, with the intent that the girls will seek to emulate their behavior. The Club formulated its "role model rule" banning single-parent pregnancies among its staff members. Chambers sued for damages. The Court of Appeals for the Eighth Circuit found the role model rule an employment practice consistent with federal law because it found it was a plausible business necessity. *Chambers v. Omaha Girls Club, Inc.*, 834 F.2d 697 (8th Cir. 1987)

OFFICE ROMANCE. Circumstances change, and misunderstandings frequently arise such that what was formerly welcomed behavior becomes harassment. Employers should also be alert to morale issues that might arise if other employees perceive favoritism shown by a supervisor toward a subordinate because of a personal relationship.

> **Example:** Ms. Rulon-Miller, an IBM® employee, dated Matt Blum, an employee of an IBM competitor. Her position at IBM did not expose her to sensitive, confidential information. After Rulon-Miller argued that her continued dating of Blum did not constitute a "conflict of interest," IBM terminated her. She sued for invasion of her privacy, and IBM defended on the grounds that her employment was at-will. Rulon-Miller prevailed in her lawsuit because there was no evidence of a conflict of interest that had helped or could help IBM's competitor. Her personal privacy interests prevailed when there was no showing of harm to the employer's business interests. *Rulon-Miller v. Int'l Business Mach. Corp.*, 162 Cal. App. 3d 241 (1984)

HEALTH-RELATED CONDITIONS. Can an employer impose health-related conditions of employment that intrude upon a worker's constitutional rights of liberty and privacy guaranteed by the Bill of Rights? Like other intrusions into privacy, the answer is that it depends upon the circumstances, including the need for the requirement and the means to achieve the purpose in a less intrusive manner. In the case of a government employer, the lifestyle requirement should be rationally related to the purpose sought to be achieved.

Example: Greg Grusendorf took three puffs from a cigarette while on a lunch break from his job as a firefighter trainee with the Oklahoma City Fire Department. He was fired that afternoon by his supervisor on the grounds that he had violated the terms of an agreement he signed as a precondition of employment that he would not smoke a cigarette, either on or off duty, for one year from the time he began work. He sued for a violation of his civil rights because the government may not unreasonably infringe upon its employees' freedom of choice in personal matters unrelated to the performance of any duties. He lost his case because of the strong public interest in the selection of firefighters. *Grusendorf v. City of Oklahoma City*, 816 F.2d 539 (10th Cir. 1987)

AI Feature: Draft an Employee Privacy Waiver

There is a direct relationship between the strength of an employee's expectation of privacy in the workplace and the outcome of a trial on that issue. The greater the expectation of privacy, the greater the likelihood the employee will prevail in litigation. When hiring and promoting employees, the employer would be well advised to obtain written authorization and ratifications from the employee that permit the employer to conduct searches of the workplace.

Using an AI program, draft a privacy waiver in favor of a private employer. Applications to work area inspections, monitoring the employee's productivity, and tracking of company-supplied devices should be included. Ensure that the waiver is compliant with federal and the law of your home state.

Key Terms

- Electronic Communications Privacy Act (ECPA), 436
- Employee Polygraph Protection Act of 1988 (EPPA), 440
- False light, 432
- Fourth Amendment, 431
- Fundamental rights, 431
- Privacy, 430
- Restatement, 430
- State action, 431
- Tort of intrusion, 432

Applying the Law

18.1 Privacy and Security. Calvin Lewis, a former employee of the St. Tammany Parish Sheriff's Office (STPSO), was promoted several times and attained the rank of captain. During this time, Lewis met Jane Doe while he was assigned to a work detail and began a relationship with her. Lewis met

Jane Doe during this time while he was assigned to a work detail and began a relationship with her. Doe, who had a prior felony conviction, then began to live together with Lewis. In 2017, Lewis learned of a social media post in which someone had commented that a "newly promoted captain" was living with a convicted felon. The STPSO terminated Lewis's employment, after concluding an internal affairs department investigation finding that he was in violation of STPSO's anti-fraternization policy. How should the conflict between the employer's interest in preserving its anti-fraternization policy and an individual right of privacy be resolved? *Lewis v. Smith*, 2019 U.S. Dist. Lexis 129848 (2019)

18.2 Free Association. A federal district court in Connecticut refused to issue an injunction regarding the imposition of discipline on a group of corrections officers for their motorcycle club membership (the Outlaws). The officers argued the discipline infringed upon their freedom of association under the First Amendment. Argue for and against the correctional officers' position. *Piscottano v. Murphy*, 317 F. Supp. 2d 97 (D. Conn. 2004)

18.3 After-Hours Employment. How extensive should the employer's power to restrict off-hours conduct be? The State of Alabama permits state employees who are paid less than $75,000 to engage in private-sector employment on their own time if no other legal prohibition or "conflict" exists (Ala. Code § 36-1-11). Do you think an employer should have the right to control after-hours conduct? If so, what limitations, if any, should apply, and how would you concretely state and measure inappropriate conduct? Alabama has chosen a monetary threshold to permit such outside employment. What do you think would be an appropriate threshold?

18.4 Private Papers. Nicole Niceforo sued her employer, UBS Global Asset Management Americas, Inc., for violations of the FLSA, FMLA, and ADA. She claimed a violation of her privacy by her former employer's review of a private notebook she maintained during her employment that was left at her desk after termination. However, because the employer maintained a "Privacy in the Workplace Policy" that stated that all materials and property in the workplace are regarded as property of the employer regardless of being marked personal or private, the court concluded that the employee could have no reasonable expectation of privacy as it related to the notebook. The employer also asserted that Niceforo's claims were waived when she abandoned the notebook following her termination. Though she lost her privacy claims, what arguments would you make on her behalf? If you were in her position, what actions would you have taken to ensure the notebook remained your private property? *Niceforo v. UBS Global Asset Mgmt. Americas*, 20 F. Supp. 3d 428 (S.D.N.Y. 2014)

18.5 First Amendment Expression. If an employer's president came into possession of an employee's "journal" or diary (it had been taken by another employee from the employee's desk), would his reading and retention of it for some hours be an invasion of privacy? Would the expectation of privacy depend upon whether the journal had been open, closed, or locked when the employee discovered it? *Ghassomians v. Ashland Indep. School District*, 55 F. Supp. 2d 675 (E.D. Ky. 1998)

18.6 Employer Investigations. Following the *Ellerth* and *Faragher* decisions (discussed in Chapter 17), it is the employer's obligation to engage in reasonable preventative and corrective measures toward combating sexual harassment in the workplace. When a sexual harassment claim is made, the company must diligently and timely investigate the matter. The investigation may disclose sometimes humiliating and embarrassing situations. Does the employer face invasion of privacy or defamation claims? Conduct an internet search to determine if a qualified privilege to conduct such investigations exists and what limitations may apply. See, e.g., *Taylor v. CAN Corp.* 782 F. Supp. 2d 182 (E.D. Va. 2010) and *Ludlow v. Northwestern University*, 79 F. Supp. 3d 824 (N.D. Ill. 2015)

18.7 Surveillance and Monitoring. Renee Gustafson was a police lieutenant supervisor at a medical center. The medical center did not have a designated female locker room for police personnel. Thus, it was common for the female officers to use a supervisor's office to change into and out of their work uniforms before and after shifts. Surveillance cameras were installed in that same office and had captured images of female workers changing. The supervisor claimed that the cameras were installed to ensure that officers were not sleeping while on duty. If the supervisor did not know that it was common for the female officers to use it as a changing room, would there still be an invasion of privacy? See, e.g., *Gustafson v. Adkins*, 803 F.3d 883 (7th Cir. 2015)

18.8 Workplace Privacy. Amber Richards was a dispatcher for the County of Los Angeles Department of Public Works. There was an allegation that Richards engaged in sexual activity with visitors in the dispatch room while on duty at night. Instead of investigating the matter, Richards's supervisor installed a hidden camera inside a fake smoke detector and recorded activities in the room continuously. The recording showed that there was evidence of Richards's having inappropriate conduct and touching with visitors. What do you think should be the result? Is there a violation of Richards's Fourth Amendment rights? See *Carter v. County of Los Angeles*, 770 F. Supp. 2d 1042 (C.D. Cal. 2011)

18.9 Intrusion on Seclusion. An insurance company had a dispute with its agent. A federal court issued a restraining order prohibiting the agent from deleting any computer data or files containing information relating to the insurer's customers and financial records. The insurer's attorneys served the agent with the restraining order at his apartment and, with the help of a consultant, copied all the data on the agent's computers. The agent explained that only a small amount of material on one computer related to the dispute. The agent claimed that he suffered from AIDS, and that he stored on his computers highly personal information, medical records, photographs, and tax returns. What are the arguments for and against his contention that he had suffered an invasion of privacy? *Dalley v. Dykema Gossett, P.L.L.C.*, 287 Mich. App. 296 (2010)

18.10 False Light. A 30-second promotional announcement of nine segments was broadcast on a television network affiliate. The purpose of the broadcast was to promote the broadcaster's investigative reporting. Within it, an employee said that an unidentified owner of a local business was cheating the city. The owner of the business was shown in one of the segments. What would he have to allege in his complaint and prove in court to be successful on a false light invasion of privacy claim? *Schivarelli v. CBS, Inc.*, 333 Ill. App. 3d 755 (2002)

PART IV: BUSINESS ORGANIZATIONS

Forming the Small Business and Operating Franchises

19

Don't sit down and wait for the opportunities to come. Get up and make them! — Madam C. J. Walker, American Businesswoman (1867-1919)

Chapter Outline

- Introduction
- Overview of Starting a Business
  - *Management Application: Conducting Market Research and Competitive Analysis*
  - *Management Application: What to Include in a Business Plan*
- Selecting the Legal Structure
- Sole Proprietorships
  - *Management Application: Trade Names*

Case 19.1: *Goodwin v. John*

- Operating Franchises
  - *Management Application: Sample Provision Regarding Franchisor Control*

Case 19.2: *DiFederico v. Marriott International, Inc.*

  - *Management Application: Exercising the Right to Terminate*
- AI Feature: Create a Business Plan

Learning Objectives

After reading this chapter, you should be able to:

1. Identify the steps that should be taken to form a business.
2. Compare and contrast the entities that can be used to form a business.
3. Describe what should be included in a business plan.
4. Discuss the advantages and disadvantages of a sole proprietorship.
5. Recognize the most common type of franchises.

Introduction

Entrepreneur
A person who initiates and operates a new business.

Entrepreneurship plays a vital role in the continued health of the U.S. economy. An **entrepreneur** is a person who initiates and operates a new business. According to the U.S. Bureau of Labor Statistics, the United States has tens of millions of entrepreneurs. Every year, approximately 600,000 to 700,000 new businesses are established. Many states have created online business guides and resources to assist their residents in planning and forming new businesses.

Example: The Texas Secretary of State provides start-up guides and resources to assist entrepreneurs at *https://www.sos.state.tx.us/corp/related.shtml.*

In addition, the U.S. Small Business Administration (SBA) has created more than 900 Small Business Development Centers (SBDCs) to provide one-stop assistance, tailored to the local community and needs of individual clients, by providing small businesses and entrepreneurs a wide variety of information, counseling, training, and technical assistance across the United States, the District of Columbia, Puerto Rico, Samoa, and the U.S. Virgin Islands.

In choosing a business organizational form, entrepreneurs should consider several important factors including (1) the difficulty of creation, (2) potential liability of individual owners, (3) tax implications, and (4) the ability to raise financing.

Part IV of the text begins our discussion of different business organizations. In this chapter, we discuss sole proprietorships and franchising. Although a franchise is not a type of business organization, entrepreneurs use franchises to quickly enter a market. In the chapters that follow, we will examine partnerships, limited liability companies (LLCs), corporations, and other business entities.

Overview of Starting a Business

While many business professionals have developed a skillset for *running* a business through training and experience, many may not possess the same level of knowledge in *starting* a business. The following series of steps should be undertaken prior to beginning a new business to establish a solid foundation for the business:

1. Planning;
2. Financial decision making; and
3. Legal compliance.

Planning

Conducting market research and performing a competitive market analysis are important first steps in creating a successful business enterprise. The information derived from such research will identify customers and their desire for a product or service.

By surveying, using focus groups, and interviewing, the entrepreneur can understand consumer behavior and learn economic trends to improve the business idea. Market research may alternatively reveal that the market is unable to support the entrepreneur's idea for a new business opportunity.

Through detailed market research, the entrepreneur should be able to describe the following characteristics about the proposed business:

1. *Consumer demand.* Are there people who want or need the product or service?
2. *Size of the market.* How many potential customers are there for the product or service?
3. *Economic factors.* What are the demographics (such as disposable income, education, and employment) of the potential customers?
4. *Location.* Where are the potential customers located? Will the business need to be located in those areas?
5. *Competitors.* Is there a similar service or product that already exists in the marketplace? How much do these services or products cost if they do exist? How is the potential service or product different from what is already in the market? How will the business displace these competitors? Essentially, the entrepreneur must determine how the business will compare to its competitors.
6. *Structure and taxation.* What is the potential liability exposure presented by this product or service? The tax considerations of operating this business and using the selected type of business entity should be evaluated as well.

Selected State Business Portals

California: *https://www.sos.ca.gov/business-programs/business-entities/*
Delaware: *https://corp.delaware.gov/*
Florida: *https://dos.myflorida.com/sunbiz/*
Kentucky: *https://onestop.ky.gov/start/Pages/default.aspx*
Nevada: *https://www.nvsos.gov/sos/businesses*
New York: *https://www.ny.gov/services/business*
Ohio: *https://www.sos.state.oh.us/businesses/*
Texas: *https://www.sos.state.tx.us/corp/related.shtml*
Washington: *https://www.business.wa.gov/site/alias__business/927/small-business-guide.aspx*
Wyoming: *http://soswy.state.wy.us/Business/Default.aspx*

For more information on starting a new business, review the U.S. Small Business Administration's website at *https://www.sba.gov/*.

Management Application Conducting Market Research and Competitive Analysis

The SBA provides the following statistical resources to assist in conducting market research and competitive analysis:

Focus	Information Provided	Reference
General business statistics	Find statistics on industries and business conditions	NAICS, FedStats, Statistical Abstract of the United States, U.S. Census Bureau
Consumer statistics	Gain information on potential customers and consumer markets	Consumer Credit Data, Consumer Product Safety
Demographics	Segment the population for targeting customers	American FactFinder, Bureau of Labor Statistics
Economic indicators	Learn unemployment rates, loans issued, and more	Consumer Price Index, Bureau of Economic Analysis
Employment statistics	In-depth employment trends in your market	Employment and Unemployment Statistics
Income statistics	Fair income rates based on earnings data	Earnings by Occupation and Education, Income Statistics
Production and sales statistics	Understand demand, costs, and consumer spending	Consumer Spending, Gross Domestic Product (GDP)
Trade statistics	Track indicators of sales and market performance	Balance of Payments, USA Trade Online
Statistics of specific industries	Review federal agency data on industries	NAICS, Statistics of U.S. Businesses

Visit the SBA website at *www.sba.gov/business-guide* and review the information for planning a business.

Business plan
A document describing the goals for a business and the strategy to achieve them.

Traditional business plan
A business plan that is comprehensive, highly detailed, and often requested by lenders and investors.

Lean start-up plan
A non-comprehensive business plan that focuses only on a few key elements.

THE BUSINESS PLAN. After completing market research and competitive analysis, the entrepreneur should prepare a business plan. The purpose of a **business plan** is to describe to third parties how the new idea will result in a profitable business. It should clearly state what problem the business is solving. Additionally, the business plan should identify opportunities for growth. If done properly, it can help persuade investors to fund the business. Thereafter, it can be used to guide decision making in the operation of the business.

There are two general types of business plans: the traditional business plan and the lean start-up plan. A **traditional business plan** contains a prominent level of detail and is commonly requested by lenders and investors when they are deciding whether to invest in or lend capital to the business. A **lean start-up plan** is less formal and focuses only on the key elements to describe the business's value proposition, infrastructure, customers, and finances. The lean start-up format is often preferred when the business is relatively simple or when the business plan is likely to change.

Management Application
What to Include in a Business Plan

Depending upon the type of business plan the entrepreneur uses, different components may be included. The following chart illustrates common components included in business plans.

Traditional Business Plan

1. *Executive summary.* Includes a mission statement, details about the product or service, and basic information about the company's leadership team, key employees, and location.
2. *Company description.* Lists competitive advantages and specifics as to what problems or issues the product or service will solve.
3. *Market analysis.* Discusses the findings of market research.
4. *Legal structure.* Details the management and organizational structure of the business.
5. *Service or product offered.* Describes the service or product offered and how it differentiates itself from those already in the marketplace.
6. *Marketing and sales strategy.* Explains how customers will be reached and the means to sell to them.
7. *Request for funds.* Summary of sources and uses of funds needed to launch and operate the business for the first year.
8. *Financial projections.* Pro forma financial projections and metrics.

Lean Start-up Plan

1. *Problems solved.* What and how this business will solve problems for its customers.
2. *Relationship activities.* Relationships contributing to the success of the business.
3. *Competitive advantage.* Contrasts itself from its competitors.
4. *Resources required.* States the business's most important assets, including staff, capital, and intellectual property.
5. *Customers identified.* Describes and profiles key customers and sales volumes.
6. *Marketing channels.* States what marketing channels will reach target customers.
7. *Revenue and costs.* Generalizes financial results obtained from operating the business.

Financial Decisions Involved in Structuring a Business

To review business plan templates of the Small Business Administration, see https://www.sba.gov/business-guide/plan-your-business/write-your-business-plan.

CALCULATING START-UP COSTS. Common start-up costs and expenses must be identified. These include the cost of leasing office space, business supplies and equipment, utilities such as telecommunications expenses, insurance, employee salaries, and marketing and sales expenses.

MAKING DECISIONS BASED ON CALCULATIONS. After calculating the start-up costs, the entrepreneur can perform a breakeven analysis, estimate profits, and begin obtaining financing.

FUNDING OPTIONS. There are three major ways in which a business can be funded: (1) self-funding, (2) attracting investors, and (3) obtaining loans.

Bootstrapping
An entrepreneur leveraging personal financial resources or financing through personal relationships to fund the business.

Self-funding is also commonly referred to as **bootstrapping**. The entrepreneur leverages personal resources, using family and friends as sources of capital. The entrepreneur retains ownership and control of the business. A significant disadvantage of self-funding is that the risks associated with the business formation are shifted to the entrepreneur and his or her family members and friends. The pressure to repay these sources may drive entrepreneurs to make rash, emotional decisions in operating the business.

Venture capitalist
An investor who invests in businesses in exchange for ownership or significant control.

Obtaining funding from investors is another option available to entrepreneurs. These investors are also referred to as **venture capitalists**. Venture capitalists typically invest in businesses that exhibit a high growth potential and often limit their investments to certain business sectors (such as information technology or pharmaceuticals). Venture capitalists often require the entrepreneur to surrender ownership majority or control of the business in return for the investment of capital.

Small business loan
A loan that is guaranteed by the Small Business Administration in the event of the borrower's default.

For more information on available SBA loan programs and eligibility requirements, https://www.sba.gov/funding-programs/loans.

The third financing option is to obtain a loan through a bank. A common type of loan is the **small business loan**, a loan guaranteed by the Small Businesses Administration (SBA) in the event of a borrower's default. Although the SBA does not lend money directly, the agency partners with lenders to provide loans to small business owners. By guaranteeing these loans, the SBA reduces risk for lenders and makes it easier for businesses to access funding. SBA-guaranteed loans typically have rates and fees that are comparable to non-guaranteed loans. Businesses must meet certain eligibility requirements to qualify for the loan programs, which are often dependent on the character of the business's ownership, location of the business, and the source of the business's income stream.

Legal Compliance in Forming a Business

Legal compliance is important to ensure that a business has been properly formed, thereby potentially protecting the entrepreneur from personal liability arising from the operation of the business. A thorough discussion of liability arising from ownership of business organizations is discussed over the next several chapters.

EMPLOYER IDENTIFICATION NUMBER. Businesses located in the United States or U.S. territories are required to pay taxes. To do so, a business must first apply for an Employer Identification Number (EIN), also known as the Federal Tax ID. The responsible party (the one who owns or controls the entity) will apply online for the EIN through the IRS. The EIN is used to pay *federal* taxes. The EIN is necessary when a business opens a bank account, applies for business licenses and permits, and for other necessary activities (such as filing the business's taxes).

Concept Summary
Tax IDs

A Taxpayer Identification Number (TIN) is an identification number used by the IRS in the administration of tax laws. One type of TIN is the Employer Identification Number (EIN), which is used to identify a business entity. For more information about business entities requiring an EIN, visit *https://www.irs.gov/businesses/small-businesses-self-employed/employer-id-numbers.*

REGISTERING THE BUSINESS. The registration process of a business will vary depending upon the business's structure and location. A business may need to register for a fictitious business name statement when the business uses a name other than the business's legal name (discussed in more detail below). Additionally, depending on the type of business entity selected, the business may need to register with the Secretary of State of the state in which the business is formed. The entrepreneur must ensure that the business is properly registered to conduct operations and avoid penalties. Obtaining assistance from an attorney and a certified public accountant who are familiar with local requirements is recommended.

LICENSES AND PERMITS. Certain business industries (such as construction) may require a license or permit to conduct business. The business may need to obtain federal and/or state permits. State and local governments may regulate the activities of a business to varying degrees. Some occupations and activities are heavily regulated, such as health care, construction, and real estate. When federal administrative agencies regulate a business, a federal license or permit is frequently required.

To obtain a state tax ID number, see the Small Business Administration website: https://www.sba.gov/business-guide/launch-your-business/get-federal-state-tax-id-numbers.

REGISTER WITH THE STATE WORKFORCE OR EMPLOYMENT SERVICES OFFICE. Each state has an agency handling employee taxation and unemployment benefits. The business must register with that agency if it will have any employees working in that state.

Selecting the Legal Structure

In addition to sole proprietorships, which are discussed below, the most utilized forms of doing business include (1) general partnerships, (2) limited partnerships, (3) limited liability companies, and (4) corporations.

The following chart provides an overview of the factors involved in selecting one of these forms of business organization. The considerations presented will be the topic of our discussion over the next several chapters.

Concept Summary
Types of Business Organizations

	Sole Proprietorship	General Partnership	Limited Partnership	Corporation	Limited Liability Company (LLC)
Creation formalities	No formalities are required to form a sole proprietorship.	No formalities are required to form a general partnership.	File a certificate of limited partnership.	File articles of incorporation.	File articles of organization.

	Sole Proprietorship	General Partnership	Limited Partnership	Corporation	Limited Liability Company (LLC)
Ownership	One person owns the business.	Two or more persons are required to own the business.	One or more general partners and one or more limited partners.	Shareholders who may be individuals or other business entities.	Members who may be individuals or other business entities.
Liability	Unlimited personal liability.	Unlimited personal liability.	General partners have unlimited personal liability. Limited partners have limited liability.	Limited liability.	Limited liability.
Taxation	The sole proprietor pays personal income taxes on the profits of the business.	Flow-through taxation (business income/debts) — flows through to individual partners.	Flow-through taxation (business income/debts) — flows through to individual partners.	Double taxation. Corporation taxed on income; shareholders taxed on distributions.	Flow-through taxation (business income/debts) — flows through to individual members.

Being your own boss is great. You get to choose which 18 hours a day you work. — Unknown

Sole proprietorship An unincorporated business entity owned and operated by one individual with no distinction between the business and the owner.

Sole Proprietorships

The simplest business organization to form is the sole proprietorship. A **sole proprietorship** is an unincorporated business entity owned and run by one individual. Due to its ease of formation, it is the most commonly used business organization in the United States. Unless the business activity requires a state or local license or permit to validly operate, an entrepreneur only needs to begin conducting business activities to form a sole proprietorship. Sole proprietorships are not considered a separate legal entity; therefore, the business and the owner of the business are treated as one and the same.

Management Application Trade Names

A trade name (also known as "doing business as" or DBA) is a name used by a business that is not the registered legal name of the businesses. If the entrepreneur elects to do business under a trade name, compliance with state and local government filing requirements is necessary. States require that businesses that operate under a trade name file a fictitious business name statement. The purpose of such filing is to create a public record of the persons operating under the trade name. Each state provides its own unique fictitious name registration requirements.

Example: See Florida's trade name registration requirements at *https://dos.myflorida.com/sunbiz/start-business/efile/fl-fictitious-name-registration/*.

Advantages of the Sole Proprietorship

One of the biggest advantages of a sole proprietorship is the ease of formation. Because there are no formalities required to form a sole proprietorship (unless a business permit or license is required), starting a business in this manner is easier and less costly than forming a partnership, limited liability company, or corporation. Additionally, with a sole proprietorship, the business owner owns the entire business. As a result, they have the right to receive all the profits of the business.

As the sole owner, they also have great flexibility in managing the business. For a sole proprietor, decisions regarding employees, operational issues, and business opportunities (such as purchasing other assets or selling the business) can be made quickly. Unlike in other business forms, approval by others is not required to make such decisions.

Since the sole proprietor is not a separate legal entity, the profits and losses of the sole proprietorship pass through to the owner's personal income tax return. Therefore, the sole proprietorship as a business organization does not pay taxes. The owner reports the profits and losses from the sole proprietorship on the owner's personal income tax form (Schedule C (Profit or Loss from Business) on Form 1040 U.S. Individual Income Tax Return). The owner is also responsible for paying Social Security and Medicare taxes.

Concept Summary
Taxation of a Sole Proprietorship

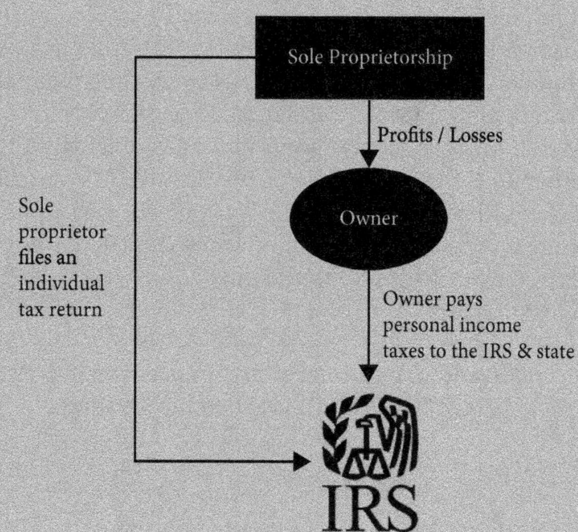

Income Taxes for Sole Proprietorships

Sole proprietors should be aware that they are taxed on all the profits of the business, regardless of whether the sole proprietor transfers the money from the business account into the sole proprietor's personal account. In the start-up years of the business as an entrepreneur grows its business, many entrepreneurs retain cash in the business to provide for the costs of growing the business and future expenses. Sole proprietors should be aware that they will be taxed on this income that they do not distribute to themselves.

Disadvantages of the Sole Proprietorship

Operating as a sole proprietorship does have a significant disadvantage. The sole proprietor is personally liable for *all* the losses or liabilities (that is, the sole proprietor has unlimited liability) incurred in the operation of the business. Therefore, all the business debts are also personal debts of the sole proprietor. To minimize this risk, a sole proprietor should procure necessary levels of liability insurance with broad protections to protect the business.

In addition, sole proprietors typically have more limited access to capital than other business entities, making growth and expansion more difficult. While corporations can raise capital from a variety of local and international sources, a sole proprietorship cannot because the investors would receive ownership in the business.

Example: Faking that your business is a business organization does not change the personal liability of a sole proprietor. The Neimans, who were homeowners, sued Edmund Tucker, doing business as Lawn Creations Franchising, LLC, for improperly recording a mechanics lien on their property for services that that they did not request. The trial court found that an individual not operating as any registered corporate entity at the time of their conduct is operating as a sole proprietorship. Tucker did not dispute that he was operating as a sole proprietorship, further rendering him liable for his unfair business practices without regard to his alleged trade name, Lawn Creations Franchising, LLC. *Nieman v. Tucker*, 159 N.E.3d 912 (Ohio Ct. App. 2020)

The following case was one of first impression in Nevada as to whether a sole proprietor is personally liable for unpaid employee wages.

CASE 19.1

A SOLE PROPRIETOR CAN BE PERSONALLY LIABLE FOR UNPAID WAGES

GOODWIN v. JOHN

624 F. Supp. 3d 1196 (2022)

United States District Court for the District of Nevada

Mathew John was the sole owner of MVJ Car Wash & Laundromat and the Valley Inn Motel. John personally owned and operated these businesses under his own name with no other employer or parent corporation. Julie Goodwin was an employee of these businesses and brought a case against John for unpaid wages. Goodwin argued that the businesses John owned were only behind fictitious names and John was the sole proprietor.

Language of the Court. *A "sole proprietorship" is a form of business in which one person owns all assets of a business, in contrast to a corporation. A "sole proprietor" refers to a single individual who owns a business, not to a sole shareholder of a corporation or to the corporate parent of a wholly owned subsidiary. A sole proprietorship has no separate legal existence or identity apart from the sole proprietor. Thus, in contrast to a corporation, a sole proprietorship has no separate existence. In other words, a "proprietorship" is not a legal entity, but merely a name under which the owner, who is the real party in interest, does business.*

Mr. John confirmed that he owns and operates the Valley Inn Motel personally, in his individual name; and, owns and operates the car wash and laundromat, and holds the business licenses for these entities in his name. . . . The overwhelming evidence demonstrates the motel and car wash/laundromat were run as sole proprietorships. Defendant presented and currently offers nothing to the contrary.

The Nevada Supreme Court has not reached the issue of whether a sole proprietorship is an employer under Nevada law for purposes of enforcement of employment rights. When the Court is faced with an issue of first impression under Nevada law, the Court must use its best judgment to predict how the Nevada Supreme Court would resolve the question presented.

The Court finds that the applicable Nevada statute defines an employer as "having control or custody of any employment, place of employment or any employee," would capture within it an individual operating a sole proprietorship that controls and has custody of a place of employment and an employee such as Plaintiff.

There is no employer other than Mr. John with respect to the Valley Motor Inn and the MVJ Car Wash & Laundromat. There is no parent corporation, partnership or limited liability company to which Plaintiff could look for relief. There is no evidence of any formal business enterprise with investment in or otherwise operating the motel, car wash or laundromat. There is only Mr. John who, as the sole proprietor and owner and operator of these business propositions, can be sued for alleged wrongdoing.

The above analysis does not hold true for MV John Corporation, sued along with Mr. John individually, the Valley Motor Inn, and the MVJ Car Wash & Laundromat. To reach Mr. John's personal assets for satisfaction of a judgment entered against MV John Corporation, Plaintiff must prove she can pierce the corporate veil of this entity. Plaintiff presented neither evidence nor argument to support piercing the MV John Corporation veil. Thus, the Court finds Mr. John's personal assets cannot be reached in an effort to collect a judgment against the MV John Corporation.

Decision. The plaintiff could recover unpaid wages due from the unincorporated businesses, but not from Mr. John, as a shareholder of an incorporated business.

Focus on Ethics

Given the choice, why wouldn't a businessperson incorporate to avoid exposure for unpaid employee wages? If the corporate shield could not be pierced, is it likely that Ms. Goodwin would recover her wage claim if the corporation could not pay the claim? What advice would you give Ms. Goodwin as a result of this decision?

Concept Summary Sole Proprietorships

Advantages of a Sole Proprietorship	Disadvantages of a Sole Proprietorship
Easy to create a sole proprietorship.	Sole proprietor has unlimited personal liability for all the business's debts and losses.
Sole proprietor has complete ownership of the business and receives all profits.	More limited access to capital than other business organizational forms.
No tax at the business organization level (pass-through taxation to the sole proprietor's personal income tax return).	
Sole proprietor retains flexibility in the operation and management of the business.	

Operating Franchises

Another way of operating a business is through franchising. A **franchise** is a business arrangement in which the owner of intellectual property (such as trademarks, copyrights, or trade names) grants a license to another person to use such intellectual property in the sale of goods or services. The purchaser of a franchise is known as a **franchisee**, while the seller of the franchise is known as the **franchisor**. When doing business as a franchise, the franchisee operates as an independent business from the franchisor and can choose any business organizational form (such as a corporation) while enjoying the benefits of the goodwill associated with the regional or national brand of the franchisor.

Franchise
A business arrangement in which the owner of intellectual property (the franchisor) grants a license to another (the franchisee) to use the franchisor's trade name and trademarks in the distribution and sale of goods or services.

> **Example:** Subway® is one of the largest franchisors in the world. An entrepreneur can obtain a franchise through Subway to own and operate its own Subway store. In such cases, Subway is the franchisor and the entrepreneur, either personally or through an entity, is the franchisee

Franchisee
A party granted a franchise and license to use the intellectual property of a franchisor.

Franchisor
A party who grants a franchise and license to use its intellectual property to another (a franchisee).

Franchises account for a significant portion of all retail sales and services in the United States. The benefits of franchising to a prospective franchisee include:

- Owning their own business while utilizing the resources of the franchisor's network;
- Franchisor typically provides in-depth training to operate the business;
- Lower failure rate than other start-up businesses; and
- Using the established goodwill of the franchisor (such as reputation and an established customer base).

The franchisor also realizes advantages with the franchise model:

- Ability to expand to new markets using the capital investments of the franchisees;
- Predictable receipt of revenue streams (such as through royalty payments) from the franchisees; and
- Growth of brand image and presence.

Types of Franchises

While there are various means of franchising a business, most often the franchise will be operated under one of these classifications:

- Product distributorship;
- A chain-style business; or
- A manufacturing arrangement.

Distributorship franchise
A type of franchise in which a manufacturer (the franchisor) licenses the ability to sell its products to a distributor (the franchisee).

PRODUCT DISTRIBUTORSHIP. In a **distributorship franchise**, a manufacturer (the franchisor) licenses the ability to sell its product to a distributor (the franchisee). Oil and gasoline distribution companies, automobile dealerships, and consumer beverage companies are common examples of distributorship franchises. A franchisor may also limit the franchisee's operations to an exclusive territory. This allows the franchisor to execute franchise agreements with many distributorships (franchisees) within discrete exclusive sales territories.

A product distribution franchise is like a supplier-dealer (retailer) relationship, but in the franchise context a franchisee is required to follow the guidelines of the franchisor. Typically, the guidelines include an agreement to sell the franchisor's brand exclusively.

Example: Automobile dealers selling a brand of vehicles must receive permission to sell another brand of vehicles. For example, a Ford® dealer would need the manufacturer's consent to sell new vehicles from a competing manufacturer.

In a supplier-dealer arrangement, the dealer may carry competing brands.

Example: Costco® sells Michelin® and Goodyear® branded tires at its tire centers.

Chain-style franchise
A type of franchise in which the franchisee conducts business under the franchisor's trade name.

CHAIN-STYLE BUSINESS OPERATIONS. In a **chain-style franchise**, a franchisee conducts business under the franchisor's trade name. Typically, the franchisee must follow the franchisor's directives relative to the operation of the franchisee's operation. Often, franchisees are required to purchase supplies, materials, and equipment from the franchisor to ensure the goods are uniform and of consistent quality. Chain-style franchising is common with fast food restaurants (such as Pizza Hut) and service-related businesses (such as Marriot International®). One source of wealth for franchisors is the ownership of land. Many franchisors under a chain-style franchise will purchase the land and then rent the premises to the franchisee to operate its business.

Example: Marriott International, Inc. is a chain-style franchise that franchises its trade name to franchisees to operate Marriott® hotels.

Manufacturing arrangement
A type of franchise agreement whereby the franchisor provides the franchisee the formula or ingredients needed to make a particular product.

MANUFACTURING OR PROCESSING-PLANT ARRANGEMENTS. In a **manufacturing arrangement** (also known as a processing-plant arrangement), the franchisor supplies the franchisee a formula or ingredients needed to manufacture a particular product. The franchisee will then sell the product according to the franchisor's standards at either the wholesale or retail level. This type of franchise is often associated with soft drink companies that have franchisees produce, bottle, and distribute their beverages.

Example: Keurig Dr. Pepper Inc. owns the "secret formula" for making Dr. Pepper®. Keurig Dr. Pepper sells its concentrate to regional bottling companies that produce and distribute Dr. Pepper.

Franchise Disclosure Laws

A franchisor licenses its intellectual property to a franchisee through a contract. Article 2 of the Uniform Commercial Code (UCC) applies to the sale of such contracts (see Chapters 26 through 28). In addition to contract law governed by Article 2 of the UCC, due to instances where franchisors mislead, failed to disclose, or embellished the success of the franchise to prospective franchisees, both the federal government and several states have enacted mandatory disclosure requirements that franchisors must make to prospective franchisees. Several of these disclosures are discussed below.

FTC FRANCHISE RULE. The Federal Trade Commission (FTC), a federal administrative agency that regulates franchising, adopted the **FTC Franchise Rule** to prevent unfair and deceptive practices in the franchising industry. The FTC Franchise Rule requires franchisors to make certain presale disclosures to a prospective franchisee to allow the prospective franchisee to fairly consider the risks of the prospective franchise.

FTC Franchise Rule A rule published by the FTC to facilitate informed decisions and prevent deception in the sale of franchises.

Review the FTC Franchise Rule Compliance Guide at https://www.ftc.gov/system/files/documents/plain-language/bus70-franchise-rule-compliance-guide.pdf.

The required disclosures vary depending upon whether the earnings projected are based on actual or hypothetical data. If a franchisor makes sales or earnings projections based on *actual data* such as sales, income, or profits of an existing franchise, the following must be disclosed:

- The number and percentage of the franchisor's actual franchises that have obtained such results; and
- A cautionary statement in at least 12-point boldface typewritten font stating there is no assurance that the franchisee will obtain the same results and that by relying upon the disclosed figures, the franchisee has accepted the risk of not being as successful as other franchises.

If a franchisor instead makes sales or earnings projections based on *hypothetical data*, the following must be disclosed:

- The assumptions underlying the estimates;
- The number and percentage of actual franchises that have obtained such results; and
- A cautionary statement in at least 12-point boldface typewritten font stating that the figures are only estimates of what the franchisor forecasts the franchisee may earn and that there is no assurance of such revenues. The statement should also state that by relying upon these estimates, the franchisee assumes the risk of the investment.

If the FTC disclosure rules are violated by a franchisor, the franchisor may be subject to an injunction against further franchise sales, civil fines, and an FTC civil action on behalf of injured franchisees to recover damages.

STATE DISCLOSURE LAWS. Most states have adopted additional franchise laws requiring franchisors to register and deliver disclosure documents to prospective franchisees. Under these state franchise laws, franchisees are given important legal rights, including the right to bring private lawsuits for violation of the state disclosure requirements.

Franchise Disclosure Document (FDD) A uniform disclosure document that requires franchisors to make disclosures of 23 specific items to prospective franchises. States may require the franchisor register the FDD with a state department prior to offering a franchise for sale.

While state legislation may vary, over 13 states have adopted the **Franchise Disclosure Document (FDD)**. The FDD is a uniform disclosure document that requires franchisors to make disclosures of 23 specific items to prospective franchisees. States may require the franchisor to register the FDD with a state department prior to offering a franchise for sale. The FDD disclosures primarily relate to information about the franchisor, such as how long the franchisor has been in business, a description of the executives of the franchise and their experience, initial and ongoing franchise costs, reasons permitted for the termination of the franchise, and any territory or customer restrictions. The FDD also requires that financial information such as financial statements be provided to prospective franchisees.

> **Example:** The State of Illinois has enacted the Franchise Disclosure Act of 1987, which applies to the sale of franchises.

The Franchise Agreement

Franchise agreement A legal document that establishes the terms and conditions of the relationship between the franchisor and the franchisee.

Once a prospective franchisee has selected a franchise to run, the franchisee will apply to the franchisor for a franchise opportunity. After review of the franchisee's financial and employment history and other requested information, the parties enter into a franchise agreement. The **franchise agreement** establishes the terms and conditions of the relationship between the franchisor and the franchisee. If any of the contractual terms are not performed by either party, the non-breaching party may sue for breach of contract. Most states require franchise agreements to be in writing. Franchise agreements often will address the topics discussed below.

COST OF THE FRANCHISE. The franchisee will pay an initial fee to obtain the rights to use the intellectual property of the franchisor (a license from the franchisor). In addition, during the operation of the franchise, the franchisee will pay the franchisor a royalty fee (often a percentage of its gross sales). Frequently, there are additional fees to be paid, including franchisor costs for marketing and advertising. The franchisee may also be required to purchase or lease fixtures, equipment, and supplies from the franchisor.

> **Example:** The UPS Store® requires a 5 percent royalty fee of all gross sales plus gross commissions from the store (known as "STR"), plus 1 percent of STR for marketing, plus 2.5 percent of STR for national advertising fees, and annual technology and development and support fees as part of the cost of owning a franchise.

BUSINESS PREMISES. The franchise agreement will determine whether the franchisee must lease or purchase the business premises. Sometimes, franchisors purchase the land and require the franchisee to lease the premises. The appreciation of land value and rental income is a significant source of wealth and income creation for franchisors. A franchisee will also often have to pay for tenant improvements to construct or remodel business premises to meet the franchisor's requirements. The franchise contract will likely include routine maintenance requirements for the business.

> **Example:** 7-Eleven, Inc.® purchases and pays for the ongoing cost of the land, building, and store equipment in exchange for a share of the gross profit of the store as part of its franchise agreements.

FRANCHISEE'S TERRITORY. The territory in which the franchisee will operate is discussed in the franchise agreement. Some agreements may provide a franchisee with exclusive territorial rights to operate in a specific geographic area. These rights protect the franchisee from competition with other operators franchised by the same franchisor in that geographic area. If the franchise agreement does not provide for exclusive rights, a franchisor can locate additional franchises within that specified area.

Example: Taco Bell® franchise agreements do not provide territorial protection or exclusivity for its franchisees.

NONCOMPETITION CLAUSES. Franchisors will expect the franchisee's commitment to the franchise operation. Accordingly, most franchise agreements contain a noncompetition clause. This clause will prohibit a franchisee from operating a competing business to that of the franchisor in a specified area during the term, and for a specified time after, the termination of the franchise.

Example: Pla-Fit Franchise, LLC (DBA Planet Fitness®) franchise agreements provide for a two-year covenant not to compete from the termination, transfer, or non-renewal of the franchise agreement within 15 miles of the business location and any other Planet Fitness.

CONTROL REQUIREMENTS. While the franchisee has control over its day-to-day operations, franchise agreements will detail the quality control standards the franchisee is expected to maintain and provide the franchisor the right to make periodic inspection of the premises to protect the franchisor's goodwill (name and reputation). A franchisee's failure to meet these standards may result in termination of the franchise agreement.

While franchisors will seek to maintain quality control standards over its franchisees, too much control may create liability for the franchisor. Franchisor and franchisees are separate legal entities and the franchisor deals with a franchisee as an independent contractor. As such, franchisees are generally not the agents of the franchisors. Each party is liable for their own torts and contractual breaches.

A franchisor will have liability for the acts of the franchisee where there is actual or apparent agency authority. Actual agency, while rare, arises where under the franchise agreement, the franchisor expressly agreed to make the franchisee its agent. Apparent agency arises when a third person believes the franchisee is the agent of the franchisor. Apparent agency can arise under a franchise where:

- Under the franchise agreement or the operations manuals, the franchisor controlled the day-to-day operations of the franchised business; and,
- The franchise agreement or the operations manual controlled how the plaintiff was injured.

The greater the degree of control exercised by the franchisor, the greater the likelihood that the franchisor will be held liable for the plaintiff's damages under apparent authority. The franchisor must therefore balance the desire to control the franchisee to maintain quality standards while avoiding liability under apparent authority.

Management Application
Sample Provision Regarding Franchisor Control

Franchisee must implement and abide by Franchisor's requirements and recommendations directed to enhancing substantial System uniformity. The following provisions control with respect to products and operations.

A. **Authorized Menu.** Franchisee's business must be confined to the preparation and sale of only such Menu Items and other food and beverage products as Franchisor designates and approves in writing from time to time for sale by Franchisee's Restaurant. Franchise must offer for sale from the Restaurant all items and only those items listed as Menu Items and other approved food and beverage products. Franchisor has the right to make modifications to these items from time to time, and Franchisee agrees to comply with any modifications. Franchisee may not offer or sell any other product or service at the Authorized Location without Franchisor's prior written consent.

B. **Authorized Products and Ingredients.** Franchisee must use in the operation of the Restaurant and in the preparation of Menu Items and other food and beverage products only the proprietary sauces and mixes and other proprietary and non-proprietary ingredients, recipes, formulas, cooking techniques and processes and supplies, and must prepare and serve Menu Items and products in such portions, sizes, appearance, taste and packaging, all as Franchisor specifies in Franchisor's most current product preparation materials or otherwise in writing. Franchisor will supply to Franchisee a copy of the current product preparation materials prior to opening the Restaurant. Franchisee acknowledges and agrees that Franchisor may change these periodically and that Franchisee is obligated to conform to the requirements. All supplies, including containers, cups, plates, wrapping, eating utensils, and napkins, and all other customer service materials of all descriptions and types must meet Franchisor's standards of uniformity and quality. Franchisee acknowledges that the Restaurant must at all times maintain an inventory of ingredients, food and beverage products and other products, material and suppliers that will permit operation of the Restaurant at maximum capacity.

Source: Gregory Battersby & Charles Grimes, *License Agreements: Forms and Checklists* (Wolters Kluwer, 2d ed. 2020).

How should a franchisor balance between controlling franchisee operations to ensure quality assurance at the retail level and risking liability for the acts and omissions of the franchisee by exercising too much control over those operations?

In the following case, a third party sought to hold a franchisor liable for harm arising from a terrorist attack on the theory that the franchisor controlled the franchisee's security procedures—the instrumentality that led to the death of a family member.

CASE 19.2

A FRANCHISOR IS NOT LIABLE IF IT DID NOT CONTROL THE INSTRUMENTALITY THAT CAUSED THE HARM

DiFEDERICO v. MARRIOTT INTERNATIONAL, INC.

677 F. App'x 830 (2017)

United States Court of Appeals for the Fourth Circuit

On September 20, 2008, Albert DiFederico died after terrorists attacked the Marriott Islamabad Hotel, in which he was a hotel guest. The Marriott Islamabad Hotel (Islamabad) was a franchisee of Marriott International (Marriott). It was owned and operated by Hashwani, Inc., a Pakistani company. During the terrorist attack, a truck carrying 1,320 pounds of explosives turned into Islamabad's driveway and crashed into the hotel's fortified gate barrier. The barrier stopped the truck from moving any closer to the hotel. Shortly thereafter, the explosives from the truck detonated, setting fire to the fourth floor of the hotel, where DiFederico died. His widow and children later sued Marriott in federal court in Maryland, where the company is headquartered, alleging that Marriott exercised sufficient control over the Islamabad's security protocols to render it liable for Mr. DiFederico's death. The federal district court held that Marriot was not liable for DiFederico's death, and the family appealed.

Language of the Court. *In order to maintain a license to use the Marriott name, franchised hotels must adhere to a set of standards that Marriott establishes. A franchised hotel must meet Marriott's Crisis Management Standards ("Standards"). The Standards delineate the minimum-security standards a franchised hotel must meet based on its level of threat risk. Marriott also has a Crisis Management Plan ("Plan") that it requires company owned hotels to meet. Unlike the Standards, however, franchised hotels need not adhere to the Plan. Instead, the Plan is "distributed to franchised hotels . . . because the contents of this manual may help the franchised hotels in developing or improving their Local Crisis Management Plan." Similarly, Marriott-owned hotels operating internationally must meet Marriott's International Lodging Crisis Plan ("International Plan"). Franchised hotels receive the International Plan, but do not need to meet its requirements.*

Marriott audits its franchised hotels twice a year to ensure the Standards are met. But Marriott takes no further steps to ensure that the franchised hotels are safe. The audit report itself is a one-page, double-sided, yes/no checklist with a short space for comments, confirming that the relevant security requirements, depending on the hotel's threat condition, are met: for example, whether there is a current, local crisis management plan on file; whether anyone is taking photographs of the hotel; whether the roof access is locked.

Marriott does not even have to review or approve a franchised hotel's local crisis management plan. It just needs to know that the hotel has one. Marriott requires franchised hotels to send its employees to mandatory Marriott training programs. These programs cover topics like hospitality, management skills, and conflict resolution. But Marriott provides franchised hotels with no training programs on security protocols or threat assessment.

The Islamabad is a franchisee of Marriott. As a franchisee, the Islamabad has to meet Marriott's Standards. Hashwani, the company that owns and manages the Islamabad, also received Marriott's Plan and International Plan, but it did not need to implement those plans. Hashwani is otherwise responsible for hiring, training, and managing the Islamabad's security staff.

Whether a franchisor controlled the instrumentalities of an injury is a highly fact intensive question. The facts here demonstrate that Marriott lacked sufficient control over the instrumentality leading to Mr. DiFederico's death—namely, the Islamabad's security protocols. Marriott did not hire any of the Islamabad's security employees. It did not provide any security training, either mandatory or optional, to the Islamabad's employees. Contrary to Plaintiffs' assertions, it did not develop or carry out a specific security plan for the Islamabad. It did not even review the Islamabad's local crisis management plan.

Mr. DiFederico's death was tragic. But ultimately, Hashwani—not the Marriott—had control over how Hashwani's employees would respond to the fire or bombing that killed Mr. DiFederico. Marriott never trained the Islamabad's employees on how to respond to such a situation; it never established a plan for such a situation; it never even reviewed the plan that Hashwani developed. As a matter of law, Marriott did not control the instrumentalities that led to Mr. DiFederico's death.

Decision. Marriott, as franchisor, was not liable for the death of Mr. DiFederico.

Focus on Ethics

Would the result be the same if there had been a uniform industry standard governing hotel security that Marriott enforced? Is this decision equitable if the family is without an effective remedy for their loss?

Terminating a Franchise

Routinely, franchise agreements provide that the franchisor can terminate the franchise for cause. Commonly, termination for cause results when the franchise fails to meet sales quotas, the franchisee fails to meet quality control standards, the franchisee dies or becomes permanently disabled, or the franchisee materially breaches the franchise contract. Unless terminated for cause, the franchise agreement will often establish a duration for the franchise (often tied to the term of the lease for the business premises).

If there is reason to terminate the franchise relationship, prior written notice must usually be given to the other party within the period stated in the agreement or as required by law. If no duration is stated, the notice must be given within a reasonable time following the event triggering the termination. Once notice is given, the franchisee may be given the opportunity to cure the breach. If the breach can be cured, the franchisee may avoid termination of the franchise agreement. The right to cure, if any, is stated in the franchise agreement. The following excerpt from a franchise agreement provides such a provision.

Management Application Exercising the Right to Terminate

A franchise agreement might contain the following language:

> Franchisee may terminate this Agreement as a result of material breach by Franchisor of a material provision of this Agreement provided that: (i) Franchisee provides Franchisor with written notice of the breach identifying the grounds of the breach; and (ii) Franchisor fails to cure the breach within thirty (30) days after Franchisor's receipt of the written notice. If Franchisor fails to cure the breach, the termination will be effective sixty (60) days after Franchisor's receipt of Franchisee's written notice of breach.

If the franchisee is exposed to such risk, what terms should it negotiate with the franchisor at the time of entering into the franchise?

Wrongful Termination

To prevent unnecessary hardship resulting from a termination, both case law and statutory law have noted the importance of the duties of good faith and fair dealing owed by the franchisor to the franchisee. The franchisee who has invested substantial time and money in the franchise may sue for wrongful termination where a franchisor acted in bad faith and unfairly terminated a franchise. In addition, termination at-will clauses in franchise agreements have been held to be void as unconscionable.

> **Example:** United Vintners® distributed and imported wine and other alcoholic beverages. It entered into a distribution agreement with Lee Beverage Company, Inc., whereby Lee would distribute on an exclusive basis United's beverages in Wisconsin. When United drastically reduced the product lines distributed by Lee, Lee sued United on the theory that it had terminated its agreement without good cause and without proper notice. A federal court agreed and awarded damages to Lee. *Lee Beverage Co., Inc. v. I.S.C. Wines of California, Inc.*, 623 F. Supp. 867 (E.D. Wis. 1985)

AI Feature: Create a Business Plan

Use an internet search engine to research a business opportunity you would like to pursue. Then, using an AI program, prepare a lean startup business plan for that business.

Key Terms

- Bootstrapping, 458
- Business plan, 456
- Chain-style franchise, 466
- Distributorship franchise, 465
- Entrepreneur, 454
- Franchise, 465
- Franchise agreement, 468
- Franchise Disclosure Document (FDD), 467
- Franchisee, 465
- Franchisor, 465
- FTC Franchise Rule, 467
- Lean start-up plan, 456
- Manufacturing arrangement, 466
- Small business loan, 458
- Sole proprietorship, 460
- Traditional business plan, 456
- Venture capitalist, 458

Applying the Law

19.1 Sole Proprietorships. Greg Carter owned and operated as a sole proprietorship three retail stores in West Virginia. Carter then incorporated it as Carter Enterprises, Inc. At the point of incorporation, Carter owed Ashland Specialty Company $426,744.41 for unpaid purchases incurred while Carter was operating as a sole proprietorship. What liability does Carter have for the debts owed to Ashland Specialty Company? *Carter Enterprises, Inc. v. Ashland Specialty Co.*, 257 B.R. 797 (S.D. W. Va. 2001)

19.2 Liability. Thomas Clardy and James Kervin were racing their automobiles one night. During an attempt to pass Kervin, Clardy went into the opposite lane and struck Norma Hoffman, killing both Hoffman and him. Thomas owned as a sole proprietorship a real estate company, known as Clardy Realty. After Clardy's death, his widow incorporated Clardy Realty. Hoffman's mother sued Clardy Realty. Is the tort liability of Thomas Clardy enforceable against the newly incorporated business? *Clardy v. Sanders*, 551 So. 2d 1057 (Ala. 1989)

19.3 Successor Liability. Constance Barr owned The Stone Scone as a sole proprietorship and secured a $100,000 line of credit from Fleet Bank, which was later acquired by Bank of America (BoA). Barr argued against personal liability for overdue payments, citing The Stone Scone's change in status from a sole proprietorship to an LLC, despite not notifying her creditors. However, the court stated that an individual doing business as a sole proprietor, even if the business operates under a different name, remains personally liable for all the obligations of the business. Thus, as the sole proprietor of The Stone Scone, Barr is personally liable for the debts incurred on the Fleet Bank credit line. The fact that The Stone Scone converted to an LLC after the line of credit was opened does not alter Barr's individual liability. The Supreme Judicial Court of Maine held that Barr remained personally liable as a sole proprietor for the debts and that a subsequent conversion of the business operation into an LLC did not alter her personal liability. *Bank of America, N.A. v. Barr*, 9 A.3d 816 (2010)

19.4 Franchise Agreement. Mamilove, LLC, and its officers, Michele and Lorraine Reymond, sought rescission of a franchise agreement and damages for claims related to their negotiations for, and ultimate purchase of, a daycare franchise. They claimed that before executing the franchise agreement they were given oral financial representations by the franchisor, Legacy Academy, Inc. Ten years after signing it, the franchisees sued the franchisor to rescind the agreement and for fraud damages. They claimed they never read the franchise agreement. The franchisor defended the suit on the grounds that the agreement disclaimed any pre-contract representations between the parties through a merger clause (discussed in Chapter 13). The representations included those of higher gross sales than the plaintiffs realized during their operation of the franchise. What result in this case? Did their failure to read the franchise agreement affect the outcome? Conduct research using an internet search engine to identify what financial information should be included in franchise disclosure documents. *Legal Academy v. Mamilove, LLC*, 771 S.E.2d 868 (Ga. 2015)

19.5 Franchisor Liability. Thomas Nearhood was exercising at a franchised location of Anytime Fitness® location. While performing squat exercises on a Smith machine, the weighted bar of the machine fell on him, causing serious internal injuries. Nearhood sued against Anytime Fitness, Inc., the franchisor of the gym, in addition to the franchisee and the manufacturer of the machine. As to the franchisor, Nearhood argued that it was liable because it allowed its franchisee to possess a dangerous instrumentality. Nearhood contended that the franchisor assumed responsibility because the electronic key system used by Anytime Fitness's franchisees ensured almost universal gym access. In the franchise agreement, a provision stated that the franchisee would always be responsible for the conduct of the day-to-day operation of its fitness center and that the mandatory standards, specifications, and policies established by the franchisor were not aimed at the day-to-day operation of the franchisee's business. Should the franchisor be held liable? *Nearhood v. Anytime Fitness*, 191 So. 3d 707 (La. Ct. App. 2016)

19.6 Franchisor Control. Turnway Donuts, Inc. entered into a franchise agreement with Dunkin' Donuts, Inc.® to operate a franchise. Dunkin' Donuts required that the donut store be open 24 hours a day. The franchise agreement stated that Dunkin' Donuts maintains a continuing advisory relationship, which includes periodic inspections to determine whether franchisees maintain the store in conformity with the Dunkin' Donuts standards manual. Dunkin' Donuts sent a series of articles on safety and security matters to its franchisees, including an internal newsletter offering several suggestions. Wendy Wu was working alone at 1:00 A.M. when two teenagers entered the store and brutally attacked her. At the time of the attack, the alarm system was not working and there was no videotape in the security camera. Should Dunkin' Donuts be liable for Turnway's allegedly negligent provision of security? *Wendy Wu v. Dunkin' Donuts, Inc.*, 105 F. Supp. 2d 83 (E.D.N.Y. 2000)

19.7 Good Faith and Fair Dealing. Buddy House was engaged in the construction business, and he enjoyed a long and rewarding relationship with Holiday Inn®. House created Hotel Associates, Inc. (HAI) expanding his business to include hotel ownership and operations. At Holiday Inn's request, HAI investigated a hotel in Texas to determine the cost of possible conversion to a Holiday Inn. House bought the hotel property and signed a ten-year franchise agreement. Before the ten years had passed, Holiday Inn had developed a plan to license a different local hotel as a Holiday Inn instead of renewing the franchise agreement with HAI. House was unaware of this plan and applied for an extension of his franchise. Holiday Inn asked for substantial renovations, leading HAI to spend $3 million on the renovations. Holiday Inn voted not to renew HAI's lease, and instead granted the franchise to the other hotel. HAI continued to operate the Holiday Inn franchise through the end of the ten-year agreement, and then sold it for $5 million. Did Holiday Inn breach its contract or commit a fraud against HAI? *Holiday Inn Franchising, Inc. v. Hotel Associates, Inc.*, 2011 Ark. App. 147 (2011)

19.8 Terminating Franchises. Dairy Mart, Inc.® approved Zapatha's franchise ownership request and presented him with a franchise agreement. The agreement contained a termination clause providing that after 12 months, either Zapatha or Dairy Mart could terminate by providing 90 days' written notice. If Dairy Mart terminated the agreement without cause, it would be required to purchase all Zapatha's remaining inventory at 80 percent of its market value. Four years later, Dairy Mart presented Zapatha with a new and more detailed franchise agreement. After Zapatha informed Dairy Mart that he would not sign a new agreement, Dairy Mart gave written notice that it was terminating Zapatha's franchise agreement within 90 days. Did Dairy Mart follow correct procedures to terminate the franchise agreement? Was this termination considered for cause or without cause? *Zapatha v. Dairy Mart, Inc.*, 408 N.E.2d 1370 (Mass. 1980)

19.9 Wrongful Termination. Russell and Nancy Zeidler owned and operated an A & W franchise pursuant to a franchise agreement with A & W Restaurants, Inc.® The Zeidlers' business operation was not a success, and the restaurant lost money every year of the operation. The Zeidlers had failed to maintain and run their restaurant according to the A & W health and sanitation standards, and they had let their liability insurance lapse. Before the term of the franchise agreement had expired, the Zeidlers closed their restaurant. Upon hearing of the closing of the franchise, A & W sent a letter formally terminating the franchise agreement. Do the Zeidlers have a claim for wrongful termination? *Zeidler v. A & W Restaurants, Inc.*, 301 F.3d 572 (7th Cir. 2002)

19.10 Opportunity to Cure. George operated a Mobil-branded gasoline station under a franchise agreement with ExxonMobil Corporation®. Exxon assigned the contract to Buchanan Energy, causing a rental dispute between Buchanan and George. Buchanan then terminated the franchise agreement because George failed to make a rent payment. George always claimed that it was ready, willing, and able to pay rent, but that Buchanan failed to accept payment. Does George have a claim for wrongful termination? Discuss. *Oshana v. Buchanan Energy*, 2012 U.S. Dist. LEXIS 16920 (N.D. Ill. 2012)

Partnerships

20

As they say on my own Cape Cod, a rising tide lifts all the boats. And a partnership, by definition, serves both partners, without domination or unfair advantage. Together we have been partners in adversity; let us also be partners in prosperity. — John F. Kennedy, Thirty-fifth President of the United States (1917-1963)

Chapter Outline

- Introduction
- Forming and Operating a Partnership
  - *Management Application: Checklist for Drafting a Partnership Agreement*
- Rights of Partners
  - *Management Application: Management Committee in a Partnership*
  - Management Application: Charging Order Form
- Authority of Partners
- Duties and Liabilities of Partners

Case 20.1: *McBeth v. Carpenter*

- Dissociation and Termination
  - *Management Application: Notice of Buyout and Estimated Payment for Partnership Interest*
- Types of Partnerships

Case 20.2: *Doctors Hospital at Renaissance, Ltd. v. Andrade*

Case 20.3: *Apcar Investment Partners VI, Ltd. v. Gaus*

- AI Feature: Draft an Agreement to Purchase a Partner's Interest

Learning Objectives

After studying this chapter, you should be able to:

1. List the key characteristics of all partnerships.
2. Describe the role of a partner within a partnership.
3. Discuss the rights and fiduciary duties of partners.
4. Distinguish among the different types of partnerships.

Introduction

For businesses owned by more than one person, the common types of business entities are partnerships, limited liability companies, and corporations. The decision as to which form to use depends on many factors, such as relationships among owners, the desire of a business owner to direct the management of the enterprise, the ease of raising capital for the business, and the need to limit personal liability for the debts and obligations of the business.

United States law recognizes several forms of partnerships: general partnerships, limited liability partnerships, limited partnerships, and limited liability limited partnerships. General partnerships allow those with varying skills and resources to combine for the operation of an enterprise in which they will benefit from the combination.

While general partnerships are the most common form of partnerships, the other forms, including the limited liability partnership, limited partnership, and limited liability limited partnership, offer a shield of limited liability for their owners (although the limited liability limited partnership form is not commonly utilized). Today, law firms and accounting firms often operate in the limited liability partnership form, while limited partnerships are commonly utilized in real estate investing and movie production investments. In this chapter, we will examine each of these forms of partnership.

Forming and Operating a Partnership

Unlike other forms of business organization, a general partnership is not formed by filing a document with a public agency. That is, few or no formalities are required to form a partnership.

A partnership is a creature of both contract and statute. The Uniform Law Commission (also known as the National Conference of Commissions on Uniform State Laws) (ULC) drafts model legislation for different areas of statutory law. The model legislation governing partnership law includes the Uniform Partnership Act (UPA) as well as the revisions to the UPA known as the **Revised Uniform Partnership Act (RUPA)**. The UPA was first adopted by the ULC in 1914 and was subsequently adopted by all states but Louisiana.[1] The most recent version of the UPA, RUPA, was enacted in 1997 and later amended in 2011 and 2013. For the purposes of this text, the term "RUPA" will be used to refer to the 1997 Act. States are free to make changes to these Acts and do not have to adopt amendments to them. In the absence of an express agreement between the partners, such as a partnership agreement, the UPA or RUPA governs the operation of all partnerships.

Revised Uniform Partnership Act (RUPA)
A revised model act that codifies partnership law. Most states have adopted the RUPA in whole or in part.

Partnership
A voluntary unincorporated association of two or more persons to conduct as co-owners a business for profit.

Definition of a Partnership

Most states have adopted the RUPA. The rest of the states, except for Louisiana, follow the UPA. Under RUPA, a **partnership** is "an association of *two or more* persons to carry on as co-owners of a business for profit."

1. Although Louisiana is the only state that has not adopted either the UPA or RUPA, many of its state statutes governing partnership law are similar to the UPA and RUPA.

Under the RUPA, a partnership requires two or more persons to manifest an intention to associate as co-owners of a business for profit. A person cannot be forced to become a partner, and other partners cannot be forced to accept another person as a partner. Adding another partner to the partnership requires the consent of all the current partners. The term "persons" includes both natural persons as well as artificial persons (such as corporations and other business organizations) who may serve as a partner. A "business" is any trade, occupation, or profession. The RUPA states that, with certain exceptions, "[a] person who receives a share of the profits of a business is presumed to be a partner in the business. . . ." Exceptions to this rule include the payment of profits for (1) repayment of the debt, (2) compensation, or (3) rent.

Example: Sheryl is employed as a salesperson in Company A. As part of Sheryl's compensation, Sheryl is paid 10 percent of the profits she generates from her sales. While Sheryl receives a portion of the profits from Company A, Sheryl is not a partner because she is receiving profits as part of her compensation with Company A.

Creation of Partnerships

Partnerships are formed either by contract or by conduct of the parties. Frequently, they are formed by an agreement between or among the partners. This agreement is known as a **partnership agreement** or the **articles of partnership**. Many partnerships have detailed partnership agreements, excerpts of which are presented in this chapter, which set forth the rights and duties of the partners operating the partnership. The partners may agree upon any terms they wish, so long as they are not illegal or against public policy.

Partnership agreement (articles of partnership) A writing setting forth the rights and duties of the partners with respect to the partnership business.

Partnership agreements may be *oral*, *written*, or *implied by conduct*. However, there are some partnership agreements that, to be enforceable, must be in writing to comply with the Statute of Frauds. Where a partnership agreement is not in writing and is required to be under the Statute of Frauds, the state partnership laws apply (usually the RUPA or UPA). Several types of partnership agreements that under the Statute of Frauds must be in writing to be enforceable are:

1. Partnerships created for the purchase and sale of an interest in land;
2. Partnerships involving the sale of *goods* for $500 or more, where one or more of the parties is a merchant;
3. Partnerships involving the lease of *goods* with payments totaling $1,000 or more; and
4. Partnerships whose duration (term) is longer than a year.

Example: Mia and Logan form a partnership to purchase and develop real estate. Their partnership agreement must be in writing to be enforceable under the Statute of Frauds.

The RUPA (or UPA if the state has not adopted RUPA) will govern all other matters not addressed in a partnership agreement. The RUPA allows partners to alter or opt out of any statutory rules, except that the partners may not:

1. Unreasonably restrict access to the books and records;
2. Eliminate the duties of loyalty and good faith and fair dealing;

3. Unreasonably reduce the duty of reasonable care;
4. Vary the power to dissociate;
5. Waive or vary the right to seek court removal of another partner;
6. Vary the right to dissolve and wind up;
7. Restrict third-party rights; or
8. Vary the law applying to a limited liability partnership (LLP).

Management Application Checklist for Drafting a Partnership Agreement

- ■ Introductory Clauses
  - ☐ Provide the partnership name
  - ☐ Identify names and addresses for all partners
  - ☐ Include the address of the principal place of the partnership's business
  - ☐ Identify the registered agent for service of process and the registered office of the partnership
  - ☐ State length of partnership or identify that it is a "partnership at will"
  - ☐ Explain the purpose and powers of the partnership
- ■ Capital Contributions and Allocation of Profits and Losses
  - ☐ State the capital contributions of each partner
  - ☐ State whether additional capital contributions of the partners will be required and identify the terms and conditions associated with a partner loaning money to the partnership
  - ☐ Identify partners who are entitled to be paid compensation in addition to their profit distributions, and the method of calculation
  - ☐ Provide how profits and losses to each partner will be calculated
- ■ Management, Control, Liability
  - ☐ Identify partnership structure and the roles and responsibilities of any managing partners
  - ☐ Identify the voting power that is tied to each partner's percentage of interest in the partnership
  - ☐ Provide whether partners may engage in one or more non-competing businesses that do not interfere with partnership business
  - ☐ State the grounds for removal of a partner and the effect of such a removal
  - ☐ State the effect of a withdrawal of a partner, as well as the rights and limitations of a withdrawal
  - ☐ State whether a partner's liability for the partnership's obligations is limited
  - ☐ Provide if the partnership will indemnify any of the partners for future claims related to the partnership
- ■ Financial and Accounting Matters
  - ☐ Specify which partner(s) is/are authorized to sign checks and any limitations regarding amount
  - ☐ Identify the partner tasked with the authority to act for and on behalf of the partnership regarding tax matters
  - ☐ State that each partner has the right to access books and records, as well as to a full accounting
  - ☐ Identify any existing partnership property, the manner in which title is or will be held, and the method for determining its value

- ☐ Identify the method to calculate a value for the partners interest in the partnership
- ■ Amendment and Termination of Partnership
  - ☐ State the way an amendment may be made and the vote necessary to pass an amendment
  - ☐ Identify the events or conditions that may give rise to the termination of the partnership liquidation
  - ☐ Identify the procedure for winding up the partnership
  - ☐ Obtain signatures from each partner

Partnership as a Separate Entity

A partnership is treated as a separate entity from the partners themselves. Each partner is a fiduciary and an agent of the partnership entity, and title to real property can be acquired by the partnership. In addition, the partnership assets belong to the partnership entity and are not considered individual assets of the partners. Finally, the partnership can sue or be sued in its own name.

Duration of the Partnership

The duration of the partnership is usually stated in the partnership agreement. Many partnerships are partnerships at will. A **partnership at will** is a partnership with no specified fixed duration and can be dissolved at any time without liability. **Partnerships for a term** are partnerships that have a limited duration. If a partner withdraws from a partnership for a term before the dissolution date, that partner can be held liable for any resulting losses suffered because of the withdrawal (such as the acceleration of the maturity of partnership debts).

Partnership at will
A partnership of no fixed duration that may be dissolved at any time without liability.

Partnership for a term
A partnership that has a limited duration.

> **Example:** A partnership agreement may provide: "The Partnership shall commence as of the date of the execution of this Agreement and shall continue thereafter for a term of 7 years." This is a partnership for a term.

Pass-through entity
An entity that does not pay income taxes because the entity's income and losses pass through to the owners of the entity, who then pay income taxes on their personal income tax returns.

Tax Treatment of Partnerships

Partnerships are pass-through entities for federal income tax purposes. A **pass-through entity** is a business entity that does not pay any income taxes. Pass-through entities enjoy a special tax treatment that reduces the effects of double taxation—one at the entity level and the second on the owner's individual returns. In a partnership, the entity's income or losses are passed through to the entity's owner (in this case, the partners), who then recognize the income or loss based on their profit and loss allocations under the partnership agreement.

While the partnership has no tax liability, it must file an information return with the Internal Revenue Service (IRS). In this filing, the IRS is provided with the partnership's profits, losses, expenses, and deductions recognized from its operations. While not paying income taxes, the partnership is required to pay all employment taxes on wages paid.

Review the IRS website for informational returns at https://www.irs.gov/businesses/small-businesses-self-employed/a-guide-to-information-returns.

Concept Summary
Taxation of a Partnership

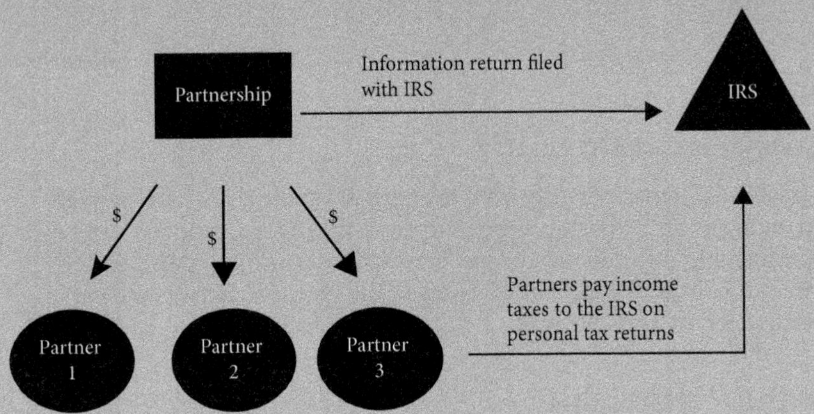

Rights of Partners

The rights of partners within a partnership include the rights to (1) participate in management; (2) use and possess partnership property for partnership purposes; (3) have a transferable interest in the partnership; (4) share in any distributions; (5) select and admit partners; and (6) seek enforcement of any of these rights. Absent the partnership agreement providing otherwise, the following default rules apply to partnerships.

Right to Participate in Management

Unless otherwise agreed, each partner has an equal right to manage the partnership (that is, one vote per partner). The vote of the majority, regardless of each partner's capital contributions, governs the actions and decisions of the partnership in any matters relating to the ordinary course of the partnership business. Acts outside of the ordinary course of the partnership business, such as selling the business and amending the partnership agreement, require the consent of all partners. However, the partners may agree to unequal voting rights.

> **Example:** A, B, and C form a partnership. They agree that A will have three votes, B will have five votes, and C will have seven votes.

Large partnerships commonly engage in this practice, having different voting classes of partners with different management rights. For example, law firms and accounting firms may divide their partners into multiple classes, such as equity partners, non-equity partners, and managing partners.

In partnerships with many partners, partners may form a management committee responsible for making decisions on behalf of the partnership. A sample management committee provision is shown below.

Management Application
Management Committee in a Partnership

The following provision is excerpted from a partnership agreement dealing with management rights of partners in the partnership:

Partnership Committees.

(a) For organizational purposes, the Partners shall form a management committee of the Partners (the Partnership Management) responsible for the planning, oversight, and approval of the policies and strategies of the Company and any other actions not expressly delegated to another committee, body, officer, or other representative of the Partnership or otherwise retained or reserved for the Partners under this Agreement. At any time after the date hereof, the Partners may form one or more other committees of the Partners to be responsible for planning, oversight, and control, and approval over such matters as delegated to such committee by the Partners.

(b) Each Partner is entitled to representation on every committee established hereunder in proportion to his or her respective Partnership Interest and each Partner will appoint in writing one (or more) of its duly authorized agents to act for the Partner on each committee of the Partners. One such agent(s) of each Partner will be given the authority by such Partner to vote on behalf of the Partner on any issue within the committee's responsibility. The collective representatives of each Partner on a committee will be entitled to one vote (or a fraction thereof) per percent (or a fraction thereof) of Partnership Interest held by such Partner, as reflected in the transfer records of the Company. Any person may serve as a representative for more than one Partner.

Source: Andrew Johnston, *Contemporary Corporation Forms* (Wolters Kluwer, 2d ed. 2020).

Right to Use and Possess Partnership Property

Partners contribute money and property to the partnership. These contributions are used in the partnership enterprise and are commonly referred to as contributed **capital**. Note that a partnership capital account not only represents the partners' capital contributions, but also the profits and losses earned and allocated to the partners, and distributions from the partnership. The partnership may create separate partnership capital accounts for each partner; or combine all partners into one account with separate ledgers attributing the transactions to each partner. A partner is not entitled to the return of the partner's capital contribution or interest on the contributed capital. The partner's agreement may provide otherwise.

Partnership property is a property that is used for a partnership purpose. Such property results from capital contributions by the partners and acquisitions of property

Partnership capital
The equity or undistributed balance allocated to the partners.

Partnership property
Assets used for a partnership purpose, including capital contributions by partners and acquisitions of property made by the partnership.

made by the partnership. Partnership property is owned by the partnership and not the individual partners. A partner is not a co-owner of partnership property and has no transferable interest in partnership property. That is, a partner cannot make an individual assignment of their right in specific partnership property.

Because the partnership owns partnership property, a partner's interest in partnership property is not subject to attachment by a partner's creditors. It is subject to attachment only when a claim against the partnership exists. The creditors and heirs of an individual party do not have a right to specific partnership property or in the partnership itself as a partner. To attach a partner's transferable interest in the partnership, creditors must obtain a court-ordered lien on the partner's distributions, known as a **charging order**.

Charging order
A court order granted to a judgment creditor to attach distributions made from a business organization, such as a partnership to a member, partner, or owner of the organization.

Example: RJ is a partner in the RJF Partnership, a profitable business. Following a judgment issued against him on a commercial loan, the lender may seek payment by attaching his partnership interest. As part of its collection efforts, the lender will secure a charging order on that interest to ensure partnership distribution payments are made to it instead of RJ.

Management Application Charging Order Form

COURT NAME
JURISDICTION
Court Address
City, ST ZIP Code

PLAINTIFF'S NAME, Plaintiff, vs. DEFENDANT'S NAME, Defendant	Case No.: Number CHARGING ORDER

The motion of _______, judgment creditor, for an order to charge a partner's interest came on regularly before this court on _______, 20__. The court having considered the motion and good cause appearing:

IT IS ORDERED THAT the interest of _______, judgment debtor, in the _______ partnership whose address is _______ is hereby charged with the unpaid balance of the judgment in this matter, entered on _______ in favor of _______ and against _______ for the sum of $_______ plus interest at the rate of 10 percent per annum from the date of entry.

IT IS FURTHER ORDERED that the _______ partnership and its partners shall pay any money or property due or to become due to _______ be paid directly to _______ until the remaining balance of the judgment, plus costs and interest, is fully and finally paid.

Dated this day of [month, 20__].

____
Judge of the Above-Entitled Court

Right to a Transferable Interest

Each partner has an economic interest in the partnership — distinct from the property the partnership may own. A partner's economic interest is considered personal property and may be assigned or transferred to others. If assigned, the person receiving the assigned interest does not receive all the rights of the transferor-partner. The transferee (that is, the person receiving the partner's interest) is not entitled to participate in the management or conduct of the partnership business, acquire access to any information concerning partnership transactions, or inspect the partnership books or records. Lacking management rights, the transferee is entitled only to financial rights, such as profits or losses. If the transfer is to an existing partner, the transferee retains the full rights afforded an initial partner.

> **Example:** Kaitlyn is a partner in a real estate partnership, which is highly profitable. As a result of a marital property settlement arising from her divorce, she transfers her economic interest in the partnership to her ex-spouse. The ex-spouse, as transferee, will have the right to the profits and losses of the partnership but will not have the right to manage or vote partnership matters.

Right to Share in Distributions

A partner is expected to devote their full time and services to a partnership; therefore, a partner is not entitled to be compensated for services rendered to the partnership, except for winding up its business. Nevertheless, a partnership agreement will provide compensation for the active managers of the partnership.

> **Example:** Alexis is the managing partner of a mid-market accounting and tax advisory firm. The partnership agreement may provide that as the managing partner, she is entitled to compensation for her management services to the firm.

Instead of compensation, partners are entitled to partnership distributions. A **distribution** is a transfer of money or other partnership property from the partnership to a partner in the partner's capacity as a partner. Each partner is entitled to an equal share of the profits and not by their capital contributions. If there are any losses, each partner is charged a share of the losses and will bear them in a proportion *identical* to that in which they share profits, absent an agreement to the contrary. Therefore, partnership agreements can provide different allocations for profits and losses.

Distribution
A transfer of money or other partnership property from the partnership to a partner in the partner's capacity as a partner.

> **Example:** Brian and Leigh form a partnership. Brian contributes $60,000, while Leigh contributes $40,000. They can agree that Brian would receive 60 percent of the profits and 40 percent of the losses while Leigh would receive 40 percent of the profits and 60 percent of the losses. However, if they do not agree on the sharing of profits and losses, each will have an equal one-half share of both the profits and losses.

Right to Choose Partners

Since a partner cannot be forced to accept another partner of whom they did not approve, consent of all partners is required for admission of a new partner. Partnership agreements may provide for partners to be admitted to a partnership by a less-than-unanimous vote.

Other Partner Rights

INSPECTION RIGHTS. Partners have access to a partnership's books and records. Former partners also have inspection rights but are generally limited to inspecting the books and records pertaining to the time they were partners.

> **Example:** An inspection rights clause may be stated as: "**Books and Records.** The managing partners of the Partnership will keep correct and complete books and records of account, including the role of all Partners, their names and addresses and the number and class of the interest held by each. In addition, the minutes of the proceedings of the meetings (and any actions by written consent of) the Partnership and the Partners and the committees at its principal place of business in Miami, Florida."

RIGHT TO AN ACCOUNTING OF PARTNERSHIP ASSETS OR PROFITS. Another important right a partner holds is the ability to demand an accounting of the partnership's affairs. An accounting determines each partner's investment, distributions, and share of gains and losses. Distinct transactions are identified, such as the contribution of funds to the partnership, withdrawal of funds or of assets, prior allocations of profits and losses, and tax reporting matters. As a result, the capital accounts of each partner's share in the partnership can be calculated.

Often, a partnership agreement will provide for the right to a pre-dissolution accounting. Under the RUPA, each partner has a right to an accounting when (1) the other partners wrongfully exclude them from the partnership business or possession of partnership property; (2) a partner makes a profit because of a breach of their fiduciary duty; or (3) some circumstances would make accounting just and reasonable. The purpose of accounting is to produce a comprehensive and effective settlement of partnership affairs. A partner has a broad right to sue the partnership and the other partners for harm identified in the accounting.

> **Example:** A managing partner has concealed payments to a related person for services rendered without knowledge of the other partners. The partners may demand an accounting to establish if the breach of fiduciary duty has resulted in damages to the partnership.

Concept Summary
Partner Rights

- Right to *use and possess partnership property*
- Right to have a *transferable interest*
- Right to *share in partnership distributions*
- Right to *participate in management* of the partnership
- Right to *select partners*
- Right to *inspect* the partnership books and records
- Right to *demand an accounting* of partnership assets or profits

Authority of Partners

Agency law is the source for partner rights, duties, and liabilities. Each partner is an agent of every other partner and an agent in any business transaction within the scope of the partnership agreement. Every act of a partner that involves the partnership's business binds the partnership. These rules may be limited by agreement.

A partner's status creates *apparent authority* to act as an agent of the partnership for transactions that are in the ordinary course of the business of the partnership. If the partner acts within the scope of their authority, the partnership will be legally bound to honor the partner's commitments to third parties. However, if a partner acts *without actual authority* on a matter not within the apparent scope of the partnership business, neither the partnership nor the other partners are bound by the act, absent the ratification of the other parties. However, the partner who entered into such an act is bound by the agreement.

Duties and Liabilities of Partners

Fiduciary Duties

Fiduciary duties are the legal duties owed by the partners to the other partners and the partnership. Essentially, they define the obligation to act solely in the interests of others. State laws will define those duties, but those laws are not uniform in their treatment of what is permissible partner conduct. They may vary by industry, such as those for real estate and those for the investment advisory industry. For example, the RUPA provides that there are only *two* duties owed by partners to the partnership and the other partners — the duties of loyalty and care.

DUTY OF LOYALTY. The duty of loyalty requires that a partner may not profit directly or indirectly at the expense of the partnership. A partner who breaches the duty of loyalty is liable for damages caused by the breach and must disgorge any profits made from the breach. Without the consent of the other partners, the partner may not:

- Compete with the partnership;
- Pursue business opportunities from which the partnership might have benefitted or that the partnership required;
- Disclose confidential information of the partnership;
- Misuse partnership property for personal gain; or
- Engage in transactions involving conflicts of interest.

Example: A partner in a restaurant decides that she could operate a restaurant more profitably than the one operated by the partnership and opens a competing restaurant. If she has not obtained the consent of all the partners, this partner has breached her duty of loyalty to the partnership.

In a landmark case, Justice Cardozo, an eminent former Associate Justice of the United States Supreme Court, rendered the majority opinion in *Meinhard v. Salmon* when he sat on the Court of Appeals of New York. The case provides a famous example of the breach of the duty of loyalty.

Landmark Case
Meinhard v. Salmon, 164 N.E. 545 (1928)

In this landmark case, Walter Salmon negotiated a 20-year lease for a hotel in New York City. Salmon intended to convert the building into shops and offices, and to help fund the cost of the project, Salmon entered into an agreement with Morton Meinhard to share the profits and losses of the joint venture (in most states, joint venture law is the same as the law of partnerships).

A few months before the end of the lease term, the building owner approached Salmon about another business opportunity, which involved constructing a single, new building across the entire property. Salmon agreed and executed a new lease in the name of his own business without informing Meinhard. Meinhard sued Salmon for a breach of the duty of loyalty.

The court held that Salmon breached his fiduciary duty to Meinhard by failing to inform Meinhard of the business opportunity. Justice Cardozo stated that "joint venturers, like copartners, owe to one another the duty of the finest loyalty. Many forms of conduct permissible in a workaday world for those acting at arm's length are forbidden to those bound by fiduciary ties. A trustee is held to something stricter than the morals of the marketplace. Not honesty alone, but the punctilio of an honor the most sensitive, is then the standard of behavior." Partners cannot secretly take advantage of business opportunities for themselves alone.

Consider the behavior exhibited by a general partner in the following case. While the case involves a limited partnership, the duties of a general partner remain the same.

CASE 20.1

A PARTNER OWES A DUTY OF LOYALTY TO THE OTHER PARTNERS AND MUST REASONABLY BELIEVE THEY ARE ACTING IN THE BEST INTEREST OF THE PARTNERSHIP

McBETH v. CARPENTER

565 F.3d 171 (2009)

United States Court of Appeals for the Fifth Circuit

James Carpenter entered into a contract with Austin Estates, L.P., for the purchase of real property located in Travis County, Texas. Unable to raise the necessary funds to complete the transaction, Carpenter contacted Sandra McBeth and her then-husband, James Reynolds, seeking their interest in making an investment in the proposed purchase. A partnership agreement was subsequently executed, forming StoneLake Ranch, with the goal of acquiring the Travis County property.

Pursuant to the agreement, McBeth and Reynolds deposited $300,000 in escrow and thereafter deposited an additional $500,000—in $100,000 increments—to obtain five separate extensions on the deadline to close on the property. However,

StoneLake Ranch was not able to complete the sale. Nonetheless, without notifying McBeth or Reynolds, Carpenter directed the money in escrow to be distributed to Austin Estates, L.P.

Subsequently, Carpenter began negotiations with other potential investors—excluding McBeth and Reynolds—even though the StoneLake Ranch partnership had not yet been dissolved. Carpenter, along with the newly secured investors, eventually purchased the property through an entity with which Carpenter was affiliated. The property was then sold for a profit of $140,000. McBeth and Reynolds sued Carpenter for breach of fiduciary duties owed to the partnership. Carpenter argued that he owed no fiduciary duties to the plaintiffs. The district court ruled in favor of McBeth and Reynolds, finding Carpenter breached his fiduciary duties, entitling them to $875,000 in damages.

Language of the Court. *Under Texas law, partners owe trust obligations to the partnership, having a duty of loyalty and due care as well as being under an obligation to discharge their duties in good faith and in reasonable belief that they are acting in the best interest of the partnership. Texas courts have long held that it is self-evident that a managing partner in a general partnership, owes his co-partners the highest fiduciary duty recognized in the law.*

Partners owed trust obligations to the partnership, having a duty of loyalty and due care as well as being under an obligation to discharge their duties in good faith and in reasonable belief that they are acting in the best interest of the partnership. A review of the record reveals that Carpenter was in a position of control in the StoneLake Partnership and therefore owed McBeth and Reynolds the highest fiduciary duty recognized in the law.

The partnership agreement between them specifically stated that "Carpenter retains the exclusive right to manage all contracts and agreements relating to the land." When the parties entered into the StoneLake partnership, Carpenter signed this agreement in his capacity as general partner of StoneLake.

McBeth and Reynolds had sufficient funds to close the land purchase transaction, but Carpenter did not inform them of the need for additional financing to complete the sale. Instead, the jury was presented with evidence that Carpenter, without dissolving the partnership, secured alternate investors, purchased the property, and turned a profit. In sum, a review of the record discloses that the jury had ample evidence from which to conclude that Carpenter breached his fiduciary duties.

Decision. Carpenter breached his fiduciary duties owed to McBeth and Reynolds as partners in StoneLake.

Focus on Ethics

If the partnership had been dissolved prior to Carpenter's securing additional investors, would that have changed the result? Would it be ethical if the partnership had been dissolved but Carpenter's reasons for dissolving the partnership were purely selfish—that is, to exclude McBeth and Reynolds?

DUTY OF CARE. The duty of care requires the partner to act with the *care*, *competence*, and *diligence* normally (ordinarily) exercised by an ordinarily prudent person in that situation. Under the RUPA, a partner violates the duty of care if the partner engages in grossly negligent or reckless conduct, intentional misconduct, or a knowing violation of law. Mere negligence by a partner does not breach the duty of care. A partnership agreement may change the duty of care but may not "unreasonably reduce" or waive the duty.

> **Example:** In a Delaware case, limited partners sued the general partner of Blue Bell Creameries, L.P.® for its failure to use its "best efforts" to operate the company's ice cream plants in accordance with "*the sound business practices in the industry.*" They claimed they lost a substantial portion of their investment because of Listeria contamination at the creamery plants. The general partner defended the suit, in part, on the theory that in accordance with Delaware law, the partnership agreement eliminated the general common law fiduciary duties to the entity and its limited partners. The court held that the parties' relationship was to be construed in accordance with their agreement. The court rejected the general partner's interpretation that it was required to perform its duties in good faith — one supporting its belief that it acted reasonably. Instead, the court held that the standard was a "contractual fiduciary duty" and that based on the allegations of the complaint, the case could proceed for the general partner's failure to prevent the contamination of the Blue Bell ice cream products. *Wenske v. Blue Bell Creameries, Inc.*, 2018 Del. Ch. LEXIS 221 (Del. Ch. 2018)

GOOD FAITH AND FAIR DEALING. A partner also has an obligation of good faith and fair dealing. This obligation requires the partner to act honestly, fairly, and in good faith with the other partners and the partnership. A partner may lend money to and do business with the partnership on the same basis as a non-partner without violating the duty of care; however, if the partner takes advantage of their position as a partner to negotiate more favorable terms, the partner has breached the obligation of good faith and fair dealing.

Liability of the Partners

The partnership is liable for partnership actions committed within the ordinary course of the partnership. One of the significant disadvantages of general partnerships is the liability the partners have for partnership debts. Beginning with their admission to the partnership, partners are personally liable for partnership debts in a general partnership incurred thereafter.

Joint and several liability
A doctrine under which a plaintiff may sue and collect a judgment from all the partners collectively or the partners individually.

JOINT AND SEVERAL LIABILITY. In most states, general partners are jointly and severally (that is, separately *or* individually) liable for all partnership obligations. **Joint and several liability** is a doctrine that allows a plaintiff to sue and collect a judgment from all the partners together (jointly) or one or more of the partners separately (severally). The creditor who sues selected partners can only recover the assets of those named partners in the lawsuit. Under joint and several liability, if one partner is sued and held liable for the debt, that partner can then pursue the other partners for a contribution to their share of the liability. Such action can be completed through a right to an accounting.

A partner is typically held liable to creditors for the partnership's obligations where:

1. The partnership is bankrupt;
2. Judicial attempts to collect from the partnership are unsuccessful;
3. The court determines that partnership assets are inadequate, exhaustion of its assets is unduly burdensome, or equity will be served by allowing suit against the partner; or
4. The partner decides that the creditor need not exhaust partnership assets.

One exception to joint and several liability applies to incoming partners. A partner who is newly admitted to an already existing partnership is liable for any preexisting partnership obligations incurred by the partnership before becoming a partner, but only to the extent of their investment (that is, capital contributions). The incoming partner is liable for all partnership debts after becoming a partner.

PARTNERSHIP BY ESTOPPEL. An individual who is not a partner but portrays themself as a partner to a third party will be held personally liable to the same extent as a general partner. This rule applies if the third party does not have reason to know that the individual is not actually a partner. These partners have the obligations of a partner but are not conferred any partnership rights (such as the right to receive profits).

> **Example:** Gary Chavers started a welding company called Chavers Welding and Construction (CWC), which operated as a sole proprietorship. When Gary's sons Mark and Reggie began working for their father, CWC had entered into an agreement with Epsco, Inc. (Epsco) to provide payroll and employee services. Epsco extended credit to CWC on the belief that CWC had become a partnership due to the addition of Mark and Reggie and the indication by one of the Chavers that the business was a partnership. Further, checks written to Epsco, as well as CWC's business cards, listed both Gary and Reggie as the owners. When CWC failed to pay the amount due, Epsco sued Gary, Mark, and Reggie Chavers individually, and CWC, to recover the amount due. Mark and Reggie argued they should not be held personally liable because CWC was still organized as a sole proprietorship. The court found that Mark and Reggie were jointly and severally liable for the debt to Epsco under the theory of partnership by estoppel because they had "represented themselves to Epsco as partners in an existing partnership." *Chavers v. Epsco, Inc.*, 98 S.W.3d 421(Ark. 2003)

Dissociation and Termination

Dissociation occurs at the severance of the relationship between a partner and the partnership. The dissociating partner no longer has the authority to act for the partnership and may not participate in managing the business with the remaining partners. While a partner has the power to dissociate from a partnership, that partner may not have the right to dissociate from the partnership (such as a partner who leaves before the term of the partnership has elapsed).

Dissociation
The severance of the relationship between a partner and the partnership.

Under the RUPA, after a partner withdraws from the partnership, the partnership may continue to operate without the dissociated partner. Under the UPA, a partnership is considered dissolved whenever a partner withdraws from the partnership. However, the controlling state statute must be consulted to determine if the partnership may be continued. Thus, the statute may permit dissociation without dissolution of the partnership.

If the partners no longer wish to continue the partnership or are unable to continue it without the dissociated partner, the partnership may be dissolved.

A partner's dissociation (withdrawal) does not, of itself, discharge that partner's liability for a partnership obligation incurred before dissociation. Usually, the date of the notice of dissociation by the withdrawing partner to the partnership is considered the date of dissociation.

Events Causing Dissociation

Under the RUPA, a partner may be dissociated from a partnership in the following ways.

VOLUNTARY NOTICE. A partner can be dissociated from a partnership by voluntarily giving notice of an "express will to withdraw." Once this occurs, the remaining partners decide if the partnership will continue. If the partnership does not continue, the dissociation of a partner will cause the partnership to dissolve.

OCCURRENCE OF A SPECIFIED EVENT. A partnership may be dissociated if a specified event in the partnership agreement occurs.

> **Example:** The partnership agreement provides that the partnership is formed to develop, build, and sell a commercial property. At the sale of the completed project, the partnership terminates by the occurrence of an event.

UNANIMOUS VOTE. A partner can be dissociated by a unanimous vote of the other partners. This most commonly occurs when a partner transfers all or substantially all their interest in the partnership to another person.

COURT (OR ARBITRATOR) ORDER. If the partner has engaged in wrongful conduct that affects the partnership, such as violating a fiduciary duty, a court (or an arbitrator) may order the partner to be dissociated from the partnership. The underlying litigation can be complex and lengthy.

> **Example:** In a protracted and acrimonious breakup of a Connecticut real estate property management partnership, Thomas Brennan, a founding partner, was dissociated from the partnership by order of the trial court. This is followed by claims and counterclaims relating to alleged distrustful conduct and lack of candor. The trial court ordered the dissociation of Brennan from the partnership. The state supreme court upheld the ruling. *Brennan v. Brennan Associates*, 977 A.2d 107 (Conn. 2009). Thereafter, more litigation ensued over Brennan's action to have his interest in the partnership valued and purchased by the partnership. The litigation entailed several separate appeals to the state supreme court.

OTHER EVENTS. A partner may be dissociated from the partnership upon filing for bankruptcy protection, assigning their interest in the partnership for the benefit of creditors, becoming physically or mentally incapacitated, or dying (if a natural person).

After Dissociation

Liability to the partnership for a dissociated partner and liability to the dissociated partner are concerns after dissociation. A statement of dissociation may be filed by the partnership or dissociated partner providing notice of the dissociation. The statement of dissociation is filed in the same location that the original partnership agreement was filed (often with the Secretary of State of the state). Ninety days after the dissociated partner's apparent authority and liability for future partnership obligations cease. If no statement of dissociation is filed, and the creditor lacks actual notice of the dissolution, then, typically for two years after the partner dissociates from the partnership (1) the partnership may be bound to contracts entered into by the dissociated partner under apparent authority, and (2) the dissociated partner may be liable for partnership obligations entered into by the partnership. However, a creditor who deals with the partnership for the first time after the partner's withdrawal is not entitled to notice.

> **Example:** Rachel dissociated from a partnership. Neither the partnership nor Rachel filed a notice of dissociation. If six months after her dissociation, Rachel contacts a new supplier who believes Rachel is still a partner in the partnership and executes a contract on behalf of the partnership to supply goods to the partnership, the partnership will be held liable on the new supplier contract under apparent authority.

Buyout
The purchase by the partnership of a partner's partnership interest after the partner dissociates (withdraws) from the partnership.

In addition, after a partner dissociates from the partnership, the partnership must purchase his or her partnership interest if it wishes for the partnership to continue operating. This is frequently referred to as a **buyout**. The buyout price is calculated as the amount distributable to that partner if the firm was wound up on that date.

Management Application Notice of Buyout and Estimated Payment for Partnership Interest

NOTICE OF BUYOUT AND ESTIMATED PAYMENT FOR PARTNERSHIP INTEREST

Trung Nguyen
123 Main Street
Los Angeles, CA 90089

This notice is pursuant to Section 16701 of the *California Corporations Code*.

Your written demand for payment for your interest in ABC Partnership, a California partnership from which you dissociated on December 5, 2024, was received on December 5, 2024. Since that date, no agreement has been reached between you and ABC Partnership concerning the partnership's purchase of your partnership interest.

The cash payment enclosed with this notice represents the partnership's estimate of the amount due to you for your partnership interest, plus accrued interest since the date of your dissociation, and less any offsets representing amounts that you owe the partnership.

Attached to and made a part of this notice are the following:

(1) A statement of the assets and liabilities of ABC Partnership as of the date of your dissociation.

(2) The latest available partnership balance sheet and income statement dated November 30, 2024.

(3) An explanation of the calculation used to arrive at the amount of payment for your interest in the partnership.

The enclosed payment is in full satisfaction of ABC Partnership's obligation to purchase your interest in the partnership under California law, unless, within 120 days of the date of this notice you have commenced legal action to determine the buyout price for your partnership interest.

Dated: [Date]

ABC Partnership
By:

____

XYZ, Managing Partner

Termination of the Partnership

Dissolution The formal disbanding of a partnership through either the acts of the partners, operation of law, or a judicial decree.

The termination of a partnership (also known as **dissolution**) is the formal disbanding of a partnership. The acts causing dissociation can trigger dissolution if the remaining partners are unable to or do not wish to continue the partnership. Dissolution can occur through the acts of the partners, by operation of law (such as the expiration of time in a partnership for a term), or by a judicial decree.

During the dissolution process, each partner must exercise good faith to the other partners and the partnership. During dissolution, the partnership collects and preserves partnership assets, pays its debts, and accounts to each partner for the value of their interest in the partnership.

CREDITORS' CLAIMS. As the partnership is dissolving, creditors of the partnership and creditors of the individual partners can make claims on the partnership's assets. Under the RUPA, a partnership's assets are first applied to pay the debts of non-partner creditors, then partner creditors, followed by a return of capital contributions and then distribution of any profits.

If the partnership's liabilities exceed its assets, the partners will generally bear the losses in the same proportion in which they shared the profits, absent an agreement to the contrary.

Dissociation or Dissolution

While many state statutes will have similar provisions governing dissociation and dissolution, they are not identical. Understanding the applicable statute is important when a dispute arises between partners regarding whether a partnership should dissociate or continue to operate. If the partners cannot reach an agreement on their own, the court may be required to decide which action should be taken. The court will reach its determination based upon the state's partnership statute.

Dissolution of a partnership requires the court to determine if dissolution is appropriate under the circumstances. Among its considerations, the court will review the following:

- If the economic purpose of the partnership is likely to be unreasonably frustrated;
- If another partner has engaged in conduct relating to the partnership business that makes it not reasonably practicable to carry on the business in partnership with that partner; and
- If it is reasonably practicable to carry on the partnership business in conformity with the partnership agreement.

When considering dissociation, the court will consider if the dissociating partner:

- Engaged in wrongful conduct that adversely and materially affected the partnership business;
- Willfully or persistently committed a material breach of the partnership agreement or of a duty owed to the partnership or the other partners; or
- Engaged in conduct relating to the partnership that makes it not reasonably practicable to carry on the business in partnership with the partner.

Wrongful Dissociation or Dissolution

Partners do not always have the right to dissociate. If a court finds that a partner has wrongfully dissociated from the partnership and the dissociation results in dissolution, the partner will be forbidden from participating in the winding up of the partnership. A dissociation is wrongful when it constitutes a breach of the partnership agreement. Additionally, a wrongful dissociation will occur when a partner ignores his or her duties under the partnership agreement. The partner is liable to the partnership (and the other partners) for damages caused by the wrongful dissociation.

Types of Partnerships

As noted in the introduction to this chapter, there are four forms of partnership: (1) general partnerships; (2) limited partnerships; (3) limited liability partnerships; and (4) limited liability limited partnerships.

General Partnerships

A **general partnership** is an unincorporated business association of *two* or more persons (natural or artificial) who engage in a business for profit. All the partnership rules discussed above in this chapter apply to general partnerships. Each partner has equal control in the partnership and unlimited personal liability for the partnership's debts. One way a general partner can protect itself is by forming a corporation (or LLC) to be the general partner in the partnership.

General partnership An unincorporated business association of two or more persons who engage in a business for profit.

Limited Partnerships

Limited partnership
A partnership consisting of one or more general partners and one or more limited partners whose liability is limited to the amount of their investment.

Certificate of limited partnership
A document that must be filed with a public official that forms a limited partnership under the state statute.

A limited partnership is an entity that is formed pursuant to state statute. A **limited partnership** is a partnership consisting of one or more general partners and one or more limited partners. Any person (natural or artificial) may be a general or limited partner, and the same person can be both the general and a limited partner. A person that is both a general and limited partner has the rights, powers, duties, and obligations pertaining to each of those capacities.

Unlike a general partnership, which can be formed without filing any formal documents, a limited partnership requires the filing of a **certificate of limited partnership** with a public official according to the relevant state law. The certificate of limited partnership must state the name of the limited partnership, its mailing address, the limited partnership's registered agent for service of process and the address, and the name and address of each general partner.

The Uniform Law Commission, in addition to drafting model legislation governing partnership law, drafted model legislation governing limited partnerships. Most states have adopted the Revised Uniform Limited Partnership Act (RULPA).[2]

LIABILITY. The general partner of a limited partnership is liable for partnership obligations to the same extent as the partners of a general partnership. However, like shareholders in a corporation, limited partners have limited liability for the partnership's debt. Their liability is usually limited to the amount of their capital contribution. Limited partners are personally liable for the torts they commit, either in their personal capacity or as agents of the limited partnership.

In the following case, the court considered whether a limited partnership and the general partner of that limited partnership were liable for the acts of a limited partner who acted beyond the scope of his authority.

CASE 20.2

A PARTNERSHIP IS NOT LIABLE FOR INJURY CAUSED BY A PARTNER IF THE PARTNER ACTS OUTSIDE OF THE ORDINARY COURSE OF PARTNERSHIP BUSINESS OR WITHOUT PARTNERSHIP AUTHORITY

DOCTORS HOSPITAL AT RENAISSANCE, LTD. v. ANDRADE

493 S.W.3d 545 (2016)

Supreme Court of Texas

Dr. Rodolfo Lozano treated Jessica Andrade during her pregnancy and delivered her daughter at Women's Hospital at Renaissance, Ltd. ("Hospital") in Texas. The delivery was complicated by the baby's shoulder position, which hindered

2. Most states have adopted the 1976 revision to the Limited Partnership Act. About half of the states have adopted the amendments proposed in 2001, which make the RULPA more flexible and stable for organizing limited partnerships.

labor. Dr. Lozano allegedly engaged in excessive twisting during delivery to dislodge the shoulder, which resulted in permanent injury including nerve damage and permanent paralysis of one of the baby's arms.

The Andrades sued Dr. Lozano as well as both Doctors Hospital at Renaissance, Ltd. (a limited partnership that owned and operated Women's Hospital at Renaissance, Ltd.) ("Renaissance"), and RGV Med, LLC (the general partner of Doctors Hospital at Renaissance, Ltd.), alleging vicarious liability for the doctor's negligence. Dr. Lozano was an independent contractor at the hospital and a limited partner in Doctors Hospital at Renaissance, Ltd. The Andrades subsequently settled with Dr. Lozano. Renaissance and RGV Med, LLC, moved for summary judgment, arguing that they were not liable for Dr. Lozano's conduct because he was not acting within the scope of the partnership or with partnership authority when providing obstetrical care to Ms. Andrade. The trial court denied the motions, and the decision was appealed. On appeal, the appellate court affirmed. But the remaining defendants appealed to the Supreme Court of Texas, which granted review.

Language of the Court. *Renaissance and RGV Med argue that Renaissance is in the business of providing and operating medical facilities, not practicing medicine. Therefore, in providing medical treatment at the Hospital, Dr. Lozano was not acting on behalf of the partnership or carrying out ordinary partnership business. Renaissance and RGV Med further argue that the Renaissance partnership agreement forbids limited partners from acting on the partnership's behalf. As such, Dr. Lozano could not have been acting with Renaissance's authority when he delivered the Andrade baby. The Andrades counter that the partnership agreement is very broad and encompasses Dr. Lozano's provision of obstetrical services as an agent of Renaissance, even if the partnership does not practice medicine. The Andrades urge that they have raised a fact issue as to whether Dr. Lozano was acting in the ordinary course of partnership business, or with the partnership's authority, and that the trial court properly denied summary judgment.*

The applicable partnership statute renders Renaissance liable for the conduct of a limited partner only if he was acting in the ordinary course of the partnership's business or with partnership authority. Dr. Lozano was doing neither when providing medical care to Jessica Andrade and her daughter, so Renaissance cannot be liable for his conduct.

The record conclusively demonstrates that the ordinary course of Renaissance's business does not include the provision of medical care. Only a person, not a partnership, may be licensed to practice medicine. Corporate entities that exert control over a doctor's practice of medicine may be engaged in the unlawful practice of medicine without a license.

The partnership agreement states that the purposes of the limited partnership are to develop, construct and operate health care facilities. On its face, the partnership agreement does not contemplate the inclusion of illegally practicing medicine in the ordinary course of the partnership business. Renaissance, as the operator of the hospital, may be in the business of providing facilities, support staff, and supplies to assist doctors in the provision of medical care, without engaging in the illegal practice of medicine by a business entity.

The partnership agreement does not give the limited partners any authority to provide medical care at partnership-owned facilities. In fact, the partnership agreement does not give the limited partners any specific authority to act on the partnership's behalf at all. Consistent with its organization as a limited partnership instead of a general partnership, the limited partnership agreement expressly authorizes the general partner to act on behalf of the entity, but not the limited partners.

Here, Dr. Lozano's medical care was neither in the ordinary course of Renaissance's business nor conducted with its authority. When limited partners who are also doctors practice medicine at the Hospital, they are not acting under separate admitting privileges, not with any authority of the partnership. These doctors have the same authority to practice medicine under their own medical license as other doctors who are not also Renaissance limited partners. As such, Renaissance cannot be liable for Dr. Lozano's alleged negligence in providing medical care at the Hospital.

Unlike a person doing business with a corporation, a person doing business with a limited partnership always has recourse against any general partner in the same manner as partners are liable for the liabilities of a partnership without limited partners. Therefore, whether RGV Med is vicariously liable for Dr. Lozano's actions depends exclusively on whether Renaissance is liable. Because we hold that Renaissance cannot be liable for Dr. Lozano's alleged negligence, RGV Med also cannot be liable as Renaissance's general partner.

Decision. The Texas Supreme Court reversed the decision of the court of appeals. Renaissance and RGV were not liable for Dr. Lozano's negligence because while providing medical facilities at the Hospital, Dr. Lozano was not acting on behalf of the limited partnership or carrying out its ordinary partnership business as a medical facility.

Focus on Ethics

For cases where a doctor has insufficient malpractice insurance limits to compensate the plaintiff, are there public policy changes you would recommend?

MANAGEMENT. In a limited partnership, there may be one or more general partners who manage the business of the partnership. As managers, these partners owe fiduciary duties to the partnership and the other partners, including the duty of loyalty and the duty of reasonable care. The general partner can be an individual or a business entity such as a corporation.

Limited partners are the capital investors in the partnership and do not have management responsibility. They may become liable as general partners if they participate in the control or management of the partnership business or when a third-party creditor extends credit to the limited partnership under the reasonable belief that the limited partner is a general partner in the limited partnership. In such cases, the limited partner is treated as a general partner to that third-party creditor only. A limited partner may act as a director, officer, or employee of the general partner in the limited partnership without adversely affecting their status as a limited partner in the limited partnership. Note that a limited partner may also be a general partner at the same time, perhaps because the person wishes to invest in the partnership and realize the rewards of being a limited partner investor. In such cases, a limited partner who is also a general partner can be held liable. In all cases, a partner can still be liable for their own conduct that harms a third party.

The Status of the Permissible Limited Partner Activities

There are "safe harbor" exceptions to the exercise of control by a limited partner over a limited partnership (LP). Among those provided by RULPA § 303(b)-(c) are doing one or more of the following:

- Being a contractor for or agent or employee of the LP or of a general partner, or being an officer, director, or shareholder of a general partner that is a corporation
- Consulting with or advising a general partner with respect to the business of the LP
- Acting as a surety for the LP or guaranteeing or assuming a specific obligation of the LP
- Proposing, approving, or disapproving by vote or otherwise one or more of the following matters pertaining to the LP:
  - ☐ Dissolution and winding up
  - ☐ Sale, exchange, lease, mortgage, or other transfer of all or substantially all the LP assets
  - ☐ Incurrence of debt other than in the ordinary course of its business
  - ☐ Change in the nature of the business
  - ☐ Admission or removal of a general partner
  - ☐ Admission or removal of a limited partner
  - ☐ Matters that the partnership agreement states in writing may be subject to the approval or disapproval of limited partners.

However, the right of control test is outdated. Under the RULPA (2001), the "control rule" was eliminated by providing that the limited partner is not liable for the obligation of the LP "solely by reason of being a limited partner, even if the limited partner participates in the management and control of the limited partnership." This form of the Act provides a full, status-based liability shield, eliminating the "control rule." It brings limited partners in parity with LLC members, LLP partners, and corporate shareholders. Thus, it is important for a business investor to ensure that they know under what Act the organization is operating.

CONTRIBUTION. Limited partners contribute cash or other property and receive an interest in the partnership, but unlike general partners, they do not enjoy management rights. They are not personally liable for the partnership debts beyond the loss of their investment. General partners also have the right to contribute cash or other property and receive an interest in the partnership.

MISCONDUCT. A limited partner may have personal liability to the *partnership* for a breach of fiduciary duty (the duty of care and loyalty).

Example: A limited partner may be personally liable to the partnership for misappropriating a partnership opportunity, asset, or interest.

PROFIT AND LOSS SHARING. Unless otherwise provided in the partnership agreement, partners in a limited partnership will receive profits and losses in proportion to their respective capital contributions.

TRANSFERRING OF PARTNERSHIP INTERESTS. Like other partnerships, unless agreed otherwise, a partner may transfer their financial rights in the partnership but may not transfer management (or governance) rights. This rule applies regardless of whether the partner is a general partner or a limited partner.

DISSOCIATION AND DISSOLUTION. Unless the limited partnership agreement provides otherwise, a general partner in a limited partnership has the power to withdraw at any time. Since the general partner(s) manage the limited partnership, a general partner's withdrawal or dissociation from a limited partnership may trigger dissolution of the limited partnership. The limited partnership can avoid dissolution upon the withdrawal of a general partner upon the occurrence of any of the following events:

1. At least one general partner remains;
2. The partnership agreement allows the remaining general partners to continue the limited partnership; or
3. All the remaining partners (limited and general) agree to continue the partnership, in writing and within 90 days after the dissociation of the general partner (they must also elect a general partner if there is not one).

Unless the limited partnership agreement states a limited partnership term, a limited partner can withdraw from a limited partnership after providing six months' notice. Most limited partnership agreements specify a term that effectively eliminates the right of a limited partner to withdraw from the limited partnership. To dissolve a limited partnership, all the partners in a limited partnership must consent.

Limited Liability Partnerships

Limited liability partnership (LLP) A partnership in which all the partners are general partners and no partner is personally liable for the debts, obligations, or liabilities of the partnership.

A **limited liability partnership (LLP)** is a type of general partnership often used by professional service organizations (especially accountants and attorneys). LLPs are composed of general partners who enjoy limited liability for the debts of the partnership or wrongdoings of other partners in the partnership. No partner is personally liable for the debts, obligations, and liabilities of the LLP. As a result, many professional service practices across the country have adopted the LLP form of doing business. Some states require LLPs to provide security for potential claims (such as malpractice insurance at specified amounts). No partner is liable for the negligence of another partner unless they supervised the individual who committed a wrongful act.

To commence or convert a general partnership to an LLP, the partnership must file a statement of qualification with the state. All states have enacted an LLP statute. While a limited liability partnership shields partners from individual liability, this protection is only afforded if the partners comply with the state's statutory requirements. In the following case, the court addressed what happens to the partners' limited liability when the LLP fails to renew its statement of qualification with the state.

CASE 20.3

PARTNERS OF AN LLP CAN BE HELD INDIVIDUALLY LIABLE WHEN THEY HAVE FAILED TO MAINTAIN ITS STATUS AS A REGISTERED LLP

APCAR INVESTMENT PARTNERS VI, LTD. v. GAUS

161 S.W.3d 137 (2005)

Court of Appeals of Texas

Smith & West, LLP registered as a domestic limited liability partnership under Texas law in 1995. In 1999, MR Partners I, Ltd., as landlord, and Smith & West, LLP, as tenant, entered into a commercial lease. Under the lease, Smith & West, LLP, rented office space from MR Partners I, Ltd., for a term of 60 months.

MF Partners assigned its interest in the lease to Apcar. Thereafter, the partners at Smith & West, LLP, failed to renew its initial registration as an LLP. Smith & West, LLP, then stopped paying rent under the lease and abandoned the leased premises. Apcar sued the LLP and the two partners in the LLP, Gaus and West, individually to collect the rent. Gaus and West defended, claiming Texas law provided protection for partners of an LLP because there was no need for strict compliance with the registration requirements.

Language of the Court. *The clear language of Texas law supports Apcar's position that Gaus and West are not protected from individual liability for the lease obligations. Under Texas law, the initial registration would expire one year after the date of registration unless renewed in accordance with Subdivision (7) of the Texas Code. Gaus and West registered the partnership in 1995, and the LLP's initial registration expired on March 6, 1996.*

Smith & West, LLP entered into the lease three years after its status as a registered limited liability partnership expired. Texas law only protects partners from individual liability for debts and obligations that are incurred while the partnership is a registered limited liability partnership. Smith & West, LLP was not a registered limited liability partnership when it incurred the lease obligations; therefore, Gaus and West are not protected from individual liability for the lease obligations.

Texas law does not contain a "substantial compliance" section, nor does it contain a grace period for filing a renewal application. We hold that a partnership must follow the registration requirements of the relevant Texas state law for its partners to receive protection from individual liability. We have determined that Gaus and West, as partners in Smith & West, LLP, may be individually liable for Smith & West, LLP's lease obligations because Smith & West, LLP was not a registered limited liability partnership when it incurred the lease obligations.

Decision. The two partners, Gaus and West, were found individually liable for the lease obligations because of their failure to renew Smith & West, LLP's status as a limited liability partnership.

Focus on Ethics

As a matter of policy, should there be a grace period or a substantial compliance provision in a state's limited liability partnership statute to prevent a situation such as occurred in this case?

Limited Liability Limited Partnerships

Limited liability limited partnership (LLLP) A partnership that fully shields the partners from any liability and is characteristically like a corporation.

Another variation of partnerships is the **limited liability limited partnership (LLLP)**. An LLLP is a partnership composed of at least one general partner(s) and at least one limited partner(s). Generally, it has the same formation requirements as an LLP; however, where LLLPs are provided by state statute, they are not limited to professionals. In addition, how partner liability is treated is different from that of an LLP. In some states, LLP statutes retain a partner's joint and several liability for partnership obligations. In others, partners not associated with the negligent act or omission are not liable. The purpose of an LLLP is to eliminate this automatic liability.

An LLLP is an entity shielding both its limited and general partners from automatic, vicarious liability while still enjoying the tax-favored treatment of a partnership. The LLLP provides a full liability shield and acts like a corporation, which is the subject of Chapter 22. Corporations are stand-alone entities that offer protections to their shareholders, and the LLLP is similar in nature.

Although operating an LLLP may provide tax benefits and limited liability to all partners, it is not a common way of operating a business. Many states offer the LLLP as a business organization option. If the state does not provide for an LLLP statute, the owners may resort to other forms of doing business, such as LLPs, LLCs, or corporations.

Example: CNN® (Cable News Network) is a limited liability limited partnership.

AI Feature: Draft an Agreement to Purchase a Partner's Interest

After reading this chapter, use an AI program to draft the purchase of a partner's interest. Ensure that the following terms are addressed:

- How the purchase price is calculated (include a provision addressing accounts receivable, allowance for bad debt);
- Include as an exhibit to the agreement a promissory note incorporating the payment terms;
- Indemnification to address uninsured claims made against the partnership after withdrawal for prior negligent acts of the withdrawing partner;
- The right to offset against the balance due under the note for such uninsured claims, and;
- Any other terms you believe will provide for a fair and equitable transaction.

Key Terms

- Buyout, 493
- Certificate of limited partnership, 496
- Charging order, 484
- Dissociation, 491
- Dissolution, 494
- Distribution, 485
- General partnership, 495
- Joint and several liability, 490
- Limited liability limited partnership (LLLP), 502
- Limited liability partnership (LLP), 500
- Limited partnership, 496
- Partnership, 478
- Partnership agreement (articles of partnership), 479
- Partnership at will, 481
- Partnership capital, 483
- Partnership for a term, 481
- Partnership property, 483
- Pass-through entity, 481
- Revised Uniform Partnership Act (RUPA), 478

Applying the Law

20.1 Research the Law. Using an internet search engine, research whether your home state follows the UPA (Uniform Partnership Act) or the RUPA (Revised Uniform Partnership Act). Summarize the rights and duties of partners under the law of that state. Are these default rules, as adopted by that state, adequate to resolve disputes not addressed in a written partnership agreement?

20.2 Partnership Creation. Norman Sweet was an employee of Paul Vohland's nursery. After many years, Sweet sued for a partnership interest. He testified that Vohland told Norman that he would not have to punch a time clock, would be paid on a commission basis, and that he would have a type of interest in the business. While Sweet testified that he intended to enter into a partnership, Vohland denied that and claimed that Sweet was merely an employee, working on a commission. There was no contention that Sweet made any contribution to capital, nor did he claim any interest in the real estate, machinery, or motor vehicles. The parties had never discussed losses. Paul filed tax returns that listed Norman's share of the profits as a "commission." Paul managed the business's finances and property, while Norman ran the operations of the nursery itself. What evidence supports the finding that a partnership had been formed? *Vohland v. Sweet*, 433 N.E.2d 860 (Ind. Ct. App. 1982)

20.3 General Partnerships. Family members formed a general partnership known as 3-D. The partnership's sole asset was a building that had been converted from a residence into offices. Some portion of the property had been rented by a law firm since 1981 on a month-to-month basis. From time to time, the property was rented on similar arrangements to others. In 1993, two of the partners began renting and using the property at below fair market value. Even though they are family members, have they breached any fiduciary duties arising from this activity? *Enea v. Superior Court*, 132 Cal. App. 4th 1559 (2005)

20.4 Partnership Rights. Milford Plaza Associates and Northmon Investment Company were partners in a partnership that owned as its only asset a parcel of real property. Milford sought to commit the partnership to a 99-year lease of the property. Northmon objected, but Milford proceeded. The partnership agreement set a partnership termination date of 2075, years before the proposed 99-year lease would end. Can Milford make a significant business decision over the objections of other partners? What are Northmon's rights? *Northmon Investment Co. v. Milford Plaza Associates*, 727 N.Y.S.2d 419 (2001)

20.5 Fiduciary Duties. The St. David's Health Care System, Inc. (the "System") operated St. David's Medical Center in Austin, Texas. The System was also the sole shareholder of St. David's Support Corporation. In the early 1980s, the Board of Trustees of the System ("Board") began considering an expansion of the hospital's facilities and services. Upon learning of the project, Alfred Hughes approached the System, proposing to arrange financing for the new facilities. Under his proposal, Hughes and his affiliates would form (1) a master limited partnership, interests of which would be sold to the public; and (2) operating partnerships, interests of which would be sold to physicians. The master limited partnership would fund the construction of the facilities and then lease them to the operating partnerships, which would operate the two hospitals. After accepting Hughes's financing proposal, the Board became dissatisfied, so it decided to take over the development of the project. It gave Hughes a "royalty interest" in the operating partnerships, which was less than one-half of one percent ownership. In 1991, a problem arose concerning the operation of the two hospitals. The Board decided to sell all operating partnership assets and dissolve both operating partnerships. The Board did not provide notice of the sale to the Hughes partners because their shares were of little economic value. Has the Board breached any fiduciary duties toward the Hughes partners? *Hughes v. St. David's Support Corp.*, 944 S.W.2d 423 (Tex. App. 1997)

20.6 Limited Partner Liability. Union Properties, Inc. was the general partner of Commercial Investors, a limited partnership. Mannon and Baxter were limited partners of Commercial Investors, but they were also co-owners and directors of Union Properties. A contractor sued when the limited partnership breached its contract. Noting that the limited partners were also the officers, directors, and shareholders of the corporate general partner, the contractor sought to impose general liability upon the limited partners, claiming that they exercised the day-to-day control of the partnership through the general partner and were therefore liable to it. Can the limited partners be held liable when the general partner was a corporation controlled by the limited partners? Discuss. *Frigidaire Sales Corp. v. Union Properties, Inc.*, 562 P.2d 244 (Wash. 1977)

20.7 Partnership Property. Padgett Carroll and Walter Fulton were partners in a trucking company called C & F Trucking. Carroll purchased a trailer for the partnership. The invoice listed C & F as the purchaser, and the trailer's certificate of title listed C & F as the owner. In December of that year, Fulton petitioned for personal bankruptcy and listed the trailer as a personal asset. Did Fulton have any rights to the trailer? *In re Fulton*, 43 B.R. 273 (Bankr. M.D. Tenn. 1984)

20.8 Partnership by Estoppel. Kelley and Galloway were partners in an accounting business. Smith joined the firm, but no partnership agreement existed among them. At the end of each year, Smith was paid a bonus out of the profits of the business. While Smith was with the firm, the firm held him out to the public as a partner. Smith was designated a partner in contracts with third parties, and partnership tax returns listed him as such. Smith had no authority to hire or fire employees or to make purchases for the firm, took no part in the management, did not sign any notes when the firm was borrowing money, and was not obligated to stand any losses of the firm. Under the doctrine of partnership by estoppel, should the court find that Smith is a partner? Explain your conclusion. *Smith v. Kelley*, 465 S.W.2d 39 (Ky. 1971)

20.9 Wrongful Dissociation. A family farming partnership held a meeting at which they determined they were going to convert the partnership to an LLC. Kelly Giles, one of five general partners, was unable to attend the meeting, but later received notice of the partnership's determination to convert to an LLC. Kelly then requested production of all the partnership books and records but was not satisfied with the records that were provided for him. He harbored animosity towards the other partners, distrusted them and used threatening language against them. He then filed suit, asking the court to force the partnership to turn over all the requested documents. In response, his partners filed a counterclaim, seeking to dissociate Kelly from the partnership. Does the family have the right to dissociate Kelly? Does Kelly have a claim for wrongful termination? Discuss. *Giles v. Giles Land Co., L.P.*, 279 P.3d 139 (Kan. Ct. App. 2012)

20.10 Partnership Dissolution. Collins and Lewis each owned a 50 percent interest in a partnership formed to own and operate a cafeteria. Their partnership agreement provided that Collins would provide funds to build and open the cafeteria, while Lewis would oversee the construction of the cafeteria and manage it once it opened for business. Soon after the cafeteria opened, Collins discovered that the expenses far exceeded the receipts. Collins demanded that Lewis immediately make the cafeteria profitable, or he would cut off additional funding. Lewis tried, but failed, to find financing to buy out Collins. Collins then filed suit, seeking dissolution of the partnership. Can Collins legally force the dissolution of the partnership when, but for his actions, Lewis could have performed his required duties? *Collins v. Lewis*, 283 S.W.2d 258 (Tex. Civ. App. 1955)

LLCs and Other Business Organizations

21

Success is not final; failure is not fatal: It is the courage to continue that counts. — Winston Churchill, Prime Minister of the United Kingdom (1874-1965)

Chapter Outline

- Introduction
- Formation of an LLC
  - *Management Application: Certificate of Formation*
- Characteristics of an LLC

Case 21.1: *Demir v. Schollmeier*

  - *Management Application: IRS Form 8832 — Entity Classification Election*
  - *Management Application: Choosing the Management Form*
  - *Management Application: Limited Partnership Compared to an LLC*
  - *Management Application: Excerpted Operating Agreement for Member-Managed LLC*
- Liabilities Relating to an LLC
- Fiduciary Duties

Case 21.2: *Veira v. Harris (In Re JK Harris & Co., LLC)*

- Dissociation and Dissolution of an LLC

Case 21.3: *Vila v. BVWebTies LLC*

  - *Management Application: Excerpted Operating Agreement — Purchase of Membership Interest Clause*
- Other Business Organizations
- AI Feature: Fiduciary Duties in LLCs

Learning Objectives

After studying this chapter, you should be able to:

1. Explain how LLCs are formed.
2. State the advantages of operating a business as an LLC.
3. Understand the fiduciary duties arising from the two methods for managing an LLC.
4. Explain the advantages of forming a joint venture.
5. Distinguish the characteristics of joint stock companies, syndicates, and cooperatives.

Introduction

Limited liability company (LLC) A hybrid form of business organization combining the liability shield of a corporation with the federal tax treatment of a partnership.

Member An owner of an LLC.

This chapter introduces the **limited liability company (LLC)** and specialized business organizations including joint ventures, syndicates, and cooperatives. An LLC is a statutorily authorized noncorporate organization that, with certain exceptions, may engage in any lawful act or activity. It is a hybrid business organization with the protection of limited liability to its owners, known as **members**, similar to that of corporate shareholders and with the flow-through tax treatment of a partnership. Members have the freedom to structure allocations of profit and losses, distributions, management powers, and voting rights. An LLC is permitted to have any number of members, and all states permit single-member LLCs.

State statutes direct the creation and operation of LLCs. The first proposed uniform act was the Uniform Limited Liability Company Act (ULLCA), which was later revised. However, fewer than 25 states have adopted the ULLCA. Although the laws governing LLCs remain far from uniform, each state's LLC statutes share the similar characteristics discussed in this chapter.

Formation of an LLC

As a creature of statute, an LLC does not exist unless the state's statutory requirements are met. Typically, the law provides that an LLC is formed when the entity files articles of organization for that LLC with the Secretary of State of that state. Such a filing is conclusive proof that the organizer satisfied all conditions for the formation of an LLC.

Selecting where to organize is an important consideration because state laws vary as to their treatment of LLCs. The governing law of an LLC is determined primarily by the laws of the state where it is organized. For example, the laws of the state or country under which the LLC is organized govern its internal affairs, the authority of its managers and members, and the liability of a member and manager for the obligations of an LLC. To create an LLC, the actions described in the list below are required.

Articles of organization Legal document filed in the state where the limited liability company will organize.

Domestic LLC An LLC operating in the state where it was organized.

Foreign LLC An LLC operating in a different state from the state in which it was organized.

Alien LLC An LLC operating in a different country from the country in which it was organized.

1. *File articles of organization.* LLC statutes require that one or more organizers file **articles of organization**, also called the *certificate of formation*, with the Secretary of State's office. Under most state LLC statutes, the articles of organization must include the name and address of the business, the contact information of a registered agent, and details regarding the management of an LLC. If an amendment is needed, an LLC can amend its articles at any time.

   An LLC transacting business in the state in which it was organized is a **domestic LLC**. An LLC that operates in a different state from the state in which it was organized is known as a **foreign LLC**. LLCs that are formed under foreign laws and are operating in a state are known as an **alien LLC**.
2. *Name.* LLC statutes often require the name of the company to include the words *limited liability company* or the abbreviation *LLC*. An LLC's name must

be different from any other business names that are already in existence in the state of formation and any other states where the LLC may qualify to do business.

3. *Contributing capital and membership interests.* Members may contribute cash, property, services, a promissory note, or other assets to an LLC as a capital contribution. A person may become a member of an LLC either by entering into an ownership transaction with the LLC or acquiring the interest of a current member of the LLC. The obligation to contribute capital is not excused by the member's death, disability, or other impediments. If property or services were to be contributed, but the member cannot do so, the member is obligated to contribute an equivalent sum of money.

   In exchange for the capital contribution, the LLC member will have a membership interest in the LLC. The LLC may issue a **certificate of interest**, which evidences the ownership of the membership interests in the LLC. That certificate is similar to a corporate stock certificate.

   Certificate of interest A document evidencing an ownership interest in an LLC.

   A membership interest is a member's rights in the limited liability company, including the member's transferable interest, any right to vote or to participate in management, and any right to information concerning the business and affairs of the limited liability company.

   The articles of organization or operating agreement (discussed below) may permit different classes of membership interests. Either document may provide for specific classes to be senior to other classes and may designate specific classes of members for voting purposes. Accordingly, an LLC may be structured to accommodate differing types of membership interests and interests issued at different times during the term of the LLC.

Example: Some classes of membership interest may have the right to vote, and other classes of membership interest may not.

4. *Voting.* In most states, unless otherwise agreed, members have voting rights in proportion to their capital contributions to the LLC. Other states provide that the voting power will be in proportion to a member's share of the profits and losses of the LLC.
5. *Operating agreement.* An **operating agreement** is an agreement among the LLC members that memorializes the members' decisions on how the LLC will be operated, financed, and managed. Many states do not require LLCs to adopt an operating agreement. In those states, the LLC will be governed by a state statute. It is good business practice to create an operating agreement to provide more assurance and certainty among the members with respect to their respective rights and duties.

   Operating agreement A contract governing the LLC's affairs and setting forth the rights and duties of the members.

   Common provisions contained in the operating agreement include:

   - Identification of the manager or managers of the company;
   - The process by which managers are chosen or removed;
   - The way profits and losses are divided or allocated among the members;
   - The acts triggering dissociation and dissolution; and
   - Whether formal member meetings are required.

Management Application Certificate of Formation

CERTIFICATE OF FORMATION

OF

CHRYSLER GROUP INTERNATIONAL SERVICES S.A. LLC

This Certificate of Formation of Chrysler Group International Services S.A. LLC, dated as of May 18, 2009, is being duly executed and filed by Giorgio Fossati, as an authorized person, to form a limited liability company under the Delaware Limited Liability Company Act (6 Del. C. § 18-101, *et seq*).

1. *Name.* The name of the limited liability company formed hereby is Chrysler Group International Services S.A. LLC (the "*Company*").
2. *Registered Office.* The address of the registered office of the Company in the State of Delaware is c/o The Corporation Trust Company, 1209 Orange Street, Wilmington, New Castle County, Delaware, 19801.
3. *Registered Agent.* The name and address of the registered agent for service of process on the Company in the State of Delaware is The Corporation Trust Company, 1209 Orange Street, Wilmington, New Castle County, Delaware, 19801.

IN WITNESS WHEREOF, the undersigned has executed this Certificate of Formation as of the date first above written.

/s/ Giorgio Fossati

Name: Giorgio Fossati
Title: Authorized Person

Concept Summary Forming an LLC

To form an LLC, the following steps are taken:

1. Select a state in which to organize the LLC.
2. Draft and execute the articles of organization.
3. Deliver the document to the state's Secretary of State. If the document complies with the statute, the Secretary of State will file the document.
4. After the document is filed, the LLC comes into existence and one or more people become the initial members.

Conversion of an Existing Business to an LLC

Other forms of business organizations can be converted to an LLC if all the owners consent. The requirement for unanimous consent can be modified through the operating agreement. The process is relatively simple: The parties execute a document describing and authorizing the conversion and a required filing is made with the state's Secretary of State.

Pre-Formation Contracts

Prior to the organization of the LLC, the future members of the LLC may enter into contracts on behalf of the yet-to-be-organized LLC. These contracts are known as pre-formation contracts. Most states will apply the state's corporation laws to determine who is liable for these pre-formation contracts. In such instances, the LLC is not liable under the contract until it adopts the contract (such as through a resolution by the LLC); however, the person who executed the contract on behalf of the yet to be formed LLC will be personally liable for that contract. That person will continue to have liability until they are released from such liability.

Once the LLC has adopted a contract, the contract with the third party should be amended to release the organizer (or other person who executed the contract on behalf of the yet to be formed LLC) from liability and substitute the LLC in its place. This process is the same as the substitution of a corporation in lieu of the corporation's promoter, discussed in Chapter 22.

Jurisdictional Concerns

In Chapter 3, we reviewed how a court exercises its jurisdiction over business entities in litigated matters. For diversity jurisdiction in federal court, a corporation is considered a citizen of the state in which it is incorporated and the state of its principal place of business. In contrast, federal and state courts have interpreted LLCs to be citizens of every state in which the members themselves are residents. Thus, if an LLC has many members who are residents of different states, courts consider the LLC to be a resident of each of those states.

Due to this treatment, an LLC may be sued in a jurisdiction that may have laws unfavorable to its position as a defendant in that lawsuit. In turn, this rule of procedure may prevent the LLC from suing in federal court based upon diversity of citizenship jurisdiction. Recall from Chapter 3 that diversity jurisdiction empowers a federal court to hear a civil case if there is complete diversity among the parties to the litigation and the amount in controversy exceeds $75,000. If diversity of citizenship is lacking, the matter will proceed in a state court having jurisdiction over the parties and the subject matter of the lawsuit.

> **Example:** If Daren, a citizen of Washington, wishes to sue an LLC organized in the State of Arizona but having members in the States of Arizona, California, Oregon, and Washington, Daren will not be able to sue in federal court under a diversity of citizenship jurisdiction because both the plaintiff and defendant would be from the same state, as the courts would consider the LLC a citizen of Washington as well since a member lives in that state.

Characteristics of an LLC

The LLC has been an increasingly popular form of doing business because it offers many advantages, including (1) limited personal liability of the members, (2) tax benefits, and (3) the ability to attract foreign investors.

Limited Liability

Members of an LLC enjoy limited liability. In the absence of a member executing a personal guarantee for the obligations of the LLC to third parties, the member's financial risk is limited to their capital contribution. The members will otherwise have no personal liability for the debts of the LLC. The following case discusses a member's liability for the company's debts and obligations.

CASE 21.1

A MEMBER OF AN LLC IS NOT INDIVIDUALLY LIABLE TO ANOTHER MEMBER FOR THE COMPANY'S OBLIGATIONS

DEMIR v. SCHOLLMEIER

199 So. 3d 442 (2016)

Florida District Court of Appeals

Avrupa, LLC, was a limited liability company formed for the purpose of managing and operating a nightclub on Miami Beach known as "Club Sin." Tulga Demir, Tugend Demir (Tulga's brother), and Georg Schollmeier entered into an LLC operating agreement. The agreement provided that the three would become members of Avrupa, LLC, and Schollmeier would contribute $400,000 for a 20 percent interest, and Demir and Tugend would each contribute $1 million for a 40 percent interest each in the company.

The agreement provided that "contributions can be made to Avrupa's LLC's bank account." Section 3 of the agreement also provided that "Schollmeier may decide to withdraw from ownership of Avrupa, in which case Schollmeier's contribution of $400,000 shall be reimbursed." Additionally, section 1 of the agreement, which was titled Limited Liability Company Agreement, stated "this Agreement is a limited liability agreement under and as provided in the Act." The agreement was signed by Demir, Tugend, and Schollmeier as "the Members" of Avrupa, LLC.

In January 2007, Schollmeier wired $375,000 into Avrupa's bank account. Club Sin opened in February 2007 and closed less than two months later. In May 2007, Schollmeier sent Demir notice of his election under the contribution agreement to withdraw as a member of the company and demanded that Demir wire $400,000 into Schollmeier's bank account pursuant to the agreement. After Demir refused, Schollmeier sued both Demir and Tugend directly (instead of the LLC), seeking $400,000 in damages for breach of contract. (Note that Schollmeier only wired

$375,000 to Avrupa, LLC.) The trial court granted Schollmeier's motion for summary judgment, finding Demir personally liable for breaching the agreement. Demir appealed.

Language of the Court. *The record is clear that Demir, Tugend, and Schollmeier set out the parameters of their relationship and its accompanying obligations through the creation of a limited liability company with a governing operating agreement. Limited liability is one of the paramount reasons for forming an LLC. It is precisely those layers of protection from personal liability that preclude Schollmeier from recovering from Demir individually.*

An operating agreement is a contract. Thus, if Demir owed a financial duty directly to Schollmeier under the terms of the Agreement, Schollmeier could recover under a breach of contract claim. However operating agreements establish a more complicated and nuanced set of contractual rights and duties. Operating agreements govern the relations among the members, the managers, and the LLC itself, as well as the effect of these relations on third parties. This distinction is important because the signing parties to an operating agreement may very well decide that no individual member owes the other members any duties whatsoever, and that those duties are owed only to the company.

The agreement reads that when Schollmeier withdrew from ownership in Avrupa, his capital contribution to the company was to be reimbursed by the company. To read these provisions to mean that the individual members of Avrupa are required to reimburse a capital contribution explicitly made to only the company is to read more into the Agreement than what its members agreed upon.

Conspicuously missing from the operating agreement is any provision stating that members shall be directly liable to each other for breaches of the terms of the operating agreement. Absent such a stipulation, we presume individual members are not liable for obligations or decisions of the company, as limited liability is one of the paramount reasons for forming an LLC. The Agreement does not contain any provision or language indicating that any member of Avrupa would be personally liable to any other member for the Company's obligations, including the reimbursement of capital contributions made to the company. If the parties intended such as result, the terms needed to be explicit.

Decision. Because the company's operating agreement did not authorize a member to bring a direct action against another member for a breach of its terms, Schollmeier was not entitled to reimbursement of his capital contribution to Avrupa from Demir. The appellate court held the trial court erred in granting summary judgment in Schollmeier's favor and reversed the trial court's order.

Focus on Ethics

Is it ethical for Schollmeier to seek $400,000 from Demir personally when he only contributed $375,000 to the LLC?

SETTING ASIDE THE LLC LIABILITY SHIELD. A substantial majority of corporations and other entities whose veils have been pierced by court order have been single-owner entities. This is because it is generally easier to prove an "alter ego" veil-piercing claim against a single-owner entity than against a multi-owner entity. (An "alter ego" argument is an argument that an entity is completely dominated by its owner and thus should not be treated as if it were separate from its owner. Plaintiffs are highly likely to raise this argument against single-owner entities.) This concept will be further discussed in Chapter 22.

Tax Benefits

The IRS disregards the LLC as a taxable entity and will tax an LLC as a partnership unless the LLC elects to be taxed as a corporation. With partnership taxation the profits and losses are "passed through" from the LLC to the members, who report the results on their individual tax returns. Commonly, the choice is to be taxed as a partnership because corporations are subject to "double taxation." The corporation is required to pay income taxes on the profits it realizes and when it distributes those profits to shareholders (through dividends), the shareholders must recognize on their individual tax returns the amount they receive as income.

In the states that permit a single-member LLC, the IRS taxes the LLC as a sole proprietorship unless the company specifically elects for taxation as a corporation.

While there are tax benefits to operating as an LLC, states may assess an annual fee on the gross income of the LLC attributable to that state. The gross receipts taxes are not as high as corporate income taxes, but this additional tax is in addition to the yearly minimum franchise tax paid to the state.

Example: In the state of California, a gross receipts tax is due for the following amounts when total income is:

$0 - $249,999	No fee
$250,000 - $499,999	Fee is $900
$500,000 - $999,999	Fee is $2,500
$1,000,000 - $4,999,999	Fee is $6,000
$5,000,000 or more	Fee is $11,790

Management Application IRS Form 8832—Entity Classification Election

The IRS taxes an LLC as a partnership unless it elects otherwise. A partnership also has the option of electing to be taxed as a corporation. The relevant form to change the tax treatment is the IRS Form 8832, shown below.

Form **8832**
(Rev. December 2013)
Department of the Treasury
Internal Revenue Service

Entity Classification Election

▶ **Information about Form 8832 and its instructions is at *www.irs.gov/form8832*.**

OMB No. 1545-1516

Type or Print

Name of eligible entity making election | **Employer identification number**

Number, street, and room or suite no. If a P.O. box, see instructions.

City or town, state, and ZIP code. If a foreign address, enter city, province or state, postal code and country. Follow the country's practice for entering the postal code.

▶ Check if: ☐ Address change ☐ Late classification relief sought under Revenue Procedure 2009-41
☐ Relief for a late change of entity classification election sought under Revenue Procedure 2010-32

Part I Election Information

1 **Type of election** (see instructions):

a ☐ Initial classification by a newly-formed entity. Skip lines 2a and 2b and go to line 3.
b ☐ Change in current classification. Go to line 2a.

2a Has the eligible entity previously filed an entity election that had an effective date within the last 60 months?

☐ **Yes.** Go to line 2b.
☐ **No.** Skip line 2b and go to line 3.

2b Was the eligible entity's prior election an initial classification election by a newly formed entity that was effective on the date of formation?

☐ **Yes.** Go to line 3.
☐ **No.** Stop here. You generally are not currently eligible to make the election (see instructions).

3 Does the eligible entity have more than one owner?

☐ **Yes.** You can elect to be classified as a partnership or an association taxable as a corporation. Skip line 4 and go to line 5.
☐ **No.** You can elect to be classified as an association taxable as a corporation or to be disregarded as a separate entity. Go to line 4.

4 If the eligible entity has only one owner, provide the following information:

a Name of owner ▶ ....
b Identifying number of owner ▶ ....

5 If the eligible entity is owned by one or more affiliated corporations that file a consolidated return, provide the name and employer identification number of the parent corporation:

a Name of parent corporation ▶ ....
b Employer identification number ▶ ....

For Paperwork Reduction Act Notice, see instructions. Cat. No. 22598R Form **8832** (Rev. 12-2013)

Foreign Investors

Foreign investors are eligible to own membership in LLCs. Other business formations, such as the S corporation (discussed in Chapter 22), do not allow for investment by a nonresident alien. Thus, the ability to attract investments from foreign investors provides an LLC with additional means of securing funding that would not be available in another business form, such as an S corporation.

The Series LLC

A few states permit the formation of a series LLC. A series LLC allows a *single* LLC to hold separate assets in a separate "series" and provides for the limitation of liabilities among the separate series. A series LLC is analogous to a honeycomb whereby separate cells (series) cluster to form the honeycomb. In a series LLC, the articles of organization allow for unlimited segregation of membership interests, assets, and activities into independent series or cells. Each series operates as if they were separate LLCs with distinct names and financing and separate accounting records.

A series LLC may have different members and managers in each series. The principal benefit of the series LLC is that it tries to insulate the liabilities of one series from the assets held in other series. This ability to place multiple assets in a single LLC, yet insulate the liabilities associated with those assets, eliminates the administrative burden and expense of forming multiple LLCs. Despite its advantages, not all state legislatures and courts are uniform in extending the liability shield to the assets held in other series within the single LLC.

> **Example:** An owner of several residential properties that are rented may seek to form a series LLC. Each of the rental properties will be its own series under the series LLC. In the event that a tenant files suit against the owner of the property, only that series in the LLC will be impacted. The other series in the LLC will not be liable for the debt.

In contrast, in the absence of veil piercing noted above, the courts of all states will respect the liability shields of single-member LLCs, since, among other considerations, (1) all of these states have their own LLC acts; (2) all of these acts provide for single-member LLCs; and (3) most or all of these acts contain express provisions recognizing the liability shields of LLCs formed under other LLC acts.

Profits and Losses and Distributions

Unless otherwise agreed, the ULLCA provides that each member has a right to an equal share of profits and losses. Because this default rule may be unfair to those who contribute more capital, it is often modified either by state law or by the operating agreement to require profit distributions be allocated in proportion to members' capital contributions.

> **Example:** If A contributed $10,000 and B contributed $90,000, A would be allocated 10 percent of the profits and B 90 percent of them.

Members in an LLC may also agree to allocate profits or losses in a proportion not equal to their respective ownership interests. In addition, the allocation of profits and the allocation of losses do not have to be in the same proportion.

Be sure you put your feet in the right place. Then stand firm. — Abraham Lincoln, Sixteenth President of the United States (1809-1865)

> **Example:** The Alabama LLC statute provides: The profits and losses, income, deductions, credits, and items of income, deduction[s], and credits of the limited liability company shall be allocated among the members in the manner provided in the operating agreement. If the operating agreement does not provide, profits and losses, income, deductions, and credits, and items of income, deductions, and credits shall be allocated on the basis of the *pro rata* value of the contributions made by each member to the extent they have been made and not returned. Ala. Code § 10-22-28.

Transferring an LLC interest

Under the ULLCA, a member's rights in a limited liability company are split into economic rights and governance rights. The economic rights, such as a member's ownership interest in an LLC, are known as **distributional interests**. Distributional interests are personal property and may be transferred like a partnership interest may be transferred. Like a partnership interest, unless otherwise provided in the operating agreement or by consent of all other members, a transfer of a distributional interest does not entitle the transferee to become a member of the LLC or to exercise any governance rights of a member (such as management rights, rights to information, and so on).

Distributional interest
The member's ownership interest in the LLC allowing the member the right to receive distributions from the LLC.

The recipient of the distributional interest only receives distributions (such as profits and losses) from the LLC to which the transferor would have been entitled and does not become a member. The transferor retains the rights of a member, other than the distributional interest, and retains all the duties and obligations of a member.

> **Example:** Hope is a 20 percent member in an LLC. The operating agreement does not provide the right to transfer membership interests. Hope thereafter transfers her distributional interest to Sydney. Sydney is not a member in the LLC but is entitled to receive Hope's 20 percent distributional interest. Hope still maintains governance rights as a member in the LLC.

Managing the LLC

The governance of an LLC includes three concepts:

- The internal management of the LLC;
- The authority of members and managers (if any) to bind the LLC to contracts; and
- The duties owed by those who manage the LLC to the members of the LLC.

INTERNAL MANAGEMENT OF THE LLC. An LLC can be managed by its members, similar to how partners manage a general partnership, or by managers, similar to corporate officers. The distinction is important because the rights to bind the LLC to contracts and fiduciary duties that are owed change based on the management of the LLC. The articles of organization or operating agreement will dictate how the LLC will be managed. If such agreements are silent as to management, the state LLC statute will provide a default form of management (usually member-managed).

In a **member-managed** LLC, all the members participate in the management of the company and act collectively. Each member has an equal right to manage the company, regardless of the member's capital contribution. Unless the state statute provides otherwise, a majority vote of the members determines business decisions.

Member-managed LLC
An LLC managed by all members.

> **Example:** A member-managed LLC is comprised of three members. Member Alicia has contributed 10 percent of the capital of the LLC, Briana has contributed 20 percent of the capital of the LLC; and Caitlin has contributed 70 percent of the capital of the LLC. While Alicia and Brianna contributed only 30 percent of the capital, in a vote of the LLC, they would each have one vote, and Caitlin would have one vote.

Manager-managed LLC
Members empower one or more managers to manage the LLC.

In a **manager-managed LLC**, a person or group of people manages the company. Managers may be members, non-members, or both members and non-members.

Frequently, in a manager-managed form, the LLC may have officers with titles much like those in a corporation, such as president and vice president.

Certain actions require the consent of all members and may not be delegated to managers. These actions include amending the articles of organization or the operating agreement; admitting new members; consenting to dissolving or merging the LLC; and the sale, lease, or disposition of all or substantially all the LLC's property.

Management Application
Choosing the Management Form

In LLCs with numerous owners or in LLCs where the nature of the business lends itself to more centralized decision making (such as manufacturing), it may be more appropriate to choose the manager-managed form of management. The authority of a manager in an LLC is broader than that of a corporate director, permitting a more streamlined and efficient management structure.

Where there are numerous owners, allowing one member in a member-managed LLC to bind the entity may not be in the best interests of the LLC where the majority of members have differing viewpoints on operating strategy.

Compensation and Reimbursement

A member in a member-managed LLC is not entitled to be compensated for rendering services on behalf of the LLC. An exception exists for members who participate in winding up the LLC. In such circumstances, those members can be compensated.

Managers in a manager-managed LLC are entitled to be compensated for their services. A member who is also a manager is entitled to compensation for their services as a manager. Both members and managers are entitled to be reimbursed for expenses incurred in the ordinary course of the LLC's business.

Management Application
Limited Partnership Compared to an LLC

The role of the general partner in a limited partnership may seem similar to that of a manager in a manager-managed LLC. They both offer flexibility and can alter the standard of care, and the fiduciary duties owed to the managers-owners. The general partner makes all of the decisions regarding the affairs of the company similar to the manager in the manager-managed LLC.

Typically, there is pass-through tax treatment of the entity. These two business entities differ in the following ways:

- Managers of an LLC are not liable for the debts and obligations of the LLC, while a general partner of a limited partnership is liable for them;
- There is no statutory requirement that managers of an LLC must be members of the entity; and
- Limited partners cannot be active participants in the entity's daily operations. Doing so can expose them to personal liability for the partnership's debts and obligations. In contrast, members of a member-managed LLC are not exposed to personal liability.

Using an internet search engine, identify the proportion of Delaware entity formations that are LLCs as compared to limited partnerships. Explain the conclusion you reach.

Management Application Excerpted Operating Agreement for Member-Managed LLC

Management Rights in Members

Except as otherwise provided in this Agreement or as otherwise agreed, management of the Company is vested in the Members in proportion to their initial capital contributions.

Members to Make Joint Decisions

No act may be taken, funds expended, decisions made, or obligations incurred by the Company except by the unanimous consent of all Members with respect to a matter within the scope of any of the following decisions:

A. The sale of all or substantially all assets of the Company;
B. A mortgage or encumbrance on all or substantially all assets of the Company;
C. Any matter that could result in a change in the amount or character of the Company's contributions to capital;
D. Borrowing of money; or,
E. Commission of an act that would make it impossible for the Company to continue its ordinary business.

Alteration of Management Responsibilities

Management responsibilities may not be altered except by the action of a majority-in-interest of all Members at a meeting called on written notice expressly describing alteration of management responsibilities as one of the purposes of the meeting.

What other important understandings should be stated in such an agreement? For example, should the fiduciary duty standards for members be reduced to allow them to invest in companies in the same or a related market?

Authority of Members and Managers

Whether a member or manager of an LLC has the power to bind the LLC to contracts will depend on which management style was adopted (manager-managed or member-managed) and the terms of the operating agreement. In a member-managed LLC, all of the members have the authority to bind the LLC to contracts. In a manager-managed LLC, only the manager(s) have the authority to bind the LLC to contracts. Members who are not managers do not have the authority to bind the LLC to contracts. However, the LLC's operating agreement can provide additional authority or place limitations on the authority of members or managers to act on behalf of the LLC.

> **Example:** A member-managed LLC's operating agreement may provide that the members must first seek approval by the other members when entering into transactions greater than $100,000.

Concept Summary
Authority to Bind an LLC to Contracts

Management Style	Contract Authority
Member-managed	All members may bind the LLC in contract.
Manager-managed	The managers may bind the LLC in contract, but the non-manager members may not.

Liabilities Relating to an LLC

An LLC is an organization distinct from its members. The assets and obligations of the LLC belong to the LLC and not the members. As a separate legal entity, an LLC can sue and be sued in its own name. It can own property and enter into and enforce contracts. It is also responsible for obeying all civil and criminal laws and regulations.

The LLC is liable for the wrongful acts or omissions caused by a member, manager, employee, or agent in the course and scope of ordinary business. Managers are not personally liable for debts, obligations, and liabilities of LLC. Many state LLC statutes allow LLCs to indemnify members from liabilities while acting in their capacity as a member. Indemnification agreements are promises by one party to compensate (and perhaps provide defense counsel for) another for the claims, losses, and lawsuits of a third party when specified events occur.

Fiduciary Duties

Certain fiduciary duties (the duty of care and duty of loyalty) are owed by managers and members to the LLC. These duties will depend on whether the LLC is organized as a manager-managed LLC or member-managed LLC. In addition, state laws vary greatly among their requirements regarding the fiduciary duties owed by members and managers. Therefore, members and managers need to be aware of varying state requirements. Further, when an LLC operates in more than one state, it is possible that the members or managers may be held to different standards in different jurisdictions.

In a member-managed LLC, the members owe these fiduciary duties to each other and to the LLC. Under the ULLCA, and the law in most states, in a manager-managed LLC, the manager(s) owe the fiduciary duties to both the LLC and to its members. In the manager-managed form of LLCs, members will want to hold the managers accountable for their actions. Managers will want rules to govern their conduct and measure their actions. However, in some states, managers owe fiduciary duties only to the LLC and not to its members.

Also, a unique aspect of LLCs is a trend among state legislatures to greatly reduce, or even eliminate, fiduciary duties in the LLC statutes. Delaware has taken the lead in allowing LLCs to limit and define fiduciary duties for members, managers, and others who might normally have fiduciary and other duties to each other and to the LLC. In effect, Delaware has allowed operating agreements to eliminate all fiduciary duties. Thus, selecting the state of formation of an LLC is important because its requirements will impact the management of the LLC. This is a significant difference when litigating breach of fiduciary duty cases.

Members who are not managers in a manager-managed LLC do not owe fiduciary duties to the LLC or other members. They are similar to a shareholder in a corporation. The two fiduciary duties of care and loyalty are discussed briefly below. For a more thorough discussion of fiduciary duties, review Chapter 15.

Duty of Care

In most states, the duty of care is the obligation to act with the care that a person in a similar position would reasonably exercise under similar circumstances. In the context of LLCs, the duty of care requires that members act in good faith and exercise reasonable care when conducting their obligations to the LLC. Managers may rely in good faith on the opinions and advice of informed consultants in exercising their duties. The business judgment rule is one in which courts presume that those persons acted on an informed basis, in good faith, and in a manner reasonably believed to be in the best interest of the LLC. This rule is discussed more fully in Chapter 23.

The duty of care for an LLC's managers in a manager-managed LLC and members in a member-managed LLC will vary from state to state. Some LLC statutes only require that managers and members operate and manage the LLC in a way that is not grossly negligent or that entails intentionally wrongful acts.

Duty of Loyalty

Like the duty of care, the duty of loyalty can vary depending upon state law. However, most states have required managers and members to refrain from acting in a manner that is adverse to the interest of the LLC. That is, the duty of loyalty prohibits managers and members of an LLC from usurping a corporate opportunity, self-dealing, or competing with the company.

The following case addresses whether the fiduciary duty of care is breached where a manager of an LLC acts with gross negligence and recklessness when authorizing member distributions in place of retiring company debt.

CASE 21.2

A MANAGER OF AN LLC BREACHES FIDUCIARY DUTIES EVEN IF UNAWARE OF THOSE DUTIES

VEIRA v. HARRIS (IN RE JK HARRIS & CO., LLC)

512 B.R. 562 (2012)

United States Bankruptcy Court for the District of South Carolina

Michelle L. Veira, acting as the Chapter 7 Trustee for three bankrupt South Carolina limited liability companies, sued John K. Harris for breaching his fiduciary duties. Harris, who owned or controlled the three companies' voting power, authorized member distributions to himself totaling over 3 million dollars while fully aware of the companies' insolvency and increasing debts. This decision allowed the companies' liabilities to exceed 30 million dollars while its assets barely reached 5 million. His actions deprived creditors of funds that could have been used for debt repayment and operational needs before the bankruptcy proceedings were commenced. In response to the suit, Harris admitted all of the factual allegations made by the Trustee in the complaint and in the Trustee's Motion and agreed that none of the facts set forth in the complaint were subject to dispute. He argued that he should not be held liable because he was not aware of his duties set forth in the South Carolina Limited Liability Company Act. The only issue raised by defendant Harris was whether his lack of knowledge constituted a defense to the Trustee's causes of action.

Language of the Court. *The duty of care requires that a manager of a limited liability company is limited to refraining from engaging in grossly negligent or reckless conduct, intentional misconduct, or a knowing violation of law. Under South Carolina law, gross negligence is the failure to exercise slight care or the absence of care that is necessary under the circumstances. Recklessness implies the doing of a negligent act knowingly; it is a conscious failure to exercise due care.*

A manager of a manager-managed company or member of a member-managed company is liable for a violation of the duty of care if they engage in grossly negligent or reckless conduct, intentional misconduct, or a knowing violation of the law. This statute is written in the disjunctive, meaning that Defendant's conduct meeting any of the four types of conduct set forth above is sufficient for the Defendant to be held liable. While the statute does provide for liability based upon a "knowing violation of the law," Defendant's knowledge of the law is irrelevant where, as here, liability is based upon gross negligence or recklessness.

By authorizing the Member Distributions, Defendant acted with gross negligence and recklessness. Defendant was aware that the Debtor limited liability companies were insolvent at all times, but nevertheless he authorized and received the member distributions from the LLCs, rather than allowing those funds to be used for debt service and ongoing operations. Even as Debtors began accruing millions of dollars in additional liabilities, Defendant continued authorizing and receiving the Member Distributions. In doing so, Defendant deprived the financially insolvent Debtors of funds that could have been used for operations, to attract investors, to persuade additional lenders, or to satisfy some of the very large claims against Debtors. The undisputed facts show that Defendant's actions in authorizing and receiving the Member Distributions in the face of Debtors' imminent financial collapse were grossly negligent and reckless. As a result of these grossly negligent and reckless actions, Defendant breached his statutory fiduciary duty of care to Debtors.

Decision. The court granted the Trustee's Motion for Summary Judgement and permitted the Trustee to recover $3,503,836.00 from Defendant Harris.

Focus on Ethics

How can managers ensure they are fulfilling their fiduciary duty to act in the best interests of the LLC and its members when making decisions about member distributions?

Ignorantia juris neminem excusat.— Latin for "Ignorance of the law is no excuse (defense)"

Concept Summary
Who Owes Fiduciary Duties?

Subject to applicable state law, under the law of many states:

- Member-Managed LLC
  - ☐ Members owe fiduciary duties to each other and to the LLC.
- Manager-Managed LLC
  - ☐ Managers owe fiduciary duties to each other and to the LLC.
  - ☐ Members who are not managers do not owe fiduciary duties to the LLC or to other members.

Dissociation and Dissolution of an LLC

Dissociation

A member always has the power to dissociate (that is, withdraw) from the LLC. Following dissociation, the member no longer participates in the business. Subject to what the operating agreement or applicable state law provides, events that trigger a member's dissociation from an LLC include voluntary withdrawal, expulsion of that member by other members, court order, bankruptcy, incompetence, and death of the member. If one member of the LLC dies, the other members may continue the business of the LLC, unless the operating agreement provides otherwise.

While a member may have the power to withdraw, a member may agree not to do so. For example, before the purpose of an LLC is accomplished, a member withdraws when not permitted to do so under the operating agreement or applicable law. That prohibited action is known as a **wrongful dissociation**.

Wrongful dissociation The withdrawal of a member from an LLC when not permitted by the operating agreement or applicable law.

A dissociated member is not entitled to usurp the information learned in the LLC or use it to the prejudice of the LLC. The former member remains liable for any debt or obligation to the company or the other members that the person incurred while a member.

Dissolution

When a member dissociates from an LLC, the dissociated member generally has no right to force the LLC to dissolve. The remaining members can choose either to continue or dissolve the company.

If the members choose not to continue the business, they must dissolve the business, which is a process under which the LLC's assets are collected, liquidated, and distributed to wind up the business. Members can preserve the LLC assets for a reasonable time to optimize their return during dissolution. Following the sale of all the LLC's assets, the proceeds first repay the debts owed to third-party creditors. After these creditors are paid, the member-creditors are paid, followed by a return of the members' capital contributions. Any remainder is then distributed to members in equal shares or in accordance with the operating agreement. The following case addresses when dissolution of an LLC is appropriate.

CASE 21.3

WHEN IT IS NOT REASONABLY PRACTICABLE FOR THE LLC TO CONTINUE DISSOLUTION IS WARRANTED

VILA v. BVWEBTIES LLC

2010 Del. Ch. LEXIS 202 (2010)

Court of Chancery of Delaware

Robert "Bob" Vila, a well-known home improvement expert, and George Hill, an experienced businessperson, formed an LLC along with HI Nominee Trust. Vila and Hill each owned 49 percent of the LLC and HI Nominee Trust owned

2 percent. As provided in the LLC agreement, Vila and Hill formed BVWebTies LLC (WebTies) for the purpose of developing and operating the website BobVila.com, a website offering home improvement advice through various forms of media, such as step-by-step videos, how-to articles, and product suggestions.

To run BobVila.com, WebTies required the use of Vila's name. Therefore, Vila and WebTies executed a formal licensing agreement that provided WebTies the right to use Vila's exclusive intellectual property rights in his name, image, and likeness, including a trademark in the name "Bob Vila." That license was cancellable by either party at will. Upon termination, the intellectual property rights reverted to Vila.

The LLC agreement provided Hill and Vila would be the initial managers of the LLC. The addition of any other manager(s) required the consent of all members (Vila, Hill, and HI Nominee Trust). Following the cancellation of Vila's syndicated home improvement television show, WebTies suffered the loss of a key advertiser, Sears, and declining income. Disagreements between the members led to different strategies for the continuance of the business. Vila sought to reinvent BobVila.com and expand WebTies's operations. Vila's vision included hiring an experienced manager, investing additional capital in WebTies, and relocating WebTies's offices. Hill, on the other hand, wanted to weather the recession by staying in business with a modest, but functioning, operation.

However, Vila engaged in several activities that constituted impermissible direct competition with WebTies (as stated in the LLC agreement). Unable to resolve the dispute about how WebTies should move forward, Villa filed a complaint seeking a judicial order of dissolution of the LLC.

Language of the Court. *This case primarily presents the question of whether it is "reasonably practicable," under Delaware law for a Delaware limited liability company to continue to operate in conformity with its LLC agreement when two coequal owners and managers whose mutual agreement is required for any company action are deadlocked as to the future direction and management of the enterprise and the LLC agreement provides no mechanism by which to break the deadlock.*

To judicially dissolve an LLC, the party seeking dissolution must prove that he is (i) a member or manager and (ii) that it is not reasonably practicable to carry on the business in conformity with a limited liability company agreement.

This case is one in which an LLC has two managers whose agreement is contractually required for WebTies to move forward with a properly authorized strategy. Neither manager can act in isolation for WebTies without the assent of the other. This sort of deadlock has classically provided the basis for a dissolution in the corporate context when a joint venture with two coequal shareholders faces a deadlock.

Neither Hill nor Vila appear to place a high value on WebTies, but they have failed to reach an agreement on how to part, this ongoing struggle being the last thing that still binds these former close friends together. Given these realities, pleas by either Hill or Vila for a lengthy winding-up will not be indulged. WebTies should be the subject of sale in an auction.

Decision. The court granted judicial dissolution of WebTies immediately to avoid a lengthy winding-up process due to the interpersonal and irreconcilable conflicts in the case.

Focus on Ethics

If you had to draft the operating agreement for this venture, what would be an appropriate mechanism to break a deadlock between two managers?

Comparing an LLC with a Partnership

	LLC	Partnership
Liability	Limited liability of the members to the loss of their investment.	It depends upon the type of partnership. There is unlimited liability for a general partnership and some form of limited liability for other types of partnerships.
Tax	Pass-through taxation.	Pass-through taxation.
Management	Can either be member-managed or manager-managed.	It depends upon the type of partnership. All partners can have an equal right to manage the partnership unless agreed otherwise.

Management Application Excerpted Operating Agreement — Purchase of Membership Interest Clause

On the occurrence of any of the following events ("Triggering Events") with respect to a Member, the Company and the other Members shall have the option to purchase all or any portion of the Membership Interest of the Member ("Selling Member") at the price and on the terms provided in Paragraph ___:

(a) The death or incapacity of a Member;

(b) The bankruptcy of a Member;

(c) The winding up and dissolution of a corporate Member, or the merger or other corporate reorganization of a corporate Member as a result of which the corporate Member does not survive as an entity;

(d) The dissociation of a Member; or

(e) Any other event that is, or that would cause, a transfer in contravention of this Agreement.

Each Member agrees to promptly give written notice of a Triggering Event to all Members.

Can you think of other events that should permit the purchase of another member's interest? Should the award of the member's interest to a spouse in a divorce proceeding be considered? In practical terms, what does "incapacity" mean? Who should make that determination?

Other Business Organizations

Joint Ventures

A **joint venture** is formed when two or more people or businesses associate together as co-owners of an enterprise to share profits and losses. However, while a partnership is created to engage in a continuous business for an indefinite or fixed period, a joint venture is formed for a single transaction or series of transactions.

Joint venture A joint undertaking in which two or more people or businesses associate together as co-owners of an enterprise to share profits and losses for a transaction or series of transactions.

Joint venturers are like partnerships. By default, joint venturers share profit and losses equally, but the parties can agree to any other profit and loss split. Moreover, each joint venture member has equal rights to manage the joint venture, and each member is bound by the same fiduciary duties as those found in partnerships. Therefore, any self-dealing by one of the members of the joint venture to the detriment of the joint venture may result in liability and payment of damages by the self-dealing member.

Joint ventures differ from partnerships in a few important respects. The members of the joint venture have less implied or apparent authority to bind the joint venture because the purpose of a joint venture is generally much narrower than the purpose and scope of a partnership. Therefore, a member of the joint venture will be limited in the ways that they can bind the other members of the co-venture. Additionally, the joint venture will terminate upon the completion of the joint venture's purpose; in contrast, a partnership will continue doing business until the partnership term has ended or the partners dissolve the partnership.

Example: Toyota® and Mazda® entered into a joint venture to build a $1.6 billion plant in the United States. This joint venture stemmed from the shared belief of the companies that U.S. demand for their vehicles had peaked and that a joint venture was the best means available to build a new plant while limiting the overall risk for both companies.

Concept Summary Comparing Partnerships and Joint Ventures

	Partnership	Joint Venture
Scope	Formed for the carrying on of a business for profit	Formed to accomplish a specific transaction, project, or series of transactions or projects
Duties Owed	Fiduciary duties owed to all partners and the partnership	Fiduciary duties owed to all joint venture members and the joint venture
Authority	Partners have actual, implied, and apparent authority to bind the partnership.	Implied and apparent authority is limited to the extent of the project or transaction.
Taxation	Pass-through taxation	Pass-through taxation
Termination	Upon completion of the partnership term or dissolution	Upon completion of the transaction, project, or series of transactions or projects

Syndicates

Syndicate
A group of persons joining to finance a project or underwrite risks of others for a price.

A **syndicate**, also referred to as an investment group, is a group of people joining together to finance a project or underwrite risks of others for a price. In many cases, parties utilize the syndicate business structure because the venture itself carries a high level of risk but also an attractive potential rate of return. Syndicates can be formed as corporations or partnerships (either general or limited). How the syndicate is structured varies greatly.

> **Example:** Since the 1680s Lloyd's of London® has provided a market where buyers and sellers of insurance may negotiate insurance policies. It operates its market by placing underwriters (those who assess and evaluate risk and who advise others to assume that risk) into groups known as syndicates. Lloyd's assigns an agent who is an expert in the insurance business to manage each syndicate on behalf of all its members.

> **Example:** Syndicates are used frequently in the issuance of public securities offerings. A group of underwriting firms forms a syndicate to purchase the securities from the issuer (the issuer is a company that is selling its securities on a stock exchange). They are purchased at a discount from the expected public offering price. The difference between the price the underwriters paid for the securities and the public offering price is the profit they realize. The underwriters own, and are

obligated to pay the issuer for, the securities regardless of whether the underwriters resell the securities to the investing public.

Joint Stock Companies

Not often employed in the United States, a **joint stock company** has characteristics of both partnerships and corporations. It is similar to a corporation in that freely transferable shares of stock based on capital contributions to the company represent ownership in the company, it exists in perpetuity, and officers and a board of directors usually manage the business.

Joint stock company An association within a business enterprise with transferable shares of stock, except that the shareholders are liable for the debts of the business.

Like a partnership, a joint stock company is formed by agreement of the members (shareholders) rather than statute. Shareholders are subject to personal liability for the debts of the joint stock company. However, unlike a partnership, the members do not owe each other fiduciary duties.

Example: In the earliest joint stock companies, a group of merchants would pool their "stocks" (the goods they had for trade) and collectively hire a ship to undertake a trade mission. When they returned, the stock of goods acquired in trade for their goods would be divided among the merchants and the "company" dissolved.

Business Trusts

Dating back to the thirteenth century, a **business trust** is a form of business organization managed by appointed trustees who hold title to the business's property for the benefit of one or more beneficiaries. Business trusts are created by a written trust agreement, setting forth the interests of the beneficiaries as well as the obligations and powers of the trustees. In some states, business trusts are either associations taxable as corporations for corporate income tax purposes or partnerships, rather than as trusts.

Business trust A form of business organization managed by appointed trustees who hold title to the business's property for the benefit of one or more beneficiaries.

Outside of the context of bankruptcy, the definitions of this entity vary greatly among the states. Commonly, business trusts allow the trustees more power over the trust property than the officers exercise in a corporation. Business trusts allow for the limited liability of the trustee, who is only liable in a fiduciary capacity to the beneficiaries.

Cooperatives

A **cooperative** has many definitions, but most frequently it is: recognized as an association that is owned and controlled by those who use its services or buy its products (known commonly as members); is democratically controlled by each owner/customer who has one vote regardless of the amount of the owner's purchases; and has the primary objective of maximizing benefits to its members rather than profits. Cooperatives may be used for a variety of purposes, including providing insurance to the members, providing discount buying of services and products needed by the members, and permitting shared processing costs (such as those formed by farmers and growers to process and market their agricultural products). If the cooperative is incorporated, the members are not personally liable to creditors.

Cooperative An association organized to provide an economic service or benefit to its members.

Example: Recreational Equipment, Inc., commonly known as REI®, provides sporting goods, camping gear, travel equipment, and clothing to the public, but members receive an annual rebate based upon the amount of goods they purchased from the cooperative.

Because cooperatives are not owned by outside investors, they typically have no duty to comply with federal (SEC) reporting requirements or provide public data on their financial activities.

AI Feature: Fiduciary Duties in LLCs

After reading this chapter, use an internet search engine to conduct research on the fiduciary duties of member-managed LLCs in Delaware. Use an AI program to consider the following scenario: Jorge is a manager of Acme Infrastructure, an airport facilities contractor. Acme is a member-managed LLC formed under Delaware law. Acme's operating agreement waives fiduciary duties among members to the maximum extent permitted under Delaware law. One of the members of the LLC, Brad, caused Acme to enter into a joint venture with Nowhere Airways. After the transaction documents have been signed, Jorge realizes that the relationship with the airline will require massive expenditures to build the requisite infrastructure at the remote airports to which Nowhere flies. Jorge believes the decision will harm Acme financially but would bolster Brad's wealth. Jorge discovers also that Brad is a substantial investor in Nowhere Airways. At no time has Brad revealed his investment in Nowhere Airways to anyone at Acme. The other members of Acme will not ratify Brad's actions in obligating Acme to contract with the airline.

Jorge decides to file a derivative lawsuit against Brad for a breach of his fiduciary duties to Acme and its members. Brad cites the waiver within the Delaware law that excuses or waives a member's fiduciary duties to the LLC or other members. Can Jorge and the other members hold Brad liable for breaching his fiduciary duties? At this point in time, what strategy do you suggest Acme pursue with Nowhere Airlines to mitigate the substantial losses it forecasts it will incur with the joint venture?

Key Terms

- Alien LLC, 508
- Articles of organization, 508
- Business trust, 529
- Certificate of interest, 509
- Cooperative, 529
- Distributional interest, 517
- Domestic LLC, 508
- Foreign LLC, 508

- Joint stock company, 529
- Joint venture, 527
- Limited liability company (LLC), 508
- Manager-managed LLC, 517
- Member, 508
- Member-managed LLC, 517
- Operating agreement, 509
- Syndicate, 528
- Wrongful dissociation, 524

Applying the Law

21.1 Research the Law. Using an internet search engine, research the uniform LLC law as adopted by your home state. Alternatively, you may review the LLC law of the State of Delaware. Has the subject law been adopted to modify a uniform LLC act? If so, have some of the duties between and among the members and managers been relaxed? What advantages are offered by the law of the state that you have studied?

21.2 To Dissolve or Not. Matthew Haley sought dissolution of Matt and Greg Real Estate, LLC (the "LLC"). Matthew and Greg were the only members of the LLC, each owning a 50 percent interest in the LLC. However, they had a falling out and wanted to separate. The LLC agreement stated it was to be managed by its two members, but it was difficult to do so since the two members deadlocked on all issues. Greg wanted the LLC to continue because the LLC agreement provided a mechanism for Matthew to dissociate and be paid the fair market value of his share of the LLC's real property. Matthew argued that because the LLC agreement needed both members to govern, a dissolution was appropriate because it would be impractical for the LLC to continue while he would remain liable as a guarantor of the LLC's mortgage. Analyze the facts and make a recommendation whether dissolution should be ordered. *Haley v. Talcott*, 864 A.2d 86 (Del. Ch. 2004)

21.3 LLC Liability. Donald Hodge, Sr., was hunting on a ladder-style deer stand when its straps, which held him up in a tree, failed. This resulted in his death. His children sued for wrongful death and named as defendants the manufacturer and seller of the deer stand, Strong Built International, LLC. Ken Killen was the LLC's sole member and manager. Can Killen be held individually liable for these claims? *Hodge v. Strong Built International, LLC*, 159 So. 3d 1159 (La. Ct. App. 2015)

21.4 Authority to Act. Michael Collins formed Kanaka Rapids Ranch, LLC. Michael and his father, E.A. Collins, were the two managers of Kanaka. E.A. Collins lived in Nevada and was not involved in the operation of Kanaka Rapids. A corporation owned by E.A. Collins deeded various properties located in Idaho to Kanaka Rapids in consideration of that corporation redeeming all the stock held by E.A. Collins. Michael Collins then deeded the conveyed properties to third parties. When E.A. Collins died, his estate on behalf of estate creditors sued seeking to set aside the land conveyances to the defendant third parties, asserting that Michael did not have the authority to convey the land on behalf of Kanaka Rapids. The estate claimed that no operating agreement existed that named Michael as manager of Kanaka Rapids, and thus he was not a valid manager and could not bind the LLC. Michael filed an affidavit in which he stated that he and E.A. had agreed that Michael would be the manager of Kanaka Rapids. Does a manager of a limited liability company need written authorization to conduct the usual business or affairs of the LLC? What type of authority does Michael have, if any? How should the court rule on whether Michael had the authority to execute these deeds to third parties? *Estate of Collins v. Geist*, 153 P.3d 1167 (Idaho 2007)

21.5 Tort Liabilities of a Member. An explosion occurred at a residence and the likely cause of the explosion was stray propane gas. The survivors and executors of the estates of those who died filed suit against Iowa Double Circle LLC, the supplier of the propane, and the two members of the LLC. Keota was one of the two member owners and owned 95 percent of the membership interests in the company. Farmland Industries, Inc., was the other member. The plaintiffs claimed Keota, through its manager Dave Hopscheidt, was negligent in failing to provide proper warnings to propane users, including the failure to warn users to install a gas detector, and to properly design the odorant added to the propane. The plaintiffs sought to hold Keota Coop liable for participating in certain torts as the designated manager of an LLC pursuant to the agreement under which it directed Hopscheidt to act for Keota in performing management services of Double Circle. Iowa law provided that a member's liability arises in contract or tort under the same or similar circumstances and to the same extent as a shareholder of a corporation may be personally liable for any debt, obligation, or liability of the corporation. How should the court rule? *Estate of Countryman v. Farmers Coop. Ass'n*, 679 N.W.2d 598 (Iowa 2004)

21.6 Fiduciary Duties of LLC Managers. A creditor of Boulder Partnership, LLC, sued the individual members and managers of the LLC, claiming that the LLC's managers authorized a distribution to the LLC's members that left the LLC insolvent and unable to repay the creditor. Do the managers of an LLC owe a fiduciary duty to the LLC's creditors? Why or why not? *Weinstein v. Colborne Foodbotics, LLC*, 302 P.3d 263 (Colo. 2013)

21.7 Fiduciary Duties. Leslie Polk and his three adult children, Dusty, Lezanne, and Yurii, formed Polk Plumbing LLC. Leslie owned 50 percent of the LLC's interest, Dusty and Yurii each owned 20 percent, and Lezanne owned 10 percent. Polk Plumbing specialized in commercial plumbing work. During one of the company's meetings, Yurii revealed that he desired to work in residential plumbing and withdrew from the company, leaving his 20 percent interest to Leslie. As a result, Leslie's interest increased to 70 percent, while Dusty and Lezanne maintained their original interest. A few years later, Leslie became dissatisfied with Dusty and Lezanne's work, and unilaterally removed them from the company by removing their access to the LLC's books, records, and offices. Dusty and Lezanne brought suit against Leslie for breach of fiduciary duty. They won because the court argued that Dusty and Lezanne served as managers of the LLC and there was no evidence of a vote. Rather, Leslie testified that he simply acted in disregard of the terms of the Operating Agreement and acted as the patriarch of the family to "fire" Dusty and Lezanne for, in his opinion, not working enough. The Alabama Supreme Court recognized that managers of an LLC owe to the company and to other members a fiduciary duty of care, and Leslie breached that duty by unilaterally "firing" his sons. *Polk v. Polk*, 70 So. 3d 363 (2011)

21.8 Fiduciary Duties of LLC Members. First Solar, LLC, was a member-managed LLC. First Solar's two members, Solar Cells, Inc., and True North Partners, LLC, each initially held 4,500 of First Solar's voting membership shares. According to First Solar's operating agreement, True North had the right to appoint three of First Solar's managers, while Solar Cells appointed two. First Solar began facing financial difficulty, and the True North managers unilaterally issued a document approving the merger of First Solar into First Solar Operating, LLC, an LLC wholly owned by True North. The day before this document was executed, a meeting of the full board of managers of First Solar was held, and the True North managers made no mention of the impending merger. By the terms of the merger, Solar Cells's interest in the surviving company would be reduced from 50 percent to 5 percent. Further, the price terms were based on a valuation that was significantly lower than prior valuations. Upon what legal theories may Solar Cells rely on to sue True North Partners? What fiduciary duties, if any, did True North Partners breach and to whom? *Solar Cells, Inc. v. True North Partners, LLC*, 2002 Del. Ch. LEXIS 38 (Del. Ch. 2002)

21.9 Member Liabilities. NetJets Aviation, Inc.® leased to LHC Communications, LLC (LHC) an interest in an airplane for a term of five years. LHC was a limited liability company whose only member-owner was Laurence Zimmerman. Zimmerman had the sole authority to make all financial decisions with respect to LHC. He often withdrew money from LHC's account for personal use and transferred money into LHC's account from his own personal account. Zimmerman did not have any written agreements with LHC regarding this commingling of funds. Many withdrawals from LHC's account were for personal expenses, including a residence, phone and cleaning bills, a car, and health insurance for his family. Much of the flight time used by LHC under the lease with NetJets was used by Zimmerman and his family for personal trips. LHC terminated the lease agreement with NetJets. The next year, LHC ceased operations. NetJets sued LHC and Zimmerman for unpaid lease obligations. Can a court pierce the corporate veil for a limited liability company? What factors should the court consider to hold Zimmerman personally liable for the debts due NetJets? *NetJets Aviation, Inc. v. LHC Communications, LLC*, 537 F.3d 168 (2d Cir. 2008)

21.10 Distribution After Member Withdrawal. Michael Lieberman was a member of Wyoming.com, LLC. Michael served Wyoming.com with a notice of withdrawal from the company, which demanded the return of his share of the current value of the company, which he estimated at $400,000. The members of Wyoming.com accepted Michael's withdrawal and elected to continue rather than dissolve Wyoming.com, but refused to return Michael's requested share of the company's current value. Absent a provision in the operating agreement on the matter, were the members of Wyoming.com obligated to buy out Michael's equity interest in the LLC? Why or why not? *Lieberman v. Wyoming.com, LLC*, 82 P.3d 274 (Wyo. 2004)

Formation and Financing of Corporations

22

Corporation: An ingenious device for obtaining profit without individual responsibility. — Ambrose Bierce, English philosopher (1842-1914)

Chapter Outline

- Introduction
- Characteristics of a Corporation
- The Incorporation Process
  - *Management Application: Why Delaware Is an Attractive State for Incorporation of Large and Publicly Held Companies*
  - *Management Application: Certificate of Incorporation for Delaware*
  - *Management Application: Bylaw Provisions Regarding Indemnification of Directors*

Case 22.1: *Caudill v. Sinex Pools, Inc.*

- Corporate Classifications
- The Corporation as a Separate Entity

Case 22.2: *MFG Healthcare Partners, Inc. v. Blue Ridge Healthcare Birmingham, LLC.*

- *Management Application: Allegations in a Complaint Asserting Alter Ego Liability*
- Financing a Corporation with Equity
  - *Management Application: Corporate Transparency Act*
- Financing a Corporation with Debt
- Other Ways to Finance a Corporation
- The S-Corp as a Tax Efficient Entity
  - *Management Application: Election by a Small Business Corporation to Be an S Corporation*
- AI Feature: Social Purpose and Public Benefit Corporations

Learning Objectives

After studying this chapter, you should be able to:

1. Describe the characteristics of a corporation.
2. Describe the steps to incorporate a business.
3. Distinguish between a *de facto* corporation and a corporation by estoppel.
4. Explain alter ego liability and piercing the corporate veil.
5. Discuss alternative ways to finance a corporation.
6. Identify the characteristics of an S corporation.

Introduction

Corporation
A legal entity created by the operation of law that is a separate entity from its owners.

A **corporation** is a legal entity created by the operation of law that is a separate entity from its owners, who are referred to as shareholders. As the most well-recognized form of business organization in the United States, the corporation has many attributes making it attractive to investors. These include insulation from the entity's debts and obligations, free transferability of shares, and continuity of existence.

A corporation is an artificial "person" and is provided similar rights to a natural person. Those rights provide that the corporation can sue and be sued, enter into contracts, own and lease property, and operate businesses. Corporations also are protected by certain constitutional protections provided to natural persons, including the right to due process with respect to its disputes and freedom from unreasonable searches and seizures.

A corporation acts through its directors, officers, and employees — all of whom are to advance the interests of the shareholders. Shareholders vote to elect directors. The directors hire officers, and the officers hire employees. We address these relationships more fully in Chapter 23.

Corporations are formed by state law. A corporation is created under the laws of the state of incorporation (the state in which it is formed). While the corporation laws of states can vary, the Model Business Corporation Act (MBCA) was created to influence and guide states in creating and implementing corporation laws. Many states have used either the MBCA or the revised version of the Act, the Revised Model Business Corporation Act (RMBCA) to help create their corporation laws. Even with a modeled uniform law, states' laws will vary and should be consulted when seeking to incorporate in a particular state.

Shareholder
An owner of shares in a corporation.

Characteristics of a Corporation

The characteristics of a corporation are:

1. Legal entity distinct from its owners;
2. Shareholder limited liability;
3. Free transferability of stock;
4. Ability to exist perpetually; and
5. Centralized management.

Legal Entity

Since a corporation is a legal entity separate and distinct from its shareholders, any property owned by a corporation belongs not to the shareholders, but to the corporation itself. Even in a situation where a single individual owns all of the shares of a corporation, there is still a separate legal existence between the corporation and the shareholder.

Limited liability
A type of liability in which the owners of a corporation will not be subject to personal liability for the debts of the corporation.

Shareholder Limited Liability

A benefit of incorporating is that shareholders have **limited liability** for the debts of the corporation. A shareholder's liability is limited to their capital investment in the corporation, and shareholders are generally not personally liable for the debts of the corporation. The exception to this rule is when a court pierces the corporate veil (discussed later in this chapter) and imposes on shareholders personal liability for the corporation's debts.

> **Example:** MRSI Corporation engaged Merdinger, Fruchter, Rosen & Company, a professional service corporation, to prepare and file MRSI's business tax returns. MRSI transferred approximately $550,000 to Stephen Corso, a shareholder in Merdinger Fruchter. Rather than use the funds to satisfy MRSI's tax liabilities, Corso diverted the funds for his own personal use. MRSI then sued Corso, in addition to the shareholders of Merdinger Fruchter, to recover the $550,000. The court held that the other shareholders had limited liability and were not liable for Corso's alleged embezzlement from the firm's client. *Souki v. Merdinger, Fruchter, Rosen & Co., P.C.*, 2003 U.S. Dist. LEXIS 10447 (S.D.N.Y. 2003)

Free Transferability of Stock

Shares in a corporation are freely transferred by way of sale, gift, or pledge (provided as a security of a loan). A transfer of stock in the corporation from one individual to another has no effect on the legal existence of the corporation. This is particularly appealing in comparison to other entities such as partnerships. The ease in which shares may be freely transferred has a positive effect on the share's market value.

Perpetual Existence

Corporations are granted *perpetual existence* unless otherwise stated in their articles of incorporation. A corporation will not terminate when a shareholder, director, or officer dies, withdraws, or is added to the corporation.

Centralized Management

Unlike other forms of business entities in which owners manage day-to-day activities, shareholders (unless they are also officers or directors of the corporation) are not involved in such decisions. Instead, shareholders vote on who will serve on the corporation's board of directors. The board of directors oversee and provide strategic guidance to the corporation. In turn, the board of directors appoints officers to run the day-to-day operations. Collectively, the board of directors and the officers are referred to as management. Although management may be composed of shareholders of the corporation, it is also possible for the two to remain separate.

The Incorporation Process

Corporations may choose to be formed in a different state than where the corporation's principal place of business is located. Other states may offer more favorable tax or liability treatment to the corporation and or its directors, officers, or shareholders. Many publicly held corporations are incorporated (formed) in Delaware because of its favorable corporate protections.

Although the procedures to incorporate may vary among states, to form a corporation articles of incorporation are filed in the state in which the corporation desires to be formed. In addition, states may have additional incorporation requirements; however, the recent trend has been to simplify the incorporation process. There are a few formalities that are consistent across all states, which are discussed below.

Selecting a State for Incorporation

Incorporation is the formation of a legal corporation. A corporation is often incorporated in the state in which it intends to be headquartered or where it intends to transact most of its business. Some states have attributes that may make incorporation in those states more attractive. These include lower corporate taxes, reduced corporate takeover abilities, strong director and officer indemnification provisions, and business-friendly courts. Businesses may incorporate in a state where they do not intend to have a physical presence or transact their business.

Example: The Walt Disney Company® is incorporated in the State of Delaware but its principal place of business (that is, its corporate headquarters) is in Burbank, California. It has operations throughout the world.

Management Application Why Delaware Is an Attractive State for the Incorporation of Large and Publicly Held Companies

The State of Delaware provides many benefits to corporations. It imposes fewer restrictions on the sale of corporate assets and the merging of businesses. Delaware also offers broad protection to officers and directors from personal liability for their acts on behalf of the corporation in comparison to other states.

Delaware offers favorable corporate taxation rates for publicly held companies, and shares owned by persons residing outside of this state are not subject to the state's taxes.

Delaware also maintains a business-centered court system known as the Court of Chancery. This court uses judges who conduct trials without juries. The Court of Chancery focuses solely on business law, resulting in judicial expertise in corporate law issues. The robust body of statutory, regulatory, and case law in Delaware offers reliability for corporate principals through its predictability and level of detail. The Delaware legislature, its administrative agencies, and courts have a strong interest in being at the forefront of matters relating to business formation and governance. In addition, the political climate within Delaware encourages legislative non-interference with the decision making of the Court of Chancery. This provides further certainty for corporations and their advisors.

Selecting a Corporate Name

In selecting a name for the corporation, most incorporation laws require that the corporate name contain words such as corporation, incorporated, limited, Corp., Inc., or Ltd. to indicate the entity is organized as a corporation. Further, the name must be distinguishable from the name of any other corporation authorized to do business within the state. Businesses can review online if a prospective corporate name is already taken and can reserve a corporation name for a short time prior to filing the articles of incorporation. Name reservation prevents another business from taking the name before the articles of incorporation are filed.

Articles of incorporation
The basic governing document of a corporation filed in the state where the corporation desires to be registered.

Incorporators and the Articles of Incorporation

The **articles of incorporation**, also referred to as the certificate of incorporation or charter, is the basic governing document of a corporation. The articles of incorporation are filed with the Secretary of State's office in the state of incorporation. The party who signs the articles of incorporation is called the **incorporator**. Under the RMBCA, a corporation is first recognized as a legal entity when the articles of incorporation are filed with the appropriate state official, usually the Secretary of State. Some states require additional filings in designated counties where the corporation will operate or maintain offices. The articles of incorporation will include the following information:

- The name of the corporation;
- The number of authorized shares the corporation can issue;
- The street address of the **registered office** (which does not have to be the same as the corporation's place of business);
- A designated **registered agent**, who is empowered to accept service of process on behalf of the corporation; and
- The name and address of the incorporator(s).

Incorporator
An individual who signs and files with the Secretary of State the articles of incorporation.

Registered office
The official address of a registered corporation and location where the registered agent receives service of process and other documents on behalf of the corporation.

Registered agent
An individual empowered to accept service of process and other documents on behalf of the corporation.

Management Application Certificate of Incorporation for Delaware

The following form corresponds to Delaware General Corporation Law § 102.

STATE OF DELAWARE CERTIFICATE OF INCORPORATION A STOCK CORPORATION

The undersigned Incorporator, desiring to form a corporation pursuant to the General Corporation Law of the State of Delaware, hereby certifies as follows:

1. The name of the Corporation is ____________________.
2. The Registered Office of the corporation in the State of Delaware is located at ____________ (street), in the City of ____________, County of ____________ Zip Code ________. The name of the Registered Agent at such address upon whom process against this corporation may be served is ____________.
3. The purpose of the corporation is to engage in any lawful act or activity for which corporations may be organized under the General Corporation Law of Delaware.
4. The total amount of stock this corporation is authorized to issue is ________ shares (number of authorized shares) with a par value of $______ per share.
5. The name and mailing address of the incorporator are as follows:
   Name ____________________
   Mailing Address ____________________

By: ____________________
(Incorporator)

Name: ____________________

Purpose of the Corporation

A corporation may be formed to engage in any lawful purpose. While not required under the RMBCA, many articles of incorporation state a purpose for the corporation. If used, a **general purpose clause** provides that the corporation may engage in any lawful activity. In other cases, a **limited purpose clause** can be inserted. Such a clause provides the specific purposes and activities that a corporation is authorized to engage. When a corporation wants to engage in other activities outside those provided for in the limited purpose clause, the articles of incorporation will need to be amended.

General purpose clause A clause within the articles of incorporation permitting the corporation to engage in any lawful activity.

Limited purpose clause A clause within the articles of incorporation that states the specific purposes and activities that a corporation may pursue.

In addition to the powers the corporation may engage in provided through the articles of incorporation, corporations have statutory and inherent powers. Powers that are provided in the state incorporation statute and state and federal laws are statutory powers. The powers provided in the articles of incorporation, statutory powers, and bylaws are express powers. The law also recognizes that the corporation has implied powers to carry out the express powers given in the articles of incorporation.

> **Example:** If the express powers stated in the articles of organization provided for the development, construction, and lease of an apartment building, the implied powers enjoyed by the corporation would include the power to execute contracts and leases for that project.

Ultra vires Actions by a corporation that exceed the scope of the powers provided in the articles of incorporation.

ULTRA VIRES* ACTS.** There may be times in which the corporation acts beyond its express, statutory, or implied powers. When a corporation engages in such actions, these acts are considered ***ultra vires, Latin for "beyond one's legal power or authority." Corporations should be careful not to engage in *ultra vires* activities, as such activities may be enjoined (prevented) by shareholders in a lawsuit against the corporation.

In addition to enjoining *ultra vires* acts, the shareholders may also sue for any damages resulting from those *ultra vires* acts.

> **Example:** A corporation's governing documents provide that the corporation shall engage in the business of manufacturing and selling microprocessors. If the directors of the corporation purchased an apartment building to rent to third-party tenants to increase the company's revenues, this act would be an *ultra vires* act. The governing documents do not allow the corporation to purchase and lease an apartment building.

Corporate Bylaws

Corporate **bylaws** are rules governing the internal management and structure of the corporation. Unlike the articles of incorporation, bylaws do not have to be filed with any government official and are more detailed than the articles of incorporation. They often contain a variety of provisions for managing the business and affairs of the corporation that are consistent with the law or articles of incorporation. Bylaws are adopted at the first organizational meeting of the board of directors and can be amended or repealed by the board of directors.

Bylaws
The rules governing a corporation's internal management and structure.

> **Example:** Bylaws often state the time and place for the annual shareholder's meetings, voting requirements for shareholders and the board of directors, and describe the duties of the corporate officers, indemnification of directors, and other related matters.

Management Application Bylaw Provisions Regarding Indemnification of Directors

Indemnification of Directors and Officers Under the Delaware General Corporation Law (DGCL)

Section 6.01. *Indemnification of Directors.* The corporation shall, to the maximum extent and in the manner permitted by the DGCL, indemnify each of its directors against expenses, judgments, fines, settlements, and other amounts actually and reasonably incurred in connection with any proceeding arising by reason of the fact that such person is or was a director of the corporation, as defined in Section 145 of the DGCL. For purposes of this Article VI, a "director" of the corporation includes any person (a) who is or was a director of the corporation, (b) who is or was serving at the request of the corporation as a director of another foreign or domestic corporation, partnership, joint venture, trust or other enterprise, or (c) who was a director of a corporation which was a predecessor corporation of the corporation or of another enterprise at the request of such predecessor corporation.

Section 6.02. *Insurance Indemnification.* The corporation shall have the power to purchase and maintain insurance on behalf of any person who is or was a director or officer of the corporation against any liability asserted against or incurred by such person in such capacity or arising out of that person's status as such, whether or not the corporation would have the power to indemnify that person against such liability under the provisions of this Article VI.

Organizational Meeting of the Board of Directors

Most states require that an organizational meeting be held to elect the initial board of directors (unless the initial board of directors are named in the articles of incorporation), adopt the corporation's bylaws, appoint the initial officers, and discuss other business matters that may arise. The adoption of the bylaws is usually one of the first items of business because bylaws describe the organization of the corporation.

Improper Incorporation

One of the benefits of a corporation is the limited liability to shareholders. But if the required steps to incorporate are not followed, a defective incorporation will occur, which may lead to personal liability of the shareholders because they may be treated as partners in a partnership. Under some circumstances, a corporate entity may still be recognized as a corporation even though it did not comply with all the necessary requirements. Two doctrines that may allow shareholders of a defectively formed corporation to continue to receive the benefit of limited liability are *de facto* corporation and corporation by estoppel.

***De facto* corporation** An improperly formed corporation that is given the temporary status of a corporation.

***DE FACTO* CORPORATION.** A ***de facto* corporation** is a corporation operating as if it were a properly formed corporation, although it has not completed all of the legal steps to become incorporated. States will often allow a *de facto* corporation where (1) the state has an incorporation statute allowing the formation of a corporation; (2) the business made a good faith attempt to substantially comply with the incorporation requirements; and (3) the business acted as if it were a corporate entity in business transactions. In such cases, a court may temporarily treat the corporation as if it were a corporation.

The *de facto* doctrine is asserted less frequently because many state statutory reforms have abolished the *de facto* corporation status. The modern trend is to require fewer technicalities to form a corporation, thereby reducing the need for *de facto* status. For example, many states have fill in the blank forms on their Secretary of State websites that are required to be completed to form a corporation. As a result of these changes, most states have provisions like the RMBCA that abolish the *de facto* doctrine. Under it, statutes expressly impose personal liability as the penalty for purporting to do business as a corporation that is not in fact incorporated.

In the following case, the court utilized a three-factor test to determine whether a corporation would be given *de facto* status.

CASE 22.1

THERE MUST BE A BONA FIDE ATTEMPT TO ORGANIZE AND COMPLY WITH STATUTORY REQUIREMENTS FOR A *DE FACTO* CORPORATION TO EXIST

CAUDILL v. SINEX POOLS, INC.

2006 Del. Super. LEXIS 18 (2006)

Superior Court of Delaware

Ken Caudill entered into a contract with Sinex Pools, Inc., to have Sinex construct an in-ground swimming pool on Caudill's property. However, Sinex breached the contract by failing to properly construct and complete the pool installation. Caudill sued Sinex Pools and Romie and Shirley Bishop, the owners of Sinex Pools, on the grounds that Sinex Pools was not recognized as a legal entity. The Bishops provided that while no forms were submitted to the Secretary of State, the Bishops did have the certificate of incorporation notarized, the bank accounts were in the name of Sinex Pools, Inc., and tax returns were filed in the name of Sinex Pools, Inc.

Language of the Court. *A corporation* de facto *is a corporation which failed to incorporate properly, despite a good faith and bona fide effort, but is nevertheless treated as a duly formed corporation. Three factors must exist for a corporation* de facto*'s creation: 1) there is a general law under which such a corporation may lawfully exist; 2) a bona fide attempt to organize under the law and colorable compliance with the statutory requirements; and 3) actual user or exercise of corporate powers in pursuance of such law and attempted organization.*

There appears to be no dispute that Sinex Pools meets two of the three requirements for a corporation de facto*'s existence. First, there is no dispute that Sinex Pools held itself out to the general public as a builder and supplier of pools, and all business was exercised in the name of the corporation. Therefore, despite not having the formal incorporation status granted by the State, its business was conducted as if that status had been granted.*

Second, there is a general incorporation statute in Delaware which would have lawfully created the corporation if Sinex Pools' had completed the appropriate documentation and filed it with the appropriate fee. As such, the sole remaining issue to be addressed by this Court is whether there was a good faith and bona fide effort by Mr. Bishop to incorporate Sinex Pools.

There was good faith and a bona fide attempt when Sinex Pools was purchased by Mr. Bishop and, shortly thereafter, Mrs. Bishop attempted to incorporate Sinex Pools by completing the appropriate and necessary documentation for incorporation. Mrs. Bishop indicates that shortly thereafter she submitted those forms to the Secretary of State to have Sinex Pools labeled an S-corporation.

In addition, Mrs. Bishop treated Sinex Pools as a corporation by establishing bank accounts in the name of Sinex Pools, obtaining an employer identification number from the IRS for Sinex Pools, taking out insurance on behalf of Sinex Pools and filing tax returns in the name of Sinex Pools. Although there is no evidence of actual submission of the incorporation documents to the Secretary of State, that fact alone is not dispositive of the issue. It is simply a factor the Court must consider in determining whether a bona fide attempt has been made.

When the Court considers all the documentation and testimony established in discovery, it finds that the only thing preventing corporate status in this case is the authorization from the Secretary of State. Sinex Pools has operated as a corporation since Mrs. Bishop bought the company, which is even evidenced by the contract at issue in this case. Contracts were executed in the name of the corporation, and there is nothing to suggest either bad faith or a deviant motive by Mrs. Bishop in the representations that were made about the business's corporate status. While the Court can only speculate why the incorporation process was not completed, the Court finds that Sinex Pools has met the criteria for a de facto *corporation status.*

Decision. Sinex Pools was given *de facto* status, and the Bishops were dismissed from the lawsuit. The case proceeded against Sinex Pools only.

Focus on Ethics

What is the policy reasoning for judicial recognition of *de facto* corporations? Why should courts afford shareholders the corporate shield from personal liability when they fail to follow the necessary procedures to incorporate?

Corporation by estoppel
A legal doctrine requiring a creditor that has dealt with the business as a corporation to look to only the assets of the business and not its owners for satisfaction of the obligations owed to them.

CORPORATION BY ESTOPPEL. The second method of avoiding personal liability under the common law in defective incorporation cases is corporation by estoppel. A **corporation by estoppel** may arise when a business has made no attempt to incorporate (it is not a *de facto* corporation) but a third person has contracted with the business and the business represented itself to the third person as a corporation. Corporation by estoppel is usually used as a defense against a claim that the owners are personally liable for the debts of the business. The corporation by estoppel doctrine does not create a corporation and is only created based on the facts of each case. Under such doctrine, a creditor that dealt with the business as a corporation must look to the "corporation's" assets rather than the assets of the shareholders.

Example: Albion Cranson was advised that Real Estate Service Bureau, Inc. ("Bureau") had been incorporated under the laws of Maryland. He became president of Bureau, and Bureau then purchased equipment from International Business Machines (IBM)®. After Bureau was unable to pay IBM for the equipment, IBM sued Cranson personally due to the failure to properly incorporate. IBM had dealt with Bureau as if it were a corporation and relied on its credit rather than that of Cranson when entering into the transaction. The court held that where one has recognized the corporate existence of an association, he is estopped to assert the contrary with respect to a claim arising out of such dealings. *Cranson v. International Business Machines Corp.*, 200 A.2d 33 (Md. 1964)

Promoter
A person who acts on behalf of a corporation prior to the corporation's formation.

Promoter Liability on Contracts

A promoter is a person who acts on behalf of a corporation prior to the corporation's formation. Liability arises when a promoter executes contracts for the benefit of the corporation, such as an office lease. The promoter is personally liable for all pre-incorporation contracts until a novation occurs. A novation occurs when the corporation executes a post-incorporation contract that expressly states the promoter is relieved of liability. Novation was discussed in Chapter 13.

Example: Jorge and Andrew are seeking to open a new restaurant and want to incorporate. Prior to the filing of the articles of incorporation, Andrew discovers the perfect restaurant location and not wanting to lose the opportunity he executes a lease in the corporation's name. Andrew has acted as a promoter and will be liable for the lease obligations.

The corporation is not bound by any pre-incorporation acts or contracts of the promoter unless it adopts or ratifies the contract of the promoter. If the corporation accepts the benefits of a promoter's contract, adoption may be implied.

Example: In the above example, if the restaurant moves into the leased space, both the corporation and Andrew are liable for the lease obligations.

Promoters often secure potential investors using stock subscription agreements. A stock subscription agreement is where an investor agrees to purchase stock in the to-be-formed corporation at a specified price in the future. The RMBCA requires that a subscription agreement be irrevocable for a period of six months, unless otherwise stated in the agreement, or all investors rescind the agreement. A publicly held corporation cannot use subscription agreements. Promoters owe a fiduciary duty to each other, the corporation, and subscribers of stock agreements.

Corporate Classifications

Corporations may be classified in a variety of ways. All corporations can be classified in the different ways that the chart below outlines.

Classification	Description
Public or Private	A *public corporation* is a corporation formed to meet a governmental or public purpose (such as a city water district). Most corporations are *private corporations*, which are created for private people and not the government.
Profit or Nonprofit (not-for-profit)	A *profit corporation* is one founded for the purpose of operating a business for profit and distributing such profit to its shareholders in the form of dividends. A *nonprofit corporation*, also known as a not-for-profit corporation, is a corporation formed for the charitable, educational, or scientific purpose for which the corporation was organized. While these corporations may earn a profit, that profit may not be distributed to their owners.
Domestic, Foreign, or Alien	A corporation is a *domestic corporation* in its state of incorporation. That corporation is considered a *foreign corporation* in every other state or jurisdiction in which it does business.

Classification	Description
	An *alien corporation* is a corporation that was incorporated in a foreign country.
Publicly Held or Closely Held	A *publicly held corporation* is a for-profit corporation whose shares are publicly traded or owned by many shareholders as required by state statutes. A *closely held corporation* (also known as a closed corporation) is a corporation whose shares are privately held by a small number of people. They are exempt from many reporting requirements of a publicly held companies.

Some corporations may also have the following classifications.

Classification	Description
Subchapter S Corporation	Closely held corporations, if they meet the qualifying requirements under Subchapter S of the Internal Revenue Code, may be treated as an S corporation. S corporations retain the advantages of corporations (such as limited liability) but can be taxed as though they were partnerships (pass-through taxation).
Professional Corporation	Some statutes allow for duly licensed professionals (such as attorneys, accountants, dentists, and physicians) to practice their professions using a specified corporate form. These corporations are identified by their initials such as P.C. (professional corporation), P.A. (professional association), or S.C. (service corporation).
Public Benefit Corporation	A type of corporation that allows for the purpose of the corporation to promote the positive impact on society, workers, the community, and the environment.
Social Purpose Corporation	A few states recognize this type of for-profit corporation, which allows a corporation to pursue a social benefit purpose but does not require the corporation to pursue such endeavors.

The Corporation as a Separate Entity

Piercing the corporate veil
A legal doctrine that may allow a shareholder to be held personally liable for a corporation's debts and obligations.

Although a corporation is a legal entity separate and distinct from its owners and provides limited liability to its shareholders, the shield from liability for shareholders is not absolute. There are situations when a court will **pierce the corporate veil** and set aside the corporate shield and hold the shareholders personally liable for corporate debts. Only third parties and neither the corporation nor its shareholders are generally allowed to set the corporate shield aside. Piercing the corporate veil is often described as the "alter ego" analysis. During "alter ego" analysis, the court is examines whether a corporation is distinct from its shareholders.

Courts vary in their willingness to pierce the corporate veil. Generally, courts consider the totality of the evidence in making this decision. No one factor controls and courts consider several factors including if the corporation was inadequately capitalized at the time of formation; if the shareholders have used the corporate entity to carry out a fraud or injustice (such as transferring assets in an attempt to avoid creditors); whether the shareholder and the corporation commingled their assets so as to not maintain a separateness of interests; and whether corporate formalities were observed, including the issuance of stock and the keeping of corporate minutes. Under the inadequate capitalization factor, most states require the corporation to have gross inadequacy of capital at the time of initial formation for the corporate veil to be pierced.

> **Example:** The Delaware Chancery Court found that the corporate veil had been pierced when a company was aware of potential liability of another company defendant a long time ago and made a deliberate decision to undercapitalize the entity. Significantly, that company had overlapping personnel with another defendant corporation. *Manichaean Capital, LLC v. Exela Techs., Inc.*, 251 A.3d 694 (Del. Ch. 2021)

Alter Ego Theory

Additionally, the corporate veil may be pierced under an **alter ego theory**. The alter ego theory is a fact intensive inquiry. While state laws vary as to the requirements, under this theory, a plaintiff must establish that there was such a unity of interest and control between two or more entities (such as a parent and subsidiary corporate structure) or between the entity and its shareholder(s) that they cannot be considered separate. The effect of proving the existence of an alter ego is that the separateness of the entities is disregarded, and they are treated as one (that is the alter ego of each other), thereby rendering both entities liable for the losses or damages incurred. One of the most common ways of establishing the alter ego theory is to demonstrate that the personal assets or business of the owner was commingled with the corporation's assets or business. These assets most often include capital, as discussed below, but may also include property, inventory, or even personnel.

Alter ego theory Permits piercing of the corporate veil when there is a unity between the corporation and another corporation or with that of the shareholder(s) such that the corporation's separateness has ceased and holding only the corporation liable would be unjust.

> **Example:** A state court listed the alter ego elements as: First, there must be such a unity of interest and ownership between the corporation and its equitable owner that the separate personalities of the corporation and the shareholder do not in reality exist. Second, there must be an inequitable result if the acts in question are treated as those of the corporation alone. "Among the factors to be considered in applying the doctrine are commingling of funds and other assets of the two entities, the holding out by one entity that it is liable for the debts of the other, identical equitable ownership in the two entities, use of the same offices and employees, and use of one as a mere shell or conduit for the affairs of the other." Other factors include inadequate capitalization, disregard of corporate formalities, lack of segregation of corporate records, and identical directors and officers. No one characteristic governs, but the courts must look at all the circumstances to determine

whether the doctrine should be applied. *Sonora Diamond Corp. v. Superior Court*, 83 Cal. App. 4th 523 (2000)

The alter ego theory has been applied to hold shareholders accountable for the corporation's debts and obligations, Members in limited liability companies have also been subject to its application.

ADEQUATE CAPITALIZATION. Perhaps the most important factor corporations can utilize to help avoid alter ego claims is by being *adequately capitalized at the time of formation.*

> **Example:** Playa Dulce Vida, S.A. (PDV) is a corporation that owns and operates two resorts in Costa Rica. Investors sued the two resorts for breach of contract and tried to pierce the corporate veil by alter ego liability in order to reach the shareholders. However, the court held that since the two resorts were initially adequately capitalized, there could be no piercing. Even though the resorts were unable to pay income distributions and needed to take out loans, the court held that doing so was not evidence of undercapitalization, but of underperformance. *Lieberman v. Corporacion Experienca Unica, S.A.*, 226 F. Supp. 3d 451 (E.D. Pa. 2016)

Other avenues of protection include maintaining adequate corporate records. Usually, this means that a corporation should regularly maintain in the ordinary course of its business separate financial records and statements, corporate minutes, and systems to ensure compliance with the law.

In the following case, the court considered whether the corporation should maintain adequate assets to pay for prospective liabilities.

CASE 22.2

CORPORATE FORM MAY NOT BE DISREGARDED MERELY BECAUSE IT IS A RELATED COMPANY

MFG HEALTHCARE PARTNERS, INC. v. BLUE RIDGE HEALTHCARE BIRMINGHAM, LLC.

542 F. Supp. 3d 1237 (2021)

United States District Court for the Northern District of Alabama, Southern Division

Blue Ridge operated nursing homes, while MGF supplied healthcare staff to them under an agreement between them. However, when Blue Ridge ceased operations, it failed to fulfill its financial obligations to MGF. Symmetry, on the other hand, provided management services to Blue Ridge, including the drafting of vendor application packets. MGF alleged that Symmetry and Blue Ridge effectively functioned as one entity, but Symmetry denied having a significant management role within Blue Ridge's operations. The issue for the court to decide was if Symmetry and Blue Ridge functioned as a single corporate entity.

Language of the Court. *Alabama law recognizes that "the corporate entity will be disregarded when it is used solely to avoid a personal liability of the owner while reserving to the owner the benefits gained through use of the corporate name." That is, courts may "pierce the corporate veil" to hold liable those who control the corporation. The party seeking to pierce the corporate veil must identify an appropriate party to whom the corporation's liability could attach. In all cases identified by this court, that party has been a "shareholder, officer, or director" of that corporate entity. In fact, Alabama law appears to strictly limit the principle of corporate veil-piercing to such entities, excluding those who are only associated with the corporation or do business with the corporation.*

MGF has presented these facts to support corporate veil piercing: (1) Symmetry and Blue Ridge maintain their headquarters in the same physical office in Florida; (2) Symmetry prepared a vendor application packet to MGF on behalf of Blue Ridge; (3) Symmetry sent invoices to Blue Ridge for management services averaging approximately $36,000/month for 21 months; and (4) Symmetry and Blue Ridge shared at least 5 common owners and therefore could not have engaged in an arm's-length transaction with each other. MGF posits that, when combined, these facts mandate a conclusion that Blue Ridge and Symmetry could not have negotiated their contract at arms' length. Symmetry admits these facts but argues they show only an ordinary business relationship between two companies within a larger conglomerate.

In short, even if Alabama law considered Symmetry a candidate for veil-piercing, MGF has failed to present enough facts to create a triable issue. MGF has presented no evidence that Symmetry financed Blue Ridge, that Blue Ridge only did business with Symmetry, that Symmetry used Blue Ridge's property as its own, or that Blue Ridge failed to observe the legal requirements of a corporation. Frankly, MGF conducted little discovery about Symmetry, taking no depositions and providing no testimony to support MGF's claims about Symmetry. In other words, MGF points at plenty of smoke, but can show no fire. Unable to show that Symmetry and Blue Ridge operated as a single corporate entity, MGF's breach of contract, subterfuge/instrumentality, and fraud claims against Symmetry fail.

Decision. The court ruled in favor of Symmetry's motion for summary judgment, as MGF failed to demonstrate that Symmetry and Blue Ridge operated as a single corporate entity.

Focus on Ethics

What do you think of the evidence MGF presented to the court? Were you convinced? What evidence should MGF have brought to evidence that Symmetry and Blue Ridge operated as one unified entity?

Management Application
Allegations in a Complaint Asserting Alter Ego Liability

There exists, and at all times herein mentioned there existed, a unity of interest and ownership among defendant(s) Able, Baker, and defendant XYZ Corporation, such that any individuality and separateness between defendant(s) Able, Baker, and defendant XYZ Corporation have ceased, and defendant XYZ Corporation is the alter ego of defendant(s) in that Able and Baker commingled defendant corporation's assets with their own.

Adherence to the fiction of the separate existence of the defendant XYZ Corporation as an entity distinct from defendant(s) Able and Baker would permit an abuse of the corporate privilege and would promote injustice in that defendants Able and Baker caused the sum of $5,000,000 to be withdrawn from the funds of defendant XYZ Corporation and distributed to themselves without any consideration to defendant XYZ Corporation, all for the purpose of avoiding and preventing attachment and execution by creditors, including plaintiff, thereby rendering defendant XYZ Corporation insolvent and unable to meet its obligations.

What other grounds for setting aside the corporation could be pled by a plaintiff?

Parent corporation The corporation owning or controlling the majority of the outstanding voting stock or other equity in another corporation.

Subsidiary The corporation over which the parent company has control.

Persuading a Delaware Court to disregard the corporate entity is a difficult task.— Harco National Ins. Co. v. Green Farms Inc., 1989 WL 110537 (Del. Ch. Sept. 19, 1989)

PARENT-SUBSIDIARY RELATIONSHIPS. When one corporation owns or controls the shares of another corporation, a parent-subsidiary relationship is created. The corporation owning or controlling the shares is known as the **parent corporation**, with the other corporation known as the **subsidiary**. A parent corporation may be liable for the debts of the subsidiary under the following circumstances:

1. Commingling of the parent and subsidiary's assets or business;
2. Failure to comply with corporate formalities (separate books and records);
3. Inadequate capitalization of the subsidiary; and
4. Parent and subsidiary hold themselves out as a single entity (as an example, for marketing purposes).

Traditionally, when there is a conflict of the law as to which state's law should apply, the "internal affairs doctrine" holds that the law of the place of incorporation should apply. Since Delaware law makes veil piercing more difficult, it is the state of formation of many large entities.

Equity security An investment representing an ownership right in the corporation in the form of common stock or preferred stock.

Financing a Corporation with Equity

To operate its business, a corporation needs working capital. One way to obtain this money is to sell equity securities. **Equity securities**, also known as stock, represent ownership rights in the corporation.

Stock Subscriptions

Stock subscriptions are agreements entered between the corporation and subscriber for the purchase of the corporation's shares. A stock subscription may be entered into before the corporate formation process is completed and constitutes an agreement to purchase the shares of the corporation upon the completion of incorporation. This is known as a *pre-incorporation* stock subscription. If the stock subscription is entered after the corporation has been incorporated, it is referred to as a *post-incorporation* stock subscription. This most commonly occurs when a corporation requires additional funding after the incorporation process has been completed.

Stock subscription
An agreement entered into by a corporation and a subscriber for the purchase of the corporation's shares.

The timing of when the agreement is entered into is an important factor when determining whether the agreement can be revoked. If the agreement is a post-incorporation subscription, it cannot be revoked by either the subscriber or the corporation. Most states allow the subscriber of a pre-incorporation stock subscription to revoke the agreement up until the time the corporation has been formed and thereby accepted the offer. Some states find that a pre-incorporation agreement constitutes a contract and therefore cannot be revoked by the subscriber unless all subscribers agree to release one another from their individual subscription agreements.

There are two forms of equity securities: (1) common stock and (2) preferred stock.

Common Stock

Common stock ownership allows shareholders to participate in management control. Before the advent of technology and electronic trading, holders of common stock were issued common stock certificates that evidenced their ownership interests in the corporation. Now, electronic registration of common stockholder ownership interests is prevalent. Because of this, many corporations no longer issue paper certificates.

Common stock
A type of equity ownership allowing shareholders to participate in management control of a corporation.

There are three important rights that common stockholders are entitled to by nature of their ownership in the corporation. Common stockholders can:

1. Vote for directors and decide other fundamental matters;
2. Participate in the distribution of dividends; and
3. Share in the distribution of net assets (equity) after dissolution and liquidation.

While most shares of stock are sold by a corporation for cash, the shares may also be issued in exchange for property or services. In instances where the shares are exchanged for services, it is permissible to withhold the shares until the services have been performed, a note is paid, or benefits are received by the corporation. However, some states do not allow a corporation to issue stock in exchange for services or an unsecured note.

Preferred Stock

Preferred stock is another type of equity security. The owners of preferred stock are given certain *preferences in rights* over common stockholders. An example of a preference is that preferred stockholders may receive a specific percentage share of any dividends before the common stockholders are paid.

Preferred stock
A type of equity ownership entitling shareholders to certain preferences in rights over common stockholders.

Cumulative stock
A type of preferred stock, where any unpaid dividends will accumulate for years of nonpayment.

Non-cumulative stock
A type of preferred stock, in which the preferred shareholders lose their dividend rights for the years in which the directors declared no dividend.

Preferred stock can either be **cumulative** or **non-cumulative**, a type of voting discussed in Chapter 23. If the preferred stock is *cumulative*, any unpaid dividends will accumulate for years of non-payment. Thus, when cumulative preferred stock is paid, current dividends plus any accumulated dividends are paid before common shareholders receive any dividends. This is different from *non-cumulative* preferred stock, in which the preferred shareholders lose their dividend rights for the years in which the directors declared no dividend.

A further classification of preferred stock is that it can either be participating or non-participating. *Participating* preferred stockholders not only receive a preference when dividends are declared, but they may also share in the common stock dividends on a pro rata basis. This is different from *non-participating* preferred stockholders, who do not share in the secondary distribution of common stock dividends on a pro rata basis.

Authorized, Issued, Treasury, and Outstanding Shares

Authorized shares
The maximum number of shares that a corporation may legally sell under its articles of incorporation.

Issued shares
Authorized shares that have been sold by the corporation.

Authorized shares refers to the number of shares provided for in the articles of incorporation. This number may be increased if the shareholders vote to amend the articles of incorporation. Authorized shares that have been sold by the corporation are called **issued shares**. Shares that have not been sold by the corporation are called non-issued shares.

Corporate financing may exist in many structures or classes of stock. These classes can be divided further into series. Each may offer different rights to the holders. For example, one class may be entitled to dividends and another not or liquidation rights (defining which classes of stockholders will be paid upon dissolution). Moreover, one class of stock may give voting rights not enjoyed by others.

> **Example:** Alphabet® (the parent company of Google®) has created three classes of shares to preserve the control of founders Larry Page and Sergey Brin. There are Class A shares, held by public investors with regular voting rights (GOOGL), Class B shares, held by the founders that have ten times the voting power compared to Class A, and Class C shares with no voting rights, normally held by employees and Class A stockholders (GOOG).

Treasury stock
Shares the corporation has issued and then repurchased that have no voting rights and are not entitled to dividends.

Outstanding shares
Shares held by shareholders.

After a corporation issues shares, it is also allowed to repurchase them. These repurchased shares are commonly referred to as **treasury stock**. Treasury stock possess no voting rights and are not entitled to dividends. Shares that are in the hands of the shareholders, whether originally issued or reissued, are referred to as **outstanding shares**. Outstanding shares may or may not include voting rights. For example, a businessperson may want to distribute non-voting shares to his or her children in order to retain control of the business yet provide for his or her estate planning.

Although repurchased shares are not afforded dividends or voting rights, there are many reasons why a corporation may wish to repurchase its shares. The two most common reasons for repurchasing are to preserve the stock price on a publicly traded exchange or because the board of directors believes the public stock price is too low and is undervalued by securities analysts.

Concept Summary
Hierarchy of Corporate Shares

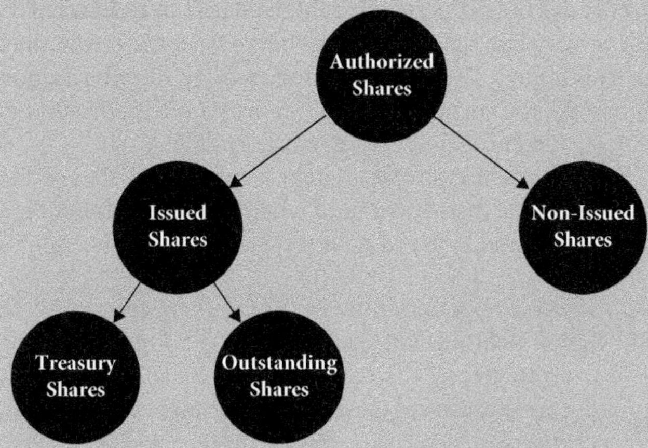

Management Application
The Corporate Transparency Act

Effective as of January 1, 2024, the Corporate Transparency Act and rules issued thereunder by the Financial Crimes Enforcement Network ("FinCEN") (collectively, the "CTA") require most U.S. entities and foreign entities registered to do business in the United States to file reports with FinCEN disclosing information about the entity and its beneficial owners (such as shareholders and members in LLCs). The intent of the legislation was to help prevent financial crimes like money laundering, corruption, and tax fraud. The collected information will lead to the preparation of a master database. All business organizations are subject to this law, except for sole proprietorships, some general partnerships, foreign entities not registered to do business in the U.S., unincorporated associations, and wealth planning trusts. It also does not apply to large operating companies, which are considered as such if they employ more than 20 full-time employees in the United States; have an operating presence at a physical address within the United States; and, have filed a federal income tax or information return in the United States for the previous year demonstrating more than $5 million in gross receipts or sales. This excludes gross receipts or sales from sources outside the United States.

Financing a Corporation with Debt

Debt security
An investment in a corporation creating a debtor-creditor relationship when the corporation borrows money from an investor. Debt securities may be in the form of a debenture, bond, or note.

Debenture
A long-term, unsecured debt instrument backed by the general credit of the borrower.

Bond
A long-term debt instrument in which the issuing company promises to pay the holders a specified amount of interest for a specified length of time and to repay the principal amount of the loan at maturity.

Note
A debt security with a short-term maturity.

Types of Debt Instruments

Instead of raising funds by issuing equity securities in the corporation, a corporation can also raise funds by issuing debt securities. A **debt security** creates a debtor-creditor relationship when the corporation borrows money from the investor to whom the debt security is issued. The investor is the *creditor,* and the corporation is the *debtor.* In this relationship, the corporation pays interest on the amount borrowed, in addition to the principal, at some stated future maturity date.

There are different types of debt securities, which are classified based on the length of the time of the instrument and whether the instrument is secured or unsecured. The following are three types of debt securities:

1. *Debenture.* A **debenture** is a *long-term, unsecured* debt instrument.
2. *Bond.* A **bond**, like a debenture, is a *long-term* debt security that is a written promise to pay a fixed sum of money at a set maturity date. However, unlike a debenture, a bond is *secured* by some form of collateral, such as a corporation's property.
3. *Note.* A **note** is a *short-term* debt instrument that can either be secured or unsecured. Commonly, the maturity is ten years or less.

Concept Summary
Major Ways to Finance a Corporation

Financing a Corporation with Equity

- Common stock — stocks without any special contract rights
- Preferred stock — stocks with contractual rights not found in common stock
  - Dividend preferences — preferred stock must receive full dividends before they proceed to common stock
  - Liquidation preferences — takes priority over common stock upon liquidation

Financing a Corporation with Debt

- Debenture — unsecured bonds that only offer the obligation of the corporation to pay them
- Bond
- Note

Other Ways to Finance a Corporation

There are other ways to finance a corporation, such as through venture capitalists (VCs), private equity, or crowdfunding.

Venture Capital

Venture capital is capital provided to new businesses by professional, outside investors—that is, venture capitalists. While providing needed capital to these new businesses, the investors face the substantial risk of losing their investment. Since this type of investment can offer the potential for above-average returns in the future, many venture capitalists are willing to invest in such businesses.

Venture capital
A type of private equity investment made by a venture capital fund that is often invested in start-up companies.

In venture capital financing, the business will transfer a portion of its ownership to the venture capitalists. In addition to providing capital, venture capitalists may also provide managerial and technical expertise to help guide the start-up.

Private Equity Capital

Private equity capital refers to funds invested by investors directly in private companies or those who engage in buyouts of companies. Private equity firms will pool funds from wealthy investors and use these funds to invest. Frequently, a private equity firm will purchase all or substantially all the ownership of a corporation. After purchasing the company, the investors improve the performance of the company and will realize their profit when they sell the company to other investors or to the public.

Private equity capital
Investments in a private corporation made by a private equity firm for a fixed period.

Crowdfunding

Crowdfunding is another way in which start-up businesses attempt to obtain financing. **Crowdfunding** is a cooperative activity in which people network and pool funds and other resources to assist a cause by means of the internet. While crowdfunding is most commonly used to raise funds for charity, a recent trend is to utilize crowdfunding to finance new start-ups. Perhaps one of the most recognized sites that triggered the crowdfunding movement is Kickstarter™. This topic is discussed more fully in Chapter 25.

Crowdfunding
A cooperative activity in which people network and pool funds and other resources to assist a cause via the internet.

> **Example:** A popular way people crowdfund by means of the internet is through websites such as GoFundMe.

Did You Know?

The word "crowdfund" is an acronym that stands for Capital Raising Online While Deterring Fraud and Unethical Non-Disclosure.

The S-Corp as a Tax Efficient Entity

S-corporation
A corporation that avoids double taxation by election and compliance with requirements under the Internal Revenue Code.

The corporations described in this chapter thus far were C corporations, commonly referred to as C-Corps. Another type of corporation, the **S corporation** (also referred to as an S-Corp or Subchapter S Corporation), is a type of entity that provides full protection to its shareholders, much like a C-Corp. The difference between the S-Corp and the C-Corp lies in how the entity is taxed.

While the C-Corp is subject to double taxation — it is first taxed at the entity level and then again at the shareholder level once distributions are made — the S-Corp is taxed like a partnership in that it is a pass-through entity. Generally, the entity pays no income tax, and thus any profits or losses are passed directly to the S-Corp's shareholders. The shareholders of the S-Corp are then taxed on their earnings. While this may seem like the ideal approach that all business owners should adopt, there are requirements to be satisfied for S-Corp status.

Owner Restrictions

The corporation must be a domestic corporation. Shareholders must be U.S. citizens or resident aliens and not a member of an affiliated group of corporations. The shareholders must be individuals, estates, or certain trusts. An S-Corp cannot have more than 100 shareholders.

Business Restrictions

There are restrictions on the type of business eligible for classification as an S-Corp. For example, foreign corporations, banks, and insurance companies cannot be structured as S-Corps.

Restrictions on the Types of Shares

While C-Corps can have multiple classes of stock (that is, common and preferred), a S-Corp is limited to a single class of stock. This restriction affects the type of debt the corporation may issue and presents an obstacle for family-owned businesses to eventually sell their shares and shift control to new owners.

Concept Summary
Taxation of C-Corps

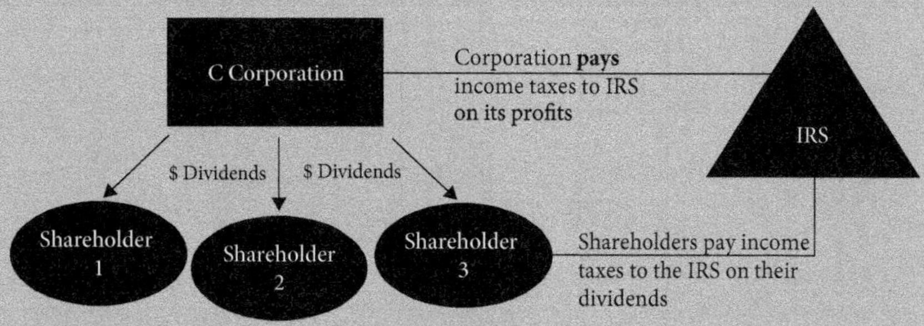

Concept Summary
Taxation of S-Corps

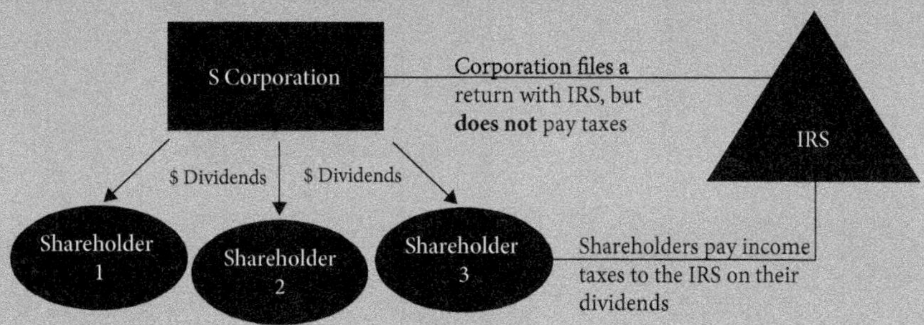

Management Application Election by a Small Business Corporation to Be an S Corporation

To classify a business entity as an S-Corp, the owners must file a Form 2553 with the IRS. Part of the form is excerpted below.

Form **2553** (Rev. December 2017) Department of the Treasury Internal Revenue Service

Election by a Small Business Corporation
(Under section 1362 of the Internal Revenue Code)
(Including a late election filed pursuant to Rev. Proc. 2013-30)
▶ You can fax this form to the IRS. See separate instructions.
▶ Go to *www.irs.gov/Form2553* for instructions and the latest information.

OMB No. 1545-0123

Note: This election to be an S corporation can be accepted only if all the tests are met under *Who May Elect* in the instructions, all shareholders have signed the consent statement, an officer has signed below, and the exact name and address of the corporation (entity) and other required form information have been provided.

Part I Election Information

Type or Print	Name (see instructions)	**A** Employer identification number
	Number, street, and room or suite no. If a P.O. box, see instructions.	**B** Date incorporated
	City or town, state or province, country, and ZIP or foreign postal code	**C** State of incorporation

D Check the applicable box(es) if the corporation (entity), after applying for the EIN shown in **A** above, changed its ☐ name or ☐ address

E Election is to be effective for tax year beginning (month, day, year) (see instructions) . . . . . . ▶ ______

Caution: A corporation (entity) making the election for its first tax year in existence will usually enter the beginning date of a short tax year that begins on a date other than January 1.

F Selected tax year:
(1) ☐ Calendar year
(2) ☐ Fiscal year ending (month and day) ▶ ______
(3) ☐ 52-53-week year ending with reference to the month of December
(4) ☐ 52-53-week year ending with reference to the month of ▶ ______
If box (2) or (4) is checked, complete Part II.

G If more than 100 shareholders are listed for item J (see page 2), check this box if treating members of a family as one shareholder results in no more than 100 shareholders (see test 2 under *Who May Elect* in the instructions) ▶ ☐

H Name and title of officer or legal representative whom the IRS may call for more information	Telephone number of officer or legal representative

I If this S corporation election is being filed late, I declare I had reasonable cause for not filing Form 2553 timely. If this late election is being made by an entity eligible to elect to be treated as a corporation, I declare I also had reasonable cause for not filing an entity classification election timely and the representations listed in Part IV are true. See below for my explanation of the reasons the election or elections were not made on time and a description of my diligent actions to correct the mistake upon its discovery. See instructions.

Sign Here Under penalties of perjury, I declare that I have examined this election, including accompanying documents, and, to the best of my knowledge and belief, the election contains all the relevant facts relating to the election, and such facts are true, correct, and complete.

▶ Signature of officer | Title | Date

For Paperwork Reduction Act Notice, see separate instructions. Cat. No. 18629R Form **2553** (Rev. 12-2017)

AI Feature: Social Purpose and Public Benefit Corporations

Using an internet search engine, identify state statutes recognizing the formation of social purpose and public benefit corporations.
Some states recognize them as flexible purpose corporations. What is emphasized in the corporate purposes of these entities? What factors other than shareholder value must directors consider in their decision making? Why should this form of entity be adopted as opposed to a nonprofit corporation? Identify which companies have adopted these organizational forms. Does your research indicate to you that the intended purposes for forming these types of entities have been realized? Having completed this research, select a mission statement and values to be upheld that will be included in the organizational documents. Use an AI program to draft the articles of formation for your organization.

Key Terms

- Alter ego theory, 547
- Articles of incorporation, 539
- Authorized shares, 552
- Bond, 554
- Bylaws, 541
- Common stock, 551
- Corporation, 536
- Corporation by estoppel, 544
- Crowdfunding, 555
- Cumulative stock, 552
- Debenture, 554
- Debt security, 554
- *De facto* corporation, 542
- Equity security, 550
- General purpose clause, 540
- Incorporator, 539
- Issued shares, 552
- Limited liability, 536
- Limited purpose clause, 540
- Non-cumulative stock, 552
- Note, 554
- Outstanding shares, 552
- Parent corporation, 550
- Piercing the corporate veil, 546
- Preferred stock, 551
- Private equity capital, 555
- Promoter, 544
- Registered agent, 539
- Registered office, 539
- S-corporation, 556
- Shareholder, 536
- Stock subscription, 551
- Subsidiary, 550
- Treasury stock, 552
- *Ultra vires,* 540
- Venture capital, 555

Applying the Law

22.1 Pre-Incorporation Liability. WinCo owns grocery stores that are divided into three geographical divisions. In 2008, Kym Nelson and WinCo's maintenance supervisor for the Portland Division discussed the possibility of Nelson's company KD3 performing concrete floor maintenance and repair work for the Portland Division stores. By January 2010, WinCo and Nelson (using the name "KD Concrete") agreed to a set of material terms, allowing KD Concrete to begin work on three test stores. On February 18, 2010, Nelson incorporated KDN to perform the WinCo contract. Jim Douty, WinCo's maintenance manager for the Boise Division, although having no authority to negotiate a new agreement on behalf of WinCo, authorized KD Concrete to perform work at specific stores in the Boise Division. In November 2011, WinCo refused to pay three invoices over concerns that KDN had overcharged WinCo for the work done. WinCo sued Nelson, KDN's sole shareholder, alleging fraud and breach of contract. Can Nelson be held personally liable for the liabilities of KDN? Explain. *KDN Management, Inc. v. WinCo Foods, LLC*, 423 P. 3d 422 (Idaho 2018)

22.2 *De Facto* Corporations. Kenneth Davenport, Dr. Gorman, and Dr. Bennett were partners doing business as Aero-Fabb Co. In January, Dr. Bennett submitted defective articles of incorporation to the state for filing. Before the certificate of incorporation was issued in the name of Aero-Fabb Corp. in June, Davenport entered into a rental agreement with Timberline Equipment Co. on behalf of Aero-Fabb. Timberline sued the defendants under the rental agreements. Who can Timberline hold liable for the rental agreements? Has a *de facto* corporation been established? *Timberline Equipment Co. v. Davenport*, 514 P.2d 1109 (Or. 1973)

22.3 Corporations by Estoppel. In 2010, 55 Day Spa, Inc., executed a three-year lease with "TY Builders LLC" to rent premises. Less than three months after the lease had been executed, William Peterson, president of 55 Day Spa, informed the managing member of TY Builders that 55 Day Spa would be vacating the premises. TY Builders commenced an action against 55 Day Spa for breach of the lease and unpaid rent. 55 Day Spa moved to dismiss the complaint on the grounds that the entities listed on the lease documents did not legally exist at the time the documents were signed. Discuss whether 55 Day Spa is likely to escape liability under the lease due to TY Builders' lack of proper incorporation. *TY Builders II, Inc. v. 55 Day Spa, Inc.*, 167 A.D.3d 679 (N.Y. App. Div. 2018)

22.4 *Ultra Vires* Doctrine. A.P. Smith Manufacturing Co. is a manufacturer of goods for use in the water and gas industries. Because of its profitability and success, the directors of A.P. Smith decided to donate $1,500 to Princeton University. This type of donation was not specifically authorized in A.P. Smith's articles of incorporation. A.P. Smith claimed that, as a corporation, it had a duty to support the public good, and that it was to the company's benefit to make sure that there was an educated public from which to attract future employees. Barlow, an A.P. Smith shareholder, filed a suit seeking a judgment declaring the contribution to be a misappropriation of corporate funds. Is the donation made by A.P. Smith *ultra vires*? What are some public policy arguments in favor of finding the donation to be within the corporation's power or authority? *A.P. Smith Mfg. Co. v. Barlow*, 98 A.2d 581 (N.J. 1953)

22.5 Alter Ego Liability. Fletcher alleged that a variety of injuries occurred due to repetitive stress from the use of keyboards manufactured by Atex, Inc. Fletcher sued Eastman Kodak Company®, Atex's parent company, under the theory that Atex was merely Kodak's alter ego or instrumentality. Several Kodak employees sat on Atex's board of directors, Atex employees regularly met with Kodak employees to discuss general business matters, and Atex could not undertake major capital expenditures, execute real estate leases, or sell stock without Kodak's approval. However, both companies always observed corporate formalities, Atex managed its own day-to-day affairs, and only one director of Kodak sat simultaneously as a director of Atex. If they can be proven, has Fletcher alleged enough facts to pierce Kodak's corporate veil? If not, what additional evidence is needed to state a claim against Kodak? *Fletcher v. Atex*, 68 F.3d 1451 (2d Cir. 1995)

22.6 Reverse Veil-Piercing. Tom Connolly was the Chapter 7 bankruptcy trustee of debtor Eugene Phillip. Phillip was the principal shareholder of Philsax, Inc., owning 51 percent of the outstanding shares. While incorporated, Philsax had no bank account, no written bylaws, and maintained no written financial statements. Philsax failed to provide written notice of board meetings, and Phillips added and removed directors at will. Connolly seeks to avoid specific transfers of real and personal property owned by Philsax by showing that Philsax was the alter ego of Phillips and that the actions taken by the corporation were actions taken by Phillips. Can Connolly "reverse pierce" the corporate veil to reach the assets of Philsax to cover Phillips' personal debts? Explain the difference between traditional piercing of the corporate veil and reverse piercing. *In re Phillips*, 139 P.3d 639 (Colo. 2006)

22.7 Corporate Liability. Gerald Marchese owned six separate business entities. He operated the companies out of a single business office. The companies shared expense accounts in common and lent funds to each other, as well as regularly lending money to Marchese for his personal expenses. None of these companies had internal governing documents such as bylaws. One of those businesses, Pepper Source, contracted with a shipping company, Sea-Land Services, Inc., for the delivery of sweet peppers. Pepper Source did not pay Sea-Land, which, in turn, sued Pepper Source. Pepper Source never defended the case and had, in fact, been dissolved for failure to pay business taxes. Sea-Land then sued Marchese and all of his companies, seeking to pierce Pepper Source's veil and collect from Marchese, and then to "reverse pierce" Marchese's other companies and collect from them. Can Sea-Land hold Marchese's other companies liable? Can Sea-Land hold Marchese liable? *Sea-Land Services, Inc. v. Pepper Source*, 941 F.2d 519 (7th Cir. 1991)

22.8 Undercapitalization. Seminole Hot Springs Corp. operated a public swimming pool at a leased facility. Seminole had no assets other than the lease, which it ultimately lost for nonpayment of its rent obligations. Cavaney was a director of Seminole, as well as the corporation's secretary and treasurer. Seminole never issued shares of stock but once proposed to issue three shares, with one going to Cavaney. Seminole's records were stored for a time at Cavaney's office, which also served at least occasionally as the corporation's mailing address. The Minton's daughter drowned in the pool that Seminole operated. The Mintons sued Seminole, and received a $10,000 judgment, which Seminole did not satisfy. The Mintons then sued Cavaney to hold him personally liable for the judgment. Will they succeed? *Minton v. Cavaney*, 364 P.2d 473 (Cal. 1961)

22.9 Preferred Stockholder Rights. MGC was a Delaware corporation that produced and distributed organic and gluten-free baked goods. MGC had authorized and issued common stock and two series of preferred stock, series A and series B. An investor, Greenmont Capital Partners I, LP, purchased series B preferred stock in MGC. Series B stockholders have special rights, including the right to a majority vote to validate any action that would alter or change the series B preferred stockholder's rights and the right to a majority vote on any amendment to the certificate of incorporation. The certificate permitted an automatic conversion of the preferred stock into common stock upon a majority vote of the preferred shares as a class, with no special rights for series B shareholders. MGC decided to seek an automatic conversion. If Greenmont Capital challenges the validity of the corporate conversion for effectively depriving the series B preferred shareholders of their special rights, what result? *Greenmont Capital Partners I, LP v. Mary's Gone Crackers, Inc.*, 2012 Del. Ch. LEXIS 236 (Del. Ch. 2012)

22.10 Piercing the Corporate Veil. Walkovszky, injured by one of Carlton's taxicabs, sought to combine the liability insurance of Carlton's various taxi companies to cover his damages. He claimed these companies operated as a single entity, aiming to hold Carlton personally responsible for the damages due to an alleged attempt to defraud the public. However, the court dismissed the case, stating that while the corporate veil can be pierced to prevent fraud, there was no evidence Carlton operated the companies in his personal capacity. The court found no grounds to hold him personally liable, as there was no indication of fraudulent behavior beyond the normal operations of multiple corporate entities. Thus, Walkovszky's attempt to hold Carlton individually accountable was unsuccessful. If the injured plaintiff cannot execute against the shareholder's assets and there is inadequate liability insurance available to pay damages to the plaintiff, is this an equitable result society should accept? *Walkovszky v. Carlton*, 223 N.E.2d 6 (1966)

Directors, Officers, and Shareholders

23

Make the best use of what's in your power and take the rest as it happens. — Epictetus, Greek philosopher (55-135 A.D.)

Chapter Outline

- Introduction
- Corporate Directors
- Corporate Officers
- Fiduciary Duties of Directors and Officers

Case 23.1: *Kamin v. American Express Co.*

- Shareholders
  - *Management Application: Call of Special Shareholder Meeting of XYZ Corporation*
  - *Management Application: How Do Investors Stay Informed?*
  - *Management Application: Climate Issues*
- Rights of Shareholders
  - *Management Application: Charging Allegations for Approving Improper Distribution to Shareholders*

Case 23.2: *Seinfeld v. Verizon Communications., Inc.*

  - *Management Application: Provision Restricting Transfer of Shares*
- Transfer of Shares
- Rights on Dissolution
- Duties and Liabilities of Shareholders
- AI Feature: Disregarding the Corporate Entity

Learning Objectives

After studying this chapter, you should be able to:

1. Describe the relationship between directors and shareholders.
2. Explain the fiduciary duties of directors.
3. Explain the fiduciary duties of officers.
4. Define the rights of corporate shareholders.
5. Describe the fiduciary duties of majority shareholders.

Introduction

In the previous chapter, the characteristics, requirements, and procedures of forming a corporation were discussed, including a discussion of the various ways a corporation may raise capital to begin its operations. This chapter continues our discussion on corporations, but the focus shifts to the rules, practices, and processes by which a corporation is directed and operated.

Recall that the shareholders are the owners of a corporation. These shareholders vote for directors to oversee the corporation. These directors appoint officers to run the day-to-day operations and hire employees. In publicly held corporations, tens of thousands of employees function with countless interactions, decisions, and other forms of communication with management, suppliers, and customers on a daily basis. When so many parties are involved, there is potential for competing interests to arise, a situation best managed through a corporate governance program.

Corporate governance The system of rules, practices, and processes by which a corporation is directed and controlled.

Corporate governance is a system of rules, regulations, and best practices by which a corporation is managed effectively while respecting social welfare. It balances the interests of a company's many stakeholders, such as shareholders, management, customers, suppliers, financiers, government, and the community. The essence of corporate governance is that the board implements internal controls to provide reasonable assurances that the corporation's objectives are realized.

This chapter addresses the relationships among the directors, officers, and the shareholders. The directors and officers owe varying duties and responsibilities to shareholders. In addition, the shareholders may be involved in the management of the corporation to the extent they can exercise rights such as voting, enjoy limited inspection rights, and be protected from the fraudulent activities of the corporation.

Corporate Directors

State corporate law statutes provide that the operation of the corporation is managed by, or under the direction of, the directors. The shareholders, as owners of the corporation, elect the board of directors, generally for an annual term. In all but small, privately held corporations, directors do not manage the day-to-day operation of the company. Instead, the officers and executive employees do so.

The corporate directors possess the most extensive authority of any position within the corporation. State law identifies what corporate actions must be approved by the board of directors. Directors exercise their authority to bind the corporation by a vote of the board. The board acts as a body because no individual director possesses the ability to act as an agent to bind the corporation.

Election of Directors

The number of directors is set forth in the corporation's articles or bylaws, subject to statutory limitations. At the time the corporation is created, the incorporators normally appoint the first board of directors. This initial board serves until the first shareholders' meeting, at which time subsequent directors are elected by a majority vote of the shareholders. Thereafter, directors are elected by shareholders at each annual meeting. If a board vacancy develops, the position is usually filled by a majority vote of the directors.

Usually, a director serves a one-year term following the annual meeting in which they were elected and continues to serve until the next annual meeting, when another election takes place. However, most state statutes allow for longer or staggered terms. Doing so allows for greater management continuity.

In many states, the shareholders may require a meeting occur for the election of directors when the time period since the last election is greater than a stated period of time, such as 15 months since the last annual meeting.

If a director fails to perform a required duty, they may be removed *for cause*. If a director is removed for cause, either the state law or bylaws of the corporation will provide how the board vacancy will be filled.

Types of Directors

There are inside directors and outside directors. An **inside director** is a person on the board of directors who is also an officer of the corporation. In contrast, an **outside director** is a person on the board of directors who does not hold a management position within the corporation. Generally, board members need not own shares in the corporation. However, many board compensation packages grant the directors the opportunity to purchase stock through favorably priced stock options.

Inside director
A person on the board of directors who is also an officer of the corporation.

Outside director
A person on the board of directors who does not hold a management position within the corporation.

Board Meetings

The board acts through validly adopted corporate resolutions. Formal meetings with recorded minutes are used by the directors to conduct business. For business to be validly conducted, there must be a quorum. A **quorum** is the minimum number of members of a board who must be present for any actions taken at the meeting to have legal effect. A quorum is usually met when the majority of the board is present. Once a quorum is present, the directors transact business by voting on corporate issues presented to them for decision. The modern trend is to also adopt resolutions in a writing signed by a minimum number of directors (without a meeting).

Quorum
The minimum number of members of a board who must be present to validly transact business.

At a properly convened meeting (that is, one following notice and with a quorum present), a majority of the directors present has the power to decide any question presented to the board. The articles or bylaws may require a greater than the majority vote of the directors.

Each corporation must keep written records of proceedings of its shareholders, board of directors, and committees of the board.

Rights of Directors

Directors are entitled to participate in all board meetings and provide their opinion in the setting of corporate policy matters.

Directors have *inspection rights* allowing them complete access to the corporation's books, records, and premises. These rights allow directors to make informed decisions regarding the company. However, they may be enjoined (that is, stopped) by a court if there are reasonable grounds to believe that the director will misuse the information to the detriment of the corporation.

In some situations (depending upon state statutes), a director may also have a *right to indemnification*. If directors are given this right, they may be eligible for reimbursement for legal costs, fees, and damages incurred in the event of a lawsuit naming them as individual defendants.

> **Example:** *Indemnification of Directors.* The corporation shall, to the maximum extent and in the manner permitted by the Delaware General Corporate Law (DGCL), indemnify each of its directors against expenses, judgments, fines, settlements, and other amounts actually and reasonably incurred in connection with any proceeding arising because of the fact that such person is or was a director of the corporation, as defined in Section 145 of the DGCL. For purposes of this Article VI, a "director" of the corporation includes any person (a) who is or was a director of the corporation, (b) who is or was serving at the request of the corporation as a director of another foreign or domestic corporation, partnership, joint venture, trust or other enterprise, or (c) who was a director of a corporation which was a predecessor corporation of the corporation or of another enterprise at the request of such predecessor corporation.

Corporate Officers

Directors do not meet frequently enough to be able to conduct all of the affairs of the corporation. Board decisions are reserved for significant policy and business decisions. The board selects officers who are delegated the authority to act on behalf of the corporation. While officers play an important role, their employment may be terminated. The authority of an officer to act on behalf of the corporation is governed by the principles of agency law, studied in Chapter 15. As discussed in that chapter, officers possess both express authority granted to them as well as implied authority to engage in any act reasonably connected with an authorized act.

> **Example:** The president of a corporation has the implied power to purchase goods and services for the corporation. Courts will recognize implied authority to act because of the office the officer holds.

A chief executive officer (CEO) or president has the implied authority to bind the corporation with respect to all matters within the ordinary course of the operation of the corporation. Such authority is broadly construed to protect third parties who rely upon the decisions made by the CEO or president.

Vice presidents of a corporation have those powers expressly granted to them by the board and the implied authority to act depending upon their activities for the corporation. For example, a vice president of corporate purchasing would impliedly have authority to make routine corporate purchases.

A corporate secretary has the power only to certify the books and records of the corporation. The secretary does not have an inherent or implied authority to bind the corporation.

The chief financial officer (CFO) has the implied authority to receive and account for the funds and properties belonging to the corporation. Like the secretary, the CFO has no implied authority to enter into contracts on behalf of the corporation. The CFO has the responsibility for ensuring the accurate and timely reporting of the financial results of the corporation, preparing financial reports, undertaking steps to raise capital, and monitoring the accounts receivable, accounts payable, and daily cash receipts.

To protect innocent third parties, the corporation is bound to any contract executed by an officer or agent who lacks express authority but nevertheless has the apparent authority to bind the corporation. An officer or agent has the apparent authority to undertake those acts that officers or agents of the same character would be authorized to undertake as a matter of custom and practice.

> **Example:** If general managers of auto dealerships are recognized within the automotive industry as having the authority to order vehicles for the new model year, the factory will be able to hold a dealership liable for its general manager's order of new vehicles despite the dealership's board directive to the general manager that they did not have that authority.

Officers and agents acting on behalf of a corporation impliedly warrant to innocent third parties their authority to bind the corporation. If the officer acts without implied authority, the corporation is not bound on a contract. The officer or agent will be liable to the third party for the third party's damages.

Fiduciary Duties of Directors and Officers

Directors and officers owe **fiduciary duties** to the corporation and the shareholders because their relationship to these parties requires confidence and trust. The fiduciary duties owed are the *duty of care* and the *duty of loyalty*.

Fiduciary duty
A standard of care imposed by law based on a relationship of trust and confidence between parties.

Duty of Care

Directors and officers owe a **duty of care** to the corporation and shareholders when performing their duties. Due care requires directors and officers to act in good faith and exercise a level of care that an ordinarily prudent person (that is, a reasonable person) would exercise in similar circumstances. Directors and officers are expected to act in the best interests of the corporation and if they fail to do so, either the directors and officers or the corporation may be held liable.

Duty of care
A fiduciary duty requiring a director or officer of a corporation to be fully and adequately informed and act with care when performing duties for the corporation.

DUTY TO MAKE INFORMED DECISIONS. The duty of care involves *process*. To determine if the duty of care has been breached, courts will review the steps the director or officer undertook prior to making the decision in question. At the very least, directors and officers must keep adequately informed by attending meetings and requesting and reading reports of officers and agents. Actions by directors or officers made without being apprised of the material facts necessary to make a decision may breach the duty of care.

DUTY TO REASONABLY SUPERVISE. Publicly held corporations must delegate work to be performed to officers, managers, and employees. The same holds true for large, closely held corporations. When such work is delegated, directors and officers are expected to exercise a reasonable amount of supervision in order to meet their duty of care.

Business judgment rule
A rule protecting directors and officers from liability for honest mistakes of judgment or bad business decisions so long as they comply with the process of remaining informed.

BUSINESS JUDGMENT RULE. Under the **business judgment rule**, directors and officers will not be liable to the corporation or its shareholders for honest mistakes of judgment or bad business decisions so long as they comply with the *process* of remaining informed.

This rule is a rebuttable presumption that directors are more able and informed than courts to make business decisions. There are three conditions in the application of this rule:

1. The directors or officers must be disinterested (undivided loyalty);
2. Reasonably diligent and informed (that is, acting with due care); and
3. Acting in good faith.

It is the directors and officers who best know the corporation's affairs, and it is not the role of the courts to substitute their business judgment for that of the directors or officers. This default rule protects corporate decision making from judicial interference. A plaintiff seeking to overturn a corporate decision has the burden of arguing that the business judgment rule should not apply. The business judgment rule is often the best protection a company can present in an action brought against a director or officer for breach of fiduciary duties.

The law imposes fiduciary duty liability upon directors and officers who are serving for any purpose, whether for a profit or nonprofit organization and regardless of whether the director or officer was compensated or serving gratuitously or as a figurehead.

Even if the corporation suffers damages because of a business decision, a court is unlikely to interfere with that decision. Consider the following case, which applies the business judgment rule.

CASE 23.1

ABSENT BAD FAITH, COURTS AND SHAREHOLDERS ARE NOT TO INTERFERE WITH THE BUSINESS JUDGMENT OF THE BOARD OF DIRECTORS

KAMIN v. AMERICAN EXPRESS CO.

86 Misc. 2d 809 (1976)

Supreme Court of New York

American Express Co. purchased stock in a company named DLJ for $29.9 million. A few years later, the stock ended up being a poor investment and had a fair market value of $4 million. Instead of selling the stock for $4 million and recognizing a $25.9 million capital loss, the American Express board of directors decided to declare a special dividend by giving all stockholders of record the DLJ shares. The shareholders did not want the dividend, but instead wanted American Express to sell the shares on the open market and use the capital loss to offset any other capital gains that the company may have had during the year. The shareholders sued to have the dividend enjoined or, in the alternative, receive monetary damages.

Language of the Court. *In actions by stockholders, which assail the acts of their directors, courts will not interfere unless the powers have been illegally or unconscientiously executed, or unless it be made to appear that the acts were fraudulent or collusive and destructive of the rights of the stockholders. Mere errors of judgment are not sufficient as grounds for equity interference; for the powers of those entrusted with corporate management are largely discretionary.*

More specifically, the question of whether or not a dividend is to be declared or a distribution of some kind should be made is exclusively a matter of business judgment for the board of directors. Courts will not interfere with such discretion unless it be first made to appear that the directors have acted or are about to act in bad faith and for a dishonest purpose. It is for the directors to say when and to what extent dividends shall be declared.

Thus, a complaint must be dismissed if all that is presented is a decision to pay dividends rather than pursuing some other course of conduct. A complaint which alleges merely that some course of action other than that pursued by the Board of Directors would have been more advantageous gives rise to no cognizable cause of action. Courts have more than enough to do in adjudicating legal rights and devising remedies for wrongs. The directors' room rather than the courtroom is the appropriate forum for thrashing out purely business questions which will have an impact on profits, market prices, competitive situations, or tax advantages. As stated by Cardozo, J., when sitting at Special Term, the substitution of someone else's business judgment for that of the directors "is no business for any court to follow."

It is not enough to allege, as plaintiffs do here, that the directors made an imprudent decision, which did not capitalize on the possibility of using a potential capital loss to offset capital gains. More than imprudence or mistaken judgment must be shown. Questions of policy of management, expediency of contracts or action, adequacy of consideration, lawful appropriation of corporate funds to advance corporate interests, are left solely to their honest and unselfish decision, for their powers therein are without limitation and free from restraint, and the exercise of them for the common and general interests of the corporation may not be questioned, although the results show that what they did was unwise or inexpedient.

Decision. The business judgment rule protected the American Express board of directors, and the court dismissed the complaint.

Focus on Ethics

Do you think it is fair for courts to give so much deference to the board of directors? How would shareholders determine if the directors had acted in bad faith? Does this rule insulate directors if they retain the advice of consultants before acting?

ADDITIONAL DEFENSES FOR DIRECTORS. Directors may be protected from shareholder suits if they dissented or abstained from the corporate action or received shareholder ratification of the alleged unreasonable conduct.

The protections of the business judgment rule are not absolute. The presumption can be rebutted if the plaintiff shows that the directors breached their fiduciary duty of care or loyalty, or otherwise acted in bad faith.

Duty of Loyalty

Duty of loyalty A fiduciary duty requiring directors and officers to subordinate personal interests to their obligation of loyalty to the corporation.

The **duty of loyalty** requires directors and officers to subordinate personal interests to their obligation of uncompromising loyalty to the corporation and its shareholders. They must act with the intent to serve those interests. For example, directors and officers cannot use corporate funds or confidential information for personal advantage.

While the duty of care arises when there is a lack of process, the duty of loyalty arises when there is some form of *interestedness* among the directors. The following are common breaches of the duty of loyalty:

1. Taking advantage of a corporate opportunity for personal gain;
   - Although the definition of corporate opportunity varies, it is typically any transaction that the corporation had or would likely have pursued (such as one within the same industry). The court will consider whether the result was unfair to the corporation.
   - The law may permit a director to take advantage of corporate opportunities when the corporation is insolvent or financially unable to pursue the investment. The director may act only after full disclosure and when the corporation has rejected the opportunity.
2. Competing with the corporation;
3. Having a personal interest that conflicts with the interest of the corporation; and
4. Insider trading.

In this situation, the director has a fiduciary duty to make full disclosure of any potential conflicts of interest that might arise in any corporate transaction.

Example: One director of an incorporated real estate investment trust (REIT) learned that another director engaged in a self-dealing transaction. However, the first director did not report to the other director and instead concealed the transaction from the rest of the board. When the shareholders brought an action alleging a violation of the duty of loyalty, both directors were found liable. *HMG/Courtland Properties, Inc. v. Gray*, 749 A.2d 94 (Del. Ch. 1999)

OVERCOMING SELF-INTEREST ISSUES. Self-interest issues may arise when a majority of the directors serving on a board have material personal interests in a transaction (or lack independence because of their relationship with other directors or shareholders). The directors will have two courses of action: (1) obtain approval for their acts or (2) prove that the transaction was fair.

Obtain Approval. When a director or officer is involved in a transaction involving self-interest and an alleged duty of loyalty violation arises, the director or officer may avoid liability if either a majority of the *disinterested* directors and officers or a majority of the *disinterested* shareholders are fully informed as to the interestedness and approve the transaction. The business judgment rule does not apply in the case of such a director because the director was not disinterested.

Apply Intrinsic Fairness Test. If prior approval for such conflicts is not obtained, an *intrinsic fairness test* is applied. It is also known as the inherently fair test and the entire fairness test. The validity of a corporate transaction approved by directors with conflicts is dependent upon a showing by the directors that the transaction was objectively fair. This test applies when the board is subject to actual conflicts of interest.

Concept Summary
Duty of Care and Duty of Loyalty

	Duty of Care	Duty of Loyalty
What Each Duty Focuses on	Ensuring that directors and officers are following a process for decision making, and not making decisions without research or deliberation.	Ensuring that directors and officers are not acting in a manner contrary to the interests of the corporation.
Applicable Test	Business judgment rule.	Intrinsic fairness test.

Director and Officer Liability

Although the business judgment rule protects directors and officers who make reasonable and informed decisions, they remain liable for their own commission of torts and crimes. As stated above, in circumstances of breaches of loyalty, directors and officers may also be sued by the corporation's shareholders. Conversely, after full disclosure, the shareholders could unanimously ratify the corporation's dealing with the interested director. In such cases, the interested director may not vote to ratify the acts in question.

Appointing Provisional Directors

Several states provide for the court appointment of a **provisional director** when the board is deadlocked, and the business of the corporation cannot proceed. The provisional director enjoys the same rights and duties as other directors. The provisional director serves until the deadlock is broken, or until removed from office by a majority of shareholders or by court order.

Provisional director
A temporary director appointed to break a board deadlock, who has the same duties and obligations as other directors.

Shareholders

Shareholder
An owner of shares in a company who has limited and indirect participation in the company's management.

Ownership in the corporation is represented by a share of stock. As owners, **shareholders** have a limited and indirect participation in the management of the corporation because that task is left to the directors and officers. The powers shareholders may exercise include the right to amend the articles of incorporation and bylaws, approve a merger or dissolution of the corporation, and approve the sale of all or substantially all the corporate assets. State laws provide that some of these powers are not absolute and require approval of the board of directors as well. Shareholders may also influence management decision making by electing or removing directors.

Annual meeting
The meeting of a company's stockholders is held each year to elect the company's directors, vote on specific corporate matters, and ratify certain actions of directors and officers.

Special meeting
A stockholder meeting that can be called to order at any time by the board of directors, shareholders of at least 10 to 20 percent of the shares, or anyone authorized to do so in the articles of incorporation.

Shareholders' Meetings

An annual shareholder meeting must occur each year. **Annual meetings** must be held for the purpose of electing directors on a date and at a time stated in or fixed in accordance with the bylaws. In addition to the election of directors, the shareholders may transact any other proper business at the annual meeting. An interim, **special meeting** can be called to address matters that must be addressed before the next annual meeting. State statutes often provide that a special meeting of shareholders may be called at any time by holders of at least 10 percent of the shares entitled to vote at the meeting. The 10 percent requirement applies to votes entitled to be cast at the meeting. If the corporation has more than one class or series of shares, the number of shares constituting this percentage may vary because different numbers of shares may be entitled to vote on different propositions.

A corporation must notify its shareholders of the date, time, and place of the meeting at least 10 days, but not more than 60 days, before the date of the meeting. In the event of a special meeting, a statement of the purpose of the meeting is required. At the special meeting, the business transacted must be limited to that purpose.

Management Application
Call of Special Shareholder Meeting of XYZ Corporation

To: *Name and title of chair of the board, president, or secretary*

The undersigned shareholders call a special meeting of the shareholders of the above-named corporation, to be held on [date] at 10:00 A.M. at [place], for the following purposes: [to approve the adoption of the following proposal: __________]. We are the holders of ____ shares entitled to cast at least ten percent (10%) of the votes at that meeting.

You are requested to cause notice of that meeting to be given within 20 days after you receive this call.

This call is made under [cite state statute and or bylaw provision].

Date: __________

____
Typed Names of Shareholders

Voting

The right to vote in corporate elections belongs to owners of shares on the applicable **record date**. Each shareholder is usually entitled to one vote for each outstanding share owned, including fractions of one vote corresponding to fractional shares. Exceptions exist for cumulative voting for directors and as otherwise provided by specific provisions in the articles restricting or eliminating voting rights. Special statutory rules often govern the voting of jointly held shares, shares held by fiduciaries, attorneys-in-fact, representatives, receivers, and pledgees, and shares held by corporations. Shareholders may exercise their voting rights through proxies or through voting agreements or voting trusts. Elections for directors need not be by ballot unless a shareholder demands election by ballot at the meeting and before the voting begins or unless the bylaws require.

Record date
The cut-off date used to determine which shareholders are entitled to vote.

TYPES OF VOTING

Regular Voting. Under the regular method of voting (also known as straight or noncumulative voting), each shareholder will vote the entire number of shares they own for each of their preferred candidates, up to the number of open positions. This allows the majority shareholders to elect the entire slate of directors.

> **Example:** Assume Shauna owns 500 shares in a corporation. There are two available director positions that are to be filled at the annual shareholders' meeting. She may cast one vote per share (500 votes) for each nominee. If there are three candidates running for director, Shauna may vote her 500 votes per candidate (1,500 votes total).

Cumulative Voting. A shareholder agreement or the articles of incorporation may provide for cumulative voting. This method of voting provides minority shareholders with a greater opportunity to elect a director of their choice. Under a **cumulative voting** procedure, a shareholder's voting power is equal to the number of directors to be elected multiplied by the number of votes to which the shareholder's shares are normally entitled.

Cumulative voting
A voting procedure that gives each voting shareholder a number of votes equal to the number of voting shares it holds multiplied by the number of directors up for election to the board of directors.

> **Example:** If a shareholder owns 125 common shares with four directors to be elected, under cumulative voting, the shareholder may cast 500 votes total (4 × 125). The shareholder may cast all votes for a single director, or they may be distributed to as many directors as the shareholder sees fit.

Concept Summary
Cumulative Voting: Example with Two Directors to Be Elected

	Number of Shares	Voting Power	Director Candidates			
			A	B	C	D
Nicole	150	300	150	150		
Sydney	150	300		150	150	

	Number of Shares	Voting Power	Director Candidates			
			A	B	C	D
Carmen	50	100				100
Nika	50	100				100
Total	*400*	*800*	*150*	*300*	*150*	*200*

In the above example, Director candidates B and D are elected to the board.

Proxy
A power of attorney allowing a specified person to vote the shares owned by a shareholder in a particular manner at a shareholders' meeting.

VOTING BY PROXY. Persons who own few shares of stock in publicly held companies often do not attend the shareholder's meeting. Shareholders may authorize another person to vote their shares at the shareholders' meeting. A power of attorney allowing a specified person to vote the shares owned by a shareholder in a particular manner is called a **proxy**. Before the shareholders' meeting, proxy materials are sent to all shareholders. Sample proxy language is found in the following example.

Example: Each Shareholder, entitled to vote at the annual shareholder meeting, may authorize another Shareholder to act for them by proxy, but no such proxy shall be voted or acted upon after eleven months from its date, unless the proxy provides for a longer period.

Various rules associated with proxies are implemented and enforced by the Securities and Exchange Commission (SEC) through Rule 14a of the 1934 Act. The SEC regulates the securities markets. Most notably, the rule requires specific disclosures be provided to the shareholders. Specific disclosures include a clear statement of the questions that will be voted upon at the meeting, conflicts of interest, and executive compensation packages.

SHAREHOLDER PROPOSALS. Shareholders can recommend or suggest that the company and/or its board of directors make changes to company policy by submitting a shareholder proposal. Shareholder proposals are submitted to the board of directors and may be included in the proxy materials that are sent to all shareholders. Not every shareholder can submit a proposal for consideration at a shareholder meeting. Under SEC Rule 14a-8, only shareholders who own at least (a) $2,000 worth of stock for at least three years, (b) $15,000 worth of stock for the last two years, or (c) $25,000 worth of stock for at least one year are eligible to submit proposals to the shareholders for adoption.

Example: John Chevedden submitted to Apache Corporation® a timely shareholder proposal. However, the proposal was still denied because he was not listed as a shareholder in Apache's records. Further, Apache could not verify Chevedden's ownership of Apache stock, the length of ownership, or the amount beneficially owned. Thus, the proposal was excluded. *Apache Corp. v. Chevedden*, 696 F. Supp. 2d 723 (S.D. Tex. 2010)

Even if shareholders meet the statutory requirements to submit a proposal, directors may exclude some proposals such as proposals that result in the violation of any state or federal law (such as materially false or misleading statements), proposals that relate to a personal claim or grievance against the company, proposals that relate to operations that account for less than 5% of the company's total assets and less than 5% of its net earnings and gross sales, and proposals that concern a matter relating to the conduct of its ordinary business operations.

Example: Shareholders of Wal-Mart® wanted the Wal-Mart directors to prepare and distribute reports about the company's equal employment opportunity and affirmative action policies. The reports would include a description of the company's efforts to advise its suppliers of these policies, as well as of its efforts to purchase goods and services from minority- and female-owned suppliers. The proposal was excluded because it concerned a matter relating to the conduct of its ordinary business operations. *Amalgamated Clothing and Textile Workers Union v. Wal-Mart Stores, Inc.*, 821 F. Supp. 877 (S.D.N.Y. 1993)

Management Application
How Do Investors Stay Informed?

In addition to information required to be provided to shareholders under state law, the SEC has adopted reporting forms that must be used by publicly held companies. These are required to be filed with the SEC pursuant to the Securities Exchange Act of 1934, which will be discussed in Chapter 25. The 1934 Act governs the regulation of the financial markets within the United States.

One of the required filings is Form 8-K. It is used in addition to filing annual reports (10-Ks) and quarterly reports (10-Qs), by which public companies report certain material events on a more current basis. Form 8-K is used to keep investors informed. If specified events, such as a government investigation or a departure of a CEO, occur, a public company will file a Current Report on Form 8-K within four business days to provide the material information to investors.

Access to SEC forms are available for review at www.sec.gov/forms. Use EDGAR, the SEC search engine, to review recent 8-K filings of a public company of your choice. What information was stated in them that would provide guidance to shareholders?

Management Application
Climate Issues

Unilever PLC® announced that it would become the first major public company to voluntarily give shareholders a vote on its efforts to reduce carbon emissions. It seeks greater shareholder engagement with shareholders on climate issues.

The company officially announced it would seek shareholder approval every three years on its carbon impact mitigation plans. The vote of the shareholders is advisory only upon the board and does not compel the company to change its processes.

Why would a company be concerned over this issue? How does this action improve corporate performance? Using an internet search engine, identify other public companies setting public targets for cutting carbon emissions. Given the expense of dramatically cutting its carbon footprint, how should the company achieve these goals? If this decision affects the use of raw materials, supply chain logistics, distribution channels, and the harm caused to the environment of its activities, how would you organize the company's approach to these issues after reviewing the efforts of other companies?

Is this policy one that is ethical? Can you identify whether this approach promotes the shareholder and/or the stakeholder theory of ethical behavior discussed in Chapter 2?

Rights of Shareholders

In addition to the right to vote their shares, shareholders have other rights available to them. A few of them are discussed below.

Preemptive Rights

Preemptive rights
In an option, security, or merger agreement, rights granted to an investor to maintain their percentage ownership by buying a proportionate number of shares of any future issue of that security.

Preemptive rights may be granted to shareholders pursuant to the articles of incorporation. Shareholders with **preemptive rights** have the first opportunity to purchase a new issue of that corporation's stock in proportion to the amount of stock that they already own. Preemptive rights allow each shareholder to maintain their proportionate ownership, voting power, and financial interests in the corporation. These rights prevent the dilution of the shareholders' voting power. The following example provides for preemptive rights.

> **Example:** A stock offering might include a preemptive rights provision such as the following: So long as the Shareholder, together with its Affiliates, owns in the aggregate at least ten percent (10%) of the issued and outstanding Shares, the Shareholder shall have a right (the "Participation Right"), subject to applicable laws or stock exchange requirements, to subscribe for its pro rata share of any Shares (other than Excluded Securities) that the Corporation may, from time to time, sell and issue after the Effective Date, whether pursuant to a public offering, private placement or otherwise (each, a "Proposed Offering").

Stock Warrants

A **stock warrant** is a right to acquire a specific number of shares from a corporation at an established price and before the warrant's expiration date. Stock warrants are issued by the company and when exercised the holder of the stock warrant receives stock from the company. Exercising a stock warrant results in the issuance of new shares that can dilute the value of existing shares of stock. They are used to raise capital and provide an additional incentive for investors if the company's stock price increases. They may also be used as long-term incentive compensation as stock warrant periods can last up to 15 years. Stock warrants are typically granted to shareholders who hold preemptive rights when a corporation issues additional shares.

Stock warrant
A right to acquire stock from a corporation at a set price and during a specified period.

Stock Options

Similar to a stock warrant, a **stock option** is a right giving the holder the opportunity to buy or sell a specific number of shares from a corporation at an established price within a specified time period. Stock options can be traded on exchanges (like stocks) and when the option is exercised, the shares of the stock are exchanged from one investor to another. Unlike stock warrants, new stock is not issued with a stock option exercise. Stock options are commonly used as part of employee compensation packages by incentivizing employees to contribute to the corporation's success and stay employed with the corporation. Generally, the option will lapse when the association between the individual holder and the corporation ends, such as termination of employment or resignation. Stock options usually have shorter expiration periods than stock warrants.

Stock option
A benefit giving the holder the opportunity to buy company stock at a discounted or fixed price.

Dividends

A **dividend** is the distribution of cash or property to shareholders because of their ownership of shares. Shareholders ordinarily have no right to receive dividends, and a declaration of dividends is an exercise of business judgment reserved to the board of directors. State laws may dictate compliance with solvency requirements to ensure that the corporation will remain in good standing prior to distributing dividends.

Dividend
A sum of money paid regularly by a company to its shareholders out of its profits.

> **Example:** A common test used by several states is the quick-ratio test, often referred to as the acid-test ratio. This test determines whether a company has enough short-term assets on hand to cover its immediate liabilities and enjoys sufficient excess capital to issue dividends to the shareholders.

Dividends that cause the corporation to become insolvent must be returned if the shareholder knew that the dividends were illegal at the time of payment. Issuing illegal dividends can subject the board of directors to personal liability for the payment of the value of those dividends.

If the directors do not declare a dividend, shareholders are not left without a remedy. Shareholders may sue to have a court compel the directors to declare dividends. Because the directors' decision is protected by the business judgment rule, shareholders have the burden of proving that the directors acted unreasonably such that their conduct was an abuse of their discretion.

Management Application
Charging Allegations for Approving Improper Distribution to Shareholders

Plaintiff is informed and believes, and on that basis alleges, that on or about June 15, 2024, defendant Directors and Officers approved a distribution of the corporation's cash to its shareholders by declaring a dividend in an amount of $1.40 per share on 500,000 outstanding Preferred Series A shares, which amounts in the aggregate of $700,000 were actually transferred to holders of those shares on June 30, 2024.

Plaintiff is informed and believes, and on that basis alleges, that the distribution alleged in Paragraph 5 of this complaint was contrary to law in that the corporation, as a result of making the distribution, will be likely to be unable to meet its liabilities as they mature.

Inspection Rights

Inspection right
A right owed to shareholders allowing them to inspect a corporation's books and records for a proper purpose.

Shareholders are entitled to examine limited corporate records for a *proper purpose*, if a request is made in advance. Not every shareholder is entitled to **inspection rights**. Some states require shareholders to hold shares for a minimum period immediately preceding the demand to inspect or to hold a minimum number of outstanding shares.

> **Example:** Some courts conduct a three-part test to determine proper purpose. The plaintiffs must make their demands in good faith, with reasonable particularity, and the documents must be directly connected to the alleged proper purpose. In a stock accounting case, the plaintiffs requested corporate documents to determine the option price of their shares in order to sell them. The request was made in good faith, as selling is a standard market activity. The plaintiffs satisfied reasonable particularity by specifying which documents they needed, and the requested documents were directly connected to gauging the price of their options. *Dewey v. Bechthold*, 387 F. Supp. 3d 919 (W.E.D.C. 2019)

The corporation may prevent potential abuses of these inspection rights. For example, a corporation can refuse to grant access to a shareholder if the corporation has reason to believe that the purpose of the demand is to acquire trade secrets or other confidential corporate information.

In the following case, a shareholder of Verizon attempted to compel production of the company's books and records without credible evidence.

CASE 23.2

SHAREHOLDERS MUST HAVE PROPER PURPOSE TO INVOKE THE RIGHT TO INSPECT THE CORPORATION'S BOOKS AND RECORDS

SEINFELD v. VERIZON COMMUNICATIONS, INC.

909 A.2d 117 (2006)

Supreme Court of Delaware

Seinfeld is a beneficial owner of approximately 3,884 shares of Verizon. Seinfeld brought suit against Verizon to compel the company to produce, for his inspection, its books and records related to the compensation of Verizon's three highest corporate officers from 2000 to 2002. Seinfeld claimed that their executive compensation, individually and collectively, was excessive and wasteful. Seinfeld's claim is based on his own calculations, which indicate that the three executives' compensation totaled $205 million over three years. However, during his deposition, Seinfeld acknowledged that he had no factual support for his claim that mismanagement had taken place. He admitted that the three executives did not perform any duplicative work, and he conceded he had no factual basis to allege that the executives "did not earn" the amounts they were paid under their employment agreements. Seinfeld also admitted "there is a possibility" that the $205 million executive compensation amount he calculated was wrong.

Language of the Court. *Stockholders' rights to inspect the corporation's books and records were recognized at common law because "[a]s a matter of self-protection, the stockholder was entitled to know how his agents were conducting the affairs of the corporation of which he or she was a part owner." The qualified inspection rights that originated at common law are now codified in the Delaware Code, which provides, in part:*

> *(b) Any stockholder, in person or by attorney or other agent, shall, upon written demand under oath stating the purpose thereof, have the right during the usual hours for business to inspect for any proper purpose.*

This statute provides stockholders of Delaware corporations with a "powerful right." By properly asserting that right, stockholders are able to obtain information that can be used in a variety of contexts. Stockholders may use information about corporate mismanagement, waste or wrongdoing in several ways. For example, they may: institute derivative litigation; "seek an audience with the board [of directors] to discuss proposed reform or, failing in that, they may prepare a stockholder resolution for the next annual meeting, or mount a proxy fight to elect new directors."

The settled law of Delaware required Seinfeld to present some evidence that established a credible basis from which the Court of Chancery could infer there were legitimate issues of possible waste, mismanagement or wrongdoing that warranted further investigation. Seinfeld argues that burden of proof "erects an insurmountable barrier for the minority shareholder of a public company." We have concluded that Seinfeld's argument is without merit.

Decision. *The issue before us is quite narrow: Should a stockholder seeking inspection be entitled to relief without being required to show some evidence to suggest a credible basis for wrongdoing? We conclude that the answer must be no.*

Focus on Ethics

The court in *Seinfeld* rejected Seinfeld's argument that the burden of proof is overly challenging for minority shareholders. Yet are there ethical considerations that might lend weight to Seinfeld's argument, such as disparities in financial and legal resources?

Derivative Actions

Derivative action A claim brought by a shareholder on behalf of the corporation against the corporation's management or board of directors.

Sometimes a corporation may be harmed by one of more of the corporation's own directors or officers. A **derivative action** allows shareholders on behalf of a corporation to file a suit for harm suffered by the corporation. Derivative actions often arise from fraud, self-dealing, or other breaches of fiduciary duties by members of the board of directors or management. Any recovery of money from a derivative action goes to the corporation and not the shareholders who bring the suit. The successful shareholders who filed the derivative action are entitled to the reasonable expenses, including attorneys' fees, incurred in the lawsuit. A derivative suit can be brought if the plaintiff:

1. Is a current shareholder and owned the stock at the time of the wrongful act; and
2. Made a written demand to the board of directors of the corporation requesting the board to commence a lawsuit to recover damages, and the board takes no action within 90 days of receiving the demand; or no written demand is required when making a written demand would be futile because a majority of the board has been accused of wrongdoing.

Transfer of Shares

Shareholders generally have the right to transfer their stock to another person unless there are valid restrictions on their transferability. If the restrictions exist, they must be set forth in the bylaws or in a shareholders' agreement and they must be reasonable.

Management Application
Provision Restricting Transfer of Shares

Why would shareholders agree to the following terms?

Each Stockholder agrees that he, she or it will not directly or indirectly, prior to the termination of this Agreement:

(i) Transfer, assign, sell, sell short, gift-over, pledge, encumber, hypothecate, exchange or otherwise dispose (whether by sale, liquidation, dissolution, dividend or distribution), or offer or solicit to do any of the foregoing, of any or all of the Shares and/or any debt or similar securities that are convertible into Shares of the Company held by him, her or it, including any additional Shares and/or any debt or similar securities that are convertible into Shares of the Company which Stockholder may subsequently acquire, including all additional Shares which may be issued to Stockholder upon the exercise of any options, warrants or other securities convertible into or exchangeable for securities of the Company.

Source: Andrew Johnston, *Contemporary Corporation Forms* (Wolters Kluwer, 2d ed. 2020).

Rights on Dissolution

Shareholders own the residual interest in the income and assets of the corporation. Upon dissolution, the corporation will first satisfy contractual claims owed to parties such as employees and creditors before distributing any remaining assets to shareholders in proportion to their share ownership. Shareholders who own preferred stock are typically given priority over common stockholders when a dissolved corporation distributes its assets. In exchange for bearing the greatest risk of loss on their investments, shareholders are provided with the unique benefits of having full voting control over the business and being the beneficiaries of the fiduciary duties discussed earlier in this chapter.

Fiduciary Duties of Controlling Shareholders

A situation in which shareholders can be personally liable occurs in the context of majority or controlling shareholders. In some instances, majority shareholders owe a fiduciary duty to minority shareholders. This occurs when a single shareholder (or a few shareholders acting as a single unit) own enough shares to exercise significant control over the corporation.

Majority shareholders owe a duty to the minority shareholders not to act oppressively, fraudulently, or illegally. Additionally, a controlling shareholder is subject to the corporate opportunity doctrine discussed under the duty of loyalty, but the rule is not as strictly applied as the rules that apply to directors and officers. The entire fairness standard of review discussed above with reference to directors also governs self-dealing transactions involving controlling shareholders. This principle has been applied in the context of both publicly held and close corporations.

> **Example:** Controlling shareholders may not use their voting power to promote opportunities that benefits them alone to the exclusion of the minority shareholders. *Jones v. H.F. Ahmanson & Co.*, 1 Cal. 3d 93 (1969)

AI Feature: Disregarding the Corporate Entity

Using an internet search engine, research the law of your home state for what elements and factors courts apply in determining whether to strip a corporation of its legal protections. Are there limitations as to whom the piercing of the corporate veil will apply? For example, is it limited to just shareholders, officers, and/or directors of corporate entities? Can it be extended to nonshareholders, such as a related company of the target defendant? Following that research, use an AI program to draft the allegations you would include in a court complaint to disregard a corporate entity to reach those in control of the target defendant.

Key Terms

- Annual meeting, 572
- Business judgment rule, 568
- Corporate governance, 564
- Cumulative voting, 573
- Derivative action, 580
- Dividend, 577
- Duty of care, 567
- Duty of loyalty, 570
- Fiduciary duty, 567
- Inside director, 565
- Inspection right, 578
- Outside director, 565
- Preemptive rights, 576
- Provisional director, 571
- Proxy, 574
- Quorum, 565
- Record date, 573
- Shareholder, 572
- Special meeting, 572
- Stock option, 577
- Stock warrant, 577

Applying the Law

23.1 Research the Law. Using an internet search engine, examine the efforts of states to compel diversity on the corporate boards of their state-based companies. Identify publicly held companies whose board of directors reflect diversity among its members. Next, identify those states which have required or are considering board diversity legislation. For example, California's AB 979 requires the following: California-headquartered public companies shall have at least one director on their boards who is from an underrepresented community, defined as "an individual who self identifies as Black, African American, Hispanic, Latino, Asian, Pacific Islander, Native American, Native Hawaiian, or Alaska Native, or who self identifies as gay, lesbian, bisexual, or transgender." The law mandates also that the number of directors from underrepresented communities be increased depending on the size of the board. What policies are served by this effort to increase diversity, equity and inclusion on such boards? Why have corporations been reluctant to act on their own to accomplish these ends?

23.2 Proper Purpose? Saito was a shareholder of McKesson. In 1998, McKesson merged with HBOC, Inc. and became McKesson HBOC, Inc. After the merger was effectuated, McKesson HBOC, Inc. reduced its revenues by $327 million in the following year due to accounting irregularities. This triggered several lawsuits by McKesson shareholders, including one by Saito as a plaintiff in a derivative action. During pretrial discovery, Saito demanded an inspection of the books and records of McKesson. More specifically, Saito demanded access to 11 categories of documents, including those relating to the merger and the financial condition of HBOC prior to the merger. In essence, Saito and the other shareholders wanted to examine the books and records in order to determine if any accounting irregularities had occurred in connection with the merger of McKesson and HBOC. The Delaware Court of Chancery determined that Saito's claim had proper purpose and deemed that the documents were a necessary and essential component to satisfy Saito's proper purpose. *Saito v. McKesson HBOC, Inc.*, 806 A.2d 113 (2002)

23.3 Direct or Derivative Action. Derivative claims are brought by shareholders on behalf of the corporation to recover for harm done to the corporation. Parametric Sound Corporation was a small, publicly held company that contemplated a merger with Turtle Beach, a larger, privately owned company. After negotiations, Parametric and Turtle Beach agreed to merge. As a result of the merger, the original Parametric shareholders were left with a significantly smaller stake in the company, and a new board of directors was elected. The original minority shareholders consolidated in the district court for breach of fiduciary duties against Parametric's new board. The court held that the claims were derivative, not direct, and therefore that the plaintiffs lacked standing to sue. *Parametric Sound Corp. v. Eighth Judicial District Court in and for County of Clark*, 401 P.3d 1100 (2017)

23.4 Duty of Loyalty. Nancy Harris was the President of the Northeast Harbor Golf Club. The club's major asset was a golf course. During Harris's tenure, the board occasionally discussed the possibility of developing some of the club's real estate. Although Harris was in favor of this, the rest of the board expressed no interest. Then, a listing broker informed Harris that there was a property available. The property consisted of three noncontiguous parcels located among the fairways of the golf course. The broker contacted Harris because he believed the club would be interested in buying the property to prevent development by others. However, Harris eventually purchased the property herself and did not disclose her plans to purchase the property to the club. Did Harris violate any fiduciary duties? Explain. *Northeast Harbor Golf Club, Inc. v. Harris*, 661 A.2d 1146 (Me. 1995)

23.5 Duty to Monitor. P&B Corporation was in the business of serving as a reinsurance broker, holding millions of dollars of client money in trust. Charles, Jr., and William Pritchard were inside directors of P&B Corporation, and their mother, Mrs. Lillian Pritchard, served as an outside director. Lillian Pritchard was unfamiliar with the rudiments of the corporation's business, never read annual reports, and visited the corporate offices only once during her five-year tenure on the board because she was in poor physical health. Without her knowledge, her two sons began withdrawing substantial sums from the client trust account and failed to return them or pay any interest. Eventually, P&B Corporation went bankrupt. Is Lillian Pritchard liable in a derivative action brought by P&B creditors for the acts of her sons? What steps should an outside director take to protect themselves from such claims? *Francis v. United Jersey Bank*, 432 A.2d 814 (N.J. 1981)

23.6 Diversion of Corporate Opportunities. James Porter was vice president and chief scientist of Energy Resources Corporation, Inc. (ERCO), a science and engineering company that provided products and services in the energy and environmental fields. While attending a meeting to deliver a paper on fluidized bed combustion, Porter met with two colleagues from Howard University. This led to an opportunity for a joint proposal to the U.S. Department of Energy (DOE) by Howard and ERCO for a development grant involving staged fluidized bed combustion of coal. When the Howard scientists expressed reservations about working with ERCO because the DOE would be more favorable to a minority subcontractor, Porter informed ERCO that the company was no longer in consideration for the Howard deal. Porter then left ERCO and formed his own company, where he began work on the research project with Howard. What defenses could Porter assert in a breach of the duty of loyalty claim by ERCO? *Energy Resources Corp., Inc. v. Porter*, 438 N.E. 2d 391 (Mass. App. Ct. 1982)

23.7 Provisional Director. Two original owners of the corporation issued new stock, constituting half the stock of the corporation, to two new investors, after which the four investors executed a shareholders' agreement providing that the shareholders had power with respect to the daily management and administrative decisions of the corporation but that the board of directors retained such mandatory duties as are imposed on them by the law as directors. When the board subsequently became deadlocked, with the original investors disagreeing with the new investors over various matters relating to the future direction and operation of the corporation, including whether it should be sold, the new directors petitioned for the appointment. Should the court grant or deny the petition and why? *In re Annrhon, Inc.*, 17 Cal. App. 4th 742 (1993)

23.8 Cumulative Voting. At a time when it owned 28.4 percent of craigslist®, eBay® had entered into a stockholders' agreement with the majority shareholders. That agreement provided that if eBay chose to compete with craigslist, it would lose certain consent rights that gave it the right to approve or disapprove certain corporate actions at craigslist. In response to eBay's launch of a competing online ad site, the majority shareholders acting as directors implemented, among other things, a staggered board that made it impossible for eBay to unilaterally elect a direct to the craigslist board. eBay sued asserting that the directors and controlling stockholders, breached their fiduciary duties owed to eBay as a minority investor. What result? *eBay Domestic Holdings v. Newmark*, 16 A.3d 1 (Del. Ch. 2010)

23.9 Controlling Shareholders. Former minority shareholders of SinglePoint Financial, Inc. sued the corporation's former directors and controlling shareholder alleging breach of fiduciary duty. They argued that the defendants had entered into a self-dealing transaction in which the controlling shareholder forgave the corporation's debt to him in exchange for being issued stock whose value exceeded the value of the forgiven debt. After the debt conversion, the company was acquired by another company. They sued to recover the value of which they claimed to have been wrongfully deprived in the debt conversion. Could the minority shareholders sue for their damages because of a breach of fiduciary duties by the controlling shareholder? *Gentile v. Rossette*, 906 A.2d 91 (Del. 2006)

23.10 Business Judgment Rule. In 1995, the Walt Disney Company™ (Disney) hired Michael

Ovitz to serve as its president. Ovitz's employment contract was negotiated by Disney's CEO and chairman, Michael Eisner, and was approved by the 1995 board of directors after receiving advice from a corporate compensation expert. According to the contract, Ovitz would receive a $1 million annual salary, a bonus, and stock options that permitted Ovitz to purchase 5 million shares of Disney common stock. If Ovitz left his position at Disney through no fault of his own, he was entitled to a severance package that included a $10 million termination payment, his remaining salary under the initial five-year term of his employment, the amount of probable bonuses, and immediately exercisable stock options for 3 million Disney shares. In 1996, just 14 months after Ovitz was hired, the new board of directors terminated his employment on a non-fault basis. Ovitz then received nearly $140 million under his severance package, as well as the value of his stock options. Are the actions of Eisner and the Disney directors protected under the business judgment rule? Why or why not? *Brehm v. Eisner*, 746 A.2d 244 (Del. 2000)

Mergers and Acquisitions

24

And while the law of competition may be sometimes hard for the individual, it is best for the race because it ensures the survival of the fittest in every department. — Andrew Carnegie, industrialist and philanthropist (1835-1919)

Chapter Outline

Learning Objectives

After studying this chapter, you should be able to:

1. Describe what should be included in a letter of intent.
2. Explain the process of mergers and acquisitions.
3. Differentiate between a merger and an asset purchase.
4. Recognize whose approvals are required to proceed with a merger or acquisition.
5. Discuss the characteristics of a short-form merger.
6. Explain a hostile takeover and defenses to it.

Introduction

In this chapter, we review the theory and practice of acquiring the assets or stock of a business. Sometimes known as a merger and acquisition. The subject matter of this chapter provides an overview for structuring a business acquisition. A privately held business involves fewer considerations and complications than a publicly held company, but many of the same processes are applied in both contexts.

The transaction frequently begins with the execution of a letter of intent and a nondisclosure agreement executed by the principals of the parties. Subject to publicly held companies' reporting requirements, this activity often remains known only to the parties until some point in the transaction when a definitive agreement is executed. In this chapter, we cover the elements of a successful acquisition and provide examples from actual practice.

The Beginning: The Letter of Intent

The Letter of Intent

Letter of intent
A document setting forth anticipated terms in the beginning stages of a transaction that commonly is not legally binding upon the parties.

The **letter of intent**, also referred to as a *term sheet* or *memorandum of understanding*, sets forth the essential terms of the merger or acquisition in the beginning stages of negotiations. The parties often use a letter of intent in complicated transactions to maintain principal transaction points throughout the process. A letter of intent is not legally binding on the parties (unless otherwise agreed) and is superseded by a definitive agreement once the negotiations are complete.

Management Application Advantages and Disadvantages of a Letter of Intent

Advantages

- Gauges the seriousness of the parties.
- Compels the parties to identify important terms and key issues, such as asset or stock sale, management retention and employee benefits, at an early stage.
- Provide assurances to seller of buyer's financing sources.
- Can be used to lock-in a prospective seller from speaking with and soliciting offers from other prospective buyers (no-shop clause).

Disadvantages

- Announcing the prospective transaction to the public may be required by federal securities laws if the company is a publicly held corporation.
- Costs additional time and money to negotiate a letter of intent.
- If not specified, it may be a binding agreement.

Management Application
Excerpted Letter of Intent

Below is an excerpted sample letter of intent with a confidentiality provision. Read the provisions of the letter and answer the questions that follow.

Prospective Seller
Target Co, Inc.
Address
RE: Letter of Intent Between Buyer Co, Inc. and Target Co, Inc.

Dear [name]:

This letter ("Letter of Intent") will confirm the mutual intentions of Buyer Co, Inc. (Buyer) agrees to purchase all of the issued and outstanding common stock of Target Co., Inc. (Seller). The Effective Date of this Letter of Intent is ____________.

Section I of this Letter of Intent summarizes the principal terms proposed in our earlier discussions. This Letter of Intent is not binding upon either of the Parties. These principal terms are subject to the execution and delivery by the Parties of a definitive Stock Purchase Agreement and other documents related to these transactions.

Section II of this Letter of Intent contains several covenants by the Parties, which shall be legally binding upon the execution of this Letter of Intent by the Parties. The binding terms in Section II below are enforceable against the Parties, regardless of whether the contemplated agreements or transactions are executed.

Section I: Proposed Terms

1. *Stock Purchase.* The Parties will execute a Stock Purchase Agreement, pursuant to which Buyer will purchase all the outstanding shares in the amount of 1,000,000 shares of the Company's Common Stock (the "Shares") from the schedule of Shareholders attached hereto for a total purchase price of not less than twenty-million dollars ($20,000,000) for the Shares.
2. *Representations of the Parties.* [In this section, the following will be stated: Seller will represent the accuracy of its financial statements, a closing date will be stated, the business will be conducted consistent with previous practices, and certain debts will be paid in full by the Seller prior to closing.]
3. *Employment Agreements.* At closing, the Company will enter into individual employment agreements with [Names of Executives], who are employed by the Seller, for one (1) year terms at annual compensation levels of $300,000. The agreements will contain such other terms and conditions as are reasonable and customary in the type of transaction contemplated hereby. [Shareholders may also be key executives.]

Section II: Binding Terms

[In this section, binding, enforceable terms are stated that will survive (that is, continue to be enforceable) even if the transaction does not close.]

No-Shop Provision. Seller is not negotiating with any other party for the sale of its stock or assets and has not entered into any understanding about a sale, whether binding or not, and, unless its negotiations

with Buyer terminate earlier, it will not negotiate for the sale of or offer to sell to any other party without Buyer's consent.

Confidentiality. Prior to Closing, neither Party nor their Representatives shall make any public statement or issue any press releases regarding the proposed agreements, the proposed transactions described herein, or this Letter Agreement without the prior written consent of the other Party, except as such disclosure may be required by law. If the law requires such disclosure, the disclosing party shall notify the other Party in advance and furnish the other Party a copy of the proposed disclosure.

[A lengthy definition of what constitutes "Confidential Information" will be stated.] Notwithstanding the foregoing, the Parties agree that certain disclosures regarding the agreements, the proposed transactions, the Confidential Information received from the other Party or under this Letter Agreement may be required to be made to each Party's representatives and to any other party whose consent or approval may be required to complete the agreements and the contemplated transactions. Buyer and its employees, affiliates, and agents will (a) treat all information received from Seller confidentially, (b) not disclose such information to third parties without the prior written consent of Seller, except as such disclosure may be required by law, (c) not use such information for any purpose other than the consideration of the matters contemplated by this Letter of Intent, including related due diligence, and (d) return to the Seller all Confidential Information received from Seller if the contemplated transactions do not take place.

Non-Solicitation. For a period of two (2) years following the effective date of this Letter of Intent, Buyer and its employees, affiliates, and agents agrees not to directly or indirectly, solicit for employment by them or any company owned or controlled by them, or any company with which any of them has any financial, management, or ownership interest any employees of Seller. This provision does not prohibit them from hiring employees of the Seller if such employees have themselves voluntarily solicited the employment without prompting from these persons.

Why would the parties require binding terms for the "No-Shop," "Confidentiality," and "Non-Solicitation" provisions? Thinking about a hypothetical business, what would you consider as protectible confidential information? What other terms and conditions would you insert in this document?

Due Diligence

Due diligence The process of identifying risks posed by a potential transaction.

The parties to a merger or acquisition conduct **due diligence**. Its function is to assess the potential risks posed by the potential transaction by examining all relevant aspects of the business to be purchased or merged with. Depending on the target company's size, the due diligence process can take many months to complete.

There are many considerations the acquirer must address, and this may involve specialists such as accountants, investment bankers, and valuation experts. It may also involve legal counsel specializing in the following areas: corporate and transactional, antitrust, intellectual property, real estate (and, perhaps, environmental), tax, employment, pension, and labor (if there are unionized employees among those employed by the target), and securities law.

Management Application
Preliminary Due Diligence List

While a due diligence list may run dozens of pages in length, the following is representative of its content:

Financial Information Review

1. Five years of historical balance sheets.
2. Five years of historical income statements with as much specific detail (breakdown of revenues and operating expenses) as possible.
3. Details of selling, and general and administrative expenses over the last five years.
4. Latest interim financial statements.
5. Original budgets/forecasts for the past three years, if available.
6. Projection of sales, by major customer, for the current fiscal year (actuals for last year).
7. A schedule of all machinery, equipment, and other fixed assets showing cost, accumulated depreciation, and net book value for each asset.
8. Estimate of the fair market value of any fixed assets owned by the company.
9. Accounts receivable as of the end of the past 12 months (one detailed, the remainder in summary).

Distribution and Marketing Review

Are all sales outright sales, or are there consignment sales?

1. A list of the top 100 customers for the past five years with the percentage of revenues that they contributed.
2. Copies of all patents, service marks, copyrights, trademarks, and other intellectual property, including internet addresses and web pages, if any.

Management and Operations Review

1. Details of all significant purchase and leasing contracts.
2. A copy of all management employment contracts and/or collective bargaining agreements.
3. An organization chart showing the name and title of key employees, and job descriptions and resumes of key employees/management.
4. Copies of all incentive compensation and bonus programs, listing, by individual, any amounts paid in the last two years.
5. Describe any pension plans, profit-sharing plans, or other significant benefits available to the company's employees.

General

Provide the following:

1. Federal and state tax returns for the past three years.
2. Corporate articles of incorporation, bylaws, and minutes.
3. Executed copies of all debt agreements, bank accounts, and lines of credit.
4. Names and addresses of attorneys and accountants.
5. Description of all material pending claims, lawsuits, and disputes.

Management Application
Due Diligence Regarding IT and Privacy

Data is rapidly becoming a significant corporate asset for most companies. In an M&A transaction, sellers will want to maximize the value of their data, while buyers will want to limit risks from the acquisition. Attorneys for both sides of the transaction must often perform an appropriate and comprehensive cybersecurity and data privacy due diligence. Understanding the data environment will help attorneys draft appropriate provisions in the M&A agreement.

The following are examples of IT and privacy due diligence requests:

- Disclosure of the target's cybersecurity policies and procedures.
- Disclosure of insurance claims resulting from privacy, information security, or data breaches, within the past three years.
- Disclosure of any prior breaches of cybersecurity systems and descriptions of the response.
- Disclosure of any litigation regarding failure to protect personal information or for violations of an individual's privacy.
- Access to employees responsible for ensuring cybersecurity procedures.

Using an internet search engine, conduct research to identify prior data breaches of publicly traded companies. Research whether their share prices fell as a result and how long it took to restore the company's share price to prior levels.

Mergers, Consolidations, and Share Exchanges

Merger
An acquisition in which two companies combine into one legal entity.

Corporations may be combined with other business entities through several methods including mergers, consolidations, and share exchanges. These methods are discussed in the following paragraphs.

Target corporation
An acquired corporation is legally absorbed into another corporation and ceases to exist.

Surviving corporation
Following a merger, either the target or acquiring corporation survives. The other corporation is dissolved.

Mergers

A **merger** of two or more corporations is a combination in which one corporation (that is, the **target corporation**) is legally acquired and absorbed into another (that is, the **surviving corporation**). When a merger is complete, the target corporation no longer exists. As a result of the merger, the surviving corporation acquires all of the target corporation's rights, duties, assets, and liabilities.

> **Example:** The risks of an acquisition are not always appreciated by corporate boards. German multinational Bayer® underestimated the risks of acquiring Monsanto®, a U.S. seed and agricultural chemical company, for $63 billion. Monsanto had sold a weed killer known as Roundup®. After the merger, American

juries held the product was responsible for personal injuries and deaths. Given the size of the resulting verdicts, Bayer sought to contain the damage by attempting to settle the many pending lawsuits, selling business divisions, and shrinking its workforce.

FIGURE 24.1: Mergers

Consolidations

Similar to a merger, a **consolidation** is the combination of two or more corporations to create a new legal entity. A consolidation differs from an ordinary merger in that neither of the original corporations survive. The new entity created after a consolidation acquires all of the formerly existing corporations' rights, duties, assets, and liabilities.

Consolidation
The combination of two or more corporations to create a new legal entity, with neither of the original corporations surviving.

FIGURE 24.2: Consolidations

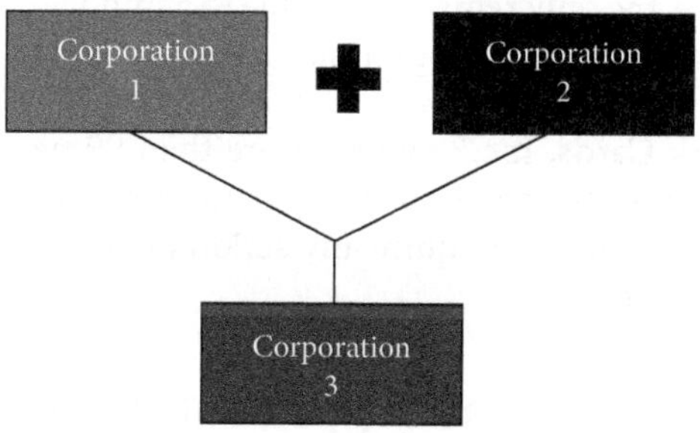

Share Exchanges

In a **share exchange**, some or all of the shares of one corporation are exchanged for some or all of the shares of another corporation. A wholly owned subsidiary arises when one corporation (parent corporation) owns all of the shares of another corporation (subsidiary corporation). Many tech sector acquisitions have occurred by the acquiring company using its stock to acquire that of the target corporation. The difference between this type of transaction and a merger or acquisition is that in a share exchange, both corporations continue to exist.

Share exchange
A transaction in which some or all of the shares of one corporation are exchanged for some or all of the shares of another corporation.

> **Example:** From an SEC filing for a Share Exchange involving the World of Jeans & Tops® ("WOJT"), the shareholders of WOJT ("Shareholders"), and Tilly's, Inc.® ("Tilly's"): *Exchange.* On the terms and subject to the conditions set forth in this Agreement, at the Closing (i) Shareholders will sell, convey, transfer and assign to Tilly's, free and clear of all liens, pledges, encumbrances, changes, restrictions or known claims of any kind, nature or description, and Tilly's will purchase and accept from Shareholders, twenty million (20,000,000) currently issued and outstanding shares of common stock of WOJT, in the aggregate (the "WOJT Shares"),

in the individual amounts as set forth on Schedule A, and (ii) in exchange for the transfer of such securities by the Shareholders, Tilly's will sell, convey, transfer and assign to Shareholders, and Shareholders will purchase and accept from Tilly's, twenty million (20,000,000) shares of newly-issued shares of Class B common stock of Tilly's, par value $0.001, in the aggregate (the "Tilly's Shares"), in the individual amounts as set forth on Schedule A (such exchange referred to herein as the "Exchange"). Upon completion of the Exchange, all of the shares of capital stock of WOJT shall be held by Tilly's.

Short-Form Mergers

Short-form merger A merger in which a subsidiary merges into a parent that already owns most of the subsidiary's shares.

Another type of merger, known as the **short-form merger**, involves a merger between a parent corporation and its subsidiary. To conduct a short-form merger, the parent corporation must own at least 90 percent of the outstanding shares of each class of the subsidiary corporation's stock. Only the approval of the board of directors of the parent corporation is required. No approval is required of the shareholders of either corporation. Once approved, the merger plan is filed with the state, and shareholders of the subsidiary corporation receive copies of the plan. Short-form mergers are less expensive and time-consuming than ordinary mergers.

Minority shareholders may attempt to challenge a short-form merger. However, absent fraud or illegality, the only remedy available to a minority shareholder objecting to the short-form merger may be an appraisal.

Example: Hallmark Cards, Inc.® owned more than 90 percent of Crown Media Holdings, Inc.® Hallmark exercised its right to undertake a short-form merger with Crown. Doing so did not require any action or consent by Crown's board of directors or shareholders.

Shareholder Approval and Appraisal Rights

Except for the short-form merger, in a merger or consolidation following the recommendation and approval from the board of directors of both companies, the shareholders of both corporations must approve a merger or consolidation plan. A shareholder vote is required in a merger or consolidation transaction because it is considered an *extraordinary matter*. Extraordinary matters require approval from both the board of directors and the shareholders because they contemplate a fundamental change to the corporation.

In a share exchange, following the recommendation and approval from the board of directors of both companies, the shareholders of the company whose shares are being exchanged (e.g. subsidiary) must approve.

Appraisal right The right of a dissenting shareholder in a merger transaction to have their shares appraised and be paid the fair value of those shares by the corporation.

The law provides a remedy to shareholders who disapprove of a merger or consolidation and are outvoted by other shareholders. An **appraisal right** gives a dissenting shareholder the right to demand that the corporation buy its shares at a judicially determined fair market value. Dissenting shareholders are thus able to avoid becoming shareholders of a corporation different from the one in which they originally invested. Appraisal rights are typically allowed in mergers, consolidations, share exchanges, short-form mergers, and sales of substantially all of the corporate assets not in the ordinary course of business.

The availability of shareholder appraisal rights depends on strict adherence to requirements designated by state law. A dissenting shareholder must follow state procedures for such an appraisal, or the right to obtain one is lost and the shareholder must concede to the merger transaction. However, dissenting shareholders otherwise have the option to sell their shares in the open market due to the transferability of shares.

Concept Summary
Appraisal Process

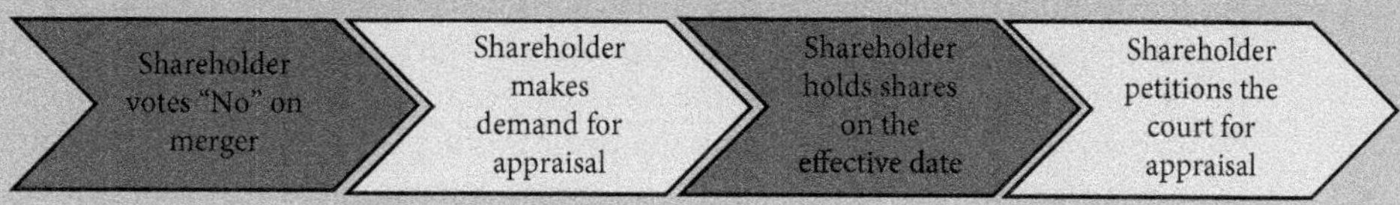

Management Application
Dissenting Shareholder's Demand for Purchase of Shares

Demand for Purchase of Shares

To XYZ Corporation:

1. I am the owner of 10,000 of the common shares of XYZ Corporation. These shares are held of record in my name and are evidenced by Certificate No. 12345.
2. I demand that XYZ Corporation purchase 10,000 of these shares for cash at the price of $25 per share. This price is the fair market value of these shares as of November 14, 2022, the day that XYZ Corporation has stated is the day before the first announcement of the terms of the proposed reorganization between XYZ Corporation and ABC Inc.
3. I submit the certificate representing the shares for which I make this demand for purchase for the purpose of stamping or endorsing the certificate with a statement that the shares are dissenting shares. The certificate is to be returned to me at the address stated below.

Dated: December 1, 2024

____
Name of Shareholder

____
Address

CASE 24.1

DISSENTING SHAREHOLDERS IN A MERGER TRANSACTION ARE ENTITLED TO PAYMENT OF THE FAIR VALUE OF THEIR SHARES

ATHLON SPORTS COMMC'NS, INC. v. DUGGAN

549 S.W.3d 107 (2018)

Supreme Court of Tennessee

Athlon Sports Communications, Inc.® ("Athlon") was a private, closely held corporation based in Tennessee that published special-interest sports magazines, websites, and related products. Stephen Duggan is the former CEO and director of Athlon. After experiencing financial difficulties, Athlon developed a merger plan. Under the plan, some Athlon shareholders, including Duggan, would not be invited to participate in the new corporation. An investment banker performed a valuation of the company prior to the planned merger, opining that the fair market value was zero and rendering a fairness opinion recommending that all shares of Athlon stock not converted into shares of the new corporation be canceled and that the owners of those shares be paid at a rate of $0.01 per share. The Athlon board of directors convened to discuss the proposed merger, and the plan was accepted after increasing the compensation of the canceled shares to $0.10 per share.

On August 10, 2012, the planned merger was consummated. Pursuant to the Tennessee dissenters' rights statutes, Athlon was required to compensate Duggan and the other non-participating shareholders for the fair value of their shares. In October 2012, Athlon sent the dissenting shareholders a fair value payment check for $0.10 per share, plus interest. Duggan rejected the offer and demanded $6.18 per share, which was rejected by Athlon. Athlon then filed suit against the dissenting shareholders for judicial appraisal of the fair value of the shares as of the date of the merger. The trial court and appellate court concluded that the fair value of the dissenting shareholders' stock at the time of merger was no greater than the $0.10 per share amount paid by Athlon. The dissenting shareholders appealed, arguing that the lower courts erred in relying exclusively on one method for determining the share value.

Language of the Court. *Under the common law, fundamental corporate changes such as a merger could be implemented only upon a unanimous vote of the corporation's shareholders. The common law rule protected minority shareholders by giving veto power to any single shareholder as to such corporate changes. Over time, corporations evolved into more democratic organizations, subject to majority rule. Now, unanimous shareholder consent is not required; corporations may effect fundamental changes by majority approval. This evolution left minority shareholders vulnerable to abuse at the hands of the majority shareholders, particularly in closely-held corporations.*

When unanimous approval was no longer required, and shareholders effectively lost their individual right to veto corporate changes, the appraisal remedy was provided to them in return. The so-called appraisal remedy protects minority shareholders who dissent from certain corporate actions by allowing them to force the corporation to purchase their shares at a judicially determined price. Every state now has statutes that provide some form of appraisal remedy; these are referred to as "dissenters' rights" statutes. As initially conceived, the appraisal remedy was intended to address concerns that a shareholder could be forced into continued ownership in a corporation fundamentally different from the one the shareholder had joined. Historically, the goals of the appraisal remedy were to give minority shareholders a "quid pro quo" for the loss of veto power as well as liquidity "and a 'way out' of an involuntarily altered investment." In modern times, the purpose of the appraisal remedy has shifted away from giving minority shareholders a "way out" of the corporation and towards protecting them from being forced out without due compensation.

Under Tennessee's statutory scheme, a shareholder is entitled to dissent from, and obtain payment of the fair value of the shareholder's shares in the event of a plan of merger such as the one in the instant case. Once the merger or other proposed corporate action is effectuated, the corporation must pay the dissenters the amount the corporation estimates to be the fair value of each dissenters' shares, plus accrued interest, accompanied by certain documentation regarding its calculation of the amount paid. If a dissenting shareholder disagrees with the "fair value" paid by the corporation, the dissenter may retain the amount received and notify the corporation in writing of his own estimate of "fair value," or the dissenter may simply reject the offer and demand payment of fair value. If the shareholder's demand for "fair value" remains unresolved, the corporation shall commence a proceeding within two months after receiving the payment demand and petition the court to determine the fair value of the shares and accrued interest.

Our dissenters' rights statutes do not require any particular valuation method for a dissenting shareholder's stock, and neither should this Court. There are now several widely-recognized valuation methods, a few of which were identified and applied by the experts in this case. We adopt the more open approach, which allows proof of value by any techniques or methods which are generally considered acceptable in the financial community and otherwise admissible in court.

Decision. The Supreme Court of Tennessee reversed the lower court's decision and held that dissenters' rights statutes do not require a specific valuation method for determining fair value of shares.

Focus on Ethics

Is the appraisal standard of "fair value" compensation an ethical standard to compensate minority shareholders in close corporations?

Acquisitions

Stock Purchases

Stock purchase The acquisition of all or a controlling interest in the target corporation's outstanding stock from the target's shareholders.

A **stock purchase** is the acquisition of the target corporation's outstanding stock from the target's shareholders. For privately held target corporations, it is often accomplished through a stock purchase agreement executed by the acquiring corporation and the shareholders of the target corporation. In the context of a publicly held company, in which there are many shareholders, the acquiring corporation submits what is known as a *tender offer*, discussed later in this chapter.

If the entirety of its outstanding stock is purchased, the target corporation becomes a wholly owned subsidiary of the acquiring corporation. As a result, the acquiring corporation acquires all of the assets and liabilities of the target.

Management Application
Stock Purchase Agreement Excerpt

Agreement of Purchase and Sale of Stock

This Agreement is made as of ____________, at __________, Ohio, among__________, Buyer, a resident of __________, Ohio, _________ and _________________ (collectively Shareholders), residents of _______, Ohio; and XYZ, Inc., an Ohio Corporation ("Corporation"), having its principal office at________________, ____________, Ohio. In this Agreement, Shareholder and Corporation are collectively referred to as Selling Parties.

Recitals

A. Shareholder represents that Shareholder owns all the outstanding stock of Corporation;

B. Buyer desires to purchase from Shareholder, and Shareholder desires to sell to Buyer, all the outstanding stock of Corporation (the Shares); and

C. Corporation desires that this transaction be consummated.

In consideration of the mutual covenants, agreements, representations, and warranties contained in this agreement, the parties agree as follows:

1. *Incorporation.* The foregoing preamble and recitals are incorporated herein as if set forth in full.
2. *Sale and Transfer of Shares.* Subject to the terms and conditions set forth in this Agreement, on the closing date, Shareholder will transfer and convey the Shares to Buyer, and Buyer will acquire the Shares from Shareholder.

3. *Consideration from Buyer at Closing.* As full payment for the transfer of the Shares by Shareholder to Buyer, in accordance with the provisions this Agreement, Buyer must deliver the following at the closing:
   a. Buyer's promissory note, dated as of the closing date, in the principal amount of $1,000,000 (subject to adjustment pursuant to Paragraph __). This note must be in the form of Exhibit "A."
   b. This note will, in addition, be secured by a pledge of the Shares under a security agreement in the form of Exhibit "B," which will be executed and delivered by Buyer to Shareholder on the closing date. Shareholder will be the pledge holder, and Buyer will deliver to Shareholder on the closing date a certificate or certificates representing all the Shares registered in Buyer's name, together with an undated assignment of the Shares in blank executed by Buyer.
4. *Buyer's Payment for Noncompetition Covenant.* In addition to the foregoing payment for the Shares, the parties acknowledge that Shareholder is also entitled to the payment of $10,000.00 for a noncompetition covenant.

To protect the Buyer from undisclosed liabilities of the Corporation, what provisions would you include in a stock purchase agreement? For example, from what risks would the Buyer want the Seller to indemnify it?

Asset Purchases

A corporation engages in an **asset purchase** when it acquires all or substantially all of the assets of another corporation. An asset purchase is unlike a traditional merger or consolidation because the acquiring corporation obtains the assets of a target corporation without any accompanying liabilities, except for those liabilities that are specifically acquired (such as accounts payable or equipment leases) or where successor liability arises (discussed below).

Asset purchase
A transaction in which a corporation acquires all or substantially all the assets of another business entity.

Example: *Purchase of Assets.* Subject to the terms and conditions in this Agreement, Seller agrees to sell, assign, and transfer to Buyer, and Buyer agrees to purchase all of Seller's tangible and intangible properties, wherever located, including all unknown and contingent rights, Seller's corporate name, goodwill, insurance and other contract benefits, cash and cash equivalents, inventories, accounts receivable, and all other assets as used in Seller's business, and a complete and accurate list of all of such assets is set forth in Exhibit A to this Agreement.

Example: In 2019, The Walt Disney Company® acquired most of the assets of 21st Century Fox®. To obtain regulatory approval in the United States and foreign countries, some of Fox's assets could not be acquired by Disney or were to be divested following the closing of the asset purchase transaction.

Management Application
Asset Purchase Agreement Excerpt

Asset Purchase Agreement

This Asset Purchase Agreement ("Agreement") is made and entered into this twentieth (20th) day of May, 2025, between and among ABC Corp., a Delaware corporation (the "Buyer"), XYZ, Inc., a Maryland corporation (the "Seller"), and [Shareholder Names] individually (each a "Shareholder" and collectively, the "Shareholders").

Recitals

A. Seller is engaged in the textile manufacturing business and activities related thereto (herein referred to as the "Corporation" or "Business"); and

B. Seller and the Shareholders (constituting all of the beneficial shareholders of the Seller) desire to sell, convey, transfer, assign, and deliver to Buyer the Business. and Buyer desires to purchase the Business and such assets, properties, and operations, on the terms and subject to conditions contained in this Agreement, and other agreements related hereto.

In consideration of the mutual covenants, agreements, representations, and warranties contained in this Agreement, the parties agree as follows:

1. *Incorporation.* The foregoing preamble and recitals are incorporated herein as if set forth in full.
2. *Sale of Assets.* Subject to the terms and conditions set forth in this Agreement, Seller, agrees to sell, convey, transfer, assign and deliver to Buyer, and Buyer agrees to purchase from Seller, the following [describe assets].
3. *Purchase Price.* The purchase price to be paid by the Buyer for the Assets to be sold, transferred, and conveyed by the Seller pursuant to this Agreement at the closing date shall be:
   a. Cash in the amount of Four Million Dollars ($4,000,000), paid by cashier's check or wire transfer; and
   b. One promissory note for the principal amount of Three Hundred Twenty-Five Thousand Dollars ($325,000).
4. *Lease, Rent, Excise and Property Taxes.* Seller shall pay all lease payments, rent due, sales and use taxes arising out of the operation of the Seller's business and shall pay the same portion pro-rated as of the closing date. In addition, Seller shall pay its portion pro-rated as of the closing date of all state and local real and personal property taxes of the business. Buyer shall not be responsible for any business occupation, withholding or similar tax or any taxes of any kind related to any period before the closing date.
5. *Consent of Third Parties.* Buyer and Seller shall use their respective reasonable commercial efforts to obtain, or to cause to be obtained, any consent, substitution, approval, or amendment required to transfer all rights and obligations under any contracts, leases, licenses, governmental permits, certificates, approvals, authorizations or other rights or obligations, or liabilities.

If this were a closely held corporation, would the buyer desire the selling shareholders to execute a covenant not to compete? Why? Using an internet search engine, research to what extent these agreements are enforceable. What if the Buyer moved to a state where such covenants did not receive strong enforcement? What would you want to include in the agreement in such an event?

Management Application
Drafting a Purchase Agreement

When the material terms of the merger or acquisition transaction have been established, legal counsel will prepare the legal documents memorializing the transaction. The purchase agreement sets forth those terms, which may include the following:

- Identification of the assets or stock being purchased, the purchase terms, and potential collateralization to ensure payment to seller; and schedule for closing (and provisions for extension of the closing date);
  - ☐ If an asset sale, which liabilities are to be assumed, and which are to remain with the target.
  - ☐ If an asset sale, address the possibility of sales taxes.
  - ☐ If an asset sale, the need to recapture tax credits and depreciation.
  - ☐ If an asset sale, the possibility of having to give notices to creditors to comply with the bulk sales law under Article 6 of the UCC (which allows them to be paid at closing). Each state has its own requirements for this notice, which relieves the buyer from post-closing liabilities for the acquired assets.
  - ☐ If an asset sale, are all the leases, licenses, and franchises transferable to the buyer?
- The nature and scope of the parties' pre-closing representations and warranties;
- Conditions precedent and concurrent to be satisfied prior to closing (this activity includes completion of the due diligence of the parties and obtaining third-party consents (such as landlord's consent to assign leases));
- The terms of the seller's indemnification for breaches discovered post-closing;
- Representations and warranties of the parties that will survive the closing (that is, those that will be enforceable following the closing);
- Employment and retention agreements for key personnel (include covenants not to compete);
- Payment of break-up fees (discussed below); and
- Remedies for breach of the contract. These may include terms for offset (reduction) to the sales price if the post-closing buyer discovers that the seller's material representations to the buyer were false. The buyer may invoke the benefits of indemnification provisions.

Are there other terms and conditions that you can suggest to include?

Approvals Required

STOCK PURCHASES. For private corporation stock purchases, approval is required from the board of directors and the shareholders of both the acquiring and selling corporations. The same approvals are needed for publicly held corporations; however, if the target corporation's board of directors opposes the transaction, the acquiring corporation can seek shareholder approval directly, leading to a hostile takeover (discussed below). In both cases, the shareholders of both corporations and the board of directors of the acquiring entity must approve the acquisition.

ASSET PURCHASES. For the *acquiring* corporation, purchasing another corporation's assets does not alter its corporate structure. Unless required by law or a shareholder agreement, the acquiring corporation only needs board of director approval for an asset purchase.

In contrast, the *selling* corporation must obtain approval from both its board of directors and shareholders, as the sale of all or substantially all of its assets is considered an *extraordinary matter* that changes the legal entity. Additionally, most state statutes grant the selling corporation's shareholders appraisal rights.

Successor Liability

Successor liability Debts of the predecessor business entity that are attributable to the successor business entity.

In some circumstances, the debts of the predecessor business entity are attributable to the successor business entity. This circumstance is known as **successor liability**. Successor liability can arise when one business entity transfers all or substantially all its assets to another business entity.

A corporation acquiring the assets of another corporation will not be responsible for the seller's liabilities, unless:

- The buyer either impliedly or expressly assumes the seller's liabilities;
- The transaction is a merger or consolidation;
- The buyer continues in the same line of business as the seller under the same management; or
- The transaction was entered into fraudulently with an intent to escape liability.

The following case considers the issue of liability for the predecessor's debts and obligations.

CASE 24.2

CORPORATE LAW GENERALLY FAVORS THE FREE TRANSFER OF ASSETS AND DISFAVORS SUCCESSOR LIABILITY

NATIONWIDE MUTUAL INSURANCE CO. v. EAGLE WINDOW & DOOR, INC.

818 S.E. 2d 447 (2018)

Supreme Court of South Carolina

In 1999, Renaul and Karen Abel contracted with Gilliam Construction Company, Inc. for the construction of a house. In constructing the house, Gilliam used windows manufactured by Eagle & Taylor, doing business as Eagle Window & Door, Inc. Later, the Abels discovered damage from water intrusion around the windows. The Abels sued Gilliam for the alleged defects and settled with Gilliam and its insurer, Nationwide Mutual, for $210,000. Nationwide and Gilliam then initiated a contribution action seeking repayment of the settlement proceeds from Eagle.

Eagle & Taylor was a wholly owned subsidiary of AAPC. In 2000, AAPC filed for reorganization and placed substantially all of its assets of Eagle Window & Door, Inc. up for auction, where Linsalata was the successful bidder. Linsalata formed EWD Acquisition Co. to purchase and take title to the assets. After the assets were conveyed, EWD Acquisition Co. formally changed its name to Eagle Window & Door, Inc., the entity against which Nationwide and Gilliam pursued their contribution claim.

Eagle defended the contribution suit on the basis that no successor liability flowed from Eagle & Taylor, the entity responsible for the manufacture and sale of the defective windows. Nationwide claimed Eagle should be considered a "mere continuation" of Eagle & Taylor because it held a substantially similar name, produced the same products in the same facility, and benefitted from the brand's history by holding itself out as the successor entity. The trial court ruled in favor of Nationwide, and the court of appeals affirmed. Eagle appealed.

Language of the Court. *Ordinarily, in the absence of a statute, a successor or purchasing corporation is not liable for the debts of a predecessor or seller unless: (1) there was an agreement to assume such debts; (2) the circumstances surrounding the transaction amount to a consolidation or merger of the two corporations; (3) the successor company was a mere continuation of the predecessor; or (4) the transaction was entered into fraudulently for the purpose of wrongfully defeating creditors' claims. In this case we are concerned only with the third exception—mere continuation.*

Eagle & Taylor was a wholly-owned subsidiary of AAPC at the time of the asset sale, meaning AAPC held 100% of the corporation's stock. After the sale, AAPC did not acquire any shares in the newly-formed Eagle corporation, nor did it possess any ownership in Linsalata. There was no commonality of ownership between the predecessor and successor entities, and none of the officers of Eagle & Taylor (who went on to become officers of Eagle and are the only possible source of shareholder commonality between Eagle and Eagle & Taylor) possessed any ownership interest in the predecessor prior to the sale. While officers were given shares in Eagle after the acquisition, none of them owned any shares in Eagle & Taylor. The sole director of Eagle & Taylor had no role with Eagle after the acquisition. Thus, the record indicates the corporate officers were the only group with commonality between Eagle and its predecessor, while no continuity existed with directors and shareholders. Because there was no commonality of shareholders and directors between Eagle and Eagle & Taylor, we reverse the court of appeals' finding of successor liability.

We recognize the mere continuation test is a strict one, but we temper our holding by noting it is not completely inflexible. While commonality of ownership is a keystone of the analysis and almost always sufficient to establish mere continuation when paired with common directors and officers, we stress control is an essential consideration as well. Typically, ownership and control are found in tandem; however, there may be instances where directors or officers—lacking ownership—exert such control and influence over a corporation that their continued presence after a corporate acquisition is sufficient to establish successor liability. Although the mere continuation test is a high burden for a plaintiff to meet, it is intentionally so, as corporate law generally favors the free transfer of assets and disfavors successor liability. However, our successor liability doctrine affords protection for plaintiffs in those cases where a corporate sale is driven by a desire to escape the predecessor's liabilities and obligations. Where the changing of corporate hats is tainted by such fraudulent intent, the successor corporation remains liable, even when the test for mere continuation is not otherwise satisfied.

Decision. The Supreme Court of South Carolina reversed the court of appeals and held that Eagle did not assume the liabilities of Eagle & Taylor.

Focus on Ethics

Is this a fair result to the unpaid creditors of Eagle & Taylor? As a business executive, what operational practices would you adopt to mitigate the risks of non-payment?

Management Application Role of Representation and Warranty Insurance

Representations and warranties insurance policies ("RWI") have been increasingly used in M&A transactions. Under an RWI policy, the insured may recover directly from an insurer for losses from breaches of the representations and warranties in an agreement. That is, the insured can shift the risk of such losses from the other party to an insurer.

RWI policies can benefit both sellers and buyers in an M&A transaction. The seller is able to limit or eliminate their liability for breaches. The buyer may be able to shorten negotiations over an acquisition agreement, which may allow them to be more competitive against other buyers.

Typically, when RWI is used in M&A transactions, there are several issues that the buyer and seller will negotiate. The following are select examples of what may be negotiated:

- Who will pay for the insurance?
- Will the seller's representations and warranties expire after closing?
- Will the seller be liable for losses in excess of the RWI policy?

Takeovers

Takeover
Obtaining controlling interest in a target corporation.

A **takeover** is the acquisition of control over a target corporation through the purchase of a substantial number of the voting shares of the target corporation. One underlying assumption in our discussion so far was that the business transactions were mutually agreed upon by the directors of both corporations. However, with respect to publicly held corporations, when the target corporation's board of directors opposes the proposed transaction, another approach may be pursued.

After rejection from the target corporation's board of directors, the acquirer can make an offer to the *shareholders* of the target corporation to purchase their shares at a stated price. In doing so, the acquiring corporation is attempting a **hostile takeover.** Alternatively, the acquirer through shareholder voting may seek to replace enough of the target's board members with others who favor the takeover.

Hostile takeover
An acquisition or merger accomplished without the approval of the board of directors of the target corporation.

Tender Offers

In a hostile takeover, the acquiring corporation makes a **tender offer** directly to all shareholders of the target corporation to purchase their shares of stock. Often, the offer is limited to a certain percentage of the outstanding shares. To induce the shareholders to accept the tender offer, the acquiring corporation usually offers a higher price than the current market price of the target corporation's shares.

Tender offer
A public, open offer, or invitation by a prospective acquirer to all shareholders of a publicly held corporation to sell their shares at a specified price during a specified time.

> **Example:** Subject to the condition that the acquirer purchases at least a percentage of a target's shares (such as 51%), the acquirer offers a higher price per share than the market price for the shares on a public exchange. This motivates current shareholders to sell their shares — presumably for a gain.

Tender offers are subject to strict regulation in order to protect investors. In addition, these regulations offer target companies guidance on how to respond to a tender offer. The Williams Act, an amendment to the Securities Exchange Act of 1934, establishes requirements for individuals, groups, or businesses that seek to acquire stocks to take control of the target company. For example, the Williams Act may require disclosure of the identity of any beneficial owner and their intentions regarding the target company. Further, the Williams Act also governs the timing and procedures of tender offers. This allows managers and shareholders to make decisions regarding the tender offer without unreasonable time pressure.

Concept Summary
Mergers and Tender Offers

- A **merger** is a transaction whereby two companies are combined to form a single entity. Their operations become integrated.
- In comparison, under a **tender offer,** the acquirer purchases the shares of the target corporation from the target's shareholders.

Defending Against a Hostile Takeover

A target corporation may respond to a hostile takeover attempt in a number of ways. Management and members of the board of directors of the target corporation are often replaced following a hostile takeover. The target corporation's board may exercise some or all of the following defenses to fight a hostile takeover:

Greenmail
A defensive technique in which the target corporation repurchases its stock at a premium price from a hostile bidder threatening to take control of the company.

Self-tender offer
A target corporation's offer to redeem (buy back) its own stock from its current shareholders at a premium.

Crown jewel
A target corporation's most valuable asset that, if sold, will make the target much less attractive to a hostile bidder.

White knight
A corporation that promises to leave the target corporation and/or its management intact if it acquires the target corporation.

Lock-up option
A defensive mechanism giving a white knight the right to purchase the target corporation's crown jewel if the hostile bidder acquires a certain percentage of the target's stock.

Poison pill
A defensive strategy built into the target corporation's articles of incorporation, bylaws, contracts, or leases that makes the target less attractive.

- *Greenmail.* **Greenmail** is a defensive technique in which the target corporation repurchases its stock at a premium price from a hostile bidder threatening to take control of the company. This strategy may prove unsuccessful if the hostile bidder utilizes the newly acquired greenmail to again launch a takeover attempt on the target.
- *Self-Tender.* A target corporation can launch a **self-tender offer** to redeem (buys its own stock) as a defensive measure against a takeover. Because a self-tender offer saddles the target corporation with increased debt and liabilities, it often becomes less attractive to a hostile bidder.
- *Pac-Man®.* In the Pac-Man defense, the target corporation becomes the acquiring corporation and attempts to purchase the hostile bidder before the bidder can acquire the target. This defensive strategy is possible only when the target corporation has adequate capital or access to financing to purchase the hostile bidder itself.
- *Selling a crown jewel.* Through this process, a core asset (known as a "**crown jewel**") is sold to the third-party white knight. When the hostile takeover attempt is thwarted, the core asset is repurchased at a premium from the white knight. Since the most valuable asset of the target corporation has been sold to the white knight, the hostile bidder withdraws its offer because the target corporation is less attractive.
- *White knight.* The target corporation's board may seek a competing bid from a friendly third party (that is, a **white knight**) who the board considers to be a better acquirer than the hostile bidder. A successful white knight defense will include a higher tender offer than the hostile bidder's and a third party that aligns with the target corporation's goals and is open to retaining the management of the target corporation.
- *Lock-up option.* With this defense, a target corporation gives the white knight a **lock-up option** to acquire the crown jewel if the hostile bidder gains a certain percentage ownership in the company. As with a poison pill, the lock-up option becomes exercisable by the white knight upon a triggering event (sometimes, the hostile bidder will acquire 15 to 20 percent of the target corporation's stock).
- *Poison pill.* Also known as a *shareholder rights plan*, a **poison pill** is a defensive strategy built into the target corporation's articles of incorporation, corporate bylaws, or contracts and leases. A common poison pill provides all shareholders other than the hostile bidder the right to purchase additional shares in either the target corporation or the acquiring corporation at a significant discount upon a triggering event. The right to purchase additional stock is often triggered when the hostile bidder buys stock over a certain percentage (usually as much as 15 to 20 percent of the target corporation's stock). A poison pill is an effective defensive measure because it dilutes the target corporation's stock, making the acquisition even more expensive to complete.

Concept Summary
Defending Against Hostile Takeovers

Defensive Device	Description
Greenmail	The target corporation pays the hostile bidder a premium to regain control of the company.
Self-Tender	The target corporation redeems (buys back) its own stock from shareholders at a higher price than the hostile bidder's offer.
Pac-Man	The target corporation purchases shares issued by the hostile bidder before being acquired itself.
Selling a Crown Jewel	The target corporation sells its most valuable asset to become less attractive to the hostile bidder.
White Knight	The target corporation solicits a friendly third party to submit a higher bid to its shareholders.
Lock-Up Option	The target corporation gives the white knight the right to acquire the crown jewel if the hostile bidder acquires a certain percentage ownership in the target company.
Poison Pill	The target corporation gives shareholders other than the hostile bidder the right to purchase additional company stock at a discounted price.

DEFENSIVE MEASURES AND THE BUSINESS JUDGMENT RULE. It is important to consider the legality of the defensive strategies utilized by a target corporation's board of directors when protecting the corporation from a takeover attempt. As mentioned in the last chapter, the board members of a corporation owe a fiduciary duty to the corporation and its shareholders. This duty is tested when a tender offer is made to the shareholders.

Defensive measures are examined under the *business judgment rule*, which protects the decisions of a board of directors acting on an informed basis, in good faith, and in the honest belief that the action taken was in the best interests of the corporation and its shareholders. In the context of a takeover, the defensive measures chosen by the target board must be reasonable and proportional in relation to the threat posed. The following case discusses poison pills as they relate to a takeover of the bookstore chain Barnes & Noble®.

CASE 24.3

TAKEOVER DEFENSES MUST BE REASONABLE AND PROPORTIONAL TO A LEGITIMATE THREAT

YUCAIPA AMERICAN ALLIANCE FUND II, L.P. v. RIGGIO

1 A.3d 310 (2010), *aff'd*, 15 A.3d 218 (Del. 2011)

Court of Chancery of Delaware

Billionaire investor Ronald Burkle told Leonard Riggio, the founder of Barnes & Noble, that Burkle's investment funds, Yucaipa American Alliance Fund I and II, were going to invest in Barnes & Noble, a publicly held company in which Riggio was a large investor. Burkle sought to change the company's governance, cause the company to enter into a technical partnership with a company such as Hewlett-Packard to revamp the company's product offerings, and acquire its primary competitor Borders Group, Inc.

Riggio and Burkle had invested together before. However, because that prior business endeavor had not gone well for Riggio, he preferred not to have other large holders in Barnes & Noble. Burkle still invested in Barnes & Noble.

Through Yucaipa, Burkle rapidly accumulated shares in Barnes & Noble and over a four-day period reached nearly 18 percent ownership. In response, the Barnes & Noble board of directors adopted a poison pill defense. This defense constituted the adoption of a plan by the board whereby no one outside of Riggio could purchase more than 20 percent of the outstanding stock and preventing the formation of a group of two or more large shareholders from joining together to take control of the company. Burkle objected to the poison pill and demanded that Yucaipa be permitted to buy up to 37 percent of the outstanding stock, but the board rejected such positions. Yucaipa then brought this action against the Barnes & Noble directors, claiming that the adoption of the pill was a breach of the directors' fiduciary duties.

Language of the Court. *Adoption of a defensive measure will be protected by the business judgment rule so long as: (1) the board that adopts the measure in question had "reasonable grounds for believing that a danger to corporate policy and effectiveness existed" and (2) the "defensive response was reasonable in relation to the threat posed." Thus, this court has recognized that directors must "show that their actions were reasonable in relation to their legitimate objective, and did not preclude the stockholders from exercising their right to vote or coerce them into voting a particular way." Even if a defense is not preclusive, the court must strike down the defense if the directors fail to persuade the court that defense was within the "range of reasonableness."*

There was a legitimate threat when the Barnes & Noble board was faced with a threat of a proxy contest by Burkle and also when there were threats of Burkle trying to influence Barnes & Noble's business strategy, including by the possible proposal of an M&A transaction.

As for whether or not the Rights Plan is a reasonable response to an ongoing threat, the key issue is whether the Rights Plan unreasonably inhibits the ability of Yucaipa to run an effective proxy contest. The Rights Plan is not an unreasonable device that fundamentally restricts Yucaipa from winning a proxy contest. To the contrary, the record shows that if Yucaipa makes a good merits case, it is likely to win.

By preventing the formation of a control bloc, the Rights Plan created an incentive for Yucaipa to make a value-maximizing proposal to all stockholders if it wished to gain control for itself with the board's assent, while leaving Yucaipa with the ability to run a successful proxy contest to obtain board representation if it did not choose to make an offer. Notably, Yucaipa is left the chance to gain influence by electing three directors at the next meeting, and three more at the following meeting. It just must do so by convincing other stockholders on the merits to vote for its slate, and without entering into mutual agreements about joint governance that raise the spectre of a de facto control bloc.

The Rights Plan is not an unreasonable device that "fundamentally restricts" Yucaipa from winning a proxy contest. The evidence presented shows that the board focused reasonably on the key problem of preclusion, and operated under and in conformity with the assumption that Yucaipa could not be foreclosed from running a successful proxy contest.

Decision. The adoption and use of the poison pill was a good faith, reasonable response to a threat to Barnes & Noble and its stockholders. The breach of fiduciary duty claims were dismissed.

Focus on Ethics

If the effect of adopting a poison pill harms the corporation, can the shareholders sue, claiming a violation of the director's duty of care? Why or why not?

Landmark Case *Unocal v. Mesa Petroleum*

Unocal was a landmark decision in corporate law that established a standard of review for a target corporation's board decisions in a hostile takeover situation. Under the *Unocal* standard, adoption of a defensive measure will be protected by the business judgment rule so long as (1) the board that adopts the measure in question had "reasonable grounds for believing that a danger to corporate policy and effectiveness existed"; and (2) the defensive response was "reasonable in relation to the threat posed." In the words of the court:

> When a board addresses a pending takeover bid it has an obligation to determine whether the offer is in the best interests of the corporation and its shareholders. In that respect a board's duty is no different from any other responsibility it shoulders, and its decisions should be no less entitled to the respect they otherwise would be accorded in the realm of business judgment. There are, however, certain caveats to a proper exercise of this function. Because of the omnipresent specter that a board may be acting primarily in its own interests, rather than those of the corporation and its shareholders, there is an enhanced duty which calls for judicial examination at the threshold before the protections of the business judgment rule may be conferred.

Unocal Corp. v. Mesa Petroleum Co., 493 A.2d 946 (Del. 1985)

Break-up Fees

Break-up fee Liquidated damages payment by the target corporation (seller) to the acquiring corporation (buyer) if the target withdraws from a transaction.

Related to a no-shop clause in a letter of intent is the break-up fee. A **break-up fee** or termination fee is a liquidated damages clause set forth in the acquisition agreement. It is a sum of money to be paid by the target (the seller) to the acquirer (buyer) because the intended transaction did not occur. It can be triggered because federal or state regulators oppose the transaction and will not give required approvals. Sometimes, this termination is the result of information learned during the due diligence period. At other times, it may be paid because the withdrawing party learns of a better opportunity it wishes to pursue. The sum is usually substantial because it is intended to compensate a party for the costs and time incurred in negotiation and due diligence related to the pending transaction and to incentivize the other party to close the transaction.

Reverse break-up fee Liquidated damages payment paid to the target (seller) corporation if the acquiring corporation (buyer) withdraws from a transaction.

A **reverse break-up fee** requires a sum to be paid to the target corporation by the acquirer if the acquiring corporation withdraws from the transaction. In this case, it is intended also to dissuade third parties from making competing offers. The most common reasons are that financing could not be secured or governmental approvals were not received.

> **Example:** During the pendency of Microsoft's® acquisition of LinkedIn®, Salesforce®, a competitor to Microsoft, made an unsolicited bid to acquire LinkedIn. The parties agreed to a no-shop provision with a break-up fee of $725 million if LinkedIn solicited a third-party buyer. Microsoft was forced to raise its bid since LinkedIn did not solicit the bid but received the offer from a third party. If LinkedIn had solicited and accepted the offer from Salesforce, LinkedIn would have been required to pay Microsoft $725 million as a break-up fee.

Required Approvals for Mergers and Acquisitions

In addition to federal law, mergers and acquisitions will need to comply with the requirements of the state laws applicable to the transaction. Most states follow the

Revised Model Business Corporation Act (RMBCA), which sets forth the following basic requirements:

1. Each corporation's board of directors must approve the merger or acquisition;
2. The plan must specify the terms and conditions of the transaction;
3. A majority of each corporation's shareholders must approve the plan;
4. After the plan is approved by the directors and shareholders of both corporations, the surviving corporation must file the merger or acquisition plan with the appropriate state official; and
5. The state must then issue a certificate of merger to the surviving corporation or newly formed corporation (that is, in the event of a consolidation).

Compliance with Government Regulations

FEDERAL SECURITIES LAWS. While mergers and acquisitions between small businesses usually do not raise federal securities law issues, federal securities laws must be considered when the parties involved are publicly traded on a stock exchange. As discussed in greater detail in the next chapter, a company involved in a merger will be required to comply with the following reporting obligations:

- 10-Q and 10-K reports, which are quarterly and annual reports;
- Registration statements if the buyer plans to issue new securities;
- Proxy information, if the proposed transaction requires shareholder approval for either the buyer or the seller; and
- SEC Schedule 13D, when the buyer of a publicly held company elects to make a tender offer.

To review the forms mentioned, visit the SEC website at https://www.sec.gov/forms.

ENVIRONMENTAL LAWS. Depending on the industry in which the parties involved do business, there may be disclosure requirements. For example, if the parties deal with hazardous substances, federal laws such as the Emergency Planning and Community Right-to-Know-Act (EPCRA) require companies to provide information about the presence of extremely hazardous substances to facilitate emergency planning.

FEDERAL ANTITRUST LAWS. Federal antitrust laws, which are discussed in Chapter 35, are primarily aimed at ensuring that there is healthy competition in the marketplace so that customers are protected. When firms dominating an industry decide to merge, there may be antitrust issues.

> **Example:** AT&T® and T-Mobile® wanted to merge in a stock and cash transaction valued at $39 billion. However, U.S. regulators decided that the transaction was against the public interest, arguing that by eliminating a major competitor in the mobile phone market, subscription fees and phone bills were likely to rise. Existing competitors — AT&T, Verizon Wireless, and Sprint — would have less incentive to improve their services. A few years later, when requested to approve the T-Mobile and Sprint merger valued at $26.5 billion, regulators at the Justice Department and the Federal Communications Commission approved the acquisition. The rationale was that the resulting organization, T-Mobile, would possess the resources to pursue the development and rollout of 5G wireless systems

LABOR AND EMPLOYMENT LAWS. A buyer and its legal counsel must address various federal and state labor and employment laws as part of the due diligence process. After a merger or acquisition transaction is completed, retirement plans and pensions of existing employees may be affected. The buyer should review the retirement plans and their summary plan descriptions. This review allows the buyer to include specific and detailed provisions with respect to the handling of employee benefits in the purchase agreement.

Special Purpose Acquisition Company (SPAC)

Special Purpose Acquisition Company (SPAC) A publicly traded investment company formed by experienced investors that will arrange for the acquisition of operating companies.

To review a S-1 Registration Statement, see https://www.sec.gov/forms.

A **special purpose acquisition company**, or SPAC, does not operate a business but is formed solely to raise capital through an initial public offering (IPO) to acquire an existing company. SPACs are also referred to as "blank check companies."

The process starts with forming a corporation by a group of initial stockholders. This corporation is formed by a small group of sophisticated investors with experience or knowledge in a particular industry who will initially hold 100 percent of the common equity of the SPAC. They seek to purchase companies within that targeted industry, and they will also, at least in part, serve as the management of the SPAC during the period the SPAC is searching for prospective target operating companies. A SPAC will file a registration statement on Form S-1 (a "Registration Statement") under the Securities Act of 1933, as amended (the "Securities Act"), to register the IPO of its securities.

To raise the capital needed, these investment companies list their shares in the stock market. Investors in SPACs range from individual investors to private equity funds. Investment banks will identify merger and acquisition opportunities or help the SPAC sponsors obtain access to their investor relationships.

In order to reduce the disclosures required under federal securities law, the investors are not aware of what company will be purchased. At an early point in the process, the SPAC will seek the assistance of underwriters and institutional investors, which will be required for the IPO. The monies raised as a result of the IPO must be placed in a trust account and expended only for the purchase of the target company. The acquisition must be completed within two years or the SPAC must be liquidated and the monies sitting in trust must be returned to the investors. Once the acquisition occurs, the SPAC is listed on a securities exchange. Non-institutional investors (that is, individuals) have access to this type of opportunity, but they do not have any knowledge of the target company that the SPAC managers are pursuing. The investors are speculating on an investment whose details are not known to them until the transaction is completed.

Example: Stock in Richard Branson's Virgin Galactic® was purchased by a venture capitalist's SPAC. It merged with the SPAC and is now trading under its new name and ticker symbol, SPCE.

AI Feature: Why Corporate Mergers Fail

Using an internet search engine, identify the common reasons why corporate mergers and acquisitions (M&A) fail to reach their potential. What impact does culture have upon the planning and implementation of a merger or acquisition upon each side to the transaction? Think of two publicly traded companies that would make suitable merger or acquisition candidates. Based upon your internet research, what action plan would you execute to minimize the past M&A mistakes of others? Then, use an AI program to prepare a memorandum identifying the advantages of the merger or acquisition you propose. Include the initiatives you would undertake to increase the chances for success of your proposed transaction.

Key Terms

- Appraisal right, 594
- Asset purchase, 599
- Break-up fee, 610
- Consolidation, 593
- Crown jewel, 606
- Due diligence, 590
- Greenmail, 606
- Hostile takeover, 605
- Letter of intent, 588
- Lock-up option, 606
- Merger, 592
- Poison pill, 606
- Reverse break-up fee, 610
- Self-tender offer, 606
- Share exchange, 593
- Short-form merger, 594
- Special Purpose Acquisition Company (SPAC), 612
- Stock purchase, 598
- Successor liability, 602
- Surviving corporation, 592
- Takeover, 604
- Target corporation, 592
- Tender offer, 605
- White knight, 606

Applying the Law

24.1 Research the Law. Using an internet search engine, research the acquisition by Snapfish, LLC®, a personalized photo printing service, of CafePress®, a retailer of customizable merchandise and personalized gifts. What benefits would the companies enjoy following a merger? Identify the approvals required to complete the transaction.

24.2 Research the Law. Using an internet search engine, identify two pending mergers and acquisitions in the news. Discuss the types of mergers being considered and if the target corporations are considering any defensive measures. Alternatively, you may wish to review why certain transactions were conducted by Special Purpose Acquisition Companies (SPACs).

24.3 Research the Law. Under Delaware law, the duty of the board of directors changes from preservation of the corporate entity to maximization of the company's value at a sale for the shareholders' benefit when the sale of the company is inevitable. What is the rationale for placing enhanced scrutiny on the directors beyond the business judgment rule? See *Revlon, Inc. v. MacAndrews & Forbes Holdings, Inc.*, 506 A.2d 173 (Del. 1986)

24.4 Letter of Intent. Johnson & Johnson® claimed that Guidant Corporation® breached a no-shop provision of its merger agreement between the two parties. J&J had also entered into a licensing agreement with Abbott Laboratories to grant Abbott a non-exclusive license to certain patents of Guidant after the merger. Boston Scientific Corporation ("BSC") made a competing bid for Guidant, regarded as superior by the Guidant board, which terminated the J&J agreement. The merger agreement between J&J and Guidant prohibited Guidant from soliciting acquisition proposals but allowed Guidant to consider unsolicited superior proposals and to provide information to the parties making unsolicited inquiries. J&J claimed that Guidant violated this no-shop provision because it provided Abbott due diligence materials without first receiving an unsolicited inquiry from Abbott. J&J did not terminate the agreement based on the alleged breach of contract and it received, pursuant to its merger agreement with Guidant, a termination fee after BSC acquired Guidant. J&J claimed it was entitled to further damages because Guidant breached. Should J&J be entitled to further damages? *Johnson & Johnson v. Guidant Corp.*, 525 F. Supp. 2d 336 (S.D.N.Y. 2007)

24.5 Short-Form Mergers. Unocal Corporation® was an earth resources company primarily engaged in the exploration for and production of crude oil and gas. Unocal owned approximately 96 percent of the stock of Unocal Exploration Corporation (UXC), an oil and gas company based in the Gulf of Mexico. In 1991, the boards of Unocal and UXC began considering a possible merger between the two companies. The UXC special committee, consisting of three directors who were also Unocal directors, consulted with financial and legal advisors and met four times before approving a merger exchange ratio of .54 shares of Unocal stock for each share of UXC. After the merger was announced, UXC's minority shareholders filed a class action asserting that Unocal and its directors breached their fiduciary duties of entire fairness and full disclosure. What type of merger is involved in this instance? How does that affect the remedies available to the minority shareholders? *Glassman v. Unocal Exploration Corp.*, 777 A.2d 242 (Del. 2001)

24.6 Asset Purchases. Christo Dritsas filed a suit against Hobart Corporation® alleging that he was exposed to asbestos while cleaning Vulcan-brand ovens, grills, and broilers while working as a short-order cook and chef. The kitchen equipment he claimed to have worked with was manufactured by Vulcan-Hart Corporation before 1986. In 1986, Hobart acquired certain assets from Vulcan-Hart. How should the court rule if Hobart moves for summary judgment on the basis that Hobart is not responsible for the liabilities of Vulcan-Hart? *Dritsas v. Amchem Products, Inc.*, 169 A.D.3d 526 (N.Y. App. Div. 2019)

24.7 Appraisal Actions. P3 Biglari Holdings was a company that franchises and operates two restaurant chains. P4 The Lion Fund and Lion Fund II were private limited partnerships that owned substantial holdings in Biglari Holdings. Biglari Holdings used company funds to purchase additional shares of the Lion Funds. The Lion Funds then used the funds to purchase additional shares of Biglari Holdings. These actions allowed S. Biglari, the sole owner of the general partner of the Lion Funds, to gain control over 54.7 percent of the voting stock of Biglari Holdings. The state's dissenters' rights statute allowed a shareholder to dissent from certain corporate actions, including a merger, and obtain payment for the fair value of their shares. Was this a fair result? Why couldn't the dissenters block Biglari's transaction and retain their shares? *Hipps v. Biglari Holdings, Inc.*, 136 N.E.3d 629 (Ind. 2019)

24.8 Poison Pill. John McGlade, president and CEO of Air Products & Chemicals, Inc.® (Air Products), privately approached Peter McCausland, founder and CEO of Airgas, Inc.® (Airgas), about a potential acquisition or combination. After being denied, Air Products went hostile, launching a public tender offer for all outstanding Airgas shares. Air Products offered its "best and final" offer of $70 per share, although the Airgas board remained adamant that Airgas was worth at least $78 per share. The Airgas board blocked the bid with a poison pill defense, which would be triggered if any party acquired 15 percent of the Airgas stock. Is the Airgas board liable for adopting a poison pill defense and preventing Airgas stockholders from deciding for themselves if they want to accept Air Products' tender offer? *Air Products and Chemicals, Inc. v. Airgas, Inc.*, 16 A.3d 48 (Del. Ch. 2011)

24.9 Poison Pill. Richardson-Vicks Inc.®, the makers of Vicks Vaporub, was resisting a takeover attempt by a newly formed subsidiary of Unilever® owners of, among others, Lever Bros., a household products company. Unilever proposed acquiring all Richardson-Vicks shares at $54 per share. That offer was refused. Unilever, which owned 100,000 shares of Richardson-Vicks stock sued under the Williams Act and made a tender offer for all outstanding shares of Richardson-Vicks common stock, at a cash price of $56 per share if the Richardson-Vicks board of directors approved the offer and $48 if it did not. The target corporate board adopted a poison pill whereby it involved the distribution of preferred stock with disproportionate voting rights, which made it impossible for Unilever to acquire the company. Should this practice be permitted? If not, why? *Unilever Acquisition Corp. v. Richardson-Vicks, Inc.*, 618 F. Supp. 407 (S.D.N.Y. 1985)

24.10 Investment Banker Opinions. When arguing that a hostile tender offer is financially inadequate, target boards often rely solely upon the opinions of their investment bankers. Why might fairness opinions provided by the target management's own bankers be unreliable? Should the reports of investment bankers be enough to protect the board from liability in exercising their business judgment regarding the adequacy of a tender offer bid?

Securities Laws and Investor Protection

25

Money is a terrible master but an excellent servant—P. T. Barnum, American Businessman and Politician (1810-1891)

Chapter Outline

- Introduction
- The Securities and Exchange Commission
- What Is a "Security"?

Case 25.1: *SEC v. Edwards*

- The Securities Act of 1933
  - *Management Application: Registration Statements (Form S-1)*
- The Securities Act of 1934
  - *Management Application: Form 8-K*

Case 25.2: *Kuebler v. Vectren Corp.*

- *Management Application: Tender Offers versus Proxy Solicitations*

Case 25.3: *Lorenzo v. Securities and Exchange Commission*

- State Securities Laws
- Protecting Investors Through Corporate Governance
- AI Feature: Form 8-K

Learning Objectives

After reading this chapter, you should be able to:

1. Define when an investment is a security.
2. Distinguish between the two major statutes regulating publicly traded securities.
3. Discuss the common exemptions from registration.
4. Explain insider trading and why it is unlawful.
5. State how investors are protected by corporate governance.

Introduction

After the 1929 market crash, Congress's concern about the new-issue securities market led to the enactment of the Securities Act of 1933 (1933 Act) and the Securities Exchange Act of 1934 (1934 Act), as well as the creation of the Securities and Exchange Commission (SEC) to provide for federal regulation of the country's securities exchanges.

The 1933 and 1934 Acts serve as the foundation of federal securities laws. Congress has reacted to financial scandals with the enactment of the Sarbanes-Oxley Act of 2002 and the Dodd-Frank Wall Street Reform and Consumer Protection Act. However, the regulatory landscape is not yet complete. The federal government continues to implement policies and issue administrative rules to best protect investors by instilling confidence in the integrity of the U.S. financial markets.

This chapter explores the major federal securities laws affecting publicly held companies. Securities laws are also addressed in Chapter 42, which deals with accountants' liabilities and those provisions of the securities laws that apply to the accounting and auditing profession.

The Securities and Exchange Commission

Securities and Exchange Commission (SEC) A federal, independent regulatory agency that administers and enforces federal securities laws. *SEC: https://www.sec.gov.*

The **Securities and Exchange Commission (SEC)** is an independent regulatory agency tasked with administering the provisions of the 1933 and 1934 Acts. Generally, the 1933 Act regulates the initial sales of stock to the public and the 1934 Act governs the subsequent stock trading along with the securities exchanges, brokers, and dealers. The SEC was created as part of the 1934 Act and delegates the authority to enforce federal securities laws.

As a federal administrative agency (administrative agencies are discussed in Chapter 34) with both quasi-legislative and quasi-judicial authority, the SEC can issue rules and regulations. With its delegated powers, it may conduct investigations; issue subpoenas for producing witnesses, books, and records; and hold administrative hearings regarding securities law issues.

What Is a "Security"?

Security A broadly defined term encompassing a breadth of investments, including stocks and bonds.

A **security** is broadly defined by the federal securities laws. Federal securities laws define securities to include, but not be limited to, the following:

1. *Instruments commonly known as securities.*

   Example: Common and preferred stocks, treasury stocks, bonds, debentures, certificates of deposit, stock options, and stock warrants.

2. *Any fractional undivided interest in oil, gas, or other mineral rights.*
3. *Privileges on security. These include any put, call, straddle, option, or privilege on any security.*

4. *Investment contracts.* Under the *Howey* test articulated by the United States Supreme Court in *SEC v. W.J. Howey Co.*, 328 U.S. 293 (1946), a contract, transaction, or scheme is an investment contract, and therefore a security, if there is:

    a. An investment of money;
    b. In a common enterprise;
    c. With the reasonable expectation of profits; and
    d. Derived primarily from the managerial efforts of others.

Example: A member in a member management LLC does not have a security under an investment contract because the member's efforts will create profit. A member in a manager-managed LLC, however, would have a security under an investment contract because that member would obtain profits through the managers' efforts.

Courts will apply the *Howey* test to determine whether what was sold is a "security." In the following case, the Court considered whether an investment scheme promising a fixed rate of return was a security subject to federal securities laws.

CASE 25.1

AN INVESTMENT SCHEME PROMISING A FIXED RATE OF RETURN CAN BE AN "INVESTMENT CONTRACT" AND A SECURITY SUBJECT TO THE FEDERAL SECURITIES LAWS

SEC v. EDWARDS

540 U.S. 389 (2004)

Supreme Court of the United States

Charles Edwards was the chairman, CEO, and sole shareholder of ETS Payphones, Inc. (ETS). ETS sold payphones to the public through independent distributors. The payphones were offered in a package with a site lease, a five-year leaseback and management agreement, and a buyback agreement. Under the leaseback and management agreement, purchasers received $82 per month, a 14 percent fixed annual return. Purchasers were not involved in the day-to-day operation of the payphones they owned. Under the buyback agreement, ETS promised to refund the full purchase price of the package at the end of the lease or within 180 days of a purchaser's request.

Unfortunately, the payphones did not generate enough revenue for ETS to make the payments required under the leaseback agreements, so the company applied funds received from new investors to pay its obligations. In September 2000, ETS filed for bankruptcy protection. The SEC then brought a lawsuit alleging ETS had violated the registration requirements of the 1933 Act. ETS argued that the payphone sale-and-leaseback arrangement was not an investment contract subject to federal securities laws.

The federal district court held that the payphone sale-and-leaseback arrangement was an investment contract within the meaning of the federal securities laws. The Court of Appeals reversed, holding it was not an investment contract for two reasons: (1) legal precedent required that an investment contract offer either capital appreciation or a participation in the earnings of the enterprise, and would exclude schemes offering a fixed rate of return from the definition of a security; and (2) legal precedent also required that the return on the investment be derived solely from the efforts of others and in this case, that requirement was not satisfied when the purchasers had a contractual entitlement to the return. The SEC appealed to the Supreme Court.

Language of the Court. *Congress's purpose in enacting the securities laws was to regulate investments, in whatever form they are made and by whatever name they are called. To that end, it enacted a broad definition of "security" sufficient to encompass virtually any instrument that might be sold as an investment. The 1933 and 1934 Acts define "security" to include "any note, stock, treasury stock, security future, bond debenture,* investment contract, *or any instrument commonly known as a "security." "Investment contract" is not itself defined.*

The test for whether a particular scheme is an investment contract requires us to look to whether the scheme involves an investment of money in a common enterprise with profits to come solely from the efforts of others. This definition embodies a flexible rather than a static principle, one that is capable of adaptation to meet the countless and variable schemes devised by those who seek the use of money of others on the promise of profits.

When Congress included "investment contract" in the definition of security, it was using a term the meaning of which had been crystallized by the state courts' interpretation of their "blue sky" laws. The state courts had defined an investment contract as "a contract or scheme for the placing of capital or laying out of money in a way intended to secure income or profit from its employment" and had uniformly applied that definition to a variety of situations where individuals were led to invest money in a common enterprise with the expectation that they would earn a profit solely through the efforts of the promoter or a third party. Thus, when we held that "profits" must "come solely from the efforts of others," we were speaking of the profits that investors seek on their investment, not the profits of the scheme in which they invest. We used "profits" in the sense of income or return, to include, for example, dividends, other periodic payments, or the increased value of the investment.

There is no reason to distinguish between promises of fixed returns and promises of variable returns for purposes of the test. In both cases, the investing public is attracted by representations of investment income, as purchasers were in this case by ETS' invitation to "watch the profits add up." A promise of a fixed return does not preclude a scheme from being an investment contract.

Decision. The Supreme Court reversed the Court of Appeals and held an investment scheme promising a fixed rate of return can be an investment contract and a security under the federal securities laws.

Focus on Ethics

In light of improved investor access to company information through technology, do you think the concept of fairness should continue to be relevant in interpreting securities laws? What was Congress's purpose in enacting the securities laws?

The definition of a security is constantly expanding to encompass more legal instruments as individuals seek to craft them in a manner that avoids the tax liabilities that accompany buying and selling securities. Using the *Howey* test, a general partnership interest is not treated as a security because general partners have equal rights to manage and control the business. Therefore, the final prong of the *Howey* test is not met. However, demonstrating the expansive definition of a security, the United States Court of Appeals for the Ninth Circuit, the court held that "dressing an investment contract in the trappings of a general partnership interest does not immunize that interest from the federal securities laws." If the general partnership interests are "stripped of the hallmarks of a general partnership and marketed as passive investments," they qualify as securities. *SEC v. Schooler*, 905 F.3d 1107 (9th Cir. 2018)

The Securities Act of 1933

Securities Act of 1933
Federal law mandating the disclosure of important financial information to enable investors to make informed decisions about whether to purchase a company's securities.

Elements of the 1933 Act

The 1933 Act has four characteristics:

1. Registration of securities and mandatory disclosures filed with the SEC;
2. SEC review of those filings, at the end of which the sale of securities may begin;
3. Mandatory delivery of a prospectus to every prospective investor; and
4. Civil liabilities for false or misleading statements or omissions.

Registration
The act of filing the appropriate documentation with the SEC for any offer or sale of securities to the public unless a specific exemption applies.

Registration Under the 1933 Act

Registration is required by the 1933 Act for any offer or sale of securities to the public unless a specific exemption from registration applies. The **issuer** of securities, which is the individual or the business that is offering the securities for sale to the public, must prepare and file a registration statement. The form for registering securities with the SEC is Form S-1. The registration statement is filed electronically using the EDGAR system.

Issuer
An individual or business offering the securities for sale to the public.

A **registration statement** is a complete disclosure to the SEC of all material information that relates to the securities being issued. Generally, the registration statement requires the following:

Registration statement
A complete disclosure to the SEC and potential investors of all material information that relates to the securities being issued.

1. A description of the issuer's business, property, and competitors;
2. A description of the significant provisions of the security that is to be offered for sale, its relationship to the other securities of the issuer, the distribution plan, and how the proceeds will be used;

3. A description of how much of the securities are owned by insiders (directors and officers) and any transactions with these insiders; and
4. A list of risk factors and any significant legal proceedings.

In addition, a registration statement must contain the following financial information and disclosures:

1. The issuer's most recent audited financial statements;
2. Management's discussion and analysis (known as MD&A), where the company's management addresses the company's performance with qualitative and quantitative measures, discuss compliance, risks, and future plans); and
3. Any changes regarding the issuer's independent public accountant within the last two fiscal years.

Once this information has been provided, a majority of the issuer's directors, the CEO, the CFO, and the chief accounting officer must execute the registration statement. After their signatures are obtained and the registration statement is filed, the statement becomes effective on the twentieth day after filing unless the SEC requires additional information to be disclosed (the waiting period). If the registration statement is amended, a new 20-day waiting period begins. The SEC does not review the accuracy of any information provided in the registration statement, but instead verifies that that appropriate information and disclosures were provided by the issuer. During this waiting period, the securities can be offered for sale but cannot be legally sold. The prospectus (discussed below) can also be distributed to prospective purchasers. After the waiting period the securities can be sold to the public.

An exception to the waiting period arises for well-known seasoned issuers who can skip the registration waiting period and file a registration statement the day they announce a new offering. A **well-known seasoned issuer (WKSI)** is a firm that has issued at least $1 billion in securities in the last three years or has outstanding stock valued of at least $700 million or more in the hands of the public.

Well-known seasoned issuer (WKSI)
A firm that meets certain thresholds and can file a registration statement with the SEC the day they announce a new offering.

Example: The Goldman Sachs Group, Inc.®, Morgan Stanley®, and J.P. Morgan Chase & Co.® are a few examples of firms that have met the well-known seasoned issuer qualifications.

A **prospectus** must also be filed by the corporation after the registration statement has been filed. The prospectus contains similar information to the registration statement, but the prospectus is used as a selling tool by the issuer. The purpose of the prospectus is to supply sufficient facts that will assist an interested investor in making an informed decision about their potential investment. The prospectus also protects the issuer from any claims that it did not disclose enough information or risks about the security offered.

Prospectus
A legal document providing investors with information and assessment of risk factors relating to the offering of a security for sale.

Example: An example of a company that recently went public is The Honest Company, Inc.® with the ticker symbol HNST. The Honest Company was founded by actress Jessica Alba after she suffered a severe allergic reaction to laundry detergent when she was pregnant with her first child. The company is dedicated to developing clean, sustainable, effective products.

Between the final registration statement and the filing of the prospectus, the underwriters (investment banks who assist the issuer in selling the securities to the public) begin their sales efforts. Company executives and investment bankers make presentations to prospective investors. This is known as a "road show." The investment bank can solicit offers for the sale of the securities but may not sell the securities during this period.

All securities transactions, even those exempt from registration, are subject to the antifraud provisions of the federal securities law. Those responsible for the filing along with the corporation will be responsible for false or misleading statements relative to the securities offered, or the offering itself. The government enforces the federal securities laws through criminal, civil, and administrative proceedings. Private parties can also take actions under certain securities laws.

An issuer who sells a security and fails to meet the registration statement or prospectus requirements and does not have an exemption (exempt security or exempt transaction), sells an unregistered security. Section 12(a)(1) of the 1933 Act imposes liability on anyone who sells a security that is neither registered nor exempt from registration. The purchaser may demand rescission, the return of their investment, and interest in exchange for the stock. If the purchaser no longer owns the security, the purchaser may sue for damages.

Management Application
Registration Statements (Form S-1)

Visit the SEC's EDGAR (Electronic Data Gathering, Analysis, and Retrieval) database via the internet and search for Company Filings. Use the search tool to find the registration statements (labeled S-1) for Lyft, Inc.® and Uber Technologies, Inc.® In the table of contents for each document, select the section titled "Risk Factors." Compare the risk factors for both companies and be prepared to discuss the similarities and differences with the class.

See, https://www.sec.gov/edgar/search/.

Registration Exemptions Under the 1933 Act

Under the federal securities laws, any offer or sale of a security must either be registered with the SEC or meet an exemption. There are registration exemptions that apply to specific securities and exemptions that apply to specific transactions.

EXEMPT SECURITIES. Certain securities are exempt from the SEC registration requirements. These securities are thought to not pose the same risk as the securities requiring registration. Exempt securities include, but are not limited to, the following:

- Government-issued securities (such as municipal bonds).
- Securities issued by nonprofit issues such as universities and charitable and religious institutions.
- Securities of financial institutions (such as banks).

- Generally, most secondary trading (that is, retail trading through brokerages) is exempt. Also exempt are stock dividends, stock splits, and securities issued in a corporate reorganization in which one security is exchanged for another security.

EXEMPT TRANSACTIONS. In addition to certain securities being exempt from the registration requirements, certain types of transactions are exempt from the registration requirements. Exempt transactions include: (1) intrastate offering exemptions, (2) Regulation A transactions, (3) Regulation D transactions, and (4) Jumpstart Our Business Startups (JOBS) Act transactions. These exemptions and their requirements are discussed below.

Intrastate Offering Exemptions. The 1933 Act exempts from registration intrastate offers and sales if certain requirements are met. The exemption originates from an assumption that local investors are more sufficiently aware of conditions within the state to understand the risks associated with such an investment. There is no limit on the amount of capital raised or the number of offers or sales. To determine if the intrastate offering exemption is available, the SEC adopted Rule 147 and Rule 147A.

Rule 147. Under Rule 147, if the following requirements are met, no registration is required under the 1933 Act:

- The issue of securities is made in the same state where the issuer is incorporated;
- The principal place of the issuer's business is in-state. The issuer shall be deemed to have its principal place of business in the state in which the officers, partners, or managers of the issuer primarily direct, control, and coordinate the activities of the issuer;
- The issuer is "doing business" in the state. Doing business is met where the issuer meets one of the following tests:
  - At least 80 percent of the net proceeds from the sale of securities are to be used in-state;
  - At least 80 percent of the issuer's assets are located in-state;
  - At least 80 percent of the issuer's gross revenues are derived from in-state activities; or
  - A majority of the issuer's employees are based within the state.
- All offers and sales are limited to in-state residents or persons who the issuer reasonably believes are in-state residents. This restriction limits the solicitation and advertising of the issue prohibiting internet advertising;
- The securities cannot be resold to nonresidents until six months after the initial sale; and
- The issuer takes precautionary measures to comply with resale restrictions (including legends, stop transfer instructions, and disclosure to purchasers).

Rule 147A. In addition to Rule 147, the SEC adopted a new intrastate offering exemption, Rule 147A, to modernize Rule 147 for current business practices and communication methods. The new Rule 147A is less restrictive and differs from Rule 147 by allowing issuers to make offers accessible to out-of-state residents (internet advertising). It also allows the issuer to be incorporated in a state different from its principal place of business. While out-of-state residents can see the offers, the issuer can only sell securities to in-state residents. Aside from these two caveats, the provisions in Rule 147 and Rule 147A are substantively the same, including the six-month resale restriction and precautionary measures.

> **Example:** A corporation incorporated in Delaware but operating and with a principal place of business in Texas can offer the sale of securities over the internet. The securities must be sold to Texas residents and the corporation must meet at least one of the "doing business" requirements noted in Rule 147.

Concept Summary Intrastate Offering Exemptions from Registration

Requirement	Rule 147	Rule 147A
Issuer Residency	■ Incorporated in-state and principal place of business in state	■ Principal place of business in state
Doing Business	■ 80% of revenues, assets, or net proceeds, or majority of employees are within the state	■ Same as Rule 147
Type of Investor	■ Principal residence or issuer's reasonable belief	■ Same as Rule 147
Resales	■ Six months after sale	■ Same as Rule 147
Precautions	■ Legend on certificates ■ Stop transfer instructions ■ Written representation from purchaser ■ Disclose legend to offerees/purchasers	
Internet Advertising	■ No	■ Yes

Regulation A Exemption. Regulation A allows for issuers to publicly offer up to either $20 million (Tier 1) or $75 million (Tier 2) of securities in any 12-month period without full registration. An issuer conducting a Tier 2 offering under Regulation A has additional requirements, such as limiting the amount of money a non-accredited investor may invest to ten percent (10%) of the non-accredited investor's annual income or net worth. An **accredited investor** includes most institutional investors and individuals with a certain income level or net worth threshold. Other than the offering amount limitations, there is no restriction on the amount of securities an accredited investor may invest in a Tier 1 or Tier 2 offering.

Accredited investor A natural person with a net worth exceeding $1 million (excluding principal residence) and with annual income of $200,000 for two years for single individuals or $300,000 for two years for joint filers.

Issuers must file an offering circular on Form 1-A with the SEC, subject to SEC review and comment. An offering circular requires fewer disclosures than a registration statement and therefore is less costly. Securities sold in reliance on Regulation A can be freely resold.

For the requirements of Form 1-A, visit https://www.sec.gov/files/form1-a.pdf.

Regulation D Exemptions. Regulation D has three exemptions: (1) Rule 504, (2) Rule 506(b), and (3) Rule 506(c).

Rule 504 Exemption. The small offering exemption under Rule 504 allows issuers to sell up to *$10 million* of securities during a 12-month period to *any number or* accredited and non-accredited investors without having to register and without having to provide specific financial information. Rule 504 is not available for investment companies such as mutual funds. The issuer may not use general solicitation or advertising to market the securities. The securities purchased in a Rule 504 offering cannot be resold for either six months or a year without registration.

Rule 506(b) Private Placement Exemption. Rule 506(b) provides a *safe harbor* for a private placement of securities. In a Rule 506(b) offering, an unlimited number of securities may be purchased by an *unlimited number* of accredited investors and *up to 35* non-accredited investors, so long as these purchasers or their representatives are experienced and sophisticated investors. However, an issuer relying on Rule 506(b) is not allowed to generally advertise or solicit investor interest in the offering and must provide certain disclosures to non-accredited investors.

Concept Summary Regulation D Exemptions from Registration

Requirement	Rule 504	Rule 506
Maximum Offering Amount	■ $10 million	■ Unlimited
Maximum Number of Investors	■ Unlimited	■ 506(b) □ 35 non-accredited □ Unlimited accredited ■ 506(c) □ Unlimited accredited
Manner of Offering	■ No general advertising/ solicitation	■ 506(b): No general advertising/ solicitation ■ 506(c): General advertising and solicitation permitted if all investors are accredited, and issuer takes reasonable steps to verify
Disclosure Obligation	■ None	■ Disclosure to non-accredited investors (should be given to accredited investors as well)

Rule 506(c) Exemption. Under Rule 506(c), an issuer can broadly solicit and advertise the offering so long as the investors are all accredited investors, and the issuer takes reasonable steps to verify their accredited status. The issuer can issue an unlimited number of securities to these investors.

Jumpstart Our Business Startups (JOBS) Act. The Jumpstart Our Business Startups (JOBS) Act was signed into law to encourage the funding of small businesses in the United States. The JOBS Act sought to improve small business funding by relaxing securities regulations, allowing companies to use crowdfunding to issue securities using the rule entitled Regulation CF. The hope was that the Act would make it easier for companies to not only go public, but also raise private capital, thereby allowing companies to remain private for a longer period.

JOBS Act A federal law passed to encourage funding of U.S. small businesses by easing compliance with securities regulation requirements.

Regulation CF is the set of rules and forms that enables eligible companies to offer and sell securities through crowdfunding. It requires all transactions to take place online through an SEC-registered intermediary, either a broker-dealer or a funding portal. Through Regulation CF, companies may sell up to $5 million worth of shares in a 12-month period to any person. Individual investors have purchase limitations. If an investor has an annual income or net worth greater than or equal to $107,000, then the investor can invest 10 percent of the greater annual income or net worth, not to exceed $107,000. If an investor has an annual income or net worth of less than $107,000, then the investor can invest the greater of (1) $2,200 or (2) 5 percent of the greater of either annual income or net worth. There is no limit to the number of non-accredited investors allowed to purchase the company's shares.

Civil Liability Under the 1933 Act

An issuer may be subject to civil liability under the 1933 Act if it does not comply with the Act's registration statement requirements.

SECTION 11. Section 11 of the 1933 Act imposes civil liability on issuers for material misstatements or omissions of fact on registration statements. The issuer and persons who assisted in preparing the registration statement (such as attorneys and accountants) can be held liable for their intentional and negligent misstatements or omissions. If these elements are established, the purchaser of the securities can recover monetary damages measured by the amount of the purchaser's loss.

Everyone but the issuer can assert a due diligence defense. These persons can avoid liability if they can show they had reasonable grounds to believe, and did believe, the statements contained in the registration statement were true and there was no omission of a material fact.

SECTION 12. Section 12 of the 1933 Act imposes civil liability against any person who violates the provisions of selling an unregistered security. This can arise when:

1. No registration statement was in effect when the plaintiff purchased a security;
2. A registered security was sold, but without delivery of a final prospectus or without a current prospectus; or
3. An offer to sell securities was made *prior to* a required registration.

Criminal Liability Under the 1933 Act

The civil liability mentioned in the previous section gives the public a private remedy to sue. Criminal sanctions can also be imposed upon those who willfully violate any of the provisions or rules and regulations of the 1933 Act. If convicted, a wrongdoer can face monetary fines and up to five years in prison.

The Securities Act of 1934

Securities Exchange Act of 1934
Federal law governing the secondary trading of securities in the United States.

While the 1933 Act regulates the initial offering of securities by requiring a registration statement to be filed with the SEC prior to a sale or offer to sell, the **1934 Act** primarily governs dealings in securities *after* their initial offering. The 1934 Act provides for the registration of certain companies with the SEC, the annual and quarterly reporting to the SEC, along with the regulation and registration of securities exchanges, brokers, and dealers.

Registration Requirement Under the 1934 Act

The registration and reporting requirements under the 1934 Act are in addition to those under the 1933 Act and are not meant to be a substitute for them. The following companies, known as Section 12 companies, are required to register under the 1934 Act:

For the requirements of Form 10-K, see, https://www.sec.gov/files/form10-k.pdf.

1. Companies that list securities on a national securities exchange; and
2. Companies that have at least 500 shareholders of equity securities and total gross assets greater than $10 million.

Proxy solicitation
A request that a corporate shareholder authorize another person to cast the shareholder's vote at a corporate meeting.

PERIODIC REPORTING UNDER THE 1934 ACT. After registration, an issuer must periodically file reports with the SEC. Each form has a specific purpose and required content. Forms used for periodic reporting include Forms 10-K (annual reports), 10-Q (quarterly reports), and 8-K (reports filed within four business days upon the happening of a material event).

Tender offer
A public, open offer or invitation by a prospective acquirer to all shareholders of a publicly held corporation to sell their shares at a specified price during a specified time.

Information is the currency of democracy.—Thomas Jefferson, Third President of the United States (1743-1826)

Regulation of Proxy Statements

SECTION 14. When shareholders of a corporation vote on matters, they can usually do so by attending a shareholders' meeting or by proxy. As discussed in Chapter 23, a proxy is a power of attorney given by a shareholder to another that authorizes that person to exercise the shareholder's voting rights.

Under Section 14(a) of the 1934 Act, **proxy solicitation** is unlawful if it contains a false or misleading statement of a material fact or an omission of a material fact. If there is a shareholder who reasonably relies on such a statement or omission, the proxy solicitor is subject to liability.

Under Section 14(e), it is illegal for any person to make a material misstatement or omit a material fact with respect to a tender offer. A **tender offer** is a public, open offer or invitation by a prospective acquirer to the shareholders of another corporation to tender their shares for a specified price.

Determining whether something is a "material misstatement" is a question of fact and requires an intensive analysis by the court. The central issue is not if the particular statements, taken separately, are true. Rather, a court will determine whether the representations, taken as a whole and in context, would have misled a reasonable investor. The following case deals with this analysis.

CASE 25.2

A STATEMENT IS FALSE OR MISLEADING IF THE REPRESENTATION WOULD HAVE MISLED A REASONABLE INVESTOR

KUEBLER v. VECTREN CORP.

13 F.4th 631 (2021)

United States Court of Appeals for the Seventh Circuit

Vectren Corporation, an Indiana public utility and energy company, merged with CenterPoint Energy, Inc., a public utility holding company. In 2017, Vectren explored the possibility of a merger. Then in 2018, Vectren retained Merrill Lynch, a financial advisor. Merrill Lynch was instructed by Vectren's board to tell potential buyers that the board's preference was that a substantial portion of the transactions have consideration paid in cash.

Vectren narrowed down to four contenders: CenterPoint and three others, referred to as Bidders A, B, and D. All four submitted non-binding proposals. CenterPoint proposed an all-cash transaction at $70.00 per share. Bidder A proposed a price of $72.50 per share with up to 83 percent in cash. Bidder B proposed an all-cash price range of $73.00 to $75.00. Bidder D proposed a price range of $65.00 to $70.00 paid in an unspecified combination of cash and stock.

In early April, CenterPoint and Bidder A submitted new offers. The Vectren board told management to continue negotiating with both Bidder A and CenterPoint and to tell them that the board was not ready to move forward at less than $72.00 per share, strongly preferring an all-cash or substantially all-cash deal.

On April 16, CenterPoint and Bidder A submitted their final offers. Two days after, Merrill Lynch told CenterPoint that Vectren wanted to move forward if CenterPoint was willing to negotiate on the final price per share and on other terms. The Vectren board pushed for an offer of at least $72.00 per share. CenterPoint said it was prepared to offer that price, and a meeting was then held. Following the meeting, Merrill Lynch reviewed the financial aspects of the transaction, providing its opinion that the $72.00 per share price was fair. The Vectren board unanimously adopted the merger agreement, and Vectren and CenterPoint executed the agreement.

On June 18, Vectren filed its preliminary proxy statement, leading six shareholders to sue Vectren and the board, alleging that the statement was misleading by omitting key information. All seven suits alleged violations of Section 14(a) of the Securities Exchange Act. The District Court held that the omitted Business Segment Projections and Unlevered Cash Flow Projections was immaterial in light of the overall information disclosed.

Language of the court. *Plaintiffs briefly address the Business Segment Projections, arguing that they were material because they were a key input in Merrill Lynch's discounted cash flow analysis. This argument misses the point. We assume that Merrill Lynch used the Business Segment Projections in its discounted cash flow analysis, but that fact does not automatically render them material for purposes of Section 14(a). Two indisputable facts make the point. First, CenterPoint was offering to acquire Vectren as a whole enterprise, not in individual business segments. Second, plaintiffs owned shares in Vectren as a whole enterprise also, not individual business segments. The proposed merger did not give shareholders the option of selling separate interests in separate business lines. Plaintiffs thus failed to allege a substantial likelihood that a reasonable shareholder would have viewed the Business Segment Projections as significantly altering the total mix of available information material to whether to vote for or against the proposed merger.*

The goal is to strike the proper balance between "not enough" information and an "avalanche" of information.

This is the fundamental defect in plaintiffs' allegations of materiality. The materiality standard requires courts to assess the value of the omitted information in light of all the information made available to shareholders. Plaintiffs were therefore required to identify circumstances under which disclosure of the Unlevered Cash Flow Projections would plausibly have affected their votes for or against the merger, which would have required that those omitted numbers, if disclosed, would have shown that their Vectren shares were undervalued in the merger. Plaintiffs have not done so.

As a final note on materiality, we emphasize that shareholders are not entitled to the disclosure of every financial input used by a financial advisor so that they may double-check every aspect of both the advisor's math and its judgment.

Decision. The appellate court affirmed the District Court's decision, which found that the plaintiffs did not argue plausibly the materiality of the omitted projections.

Focus on Ethics

Based on the language of the court, "The goal is to strike the proper balance between "not enough" information and an "avalanche" of information." Do you think finding this balance takes on a subjective approach in court? Based on the language of the court, should the "subjective" nature of valuation serve as a defense to a claim that the company violated federal securities laws? Why or why not? Does the concept of what is "fair" or "ethical" have a place in these evaluations, or should they be based principally on quantitative analyses?

Management Application
Tender Offers versus Proxy Solicitations

The last chapter discussed the role of tender offers in M&A transactions. Aside from tender offers, proxy solicitations are another option for a buyer seeking to gain control of a target company. There are several merits for either method; however, timing is a concern for the buyer.

Tender offers have the advantage of shorter timing. Tender offers may close within 20 business days from the date of commencement. Further, there is no requirement to file with the SEC tender offer documents prior to the commencement of the tender offer. That is, it is possible for the buyer to have control of the target at the conclusion of the tender offer.

Proxy solicitations require review by the SEC. This review requires proxy materials to be submitted, and the review may take up to 10 to 30 days. After the review, the proxy materials are then sent to shareholders. Depending on the applicable state law and the target company's bylaws, the shareholder's meeting may not occur until several days after the proxy materials are distributed to shareholders. At a minimum, shareholders must have 20 days after receiving the proxy materials to review the materials and submit their proxy. That is, a buyer may gain control of the target company 45 to 60 days after the proxy materials are submitted to the SEC.

Statutory Insider Reporting and Short-Swing Profits

SECTION 16. Under Section 16(a), statutory insiders are required to file reports with the SEC. Section 16(a) defines a **statutory insider** as a director, officer, or any person who beneficially owns more than 10 percent of the stock of a corporation that is either publicly held or registered with the SEC. These insiders must report the following:

Statutory insider
A director, officer, or any person who beneficially owns more than 10 percent of the stock of a corporation that is publicly held or registered with the SEC.

1. An initial statement of ownership within ten days of becoming a director, officer, or beneficial owner;
2. A statement within two business days of the statutory insider engaging in a transaction involving the company's equity securities; and
3. An annual statement within 45 days after the company's fiscal year has ended.

Failure to meet these reporting deadlines will subject the statutory insiders to administrative and criminal action.

Under Section 16(b), statutory insiders may also be sued by the company or shareholders for short-swing profits. A **short-swing profit** results from the purchase and sale (or sale and purchase) of the issuer's stock by an insider within a six-month period. The profit is calculated by taking the difference between the highest sales price and the lowest purchase price during the period. Insiders who have short-swing profits are held strictly liable and must disgorge such profits back to the issuer.

Short-swing profit
A profit resulting from the purchase and sale (or sale and purchase) of the issuer's stock by a statutory insider within a six-month period. Under Section 16(b), the profits are recoverable by the corporation.

Example: The president of a company sells 10,000 shares of stock for $50 a share on June 1st of a year. If the president had purchased 10,000 shares of stock on February 1st of the same year for $35 a share, the president is liable for $150,000 of short-swing profits (10,000 shares × ($50 – $35)).

Example: The president of a company owns 10,000 shares of stock. On February 1st, the president sold 10,000 shares for $50 a share. Thereafter, on June 1st, the president purchases 10,000 shares of stock for $35 a share. The president is liable for short-swing profits and must pay the company $150,000 (10,000 shares × ($50 – $35)). In this case, the president avoided a loss of $150,000 by not keeping the shares.

SECTION 18. Under Section 18(a), a person or a corporation can be held civilly liable for any SEC filing containing a materially false or misleading statement or omission. Damages are typically measured by the difference between the price paid or received for the security and the value it would have had if the materially false or misleading statement had not been made.

Section 10(b) and Rule 10b-5

Section 10(b) of the 1934 Act
Provision of the 1934 Act prohibiting manipulative and deceptive practices in connection with the purchase or sale of a security.

Rule 10b-5 of the 1934 Act
A regulation enacted by the SEC targeting securities fraud through the use of the mail, interstate commerce, or a national securities exchange.

SECTION 10(b) AND SEC RULE 10b-5. One of the most important sections of the 1934 Act is Section 10(b). This section prohibits fraud (manipulative and deceptive devises) in connection with the purchase and sale of any form of a security, whether registered or not. Therefore, securities sold over stock exchanges, in the over-the-counter market, and even private party transactions are covered by this act.

The SEC adopted Rule 10b-5 to implement that part of the Act. Under the anti-fraud provision of Rule 10b-5, it is unlawful for a party to use the mail, interstate commerce, or a national securities exchange to defraud any person in connection with the purchase or sale of a security. The SEC can sue for violation of this provision. Private parties may also sue, because the Supreme Court has implied a private cause of action for its violation. Rule 10b-5 prohibits the following in connection with the sale (or purchase) of a security:

1. Employing any device or scheme with the intent to defraud;
2. Making any untrue statement of a material fact or omitting a material fact that would be necessary to make a statement not misleading; or
3. Engaging in any act or business practice that would deceive or defraud an investor.

Any person who violates this rule can be sued for damages, whether or not that person actively participated in the purchase or sale of the security, thus extending liability to accountants, lawyers, underwriters, and executives. The elements necessary to show a violation of this act are as follows:

Scienter
Having the intent to deceive or defraud another.

- *Scienter.* The plaintiff must prove that the misrepresentation or omission of material fact occurred through either intentional or reckless conduct by the defendant. Negligent acts or omissions are insufficient to show scienter is material if there is a substantial likelihood that a reasonable investor would consider it important to an investment decision.

Example: Material information could include: a proposed asset or stock purchase of the corporation; significant changes to the company's financial condition; earnings per share reports prior to public dissemination; dividend changes; significant intellectual property creations or claims made by third parties.

- *Reliance or fraud on the market.* A successful plaintiff must prove they justifiably relied on the *misstatements of material fact* and, as a result, suffered damages. Alternately, fraud can occur through *omission of a material fact*, when the plaintiff does not have to prove reliance, because it is assumed to have occurred.
  If the defendant made a fraudulent statement or omitted material information in public pronouncements, *every* investor could sue if it could be shown that the statement affected the market. This is known as the "fraud on the market" theory, adopted by the Supreme Court in *Basic, Inc.* It presumes the plaintiff's reliance upon the deceit is only available when the security is publicly held.
- *Purchase or sale of a security.* Rule 10b-5 covers both buyers and sellers. The information must relate to one of these actions. This action gives the plaintiff standing to sue. Someone who has not invested in the security may not sue under this rule.
- *Damages.* Purchasers or sellers of securities must show economic losses were suffered.
- *Causation.* The economic loss must have been caused by the misstatement of a material fact.

Example: A football coach overheard a man tell his wife about a company's plans to liquidate a major subsidiary. The coach recognized the man as the company's chairman. The coach bought stock in the subsidiary on the basis of this material non-public information. In this case, the coach did not violate Rule 10b-5. While the coach possessed material non-public information, the information was overheard in a public place. The act of the chairman was negligent and did not meet the elements of scienter. *SEC v. Switzer*, 590 F. Supp. 756 (W.D. Okla. 1984)

In the following case the Supreme Court addressed whether the dissemination of false or misleading statements with intent to defraud falls within the scope of SEC Rule 10b-5.

CASE 25.3

A PERSON OR ENTITY DISSEMINATING FALSE OR MISLEADING STATEMENTS WITH INTENT TO DEFRAUD VIOLATES RULE 10B-5

LORENZO v. SEC

587 U.S. 71 (2019)

Supreme Court of the United States

Francis Lorenzo was the director of investment banking at Charles Vista, LLC, an SEC-registered brokerage firm in New York. As director, Lorenzo sent two emails to prospective investors. The content of the emails was provided by Lorenzo's boss and discussed a potential investment in a company with "confirmed assets" of $10 million. In reality, Lorenzo knew that the company had recently disclosed that its total assets were valued at less than $400,000.

In 2015, the SEC found that Lorenzo had violated Rule 10b-5 and Section 10(b) of the Exchange Act by sending false and misleading statements to investors with intent to defraud. As a sanction, the Commission fined Lorenzo $15,000, ordered him to cease and desist from violating the securities laws, and barred him from working in the securities industry for life.

On appeal, the District of Columbia Circuit decided Lorenzo could not be held liable as a "maker" under subsection (b) of the rule. The United States Supreme Court granted *certiorari* to determine whether someone who is not a "maker" of a misstatement can nevertheless be found to have violated the other subsections of Rule 10b-5, when the only conduct involved concerns a misstatement.

Language of the Court. *In* Janus Capital Group, Inc. v. First Derivative Traders, *we examined Rule 10b-5(b), which forbids the making of any untrue statement of a material fact. We held that the maker of a statement is the person or entity with ultimate authority over the statement, including its content and whether and how to communicate it. We said that without control, a person or entity can merely suggest what to say, not "make" a statement in its own right. And we illustrated our holding with an analogy: "When a speechwriter drafts a speech, the content is entirely within the control of the person who delivers it. And it is the speaker who takes credit—or blame—for what is ultimately said." On the facts of* Janus, *this meant that an investment adviser who had merely participated in the drafting of a false statement made by another could not be held liable in a private action under subsection (b) of Rule 10b-5.*

After examining the relevant language, precedent, and purpose, we conclude that dissemination of false or misleading statements with intent to defraud can fall within the scope of subsections (a) and (c) of Rule 10b-5, as well as the relevant statutory provisions. In our view, that is so even if the disseminator did not "make" the statements and consequently falls outside subsection (b) of the Rule.

We see nothing borderline about this case, where the relevant conduct consists of disseminating false or misleading information to prospective investors with the intent to defraud. And while one can readily imagine other actors tangentially involved in dissemination—say, a mailroom clerk—for whom liability would typically be inappropriate, the petitioner in this case sent false statements directly to investors, invited them to follow up with questions, and did so in his capacity as vice president of an investment banking company.

As for Lorenzo's suggestion that those like him ought to be held secondarily liable, this offer will, far too often, prove illusory. In instances where a "maker" of a false statement does not violate subsection (b) of the Rule (perhaps because he lacked the necessary intent), a disseminator of those statements, even one knowingly engaged in an egregious fraud, could not be held to have violated the "aiding and abetting" statute. That is because the statute insists that there be a primary violator to whom the secondary violator provided "substantial assistance." And the latter can be "deemed to be in violation" of the provision only "to the same extent as the person to whom such assistance is provided." In other words, if Acme Corp. could not be held liable under subsection (b) for a statement it made, then a knowing disseminator of those statements could not be held liable for aiding and abetting Acme under subsection (b). And if, as Lorenzo claims, the disseminator has not primarily violated other parts of Rule 10b-5, then such a fraud, whatever its intent or consequences, might escape liability altogether.

That is not what Congress intended. Rather, Congress intended to root out all manner of fraud in the securities industry. And it gave to the Commission the tools to accomplish that job.

Decision. The Supreme Court affirmed the decision of the Court of Appeals that Lorenzo was liable for disseminating false or misleading statements with intent to defraud under Rule 10b-5. By sending emails he understood to contain material untruths, he employed a device, scheme, and artifice to defraud within the meaning of SEC Rule 10b-5.

Focus on Ethics

Should Lorenzo have been held primarily liable under Rule 10b-5 for disseminating the emails, even though he did not "make" the false statements? He did so at the direction of his boss, who supplied the content and "approved" the messages. Is this fair? Explain.

Insider Trading. An important goal of Rule 10b-5 is to prevent insider trading. **Insider trading** involves the purchase or sale of securities by insiders. **Insiders** are individuals who have access to material, non-public information. As insiders can possess material non-public information, it is unfair and unethical to allow them to take advantage and trade in securities using this knowledge over the public and other shareholders.

An insider under Rule 10b-5 is much more broadly defined than a statutory insider under Section 16(b). An insider under Rule 10b-5 includes anyone who has access to or receives non-public information. The broad coverage of insiders includes officers, directors, consultants, agents, lawyers, auditors, bankers, and all employees at all levels of the company (full time and part time). Insiders also include anyone who owes a fiduciary duty to the company. An insider will be held liable if they use the inside information for an improper purpose.

> **Example:** Armaan is an attorney for Big Corporation. Armaan has been brought into recent meetings to address a significant products liability issue that the corporation must handle. The impact of the litigation will reduce Big Corporation's earnings for the next year or two. Armaan is an insider who possesses material, non-public information.

Insider trading
The purchase or sale of securities by individuals who have access to material, non-public information that provides an unfair advantage to those traders.

Insider
Anyone who has access to or receives material non-public information about a company due to their position or relationship with the company.

Tipper-Tippee Liability. In addition to insiders, SEC Rule 10b-5 has been extended to cover transactions involving outsiders. Outsiders are persons who receive material, non-public information from an insider. The insider who provides the material, non-public information is a **tipper**. Tippers are liable if they breached a fiduciary duty to the corporation whose shares are involved in the trading by tipping material, non-public information. To be liable, a tipper must be shown to:

Tipper
A person who gives non-public information to someone else to trade on.

1. Owed and breached a fiduciary duty to the corporation whose shares are involved in the trading; and
2. Had the requisite intent to deceive, manipulate, or defraud; and personally benefitted from the tip.

Example: Maher Kara was a former investment banker at Citigroup®. Maher shared inside information about Citigroup with Michael Kara, who traded on the information and who also happened to be Maher's brother. Maher was liable as a tipper because by disclosing confidential information as a gift to his brother, he breached his duty of trust and confidence to Citigroup and its clients. *Salman v. United States*, 580 U.S. 39 (2016).

Tippee
A person who receives non-public information and trades on that information.

A **tippee** is a person who receives material non-public information from a tipper and trades on the information. Tippers are liable for the profits made by the tippee. A tippee will be liable for acting on the material, non-public information if they know or should have known that the information was not public.

Misappropriation Theory Liability. Tipper-tippee liability arises when a tipper breached a fiduciary duty to the corporation whose shares were involved. The misappropriation theory expanded liability to outsider's misappropriation of information. Under the **misappropriation theory**, outsiders can be held liable for trading in a security on the basis of material non-public information that is obtained by a breach of duty of trust or confidence *owed to the person who is the source* of the information. The misappropriation theory often arises from nonbusiness relationships, such as friendships.

Misappr-opriation theory
An SEC rule that imposes liability on outsiders who trade on material, non-public information that was gained by a breach of a duty of trust or confidence owed to the person who is the source of the information.

Example: Scott Rocklage was the CEO of a publicly traded biotechnology company. After learning that one of the company's key drugs had failed its clinical trial, Mr. Rocklage phoned his wife and conveyed the results to her. She was told to keep the results confidential, and the couple had a of sharing non-public information about the company without trading on the information. Unbeknownst to Scott Rocklage, his wife had a preexisting understanding with her brother, that she would inform him with "a wink and a nod" if she learned significant negative news about the company. On the first possible trading day after he was tipped off, her brother sold all his shares of stock in the company. Mrs. Rocklage was held liable under the misappropriation theory. *SEC v. Rocklage*, 470 F.3d 1 (1st Cir. 2006)

The Supreme Court's decision in *SEC v, Jarkesy*[1], created a significant development in securities law enforcement. The court held that under the Seventh Amendment, the SEC must bring civil-penalty actions for securities fraud in federal

1. 603 U.S. ___ (2024).

court, where the defendant is entitled to a jury, and cannot do so in an in-house administrative hearing. Despite this right to litigate in federal court, it is expected that those subject to SEC investigations will continue to settle in the SEC's administrative forum because it is perceived that the sanctions will be less than those issued by a federal court.

Civil Liability under 10(b) and 10b-5. Violations of Section 10(b) of the Securities Exchange Act of 1934 and SEC Rule 10b-5 can result in the SEC bringing a civil action against individuals or entities that have engaged in fraudulent activities involving the purchase or sale of securities. This includes trading while in possession of material non-public information. Penalties for such violations can include:

- Rescission of the Securities Contract.
- Disgorgement of Profits: The violator may be required to return any profits gained from the illegal activities.
- Civil Penalties: The court may access civil penalties up to three times the amount of the profits gained or losses avoided.
- Other Damages: The court can impose additional damages to compensate the affected investors for their losses.

Criminal Liability Under the 1934 Act

SECTION 32. While Section 18(a) imposes *civil* liability for materially false or misleading statements or omissions in any SEC filing, Section 32(a) imposes *criminal* liability when a party willfully and knowingly makes a materially false and misleading statement in a document filed with the SEC. In some cases, reckless disregard for the truth or falsity of a statement can be enough to constitute a willful violation.

If found to be in violation of the 1934 Act, an individual can be penalized with a fine of up to $5 million, 20 years in prison, or both. If the violator is not a natural person, such as a corporation, the maximum fine for a violation is $25 million.

Review the fines that have been recently collected by the SEC's Division of Enforcement at https://www.sec.gov/newsroom/press-releases.

State Securities Laws

Similar to the federal securities laws, every state has its own securities laws regulating the offer and sale of securities within the state. These state securities laws are known as "blue sky laws." These laws apply primarily to intrastate transactions (that is, those that occur solely within the state).

Blue sky laws
State laws and regulations intended to protect securities investors from fraud.

State Regulators of Securities Laws

States have their own regulators that can enforce the provisions of the state securities laws. These regulators can conduct investigations, issue subpoenas, bring administrative proceedings, impose penalties, sue for injunctive or declaratory relief, and make referrals to the state attorney general for criminal prosecution. In some cases, a violation can lead to simultaneous enforcement by the SEC.

Federal and State Securities Laws

Companies must comply with both federal and state securities laws. While there are situations in which the two bodies of law may be the same, sometimes they differ. When they do, companies must still comply with both laws, as an exemption under federal law is not necessarily an exemption under state law, and vice versa.

Protecting Investors Through Corporate Governance

Corporate governance The system of rules, practices, and processes by which a corporation is directed and controlled.

Securities law is only one way to protect investors. Another is through effective corporate governance. **Corporate governance** is the system of rules, practices, and processes by which a corporation is directed and controlled. It requires that corporate officers and directors balance the interests of many stakeholders—including shareholders, employees, customers, banks, the government, and the public, among others.

Sarbanes-Oxley Act and Corporate Governance

The Sarbanes-Oxley Act was passed by Congress in 2002 following a series of corporate and accounting scandals. Comprehensive in scope, part of Sarbanes-Oxley deals with corporate governance by imposing strict disclosure requirements and penalties to *publicly held* companies for violations of securities laws. For example, the Act imposes liability upon the CEO and CFO if the company's financial statements or reports contain material misrepresentations or omissions.

Sarbanes-Oxley altered the duties and responsibilities of the board of directors by setting forth the following standards of best practices:

1. Requiring the CEO and CFO to certify the company's financial statements;
2. Requiring companies to have management assessments and have in place a set of internal controls, as well as requiring management to file a report on that assessment;
3. Requiring the board to establish an independent audit committee, in which at least one member must have financial expertise and the authority to hire and fire the auditor; and
4. Prohibiting most loans to executive officers and directors.

These requirements encourage greater transparency from the corporation, intending to increase shareholder and investor confidence.

CERTIFICATION. Section 302 of Sarbanes-Oxley provides that the SEC must adopt rules requiring the CEO and CFO to certify periodic reports filed with the Commission. In certifying a report, such as a Form 10-K or Form 10-Q, the officers must represent that:

1. The report does not contain any material misstatement or omission according to their knowledge; and
2. The report fairly represents the financial condition and cash flow of the company.

INTERNAL CONTROL. Section 404 of Sarbanes-Oxley requires the company's annual report, Form 10-K, to contain an "internal control report" stating the responsibility of management for establishing and maintaining an adequate internal control structure and procedures for financial reporting.

AUDIT COMMITTEE. Under Sarbanes-Oxley, companies must establish an independent audit committee to increase the committee's general financial expertise and prevent accounting scandals. A company must include a financial expert on its audit committee or provide a reasonable explanation for the expert's absence to the SEC.

Under Section 301 of Sarbanes-Oxley, the primary function of the audit committee is to enhance the independence of the audit function and ensure objective and accurate financial reporting. As a result, the committee is directly responsible for hiring, monitoring, and firing the outside auditor.

PROHIBITION OF LOANS. Publicly held companies are prohibited from making either direct or indirect loans to any director or executive officer.

AI Feature: Form 8-K

Identify a publicly held company that has recently reported adverse news to the market. Review the company's filings by visiting the SEC's EDGAR database at *https://www.sec.gov/search-filings*. Use the search tool to find the company's most recent Form 8-K (labeled 8-K). Then, use an AI Program to compare this company with the most recent Form 8-K of a competitor. Be prepared to discuss your findings.

Key Terms

- Accredited investor, 625
- Blue sky laws, 637
- Corporate governance, 638
- Insider, 635
- Insider trading, 635
- Issuer, 621
- JOBS Act, 626
- Misappropriation theory, 636
- Prospectus, 622
- Proxy solicitation, 628

- Registration, 621
- Registration statement, 621
- Rule 10b-5 of the 1934 Act, 632
- Scienter, 632
- Section 10(b) of the 1934 Act, 632
- Securities Act of 1933, 621
- Securities Exchange Act of 1934, 628
- Securities and Exchange Commission (SEC), 618
- Security, 618
- Short-swing profit, 631
- Statutory insider, 631
- Tender offer, 628
- Tippee, 636
- Tipper, 636
- Well-known seasoned issuer (WKSI), 622

Applying the Law

25.1 Definition of a Security. Robert Dillie controlled Mid-America Foundation, which sold charitable gift annuities through financial planners, insurance agents, and others. The foundation's marketing literature assured investors that they would receive a lifetime stream of income, with the money remaining at their death directed to a charity designated by the investor. In all, the foundation raised $55 million from the sale of more than 400 charitable gift annuities. Robert Dillie used the proceeds for personal expenses, such as retiring his gambling debts. Are these annuities subject to the securities laws? Why should this opportunity be considered a security? *Warfield v. Alaniz*, 569 F.3d 1015 (9th Cir. 2009)

25.2 Form 8-Ks. Atossa develops and markets products used to detect precancerous conditions that foreshadow the development of breast cancer. On December 20, 2012, Atossa filed a Form 8-K report with the SEC that stated that "[t]he proceeds from the IPO will enable us to accelerate the national roll-out of our first FDA-cleared and marketed product, the ForeCYTE Breast Health Test for breast cancer risk assessment." In an interview, the Atossa CEO answered a question about the ForeCYTE test by saying that, "[i]t has gone through all of the FDA clearance process." In reality, the FDA had sent a warning letter to Atossa that the ForeCYTE test still required FDA approval due to a new modification. When Atossa did not receive FDA clearance and publicly announced a recall, Atossa's share price plummeted by more than 46 percent. Atossa shareholders filed a class action lawsuit alleging Section 10b violations. Was Atossa required to submit a Form 8-K with the SEC regarding the FDA warning letter? If so, what information should have been disclosed? *In re Atossa Genetics Inc. Securities Litig.*, 868 F.3d 784 (9th Cir. 2017)

25.3 Promotions. Norstra Energy, Inc. was in the business of oil drilling, exploration, and extraction. In order to promote the sale of Norstra's stock, the company hired a stock endorser by the name of Eric Dany to prepare various promotions, including a "marketing piece" and a "landing page" on the internet site to which readers would be directed. The completed promotional materials urged investors to "turn $5,000 into $60,000,000 as Norstra drills wells on its *overlooked* and *underpriced* Bakken Resource!" The materials stated that Norstra Energy could be sitting on top of as much as "8.5 billion barrels of oil" and advised that investors could obtain a return of 5,000 percent on their investment. If the SEC pursues an action against Dany for a Rule 10b-5 violation, what are Dany's best arguments in defense of his promotional statements? *SEC v. Norstra Energy Inc.*, 202 F. Supp. 3d 391 (S.D.N.Y. 2016)

25.4 Reading Between the Lines. Avaya Inc. sells communications products and services. Avaya released financial results for a financial year-end and issued a press release that stated in part: "We have entered the new year *well positioned* to translate our ongoing success in the marketplace into enhanced shareholder value." Then, in a conference call for analysts and investors, Avaya (through its president) said: "We are a stronger, more competitive organization that enjoyed significant potential to further build shareholder value." A year later, Avaya announced that it would be unable to meet its previously stated goals for growing revenues and blamed internal problems for failing to do so. Regardless, Avaya made public statements saying that the financial results "position Avaya" to meet goals for the year and that the company was "on track" to meet projections. What constitutes a misleading statement and is one present here? *Institutional Investors Group v. Avaya, Inc.*, 564 F.3d 242 (3d Cir. 2009)

25.5 Registration Requirement. Capital Cove Bancorp LLC was a real estate and investment services firm focused primarily on real estate–owned properties. Since early 2012, CCB had raised nearly $1.9 million through unregistered securities offerings of two private investment funds. The CEO directly offered securities related to the funds when he personally solicited investors by telephone and email, and no registration statement had ever been in effect for the funds. The company raised the money from at least 17 investors located in California and New Jersey, representing that it would invest the proceeds in real estate. Instead, CCB misappropriated those investments for the personal use of the CEO. What must the SEC establish to state a claim for CCB's violation of the registration requirements of the 1933 Act? Based on the facts as stated, can CCB claim any exemptions from registration? *SEC v. Capital Cove Bancorp LLC*, 2015 U.S. Dist. LEXIS 174856 (C.D. Cal. 2015)

25.6 Ponzi Scheme. John Bravata and Richard Trabulsy operated BBC Equities, LLC and Bravata Financial Group, LLC. BBC Equities and Bravata Financial solicited contributions from individuals, representing that the money contributed would be invested and specific returns would be realized. Nearly 440 individual investors transferred to BBC Equities and Bravata Financial funds, totaling $55.2 million. Neither Bravata nor Trabulsy was a registered securities broker or dealer at the time. The returns paid to earlier investors did not come from proceeds earned by the companies' investments, but rather from funds contributed by later investors (known as a pyramid or Ponzi scheme). Bravata and Trabulsy used the investors' money to purchase several personal luxury items. Discuss the potential securities law violations that Bravata and Trabulsy have committed. *USSEC v. Bravata*, 3 F. Supp. 3d 638 (E.D. Mich. 2014)

25.7 Short-Swing Profits. James Mercer sued Rajat Gupta, a former director of Goldman Sachs, pursuant to Section 16(b) of the 1934 Act, for short-swing profits. On three separate occasions, Gupta provided material, non-public information about Goldman Sachs to Raj Rajaratnam, founder of a hedge fund called Galleon Group. Rajaratnam immediately made several trades in Goldman Sachs securities on the information. Gupta had also invested in the hedge fund, and as an added benefit, also profited from Rajaratnam's trade. Is he liable under Section 16(b)? If not, is there any violation of the 1934 Act? *Mercer v. Gupta*, 880 F. Supp. 2d 486 (S.D.N.Y. 2012)

25.8 Section 10b. STTX processes flat-rolled steel to specific requirements for customers in steel-consuming industries. David Stitt was the general manager for STTX's Northeast Region. Stitt was friends with John Monroe, a Pennsylvania car sales manager, and Somers, a commodities trading advisor. In the week prior to STTX's public announcement of its acquisition by Mitsui & Co. USA Inc., Stitt made a series of phone calls, one of which was to Monroe. Following the phone call, Monroe immediately called Somers and his financial advisor, Mr. Waldron. That same day, Somers bought 2,000 shares of STTX stock. Eight days later, Somers sold his STTX stock, generating a profit of approximately $20,000. Should Stitt be considered an insider such that Somers can be held liable under the tippee insider trading theory? Why or why not? *SEC v. Carroll*, 9 F. Supp. 3d 761(W.D. Ky. 2014)

25.9 Insider Trading. Paul Gianamore was a financial analyst at Credit Suisse First Boston, an investment banking firm. As a financial analyst, he had access not only to his own analytical work but to that of other analysts in the firm as well. He was thus privy to information about tender offers and proposed mergers. While Gianamore worked at Credit Suisse, he disclosed confidential, inside information to his college friend, Ryan Evans. Evans then traded on three tender offers and one merger in which Credit Suisse was involved, using his online brokerage account to make the trades. What theories of liability for insider trading under Rule 10b-5 are appropriate for Gianamore and Evans? *United States v. Evans*, 486 F.3d 315 (7th Cir. 2007)

25.10 Research the Law. Having read this chapter, using an internet search engine, research your state's securities laws to identify which transactions are exempt from state registration. Under these exemptions, the nature of the security and the type of transaction do not require regulation. For those that you identify, can you explain the public policy for the exemptions?

PART V: COMMERCIAL LAW AND TRANSACTIONS

Formation of Sales and Lease Contracts

26

Society is indeed a contract. . . . It is a partnership in all science; a partnership in all art; a partnership in every virtue, and in all perfection. — Edmund Burke, Reflections on the Revolution in France (1790)

Chapter Outline

- Introduction
- Policies Underlying the UCC
- Article 2: Sales Contracts
- Article 2A: Lease Contracts
- Forming Sales and Lease Contracts
  - *Management Application: Example of Open Price Terms*

Case 26.1: *Tourcats, Inc. v. Transp. Custom Designs, LLC*
Case 26.2: *Olah v. Ganley Chevrolet, Inc.*

- Interpretation of Contracts Under the UCC

Case 26.3: *Starbucks Corp. v. Amcor Packaging Distribution*

- Unconscionability Under the UCC
  - *Management Application: Factors Indicating Unconscionability*
- CISG Compared to the UCC
- AI Feature: Parol Evidence

Learning Objectives

After studying this chapter, you should be able to:

1. Recognize the scope of the UCC regarding the sale of goods.
2. Discuss when Articles 2 and 2A of the UCC apply.
3. Distinguish sales contracts under the UCC from those of common law.
4. Describe the requirements of the UCC's doctrine of unconscionability.
5. Identify requirements for the international sale of goods under the CISG.

Introduction

Sales and lease contracts governed by the Uniform Commercial Code (UCC) are the subject of this chapter. The UCC is a comprehensive scheme covering subjects within the commercial law context. Among its purposes is to make commercial contracting more streamlined and efficient. While the UCC was proposed by the National Conference of Commissioners on Uniform State Laws, state legislatures can amend it when adopting it. Although there is not complete uniformity, there is general agreement as to the terminology and application of the Code as adopted throughout the United States. Our study will address the general rules proposed for adoption by the states.

In the area of commercial contracts, Article 2 of the UCC deals with the sale of goods and Article 2A deals with lease contracts. Additionally, the UCC operates in concert with the common law contract principles we studied earlier (contract requirements of agreement, consideration, capacity, legality). When the UCC applies to a transaction, the provisions of the UCC provide missing information not addressed by the parties and modifies common law contract principles to better meet the needs of business. When the UCC does not apply to a contract or where the UCC is silent, common law contract rules apply.

> **Example:** General contract law applies to contracts involving services and those relating to real estate. The UCC, on the other hand, controls contracts for the sale and lease of goods regardless of whether the transaction is a consumer transaction or a commercial one.

The applications of the UCC are reflected in the following table.

TABLE 26.1: An Overview of the Articles of the UCC

Article	Coverage
Article 1 — General Provisions	Summary — Introduces definitions and deals with the rules of interpretation Subject Matter — General provisions, definitions, principles of interpretation, territorial applicability, and general rules
Article 2 — Sales	Summary — Applies to transactional goods except those intended to operate as a security transaction Subject Matter — Form, formation, readjustment of contracts, general obligations, title, creditors' rights, good faith purchasers, performance, breach, repudiation, excuse, and remedies
Article 2A — Leases	Summary — Deals with any transaction that creates a lease, regardless of the form of the transaction Subject Matter — Form and construction of a lease contract, effect of a lease contract, performance, repudiation, substitution, excuse, and default
Article 3 — Negotiable Instruments	Summary — Applies only to negotiable instruments and not money or transactions governed under Article 4 or Article 9 Subject Matter — Negotiation, transfer, indorsement, enforcement of instruments, liability, dishonor, discharge, and payment

TABLE 26.1: Continued

Article	Coverage
Article 4 — Bank Deposits and Collections	Summary — Addresses the liability of a bank in regard to presentment, payment, or collection Subject Matter — Collection of items, depositary and collecting banks, payor banks, the relationship between payor banks and customers, and collection of documentary drafts
Article 4A — Funds Transfers	Summary — Applies to funds that are transferred to make a payment to the beneficiary of the order. Additionally, payment order is discussed Subject Matter — Issue and acceptance of a payment order, execution of sender's payment order by receiving bank, and payment
Article 5 — Letters of Credit	Summary — Addresses letters of credit and the rights and obligations of the parties involved Subject Matter — Scope, requirements, issuance, amendment, cancellation, duration, issuer's rights and obligations, fraud and forgery, warranties, remedies, and transfers
Article 6 — Bulk Sales	Summary — Applies only to bulk sales and liquidation of assets Subject Matter — Provides specific forms of protections to creditors of businesses that sell merchandise from stock
Article 7 — Documents of Title	Summary — Addresses the rights and obligations involved in the carriage and storage of goods Subject Matter — Warehouse receipts, bills of lading, general obligations, negotiations, and transfer
Article 8 — Investment Securities	Summary — Sets forth the rules for the transfer of stocks, bonds, and other securities Subject Matter — Issue, issuer, transfer of certified and uncertified securities, registration, security entitlements, and transition provisions
Article 9 — Secured Transactions	Summary — Deals with security interests in personal property as created by agreements, chattel papers, and promissory notes Subject Matter — Effectiveness of a security agreement, attachment of a security interest, rights of parties to a security agreement, perfection and priority, filing, default, and transition

Policies Underlying the UCC

The UCC is to be "liberally construed and applied to promote its underlying purposes and policies," which are "(1) to simplify, clarify, and modernize the law governing commercial transactions; (2) to permit the continued expansion of commercial practices through custom, usage, and agreement of the parties; and (3) to make uniform the law among the various jurisdictions." UCC § 1-103(a). In addition, the uniform construction of the provisions of the UCC promotes these purposes. The decisions of other states having the same uniform provisions are often held as good authority in litigation arising under a state version of the UCC.

Article 2: Sales Contracts

The UCC governs the sale and lease of goods involving a merchant. The passage of title can occur at various times and is the subject of Chapter 27.

TABLE 26.2: Comparing Sales and Other Transactions

Type of Transaction	Comparison to a Sale
Bailment	The principal test used to distinguish a bailment from a sale is whether there is a binding promise to pay for the goods by the person who has been given possession. If there is a binding promise, the transaction is considered a sale. If there is no binding promise, it is simply a bailment.
Sales Agency	When a seller enters into a contract with an agent that creates an agency relationship in which the agent has the exclusive privilege of selling a particular product, a sale may be created if the agent plans to sell the goods as its own. If the agent plans to sell the goods while still allowing the seller to remain in control over the subsequent transactions, a sales agency has been created.
Option to Buy	An option to buy simply gives the individual the right to purchase the goods within a specified amount of time. A contract, on the other hand, gives rise to an obligation to buy or sell a good.
Pledge	A pledge is a type of security device. The occurrence of a sale or a pledge is determined by whether the property was transferred in order to secure an obligation. If the transfer has occurred in order to secure an obligation, it will be considered a pledge.

What Are Goods?

Goods
Property that is both "tangible" and "movable" when identified in a contract.

Article 2 of the UCC applies to the sale of moveable goods. Goods covered are characterized as most forms of tangible (property that can be touched), movable personal property. Certain items that are not considered goods and would therefore not be governed by Article 2 include:

- Money and intangible items such as patents, stocks, and bonds
- Real estate, because even though real estate is tangible, it is not movable under the definition prescribed in UCC § 2-105(1)

Even though real estate is not considered a good for purposes of the UCC, items that are severable from real estate may be classified as goods and be governed by Article 2 if the removal of these things would not cause material harm to the real estate system. For example, a small garden shed. Items that become so attached to the realty that they lose their identity separate from the real property are known as fixtures. Fixtures are considered real property and are discussed in Chapter 39.

Example: A utility provider supplied electricity to a bankrupt debtor's business. As a result of the business owner's nonpayment, the utility provider sought the payment of an administrative expense claim in the bankruptcy proceeding for the value of the electricity. The court determined that the electricity was considered a "good" because the electricity itself is tangible and was governed by Article 2 of the UCC. *In re Escalera Resources Co.*, 563 B.R. 336 (Bankr. D. Colo. 2017)

Commerce cures destructive prejudices; it is almost a general rule that wherever manners are gentle there is commerce, and wherever there is commerce, manners are gentle. — Charles-Louis de Secondat (Montesquieu), French Judge, The Spirit of the Laws (1689-1755)

What Are Sales?

Article 2 of the UCC governs sales contracts, or contracts for the sale of goods. UCC § 2-102. These rules are supported by common business practices, and where a contract does not supply a provision to address a particular issue, Article 2's default rules will apply. A **sale** is defined as a transfer of title to goods for consideration or price. UCC § 2-106(1).

Sale
A transfer of title to goods for consideration or a price.

Some sales are **mixed sales**. A mixed sale involves the sale of both a good and a service. When this happens, we need to determine whether the UCC applies. For the UCC Article 2 to apply to a mixed sales transaction, the value of the goods must be predominant when compared to the value of the services being rendered. Courts applying the predominant factor test determine if the sale of goods is the predominant part of a mixed sale on a case-by-case basis.

Mixed sales
A sale that involves both the provision of a service and a good in the same transaction.

Example: Willie Rosenfeld hired Fallsview Glatt Kosher Caterers to cater a dinner for him and 15 guests. On the night of the event, he and his friends did not show up, nor did they call to cancel. Fallsview sued him for breach of contract. He used the Statute of Frauds under the UCC as an affirmative defense, alleging that a contract for the sale of goods of more than $500 is not enforceable unless the contract was in writing, and here there was no contract in writing. The court had to determine if this agreement for a mixed sale was predominantly for the sale of goods or for services. The court found the agreement was predominately for services rendered and, therefore, the Statute of Frauds did not apply. He was liable for paying the caterer. *Fallsview Glatt Kosher Caterers, Inc. v. Rosenfeld*, 794 N.Y.S.2d (2005)

Who Is Considered a Merchant?

The UCC applies to sale and lease transactions involving one or more merchants. It applies to sale and lease transactions where both parties are merchants as well as when only one party is a merchant. When neither party is a merchant, the UCC does not apply, and the common law applies.

Example: A consumer's purchase of a television from BestBuy® is governed by the UCC; however, if the consumer purchased a television at a garage sale, the UCC does not apply.

Under Article 2, a merchant is expansively defined as any of the following:

1. A person who "deals in goods of the kind" involved in the sales contract. A merchant is not necessarily considered a merchant for all goods it sells.

Example: A retailer, wholesaler, or a manufacturer is a merchant of those goods sold in the business. However, a jewelry store that sells a used phone is not considered a merchant for the phone but is a merchant for the jewelry it sells.

2. A person who, by occupation, "holds himself or herself out as having special knowledge and skill" related to the types of practices or goods involved in the contract.

Example: A university or banks may be considered merchants under this definition.

3. A person who "employs a merchant as a broker, agent, or other intermediary" will be classified as a merchant for that transaction.

Article 2A: Lease Contracts

Many contracts across various industries involve leases of automobiles, equipment, and machinery. Article 2A of the UCC addresses these types of personal property leases and subleases of goods. In many ways, Article 2A repeats many of the terms and principles of Article 2. It is important to remember that although this article covers leases, Article 2A does not apply to leases of real property, such as those involving land or buildings.

What Is a Lease Agreement?

Lease agreement
The bargain between a lessor and a lessee with respect to the lease of goods.

Lessor
The party who transfers their right to the possession and use of the goods to the lessee under a lease agreement.

Lessee
The party who acquires the right to the temporary possession and use of goods under a lease agreement.

A **lease agreement** is defined in Article 2A as the bargain between a lessor and a lessee with respect to the lease of goods, as found in their language and as implied by other circumstances, including course of dealing and usage of trade or course of performance. A **lessor** is the party in a lease that transfers their right to the possession and use of the goods to the **lessee**. The **lessee** is the party who acquires the right to the temporary possession and use of goods under the lease. The lessor lends property to the lessee. The lessee leases the property from the lessor.

Example: Keith Powers rented used household goods. He filed for bankruptcy and the rental company wanted to repossess the goods. He claimed the contract was one for the sale of the furniture to him. The rental company believed the contracts were lease agreements. The court agreed with the rental company, finding that the contracts were lease agreements and not installment contracts because they did not indicate Powers was under any obligation to make installment payments that would ultimately allow him to exercise the option to own the goods. *In re Powers*, 983 F.2d 88 (7th Cir. 1993)

Forming Sales and Lease Contracts

Recall our discussion of offer and acceptance in Chapter 9. Article 2 and Article 2A also have their provisions regarding the offer and acceptance of sales and lease contracts. The UCC modifies the common law rules we covered in Chapter 9.

Offer

Unlike the common law of contracts, which requires offers to be definite enough for the parties to make out what the essential terms are, the UCC does not require such definiteness. Rather, under UCC §§ 2-204(3) and 2A-204(3), a valid offer exists even if one or more terms are left open if *both* of the following are true:

1. There was an intent by the parties to make a contract; and
2. The courts have a reasonably certain basis upon which they could grant an appropriate remedy.

Additionally, the UCC is tolerant of open terms, or terms that have yet to be determined by the parties. Evidence may be used to prove missing terms, or a court can just presume that the parties intended whatever is reasonable under the circumstances. Even though the UCC is tolerant of open terms, a court is unlikely to find the existence of any contract if too many terms are left open. Nonetheless, there are certain open terms that are permitted to be "read into" sales or lease contracts. This rule is known as the **gap-filling rule**; a few examples of terms that are commonly used as gap-fillers are discussed below.

Gap-filling rule
A legal practice in which a default term is inserted when a gap has been left in a contract.

OPEN PRICE TERM. A "reasonable price" will be implied at the time of delivery if a sales contract does not contain a specific price. However, if one of the parties to the contract does set a price before delivery and, therefore, there is no open price term, the price that is set must be made in good faith pursuant to the UCC.

Management Application Example of Open Price Terms

The parties hereby agree that they intend to enter into a binding contract even in the event the parties fail to agree on a price for the goods set forth above. Further, the parties agree that in the event they fail to agree on a price, the price will be a reasonable price at the time of delivery based upon the current fair market value of the goods in question.

OPEN PAYMENT TERM. If the parties to a sales contract do not agree or specify payment terms, payment will be due at the time and place at which the buyer receives the goods. UCC § 2-310(a).

OPEN DELIVERY TERM. If the parties do not agree on the time, place, and manner of delivery of the goods, the seller's place of business will be the place for delivery. If the seller does not have a place of business, the seller's residence will be the place of delivery.

OPEN DURATION TERM. Sometimes, a single contract may specify multiple, successive performances by one of the parties but fails to specify how long the parties are required to perform. In this situation, either party may terminate the ongoing relationship, but before this is done, reasonable notice to the other party must be given.

The *quantity* of goods involved in a contract cannot be read into a contract. If the quantity term is left open, a sales or lease contract will likely fail for indefiniteness because under the requirements of UCC §§ 2-204(3) and 2A-204(3), a court would have no reasonably certain basis to grant an appropriate remedy. Nevertheless, the UCC does permit two exceptions for open quantity terms. They are requirements contracts and output contracts.

Requirements contract
A contract in which the buyer agrees to purchase, and the seller agrees to sell, all or up to a stated amount of what the buyer needs or requires. Buyer also agrees to purchase exclusively from the seller.

In a **requirements contract**, the buyer agrees to purchase, and the seller agrees to sell all or up to a stated amount of what the buyer *needs* or *requires*. Additionally, the buyer agrees to purchase the goods exclusively from the supplier. Requirements contracts are normally enforceable.

> **Example:** A rubber company claimed a carbon manufacturer breached their requirements contract when the carbon manufacturer missed sending a scheduled shipment to the rubber company. The carbon manufacturer argued the contract was not a requirements contract but was simply a contract to sell a specific quantity of material. The court found the agreement was a requirements contract because it required the carbon manufacturer to supply all the material the rubber company needed and prohibited the rubber company from purchasing the material from anyone else. *BCR Rubber & Plastics, Inc. v. Continental Carbon Co.*, 876 F. Supp. 2d 1042 (N.D. Ind. 2012)

Output contract
A contract in which the seller agrees to sell, and the buyer agrees to buy, all or up to a stated amount of what the seller produces.

In an **output contract**, the seller agrees to sell, and the buyer agrees to purchase all or up to a stated amount of what the seller *produces*. Both requirement and output contracts are subject to a good faith limitation under the UCC. As a result, the amount purchased or sold under the contract must be comparable to previous requirements or output. The court will not uphold the agreement if the actual quantity is unreasonably disproportionate to previous requirements or output. UCC § 2-306(1).

> **Example:** Milk producers brought an action against a creamery alleging that the creamery had wrongfully refused to accept milk supplied under an output contract between the parties. The milk producers attempted to sell the milk on the market but were unable to find another buyer. The creamery argued that it had not entered into an output contract. The court ruled that the agreement was in fact an output contract as the milk producers had agreed to sell and the creamery had agreed to purchase "all the milk" that would be produced during the school term. *McNussen v. Graybeal*, 405 P.2d 447 (Mont. 1965)

IRREVOCABLE OFFERS. Under common law contract principles, an offer can generally be revoked at any time prior to acceptance. The exception to this rule is an option contract, in which the offeree pays consideration to the offeror in exchange for an irrevocable promise to keep the offer open for a stated period.

> **Example:** Allen submitted an offer to purchase Smith's home for $1,175,000 with a deposit of 3 percent of the purchase price and another $20,000 down. Allen agreed to pay an additional $80,000 once all contingencies were removed. Allen

paid over $100,000 in down payments, but then prior to closing two months later, Allen informed Smith he would not complete the purchase. Allen believed Smith was only entitled to keep the initial $20,000. Smith believed he was entitled to all $100,000. Allen then sued Smith for breach of contract. The court found this was not an option contract because it did not specify the period within which the option must have been exercised, or a mode of acceptance. Therefore, the court found that Smith breached the purchase agreement when he refused to refund all but the 3 percent of the purchase price. *Allen v. Smith*, 94 Cal. App. 4th 1270 (2002)

The UCC equivalent to this is known as a firm offer. A **firm offer** is an offer *by a merchant* that is irrevocable. It arises when the merchant gives *assurances* in a *signed writing* that the offer will remain open. To be effective, the firm offer must be written and signed by the offeror. Unlike common law, a merchant's firm offer does not need consideration to be irrevocable. A firm offer will be irrevocable for the stated period. However, if there is no stated period, the firm offer will stay open for a reasonable time not to exceed three months. UCC § 2-205 and UCC § 2A-205.

Firm offer
An offer by a merchant that gives assurances in a signed writing and is therefore irrevocable.

Example: Stanley Chin believed the fax he received from Ram, in combination with several oral representations made to him, created a firm offer. Stanley argues that this firm offer extended to him a four-day window in which the offer would be held open. The court found the fax itself did not contain any assurances that the quoted price would be held open. Further, the UCC will not take into consideration any alleged oral representations when determining if a firm offer exists. Therefore, the court determined no firm offer existed. *Chin v. Ram Paging Hawaii*, 103 F.3d 137 (9th Cir. 1996)

Acceptance

Unlike the mirror image rule in common law, which requires the acceptance to match the terms of the offer exactly with no modifications, the UCC has a more lenient approach to acceptance. Unless specifically agreed to by the parties, an offer to make a sales or lease contract may be accepted in any manner and by any reasonable medium of acceptance under UCC §§ 2-206(1)(a) and 2A-206(1).

Further, it is important to note that the UCC dispenses with the mirror image rule. Under the UCC, a contract is formed if the offeree's response indicates a *definite* acceptance of the offer, even if the acceptance includes terms additional to or different from those contained in the offer. This is known as the "battle of the forms" provision under UCC § 2-207. Whether the additional terms become part of the contract would depend on certain factors, such as if the parties are merchants or nonmerchants.

RULES WHEN ONE OR BOTH PARTIES ARE NONMERCHANTS. When one or both parties are nonmerchants, the contract is formed according to the terms of the original offer submitted by the original offeror and the additional or different terms are merely proposals. This means that the offeree may choose to accept these new terms if they wish but is under no contractual obligation to do so.

Example: Yvette seeks to purchase an automobile. The salesperson offers the vehicle for $35,000. Yvette responds, "I accept, but want 2 years of satellite radio included." In this case, there is a contract to sell the vehicle for $35,000. The car dealership can include the two years of satellite radio but is not under any obligation to do so.

RULES WHEN BOTH PARTIES ARE MERCHANTS. However, when both parties to the contract are merchants, the additional terms *automatically* become part of the contract unless at least one of the following conditions is present:

1. The original offer expressly limited acceptance to its terms;
2. The new terms materially change the contract; or
3. The offeror rejects the new terms within a reasonable period of time.

Courts will consider several factors to determine whether an alteration is material or not. Generally, new terms that do not create an unreasonable hardship will not be a material alteration. Courts will also look at prior dealings and see how the parties have dealt with situations involving new terms in the past. The case below discusses an example of what is and what is not considered a material alteration.

CASE 26.1

CHANGES IN A FORUM SELECTION CLAUSE ARE GENERALLY MATERIAL ALTERATIONS

TOURCATS, INC. v. TRANSP. CUSTOM DESIGNS, LLC

670 F. Supp. 3d 526 (N.D. Ohio 2023)

United States District Court for the Northern District of Ohio

Tourcats, based in Ohio, specializes in providing backstage and tour catering services to musical acts using large mobile kitchen trailers. They travel extensively across the country, covering up to 10,000 miles annually to cater to their clients during tours. Transportation Custom Designs, LLC (Transport), located in Pennsylvania, designs, manufactures, and sells custom trailers. The two parties entered into an agreement for Transport to manufacture and deliver a trailer to Tourcats. Delivery of the trailer occurred after the agreed delivery date. In addition, Tourcats discovered numerous significant defects and failures.

When the trailer was delivered it included a limited warranty with a forum selection clause, designating Pennsylvania as the jurisdiction for any disputes. Tourcats filed a lawsuit in Ohio alleging breach of contract among other claims against Transport. Transport relied upon the forum selection clause and attempted to dismiss the case due to *forum non conveniens*, asserting that the forum selection clause mandates litigation to be venued in Pennsylvania.

According to Transport, it provided Tourcats with a copy of a document titled "Limited Warranty" when it delivered the new trailer. The Limited Warranty contained the following forum selection clause: "In the event there is any claim or dispute regarding the product or the warranty, venue for litigation purposes shall be in the Court of Common Pleas of Lycoming County, Pennsylvania. The law of Pennsylvania shall govern any claims or disputes regarding the product or the warranty." Tourcats contested its agreement to this clause, arguing that it materially altered the contract under UCC § 2-207, which requires explicit consent for terms that materially alter a contract.

Language of the Court. *Relying on caselaw from other jurisdictions, the court observed that other courts had considered the placement of a forum selection clause on the back of the defendant's invoice materially altered the parties' contract. Most people want the ability to sue in their own backyard. Going to a local courthouse, accompanied by a local lawyer, to trial in front of local jurors is more appealing than litigating many states away. Moreover, given choice-of-law considerations, the place of filing can impact the substantive law that governs a case.*

The court concludes that the instant Forum Selection Clause within Transport's Limited Warranty is a material alteration of the terms of the parties' contract. Transport did not provide the Limited Warranty terms and conditions, including the Forum Selection Clause, to Tourcats until well after the parties formed their contract for the purchase of the new trailer. Thus, the Forum Selection Clause set forth in Transport's Limited Warranty was only a proposed additional term to the contract, one to which Tourcats did not agree. Because there is no binding forum selection clause applicable to this dispute, the Court will not disturb Tourcats' venue selection. Transport's Motion to Dismiss pursuant to forum non conveniens *is denied.*

Decision. A forum selection clause included in a limited warranty (as well as the limited warranty itself) provided at the time of delivery is a material alteration of the contract within the meaning of the UCC and did not become part of the contract.

Focus on Ethics

Why should the courts apply this alteration theory? If it had accepted the forum selection clause in the warranty, would the court be altering what constituted the original acceptance of the contract?

ADDITIONAL TERMS MAY BE STRICKEN. Because the additional terms *automatically* become part of the contract, there may be circumstances in which the terms that are added into the contract conflict with those already existing. In this situation, the UCC allows for a court to simply strike from the contract those terms on which the parties do not agree.

SHIPMENT OF GOODS. If the offer requires prompt shipment of goods, the offer is accepted if the seller promptly promises to ship the goods or promptly ships either conforming or nonconforming goods. Conforming goods are goods that are in line with the contract's terms, while nonconforming goods are not.

The shipment of conforming goods signals acceptance of an offer to purchase goods. If the goods are nonconforming, the contract is both created and breached by the act of shipping the nonconforming goods. However, the seller can remedy this situation by seasonably or promptly notifying the buyer that the nonconforming goods have been sent only as a favor and do not constitute acceptance. This notification from the seller to the buyer must clearly indicate that no contract has been formed.

From the buyer's or lessee's perspective, an acceptance of goods would occur after the buyer or lessee has had a reasonable opportunity to inspect the goods and:

1. Signifies that the goods are conforming;
2. Signifies the goods are nonconforming but they will retain the goods; or
3. Fails to reject the goods within a reasonable time after tender or delivery.

If the goods are nonconforming, the buyer may provide a written notice of objection to the seller.

Concept Summary Battle of the Forms

Unlike common law, acceptance under the UCC with varying terms is still valid. To determine if these terms become part of the contract the following steps are undertaken:

Step 1: Determine whether the terms are *different*. Most courts will apply the knockout rule, which states that *different terms* that conflict with each other are "knocked-out" and not included in the contract. If different terms knock each other out, apply gap-fillers to fill in missing terms.

Step 2: If the terms are *additional*, decide if both of the parties are merchants. If one or both of the parties is not a merchant, the additional terms are *proposals*, and the analysis ends there. If both of the parties are merchants, go to Step 3.

Step 3: If both parties are merchants, the additional terms become part of the contract *unless*:

- The offer expressly limits acceptance to the terms of the offer;
- The additional terms materially alter the contract; or
- Notification of objection to terms is given within a reasonable time after receiving notice.

Consideration

Under both the common law and the UCC, a contract requires consideration. However, the UCC does not require additional consideration to be given when a contract is modified. An agreement modifying a sales or lease contract needs no consideration to be binding. UCC §§ 2-209(1), 2A-208(1). In some situations, however, such a modification must be in writing to be enforceable.

Statute of Frauds

Under the UCC, the Statute of Frauds applies whenever there is an agreement for the sale of goods for $500 or more ($5,000 under the revised UCC) or there is a lease contract requiring payments of $1,000 or more. The **Statute of Frauds** requires certain types of contracts to be evidenced in writing to be enforceable. The Statute of Frauds in an Article 2 or Article 2A situation will be satisfied as long as there is "some writing sufficient to indicate that a contract for sale has been made between the parties." UCC § 2-201(1).

Statute of Frauds
A rule of contract law requiring certain contracts to be in writing to be enforceable.

SUFFICIENCY OF THE WRITING. To meet the requirements of the Statute of Frauds, the writing (which includes email and other electronic records) must (1) indicate that the parties intended to form a contract, and (2) be signed by the party against whom enforcement is sought. This means that the party who is claiming there is no contract or who owes under the contract is the party who signed the writing.

EXCEPTIONS TO THE STATUTE OF FRAUDS. There are certain exceptions to the Statute of Frauds in the UCC. UCC § 2-201(3) and UCC § 2A-201(4) provides an oral contract for the sale of goods priced at $500 or more—or an oral contract for the lease of goods involving payments of at least $1,000—will be enforceable in any of the following situations:

1. *Specially manufactured goods.* An oral contract for the sale or lease of goods will be enforceable where:
   a. the goods are *specially manufactured* for a particular buyer or specially obtained for a particular lessee,
   b. the goods must not be suitable for resale or lease to others in the ordinary course of the seller's or lessor's business, and
   c. the seller or lessor must have substantially started to manufacture the goods or have made commitments for the manufacture or procurement of the goods.

   If any of these requirements are missing, an oral contract for the sale or lease of custom-made goods will not be enforceable and will need to comply with the Statute of Frauds requirements.
2. *Admissions.* If the party against whom enforcement of the contract is sought admits in pleadings, depositions, or court proceedings that a contract for the sale or lease of goods was made, there is no need for the contract to be evidenced by a writing.
3. *Partial performance.* An oral contract for the sale or lease of goods will be enforceable and will not require a writing if payment has been made and accepted or goods have been received and accepted. With partial performance, at least one of the parties has already begun performing their end of the bargain and that performance will evidence the existence of a contract.

Under the UCC, merchants may satisfy the Statute of Frauds when a signed written confirmation is signed by one of the merchants within a reasonable time after the oral agreement occurred between the two merchants. The written confirmation must include the terms of the agreement. The merchant who receives the confirmation then has ten days to object to it before the confirmation is deemed sufficient to satisfy the Statute of Frauds.

Parol Evidence

Parol evidence Evidence of prior or contemporaneous agreement to modify, explain, or supplement the contract at issue.

The purpose of the parol evidence rule is to ensure certainty in written sales and lease contracts. Although courts tend to give deference to the contracting parties, there are times in which the express terms of a contract are not clear on their face and must be interpreted. To help with the interpretation of these ambiguous terms, parol evidence may be used to clarify the parties' intent.

Parol evidence consists of evidence that is not included in the terms of the contract, such as evidence of the parties' prior negotiations, prior agreements, or oral agreements made at the time of contract formation. When a contract completely sets forth all the terms and conditions agreed to by the parties and is intended as the final version of their contract, the contract is *fully integrated.* In such a situation, parol evidence that contradicts the terms of the contract or adds additional terms to the contract will not be allowed.

However, in situations where the writing (or record) contains some of the terms the parties agreed on but not others, the contract is partially integrated. In this situation, a court may allow evidence of *consistent additional terms* to explain or supplement the terms stated in the contract. The parties may also be allowed to submit evidence of course of dealing, usage of trade, or course of performance. Any evidence that is allowed by the courts will be interpreted together as long as they are consistent with each other. Under no circumstances will a court allow the parties to submit evidence that contradicts the contract's stated terms.

> **Example:** In a contract between a wholesaler and retailer, the court found that the contract was partially integrated, and therefore could not be contradicted by evidence of any prior agreement or of a contemporaneous oral agreement for a different price; the invoices unambiguously specified the prices, and retailer paid all but the final invoice. Therefore, the retailer was required to pay the full price of the final invoice. *Segal Wholesale, Inc. v. United Drug Service*, 933 A.2d 780 (D.C. 2007)

The next case deals with the parol evidence rule as applied to a sales contract of an automobile.

CASE 26.2

PAROL EVIDENCE BARS THE USE OF EVIDENCE WHEN SUCH EVIDENCE CONTRADICTS THE TERMS OF A FULLY INTEGRATED CONTRACT

OLAH v. GANLEY CHEVROLET, INC.

191 Ohio App. 3d 456 (2010)

Court of Appeals of Ohio

In October 2004, the Olahs made the decision to go to a Chevrolet dealership after seeing a newspaper advertisement for a new Chevy Aveo with a sales price of $7,777. They told the salesperson that they were interested in purchasing a new

Aveo and mentioned seeing the advertisement. After showing the Olahs some different vehicles, the salesperson directed the Olahs to a vehicle across the street that had a few miles on it but that they could get for a good price. The vehicle had 541 miles on it and some additional options from the base-model Aveo. The Olahs said that they did not observe a sales price sticker on the window and were told it was taken down for test driving. However, on the purchase contract, the "Rental box" was checked to put the Olahs on notice that the vehicle could have been used as a rental. Moreover, the purchase contract stated that it was "the entire agreement between the parties, and no other agreements or representation shall bind the parties."

After taking the vehicle for a test drive, the Olahs negotiated the purchase of the vehicle with the salesperson for a purchase price of $9,400. They were under the impression that the vehicle was new, and that the mileage was from test drives and dealer usage. Thus, they thought they had purchased a new vehicle with 541 miles on it and a full warranty. Later, the Olahs discovered they did not purchase a new vehicle and sued for contract breach. To help further their claim, the lower court allowed evidence that there were representations that the vehicle was new. On appeal, the court held that this evidence was barred by the parol evidence rule.

Language of the Court. *Chevrolet argues that the trial court erred by failing to apply the parol evidence rule to bar the Olahs' claims. We agree. The parol evidence rule is a rule of substantive law that has application to claims beyond those sounding in contract. The rule provides that absent fraud, mistake or other invalidating cause, the parties' final written integration of their agreement may not be varied, contradicted or supplemented by evidence of prior or contemporaneous oral agreements, or prior written agreements. This rule serves to protect the integrity of written contracts and to ensure stability, predictability, and enforceability of finalized written instruments. As such, the rule prohibits a party to a final written contract from contradicting or varying the terms thereof with evidence of prior oral representations, understandings and negotiations. Furthermore, "testimony introduced in violation of the rule, even in the absence of objection thereto, can be given no legal effect."*

In this case, the trial court erred as a matter of law by considering evidence, in violation of the parol evidence rule, of representation purportedly made prior to the written purchase contract. Indeed, the parol evidence rule may not be avoided when the inducement to sign the writing was a promise that directly contradicts an integrated written agreement. Because the Olahs's claims are predicated on evidence of prior representations that are barred by the parol evidence rule, we reverse the trial court's final judgement that was in favor of the Olahs and against Chevrolet. Thus, any impression concerning the warranty or that the vehicle was new is prohibited by the parol evidence rule because it is in contradiction to the terms of a final written contract.

Decision. The parol evidence rule barred the use of parol evidence when there was a signed contract that was fully integrated and the evidence contradicted what was in the contract.

Focus on Ethics

Why is this not a case of fraudulent misrepresentation? Is it because the purchasers of automobiles have the duty to read the terms of the contract before signing?

Interpretation of Contracts Under the UCC

The meaning or interpretation of any agreement under the UCC must consider commercial practices and other surrounding circumstances. Courts assume that the contracting parties considered the course of prior dealings and usage of trade. In some instances, courts will look to see if there was a course of performance, course of dealing, or usage of trade.

UCC § 1-303 defines course of performance, course of dealing, or usage of trade. The UCC provides that any of these terms "may give particular meaning to specific terms of the agreement and may supplement or qualify the terms of the agreement." UCC § 1-303(d). Freedom of contract is a well-respected principle of U.S. law. Subject to the limitations of law, the parties are free to negotiate the terms of a commercial sales contract.

The parties are free to vary or reject the application of the UCC to their contract except for the obligations of good faith, diligence, reasonableness, and care prescribed by the UCC. However, when a conflict arises between any of these three terms and the express terms of the agreement, UCC §§ 1-302 and 1-303 provide the resolution. Whenever the contract involves these three defined terms, they must be construed whenever reasonable as consistent with each other. When such a construction is unreasonable:

- Express terms of the contract prevail over course of performance, course of dealing, and usage of trade;
- Course of performance prevails over course of dealing and usage of trade; and
- Course of dealing prevails over usage of trade.

Course of performance
The series of conduct under a contract in which the contract involves repeated occasions for performance and opportunities for objection.

COURSE OF PERFORMANCE. Course of performance is the series of conduct under a contract in which the contract involves repeated occasions for performance and opportunities for objection by either of the parties.

Example: In 1980, Pathmark Stores Inc. entered into a lease agreement with Gator Monument Partners, LLP to rent a space in a shopping center. In 2008, Gator notified Pathmark that it was terminating the lease due to several alleged defaults. Pathmark filed a suit seeking to prevent Gator from terminating the lease. Gator stated that the alleged defaults arose out of Gator's claim that according to the lease agreement payments were to be made based on a square-footage formula, not a lump-sum formula. The court ruled in favor of Pathmark, finding course of performance applied because Gator had accepted lump-sum payments for over 28 years without complaint. *Pathmark Stores, Inc. v. Gator Monument Partners, LLP*, 2009 U.S. Dist. LEXIS 119927 (E.D. Pa. 2009)

COURSE OF PRIOR DEALING. **Course of prior dealing** describes prior conduct between the parties to a contract that establishes a common basis for their understanding. Under the UCC, a course of prior dealing between the parties is relevant in determining the meaning of the parties' agreement. It may be used to give meaning to specific terms or qualify the terms of the agreement. The following case discusses the course of prior dealing and whether certain terms have been accepted.

Course of prior dealing
Describes prior conduct between the parties to a contract that establishes a common basis for their understanding.

CASE 26.3

SOMETIMES A PRIOR COURSE OF DEALING ANALYSIS IS INAPPROPRIATE

STARBUCKS CORP. v. AMCOR PACKAGING DISTRIBUTION

2016 U.S. Dist. LEXIS 82538 (2016)

United States District Court for the Eastern District of California

In late 2011, Starbucks contracted with Amcor Packaging to purchase 9,480 wooden pallets for storing its coffee at a warehouse owned and operated by OHL. Starbucks specified that it needed the wooden pallets to be made of lumber that was dried to a moisture content of less than 19 percent. Upon delivery, OHL, acting on behalf of Starbucks, visually inspected the wooden pallets for damage but did not test the pallets for moisture content. Except for one shipment of wooden pallets that were found to be wet and returned, OHL accepted all of the pallet deliveries on behalf of Starbucks. Following the deliveries, Amcor would send invoices to Starbucks for the sale of the wooden pallets. Each invoice included a disclaimer at the bottom that limited Amcor's liability. Starbucks paid these invoices and loaded 68,000 bags of green coffee onto the wooden pallets for storage and subsequent transportation for roasting.

In February 2012, OHL personnel discovered mold growing on some of the wooden pallets. Shortly thereafter, Starbucks discovered mold on green coffee, coffee bags, and wooden pallets that were delivered from storage to where the roasting was supposed to be done. Starbucks then retained independent surveyors to investigate the source of the mold. The surveyors determined that the mold resulted from Amcor's pallets not meeting the moisture requirement. Starbucks sued Amcor, alleging claims for breach of contract.

As a defense, Amcor argued that since the companies started doing business in 2008, the parties' course of dealing indicated that Starbucks had never raised any objections to those disclaimers and, moreover, that the disclaimers had always had the same language. Amcor argued that Starbucks' failure to object constituted its assent to the disclaimers.

Language of the Court. *Course of dealing analysis is not proper in an instance where the only action taken has been the repeated delivery of a particular form by one of the parties and the parties had not taken any action with respect to the matters addressed by the disputed terms. Because a seller in multiple transactions, will typically have every opportunity to negotiate the precise terms it seeks, its failure or inability to obtain a negotiated agreement reflecting its desired terms strongly suggests that those terms are not a part of the parties' commercial bargain. Payment on an invoice in accordance with an existing oral contract does not in itself establish assent to the additional terms to the contract. For a party's performance to establish assent to a modification or addition of terms, the performance must be related to the proposed modification or addition and differ from the performance already required of the party by the existing contract.*

It cannot be said here that Starbucks' payment of Amcor's prior invoices without objection constituted a course of dealing establishing a common basis of understanding between the parties as to their respective liabilities and remedies. There is no evidence that, by paying the prior invoices, Starbucks manifested its affirmative assent to the disclaimers in the Amcor's prior invoices. Rather, Starbucks was merely performing its obligation to pay Amcor for the goods that it purchased. Consequently, the parties did not have a course of dealing from which Starbucks' assent to the disclaimers may be inferred.

Decision. Starbucks' payment of Amcor's prior invoices without objection did not constitute a course of dealing establishing a common basis of understanding between the parties as to their respective liabilities and remedies.

Focus on Ethics

As discussed in Chapter 14, parties can agree upon a liquidated damages provision. How is the disclaimer provision in this case different from that provision? Do you think this case was fairly decided?

Usage of trade
Any practice or method of dealing that is so regularly observed in the industry that parties can reasonably expect it will be observed in their transaction.

USAGE OF TRADE. Usage of trade refers to any practice or method of dealing that is so regularly observed in the industry that parties can reasonably expect it will be observed in their transaction.

Example: Bob Kincheloe bought Maury Burk's 14 cows at an auction for $15,000. A few weeks later when Bob tried to sell the cows, he learned that many of them were diseased. He brought an action against Burk for breach of implied warranty of merchantability. The court found that although Burk breached the implied warranty of merchantability, it was not applicable because usage of trade indicated that the cows were sold "as is." *Kincheloe v. Geldmeir*, 619 S.W.2d 272 (Tex. App. 1981)

TABLE 26.3: Distinguishing Between UCC and Common Law

	The UCC	Common Law
Applies to:	Contracts for the sale and lease of goods where at least one of the parties is a merchant	Contracts for services and wherever the UCC does not apply
Consideration:	Consideration for initial contract required	Consideration for initial contract required
Consideration for modifications:	Consideration not required	Consideration required
Definiteness:	Only the quantity is required to be specified	Quantity, price, time for performance, nature of the work, and identity of the parties are required
Different/additional terms:	Acceptance need not be the mirror image of the offer's terms	Acceptance must identically mirror the terms of the offer
Irrevocable offers:	An offer by a merchant is irrevocable when the merchant gives assurances in a signed writing that the offer will remain open	An offer is only irrevocable if consideration is paid in exchange for the promise to keep the offer open
Parol evidence:	Evidence of consistent course of performance, course of dealing, or usage of trade is permitted in addition to oral or written statements that are consistent with the contract	Only oral or written statements that are consistent with the contract are permitted
Statute of Frauds:	Special rules for merchants allowing signed written confirmations to be sufficient even in cases where the goods exceed $500 in value	Requires a memorandum containing the essential terms of the contract and identification of the parties

Unconscionability Under the UCC

In the context of sales and lease contracts, the UCC in Articles 2 (Sales) and 2A (Leases) have provisions that deal with unfair (unconscionable) contracts. To prove **unconscionability**, there must be proof that:

Unconscionability Contracts set aside because terms are extremely unjust or one-sided.

- There was substantial unequal bargaining power between the contracting parties;
- The dominant party misused its power in contracting; and
- Enforcing the contract would either be oppressive or manifestly unfair.

Unconscionability encompasses both *procedural* abuses in contract formation and *substantive* abuses in the contract's terms. If the elements above are proven, a court may refuse to enforce the entire contract, or any part of a contract found to be unconscionable. Article 2A provides relief and award of attorney fees for consumers.

Management Application
Factors Indicating Unconscionability

In a sales or lease contract, the most common indicator of unconscionability is *price*. To determine whether the price charged for a good or service is unconscionable, look for the following factors:

- Whether there was an adequate basis or justification for the price charged;
- The price paid by other similarly situated consumers for similar goods or services;
- Any inconveniences the party charging the price may have;
- The actual value of the goods or services;
- Whether there were any deceptive practices involved; and
- Availability of comparable alternative goods or services.

CISG Compared to the UCC

United Nations Convention on Contracts for the International Sale of Goods (CISG)
A treaty created to govern international sales contracts between firms or individuals located in different countries.

The **United Nations Convention on Contracts for the International Sale of Goods (CISG)** is a treaty created to govern international sales contracts between firms or individuals located in different countries.

The CISG will be applicable where:

1. The contract is one for the commercial sale of goods (however, the CISG does not define the term "goods");
2. The parties to the contract have their places of business in different countries; and
3. The places of business of the parties are located in countries that have ratified the Convention.

Essentially, the CISG is the international equivalent of Article 2 of the UCC. Neither the UCC nor the CISG applies to contracts for services. As discussed earlier, the UCC applies when parties to a contract for the sale of goods have failed to specify in writing certain terms such as price or delivery. Like the UCC, the CISG applies whenever the parties fail to specify in writing the precise terms of an international sale of goods contract.

OFFER AND ACCEPTANCE. Under the CISG, an offer can become irrevocable without a signed writing or record. An offer under the CISG will be irrevocable if any of the following happen:

1. The offeror states orally that the offer is irrevocable; or
2. The offeree reasonably relies on the offer as being irrevocable.

Recall that under the UCC, a contract may be formed even if the offeree's acceptance included additional terms. Under the CISG, a contract may be formed even though the acceptance contains additional terms, unless the additional terms materially alter the contract. A material alteration under the CISG, however, includes almost any change in the terms. Any additional terms that relate to payment, quality, quantity, price, time and place of delivery, liability of the parties, or dispute resolution would be considered a material alteration. Thus, it would appear as though the CISG requires acceptance to be more consistent with that of the mirror image rule under the common law.

STATUTE OF FRAUDS. The UCC has a Statute of Frauds requirement, but under the CISG, an international sales contract does not need to be evidenced by a writing or be in any particular form.

AI Feature: Parol Evidence

Roman owns a well-established seafood wholesaling business and has agreed to buy "premium" lobster from Clark Lobster and Crab, a fishing enterprise in Alaska. They have a long-term requirements contract with each other and have been doing business with each other for over a decade. Individually sourced relationships between provisioners and their customers are the nature of the business. As a result, it is difficult to switch suppliers within Roman's market area. Roman repeatedly receives deliveries of what he considers to be undersized lobsters. In response to his complaints, Clark states that market tastes have changed, and that Clark can no longer supply what Roman had received in the past as premium lobsters. Roman's restaurant customers demand larger ones than what Clark is supplying to Roman. Having read this chapter, use an AI program to assess the probability of success if Roman sues Clark for damages? What defenses could Clark assert? Could parol evidence be introduced at the time of trial; if so, to what purpose? Explain the arguments of the parties and the probable outcome of this dispute.

Key Terms

- Course of performance, 658
- Course of prior dealing, 660
- Firm offer, 651
- Gap-filling rule, 649
- Goods, 646
- Lease agreement, 648
- Lessee, 648
- Lessor, 648
- Mixed sales, 647
- Output contract, 650
- Parol evidence, 656
- Requirements contract, 650

- Sale, 647
- Statute of Frauds, 655
- Unconscionability, 661
- United Nations Convention on Contracts for the International Sale of Goods (CISG), 662
- Usage of trade, 660

Applying the Law

26.1 Statute of Frauds. Exxon Corporation® made an oral agreement with Breezevale Ltd. in which Breezevale would procure Nigerian oil development rights. Breezevale helped Exxon arrange appointments, conduct briefings, and obtain information, and it spoke with government officials on Exxon's behalf for a period of 18 months. There was no formal agreement in place as to Breezevale's compensation for its services. Breezevale wanted a more long-term relationship with Exxon but after the 18-month period, Exxon terminated its relationship with Breezevale and sent a $30,000 check to cover Breezevale's services. Breezevale sued, claiming Exxon breached the oral agreement between the two parties. Should a memorandum evidence this type of agreement pursuant to the Statute of Frauds to be enforceable? Why or why not? *Exxon Corp. v. Breezevale Ltd.*, 82 S.W.3d 429 (Tex. App.–Dallas 2002)

26.2 Firm Offer. Mid-South Packers, Inc.® and Shoney's, Inc.® engaged in negotiations for the sale by Mid-South to Shoney's of various pork products, including bacon and ham. Mid-South submitted a letter styled "Proposal" that set forth prices and terms at which Mid-South would supply Shoney's with several types of meat. The letter also provided that Shoney's would be informed 45 days prior to any adjustment in price. The letter contained neither quantity nor durational terms. Shoney's expressed neither assent to nor rejection of the prices outlined in the letter. Shoney's estimated its needs from Mid-South at 80,000 pounds of meat per week. Mid-South asserts that the proposal was at most a "firm offer." Mid-South argues that under UCC § 2-205, a firm offer is irrevocable despite a lack of consideration "during the time stated or if no time is stated for a reasonable time; but in no event may such period of irrevocability exceed three (3) months." Thus, Mid-South contends that under any construction of the document, the offer must have expired three months after April 17, 1982, the date of the letter proposal, or on approximately July 17, 1982; therefore, it asserts the right on August 12, 1982, to increase the selling price without notice. Who prevails and why? *Mid-South Packers, Inc. v. Shoney's, Inc.*, 761 F.3d 1117 (5th Cir. 1985)

26.3 Mixed Sales. Contractor Dennis Ceola sued Homeowner Willard Robertson for breach of an oral contract for the purchase and installation of tile during the construction of Robertson's house. On appeal the issue was whether the Statute of Frauds applied. Was it a contract for the sale of goods or was it a personal service contract? Did UCC § 2-201 apply to this contract? *Robertson v. Ceola*, 501 S.W.2d 764 (Ark. 1973)

26.4 Prior Dealings. WPS was a manufacturing company that was solicited to present a proposal to Expro Americas to receive a contract to make gas compressors. Expro Americas sent purchase orders to WPS. WPS approved one and conditionally approved another. Further negotiations continued, with WPS adding terms; however, Expro Americas needed this equipment in about five months' time. Subsequently, WPS requested a release to proceed, and that Expro Americas would assume responsibility for the cancellation costs. After the release was granted, more negotiations continued. But, as fate would have it, Expro Americas did cancel, and argued that all these additional terms requested by WPS were material alterations to the contract. Is there conduct to establish a common basis for an understanding between WPS and Expro Americas? *WPS, Inc. v. Expro Americas, LLC*, 369 S.W.3d 384 (Tex. App. 2012)

26.5 Contracts Between Merchants. Farmer Lindgren stated the following in his deposition: He agreed over the phone to sell soybeans and corn to Glacial Plains in four transactions. First, they discussed that Lindgren would deliver 9,000 bushels of soybeans, followed by another 10,000 bushels of soybeans. Then, Lindgren was to deliver 65,000 bushels of corn. Finally, a year later Lindgren was to deliver another 30,000 bushels of corn. Immediately after this conversation, Glacial Plains sent out four written contracts. Farmer Lindgren sent out both deliveries of soybeans and partially performed on the first delivery of corn. However, Lindgren realized that he had never signed any of the contracts and concluded they were unenforceable. So, he decided to sell the rest of his corn to another grain dealer. Farmer Lindgren argues that oral corn agreements are not enforceable because they violate the Statute of Frauds. Is there a way for oral agreements to be enforceable under the Statute of Frauds? *Glacial Plains Co-op. v. Lindgren*, 759 N.W.2d 661 (Minn. Ct. App. 2009)

26.6 Partially Integrated Contract. Nstein Technologies Corp. moved to dismiss a case on the grounds that the plaintiff's pleading failed to state a claim, because the underlying agreement failed to comply with the Statute of Frauds. In this case, Al-Bawaba.com, presented to the court a multitude of emails from Denis, an authorized agent of Nstein, with regard to a specific agreement. One particular email was made with the intent to confirm their oral agreement for three years. In this email, the defendant stated that it had a product for the plaintiff and would extend a two-week free trial. Moreover, Nstein requested that Al-Bawaba send over its "articles" for testing and the email was signed "Thank you in advance, Denis." Is this enough to satisfy the Statute of Frauds? *Al-Bawaba.com, Inc. v. Nstein Techs. Corp.*, 19 Misc. 3d 1125(A) (N.Y. Sup. Ct. 2008)

26.7 Personal Property. Blasini, LLC agreed to buy the personal property attached to its lease of the Attic Bar & Grill. However, Blasini did not purchase the personal property outright from Cheran Investments. Rather, it bought the property with a down payment and then had to make monthly installment payments. Unfortunately, a fire damaged the personal property inside the Bar & Grill before Blasini had finished fully paying for the property. Who has title to the personal property? To whom should the insurance proceeds be paid? *Nautilus Ins. Co. v. Cheran Investments, L.L.C.*, 2016 Neb. App. LEXIS 98 (Neb. Ct. App. 2016)

26.8 Open Price Term. Two Brothers and ten other gasoline retailers sued Valero®, which distributes gasoline to retailers in the Phoenix, Arizona, market. Agreements with Valero stated that the retailers "shall pay to [Valero] that price specified by [Valero] from time to time[.]" The agreements did not explain or limit how Valero would set fuel prices. The retailer contended that Valero orally promised that it would charge them a fuel price in line with discount brands and Valero-owned stations so that the gas stations would remain competitive and profitable. The agreements between the retailers and Valero were fully integrated. If Valero charged the retailers a higher price than it charged its own stations, did Valero fail to set a price in good faith? *Two Bros. Distrib. v. Valero Mktg. & Supply Co.*, 769 Fed. Appx. 408 (9th Cir. 2019)

26.9 Superior Right of Possession. Max Ellis Alexander agreed to purchase hay from the Wagners. However, when the payment would be due was never specified in the agreement. The Wagners assumed that, in accordance with their usual dealings, Alexander would pay when he received the hay. After the agreement was made, Alexander left his truck and trailer for it to be filled with the hay. Upon his return to pick up the hay, Alexander got into an argument with the Wagners about the quantity of the hay that he was supposed to be sold. Instead of paying for the hay, Alexander drove off in his truck and trailer with the hay. Who has the superior right of possession? *State v. Alexander*, 64 P.3d 1148 (Ore. App. 2003)

26.10 Material Alteration. Duro Textiles, a Delaware corporation, ordered blue dye from Sunbelt, a South Carolina corporation, in 2011. When Duro used the dye, it caused random blue spots on its products, resulting in $550,000 in losses. Duro sued Sunbelt, which attempted to dismiss the case based on a forum selection clause in its invoice, designating South Carolina courts for disputes. Duro argued the forum selection clause was not part of their contract because it materially altered the terms, requiring Duro to litigate in South Carolina. According to your understanding of materially altering terms under UCC § 2-207, explain the court's ruling. *Duro Textiles, LLC v. Sunbelt Corp.* 12 F. Supp. 3d 221 (2014)

Title and Risk of Loss

27

The great and chief end, therefore, of men's uniting into commonwealths, and putting themselves under government, is the preservation of their property. — John Locke, The Second Treatise on Government (1632-1704)

Chapter Outline

Learning Objectives

After studying this chapter, you should be able to:

1. Identify the requirements for the passage of title.
2. Explain how circumstances of delivery may affect the passage of title.
3. Identify the problems associated with the acquisition of imperfect title.
4. Identify when risk of loss will transfer given the circumstances of a transaction.
5. Explain what it means to possess an insurable interest in an item.

Introduction

This chapter addresses the passage of title to goods from a seller to a buyer under the UCC. Sales contracts may be executed weeks or months prior to the transfer of title of the goods. Who is responsible for the goods during that time, what happens if they are damaged during shipment, and when does the risk of loss transfer between the buyer and seller are discussed in this chapter.

Prior to the UCC, the rights and duties of the parties to a sales contract could be determined by analyzing which party had title to the goods at the time of the loss. With the enactment of the UCC, prior case law was altered by virtually eliminating title as a factor in such determinations. Almost all sales matters are now covered by specially tailored narrow rules, and title is rarely employed in the solution of cases governed by the UCC. The creation of the UCC has led to increased focus being placed on concepts such as identification of goods, risk of loss, and insurable interest. These concepts and more will be discussed in this chapter. Finally, the rules associated with the passage of title are not applicable to leased goods, because the title to leased goods will always remain with the lessor or owner, not with the lessee or temporary possessor of the goods.

UCC § 2-401 governs the passage of title. While its terminology is daunting, we will study the following elements of this Code section:

- Title to goods cannot pass under a contract for sale before their identification to the contract.
- On identification of the goods to the contract, unless otherwise explicitly agreed, the buyer acquires a "special property" in the goods.
- Any reservation of title by the seller in goods shipped or delivered to the buyer is limited in effect to a reservation of a security interest. Subject to the foregoing, title to the sold goods passes as the parties explicitly agree.
- Unless otherwise explicitly agreed, passage of title is controlled by UCC § 2-401(2) when there is to be physical delivery of the goods and by UCC § 2-401(3) when delivery is to be made without moving the goods.

The buyer's rejection of the goods, whether or not justified, or the buyer's justified revocation of acceptance reverts title to the seller. UCC § 2-401(4).

Identification of Goods

Title to goods cannot pass under a contract for sale before their identification in the contract. UCC § 2-401. Although identification is not specifically defined by the UCC, it means the designation of particular existing goods as the goods to which the contract refers. **Identification** occurs in a sales or lease contract when specific goods are recognized as the subject matter of the contract.

Identification
Time when specific goods are recognized as the subject matter of the contract.

In addition to allowing title to pass from the seller to the buyer, identification allows the **risk of loss** to pass from the seller to the buyer. When the risk of loss passes, the buyer gains the right to insure the goods, thereby allowing the buyer to recover if third parties damage the goods. This concept of the right to insure is known as having an insurable interest. Insurable interest and risk of loss are closely related commercially. The concept is important because for an insurance policy to be enforceable, the owner of the policy must have an insurable interest in the insured property. This concept will be discussed in more detail later in the chapter.

A contract of sale cannot redefine insurable interest to validate or invalidate insurance carried by either the buyer or the seller with respect to the goods. However, the contract can provide a basis for establishing an insurable interest in either party by allocating the risk of loss (UCC §§ 2-303, 2-509(4)) or providing for other liabilities or rights on which an insurable interest can be based. A practical method of insuring a seller for the unpaid balance of the price in the event the goods are destroyed or lost after delivery to the buyer is to obtain an insurance policy that names both the buyer and the seller as insureds, with benefits payable according to their respective interests. The sales contract can require either party to obtain such a policy.

Through the use of a sales agreement, parties are free to negotiate the time at which they wish for the goods to be identified, if these goods are already in existence. When the goods are not in existence, identification depends on the type of good being transferred. If the parties fail to specify a time for identification, the UCC will control.

Goods Already in Existence

UCC § 2-501(1) states that if the goods are already in existence, identification takes place at the time the contract is made.

> **Example:** When a wholesaler executes a contract to sell the local grocery store 100 bushels of apples with the SKU number 775463, identification has taken place, and the local grocery store now has an insurable interest in the apples.

Future Goods

Future goods are those not in existence at the time the contract is formed. There can be no present sale of future goods; a purported present sale of such goods or any interest in them operates only as a contract to sell. UCC § 2-105(2). If the subject matter of the contract deals with future goods, identification is dependent on the type of goods being transferred, as described below:

Future goods
Goods that are not in existence at the time the contract is formed.

- Sales or lease contracts for the transfer of crops to be harvested within 12 months or the next harvest season, whichever is longer, will be identified when the crop is planted or when it begins growing.
- Sales or lease contracts for unborn animals that are to be born within 12 months of contracting are identified when the animals are conceived.
- Sales or lease contracts for any other future good will be identified when the goods are shipped, marked, or designated by the seller or lessor. UCC § 2-501(1)(b)-(c).

Goods Part of a Larger Mass

When goods are part of a larger mass, they are typically identified at the time the goods are marked, shipped, or designated by the seller as the subject matter of the transaction.

An important exception to this rule includes the sale of fungible goods. **Fungible goods** are those goods whose individual units are alike such that they are regarded as commercially interchangeable.

Fungible goods
Goods whose individual units are alike such that they are regarded as commercially interchangeable.

> **Example:** Oil, gold, and other precious metals, unopened items of consumer products on store shelves such as boxes of oatmeal or cereal are examples of fungible goods. Diamonds are not fungible because each diamond is unique, and its characteristics will increase or decrease the diamond's value.

Where multiple owners hold fungible goods as tenants in common (each owner has an undivided interest in the property), the owner-seller will not have to separate the goods in order to pass title and risk of loss onto the buyer. The buyer will then replace the seller as a tenant in common of the fungible goods. UCC § 2-105(4).

> **Example:** A number of corn farmers store their harvested corn in a silo operated by a cooperative. Each will have a proportionate ownership interest in the stored corn.

The Passage of Title

Title
Evidence of ownership of property passed by an instrument or court order.

UCC § 2-401 sets forth the standard rules for the passage of title once the goods have been identified. **Title** is the evidence of ownership of property passed by an instrument or court order. As with other sections of the UCC, the parties may deviate from the Code provisions and expressly agree when title passes. Unless otherwise agreed, UCC § 2-401(2) provides that the buyer receives title to the goods at the time and place the seller delivers the goods to the buyer.

> **Example:** The Hummels bought a car from Raisor Pontiac on June 3, paying half the down payment and the remainder the next day when they received the car. On June 5, they were in a fatal accident with the Lyons. Title to the vehicle transferred six days after the accident. The families of the deceased sued Raisor Pontiac's insurers, claiming Raisor still held title at the time of the accident. The court ruled that since the Hummels took possession of the car upon delivery, they held title, barring the families from suing Raisor's insurers. *O'Donnell v. American Employers Ins. Co.*, 622 N.E.2d 570 (Ind. Ct. App. 1993)

The following case discusses how passage of title affects liability to third parties.

CASE 27.1

THE ABSENCE OF A CERTIFICATE OF TITLE DOES NOT INVALIDATE A SALE

UNIVERSAL UNDERWRITERS INS. CO. v. WINTON

818 F.3d 1103 (2016)

United States Court of Appeals for the Tenth Circuit

In the early morning of November 11, 2007, Sofia Roberts caused an automobile accident that severely injured two people and resulted in the death of five people, including herself. At the time of the accident, Roberts was driving a vehicle, a Chrysler 300, that she had obtained from the Marc Heitz Auto Valley (Heitz) dealership on November 9. The vehicle was delivered to Heitz by Bob Moore Auto Group (Moore) earlier that same day. Roberts's estate settled lawsuits with the survivors and one victim for $3 million each and another victim for $5 million. Roberts's insurer on her automobile policy contributed the policy limit of

$50,000. The judgment was enforceable against other applicable insurance policies. Universal, Phoenix, and National, the three insurance carriers (the Insurers) for Heitz and Moore, sued the victims seeking a declaratory judgment that the Insurers were not liable for the judgment because the dealership did not own the vehicle at the time of the accident. The district court ruled in favor of the Insurers, finding they were not liable. The victims appealed.

Language of the Court. *The Victims concede that Ms. Roberts was covered under Moore's primary policy issued by Phoenix and its umbrella policy issued by National only if Moore owned the Chrysler at the time of the accident. Although it is undisputed that Moore delivered the Chrysler to Heitz on Friday, November 9, 2007, two days before the accident, the Victims rely on the failure of Moore to transfer the vehicle certificate of title until the day after the accident. We hold that Moore did not own the vehicle even though it had not transferred the title certificate.*

Under the Oklahoma version of the Uniform Commercial Code, "Unless otherwise explicitly agreed title passes to the buyer at the time and place at which the seller completes his performance with reference to the physical delivery of the goods, despite any reservation of a security interest and even though a document of title is to be delivered at a different time or place. . . ." This supports the proposition that "motor vehicle certificates of title are not necessarily controlling of ownership of an automobile. Thus, despite the failure to convey a certificate of title, "the sale of an automobile is complete upon the delivery of the car with intent to sell."

It is "unnecessary for a dealer to deliver a certificate of title before conveying ownership and . . . the absence of the certificate of title does not invalidate the sale." The ownership of the Chrysler passed to Heitz from Moore when Heitz took possession on November 9, 2007. Because Moore was not the owner of the vehicle at the time of the accident, the Phoenix and National policies did not cover Ms. Roberts.

Decision. The court of appeals affirmed the trial court's finding that the Insurers were not liable to the victims because the victims no longer had an ownership interest in Roberts's vehicle.

Focus on Ethics

Assume the law was different and title passed only upon the receipt of the certificate of title. How might this affect the way in which business is transacted? Do you believe this would be beneficial or overly burdensome to interstate commerce?

Tender

Under the UCC, the buyer's payment for the goods is conditioned on the seller's "tender" of the goods for the delivery. The word "tender" is given particular legal significance as defined by the UCC. Under the UCC, tender means that the goods are made available to the buyer.

Shipment versus Destination Contracts

Shipment contract
A sales contract that allows or obligates the seller to ship the goods by carrier; allows the seller to mitigate risk by passing title to the buyer at the time and place of shipment.

Absent an express agreement to the contrary, the circumstances of the delivery may determine when title has passed from the seller to the buyer. A **shipment contract** is a type of sales contract that authorizes or obligates the seller to ship the goods by carrier (a company that transports goods). Shipment contracts allow the seller to mitigate the potential risk of loss in the transaction. Under a shipment contract, the title to goods passes to the buyer at the time and place of shipment. Sellers usually prefer not to be responsible for goods while they are in transit. Unless the contract states otherwise, a shipment contract is presumed.

> **Example:** Pestana agreed to purchase 64 watches from Karinol Corp. The purchase agreement did not include any clauses regarding the risk of loss. However, the bottom of the contract stated, "Please send the merchandise in cardboard boxes strapped with metal bands via air parcel post to the following address. . . ." Pestana paid a 25 percent down payment for the goods. Karinol delivered the goods to a common carrier, but the goods were subsequently lost in transit. Pestana sued Karinol to recover the purchase price. The court found Karinol not liable, finding that the purchase agreement constituted a shipment contract; therefore, Karinol fulfilled its obligations of delivery and thus the risk of loss had shifted to Pestana. *Pestana v. Karinol Corp.*, 367 So. 2d 1096 (Fla. Dist. Ct. App. 1979)

Management Application
Delivery Terms for a Shipment Contract

The above-mentioned goods are sold Free Alongside Ship (FAS) to 1234 Acme Way, Acme, Washington 98001. Seller agrees to deliver the goods to the vessel named by the Buyer at the specified loading time. Notification of the Buyer's chosen vessel must be provided to the Seller no later than seven (7) days prior to the loading date. It is the responsibility of the Seller to procure all documents that are necessary for the Buyer to obtain a bill of lading for the goods.

Destination contract
A sales contract that allows the buyer to mitigate risk by having title pass to the buyer only when the goods are tendered at destination.

A **destination contract** is a type of contract that obligates the seller to tender the goods to the buyer or to a location specified by the buyer. This allows the buyer to mitigate some of the transactional risk because title does not pass to the buyer until the seller tenders delivery of the goods at the specified location.

> **Example:** Baumgold Bros. was a jewelry wholesaler that contracted with Fox for the sale of a small amount of diamonds. Fox requested that the diamonds be delivered by Baumgold to his office, but they never arrived. The court determined that by the seller agreeing to deliver the goods to a particular destination established by the buyer, the parties had created a destination contract. Therefore, the risk of loss remained with Baumgold. *Baumgold Bros., Inc. v. Allan M. Fox Co., East*, 375 F. Supp. 807 (N.D. Ohio 1973)

Concept Summary
Shipment versus Destination Contracts

Type	Description
Shipment Contract	Title passes to the buyer at the time of shipment. Buyer bears the risk of loss once the goods are delivered to the carrier.
Destination Contract	Title does not pass to the buyer until the seller tenders delivery of the goods at the buyer's specified location. Seller bears risk of loss prior to buyer's receipt of the goods.

Who Tenders First?

Whether a shipment or destination contract is involved, the seller is the first to tender because it must first make the goods available to the buyer before the buyer's obligation to pay arises. However, the parties are free to contract around this presumption and require the buyer to make a full or partial payment prior to the seller tendering the goods.

Documentary Transaction

A **documentary transaction**, often known as a documentary sale, is a type of contract for the sale of goods in which possession and ownership of the goods are transferred from a seller to buyer without the seller moving the goods. Title is transferred through the negotiation and delivery of a negotiable document of title. This allows for the instantaneous ownership and the right to possession to be transferred to another. Taking possession of goods is not required to accomplish placing the buyer with title. This process is traceable to ancient traders who would exchange receipts for goods and allow the goods to be sold and resold among them without ever disturbing the goods while they remained in storage.

Documentary transaction
A sales transaction in which receipt of a document gives buyer legal title to the goods accounted for in the sales contract.

> **Example:** Fields signs a contract to purchase lumber from LumberMart. The contract provides that Fields will pick up the lumber at LumberMart. In this case, title passes to Fields upon the execution of the contract by both parties.

Document of title
A writing authorizing the holder to receive the goods it covers.

A negotiable **document of title** is a document that evidences the ownership of goods it represents. It entitles the party who possesses the document to possess the goods. The documents of title are created out of a special "bailment" relationship between the owner of personal property, the bailor, and the one to whom possession is entrusted, the bailee. A **bailment** is a relationship involving two aspects of the goods—the first is the right of ownership (the bailor) and the second is the right to possession (the bailee). Bailment is discussed further in Chapter 38.

Bailment
The possession of personal property by someone who is not the true owner, without transfer of title, for a particular purpose.

Two common examples of documents of title are bills of lading and warehouse receipts. In either case, the document of title will pass from the seller to the buyer when and where the document is delivered. A **bill of lading** serves as a receipt for the goods and acts as the contract between the seller and the carrier for the transportation of the goods to a specified location. You receive a copy of a bill of lading when goods you order are delivered to your residence by a common carrier.

Bill of lading
A document indicating receipt of goods by a carrier and the contract for the transportation of those goods.

Sample Form
U.S. Government Bill of Lading

U.S. GOVERNMENT BILL OF LADING
INTERNATIONAL AND DOMESTIC OVERSEAS SHIPMENTS

B/L NUMBER

TRANSPORTATION COMPANY TENDERED TO | SCAC | DATE B/L PREPARED

DESTINATION NAME AND ADDRESS | SPLC *(Dest.)* | SPLC *(Orig.)* | ORIGIN NAME AND ADDRESS

CONSIGNEE *(Name and full address of installation)* | GBLOC *(Cons.)* | SHIPPER NAME AND ADDRESS

APPROPRIATION CHARGEABLE | BILL CHARGES TO *(Dept./agency, bureau/office mailing address and ZIP code)* | AGENCY LOC CODE

VIA *(Route shipment when advantageous to the Government)*

MARKS AND ANNOTATIONS

PACKAGES		HM	DESCRIPTION OF ARTICLES *(Use carrier's classification or tariff description if possible; otherwise use a clear nontechnical description.)*	19. WEIGHTS* *(Pounds only)*	FOR USE OF BILLING CARRIER ONLY		
NO.	KIND				Services	Rate	Charges
			CLASSIFICATION ITEM NO.		TOTAL CHARGES		

TARIFF/SPECIAL RATE AUTHORITY | CARRIER WAY/FREIGHT BILL NO. AND DATE

STOP THIS SHIPMENT AT

FOR

CARRIER'S PICKUP DATE *(Year, month, and day)*

MODE

FURNISH INFORMATION ON CAR/TRUCKLOAD/CONTAINER SHIPMENTS

SEAL NUMBERS	LENGTH/CUBE		MARKED CAPACITY		DATE FURNISHED
	ORDERED	FURNISHED	ORDERED	FURNISHED	
APPLIED BY:					
ESTIMATE	NO. OF CLS/TLS	TYPE RATE	PSC	REASON	

This U.S. Government shipment is subject to terms and conditions of 41 CFR 102-117 and CFR 102-118.

CERTIFICATE OF CARRIER BILLING -- CONSIGNEE MUST NOT PAY ANY CHARGES

DELIVERED ON *(Year, month, and day)*

FOR USE OF ISSUING OFFICE

ISSUING OFFICE *(Name and complete address)* | GBLOC | ISSUING OFFICER

CONTRACT/PURCHASE ORDER NO. OR OTHER AUTHORITY | DATED

FOB POINT NAMED IN CONTRACT

*Show also cubic measurements for shipments via air, truck or water carrier in cases where required.

AUTHORIZED FOR LOCAL REPRODUCTION

STANDARD FORM 1103 (REV. 9/2003)
Prescribed by GSA/FMR 102-118

A **warehouse receipt** is issued by a warehouse evidencing title to goods stored with another. Although these two documents are different, both will pass title to the buyer upon delivery of the document.

Warehouse receipt
A document evidencing title to goods stored with another.

Global Application
International Documentary Transactions

International transactions for the sale of goods are documentary in nature. These are the processes by which the transaction will occur:

- The seller and the buyer enter into a sales contract for the sale of goods (or one for predominantly goods when some services are also being provided);
- The seller procures the goods and delivers them to a carrier;
- The buyer procures a letter of credit from its bank to arrange for payment of the goods;
- The carrier loads the goods (on a ship, truck, etc.) and issues a bill of lading to the seller;
- The seller presents the bill of lading and other documents such as an invoice and insurance certificates to the seller's bank, which acts in coordination with the buyer's bank;
- The seller's bank examines the documents to ensure that they conform to the letter of credit issued by the buyer's bank;
- The seller's bank forwards the seller's documents to the buyer's bank;
- The buyer's bank examines the documents to ensure that they conform to the letter of credit issued by the buyer's bank; if so, the buyer's bank issues payment to the seller's bank (at which time the seller's bank will pay the seller);
- The buyer's bank forwards the documents to the buyer and debits the buyer's account, or the buyer pays the bank for the sums sent to the seller's bank;
- The buyer presents the bill of lading to carrier; and
- The carrier delivers the seller's goods to the buyer at the delivery point.

Acquisition of Imperfect Title

Transactions do not always go smoothly. This section addresses what happens when a party who has purchased goods with imperfect title attempts to sell or lease the goods to a third party. Imperfect title occurs when the original seller is not the rightful owner of the goods. The UCC addresses this problem by identifying the rights of the two parties who are both contesting ownership of the goods. UCC §§ 2-402, 2-403. Generally, the buyer acquires the same title the seller possessed.

Void title
Title in which the purchaser acquires no ownership interest, usually because the goods were stolen.

VOID TITLE. When a buyer purchases goods from a seller who, unbeknownst to the buyer, has stolen the goods, the buyer's title is typically considered void. Even though the buyer had no knowledge the goods were stolen, the buyer will not acquire title. This allows the true owner of the goods to recover them from the buyer.

Example: Alfonso Candela purchased a vehicle from Port Motors Inc. (Port). A few days later his vehicle was seized by law enforcement as a suspected stolen vehicle. Candela then sued Port for breach of warranty of title. Port claimed it had no knowledge that the car was stolen and thus should not be liable to Candela. The court concluded that if the car was in fact stolen, it does not matter whether Port knew it was stolen or not. The court reasoned that if Port did purchase the vehicle from the car thief, Port's title would be void, and thus Port could not convey good title to Candela. *Candela v. Port Motors Inc.*, 208 A.D.2d 486 (N.Y. App. Div. 1994)

Voidable title
Title in which the purchaser may receive good title to the goods so long as the purchaser did not have notice that valid title belonged to another party.

Good faith purchaser
A purchaser who did not have prior notice of the claims of another having valid title to the goods.

VOIDABLE TITLE. Unlike a void title, **voidable title** gives the seller the ability to transfer good title to a purchaser so long as they are a good faith purchaser. A **good faith purchaser** is a purchaser who did not have prior notice that someone other than the seller holds valid title to the goods in question. Additionally, the good faith purchaser must give legally sufficient consideration in exchange for the goods to obtain voidable title. The true owner of the goods could file a claim against the seller who obtained voidable title of the goods, but the true owner cannot recover the goods from the good faith purchaser. UCC § 2-403(1).

The seller will possess voidable title of the goods being sold if they were (1) obtained through fraud, (2) paid by use of a check to which the funds were insufficient, or (3) purchased by the seller on credit while insolvent. The UCC deems a party to be insolvent when the party is unable to pay its debts in the ordinary course of business, fails to pay its debts as they come due, or is insolvent as defined by federal bankruptcy law.

Example: James Foley traded his truck with Karl Rudolph in exchange for a front-end loader. Rudolph then pledged the truck as security for a loan. When Rudolph failed to pay the loan, the truck was seized by the creditor and sold to a bona fide purchaser in exchange for partial satisfaction of the loan. Foley then learned that the front-end loader he had received in exchange for the truck had been stolen, and he returned it to its original owner. Foley brought an action against the secured creditor Rudolph to recover the value of the truck. The court held in favor of the creditor, finding that even though Rudolph, who had voidable title to the truck, did not sell it to the creditor, using it as collateral had the same effect and thus the creditor obtained valid title to the vehicle. *Foley v. Production Credit Ass'n of Fourth Dist.*, 753 S.W.2d 876 (Ky. App. 1988)

Concept Summary
Void Title Compared to Voidable Title

Type	Description
Void Title	Occurs when a buyer purchases stolen goods from a seller. Even if the buyer had no knowledge that the goods are stolen, the buyer will not acquire title to the goods.
Voidable Title	A good faith purchaser may acquire title to the goods even though they were obtained by the seller through use of (1) fraud, (2) a check with insufficient funds, or (3) credit despite the seller being insolvent. The good faith purchaser will hold title to the goods over all except for the true owner of the goods.

Sales by Merchants

THE ENTRUSTMENT RULE. The UCC contains special rules for the sale of goods between a merchant and a buyer. Recall from Chapter 26 a merchant is a person who deals in goods of the kind involved in the sales contract. The UCC created the **entrustment rule**, which states that a merchant has the power to transfer all rights to a buyer in the ordinary course of business, so long as the goods entrusted to the merchant are of the kind in which the merchant deals. UCC § 2-403(2).

Entrustment rule
A UCC rule by which a merchant has the power to transfer all rights to a buyer in the ordinary course of business so long as the goods entrusted to the merchant are the kind in which the merchant deals.

Entrusted goods are those that have been given to the merchant or purchased and left with the merchant to be delivered later. UCC § 2-403(3). Additionally, there is a similar rule for leased goods found in Article 2A of the UCC. UCC § 2A-305(2). Essentially, this rule gives innocent purchasers the ability to obtain legitimate title to the goods they have purchased from merchants, regardless of whether the merchants have good title or not.

The UCC defines a person as a buyer in the ordinary course of business where:

1. The person buys goods in good faith;
2. The goods are obtained without knowledge that the sale violating another person's rights in the goods;
3. The goods are bought in the ordinary course of business from a merchant (other than a pawnbroker) selling goods of that kind; and
4. The sale is consistent with the customary practices in the type of business in which the seller engages. UCC § 1-201(9).

The next case considers the entrustment rule in the context of stolen equipment. It involves an action brought for replevin. Replevin is an action for repossession of personal property wrongfully taken or detained. If granted, the plaintiff retains possession until the court decides who owns the property. Additionally, the court also issues a money judgment relating to the plaintiff's damages. Such was the following case filed over replevin claim for a rare 1934 Pierce Arrow coupe ("Pierce Arrow") and disputes over its ownership. The question in this case was whether Gary Disco, an antique car trader and restorer, had the right to convey title to the Pierce Arrow without the consent of Richard Richmond (the original owner).

CASE 27.2

THE ENTRUSTMENT RULE ONLY APPLIES WHEN THE SELLER IS A MERCHANT "WHO DEALS IN GOODS OF THE KIND AT ISSUE"

RICHMOND v. F-40 RESTORATION, LLC

467 F. Supp. 3d 20 (2020)

United States District Court for the District of Connecticut

Robert Richmond (Richmond), an antique car collector, resided in Australia. He was referred to Gary Disco for restoration work in the United States. Richmond hired Disco to help him purchase, restore, and prepare for shipment approximately 19 vehicles during the course of their relationship. Richmond purchased the Pierce Arrow for $98,000 from Gould, with logistical assistance from Dicso, who did not provide financial contribution but helped with storage arrangements. Over time, the business relationship between Richmond and Dicso soured. Without Richmond's consent, Dicso transferred title of the car to himself and subsequently sold it to Gullwing for $62,500. Gullwing then sold it to F-40 for $110,000, and F-40 later sold it to Sotheby's for $250,000.

Richmond soon learned of the actions of Dicso and the other buyers. Richmond claimed ownership of the Pierce Arrow. F-40 was the current holder of the title procured by Dicso, and the Pierce Arrow was currently in its possession. Richmond sued for replevin and conversion. The district court decided the summary judgment motion for the replevin cause of action.

Language of the Court. *This case represents one of those rare but unfortunate cases where although all parties ostensibly acted in good faith one is doomed to incur the losses occasioned by a bad actor, who is himself, not a party to the litigation.*

Here, the Defendants assert that Richmond entrusted the Pierce Arrow to Dicso, a "merchant," and therefore bore the risk that Dicso, as a merchant, would then put the Pierce Arrow into the stream of commerce by selling it to "a buyer in the ordinary course of business" (e.g., Gullwing). This defense raises two intertwined issues: first, whether Dicso was a "merchant who deals in goods of the kind" at issue and, second, whether Dicso was "in the business of selling goods of [the] kind." The Defendants contend that because there is evidence that Dicso worked in the antique car industry and previously sold antique cars, summary judgment on their entrustment defense is inappropriate. Richmond disagrees, arguing that to prevail in this defense the Defendants must establish that Dicso regularly sold antique cars, which they cannot do because he did not.

The undisputed facts establish that Richmond purchased the Pierce Arrow from Gould for $98,000, at which point he was the vehicle's owner. As the owner, Richmond has both a property interest in and the right to immediate possession of the Pierce Arrow.

The UCC provides that "[a]ny entrusting of possession of goods to a merchant who deals in goods of that kind gives him power to transfer all rights of the entruster to a buyer in ordinary course of business." A "merchant" is defined in relevant part as "a person who deals in goods of the kind or otherwise by his occupation holds himself out as having knowledge or skill peculiar to the practices or goods involved in the transaction. . . ." A "buyer in the ordinary course" is defined in relevant part as "a person that buys goods in good faith, without knowledge that the sale violates the rights of another person in the goods, and in the ordinary course from a person . . . in the business of selling goods of that kind."

There is no evidence that Dicso regularly engaged in the sale of antique cars. Dicso was in the business of car restoration, and he has specifically disavowed ever having a dealer's license or ever being in the business of selling new or used motor vehicles. Aside from the sale of the Pierce Arrow, the record reflects only one other car sale made by Dicso. Notably, Dicso did not sell that vehicle as a foray into the world of antique car dealing. Rather, he sold it for the same reason he sold the

Pierce Arrow; to address his significant financial troubles. Under these facts and circumstances, no reasonable jury could conclude that Dicso was a merchant "who deals in goods of the kind" at issue.

Decision. The court granted summary judgment to Richmond on his claim of replevin, allowing him to recover the 1934 Pierce Arrow coupe because Dicso was deemed not a merchant.

Focus on Ethics

Is it fair that F-40 is deprived of the special vehicle? How do you think the court would have acted if Dicso was deemed a merchant?

Risk of Loss

Risk of loss is a term used to identify which party will bear the risk if goods are damaged between the sale and the delivery of the goods. Risk of loss may not always pass with title under the UCC. The time at which risk of loss transfers between the seller and the buyer will depend on the contents of the contract between the parties. Commonly a contract will specifically state when risk of loss will pass between the parties. However, when the contract does not expressly state when the risk of loss passes, the court will utilize the following rules to interpret the terms of the contract to determine when the risk of loss passes.

Risk of loss
A term used to identify which party will bear the risk if the goods are damaged between the sale's completion and the delivery of the goods.

Carrier Contracts

Goods are often transported from seller to buyer by means of a common carrier. A **common carrier** is a party, usually a company that provides for the transportation of goods for a fee established or regulated by the government. When a contract for the sale of goods involves the use of a common carrier but fails to specify when the risk of loss will pass, the courts begin their analysis by reviewing delivery terms stated in the contract.

Common carrier
A commercial enterprise providing transportation of persons or goods for a fee.

> **Example:** Old Dominion Freight Line® is a common carrier that transports goods nationwide.

The terms of delivery allow the court to determine when the risk of loss will pass, as well as which party is required to pay the cost associated with the delivery of the goods. Common delivery terms and when the risk of loss transfers are stated in the table below. If the contract fails to include one of these terms, the court will decide if the transaction involves a shipment or a destination contract.

Concept Summary
Common Delivery Terms

Term	Description
FCA — Free Carrier	■ Buyer will arrange for carriage or may ask the seller to do it on their behalf for a fee. ■ Title and risk of loss transfers to the buyer when the seller delivers the goods to the carrier. Buyer has a duty to pay when the goods have been delivered to the carrier.
FOB — Free on Board at a named place	■ If FOB point of shipment, the seller arranges for the shipment of goods and bears the expense and risk of loss until the goods are tendered to the carrier. The buyer bears the risk of loss during transit. ■ If FOB place of destination, the seller bears the expense and risk of loss until the goods are tendered to the buyer at the place of destination.
FAS — Free Alongside Ship	■ The seller to deliver the goods and bears the expense and risk of loss until the goods are tendered to the named vessel or the dock designed by the buyer. ■ The buyer bears the shipping cost and the risk of loss during transit.
CFR — Cost and Freight	■ A pricing term indicating that carriage and freight are arranged by seller and factored into the sales price of the goods. ■ Seller bears expense and risk of loss until goods are tendered to the carrier. ■ Buyer bears the risk of loss during transportation. ■ Buyer has duty to pay when the goods reach the buyer's port of destination.
CIF — Cost Insurance and Freight	■ A pricing term indicating that carriage, insurance, and freight are arranged by seller and factored into the sales price of the goods. ■ Seller bears expense and risk of loss until goods are tendered to the carrier. ■ Buyer bears the risk of loss during transportation. ■ Buyer has duty to pay when the goods reach the buyer's port of destination.

CASE 27.3

GIVING SHIPPING INSTRUCTIONS DOES NOT CONVERT A SHIPPING CONTRACT TO A DESTINATION CONTRACT

DEITER v. COONS

394 P.3d 87 (2016)

Supreme Court of Idaho

Patty Anderson posted an ad on Craigslist seeking the sale of her granddaughter's 4-H steer. She was contacted by Joseph Deiter, who only wanted to purchase meat from half of the steer. Anderson prepared a handwritten contract that stated the steer would be slaughtered and delivered to Don's Meats where it would be weighed, portioned, and available to pick up thereafter. Deiter paid a $100 deposit for his share of the meat. Mrs. Kirk purchased the other half of the steer. Anderson contacted Janak, Inc., a mobile slaughtering business, to slaughter the steer and deliver it to Don's Meats. Both purchasers picked up their meats from Don's Meats, where the meat was also processed. However, after eating the meat Deiter's family became ill due to the meat being infected with *E. coli* bacteria. Deiter then sued Anderson, believing she was liable for the meat's exposure to *E. coli* bacteria. The trial court ruled in her favor, finding she was not liable. Deiter then appealed to the Supreme Court of Idaho.

Language of the Court. *If the parties intend that delivery be made to a carrier, a request in the buyer's letter to the seller that the goods be shipped to the buyer's residence is a mere shipping instruction that does not convert the contract to a destination contract, and the risk of loss passes to the buyer at the time the goods are delivered to a carrier, such as the postal service.*

Anderson was not liable because under the Idaho Uniform Commercial Code, title to the steer passed to Mr. Deiter and Mrs. Kirk when possession was transferred to Mr. Janak.

The Deiter Contract did not expressly require Ms. Anderson to deliver the steer to any place. "The parties must explicitly agree to a destination contract; otherwise the contract will be considered a shipment contract." There was nothing in the contract regarding risk of loss if the carcass was taken to the wrong place. Moreover, a "ship to" term has no significance in determining whether a contract is a shipment or destination contract for risk of loss purposes. Because the contract in this case was a shipment contract, title passed to Mr. Deiter and Mrs. Kirk at the time and place that Ms. Anderson completed her performance with reference to the physical delivery of the goods. Once possession of the steer was delivered to Mr. Janak, there was nothing more for Ms. Anderson to do under the contract with respect to the physical delivery of the goods.

Mr. Janak had agreed to transport the carcass to Don's Meats, where the Deiters were to pick up their portion of the meat after it was processed. As the contract stated, "When the meat has been cut + wrapped by Don's Meat Joseph and Melinda Deiter will pay Sharon Coons 45¢ /lb. for that service and will pick up their half of the beef." Once Ms. Anderson delivered possession of the steer to Mr. Janak, Mr. Deiter became the owner of a one-half interest in the steer, and Mrs. Kirk became the owner of the other one-half interest.

Decision. The Supreme Court of Idaho affirmed the trial court's ruling that Ms. Anderson was not liable because the risk of loss had transferred to Deiter at the time the steer was delivered to Janak, Inc.

Focus on Ethics

While illness was an unfortunate consequence, do you think the court made the right decision? Does the Idaho version of the UCC adequately protect the interests of the parties in this instance?

SHIPMENT CONTRACTS AND RISK OF LOSS. As previously discussed, shipment contracts allow the seller to mitigate some of its potential risk. In a shipment contract the risk of loss passes to the buyer upon the goods being delivered to the common carrier. Thus, the seller is not responsible for the goods reaching the final destination, thereby reducing the time for which the seller may be liable for any loss.

> **Example:** Ladex Corp. entered into a contract with Santeri Fisheries de Hondouras, S.A. (Santeri) for the purchase of 175 cartons of frozen shrimp. The shrimp were delivered to Transportes Aereos Nacionales, S.A. (TAN) by Santeri. The shrimp arrived at Miami International Airport and were loaded onto a truck bound for Ladex's warehouse. The truck never arrived and was believed to have been hijacked. Ladex filed a claim against TAN seeking recovery of the $37,328.50 paid for the shrimp. The court found TAN was not liable to pay Santeri, finding that Ladex and Santeri had formed a shipment contract in which title and risk of loss passed to Ladex when Santeri delivered the goods to TAN. *Ladex Corp. v. Transportes Aereos Nacionales*, 476 So. 2d 763 (Fla. 3d Dist. App. 1985)

DESTINATION CONTRACTS AND RISK OF LOSS. Conversely, a **destination contract** allows the buyer to mitigate its potential risk by delaying the risk of loss passing to the buyer until the goods are tendered to the buyer at a specific location. Thus, if the goods are damaged or destroyed at any point prior to the buyer's receiving them, the seller will bear the loss. UCC § 2-401(2)(b). Under the UCC, this is known as *the tender of delivery*, meaning the seller has tendered or placed the goods in the buyer's possession or in an agreed upon location in which the goods are available to the buyer. UCC § 2-503(1).

Management Application
What If the Goods Never Arrive?

Issue	Result
Parties entered into a destination contract, but the goods never arrived.	Under UCC §§ 2-324 and 2-613, in instances where the goods do not arrive it will be treated as if there was no contract formed between the parties. Therefore, neither the seller nor the buyer will be liable. The seller will only be liable if the seller caused the non-arrival to occur.

> **Example:** June Ashton, an interior designer, entered into a contract with Stark Carpet Corporation for the purchase of carpeting on behalf of a client. The carpeting was to be shipped from England where it was being woven and then sent to Ashton in Chicago. The dates for delivery were not met. Ashton cancelled the order. She sued Stark for failing to deliver the carpet timely. Stark sued Ashton

for the unpaid balance asserting it had tendered the goods to Ashton because they arrived the day following the order cancellation and title had already passed to Ashton. The court found that title had not passed to Ashton, as the contract was a destination contract. The court reasoned that Stark's agreement to deliver the carpet to Ashton in Chicago meant that title did not pass until delivery. *June G. Ashton Interiors v. Stark Carpet Corp.*, 491 N.E.2d 120 (Ill. App. Ct. 1986)

Delivery Without Movement of the Goods

Sometimes, a sale or lease contract will not require the goods to be moved. In these situations, either the buyer will pick up the goods directly from the seller or a bailee will hold the goods.

A bailment is the possession of personal property by someone who is not the true owner, without the transfer of title, for a particular purpose. The party who by means of a document of title, such as a bill of lading or warehouse receipt, acquires possession of the goods is the bailee. The bailee may also be required to deliver the goods, if required by the agreement.

GOODS HELD BY SELLER. When the seller retains possession of the goods until they are delivered, the risk of loss does not pass until the buyer takes possession of the goods. UCC § 2-509(3). In this situation, a document of title will not be used. Whether or not the seller is a merchant will determine the time at which risk of loss passes. If the seller is a merchant, the merchant bears the risk of loss until the buyer takes physical possession of the goods. If the seller is not a merchant, the risk of loss will pass to the buyer on tender of delivery. UCC § 2-509(3). Therefore, as soon as the seller makes the goods available to the buyer and provides notice that the goods are ready to be picked up, risk of loss passes to the buyer. Additionally, the rules are the same when dealing with contracts for the lease of goods. UCC § 2A-219(2)(c).

Example: John Caudle agreed to purchase a house trailer from Sherrard Motor Company. The contract stated Caudle would make a down payment of $2,685 and the remaining $4,005 would be paid in the form of a note payable to Sherrard. Before the trailer was ready for Caudle to take possession, he received a call and was required to return home to Dallas immediately. Caudle told Sherrard he would return later to take possession of the trailer. Before Caudle picked up the trailer, it was stolen from Sherrard's place of business. Caudle then immediately stopped payment on the check for the down payment. Sherrard then sued Caudle for the contract price. Sherrard contended that the risk of loss passed to Caudle before the trailer was stolen. The court found that risk of loss remained with Sherrard, a merchant, until Caudle took physical possession of the trailer, which never occurred. Therefore, the court found Caudle was not liable to pay Sherrard the contract price. *Caudle v. Sherrard Motor Co.*, 525 S.W.2d 238 (Tex. Civ. App. 1975)

GOODS HELD BY BAILEE. Goods may be sold by a seller to a buyer that are in the possession of a bailee (such as at a logistics company's warehouse). When a bailee holds the goods, the occurrence of any one of the following will pass risk of loss to the buyer because tender of delivery occurred when:

- Buyer receives from seller a negotiable document of title for the goods (such as a warehouse receipt or bill of lading);
- Bailee recognizes the buyer's right to possession of the goods; or
- Buyer obtains the nonnegotiable document of title, and the buyer is given reasonable time to present the document and demand the goods from the bailee. The bailee's refusal to honor the document will result in the risk of loss remaining with the seller. UCC §§ 2-503(4)(b), 2-509(2).

Goods that are to be leased may also be held by a bailee. Risk of loss will pass to the lessee when the bailee recognizes the lessee's right to possess the goods. UCC § 2A-219(2)(b).

Example: O.C.T. Equipment (O.C.T.) agreed to purchase four tractors from Shepherd Machinery Co. O.C.T. wired the payment to Shepard, and Shepard delivered the tractors to Keen, a bailee. One of the tractors was damaged while in possession of the bailee. After finding out the tractor was damaged, O.C.T. refused delivery and sought reimbursement of the purchase price. After Shepard refused to refund the money, O.C.T. filed a suit alleging Shepard had breached their contract. The court found that Shepard was liable and thus must refund O.C.T. The court reasoned that Shepard bore the risk of loss at the time the damage occurred because the bailee had not yet acknowledged O.C.T.'s right to possession nor had the tractor been made ready for delivery. *O.C.T. Equipment Inc. v. Shepard Machinery Co.*, 95 P.3d 197 (Okla. Civ. App. 2004)

Risk of Loss upon Breach of Contract

The transfer of risk of loss will be altered when the sales or lease contract for the goods is breached. Typically, the party who has breached the contract will bear the risk of loss.

BREACH BY SELLER OR LESSOR. Often a breach will occur because goods supplied by the seller or lessor are considered nonconforming and the buyer rejects the goods. **Nonconforming goods** are those that do not meet the specifications of the contract. The risk of loss will not pass to the buyer if the goods supplied by the seller or lessor are nonconforming.

Nonconforming goods
Goods that do not meet the specifications of the contract.

Example: A buyer orders 1,000 clear cell phone cases. The contract provides FOB seller's warehouse (buyer would have risk of loss during transportation). The seller transports 1,000 blue cell phone cases which are damaged during transit. As the seller transported nonconforming goods, the risk of loss remained with the seller.

Even if the goods are nonconforming, risk of loss may still pass to the buyer if either of the following occurs:

- The seller cures any defects by either repairing, replacing, or discounting the goods; or
- The buyer waives the right to reject the goods by accepting them regardless of the defects.

A buyer who accepts goods only to realize later that there is a defect can revoke its acceptance of the goods. The buyer's revocation of acceptance will allow the risk of loss to pass back to the seller if the buyer's insurance does not cover the loss. UCC § 2-510(2). Under Article 2A of the UCC, leases are subject to a similar rule.

> **Example:** Stanley Jakowski entered into a contract with Carole Chevrolet, Inc., for the sale of a vehicle. The parties agreed the car would be undercoated and the paint would be finished with a polymer coating before delivery. The vehicle was delivered to Stanley without the required coatings. The day after receiving the vehicle Stanley returned to the dealership to have the coatings applied. While at the dealership for the coatings, the vehicle was stolen and was never recovered. Carole Chevrolet refused to provide a replacement vehicle or refund the purchase price. Carole Chevrolet claims the risk of loss passed to Stanley upon his acceptance of the vehicle. The court found that Stanley had not accepted the vehicle given that when he learned the vehicle was not in conformance with the terms of the contract the defect was never cured. Therefore, the risk of loss remained with Carole Chevrolet, thereby entitling Stanley to a refund of the purchase price. *Jakowski v. Carole Chevrolet, Inc.*, 433 A.3d 841 (N.J. 1981)

BREACH BY BUYER OR LESSEE. In most situations, a breach of the contract by the buyer or lessee (such as refusing to take delivery of the conforming goods) will result in the immediate shift of the risk of loss to the buyer or lessee. However, there are three important limitations under which this rule operates:

- The goods specified for the contract must have already been identified by the seller or lessor;
- After the seller or lessor has learned of the breach, the buyer or lessee will only bear the risk of loss for a commercially reasonable time; and
- The buyer or lessee will only be liable to the seller for the portion of the loss not covered by the seller's insurance. UCC §§ 2-510(3), 2A-220(2).

Insurable Interest

It is common for parties involved in a contract for the sale or lease of goods to obtain insurance coverage to protect an insured against any loss, damage, or destruction of the goods. Only persons with a legally sufficient interest in the goods may purchase a valid insurance policy. What qualifies as a "sufficient interest" is not determined by the UCC, but instead by state insurance laws. However, the UCC does provide rules concerning the insurable interest of goods. An **insurable interest** will exist when a party has a legal interest in goods. An insurable interest allows that party to purchase insurance to mitigate financial loss in the event the item is damaged or destroyed.

Insurable interest A legal stake in the value of an item that allows a party to purchase insurance to mitigate loss in the event the item is damaged or destroyed.

Insurable Interest of Buyer or Lessee

A buyer or lessee possesses an insurable interest in identified goods. The identification of the goods by the seller or lessor creates an immediate insurable interest for the buyer or lessee, thus allowing the buyer or lessee to procure the requisite insurance coverage prior to the risk of loss being passed. UCC §§ 2-501(1), 2A-218(1). Recall the rules for determining when identification occurs that were discussed earlier in this chapter.

Insurable Interest of the Seller or Lessor

The insurable interest of a seller or lessor will exist during the time in which the seller or lessor holds title to the goods. However, if the seller has a security interest in the goods, it will still have an insurable interest even after the title passes. UCC § 2-501(2). This allows the seller and the buyer to both possess an insurable interest in the goods at the same time. In a contract for leased goods, the lessor will possess an insurable interest in the goods unless the lessee has exercised a purchase option, thereby passing the risk of loss to the lessee. UCC § 2A-218(3).

AI Feature: Damages in Transit

After reading this chapter, you should be able to contrast shipment contracts with destination contracts. Using an internet search engine, conduct research to determine if there is a strong presumption under the UCC favoring shipment contracts. If one party desired a shipment contract, how would it be known and become part of the contract?

Use an AI program to analyze the following facts and draft a clear form of a destination contract. Windows, Inc. is a fabricator and seller of windows, and Jordan Systems, Inc. is a construction subcontractor, which contracted to install window wall panels at an air cargo facility at John F. Kennedy Airport in New York City. Jordan ordered custom-made windows from Windows. The purchase contract specified that the windows were "to be shipped properly crated/packaged/boxed suitable for cross-country motor freight transit and delivered to New York City." Additionally, the contract referred to the specific job site, "Nippon Cargo, JFK Airport, N.Y." Windows constructed the windows according to Jordan's specifications. It arranged to have them shipped to Jordan by a common carrier, Consolidated Freightways Corp., and delivered to Consolidated intact and properly packaged. During the course of shipment, however, the goods sustained extensive damage. Much of the glass was broken and many of the window frames were gouged and twisted. Jordan's president signed a delivery receipt noting that approximately two-thirds of the shipment was damaged due to "load shift."

Jordan did not pay Windows for either the first shipment of damaged windows or a second, intact shipment. Windows filed suit to recover payment from Jordan for both shipments. Jordan counterclaimed, seeking incidental and consequential damages resulting from the damaged shipment. Windows then brought a third-party claim against Consolidated, which removed the suit to the United States District Court for the Eastern District of New York.

What are the arguments to be made that this is a shipment contract relieving Windows of liability to Jordan. What are the arguments to be made that is a destination contract? What language would you draft to create an unambiguous destination contract? Is the carrier relieved of liability? *See, Windows, Inc. v. Jordan Panel Sys. Corp.*, 177 F.3d 114 (2d Cir. 1999)

Key Terms

- Bailment, 673
- Bill of lading, 673
- Common carrier, 679
- Destination contract, 672
- Documentary transaction, 673
- Document of title, 673
- Entrustment rule, 677
- Fungible goods, 669
- Future goods, 669
- Good faith purchaser, 676
- Identification, 668
- Insurable interest, 685
- Nonconforming goods, 684
- Risk of loss, 679
- Shipment contract, 672
- Title, 670
- Voidable title, 676
- Void title, 676
- Warehouse receipt, 675

Applying the Law

27.1 Research the Law. Using an internet search engine research the differences between a negotiable bill of lading and a nonnegotiable bill of lading. Are there any instances in which a contracting party would prefer one over another?

27.2 Bill of Lading. What happens if parties to a contract have an "off record" agreement that understates the value of goods and is in an amount that is different from the bill of lading? What legal consequences are foreseeable? *Dictor v. David & Simon, Inc.*, 106 Cal. App. 4th 238 (2003)

27.3 Shipment or Destination Contract. A seller places an address label on the package and directs the carrier to "ship to" a particular destination. Is this enough to establish a destination contract? *Wilson v. Brawn of California, Inc.*, 132 Cal. App. 4th 549 (2005)

27.4 Ownership. Timothy Allen commissioned Indy Route 66 Cycles (Indy) to make a custom motorcycle. In April 2007, Indy finished building the custom motorcycle. Two years later, Tim was arrested for drug trafficking and the government seized the motorcycle from the garage of an Indiana home owned by Tim's sister. First, the government alleged that the motorcycle was subject to civil forfeiture because it constituted proceeds of drug trafficking, and the property was involved in a money laundering transaction. Second, Indy claimed it owned the motorcycle based on the Certificate of Origin and claims it never delivered the motorcycle. Rather, Indy suggested it was keeping it in storage until Tim could finish paying for it in full. Under the UCC, what determines who owns the motorcycle as between Indy and Tim? Should the government be able to seize the motorcycle? *United States v. 2007 Custom Motorcycle*, 2011 U.S. Dist. LEXIS 10230 (D. Ariz. 2011)

27.5 Entrustment. Christopher Crowe stole nearly $920,000 worth of IT equipment from Vectren and sold it to Nextday for $228,609. Nextday knew the goods were stolen but refused to return them when informed by the police. Vectren's insurer, Great American Insurance Company, sued Nextday for the stolen goods' value. Nextday claimed it had valid title under the Uniform Commercial Code's entrustment rule, but the court disagreed. Nextday was found liable for conversion (civil theft) and ordered to pay $593,447.55 plus interest to Great American Insurance Company. Is it fair that Nextday must reimburse the insurance company even though it did not take the equipment from Vectren's premises? Why wasn't Crowe sued for damages? *Great*

American Ins. Co. v. Nextday Network Hardware Corp. 2016 U.S. Dist. LEXIS 25044

27.6 Shipment or Destination Contract. Windows Inc. (Windows) was a fabricator and seller of windows, based in South Dakota. Jordan Systems Inc. (Jordan) was a construction subcontractor that contracted Windows to install window wall panels at an air cargo facility at the John F. Kennedy Airport in New York City. The purchase contract specified that the windows were to be shipped properly packaged for cross-country motor freight transit and "delivered to New York City." Windows arranged to have the products shipped to Jordan by a common carrier and delivered the product to the carrier intact and properly packaged. Unfortunately, the goods sustained extensive damage while being shipped. In fact, much of the glass was broken and many of the window frames were gouged and twisted. Jordan's president signed the delivery receipt; however, he noted that almost two-thirds of the shipment was damaged. Subsequently, Jordan ordered a second shipment from Windows, which was delivered in good condition. Jordan did not pay Windows for any of the shipments. Was this a destination contract or a shipment contract? Why? Who assumed the risk of loss? *Windows, Inc. v. Jordan Panel Sys. Corp.*, 177 F.3d 114 (2d Cir. 1999)

27.7 Risk of Loss. Israel Martin entered into a contract with Melland's Inc., a farm implement dealer, to purchase a truck and a haystack mover. Martin was given trade-in value for his old unit, which left a balance of about $18,000 to be paid. The agreement provided that Martin would mail or bring in the title to the old unit and give it to Melland's. Martin mailed the certificate of title; however, he could retain use and possession of the old unit until the new unit was ready. The new unit was not expected to be ready for two or three months. In addition, Melland's performed minor repairs to the trade-in unit on two occasions without requiring Martin to pay a fee for the repairs. Unfortunately, fire destroyed the trade-in unit. The parties did not have an agreement regarding insurance or the risk of loss on the unit. Must Martin or Melland's bear the risk of loss? Why? *Martin v. Melland's Inc.*, 283 N.W.2d 76 (N.D. 1979)

27.8 Issue of Title. Kenneth James West agreed to sell his 1975 Corvette to a man representing himself as Robert Wilson. West signed over the Corvette's title to Wilson and gave him the car in exchange for a cashier's check. Ten days later West learned that the cashier's check was forged. Subsequently, West filed a stolen vehicle report with the police. The police did not locate Wilson or the Corvette, and the case went cold. Nearly two and a half years later, West asked the police to run a check on the Corvette's vehicle identification number. The police check yielded the name and address of Tammy Roberts. It turns out that Roberts, who held the certificate of title to the Corvette, had purchased the vehicle from her brother, who in turn had purchased it in response to a newspaper ad. Unsurprisingly, West filed a suit against Roberts to establish legal ownership of the Corvette. Who has proper title? Why? *West v. Roberts*, 143 P.3d 1037 (Colo. 2006)

27.9 Third-Party Contractor. Can a third-party contractor be entitled to receive the benefit of a liability limitation in a contract between a shipper and a carrier where the contract does not extend the limitation to third parties? *Royal & Sun All. Ins., PLC v. Int'l Mgmt. Servs. Co.*, 703 F.3d 604 (2d Cir. 2013)

27.10 Risk of Loss. In response to Gary Newman dba Lakeview Mobile Homes' advertisement of "trailer, complete set-up," Mike Moses, along with his uncle, made several trips to Lakeview Mobile Homes and agreed on February 7, 1981, to purchase a used mobile home. On February 9, 1981, Newman delivered the mobile home to Moses's rented lot, blocked, and leveled the mobile home, removed the tires and axles, and connected the sewer and water pipes. On the same date, Moses's fiancée cleaned the interior of the mobile home and moved some kitchen utensils and dishes into the mobile home. She inspected the home and discovered a broken window and water pipe. Moses called these conditions as well as the lack of door keys to Newman's attention. On the afternoon of February 10, a windstorm destroyed the mobile home. Had the risk of loss shifted from the buyer to the seller? *Moses v. Newman*, 658 S.W.2d 119 (Tenn. Ct. App. 1983)

Performance and Breach of Sales and Lease Contracts

28

Many, while performing the foulest deeds, use the fairest words. — Democritus, Greek philosopher (470-370 B.C.)

Chapter Outline

- Introduction
- Obligations of Contracting Parties
  - *Management Application: Requirement of a Single Delivery*
  - *Management Application: Seller's Notice of Intent to Cure*
  - *Management Application: Demand for Assurances*
  - *Management Application: Contractual Language for Buyer's Right to Inspection*
- Anticipatory Repudiation
  - *Management Application: Response to Repudiation*
- Remedies of the Seller or Lessor
- Remedies of the Buyer or Lessee
- An Introduction to Warranties
- Express Warranty
- Implied Warranties

Case 28.1: *French v. Ben's Supercenter, Inc.*
Case 28.2: *Impact Finishing, Inc. v. Wild Card, Inc.*

- Warranty Disclaimers
  - *Management Application: Disclaimers of Express and Implied Warranties*
- Magnuson-Moss Warranty Act
- Warranties of Title and Possession
- AI Feature: Social Media Influencers and Puffery

Learning Objectives

After studying this chapter, you should be able to:

1. Describe remedies for the breach of sales or lease contract.
2. Explain express warranties and their functions.
3. Describe the types of implied warranties.
4. Describe how the Magnuson-Moss Warranty Act applies to consumer products.
5. Identify the warranties of title and possession.

Introduction

Having discussed the formation of sales and lease contracts in Chapter 26, in this chapter we will discuss the performance and breach of such contracts. Our discussion includes warranties, whose protections are intended to protect both buyers and lessees.

Obligations of Contracting Parties

The obligations of the parties to a sales or lease contract will vary depending upon the terms and meaning of their agreement. When the terms are vague or ambiguous, courts will apply the default provisions of the UCC to determine which party's interpretation will meet the requirements of good faith and commercial reasonableness.

Good Faith Provision of the UCC

Good faith provision A general presumption that the parties to a contract will deal with each other honestly, fairly, and in good faith, so as not to destroy the right of the other party or parties to receive the benefits of the contract.

The UCC's **good faith provision** states that every duty or contract under the UCC includes an obligation of good faith in relation to its performance or enforcement. UCC § 1-304. This provision cannot be disclaimed, or waived, by the parties. When applied to a merchant, the UCC defines good faith as "honesty in fact and the observance of reasonable commercial standards of fair dealing in the trade." UCC § 2-103(b). This imposes a higher standard of performance or duty on a merchant than is required for a party that is not a merchant.

If a detail related to the performance of the contract is not specified in the agreement, the good faith provision requires the parties to exercise good faith and commercial reasonableness in specifying these details later.

Seller or Lessor's Obligations

Under a sales or lease contract, a seller or lessor's primary obligation is to deliver or tender delivery of conforming goods to the buyer or lessee. In order for goods to be considered conforming, they must comply in every way with the description of the goods set forth in the agreement. When the seller or lessor makes the goods available and provides the requisite notice to the buyer or lessee, this is known as **tender of delivery**. UCC §§ 2-503(1), 2A-508(1). In order for the tender to be considered proper, it must take place at a reasonable time and in a reasonable manner. This requires that the tender must take place at a reasonable time of the day or night and the goods must be available for a reasonable period of time to allow the buyer or lessee to take possession of them unless the parties have agreed otherwise. UCC § 2-503(1)(a).

Tender of delivery Refers to an offer of goods by a seller to a buyer by putting or holding them at the disposition of the buyer and giving the buyer notification reasonably necessary for taking delivery.

Typically, when a transaction for goods is contemplated by contract, the goods are to be delivered in a single delivery, unless the parties have agreed to have the goods delivered in installments. UCC §§ 2-307, 2-612, and 2A-510.

When a contract is silent in regard to the place where the goods are to be delivered by the seller, the UCC will control this term. In such case, the UCC allows for the delivery to take place at either the seller's place of business or the seller's residence if it has no place of business. UCC § 2-308(a). Further, the UCC provides that if at the time of contracting both parties know the goods are not located at the seller's business, delivery will be proper at the location of the goods. UCC § 2-308(b). Keep in mind that if the contract provides that delivery may take place in another location, delivery can be proper at the agreed-upon location.

Management Application
Requirement of a Single Delivery

The parties agree, notwithstanding any prior dealings, usage of trade, other provisions provided herein, or applicable law to the contrary, that all of the goods referred to in this contract shall be delivered in a single delivery on July 1, 2025.

PLACE OF DELIVERY. If the parties to the contract fail to provide a term regarding the place of delivery, the UCC allows delivery to be considered proper if made to any of the following:

- Seller's place of business;
- Seller's residence, but only if the seller does not have a physical business location, UCC § 2-308(a); or
- The location of the goods, so long as at the time of contracting both parties know that the goods are not located at the seller's business, UCC § 2-308(b).

DELIVERY BY COMMON CARRIER. Frequently, a contract will include delivery terms, such as FOB, FAS, or CIF (discussed in Chapter 27), which indicate the parties' intention to have the goods delivered by a **common carrier**. These common carriers enter into contracts with sellers, thereby agreeing to deliver the goods on behalf of the seller. Agreements between sellers and common carriers are either shipment or destination contracts.

Common carrier
A person or company that transports goods or passengers on regular routes at set rates.

Recall from Chapter 27 that *shipment contracts* allow the seller to contract with a carrier to take on the seller's obligation of delivering the goods to a specified location. Additionally, shipment contracts mitigate the seller's risks by passing title to the buyer at the time of shipment. There is a general presumption that all contracts for the sale of goods are shipment contracts unless stated otherwise. When the parties have entered into a shipment contract, there are several things that the UCC requires the seller to do. Unless the parties agree otherwise, UCC § 2-504 requires the seller to do the following:

1. Delivers the goods to the common carrier;
2. Contract with the common carrier for the transportation of the goods in a manner that is reasonable. What is reasonable will be determined by the type of goods and their value;
3. Obtain and promptly deliver or tender to the buyer all the documents necessary for the buyer to receive possession of the goods from the carrier; and
4. Provide the buyer with prompt notice that the goods have been shipped.

When the parties agree to a *destination contract*, the seller must deliver the conforming goods to the buyer at a specified location. Under these circumstances, the seller is required to give the buyer reasonable notice of the delivery and make the goods available to the buyer for a reasonable amount of time. Upon delivery, the seller must present the buyer with any necessary documents of title, at which time title to the goods will pass from the seller to the buyer.

Perfect tender rule A common law principle requiring that the seller deliver goods in perfect conformity with the description in the contract.

THE PERFECT TENDER RULE. Unlike under common law where substantial performance is considered sufficient performance of the contract, the UCC requires strict compliance with the contract's terms. Therefore, under the UCC substantial performance will not be enough to prevent a party from being found liable for breach of contract. The perfect tender rule states that when the goods fail to comply with their specific description or terms of delivery, the buyer is able to:

- Accept the goods,
- Reject the goods, or
- Accept part of the goods while rejecting another part of the goods.

However, if the goods conform to the description in every aspect, the buyer or lessee will not have a right to reject the goods, in whole or in part. UCC §§ 2-601, 2A-509.

> **Example:** Alaska Pacific Trading Company (ALPAC) and Eagon Forest Products, Inc. (Eagon) contracted to sell and buy logs. The delivery date passed with no shipment, leading Eagon to cancel the contract and allege that ALPAC had breached. ALPAC brought an action for breach of contract. The court ruled in favor of Eagon, finding under the applicable perfect tender rule that ALPAC breached its duty under the contract and releasing Eagon from its duty to accept the logs. *Alaska Pacific Trading Co. v. Eagon Forest Products, Inc.*, 933 P.2d 417 (Wash. Ct. App. 1997)

Exceptions to the Perfect Tender Rule

In order to deal with the strict requirements of the perfect tender rule, several exceptions have been created to allow these transactions to remain efficient, as discussed below:

BY AGREEMENT. Given the courts' deference to the terms of contracts between parties, the parties may waive the perfect tender rule, thereby not rejecting the nonconforming goods, so long as the seller or lessor can replace or repair the goods within a reasonable amount of time.

Right to cure Provision of the UCC that allows the seller or lessor to cure nonconforming goods in limited circumstances.

THE RIGHT TO CURE. The UCC allows a seller or lessor the **right to cure** nonconforming goods so long as the following are true:

1. The delivery of the goods was rejected due to nonconformance;
2. The time allocated for performance has not yet expired;
3. The seller or lessor has provided the buyer or lessee with timely notice of their intention to cure the defect; and
4. The defect can be cured within the time allocated for performance. UCC § 2-508.

Management Application
Seller's Notice of Intent to Cure

To: Buyer

PLEASE TAKE NOTICE that in response to your notice of rejection dated January 23, 2025, Seller intends to ship additional goods. These goods shall conform in all respects to the terms of our contract dated August 18, 2025, and therefore will satisfy the objections stated in the notice of rejection. Shipment of such goods will occur in accordance with the terms of our contract. This notice of Seller's intent to cure has been made in good faith. It is done with the intention of avoiding further disputes and does not constitute an admission that Seller has breached our contract or effectuated an improper tender.

____
Seller's signature

SUBSTITUTION OF CARRIERS. When the intended method of delivery becomes unavailable for reasons not under the control of either party, the parties may agree to use a commercially reasonable substitute to effect delivery. UCC § 2-614.

> **Example:** Buyer and Seller enter into an agreement for the sale and delivery of a vehicle. The contract provides FOB buyer's address which is 1,500 miles from Seller. Delivery is through rail freight transportation. After execution of the contract, a severe earthquake caused the rail route to be impacted. The Seller can substitute a commercial carrier to transport the goods through the highway.

THE RIGHT OF ASSURANCES. If one party has reasonable grounds to believe the other party will not perform under the contract, the party may demand adequate assurance of performance from the other party. The demand must be made in writing. Receipt of the demand suspends the demanding party's need to perform until the proper assurances are received. UCC §§ 2-609, 2A-401.

Right of assurances The right to demand adequate assurance of the performance of obligations under a contract when there are reasonable grounds to believe the party will not perform.

> **Example:** Buyer and Seller enter into an agreement for the purchase of Seller's last 100 bales of hay. A few days later, Buyer learns from the owner of a neighboring ranch that Seller agreed to sell the 100 bales to him instead for a higher price. Buyer may then demand assurances from Seller by stating he will not pay for the hay until it is actually delivered.

INSTALLMENT CONTRACTS. An **installment contract** allows a single contract to authorize multiple deliveries to be accepted and paid for separately. UCC §§ 2-612, 2A-510. The perfect tender rule is relaxed with respect to installment contracts. The buyer may only reject the installment if the nonconformity substantially impairs the value of the goods in that installment. However, the buyer will not be able to terminate the entire contract based on one installment that suffered substantial impairment. The right to terminate the entire contract will only arise if the nonconformity that occurs

Installment contract A single contract that authorizes multiple deliveries to be accepted and paid for separately.

in one or more installments substantially impairs the value of the entire contract. If it would not be in the buyer's interest to terminate the entire contract, the buyer can instead make a demand for assurances as discussed above.

Management Application
Demand for Assurances

To: Buyer

Recent events have raised our concerns regarding your ability and/or willingness to complete performance of our contract dated August 31, 2022. You failed to pay the sums due for the lots delivered by our company to you on September 1, 2025, and November 1, 2025. Under the provisions of applicable law, we may demand your assurances under these circumstances. We request that you provide assurance by posting a letter of credit in addition to the amount due for the two unpaid deliveries (copies of the related invoices are enclosed herewith). Until your assurances have been received, we will suspend the performance of our obligations under this contract. Failure to receive your assurances by December 10, 2025, will be deemed a breach of the contract under applicable law.

____
Seller's signature

Commercial impracticability A legal concept making performance of the contract impracticable due to circumstances that were not foreseen by either party during the formation of the contract.

COMMERCIAL IMPRACTICABILITY. Circumstances may arise that were not foreseen by either party during the formation of the contract that make performance **commercially impracticable**. The seller or lessor is required to notify the buyer or lessee as soon as practicable under the circumstances. UCC §§ 2-615, 2A-405.

> **Example:** Seller agrees to sell 1,000 pounds of fresh fish to the buyer. However, a large oil spill kills all the fish stock. Due to the oil spill, the seller will be unable to perform the obligations of the contract without incurring extravagant expense obtaining replacement stocks. Seller may assert an impracticability defense.

Partial performance When a party is only able to execute part of their performance under the contract.

COMMERCIAL IMPRACTICABILITY AND PARTIAL PERFORMANCE. Often the unforeseen circumstances that cause commercial impracticability result in only **partial performance**. This usually requires the seller or lessor to distribute the available goods. UCC §§ 2-615(b), 2A-405(b). The buyer or lessee must receive notice of the impracticability and will then have the right to accept or reject the goods. UCC §§ 2-615(c), 2A-405(c).

> **Example:** In the example above, if the seller had already acquired five hundred pounds of the specified fish inventory before the oil spill occurred, the seller must distribute it to the buyer.

DESTRUCTION OF IDENTIFIED GOODS. When an unexpected event results in the **destruction of identified goods** through no fault of either party, each of the parties will be excused from performance so long as the goods were identified when the contract was formed. UCC §§ 2-613, 2A-221. In the event that only part of the goods was destroyed, the buyer can choose to either void the contract or accept the available goods subject to a reduction of the contract price.

Destruction of identified goods Excusal from performance when goods that were identified when the contract was formed are destroyed as a result of unexpected events.

Example: Buyer and Seller enter into a contract for the purchase of 200 laptop computers that had been identified by their serial numbers; however, before shipment, the seller's warehouse was destroyed along with all of its contents. In this case, both parties are excused from performance.

DUTY OF COOPERATION. When one party fails to cooperate, the UCC allows the other party to suspend their performance while avoiding liability. The rule also allows the noncooperating party to be subject to a suit for breach of contract. UCC § 2-311(3).

Duty of cooperation The act of suspending performance under a contract while avoiding liability when the other party fails to cooperate.

Example: Buyer contracts with Seller, by which Seller agrees to deliver 300 chairs to various fast-food restaurants owned by Buyer throughout the city by July 31. Seller attempts to contact Buyer to find out to what locations the deliveries are to be made, but Buyer never returns Seller's many calls. If Seller does not make the deliveries by July 31, it cannot be held liable due to Buyer's failure to cooperate.

Buyer or Lessee's Obligations

PAYMENT. Generally, the buyer or lessee's obligation under a sales or lease contract is simply to pay for the goods as specified by the contract. In the absence of a specific agreement, the buyer or lessee is required to pay for the goods at the time and place they are received. UCC §§ 2-310(a), 2A-516(1).

When the buyer or lessee pays using credit, they must pay in accordance with the credit terms rather than when the goods are received. The terms typically establish a credit period, usually of 60, 90, or 120 days, and generally the credit period begins on the day the goods are shipped. UCC § 2-310(d). The contract may also specify the payment method the parties may use in the transaction; however; if the seller demands the payment be made in cash the seller must give the buyer a reasonable opportunity to obtain the amount specified. UCC § 2-511.

INSPECTION. A buyer or lessee will have the right to inspect the goods within a reasonable time prior to making a payment unless the parties specify otherwise.

Essentially, this precaution allows the buyer or lessee to ensure the goods are in conformity with the terms of the contract before payment occurs. Under the UCC, a buyer or lessee's opportunity to inspect the goods is a condition precedent to the seller's right to enforce payment. UCC §§ 2-513(1), 2A-515(1). This means the seller cannot enforce the terms of payment under the contract until the buyer has inspected the goods. When the goods are not in conformity with the terms of the contract, the buyer or lessee is not obligated to pay.

The cost of such an inspection is the responsibility of the buyer unless the goods are not in conformity with the terms of the contract. If the goods are nonconforming, the buyer may seek to be reimbursed for the inspection costs in the form of incidental damages.

Management Application Contractual Language for Buyer's Right to Inspection

The parties agree that the Buyer shall have the right and shall be given the opportunity to inspect the goods immediately upon the goods being ready for shipment. After Buyer receives notification of the goods' availability, the Buyer shall be given three (3) days to inspect the goods. Buyer's failure to inspect the goods under these terms will constitute a waiver of the Buyer's right of inspection.

The buyer has no right to inspect goods when the sales contract states that delivery will be made COD (cash on delivery — that is, when payment is made upon delivery of the goods instead of in advance).

ACCEPTANCE. Acceptance may be demonstrated by the buyer, after a reasonable opportunity for inspection, in the following manner:

- Buyer or lessee uses words or conduct to indicate to the seller or lessor that the goods are in conformity or that the buyer or lessee will keep the goods regardless of their nonconformity, UCC §§ 2-606(1)(a), 2A-515(1)(a);
- Buyer or lessee fails to reject the goods in a reasonable amount of time, UCC §§ 2-602(1), 2-606(1)(b), 2A-515(1)(b); or
- In a transaction between the buyer and seller, the buyer performs an act that is contrary to the seller's ownership of the goods, such as reselling the goods, UCC §§ 2-606(1)(c).

PARTIAL ACCEPTANCE. The buyer or lessee may take partial acceptance of goods where some of the goods delivered are not in conformity with the terms of the contract and the seller or lessor has failed to cure the nonconformity. UCC §§ 2-601(c), 2A-509(1). This rule also applies when the nonconformity was not reasonably discoverable prior to acceptance.

Anticipatory Repudiation

Anticipatory repudiation Informing the other party to a contract that a party they will not be able to perform the contract when performance is due.

Anticipatory repudiation occurs when a party will communicate or demonstrate to the other party before their contractual performance is due that they will not perform the contractual duties.

Responses to Repudiation

The nonbreaching party has two possible responses when anticipatory repudiation occurs:

1. Pursue a remedy, thereby treating the repudiation as a final breach.
2. Wait to determine if the breaching party will honor the contract despite their statements or conduct indicating their intention to renege. UCC §§ 2-610, 2A-402.

Regardless of the response the nonbreaching party chooses, the nonbreaching party may suspend their own performance without risk of liability.

> **Example:** Henry Linke agreed to sell Sawyer Farmers' Cooperative Association 5,000 bushels of grain; however, a few weeks later Linke's wife called Sawyer to inform them the grain would not be delivered. The cooperative neither accepted nor denied the repudiation. Later, the cooperative sued Linke for breach of contract. Linke argued that he had not breached the contract because the cooperative never accepted the repudiation. The court held that the aggrieved party need not accept the repudiation for it to constitute a breach; therefore the Linkes' anticipatory repudiation closed the contract and the cooperative was entitled to damages. *Sawyer Farmers Cooperative Ass'n v. Linke*, 231 N.W.2d 791 (N.D. 1975)

Management Application Response to Repudiation

To: Seller

PLEASE TAKE NOTICE that Buyer regards the letter you sent dated April 13, 2025, informing us there would be an indefinite delay of future shipment to be an anticipatory repudiation of our contract entered into on February 26, 2025, which has left us unable to fulfill the order of our customer under those circumstances. Please be advised we have made the necessary arrangements to obtain similar goods from a competitor and due to this material change, this repudiation must be treated as final and therefore any attempted retraction of it by you will not revive our contract.

____

Buyer's signature

Retraction of Repudiation

A breaching party may retract the repudiation of a contract by any method that clearly indicates the party's intention to perform the contract. After the repudiation is retracted, all rights of the repudiating party are reinstated to their original form. However, a redaction may not occur if after the initial repudiation, the nonbreaching party indicated that the repudiation was final. UCC §§ 2-611, 2A-403.

Remedies of the Seller or Lessor

The remedies available to a seller or lessor upon a breach by the buyer or lessee will depend upon the circumstances. The most relevant factor is the identity of who has possession of the goods and whether the buyer or lessee has rejected or accepted them.

When the Goods Are in the Possession of the Seller or Lessor

Several remedies are available to the seller or lessor when the goods have not been delivered to the buyer or lessee at the time of the breach, including:

- Rescinding the contract;
- Discontinuing delivery of the goods;
- Reselling the goods;
- Recovering the purchase price; and
- Suing for damages arising from buyer's nonacceptance of the goods.

RESCINDING THE CONTRACT. When the buyer or lessee breaches the contract, the seller or lessor may rescind the contract. UCC §§ 2-703(f), 2A-523(1)(a). This effectively cancels the contract between the parties. However, for the rescission to be effective, the seller or lessor must provide notice to the buyer or lessee of the cancellation. Once notice is given, the remaining obligations of the seller or lessor are dismissed; however, this is not the case for the buyer or lessee. Due to the buyer or lessee's breach of the contract the seller or lessor may also sue to obtain additional remedies that are available under the UCC.

DISCONTINUING DELIVERY. When a buyer or lessee has breached the contract, the seller or lessor can withhold or discontinue the performance of any remaining obligations while the buyer or lessee is in breach. UCC § 2-703(a), 2A-523(1)(c). This right includes refusing to deliver the goods to a buyer or lessee who is insolvent unless the insolvent buyer or lessee can pay cash, then, the goods must be delivered. UCC §§ 2-702(1), 2A-525(1).

RESELLING THE GOODS. If the seller or lessor is still in possession of the goods at the time the buyer or lessee breaches the contract, the seller or lessor has the option to resell or dispose of the goods. This typically requires the seller or lessor to notify the buyer or lessee of the resale unless the goods are perishable or subject to an imminent decline in value. UCC §§ 2-706(2)-(3).

If the goods are resold, the seller or lessor keeps any resulting profits. UCC §§ 2-703(d), 2A-523(1)(e). If the resale results in a loss, the seller or lessor may sue the buyer or lessee to recover the difference between the contract price and the sales price, in addition to any incidental damages. UCC §§ 2-706, 2A-530. Recall from Chapter 14 that incidental damages are expenses that were incurred in caring for the goods after the buyer or lessee's breach. In either case, the seller or lessor must make the resale in good faith and in a commercially reasonable manner in an effort to mitigate damages.

Essentially, this means the seller or lessor should attempt to obtain the highest price possible.

If at the time of the breach the goods are unfinished, the seller or lessor has two options. They may stop the construction of the goods and sell the components or materials for scrap, or the construction of the goods can be completed, and the finished goods can be resold, with the buyer or lessee remaining liable for the difference between the contract price and the sales price. Once again, the resale must be made in good faith and in a commercially reasonable manner.

RECOVERING THE PURCHASE PRICE. A seller or lessor who has not been paid may sue to recover what is due under the contract. UCC §§ 2-709(1), 2A-529(1). Additionally, incidental damages are recoverable. In the event the goods are resold, the net proceeds of the sale must be used to offset the damages owed by the buyer or lessee. In instances where the seller or lessor is unable to find a new buyer, the goods are required to be set aside for the buyer or lessee.

SUING FOR DAMAGES ARISING FROM NONACCEPTANCE. When a buyer or lessee wrongfully refuses to accept the goods or repudiates the contract, the seller or lessor is entitled to bring an action for recovery of the damages incurred as a result. The damages are the difference in the contract price and the market price at the time the goods were tendered, in addition to any incidental damages sustained. UCC §§ 2-708(1), 2A-528(1).

When the Goods Are in Transit to Buyer or Lessee

Once the goods are delivered to a common carrier or a bailee (such as a warehouse), the seller or lessor's ability to prevent the goods from being delivered to the buyer or lessee is more limited and only arises in the following circumstances:

- Insolvency of the buyer;
- Breach by the buyer; and
- Right to stop delivery.

INSOLVENCY OF THE BUYER. If the seller or lessor learns that the buyer or lessee is insolvent while the goods are in transit, the seller or lessor can prevent the carrier or bailee from delivering the goods. The seller or lessor has this ability regardless of the size of the shipment. UCC §§ 2-705(1), 2A-526(1).

BREACH BY THE BUYER. If the buyer or lessee simply breaches or repudiates the contract but is not insolvent, the seller or lessor can only prevent the carrier or bailee from delivering the goods if the quantity of the shipment amounts to at least a carload, truckload, or planeload, or constitutes a larger shipment. UCC §§ 2-705(1), 2A-526(1).

RIGHT TO STOP DELIVERY. There are certain requirements that the seller or lessor must meet in order to properly prevent delivery to the buyer or lessee. First, the seller or lessor must timely notify the carrier or bailee and give instructions as to whether the goods are to be held or returned to the seller or lessor. The carrier or bailee must then follow those instructions; however, the seller or lessor is liable for any additional costs to the carrier or bailee as a result. UCC §§ 2-705(3), 2A-526(3). However, the seller or lessor no longer has the ability to stop the delivery of the goods when any of the following occur:

- The buyer or lessee receives the goods;
- The carrier or bailee has acknowledged the rights of the buyer or lessee; or
- The buyer or lessee has been given ownership rights to the goods because of the proper transfer or a negotiable document of title for the goods. UCC § 2-702.

If following these requirements results in the seller or lessor reclaiming the goods, the remedies of sellers and lessors when the goods are in their possession may also be sought.

When the Goods Are in the Possession of the Buyer or Lessee

In most instances, when the buyer or lessee is in possession of the goods, the seller or lessor will only be able to sue. The seller or lessor may seek recovery of both the purchase price of the goods and any incidental damages incurred because of the breach. UCC §§ 2-709, 2A-529(1).

There are, however, some limited situations in which the seller or lessor has the right to recover the goods from the buyer or lessee. The seller can demand the return of the goods if the seller discovers the buyer is insolvent and the buyer received the goods on credit. UCC § 2-702(2). Typically, the demand for the return of the goods must be made by the seller within ten days of the buyer's receipt of the goods. As discussed in the previous chapter, the seller's right to reclaim the goods will be ineffective if the goods have been sold by the original buyer to a good faith purchaser or a buyer in the ordinary course of business. A lessor, on the other hand, may reclaim the goods if the lessee has failed to make payments when they come due. UCC § 2A-525(2).

Remedies of the Buyer or Lessee

A contract for the sale or lease of goods is breached by the seller or lessor if they fail to deliver the goods, deliver nonconforming goods, tender the goods improperly, or refuse to deliver the goods. In any of these instances, the UCC provides the buyer or lessee with several remedies. The facts surrounding the breach will determine the available remedies to the buyer or lessee. The relevant facts for determining the remedy are whether the seller or lessor refused to deliver the goods or whether nonconforming goods were delivered.

Refusal to Deliver the Goods

The remedies that are available to the buyer or lessee when the seller or lessor has refused to deliver the goods, or the buyer or lessee rightfully rejects the goods include:

- Rescinding the contract;
- Obtaining possession of the goods that have been paid for when seller or lessor is insolvent;

- Suing for specific performance;
- Purchasing replacement goods and seeking damages from seller;
- Suing for replevin; and
- Suing for damages.

RESCINDING THE CONTRACT. When the seller or lessor breaches the contract by either failing to properly deliver the goods or repudiating the contract, the buyer or lessee can rescind the contract. UCC §§ 2-711(1), 2A-508(1)(a). Once the buyer or lessee provides notice of the cancellation to the seller or lessor, the remaining obligations of the buyer or lessee under the contract will be discharged. However, due to the seller or lessor's breach, the buyer or lessee can also sue to obtain additional remedies under the UCC.

OBTAINING POSSESSION OF THE GOODS. The buyer or lessee will have the right to obtain the goods in the event that the seller or lessor becomes insolvent, and the buyer or lessee has paid for the goods in full or even partially. The buyer or lessee only has this right if the goods are identifiable in the contract. Additionally, if only a partial payment has been made by the buyer or lessee, the remaining balance must be paid to the seller or lessor. UCC §§ 2-502, 2A-522.

Expenses incurred in the handling of the goods such as shipping, repairs, and putting goods in workable condition, and in obtaining cover have been deemed incidental.

SPECIFIC PERFORMANCE. Specific performance is a court-ordered remedy compelling the parties to perform their contractual obligations. The buyer or lessee will be able to obtain specific performance if:

- There was a valid and enforceable contract, definite and certain;
- The buyer or lessee has satisfied all the conditions, or the conditions were excused;
- Legal remedies (damages were insufficient) because the goods were unique; and
- The remedy is feasible, meaning the court does not have to constantly supervise the transaction to ensure performance.

In most situations, monetary damages are adequate to place the injured party in the position they would have been in had the contract been performed. Therefore, specific performance arises when the goods in question are unique such that an adequate replacement cannot be obtained.

PURCHASING REPLACEMENT GOODS AND SEEKING DAMAGES. The act of purchasing replacement goods is known as "obtaining cover." Obtaining cover is an appropriate remedy when the seller or lessor either repudiates the contract, fails to deliver the goods, or when the buyer or lessee rightfully rejects the goods. The buyer or lessee is required to act in good faith when seeking substitute goods. Additionally, the buyer or lessee must not unreasonably delay the pursuit of the substitute goods. Once the substitute goods are obtained, the buyer or lessee may seek to recover the following damages:

1. The difference between the cost of the substitute goods and the contract price;
2. The incidental damages resulting from the breach; and

3. Any consequential damages necessary to compensate for the indirect losses occurring due to the breach that were foreseeable at the time of contracting.

The buyer or lessee is not required to obtain cover, but if they do not, a claim against the breaching party for consequential damages (lost profits) would be unavailable. Moreover, the failure to obtain a substitutable good can persuade a court that in failing to do so, the buyer failed to mitigate their damages—a duty that each non-breaching party to a contract must observe.

Replevin
A procedure in which seized goods are provisionally restored to a buyer depending on a court's determination of the rights of the parties concerned.

SUING FOR REPLEVIN. On occasion, the title to goods is disputed by the parties. **Replevin** is an action for the repossession of personal property wrongfully taken or withheld by a wrongdoer. The plaintiff gives security for and holds possession of the property until the court decides the ownership of the property. The elements of a cause of action for replevin are as follows:

- The buyer or lessee must pay for the goods, in part or in full, and the seller fails to deliver the goods; and either
  - The seller becomes insolvent (liabilities exceeds assets) within ten days; or
  - The goods were for personal, family, or household purposes;

  or,
- The goods were specifically identified in the contract and the plaintiff was unable to find an adequate substitute good.

SUING FOR DAMAGES. The buyer or lessee may sue to recover damages if the seller or lessor either fails to deliver the goods or repudiates the contract. The buyer or lessee is then entitled to seek the difference between the contract price and the market price of the goods at the time the breach occurred. Incidental and consequential damages are also recoverable; however, these damages will be offset by any expenses that were not incurred by the buyer or lessee due to the breach. UCC §§ 2-713, 2A-519.

Delivery of Nonconforming Goods

When the seller or lessor delivers nonconforming goods or fails to properly tender the goods under the contract, the remedies that are available to the buyer or lessee under the UCC will depend on the actions taken by the buyer or lessee following the breach. When a breach occurs due to delivery of nonconforming goods or improper tender, the buyer or lessee may either reject the goods, revoke acceptance of the goods, or accept the goods and recover damages.

REJECTION OF THE GOODS. The UCC requires that both the goods themselves and the tender of the goods conform to the contract in all aspects. The failure to be in such conformity gives the buyer or lessee the ability to reject the goods completely or partially. UCC §§ 2-601, 2A-509. Several options are available to the buyer or lessee when they reject the goods. The buyer or lessee may then either obtain substitute goods (cover), rescind the contract, or simply sue for damages based on an action for breach of contract.

Timeliness and Identification. To seek the remedies discussed above, the goods must be rejected in a reasonable amount of time and the buyer or lessee must also provide timely notice to the seller or lessor of the rejection. The failure to reject the goods in a reasonable amount of time will constitute acceptance by the buyer or lessee.

The buyer or lessee cannot simply reject the goods because they no longer wish to purchase them; they can only reject them if there is a specific defect that the seller or lessor should have been aware of upon reasonable inspection of the goods prior to shipment. If the buyer or lessee fails to indicate these specific defects, they will be unable to use these defects as the basis for rejecting the goods. UCC §§ 2-605, 2A-514.

REVOCATION OF ACCEPTANCE. Once the goods have been accepted by the buyer or lessee, the option of rejecting the goods no longer exists. However, the UCC does permit the buyer or lessee to obtain other remedies by revoking their acceptance of the goods under certain circumstances.

Revocation of acceptance may occur when the nonconformity of the goods creates a substantial impairment of the value and one of the following factors is present:

1. The acceptance was given under the reasonable belief that the nonconformity at issue would be cured, but the cure failed to occur within a reasonable amount of time, UCC §§ 1-608(1)(a), 2A-517(1)(a); or
2. The nonconformity of the goods was not discovered by the buyer prior to acceptance due to the difficulty of such a discovery, or the buyer or lessee did not inspect the goods due to assurances given by seller or lessor indicating the goods were in conformity, UCC §§ 2-608(1)(b), 2A-517(1)(b).

ACCEPTANCE AND RECOVERY OF DAMAGES. Buyers or lessees not meeting the standards for revocation can retain the goods and sue for the damages resulting from the seller or lessor's breach. The buyer or lessee is required to notify the seller or lessor of the breach within a reasonable amount of time. UCC §§ 2-607(3), 2A-516(3). Since a "reasonable amount of time" is not defined by the UCC, the parties to sales and lease contracts will include a provision specifying the amount of time the party has to give notice of the breach.

The damages associated with nonconforming goods are the difference between the value of the goods warranted under the contract and the value of the goods accepted. UCC §§ 2-714(2), 2A-519(4). Incidental and consequential damages may also be awarded to the buyer or lessee depending on the circumstances. If the buyer or lessee still owes payments to the seller or lessor for the goods, the UCC permits the damages to be deducted from the amount that remains due. UCC §§ 2-717, 2A-516(1).

Concept Summary
Remedies Under the UCC

Type of Breach	Remedy
Seller breaches, seller in possession of goods	Buyer is entitled to the greater of: The difference of the market price at the time the breach is discovered and the contract price OR The difference between a reasonable replacement price and the contract price

Type of Breach	Remedy
Seller breaches, buyer in possession of goods	The buyer is entitled to the fair market value of the goods under the terms of the contract, and the fair market value OR the cost to remedy the goods
Buyer breaches, seller in possession of goods	The seller may recover the difference between the contract price and the price at which the goods were resold, and may also sue to recover other damages associated with the breach (incidental)
Buyer breaches, buyer in possession of goods	Seller may sue for breach of contract and recover any damages resulting from the breach

An Introduction to Warranties

The common law rule of *caveat emptor*, or "let the buyer beware," was the governing law for sales and lease contracts. This principle simply meant that the buyer was responsible for determining the quality of the goods in question prior to their purchase or lease. Today, Article 2 and Article 2A of the UCC provide several warranties from the seller of goods to buyers and lessees.

These warranties are assurance that the goods are in conformity with the sales or lease contract and commonly accepted standards of quality. The warranties may be stated in the sales agreement, or they may be implied by the operation of the law. If the warranty is breached, the buyer or lessee can sue the seller for damages.

Express Warranty

Express warranty
A seller/lessor asserts that the goods being sold or leased meet certain standards related to the good's description, quality, condition, or performance.

In an **express warranty**, a seller or lessor asserts that the goods being sold, or leased meet certain standards related to the good's description, quality, condition, or performance. UCC §§ 2-313(1), 2A-210(1). These warranties do not have to be included in the sales agreement, as they may be either written, oral, or inferred by the seller's conduct. The seller or lessor does not even have to intend to make the warranty for one to exist. UCC §§ 2-313(2), 2A-210(2). It is important to note that the seller or lessor is not required to make any express warranties to the buyer or lessee.

There is no requirement for sellers or lessors to make express warranties; however, they are typically made to persuade the consumer to purchase or lease the goods.

How Express Warranties Are Created

Under UCC §§ 2-313 and 2A-210, an express warranty will be created when a seller or lessor indicates the goods will be in conformance with any of the following representations:

- Any affirmation of fact or promise related to the goods
    - **Example:** Statements such as "the band of the ring is made of pure platinum and is not susceptible to scratches," would create an express warranty.

- Any description of the goods
  - **Example:** The statement by a seller that a coffee table is "made entirely from Brazilian Nut wood" is an example of a description that would constitute an express warranty.
- Any sample or model of the goods
  - **Example:** A sample of the coffee beans taken from the seller's most recent harvest would create an express warranty.

When any of these express warranties were a contributing factor in the buyer or lessee's purchasing or leasing of the product, the buyer or lessee can recover for a breach of express warranty. UCC §§ 2-313(1), 2A-210(1). To create an express warranty, the buyer or lessee must consider the representation made by the seller or lessor to be part of the basis of the bargain. What constitutes the basis of the bargain is a fact that will vary on a case-by-case basis, because the UCC does not define the basis of the bargain.

Opinions and Statements of Value

Opinions and statements of value Statements made by the seller or lessor regarding the presumed value of the goods or an opinion or recommendation related to the goods do not create an express warranty.

Express warranties can only be created by statements of fact. Statements that are made by the seller or lessor regarding the presumed value of the goods or an opinion or recommendation related to the goods will not create an express warranty. UCC §§ 2-313(2), 2A-210(2).

> **Example:** Kevin Wilson sued David Russell, for fraudulent misrepresentation regarding the condition of the motorcycle he sold to Wilson in "as is" condition. Wilson claimed that prior to the sale Russell told him it was "in fine working order." Wilson also drove the motorcycle on a short test drive during which the engine sputtered. After his purchase, a mechanic informed him that it would cost as much as he paid for the bike to have it restored to operating condition. Russell refused to refund the purchase price to Wilson. Russell asserted that all warranties were disclaimed by the "as is" sale. The court held that such a clause does not exclude a prior express warranty and remanded the case to the trial court. But Russell's other statements regarding the bike's condition were statements of opinion and did not rise above the level of mere sales talk or puffery. *Russell v. Wilson*, 991 So. 2d 745 (Ala. Civ. App. 2008)

Sales puffery is defined by the Federal Trade Commission as a "term frequently used to denote the exaggerations reasonably to be expected of a seller as to the degree of quality of the product the truth of which cannot be precisely determined." Distinguishing between an express warranty and sales puffery can be difficult, so a court looks to the buyer's or lessee's reasonableness in relying on the statements of the buyer or lessee to determine if it constitutes an express warranty or puffery.

> **Example:** John Serbalik purchased a new vehicle from Queensberry Motors that began exhibiting mechanical problems soon after its purchase. Serbalik sued Queensberry for fraud and deceptive selling practices because the salesperson had told him the vehicle was "luxurious and would perform excellently." The court found Serbalik failed to present any basis for concluding that the salesperson's comments, which were not made in response to any particular question or concern expressed by plaintiff, were anything more than innocent puffery. *Serbalik v. General Motors Corp.*, 246 A.D.2d 724 (N.Y. 1998)

Breach of Warranty Damages

Under the UCC, a buyer or lessee may sue the seller or lessor to recover compensatory damages for a breach of warranty. The amount recoverable by the buyer or lessee is the difference between the value of the goods at the time of acceptance and the value the goods would have had they been warranted. UCC §§ 2-714(2), 2A-508(4). The UCC does allow for additional damages to be recovered under certain circumstances.

Implied Warranties

Implied warranty
A warranty not expressly provided for in the sales or lease contract, but which is instead implied by law given the circumstances of the transaction.

Implied warranties are those that are not expressly stated in the sales or lease contract but are, instead, implied by law given the circumstances of the transaction. For a buyer or lessee to be successful on a claim of breach of implied warranty, they must prove the existence of an implied warranty and its breach caused the damage the buyer or lessee incurred. Several implied warranties are discussed below.

Implied Warranty of Merchantability

Implied warranty of merchantability
A warranty not expressly provided for in the sales or lease contract that assures the goods are at least of average quality, properly packaged and labeled, and fit for the ordinary purposes they are intended to serve.

A sales or lease contract will contain an **implied warranty of merchantability** when the seller or lessor is a merchant of the type of goods involved in the transaction. UCC §§ 2-314(1), 2A-212(1). For the implied warranty of merchantability to apply, the following conditions must be met:

- The quality of the goods would pass without objection in the trade;
  - **Example:** The goods are required to be of such a quality that other users of this type of good would not object to their quality.
- Goods that are fungible are required to meet a fair average standard of quality;
  - **Example:** If the goods are to be classified as a particular grade, they must meet the average standard of quality of that grade.
- The goods must be fit for the ordinary purpose for which the goods are to be used;
  - **Example:** The good must be able to safely perform the function for which it was created.
- The goods must be of an even kind, quality, and quantity within each unit;
  - **Example:** All the goods contained in a package or box must be consistent with each other.
- The goods are adequately contained, packaged, and labeled;
  - **Example:** The implied warranty extends to the packaging as well as the goods contained inside.
- The goods must conform to the promise or affirmations made on the label or container.
  - **Example:** The goods must have the ability to be used safely in accordance with the instructions on the label or container.

The implied warranty of merchantability will not apply in instances in which it has been properly disclaimed or where the seller is not a merchant. Disclaimers of warranties are discussed below.

Implied Warranty of Fitness for Human Consumption

The UCC provides within the implied warranty of merchantability an **implied warranty of fitness for human consumption**. This implied warranty applies to food that is sold at retail for immediate human consumption, such as in restaurants, coffee shops, bars, and grocery stores. There are two tests that may be applied to determine if a breach of the implied warranty of fitness for human consumption has been breached:

Implied warranty of fitness for human consumption
A warranty not expressly provided for that applies to food that is sold for immediate human consumption.

- *Consumer expectation test.* The modern view is to use the consumer expectation test, which is adopted by most states. This test requires the court to ask what a consumer may expect to find or not find when consuming their food or drink.
  - **Example:** The implied warranty would be breached if a consumer were injured by a chicken bone that was found in his chicken burrito. In this case, a consumer would expect the chef or cook to have removed all the bones from the chicken before putting it in the burrito. The implied warranty would not be breached if a consumer is injured by a fish bone found in her salmon dinner. This is because the consumer would expect to find a bone in her fish dinner.
- *Foreign substance test.* Under this test, a consumer's food or drink will be deemed unmerchantable if the consumer is injured due to a foreign substance in the food or drink.
  - **Example:** The implied warranty would be breached if a consumer were injured by a rock that was found in his chicken burrito, because the rock is a foreign object in the burrito.

Implied Warranty of Fitness for a Particular Purpose

Another implied warranty of the UCC is the **implied warranty of fitness for a particular purpose**. This implied warranty arises when the seller or lessor has provided the buyer or lessee with assurances that the goods will meet the specific needs of the buyer or lessee.

Implied warranty of fitness for a particular purpose
A warranty not expressly provided for in a sales or lease contract that assures the goods will meet the specific needs of the buyer or lessee.

When the goods fail to meet the buyer or lessee's expressed needs, the implied warranty of fitness for a particular purpose has been breached. Unlike the implied warranty of merchantability, the implied warranty of fitness for a particular purpose applies to both merchants and nonmerchants. The implied warranty of fitness for a particular purpose will apply if at the time of contracting the following occurred:

1. The seller has reason to know the buyer's particular purpose for buying the goods; and,
2. The buyer purchases the goods in reliance of the seller's representation, based upon the seller's skill or judgment. UCC §§ 2-315, 2A-213.

Example: A boy and his mother filed a suit against a manufacturer to recover damages for the loss of the boy's right eye. The boy, a baseball player, lost his eye after a baseball shattered the sunglasses he was wearing. The sunglasses, which were manufactured by the defendant, sent sharp splinters into the boy's right eye when they were hit by a baseball. The boy's coach had allowed team members to wear the sunglasses because they were guaranteed for life against breakage and specifically advertised for baseball players. The defendant manufacturer was held to be in breach of its implied warranty of fitness for a particular purpose. *Filler v. Rayex Corp.*, 435 F.2d 336 (7th Cir. 1970)

Multiple Warranties

Sometimes more than one warranty will be made in a single transaction. In these cases, the UCC states that both warranties will apply if they are consistent with each other. UCC §§ 2-317, 2A-215. As a result, the warranties discussed above may all be present in the same transaction, and the court will find they all apply so long as they do not contradict each other. However, if the warranties are contradictory, the express warranties take precedence over any inconsistent implied warranty, other than the implied warranty of fitness for a particular purpose.

CASE 28.1

SELLER'S KNOWLEDGE OF PLAINTIFF'S RELIANCE IS NOT REQUIRED FOR IMPLIED WARRANTY OF FITNESS CLAIMS

FRENCH v. BEN'S SUPERCENTER, INC.

2016 Mich. App. LEXIS 2210 (2016)

Court of Appeals of Michigan

On May 21, 2011, John French (French) met with a salesperson of Ben's Supercenter, Todd Katz (Katz), and discussed, at length, his desire to purchase an outdoor wood furnace for his home. French ultimately purchased a wood furnace for $12,000. The furnace was then delivered to French's property by employees of Ben's Supercenter, and French subsequently installed the furnace. By Christmas that year, French began to experience issues with the furnace's performance after using it for only three weeks. French then contacted Katz for assistance, but Katz was unable to determine the issue. Nevertheless, French continued to use the furnace to heat his house through the winter months. In spring of 2013, French and Katz met to discuss the furnace's problems. Katz contacted the manufacturer and received a kit that was intended to solve the furnace's issues. The kit did not fix the furnace's problems. Katz continued to contact the manufacturer in an attempt to solve the problems related to French's furnace. French retained a lawyer who notified Katz and the owner of Ben's Supercenter that French wanted either a full refund of the purchase price or a new furnace. Neither Katz nor the store's owner responded to French's attorney. French filed suit against Ben's Supercenter in May. His lawsuit included a claim for the breach of implied warranty of fitness for a particular purpose. French moved for summary judgment, which the court granted. French was awarded damages in the amount of the purchase price, interest, and attorney's fees and costs. Ben's Supercenter appealed.

Language of the Court. *The implied warranty of fitness for a particular purpose, as follows where the seller at the time of contracting has reason to know* *any particular purpose for which the goods are required and that the buyer is relying on the seller's skill or judgment to select or furnish suitable goods, there is unless excluded or modified under the next section an implied warranty that the goods shall be fit for such purpose. Under this section the buyer need not bring home to the seller actual knowledge of the particular purpose for which the goods are intended or of his reliance on the seller's skill and judgment, if the circumstances are such that the seller has reason to realize the purpose intended or that the reliance exists. The buyer, of course, must actually be relying on the seller.*

Here, we agree with the trial court that there is no genuine issue of fact concerning whether the circumstances were such that Katz had reason to realize that reliance existed. Plaintiff's deposition testimony establishing his actual reliance on Katz is overwhelming. Katz's deposition testimony is equivocal at best. Katz has also acknowledged that he was so highly involved in the sale that he took the plaintiff out to lunch as part of the sales process. And, although we agree that Katz's opinion that plaintiff was sharp and had a good understanding of what he wanted has some relevance to this issue, we do not think it sufficient to provide a basis on which reasonable minds could disagree, given everything stated above. Under these circumstances, Katz had every reason to realize that plaintiff was relying on him.

Defendant also argues that it disclaimed the implied warranty of fitness. In contrast with the implied warranty of merchantability, there is no such requirement with the implied warranty of fitness for a particular purpose. Rather, language to exclude all implied warranties of fitness is sufficient if it states, for example, that "There are no warranties which extend beyond the description on the face hereof." However, similar to the implied warranty of merchantability, in order to disclaim the implied warranty of fitness for a particular purpose, the disclaimer must "be by a writing and conspicuous."

Although the language of this disclaimer appears sufficient to exclude the implied warranty of fitness for a particular purpose, it is presented in such a way that it does not meet the statute's "conspicuous" requirement, because it is in a font no larger than the fonts appearing on the rest of the page, not set off from the surrounding text, and not in all capital letters, bold, or a different color ink.

Decision. The Court of Appeals of Michigan affirmed the trial court's ruling that Ben's Supercenter had breached the implied warranty of fitness for a particular purpose.

Focus on Ethics

Is it proper for a court to consider factors like font size, fonts, italics, bolding of terms, and capitalization in such determinations? What would you do with respect to selling goods and disclaiming warranties for them?

CASE 28.2

A BUYER IS NOT REQUIRED TO PAY FOR REJECTED NON-CONFORMING GOODS BUT MUST PAY FOR GOODS ACCEPTED

IMPACT FINISHING, INC. v. WILD CARD, INC.

2024 U.S. Dist. LEXIS 15030 (2024)

United States District Court for the Northern District of Texas

In May 2021, Wild Card hired Impact Finishing, Inc. to produce 8.1 million trading cards for their Blaster Project, aiming for completion by September 2021. Impact delivered 9.1 million cards by October 2021, but Wild Card rejected 460,000 cards due to defects like color discrepancies and scratches. Despite agreements to replace the cards, Impact faced delays, prompting Wild Card to spend $320,000 on reproducing the rejected cards with another printer.

After completing the project, Impact invoiced Wild Card for additional costs beyond the original scope. Wild Card withheld payment totaling $641,636.59, citing issues with the project and defects in the delivered goods. Wild Card had the right to reject nonconforming goods and was not obligated to pay for them, which it claimed justified its withholding of payment. Each company sued the other for their cost overruns. The federal district court considered cross-motions for summary judgment.

Language of the Court. *While there are a myriad of claims asserted in this case, this lawsuit is about a contract between Impact and Wild Card. Wild Card is in the sports trading card business. Impact is in the printing business. In substance, Impact promised to produce trading cards for Wild Card, and Wild Card promised to pay Impact for those goods. Impact claims that it produced and delivered quality trading cards to Wild Card and that Wild Card breached the contract by failing to pay for the cards. Wild Card's position is that Impact breached the contract by failing to produce quality cards, and, therefore, Wild Card was under no obligation to pay.*

Here, the evidence establishes that Impact and Wild Card each breached the contract as a matter of law. Wild Card breached the contract because it accepted, but did not pay for, a portion of the goods; Impact breached the contract by delivering nonconforming goods that Wild Card properly rejected or revoked.

Wild Card breached the contract as a matter of law because there is no genuine dispute that it accepted, but did not pay for, approximately 8.6 million cards delivered by Impact.

The Court further concludes that Impact likewise breached the contract with respect to the 460,000 cards that were returned to it. Impact delivered 460,000 nonconforming cards; Wild Card either rightly rejected or revoked its acceptance as to these cards. And Impact either did not have an opportunity to cure, or if it did, failed to timely cure its nonconforming delivery. As such, Impact breached.

Decision. The court held that both parties had breached the contract and awarded damages to both parties.

Focus on Ethics

Consider the numerous arguments and substantial attorney's fees involved in this case of accusations and counteraccusations. Why did this dispute consume so much time and resources? Ethically, was it fair of Wild Card to accept the conforming cards, sell them to retailers, and, yet, not pay Impact? How would you have structured the contract to minimize the risk of liability for each party?

Concept Summary
Types of Warranties

Warranty	Creation	Description	UCC Provisions
Express warranty	Made by seller or lessor (written, oral, or inferred)	Applies when a seller or lessor indicates the goods will be in conformance with any of the following: 1. Any affirmation of fact or promise related to the goods 2. Any description of the goods 3. Any sample or model of the goods	§§ 2-313(1) & 2A-210(1)
Implied warranty of merchantability	Implied by law so long as the seller or lessor is a merchant	Applies when seller or lessor is a merchant of the type of goods in the transaction and all six elements are met	§§ 2-314(1) & 2A-212(1)
Implied warranty of fitness for human consumption	Implied by law	Applies to food that is sold for immediate human consumption. Courts will use either the consumer expectation test or the foreign object test.	§§ 2-314(1) & 2A-212(1)
Implied warranty of fitness for a particular purpose	Implied by law	Applies when the seller or lessor has provided the buyer or lessee with assurances that the goods will meet the specific needs of the buyer or lessee	§§ 2-315 & 2A-213

Warranty Disclaimers

The UCC permits warranty disclaimers to exclude or limit warranties. The way in which a particular warranty must be disclaimed will vary; therefore, the seller or lessor will have to provide a specific disclaimer for each type of warranty they wish to exclude or limit. Some disclaimers may be made orally, while others are required to be in writing. To be valid all written disclaimers must be conspicuously displayed. The term "conspicuous" has been interpreted by the courts to mean that a reasonable person would be put on notice by the disclaimer. UCC §§ 2-316, 2A-214.

> **Example:** Courts have found a disclaimer to be conspicuously displayed when it contains a heading in a larger font, a different style, uppercase letters, or a different color than the rest of the contract.

Since the purpose of the UCC is to make business transactions easier, the UCC provides that disclaimers should be construed reasonably and found to be enforceable unless they are unreasonable under the circumstances.

> **Example:** NuWave, the manufacturer of a pressure cooker, argued that it disclaimed any implied warranty of merchantability in its instruction manual, but its motion to dismiss was denied. "To begin with, the disclaimer appears on the thirtieth page of a busy and colorful owner's manual — sandwiched just between a troubleshooting guide and a page titled 'Pressure Cooking Notes' and then followed by another thirty plus pages of recipes. NuWave correctly asserts that a conspicuous writing need not necessarily be in colored ink or call a reader's attention in a specific way, but their argument fails to consider the Manual as a whole." *Partin v. NuWave*, 603 F. Supp. 3d 280 (E.D. Va. 2022)

Express Warranties

To limit an express warranty, the warranty disclaimer and the warranty itself must be reasonably construed together. It is not sufficient to simply state that there are "no warranties, express or implied." The seller or lessor can disclaim any and all oral express warranties made by including a statement indicating such in a written contract. However, this contract must be in clear, unambiguous language and brought to the attention of the buyer or lessee at the time the contract is formed. UCC §§ 2-316(1), 2A-214(1). Any instance in which a warranty is disclaimed requires the buyer or lessee to be made aware of the disclaimer at the time the contract is formed.

> **Example:** At car dealerships, there will often be a notice next to the sticker price of a used car indicating whether there is still a factory warranty. For used cars that no longer have a warranty, the dealer will indicate that the car is sold "As Is — No Warranty."

Implied Warranties

A seller or lessor who wishes to disclaim all implied warranties may do so by stating that the good is being sold or leased "as is," "with all faults," or any other similar language that indicates no implied warranties exist. If a seller or lessor seeks to limit only the implied warranty of merchantability, the disclaimer must specifically mention "merchantability" in the disclaimer so that the intent of the provision is clear to the buyer or lessee. A disclaimer for the warranty of merchantability need not be in writing. In contrast, instances where the seller or lessor wishes to disclaim only the implied warranty of fitness for a particular purpose do not need to include the term "fitness" and may instead use general language. A disclaimer for the warranty of fitness for a particular purpose must be in writing.

There are instances in which conduct will disclaim a warranty. For example, when a buyer or lessee is given the opportunity to fully inspect the goods, there will no longer be an implied warranty for any defect that a reasonable examination would reveal. Further, any defects that are discovered upon examination will prevent the buyer from later claiming there was a breach of an implied warranty as to that defect. UCC §§ 2-316(3)(b), 2A-214(3)(a).

Management Application Disclaimers of Express and Implied Warranties

Disclaimer of Express Warranty

THE AFOREMENTIONED WARRANTIES HAVE BEEN MADE IN LIEU OF ALL OTHER EXPRESS WARRANTIES AND NO STATEMENTS OR REPRESENTATIONS OTHER THAN THOSE EXPRESSED HEREIN HAVE BEEN MADE OR RELIED ON.

Disclaimer of Implied Warranty

The goods sold under this contract shall be purchased "AS IS," AND "WITH ALL FAULTS." ADDITIONALLY, SELLER DOES NOT WARRANT THE GOODS ARE OF MERCHANTABLE QUALITY OR THAT THEY MAY BE USED FOR ANY PARTICULAR PURPOSE.

Research the law of your state for required language to disclaim such warranties.

Magnuson-Moss Warranty Act

Magnuson-Moss Warranty Act
A federal statute that governs warranties on consumer products and prohibits sellers or lessors who make express warranties from disclaiming or modifying the implied warranties of merchantability and fitness for a particular purpose.

The **Magnuson-Moss Warranty Act** is a federal statute that governs warranties on consumer products and is administered by the Federal Trade Commission (FTC). As previously mentioned, a seller or lessor is not required to make any express warranties to a buyer or lessee. However, consumer transactions involving express warranties must comply with this Act. Additionally, the Act states that a seller or lessor of consumer products who makes express warranties may not disclaim or modify the implied warranties of merchantability or fitness for a particular purpose.

Full warranty
A warranty guaranteeing that a defective product is to be replaced or repaired free of charge during the duration of the warranty.

Limited warranty
A warranty limiting the scope of the warranty in some manner.

The Act labels express warranties as either full or limited. A **full warranty** is one in which it is guaranteed that a defective product is to be replaced or repaired free of charge during the duration of the warranty. The time for which the warranty is operative must be indicated. The more commonly used **limited warranty** will limit the scope of the warranty in some manner. For example, a warranty that stipulates that only certain defects will be repaired or replaced would constitute a limited warranty.

The Act contains specific provisions related to dispute resolution. For example, it establishes the use of arbitration to resolve the parties' disputes. Additionally, the Act specifically states the damages available to the buyer or lessee. A plaintiff who is successful in their claim may recover damages, costs, and attorney's fees.

Warranties of Title and Possession

Special warranties are automatically imposed on sellers and lessors of goods by the UCC. The following subsections discuss the warranty of good title, the warranty of no security interest, and the warranty against infringements.

Warranty of good title
A special warranty that states the seller of a good warrants that they have valid title to the goods being sold and therefore the transfer of title is rightful.

Warranty of no security interests
A special warranty in which the seller of the goods will automatically warrant the goods being sold are free of any third-party security interest, lien, or other encumbrances of which the buyer is unaware.

Warranty against infringements
A special warranty that states that a seller or lessor who is a merchant that regularly sells or leases the type of goods provided for in the transaction warrants that the goods are not subject to any third-party copyright, trademark, or patent.

Warranty of Good Title

The **warranty of good title** states that the seller of a good warrants they have valid title to the goods being sold and the transfer of title is rightful. UCC § 2-312(1)(a), 2A-211(1). When a seller transfers goods without proper title, they will be in breach of the warranty of good title. This warranty may be disclaimed by the seller if this is done by use of specific language. UCC § 2-312(2). The general language of "as is" or "with all faults" will not be sufficient to disclaim either the warranty of good title or the warranty of no security interests.

> **Example:** Edwin Godwin purchased a used car from Leon Murdock, a used car dealer, in which Godwin received an express guarantee of a clear title. Three years later, Godwin was contacted by law enforcement who believed the vehicle to be stolen. After inspection by law enforcement determined the vehicle was in fact stolen, the vehicle was seized, and Godwin filed a claim against Murdock for breach of warranty of good title. The court ruled in favor of Godwin, finding that he was entitled to the market value of the vehicle. *Murdock v. Godwin*, 269 S.E.2d 905 (Ga. Ct. App. 1980)

Warranty of No Security Interests

Under the **warranty of no security interests**, sellers of goods automatically warrant the goods they are selling are free of any third-party security interest, liens, or other encumbrances of which the buyer is unaware. UCC § 2-312(1)(b).

Warranty Against Infringements

The **warranty against infringements** states that a seller or lessor who is a merchant that regularly sells or leases the type of goods provided for in the transaction will automatically warrant that the goods are not subject to any third-party copyright, trademark, or patent. UCC §§ 2-312(3), 2A-211(2).

Example: Chemtron, Inc.® brought a claim against Aqua Products, Inc.® for infringing on Chemtron's patents. Aqua claimed it did not infringe on the patent because the patent for a dishwasher's soap dispenser was sold to it by Viking, Inc., and thus the warranty against infringements barred Aqua's liability and Viking must be held liable. The court disagreed, finding that Viking transferred clear title of the patent to Aqua and Aqua had subsequently used the patent to create a non-infringing good to be used in an infringing device, and thus liability rested solely with Aqua. *Chemtron, Inc. v. Aqua Products, Inc.*, 830 F. Supp. 314 (E.D. Va. 1993)

AI Feature: Social Media Influencers and Puffery

Using an internet search engine, research if social media influencers violate the law by failing to disclose a paid relationship with a brand. Is their promotion of a brand mere puffery? Is it a false representation in the advertising that may invoke an express warranty? Are promoters engaging in consumer fraud under the Federal Trade Commission Act and state consumer protection statutes? Then, using an AI program, draft a disclosure statement to be placed within an advertisement that the influencer is being paid for the endorsement.

Key Terms

- Anticipatory repudiation, 696
- Commercial impracticability, 694
- Common carrier, 691
- Destruction of identified goods, 695
- Duty of cooperation, 695
- Express warranty, 704
- Full warranty, 714
- Good faith provision, 690
- Implied warranty, 706
- Implied warranty of fitness for a particular purpose, 707
- Implied warranty of fitness for human consumption, 707
- Implied warranty of merchantability, 706
- Installment contract, 693
- Limited warranty, 714
- Magnuson-Moss Warranty Act, 713
- Opinion and statements of value, 705
- Partial performance, 694
- Perfect tender rule, 692
- Replevin, 702
- Right of assurances, 693
- Right to cure, 692
- Tender of delivery, 690
- Warranty against infringements, 714
- Warranty of good title, 714
- Warranty of no security interests, 714

Applying the Law

28.1 Implied Warranty. Edward Lariviere sued the manufacturer of a wooden stepladder that he was using as an ironworker. When the ladder broke, he suffered injuries. He sued the retail seller, the owner of the ladder, and the manufacturer. Left at the time of appeal was only the manufacturer who claimed it was not in privity (that is, in contract) with Lariviere to permit him to sue for damages. He claimed he was a beneficiary of any implied warranty of merchantability that the seller may have given to the purchaser of the ladder. How should the court rule? *Lariviere v. Dayton Safety Ladder Co.*, 525 A.2d 892 (R.I. 1987)

28.2 Disclaimer of Warranty. The Commonwealth of Massachusetts sued a contractor which had supplied and installed asbestos-containing products in several state-owned buildings. The state sued, seeking damages for the costs of removing those materials under a theory of breach of an implied warranty of merchantability. The court found that the contract specifications were not specific enough for the contractor to disclaim them. What language should have been insisted upon in the contract by the contractor to avoid such liability? *Commonwealth v. Johnson Insulation*, 682 N.E.2d 1323 (Mass. 1997)

28.3 Anticipatory Repudiation. Bausch & Lomb, Inc.® (B & L) entered into a contract with Sonomed Technology, Inc.® The contract involved the purchase and distribution of ophthalmic diagnostic instruments manufactured and supplied by Sonomed. Their contract limited the ability of an aggrieved party to terminate the agreement by providing that, upon the occurrence of a material breach, the aggrieved party could cancel the agreement only upon 30 days' notice, during which time the breaching party could attempt to effect a cure. After alleging that Sonomed wrongfully sold products within B & L sales territories and did not deliver products in accordance with the contract, by a letter dated October 23, B & L stopped further product purchases and asserted its contractual duties to Sonomed were at an end. Sonomed asserted that B & L's refusal to purchase products from Sonomed was an anticipatory breach and repudiation of their agreement. Sonomed also demanded that B & L provide "assurance of your willingness to live up to all the terms of the Agreement by 1:00 P.M. Friday, November 6," two days following B & L's receipt of the November 3 letter (in which Sonomed asserted their agreement remained in full force "except to the extent B & L had repudiated it"). B & L did not respond to the November 3 letter by November 6. Did Sonomed materially breach the contract because it failed to abide by the 30-day notice provision, or was compliance excused? *Bausch & Lomb, Inc. v. Bressler*, 977 F.2d 720 (2d Cir. 1992)

28.4 Conspicuous Disclaimer. Kelley Metal Trading Company sued Al-Jon/United for breach of the implied warranties of fitness and merchantability. The defendant argued that they had been disclaimed. In response, Kelley contended that the disclaimer was invalid because it was not conspicuous. If the disclaimer language was in the same size type and ink color as the other provisions and not in capital letters or contrasting type in terms of style or shade." Was the disclaimer conspicuous? *Kelley Metal Trading Co. v. Al-Jon/United*, 812 F. Supp. 185 (D. Kan. 1993)

28.5 Breach of Contract. Tower City Grain, the buyer, under contract for the purchase of grain brought action against the Richmans, the sellers, to recover for alleged breach of contract for refusing to deliver grain. However, evidence was entered finding that buyer's lack of available storage space resulted only because of the buyer's acceptance of other grain subsequently contracted for, and the buyer delayed approximately seven months in accepting more grain from the Richmans. Was the buyer's delay unreasonable so that the sellers were excused from performing? *Tower City Grain Co. v. Richman*, 262 N.W.2d 22 (N.D. 1978)

28.6 Justified in Treating the Contract as Cancelled. In April 1979, the parties entered into a written agreement whereby Hummel agreed to sell a Quonset-type building to Robert Keller. The contract provided a purchase price of $3,500, with

$2,000 to be paid April 25, 1979, and the balance of $1,500 to be paid before the structure was moved or by April 15, 1980, whichever came first. Further, the terms of the contract set the rate of interest for the unpaid amount at 5 percent. The contract stated that Keller could use the Quonset for storage of grain until the time of its removal from the premises and that the building could be removed at any time, but no later than April 15, 1982. Keller paid the $2,000 down payment and subsequently stored approximately 10,000 bushels of wheat from his 1979 crop in the Quonset. It was not disputed that Keller failed to pay the balance due on the contract by April 15, 1980. Hummel contended that Keller informed him that he no longer had any use for the building and that, therefore, Hummel was justified in treating the contract as cancelled. Keller disputed Hummel's contention and said that he informed Hummel, shortly after he had missed payment on April 15, 1980, that he intended to remove and sell his grain in the summer of 1980 and use the proceeds to pay the balance due on the contract, but that Hummel denied him access to the Quonset. Was the contract cancelled when Keller failed to pay? *Keller v. Hummel*, 334 N.W.2d 200 (N.D. 1983)

28.7 Wrongful Death and the Implied Warranty of Fitness for a Particular Purpose. John Bonfilio died because of a head injury sustained the day before while he was riding a motorcycle that collided with a car at an intersection in Lexington, Massachusetts. His surviving mother sued for damages. The defendant was the manufacturer of the protective helmet that the decedent was wearing prior to the collision. At the close of all the evidence on the issue of liability, the district court directed a verdict for the defendant, and the plaintiff appealed. The helmet's "fastening device" involved two straps. The inner strap was made of a leatherette material and consisted of two pieces, one attached to each side of the helmet by rivets and then joined in the center with three snap fastenings. The outer strap was made of two pieces of nylon fabric that could be joined at one side with metal buckles. In her claim the plaintiff stressed the condition of the straps when the helmet was found after the accident and the fact that the decedent was observed wearing the helmet immediately prior to impact. The essence of the plaintiff's claim was that the reconstructed sequence of events was the proximate cause of the decedent's death and was the result of negligent design of the helmet's "retention system" by the defendant. May the plaintiff pursue a breach of the warranty of fitness claim? *Carlson v. Am. Safety Equip. Corp.*, 528 F.2d 384 (1st Cir. 1976)

28.8 Damages. In May of 1998, Frank Coghlan purchased an Aquasport®205, a fishing boat with a retail price of approximately $28,000. He and others filed a class action alleging that starting in 1996, the defendant manufacturer and sellers changed their advertising strategy to emphasize the fiberglass construction of their fishing boats. According to the plaintiffs, the marketing logic behind this shift in emphasis was that a fiberglass construction is "a characteristic desirable to fishermen because, among other things, the boats would not rot and would retain their value." Plaintiffs alleged, and the defendants conceded, that the Aquasport 1998 brochure contained the following excerpts: "Since 1964, Aquasport has given fishermen more for their dollar than any other brand. More innovation. More features. More performance. More value. More of everything you look for in a fishing boat. You can pay a lot more for a boat, but why? Aquasport's got it all. More innovation.... And, believe it or not, the first to introduce an all fiberglass fishing boat. That's right, the first to get the wood off and out." The defendants acknowledged that the brochure contained the statement that the 1998 Aquasport line, with one exception, has a "self-draining, non-skid fiberglass deck." The plaintiffs subsequently discovered that the deck of their Aquasport 205 was composed of one and a half inches of plywood encased within fiberglass. Disappointed that they were not the owners of a truly "all fiberglass fishing boat," the plaintiffs sued for breach of contract and in tort. Essentially, the plaintiffs sued alleging a breach of warranty over the claims made (negligent misrepresentation). Who will prevail and why? *Coghlan v. Aquasport Marine Corp.*, 73 F. Supp. 2d 769 (S.D. Tex. 1999)

28.9 Damages for Breach. H & H Meat Products Company, Inc. (H & H) sold its cattle hides as a byproduct of its meat processing and packing business. Laredo Hides Company, Inc. (Laredo Hides) purchased those hides and shipped them to tanneries in Mexico. In their contract, the terms were to be cash upon delivery with at least two deliveries a month. There was a dispute over whether payment was delivered as required by the contract. The court held that H & H had repudiated the contract with Laredo Hides. To what damages would Laredo Hides be entitled? *Laredo Hides v. H & H Meat*, 513 S.W.2d 210 (Tex. Civ. App. 1974)

28.10 New Vehicle Warranty. In December of 2009, Kuns purchased a new 2010 Mercury Mariner® from the Liberty Ford dealership in Vermillion, Ohio. About a year later, as Kuns's husband was closing the rear liftgate, its glass window suddenly exploded and shattered. After looking over the warranty supplied by Ford®, Kuns and her husband determined that it would not cover the broken window, so they took the car to a repair shop not associated with Ford to have the glass replaced. Then, just over a month after the first incident, the rear window shattered again, this time while Kuns's daughter was closing the liftgate. At this point, Kuns became aware that other owners of the 2010 Mariner had experienced similar breakages, and she asked the dealership to replace the window at no charge to her. The dealership initially refused, explaining that the initial repair had not been made by a Ford-authorized entity, but after Kuns spoke with another Ford representative by phone and threatened to stop making payments on the vehicle, Ford agreed to replace the window. Liberty Ford then completed the repair. Was the dealership's initial refusal reasonable under the Magnuson-Moss Warranty Act enacted by Congress? *Kuns v. Ford Motor Co.*, 926 F. Supp. 2d 976 (N.D. Ohio 2013)

29

Negotiable Instruments: Creation, Transferability, and Liability

'Tis money we need; for without money nothing can be done. — Demosthenes, Athenian orator (384-322 B.C.)

Chapter Outline

- Introduction
  - *Management Application: Assignment of Negotiable Instrument Provision*
- Purposes of Negotiable Instruments
- Types of Negotiable Instruments
  - *Management Application: Promissory Note*
- Requirements for Negotiable Instruments
- Transfer, Negotiation, and Indorsement of Instruments
- Holder in Due Course (HDC)

Case 29.1: *Buckeye Check Cashing, Inc. v. Camp*

- Liability of the Parties
- Defenses, Limitations, and Discharge of Negotiable Instruments

Case 29.2: *Georg v. Metro Fixtures Contractors, Inc.*

- AI Feature: Effects of a Material Alteration of a Negotiable Instrument

Learning Objectives

After studying this chapter, you should be able to:

1. Describe a negotiable instrument and its purposes.
2. Identify and explain the types of negotiable instruments.
3. Identify the requirements for the creation of negotiable instruments.
4. Describe how negotiable instruments are transferred.
5. Explain how a party becomes a holder in due course.
6. Recognize the allocation of risk to the parties to a negotiable instrument.
7. State the defenses to enforcement of a negotiable instrument.
8. Describe how a negotiable instrument may be discharged.

Introduction

Negotiable instrument
A signed document stating that a specified sum is payable to an identified person on either a predetermined date or on demand.

If not for negotiable instruments, trade as we know it would not exist. A **negotiable instrument** is a signed document stating that a specified sum is payable to an identified person on either a predetermined date or on demand. Negotiable instruments are used in substitution of cash or as an extension of credit. The most common example of a negotiable instrument is a check.

Article 3 of the Uniform Commercial Code (UCC) sets forth the rules for creating, transferring, and enforcing negotiable instruments. Additionally, the UCC discusses the liabilities arising from the use of negotiable instruments.

The important characteristic of negotiable instruments is their transferability. The transferability of a negotiable instrument is essential for the instrument to be accepted as a substitute for cash or a credit extension. This chapter will discuss the types of negotiable instruments, their creation, their transferability, and resulting liabilities.

> **Example:** To settle a lawsuit against it, Westview Concrete (Westview) issued coupons to a number of other concrete companies. The coupons stated they were "redeemable by the holder of the coupon" and could be presented for redemption at a specified time. When the time came, a coupon was presented to Westview by Kenneth Klingshirn for a value of $1,470. When presented, Westview agreed to redeem the coupon; however, Westview offset the value of the coupon with a debt that was owed to it by Klingshirn Corporation. As a result, Kenneth Klingshirn was only paid $375.03. Kenneth Klingshirn sued, claiming he was entitled to the full $1,470. The court agreed and found that the debt was owed by the corporation and not by Kenneth personally. Additionally, the court found the coupon was a negotiable instrument and had been validly transferred to Kenneth by Klingshirn Corporation, thereby making Kenneth the holder of the coupon and entitled to its full value. *Klingshirn v. Westview Concrete Corp.*, 680 N.E.2d 691 (Ohio Ct. App. 1996)

Management Application Assignment of Negotiable Instrument Provision

October 19, 2025

For the value received, I assign to ABC, Assignee, all my rights, title, and interest in a promissory note dated June 27, 2025, made by DEF and made payable to GHI in the amount of $9,500.00.

ASSIGNOR

____

GHI

Purposes of Negotiable Instruments

The most common purposes for negotiable instruments are for payment of an obligation or maintenance of records:

PAYMENT OF AN OBLIGATION. Negotiable instruments are used in substitution of cash because it is typically uncommon, and unsafe, for merchants or buyers to carry large sums of cash with them. Over time, various types of checks were created to facilitate the purchase and sale of goods. Additionally, negotiable instruments can function as an extension of credit by allowing a buyer to accept the goods now while promising to pay the seller for the goods later.

MAINTENANCE OF RECORDS. Negotiable instruments are commonly used as recordkeeping devices. For example, most banks will provide customers with an online copy of all the checks the customer wrote and deposited. This allows the records to be easily accessed when various accounting statements or tax returns need to be prepared.

Types of Negotiable Instruments

The UCC identifies the following as negotiable instruments: (1) drafts, (2) checks, (3) promissory notes, and (4) certificates of deposit. Drafts and checks are orders to pay, while promissory notes and certificates of deposit are promises to pay.

Drafts

A **draft** is an instrument between three parties that acts as an unconditional written order in which the **drawer of the draft** orders the **drawee of the draft** (acceptor of the draft) to pay a third party, known as the **payee of the draft**. Drafts will always include an order for a payment to be made. There are various types of drafts, but the two most commonly used in business transactions are time and sight drafts.

TIME DRAFTS AND SIGHT DRAFTS. A **time draft** is a draft that is payable at a specified future date. The obligation to be paid begins when the payee meets all the conditions of the transaction and presents the draft to the drawee; however, the payee typically does not get paid until the date specified on the draft.

> **Example:** A time draft may state an exact date for payment, such as "April 17, 2025," or it may state that payment is due "within 30 days of presentation."

A **sight draft** is payable on sight. Typically, a sight draft is preferred because it allows the payee to receive payment immediately. However, in both situations, an obligation to be paid is created the moment the draft is presented to the drawee. Therefore, if the payee is not paid by the date stated on the time draft, they will have to sue to obtain payment, which increases the riskiness of the transaction.

> **Example:** A sight draft may state that it is payable "on demand" or "on sight."

Draft
An instrument between three parties that acts as an unconditional, written order in which the drawer orders the drawee to pay the payee.

Drawer of the draft
The party who writes the order for a draft.

Drawee of the draft
The party required to pay the money as stated in the draft. May also be called the acceptor of the draft.

Payee of the draft
The party who receives the money from the draft.

Time draft
A draft that is payable at a specified future date.

Sight draft
A draft that is payable on sight.

EXHIBIT 29.1: Time Draft

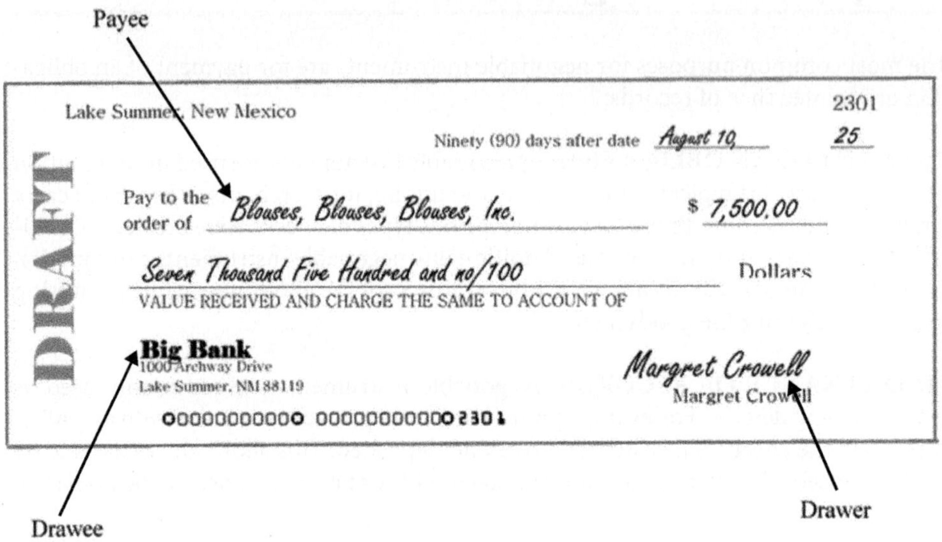

EXHIBIT 29.2: Sight Draft

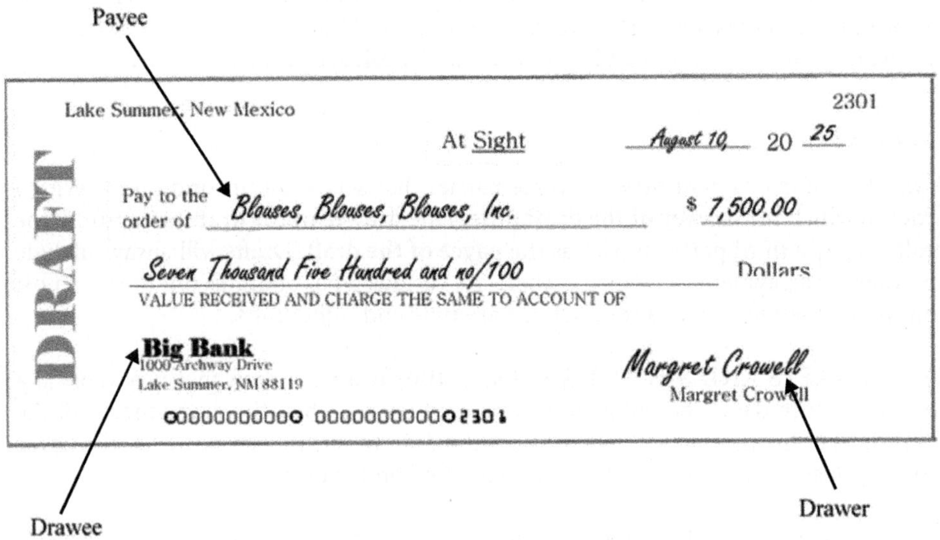

Trade acceptance
A type of sight draft that is created when credit for the sale of goods is extended to the buyer from the seller.

A type of sight draft known as a **trade acceptance** is created when credit for the sale of goods is extended to the buyer from the seller. In this situation, the seller would be considered both the drawer and the payee, while the buyer is the drawee. A trade acceptance is considered a three-party instrument because the three legal positions remain, even though only two parties are involved. This type of draft poses a risk for the seller because there is no third party to assure the buyer's ability to pay back the credited amount.

Similar to a trade acceptance is a **banker's acceptance**. This instrument orders the buyer's bank to pay the specified amount, thereby reducing the risk to the seller. Banker's acceptances are commonly used in international transactions.

Banker's acceptance
A type of sight draft that is commonly used in international transactions and requires the buyer's bank to pay the amount owed.

Checks

Checks are the most common type of draft. Like all other drafts, a **check** is an order to pay and is a three-party instrument. However, the drawee of the check is a financial institution with whom the business or individual has a checking account. Under these circumstances, the business or individual with the checking account that writes the check is the drawer. The financial institution is the drawee and the person to whom the check is entitled is the payee.

Check
A type of draft drawn by a financial institution as an order to pay.

Promissory Note

A **promissory note** is an unconditional written promise made by one party (maker or borrower) to another party (payee or lender). Promissory notes indicate an extension of credit has been issued and that a promise to repay the debt exists. Notes differ from drafts because notes are promises to pay, not orders to pay. Additionally, notes are a two-party instrument. However, like drafts, notes can be payable at a specified time (time note) or on demand (demand note) and can be transferred to other parties.

Promissory note
A two-party instrument that includes an unconditional written promise made by one party (maker or borrower) to another party (payee of lender).

Management Application Promissory Note

Oklahoma City, Oklahoma
$250,000.00 **March 2, 2025**

For value received, the undersigned, Jacoby Wallace on behalf of Wallace's Hardware, Inc. (Maker), promises to pay to the order of Jax Anderson (Holder), or his assigns, the principal sum of $250,000.00, with interest from and after the date of his Note at the rate established by Big O.K.C. Bank each month at its prime rate or reference rate.

A security agreement dated March 2, 2025, secures the indebtedness evidenced by this note.

Interest only shall be payable on April 31, 2025, and on the last day of each month thereafter, until March 31, 2033, at which time the entire unpaid balance of principal and interest shall be due and payable.

All such payments of this Note shall be payable in lawful money of the United States of America. Holder shall have the option to apply the payments on this Note in any order it determines, including, but not limited to, costs, late charges, fees, or expenses incurred in collecting any accounts due hereunder, past due interest, currently due but unpaid interest and outstanding principal.

All liabilities of the Maker to the Holder, including this note, will, at the option of the holder, mature and become due and payable immediately without presentment or notice, which rights are expressly waived if:

1. Maker fails to make the required payment when due.
2. Maker or any endorser, surety, or guarantor of this Note:

   a. Fails, after demand, to furnish financial information or to permit inspection of any books or records,
   b. Suspends business,
   c. Becomes insolvent or offers settlement to any creditors,
   d. Files a petition in bankruptcy, either voluntarily or involuntarily,
   e. Institutes any proceeding under any bankruptcy or insolvency laws relating to relief of debtors,
   f. Gives notice of any intended bulk sale,
   g. Makes an assignment for the benefit of creditors,
   h. Makes a false statement or representation either orally or in writing, fails to furnish information, or fails to permit inspection of any books or records on demand of the Holder, or
   i. Fails any obligation when due.
3. Holder discovers that any misrepresentation was made by or on behalf of Maker to obtain credit or an extension of credit.
4. Any legal action is commenced against Maker or any endorser, surety, or guarantor including:
   a. Entry of judgment,
   b. Issuance of a writ of attachment, order of garnishment, or similar process.

The maker agrees that if any legal action is necessary to enforce this Note, the prevailing party will be entitled to reasonable attorney's fees in addition to any other relief to which that party may be entitled. This provision is applicable to the entire Note.

MAKER

Jacoby Wallace
By: Jacoby Wallace, President of
and on behalf of Wallace's
Hardware, Inc.

Are there other terms of acceleration you would insert in this instrument to protect the lender?

Certificate of Deposit

Certificate of deposit (CD)
A type of note that contains a fixed maturity date and a specified interest rate and includes terms restricting the use of the deposited funds until the maturity date.

A **certificate of deposit (CD)** is a type of negotiable instrument. A CD is a document stating a fixed maturity date and a specified interest rate; however, the funds deposited are restricted until the maturity date. These funds may be accessed (withdrawn) but will be subject to substantial penalties if this is done before the maturity date. CDs may have a fixed or adjustable interest rate. Interest rates are higher for CDs with a longer term to compensate investors for their inability to use these funds until the maturity date.

A CD is another two-party instrument, like a promissory note; however, under these circumstances, the bank is the borrower (maker of the certificate deposit), and the investor is the lender (payee of the certificate deposit). Additionally, CDs are a promise to pay, not an order to pay.

EXHIBIT 29.3: Certificate of Deposit

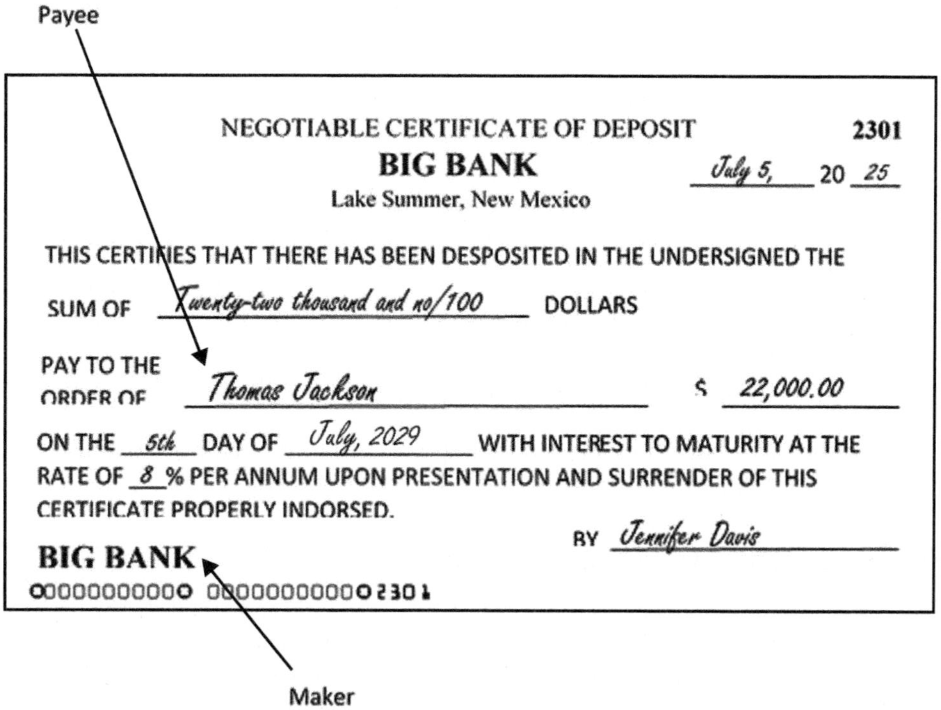

NEGOTIABLE CERTIFICATE OF DEPOSIT 2301
BIG BANK July 5, 20 25
Lake Summer, New Mexico

THIS CERTIFIES THAT THERE HAS BEEN DESPOSITED IN THE UNDERSIGNED THE

SUM OF Twenty-two thousand and no/100 DOLLARS

PAY TO THE ORDER OF Thomas Jackson $ 22,000.00

ON THE 5th DAY OF July, 2029 WITH INTEREST TO MATURITY AT THE RATE OF 8 % PER ANNUM UPON PRESENTATION AND SURRENDER OF THIS CERTIFICATE PROPERLY INDORSED.

BY Jennifer Davis

BIG BANK

00000000000 00000000000 2301

Requirements for Negotiable Instruments

For an instrument to be considered negotiable, it must meet the following requirements of UCC § 3-104(a):

1. Be in writing;
2. Be signed by the maker or the drawer;
3. Be an unconditional promise or order to pay;
4. State a fixed amount of money;
5. Be payable on demand or at a definite time; and
6. Be payable to order or bearer.

Be in Writing

To demonstrate the necessary level of certainty, negotiable instruments must be in the form of a writing. UCC § 3-103(a)(6), (9). Therefore, the writing must meet the following requirements:

1. *Permanency.* The writing must be documented on a material that demonstrates its permanence, such as paper. This is necessary to promote transferability and deter fraud.

Example: An audio recording would not be considered a negotiable instrument because it is not a writing. Additionally, if Damion were to write in the snow, "I promise to pay $1,000 to the order of Steven," this would not be a negotiable instrument because it lacks permanence because the snow will either melt or be covered with more snow.

2. *Portability.* This requirement is not explicitly stated in the UCC; however, it is implied that a writing that is not movable will not possess the necessary characteristic of transferability. If the writing is on something easily conferred in the ordinary course of business, it will be considered portable.

Example: If Jordyn writes, "I promise to pay $1,500 to the order of Brianne" on a large piece of timber, it would not be considered portable.

Signed by the Maker or the Drawer

The UCC requires a note or CD to be signed by the maker, and similarly the drawer must sign a check or draft. UCC § 3-103(a)(3). Until the maker or drawer signs the instrument, they will not be liable on the instrument. This signature may be placed anywhere on the face of the instrument, although most commonly, it is in the lower right corner. Alternatively, an authorized agent of the maker or drawer may sign the instrument on their behalf. UCC § 3-401(a).

Signature
Any symbol adopted or executed by a party with the intent to authenticate a writing.

What constitutes a **signature** has been broadly defined by the UCC. Essentially, any symbol adopted or executed by the party with the intent to authenticate a writing will be deemed a signature. UCC § 1-201(37). A signature need not be made by hand, as the use of some device (stamp, print, etc.) that has been adopted by the signer will suffice.

When the maker or drawer appoints an agent to sign the negotiable instrument on their behalf, the representative's signature binds the maker or drawer in the same manner as if the maker or drawer had signed the instrument themselves. This means that the maker or drawer will be liable for the negotiable instrument signed by the agent on their behalf. However, for the agent to prevent being found personally liable on the negotiable instrument, their signature must clearly disclose (1) their agency status and (2) the identity of the maker or drawer. UCC § 3-402(b).

Example: If a corporate officer is signing a promissory note on behalf of the corporation they work for, the corporate officer should include their title, such as "Chief Financial Officer of ABC, Inc." below their signature in order to prevent becoming personally liable for the instrument

Taylor Hanson
Taylor Hanson
Chief Financial Officer, ABC Inc.
Date: August 20, 2025

Be an Unconditional Promise or Order to Pay

The face of the writing must contain either an unconditional order or a promise to pay. An unconditional order to pay will apply when the negotiable instrument is a draft of the check. Conversely, an unconditional promise to pay will apply when the negotiable instrument is a note or CD.

To meet the requirement of being an *unconditional* promise or order to pay, the obligation to pay cannot be contingent on another event occurring or not occurring.

ORDER TO PAY. To be negotiable, the draft or check is required to demonstrate the drawer's unconditional order to pay the payee. This requires the use of specific language, most importantly the use of the word *pay*. Benefit of the payment can be ordered to one or more parties, either in the form of "to Cole and Nevaeh" or "to Cole or Nevaeh."

> **Example:** A check or that includes the phrase "Pay to the order of" is adequate to make the instrument negotiable.

PROMISE TO PAY. To be negotiable, the promissory note requires the maker's unconditional promise to pay to be included in the writing. Simply acknowledging that money is owed to a party will not be sufficient to create a negotiable instrument. For example, telling someone, "I owe you $500," will not constitute an unconditional promise to pay.

> **Example:** An instrument that includes "I promise to pay ABC $500 by January 26, 2027" would be considered a negotiable instrument.

A CD does not require an express promise to pay because the bank's promise to repay the holder of the certificate has been plainly stated within the terms of the CD.

UNCONDITIONAL. When a promise or order is conditioned on another promise or the occurrence of an event, a negotiable instrument will not be created. This is because the person holding the instrument would incur all the risk that the required promise or event would not occur. Contract law principles will apply when a document contains a conditional promise.

The presence of any one of the following will make a promise or order conditional and, therefore, not negotiable: (1) it contains an express condition to payment, (2) another writing governs the promise or order, or (3) the rights of obligations with respect to the promise or order are stated in another writing. However, merely referencing another document in the promise or order is not enough to make it conditional. UCC § 3-106(a).

> **Example:** If an instrument instructs, "Pay to the order of Sofia Rodriguez if she obtains 100,000 retweets by June 19, 2026," it would not be considered a negotiable instrument because the statement contains an express condition to payment.

State a Fixed Amount of Money

Negotiable instruments are also required to state a fixed amount of money with certainty. This amount is to be paid at any time at which the instrument is considered payable. UCC § 3-104(a). To be considered a *fixed amount*, certainty as to the value of the instrument is required and must be determinable from the face of the instrument.

> **Example:** An instrument that states, "Pay to the Order of Dwayne Williams in the amount of $65,050.09" is a negotiable instrument.

Instruments that include the payment of interest may be stated as either a fixed or variable amount. If the interest is fixed, the instrument should state something like the following: "Interest to be payable at the rate of 5% of the principal amount." A variable interest rate, although not ascertainable from the instrument alone, is still sufficient if it is established by means of a formula or another source indicated in the instrument. For example, "interest is to be payable subject to the *Wall Street Journal*® (WSJ) Prime Rate published on the first business day of each month during the term of this instrument" is an example of a variable rate. When an instrument indicates interest is to be paid, but an interest rate cannot be ascertained based on the instrument, the interest will be payable at the *legal rate of interest* (a rate established by statute) and will be considered negotiable.

Additionally, this requirement also compels the fixed amount of the negotiable instrument to be payable in money. Under the UCC, money is defined as a "medium of exchange authorized or adopted by a domestic or foreign government as part of its currency." UCC § 1-201(24). This definition has been interpreted to mean any instruments that call for payment, either partially or fully, in the form of something other than money are not negotiable. Orders or promises for payment in the form of a precious metal such as gold or silver will be considered nonnegotiable because these metals are not recognized mediums of exchange under U.S. law.

> **Example:** An instrument that states it is "payable in $8,500 in Canadian dollars" is a negotiable instrument.

Be Payable on Demand or at a Definite Time

For an instrument to be negotiable, it is necessary to know when the maker, drawee, or acceptor is required to pay. As set forth in UCC § 3-104(a)(2), the instrument must be payable either on demand or at a definite time. The time of payment is to be stated on the face of the instrument. Knowing when payment is due is particularly important for the purposes of calculating the correct amount of interest that is to be paid.

PAYABLE ON DEMAND. A demand instrument is an instrument that is payable on demand. A demand instrument will be indicated using the phrases "payable on demand" or "payable on presentation." UCC § 3-108(a). In some instances, when payment is due can be determined by the nature of the instrument. For example, checks by their nature are payable on demand, UCC § 3-104(f), while other instruments, such as drafts, CDs, and notes, will be payable on demand unless otherwise specified in the instrument. UCC § 3-108(a).

PAYABLE AT A DEFINITE TIME. For an instrument to be negotiable, the only other option is for it to be payable at a definite time. An instrument is payable at a definite time if on its face it states it is payable (1) on a specific date, (2) within a defined period of time after being presented for payment, or (3) on a date or time that is readily ascertainable at the time the promise or order is issued. UCC § 3-108(b). If the instrument is payable at the time of an uncertain event, it is not negotiable.

ACCELERATION CLAUSE. An **acceleration clause** may be provided for in the instrument to allow the payee to demand full payment (entire principal amount plus any interest) upon the occurrence of a certain event, such as a default.

Acceleration clause
A clause in the instrument that allows the payee to demand full payment upon the occurrence of a certain event.

> **Example:** "In the event of default in the payment of any of the said installments or said interest when due as provided herein, the holder of this note may declare the entire principal sum then unpaid immediately due and payable."

The UCC states that instruments containing an acceleration clause are negotiable for two reasons: (1) the precise value of the instrument can be ascertained, and (2) the instrument will be payable on a specified date if the event causing the acceleration does not occur. UCC § 3-108(b)(ii).

EXTENSION CLAUSE. Conversely, the maker or drawer of the instrument might wish to have an **extension clause** within the instrument. UCC § 3-108(iii), (iv). An extension clause allows the maker or drawer to extend the instrument's date of maturity to a time in the future. However, for it to be negotiable, the period for which the extension is granted to the maker or drawer must be clearly stated in the instrument. On the other hand, if the instrument holder wishes to extend the time of payment, the extension of the maturity date need not be specified in the instrument.

Extension clause
A clause in the instrument that allows the maker or drawer to extend the instrument's date of maturity to a time in the future.

> **Example:** "Drawer shall have the right, at its option, to extend for any period of time by giving notice of such extension to Lender at least fifteen (15) days prior to the originally scheduled Stated Maturity Date."

For an overview of the requirements of negotiable instruments, see, https://nacm.org/pdfs/articles/Negotiable_Instruments.pdf.

Payable to Order or Bearer

Negotiable instruments would serve little practical purpose as a substitute for cash or credit if they were unable to be transferred. Therefore, UCC § 3-104(a)(1) requires the instrument to be "payable to order or a bearer" either when the instrument is issued or when it comes into possession of the holder. If an instrument fails to meet this requirement, it is not negotiable.

ORDER INSTRUMENTS. Under UCC § 3-109(b), an **order instrument** is one that is payable to either (1) the order of an identified person or (2) to an identified person or order. The person who has been identified may then transfer the instrument to whomever they choose.

Order instrument
An instrument that is made payable to either the order of an identified person or to an identified person or order.

> **Example:** The use of the word "order" is of paramount importance in negotiable instruments. If an instrument simply states "Payable to Jameis Weaver" or "Pay to Jameis Weaver," it will not be considered negotiable, whereas an instrument that says "Payable to the order of Jameis Weaver" or "Pay to the order of Jameis Weaver" would be considered negotiable.

Do not overlook the role that the signature requirement plays in conjunction with order instruments. Since the instrument requires a signature or indorsement of the payee to be transferred, it is essential that the person specified in the instrument is identified with certainty.

Example: An instrument made "payable to the order of my best friend ever" would not be negotiable because it lacks identification of the payee with reasonable certainty. However, if the instrument stated, "payable to the order of my best friend, Brianna Hart," it would be negotiable because the payee can be ascertained with reasonable certainty.

Bearer instrument An instrument that is made payable to whomever is in physical possession and presents it for payment when it is due.

BEARER INSTRUMENTS. A **bearer instrument** is payable to whomever is in physical possession and presents it for payment when it is due. Here, the instrument does not identify a particular payee; therefore, the maker or drawer agrees to pay whoever presents the instrument for payment. UCC § 3-109(a). Bearer instruments contain language such as "payable to bearer," "payable to the order of the bearer," "payable to cash," or "payable to the order of cash." Additionally, the instrument might indicate that it is not payable to a specific person and, therefore, would be considered a bearer instrument.

Example: The following are common phrases used to indicate the instrument is a bearer instrument: "payable to bearer," "payable to the order of bearer," "payable to Blue Bottle, Inc., or bearer," "payable to the order of cash," or "payable to cash."

Concept Summary
Conditions and Omissions That Do Not Affect Negotiability

As discussed above, there are certain requirements for an instrument to be considered negotiable. Other factors often mislead contracting parties into thinking that an instrument is not negotiable. Listed below are conditions and omissions that do not affect negotiability:

1. *Place of payment.* Whether an instrument specifies a place of payment has no effect on negotiability.
2. *Interest.* Unless otherwise provided in the instrument, the amount owed on an instrument is not payable with interest.
3. *Dates.* Whether an instrument is undated, antedated, or postdated has no effect on negotiability.
4. *Contradictory terms.* Contradictory terms will not make an instrument non-negotiable. If such terms exist, typewritten terms prevail over printed terms, handwritten terms prevail over both typewritten and printed terms, and words prevail over numbers.

Transfer, Negotiation, and Indorsement of Instruments

As previously stated, the transferability of negotiable instruments has been essential in making trade what it is today. When a negotiable instrument has been issued, it may be transferred to another party by assignment or negotiation.

Transfer by Assignment

As you may recall from Chapter 13, an assignment is the transfer of a contractual right, and under the doctrine of assignment, these rights are freely transferrable. The rights that the transferor (assignor) transfers to the transferee (assignee) are limited to the rights originally belonging to the transferor. Therefore, any defense that could be brought against the assignor can also be brought against the assignee. Similarly, in the case of negotiable instruments, the same principles apply when a transfer by assignment occurs. When a transfer by assignment occurs, the transferee is an assignee but does not become a *holder* of the instrument.

Transfer by Negotiation

Unlike an assignment, when a **negotiation** of an instrument occurs, the transferee will become a holder. UCC § 3-203(a). When a transfer by negotiation occurs, a holder is created, and this holder is entitled to at least all the rights of the transferor. UCC § 3-203(b). However, unlike transfers by assignment, the holder created in a transfer by negotiation may receive more rights than the previous holder of the instrument had. This holder is known as a holder in due course. UCC §§ 3-202(b), 3-305. The holder in due course (HDC) has more rights than the transferor because the HDC will not be subject to many of the defenses that could be asserted against the transferor. HDCs will be discussed in more detail later in this chapter.

Negotiation
A type of transfer of the possession of a negotiable instrument to a person who becomes the holder.

It is important to note that if a transfer by negotiation fails to meet any of the requirements of a negotiable instrument set forth above, the transfer will instead become an assignment.

There are two ways in which transfers by negotiation occur. The type of method used depends upon whether the instrument is an order instrument or a bearer instrument.

NEGOTIATING AN ORDER INSTRUMENT. An instrument that is payable to a specific payee who can indorse it is known as an order instrument. UCC § 3-201(b) requires an order instrument to be negotiated by delivery with all necessary indorsements. Therefore, there must be both delivery and indorsement for a transfer by negotiation of an order instrument to be valid.

> **Example:** Assume Big Corp. issues a check "to the order of Jon Thompson" for the landscaping work completed by Jon. Jon would have to take the check to the bank, sign the back of the check with his name (indorsement), hand the check to

the teller (delivery), and collect the cash. By completing these steps, Jon will have negotiated the check to the bank pursuant to UCC § 3-201(b).

NEGOTIATING A BEARER INSTRUMENT. When an instrument is not payable to a specified payee or indorsee, it is known as a bearer instrument. A bearer instrument is one that is negotiated by delivery but is not required to be indorsed. UCC § 3-201(b). However, it is important to note that the use of this type of instrument increases the risk that the wrong person will be paid if the instrument is lost or stolen.

Example: Kali writes a check "payable to cash" and gives it to Ian (delivery). If the check is stolen, the thief has possession of the check but none of the rights transfer to the thief. However, if the thief then delivers the check to a party who has no reason to believe the check is stolen, the rights of the check will be transferred to that third party. When the innocent third party receives the rights, Ian will no longer hold any rights to the check. This means Ian would not be able to recover the money from the innocent party. The only person Ian could pursue to recover his money would be the thief.

Indorsements

Indorsement
A signature on the instrument to transfer ownership of the instrument.

When order instruments are negotiated, they must be indorsed. Indorsements are not required for bearer instruments. An **indorsement** is a signature required on the instrument in order to transfer ownership of the instrument. An indorsement may but is not required to include additional words or directions. If there is no room on the instrument for the indorsement, it can be made on a separate piece of paper, if it is securely fixed to the instrument itself. UCC § 3-204(a). The individual who transfers the instrument by signing it and then delivering it to the other party is known as the indorser. The person to whom the instrument is indorsed and delivered is the indorsee.

There are four categories of indorsements: blank, special, qualified, and restrictive. The characteristics of a single indorsement are not limited to a single category—it is quite possible, even common, for an indorsement to be classified as more than one of the following categories at a given time.

Blank indorsement
An indorsement that does not specify the indorsee.

BLANK INDORSEMENTS. An indorsement that does not specify the indorsee is known as a **blank indorsement**. These indorsements may simply contain a signature.

A blank indorsement modifies the order instrument into a bearer instrument, which can be presented by anyone in exchange for the payment due. When a bearer's instrument is lost or stolen, there is an increased risk that a wrongful party will receive the payment instead of the intended party.

Special indorsement
An indorsement that contains the signature of the indorser and specifies the person to whom the instrument will be made payable.

SPECIAL INDORSEMENT. A **special indorsement** contains the signature of the indorser and specifies the person to whom the instrument will be made payable. Phrases such as "pay to the order of . . ." and "pay to . . ." are adequate to create a special indorsement. A special indorsement creates an order instrument, which will require both indorsement and delivery.

EXHIBIT 29.4: Blank Indorsement

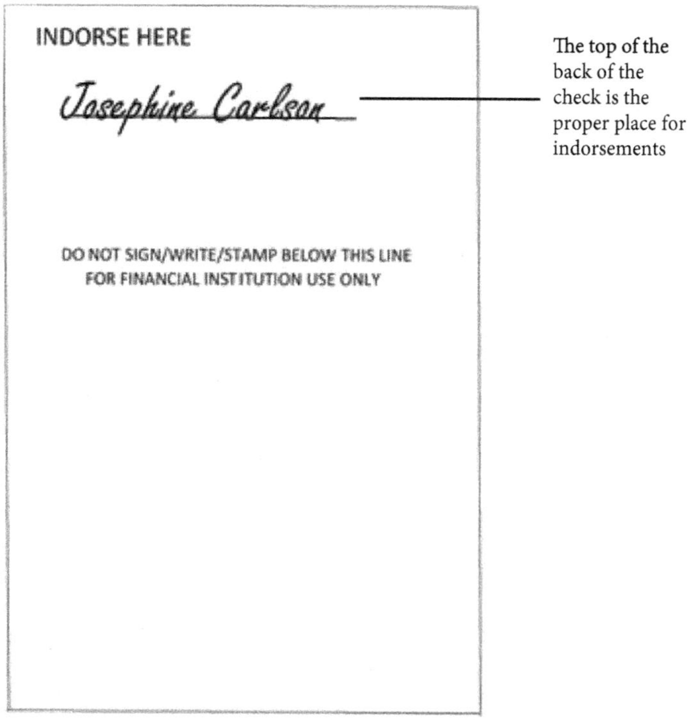

Special indorsements alleviate the risks associated with the loss or theft of an instrument, which is why special indorsements are preferred. A blank indorsement can be changed into a special indorsement by adding words identifying the indorsee above the signature of the indorser. This alteration will be sufficient to change a bearer instrument into an order instrument.

> **Example:** A check is made payable to Josephine Carlson. She indorses the check in blank by only signing her name and delivers the check to Ben Moore. Moore knows he will not be able to cash the check for several days and is worried about what would happen to the check if he were to misplace it. Therefore, he places "Pay to Ben Moore" above her name. Adding this phrase converts the blank indorsement into a special indorsement.

QUALIFIED INDORSEMENT. Typically, the mere act of an indorser indorsing an instrument signifies an implied promise to pay the amount of the instrument to the holder or any subsequent holder if for any reason the drawer or maker defaults on the payment. UCC § 3-415(a). Such instruments are referred to as *unqualified indorsements*, which signifies the indorser is guaranteeing the payment of the instrument as well as transferring it to the indorsee.

A **qualified indorsement** can be used to disclaim or limit liability when an indorser does not want to be liable on the instrument. If an indorser uses a qualified

Qualified indorsement
An indorsement on a negotiable instrument that disclaims or limits liability when an indorser does not want to be liable on the instrument.

EXHIBIT 29.5: Special Indorsement

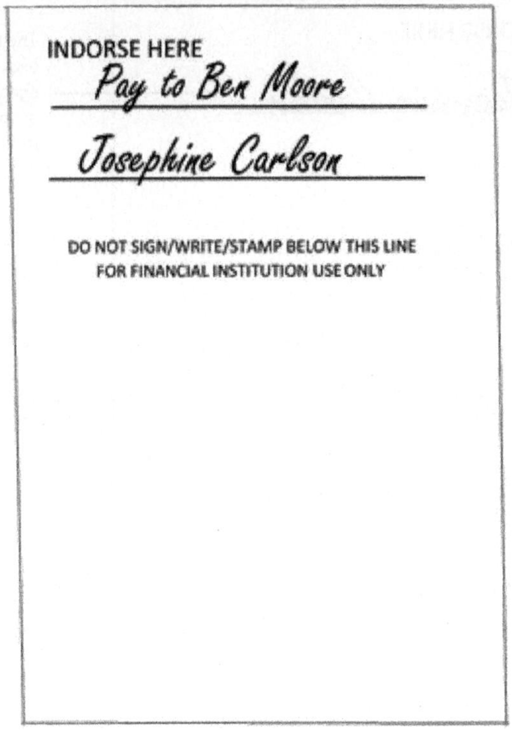

EXHIBIT 29.6: Qualified Indorsement

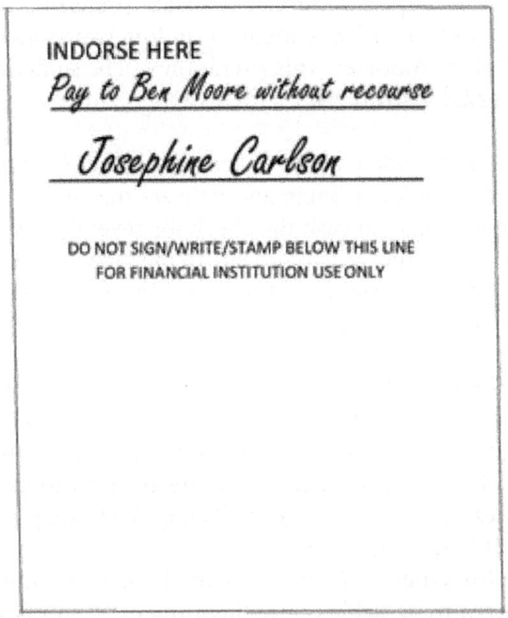

indorsement, they are not providing any guarantee to make payment to the maker or drawer, essentially leaving the holder *without recourse.* Without recourse means that the holder cannot recover from the indorser unless the indorser failed to fulfill one of the transfer requirements. Qualified indorsements are commonly found in situations in which an instrument has been signed by someone acting as a representative or agent of another.

There are two types of qualified indorsements, special and blank. **Special qualified indorsements** generate order instruments that are negotiated by indorsement and delivery. The name of the indorsee and the phrase "without recourse" are included on special qualified indorsements. **Blank qualified indorsements**, on the other hand, produce bearer instruments that are negotiated by delivery and do not require indorsement.

Special qualified indorsement
An indorsement that creates order instruments that are negotiated by indorsement and delivery.

Blank qualified indorsement
An indorsement that produces bearer instruments that are negotiated by delivery and do not require indorsement.

INDORSEMENTS USING RESTRICTIVE LANGUAGE. Although most instruments do not possess any instructions or conditions accompanying the payment of the funds, those that do are called **restrictive indorsements**. As the name implies, restrictive indorsements restrict the rights of the indorsee to a certain extent. Restrictive indorsements do not prevent further negotiation of the instrument, they simply dictate additional terms relating to the funds. Various forms of restrictive indorsements can be found in practice, many of which are beyond the scope of this text. The most common ones are discussed below.

Restrictive indorsements
Negotiable instruments that possess instructions and conditions regarding the payment of funds.

EXHIBIT 29.7: Restrictive Indorsement

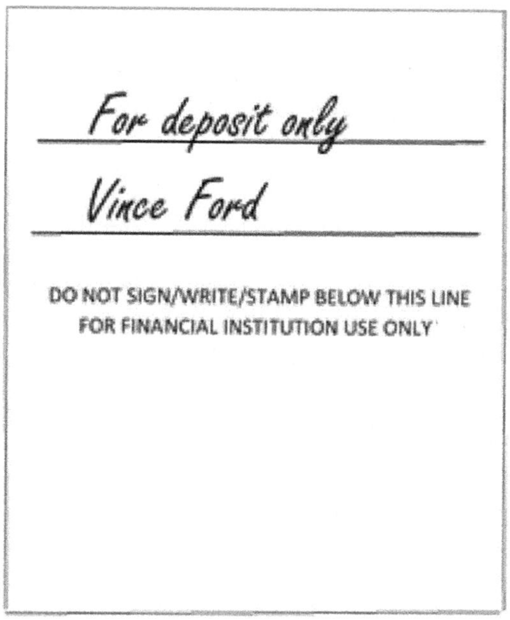

Other Types of Indorsements
Conditional Indorsements

A conditional indorsement occurs when payment is dependent on the happening of a specific event stated in the indorsement.

> **Example:** Blake Michaels indorses a check "Pay to Bob Bulloch if he finishes the electrical work on my home by October 3, 2025" and signs his name on the instrument. This will create a conditional indorsement.

Indorsements for Deposit

An indorsement for deposit makes the indorsee a collecting agent for the indorser. This occurs most frequently in situations where the indorsee is a bank. The instrument will be prohibited from any further negotiation except by the bank when it is indorsed "for deposit only."

Trust Indorsements

Another common condition occurs when the indorsement is to an individual who is to hold or use the funds to benefit the indorser or a third party. This is known as a trust indorsement. Trust indorsements may also be referred to as agency indorsements.

> **Example:** Following a bankruptcy proceeding, Quinn owes money to a creditor. Quinn can indorse a check that was made out to him by a third party, "Pay to my attorney, Isabel Thomas, in trust for Helen Dupree (creditor)." Quinn's attorney may then pay the creditor the stated amount on his behalf.

Misspelled or Incorrect Name

If the name of the payee or indorsee is misspelled in a negotiable instrument, the UCC provides a few options. The payee or indorsee may indorse the instrument using the misspelled name, the correct name, or both. UCC § 3-204(d).

> **Example:** If Karl Johansen receives a check made payable to "Karl Johanson," Karl has the option to indorse the check by signing either "Karl Johansen," "Karl Johanson," or both.

Multiple Payees or Indorsees

It is common for instruments to be payable to two or more payees or indorsees. The answer to the question of "Who must sign the instrument?" is different depending on whether the instrument is jointly or alternatively payable. A jointly payable instrument requires the signature of both payees or indorsees. Instruments that are jointly payable will include the word *and*, indicating both signatures are needed.

> **Example:** An instrument that states "Payable to the order of ABC and DEF" will require signatures of both parties.

Conversely, an instrument that is alternatively payable only needs to be signed by one of the payees or indorsees. These instruments will include the word *or*, indicating that either party's signature will be sufficient.

> **Example:** An instrument that states "Payable to George or Martha Washington" will only require the signature of one of the parties.

When it is unclear whether an instrument is jointly or alternatively payable because a slash mark (/) is used, courts have interpreted this to mean that the instrument is payable in the alternative. Therefore, a / is read as if it were an "or" and either party's signature is sufficient.

> **Example:** An instrument that states "Payable to Martha/Anne Washington" will only require the signature of one of the parties.

Holder in Due Course (HDC)

One of the most important distinctions in the law of negotiable instruments is the difference between a holder and a holder in due course. A **holder**, as defined by UCC § 1-201(21), means a person in possession of a negotiable instrument that is payable to either the bearer or the identified person that is in possession of the instrument. A holder is essentially an assignee, which means the holder is still subject to all the claims and defenses that could be asserted against the transferor in the event of an action being brought against them.

Holder
A person in possession of a negotiable instrument that is payable to either the bearer or the identified person that is in possession of the instrument.

A **holder in due course (HDC)**, on the other hand, possesses the negotiable instrument free and clear of most of the claims and defenses that could have been brought against the transferor. Because of this, an HDC may acquire superior rights to the instrument than the transferor had at the time of transfer.

Holder in due course (HDC)
A person who possesses the negotiable instruments free and clear of most of the claims and defenses that could have been brought against the transferor.

> **Example:** Susan executes a $2,500 note to Jared in exchange for three precious stones. Jared then negotiates the note to Erin, who promises to pay Jared for it in 60 days. Forty days later, Erin finds out that Jared has breached his agreement with Susan by giving her inauthentic stones, and for that reason, Susan to honor the $2,500 note. Erin will want to hold Susan liable on the note, but she will only be able to do so if she meets the requirements necessary to meet HDC status. If Erin is unable to show she has obtained HDC status, any defense Susan uses against Jared, she can also use it against Erin.

Obtaining HDC Status

Before a transferee is considered a holder in due course there are a few requirements that the UCC has established that the transferee must meet: The person must be the holder of a negotiable instrument that was taken:

1. For value;
2. In good faith;
3. Without notice that it is overdue, dishonored, or encumbered in any way; and
4. Bearing no apparent evidence of forgery, alterations, or irregularity. UCC § 3-302(a)(2).

The subsections below will discuss each requirement at length.

VALUE. To qualify as an HDC, the UCC requires the holder to have given value for the negotiable instrument. UCC § 3-302(a)(2)(i). There are several ways in which the holder can give something of value, including:

- Performance of the promise for which the instrument was transferred.
- Acquiring a security interest or other lien in the instrument, other than one obtained by means of a judicial proceeding.
- Taking the instrument in payment of or as security for a prior claim.
- Giving a negotiable instrument as payment.
- Giving an irrevocable obligation as payment. UCC § 3-303(a).

If only a promise to perform has been given and no performance has yet occurred, no value has been given, and the person will not be considered an HDC. Similarly, the promise to give something of value does not meet the requirement and that person will also not be considered an HDC.

> **Example:** Suppose Carly executes a note payable to Jessie for $10,000 in exchange for his car, to be paid in equal installments over the course of five months. Jessie really needs the money right now, so he agrees to transfer the note to Rachel in exchange for $8,000. Under these circumstances, Rachel is a holder in due course because she has given value for the negotiable instrument.

GOOD FAITH. The UCC also requires that the holder take the instrument in good faith to be an HDC. UCC § 3-302(a)(2)(ii). The UCC defines good faith as honesty in fact and the observance of reasonable commercial standards of fair dealing. UCC § 1-201(20). Simply put, the holder must have acted properly while obtaining the instrument. The requirement of good faith only applies to the holder; therefore, even if any other party acts in bad faith during the transfer of the document, the holder will still become an HDC.

In order to determine if a holder acted in good faith, the court applies a subjective test to determine the holder's actual belief. If the court determines the holder actually believed the instrument was not defective, the holder can become an HDC.

In the following case, the court was asked to determine if a check-cashing company had acted in good faith when it cashed a postdated check.

CASE 29.1

THE REASONABLE COMMERCIAL STANDARD MAY BE APPLIED IN DETERMINING IF A PARTY ACTED IN GOOD FAITH

BUCKEYE CHECK CASHING, INC. v. CAMP

825 N.E.2d 644 (2005)

Court of Appeals of Ohio

On or about October 12, 2003, Shawn Sheth began negotiating with James Camp for Camp to complete various services for Sheth by October 15, 2003. When the negotiations concluded, Sheth issued Camp a check for $1,300. The check issued by Sheth was postdated to October 15, 2003, meaning Camp should not be able to cash the check before that date. On October 13, 2003, Camp negotiated the check to Buckeye Checking, Inc. and subsequently received a payment of $1,261.31. Sheth contacted his bank on October 14, 2003, to cancel the check, as he feared Camp did not intend to provide the services to which he had agreed. Unaware that the check had been canceled, on October 14, 2003, Buckeye deposited the check with its own bank. Buckeye believed the check would not be received until the next day. However, due to the check being canceled Sheth's bank dishonored the check immediately. Buckeye brought suit against Camp after he was unable to obtain payment from Sheth directly. The trial court ruled in favor of Buckeye, finding it was a holder in due course and therefore entitled to payment despite the fact that Sheth had canceled the check. Sheth appealed.

Language of the Court. *At issue in the instant appeal is whether Buckeye acted in "good faith" when it chose to honor the postdated check originally drawn by Sheth. UCC 1-201 defines "good faith" as "honesty in fact and the observance of reasonable commercial standards of fair dealing."*

In 1994, however, the Ohio legislature amended the definition of "good faith" to include not only the subjective "honesty in fact" test, but also an objective test: "the observance of reasonable commercial standards of fair dealing." A holder in due course must now satisfy both a subjective and an objective test of good faith. What constitutes "reasonable commercial standards of fair dealing" for parties claiming holder-in-due-course status, however, has not heretofore been defined in the state of Ohio.

Under a purely subjective "honesty in fact" analysis, it is clear that Buckeye accepted the check from Camp in good faith and would therefore achieve holder-in-due-course status. When the objective prong of the good faith test is applied, however, we find that Buckeye did not conduct itself in a commercially reasonable manner. While not going so far as to say that cashing a postdated check prevents a holder from obtaining holder-in-due-course status in every instance, the presentation of a postdated check should put the check cashing entity on notice that the check might not be good. Buckeye accepted the postdated check at its own peril. Some attempt at verification should be made before a check-cashing business cashes a postdated check. Such a failure to act does not constitute taking an instrument in good faith under the current objective test of "reasonable commercial standards."

When Buckeye decided to cash the postdated check presented by Camp, it did so without making any attempt to verify its validity. This court in no way seeks to curtail the free negotiability of commercial instruments. However, the nature of certain instruments, such as the postdated check in this case, renders it necessary for appellee Buckeye to take minimal steps to protect its interests. That was not done. Buckeye was put on notice that the check was not good until October 15, 2003. "Good Faith," as it is defined in the UCC and the Ohio Revised Code, requires that a holder demonstrate not only honesty in fact but also that the holder act in a commercially reasonable manner. Without taking any steps to discover whether the postdated check issued by Sheth was valid, Buckeye failed to act in a commercially reasonable manner and therefore was not a holder in due course.

Decision. The court reversed the judgment of the trial court, finding Buckeye was not a holder in due course and not entitled to payment from Sheth.

Focus on Ethics

Is the "reasonable commercial standard" a fair burden to place on a party claiming holder-in-due-course status?

NOTICE. To qualify as an HDC, the person must show the taking of the instrument occurred without notice of any one of the following:

1. It is overdue.
2. It has been dishonored.
3. It is issued as part of a series which has at least one instrument that has an uncured default.
4. It contains an unauthorized signature or has been altered.
5. Another person has claim to it or a defense against the instrument.
6. The instrument is so irregular or incomplete as to call into question its authenticity.

The UCC defines notice as (1) actual knowledge of the defect, (2) receipt of written notice, or (3) when the person has reason to know a defect exists, given the facts and circumstances known to them at the time in question. UCC § 1-202(a). This notice must be received "at a time and in a manner that gives a reasonable opportunity to act on it." UCC § 3-302(f).

Overdue. Some instruments contain a stated due date, and these instruments are known as time instruments. When a time instrument is not paid on the specified due date, it is considered overdue. Typically, the instrument will become overdue the following day.

> **Example:** If an instrument is due on February 12, 2025, the note must be acquired by the transferee by 11:59 P.M. on February 12, 2025, for the transferee to obtain HDC status. If the instrument is acquired after 11:59 P.M. on February 12, 2025, the party will simply be a holder.

Dishonored. When an instrument is presented for payment in a timely manner for payment and the payment is refused, the instrument becomes dishonored. A person will be considered to have notice if they either have actual knowledge of the instrument being dishonored or know facts that would lead them to believe the instrument has been dishonored.

> **Example:** If an instrument has been marked by a bank stating that payment was refused, any subsequent acquirer will not obtain HDC status.

Claims or Defenses. If a holder has notice of any claims to the instrument or defenses against it, they will not qualify as an HDC. UCC § 3-302(a)(2).

NO EVIDENCE OF FORGERY, ALTERATION, OR IRREGULARITY. The last requirement states that a holder will not qualify as a HDC if the instrument exhibited any apparent evidence of forgery, alteration, or was so irregular or incomplete as to call into question its authenticity. UCC § 3-302(a)(1). The facts and circumstances of each case will determine whether a forgery or alteration was apparent and whether the irregularities or incompleteness of the instrument call into question its authenticity. In cases where the forgery or alteration was not apparent, the holder will become an HDC.

Becoming a Holder Through an HDC

When a person receives her title from an HDC but is not one herself, she may still be able to receive the rights and privileges of an HDC. This rule is commonly known as the shelter principle. In an effort to assist HDCs in the transfer of instruments, the rule states that so long as a holder can trace their title back to an HDC, no matter how far back, the holder will receive all the rights of the HDC. UCC § 3-203(b). However, the holder must still meet the requirements of good faith and notice to obtain the HDC rights. Therefore, if the holder partook in any fraud to obtain the instrument or had notice of an inconsistency, the holder will not receive the rights and privileges of the HDC.

Liability of the Parties

Various types of liability may arise under the law of negotiable instruments. Most commonly, these relate to a person's signature or the warranties that result when an instrument is presented for negotiation. Both signature and warranty liability are discussed below.

Signature Liability

Signature liability Contractual liability imputed to the signer of an instrument.

In most cases, when a person signs an instrument, they become contractually liable on that instrument. This is known as **signature liability**. This rule does not apply to a qualified indorsee who has indorsed the instrument "without recourse." Every party who signed an instrument will be contractually liable when payment is due. The degree to which a party is liable depends upon whether they are subject to primary or secondary liability.

Primary liability When a party is absolutely required to pay the instrument.

PRIMARY LIABILITY. When a party is required to pay the instrument, the party is subject to **primary liability**, unless the party asserts a legal defense to payment. UCC §3-305. Primary liability applies only to the makers and acceptors of instruments. For example, when the maker of a promissory note signs the note, they have made an unconditional promise to pay the specified amount by the date stated in the note. If the promissory note was incomplete at the time it was signed, the maker is still obligated to pay according to the note's terms or any terms that were agreed upon by the parties. UCC § 3-412.

Certified check Type of check by which the bank certifies that the customer has the necessary funds in the customer's account to make the payment stated on the check and also verifies the signature is genuine.

Typically, a draft or check does not result in a party becoming primarily liable because these instruments are orders to pay. This means that a drawee who refuses to pay a draft or check is not liable to the payee unless the instrument is wrongfully dishonored (in these situations the drawee could be liable to the drawer for some damages). However, when dealing with trade acceptances and certified checks, the acceptor (drawee) becomes primarily liable when they signify acceptance by signing the instrument and then fail to pay when due.

Secondary liability Liability that applies to a drawer or indorser only when the person responsible for the payment denies the holder the payment.

SECONDARY LIABILITY. **Secondary liability** applies to a drawer or indorser only when the person responsible for the payment denies the holder the payment when due. Therefore, the drawer or indorser's liability does not begin until after the drawee has refused to pay or accept the instrument. UCC §§ 3-412, 3-415.

> **Example:** Jim writes a check from his account with State Bank and makes the check "payable to the order of Darrel." When Darrel presents the check for payment and State Bank refuses to pay it, Darrel can still collect the amount payable from Jim because as the drawer, Jim is still liable on the check due to secondary liability.

Indorsees can protect themselves from becoming secondarily liable on an instrument by making a qualified indorsement "without recourse." Drawers can protect themselves in a similar manner by drawing the instrument "without recourse;" however, this does not apply when the draft is a check. UCC § 3-414(e).

The following events must occur for parties to become secondarily liable on a negotiable instrument:

1. The instrument is properly and timely presented;
2. The instrument is dishonored; and
3. The party that is secondarily liable is given timely notice of the dishonor.

Presentment. When an instrument is presented, it signifies a demand for acceptance or payment of an instrument to the liable party by the holder. Proper **presentment** occurs when a holder presents the instrument to the appropriate party in a timely fashion and provides reasonable identification if it is requested. UCC §§ 3-415(e), 3-502(b). Presentment will be deemed effective when the demand for payment or acceptance is received by the person to whom it was presented. UCC § 3-501. This presentation can be made by any commercially reasonable means, such as written, oral, or electronic communication. UCC § 3-501.

Presentment
The act of presenting the documents of the transaction to the appropriate bank to receive the money due under the negotiable instrument.

Presentment must also be timely. If the instrument is not presented on time, the presentment will be deemed improper and any unqualified indorsers will no longer be secondarily liable. This is the most common reason a presentment is found to be improper.

Concept Summary
Procedural Guide to Presentment and Acceptance

1. If presentment has not been excused, presentment is made to enforce the obligations of both the drawer and endorser.
2. Presentment is made to either the maker, acceptor, drawee, or any other payor (or more than one).
3. Presentment is made either at the place of payment specified in the instrument or at the address of the drawee or maker if no place is stated.
4. Presentment can be made by any commercially reasonable means and within a reasonable period.
5. If required, present either the instrument or identification.
6. Advise the holder that the person making presentment may be required to sign or surrender the instrument if paid in full.
7. If a draft is involved, obtain the drawee's acceptance in the form of the drawee's signed agreement to pay the draft as presented, written on the draft.

Dishonor. When a required acceptance or payment is refused or cannot be obtained in the designated amount of time after the presentment is made, an instrument is deemed dishonored. UCC § 3-502.

However, sometimes a bank's refusal to pay will not dishonor an instrument. This may occur in situations where the instrument is presented after a stated cut-off time. For example, if an instrument states that it must be presented by 12 P.M., the bank can wait until the following business day to pay without dishonoring the instrument. If a holder fails to provide reasonable identification or sign a receipt for the payment, the bank's refusal will not constitute a dishonor of the instrument.

Notice. Proper notice of an instrument being dishonored must be given to the parties that are secondarily liable for them to be held liable. Notice may be given by any person, by any commercially reasonable means, such as written, oral, or electronic communication, so long as it identifies the instrument and indicates that the instrument has been dishonored or that it has not been paid or accepted. A bank must provide notice by midnight of the day following the day on which the bank receives the notice of dishonor. Any party, other than a bank, must provide notice within 30 days following the date on which they receive the notice of dishonor. UCC § 3-503.

Unauthorized Signatures

Unauthorized signature
A signature on a negotiable instrument signed by an agent without the authority of the principal or that is forged.

An **unauthorized signature** may arise on a negotiable instrument when a person forges someone else's signature or when an agent signs an instrument on behalf of their principal without the authority to do so. Generally, unauthorized signatures are treated as being invalid, meaning the unauthorized signature will not bind the party who had their name wrongfully signed.

> **Example:** Suppose a corporation's bookkeeper left blank checks on the top of his desk when he left for lunch. While the bookkeeper was at lunch, an employee from the marketing department walked past the bookkeeper's desk and took the blank checks. The marketing employee writes checks to herself for various amounts from the corporation's account and signs the bookkeeper's name. This would constitute an unauthorized signature.

There are two ways in which an unauthorized signature will bind the person whose name is signed. The first occurs when the party who had their name signed ratifies or approves the signature. UCC § 3-403(a). Second, when negligence of the party whose name was forged substantially contributed to the forgery, the court may not allow the party to deny the effectiveness of the unauthorized signature. UCC §§ 3-115, 3-406, 4-401(d)(2).

Special Rules for Forged Instruments

The general rule concerning an instrument with a forged or unauthorized indorsement is that the burden of loss will fall on the first party to take or accept the instrument. This is because that party is in the best position to prevent the loss.

> **Example:** A bank may be held liable for issuing payment on an instrument that bears a forged signature where the bank did not request the holder to present identification.

There are two exceptions to this rule that result in the loss falling on the drawer or maker instead of the first party to accept the instrument. These exceptions are applicable in situations where the indorsement is made by an imposter or a fictitious person.

IMPOSTER RULE. An imposter is an individual who pretends to be another person to deceive the maker or drawer into issuing an instrument in the name of the person they are impersonating. When a maker or drawer believes the imposter is the party named on the instrument at the time of issue, the imposter's indorsement will not be treated as unauthorized if the instrument is transferred to a party who takes the instrument in good faith. UCC § 3-404(a). The maker or drawer will be liable to the party who takes this instrument in good faith because the maker or drawer intended the imposter to receive the instrument.

FICTITIOUS PAYEE RULE. When a person does not intend the person identified as the payee of an instrument to have any interest in the instrument, the payee is known as a fictitious payee. Under these circumstances, the maker or drawer will be liable on the instrument. A fictitious payee can be either a person or entity that does not exist or a party that exists but has not acquired any interest in the instrument. The UCC does not treat the payee's indorsement as forgery under these circumstances, therefore allowing the maker or drawer to be held liable.

> **Example:** Bailey is the controller for ABC Corp. and is authorized to sign checks on behalf of the company. Bailey writes a check payable to Clean Corp. in the amount of $500, citing the payment was in exchange for cleaning. However, ABC never hired Clean Corp. Bailey took the check to Clean Corp., forged its indorsement, and named herself as the indorsee. She then cashed the check at a check cashing business. Under the fictitious payee rule, ABC Corp. is still liable because it was in a better position to prevent the fraud.

Warranty Liability

Transferors may also be found liable under the theory of warranty liability in addition to signature liability. **Warranty liability** arises when a transferor breaches an implied warranty that was made in the negotiation of the instrument. Warranty liability is implemented when the transferor signed the instrument. These implied warranties only arise when a negotiable instrument is transferred because implied warranties are not made upon the original issuance of the instrument. Warranties will fall into one of two categories, either transfer warranties or presentment warranties. These warranties shift the burden of liability back to the party who dealt with the wrongdoer. This is because that party was in the best position to prevent the loss.

Warranty liability Liability that arises when a transferor breaches an implied warranty that was made in the negotiation of the instrument.

TRANSFER WARRANTIES. When an instrument is transferred for consideration, certain warranties are made to the transferee by the transferor. Additionally, when the transfer occurs by indorsement, all subsequent transferees and holders who take the instrument in good faith will receive the same warranties. UCC § 3-416 recognizes the following transfer warranties:

- The transferor is authorized to enforce the instrument;
- All the signatures are authentic and authorized;
- The instrument has not been altered;
- No defense or claim by any party may be asserted against the transferor; and
- The transferor possesses no knowledge of any bankruptcy proceeding against the maker, acceptor, or drawer of the instrument.

Instruments other than checks may disclaim transfer warranties. UCC § 3-416(c). If an indorsement states, "without recourse," the above-mentioned transfer warranties have been disclaimed. Only transferees who take an instrument in good faith may recover damages in the event of a breach of transfer warranties, but recovery is limited to the amount of the instrument, expenses, and any interest accrued. UCC § 3-416(b).

Presentment warranties Warranties regarding payment and acceptance made to the person who pays or accepts an instrument in good faith.

PRESENTMENT WARRANTIES. When presenting instruments for payment or acceptance, the person presenting the instrument makes **presentment warranties** to the person who pays or accepts the instrument in good faith. UCC § 3-417 includes the following presentment warranties:

- The individual seeking payment or acceptance is entitled to enforce the instrument or is authorized to obtain payment or acceptance of the instrument on behalf of the person entitled to enforce the instrument;
- The instrument has not been altered; and
- The individual seeking payment possesses no knowledge that the signature of the issuer for the instrument is unauthorized.

Presentment warranties seek to protect the party being presented the instrument by shifting the liability back to the party who had the best opportunity to prevent the loss.

Additionally, when the presenter is an HDC, the second and third presentment warranties will not apply to makers, acceptors, or drawers. This is because a drawer or maker will be able to recognize their own signature, and a maker or acceptor will recognize if material alterations have been made to the instrument.

Defenses, Limitations, and Discharge of Negotiable Instruments

A party who would otherwise be primarily or secondarily liable to pay a negotiable instrument can sometimes use a defense to prevent the holder from collecting. The two categories of defenses are universal and personal defenses.

Universal Defenses

Universal defense A defense from payment liability against all holders, including HDCs.

A **universal defense** can be used against all holders, including HDCs, to prevent the payment of a negotiable instrument. The following list discusses the most important of these universal defenses:

1. *Fraud in the execution.* When a person is tricked into signing a negotiable instrument under the assumption, they are actually signing something else, fraud in the execution of the instrument is committed against the signer. UCC § 3-305(a)(1). The instrument is deemed to be void. This defense cannot be asserted if a reasonable examination would have revealed the true nature of the instrument and its terms.
2. *Illegality, incapacity, or extreme duress.* Instruments that are signed because of illegal conduct are void. Equally, someone who has been deemed mentally incompetent or found to be under extreme duress, such as the threat of immediate violence, will not be liable on the instrument, and it is void.
3. *Forged signature.* Unless ratified or due to negligence, a forged signature cannot bind the person whose name was used. UCC § 3-403(a). An instrument with a forged signature will normally not impose liability upon the person whose name was used.

4. *Material alteration.* When the terms of an instrument are altered in a way that changes the obligations of the parties, a material alteration has occurred. A material alteration can be a complete defense against an ordinary holder but will only function as a partial defense against an HDC. The UCC describes any unauthorized changes that affect the obligations of the parties, which includes the completion of an instrument. UCC § 3-407(a).
5. *Discharge due to bankruptcy.* The purpose of bankruptcy proceedings is to relieve the debtor of all outstanding debts, even negotiable instruments. Regardless of the status of the holder, a discharge in bankruptcy will function as a universal defense against liability on the instrument. UCC § 3-305(a)(1).
6. *Minority.* Since minors cannot enter into valid contracts, unless otherwise permitted by state law, minors who obtain a negotiable instrument can declare the instrument void as a defense to liability under the instrument. UCC § 3-305(a)(1)(i). If the minor misrepresented their age, this defense will not be available.

PERSONAL DEFENSES. A **personal defense** can be used to deny payment of a negotiable instrument against an ordinary holder but cannot be used against an HDC or a holder with the rights of an HDC.

Personal defense
A defense from payment liability against all holders, but not including HDCs.

1. *Breach of contract or warranty.* When the contract underlying the instrument is breached, the maker of the note can refuse to pay the holder. Additionally, the drawer of the check can repudiate payment.
2. *Failure to provide consideration.* Failure to provide adequate consideration can sometimes be used as a defense to enforcement. UCC § 3-303(b).
3. *Fraud in the inducement.* When a negotiable instrument is issued based on false statements, the issuer of the instrument has a defense against enforcement of the instrument, unless the holder is an HDC.
4. *Illegality, incapacity, or ordinary duress.* An instrument may be deemed *voidable* due to illegality, incapacity, or ordinary duress. A contract that is voidable is still a valid contract but could still be set aside by the court. But a contract that has been found void is invalid from the time of creation and is unenforceable.

CASE 29.2

A PARTY MAY BE CONSIDERED A HOLDER IN DUE COURSE IF THEY ACCEPT A CHECK WITHOUT NOTICE THAT THE AGENT LACKED AUTHORITY TO SIGN

GEORG v. METRO FIXTURES CONTRACTORS, INC.

178 P.3d 1209 (2008)

Supreme Court of Colorado

Cassandra Demery (Demery) was employed by Freestyle Sports Marketing Inc. (Freestyle) as a bookkeeper for several years before Freestyle discovered that Demery had embezzled over $200,000 for her personal use and failed to pay $240,000 in state and federal taxes on Freestyle's behalf. When Freestyle learned of this, her employment was terminated, and the company threatened to notify the authorities if she did not pay them back. Demery then took a job as a bookkeeper for Metro Fixtures Contractors, Inc. (Metro), which was owned by her parents. As the bookkeeper for Metro, Demery wrote a check to Freestyle for $189,000. Demery included on the check that it was for "deposit only" and provided Freestyle's account number before depositing the check in Freestyle's bank account. Demery then called and told Clinton Georg (Georg), Freestyle's president, that her parents had given her a loan from their company so she could pay back her debts. Demery also informed Georg that the funds had been deposited to Freestyle's bank account. After Georg confirmed the payment had been made, he used these funds to pay Freestyle's outstanding taxes.

Two years later, Metro discovered the transaction Demery made with Freestyle and proceeded to file suit against Georg and Freestyle claiming theft, conversion, and unjust enrichment, among other things. Freestyle moved for summary judgment on the basis that it was a holder in due course. The trial court agreed and granted the motion. Metro appealed to the court of appeals and asserted the negotiable instrument was an unauthorized forgery and therefore Freestyle was not entitled to the payment. The court of appeals partially reversed, and Freestyle appealed to the Supreme Court of Colorado.

Language of the Court. *An otherwise authorized signature on a negotiable instrument is not converted into an unauthorized forgery when an agent, authorized to sign negotiable instruments in his principal's name, abuses that authority by negotiating the instrument to a holder in due course for the agent's own personal benefit.*

In the case before us, Demery was Metro's agent, specifically its employee. As a bookkeeper for Metro, Demery's authority included the power to write checks on Metro's behalf. Despite the fact that Metro did not specifically authorize Demery to write a check to Freestyle, Metro placed her in a position to do so. Subsequently, Demery informed Freestyle that she had obtained authority from Metro's owners, her parents, to issue the check and had directly deposited the funds into Freestyle's account. Freestyle verified with its bank the deposit of these funds into its account and then, relying on the availability of those funds, paid the delinquent taxes to the state and federal authorities.

Finally, Freestyle had no notice that Demery lacked authority to issue the check or that it was forged. The undisputed facts are that Demery was Metro's bookkeeper and had authority to issue the check. . . . Metro's owner, Demery's father, testified that he had no reason to believe Freestyle knew that the check had been forged. Demery also testified that she had no reason to believe Freestyle knew that the check was forged.

Demery acted as a bookkeeper for Metro for several years. Metro was in the best position to have instituted internal procedures and mechanisms regarding the company's accounting. Attesting to its lack of internal procedure, Metro did not uncover the embezzlement until two years after Demery deposited the check into Freestyle's bank account. Freestyle was not in a position, as a third party, to dictate Metro's internal control procedures to prevent employee theft.

Decision. The court determined Freestyle was a holder in due course and not liable for Metro's claims of theft, conversion, or unjust enrichment.

Focus on Ethics

Would the result be different if Demery did not have a familial relationship with the owners of Metro? Why or why not?

Discharge of Liability

There are various ways in which a party may be discharged or relieved from liability of a negotiable instrument, such as payment, cancellation, or material alteration. Discharge of liability occurs when the party primarily liable on the instrument pays the holder the full amount required under the instrument. This will relieve all parties of liability. However, when any other party makes payment on an instrument, only that party and subsequent parties will be discharged of liability. UCC § 3-602.

When the holder intentionally cancels the instrument, all parties will be discharged of liability. UCC § 3-604. A party can cancel an instrument in two ways: either by indicating on the instrument's face or indorsement their intent to cancel the contract or by destroying the instrument with the intent of terminating the obligation. If the instrument is destroyed by accident or by a third party without authorization, the instrument will not be considered canceled.

Finally, when a material alteration to the instrument occurs, the party affected by the alteration will be discharged from liability. UCC § 3-407(b). Under this scenario, an HDC could still attempt to enforce the instrument against the maker or drawer but only based upon the instrument's original terms.

AI Feature: Effects of a Material Alteration of a Negotiable Instrument

After reading the law relating to a material alteration of a legal instrument, research the topic using an internet search engine. Then, using an AI program reach a conclusion as to whether the following mortgage is binding upon the borrower. Assume Able, a co-owner of real property, executed a $500,000 promissory note and mortgage in favor of Figueroa National Bank. At all material times, Able and Baker were co-owners of the real property. Should foreclosure proceedings of the mortgage following default under Able's note be enjoined (stopped)—because Baker's name was added as a borrower to the mortgage without Baker's authority by the attorney acting on behalf of the Bank? Does Baker have contractual liability to the Bank?

After reaching your conclusion, identify and explain the public policies underlying the law of material alteration of a negotiable instrument.

Key Terms

- Acceleration clause, 729
- Banker's acceptance, 723
- Bearer instrument, 730
- Blank indorsement, 732
- Blank qualified indorsement, 735
- Certificate of deposit, 724
- Certified check, 742
- Check, 723
- Draft, 721
- Drawee of the draft, 721
- Drawer of the draft, 721
- Extension clause, 729
- Holder, 737
- Holder in due course (HDC), 737
- Indorsement, 732
- Negotiable instrument, 720
- Negotiation, 731
- Order instrument, 729
- Payee of the draft, 721
- Personal defense, 747
- Presentment, 743
- Presentment warranties, 746
- Primary liability, 742
- Promissory note, 723
- Qualified indorsement, 733
- Restrictive indorsement, 735
- Secondary liability, 742
- Sight draft, 721
- Signature liability, 742
- Signature, 726
- Special indorsement, 732
- Special qualified indorsement, 735
- Time draft, 721
- Trade acceptance, 722
- Unauthorized signature, 744
- Universal defense, 746
- Warranty liability, 745

Applying the Law

29.1 Liability. Plaintiffs, who were investors in Third Eye Systems, LLC, wrote checks payable to Third Eye Systems, LLC in 2000 to purchase their investment units. Nine of the checks indicated "Third Eye Systems, LLC" as the payee; one of the checks indicated "Third Eye," and one indicated "Third Eye Systems." The checks were not negotiated by Third Eye Systems, LLC, but by a different entity, Third Eye Systems Holdings, Inc., which presented the checks for deposit into its account at U.S. Bank. Subsequently, U.S. Bank accepted the checks for deposit, which were marked with various endorsements, but they were not properly endorsed to transfer title from Third Eye Systems, LLC to Third Eye Systems Holdings, Inc. According to plaintiffs, they were damaged when the funds from their checks were deposited into the account of Third Eye Systems Holdings, Inc., because among other things, Third Eye Systems, LLC was worth 75 percent less without the funds from Plaintiffs' investments. Further, Plaintiffs claimed that because they did not have ownership of Third Eye Systems Holdings, Inc., they could not access its assets (which were purchased using Plaintiffs' funds) to recoup their eventual losses from their investments. Should there be any liability on the part of U.S. Bank? Why or why not? *Mills v. U.S. Bank*, 166 Cal. App. 4th 871 (2008)

29.2 Payee. A check is made out to "Cash." Is this a bearer instrument, or did the drawer of the check intend for someone named "Cash" to obtain a beneficial interest in the check? *Bascal v. Nat'l City Bank*, 262 N.Y.S. 839 (1933)

29.3 Valid or Not? Derrick and Sonly Stoudemire sued HSBC Bank USA to rescind a foreclosure and quiet title transaction. They alleged that Wells Fargo's assignment of their security deed (a mortgage like device) was ineffective so that HSBBC did not have the legal right to foreclose. There was an irregularity as to the notary seal and they asserted the assignment was therefore void. Who prevails? *Stoudemire v. HSBC Bank USA*, 333 Ga. App. 374 (2015)

29.4 Buyer a Holder in Due Course? Triffin purchased a dishonored postdated check from a check cashing service. Was Triffin, the buyer of the check, a holder in due course? *Triffin v. Liccardi Ford, Inc.*, 10 A.3d 227 (N.J. Super. 2011)

29.5 Embezzlement. City Rentals discovered that its former bookkeeper, Robin Bauer, had embezzled several hundred thousand dollars from the company. Bauer was convicted in a criminal case and ordered to pay $200,000 in restitution. During the commission of the criminal offense, Bauer forged several checks drawn on City Rentals' bank account and issued them to various people, including Kesler. Kesler had lent money to Bauer on several occasions in the form of personal loans. Moreover, Kesler stated that unbeknownst to him at the time, Bauer made these deposits and payments using City Rentals' checks. Kesler explained that he never saw or endorsed the checks Bauer deposited in his account. In fact, Kesler denied having any prior knowledge that the checks used by Bauer had been paid from City Rentals' funds. However, after becoming aware of Bauer's embezzlement, City Rentals notified Kesler that Bauer had forged the checks issued to him and demanded that he return the funds. Kesler refused City Rentals' demands. As a result, City Rentals sued Kesler. Will the court likely hold that Kesler has to return the funds? *City Rentals, Inc. v. Kesler*, 946 N.E.2d 785 (Ohio 2010)

29.6 Imposter Rule. American General Financial Services was contacted by telephone by a man, who was later revealed to be an imposter posing as Ronald E. Wilder. The imposter sought a $20,000 loan. American General ran a credit check on Wilder and, based on the information provided to them, found him to have excellent credit. American General asked the imposter to send tax returns, which he did. The district manager of American General approved the loan after verifying the tax returns and learning that the supposed purpose for the funds was to renovate a property he owned. The loan was approved, and the imposter arrived at noon to collect the check. American General checked for proper identification, a driver's license. After meeting with the branch manager and the customer account specialist for a brief time, the imposter left with a $18,000 check. The imposter went to State Security Check Cashing Inc. There, the employee who was working at that time checked his driver's license, reviewed the loan documents, and called the compliance officer because the check amount was rather large. The compliance officer instructed the employee to check the date, name of payee, address on the license, loan paperwork, and if the check matched other checks they had from the same issuer. Then, the compliance officer approved the cashing of the check, and the imposter left with the cash. On the next business day, all parties became aware of what happened, and the real Ronald E. Wilder completed an affidavit of forgery. American General placed a stop payment on the check. State Security filed a claim against American General for the face value of the check, plus interest, asserting that it was a holder in due course of American General's check. Who is likely to prevail? Why? *State Sec. Check Cashing, Inc. v. Am. Gen. Fin. Servs. (DE)*, 409 Md. 81 (2009)

29.7 Signature Liability. Donald Galt obtained a loan from Alaska Mutual Bank for $912,000 on behalf of Woodside Construction, of which he was an officer. The loan was evidenced by a promissory note, a deed of trust, a loan agreement, and a contract of guaranty. The note bore Galt's signature below the name of the corporation, on the line designating his representative capacity as president. It also bore Galt's signature above the name of the corporation with no representative capacity designated. The contract of guaranty bore Galt's signature below the name of the corporation, on the line designating his representative capacity, and then bore his signature on a line where no representative capacity was indicated. He did not sign on the line designated for his signature as guarantor. When an authorized representative signs his own name to an instrument are they personally liable for failing to state their representative capacity as Galt had failed to do? *FDIC v. Woodside Constr., Inc.*, 979 F.2d 172 (9th Cir. 1992)

29.8 Physical Possession of the Original Note. In August 2006, Turner obtained a $1 million mortgage loan, secured by real property he owned in Boulder County. As part of the transaction, Turner executed and delivered that note to Valley Vista Mortgage Corporation. This note was negotiated many times. Valley Vista endorsed the note to DB Structured Products. Then, DB Structured Products assigned it to MortgageIT, who turned around and assigned it to IndyMac Savings Bank. Next, IndyMac purportedly assigned it to Countrywide Home Loans, which endorsed it blank. However, the FDIC took over IndyMac, and eventually it assigned that note to CIT Bank, who had physical possession of the note. As it turns out, Turner failed to make his mortgage payments and was in default. CIT Bank demands repayment. Is CIT Bank the current holder of the note? *CIT Bank, N.A. v. Turner*, 2016 U.S. Dist. LEXIS 160294 (D. Colo. 2016)

29.9 Substitute Checks. Zions First National Bank is a national banking association with its principal place of business in Salt Lake City, Utah. Moto Diesel Mexicana (MDM) is a company located in Aguascalientes, Mexico. In December 2007, MDM wrote eight checks to a Zions customer, Casa de Cambio Majapara S.A. (Majapara), which is also located in Mexico. The MDM checks were drawn on its checking account at Comerica Bank in Detroit, Michigan. Majapara electronically deposited the checks, which totaled $2 million, into its account at Zions. Then, Zions sent the checks out for collection to Comerica. In the meantime, Zions granted Majapara provisional credit for the checks. Subsequently, Majapara withdrew the full amount from its Zions account. Thereafter, Comerica returned the checks to Zions unpaid because there were insufficient funds in MDM's account. Majapara's account was left in overdraft status and Zions suffered a loss of $2 million. Further, Majapara had filed for bankruptcy, so Zion was unable to collect. As a result, Zion filed a complaint against MDM as a holder in due course of the checks. Is Zion a holder in due course of the checks? *Zions First Nat'l Bank v. Moto Diesel Mexicana, S.A. de C.V.*, 2011 U.S. Dist. LEXIS 72989 (E.D. Mich. 2011)

29.10 Holder in Due Course. Cordelia Smith was appointed the guardian of the property of her child, Clifton Smith, by the court in the District of Columbia where they were then residing. They moved to Maryland and used the proceeds of a settlement, with respect to the injuries Clifton had sustained, to buy a home. While living in Maryland, Cordelia contacted a mortgage broker for the purpose of securing financing for her bills with the property of Clifton's estate in Maryland. The property was titled "Cordelia Smith, Guardian of Clifton Dominick Smith, a Minor Child," and was used as collateral security for the repayment of the promissory note. Cordelia obtained a loan of $69,000, and then almost immediately she refinanced it to receive the sum of $93,500. Moreover, Cordelia obtained these loans by the execution of a promissory note collaterally secured by a deed of trust and the guardianship property. All the instruments for the financing and refinancing were executed by Cordelia in her capacity as Guardian of the Property of Clifton Dominick Smith, a Minor Child. However, Cordelia neglected to obtain permission from the court in the District of Columbia, which required that she get approval for transactions involving the real property of her ward. Cordelia did not get permission, but the loan was still processed, and the promissory note and deed of trust were assigned by the original creditor to Contimortgage Corporation. M & T subsequently succeeded Contimortgage's interest. It was established that M & T was a holder in due course. Can M & T demand payment for default and foreclose on the home, even though Cordelia was required to get the court's permission before she engaged in any real property transactions for Clifton? *Hand v. Manufacturers & Traders Tr. Co.*, 952 A.2d 240 (Md. 2008)

Banking

30

It is not by augmenting the capital of the country, but by rendering a greater part of that capital active and productive than would otherwise be so, that the most judicious operations of banking can increase the industry of the country. — Adam Smith, economist, philosopher, and author (1723-1790)

Chapter Outline

- Introduction
- Checks
- The Bank and Customer Relationship
- Duty to Honor Checks

Case 30.1: *Aliaga Medical Center, S.C. v. Harris Bank N.A.*

  - *Management Application: Criminal Liability*

- Duty to Accept Deposits

Case 30.2: *Shahin v. Delaware Federal Credit Union*

- The Collection Process
- Electronic Funds Transfers
- Letters of Credit
  - *Management Application: Irrevocable Letter of Credit*
- AI Feature: Stale Checks

Learning Objectives

After studying this chapter, you should be able to:

1. Identify the different types of checks and the purposes of each.
2. Determine when a bank may properly dishonor a check without liability to the consumer.
3. Identify a bank's duties under the UCC when it comes to forged and altered checks.
4. Explain the collection process for deposited checks.
5. Describe the types of electronic fund transfers.
6. Explain the purpose and structure of a letter of credit transaction.

Introduction

Everyday transactions require an exchange of goods or services for some form of consideration, and often the consideration is the payment of money. Our personal transactions are simple, but commercial transactions require more complex banking relationships. For those transactions, banks play an important role, whether acting as facilitators or intermediaries. This chapter discusses the role of banks in commercial transactions and familiarizes the reader with common banking terminology and processes.

Checks

Although far more people use debit cards and smartphones for day-to-day transactions, checks are still employed in transacting business. The UCC, specifically Articles 3 and 4, regulates the use of checks. When a conflict between Articles 3 and 4 arises, Article 4 will override Article 3 as to the law to be applied.

As mentioned in Chapter 29, checks are the most common type of a draft. A check is a type of draft drawn by a financial institution as an order to pay. The amount that the bank will be required to pay is fixed by the amount stated on the check. Article 4 defines a bank as "a person engaged in the business of banking, including a savings bank, savings and loan association, credit union, or trust company." If the check is managed by an institution that is not of the type stated in the rule, the rules of Article 4 will not apply to the check.

EXHIBIT 30.1: Check

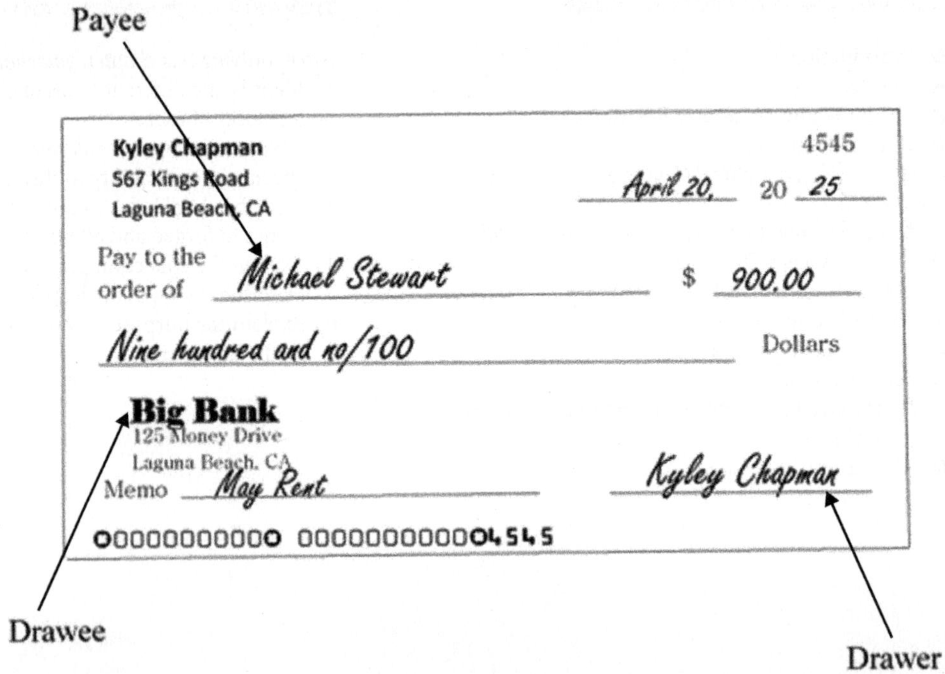

Additionally, recall from Chapter 29 that the person writing the check is known as the drawer, while the person to whom the check is made payable is the payee. The bank will be the drawee because it is the party required to pay the money as stated on the check.

In some instances, the financial institution will be both the drawer and the drawee. These types of checks are known as **cashier's checks**. A bank customer will purchase a cashier's check from the bank by paying the bank the amount of the check and indicating to whom the check will be payable. The bank will be the drawer instead of the customer, as well as the drawee. This means that the bank is liable for the payment of the check. This greatly reduces the payee's risk of not receiving payment due to insufficient funds in the drawer's bank account. Cashier's checks are often treated as a guaranteed payment because the bank, instead of the buyer, is responsible for paying the amount.

Cashier's check
A type of check in which the financial institution will be both the drawer and the drawee, thereby reducing the payee's risk of nonpayment.

A **certified check** is another type of check by which the bank certifies that the customer has the necessary funds in their account to make the payment stated on the check and the signature is genuine. The bank sets aside the amount specified on the check and uses this money only for the payment of the certified check. Often, the certifying bank will stamp the word "certified" on the check. A certified check will reduce the risks associated with the transaction for the payee because the bank has ensured the payee will be paid. If payment is not received, the UCC permits the payee to sue both the bank and the customer.

Certified check
Type of check by which the bank certifies that the customer has the necessary funds in the customer's account to make the payment stated on the check and also verifies the signature is genuine.

Another type of check that can be obtained from a bank is known as a traveler's check. A **traveler's check** is a check in a prepaid, fixed amount that acts like cash to purchase items while traveling. Traveler's checks may be exchanged anywhere for cash and are available in a variety of fixed amounts in all major currencies. Some banks may charge a small fee to issue traveler's checks. When a check is reported lost or stolen, the bank will cancel the check and issue the customer a new one. Traveler's checks are a safe alternative to carrying large amounts of cash in foreign countries.

Traveler's check
Type of check that is a prepaid, fixed amount that acts as cash for use when traveling in foreign countries.

Concept Summary
Types of Checks

Type of Check	Who Signs?	Who Is Liable for Payment?
Cashier's check	The bank	The bank
Certified check	The customer signs the check while the bank provides the payee with written acknowledgment	The bank and customer
Traveler's check	The bank	The bank

The Bank and Customer Relationship

There are three different relationships that are created between the bank and the customer when the customer first opens an account with the bank.

Contractual Relationship

A customer-bank relationship begins with the execution of account documents setting forth the rights and obligations of both the customer and the bank. Upon signing these documents, the customer has entered into a contractual relationship with the bank. Both parties to the check (customer and bank) will owe duties to each other. The various rights and obligations of the parties will be discussed in detail in subsequent sections of this chapter.

Creditor-Debtor Relationship

A creditor-debtor relationship begins once the customer makes a deposit into their bank account. Upon making the deposit, the customer becomes the creditor, and the bank becomes the debtor. The bank is only a debtor to the extent of the deposits made by the customer.

Agency Relationship

The agency relationship between the bank and the customer will arise in two ways. The first occurs when the customer makes a deposit into their account. Once this occurs, the bank has an obligation to collect the funds from the drawee bank and transfer this amount into the customer's account. The agency relationship also arises when the customer writes a check from their bank account. By writing this check, the customer is ordering the bank to pay the holder of the check the amount stated on the check once the holder presents the check for payment.

Duty to Honor Checks

A bank or financial institution providing checking services must agree to honor the checks written by its customers, subject to certain requirements such as sufficient funds in the customer's account to cover the amount of each check. UCC § 4-401(a).

Typically, the customer will enter into an agreement with the bank whereby the customer agrees to maintain a balance sufficient to cover all checks written by the customer. If the check is dishonored, the customer may be liable to the payee or the check's holder in a civil suit. If it can be proven that the customer acted with the intent to defraud, the customer may be subject to a criminal penalty for writing a bad check.

When a check for insufficient funds is properly dishonored by the bank, the bank will not be liable to the customer. Dishonoring a check for insufficient funds is one of the many ways a bank may refuse payment. Additional reasons, such as account overdrafts, postdated checks, and stale checks, are discussed below.

If a drawee bank acts wrongfully in failing to honor a check, the drawee bank will be liable to its customer for the damages that occur as a result of its refusal to pay. UCC § 4-402(b). If an item that is not properly payable is wrongfully charged against the customer's account, the UCC imposes strict liability upon the bank for the customer's damages. It is easy for the customer to prevail on such a claim, as the customer does not have to show the bank acted negligently or was in breach of a contractual obligation.

Example: A physician whose bookkeeper had been embezzling funds from his account over a seven-year period sued Fleet Bank® for negligently paying the forged checks. It took the physician seven years to realize the funds were being embezzled; however, the physician immediately notified the bank as soon as he discovered the employee's actions. Although the physician failed to comply with his duties to examine his bank statements for error, the court found that the physician was not precluded from bringing a claim against the bank for the bank's failure to exercise reasonable care. *Monreal v. Fleet Bank*, 735 N.E.2d 880 (N.Y. 2000)

Account Overdrafts

A bank has two options when the drawer does not have enough money in their account when a check is presented for payment by the bank from the customer-depositor's account. The first option is to dishonor the check; in doing so the bank will notify the drawer that the check has been dishonored and return the check to the holder. Upon returning the check to the holder, the bank will mark the check "insufficient funds." The holder of the check may try to present the check again, on the chance the drawer has deposited more money into that account. If once again there are not sufficient funds, the holder may pursue recourse from the drawer of the check.

The second option allows the bank to pay the check despite an insufficiency of funds in the drawer's account. Known as an **account overdraft**, under this option the bank then charges the depositor's account for the amount that was due along with a fee for the overdraft. UCC § 4-401(a). Generally, the overdraft and the fee will be deducted from the customer's next deposit. If the drawer is unable to fulfill their obligation, the bank will be able to sue the customer in order to recover this amount. To prevent overdrafts and their subsequent fees, many banks allow their customers to obtain overdraft protection for their accounts. When an overdraft protection agreement is formed, the bank's failure to honor a check due to insufficient funds of the drawer would be treated as a wrongful dishonor because it would be in breach of the overdraft protection agreement. UCC § 4-402(a).

Account overdraft
The act of a bank paying a check despite insufficient funds in the drawer's account.

Stop Payments

To prevent a potential overdraft, fraudulent transaction, or for any valid, legal reason, a bank customer may order their bank to not pay a particular check. This is known as a **stop payment**. Only the account holder, the customer, can order the bank to do a stop payment. UCC § 4-403(a). Additionally, the customer cannot order the bank to stop payment on the check once it has been accepted by another bank. Generally, the customer is required to provide the bank with adequate notice of the stop payment order. The manner and timing of the notice will typically be set forth in the bank's agreement with the customer; however, the UCC provides for certain requirements, such as the length of time the order is effective, depending upon the way the notice is given. UCC § 4-403(b). If the stop payment notice is given orally, it will only be effective for 14 days. However, if the customer wishes to stop the payment for a longer period, the notice must be provided to the bank in writing. A written notice is binding for six months and may be renewed by the customer. If the bank pays the check despite timely notice to stop payment, the bank will be required to recredit the customer's account and pay or waive the resulting overdraft fees that are incurred.

Stop payment
The act of a bank customer ordering the bank to not pay a particular check.

Example: George Dixon telephoned the bank to place a stop payment on a check he had written the prior day. Dixon gave the bank employee the correct account number, check number, and payee of the check; however, Dixon misstated the check amount as $1,828.73 when the correct amount of the check was $1,868.15. A few weeks later Dixon received his bank statement and learned the check was cashed despite his attempt to stop the payment. Dixon sued the bank after the bank refused to credit him for the transaction. The court found that Dixon had supplied the bank with sufficient information regarding the check he wished to stop, and the bank was liable for Dixon's losses. *First State Bank of Warren v. Dixon*, 728 S.W.2d 192 (Ark. 1987)

Postdated Checks

Postdated check
A check in which a future date is put on the check rather than the date the check is written.

A **postdated check** is one on which a future date is stated on the check rather than the date on which the check was written. A person will postdate a check because they do not want the check to be cashed or deposited until sometime in the future. If the customer wants to prevent the depositing or cashing of the check until the date specified, the customer must notify the bank in enough time to for the bank to prevent the deposit from occurring. If the bank does not act on the customer's timely notice and charges the customer's account before the date specified on the check, the bank may find itself liable to the customer for any damages that have been incurred. UCC § 4-401(c).

Most banks will set out in their disclosures whether a postdated check will be honored; however, most banks typically honor postdated checks. The UCC specifically gives banks the right to honor a written check even though the check states a future date. UCC § 4-401(c).

Stale Checks

Stale check
A check that is presented to the customer-depositor bank six months after it is dated.

When the payee or holder of the check fails to present the check to its bank in six months, the check will be considered a **stale check**. UCC § 4-404. When a check becomes stale, the bank is no longer under an obligation to pay it. However, a bank may charge the drawer's account if it pays the stale check in good faith. It is often in the bank's best interest to consult the customer prior to paying a stale check; otherwise, the bank may find itself liable to the customer for the amount of the check and other damages. The following case illustrates what may happen when the bank decides to honor a check that has become stale.

CASE 30.1

WRITING "VOID AFTER" MAY NOT BE SUFFICIENT TO PRECLUDE A BANK FROM HONORING A CHECK PRESENTED AFTER THE DATE INDICATED

ALIAGA MEDICAL CENTER, S.C. v. HARRIS BANK N.A.

21 N.E.3d 1203 (2014)

Appellate Court of Illinois

Aliaga Medical Center (Aliaga) opened two business checking accounts with Harris Bank (Harris), first in December 2003 and again in November 2010.

In both instances, Aliaga received a Harris Bank Handbook for Personal and Business Deposit Accounts (Agreement). In both instances, Aliaga acknowledged its receipt of the Agreement and agreed to be governed by its terms. The Agreement stated that if Aliaga wished to stop payment on a check it had written it needed to give Harris notice either in person, over the phone, in writing, or via Harris's online banking platform. The agreement also stated that Harris reserved the right to pay a stale check. Lastly, the agreement stated that Harris would not be liable for any errors unless the errors were brought to its attention within 60 days.

On July 10, 2010, Dr. Aliaga wrote a check for $50,000 to his wife, whom he was currently divorcing. On the face of the check it stated, "void after 90 days." Despite this, Harris honored the check on December 30, 2010. Dr. Aliaga never notified Harris that he wished to have the check stopped. In January 2011, Harris sent its monthly statement for December 2010; however, Aliaga failed to notify Harris of the improper check payment within the 60-day time frame established in the Agreement. Additionally, Aliaga waited nearly two years after the December 2010 statement was sent before disputing the check with Harris. Harris moved to dismiss Aliaga's lawsuit because it was barred by the Agreement. The court granted the motion and dismissed the case. Aliaga appealed to the Illinois Appellate Court.

Language of the Court. *Aliaga does not dispute the applicability of the various contractual provisions on which Harris relies, but argues that the use of the printed word "void" on the check and the passage of time somehow took it outside the scope of the account agreement.*

Harris had the right to pay the check despite the "void after 90 days" language because Aliaga failed to properly stop payment of the check. Under the parties' agreement, if Aliaga did not want Harris Bank to pay a check it had written, then Aliaga had to comply with certain requirements. In particular, Aliaga must order Harris Bank either in person, online, or in writing to stop payment of a check by including an "account number, the number and date of the check, the name of the payee, and the amount" by a certain deadline and also pay a stop payment fee.

Here, Aliaga acknowledges that it did not comply with the stop payment provisions of the agreement. Without the required stop payment order, Harris Bank maintained its right to honor the check. Therefore, the check's "void" language did not suffice to stop payment because the agreement contains no exception for such language on checks.

Even if Aliaga is correct that the stop payment provision of the agreement was neither exclusive nor meant to override the UCC, the "void" notation was ineffective because it did not comply with section 4-403(a) of the UCC by providing notice "at a time and in a manner that affords the bank a reasonable opportunity to act on it." Here, Aliaga admitted that it did not provide the check bearing the language "void" directly to Harris Bank; it was first transmitted to the payee of the check. Thus, Aliaga neither knew when the check would be received at Harris Bank nor the means by which it would be processed once it was received.

Furthermore, under the parties' agreement, Harris Bank specifically "reserved the right to pay a stale check." Aliaga's contention that this provision is inapplicable because the check "was not stale but instead it was void" is without merit.

The effect of a bank customer writing "void after 90 days" on a check has been described as making the check stale after the initial 90-day period. Aliaga has not cited to any case nor identified any other authority supporting its proposition that there is a substantive difference between stale checks and those marked void after a certain time.

Decision. The Illinois Appellate Court affirmed the trial court's ruling. It held that Harris was permitted to pay the check despite the indication it was to be considered void after 90 days of its date.

Focus on Ethics

Is it fair that Harris still had the right to pay the check even though it stated, "void after 90 days"?

Forged Checks

Forged check
A check in which the drawer's signature is forged or unauthorized.

Chapter 29 discussed forged indorsements and provided the burden of loss will fall on the first party to take or accept the instrument. In the case of checks, a bank is usually the first party to accept the instrument. Thus, the bank would be liable for accepting a **forged check**. The bank will typically be required to re-credit the customer's account for the amount paid due to the forged check.

Example: Dominque writes a $350 check "to the order of Michelle." Suzy steals the check, forges Michelle's indorsement, and cashes the check. When the check is presented by Suzy's bank to Dominque's bank for payment, the bank pays it and deducts the $350 from Dominque's account. In this instance, the bank must recredit the $350 to Dominque's account because it did not carry out Dominque's order to pay "to the order of Michelle."

In the above example, Dominque's bank has recourse. It may still recover from the bank that cashed the check when Suzy presented it, under the theory of breach of warranty. UCC § 4-207(a)(2). The bank that accepted the check from Suzy also could recover from Suzy; however, it may be difficult to locate a forger and the forger may not have the funds to pay any resulting judgment entered against her.

In all cases, the customer will have a duty to promptly report forged indorsements. If the forged document is not reported within a year of the forged check becoming discoverable to the customer, the bank will be absolved of liability. UCC § 4-406(f).

Example: Robert Napleton had a checking account with Great Lakes Bank. In late October of 2007, an unknown person stole a personal check from Napleton and made it payable to a third-party company. Great Lakes paid the check and debited Napleton's account $7,500. The withdrawal appeared on Napleton's statement in November 2007, but Napleton did not discover the forgery until March 2008. Napleton then notified Great Lakes and sought to be reimbursed; however, Great Lakes refused to reimburse the check and claimed Napleton failed to promptly notify the Bank. Napleton sued Great Lakes for conversion and breach of contract. The court found that Napleton's failure to notify the bank of the forged check within 30 days after the monthly statement was mailed to him precluded claims against bank. *Napleton v. Great Lakes Bank, N.A.*, 945 N.E.2d 111 (Ill. App. 2011)

Altered Checks

An **altered check** is one that has been changed from the way the customer had written it. Most commonly, a check will be altered to state a higher payment than was intended by the customer.

Altered check
A check that has been changed from the way the customer has written it.

Banks have a duty to inspect each check prior to making a final payment. When a bank fails to detect an alteration, it is liable to the depositor for the loss because the bank failed to pay as the customer ordered. The bank incurs the loss for the difference between the amount paid and the original amount the customer had written. UCC § 4-401(d)(1).

Example: If the customer writes a check for $100 and it is altered to show $1,000, the customer will only be charged the $100. The bank will be responsible for covering the $900 difference.

Negligence

Negligence on the part of the customer may result in the bank not being liable for honoring an altered check or forged indorsement. In instances where the customer was careless in writing the check by leaving dollar amount blank to be filled in by someone else, the customer will have no claim against the bank.

Example: When 20 forged checks were accepted by a bank over a 10-month period, the court found the bank was not liable because the customer failed to exercise due care by not examining the first four checks that were returned to the customer as cancelled. *Airco Supply Co. v. Albuquerque Nat'l Bank*, 360 P.2d 386 (N.M. 1961)

Management Application Criminal Liability

If the party responsible for the forged indorsement or altered check is located, they may be criminally liable for their actions. Forgery is considered a felony in all fifty states, but the punishment for forgery varies. The most common penalties for forgery include imprisonment, fines, and compensation paid to the victims. Forgery charges are usually prosecuted in state courts. However, certain types of forgeries are considered felonies under federal law, such as when the forgery amounts to identity theft, which includes the false application of loans and credit cards or the fraudulent withdrawal from bank accounts.

Duty to Accept Deposits

Banks have a duty to accept a customer's cash and check deposits and make them available for use by the customer within a certain time frame. Additionally, the bank has a duty to collect the payment of checks that are payable or have been indorsed to the bank's customers and then deposit the funds into the customer's account.

The time frame within which the bank must make the funds available to the customer is subject to the Expedited Funds Availability Act. This Act was enacted to create a uniform hold period on deposits made to commercial banks. Additionally, the Act regulates the ability of these banks to use deposit holds on customers.

According to the Act, cash, electronic payments, and most check deposits are generally required to be made available for withdrawal by the next business day following the banking day on which the deposit was received. In order to qualify for next-day availability, the deposit must be made at a staffed teller station and deposited into the account of the payee of the check. In situations where the check deposit will not be available the next day, the bank is required to make $200 of the deposit available for withdrawal the next day. If the amount the customer deposited is less than $200, the full amount of their deposit will also be made available the next business day.

Deposits made to nonproprietary ATMs (automated teller machines)—ATMs that are not owned by the bank receiving the deposit—are permitted to be subject to a five-day hold. This includes deposits of cash. In situations where the bank will need to place a longer hold on the deposit, the bank is required to notify the customer. Failure to properly notify the customer will preclude the bank from assessing any overdraft fees against the customer if the overdraft would not have occurred but for the delay.

In addition to the requirements set forth by the Expedited Funds Availability Act, the Check Clearing in the 21st Century Act (Check 21) states that as soon as a bank receives the funds, the bank must credit the customer's account. Check 21 was enacted by Congress to make check processing faster and more efficient by creating a new negotiable instrument called a substitute check. The substitute check is a paper reproduction of the front and back of the original check that carries the same legal weight as the original paper check. Banks can then process the check electronically or deliver a substitute check to a bank that desires to receive paper checks.

CASE 30.2

THE GENERAL BANK-CUSTOMER RELATIONSHIP DOES NOT GIVE RISE TO A FIDUCIARY DUTY

SHAHIN v. DELAWARE FEDERAL CREDIT UNION

602 F. App'x 50 (2015)

United States Court of Appeals for the Third Circuit

On May 10, 2010, Nina Shahin (Shahin) deposited a check for $2,500 in her checking account at Delaware Federal Credit Union (DelOne). This particular check was drawn from her daughter's account at Wells Fargo Bank in Portland, Oregon. DelOne placed a two-business day hold on the check to verify it and then placed a 15-day "non-verified" hold on the check because the bank employees noticed that the signature did not appear to match the handwriting on the rest of the check, and it could not be immediately verified by Wells Fargo. Subsequently, Shahin received a letter the next day advising her of the hold and informing her the funds would be available as of June 1, 2010. During this time, payments made by Shahin to Bank of America were denied for insufficient funds. DelOne then transferred funds from Shahin's savings account to cover the payments. DelOne penalized Shanin for her overdrafts with two $30 fines and $6 in total fees.

Shanin proceeded to file claims against DelOne for violation of the Expedited Funds Availability Act, alleging DelOne failed to provide her with proper notice as required and also failed to grant her timely access to her funds. Shanin sought $100,000 in damages under the belief that DelOne breached its fiduciary duty to her. Both parties filed for summary judgment and the federal district court granted Shanin's motion and awarded her the overdraft fines and fees, in addition to $1,000 for violating the notice requirement. Shanin appealed, arguing that the district court failed to award her sufficient damages.

Language of the Court. *A depository institution that fails to comply with the notice provision of § 229.13(e) with respect to any person:*

> *(a) . . . IS LIABLE TO THAT PERSON IN AN AMOUNT EQUAL TO THE SUM OF—*
>
> *(1) Any actual damage sustained by that person as a result of the failure;*
>
> *(2) Such additional amount as the court may allow, except that—*
>
> *(i) In the case of an individual action, liability under this paragraph shall not be less than $100 nor greater than $1,000; and . . .*
>
> *(3) In the case of a successful action to enforce the foregoing liability, the costs of the action . . .*

Shahin asserted only that DelOne imposed $60 in NSF charges and $6.00 in transfer fees. The summary judgment record supported the District Court's finding that DelOne was liable to Shahin for the NSF and "overdraft" fees it imposed; those actual damages totaled $66.00. At the summary judgment stage, Shahin failed to argue or provide evidence to support any other claim for actual damages.

DelOne was subject to liability to Shahin for penalties under § 229.21(a)(2). Its offer of judgment in the amount of $1,000 was the maximum amount allowable under that provision. Having succeeded on her notice claim, Shahin was entitled to recover the costs of the action, in addition to her damage and penalty awards, under § 229.21(a)(3). However, pursuant to Rule 68(a), if an offer of judgment is unaccepted, and "the judgment that the offeree finally obtains is not more favorable than the unaccepted offer, the offeree must pay the costs incurred after the offer was made."

We agree with the District Court that Shahin failed to properly plead her breach of fiduciary duty claim. To the extent the complaint can be construed to state a claim for common law breach of fiduciary duty, we note that the banker/customer relationship is one of creditor to debtor, which does not give rise to a fiduciary relationship. The relation between a bank and a mere general depositor of funds is that of debtor and creditor and is in no sense of a fiduciary nature.

Decision. The U.S. Court of Appeals agreed with the district court that Shahin failed to properly plead her breach of fiduciary duty claim.

Focus on Ethics

Banks deal with a substantial number of deposits and withdrawals daily. Do you think the bank should have done more in this case to notify Shahin, or do you agree with the decision? Why or why not?

The Collection Process

Depository bank The bank that receives the check for payment.

Payor bank The bank of the drawee.

Intermediary bank A bank to which the check is transferred during the collection process that is not the payor or depository bank.

Whether or not the parties to a transaction have the same bank, the collection process will follow Article 4 of the UCC. The bank that receives the check for payment is called the **depository bank**. Conversely, the bank of the drawee is the **payor bank**. If the check is transferred to a bank that is not the payor or depository bank at any time during the collection process, this bank is known as an **intermediary bank**. It is common for a bank to assume more than one of these roles during the collection process.

When the collection taking place is between customers of the same bank, that bank will be acting as both the depository bank and the payor bank. The item that is payable in this scenario is called an "on-us item." Article 4 of the UCC states that if the bank has not dishonored the check by the beginning of business hours of the second banking day after being received, the check is considered paid. UCC § 4-215(e)(2). Generally, when a bank is dealing with on-us items, the bank will issue a provisional credit, which is a temporary credit applied to the payee's account.

The collection process is slightly more complicated when a check is collected between customers from different banks. The depository bank will be in receipt of a check that is payable to another bank, and the depository bank must plan to present the check to the payor bank. This presentation may occur directly or indirectly by means of intermediary banks. Each bank taking part in the collection process is required to pass the check on prior to midnight of the next banking day following the receipt of the check. UCC § 4-202(b). Days in which the bank engages in substantially all its banking functions are deemed to be "banking days."

Deferred posting is commonly used by banks and is permitted by the UCC. Deferred posting occurs when a bank sets an afternoon cutoff time of 2:00 P.M. or later and any checks received after the cutoff time are treated as though they were received at opening of the next business day. UCC § 4-108.

Example: Suppose Big Bank establishes a cutoff time of 3:00 P.M. If Amelia goes to Big Bank at 3:45 P.M. on Tuesday to deposit her check, the posting of the check will be deferred until the opening of Big Bank on Wednesday. Therefore, Big Bank's deadline will be midnight Thursday.

Unless a payor bank returns or dishonors a check by midnight on the next banking day after receiving the check the liability for payment of the face value of the check will fall on the payor bank. UCC § 4-302.

Example: Campbell opened an account with Citibank® on a Friday and deposited over $17,000 into the account. Upon her deposit, Campbell was assured the funds would be available to her the next day, Saturday, and Campbell relied on this assurance as she had travel plans the next day. However, on Saturday when she tried to withdraw from an ATM, Campbell was informed she had insufficient funds. Upon calling Citibank, Campbell learned a hold had been placed on her account. Campbell's access to the funds was restored on Monday. Campbell sought damages against the bank for failure to timely make funds available under UCC § 4-302 and claimed that she was fired because of the stress she suffered due to her inability to access the funds. The court found that Citibank did not violate UCC § 4-302, which only requires that the funds be accepted by the next banking day, which would have been Monday in this case, not Saturday. Therefore, although Citibank may have breached its contract with Campbell by not having the funds accessible by Saturday, UCC § 4-302 was not breached. Further, the court held that even if Citibank had violated UCC § 4-302, Campbell's recovery would be limited to the amount of the check. *Campbell v. Citibank, N.A.*, 302 A.D.2d 150 (NY. App. Div. 2003)

TABLE 30.1: Summary of Important Article 4 Rules

UCC § 4-202 Responsibility for Collection or Return	Each bank taking part in the collection process is required to pass the check on to the next party prior to midnight of the next banking day following the receipt of the check.
UCC § 4-401 Charge Against Account	A bank may charge the customer's account for all properly payable checks, potentially even an overdraft.
UCC § 4-402 Wrongful Dishonor	A bank that wrongfully dishonors a check will be liable to the customer for the damages that occur as a result of its refusal to pay.
UCC § 4-403 Stop Payment Orders	A bank will be liable for payment despite a timely stop payment order. Oral orders act to bind the bank 14 days but can be extended if subsequently put in writing. A written order is good for six months and may be renewed.
UCC § 4-404 Stale Checks	A check becomes stale if the payee fails to present the check to the bank in six months. When the check becomes stale, the bank is no longer obligated to pay it.
UCC § 4-406 Customer's Duty to Examine Statements	The customer is required to examine their account statements and notify the bank of any potential unauthorized signatures or alterations. If the bank exercised reasonable care and the customer failed to examine their statements or report the issue within 30 days, the bank will not be found liable for paying a forged or altered check.
UCC § 4-406(f) Statute of Limitations	If more than one year has passed since receiving the bank statement, the customer is precluded from asserting a cause of action against the bank for a forged or altered check. This deadline applies even if the bank acted negligently.

The Clearing of Checks

Clearing a check is the process of moving funds from one account to another. Once the check has been deposited it will need to be transferred to a clearing system or clearinghouse, which will then communicate with the bank from which the check was drawn. The Federal Reserve operates as a clearinghouse through which financial institutions exchange financial instruments such as checks and drafts. The clearinghouse acts as an intermediary between the two banks rather than requiring them to collaborate directly with each other. Most banks in the United States have accounts with the Federal Reserve System (the Fed).

> **Example:** Instead of a bank transferring a check directly to another bank for collection, member banks can submit the check to the clearinghouse for collection. The clearinghouse then debits the account of the depositary bank and credits the account of the payor bank in accordance with the collection and payment of checks.

Presenting a Check Electronically

Check 21 has increased efficiency in banking by replacing the physical transfer of paper checks with the process of presenting checks electronically. Electronic presentment can be completed within the day of deposit, thereby making the funds accessible to the customer sooner. When a check is presented electronically, the information on the check is encoded, then transmitted to the other bank at which time that bank will process the information. Once the check is encoded, the physical form of the check may be retained by the bank while only the check's image or payment description is presented electronically. UCC § 4-110.

Regulation CC, which works in conjunction with the Expedited Funds Availability Act to regulate the availability of funds, requires a returned check to be encoded with certain information such as the depositary bank's routing number and the amount of the check. Additionally, Regulation CC requires the check to be returned within the time frame required by the UCC.

It is important to note that electronic presentment carries with it certain warranties. For example, the act of a bank encoding the check's information for electronic presentment will warrant to any payor or subsequent bank that the encoded information is correct. UCC § 4-209. Additionally, a bank that retains the check and presents the check's image or payment description electronically warrants that the presented information is correct.

Electronic Funds Transfers

Electronic funds transfer (EFT)
A transfer of funds where the money is electronically transferred from one bank account to another by means of a computer-based system.

An **electronic funds transfer (EFT)** is one in which money is electronically transferred from one bank account to another by means of a computer-based system. The electronic transfer of funds is governed by Article 4A of the UCC when commercial funds are involved. For EFTs relating to consumer funds, the Electronic Fund Transfer Act (EFTA) will govern. EFTs do not require any action by the staff of either bank or may occur between multiple banks in a single transaction.

Although the convenience of transferring funds electronically is undeniable, it does pose a few concerns. First, the chances that a person's private banking information may be tampered with are greatly increased. Second, it can be difficult to stop a payment that has been made through electronic banking. Additionally, the reversing of an electronic transfer of funds once it has occurred is not allowed by the EFTA. Lastly, there are various restrictions placed on accounts in terms of the amount of money and the number of transactions that can take place per day. Most businesses believe the benefits, particularly those related to cash management and convenience, outweigh the potential drawbacks of using EFTs.

Types of EFT Systems

Most banks offer EFT services to their customers in a variety of ways. The most common types of EFT systems are set forth below:

1. *Automated teller machines.* When a bank customer inserts an ATM or debit card and enters their personal identification number (PIN) into the machine, the customer will gain access to their bank accounts. The customer can conduct various banking transactions, such as depositing checks and cash, transferring funds between accounts, and withdrawing cash.
2. *Direct deposits and withdrawals.* Banks can allow a customer to give the authorization to allow direct deposits to be made into their account by another party, usually from an employer or the government. In a similar fashion, the customer may also authorize the bank to make automatic payments to a party in a specified amount and on a recurring basis.
3. *Online payment systems.* Most banks have established some form of online banking system that allows their customers to transfer funds between accounts and make payments to a third party.
4. *Point-of-sale systems.* Customers may transfer their funds to merchants through online terminals, which has the same effect as the customer's using their debit card.

Consumer Protections

To protect consumers, the Electronic Fund Transfer Act (EFTA) governs the financial institutions that facilitate electronic fund transfers for consumer accounts. Consumer accounts are those that are personal in nature or are used for family or household purposes.

The EFTA sets forth the basic rights, liabilities, and responsibilities of those who use EFT systems. Further, the Act provided the Federal Reserve Board with the authority to establish the rules and regulations used to carry out the provisions of the Act. These rules and regulations are known as Regulation E.

The EFTA protects consumers by setting forth the disclosure requirements of financial institutions. The Act requires financial institutions to inform all consumers of their rights and responsibilities regarding EFT systems. The following examples are within the required disclosures:

1. Financial institutions must provide the consumer with written notice of the consumer's liability for any unauthorized transfers. However, if the

financial institution imposes no liability on the consumer, it need not provide a disclosure.

Example: The EFTA has limited the liability that can be imposed on a consumer for transfers resulting from their debit card being lost or stolen to $50, so long as the card is reported lost or stolen within two business days of learning it was missing.

2. A financial institution must disclose, in detail, any limitations regarding the frequency and dollar amount of transfers per account.

Example: It is common for a bank to limit the amount of money that a customer may withdraw from an ATM per day; common amounts range from $100 to $500 depending upon the account.

3. Limitations on the amount of time a consumer has to challenge and correct errors.

Example: Under the EFTA, the consumer has 60 days to challenge or correct errors.

4. Financial institutions must provide the customer with a list of all the transactions that took place pertaining to their account.

Example: Financial institutions must provide their customers with monthly statements of the transactions that took place regarding EFTs. The statement must include the date of transfer, the amount, the names of the parties involved, and any fees that were incurred.

If a bank's violation of the EFTA results in a consumer's incurring a monetary loss, the consumer may sue to recover the actual damages as well as punitive damages up to $1,000. In situations where the consumer has not incurred any actual damages, the bank may still be liable for the legal fees and punitive damages if it is determined that the bank failed to act in accordance with the procedures of EFTA's provisions on resolving errors.

Wire Transfers

Wire transfers
A type of EFT between one bank or financial institution and another where no physical transfer of money takes place.

Funds may also be transferred electronically between commercial parties by wire. **Wire transfers** are a type of EFT between one bank or financial institution and another where no physical transfer of money takes place. The sender of the wire transfer will pay the necessary amount and transaction fees up front. The information is then transmitted from the sender's bank to the recipient's bank. When the recipient's bank receives all the necessary information, it will then use its reserve funds to deposit the stated amount into the recipient's account. The two banks will then settle the payment of the funds once the funds are in the possession of the recipient. This process usually takes one to two days. If timely submitted, wire transfers within the United States are usually processed and deposited on the same day they are received. International transfers should be completed within no more than two business days.

Letters of Credit

A primary concern of sellers, whether in a domestic or international transaction, is getting paid. Transacting internationally brings additional risks relating to securing payment from the buyer. Separation by geography between the parties, as well as currency fluctuations, increase that risk of non-payment. As a result, the parties commonly use a letter of credit in both domestic and international transactions. Banks play a critical role in letter of credit transactions.

A **letter of credit** is a document in which a promise is made by the issuer, most commonly a bank, to honor the drafts or documents that are presented for payment. The issuer will only pay when the terms of transaction are met. The letter of credit is separate from the sales contract but should contain the same terms. The sales contract cannot be referenced in the letter of credit—to do otherwise would undermine the separateness of the documents.

Letter of credit
A document in which a promise is made by the issuer to honor the drafts or documents that are presented for payment.

A letter of credit transaction seeks to alleviate the fears of both parties. The purpose of a letter of credit is to provide the parties with certain assurances. The seller is worried that it will not be paid and wishes to avoid delivering the goods until it knows payment will be received. The buyer, on the other hand, does not want to pay the seller until it knows the seller has shipped the goods.

Issuing a Letter of Credit

Usually, the buyer requests its bank to issue a letter of credit. The buyer's bank is commonly known as the **issuer** or **issuing bank**. When the issuer agrees to issue a letter of credit, it will verify the buyer has sufficient funds to reimburse the bank for the transaction. The issuing bank will also verify the seller has met the conditions necessary to receive payment. The seller is also known as the **beneficiary** because the letter of credit is a contract between the issuing bank and the buyer, not the buyer and the seller. The buyer must promise to reimburse the issuing bank for the amount stated in the letter of credit. Additionally, the issuing bank will typically charge the buyer a certain percentage of the sales prices in fees, usually between 1 to 2 percent. Typically, the buyer and the issuing bank will be in the same jurisdiction.

Issuer or Issuing bank
The buyer's bank in a letter of credit transaction.

Beneficiary
The seller in a letter of credit transaction.

Often the terms of the letter of credit will require that the seller procure its own bank in the seller's jurisdiction to manage the transaction. This is known as a **confirming bank**. Having a confirming bank involved in the transaction will benefit both the issuing bank and the seller. The issuing bank will benefit by working with a confirming bank because they are both sophisticated parties that understand the requirements for letter of credit transactions. Sellers benefit from the existence of a confirming bank because the confirming bank will be liable to reimburse the seller should the buyer fail to pay for the goods.

Confirming bank
A bank in the seller's jurisdiction that manages the letter of credit transaction.

Once the seller receives the letter of credit from the issuing bank, the seller prepares the goods for shipment. In instances where a confirming bank is involved, the issuing bank sends the confirming bank a confirmation of the letter of credit. In most cases, the letter of credit will require the seller to deliver a **bill of lading** as evidence to the confirming bank that the goods have been shipped. Additionally, other documents may need to be included with the bill of lading when the seller presents them to the issuing bank. If this is the case, the letter of credit will state which documents are necessary. The seller presents these documents to its confirming bank in order to receive the money

Bill of lading
A document indicating receipt of goods by a carrier and the contract for the transportation of those goods.

due under the letter of credit, a process known as presentment. The confirming bank then presents these same documents to the issuing bank through the same process, at which time the confirming bank will be paid by the issuing bank. The same process continues with the issuing bank and buyer. The buyer will reimburse the issuing bank, and, in turn, the buyer will receive the bill of lading, which gives the buyer title to the goods shipped by the seller.

Concept Summary
Letter of Credit Transactions

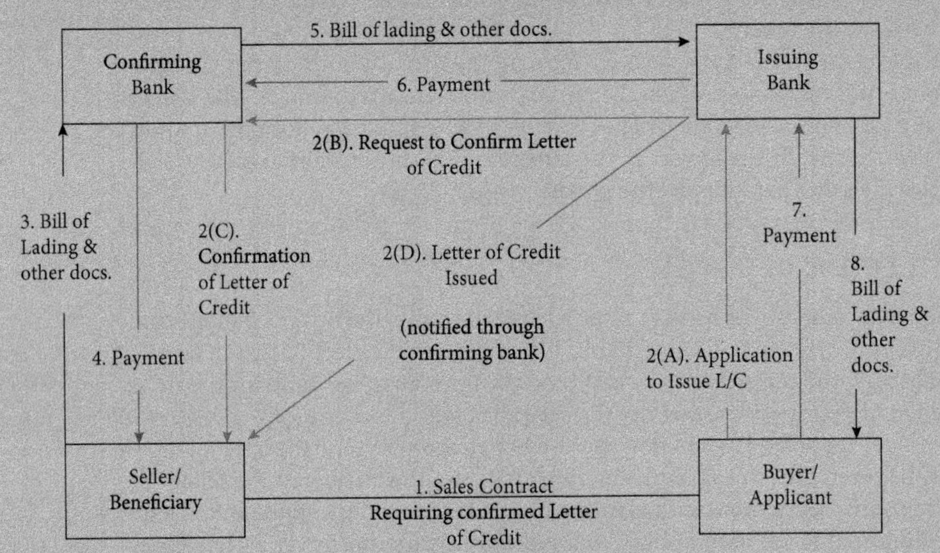

Proper Presentment

Uniform Customs and Practice for Documentary Credits (UCP 600) A uniform law that governs letter of credit transactions.

Letter of credit transactions are governed by both Article 5 of the UCC and the **Uniform Customs and Practice for Documentary Credits (UCP 600)**. Both require the demand for payment to strictly comply with the terms of the letter of credit. However, the rules of strict compliance have been recently tempered. For example, despite the UCC § 5-108 adoption of a standard of strict compliance, the presentment documents are not required to be mirror images of each other. However, the bank must still be able to determine that the documents constitute a complying presentation before accepting the demand for payment.

Similarly, the UCP 600 embraces a case-by-case approach and expressly refutes the requirement that the documents be identical. Instead, it adopts a standard of review based upon the materiality of the discrepancy. If the bank determines the discrepancy is material, it may reject the demand for payment. On the other hand, if the bank believes the discrepancy is immaterial, it must accept the demand for payment.

In determining the materiality of the discrepancy, the bank is required to use common sense and may only consult the documents in so deciding. The bank is not required to do any further investigating beyond the documents. Additionally, the bank may not request the parties to review whether the discrepancy is material, but it may ask the party it represents to waive the requirement of strict compliance.

> **Example:** A court was asked to determine if the discrepancies on the documents justified a bank's refusal to pay. The documents included several errors, including the misspelling of the city of destination, the absence of stamps indicating "originals," and certain documents being dated one day apart. Despite these discrepancies, the court determined that the documents constituted complying presentation under the relaxed strict compliance standard. *Voest-Alpine v. Bank of China*, 142 F.3d 887 (5th Cir. 1998)

If a confirming bank accepts a demand in which the documents do not meet the requirements of strict compliance, it may find itself unable to recover from the issuing bank the money it has already paid to the seller. This is because the issuing bank will have the opportunity to deny the demand for payments if it finds the documents do not comply strictly. Thus, the only available recourse for the confirming bank is to sue the issuing bank for wrongfully rejecting its demand for payment. Note that a bank may also be found liable for wrongfully dishonoring a letter of credit.

The prevailing standard established by the courts for examining documents relating to a letter of credit is the **rule of strict compliance**. According to this doctrine, the terms of the documents presented to the issuing bank must strictly conform to the requirements of the letter of credit and the UCP 600. There is a developing standard of a "functional standard" of compliance. However, the following example is one of strict compliance.

Rule of strict compliance
A doctrine that entitles a bank to reject documents that do not strictly comply with the terms of a letter of credit.

> **Example:** The North Carolina National Bank issued an irrevocable letter of credit on behalf of its customer, Adastra Knitting Mills. It promised to honor 60-day time drafts of Courtaulds North American, Inc. for up to $135,000 covering shipment of 100 percent acrylic yarn. Courtaulds presented its draft together with a commercial invoice describing the goods as "Imported Acrylic Yarns." The packing list stapled to the invoice described the shipment as "Cartons marked: 100% Acrylic." The bank refused the draft because of the discrepancy between the letter of credit and the invoice. In the meantime, the buyer (Adastara Knitting Mills) had filed for bankruptcy and the court-appointed trustee would not waive the discrepancy—it wanted the bankruptcy estate to retain the funds and not pay them over to the supplier. The documents were returned and Courtaulds sued the bank. On appeal to the federal Fourth Circuit, the bank prevailed. The description of the goods in the invoice did not match the description of the goods in the credit, and the difference was not cured by the packing list. *Courtaulds North America, Inc. v. North Carolina National Bank*, 528 F.2d 802 (4th Cir. 1975)

It is important to note that the letter of credit is independent of the sales contract underlying the transaction between the buyer and seller. The independence of these two documents means that the banks will not inquire as to whether the contractual obligations or conditions have been satisfied. The banks are responsible only for making a proper presentment. If the goods are not in compliance with the sales contract, the buyer's only recourse will be to make a claim against the seller directly, as it cannot attempt to recover from any of the banks involved in the letter of credit.

Management Application Irrevocable Letter of Credit

Sir or Madam:

At the request of John Doe of 123 Main Street, we hereby establish our Irrevocable Letter of Credit in your favor up to an aggregate amount of $50,000, U.S. DOLLARS, to expire at our counters on December 31, 2028. This letter of credit is available for payment against your draft(s) at sight drawn on XYZ Bank, accompanied by this original Standby Letter of Credit and the following document[s]: bill of lading.

We agree with you that all draft(s) drawn under and in compliance with this letter of credit will be honored on presentation to us as specified in this letter.

This credit is subject to the Uniform Customs and Practice for Documentary Credits, International Chamber of Commerce Publication No. 500. The number and the date of the credit and the name of our bank must be quoted on all drafts required.

Please examine this instrument carefully. If you are unable to comply with the terms or conditions, please communicate with your buyer to arrange for an amendment. This procedure will facilitate prompt handling when documents are presented.

_____________ [*signature*]
Authorized Signature

What purposes does this instrument serve?

AI Feature: Stale Checks

After reading this chapter, use an internet search engine to review the time limit of presenting a stale check in your home state. Then, use an AI program to determine the time limit for doing so in three other jurisdictions. What is the law if the stale check is drawn on an overseas bank?

Key Terms

- Account overdraft, 757
- Altered check, 761
- Beneficiary, 769
- Bill of lading, 769
- Cashier's check, 755
- Certified check, 755
- Confirming bank, 769
- Depository bank, 764
- Electronic funds transfer (EFT), 766
- Forged check, 760
- Intermediary bank, 764
- Issuer or Issuing bank, 769
- Letter of credit, 769
- Payor bank, 764
- Postdated check, 758
- Rule of strict compliance, 771
- Stale check, 758
- Stop payment, 757
- Traveler's check, 755
- Uniform Customs and Practice for Documentary Credits (UCP 600), 770
- Wire transfers, 768

Applying the Law

30.1 Research the Law. Using an internet search engine, research the law in your state and determine the applicable statute of limitations for filing a lawsuit for reimbursement of a forged check.

30.2 The Extent of a Bank's Rights. Paul Miller received Supplemental Security Income (SSI) benefits via direct deposit into his checking account with Bank of America®. In January, Bank of America erroneously credited $1,799.83 to Miller's account. Two months later, and without Miller's authorization, the bank reversed the credit, causing a negative balance in Miller's account that also depleted his most recent SSI payment as soon as it was directly deposited. From time to time, Miller overdrew his account, and the bank recouped those overdrafts and associated insufficient funds fees from his directly deposited public benefit funds Did the bank have a right to recoup overdrafts and insufficient funds from the SSI benefits, or it is limited to only other types of deposits? *Miller v. Bank of America*, 207 P.3d 531 (Cal. 2009)

30.3 Writing Checks to Yourself. JAG Orthopedics alleged Lydia Vecchio Ferrante, JAG Orthopedics' officer manager from September 2009 to June 2014, misappropriated and embezzled hundreds of thousands of dollars from JAG Orthopedics by (1) writing checks to herself well in excess of her monthly salary of $4,000; (2) obtaining, without authorization from JAG Orthopedics, a debit/credit card tied to its checking account and charging items for her own personal use; (3) forging the signature of JAG Orthopedics' owner and president, Andrew Miller, M.D., on checks made out in her name; and (4) misappropriating funds from a checking account that it had closed prior to the misappropriation. Effectively, these checks and the actions committed by Ferrante were paid out by the bank. Do the bank's actions of paying the forged checks violate the UCC? *JAG Orthopedics, P.C. v. AJC Advisory Corp.*, 48 Misc. 3d 1213(A) (N.Y. Sup. Ct. 2015)

30.4 Unauthorized Transactions? Royal Arcanum is a New York not-for-profit corporation. According to the minutes of a meeting in 1989, two officers must sign all checks. Frank Vassall, William Herrnkind, and Joseph Rugilio were authorized to sign the checks. About 14 years later, the name listed on the monthly account statements was changed to Herrnkind and included only him. Royal Arcanum then opened up a new account, with the same bank, which had a signature card that listed Herrnkind as the sole authorized signatory. Herrnkind was able to withdraw funds from the bank and function as the sole signatory. In 2008, Royal Arcanum filed an action against Herrnkind and the bank. Royal Arcanum claimed that two signatures of its officers were required for withdrawal of funds. As such, Royal Arcanum asserts Herrnkind's single signature was an unauthorized signature. Is Royal Arcanum correct? *Royal Arcanum Hosp. Ass'n of Kings Cnty., Inc. v. Herrnkind*, 35 Misc. 3d 1205(A) (N.Y. Sup. Ct. 2012)

30.5 Forgery. In January 2003, Enchantment RV hired an employee to assist with bookkeeping and to help balance the accounts of Enchantment's combined companies. In February 2003, the new employee began forging checks on their accounts held at a bank. Between February 2003 and October 2004, the employee forged 211 checks, mostly payable to herself or to "cash," stealing $283,546.85 from Enchantment. About a year and half into the scheme, Enchantment discovered the forgeries and notified the bank. The bank refused to repay Enchantment for any of the losses. According to the bank, it had provided statements monthly, including photocopies of canceled checks, to Enchantment for its various accounts. Thus, the bank believed that it had relieved itself of its obligation to pay under the UCC. Enchantment brought an action against the bank. Who is likely to prevail under the UCC? Why? *Associated Home & RV Sales, Inc. v. Bank of Belen*, 294 P.3d 1276 (N.M. Ct. App. 2012)

30.6 Withdrawal by Estranged Husband. Spouses were getting divorced, and the wife had a separate bank account. However, the husband gained access to the account through a signature card that bore both their signatures. As a result, the husband was able to make withdrawals from the account. Both parties received notice through monthly online statements. When the wife later complained about "unauthorized withdrawals," the bank claimed that the wife could have notified the bank within the required 30-day window. Can the wife still bring a claim against the bank? *Kaplan v. JPMorgan Chase Bank, N.A.*, 2015 WL 2358240 (N.D. Ill. 2015)

30.7 Duty of Ordinary Care. A law firm maintained its client trust account at Busey Bank®. On May 25, the law firm deposited into its trust account a check from one of its clients in the amount of $350,000. The check was drawn on the account of Intact Insurance Company at Royal Bank of Canada® in Toronto, Ontario. The check was marked as follows: "US Funds" and "This cheque contains a true security watermark—hold at an angle to view." On June 6, the law firm transferred $210,000 from its trust account to the client who provided the $350,000 check. In addition, on June 8, the law firm transferred $60,000 from the trust account to the client. However, the $350,000 check from its client was returned to Busey Bank uncollected, and Busey Bank notified the law firm and charged back $350,000 to the law firm's account the same day. As a result, the law firm filed an action against Busey Bank, alleging the bank breached its duty of ordinary care regarding the $350,000 fraudulent check the law firm deposited and drew against. The check was later determined to be uncollectible. Did the bank breach its duty of ordinary care? *Dixon, Laukitis, & Downing, P.C. v. Busey Bank*, 993 N.E.2d 580 (Ill. App. Ct. 2013)

30.8 Requiring Customer to Discover and Report Customer's Unauthorized Signature. Century opened a corporate checking account with BancorpSouth®, and the authorized signors on the account were Clarence Chapman Jr. and Jo Lynn Chapman. About two months later, Century's newly hired bookkeeper, Vicki Smith, began forging checks drawn on Century's corporate account with BancorpSouth. The checks were made payable to vendors who did business with Century; however, the spellings of the vendor's names were altered. In addition, Vicki, who was not authorized to sign checks, forged the authorized signor's names. About a year and $450,002.55 later, the forgeries ended. Century requested BancorpSouth provide them with bank statements for the past year, because Smith had destroyed all of the bank statements to conceal the fraud. Moreover, Century requested that BancorpSouth only pay checks that were signed by authorized signors. Further, Century sued BancorpSouth for breach of warranty. Will Century prevail in its suit? *Century Const. Co., LLC v. Bancorpsouth Bank*, 117 So. 3d 345 (Miss. Ct. App. 2013)

30.9 Letter of Credit. Uniloy contracted with MAB LLC to manufacture two plastic bottling machines for MAB's use. The total price of the machines was $1,320,050. After making a $132,050 down payment on the machines, MAB obtained $800,000 of the outstanding balance of the purchase price from a venture capital firm. MAB remained responsible for the remaining outstanding balance of $388,000. As a condition to obtaining the venture capital funding, MAB was required to obtain a letter of credit to cover the $388,000 for which it remained responsible. PNC Bank® issued a letter of credit to Uniloy on behalf of MAB and required Uniloy to present to the Bank: (1) a dated signed certification by an authorized Uniloy representative stating that Uniloy had not received payment from MAB within 60 days of shipment; (2) copies of the unpaid invoices for the merchandise described above; and (3) a copy of the bills of lading for the merchandise described evidencing the shipment date. After Uniloy shipped the machines to MAB, MAB failed to pay the remaining $388,000 of the purchase price. Subsequently, Uniloy sent a demand for payment under the letter of credit to PNC Bank a couple of days before the expiration of the 60 days. Upon review of the documents submitted by Uniloy, PNC Bank discovered that the signed certification was undated, the serial number was different from what was originally specified, and the bills of lading had incorrect serial numbers. The bank faxed a notice of discrepancies to Uniloy stating that it was refusing to honor Uniloy's request due to the discrepancies between the documents submitted and the letter of credit. However, before contacting MAB, the 60 days within which the statement had to be received by the bank had passed. Uniloy sued PNC Bank, arguing that the discrepancies were minor and that it was entitled to payment from the bank under the letter of credit. How should the court rule, and why? *Uniloy Milacron Inc. v. PNC Bank, N.A.*, 2008 U.S. Dist. LEXIS 33063 (W.D. Ky. 2008)

30.10 Inconsistent Bill of Lading. Broadway National Bank asserted that it properly dishonored E & H Partner's drafts on a letter of credit, because the bank could not properly match the invoice numbers and merchandise descriptions among submitted documents. Broadway asserted: "Merchandise on commercial invoice are [sic] different from the bill of lading." According to the bank, the bills of lading in question did not describe the merchandise listed on the invoices in sufficient detail. For example, one invoice demanded payment for remote color TVs, but the bill of lading submitted along with that invoice failed to describe the merchandise in that manner. Rather, it simply listed the item numbers of the goods being shipped. Broadway contended that these omissions on the bills of lading constituted fatal discrepancies. Is Broadway correct in its contention? *E & H Partners v. Broadway Nat'l Bank*, 39 F. Supp. 2d 275 (S.D.N.Y. 1998)

Creditors' Rights and Secured Transactions

31

Weep, moneylenders, yourselves and your money and your interest's interest. — Aristophanes, Greek playwright (445-386 B.C.)

Chapter Outline

- Introduction
- Liens, Garnishments, and Guaranties
  - *Management Application: Claim of Lien on Real Property*
- Secured Transactions
  - *Management Application: Security Agreements*

Case 31.1: *Altair Global Credits v. P.R. AAA Portfolio Bond Fund, Inc. (In re Fin. Oversight & Mgmt. Bd.)*

  - *Management Application: What Happens When There Is a Name Change?*
- Priorities, Rights, and Duties of Parties
- Defaults and Remedies

Case 31.2: *Icon Agents, LLC v. Kanza Construction, Inc.*

- AI Feature: Draft a Personal Guarantee

Learning Objectives

After studying this chapter, you should be able to:

1. Describe the ways unsecured creditors may collect debts and judgments.
2. Explain how to create and perfect a security interest.
3. Explain the how to perfect a security interest.
4. Describe the remedies available to secured creditors following a default.

Introduction

In the next few chapters, we will review the collection of debts and judgments as they relate to consumer and commercial claims. In the first part of this chapter, the remedies of unsecured creditors are discussed. The types of involuntary liens that can be

Debtor
The person or institution that owes a sum of money.

enforced against the **debtor's** (the person who owes a sum of money) property and the rights and duties of guarantors and sureties are explained. Then, we review the subject of secured transactions—transactions in which personal property is used to collateralize the repayment of debts and obligations.

Liens, Garnishments, and Guaranties

Both the common law and the Uniform Commercial Code (UCC) provide rights and remedies for creditors. We first discuss the rights and remedies available under the common law (that is, state statutory law) and then discuss the rights and remedies contained in the UCC.

Liens

Lien
A legal instrument by which property acts as a security for the repayment of a debt.

Creditor
The person or institution to whom money is owed.

A **lien** is an encumbrance on (or a claim against) either real or personal property securing the repayment of a debt. If the property owner defaults on the obligation, a lien may be used by the **creditor** (the person who is owed money) to force the sale of the property, with the proceeds of the sale used to compensate the creditor. Liens are important to creditors as they establish priority among competing creditors seeking payment from a defaulting debtor. Common types of liens include mechanic's liens, artisan's liens, and judicial liens.

> **Example:** A mortgage is a lien that encumbers real property.

Mechanic's lien
A lien recorded on the title to real property by a contractor, subcontractor, or material supplier for unpaid sums owed under a construction-related contract.

MECHANIC'S LIENS. Those persons hired to perform work or furnish materials or equipment to improve a third-party owner's real property are entitled to record a type of lien known as a **mechanic's lien**. This lien arises from the construction or other improvement of real estate. Every state has enacted laws relating to mechanic's liens.

State constitutions, statutes, and case law establish who is entitled to record a mechanic's lien. The most common examples of those who are entitled by law to record this lien are contractors, subcontractors, sub-subcontractors (a subcontractor to a subcontractor), material suppliers (those who supply materials to a project), equipment rental companies, surveyors, and designers (including architects and engineers). A mechanic's lien claimant who does not receive payment is allowed to record a mechanic's lien (an encumbrance) on the title to the real property upon which work was performed. Mechanic's liens must be recorded in the appropriate local recording office within a permitted period of time following the completion of the project. If the property owner fails to timely pay the mechanic's lien claimant, the holder of the mechanic's lien can foreclose on the property and use the proceeds to pay the debt owed. Additionally, a discharge or release of the lien should be recorded when a mechanic's lien has been recorded and the debt has been paid.

> **Example:** Allen Edmonds® Corporation (Allen Edmonds) entered into a ten-year lease with Plaza Frontenac (Plaza) for a storefront space in a shopping mall. The lease required Allen Edmonds to make certain improvements to the premises. Allen Edmonds employed both Crafton Contracting Company (Crafton) and Vogel Sheet Metal and Heating (Vogel) to make the improvements. Allen Edmonds never paid Crafton and Vogel, who then recorded mechanic's liens on

the title to the mall property. The court found the mechanic's liens were enforceable against the mall owner as the landlord and operator because Allen Edmonds was acting as the agent of Plaza since the improvements were a requirement of the lease. *Crafton Contracting Co. v. Swenson Construction Co., Inc.*, 495 S.W.3d 178 (Mo. Ct. App. 2016)

Some states require that a contractor's notice to owner be provided by the general contractor prior to the execution of a construction contract. The general contractor is also required to deliver a copy of the same to each subcontractor on the project.

Management Application
Claim of Lien on Real Property

Recording Information:
Assessor's Parcel No.:

NOTICE OF LIEN
(Nev. Rev. Stat. § 108.226)

The undersigned claims a lien upon the property described in this notice for work, materials or equipment furnished to the improvement of the property:

1. Name and address of the person claiming the claim of lien on real property:
____
2. The total amount of the original contract is: $ __________
3. The total amount of all payments received to date is: $ __________
4. The amount of the lien, after deducting all just credits and offsets, is: $ __________
5. The name of the owner, if known, of the property is: __________
6. The name of the person by whom the lien claimant was employed or to whom the lien claimant furnished or agreed to furnish work, materials or equipment is:
____
7. A brief statement of the terms of payment of the lien claimant's contract is:
____
8. A description of the property to be charged with the lien is:
____

Dated: __________

____
(Lien Claimant)

By: Owner/President
(Print or Type Name/Title)

Notarization of Signature of Lien Claimant

Similarly, when the lien claimant has been paid or settled the dispute, the claimant will execute for recordation on the title to the improved real property a release of the foregoing lien.

Artisan's lien
A lien for the unpaid labor and materials that have been furnished by a creditor to improve or repair personal property of the debtor.

ARTISANS' LIENS. When a creditor is not paid for the labor and materials that have been furnished to improve or repair *personal property*, the creditor may be able to recover the property through an **artisan's lien**. Unlike a mechanic's lien, an artisan lien is possessory. This requires the creditor as the artisan to retain possession of the debtor's property until the obligation is paid. Additionally, the parties must have either expressly or implicitly agreed that the creditor would provide a service in exchange for a cash payment. The lien will remain so long as the lienholder retains possession of the property. Once possession of the property is released, the lien is terminated. Creditors of this type are permitted to foreclose on the debtor's personal property and to sell property in order to retire the debt due.

> **Example:** Helen takes her mechanical watch to a jeweler for cleaning. The law automatically gives the jeweler an artisan's lien on the watch in the amount of the cleaning costs. If Helen fails to pay for the services rendered, the jeweler can sell the watch and use the proceeds to pay for the cost of the cleaning. Helen is entitled to the balance of the proceeds, if any.

Judicial lien
A lien obtained by judgment allowing the creditor to collect on a debt.

JUDICIAL LIENS. Creditors also have the option to file a lawsuit against a debtor. When successful, the creditor will receive a judgment for the amount of the debt plus any interest accrued or legal costs expended. A **judicial lien** may be recorded or filed with a governmental office to reflect the outstanding judgment. Often, the debtor does not willingly pay the judgment against them, thus requiring the debtor's nonexempt property interests to be seized and sold to satisfy the debt.

Writ of attachment
A pre-judgment court order to seize a property interest of a debtor.

Writ of execution
A post-judgment court order to seize a property interest of a debtor.

There are two ways a creditor can request the court to issue an order to seize a property interest of the debtor. If the creditor fears the debtor will destroy or cause harm to the property, the creditor may request a **writ of attachment**. If granted, the attachment of the property will occur at the time at which a lawsuit is filed or shortly thereafter. Since a writ of attachment is issued prior to judgment, due process of the law requires that the debtor receive proper notice and a meaningful hearing on the issue before the property may be seized. A **writ of execution** can be issued after the judgment. In this instance, the court orders the sheriff to take possession of the debtor's property for the eventual public sale.

> **Example:** A purchaser of medical equipment leases brought an action seeking a pre-judgment writ of attachment against the seller. The purchaser alleged that the seller breached the contract. The court denied the request for a writ of attachment because the court believed that the purchaser failed to demonstrate a likelihood of success on the merits and that the purchaser's remedy would otherwise be lost and failed to satisfy the indebtedness requirement necessary to obtain the writ. *First Guaranty Bank v. Republic Bank, Inc.*, 303 F. Supp. 3d 1200 (D. Utah 2017)

	Writ of Attachment	Writ of Execution
Timing	Prior to judgment by the court	After judgment by the court
Procedures	1. Creditor files claim against debtor in court. 2. Separate hearing held on the issue. 3. If granted, the creditor will post a bond for court costs, the value of the property to be attached, and the value of the loss debtor will incur by not being able to use the property. 4. Writ of attachment issued. 5. Sheriff or other officer seizes property.	1. Creditor files claim against debtor in court. 2. Creditor prevails. 3. Writ of execution is granted. 4. Court order issued directing the sheriff to seize and sell the debtor's nonexempt property.
Result	Property is held in official custody until a final judgment is rendered by the court. If creditor prevails in their claims against the debtor, the debt may be satisfied through the sale of the seized property.	Profits derived from the sale of the property will be used to satisfy the judgment, any interest accrued, and the cost of the sale. Any money that remains will go to the debtor.

Garnishment

A creditor may also have the option to obtain a garnishment. A **garnishment** allows the creditor to collect on the debt by seizing the debtor's property that is held by a third party. Garnishments are common for seizing wages or funds held in the debtor's bank. Often, a garnishment proceeding will result in the debtor's employer receiving a court order requiring an apportionment of the debtor's wages be paid to the creditor to satisfy a debt.

Garnishment
A court order allowing a creditor to collect on a debt by seizing the debtor's wages or funds held by a third party.

> **Example:** A creditor who obtains a favorable judgment against a debtor can have an order sent from the court to the debtor's employer. The employer will then be directed to remove a portion from the debtor's check every pay period and send it to the court that issued the judgment. The court will then make sure the creditor receives the money.

The procedural requirements for obtaining a garnishment vary from state to state. Commonly, garnishments are post-judgment remedies; however, they may be obtained pre-judgment, after a hearing before the court. In some states, the creditor only needs to obtain a single order of garnishment, as it allows the debtor's wages to be garnished until the entirety of the debt is paid off. Other states require the creditor to request a new order of wage garnishment for each pay period. There are both state and federal limits placed upon the amount that can be seized through garnishments.

To review more information concerning wage garnishments, see https://www.dol.gov/general/topic/wages/garnishments.

Sureties and Guarantors

When a third person promises to pay a debt that is owed by another party (the debtor), this relationship is known as a suretyship or guaranty. A suretyship or guaranty results in the third party's assets and income being used as a security for the repayment of a debt—for example, a parent may guarantee a Stafford student loan. If the debtor fails to pay its obligation, the creditor may pursue payment from the third party.

Suretyship
The relationship between the surety, the principal debtor, and the creditor in which the creditor may seek payment from the surety at the maturity date.

SURETY. A **suretyship** arises when a third party promises the creditor will be responsible for the debtor's obligation. Thus, an express contract between the creditor and the surety is created and the surety is primarily liable to the creditor for the debt. As a result, when the debt becomes due the creditor may seek payment from the surety. The creditor does not have to first attempt to collect from the debtor. However, the surety is entitled to seek reimbursement from the debtor for sums paid on behalf of the debtor.

> **Example:** Steven agrees to be Derek's surety on a loan from Leanne. Steven and Leanne enter into an express contract and six months later the debt is due. Leanne contacts Steven, asking him to honor the suretyship before she seeks payment from Derek. As a surety, Steven must pay Leanne the amount owed. Steven may then seek reimbursement from Derek.

Guaranty
The relationship between the guarantor, the principal debtor, and the creditor, in which the creditor may seek payment from the guarantor only after attempting to collect from the debtor

GUARANTY. Unlike a suretyship, a **guaranty** holds the third party secondarily liable for the debt. Thus, the guarantor is not liable to pay for the debt until after the debtor has defaulted. Additionally, the creditor is generally required to attempt to collect from the debtor before pursuing payment from the guaranty.

> **Example:** Assume the same facts as in the example above, except this time Steven's sister Gabriella has agreed to be Derek's guarantor. When the debt becomes due, Leanne must first try to collect from Derek before requesting Gabriella to pay.

Requirements. Guaranty contracts between guarantors and creditors generally must be in writing to be enforceable under the Statute of Frauds. Traditionally, under common law, suretyships did not need to be in writing; however, some states now require a writing for the suretyship to be enforceable.

Releases. Guarantors and sureties may both be released from their obligations upon the happening of a specific event, including the following:

1. *Payment.* The payment of the debt obligation by the debtor, or by another party on the debtor's behalf, results in the guarantor or surety being released from the obligation.
2. *Surrender of property.* The obligation of the guarantor or surety will be discharged if the creditor surrenders the property to the debtor or if the creditor impairs the property without the consent of the guarantor or surety.
3. *Material modification.* If material changes to the guaranty or surety are made without the guarantor or surety's consent, the guarantor or surety will be discharged of the obligation.

Defenses. Generally, any of the defenses that the debtor may assert to avoid liability may also be asserted by the guarantor or surety. There are a few defenses not available to the guarantor or surety, including the statute of limitations or the debtor's incapacity or bankruptcy. Additionally, some defenses are only available to the guarantor or surety. These defenses include the bankruptcy of the guarantor or surety, or if the guarantor or surety was fraudulently induced into guaranteeing the debt. To reduce instances of fraud, most states require the creditor to inform the guarantor or surety of any material facts that substantially increase the likelihood that the guarantor or surety will be liable for the debt. The failure to properly inform the third party of the change may make the underlying surety or guaranty voidable.

Surety or Guarantor's Rights. When a guarantor (or surety) pays the debt, the guarantor is entitled to certain rights against the debtor. The **right of subrogation** is the assumption by a third party of another party's right to collect a debt or damages. Essentially, the guarantor will stand in place of the creditor and may seek all available legal remedies. The guarantor also has the **right of reimbursement** from the debtor. This means the guarantor has the right to be repaid by the debtor for all costs and expenses incurred during the guaranty, in addition to the amount paid to the creditor by the guarantor. When there are two or more guarantors (or sureties), the **right of contribution** states that a guarantor who pays more than their proportionate share of the liability will be entitled to recover the amount in excess of their obligation from the other co-guarantors.

Right of subrogation The rights the creditor has against the debtor become the legal right of the guarantor/surety upon repayment of the debt by the guarantor/surety.

Right of reimbursement The right to be repaid by the debtor for all costs and expenses incurred during the guaranty upon repayment of the debt by the guarantor/surety.

Right of contribution The right of repayment by co-guarantors when one guarantor/surety pays in excess of their proportionate share of the liability.

> **Example:** Multiple guarantors signed four separate agreements that guaranteed the payment of a \$5.2 million bank loan to a real estate company. The real estate company ultimately defaulted on the loan and the bank sued all of the guarantors for the unpaid loan balance. One of the guarantors (Dunbar) settled with the bank for \$150,000, while another guarantor (Kroona) was sued, and a judgment was entered for the bank for \$400,000. Kroona filed an action seeking contribution from the guarantors who settled with the bank. The court found Kroona was entitled to contribution from the other guarantors because a common liability was shared between them even though they had signed separate guaranties. *Kroona v. Dunbar*, 868 N.W.2d 728 (Minn. Ct. App. 2015)

Concept Summary
Rights of the Guarantor and Surety

Term	Definition
Right of subrogation	The assumption by a third party of another party's right to collect a debt or damages.
Right of reimbursement	The right to be repaid by the debtor for all costs and expenses incurred during the guaranty upon repayment of the debt by the guarantor/surety.
Right of contribution	The right of repayment by co-guarantors when one guarantor/surety pays in excess of their proportionate share of the liability.

Secured Transactions

Secured transaction Transaction where the payment has been secured by the debtor's personal property.

The term "**secured transaction**" applies to any transaction, regardless of its form, that is intended to create a security interest in personal property or fixtures, including goods, documents, instruments, general intangibles, chattel paper, or accounts. The security interest is designed to protect the secured party in the event that the debtor fails to pay or perform the underlying obligation. In addition, the term "secured transaction" applies to any sale of an account of chattel paper. UCC § 9-102(a)(11). Taking personal property to collateralize a debt is the subject of the remainder of this chapter.

Article 9 of the UCC contains numerous terms that are to be used in documents involving secured transactions. These terms have been adopted by all states and include those in the table below.

Term	Definition
Debtor	The person or institution that owes a sum of money
Creditor	The person or institution to whom money is owed
Secured Transaction	Transaction where the payment has been secured by the debtor's personal property
Collateral	The personal property, tangible or intangible, used to secure the transaction

The Nature of a Secured Transaction

Collateral The personal property, tangible or intangible, used to secure the transaction.

A secured transaction creates two kinds of rights. First, it creates a "security interest," which is an interest in personal property, fixtures, accounts, or chattel paper, otherwise known as "**collateral**." The security interest secures the payment or performance of an obligation and gives the person in whose favor the security interest was created the right to repossess and retain or dispose of the collateral. Security interests come in many forms, such as pledges, assignments, personal property mortgages, deeds of trust, inventory liens, conditional sales, and leases or consignments intended as a security.

Second, a secured transaction creates a right to be paid first among creditors to the extent that the collateral has value.

Security agreement A document providing a lender with a security interest in a specified asset of the debtor that has been pledged as collateral.

Secured party The person in whose favor the security interest is created.

An agreement that creates or provides for a security interest is known as a **security agreement**. The person in whose favor the security interest is created is typically the lender or seller of the collateral and is referred to as the "**secured party**." The debtor is the person who owes the payment or other performance of the secured obligation. The debtor usually owns or has the right to possess the collateral. If the debtor and the owner of the collateral are not the same person, the term "debtor" may refer to the owner of the collateral, the person owing the obligation, or both depending on the context. The term "debtor" has also been held to include a guarantor.

Creation of a Security Interest

Default is not a term that is defined within Article 9 of the UCC. Instead, what will constitute a default is generally provided for in the security agreement. However, a default is commonly considered as the failure to make timely payments on a related loan obligation. When the debtor defaults, the concerns of the creditor will vary depending on whether the creditor is in possession of the property that was used to secure the loan. If the creditor is in possession, the creditor's concern will generally be whether or not the property can be sold for an amount that will satisfy the debt. Additionally, the creditor must determine if they have priority over another creditor who has rights to the same collateral. When the creditor is not in possession of the collateral, the creditor will first have to determine the best way to gain possession of the collateral.

Many of the creditor's concerns can be alleviated by the creation and perfection of a security interest. The protection garnered from being a secured creditor occurs upon obtaining a security interest in the collateral. The first step is to identify how a security interest is created.

REQUIREMENTS. There are three requirements to create a security interest in the debtor's collateral.

1. In instances where the creditor is not in possession of the collateral, the parties must have created a written or authenticated security agreement clearly describing the collateral to be subject to the security interest. This written agreement must be signed or authenticated by the debtor to be enforceable;
2. The secured party (creditor) must give the debtor something of value; and
3. The debtor is required to have property rights in the collateral.

When these requirements are met, the rights of the creditor attach to the collateral. Attachment creates an enforceable security interest in the collateral.

Security Agreement. The security agreement is a document gives the creditor a security interest in specific asset(s) of the debtor. Security agreements are required when the creditor is not in possession of the collateral. The security agreement must be written or authenticated, must sufficiently describe the collateral, and must be signed by the debtor.

In this context, authenticate means that the document signifies an intent to adopt or accept the record by signing or adopting a symbol on an electronic record, which confirms that intent. UCC § 9-102(a)(7).

Management Application Security Agreements

1. FOR VALUABLE CONSIDERATION, ________________ (hereinafter called "Debtor") hereby grants to ________________ (hereinafter called "Secured Party"), a security interest in and to all of Debtor's inventory (including raw materials and work in process), equipment, accounts, contract rights, general intangibles, furniture, fixtures, leaseholds, paper, documents, goods, instruments, patents, trademarks, copyrights, goodwill, and all other personal property, wherever located, now owned or hereafter acquired,

and all products, proceeds, additions, and accessions of any of such items. The foregoing property is hereafter sometimes referred to as the "collateral."

2. The term "Account" as used herein shall refer to and include all rights to payment for goods sold or leased or for services rendered, all sums of money or other proceeds due or becoming due thereon, all instruments pertaining thereto, all guarantees and security therefore, and all goods giving rise thereto and the rights pertaining to such goods, including the right of stoppage in transit and all related insurance. There shall further be included in the definition of the word "Account" all other rights of Debtor to the payment of money, including without limitation amounts due from affiliates, tax refunds, and insurance proceeds, all files, records and writings of the Debtor, or in which it has an interest, in any way relating to the foregoing property. The persons obligated on such accounts shall hereinafter be called "Account Debtors."

3. The security interest hereby granted shall secure the Secured Party for all debts of Debtor to Secured Party of whatever nature, whether matured or unmatured, direct or indirect, absolute or contingent, now or hereafter existing, including future advances of credit, or arising or contracted or incurred or owing to or acquired by Secured Party by assignment, negotiation, transfer, or otherwise, including without limitation, notes, drafts, unpaid accounts payable, guaranties, and other debts. All such obligations of Debtor are hereinafter called "Indebtedness."

4. Debtor has executed and delivered a financing statement and authorizes Secured Party to sign the same and to file the same in accordance with law. Debtor agrees to execute and deliver to Secured Party such further financing statements, renewal statements and other documents as may be requested by Secured Party from time to time for the purpose of perfecting the security interest created hereby, evidencing Debtor's indebtedness, or otherwise effectuating the purpose of this Agreement.

5. Debtor at any time upon request of Secured Party will permit secured Party to examine, inspect, and check the collateral, or any part thereof. Debtor will do all acts which may be necessary to maintain, preserve and protect the collateral; also, Debtor will not cause or permit any waste or unusual or unreasonable depreciation thereof, or any act for which said collateral might be confiscated. Debtor will keep the collateral insured against fire, theft, and such other risks as secured Party may designate, in companies and amounts acceptable to Secured Party, and upon Secured Party's request will deliver the policies evidencing such insurance to Secured Party. In the absence of any designation of amount by Secured Party, Debtor shall maintain such insurance in an amount sufficient to cover the indebtedness to Secured Party plus any amounts owing to all other creditors holding a lien or security interest in any of the collateral. The collateral shall not, without the consent of Secured Party, be moved from Debtor's premises except as such movement may be required as a part of the processing by Debtor of such collateral or by a sale of inventory in the normal course of business. Debtor from time to time at the request of Secured Party will deliver to Secured Party an inventory of merchandise and equipment showing its location and detail as secured Party may require.

6. Failure by the Debtor in the performance of any covenant or agreement herein or in the discharge of any liability or obligation to Secured Party, or the happening of any of the events specified in Paragraph 9 of this Agreement, shall constitute an event of default under this Agreement. Upon the occurrence of any such event of default, Secured Party shall have all of the rights and remedies of a Secured Party under applicable law and all rights provided herein, and in any other applicable security, all of which rights and remedies shall, to the full extent permitted by law, be cumulative. Without limiting the generality of the foregoing, upon the occurrence of any such event of default, the Secured Party shall have the right, but not the obligation, to take possession of the collateral or any part thereof, and Debtor promises and agrees to deliver possession thereof to Secured Party immediately upon Secured Party's request. Debtor grants to Secured Party a right of entry to obtain possession of the collateral, which after such taking may be stored on the premises of Debtor without cost to Secured Party. In the event that Secured Party under the foregoing provisions should take possession of any of said collateral and sell, or propose to sell, the same, Secured Party is authorized to use any trademark, trade name, service mark, trade dress, logo, or trade style utilized by Debtor without compensation to Debtor.

Debtor promises and agrees upon request of Secured Party to assemble the collateral and to make it available to Secured Party at a place to be designated by Secured Party. Any notice of sale, disposition, or other intended action by Secured Party sent to Debtor at least five (5) days prior to such action shall constitute reasonable notice to Debtor.

7. The parties acknowledge their equality of bargaining position, and that this transaction is a non-consumer transaction. The parties further recognize and acknowledge that the commercial necessities of this transaction make it imperative that Debtor agrees, and Debtor does so agree, that in the event of a default as described in this Agreement, in addition to the remedies contained in this paragraph, as well as all other remedies specified in this Agreement or provided by law, Secured Party shall have the right to cause a receiver to be placed on Debtor's premises, which said receiver shall be authorized to conduct the business of the Debtor in Debtor's name, said receiver shall not be liable for any losses incurred in the operation of Debtor's business, it being acknowledged by all parties that any loss which might occur during the operation of a receivership would be offset by the value of maintaining the business as a going business.

8. The rights, powers, and remedies given to Secured Party by this Agreement shall be in addition to all rights, powers, and remedies given to Secured Party by virtue of any statute or rule of law. Any forbearance or failure or delay by Secured Party in exercising any right, power, or remedy hereunder shall not be deemed to be a waiver of any such right, power, or remedy, and any single or partial exercise of any right, power, or remedy shall not be a waiver of any other right, power, or remedy unless such right is specifically waived by an instrument in writing executed by Secured Party. The waiver of any, default hereunder shall not be a waiver of any subsequent default. The grant of any right, power, or remedy by this Agreement shall not be interpreted so as to impose upon Secured Party any affirmative obligations not otherwise imposed by law, and Secured Party shall have no obligation to exercise any right, power, or remedy granted by law or by this Agreement.

9. At the option of Secured Party, and without necessity of demand or notice, all or any part of the Indebtedness shall immediately become due and payable, irrespective of any agreed maturity date, upon the happening of any of the following events:

(a) Failure by Debtor to keep or perform any of the terms, conditions, provisions, or warranties of this Agreement;
(b) Default by Debtor in the payment of any part of the Indebtedness when due;
(c) Any deterioration or impairment of the collateral or any part thereof, or any decline or depreciation in the value or market price thereof (whether actual or reasonably anticipated), which causes the collateral in the judgment of secured Party to become unsatisfactory as to character or value;
(d) The levy of any attachment, execution, or other process against Debtor or the entry of an order by any court enjoining either temporarily or permanently the transfer, either in the ordinary course of business or otherwise, of all or any portion of any of Debtor's, assets;
(e) The death, termination of business, insolvency, failure in business, the making of a limited or general assignment for the benefit of creditors, the filing of any petition under any bankruptcy law of the United States of, by, or against Debtor or any guarantor of the Indebtedness or any part thereof; or
(f) The foreclosure by any other person or entity of any other lien or security interest in all or any part of the collateral, regardless of whether such lien or security interest was at any time known to Secured Party or existed at the time of the execution of this Agreement.

10. In case of default by Debtor under any of its obligations hereunder, in addition to any other sums for which Debtor shall be liable, Debtor will pay to Secured Party all attorneys' fees, court costs, or other expenses which Secured Party shall have expended or incurred in enforcing Debtor's obligations hereunder, or in connection with any Accounts, against Debtor, any Account Debtor, or any Guarantor of Debtor or of any Account Debtor.

11. It is agreed and understood that although this Security Agreement secures Secured Party for the obligations of Debtor to pay for merchandise which Debtor has purchased and/or will purchase from Secured Party in the future, this Agreement shall not constitute an obligation upon Debtor to purchase any goods, wares, or merchandise from Secured Party nor shall it constitute an obligation on Secured Party to sell to Debtor any goods, wares, or merchandise.

12. Any notices or communications provided for to be given in this Agreement shall be sent by either party to the address set forth below, or to such other address as may be substituted in writing by either party from time to time.

13. All rights of Secured Party hereunder shall inure to the benefit of its successors and assigns; all obligations of Debtor shall bind Debtor's heirs, executors, administrators, personal representatives, successors, and assigns. If there is more than one Debtor, their obligations hereunder shall be joint and several.

14. This Agreement, and all transactions between Secured Party and Debtor, or any guarantor of Debtor's obligations, shall be governed by the law of the State of ______ which is applicable to contracts executed and wholly performed in the State of _______, regardless of where this Agreement shall be executed, such transactions shall be performed, or Debtor shall reside or do business.

15. Should any paragraph, clause, or provision of this Agreement be found invalid, void, voidable, or unenforceable, such decision shall affect only the paragraph, clause, or provision so found, and all remaining paragraphs, clauses, and provisions of this Agreement shall remain fully valid and enforceable,

IN WITNESS WHEREOF Debtor and Secured Party have caused this Agreement to be executed this day of ________________

DEBTOR PARTY: ____________________

By: ____________________

____

Title

SECURED PARTY: ____________________

By: ____________________

____

Title

What other events of default should be stated in paragraph 9?

The description of the collateral must reasonably identify the property used as collateral. For example, a security agreement stating "all of a debtor's personal property" would not be found to reasonably identify the collateral. UCC § 9-108(c). The description is sufficient so long as it furnishes a reasonable basis for identification of the property. UCC § 9-108(b). The purpose of the description is to protect third parties from attempting to secure an interest in property that has already been secured by another creditor.

> **Example:** A debtor used eight pieces of equipment as collateral; however, the pieces of equipment were used as security interests for multiple different creditors. As a result, the debtor sought to determine the secured status of the various creditors. The court determined that one of the creditors was an unsecured creditor because for one of the specific pieces of equipment, both the model number and serial number were mislabeled on the financing statement and security agreement. Thus, the description was insufficient because a potential purchaser of that piece of equipment in dispute could easily assume that the equipment was not covered by either the security agreement or the financing statement. *In re Pickle Logging, Inc.*, 286 B.R. 181 (Bankr. M.D. Ga. 2002)

Something of Value Given to Debtor. The secured party is required to give something of value to the debtor. Value is a broad term including anything that is given as consideration under contract law, which was discussed in Chapter 10. This consideration, or bargained-for exchange, consists of a commitment to extend credit, and an antecedent debt.

> **Example:** Mateo buys farming equipment from Yuri on credit. If Mateo fails to pay Yuri on time, Mateo and Yuri can enter into a security agreement that gives Yuri a security interest in the farming equipment.

Debtor Must Have Rights in Collateral. The debtor is required to have **rights in the collateral**, meaning the debtor must possess either a current or future ownership interest in or the right to take possession of the collateral. A future ownership interest is sufficient because the debtor is not required to have title to the collateral at the time it is used to secure the transaction.

Rights in the collateral
Debtor possesses a current or future ownership interest in or the right to take possession of the collateral.

> **Example:** Robert's Retail Store sells clothes, cologne, and accessories for men. It entered into a security agreement with Coco's Cologne, a vendor of cologne. As collateral, Robert's Retail Store pledges its future inventory until the loan is repaid. If Robert's Retail Store does not repay the loan from Coco's Cologne, Coco's Cologne is entitled to use any future inventory, such as clothes and accessories, as a form of repayment.

Scope of a Security Interest

The collateral that a security interest covers can include assets that the debtor currently has in its possession as well as assets that the debtor will own in the future. The scope of the security interest can include the future collateral of the debtor through sale or exchange proceeds, after-acquired property, future advances which are discussed in the below paragraphs.

PROCEEDS. Unless the security agreement provides otherwise, when a debtor sells or exchanges collateral subject to a security agreement, the secured party has an automatic right to the benefits of proceeds that are derived from the sale or exchange. UCC § 9-204(a).

> **Example:** A car dealer finances its acquisition of inventory through a lien on the title of the vehicles. When the car dealership sells one of the cars that was used as collateral and is paid in full with a $20,000 payment, the creditor has a right to the proceeds of that $20,000 sale under the proceeds of a security interest.

AFTER-ACQUIRED PROPERTY. A security interest may also attach to property that is acquired by the debtor after the security agreement has been executed. UCC § 9-204. This after-acquired property often takes the form of debtor's inventory. Additionally, many states do not necessarily require that the security agreement contain an "after-acquired property clause" for the security interest to attach to the after-acquired property. Instead, this is a question of fact for the court to determine based on the circumstances surrounding the collateral. However, having a security agreement that contains such a provision is recommended to provide clarity and avoid potential disputes.

> **Example:** Using the example above, after the sale of the vehicle and receipt of $20,000 cash payment, the car dealer acquires additional vehicles as collateral to sell. These additional vehicles are collateral under the security agreement under an after-acquired property clause

FUTURE ADVANCES. Debtors may establish a line of credit by which the creditor will advance additional funds or credit against the debtor's secured personal property. The security agreement may provide those future advances will be subject to the security interest in the collateral. UCC § 9-204(c). There is no need to execute a new security agreement for each future advance made.

> **Example:** Using the car example above, if the car dealership had a $2 million line of credit and borrowers $50,000 to pay wages and salaries one month that is secured by the title of the vehicles. The following month, the car dealership borrows $250,000 for additional inventory of vehicles. This loan can be secured by the title of the vehicles under a future advances clause.

Floating lien
A legal claim to a set of assets that are subject to change over time.

THE FLOATING LIEN CONCEPT. A security agreement that provides for a security interest to attach to property that is acquired after the security agreement was signed by the debtor, proceeds from the sale of the collateral and future advances of credit to the debtor by the creditor or a combination of these is known as a **floating lien.**

Floating liens are commonly used in the context of financing a business's inventory. Given that a business's inventory is constantly changing, the creditor is not interested in any specific units of inventory; therefore, the lien floats from unit to unit as the inventory is bought and sold.

Perfection of a Security Interest

Perfection
Process of ensuring that a security interest is protected against the claims of another creditor seeking to obtain payment on a debt from the same collateral.

The **perfection** of a security interest is extremely important in instances where the debtor has borrowed from more than one creditor and secured the debt with the same collateral. Having the security interest perfected allows the secured party to be protected against the claims of another creditor who seeks to obtain payment on a debt from the same collateral. The creditor with the perfected security interest will prevail against the creditor with an unsecured interest.

Usually, perfection is obtained through the filing of a financing statement, but there are instances in which perfection occurs without a financing statement being filed.

Perfection through filing
Process of perfecting a security interest by following the necessary steps when filing a financing statement.

Perfection Through Filing of Financing Statement

Perfection through filing occurs when a financing statement is presented to the appropriate government office and the requisite filing fee is paid or the financing statement is accepted by the filing officer. UCC § 9-521. Most filings occur electronically, as most states now use electronic filing systems. UCC § 9-102(a)(18). It is entirely permissible for the financing statement to be *filed* before the security agreement has been made or a security interest has attached. UCC § 9-502(d).

In the following case, amended financing statements permitted bondholders to retain a secured creditor position.

CASE 31.1

A FINANCING STATEMENT MUST CONTAIN A DESCRIPTION OF THE COLLATERAL TO BE PERFECTED

ALTAIR GLOBAL CREDIT OPPORTUNITIES FUND (A), LLC V P.R. AAA PORTFOLIO BOND FUND, INC. (IN RE FIN. OVERSIGHT & MGMT. BD.)

914 F.3d 694 (2019)

United States Court of Appeals for the First Circuit

In 2008, Puerto Rico's Employee Retirement System issued bonds bought by various bondholders ("Bondholders"). The Bondholders claimed a right to this property as security. In 2017, Puerto Rico's Employee Retirement System sued for declaratory relief related to the validity, breadth, and perfection of the Bondholders' claims as to the System's property that served as collateral for the bonds. The district court ruled against the Bondholders, holding that their claim wasn't properly secured under the law because their 2008 filing lacked a sufficient description of the collateral.

Language of the Court. *The Bondholders argue that the initial 2008 Financing Statements perfected their security interest. Under the former version of Article 9 operative in 2008,*

> *[a] financing statement is sufficient if it [1] gives the names of the debtor and the secured party, [2] is signed by the debtor, [3] gives an address of the secured party from which information concerning the security interest may be obtained, [4] gives a mailing address of the debtor and [5] contains a statement indicating the types, or describing the items, of collateral.*

There is no dispute that the 2008 Financing Statements met the first four requirements. . . . Instead our discussion is limited only to whether the 2008 Financing Statements "contain a statement indicating the types, or describing the items, of collateral," as required by the then-existing statute.

The 2008 Financing Statements do not describe even the type of collateral, much less the items, at issue. In addition, the referenced document—the Resolution—was held in a different location from the UCC filing office, and the 2008 Financing Statements (including the attached Security Agreement) contain no indication of the referenced document's location or how to find it.

This at best gives an interested party notice about an interest in <u>some</u> undescribed collateral, but does not adequately specify <u>what</u> collateral is encumbered.

We agree with the district court on the particular facts here that the UCC financing statements filed in 2008 did not perfect the Bondholders' security interest, as they lacked a sufficient description of collateral. But we find that the financing statement amendments filed in 2015 and 2016 satisfied the filing requirements for perfection when read in conjunction with the 2008 Financing Statements.

Decision. The appeals court agreed with the trial court that while the 2008 filing statement was insufficient, when viewed in conjunction with the amended 2015 and 2016 filings, the documents satisfied the description requirement to perfect the Bondholders' security interest.

Focus on Ethics

If a bond default had occurred before the amended statements were filed, who would have been harmed? If that had occurred, is it ethically justifiable to move the Bondholders to an unsecured position?

The purpose of filing the financing statement is to give public notice of the security interest to third parties. While the security agreement itself cannot be filed as a financing statement, the information it contains can be used to create the financing statement. It is important to note that a financing statement is distinct from a security agreement and cannot serve as a replacement for it. A financing statement must include the names of both the debtor and the secured party, as well as a description of the collateral. The UCC provides a uniform financing statement form that can be used in all states, as outlined in UCC § 9-521.

DEBTOR'S NAME. A financing statement must be filed under the name of the debtor because this allows a subsequent potential creditor to learn of an already existing security interest in the collateral. UCC § 9-502(a)(1). Minor errors and omissions, even those regarding the debtor's name, will not be considered misleading, so long as a search of the filing office's records, using its standard search methods, would disclose the filings. UCC § 9-506(c).

Example: Am-Pac filed a proof of claim for $130,130.13 against Jim Ross Tires, Inc. (Tires) as evidenced by three financing statements. However, the trustee of Tires argued that one of the financing statements was inadequate because it failed to properly list the debtor's name. Later, Tradition Bank filed a secured claim for $63,033.56 against Tires as evidenced by two financing statements. The trustee for Tires again asserted one of the financing statements failed to properly list the debtor's name and was therefore inadequate. As a result, the court determined that the misstatement of the debtor's name on both financing statements was considered "seriously misleading" as a matter of law and therefore were ineffective to grant security interests in the collateral of Tires. *In re Jim Ross Tires, Inc.*, 379 B.R. 670 (Bankr. S.D. Tex. 2007)

The sufficiency of the name provided for the debtor will vary depending upon the type of entity. UCC § 9-503. When the debtor is a corporation, the name of the debtor that should appear on the financing statement is the name found on the public record of the jurisdiction in which the debtor is organized. UCC § 9-503(a)(1). When the debtor is a trust or the trustee of property that is held in trust, this information must be disclosed in the financing statement and must include the name of the trust as it appears in its formation documents. UCC § 9-503(a)(3). The organizational name of a business entity, and not merely its trade name, should identify a business entity. UCC § 9-503(a)(4)(A).

When an association of individuals do not have a collective name, the individuals of the organization will be named in the financing statement. Sometimes, a business

FIGURE 31.1: Excerpt of UCC Financing Statement

UCC FINANCING STATEMENT
FOLLOW INSTRUCTIONS

A. NAME & PHONE OF CONTACT AT SUBMITTER (optional)

B. E-MAIL CONTACT AT SUBMITTER (optional)

C. SEND ACKNOWLEDGMENT TO: (Name and Address)

SEE BELOW FOR SECURED PARTY CONTACT INFORMATION

THE ABOVE SPACE IS FOR FILING OFFICE USE ONLY

1. DEBTOR'S NAME: Provide only one Debtor name (1a or 1b) (use exact, full name; do not omit, modify, or abbreviate any part of the Debtor's name); if any part of the Individual Debtor's name will not fit in line 1b, leave all of item 1 blank, check here ☐ and provide the Individual Debtor information in item 10 of the Financing Statement Addendum (Form UCC1Ad)

1a. ORGANIZATION'S NAME			
OR 1b. INDIVIDUAL'S SURNAME	FIRST PERSONAL NAME	ADDITIONAL NAME(S)/INITIAL(S)	SUFFIX
1c. MAILING ADDRESS	CITY	STATE / POSTAL CODE	COUNTRY

2. DEBTOR'S NAME: Provide only one Debtor name (2a or 2b) (use exact, full name; do not omit, modify, or abbreviate any part of the Debtor's name); if any part of the Individual Debtor's name will not fit in line 2b, leave all of item 2 blank, check here ☐ and provide the Individual Debtor information in item 10 of the Financing Statement Addendum (Form UCC1Ad)

2a. ORGANIZATION'S NAME			
OR 2b. INDIVIDUAL'S SURNAME	FIRST PERSONAL NAME	ADDITIONAL NAME(S)/INITIAL(S)	SUFFIX
2c. MAILING ADDRESS	CITY	STATE / POSTAL CODE	COUNTRY

3. SECURED PARTY'S NAME (or NAME of ASSIGNEE of ASSIGNOR SECURED PARTY): Provide only one Secured Party name (3a or 3b)

3a. ORGANIZATION'S NAME			
OR 3b. INDIVIDUAL'S SURNAME	FIRST PERSONAL NAME	ADDITIONAL NAME(S)/INITIAL(S)	SUFFIX
3c. MAILING ADDRESS	CITY	STATE / POSTAL CODE	COUNTRY

4. COLLATERAL: This financing statement covers the following collateral:

5. Check only if applicable and check only one box: Collateral is ☐ held in a Trust (see UCC1Ad, item 17 and Instructions) ☐ being administered by a Decedent's Personal Representative

6a. Check only if applicable and check only one box: ☐ Public-Finance Transaction ☐ Manufactured-Home Transaction ☐ A Debtor is a Transmitting Utility

6b. Check only if applicable and check only one box: ☐ Agricultural Lien ☐ Non-UCC Filing

7. ALTERNATIVE DESIGNATION (if applicable): ☐ Lessee/Lessor ☐ Consignee/Consignor ☐ Seller/Buyer ☐ Bailee/Bailor ☐ Licensee/Licensor

8. OPTIONAL FILER REFERENCE DATA:

FILING OFFICE COPY — UCC FINANCING STATEMENT (Form UCC1) (Rev. 07/01/23) will use a trade name that is not the legal name of the business. The listing of a trade name is not sufficient for perfection through filing and the debtor's actual name must also be included. UCC § 9-503(c).

Management Application What Happens When There Is a Name Change?

As depicted above, only three pieces of information are provided on the financing statement — the debtor's name, the name of the secured party, and a description of the collateral. As previously discussed, Article 9 of the UCC requires that inputting the debtor's name into an official database will result in finding the financing statement, and even if there are slight errors, this will not render the financing statement misleading. If a secured party ensures the debtor's name is accurately stated on the financing statement, the debtor may change its name later without affecting the financing statement.

When the name change takes place after the financing statement has been filed, any subsequent searches under the new and correct debtor name will likely not reveal financing statements filed under the old name. When this occurs, the financing statement is no longer in compliance with Article 9 and is rendered misleading. The secured party will maintain its interest in the property acquired before the name change and for a four-month period following the financing statement's becoming misleading. However, in order to protect the security interest in any after-acquired collateral, the secured party must file an amendment by the end of the four-month period. This amendment will simply add a new name, the debtor's new name, to the record.

DESCRIPTION OF COLLATERAL. As previously stated, both the security agreement and the financing statement must include a description of the collateral. Including the description of the collateral on the financing statement allows subsequent creditors to obtain notice as to what property of the debtor is already subject to a perfected security interest.

The description of the collateral may vary between the two documents, as the description in the security agreement must be more exact than the financing statement. For example, it is permissible for a financing statement to include terms like "all of debtor's personal property"; however, recall that this phrasing was not permissible for the security agreement. UCC § 9-504.

LOCATION OF FILING. The majority of states require the financing statement to be filed with the appropriate state office where the debtor is located. In circumstances where the collateral is located in a different state than the debtor, the filing still must occur in the state where the debtor, not the collateral, is located. UCC § 9-301. Determining the location of the debtor will depend on the debtor's type of entity:

- Individual debtors are located in the state of their principal residence.
- For an organization that is registered with the state (corporation or limited liability company), the debtor's location is the state in which the organization is registered.

- All other entities are located in the state in which the business is located. However, if the business has multiple offices, the place where the debtor manages the affairs and operations of the office is the proper location.

WHEN A FILING IS IMPROPER. If a financing statement filing is improper, such as by being filed in the wrong jurisdiction, the security interest is unperfected. In the event of the debtor's bankruptcy or a contest with a duly perfected lienholder, the secured party will be treated as an unsecured creditor. Other creditors will enjoy a superior right to the collateral ahead of the unsecured creditor. For example, the collateral may be seized by the secured creditor(s) and the debtor will not have any remaining assets to pay the unsecured creditor.

Perfection Without Filing

There are two exceptions to the necessity of filing a financing statement to perfect a security interest. The first is when the collateral is transferred to the secured party's possession. The second is when the security interest is perfected upon attachment. UCC § 9-309. In instances of perfection upon attachment, the security interests are automatically perfected when they are created. One of the most common instances of perfection on attachment, a purchase-money security interest, is discussed below.

PERFECTION BY POSSESSION. The UCC does not require that a security agreement be in writing, so long as possession of the collateral is transferred to the secured party. UCC §§ 9-310, 9-312(b), 9-313. Some items are commonly transferred into the possession of the creditor as collateral for a loan (jewelry, electronics, stocks, bonds, and negotiable instruments).

> **Example:** A purchaser of stock was deemed to have a perfected security interest in the stock of a closely held corporation at the time when the company's attorney acquired possession of the certificate on behalf of the purchaser. The stock purchase agreement between the company and the purchaser made it clear that the stock was given as a security for the payment of a note. Therefore, the court determined the purchaser was a secured party entitled to payment prior to any unsecured creditors. *In re Webber*, 350 B.R. 344 (Bankr. S.D. Tex. 2006)

Transferring possession of the collateral may not be possible given the nature of the collateral. Additionally, the transfer of possession is impractical because the collateral in question must remain in the debtor's possession to generate income in order to service the debt.

> **Example:** A debtor who gives a creditor a security interest in the debtor's inventory would not transfer possession of the inventory to the creditor. The debtor needs the inventory to sell to customers.

Purchase-money security interest (PMSI) A security interest in a consumer good that is automatically perfected from the moment the good is purchased on credit.

PERFECTION UPON ATTACHMENT: THE PURCHASE-MONEY SECURITY INTEREST. The UCC provides for many types of security interests that are automatically perfected from the moment they are created. The seller does not need to take any further action to perfect their interest. The most common of these interests is the **purchase-money security interest (PMSI)** in consumer goods. In this context, consumer goods constitute items that are purchased primarily for personal, family, or household use. When one of these goods is purchased on credit, a PMSI is created. The party extending the credit to the debtor to purchase the goods may be either the seller or a financial institution, such as a bank or credit union, provided that the credit is specifically extended for the purchase of that item. If the goods are purchased using a credit card, neither the seller nor the credit card company would be PMSI creditors, as the credit card is a general line of credit and not specifically used for the purchase of the goods.

> **Example:** If Home Depot® were to finance the installation of kitchen cabinets in a residence and received a security interest in the cabinets as a fixture, and if the homeowner were to obtain another loan for which the cabinets served as collateral, Home Depot, as the PMSI creditor, would have priority. This priority is due to the purchase-money security interest rules.

> **Example:** In the example above, if the homeowner purchased the cabinets at Home Depot and financed the cabinets using a credit card, neither Home Depot nor the credit-card company would be PMSI creditors because the credit card is not used specifically for the purchase of the cabinets but is a general line of credit.

EXCEPTIONS TO AUTOMATIC PERFECTION. There are two exceptions to the rule of automatic perfection for PMSI that may apply:

1. The security interest is one that is subject to other federal and state laws that require subsequent actions in order for the interest to be perfected. UCC § 9-311. The most common exception occurs in regard to vehicles and machinery, as many states have certificate-of-title statutes requiring additional steps.
2. The PMSI pertains to a non-consumer good. When the PMSI is for a non-consumer goods such as inventory for a business, it will not be automatically perfected. UCC § 9-324.

THE CLASSIFICATION OF COLLATERAL. Classification of the collateral affects how a security interest is perfected. These distinctions are presented in the chart below:

Concept Summary
Classification of Collateral

Tangible Collateral (Property that is capable of being touched or moved at the time at which the security interest attaches)

	Definition	Manner of Perfection	UCC Provisions
Consumer Goods	Goods that are primarily bought and sold for personal, family, or household uses. UCC § 9-102(a)(23).	When there is a purchase-money security interest—attachment is adequate. Automobiles, boats, and trailers—must be in compliance with certificate-of-title statutes. Other consumer goods—by filing or possession.	UCC §§ 9-301, 9-303, 9-309(1), 9-310(a), 9-313(a)

	Definition	Manner of Perfection	UCC Provisions
Equipment	Goods that are not inventory or farm products, which are primarily bought and sold for a business purpose. UCC § 9-102(a)(33).	By filing or possession by secured property.	UCC §§ 9-301, 9-310(a), 9-313(a)
Farm Products	Goods including crops, livestock, supplies, and products produced in a farming operation. UCC §§ 9-102(a)(34).	By filing or possession by secured property.	UCC §§ 9-301, 9-310(a), 9-3, 9-313(a)
Inventory	Goods, other than farm products, held for sale or by service or lease under contract, including raw materials used in production and work in progress. UCC § 9-102(a)(48).	By filing or possession by secured property.	UCC §§ 9-301, 9-310(a), 9-313(a)
Intangible Collateral (Property that does not have a physical presence)			
	Definition	**Manner of Perfection**	**UCC Provisions**
Accounts	A right to receive payment in exchange for real, personal, tangible, or intangible property, including insurance policies and services rendered. UCC § 9-102(a)(2).	Filing typically required, other than specific assignments that can be perfected by attachment.	UCC §§ 9-301, 9-309(2) & (5), 9-310(a)
Deposit Accounts	An account (demand, time, savings, passbook, etc.) is kept with a bank. UCC § 9-102(a)(29).	Perfection by means of control, such as a bank maintaining the deposit account.	UCC §§ 9-104, 9-304, 9-312(b), 9-314(a)
Chattel Paper	A record, either written or electronic, constituting evidence of both a security interest in goods and a financial obligation. UCC § 9-102(a)(11).	By filing or possession by secured property.	UCC §§ 9-301, 9-310(a), 9-312(a), 9-313(a), 9-314(a)
Negotiable Instruments	Documents such as checks, notes, CDs, drafts used to evidence the right to be paid that are typically transferred upon delivery. UCC § 9-102(a)(47).	By filing or possession, although promissory notes may be perfected by attachment.	UCC §§ 9-301, 9-309(4), 9-310(a), 9-312(a) & (e), 9-313(a)

DURATION OF PERFECTION. A properly filed financing statement is effective for five years from the date of its filing. UCC § 9-515. However, a continuation statement can be filed within six months prior to the date of expiration. The continuation statement will render the filing valid for an additional five years after the date of expiration of the first five-year period. Continuation statements may be filed endlessly. In theory, a financing statement could be effective forever.

If the continuation statement is not filed within the six months prior to the expiration of the financing statement, at the end of the five-year period the perfection will terminate. When the security interest becomes unperfected, if the collateral is purchased for value by a party without knowledge of the security interest, the buyer will take it free of the security interest. UCC § 9-515(c). However, the creditor's interest can be re-perfected even following a lapse of the financing statement.

> **Example:** Bank One® was able to re-perfect its security interest in debtor's assets including inventory, chattel paper, and equipment, by filing a second financing statement subsequent to the lapse of the initial financing statement. The court found Bank One had re-perfected its security interest even though at the time the bankruptcy petition was filed the initial financing statement had lapsed. The court determined that Bank One was in possession of a perfected security interest in the debtor's assets. *In re Aliquippa Machine Co., Inc.*, 343 B.R. 145 (Bankr. W.D. Pa. 2006)

Priorities, Rights, and Duties of Parties

Conflicting interests in the same collateral are resolved by detailed UCC rules. Usually, the party perfecting the security interest first has priority, but there are exceptions to this rule. The UCC will also impose additional rights and duties, in addition to those contained in the security agreement.

Priority

The general rule is that when more than one interest in the same collateral has been perfected, the security interest that is the first to perfect will have priority over any of those perfected later in time. When two parties have a claim in the same collateral, but only one of the interests has been perfected, the perfected interest will have priority. If neither of the interests has been perfected, the security interest that attached first will have priority. A PMSI in consumer goods takes priority over other security interests, without the need for filing a financing statement.

Here is a summary of the UCC's rule of priority in different circumstances:

Situation	UCC Section	Who Has Priority?
A PMSI in consumer goods versus a perfected security interest	§ 9-324(a)	The PMSI creditor in consumer goods.
A perfected security interest versus unsecured creditors and unsecured security interests	§ 9-322(a)(2)	The party with the perfected secured interest will have priority over most other creditors.

Situation	UCC Section	Who Has Priority?
Two conflicting perfected security interests	§ 9-322(a)(1)	The party to perfect the interest first.
Two conflicting unperfected security interests	§ 9-322(a)(3)	The first party to attach.

Exceptions

Sometimes, a secured party's interest in the collateral of a defaulting debtor is not protected against a third-party claim. PMSI creditors (discussed above), buyers in the ordinary course of business (discussed below), as well as buyers of securities, instruments, chattel paper, documents, or farm products may have priority over the secured party in certain circumstances, including in the proceeds of the sale of the collateral.

BUYERS IN THE ORDINARY COURSE OF BUSINESS. One common exception is a buyer in the ordinary course of business. The UCC defines a buyer in the ordinary course of business as a person who, in good faith and without knowledge of a sale violating another's rights in the goods, purchases goods in the ordinary course of business from a person who is in the business of selling goods of that type. UCC § 1-201(9). If buyers were unable to purchase the goods free and clear of a security interest, they would not purchase the goods at all.

> **Example:** A construction company that purchased a used crane from a crane dealer was a buyer in the ordinary course of business, allowing the construction company to purchase the crane free and clear of the security interest held by the dealer's lender in its inventory. *Financial Federal Credit, Inc. v. Ramar Crane Services, LLC*, 604 F. App'x 38 (2d Cir. 2015)

Rights and Duties

In addition to those rights and duties stated in the security agreement, the UCC also provides some additional features when parties use a financing statement:

1. *Information requests.* At the time of filing, a secured party may request that a filing officer include the file number, date, and time of the original filing on the copy. UCC § 9-523(a). A copy must be sent by the filing officer to the person indicated by the secured party.

   If a party is considering procuring a security interest from a potential debtor, they may request the filing officer to provide a certificate identifying all perfected financing statements in the property of that debtor.
2. *Amendment.* The information contained in the financing statement can be amended. Pursuant to UCC § 9-512, collateral may be added or deleted as stated in the financing statement. An amendment may add a debtor. UCC § 9-512(d).

   While most amendments are effective upon the filing of the amendment, they are not effective if they delete all debtors or all secured parties of record. Thus, an amendment cannot leave a financing statement without a debtor or secured party. UCC § 9-512(e).

3. *Assignment.* Generally, the secured party may assign its security interest. This can be done from the very beginning in the initial financing statement by including a provision that would grant the secured party the power to authorize an amendment to the financing statement by providing the name and mailing address of the assignee in substitution of the name and address of the secured party. UCC § 9-514(a).

   Another way in which the secured party can have the power to assign is by filing an amendment of the financing statement that (1) identifies the initial financing statement by reference to its file number; (2) provides the name of the assignor (secured party); and (3) provides the name and mailing address of the assignee. UCC § 9-514(b).
4. *Release.* The secured party has the discretion to release a portion, or all of the collateral specified in a financing statement. This action terminates a security interest in the collateral.

Request for an accounting
Debtor's right to ask the creditor to provide an accounting of any unpaid obligations that are secured by the collateral.

5. *Accounting or confirmation request from debtor.* The debtor may **request an accounting**. The debtor can request the creditor (secured party) to provide a calculation of the unpaid obligations secured by collateral. In other words, the debtor can ask the secured party, "How much do I still owe you?"

   If the secured party receives such a request, they must typically respond within 14 days. UCC § 9-210(c)-(d). A debtor is allowed one request free of charge during any six-month period. For additional responses, the secured party may require a payment from the creditor not to exceed $25. UCC § 9-210(f).

Termination statement
Creditor-issued document confirming that the debt or obligation of the debtor has been repaid. Releases its security interest in the collateral.

6. *Termination statement.* Once the debtor has satisfied its obligations to the creditor, the debtor should insist that a termination statement be filed. The purpose of the **termination statement** is to allow the debtor to "clean up" their record and remove evidence of security interests that have already been satisfied. Typically, the creditor is only required to file a termination statement if the debtor makes such a demand. However, when consumer goods have been secured by the security interest, the creditor must file the termination statement within either 20 days of receiving the debtor's demand or within a month of the final payment, whichever is earlier. UCC § 9-513(b).

   If the secured party fails to provide or file a termination statement when it is obligated to do so, the secured party can be liable for minimum statutory damages of $500. UCC § 9-625(e)(4). In addition, the debtor can also recover for any actual damages suffered because of the secured party's failure to comply with this requirement. UCC § 9-625(b).

Example: Debtor was unable to obtain a favorable 7 percent loan from Lender because of an outstanding financing statement because Creditor neither provided nor filed a termination statement when obligated to do so. As a result, Debtor ended up having to pay 9 percent interest. Under the UCC, Debtor could recover damages equal to the extra 2 percent interest they would have to pay under the new loan.

Defaults and Remedies

Default
When a borrower fails to observe their duties and promises as set forth in an agreement.

A **default** occurs when a borrower fails to observe their duties and promises as set forth in an agreement. In the context of secured transactions, this generally means that the debtor did not pay the creditor. However, the UCC does not define or specify what exactly constitutes a default or when it occurs. Thus, either general contract law or the security agreement will determine when a default occurs. Defaults and the remedies available to the creditor will be discussed in the context of real property in the following chapter, while the discussion of default in this chapter focuses on personal property.

After default, any applicable provisions of the UCC govern the rights and remedies of the parties. There are three primary remedies the creditor is entitled to upon default by the debtor: (1) repossession, (2) strict foreclosure, and (3) sale of collateral.

Repossession

A creditor is entitled upon default to **repossession**. Repossession is the secured party's taking possession of the collateral on default. Following repossession, the secured party may either keep the collateral (strict foreclosure) or sell the collateral and use the proceeds from the sale of the collateral to decrease the debt owed.

Repossession
A remedy in the event of a default that allows the secured party to take possession of the collateral.

> **Example:** Consumer purchased a used vehicle from Oyster Point Dodge (Oyster). Three weeks later the consumer's credit application was rejected. Oyster did not inform the consumer of the rejection. Shortly thereafter, the consumer made his first monthly payment for the vehicle. A few days later, Oyster asked the consumer to return to the dealership. While at the dealership, Oyster took possession of the car, and the consumer was reimbursed for his monthly payment. In a subsequent action by the consumer, the court found that the repossession of the used vehicle was improper because the consumer was not in default at the time of repossession. *Padin v. Oyster Point Dodge*, 397 F. Supp. 2d 712 (E.D. Va. 2005)

If repossession can occur without "breaching the peace," the taking is allowed without judicial process. UCC § 9-609. The phrase "breaching the peace" is not defined in the UCC and is left to the courts to decide on a case-by-case basis. Typically, an act will be found to breach the peace if a trespass on land, assault or battery, or breaking and entering occurs while the creditor is attempting to repossess the collateral.

Strict Foreclosure

Strict foreclosure, also known as acceptance of collateral, permits the secured party, after default and repossession, to retain the collateral in full or partial satisfaction of the debt owed by the debtor without selling or disposing of the collateral. UCC § 9-620(a).

Strict foreclosure
Creditor's acquisition of the debtor's interest without a sale or disposition.

If the secured party elects to retain the collateral, it must comply with two requirements. First, the secured party must provide notice to the debtor that it will retain the collateral. Second, the secured party must provide notice to other secured parties who claim an interest in the collateral that the secured party knows of, unless the collateral is consumer goods. Any secured party who has received this notice has 20 days to object; if no objection is made, the original secured party may retain the collateral. UCC §§ 9-620(a), 9-621.

Sale of Collateral

Another remedy available to the creditor upon default is to permit the sale, lease, license, or other disposition of any collateral at the time of default or following any commercially reasonable preparation or processing. UCC § 9-610(a). When the secured party (creditor) disposes of the collateral after default, the security interest under which the disposition occurred is discharged.

The sale of the collateral can take place at either a public sale (auction) or a private sale, so long as all aspects of the sale are "commercially reasonable." UCC § 9-610(b). Once the collateral has been sold, the proceeds from the sale are applied in the following order:

1. To cover any reasonable expenses incurred because of the secured party's repossession, storage, and resale of the collateral;
2. To pay the balance of the debt owed to the secured party;
3. To pay the debts owed to any other lienholders who have made the requisite written or authenticated demands; then
4. Any remaining proceeds from the sale will go to the debtor, unless the collateral is in the form of accounts, promissory notes, or chattel paper.

If the secured party does not receive cash for the deposition of the collateral, the secured party must determine the value of the proceeds received. This amount must then be applied to the debt that is outstanding in a commercially reasonable manner. UCC §§ 9-608(a), 9-615(c).

PROCEDURES TO SELL THE COLLATERAL. The UCC requires the secured party to provide notice of the sale to the debtor and all secured parties in that collateral. This notice occurs prior to the sale unless the goods are perishable or the value of the goods will diminish rapidly. UCC § 9-611(b),(c). This right to notice may be waived by the debtor after the default has occurred. UCC § 9-624(a).

The property must be sold or otherwise disposed of in a commercially reasonable manner. UCC § 9-610(b). Failure to dispose of the collateral in a commercially reasonable manner may negatively affect the collateral's sales price. Failure to use a commercially reasonable manner to dispose of the collateral will result in the court decreasing the amount the secured party is entitled to upon a deficiency judgment. UCC § 9-626(a)(3).

In the following case, the court considered whether the disposition of collateral occurred in a commercially reasonable manner.

CASE 31.2

FORECLOSURE UPON THE COLLATERAL MUST BE COMMERCIALLY REASONABLE

ICON AGENTS, LLC v. KANZA CONSTRUCTION, INC.

364 P.3d 579 (2016)

Court of Appeals of Kansas

In March 2012, Kanza Construction, Inc. (Kanza) received a $12.5 million loan from Icon Agents, LLC (Icon), which was secured by equipment owed by Kanza and guaranties from its owners Steve and Mary Hutchinson. The loan was made by a group of lenders, who appointed Icon as their agent for the transaction. Part of Icon's duties as agent included holding the collateral and enforcing the loan agreement against Kanza and the Hutchinsons on behalf of the lenders. Icon perfected its security interest in Kanza's property. Within a month of the closing, Kanza defaulted. In June 2012, Icon made written demands upon Kanza and the Hutchinsons as guarantors, requesting payment and delivery of the collateral. Kanza agreed with a third party to sell its collateralized equipment. Three auctions took place between August and December of 2012, but a significant amount of the balance remained unpaid. Icon sent a final demand in January 2013, requesting payment and possession of the remaining collateral. The remaining collateral was sold in March 2013, but an outstanding balance still remained. Icon filed suit against Kanza to recover the remaining amount due. The trial court entered a deficiency judgment in favor of Icon for $7,224,613.59 and found that the collateral had been sold in a commercially reasonable manner. The Hutchinsons appealed arguing that no evidence had been offered to support the commercially reasonable value of the assets sold at auction.

Language of the Court. *Our Supreme Court set out nine nonexclusive factors to consider in determining whether a sale was commercially reasonable:*

(1) *the duty to clean up, fix up, and paint up the collateral;*
(2) *whether disposition was made public or private;*
(3) *whether the collateral was disposed of wholesale or retail;*
(4) *whether the collateral was disposed of by unit or in parcels;*
(5) *the creditor's duty to publicize the sale;*
(6) *the length of time the collateral is held prior to the sale;*
(7) *the creditor's duty to give notice of the sale to the debtor and competing secured parties;*
(8) *the actual price received at the sale; and*
(9) *other factors such as the number of bids received and the method employed to solicit bids.*

The determination of whether such a sale is commercially reasonable must be made on a case-by-case basis considering the factors and the aggregate of circumstances shown. The fact that a better price could have been obtained at a different time or by using a different method is not sufficient to show that the sale was not commercially reasonable.

The Hutchinsons argue that absent evidence of the exact value of the equipment sold there is "no way to determine the commercial reasonableness of the price received at the fire sale auction." But our UCC statute on commercially reasonable dispositions expresses the factors establishing a commercially reasonable sale in the alternative.

Here, the evidence at trial established that the sale was conducted in the usual manner for the market for such equipment and was in conformity with reasonable commercial practices among dealers in the type of property that was being sold. There was testimony that Icon selected Ritchie Brothers to perform the sale based on its experience auctioning heavy and rail equipment. There were at least 200 rail-related companies that had either attended its sales or were part of its database of equipment buyers. There was testimony that Ritchie Brothers is the world's largest industrial auction company, conducting several auctions a year at each of its auction sites where it assembles heavy equipment from numerous sources. It establishes set auction dates in order to permit it to assemble a sufficient volume of equipment to attract buyers. Ritchie Brothers had prior experience selling railroad construction equipment. Icon introduced exhibits showing data from the sale as well as marketing that occurred prior to the sale. Icon presented evidence of the sale price of each and every item of collateral sold at the auction and compared those prices to certain values asserted by Hutchinson.

There was substantial evidence to support the conclusion that the sale was conducted in a commercially reasonable manner.

Decision. The Court of Appeals of Kansas affirmed the trial court's decision, finding Icon was entitled to a deficiency judgment for the amount due and that the collateral had been sold in a commercially reasonable manner.

Focus on Ethics

Does the fact that Kanza defaulted on the loan within a month raise any red flags? Should the lenders have known Kanza would be unable to repay the loan?

Deficiency Judgment

Often, the debtor will still owe money to the creditor after the creditor has retained or sold the collateral. Normally, the debtor will still be liable for the amount that is due. To collect, the creditor obtains a deficiency judgment from a court. However, often this does not result in the creditor's receiving the remaining balance, as debtors who default on the loan in the first place often cannot pay the deficiency judgment resulting in a "paper judgment," meaning the creditor receives no payment; it is uncollectible.

Debtor's Right of Redemption

Right of redemption Right of the debtor to free the collateral from the security interest upon fulfilling all obligations and paying any reasonable expenses.

Unless the debtor waives its rights in the collateral following defaulting, the debtor has a **right of redemption**. The right of redemption allows the debtor to regain possession and ownership of the collateral, free of the security interest. To accomplish this the debtor must pay the amount owed to the secured party, as well as reasonable expenses and attorneys' fees incurred by the secured party as a result of the debtor's default.

Consumer Goods

The UCC treats consumer transactions differently than business transactions. The purpose is to afford special protections to consumer transactions. When the collateral is a consumer good, the secured party must sell the collateral within 90 days if the debtor has paid more than 60 percent of the amount due if the interest is not a PMSI. UCC § 9-620(e). Otherwise, the secured party is liable to the debtor for damages. UCC § 9-625(b). After default, the secured party may require the debtor to waive the sale of the secured goods. UCC § 9-624.

AI Feature: Draft a Personal Guarantee

Having read this chapter, conduct research using an internet search engine to determine what provisions a creditor should insert within a written guarantee of debt agreement. Then, using an AI program, draft one for an electrical supply house that obtains a personal guarantee with respect to all its corporate customer accounts. Ensure that the following provisions are addressed:

- There is consideration given for the guarantee.
- What happens when the credit limits need to be increased?
- Does the supply house have to sue the debtor corporation before proceeding against the guarantor?

Ensure that all waivers by the guarantor you choose to insert are lawful under the laws of your home state.

Key Terms

- Artisan's lien, 780
- Collateral, 784
- Creditor, 778
- Debtor, 778
- Default, 800
- Floating lien, 790
- Garnishment, 781
- Guaranty, 782
- Judicial lien, 780
- Lien, 778
- Mechanic's lien, 778
- Perfection, 790
- Perfection through filing, 790
- Purchase-money security interest (PMSI), 795
- Repossession, 801
- Request for an accounting, 800
- Right of contribution, 783
- Right of redemption, 804
- Right of reimbursement, 783
- Right of subrogation, 783
- Rights in the collateral, 789
- Secured party, 784
- Secured transaction, 784
- Security agreement, 784
- Strict foreclosure, 801
- Suretyship, 782
- Termination statement, 800
- Writ of attachment, 780
- Writ of execution, 780

Applying the Law

31.1 Research the Law. Using an internet search engine, research those security interests listed in the UCC that are automatically perfected at the time of creation.

31.2 Research the Law. Using an internet search engine, research the law in your state to determine who may record a mechanic's lien upon real property. What procedures are required by your state to obtain a security interest in personal property?

31.3 Who Has Priority? In 2005, Ag Venture made a $457,000 loan to Montagne Heifers, Inc. (MHI). MHI was owned by Michael Montage, with his wife and son being shareholders and employees. The loan from Ag Venture was secured by collateral in the form of MHI's livestock, inventory, farm products, equipment, accounts, and proceeds. A year after the loan, Michael separated from his wife. The separation agreement between Michael and his wife gave her money and some parcels of land. Then in 2007, Michael gave his son a $100,000 promissory note in exchange for his shares in MHI. This note also listed MHI's livestock, inventory, equipment, and proceeds as collateral. In 2008, when Michael filed for bankruptcy, a dispute arose between Ag Venture, the son, and the ex-wife regarding which party was entitled to the proceeds from a $500,000 sale of livestock in 2007. Assuming the sale occurred after Michael acquired his son's shares, whose security interest has priority? *In re Montagne*, 417 B.R. 214 (Bankr. D. Vt. 2009)

31.4 Security Interest. Yamaha Motor Corporation, U.S.A.® entered into a dealer franchise agreement with Tri-City Motors & Sports. The dealer executed a security agreement with Yamaha granting Yamaha a security interest in all motorcycles, and their proceeds, sold to the dealer on credit. A financing statement was filed. Several years later a bank was notified that Yamaha was considering entering into an inventory financing agreement with the dealer. The bank requested a repurchase agreement from Yamaha whereby it could sell any motorcycles back to the manufacturer which it found necessary to repossess from Tri-City. Yamaha agreed to this arrangement and a security interest in the dealer's motorcycles was given by the dealer to the bank. The Tri-City sold the dealership franchise along with inventory to Lakeside Motors. The checks of Tri-City to Yamaha for inventory dated a few days prior to the sale were refused for payment because of insufficient funds in the dealer's account. The Lakeside Motors and the bank entered into a security agreement covering the inventory supplied by Yamaha. Upon the eventual sale of the inventory, Lakeside Motors paid the debt it owed to the bank but did not pay Yamaha. Yamaha waited two years before suing to recover the sums due from Tri-City. The trial court held that Yamaha had not acted seasonably to protect its rights. Yamaha appealed, arguing that its security interest was prior to the interest of the bank. How should the court rule? *Yamaha Motor Corp. v. Tri-City Motors & Sports, Inc.*, 171 Mich. App. 260 (1988)

31.5 Lapsed Security Interest. In January of 2011, The Thoman Trust perfected a security interest in the farm equipment and vehicles that it sold to Ronald Novak, The Trust did not file a continuation statement for its financing statement. It lapsed on January 14, 2016, five years after its statement's original filing date. At the time Novak filed bankruptcy in October 2017, Novak owed First National Bank more than $840,000, To secure that debt, Novak gave the Bank security interests in all his assets, including the Trust collateral. The Bank filed a financing statement on January 7, 2014. What advice did the court share with respect to conflicting security in the same collateral? *First National Bank and Trust v. Novak (In re Novak)*, Bankr. LEXIS 2586 (Bankr. D. Kan. 2018)

31.6 Holder of a Perfected Security. United Thrift Stores was a retailer of home appliances to consumers. When United Thrift filed for bankruptcy, Redisco sought to reclaim the assets listed in its security agreement with United Thrift. Redisco had filed a financing statement that listed Redisco as a secured creditor to the debtor United Thrift. The trial court determined that Redisco was not a perfected secured creditor because the company filed before it had created a security agreement. On appeal, how should the court rule? *In the Matter of United Thrift Stores, Inc., Bankrupt*, 242 F. Supp. 714 (1965)

31.7 DBA as the Debtor's Name. Over the years, Hastings State Bank made several loans to EDM, in excess of $4.5 million. As a result, Hastings filed a financing statement with the Nebraska Secretary of State. In its financing statement, Hastings identified the debtor as "EDM CORPORATION D/B/A EDM EQUIPMENT." Would that financing statement likely be sufficient to provide the name of the debtor, as required for a financing statement to perfect the bank's security interest in most states? *In re EDM Corp.*, 431 B.R. 459 (B.A.P. 8th Cir. 2010)

31.8 Lien Creditor's Constructive Trust in Lathe or Seller's Security Interest? There are two competing claims to the right of possession of an industrial lathe that was purchased with stolen funds. First, in May 2010, Davis-Lynch filed a motion to enforce a constructive trust on all equipment purchased by Hanna-Skye with the stolen funds. A constructive trust arose in favor of Davis-Lynch in June 2009 after Hanna-Skye made partial payments for the lathe using Davis-Lynch's stolen funds and when Marathon transferred the lathe to Hanna-Skye. A person claiming equitable ownership under a constructive trust was a lien creditor with respect to the property covered by the trust. Accordingly, Davis-Lynch became a lien creditor with rights to the lathe seven months before Marathon perfected its security interest in February 2010. Next, on November 12, 2010, Marathon sued Davis-Lynch in Texas state court, alleging Marathon had a superior security interest to the lien creditor in the lathe. Marathon and Davis-Lynch filed competing traditional motions for summary judgment. Whose competing claim is likely to prevail? *Marathon Mach. Tools, Inc. v. Davis-Lynch, Inc.*, 400 S.W.3d 133 (Tex. App. 2013)

31.9 Estopped from Denying the Creation of a Security Interest. Debtor transferred $170,000.00 from its checking account for the purposes of opening a certificate of deposit in the name of the Debtor's subsidiary, Terrabon Research Company LLC. Thereafter, the subsidiary assigned, transferred, and pledged all of its interest in the CD to Comerica as security for the subsidiary's present and future indebtedness to Comerica. In fact, it was Gary Luce, the chief executive officer of the Debtor and the subsidiary and agent of the subsidiary, who executed the assignment on the subsidiary's behalf. As such, Comerica issued a $170,000.00 letter of credit on the subsidiary's behalf. Here, the Debtor argued that only it owned the security interest, and not the subsidiary. However, Comerica argued that even if the Debtor, not the subsidiary, owns the CD, the subsidiary nevertheless had sufficient rights and displayed apparent authority as to be able convey and create a security interest. Comerica argued that both the Debtor and the subsidiary created a security interest. Who is likely to prevail? Why? *Sommers v. Comerica Bank, N.A. (In re Terrabon, Inc.)*, 2013 Bankr. LEXIS 4965 (Bankr. S.D. Tex. 2013)

31.10 Action for Equitable Contribution. Smith and Kleynerman were each 50 percent shareholders in EMW. They both executed a promissory note in favor of the bank in the amount of $379,093.42, plus interest, payable in monthly installments. Moreover, Smith and Kleynerman were each personally liable for EMW's obligation to the bank pursuant to continuing guarantees. Unfortunately, EMW eventually ceased generating revenue and was unable able to make payments on its obligations to the bank; however, for a period of time thereafter, Smith and Kleynerman made payments to the bank on EMW's behalf by utilizing revenue from another business and from personal resources. Ultimately, they were unable to continue paying back EMW's debt, and EMW defaulted on its payments on the promissory note. EMW owed approximately a total, including interest, of approximately $539,400. First, Smith settled with the bank as to the amount due of around $240,000, which Smith paid. After Smith's settlement, Kleynerman was released from his obligation by the bank by only paying around $10,000. Smith then demanded contribution from Kleynerman, because Smith paid more than his fair share because the original amount owed was $379,093.42. Will Kleynerman have to contribute anything, other than attorney's fees? Why or why not? *BMO Harris Bank, N.A. v. European Motor Works*, 372 Wis. 2d 656, 668 (Ct. App. 2016)

Financing, Defaults, and Foreclosures of Real Property

32

Thieves respect property. They merely wish the property to become their property, that they may more perfectly respect it. — G.K. Chesterton, English writer (1874-1936)

Chapter Outline

- Introduction
- Introduction to Mortgages
- The Mortgage Process
- Mortgage Creation and Terms
  - *Management Application: Secured Promissory Note*
- Predatory Lending

Case 32.1: *Bank of Am. Corp. v. City of Miami*

- Types of Loan Payments
- Taking Subject to and Assuming Mortgages
- Deeds of Trust
- Default
- Installment Land Sale Contracts

Case 32.2: *Bean v. Walker*

- AI Feature: Draft a Default Clause for a Commercial Mortgage

Learning Objectives

After studying this chapter, you should be able to:

1. Describe the differences between mortgages and deeds of trust.
2. State the essential terms of notes and mortgages.
3. Describe the various types of mortgages.
4. Understand the differences between taking subject to and assuming a mortgage.
5. Explain how foreclosure of real property occurs.

Introduction

We begin this chapter's discussion with a review of financing the purchase and sale of real property. Unless a buyer purchases a property using cash, a lender will be required to extend credit to the borrower to provide financing for the purchase. This process involves creation of a mortgage, deed of trust, or land sale installment contract, which are discussed in this chapter.

Introduction to Mortgages

FIGURE 32.1: A Mortgage

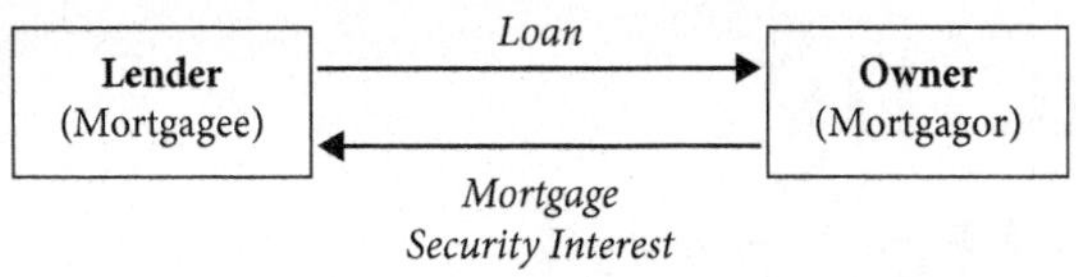

Mortgage
A real estate security instrument. Borrower retains title but gives a lien interest and note to the lender.

Hypothecated
To pledge real property as security without giving up possession to guarantee the repayment of the loan.

Mortgagor
The owner-borrower in a mortgage agreement.

Mortgagee
The lender or creditor in a mortgage agreement.

When a party does not purchase a property using all cash, it must borrow all or a portion of the purchase price. A **mortgage** is a two-party instrument financing arrangement in which one person, usually the purchaser, borrows money from a lender. It creates a lien on the borrower's property. Most states use mortgages to secure a real estate loan; however, some states may create their own unique requirements for a mortgage's creation and enforcement. States may also use other instruments in lieu of a mortgage, such as the deed of trust, discussed later in this chapter.

When real property is subject to a mortgage, it is **hypothecated**. That means the property is pledged as security to guarantee the repayment of the loan. The borrower retains possession of the property during the mortgage term. The owner-borrower is the **mortgagor**, and the lender or creditor is the **mortgagee**. If the borrower fails to fulfill an obligation, the borrower defaults on the loan. The lender can then foreclose on the property and sell it at a public auction.

The Mortgage Process

Obtaining a mortgage can be painless, exceptionally time consuming, or somewhere in the middle. Current market conditions, available financing, and the applicant's financial position affect the experience.

FIGURE 32.2: The Mortgage Process

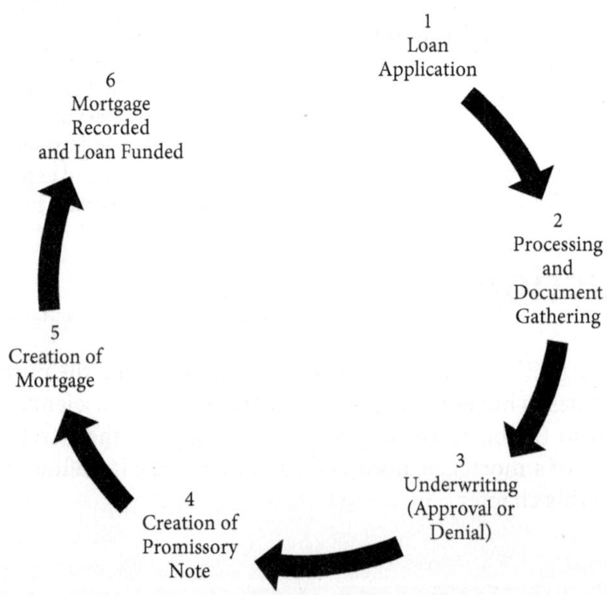

Loan Application

The first step in obtaining a mortgage loan is the application. Many people utilize mortgage bankers, who are also known as mortgage loan originators (MLOs), loan officers, or loan specialists. Mortgage bankers do not lend money directly; they act as intermediaries, gathering the applicant's information and shopping the applicant to potential lenders. The mortgage banker then provides the applicant with a list of potential lenders who would agree to provide a loan to the applicant, as well as those lenders' financing terms.

Once a lender is selected, the mortgage banker submits the loan application to the lender and facilitates the funding and closing of the transaction. One of the benefits of using a mortgage banker is the access to potentially lower interest rates. Rather than utilizing a mortgage broker, an applicant can also apply for a loan directly from a bank, credit union, or other financial institution.

Many people prefer to use a bank or credit union directly because they have an established relationship with the bank or credit union, feel a sense of trust, or prefer the ease of gathering documentation if the business holds the applicant's checking, savings, or other investment accounts.

Underwriting

The lender's process of analyzing documentation, assessing the value of the real property, and approving the loan is called underwriting. In underwriting, the borrower's creditworthiness; the property's condition, location, and current use; other relevant economic influences; and the laws pertaining to the foreclosure procedures available to the lender become part of the decision to make the loan.

Approval or Denial

Once underwriting has been completed, the loan is either approved or denied. Federal law requires the lender to disclose the specific reasons for a loan's denial. If the loan has been approved, a promissory note and its security instrument (such as a mortgage or deed of trust) are issued.

Mortgage Creation and Terms

Two documents exist with nearly every mortgage. The first is the promissory note, and the second is the mortgage.

Creation of a Promissory Note

The **promissory note** is the borrower's promise to repay the money borrowed. A borrower who defaults on the repayment may be personally liable for the debt owed. The promissory note is the contract between the parties to repay the obligation. The person who borrows money and enters into the promissory note is called the maker or the **debtor**. The person who provided the financing is known as the **payee**. The note may or may not be secured by a mortgage or deed of trust.

Promissory note
An executed (signed) instrument acknowledging a debt and promising to pay a creditor.

Debtor
A person who executes (signs) a note or contract and is primarily liable for repayment.

Payee
A person who receives payment under a note or negotiable instrument.

The promissory note does not create an interest in land, but it serves the important function of showing that the borrower is indebted to the creditor. The promissory note because it contains a fixed, determinable date of payment, is a negotiable instrument. As negotiable instruments, promissory notes can be sold, transferred, or conveyed to another.

Management Application
Secured Promissory Note

$________________
[Date]____________

FOR VALUE RECEIVED, _______ (hereinafter "Borrower"), promises to pay to _______ (hereinafter "Lender") at the following address at _______, or at such place as Lender may from time to time designate in writing, in legal tender of the United States of America, the unpaid principal amount _______ ($_______), together with interest on the unpaid principal balance from time to time outstanding at the rate of _______ (_______%) per annum, simple interest accruing monthly (hereinafter "Note").

This Note shall be subject to the following additional provisions:

1. *Payment of Principal and Interest.* Principal and interest shall be payable in consecutive monthly installments of _______ dollars ($_______) or more on the first day of each month beginning _______. Such payments shall continue until the entire indebtedness evidenced by this Note and all accrued and unpaid interest is fully paid, with any unpaid principal and interest due and payable on _______ (the Maturity Date).

   Each payment under this Note shall be credited in the following order: (a) costs, fees, charges, and advances paid or incurred by Lender or payable to Lender and interest under any provision of this Note in such order as Lender, in its sole and absolute discretion, elects; (b) interest payable under the Note; and (c) principal under the Note.

2. *Prepayment.* Prepayment in whole or part may occur at any time hereunder without penalty; and provided further that any such partial prepayment shall not operate to postpone or suspend the obligation to make and shall not have the effect of altering the time for payment of the remaining balance of the Note as provided for above, unless and until the entire obligation is paid in full. All payments received hereunder shall be applied, first, to any costs or expenses incurred by Lender in collecting such payment or to any other unpaid charges or expenses due hereunder; second, to accrued interest; and third, to principal.

3. *Default and Acceleration.* On (a) Borrower's failure to pay any installment or other sum due under this Note when due and payable (whether by extension, acceleration, or otherwise), (b) any breach of any other promise or obligation in this Note or in any other instrument now or hereafter securing the indebtedness evidenced by this Note, or (c) if all or any part of the property or any interest in the property is sold or transferred without Lender's prior written consent, then, and in any such event, Lender may, at its option, declare this Note (including, without limitation, all accrued interest) due

and payable immediately regardless of the Maturity Date. Borrower expressly waives notice of the exercise of this option.

4. *Late Charge.* Borrower acknowledges that default in the payment of any sum due under this Note will result in losses and additional expenses to Lender in servicing the indebtedness evidenced by this Note, handling such delinquent payments, and meeting its other financial obligations. Borrower further acknowledges that the extent of such loss and additional expenses is extremely difficult and impractical to ascertain. Borrower agrees that, if any payment due under this Note is not made within ____ days when due, a charge of _____ cents ($0.__) for each dollar ($1.00) that is not paid when due would be a reasonable estimate of expenses so incurred (the Late Charge).
5. *Interest on Interest.* If any interest payment under this Note is not paid when due, the unpaid interest shall be added to the principal of this Note, shall become and be treated as principal, and shall thereafter bear like interest.
6. *Notice.* Any notice or demand to be given to the parties hereunder shall be deemed to have been given to and received by them and shall be effective when personally delivered or when deposited in the U.S. mail, certified or registered mail, return receipt requested, postage prepaid, and addressed to the party at the addresses set forth above, or at such other address as the one of the parties may hereafter designate in writing to the other party.
7. *Waiver.* The Borrower, endorsers, and all other persons liable or to become liable on this Note, waive presentment for payment, protest, demand, notice of protest, notice of dishonor, and notice of nonpayment, and expressly agree that this Note, or any payment hereunder, may be extended from time to time by the Lender without in any way affecting its liability hereunder.
8. *Collateral.* This Note is secured pursuant to the terms of the Mortgage between Borrower and Lender dated of even date herewith. The entirety of the terms and conditions of the Mortgage executed by Borrower concurrently herewith is incorporated herein as if set forth in full.
9. *Miscellaneous.* This Note shall be governed and construed in accordance with the Laws of the State of ___________. This Note shall bind and inure to the benefit of Borrower's and Lender's successors and assigns. Time is of the essence for every obligation under this Note. If any court of competent jurisdiction holds any provision of this Note to be illegal, unenforceable, or invalid in whole or in part for any reason, the validity and enforceability of the remaining provisions, or portions of them, will not be affected. Any rule of construction to the effect that ambiguities are to be resolved against the drafting party shall not apply in interpreting this Note. In the event any action is required to enforce the terms of this Note, the prevailing party is entitled to recover their reasonable attorney fees, costs, and expenses in such collection action.

EXECUTED as of the date first written above.

Borrower:

By: ____________________________

Print Name: ____________________

Creation of a Mortgage

The mortgage is a document that gives the lender the right to have the property sold to repay the loan (the promissory note) if the borrower defaults under the terms of the note. The mortgage is recorded on the title to the property and creates an interest in land. Because a mortgage affects an interest in land, the Statute of Frauds requires that it be evidenced by a writing to be enforceable.

With a promissory note and mortgage, a lender can, subject to purchase money mortgage exceptions (discussed later in this chapter), sue a borrower to collect against the promissory note and foreclose on the property that secures the mortgage. This provides the lender with a higher degree of protection in lending money.

Mortgage Terms

While most lenders provide mortgages in a standardized form, a mortgage requires an expression of intent by the parties to create a security interest in the property pledged as collateral for a promissory note. Because mortgages are subject to state law, states may impose additional requirements and terms for a valid mortgage.

First and Second Mortgages

First mortgage The mortgage that is recorded first in time.

Second mortgage The mortgage recorded next in time after a first mortgage is recorded.

The same piece of real property can be used as collateral for more than one loan. The **first mortgage** is the one that is recorded first in time. The **second mortgage** is the mortgage recorded next in time. It is possible to have additional mortgages — third mortgages, fourth mortgages, and so on — but this is not common. Second mortgages have a "junior" position behind the first mortgage. If the first mortgage lender forecloses its lien, the second mortgage lien is terminated at the foreclosure sale (but not the related debt owed to the lender). Compared to first mortgages, second mortgages (and third mortgages, fourth mortgages, and so on) are usually offered for shorter periods of time and have higher interest rates than first mortgages to compensate for the increased risk.

Predatory Lending

Predatory lending A term used to describe illegal and abusive lending practices.

Predatory lending is the term used to characterize unfair and deceptive mortgage practices directed at consumers by unscrupulous lenders who prey upon the poor, the undereducated, and the naïve. The following are some, but not all, of the practices considered predatory by the Mortgage Bankers Association:

- Steering borrowers to high-rate lenders
- Structuring high-cost loans with payments the borrower cannot afford
- Falsifying loan documents
- Making loans to those lacking mental capacity
- Forging signatures on loan documents
- Making adverse changes to the loan terms at closing
- Falsely identifying the loan as a line of credit or open-end mortgage

- Charging excessive prepayment penalties or excessive charges for preparing loan releases
- Failing to provide accurate loan balance and payoff amounts, including failing to respond promptly to an inquiry for a loan payoff

In the following case, the City of Miami, Florida, sued Bank of America and Wells Fargo for predatory lending practices. Miami alleged that these banks violated the Fair Housing Act by unfairly imposing predatory conditions on loans granted to minority borrowers.

CASE 32.1

PROXIMATE CAUSE IS THE STANDARD FOR REVIEWING VIOLATIONS OF THE FAIR HOUSING ACT

BANK OF AMERICA CORP. v. CITY OF MIAMI

581 U.S. 189 (2017)

Supreme Court of the United States

The City of Miami, Florida, sued Bank of America and Wells Fargo for discriminatory lending practices, specifically for offering riskier mortgage loans to minority borrowers with more predatory conditions. Miami argued that the banks unjustly enriched themselves by taking advantage of benefits conferred by the city, that their actions denied the city of expected property and tax revenues, and cost the city money that it would not have had to pay had the banks not engaged in these predatory lending practices. The banks argued that Miami's claims are not covered under the Fair Housing Act (FHA) and lacked the element of causation.

The district court dismissed the FHA claims and held that Miami did not fall within the "zone of interests" the statute was meant to protect and did not have standing to sue. The court also held that Miami had not adequately shown that the banks' conduct was the proximate cause of the harm the city claimed to have suffered. The Court of Appeals for the Eleventh Circuit reversed and held that plaintiffs did have standing to sue and that Miami had sufficiently shown that the banks' actions were the proximate cause of the harm because the harm was reasonably foreseeable as a result of the actions.

Language of the Court. *The City of Miami brought lawsuits in federal court against two banks, Bank of America and Wells Fargo. The City's complaints charge that the Banks discriminatorily imposed more onerous, and indeed "predatory," conditions on loans made to minority borrowers than to similarly situated nonminority borrowers. Those "predatory" practices included, among others, excessively high interest rates, unjustified fees, teaser low-rate loans that overstated refinancing opportunities, large prepayment penalties, and—when default loomed—unjustified refusals to refinance or modify the loans. Due to the* *discriminatory nature of the Banks' practices, default and foreclosure rates among minority borrowers were higher than among otherwise similar white borrowers and were concentrated in minority neighborhoods.*

The Eleventh Circuit concluded that the City adequately pleaded that the Banks' misconduct proximately caused these financial injuries. The court held that in the context of the FHA "the proper standard" for proximate cause "is based on foreseeability." The City, it continued, satisfied that element: Although there are "several links in the causal chain" between the charged discriminatory lending practices and the claimed losses, the City plausibly alleged that "none are unforeseeable."

We conclude that the Eleventh Circuit erred in holding that foreseeability is sufficient to establish proximate cause under the FHA. As we have explained, proximate cause "generally bars suits for alleged harm that is 'too remote' from the defendant's unlawful conduct." In the context of the FHA, foreseeability alone does not ensure the close connection that proximate cause requires. The housing market is interconnected with economic and social life. A violation of the FHA may, therefore, "'be expected to cause ripples of harm to flow'" far beyond the defendant's misconduct. Nothing in the statute suggests that Congress intended to provide a remedy wherever those ripples travel. And entertaining suits to recover damages for any foreseeable result of an FHA violation would risk "massive and complex damages litigation."

Decision. The Supreme Court ruled that Miami failed to show that the actions of the banks were sufficiently related to the alleged violations, stating that foreseeability, alone, is insufficient to prove proximate cause.

Focus on Ethics

Is it ethical to restrict FHA lawsuits to proximate cause when the consequences, while not always direct, still result in significant real-world impacts?

Types of Loan Payments

The types of loan payments discussed in the subsections below have been commonly used in the real estate industry.

Fixed-Rate Mortgages (Amortized Loans)

Fixed-rate mortgages, also known as amortized loans, have a fixed interest rate for the life of the loan. Most residential mortgages in the United States are amortized (repaid in regular payments over a given time) for the life of the loan, often with 30-year fixed rates, but it is common to find 15-, 20-, and 40-year maturity dates. Usually, the shorter the maturity date, the lower the interest rate charged. With fixed-rate mortgages, the monthly payment remains the same throughout the duration of the loan. The monthly payment pays both interest and principal throughout the duration of the loan.

Adjustable-Rate Mortgages

Adjustable-rate mortgages (ARMs) are mortgages in which the interest rate and the monthly payments may be adjusted periodically. The interest rate is tied to an agreed upon lending index at the time the loan is made.

> **Example:** A borrower may obtain a 30-year 7/1 ARM at 6.50 percent. This means the principal and interest are paid over a 30-year term. The 7/1 means the loan is fixed at 6.50 percent for the first seven years and then adjusts to a new interest rate at the end of each year thereafter until the loan is paid in full.

The loans have interest rate caps. The caps can limit the maximum interest rate increase in any one period or can cap the total amount that the interest rate may increase to over the life of the loan. These amounts are stated in the promissory note.

Interest-Only Mortgages (Straight Loans)

Straight loans, commonly known as interest-only loans, are loans in which the borrower pays only interest during the loan period, which is usually three to five years. No principal is paid during the loan period. Instead, either the loan with principal and interest is amortized over the remaining loan term (often 25 to 27 years), or at the end of the loan period, the principal balance is due.

Piggyback Mortgages

With a piggyback mortgage, a borrower takes out two mortgages for the property at the same time. Usually, the first mortgage is taken out at 80 percent of the purchase price so that the borrower does not have to pay PMI. At the same time, the borrower takes out a second mortgage on the property to cover the balance of the purchase price or a portion of the purchase price, with the remainder being a cash payment. The second mortgage's interest rate is generally higher than that of the first mortgage.

> **Example:** A common piggyback mortgage is an 80-10-10. The borrower takes out an 80 percent first mortgage, the second mortgage covers the next 10 percent of the purchase price, and the borrower pays 10 percent down on the home to cover the balance of the purchase price.

Taking Subject to and Assuming Mortgages

At times, a property is sold without paying the balance due on the existing mortgage. This occurs when the purchaser takes "subject to the mortgage" or when the purchaser assumes the mortgage.

Taking Subject to a Mortgage

Taking subject to a mortgage
When a purchaser buys real estate aware of a mortgage and makes payments on the mortgage but does not agree to become personally liable to repay the mortgage debt.

If an existing mortgage does not contain a due-on-sale clause, a buyer may purchase a home subject to the mortgage. When **taking subject to a mortgage**, the buyer takes title to the property but is not personally liable for payment of the mortgage debt. The seller remains liable for the payments on the mortgage. If the mortgage goes into default, the lender may foreclose. The lender may enforce payment only against the original owner.

> **Example:** George purchased a home and secured a 30-year mortgage at a fixed rate of 4.25 percent. Ten years later, after interest rates had risen to 7.75 percent, George sold the home to William, who purchased the home subject to George's existing mortgage. George will still be liable to the original lender if William defaults with regard to the terms of the mortgage.

Assuming an Existing Mortgage

Assume an existing mortgage
When a purchaser agrees to become personally liable for an existing mortgage obligation in a real estate purchase.

Instead of purchasing a home subject to a mortgage, a new purchaser might **assume an existing mortgage**. When assuming a mortgage, the buyer takes over an existing mortgage from the seller. The buyer becomes personally liable for the mortgage payments, while the original owner remains liable for the repayment of the loan.

The original owner may have the lender consent to a release of liability and may request that the lender substitute the new purchaser in place of the original mortgagor.

FIGURE 32.3: Taking Subject to a Mortgage

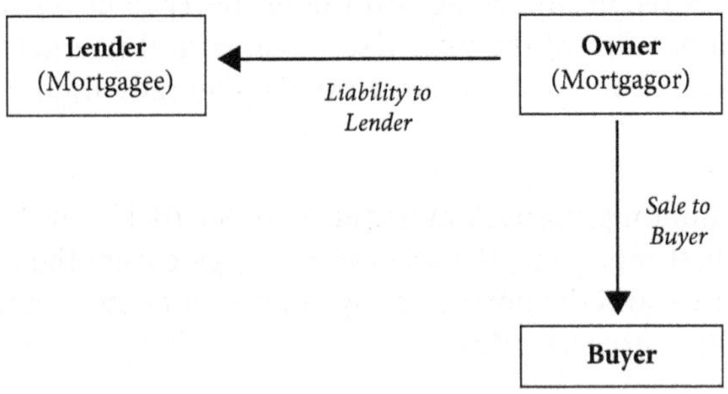

FIGURE 32.4: Assuming an Existing Mortgage

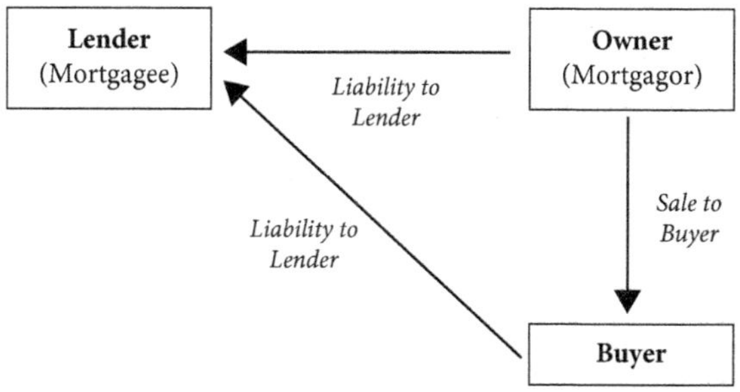

Concept Summary
Taking Subject to a Mortgage and Assumption of Mortgage

Issue	Subject to Mortgage	Assumption of Mortgage
Can the lender sue original owner?	Yes	Yes, unless a novation
Can the lender sue the buyer?	No	Yes
Can the lender foreclose on the property?	Yes	Yes

Deeds of Trust

A minority of jurisdictions allow the use of a promissory note and deed of trust. A **deed of trust** is similar to a mortgage, but it involves three parties. Under the deed of trust, the lender is the **beneficiary**. The beneficiary does not have actual ownership of the property but instead has a lien against it. The borrower or property owner is the **trustor**. The trustor holds equitable title which allows the trustor to occupy and use the property. The trustor conveys legal title to a third party known as the **trustee** (usually a financial institution). Legal title provides the trustee the authority to sell the property in the event of the borrower's default. The trustee holds the deed of trust for the beneficiary's benefit until the underlying obligation on the note is paid in full. When the loan is paid, the trustee files a written reconveyance with the local public recorder's office; this returns the legal title to the trustor.

Lenders benefit from deeds of trust because, compared to the traditional mortgage foreclosure process, such a setup enables a swift, inexpensive sale of the property in the event of a default.

Deed of trust
A three-party instrument financing arrangement that involves a beneficiary, a trustor, and a trustee.

Beneficiary
The lender identified in a deed of trust.

Trustor
The property owner or party to a deed of trust.

Trustee
The party to a deed of trust who holds (legal) title until the underlying obligation is paid in full.

FIGURE 32.5: Deed of Trust

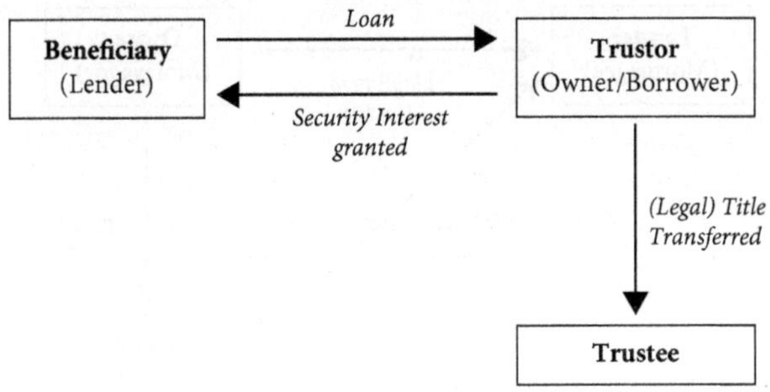

TABLE 32.1: Mortgages versus Deed of Trust

	Mortgage	Deed of Trust
Parties Involved	Mortgagor — Borrower Mortgagee — Lender	Trustor — Borrower Beneficiary — Lender Trustee — Disinterested Third Party
Foreclosure Method	Judicial (court action is required)	Judicial or nonjudicial means
Benefits	Right to deficiency judgments against borrower	Quicker and cheaper to obtain title than through mortgage foreclosure process
Detriments	More costly and time consuming than nonjudicial foreclosures	Usually, no right to a deficiency judgment when nonjudicial foreclosure is used

Default

Default
A debtor's failure to fulfill an obligation to pay the creditor.

A **default** occurs when the borrower fails to observe their duties and promises. A loan is in default when the borrower fails to make the mortgage payments when they become due. Generally, a lender won't declare a borrower in default until the borrower fails to make payment for at least 90 days. However, depending on the terms of the loan, the borrower may face significant late fees associated with the untimely payment.

When default occurs, the property may be subject to what is known as pre-foreclosure proceedings. In pre-foreclosure proceedings, the lender begins by filing a default notice on the property. This notice informs the borrower that the lender intends to proceed with foreclosure actions if the debt is not paid. The pre-foreclosure proceedings generally last anywhere from three to ten months depending on the state and the terms of the mortgage. The pre-foreclosure stage presents the borrower with two options: either pay off the debt or sell the property before it goes into foreclosure.

A common way that the borrower sells the property before foreclosure is a short sale. A short sale arises when the debt on the property exceeds the fair market value of the property. Short sales often must be approved by the lender before the sale can be finalized. When the property is sold at this stage, the borrower can avoid the significant damage to their credit history that occurs because of a foreclosure. A short sale is beneficial to the lender by allowing it to avoid the costs associated with foreclosure proceedings. Generally, short sales occur when the borrower believes there is an interested party who is willing to purchase the property for a value greater than what would be obtained at a foreclosure auction.

Foreclosure

Foreclosure is the legal process of terminating the borrower's claims of ownership of the real property. They may foreclose on the property after default occurs. Only a lender whose loan is in default can foreclose. Foreclosures eliminate all junior-priority liens, enabling the lender to sell the property free and clear of liens to recover the outstanding indebtedness owed to it. Buyers who purchase property at a foreclosure sale take title to the property free of any liens, except for those that are not dischargeable (such as certain tax liens).

Foreclosure
A procedure following a default, in which property serving as security for the loan is sold, with proceeds applied to retire the debt.

Equity Redemption Rights

A borrower may be able to stop the foreclosure sale by satisfying the debt. This process is commonly known as **equity of redemption** (also known as reinstatement). It is the borrower's right to pay the indebtedness *before* the foreclosure sale occurs and thereby redeem the property. This right to reinstate the mortgage or deed of trust is guaranteed under most state laws.

Under equity of redemption, the borrower or trustor pays the amount in default at the time the foreclosure proceedings commence, plus all foreclosure costs and the trustee or attorney fees. When payment is made, the loan is considered current from the lender's perspective and is then reinstated. When a mortgage or deed of trust is reinstated, the mortgage foreclosure proceedings are canceled.

Equity of redemption
The right of a borrower to redeem (retain) the mortgaged property before a foreclosure sale occurs.

Foreclosure Sale and Statutory Redemption Rights

Following the foreclosure sale, the sheriff reports the result to the court, which can then confirm the sale. Once the court has confirmed the sale, some states give the borrower an additional right to redeem the property, called a **statutory redemption period**. During this time, the debtor has a right to repurchase the property *after* the foreclosure sale by paying the amount of money for which the property was sold, interest from the sale date at the mortgage's interest rate, and other costs allowed by statute. These other costs can include taxes and assessments paid by the purchaser from the sale date. After the expiration period for redemption, the borrower's rights in the property are terminated. The redemption period varies by state and is commonly between three months and one year. Many states extend the redemption period if the sale proceeds do not cover the debt owed to the lender.

Statutory redemption period
The right of a borrower to redeem (retain) the mortgaged property after a foreclosure sale occurs within a time period established by state law.

Trustee's sale
A type of nonjudicial foreclosure proceeding where the lender waives the right to seek a deficiency judgment against the borrower.

Foreclosure by Power of Sales (Trustee's Sale)

In states that permit nonjudicial foreclosure proceedings, the most common alternative is either a public or private trustee's sale. The process begins with the borrower being served with notice of default. This notice gives the borrower the opportunity to either pay the debt or sell the property, just like that of the pre-foreclosure process. If the debt remains unpaid, the lender then serves a notice of sale on the borrower. The notice of sale typically gives the borrower until the time of the auction or another specified date to pay the debt. If the debt is still unpaid, the property will be sold to the highest bidder. Other than the fact that a trustee's sale does not require judicial involvement, the other important distinction between a trustee's sale and foreclosure is that a trustee's sale requires the lender to waive the right to seek a deficiency judgment against the borrower if the proceeds from the sale do not cover the amount due. As a result, the lender is typically the highest bidder at trustee's sales. This allows the lender to enter into a private transaction to sell the property for a higher price at a future date.

Deficiency Judgment

Deficiency judgment
A money judgment obtained by the creditor against the borrower when the foreclosure sale does not satisfy the entire debt.

If the proceeds of the resulting sale exceed the amount of the debt, the surplus is given to the mortgagor. If the proceeds are insufficient, in some states the lender may proceed against the borrower in an action to collect the remaining balance, called a deficiency judgment. A **deficiency judgment** is a money judgment against a borrower whose foreclosed property was sold but yielded insufficient sale proceeds to pay the loan in full. Only the party foreclosing is entitled, if available, to a deficiency judgment. Deficiency judgments are available for judicial foreclosures but not for non-judicial foreclosures. Thus, the method of foreclosure used makes a big difference to both the lender and the borrower.

Purchase money mortgage
A loan by a lender or seller to finance all or a portion of the purchase price of a property.

PURCHASE MONEY MORTGAGES. Whether a deficiency judgment is available to a lender depends upon state law. In some states, antideficiency laws exist that provide that a deficiency judgment is not allowed for purchase money mortgages. A purchase money mortgage is a loan by a lender or seller in which the borrower's funds are used to finance the purchase of a one- to four-unit residential property. These laws were intended to protect homeowners and buyers who purchased overvalued properties secured by a mortgage or deed of trust.

A refinance is not a purchase money mortgage, and in states allowing deficiency judgment following foreclosure, they expose the borrower to that risk. In addition, Federal Housing Administration (FHA) and Veterans Administration (VA) loans are subject to deficiency judgments, even if they are considered purchase money mortgages. In those states permitting a deficiency judgment following a foreclosure sale, only the original borrower is liable, not the purchaser at the foreclosure sale.

Purchase money mortgages are considered nonrecourse obligations. Nonrecourse means the borrower is not liable to the lender for any deficiency following a foreclosure sale. The lender's recourse is limited to the amount realized from the sale of the real property. Lenders operating in nonrecourse states are exposed to more risk and may require stricter loan underwriting, higher loan-to-value ratios, and higher interest rates. Many states limit the application of nonrecourse debt only to purchase money mortgages.

Example: A homeowner purchases a property for $350,000. The home was purchased with 90 percent financing and a 10 percent down payment. Within three years, the home is worth $175,000, and the borrower is unable to make the monthly payments required under the loan. The bank forecloses and seeks a deficiency judgment. In states providing for a purchase money mortgage exception, the homeowner would not be liable for a deficiency judgment.

Installment Land Sale Contracts

As an alternative to a mortgage or deed of trust, property may also be bought under an installment land sale contract, also known as a contract for deed arrangement. In an **installment land sale contract**, the seller provides the financing to the buyer. The seller retains title to the property as security until the final payment is received. Payments are allocated to principal and interest similar to the allocation used for amortized mortgage payments; alternatively, the contract may involve a balloon payment. The buyer is entitled to possession of the land during the repayment period. Once the buyer has paid the seller all, or substantially all, of the purchase price agreed to in the contract, the buyer receives title to the property.

Installment land sale contract
A contract for the purchase of real property in which the seller provides financing to the buyer and retains title to the property until the final payment is received.

Installment land sale contracts are widely used in real estate transactions, including those relating to low-cost housing and vacation lots. No bank loan is necessary, the down payment can be small, and the seller may be willing to sell to persons who would not qualify for a conventional loan.

In the following case, the parties litigated their rights and duties under their installment sale contract.

CASE 32.2

INSTALLMENT LAND SALE CONTRACTS MAY BE TREATED AS EQUITY

BEAN v. WALKER

95 A.D.2d 70 (1983)

Supreme Court of New York, Appellate Division

In 1973, Carl Walker agreed to buy a home in Syracuse, New York, from Franklin Bean for $15,000. The installment land sale contract stated that the sum would be paid in monthly installments over a 15-year period at 5 percent interest. Bean retained legal title until he was paid in full. The contract provided that if Walker defaulted in making payments and failed to cure the default within 30 days, Bean could elect to call the remaining balance immediately due or elect to declare the contract terminated and repossess the house. If Bean were to choose the second option, he could retain all the money paid under the contract as liquidated damages. After falling upon hard times owing to an injury, Walker defaulted on the contract, having paid over $12,000 in principal and interest and having made substantial improvements to the house. Bean gave the 30-day notice and filed suit to eject Walker and have Bean declared the lawful owner of the property. The trial court granted summary judgment for Bean. Walker appealed.

Language of the Court. *Certain general principles may be observed. It is well settled that the owner of the real estate, from the time of the execution of a valid contract for its sale, is to be treated as the owner of the purchase money, and the purchaser of the land is to be treated as the equitable owner thereof. The purchase money becomes personal property. Thus, notwithstanding the words of the contract and implications that may arise therefrom, the law of property declares that, upon the execution of a contract for sale of land, the buyer acquires equitable title. The seller holds the legal title in trust for the buyer and has an equitable lien for the payment of the purchase price. The buyer in possession, for all practical purposes, is the owner of the property with all the rights of an owner, subject only to the terms of the contract. The seller may enforce his lien by foreclosure or an action at law for the purchase price of the property. The conclusion to be reached, of course, is that upon the execution of a contract an interest in real property comes into existence by operation of law, superseding the terms of the contract.*

The key to the resolution of the rights of the parties lies in whether the buyer under a land sale contract has acquired an interest in the property of such a nature that it must be extinguished before the seller may resume possession. We hold that such an interest exists since the buyer acquires equitable title and the seller merely holds legal title in trust for the buyer, subject to the seller's equitable lien for the payment of the purchase price in accordance with the terms of the contract. The seller may not enforce his rights by the simple expedient of an action in ejectment but must instead proceed to foreclose the buyer's equitable title or bring an action at law for the purchase price.

The effect of the judgment granted by the trial court is that Bean would have the property with improvements made over the years by Walker, along with over $7,000 in principal payments on a purchase price of $15,000, and over $4,000 in interest. The basic inequity of such a result requires no further comment. If a forfeiture would result in the inequitable disposition of property and an exorbitant monetary loss, equity can and should intervene.

Decision. The judgment was reversed. Bean as the seller must foreclose upon Walker's interest or file a lawsuit seeking to recover the purchase price.

Focus on Ethics

Should state law permit a forfeiture of all principal and interest payments made to the seller in the event of a default?

AI Feature: Draft a Default Clause for a Commercial Mortgage

Use an internet search engine to review applicable default and lender's remedies clauses for a lender to insert into a mortgage instrument. Then, use an AI program to draft a default clause. Be specific in stating what covenants, if breached, would trigger acceleration of the maturity date of the underlying promissory note. Additionally, ensure that you include the most prominent remedies available to the lender in the event of a default. If the lender is concerned about the risks posed by the loan, what other covenants and conditions would you insert into the mortgage document to protect the lender?

Key Terms

- Assume an existing mortgage, 818
- Beneficiary, 819
- Debtor, 811
- Deed of trust, 819
- Default, 820
- Deficiency judgment, 822
- Equity of redemption, 821
- First mortgage, 814
- Foreclosure, 821
- Hypothecated, 810
- Installment land sale contract, 823
- Mortgage, 810
- Mortgagee, 810
- Mortgagor, 810
- Payee, 811
- Predatory lending, 814
- Promissory note, 811
- Purchase money mortgage, 822
- Second mortgage, 814
- Statutory redemption period, 821
- Taking subject to a mortgage, 818
- Trustee, 819
- Trustee's sale, 822
- Trustor, 819

Applying the Law

32.1 Research the Law. Using an internet search engine, determine if lenders in your home state finance and collateralize real estate purchases primarily through mortgages or deeds of trust. Determine the rights of the borrower following a mortgage loan default.

32.2 Research the Law. Using an internet search engine, research the laws of your state to determine what remedies are available when default occurs under an installment land sale contract. Should the borrower be entitled to any surplus equity in the property?

32.3 Purchase Money Mortgage. Garrett Tire Center, Inc., obtained a judgment on account against Robert Herbaugh. Later, Farmers and Merchants Bank made a purchase mortgage loan to Herbaugh. The purchase money mortgage was recorded after the deed to Herbaugh had been recorded. A year later, the bank filed for foreclosure of its purchase money mortgage. Garrett Tire asserted its judgment lien was superior to the bank's purchase money mortgage lien. Whose lien should have priority and why? *Garrett Tire Center, Inc. v. Herbaugh*, 740 S.W.2d 612 (Ark. 1987)

32.4 Purchase Money Mortgage. William and Merlann Cely sold their Tucson, Arizona, home to Douglas Clark. It was encumbered by a purchase money deed of trust and a second mortgage to secure the purchase of a home in Oregon. After several years, the Celys stopped paying on the second mortgage. The holder of the note and mortgage sought payment from the sellers who, in turn, sought payment from the buyers. Are the Celys protected from a deficiency judgment on the second mortgage if the holder forecloses on that mortgage? *Cely v. DeConcini, McDonald, Brammer, Yetwin & Lacy, P.C.*, 803 P.2d 911 (Ariz. Ct. App. 2008)

32.5 Taking "Subject To." Sarah Oliver sold property to the Mirabitos and received a first mortgage (Oliver mortgage). The Mirabitos sold the property to the Beltons and conveyed a deed which contained as "subject to" clause as to the Oliver mortgage. The Beltons gave the Mirabitos a purchase money second mortgage (Belton mortgage). The Beltons sold the property to James McVeigh. The deed to McVeigh stated McVeigh was not assuming the mortgages, only that the property was subject to them. After McVeigh defaulted, the Mirabitos foreclosed on the Belton Mortgage. The holder of the Oliver mortgage sought foreclosure and named McVeigh and the Mirabitos. Had McVeigh assumed the debt owing under the Oliver mortgage? *McVeigh v. Mirabito*, 556 So. 2d 1226 (Fla. Dist. Ct. App. 1990)

32.6 Nonrecourse Loan Liability. Harry Lee and Van Why along with others secured two loans on a hotel, the second of which was from Heller Financial. During the term of the loan, six liens were recorded on the title to the property secured by the Heller loan, which were prohibitions carved out from the nonrecourse provisions of the loan. Following a default and the sale of the property, Heller only received a portion of the sums due it. Heller sued Lee and Van Why for personal obligations under the loan agreement and note. Are they personally liable for repayment of the loan because of the liens? *Heller Fin., Inc. v. Lee*, 2002 U.S. Dist. LEXIS 15183 (N.D. Ill. 2002)

32.7 Reinstatement of Mortgage. The debtors filed a chapter 13 bankruptcy petition, their third bankruptcy filing in a two-year period. The filing came 10 days following the foreclosure sale of the debtors' residence. The mortgage holder (the mortgagee), who had purchased the residence at the foreclosure sale, filed a motion for relief from the automatic stay. The debtors contended that they had a right to reinstate the mortgage and cure the default through their chapter 13 plan. Do they have such a right after the foreclosure sale, when, usually, after sale redemption of the property through a cash payment of the full amount of the mortgage debt would be required? *In re McKinney*, 174 B.R. 330 (Bankr. S.D. Ala. 1994)

32.8 Collusive Foreclosure. Loan Fund was a division of a national fraternity which assisted its local chapters regarding purchase, financing and renovations of fraternity houses. The chapter borrowed money from a third-party lender which was guaranteed by the Loan Fund. It also borrowed from Megabank for the renovation project. The chapter defaulted on these loans. When the holder of the first foreclosed, Loan Fund purchased it for a lesser sum than was due and took an assignment of all rights in the note and first deed of trust. As a result, Megabank remained in a junior position. Eventually, Loan Fund foreclosed, and Megabank's junior position was wiped out. But the bank sued to declare that extinguishing its rights was collusive and sought to reinstate its deed of trust in first position. What should the court decide? *Megabank Financial Corp. v. Alpha Gamma Rho Fraternity*, 841 P.2d 318 (Colo. App. 1992)

32.9 Predatory Lending. Fremont Bank made 50 to 60 percent of its loans to subprime borrowers. To insulate itself from borrower default losses, Fremont sold them on the secondary market. Additionally, Fremont did not interact with the borrowers directly, but through mortgage brokers who acted as independent contractors to aid the borrower in choosing their mortgage plan. The Massachusetts Attorney General sued Fremont for violating the state's consumer protection statute. The Attorney General noted four characteristics that made it almost certain that borrowers would not be able to make the loan payments: (1) the loans were adjustable, with an initial rate that applied for only three years; (2) the initial rate was three points lower than the usual mortgage rate on 30-year loans; (3) the debt-to-income ratio would exceed 50 percent after the initial period expired; and (4) the loan-to-value ratio was 100 percent. The trial judge held that Fremont, as a lender, should have recognized that loans with the first three characteristics described were doomed to foreclosure unless the borrower could refinance the loan at or near the end of the introductory rate period and obtain in the process a new low introductory rate. The trial judge granted the injunction against Fremont. On appeal, how should the court rule as to the charge of predatory lending? *Commonwealth v. Fremont Investment & Loan*, 897 N.E.2d 548 (Mass. 2008)

32.10 Land Sale Contract. Lee Hackler sold to Paul and Tina Akin a lot in Van Buren, Arkansas. Hackler executed a contract with buyers for the sale of property. The buyers then assigned their interest to the ultimate purchasers, Richard and Mae Perryman. The contract had a 12 percent interest rate and provided that a failure to make any installment would result in forfeiture and would create a landlord-tenant relationship. The Perrymans sued Hackler, claiming the contract was usurious and void as to interest due, seeking recovery for twice the interest paid, and requesting reformation of the contract. But the Perrymans had defaulted on their payments prior to the discovery of the usurious interest rate. How should the court rule? *Perryman v. Hackler*, 323 Ark. 500 (1996)

Bankruptcy

33

Creditors have better memories than debtors. — Benjamin Franklin, American polymath, Founding Father of the United States. (1706-1790)

Chapter Outline

- Introduction
- Overview of Bankruptcy Law
- Common Types of Bankruptcy Proceedings
  - *Management Application: Small Business Reorganization Act of 2019*
- Parties to a Bankruptcy Proceeding
- Bankruptcy Procedures
  - *Management Application: Selected Additional Federal Exemptions*
  - *Management Application: Strategic Planning for Delinquent Debtors*

Case 33.1: *City of Chicago v. Fulton*

  - *Management Application: Proof of Claim*

Case 33.2: *Venture Bank v. Lapides*

  - *Management Application: Nondischargeable Debts in Bankruptcy*
- AI Feature: State Bankruptcy Exemptions

Learning Objectives

After studying this chapter, you should be able to:

1. Explain the differences among Chapter 7, Chapter 11, and Chapter 13 bankruptcy proceedings.
2. Identify the parties to a bankruptcy proceeding.
3. Discuss the order of events within a bankruptcy.
4. Recognize what assets are included in the bankruptcy estate.
5. Describe the importance of the automatic stay.

Introduction

The relationship between bankruptcy and business is expansive. Businesses and individuals may find the need to file bankruptcy due to unforeseen risks they have taken, changes in market conditions, or losses caused by economic slowdowns. In this chapter, our study will address the most common types of bankruptcies available to businesses and individuals. We will provide an overview of bankruptcy law and discuss the types and process of bankruptcy proceedings.

Overview of Bankruptcy Law

Bankruptcy provides individuals and businesses with a means of settling debts they are unable to pay as they become due. Each of the federal district courts across the United States includes a bankruptcy court. The presiding decision maker in each bankruptcy case is the United States bankruptcy judge. The bankruptcy judge may decide any matter connected with a bankruptcy case. The law used in these proceedings is a uniform law known as the Bankruptcy Code. The Bankruptcy Code was established by Congress through the power given to Congress by the United States Constitution.

Creditor
The lender in a credit transaction.

Debtor
The borrower in a credit transaction.

Website for the U.S. Bankruptcy Court: http://www.uscourts.gov/services-forms/bankruptcy.

Two important parties in a bankruptcy are the creditor and debtor. A **creditor** is a person who is owed money. The **debtor** is the person who owes the money to the creditor. Unlike federal court judges, who have lifetime appointments, bankruptcy judges serve a term of 14 years.

Purpose of Bankruptcy

The bankruptcy court provides a forum in which the debtor's assets are equitably distributed to creditors. Additionally, the debtor is given a fresh start by reducing or eliminating the pre-bankruptcy debt.

Common Types of Bankruptcy Proceedings

Six types of bankruptcy cases are provided for under the Bankruptcy Code. In this chapter, we will focus on the three types that primarily relate to individuals and businesses: Chapter 7, Chapter 11, and Chapter 13. The cases are traditionally given the names of the chapters that describe them.

Chapter 7: Liquidation

Chapter 7 bankruptcy
A type of bankruptcy that results in the debtor receiving a fresh start in exchange for distributing all the debtor's nonexempt assets to the bankruptcy trustee to be liquidated and the proceeds distributed to creditors.

A **Chapter 7 bankruptcy** petition, also known as liquidation, provides the debtor with a fresh start in exchange for distributing all the debtor's nonexempt assets to the bankruptcy trustee for liquidation. The Bankruptcy Code allows debtors to keep certain exempt property. The Chapter 7 trustee converts the nonexempt assets into cash, which is then distributed to the creditors. Through this process, the debtor is discharged from most of the remaining debts. Proceedings under Chapter 7 apply to all debtors, including individuals, partnerships, and corporations. Because there is usually little or no nonexempt property available in most Chapter 7 cases, an actual liquidation of the debtor's assets may not occur. These types of cases are called no-asset cases. In most Chapter 7 cases, if the individual receives a discharge, they are released from personal liability for certain dischargeable assets.

FIGURE 33.1: Chapter 7: Individual Liquidation

Chapter 11: Reorganization

A **Chapter 11 bankruptcy** petition is known as a reorganization or restructuring. A Chapter 11 petition allows a distressed business, such as a partnership or corporation, involved in operating real estate to restructure its finances. The restructuring allows the business to continue and the creditors to be paid, though usually not in full.

Chapter 11 bankruptcy
A type of bankruptcy that results in the reorganization or restructuring of the debtor's finances.

Reorganization is primarily a negotiation process that allows the debtor and its creditors to develop a plan for the adjustment and discharge of the debts owed by the debtor. In reorganization, the debtor receives a fresh start in exchange for the debtor's paying creditors over time, in an amount greater than the creditors would have received in a Chapter 7 liquidation.

Unlike with Chapter 7 petitions, insolvency is *not* a condition for filing a voluntary petition for Chapter 11. Under a Chapter 11 proceeding, the debtor has the exclusive right to file a plan of reorganization during the first 120 days after the order of relief, unless a trustee has been appointed, in which case the debtor may file a plan at any time. Prior to any restructuring taking place, the bankruptcy trustee will investigate the entity's assets. Based on that investigation, the trustee will file a report with the court that will either recommend that the entity be reorganized or undergo Chapter 7 liquidation. The role of a bankruptcy trustee is discussed in more detail below.

Management Application Small Business Reorganization Act of 2019

The Small Business Reorganization Act of 2019 (SBRA) provides small business debtors with new options to restructure their debts while also reducing the costs associated with Chapter 11 proceedings. The SBRA makes it easier for small business debtors to maintain their businesses and streamlines business reorganizations, as governed by Chapter 11 of the Bankruptcy Code.

Small business debtors must plan to meet the Act's requirements. Small business debtors must have not more than $2,725,625 in noncontingent, unliquidated debt as of the filing of the bankruptcy petition. Further, 50 percent or more of that debt must have arisen from commercial or business activities. If qualified, the small business debtor may take advantage of the new changes to the

Bankruptcy Code and elect to be a debtor under Subchapter V of Chapter 11.

Effect of Original Chapter 11 Proceedings on Small Businesses

- Owners must contribute sufficient new money or an equivalent to retain their ownership interest.
- Original process imposed heavy costs and burdens, which was not a viable solution for small businesses operated by owners or their families.
- Strict deadlines left small businesses without enough time to restructure.
- Original process left small business debtors with many challenges by creditors.

Changes to Chapter 11 Proceeding for Qualified Small Business Debtors

- Debtor may maintain ownership without contributing any new value.
- Committee professional fees may be paid from debtor's assets.
- Quarterly fees to United States Trustee are eliminated.
- Administrative expenses can be paid over the course of proposed plan.
- Debtor has the exclusive right to file a proposed plan.
- Debtor may avoid repeated creditor challenges during the proceeding, with the exception of the confirmation hearing.

FIGURE 33.2: Chapter 11: Reorganization

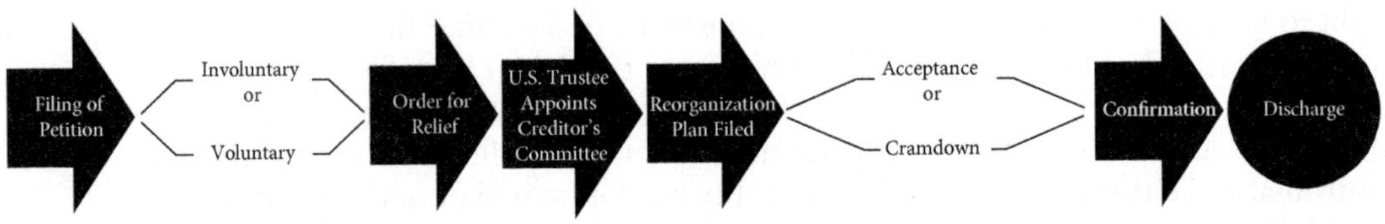

Chapter 13: Individual Repayment Plan

Chapter 13 bankruptcy
A type of bankruptcy that results in the adjustment of the individual's debts and is not available to businesses.

A **Chapter 13 bankruptcy** petition provides for an adjustment of an individual's debts. Businesses cannot file a Chapter 13 petition. It is designed for an individual who has a regular source of income. Chapter 13 is often preferable to a Chapter 7 proceeding for an individual because it enables the debtor to keep valuable assets such as his home; it also allows the debtor to propose a plan for repaying the debt over a period of three to five years.

Parties to a Bankruptcy Proceeding

The parties to the bankruptcy proceeding may include the debtor, a bankruptcy trustee (in Chapter 7 and Chapter 13 cases), a creditors' committee (in most Chapter 11 cases), a U.S. attorney (for the prosecution of bankruptcy crimes), creditors and equity holders, officers and directors of bankrupt corporations and general partners of bankrupt partnerships, and members of the limited liability companies that have filed for bankruptcy protection.

Bankruptcy Trustee

A **bankruptcy trustee**, who is often an attorney, certified public accountant, or business manager, becomes the legal representative of the bankruptcy estate. The bankruptcy trustee is *not* the same person as the U.S. Trustee. Broad powers are granted to the bankruptcy trustee, such as the following: collecting the debtor's property, performing investigations relating to the debtor's affairs, setting aside fraudulent conveyances and other preferential transfers, operating the debtor's business, hiring professionals such as accountants, filing reports, and closing the estate.

Bankruptcy trustee A legal representative of the bankruptcy estate before the bankruptcy court.

The trustee performs these services and is compensated for the fair value of the services rendered. The trustee must be qualified and receive court approval of their appointment.

U.S. Trustee

The **U.S. Trustee** is a government employee appointed by the Justice Department to perform administrative tasks for the benefit of the bankruptcy courts. The U.S. Trustee supervises the bankruptcy case and monitors the creditor's committees, disclosure statements, and other required bankruptcy duties. A trustee is required in Chapter 7 and Chapter 13 cases but not in a Chapter 11 case. However, the court may, for cause, order the appointment of a trustee, who may then be elected by the creditors.

U.S. Trustee A federal government official who handles and supervises administrative tasks within a bankruptcy case.

Debtor in Possession

Normally, there is no trustee in a Chapter 11 case; instead, the debtor continues in possession of its property as a **debtor in possession**. As a debtor in possession, the debtor enjoys the same rights and powers — as well as the obligations — of a trustee in bankruptcy.

Creditor

The Bankruptcy Code defines a **creditor** as "an entity that has a claim against the debtor that arose at the time of or before the order for relief concerning the debtor." Creditors include any person that loaned a money with the intent of being repaid, such as a bank. Creditors can also be local, state, and federal taxing authorities; lenders; landlords; secured creditors; holders of executory contracts and unexpired leases; trade creditors; and the like.

Debtor in possession The debtor in a Chapter 11 case that retains possession of their property and enjoys the same rights and powers, as well as obligations, of a trustee in bankruptcy.

Creditor's Committee

A **creditor's committee** is appointed by the U.S. Trustee in Chapter 11 cases. Creditor's committees are appointed in most, if not all, Chapter 11 cases. The members of the creditor's committee are not paid for their service. The committee is responsible for representing the interests of the unsecured creditors. Members of the creditor's committee are usually the first to know of events affecting the bankruptcy, which can provide them with invaluable knowledge.

Creditor's committee Members appointed by a U.S. Trustee in a Chapter 11 bankruptcy proceeding who are to represent the interests of the unsecured creditors.

Key Terms Used in Bankruptcy

Adversary proceeding	A lawsuit arising in or related to a bankruptcy case that is commenced by filing a complaint.
Assume	An agreement to continue performing duties under a contract or lease.
Automatic stay	An injunction that automatically stops lawsuits, foreclosures, and all collection activity against the debtor the moment a bankruptcy petition is filed.
Bankruptcy estate	All legal or equitable interest of the debtor in property at the time of bankruptcy filing.
Bankruptcy plan	A debtor's detailed description of how the debtor proposes to pay the creditor's claims over a period of time.
Claim	A debtor's assertion of a right to payment from the debtor or its property.
Discharge	The release of a debtor from personal liability for certain debts. A discharge prevents creditors owed those debts from taking any action against the debtor to collect them.
Equity	The value of a debtor's interest in property after liens and other creditor interests are considered. (For example, if a house is valued at $100,000 and is subject to a $75,000 mortgage, there is $25,000 of equity.)
Executory contract or lease	Those agreements that have duties remaining to be performed. If the agreement is an executory contract, a debtor may assume or reject the contract or lease.
Exemptions	Property owned by individual debtors that the Bankruptcy Code or state law permits the debtor to keep from unsecured creditors.
Insider	Any relative of the debtor or of a general partner, a partnership in which the debtor is a general partner, a general partner of the debtor, or a corporation of which the debtor is an officer, director, or person in control.
Preference or preferential debt payment	A debt payment made to a creditor in the 90 days prior to when a debtor files bankruptcy (or within one year, if the payment was to benefit an insider) that gives the creditor more than the creditor would receive in a Chapter 7 case.
Priority	A statutory ranking of unsecured claims that determines the order in which they will be paid, if not enough money is available to pay all of them in full.
Proof of claim	A written statement and verified documentation filed by a creditor that describes the reasons why the debtor owes the creditor money.
Secured creditor	A creditor holding a claim against the debtor who has the right to take and hold or sell certain property in partial or complete satisfaction of the creditor's claim. Holders of secured claims usually obtain some payment in the bankruptcy; this payment is generally determined by the value of the collateral securing the claim.
Secured debt	Debt backed by a mortgage, pledge of collateral, or other lien. (Examples include mortgages and deeds of trust, as well as tax liens.)

U.S. Trustee	A federal government official who handles and supervises administrative tasks within a bankruptcy case.
Unsecured claim	A claim or debt for which a creditor holds no assurance of payment, such as is present with a mortgage or deed of trust. It is a debt for which credit was extended solely based upon the debtor's future ability to pay. Unsecured claims have the lowest priority of repayment and are often discharged in bankruptcy.

Bankruptcy Procedures

Certain procedures must be followed pursuant to the Bankruptcy Code, and each of the procedures is discussed in detail below. They include the following:

1. Bankruptcy counseling and education (if required)
2. Filing of a bankruptcy petition
3. Automatic stay of most civil actions against the debtor
4. Creation of the bankruptcy estate
5. Meeting of the creditors
6. Creditors file proofs of claim
7. Debtor may execute reaffirmation agreements
8. Distribution of property (in Chapter 7 cases)
9. Discharge of debts
10. Closing of the bankruptcy estate

FIGURE 33.3: Bankruptcy Procedures

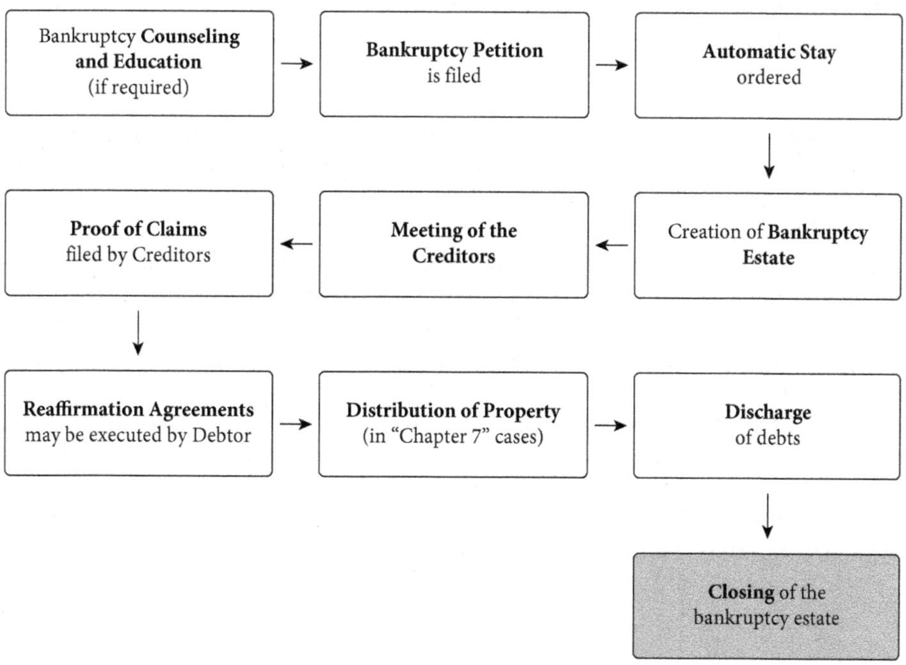

Bankruptcy Counseling and Education

With a few exceptions, individual debtors who wish to file a Chapter 7 personal bankruptcy or a Chapter 13 bankruptcy must receive credit counseling by an approved credit counseling agency within 180 days before they file a bankruptcy petition. The counseling is designed to review the debtor's financial position, provide the debtor with alternatives to filing bankruptcy, and discuss budget plans.

Once a bankruptcy petition has been filed, the debtor must also receive financial management education before their debts may be discharged. Debtor education assists the debtor in developing a budget, managing money, and using credit wisely. Debtor education must also be provided by a U.S. Trustee–approved provider.

Filing a Bankruptcy Petition

A bankruptcy case is commenced by the filing of a voluntary or involuntary petition under a chapter of the Bankruptcy Code. The filing of the bankruptcy petition triggers several consequences, including the creation of a bankruptcy estate consisting of the debtor's property, the automatic stay (discussed below), and the creation of the preference periods for avoiding certain transactions of the debtor prior to the filing date of the petition.

Voluntary petition A petition filed by the insolvent debtor.

VOLUNTARY PETITION. A **voluntary petition** triggers not only an automatic stay but also an automatic order for relief. An automatic stay is an injunction that automatically stops lawsuits, foreclosures, and all collection activity against the debtor the moment a bankruptcy petition is filed. The filing date establishes the date for pre- and post-bankruptcy debts and assets. The petition includes:

- A list of all secured and unsecured creditors.
- A list of all of the debtor's assets, including exempt assets.
- A statement of the debtor's affairs and a schedule of income and expenses.
- A schedule of executory contracts and leases; required notices to creditors and tax authorities; and debtors must also provide the trustee with a copy of filed tax returns.

Median income test A test to determine whether the debtor's familial income is above the median family income for a family of that size residing in the debtor's state.

Means test A test to determine if the debtor has adequate disposable income to pay debts in existence prior to the petition by using income derived after the filing of the petition.

Qualifying for Chapter 7. To prevent debtors from abusing use of a Chapter 7 proceeding instead of filing Chapter 13 bankruptcy, the law requires that a median and means test be used to determine if the debtor qualifies for a discharge of debts under Chapter 7 bankruptcy.

The first step is the median income test. The **median income test** determines whether the debtor's family monthly income is above the median family income for a family of that size residing in the debtor's state. If the debtor's median family income is equal to or below the state median, the debtor will automatically qualify for Chapter 7.

If the debtor's median family income exceeds that of the state median income for a family of that size, the **means test** will be conducted to determine if the debtor qualifies for Chapter 7 bankruptcy. The means test is a calculation made to verify if the debtor has adequate disposable income to pay debts in existence prior to the petition by using income derived after the filing of the petition. The disposable income is determined by subtracting certain statutorily allowed expenses (not the debtor's actual expenses) from the debtor's actual income. If the court finds that the debtor's disposable income is adequate to pay the prepetition debts, the case is usually converted to a Chapter 13 bankruptcy and the debtor is unable to use a Chapter 7 bankruptcy.

INVOLUNTARY PETITION. An **involuntary petition** can be filed only under Chapter 7 and Chapter 11. A debtor may be forced into a bankruptcy proceeding by creditors holding unsecured claims. The filing triggers the automatic stay against most creditor activity. In an involuntary Chapter 7 case, the debtor remains in possession of its business and property until the order for relief is entered or an interim bankruptcy trustee is appointed. The debtor has the right to contest the filing of the involuntary petition.

Involuntary petition A petition filed by creditors of a debtor that alleges the debtor is not paying its debts as they become due.

> **Example:** Debtors who are successful in contesting the filing of the involuntary petition may be entitled to reimbursement of the attorney's fees and costs incurred in contesting the petition. Wes Higgins invented a new fishing lure and created the business Vortex Fishing Systems with Ray Scott. Higgins and Scott were unable to work together, and Scott eventually removed Higgins from the corporation. Higgins then filed an involuntary Chapter 7 bankruptcy petition against Vortex. At trial, the petition was dismissed by the bankruptcy judge. Vortex then filed a motion seeking attorney's fees and costs. The motion was granted, and the court held that the petition was not filed in good faith, but instead by an ousted business partner attempting to force an involuntary bankruptcy in order to gain a business advantage. Therefore, Vortex was entitled to attorney's fees and costs associated with contesting the petition. *Higgins v. Vortex Fishing Systems, Inc.*, 379 F.3d 701 (9th Cir. 2004)

Automatic Stay

Once the bankruptcy petition is filed, an automatic stay arises. The **automatic stay** is one of the most important tools available to a debtor in bankruptcy, as it provides a period during which all collection activities, foreclosures, and repossessions of the debtor's property are suspended. Creditors may not pursue the debtor or the debtor's property for any debt or claim that arose before the filing of the bankruptcy petition. Criminal prosecutions against the debtor are not stayed. In addition, some personal debts continue despite the automatic stay, including child and spousal support. The stay also does not apply to lawsuits commenced against the debtor in the bankruptcy court where the debtor's bankruptcy is pending.

Automatic stay The suspension of legal proceedings against a debtor.

The bankruptcy court can penalize creditors who violate the automatic stay. The court can order the disgorgement (forced return) of the debtor's property unlawfully seized by a creditor and can award damages and attorney's fees to the debtor.

> **Example:** Jamie Aleckna attended California Coast University (CCU) and obtained a Bachelor of Science degree. After graduating, she requested her transcripts, but CCU declined to release them due to a "financial hold" placed on her account. Subsequently, Aleckna filed for Chapter 13 bankruptcy, and included in her petition was the creditor California Coast University (CCU). Aleckna claimed that for CCU to withhold her transcripts was in violation of the automatic stay.

The court agreed with Aleckna and held in her favor. In so doing, the court reasoned that withholding transcripts for payment is an action designed to collect an unpaid debt, and therefore was subject to the automatic stay. *In re Aleckna*, 543 B.R. 717 (Bankr. M.D. Pa. 2016)

RELIEF FROM THE AUTOMATIC STAY. Most creditor actions against a debtor are immediately and automatically stayed upon the filing of the bankruptcy petition. However, many exceptions to the automatic stay exist in which relief from the automatic stay is granted, including the following:

1. Commencement or continuation of any criminal action against the debtor.
2. Commencement or continuation of a civil action regarding paternity, domestic support obligations, child custody, divorce, or domestic violence.
3. A government audit to determine tax liability, a notice of tax deficiency, and a demand for tax returns.
4. Commencement or continuation of an investigation or action by a securities regulation body, and the enforcement of any resulting decision.

In the following case, creditors argued that the mere retention of estate property after filing bankruptcy does not violate the automatic stay. The creditor retained possession of automobiles seized because the owners had not paid for motor vehicle infractions. The question was whether retaining the debtors' vehicles was a failure to turn over property belonging to the debtors and violative of the automatic stay.

CASE 33.1

RETAINING PROPERTY DOES NOT VIOLATE THE AUTOMATIC STAY

CITY OF CHICAGO v. FULTON

592 U.S. 154 (2021)

Supreme Court of the United States

The City of Chicago (City) impounded each respondent's vehicle for failure to pay fines for motor vehicle infractions. Each respondent filed a Chapter 13 bankruptcy petition and requested that the city return their vehicle. The Court of Appeals affirmed all the judgments in a consolidated opinion. The court concluded that "by retaining possession of the debtors' vehicles after they declared bankruptcy," the City had acted "to exercise control over" respondents' property in violation of § 362(a)(3). The Supreme Court granted *certiorari* to resolve a split in the courts of appeals over whether an entity that retains possession of the property of a bankruptcy estate violates § 362(a)(3), the automatic stay provisions.

Language of the Court. *Under the Bankruptcy Code, the filing of a bankruptcy petition has certain immediate consequences. For one thing, a petition "creates an estate" that, with some exceptions, comprises "all legal or equitable interests of* *the debtor in property as of the commencement of the case." § 541(a)(1). Section 541 "is intended to include in the estate any property made available to the estate by other provisions of the Bankruptcy Code." One such provision, § 542, is important for present purposes. Titled "Turnover of property to the estate," § 542 provides, with just a few exceptions, that an entity (other than a custodian) in possession of property of the bankruptcy estate "shall deliver to the trustee, and account for" that property.*

A second automatic consequence of the filing of a bankruptcy petition is that, with certain exceptions, the petition "operates as a stay, applicable to all entities," of efforts to collect from the debtor outside of the bankruptcy forum. The automatic stay serves the debtor's interests by protecting the estate from dismemberment, and it also benefits creditors as a group by preventing individual creditors from pursuing their own interests to the detriment of the others. Under the Code, an individual injured by any wilful violation of the stay "shall recover actual damages, including costs and attorneys' fees, and in appropriate circumstances, may recover punitive damages."

The language used in § 362(a)(3) suggests that merely retaining possession of estate property does not violate the automatic stay. Under that provision, the filing of a bankruptcy petition operates as a "stay" of "any act" to "exercise control" over the property of the estate. Taken together, the most natural reading of these terms— "stay," "act," and "exercise control"—is that § 362(a)(3) prohibits affirmative acts that would disturb the status quo of estate property as of the time when the bankruptcy petition was filed. Taking the provision's operative words in turn, the term "stay" is commonly used to describe an order that "suspend[s] judicial alteration of the status quo."

Decision. The Supreme Court decided that mere retention of the vehicles was not an affirmative act altering the status quo and did not violate the automatic stay.

Focus on Ethics

Why is the automatic stay fair to both the debtor and creditors?

SECURED PROPERTY. In addition, a secured creditor can move for relief from the automatic stay for the following reasons:

- For "cause," including lack of adequate protection; or
- If the debtor has no equity in the property and the property is not necessary for reorganization.

Adequate protection is the relief or compensation given by a court to a secured creditor whose collateral is decreasing in value because the collateral continues to be used

Adequate protection The relief or compensation given by a court to a secured creditor whose collateral is decreasing in value because the collateral continues to be used by the debtor or is sold during the bankruptcy case.

by the debtor or is sold during the bankruptcy case. The types of adequate protection include:

- Cash payments to the secured creditor during bankruptcy (such as continuing rent or mortgage payments).
- Additional or replacement liens (increasing the secured position of the creditor so that its position is not jeopardized).
- Other relief, which may include giving the creditor priority in the distribution of payments from the estate.

Creation of the Bankruptcy Estate

When a bankruptcy petition is filed, a "bankruptcy estate" is created. The bankruptcy estate includes legal and equitable interests in the debtor's property at the time of the bankruptcy filing. The Bankruptcy Code defines the property of the estate in the broadest terms possible, as "wherever located and by whomever held." The bankruptcy estate is a legal entity separate and apart from the debtor.

Generally, property that is acquired after the bankruptcy petition remains the debtors; however, the bankruptcy estate will include certain property that the debtor becomes *entitled to receive* within 180 days of filing the bankruptcy petition. The 180-day rule was created to discourage people from filing a bankruptcy petition when they were anticipating receiving assets that could otherwise be used to pay existing creditors. After-acquired property that will be part of the bankruptcy estate include:

- Inheritances
- Gifts
- Property received from a divorce
- Life insurance proceeds

Order for relief
A court order subjecting the debtor to the control of the bankruptcy court.

In most bankruptcy cases, the filing of the petition also creates an **order for relief**. The order for relief allows the case to proceed through bankruptcy.

PROPERTY EXEMPT FROM THE BANKRUPTCY ESTATE. When filing bankruptcy, the debtor must file a financial statement that lists the debtor's assets, creditors, and exempt property. The Bankruptcy Code allows individual, not corporate, debtors to keep certain property from the bankruptcy estate. This property is called **exempt property**. The type of property considered outside of the bankruptcy estate is provided for by both federal and state law. States may require their citizens to use the exemptions available under the applicable state law. If the state does not have such a requirement, the debtor is free to choose between the state and the federal list of exempt property. The debtor cannot mix and match between the state and federal exemptions and must choose one list of exemptions. If no dollar amount is stated, the entire asset may be exempted. The attorney who represents the debtor must conduct a thorough investigation of the financial statement to make sure the debtor's representations are accurate and truthful.

Homestead exemption
An exemption preventing the forced sale of a home to pay creditors if the home does not have a certain level of equity.

Listing all the available exemptions is beyond the scope of this text, but one relevant exemption is the **homestead exemption**. A homestead exemption prevents the forced sale of a home to pay creditors if the home does not have a certain level of equity.

Different jurisdictions provide different degrees of homestead protection. If the homestead's equity exceeds the homestead exemption amount, creditors may still force the sale of a residence, but the homesteader will be able to keep the protected portion from the sale proceeds. Some examples of homestead provisions are provided below:

- California allows the greater of the following two amounts: the countywide median sale price for a single-family home in the calendar year prior to the year in which the judgment debtor claims the exemption, not to exceed $722,220; or $361,110. These amounts are subject to adjustment for inflation.
- Florida, Iowa, Kansas, Oklahoma, and Texas offer broad protections to a debtor in bankruptcy. In some cases, the homestead has no dollar limit, depending upon the size and location of the property.

Example: Florida's homestead exemption on homes has no dollar limit. However, to qualify for the Florida homestead exemption, an individual must have owned the property for 1,215 days prior to filing and have lived in Florida for at least 730 days prior to filing, and the property must be a half-acre or smaller.

- The federal homestead exemption is $27,900 ($55,800 if married filing jointly).

Management Application Selected Additional Federal Exemptions

1. Up to $4,450 in a motor vehicle.
2. Up to $700 for a single household item, and up to $14,875 in total value of household items.
3. Up to $1,875 in personal jewelry.
4. Up to $2,800 in personal books or tools used in the trade of the debtor.
5. Any life insurance contract with a loan value of up to $14,875, other than a credit life insurance contract.
6. Professionally prescribed health aids.
7. Social Security, unemployment benefits, veteran's benefits, alimony, support, and specific retirement funds.

Example: Richard Kooi was in ongoing divorce proceedings when he filed for a Chapter 7 bankruptcy. The bankruptcy court granted Mrs. Kooi relief from the automatic stay to continue the divorce proceedings. As part of the divorce judgment, Mr. Kooi was awarded all the hockey inventory from his former wife's LLC, and a cash payment of $2,700. Mr. Kooi sought to exempt the cash and property from the bankruptcy estate under the alimony and support exemption. The court rejected Mr. Kooi's argument, finding that the cash and property were part of a property division, and not properly classified as alimony. *In re Kooi*, 547 B.R. 244 (Bankr. W.D. Mich. 2016)

PREFERENTIAL TRANSFERS. The debtor's assets should be equitably distributed among all creditors. The debtor cannot prefer one creditor over another by paying one creditor more or less than other creditors prior to filing bankruptcy. The U.S. Trustee can recover payments made by a debtor to a creditor and include the sums recovered in the bankruptcy estate under certain situations.

Preferential transfer
A wrongful transfer of the debtor's property benefitting one or more creditors by allowing them to receive more than they would have otherwise received in a Chapter 7 liquidation.

Payments made to a creditor for a *preexisting* debt within the 90-day period before a debtor files a bankruptcy petition, or payments made by a debtor to an insider (an individual, partnership, or corporation with a close relationship with the debtor) within one year from filing the bankruptcy petition, are deemed **preferential transfers**. A preferential transfer requires the debtor to receive more than they would have through a bankruptcy proceeding. The trustee may void these preferential transfers.

Not all payments made by a debtor within 90 days before filing bankruptcy are deemed preferential. Creditors who receive payments within the ordinary course of business are not deemed preferential and the U.S. Trustee cannot recover the payment.

Example: Twenty days before filing bankruptcy, the debtor makes a payment to her cell phone carrier for the current month's bill. As the payment was made for a current debt and done in the ordinary course of business, this payment is not a preferential transfer.

Example: In the above example, if 20 days before filing bankruptcy, the debtor's payment to her cell phone carrier was to pay the past four months of cell phone bills, the payment was made for a preexisting debt and the U.S. Trustee could recover this payment as a preferential transfer.

Fraudulent transfer
A transfer made by the debtor with the intent to hinder, delay, or defraud a creditor.

FRAUDULENT TRANSFERS. If the debtor transfers property with the intent to hinder, delay, or defraud a creditor, the trustee may avoid this **fraudulent transfer** if it is made within two years of the filing of the bankruptcy petition. Fraudulent transfers arise when the debtor receives less than the fair market value for the property.

Example: Kudzu Marine, Inc., was a maritime company engaged in pushing tank barges loaded with fuel. As part of its business Kudzu purchased for $1.3 million a large shipping vessel (the "1801"). Kudzu failed to turn a profit and borrowed heavily to maintain operations. Prior to filing for Chapter 7 bankruptcy, the owners of Kudzu sold the 1801 for $460,711.64 to another company owned by a major shareholder of Kudzu. The trustee challenged the transfer as fraudulent. The court found in favor of the trustee and avoided the transfer, reasoning the sales price was not "reasonable equivalent value." *In re Kudzu Marine, Inc.*, 569 B.R. 192 (S.D. Ala. 2017)

Management Application Strategic Planning for Delinquent Debtors

Businesses must be aware of preferential transfer rights. When a third party is delinquent on a payment and the debt becomes preexisting, the bankruptcy court may void the preferential transfer. Assume a client owes $100,000 in preexisting debts to your company and your company, in turn, owes $60,000 to third parties (your own suppliers and vendors). If the client pays the $100,000 to your company and then files bankruptcy 45 days later your company may be obligated to return the $100,000 payment to the bankruptcy estate, even if your company already sent $60,000 in payments to the third parties.

It is prudent to be aware of delinquent debtor's credit risk. Where a company believes that a delinquent party may be on the cusp of filing bankruptcy, the company should retain the payment or not distribute a significant sum of that payment to its own creditors until after the passing of 90 days to avoid the preferential transfer window.

Meeting of Creditors

Once the court grants the order for relief, it schedules a meeting of creditors. This is usually scheduled between 10 to 30 days after the court has granted the order for relief. At the meeting of creditors, the debtor appears and submits to questioning, under oath, by the creditors regarding the debtor's assets, finances, any transfers of property prior to bankruptcy, and so forth.

With parsimony a little is sufficient; without it nothing is sufficient; but frugality makes a poor man rich. —Lucius Annaeus Seneca (Seneca the Younger), Roman Philosopher (unknown- 65 A.D.)

Proofs of Claim

Filing a **proof of claim** is usually a necessary step for the creditor to recover its share of the bankruptcy assets. The bankruptcy court provides the form known as a proof of claim.

Two types of claims can be filed against a debtor—secured and unsecured claims. Unsecured claims are then categorized as either priority claims or general unsecured claims.

Management Application
Proof of Claim

Fill in this information to identify the case:

Debtor 1 ______________________________

Debtor 2 ______________________________
(Spouse, if filing)

United States Bankruptcy Court for the: ________ District of ________

Case number ______________________________

Official Form 410

Proof of Claim

04/19

Read the instructions before filling out this form. This form is for making a claim for payment in a bankruptcy case. Do not use this form to make a request for payment of an administrative expense. Make such a request according to 11 U.S.C. § 503.

Filers must leave out or redact information that is entitled to privacy on this form or on any attached documents. Attach redacted copies of any documents that support the claim, such as promissory notes, purchase orders, invoices, itemized statements of running accounts, contracts, judgments, mortgages, and security agreements. **Do not send original documents;** they may be destroyed after scanning. If the documents are not available, explain in an attachment.

A person who files a fraudulent claim could be fined up to $500,000, imprisoned for up to 5 years, or both. 18 U.S.C. §§ 152, 157, and 3571.

Fill in all the information about the claim as of the date the case was filed. That date is on the notice of bankruptcy (Form 309) **that you received.**

Part 1: Identify the Claim

1. **Who is the current creditor?**

   ____
   Name of the current creditor (the person or entity to be paid for this claim)

   Other names the creditor used with the debtor ______________________________

2. **Has this claim been acquired from someone else?**

   ☐ No
   ☐ Yes. From whom? ______________________________

3. **Where should notices and payments to the creditor be sent?**

   Federal Rule of Bankruptcy Procedure (FRBP) 2002(g)

Where should notices to the creditor be sent?	**Where should payments to the creditor be sent?** (if different)
Name	Name
Number Street	Number Street
City State ZIP Code	City State ZIP Code
Contact phone ________	Contact phone ________
Contact email ________	Contact email ________

   Uniform claim identifier for electronic payments in chapter 13 (if you use one):

   _

4. **Does this claim amend one already filed?**

   ☐ No
   ☐ Yes. Claim number on court claims registry (if known) ______ Filed on ________ MM / DD / YYYY

5. **Do you know if anyone else has filed a proof of claim for this claim?**

   ☐ No
   ☐ Yes. Who made the earlier filing? ______________________________

Official Form 410 **Proof of Claim** page 1

Part 2: Give Information About the Claim as of the Date the Case Was Filed

6. **Do you have any number you use to identify the debtor?**	❑ No ❑ Yes. Last 4 digits of the debtor's account or any number you use to identify the debtor: ___ ___ ___ ___
7. **How much is the claim?**	$___________. **Does this amount include interest or other charges?** ❑ No ❑ Yes. Attach statement itemizing interest, fees, expenses, or other charges required by Bankruptcy Rule 3001(c)(2)(A).
8. **What is the basis of the claim?**	Examples: Goods sold, money loaned, lease, services performed, personal injury or wrongful death, or credit card. Attach redacted copies of any documents supporting the claim required by Bankruptcy Rule 3001(c). Limit disclosing information that is entitled to privacy, such as health care information. ___________________________
9. **Is all or part of the claim secured?**	❑ No ❑ Yes. The claim is secured by a lien on property. **Nature of property:** ❑ Real estate. If the claim is secured by the debtor's principal residence, file a *Mortgage Proof of Claim Attachment* (Official Form 410-A) with this *Proof of Claim.* ❑ Motor vehicle ❑ Other. Describe: ___________ **Basis for perfection:** ___________ Attach redacted copies of documents, if any, that show evidence of perfection of a security interest (for example, a mortgage, lien, certificate of title, financing statement, or other document that shows the lien has been filed or recorded.) **Value of property:** $________ **Amount of the claim that is secured:** $________ **Amount of the claim that is unsecured:** $________(The sum of the secured and unsecured amounts should match the amount in line 7.) **Amount necessary to cure any default as of the date of the petition:** $________ **Annual Interest Rate** (when case was filed)_______% ❑ Fixed ❑ Variable
10. **Is this claim based on a lease?**	❑ No ❑ Yes. **Amount necessary to cure any default as of the date of the petition.** $________
11. **Is this claim subject to a right of setoff?**	❑ No ❑ Yes. Identify the property: ___________

Official Form 410 **Proof of Claim** page 2

		Amount entitled to priority
12. **Is all or part of the claim entitled to priority under 11 U.S.C. § 507(a)?** A claim may be partly priority and partly nonpriority. For example, in some categories, the law limits the amount entitled to priority.	❑ No ❑ Yes. *Check one:*	
	❑ Domestic support obligations (including alimony and child support) under 11 U.S.C. § 507(a)(1)(A) or (a)(1)(B).	$__________
	❑ Up to $3,025* of deposits toward purchase, lease, or rental of property or services for personal, family, or household use. 11 U.S.C. § 507(a)(7).	$__________
	❑ Wages, salaries, or commissions (up to $13,650*) earned within 180 days before the bankruptcy petition is filed or the debtor's business ends, whichever is earlier. 11 U.S.C. § 507(a)(4).	$__________
	❑ Taxes or penalties owed to governmental units. 11 U.S.C. § 507(a)(8).	$__________
	❑ Contributions to an employee benefit plan. 11 U.S.C. § 507(a)(5).	$__________
	❑ Other. Specify subsection of 11 U.S.C. § 507(a)(__) that applies.	$__________
	* Amounts are subject to adjustment on 4/01/22 and every 3 years after that for cases begun on or after the date of adjustment.	

Part 3: Sign Below

The person completing this proof of claim must sign and date it. FRBP 9011(b).

If you file this claim electronically, FRBP 5005(a)(2) authorizes courts to establish local rules specifying what a signature is.

A person who files a fraudulent claim could be fined up to $500,000, imprisoned for up to 5 years, or both. 18 U.S.C. §§ 152, 157, and 3571.

Check the appropriate box:

❑ I am the creditor.

❑ I am the creditor's attorney or authorized agent.

❑ I am the trustee, or the debtor, or their authorized agent. Bankruptcy Rule 3004.

❑ I am a guarantor, surety, endorser, or other codebtor. Bankruptcy Rule 3005.

I understand that an authorized signature on this *Proof of Claim* serves as an acknowledgment that when calculating the amount of the claim, the creditor gave the debtor credit for any payments received toward the debt.

I have examined the information in this *Proof of Claim* and have a reasonable belief that the information is true and correct.

I declare under penalty of perjury that the foregoing is true and correct.

Executed on date ____________
MM / DD / YYYY

____
Signature

Print the name of the person who is completing and signing this claim:

Name ________________________
First name Middle name Last name

Title ________________________

Company ________________________
Identify the corporate servicer as the company if the authorized agent is a servicer.

Address ________________________
Number Street

____
City State ZIP Code

Contact phone ____________ Email ____________

Official Form 410 **Proof of Claim** page 3

Secured Claim
A claim secured by a valid lien on the debtor's real or personal property.

SECURED CLAIM. A **secured claim** is a claim secured by a valid lien on the debtor's real or personal property. Secured claims have priority over all unsecured claims in the right of payment from the bankruptcy estate, up to the amount of the claim and the value of the assets. Whether or not a creditor's claim is secured depends upon the rights of the creditor under state law.

UNSECURED CLAIM. An **unsecured claim** is a claim in which no property or asset serves as collateral or security for the debt.

Unsecured claim
A claim in which no property or asset serves as collateral or security for the debt.

FILING OF PROOF OF CLAIMS. Unsecured creditors in Chapter 7 and Chapter 13 cases must file a proof of claim to be entitled to receive distributions at the close of the bankruptcy. In Chapter 7 or Chapter 13 proceedings, all proofs of claim must be filed within 90 days after the initial meeting of creditors. In Chapter 11 cases, a claim is deemed filed when it has been listed by the debtor in possession or the bankruptcy trustee if the schedules filed reflect the claim.

Generally, Chapter 11 cases set a bar date (that is, a deadline) for the filing of proofs of claim. A proof of claim, once filed, is deemed an allowable claim of the estate unless the debtor or another party objects to the claim. A properly executed and filed proof of claim constitutes prima facie evidence of its validity. A person objecting to a claim in a bankruptcy has the duty to overcome that presumption.

Reaffirmation Agreements

In Chapter 7 cases, a debtor may enter into a reaffirmation agreement with a creditor. A **reaffirmation agreement** is an agreement in which the debtor agrees to continue to pay a dischargeable debt to a creditor after the discharge in bankruptcy. A reaffirmation agreement must be filed with the court prior to the time at which the bankruptcy discharge is granted.

Reaffirmation agreement
An agreement in which the debtor agrees to pay a dischargeable debt to a creditor after the discharge in bankruptcy.

> **Example:** A debtor has an automobile that was financed with an auto loan. If the debtor wishes to continue to possess the vehicle after bankruptcy, they will enter into a reaffirmation agreement with the auto lender prior to the discharge in bankruptcy.

In the following case, the court considered the validity of a reaffirmation agreement between an individual and a bank.

CASE 33.2

REPAYMENT AGREEMENTS THAT ARE NOT SUBMITTED FOR APPROVAL BY THE BANKRUPTCY COURT ARE UNENFORCEABLE

VENTURE BANK v. LAPIDES

800 F.3d 442 (2015)

United States Court of Appeals for the Eighth Circuit

Howard Lapides obtained a loan from Venture Bank, secured by a third mortgage on his home. Subsequently, Mr. Lapides filed for Chapter 7 bankruptcy protection. Shortly after filing, Mr. Lapides met with Venture Bank and executed an agreement to pay $3,000 a month for continued use of the home (the Change in

Terms Agreement). The agreement was never submitted to the bankruptcy court. Later, Mr. Lapides emerged from bankruptcy and had his debts discharged. He continued to pay between $3,000 and $3,500 a month for 12 months to Venture Bank. Mr. Lapides ceased making payments once he lost his job. Venture Bank sued Mr. Lapides for breach of contract on the loan agreement, Mr. Lapides counterclaimed asserting that the loan was discharged as part of his Chapter 7 proceeding. The bankruptcy court held in favor of Mr. Lapides, and the district court affirmed. Venture Bank appealed.

Language of the Court. *A reaffirmation agreement is one in which the debtor agrees to repay all or part of a dischargeable debt after a bankruptcy petition has been filed. Under federal bankruptcy law, reaffirmation agreements are enforceable only if they are enforceable under state law and meet the requirements of the bankruptcy code § 524(c).*

In the 1978 Bankruptcy Code, Congress sought to equalize the unequal bargaining positions of experienced creditors and unsophisticated bankruptcy debtors by enacting § 524(c) of the Code, which provides in relevant part:

> *(c) AN AGREEMENT BETWEEN A HOLDER OF A CLAIM AND THE DEBTOR IS ENFORCEABLE ONLY IF—*
>
> *(1) such agreement was made before the granting of the discharge;*
> *(2) the debtor received the disclosures;*
> *(2) such agreement has been filed with the court.*

If the Agreements violate § 524(c), they are unenforceable as a matter of law, whether or not they would be enforceable under applicable state law contract principles. It is undisputed that the post-discharge Change in Terms Agreements were not enforceable § 524(c) reaffirmation agreements, most obviously because they were entered into after Mr. Lapides' bankruptcy discharge and were not filed with the bankruptcy court.

The Agreements served no purpose other than reaffirmation agreements in which Mr. Lapides agreed to repay all his discharged personal debt. Instead of continuing to accept Howard's voluntary payments, a post-discharge arrangement both parties were free to continue, Venture Bank insisted that Mr. Lapides again promise to repay the entire discharged personal debt in order to continue the refinancing negotiations.

When a post-discharge agreement does nothing but obligate a debtor to repay a discharged debt, it is inconsistent with § 524(c), a statute declaring that agreements removing specific personal debts from the benefits of discharge must be negotiated and filed with the court before discharge, when a debtor has the protection of his bankruptcy attorney and the bankruptcy court. We simply conclude that the post-discharge Change in Terms Agreements are unenforceable because they were nothing more than reaffirmation agreements that did not comply with § 524(c).

Decision. The court found in favor of Mr. Lapides. In so doing, the court reasoned that the Change in Terms Agreement was never properly submitted to the bankruptcy court and thus was not a valid reaffirmation agreement.

Focus on Ethics

The court focused on the strict formality of requiring all reaffirmation agreements to be submitted to the bankruptcy court. Is this strict requirement unfair to creditors? Does the Bankruptcy Code unfairly favor debtors?

Distributions of Property (in Chapter 7 Cases)

In Chapter 7 cases, nonexempt property must be distributed to the debtor's secured and unsecured creditors. Secured creditors have priority over the claims of unsecured creditors and paid in full first before any assets are distributed to unsecured creditors. Any assets remaining after the distribution, while unlikely to occur, are returned to the debtor.

SECURED CREDITORS. Secured creditors are paid in full before assets are distributed to unsecured creditors. With secured creditors, two situations may arise:

1. *Oversecured secured creditor.* An oversecured secured creditor is when the value of the collateral exceeds the secured creditor's bankruptcy claim. The property is usually sold, and the creditor is paid in full (including interest, reasonable fees and costs under the security agreement). The excess funds can then be used by the second priority secured creditors or unsecured creditors.
2. *Undersecured secured creditor.* An undersecured secured creditor is when the value of the collateral is less than the secured creditor's bankruptcy claim. The property is usually given to the creditor and the creditor becomes an unsecured creditor for the remaining balance owed.

UNSECURED CREDITORS. Unsecured creditors are paid according to the priority set forth in the Bankruptcy Code. The statutory priority includes domestic support allegations (child and alimony payments), followed by bankruptcy administrative expenses, wages and salaries owed, income taxes owed, and claims for personal injuries or death caused by a debtor who was intoxicated.

Creditors in lower classes (such as bankruptcy administrative expenses or domestic support allegations) are paid once the higher class unsecured creditor is paid in full. If any class of creditor cannot be paid in full, then each of the creditors in that class is paid a proportionate amount.

Bankruptcy Discharge

A **bankruptcy discharge** releases the debtor from liability for certain specified debts. In other words, the debtor is no longer obligated to pay them. The Bankruptcy Code provides that a discharge voids any judgment against the debtor to the extent that it affects the debtor's personal liability; a discharge also stops the commencement or continuation of an action to collect or offset a debt. Debts not included in the bankruptcy, or for which a reaffirmation agreement was executed, or that cannot be discharged in bankruptcy, remain in effect after the discharge.

Bankruptcy discharge
A court order that relieves a debtor from the obligation to pay for certain debts included in the bankruptcy proceeding.

CHAPTER 7 DISCHARGE. In a Chapter 7 bankruptcy, the debtors retain the exempt property and are discharged from liabilities, debts, and obligations that were subject to the bankruptcy proceeding.

CHAPTER 11 DISCHARGE. In a Chapter 11 bankruptcy, a business entity will be discharged from its debts and liabilities that have occurred prior to the confirmation of the plan. The effect of the confirmation is to make the plan binding on all parties and to grant the debtor a discharge from those claims not provided for by the plan. Following the reorganization, the debtor is revested with all property of the estate on confirmation.

Confirmation in Chapter 11 can occur through acceptance by a class of claims. Such acceptance requires holders of more than 50 percent of those claims and representing at least two-thirds of the dollar totals to approve the plan. **Confirmation** makes the plan binding on all parties. Confirmation can also occur through a cramdown. If one or more classes of creditors object to the plan, the bankruptcy court can force those creditors to accept the plan through a **cramdown**. The requirements for a cramdown are:

Confirmation
Bankruptcy court approval of a plan of reorganization under Chapter 11.

Cramdown
A bankruptcy rule allowing the court to confirm a plan of reorganization over the objections of a class of creditors, subject to certain restrictions.

- Acceptance by at least one class of creditors;
- A finding that the plan is fair and equitable (the plan must follow the absolute priority rule of distribution and not allow payments in excess of any allowed claim); and
- A finding that the plan does not unfairly discriminate against any class of creditors (each class of creditors of equal rank in priority must receive proportionate amounts).

Example: A bankruptcy court may approve a plan that treated an unsecured trade creditor class more favorably than a general unsecured creditor class because the continued supply of the trade vendors' services and products were essential to the debtor's successful operations. In one case, the debtor had developed business relationships with these vendors over several years that could not easily be replaced. Failure to pay these vendors in full, the bankruptcy court held, would likely lead to their refusal to do business with the debtor, resulting in serious harm to the debtor's post-confirmation reorganization efforts. Discrimination among creditors was found to be reasonable. *In re Creekstone Apartments Associates, L.P.*, 168 B.R. 639 (Bankr. M.D. Tenn. 1994)

CHAPTER 13 DISCHARGE. Chapter 13 is the simplest form of reorganization available to individuals who have debt below certain thresholds for noncontingent, liquidated, unsecured debts and noncontingent, liquidated, secured debts. In consideration for retaining nonexempt assets, the debtor must formulate a plan in which the debtor is required to pay creditors not less than the value of the nonexempt assets being retained over a period of no more than five years. The debtor in a Chapter 13 case is not discharged until the plan is performed to completion.

A trustee is appointed in Chapter 13 cases, but the Chapter 13 trustee's duties differ from those of a Chapter 7 trustee. The only property that the Chapter 13 trustee deals with is the debtor's earnings, which are the source of payments under the plan. The primary duty of the Chapter 13 trustee is to make the required disbursements to creditors and monitor the debtor's performance of the plan.

Management Application Nondischargeable Debts in Bankruptcy

The Bankruptcy Code provides that certain debts arising from intentional or willful conduct are nondischargeable. Among them are the following:

- Loans obtained by material misrepresentations or omissions made by the debtor to induce the lender to make the loan.
- Claims arising from fraud, breaches of duty by a fiduciary, embezzlement, or larceny.
- Claims for willful and malicious injury, including punitive damages.

Other debts are nondischargeable as a matter of law, including:

- Debts not listed or scheduled by the debtor in the bankruptcy unless the creditor had actual knowledge of the bankruptcy in time to permit the timely filing of a proof of claim. However, when no assets exist that compel the filing of a proof of claim and no claim exists for nondischargeability, such unlisted or unscheduled debts are discharged.
- Domestic support obligations (such as child support and spousal support).
- Student loans, in the absence of an undue hardship.
- Liability for wrongful death and personal injury caused while operating a vehicle under the influence of alcohol or drugs.
- Certain claims against the debtor arising from fraud while acting in a fiduciary capacity.
- Claims for condominium fees, homeowner's association fees, or assessments that become due and payable post-petition.
- Liability for violation of federal or state securities laws and regulations arising from or relating to the sale of a security.

DEBTOR'S ACTIONS BARRING DISCHARGE. Sometimes a debtor's actions may bar (deny) discharge. Examples of debtor actions that bar discharge include:

- Making false representations when obtaining credit;
- Transferring, concealing, removing, or destroying estate property with the intent to hinder, delay, or defraud creditors within one year before the filing date;
- Falsifying, destroying, or concealing records of financial condition;
- Failing to disclose all assets;
- Failing to participate in the meeting of creditors; and
- Failing to take a credit counseling course required for personal bankruptcies (unless excused).

REVOCATION OF BANKRUPTCY DISCHARGE. A discharge can be revoked under certain circumstances. These cases often occur when the debtor has obtained the discharge fraudulently, failed to disclose that the debtor acquired or became entitled to acquire property that would constitute property of the bankruptcy estate, or committed one or several statutory acts of impropriety.

Closing of the Bankruptcy Estate

Upon the closing or dismissal of the case, the bankruptcy court continues its jurisdiction to enforce or interpret any of its orders. The bankruptcy court retains the power to reopen the case "to administer assets, to accord relief to the debtor, or for any other cause." The automatic stay terminates upon closing, except with regard to property not scheduled and not administered. Such property remains the property of the bankruptcy estate, and the debtor has no right to that property. The closing of the case terminates the trustee's services.

AI Feature: State Bankruptcy Exemptions

Using an internet search engine, identify the exemptions available to individuals filing for bankruptcy in your home state and those afforded by another state that offers generous personal exemptions. Compare those exemptions to those afforded under federal law. Then, using an AI program, compare and contrast your findings. Why are there variations in what state laws seek to protect? With the AI program, identify those states that are most generous in exempting debtor assets from the bankruptcy estate. Do those states require the debtor to be a full-time resident before being able to invoke those exemptions? What is the public perception of the strategy of moving to debtor-friendly states and then petitioning for bankruptcy?

Key Terms

- Adequate protection, 839
- Adversary proceeding, 834
- Automatic stay, 837
- Bankruptcy discharge, 849
- Bankruptcy estate, 834
- Bankruptcy plan, 834
- Bankruptcy trustee, 833
- Chapter 11, 831
- Chapter 7, 830
- Chapter 13, 832
- Claim, 834
- Confirmation, 850
- Cramdown, 850
- Creditor, 830
- Creditor's committee, 833
- Debtor, 830
- Debtor in possession, 833
- Discharge, 834

- Executory contract or lease, 834
- Exemptions, 834
- Fraudulent transfer, 842
- Homestead exemption, 840
- Insider, 834
- Involuntary petition, 837
- Means test, 836
- Median income test, 836
- Order for relief, 840
- Preference or preferential debt repayment, 834
- Preferential transfer, 842
- Priority, 834
- Proof of claim, 834
- Reaffirmation agreement, 847
- Secured claim, 846
- Secured creditor, 834
- Secured debt, 834
- Unsecured claim, 847
- U.S. Trustee, 833
- Voluntary petition, 836

Applying the Law

33.1 Research the Law. Using an internet search engine, research the exemptions from the bankruptcy estate in your home state and compare them to the federal exemptions discussed in this chapter. Which exemptions would you prefer if you filed for bankruptcy protection? Why? What conditions are imposed upon a debtor seeking to move to another state to enjoy more generous exemptions?

33.2 Discharge. William Harrington the U.S. Trustee filed an adversary proceeding seeking to revoke the Chapter 7 discharge of Anthony and Michelle Mazzone. The Mazzones requested that their tenant Robert Bost make monthly rent payments in cash. They also requested that he not take the state income tax deduction for rental payments available to Massachusetts taxpayers. The Mazzones made these requests so that the City of Methuen would not discover their illegal basement apartment and the federal and state taxing authorities would not discover their rental income which they did not declare on their state and federal income tax returns. They failed to disclose rental income in their bankruptcy schedules and lied about the rental arrangement at their meeting of creditors. How should the court rule? *Harrington v. Mazzone (In re Mazzone)*, 510 B.R. 439 (Bankr. D. Mass. 2014)

33.3 Liquidation. Nnika and Mark White (Debtors) filed for Chapter 13 bankruptcy. The Debtors' primary asset was a 100 percent ownership interest in The Law Offices of White & Associates, PLLC (White Law Firm). Debtors filed an initial Chapter 13 repayment plan, but the trustee objected, due to a substantial amount of missing and misleading documentation. Also, the debtors understated their income by using business funds to pay personal expenses, proposed unconfirmable amended plans to discourage creditor participation until after the claim bar date and failed to make payments under the plans. The trustee sought to convert the case to Chapter 7 liquidation because of the unreasonable delay caused harm to the creditors. The Debtors argued that the most recent repayment plan was superior to Chapter 7 liquidation because they offered to pay 100 percent of unsecured debts. Should the court force the Debtors to liquidate their assets? *In re White*, 542 B.R. 762 (Bankr. E.D. Va. 2015)

33.4 Automatic Stay. Crest By The Sea, LLC (Crest) is a member-managed limited liability company that designed, developed, and sold a residential community consisting of ten condominium units contained by a single building. Prior to Crest's bankruptcy petition, it was the defendant in a state law action for construction defects initiated by the Condominium Homeowner's Association (collectively, the "Association") that claimed breach of contract. Crest denied liability. While the litigation was ongoing, Crest filed for Chapter 7 bankruptcy protection, giving rise to an automatic stay that applied to the state law action. The Association filed a motion to dismiss the Chapter 7 bankruptcy petition due to bad faith by Crest, or in the alternative, a motion seeking relief from the automatic stay. Review this decision and decide if the order of dismissal was appropriate and fair to the parties. *In Re Crest by the Sea*, LLC, 522 B.R. 540 (2014)

33.5 Undue Hardship Discharge. Kristin Price (Debtor) was a 29-year-old mother of three, with a total of $56,442.37 in student loan debt. In addition, Ms. Price and her husband were separated, although he did contribute $2,000 per month in child support. Ms. Price earned a degree in sonography and passed a licensing examination. She had only been able to acquire part-time work as a sonographer. Ms. Price argued that she met the hardship discharge as to her student loans because her financial circumstances were not likely to improve and would continue for a significant time during the repayment period. The loan holder argued that Ms. Price was young and able, and her financial situation would likely improve as the job market improved. Did she meet the undue hardship standard such that her student loan debt should be discharged? *Devos v. Price*, 583 B.R. 850 (Bankr. E.D. Pa. 2018)

33.6 Bad Faith Evidence in Bankruptcy. Four creditors of Medpoint Management LLC filed an involuntary Chapter 7 petition against Medpoint. Thereafter, Medpoint claimed that it was entitled to damages against the petitioning creditors' actions because they were motivated by a bad faith desire to take control of its valuable medical marijuana certificate issued under Arizona law. The court denied the opportunity to hear evidence on the matter in part because the business was operating illegally under federal law. Was the court's decision proper? *Medpoint Mgmt., Inc. v. Jensen (In re Medpoint Mgmt., LLC)*, 2016 Bankr. LEXIS 2197 (9th Cir. 2016)

33.7 Wildcard Statutes. While suing her former employer for employment discrimination, Courtney Hall (Debtor) field for Chapter 7. In her filings, she declared that the lawsuit was of unknown value and not property of the bankruptcy estate when she for Chapter 7 protection. Can the debtor file what is known as a federal "wildcard" exemption, which allows a debtor to exempt essentially an unknown amount? Can she exempt her lawsuit from the proceedings? *In re Hall*, 453 B.R. 22 (Bankr. D. Mass. 2011)

33.8 Renewed Objections to Exemptions. Loren Brown filed for relief under Chapter 13 of the Bankruptcy Code claiming as exempt a portion of the bankruptcy's estate interest in his home. The Chapter 13 plan was confirmed without objection. Brown later elected to convert the case to a Chapter 7 proceeding. Would the Chapter 7 trustee, a party in interest to the second proceeding, have a new opportunity to object to exemptions previously claimed by the debtor? *In re Brown*, 375 B.R. 362 (Bankr. W.D. Mich. 2007)

33.9 Dischargeable Debt. Cynthia Dean and her husband were divorced in December of 1998. Since her divorce, she had not remarried. Subsequently, Dean entered into an agreement whereby she assigned to Ulysses Telegadis the remaining monthly alimony payments that she was scheduled to receive from her former husband. As consideration for the sum, Telegadis made a lump-sum payment to the debtor, and she agreed to remit the rest of her payments to Telegadis. But Dean filed for a voluntary Chapter 7 and claimed an exemption in the full amount of the remaining payments from her ex-husband's alimony. Dean sought to discharge the debt she owed to Telegadis. May she reject the contract with Telegadis? *In re Dean*, 317 B.R. 482 (Bankr. W.D. Pa. 2004)

33.10 Proof of Claim. Robert Hawxhurst sued Pettibone Corporation for personal injuries suffered when operating a baggage tractor manufactured by Pettibone. While that suit was pending, Pettibone filed a Chapter 11 proceeding. Hawxhurst failed to file a proof of claim prior to discharge of defendant's debts and later sought leave to file late proof of claim and to modify the post-confirmation injunction preventing the prosecution of his case. The court denied the motion to file a late proof of claim, from which Hawxhurst did not appeal, but permitted him to proceed against Pettibone's insurance companies. Explain. *Hawxhurst v. Pettibone Corp.*, 40 F.3d 175 (7th Cir. 1994)

Administrative Law

34

Formerly, we suffered from crimes; now we suffer from laws. — Tacitus, Roman historian (55-120 A.D.)

Chapter Outline

- Introduction
- Administrative Agencies
- Creation of Administrative Agencies
- Administrative Agency Powers

Case 34.1: *Moore v. K-Mart Corp.*

  - *Management Application: The SEC's Whistleblower Program*
  - *Management Application: Sample Letter Accompanying a Subpoena to Produce Business's Records*

Case 34.2: *Huntley v. Social Security Administration, Commissioner*

- Administrative Agencies and Judicial Deference

Case 34.3: *Loper Bright Enterprises v. Raimondo*

- Public Disclosure of Agency Actions
- AI Feature: Draft a Local Rent Control Ordinance

Learning Objectives

After studying this chapter, you should be able to:

1. Explain how administrative agencies enforce their rules and regulations.
2. Review the tests used to ensure an agency is acting in accord with the APA.
3. Define the limits of an agency's ability to interpret a statute.
4. Identify key federal statutes enacted to promote public disclosure of federal administrative agency actions.

Introduction

Administrative law
The body of law that regulates the operation and procedures of government agencies.

Regulations
Specific guidelines for conducting and enforcing policies established by laws.

Administrative agencies
Agencies created by federal, state, and local governments to enforce regulatory statutes.

Judge Henry Friendly, who served on the United States Court of Appeals for the Second Circuit, provided a good definition of administrative law: "Administrative law includes the entire range of action by government with respect to the citizen or by the citizen with respect to the government, except for those matters dealt with by the criminal law and those left to private civil litigation where the government's participation is in furnishing an impartial tribunal with the power of enforcement."[1]

This definition of administrative law encompasses broad powers and authority. **Administrative law** is defined as the body of rules, orders, and decisions issued by administrative agencies in order to regulate industries and businesses. It plays an important role across all industries and has a significant impact on virtually all businesses in the United States. In order to enforce these regulations, federal, state, and local governments create **administrative agencies**. Administrative agencies have been informally referred to as the fourth branch of the government due to the power and control they exercise in our society.

This chapter will discuss the role administrative law plays in our legal system, as well as the significant influence these rules and regulations have on business.

History of Administrative Agencies

The first federal administrative agency in the United States was the Interstate Commerce Commission, established in 1887. Congress created it to regulate railroads and address issues like discriminatory pricing practices. It marked the beginning of continuing government intervention within industry through the administrative process.

Administrative agencies became prominent in the regulation of businesses during the presidency of Franklin D. Roosevelt. Roosevelt's New Deal vastly expanded federal government programs and agency powers to generate an economic revival. With each new financial or societal crisis, the government often creates new agencies to intervene to address the underlying and persistent problems. Recent examples on the federal level are the Cybersecurity and Infrastructure Security Agency (CISA) and the Consumer Financial Protection Bureau (CFPB).

Administrative Agencies

When the government (federal, state, or local) creates a new statute, an administrative agency often will administer and enforce that statute. Sometimes, a new administrative agency is formed (such as the Securities and Exchange Commission formed after the

1. Henry J. Friendly, *New Trends in Administrative Law*, Md. B.J., Apr. 1974, at 9.

enactment of the Securities Act of 1933 and the Securities Exchange Act of 1934), but often an already existing administrative agency assumes the role of administering and enforcing the statute. The implementation of the statute is left to the administrative agency to create substantive and interpretive rules and regulations and pursue enforcement actions.

For information on federal administrative agencies, see, the US Government Manual at: https://usgovernmentmanual.gov; and an index of U.S. government department and agencies at: https://www.usa.gov/agency-index.

Federal Agencies

Federal agencies operate at the national level and can be grouped into two types: (1) executive agencies or (2) independent regulatory agencies. **Executive agencies** are those that exist within the cabinet departments of the executive branch (such as the National Park Service is within the Department of the Interior) or the Executive Office of the President (such as the Director of National Intelligence). These agencies are subject to the authority of the President because the President has the power to appoint and remove the officers of these federal agencies.

Executive agencies Agencies that exist within the cabinet departments of the executive branch.

Federal Executive Departments

Department Name	Principal Duties
Agriculture	Governs food, agriculture, natural resources, rural development, nutrition, and related issues based on public policy.
Commerce	Promotes job creation and economic growth by ensuring fair and secure trade.
Defense	Provides the military forces needed to deter war and to protect the security of the country.
Education	Promotes student achievement and preparation for global competitiveness by fostering educational excellence and ensuring equal access.
Energy	Ensures America's security and prosperity by addressing its energy, environmental, and nuclear challenges through transformative science and technology solutions.
Health and Human Services	Enhances and protects the health and well-being of all Americans by providing for effective health and human services and fostering advances in medicine, public health, and social services.
Homeland Security	Prevents terrorism and enhances our nation's security, manages borders, enforces trade laws, administers immigration laws, secures cyberspace, and ensures disaster resilience.
Housing and Urban Development	Creates strong, sustainable, inclusive communities and quality affordable homes.
Interior	Protects and manages the nation's natural resources and cultural heritage and provides scientific and other information about those resources.

Department Name	Principal Duties
Justice	Enforces the law and defends the interests of the United States, ensures public safety against threats, provides federal leadership in preventing and controlling crime, and seeks just punishment for those guilty of unlawful behavior.
Labor	Promotes and develops the welfare of wage earners, job seekers, and retirees of the United States; improves working conditions; advances opportunities for profitable employment; and assures work-related benefits and rights.
State	Shapes and sustains a peaceful, prosperous, just, and democratic world and fosters conditions for stability and progress for the benefit of the American people and people everywhere.
Transportation	Ensures a fast, safe, efficient, accessible, and convenient transportation system.
Treasury	Promotes conditions enabling economic growth and stability, strengthens national security by combating threats and protecting the integrity of the financial system, and manages the U.S. government's finances and resources.
Veterans Affairs	To fulfill President Lincoln's promise "to care for him who shall have borne the battle, and for his widow, and his orphan" by serving and honoring the people who are America's veterans.

Independent regulatory agencies Federal agencies with broad powers created by Congress, whose officers serve fixed terms and can only be removed for just cause.

The other type of federal agencies are **independent regulatory agencies** (also known as **federal administrative agencies**). These agencies are given broad regulatory powers. While the President appoints the officers who serve on these agencies, the officers serve for fixed terms and may only be removed for just cause. While independent regulatory agencies play a significant role in the federal government, they do not constitute the majority of federal agencies. Congress establishes independent regulatory agencies to have a degree of independence from presidential control, often to regulate specific sectors or activities. A chart describing selected independent agencies appears below.

Selected Independent Regulatory Agencies

Agency Name	Principal Duties
The Federal Reserve (the "Fed")	Conducts monetary policy to promote maximum employment, stable prices, and moderate long-term interest rates. Supervises and regulates banks. Maintains financial stability when confronted with systemic risks that may arise in financial markets and acts as a lender of last resort during economic crises. Operates payment systems of banks.

Agency Name	Principal Duties
Federal Trade Commission (FTC)	Protects consumers by preventing anticompetitive, deceptive, and unfair business practices. Enhances informed consumer choice and public understanding of the competitive process without unduly burdening legitimate business activity.
National Labor Relations Board (NLRB)	Protects the rights of private-sector employees to join together, with or without a union, to improve their wages and working conditions.
Securities and Exchange Commission (SEC)	Protects investors; maintains fair, orderly, and efficient markets; and facilitates capital formation.
Small Business Administration (SBA)	Aids, counsels, assists, and protects the interests of small business concerns, to preserve free competitive enterprise and to maintain and strengthen the overall economy of our nation.

State and Local Agencies

There are administrative agencies at the state and local level. **State administrative agencies** are created to administer and enforce state regulatory law. They also work alongside a federal agency to expand the scope of federal agency protections to state concerns. For example, each state has created its own department of education (a state administrative agency) to work cooperatively with the United States Department of Education (a federal administrative agency). Federal statutes preempt (override) any conflicting state or local laws, as discussed in Chapter 4; similarly, federal administrative agency regulations preempt conflicting state or local administrative agency regulations.

State administrative agencies Administrative agencies that administer and enforce state regulatory law.

Example: The Red River Authority of Texas is a Texas administrative agency that enforces the orderly conservation, reclamation, protection, and development of the water resources throughout the Red River Basin for the benefit of the public.

In addition to state agencies, many local governments create **local administrative agencies** to administer and enforce their local regulatory law. Since federal, state, and local regulations vary widely, this text will focus on federal administrative law.

Local administrative agencies Administrative agencies that administer and enforce local regulatory law and may work in coordination with a federal or state agency.

Example: The Public Art Review Board is a local administrative agency in Orange County, Florida, responsible for approving the annual Public Art Action Plan and Artist Selection Panel recommendations with respect to county capital improvement projects.

FIGURE 34.1: The Structure of Federal Administrative Law

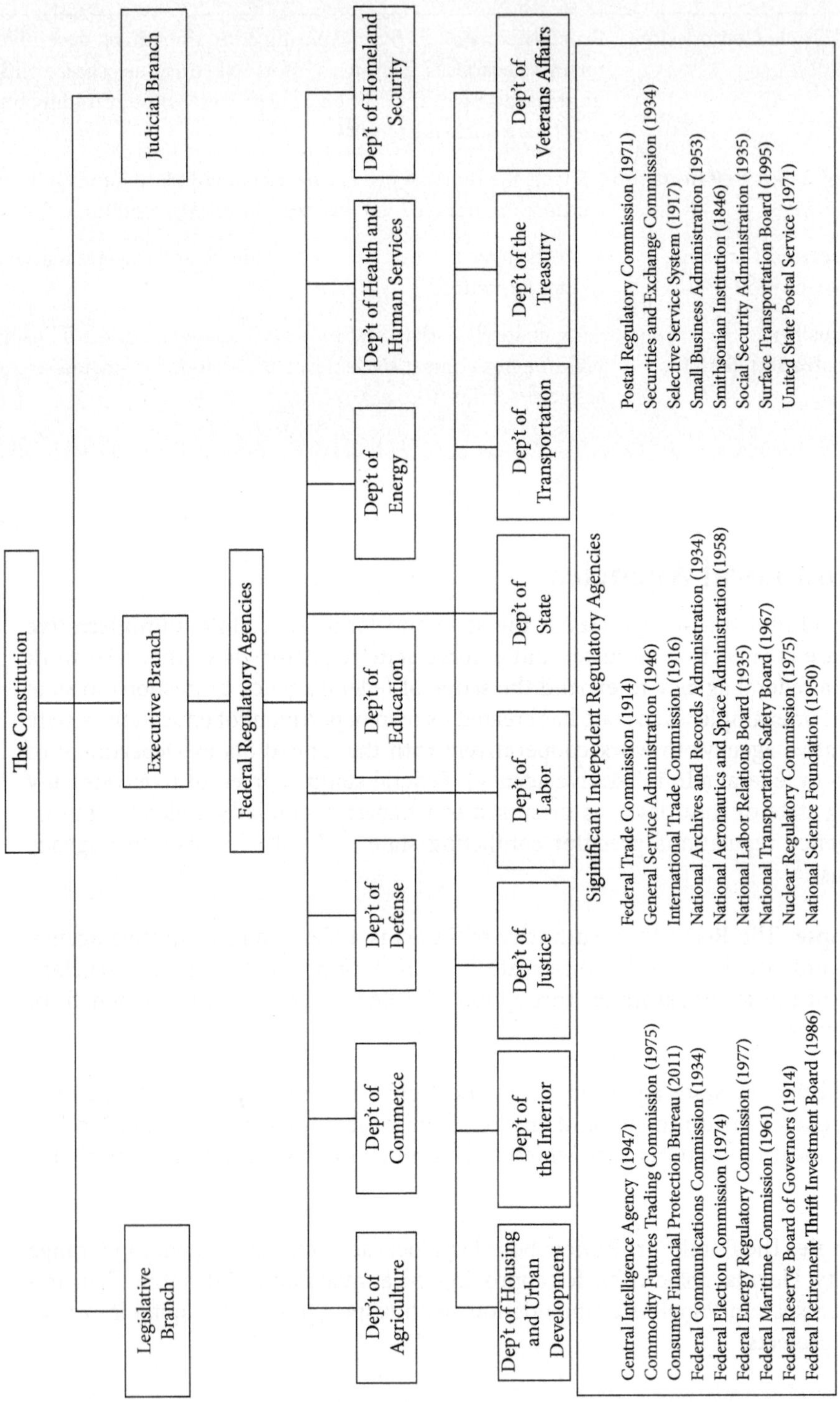

Creation of Administrative Agencies

One of the primary reasons for the growth in power of administrative agencies is the delegation of legislative authority by Congress. Congress has passed laws that outline broad goals, such as improving public health or environmental standards, but leaves the specifics to be determined by administrative agencies. This delegation allows agencies to create detailed regulations that have the force of law. The justification for expanding agency powers is due to the increasing complexity of modern life and the need for specialized expertise that agencies can provide.

The United States Constitution provides Congress the implied power to delegate its legislative authority. Congress uses such authority and can create an administrative agency through the delegation doctrine. The **delegation doctrine** provides that the administrative agency has only those legislative (adopt a rule), executive (enforce a rule), and judicial (adjudicate a dispute) powers that are delegated to it.

Delegation doctrine A principle providing an administrative agency only those legislative, executive, and judicial powers delegated to it.

To create the administrative agency, the legislature enacts **enabling legislation** creating the administrative agency and delegates the powers to it. If the delegation of authority is too vague to permit a reviewing court to determine whether the agency has acted beyond the scope of its power, the agency's actions will be deemed unconstitutional. Thus, administrative agencies are provided broad powers under enabling legislation so that they may act lawfully.

Enabling legislation A governmental statute creating an administrative agency and delegating powers to it.

Administrative Agency Powers

The enabling legislation delegates the administrative agency with certain legislative, executive, and judicial powers. Administrative agencies are therefore unusual because such power is usually divided between the three branches of government and not held by a single organization. With three separate branches of government, a system of checks and balances provides that no one branch of government can exceed its lawful authority. With administrative agencies, though, all three systems of checks and balances are housed within the agency. Administrative agency powers are discussed in the next sections.

Legislative Power

The legislative powers that have been delegated to administrative agencies can include the power to engage in rulemaking, to issue statements of policy, and to grant licenses.

RULEMAKING. One of the major functions of an administrative agency is to implement, interpret, and prescribe law and policy, a process known as **rulemaking**. The enabling statute creating the administrative agency will often provide the administrative agency with the authority to create substantive rules (or legislative rules). **Substantive rules** created by the administrative agency are laws that are as legally binding as if Congress itself had passed them. As a result, businesses and individuals must adhere to substantive rules issued by the administrative agency. Violations of substantive rules can subject the violator to civil and/or criminal liability depending on the substantive rule violated. All substantive rules are subject to judicial review.

Rulemaking The process whereby administrative agencies implement, interpret, and prescribe law and policy.

Substantive rules A legally binding rule issued by an administrative agency.

When agencies engage in rulemaking, they are required to act within the constitutional constraints set forth in the federal **Administrative Procedure Act (APA).** Congress enacted the APA in 1946 to govern the procedures that administrative agencies must follow to propose and establish regulations. Additionally, the APA establishes how federal administrative agencies may adopt various rules and regulations.

Administrative Procedure Act (APA) Enacted by Congress to govern the procedures that administrative agencies must follow to propose and establish regulations.

Informal Rulemaking. The standard process through which rules and regulations are adopted uses an informal rulemaking process known as "notice-and-comment" rulemaking. Under this form of rulemaking, the APA requires administrative agencies to follow the following process before adopting a substantive regulation:

To review the Federal Register, see https://www.federalregister.gov.

1. *Publish a general notice.* The notice is published by the federal agency in the *Federal Register*. The notice must include the time, place, and substance of the proposed rule. It must also state the legal authority from which the rule is proposed (often the enabling legislation), along with a statement of its rationale. Each day federal agencies publish documents in it.
2. *Comment period.* The proposed rule must provide sufficient time (at least 30 days) for the public to comment on the proposed rule. Such comments can include oral hearings on the proposed rule. The purpose of such comments is to allow affected persons the opportunity to express their views and opinions on the policy and potentially influence the policy. The agency then considers and reviews all of the comments received from the public. The agency must respond to significant comments made by the public by either modifying the proposed rule or explaining why the modifications were not made. If the rule is revised, the agency provides another comment period. The agency will announce its final rulemaking on the matter.
3. *Final rule is published.* The final rule is then published in the *Federal Register*. The final rule must provide a concise general statement of the rule and the rationale and purpose of the rule. Final rules are binding unless they are overturned by a court. Rules are typically overturned when the court finds the agency failed to follow the proper rulemaking procedures required by the APA.

FIGURE 34.2: The Process of Creating a Rule

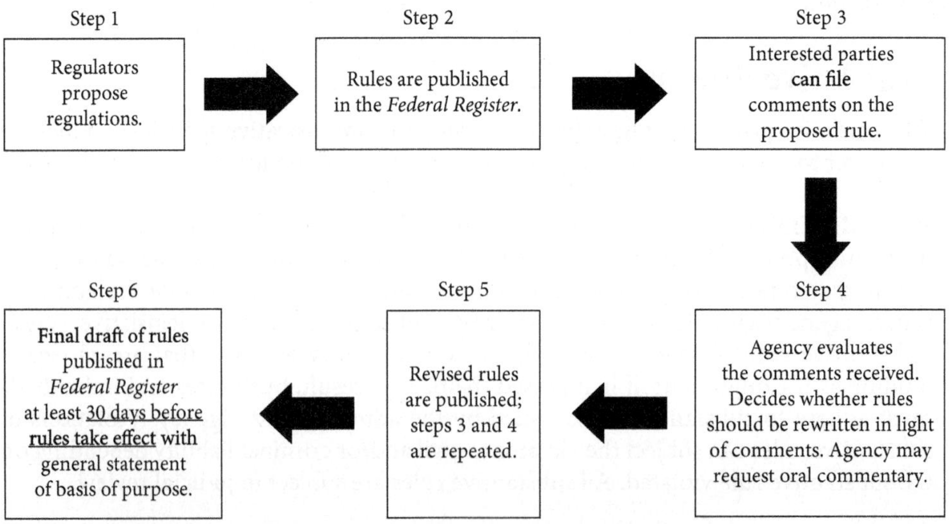

Formal Rulemaking. While informal rulemaking is more common, Congress may mandate in the enabling statute that a formal rulemaking process occur to propose and establish regulations. This process is more rigorous and time consuming than informal rulemaking and is conducted like a trial. The process required under this form of rulemaking is to: (1) publish a general notice (like the informal process), (2) provide a hearing where a formal record is created through interested parties presenting evidence and witnesses are questioned, and (3) make a decision based on the evidence and testimony provided during the hearing.

INTERPRETIVE RULES. The delegation of legislative powers allows administrative agencies to issue interpretive rules. **Interpretive rules** explain the existing language of a statute that the agency administers. Interpretive rules do not require the APA process discussed above (therefore there is no notice-and-comment procedure). Unlike legislative rules, interpretive rules are not legally binding on the public or the court system. (Moreover, the Supreme Court decision in *Loper*, discussed below, casts doubt on the effectiveness of an agency.)

Interpretive rules Rules that explain existing statutory language but are not legally binding on the public or the court system.

Example: The Department of Labor issued the following interpretive ruling regarding the Fair Labor Standards Act: "[N]o employer shall be subject to any liability for failing 'to pay minimum wages or overtime compensation' if it demonstrates that the 'act or omission complained of was in good faith and in conformity with and in reliance on any written administrative regulation, order, ruling, approval, or interpretation' of the Administrator of the Department's Wage and Hour Division, even when the guidance is later 'modified or rescinded.' " *Perez v. Mortgage Bankers Ass'n*, 575 U.S. 92 (2015)

STATEMENTS OF POLICY. Additionally, administrative agencies may issue a **statement of policy**. These statements announce the agency's methods and behaviors regarding a particular topic that the agency intends to follow in future occurrences. Like interpretive rules, they are not legally binding on the public or the court system. In addition, a policy statement is not judicially enforceable against the agency.

Statement of policy Public statements by an administrative agency that announce its methods and behaviors regarding a particular topic that the agency intends to follow in the future.

GRANTING OF LICENSES. Administrative agencies may also be authorized to grant licenses to persons in certain types of industries (such as financial services) or professions (such as lawyers, doctors, and certified public accountants). The agency has the power to determine through testing or other means whether to grant a license to an applicant.

LEGISLATIVE LIMITATIONS. The authority of Congress does not end with enacting legislation. Congress possesses the authority to investigate an agency to determine if the agency's actions are appropriate. Congress can enact legislation to affect an agency's jurisdiction or abolish the agency altogether (such as the Interstate Commerce Commission). Further, Congress can declare an agency's regulations to be inoperative, thereby freezing the agency's regulations before they have a chance to take effect.

A court may also review whether a regulation is reasonable and consistent with a statute, as was the subject in the following case.

CASE 34.1

AGENCY REGULATIONS MUST REFLECT THE INTENT OF THE STATUTE

MOORE v. K-MART CORP.

769 S.E.2d 35 (2015)

Supreme Court of Appeals of West Virginia

Jennifer Moore worked for the K-Mart Corporation for over 30 years. Moore refurbished furniture for K-Mart in a small, poorly ventilated room, which exposed her to vast amounts of furniture dust and metal dust. As a result of this exposure, Moore was diagnosed with damage to the nervous system causing numbness and pain in the extremities.

Moore subsequently filed a claim for workers' compensation and after a decision by an administrative law judge (ALJ), Moore was compensated under such action. Thereafter, Moore began receiving intravenous chelation therapy, a chemical process in which a solution is injected into the bloodstream to remove the metal from the body. The chelation therapy was successful in alleviating Moore's symptoms. Moore filed an order with the Workers' Compensation Review Board (BOR) seeking compensation for her treatment. BOR denied Moore's order for reimbursement and reversed the decision by the administrative law judge who had found that Moore was entitled to reimbursement.

BOR denied the reimbursement pursuant to a regulation that stated, "The Commission, Insurance Commissioner, private carrier or self-insured employer, whichever is applicable, will not reimburse for IV chelation therapy performed in office." Moore appealed to the Supreme Court of Appeals of West Virginia, arguing that the BOR erred in denying reimbursement for her medically necessary chelation therapy.

Language of the Court. *The sole issue we address in this appeal is whether Petitioner is entitled to receive reimbursement for medically necessary intravenous chelation therapy when the therapy was performed in her physician's office. The Workers' Compensation Act provides benefits to workers who have "received personal injuries in the course of and resulting from their covered employment." Under the Act, the term "personal injury" includes occupational disease. "One of the basic purposes of workmen's compensation legislation is to impose upon industry the cost of medical expenses incurred in the treatment and rehabilitation of workers who have suffered injuries in the course of and as a result of their employment."*

According to the agency regulation at issue, a claimant will be denied reimbursement for intravenous chelation therapy performed in an office. However, an administrative regulation is not, itself, the equivalent of a statute. "To be valid, a regulation promulgated by an administrative agency must carry out the legislative intent of its governing statutes." As a rule of statutory construction, we have repeatedly held that any rules or regulations drafted by an agency must faithfully reflect the intention of the Legislature, as expressed in the controlling legislation. Where a statute contains clear and unambiguous language, an agency's rules or regulations must give that language the same clear and unambiguous force and effect that the language commands in the statute.

K-Mart states the regulation does not require that the chelation therapy be performed in a hospital; it just prohibits reimbursement when performed in an office. This point only highlights the arbitrary nature of this portion of the regulation. Applying the plain language of the regulation, Dr. Murphy could travel to Moore's home to administer the chelation therapy, and the cost would be reimbursable. Ostensibly, Dr. Murphy could walk out of his office and meet Moore in the parking lot of his medical practice to administer the chelation therapy and the cost would be reimbursable; this asinine example reveals the absence of any rational basis for the challenged portion of the workers' compensation act. Nevertheless, we are not asked in this case to say whether we think this regulation is wise. We are asked to hold if it violates the Act. And that, we do.

Decision. The Supreme Court of Appeals of West Virginia reversed the decision of the workers' compensation review board to deny the reimbursement and found the regulation to be invalid.

Focus on Ethics

Is it ethical for an agency to compel victims of unreasonable regulations to pursue these procedural requirements to challenge arbitrary regulations? Would an expedited judicial appeals process provide a fair remedy to a claimant and an agency?

Management Application The SEC's Whistleblower Program

The enactment of the Dodd-Frank Act created the Securities Whistleblower Incentives and Protection Program, which gives monetary awards to individuals who volunteer information that leads to the SEC's successfully enforcing the law to produce monetary sanctions of $1 million or more against a violator. Since its enactment, the program has awarded hundreds of millions of dollars. The chart below depicts the process of the SEC's program.[2]

2. *https://www.sec.gov/enforcement-litigation/whistleblower-program.*

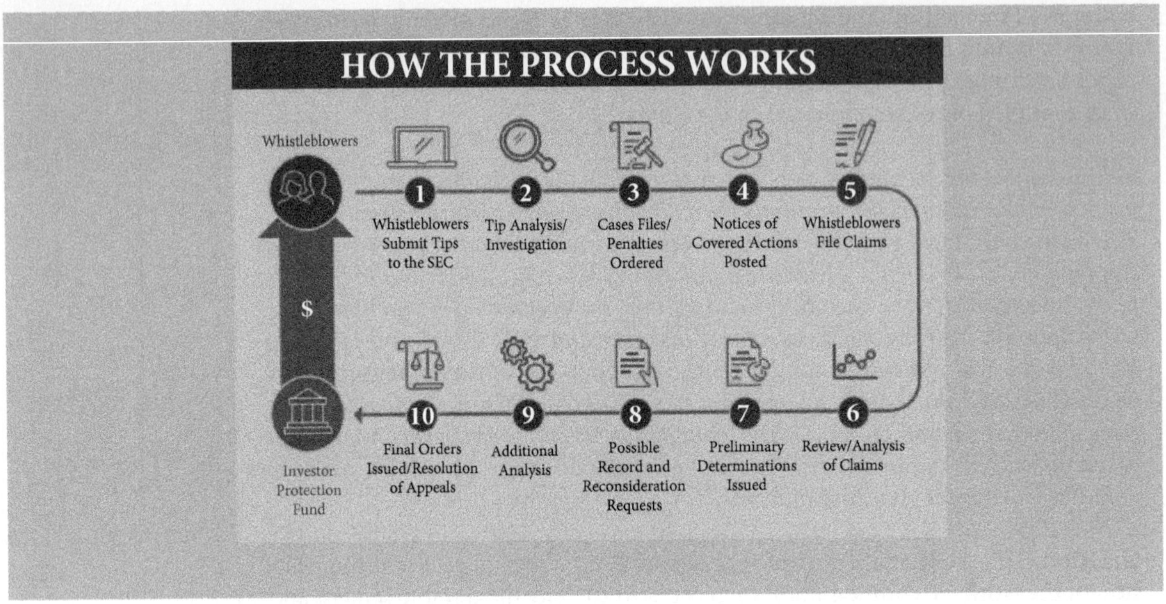

Executive Power

In addition to legislative powers, administrative agencies can be delegated executive powers. These powers can allow administrative agencies the ability to investigate and monitor compliance of the substantive rules created by the administrative agency.

To effectively perform these functions, administrative agencies must obtain information from persons and businesses under investigation. While persons and businesses may voluntarily provide the information sought, administrative agencies have the power to issue administrative subpoenas and conduct administrative searches.

Administrative subpoena
A subpoena issued by an administrative agency that allows the agency to compel the attendance of persons or production of documents, or to allow a search of the business or individual's premises.

An **administrative subpoena** compels the person or business to disclose the requested information to the administrative agency. The subpoena can provide for oral testimony to be taken or for requested documents, records, and items to be turned over to the administrative agency for review and inspection. If a person or business fails to respond to the administrative subpoena, the administrative agency can obtain judicial enforcement to force the person or business to comply with the administrative subpoena.

> **Example:** The Wage and Hour Division (WHD) of the U.S. Department of Labor is the administrative agency charged with enforcing the Fair Labor Standards Act (FLSA). The FLSA establishes minimum wage, overtime pay, and other wage-related regulations. The WHD may issue an administrative subpoena to a restaurant requiring the restaurant to provide its payroll records to review compliance with minimum wage laws.

Administrative search
A search of a business or individual's premises that is conducted by an administrative agency.

In addition, the administrative agency may monitor compliance with substantive rules by inspecting, testing, or searching the business or individual's premises under an **administrative search**.

> **Example:** A local health department will periodically inspect restaurants to ensure compliance with food safety laws.

Following the search, the administrative agency may invoke its prosecutorial power by acting against the business or individual. Many of these administrative actions are settled before the administrative agency issues a complaint against the business.

CONSTITUTIONAL LIMITATIONS ON INSPECTIONS. Administrative agencies, through their executive powers, can conduct physical searches of business premises. The Fourth Amendment to the U.S. Constitution imposes restrictions on searches. These restrictions require administrative agencies to usually obtain a search warrant; however, search warrants are not required in highly regulated industries (such as businesses that sell alcohol).

Management Application
Sample Letter Accompanying a Subpoena to Produce Business's Records

Certified Mail — Return Receipt Requested

[Date]

Name
Address
Re: Investigation of ________________________
EBSA Case No. XX-XXXXXX

Dear: __________,

This office is investigating the above-referenced matter pursuant to § 504(a)(1) of the Employee Retirement Income Security Act of 1974 (ERISA), 29 U.S.C. § 1134(a)(1), to determine whether any person has violated or is about to violate any provision of Title I of ERISA. Enclosed is a subpoena that requires you to produce certain documents and records in connection with that investigation.

Your personal appearance pursuant to this subpoena will not be required at this time provided the documents are produced on or before the date noted in the subpoena. You will be informed at a later date if your personal appearance to testify is required. Inasmuch as your appearance is not now required, please provide a cover letter with your response that identifies the documents being produced. Your cover letter should also state whether a diligent search has been made for the subpoenaed documents and that the documents transmitted constitute all documents called for by the subpoena.

The subpoena requests that documents maintained in electronic form, Electronically Stored Information (ESI), be produced in electronic form. The formats in which EBSA can accept ESI are listed in the subpoena. When producing ESI, the material should be produced as maintained on your computer system, i.e., ESI should be produced with all files, folders and sub-folders intact, and emails should be produced with all attachments intact.

If any documents called for are not furnished, please list such documents and indicate their location and the reason for their non-production.

This inquiry should not be construed as an indication that any violations of law have occurred or as a reflection upon any person involved in this matter.

If you have any questions concerning your rights and duties, you may wish to consult counsel. If you have any questions concerning the subpoena or the documents required to be produced, including the production of ESI and the appropriate format and media, please call [name of investigator/auditor] at [telephone number].

Sincerely,
Regional Director

Enclosure

Judicial Powers

While many administrative agency matters are resolved through negotiated settlements between the party and the administrative agency, when such a settlement cannot be reached, the administrative agency may be delegated the power to adjudicate the cases (that is, resolve the matter) through an administrative proceeding before an administrative law judge. To start such a process, the agency issues a formal complaint against the party. Formal complaints by an agency are public documents. Once the complaint is filed, the party served with the complaint responds to the complaint by answering the allegations in the complaint. Settlement between the parties may then occur, but if it is not successful, the administrative law judge will adjudicate the case.

Administrative law judge An appointed person who presides over hearings and adjudicates issues of administrative law.

An administrative law judge (ALJ) is a an executive official in the administrative agency who is appointed to hear the complaints filed under the agency's regulations. Although the ALJ is employed by the administrative agency, they are required to function as an impartial (unbiased) decision maker. While ALJs are not members of the judicial branch, they are given great power to hold hearings, administer oaths, obtain testimony, and render binding decisions.

Initial order Decision of the ALJ that has not yet been appealed.

Final order A decision by an ALJ not appealed by any party, or a decision reached on appeal to the board, commission, or court hearing the appeal.

The decision of the ALJ is known as an **initial order**, which is appealable by either party. The appeal is heard by the governing commission or board in charge of the agency. The decision by the governing commission or board can also be appealed to a state or federal court. A federal administrative agency's decision can be appealed at the federal court, and a state administrative agency's decision can be appealed only at the state court. Either the commission's decision or the decision of the federal court will become the final order. If neither party decides to appeal, the ALJ's decision becomes the **final order**.

Arbitrary and capricious test A test applied by a court when reviewing informal adjudications and rulemaking in which orders and regulations are overturned if there is a clear error in judgment.

ADMINISTRATIVE PROCEDURE ACT. The Administrative Procedure Act (discussed above) authorizes judicial review of administrative agency actions. An agency's decision may be set aside when a court determines the agency's regulation was "arbitrary and capricious, an abuse of discretion, or otherwise not in accordance with the law." This test is known as the **arbitrary and capricious test**. While courts have not specifically defined what constitutes "arbitrary and capricious," courts often consider the following elements to determine if an agency's decision should be set aside:

1. The agency relied on factors that Congress did not intend for it to consider;
2. The agency failed to consider an important aspect of the problem;
3. The agency explains its decision that is counter to the evidence before it; or
4. The result is so implausible that it cannot be attributed to a difference in view or the product of the agency's expertise.[3]

Most often, this test is applied to ensure that agency decisions are rational and reflect relevant factors and evidence. For example, a court may assess an agency's informal rulemaking to consider whether the agency's decision-making process was reasonable and based on substantial evidence.

In addition to the arbitrary and capricious test, enabling acts generally require courts to apply the substantial evidence test to determine if the regulation or order should be set aside. This test is also applied when the court reviews a formal adjudication (where the hearing is conducted following more formal procedures similar to a judicial-type trial) or formal rulemaking (where the rulemaking is conducted on the record after a hearing pursuant to the agency's enabling act).

The **substantial evidence test** considers whether a reasonable person considering the record as a whole (that is, reviewing the evidence from both sides) would find the agency's decision to be supported by adequate relevant evidence.

Substantial evidence test
An agency's decision is supported by such relevant evidence as a reasonable person would find adequate to support the conclusions reached.

In the following case, the court applied the substantial evidence test to support the conclusions reached in an agency adjudication.

CASE 34.2

SUBSTANTIAL EVIDENCE TEST ALLOWS ADMINISTRATIVE LAW JUDGES TO DETERMINE THE WEIGHT OF SPECIFIC EVIDENCE

HUNTLEY v. SOCIAL SECURITY ADMINISTRATION COMMISSIONER

683 F. App'x 830 (2017)

United States Court of Appeals for the Eleventh Circuit

Chris Huntley claimed that he became disabled when he began to experience shortness of breath, dizziness, poor balance, high blood pressure, left ankle pain and numbness, and sleep apnea. Huntley claimed these impairments made him unable to continue working as a heavy equipment operator and subsequently applied for disability insurance benefits. His request was first denied by the ALJ for the Social Security Administration, who found Huntley was not considered disabled according to the Social Security Act. Huntley then appealed to the U.S. District Court, arguing that the ALJ had given improper weight to the testimony of a non-examining doctor regarding the severity of his impairments over those of Huntley's examining physicians. The district court upheld the agency's finding that denial of disability insurance benefits was proper. Huntley appealed. He argued that the order affirming the Commissioner's denial of his application gave too little weight to the evaluation of two examining physicians, gave too

3. *Nat'l Ass'n of Home Builders v. Defenders of Wildlife*, 551 U.S. 664, 658 (2007).

much weight to the opinion of a non-examining physician, and substituted the opinion of medical experts for the ALJ's own opinion.

Language of the Court. *We review the Commissioner's legal conclusions de novo and her decision to deny benefits for substantial evidence. Substantial evidence is relevant evidence that a reasonable person would accept as sufficient to support a conclusion. We do not find facts anew, reweigh the evidence, or substitute our judgment for that of the Commissioner. We instead defer to the Commissioner's decision, so long as it is supported by substantial evidence, even if the evidence may preponderate against it.*

In determining whether an applicant has proved that he is disabled, the administrative law judge must complete a five-step sequential evaluation. The applicant has the burden to prove (1) that he has not engaged in substantial gainful activity, (2) he has severe impairment or combination of impairments, and (3) his impairment or combination of impairments meets or equals a listed impairment so that he is entitled to a finding of disability, or if not, (4) that he is unable to perform past relevant work in light of residual functional capacity. At the fifth step, the burden shifts to the Commissioner to determine if there is other work available in significant numbers in the national economy that the claimant can perform.

When assessing medical opinions, the administrative law judge must consider several factors to determine how much weight to give each medical opinion, including whether the physician has examined the claimant; the length, nature, and extent of a treating physician's relationship with the claimant; the medical evidence and explanation supporting the physician's opinion; how consistent the physician's opinion is with the "record as a whole"; and the physician's specialty. These factors apply to both examining and non-examining physicians. The administrative law judge must state with particularity the weight given to different medical opinions and his supporting reasons. The administrative law judge need not defer to the opinion of a physician who conducted a single examination because that physician is not a treating physician. When considering an examining, non-treating medical opinion, the more a medical source presents relevant evidence to support an opinion, the more weight the administrative law judge will give that opinion.

The decision to assign little weight to examining physicians' opinions is supported by substantial evidence. As one-time examiners, the physicians were not treating physicians, and the administrative law judge was not required to afford special deference to their opinions. Substantial evidence also supports the administrative law judge's decision to assign more weight to the non-examining physician's opinion. Although the opinion of an examining physician is ordinarily entitled to greater weight than the opinion of a non-examining physician, the administrative law judge was free to reject the opinions of the examining physicians because they were not supported by the record.

Decision. The Court of Appeals for the Eleventh Circuit affirmed the district court's opinion that the ALJ properly decided Huntley was not considered disabled under the Social Security Act and such decision was based on substantial evidence.

Focus on Ethics

Do you believe the substantial evidence test is too low a standard in ALJ decision making? Does this standard lessen the duty of an agency to provide its rationale and the factual basis for it within the record?

Administrative Agencies and Judicial Deference

The growth of federal administrative agencies has led the Supreme Court to decide the degree to which executive branch agencies may exercise legislative power in implementing broad or ambiguous statutory mandates. One of the Court's landmark decisions, *Chevron U.S.A., Inc. v. Natural Resources Defense Council, Inc.*,[4] established a two-part test for courts to follow when evaluating how a federal agency has construed a statute: (1) If Congress has directly addressed the precise question at issue, the agency must follow Congress's explicit directive; and (2) if Congress has not addressed the issue—if the statute is silent or ambiguous—the agency's interpretation will govern—as long as it is based on a reasonable construction of the statute. The *Chevron* decision instructed lower federal courts to defer to an agency's reasonable interpretation of ambiguities in a law that the agency administers.

In the following case, along with a companion case, the Court withdrew the deference principle while still giving recognition to executive agency subject matter expertise. After withdrawing the *Chevron* deference, federal courts review agency actions under the standards of the Administrative Procedure Act. APA Section 706 directs that "all relevant questions of law" are to be decided by the federal courts, and it provides no different standard when considering questions of law arising from ambiguous or incomplete statutes, which *Chevron* previously provided. In each case, the task of the court will be to "decide whether the law means what the agency says."

CASE 34.3

COURTS MUST EXERCISE INDEPENDENT JUDGMENT WHEN INTERPRETING THE MEANING OF STATUTORY AUTHORITIES

LOPER BRIGHT ENTERPRISES v. RAIMONDO

603 U.S. ___, 143 S. Ct. 2429 (2024)

Supreme Court of the United States

A group of commercial fishermen who regularly participated in a federally regulated fishery sued the National Marine Fisheries Service after the Service

4. 467 U.S. 837 (1984).

promulgated a rule that required the industry to fund at-sea monitoring programs at an estimated cost of $710 per day. The fishermen argued that a 1976 law did not authorize the Service to create industry-funded monitoring requirements and that the Service failed to follow proper rulemaking procedure. The district court granted summary judgment for the government based on its reasonable interpretation of its authority and its adoption of the rule through the required notice-and-comment procedure. The U.S. Court of Appeals for the D.C. Circuit affirmed. The Supreme Court granted *certiorari.*

Language of the Court. *Article III of the Constitution assigns to the Federal Judiciary the responsibility and power to adjudicate "Cases" and "Controversies"—concrete disputes with consequences for the parties involved. The Framers [of the Constitution] appreciated that the laws judges would necessarily apply in resolving those disputes would not always be clear. The Framers also envisioned that the final "interpretation of the laws" would be "the proper and peculiar province of the courts." To ensure the "steady, upright and impartial administration of the laws," the Framers structured the Constitution to allow judges to exercise that judgment independent of influence from the political branches. [Courts have] made clear, repeatedly, that "[t]he interpretation of the meaning of statutes, as applied to justiciable controversies," was "exclusively a judicial function."*

Congress in 1946 enacted the APA "as a check upon administrators whose zeal might otherwise have carried them to excesses not contemplated in legislation creating their offices." It specifies that courts, not agencies, will decide "all relevant questions of law" arising on review of agency action—even those involving ambiguous laws—and set aside any such action inconsistent with the law as they interpret it. And it prescribes no deferential standard for courts to employ in answering those legal questions. [The APA] makes clear that agency interpretations of statutes—like agency interpretations of the Constitution—are not entitled to deference. Under the APA, it thus "remains the responsibility of the court to decide whether the law means what the agency says."

The APA, in short, incorporates the traditional understanding of the judicial function, under which courts must exercise independent judgment in determining the meaning of statutory provisions. In exercising such judgment, though, courts may—as they have from the start—seek aid from the interpretations of those responsible for implementing particular statutes.

Rather than safeguarding reliance interests, Chevron *affirmatively destroys them. Under* Chevron, *a statutory ambiguity, no matter why it is there, becomes a license authorizing an agency to change positions as much as it likes, with "[u]nexplained inconsistency" being "at most . . . a reason for holding an interpretation to be . . . arbitrary and capricious." But statutory ambiguity, as we have explained, is not a reliable indicator of actual delegation of discretionary authority to agencies.* Chevron *thus allows agencies to change course even when Congress has given them no power to do so. By its sheer breadth,* Chevron *fosters unwarranted instability in the law, leaving those attempting to plan around agency action in an eternal fog of uncertainty.*

The deference that Chevron *requires of courts reviewing agency action cannot be squared with the APA. Four decades after its inception,* Chevron *has thus become an impediment, rather than an aid, to accomplishing the basic judicial task of "say[ing] what the law is." Given our constant tinkering with and eventual turn away from* Chevron, *and its inconsistent application by the lower courts, it instead is hard to see how anyone—Congress included—could reasonably expect a court to rely on* Chevron *in any particular case.* Chevron *was a judicial invention that required judges to disregard their statutory duties. And the only way to "ensure that the law will not merely change erratically, but will develop in a principled and intelligible fashion," is for us to leave* Chevron *behind.*

Decision. The Supreme Court overturned *Chevron*, reaffirming a court's role to interpret laws and holding that courts must not defer to the interpretations of agencies even if those interpretations are seemingly reasonable.

Focus on Ethics

Since many laws are passed with incomplete directives and uncertain meanings, does this decision unduly burden the judicial branch? Are judges equipped to deal with complex scientific problems? Should Congress act to overturn this decision?

This framework applies specifically to federal administrative agencies. State administrative agencies operate under the laws and judicial precedents of their respective state governments, which may differ significantly from the federal approach to judicial deference and agency interpretation.

Public Disclosure of Agency Actions

Congress has enacted several statutes to address the public's demands for transparency in administrative agency actions. The following statutes aim to promote public disclosure of federal administrative agency actions and seek to protect individuals and businesses from overly intrusive agency actions.

Freedom of Information Act

The **Freedom of Information Act (FOIA)** was enacted to provide the public with the right to request and access most records in the possession of a federal administrative agency. The FOIA does not apply to state and local government agencies; however, many of these records may be obtained through state public records laws. Under the FOIA, the federal agency will be required to disclose any information requested unless the request falls under an exemption to the disclosure requirement. Exemptions include protection of proprietary business information (such as trade secrets or confidential information); personal privacy (such as medical records); national security interests (documents classified by the President to be in the interests of national security); records whose disclosure would interfere with law enforcement proceedings (such as pending charges against a defendant); or where the disclosure is prohibited by law

Freedom of Information Act (FOIA) Act that provides the public with the right to request and access most records in the possession of a federal administrative agency.

(such as when a federal statute prohibits disclosure of the information). Additionally, the Act requires federal administrative agencies to publish procedures, rules, regulations, and interpretations in the *Federal Register*.

Each federal administrative agency manages its own FOIA requests. There is no formal process or form that must be completed to make a FOIA request. The decision of a federal administrative agency to refuse to disclose requested documents is subject to judicial review in a U.S. District Court.

EXHIBIT 34.1: Freedom of Information Act Request

FREEDOM OF INFORMATION ACT REQUEST

TO:____

City/Township/Municipal Government/Police Department (e.g. City of Detroit or Dearborn Police Department)

My name, information, and address to send all invoices and responses to:

Name:____

Date of Birth:____________________ Date of this FOIA Request: ____________________

Address:____

Street Address City State Zip

Telephone No.____

Arrest / Incident Date:____________________ Approx. Time of Incident:____________________

Attention: FOIA Coordinator

Pursuant to the Michigan Freedom of Information Act, MCL 15.231 et seq., I am requesting copies of the following documents. Please provide copies of all checked items in the following list:

- ☐ Copies of all police reports regarding or referencing me and/or the arrest / incident / investigation referenced above, redacting any necessary information pursuant to MCL 15.244 and producing all non-exempt portions.
- ☐ Copies of all accident reports, traffic citations, DI-177 forms, DI-93 forms, and OD-80 forms relative me or the investigation.
- ☐ All station-house videos and audio of me at the police station on or about the above date.
- ☐ All in-car and patrol car videos and audio recordings of me and/or the arrest / incident / investigation from the patrol car of the arresting officer.
- ☐ All other videos and audio recording of me from all other patrol cars, the police station, or anywhere else that recorded me, the arrest, and/or the incident in your possession or under your control.
- ☐ 911 recordings and radio dispatch recordings regarding me and/or the arrest / incident / investigation.
- ☐ All vehicle inventory sheets, tow records/slips, and a written inventory of the vehicle.
- ☐ Copies of all search warrants and supporting affidavits.
- ☐ All witness statements about me and/or the arrest / incident / investigation in your possession as of the date of this request.
- ☐ The arresting officer's disciplinary reports and citizen complaints (excluding internal disciplinary investigations and "frank discussion" materials but not final disciplinary actions).
- ☐ The following specifically described document(s):____

____

Government in the Sunshine Act

Congress enacted the **Government in the Sunshine Act** to establish the best practices to enhance the transparency of decision making of administrative agencies. The Act requires most federal agencies to announce their meetings in the *Federal Register* at least seven days in advance and be open to public observation. Like the FOIA, there are exceptions that apply. These meetings can be closed to the public when there is a discussion of possible criminal activity, when a public meeting would frustrate the implementation of future agency actions, or when agency matters involve future litigation or rulemaking. The decision of a federal administrative agency to close the meeting to the public is subject to judicial review in a U.S. District Court.

Government in the Sunshine Act
Act that enhances the transparency of decision making of administrative agencies by requiring most federal agencies to announce their meetings in the *Federal Register* at least seven days in advance and be open to public observation.

Equal Access to Justice Act

Congress enacted the **Equal Access to Justice Act** to protect individuals and businesses from harassment by federal administrative agencies. A private party who believes they have been harassed by a federal administrative agency is entitled to sue the agency and recover attorney fees and other expenses. Courts require the agency's conduct toward the aggrieved party to be extremely outrageous before they will issue an award under the Act.

Equal Access to Justice Act
Act that protects individuals and businesses from harassment by federal administrative agencies.

Privacy Act

Congress enacted the **Privacy Act** to protect individual privacy in records maintained by the federal government. This Act limits the information that a federal agency may possess regarding an individual to only that which is relevant and necessary to accomplish the purposes of the agency. Further, the Act gives individuals the right to access their records in the possession of the agency.

Privacy Act
Act that protects individual privacy in records maintained by the federal government.

Regulatory Flexibility Act

The **Regulatory Flexibility Act** represents Congress's attempt to reduce the negative effects that regulations have on the efficiency of small businesses in the United States. This law alerts small businesses about forthcoming regulations and requires a regulatory flexibility analysis to be conducted when a new regulation is determined to have serious impact upon significant numbers of small businesses.

The regulatory flexibility analysis measures the cost the proposed regulation would impose on small businesses and requires the agency to consider less burdensome regulations. The Regulatory Flexibility Act was amended by the Small Business Regulatory Enforcement Fairness Act in 1996. The amendment provides Congress 60 days to review all new federal regulations before the regulation becomes effective. As a result of this review period, small businesses that have concerns with or oppose the proposed regulations have the ability to challenge the regulation in court.

Regulatory Flexibility Act
An act created by Congress which requires the cost of proposed regulation to be measured and requires the agency to consider regulation that may be less burdensome.

AI Feature: Draft a Local Rent Control Ordinance

Use an internet search engine to review the law of a state or local government that has adopted a rent control law or ordinance. They are examples of administrative regulations enforced by an administrative agency. Rent control is price regulation imposed upon landlords through setting rental rates and regulating leases to provide affordable housing options to tenants. Such agencies can control the degree to which and how often rent can be increased, limit late fees, and the total amount chargeable to a tenant. Typically, property owners may raise rents only when the tenant does not renew the lease and has vacated the premises. In addition, many cities with such ordinances restrict the landlord's ability to evict tenants.

Use an AI program to draft a rent control ordinance. The proposed ordinance should include the following: the scope of the ordinance, the types of housing units to which it applies (e.g., single family and/or multi-family), limitations on rent increases, and the powers to create and enforce regulations of the newly formed rent control agency.

Key Terms

- Administrative agencies, 856
- Administrative law, 856
- Administrative law judge, 868
- Administrative Procedures Act (APA), 862
- Administrative search, 866
- Administrative subpoena, 866
- Arbitrary and capricious test, 868
- Delegation doctrine, 861
- Enabling legislation, 861
- Equal Access to Justice Act (EAJA), 875
- Executive agencies, 857
- Final order, 868
- Freedom of Information Act (FOIA), 873
- Government in the Sunshine Act (GSA), 875
- Independent regulatory agencies, 858
- Initial order, 868
- Interpretive rules, 863
- Local administrative agencies, 859
- Privacy Act, 875
- Regulations, 856
- Regulatory Flexibility Act, 875
- Rulemaking, 861
- State administrative agencies, 859
- Statement of policy, 863
- Substantial evidence test, 869
- Substantive rules, 861

Applying the Law

34.1 Research the Law. Using an internet search engine, research how to submit a Freedom of Information Act request to a federal agency. Review the link at *https://www.esd.whs.mil/*. How do you make such a request, and what information is needed to do so? Can you find any successful past FOIA requests to the Department of Defense or the Central Intelligence Agency? What information has been available with respect to unidentified flying objects (UFO's)?

34.2 Rulemaking. The APA distinguishes between legislative rules issued through notice-and-comment rulemaking, having the force and effect of law, and interpretative rules that advise the public of the agency's construction of the laws it administers. When a federal administrative agency first issues a rule interpreting one of its regulations, it is generally not required to follow the notice-and-comment rulemaking procedures of the Administrative Procedure Act. Does this practice deter public participation in the rulemaking process? Does it invite judicial scrutiny of agency interpretations? Consider the Supreme Court's decision in *Perez v. Mortg. Bankers Ass'n*, 575 U.S. 92 (2015)

34.3 Arbitrary and Capricious. In 2012, the U.S. Department of Homeland Security (DHS) adopted a program—known as the Deferred Action for Childhood Arrivals (DACA)—to postpone the deportation of undocumented immigrants who had been brought to the United States as children and to assign them work permits. Those permits allowed them to obtain Social Security numbers, pay taxes, and become part of American society. During the Trump Administration, DHS began a phase-out of DACA. The Supreme Court was confronted with the question if the DHS decision to so act was judicially reviewable. How and why did the Court rule? *Dep't of Homeland Sec. v. Regents of the Univ. of Cal.*, 591 U.S. 1 (2020)

34.4 Decision Maker. The Securities and Exchange Commission had historically taken the position that its ALJs are employees (rather than judicial officers) and did not need to be appointed pursuant to the Appointments Clause of the Constitution. The SEC's position, however, came under scrutiny because of its increased use of administrative proceedings enjoying a "home court" advantage when it proceeded against companies administratively rather than through court litigation. The SEC proceeded against Raymond J. Lucia and his investment advisory company, imposing a lifetime industry bar on Lucia and assessing civil penalties. Was the SEC acting unconstitutionally in that ALJs were not officers of the court? *Lucia v. SEC*, 585 U.S. 237 (2018)

34.5 Exemptions Under the Freedom of Information Act. A local newspaper was investigating municipal airport noise. As part of its research, the newspaper requested information relating to the complaints about the airport noise. The Freedom of Information Act bars disclosure when it would amount to an unwarranted invasion of privacy. Does the information sought by the newspaper invade individuals' privacy rights? *City of San Jose v. Superior Court*, 74 Cal. App. 4th 1008 (1999)

34.6 Judicial Deference. In a post-*Loper Bright* era, the State of Texas challenged a rule issued by the United States Department of Labor (the "Department") that raised the minimum salary at which executive, administrative, and professional employees (EAPs) are exempt from overtime pay under the Fair Labor Standards Act ("FLSA")—thereby changing the exemption status of millions of employees. Texas contends that the 2024 Rule's changes to the salary level for these employee exemptions exceeded the Department's authority under the FLSA and was unlawful. Notwithstanding the fact that the FLSA's language providing for the EAP Exemption makes no mention of any minimum salary component or requirement, the Department considered salary in some capacity since the FLSA's inception. Why did the court rule as it did? If the decision is appealed, how should the Court of Appeals for the Fifth Circuit rule? *State v. United States Department of Labor (DOL)*, 2024 U.S. Dist. LEXIS 114902 (2024)

34.7 New Rules. Stewart and Lynda Resnick formed POM Wonderful, LLC ("POM") to make, market, and sell pomegranate-based products. They began to collaborate with doctors and scientists to investigate the potential health benefits of consuming pomegranates, especially the capacity to improve cardiovascular health. POM's promotional materials often referenced scientific support for the claimed health benefits of its products. The Federal Trade Commission filed an administrative complaint alleging that POM had made false, misleading, and unsubstantiated representations in violation of the FTC Act. In determining whether an advertisement is deceptive, the Commission considers: (i) what claims are conveyed in the ad; (ii) whether those claims are false, misleading, or unsubstantiated; and (iii) whether the claims are material to prospective consumers. POM argued that the standard applied by the Commission was a new legal rule adopted in violation of the Administrative Procedure Act's notice-and-comment requirement for rulemaking. How should the court rule? *POM Wonderful, LLC v. Federal Trade Commission*, 777 F.3d 478 (D.C. Cir. 2015)

34.8 Disclosure? AT&T® participated in a Federal Communications Commission administered program that was created to enhance access for schools and libraries to advanced telecommunications and information services. The FCC's Enforcement Bureau investigated multiple AT&T documents including invoices, emails with pricing and billing information, names and job descriptions of employees involved, and AT&T's assessment of whether these employees had violated the company's code of conduct. Months later, CompTel®, a trade association representing AT&T's competitors, submitted a FOIA request seeking all documents and correspondence in the Bureau's file on the AT&T investigation. The Bureau concluded the information AT&T provided should be protected from disclosure because releasing it would constitute an unwarranted invasion of personal privacy. However, it explicitly stated that this applies to the individuals identified in the submissions and not to the corporation itself. Does "personal privacy" within the meaning of the Freedom of Information Act exemption encompass corporations? Why or why not? *Federal Communications Commission v. AT&T Inc.*, 562 U.S. 397 (2011)

34.9 Due Process. The Federal Communications Commission began enforcing the ban of "any obscene, indecent, or profane language" in the 1970s. Fox Television aired two live broadcasts that contained utterances of obscene words. These incidents were after the FCC declared for the first time that fleeting expletives could be actionable but before the Commission issued Notices of Apparent Liability to Fox. Did the FCC violate the network's due process rights? Why or why not? *Federal Communications Commission v. Fox Television Stations, Inc.*, 567 U.S. 239 (2012)

34.10 Arbitrary and Capricious. Michael Manin held various FAA certificates, including a first-class airman medical certificate. A first-class airman medical certificate must be renewed periodically. Manin was convicted of disorderly conduct in 1996 and 1997, which he did not report on the following years' applications believing that the disorderly charge was a minor summary offense and would not have to be reported. In late 2007, the FAA discovered the unreported convictions. The FAA immediately revoked his certificate. Manin argued that the National Transportation Safety Board's policy of considering the applicant's understanding of the disclosures required prior to deciding if the application was false was not followed. The Board rejected Manin's defense. In Manin's lawsuit, Manin argued the agency had acted arbitrarily and capriciously by not applying the intent element consistently. How should the court rule? *Manin v. National Transp. Safety Bd.*, 627 F.3d 1239 (D.C. Cir. 2011)

Antitrust and Unfair Competition

35

Competition has been shown to be useful up to a certain point and no further, but cooperation, which is the thing we must strive for today, begins where competition leaves off. — Franklin D. Roosevelt, Thirty-second President of the United States (1882-1945)

Chapter Outline

- Introduction
- Enforcement of Antitrust Laws
- The Sherman Antitrust Act

Case 35.1: *American Needle, Inc. v. NFL*

- Unlawful Restraints of Trade (Section 1 of the Sherman Act)

Case 35.2: *United States v. Apple, Inc.*

- Monopolies (Section 2 of the Sherman Act)
- The Clayton Antitrust Act
    - *Management Application: How Businesses May Violate the Robinson-Patman Act*
- Federal Trade Commission Act
    - *Management Application: Antitrust Compliance Programs*
- Exemptions from Antitrust Laws

Case 35.3: *Miranda v. Selig*

- AI Feature: Prospective Merger Analysis

Learning Objectives

After studying this chapter, you should be able to:

1. Explain the purpose of antitrust laws and why they are needed in our economy.
2. Recognize who enforces antitrust laws.
3. Distinguish between the different significant antitrust laws in the United States.
4. Identify the different activities prohibited under Section 1 and Section 2 of the Sherman Act.
5. Recognize the prohibitions under the Clayton Act.
6. Explain the exemptions to antitrust laws.

Introduction

Antitrust laws Laws enacted by Congress that regulate economic competition in the United States.

Antitrust laws are designed to regulate economic competition in the United States, promoting and protecting a competitive marketplace. Following the Civil War, the United States underwent rapid industrialization, leading to the emergence of large companies, trusts, and the accumulation of significant wealth and power. This shift resulted in monopolies dominating various industries (such as steel, oil and gas, and banking). For example, John D. Rockefeller's Standard Oil Company controlled 90 percent of the country's oil refining capacity. In response to the monopolistic practices employed by these businesses to maintain their market dominance, Congress enacted a series of laws aimed at stopping anticompetitive behavior. A commonly held business belief is that competition benefits customers in the form of improved products and services and lower prices.

Antitrust laws apply to all businesses, regardless of whether they are publicly or privately held, and irrespective of their profit levels — be it billions, millions, or thousands. It is important for business students to have a foundational understanding of antitrust laws.

This chapter focuses on a few of the important federal antitrust statutes, including the Sherman Antitrust Act, the Clayton Antitrust Act, the Robinson-Patman Act, and the Federal Trade Commission Act. It is important to note that a single business practice may violate multiple antitrust statutes.

Enforcement of Antitrust Laws

Two federal agencies share the primary responsibility for enforcing federal antitrust laws: the Antitrust Division of the Department of Justice (DOJ) and the Federal Trade Commission (FTC). Both agencies work to ensure that markets remain competitive and free from anticompetitive practices, but they have distinct roles and sometimes coordinate their efforts.

The Antitrust Division of the DOJ is responsible for enforcing the Sherman Act, the Clayton Act, and the Robinson-Patman Act. The Sherman Antitrust Act, discussed below, is the only major antitrust law that provides for criminal penalties. The DOJ has the unique authority to criminally prosecute violations of the Sherman Act. In addition, the DOJ may also bring civil enforcement actions under the Clayton Act to prevent anticompetitive mergers and practices that could harm consumers.

The FTC enforces the Federal Trade Commission Act, which prohibits unfair methods of competition and unfair or deceptive acts or practices in commerce. The FTC shares responsibility with the DOJ for enforcing certain provisions of the Clayton Act including:

- Section 2 (Price Discrimination);
- Section 3 (Exclusionary Practices);
- Section 7 (Mergers); and
- Section 8 (Interlocking Directorates).

While the DOJ and FTC have distinct areas of responsibility, they often coordinate their enforcement efforts, particularly when reviewing mergers and acquisitions. This coordination helps prevent overlapping and ensures that antitrust laws are enforced consistently across different industries.

The FTC's mission statement is "protecting the public from deceptive or unfair business practices and from unfair methods of competition through law enforcement, advocacy, research, and education."

While the DOJ and FTC have the authority to bring actions against offenders under federal antitrust laws, private parties who have been injured by such violations also have the right to sue the offending party. These private plaintiffs may seek treble damages (three times the actual damages suffered) as well as the recovery of litigation costs and attorneys' fees incurred during the prosecution of the action. In addition, private parties may sue for injunctive relief to prevent the violator from continuing to engage in anticompetitive behavior.

The Sherman Antitrust Act

In response to the large business enterprises formed after the Industrial Revolution, in 1890 Congress enacted the **Sherman Antitrust Act** (Sherman Act), which prohibited contracts, combinations, and conspiracies in restraint of trade, and monopolization, attempted monopolization, and combinations and conspiracies to monopolize.

Sherman Antitrust Act
This Act prohibits contracts, combinations, and conspiracies in restraint of trade, and monopolization, attempted monopolization, and combinations and conspiracies to monopolize.

The Sherman Act applies only to violations that result in a substantial impact on interstate commerce. Allegations of Sherman Act violations, and violations of any other federal antitrust laws, can only be brought in federal court (federal courts have exclusive jurisdiction over Sherman Act violations). States may enact additional protections to preserve local competition, and violation of these laws may be brought in state court.

The Sherman Act contains two main sections relevant to our study. Section 1 addresses restraints of trade and Section 2 addresses monopolization. Each of these sections is discussed below.

Comparing Section 1 with Section 2 of the Sherman Act

Section 1 of the Sherman Act states:

> Every contract, combination in the form of trust or otherwise, or conspiracy, in restraint of trade or commerce among several States, or with foreign nations, is declared to be illegal.[1]

Section 2 of the Sherman Act states:

> Every person who shall monopolize, or attempt to monopolize, or combine or conspire with any person or persons, shall be deemed guilty of a felony.[2]

A violation under Section 1 of the Sherman Act requires *two or more* persons to act. Actions on behalf of an individual person or business are not alone enough to violate this

1. 15 U.S.C. § 1.
2. 15 U.S.C. § 2.

section because one person cannot contract, combine, or conspire. Section 1 violations arise by the nature of the two parties acting together in an unlawful manner. Section 1 also requires that the acts affect interstate commerce (that is, they cross state lines).

While one person's actions may not violate Section 1, they may violate Section 2 of the Sherman Act. Section 2 applies to "every person." Therefore, actions by one person alone (unilateral conduct) or conduct by more than one person that monopolizes or attempts to monopolize can violate Section 2 of the Act.

Sometimes a single entity composed of multiple members may act on behalf of its members. Does this activity fall under Section 1 of the Sherman Act? The Supreme Court has taken the position that concerted action does not turn simply on whether the parties involved are legally distinct entities; instead, whether there is a concerted action is determined through a case-by-case analysis. In the following case involving the National Football League (NFL), the Supreme Court reviewed whether the actions taken by a single firm (the NFL) with 32 members can constitute a concerted action under Section 1.

CASE 35.1

AGREEMENTS MADE WITHIN A SINGLE FIRM CAN CONSTITUTE CONCERTED ACTION SUBJECT TO SECTION 1 OF THE SHERMAN ACT

AMERICAN NEEDLE, INC. v. NFL

560 U.S. 183 (2010)

Supreme Court of the United States

The NFL is an unincorporated association made up of 32 separately owned professional football teams, each with its own name, colors, logos, and ownership rights over intellectual property. Prior to 1963, the teams made their own arrangements for licensing their intellectual property and marketing trademarked items such as caps and jerseys.

In 1963, the teams formed National Football League Properties (NFLP) to develop, license, and market their intellectual property. Between 1963 and 2000, NFLP granted *non-exclusive* licenses to a number of vendors, permitting them to manufacture and sell apparel bearing team insignias. American Needle, Inc. was one of those licensees. However, beginning in 2000, the teams voted to authorize NFLP to grant *exclusive* licenses, and NFLP granted Reebok an exclusive 10-year license to manufacture and sell trademarked headwear for all 32 teams. Shortly after, it declined to renew American Needle's non-exclusive license.

American Needle filed a lawsuit, alleging that the agreements between the NFL, its teams, NFLP, and Reebok violated the Sherman Act. The NFL defended on the grounds that NFLP, the NFL, and the teams were incapable of conspiring within the meaning of Section 1 because they were a single economic enterprise with respect to the conduct challenged. The district court granted summary judgment in favor of the NFL. American Needle appealed to the United States Court of Appeals for the Seventh Circuit, which affirmed the lower court's decision. American Needle appealed the Seventh Circuit's decision to the Supreme Court.

Language of the Court. *We have a narrow issue to decide: whether the NFL respondents are capable of engaging in a "contract, combination, or conspiracy" as defined by Section 1 of the Sherman Act or whether the alleged activity must be viewed as that of a single enterprise for purposes of Section 1.*

We have long held that concerted action under Section 1 does not turn simply on whether the parties involved are legally distinct entities. As a result, we have repeatedly found instances in which members of a legally single entity violated § 1 when the entity was controlled by a group of competitors and served, in essence, as a vehicle for ongoing concerted activity.

The relevant inquiry is whether there is a "contract, combination or conspiracy" amongst "separate economic actors pursuing separate economic interests," such that the agreement deprives the marketplace of independent centers of decision making and therefore of diversity of entrepreneurial interests.

The NFL may be similar in some sense to a single enterprise that owns several pieces of intellectual property and licenses them jointly, but they are not similar in the relevant functional sense. Although NFL teams have common interests such as promoting the NFL brand, they are still separate, profit-maximizing entities, and their interests in licensing team trademarks are not necessarily aligned.

The Court of Appeals held, they constitute a single entity because without their cooperation, there would be no NFL football. It is true that "the clubs that make up a professional sports league are not completely independent economic competitors, as they depend upon a degree of cooperation for economic survival. The justification for cooperation is not relevant to whether that cooperation is concerted or independent action. A "contract, combination . . . , or conspiracy," § 1, that is necessary or useful to a joint venture is still a "contract, combination . . . , or conspiracy" if it "deprives the marketplace of independent centers of decision making."

Apart from their agreement to cooperate in exploiting property owned by the separate teams, there would be nothing to prevent each of the teams from making its own market decisions relating to purchases of apparel and headwear, to the sale of such items, and to the granting of licenses to use its trademarks. Agreements made within a firm can constitute concerted action covered by § 1 when the parties to the agreement act on interests separate from those of the firm itself, and the intrafirm agreements may simply be a formalistic shell for ongoing concerted action.

For these reasons, decisions by the NFLP regarding the teams' separately owned intellectual property constitute concerted action.

Decision. The Supreme Court reversed the lower court's decision. It held that the licensing activities for the 32 teams conducted through a single entity (NFLP) constituted a concerted action within the meaning of Section 1 of the Sherman Act.

Focus on Ethics

Is it just that exclusive dealings contracts for sports leagues violate the Sherman Act? How do you think this ruling affects the players, coaches, and customers?

Concept Summary
What Are the Required Elements for a Violation Under the Sherman Act?

Elements of a Section 1 Violation

1. An agreement between two or more persons/businesses;
2. Acts that are unreasonable restraint of competition; and
3. Such acts affect interstate commerce.

Elements of a Section 2 Violation

1. A person or business that has monopoly power in the relevant market; and
2. Any willful attempt to either gain monopoly power or preserve that monopoly power by improper means.

Unlawful Restraints of Trade (Section 1 of the Sherman Act)

Section 1 of the Sherman Act prohibits two or more persons from unlawfully restraining trade. Persons may unlawfully restrain trade through written, oral, or inferred conduct of the parties. The Sherman Act does not define the conduct declared unlawful; therefore, the court system has interpreted the prohibitions. The Supreme Court has developed two different tests to determine if actions unlawfully restrain trade: (1) *per se* violations and (2) rule of reason.

***Per se* violation** Actions that are presumed unreasonable restraints of trade and therefore unlawful under the Sherman Act.

If Section 1 of the Sherman Act were read literally, almost every contract would be prohibited under the Sherman Act. The Supreme Court has held that some actions are presumed unreasonable restraints of trade and therefore unlawful under the Sherman Act (such as horizontal agreements among competitors to fix prices). These restraints are known as ***per se* violations**. A *per se* violation occurs when the restraint is so obviously anticompetitive that the restraint is deemed to be illegal on its face. Under this rule, justifications and defenses are irrelevant.

Rule of reason An antitrust law test used to determine if an agreement constitutes an unreasonable restraint of trade.

Restraints that are not characterized as *per se* violations are examined using the rule of reason. Under the **rule of reason** analysis, only "unreasonable restraints of trade" violate Section 1 of the Sherman Act. Reasonable restraints of trade are lawful. Most antitrust claims are reviewed under the rule of reason.

The Rule of Reason

The rule of reason test was established in the landmark case *Standard Oil Company of New Jersey v. United States.*[3] Under the rule of reason, courts consider several factors to determine whether the agreement is anticompetitive and amounts to an unreasonable restraint of trade. As the Supreme Court stated in *Chicago Board of Trade v. United States*, "[t]he true test of legality is whether the restraint imposed is such as merely regulates and perhaps thereby promotes competition or whether it is such as may suppress or even destroy competition."[4] The factors the court includes in its analysis typically include:

1. The purpose and reason for the agreement;
2. The competitive structure of the industry affected by the agreement;
3. The pro- and anticompetitive effects of the agreement within the relevant product and geographic markets;
4. The company's market share and ability to implement the agreement to achieve its purpose; and
5. The history and duration of the restraint.

Example: American Express® charges higher fees to merchants than other credit card companies. It alleges these fees offset the additional expenses American Express incurs in providing superior member rewards. To compete with other credit card companies, American Express inserted "anti-steering" provisions in its contracts with merchants that prevented merchants from steering customers away from using their American Express cards at the point of sale because of the higher fees to merchants. American Express was sued for violation of Section 1 of the Sherman Act under a claim that the "anti-steering" provisions were anticompetitive. The Supreme Court applied the rule of reason test and decided in favor of American Express, holding that its actions expanded and improved the market.[5]

Horizontal Restraints

Under Section 1, trade restraint violations are categorized as either horizontal restraints or vertical restraints. A **horizontal restraint** arises when competitors in the same market agree to restrain trade. A few of the common forms of horizontal restraints include (1) price fixing, (2) horizontal market divisions, (3) trade associations, and (4) group boycotts.

Horizontal restraint
A Sherman Act violation in which competitors in the same market agree to restrain trade.

PRICE FIXING. Price fixing among competitors is a significant concern of the U.S. government. A **price-fixing agreement** is an agreement among two or more competitors to set the prices for goods or services. Price fixing includes establishing minimum or maximum prices, agreeing to lower prices, agreeing to fix a price, or stabilizing the price of a commodity or service. Horizontal price fixing is a *per se* violation of the Sherman Act.

Price-fixing agreement
An agreement between two or more competitors to fix prices or price levels, or terms and conditions of sale for goods and services.

---

3. 221 U.S. 1 (1911).
4. 246 U.S. 231 (1918).
5. *Ohio v. American Express Co.*, 138 S. Ct. 2274 (2018).

A common form of price fixing arises when competitors agree to raise the price of a product or service. It is the agreement by the competitors to raise prices that makes it subject to antitrust violations. The fact that all competitors charge the same price or use the same terms of sale is not sufficient to establish the illegal restraint of trade of price fixing because the competitors may have individually come to the same conclusion to raise the price.

> **Example:** StarKist Co.® was fined tens of millions of dollars for fixing the price of canned tuna with Bumble Bee® and Chicken of the Sea®. The three brands control approximately 80 percent of the United States canned tuna market. The companies had held meetings and exchanged information on pricing data, sales, supply, demand, and production.

This next case addresses price fixing in the publishing industry. With the advent of electronic books (e-books) at lower prices, sustaining profits through book sales has become a new concern for publishers. Publishers' attempts to protect profits have given rise to antitrust violations.

CASE 35.2

A RETAILER THAT ORCHESTRATES WITH PUBLISHERS TO RAISE E-BOOK PRICES VIOLATES THE SHERMAN ACT

UNITED STATES v. APPLE, INC.

791 F.3d 290 (2015)

United States Court of Appeals for the Second Circuit

In the publishing industry, there is a group known as the "Big Six," which comprises six of the largest publishers in the United States. These publishers sold over 48 percent of all e-books in the United States in the first quarter of 2010. However, Amazon.com Inc. (Amazon) had nearly 90 percent of the e-books industry and was charging $9.99 for certain new releases and bestselling e-books. Amazon's price point caused discontent among these publishers, since the low price point cut into their profits for hardcover books.

In 2009, Apple was getting ready for the launch of its tablet computer, iPad, and saw an opportunity to sell e-books on what became known as iBookstore. Conveniently, the Big Six operated in a close-knit industry and had no qualms about communicating about the need to act together. On a fairly regular basis, roughly once a quarter, the CEOs of the Big Six held dinners in the private dining rooms of New York restaurants, without legal counsel or assistants present, in order to discuss the common challenges they faced. Because they "did not compete with each other on price," but over authors and agents, the publishers "felt no hesitation in freely discussing Amazon's prices with each other and their joint strategies for raising those prices."

Apple contacted these publishers and entered into agreements with five of the six major publishing companies, promising to sell their e-books at a higher price point than Amazon did. In these agreements, Apple followed an "agency model" of pricing, which allowed the publishers to set prices and retain about 70 percent of their profits, which was more than what Amazon was offering at the time. Additionally, prior to entering into these agreements, Apple stated that it would only launch its iBookstore if enough of the Big Six agreed to participate.

After entering into these contracts with Apple, the publishers then went to Amazon and refused to do business with Amazon unless it changed its pricing model to be similar to Apple's. Amazon reluctantly agreed. Amazon then sent a letter to the Federal Trade Commission (FTC), complaining about the simultaneous nature of the demands for pricing agreements from the publishers who had signed with Apple. The Department of Justice (DOJ) responded, alleging that these publishers and Apple illegally conspired to adopt a pricing model all at once to retaliate against Amazon's discounting.

Language of the Court. *The Supreme Court has for nearly 100 years held that horizontal collusion to raise prices is the "archetypal example" of a* per se *unlawful restraint of trade. If successful, these conspiracies concentrate the power to set prices among the conspirators, including the power to control the market and fix arbitrary and unreasonable prices.*

The Publishers' primary objective in expressly colluding to shift the entire e-book industry to an agency model (with Apple's help) was to eliminate Amazon's $9.99 pricing for new releases and bestsellers, which the publishers believed threatened their short-term ability to sell hardcovers at higher prices and the long-term consumer perception of the price of a new book. They had grown accustomed to a business in which they rarely competed with one another on price and could, at least partially, control the price of new releases and bestsellers by releasing hardcover copies before paperbacks. Amazon, and the e-book, upset that model, and reduced prices to consumers by eliminating the need to print, store, and ship physical volumes.

The Publishers—their coordination orchestrated by Apple—combined forces to grab control over price. Once organized, they had sufficient clout to demand control over pricing, in the form of agency agreements, from Amazon and other e-book distributors. This control over pricing facilitated their ultimate goal of raising e-book prices to the price caps.

Apple understood that its proposed contracts were attractive to the Publishers only if they collectively shifted their relationships with Amazon to an agency model—which Apple knew would result in higher consumer-facing e-book prices. The use of the promise of higher prices as a bargaining chip to induce the Publishers to participate in Apple's iBookstore constituted a conscious commitment to the goal of raising e-book prices, which matches the definition of an "agreement" for Section 1 purposes.

By agreeing to orchestrate a horizontal price-fixing conspiracy, Apple committed itself to achieving an unlawful objective. This conspiracy to raise prices had its intended effect. After the Publisher defendants switched Amazon to an agency model, 85.7% of Amazon's new releases and 96.8% of their New York Times bestsellers had price increases. These sudden increases in prices reduced e-book sales. By setting new prices through collusion rather than competition, Apple and the Publishers imposed their view of proper pricing, supplanting the market's free play. This evidence is sufficient to support the conclusion that the agreement to raise e-book prices was a per se unlawful price-fixing conspiracy.

Decision. The court held that Apple conspired to fix prices and violated federal antitrust law under Section 1 of the Sherman Act and held Apple liable for $450 million in damages.

Focus on Ethics

Does this decision discourage businesses from entering other markets for fear of being held in violation of antitrust laws? Why or why not?

Horizontal market division
A restraint of trade where competitors agree to divide the market in which they will engage.

HORIZONTAL MARKET DIVISIONS. Horizontal market division, also called allocation schemes, are *per se* violations of the Sherman Act. In a horizontal market division, competitors agree to divide the market they will engage in among themselves. In this type of violation, competitors may allocate specific customers, types of customers, territories, or products among themselves.

Example: Palmer contracted to take a bar review course offered by BRG of Georgia, Inc. At the time, HBJ was the nation's largest provider of bar review materials and lecture services. BRG and HBJ entered into an agreement that gave BRG an exclusive license to market HBJ's material in Georgia and to use its trade name "BarBri." The parties agreed that HBJ would not compete with BRG in Georgia and that BRG would not compete with HBJ outside of Georgia. The United States Supreme Court held that this was a market allocation agreement between competing providers of bar review courses that illegally restrained trade in violation of the Sherman Act. *Palmer v. BRG of Georgia, Inc.*, 498 U.S. 46 (1990)

Trade associations
Where member firms and individuals who also happen to be competitors can come together and exchange price or other sensitive business data.

TRADE ASSOCIATIONS. Competitors in a relevant market may form **trade associations** in order to pursue common interests. For example, the National Association of Realtors, representing real estate agents and brokers, is the largest trade association in the United States. Trade associations are often formed to influence public policy toward positions favorable to the group members.

Within the trade associations, members, who are also competitors, may exchange pricing, conduct advertising campaigns, or establish industry standards. This conduct may raise antitrust concerns. For example, if the trade association establishes new standards that make it more difficult for new companies to enter the marketplace, antitrust may be violated. Courts generally follow the rule of reason regarding these types of horizontal actions by trade associations.

Example: The FTC brought antitrust charges against the Professional Lighting and Sign Management Companies of America, Inc. The trade association's bylaws, with which members were required to comply, restrained competition by designating a territory for each member and restricting the ability of its members to compete in the designated territory of another member. Further, members were prohibited from competing on price or soliciting or competing for customers of other members. As part of the order, the FTC required the association to revise its bylaws to remove the unlawful restraints of trade. *In the Matter of Professional Lighting and Sign Management Companies of America, Inc.*, FTC Docket No. C-4507

GROUP BOYCOTTS. Group boycotts can also raise antitrust concerns under the Sherman Act. A **group boycott** is an agreement whereby two or more competitors in a market refuse to conduct business with another person or company. Unlike many other antitrust violations that affect many people, group boycotts usually affect one or a few victims (often an upstart competitor in a marketplace). Typically, the *per se* standard is applied to horizontal group-boycott claims (such as between two or more competitors utilizing exclusionary tactics to the detriment of another business). Where the *per se* standard is not applied, the rule of reason test is used.

Group boycott
An agreement whereby two or more competitors in a market refuse to conduct business with another person or company.

Example: Toys 'R' Us® sold 20 percent of all toys in the United States from 1980 until about 2000. Toys 'R' Us competitors could not match the price or the variety of its toys. It enjoyed a strong position as the low-price leader for toy sales because its only competition came from traditional toy stores who could not or did not wish to meet its prices.

This changed with the advent of warehouse clubs like Sam's Club® and Costco®. Rather than earning profits from price mark-ups, these clubs were able to match the Toys 'R' Us prices and variety. As a result, Toys 'R' Us set forth a new policy and entered into an agreement with its suppliers that these warehouse clubs could no longer have any new or promoted products. Further, the agreement required these suppliers to give Toys 'R' Us the right of first refusal for toys, and only if Toys 'R' Us did not want the product could the supplier then sell to these warehouse clubs.

The FTC brought charges against Toys 'R' Us for orchestrating a conspiracy to boycott the warehouse clubs, and Toys 'R' Us was held liable for a *per se violation* under the Sherman Act. *Toys 'R' Us, Inc. v. FTC*, 221 F.3d 928 (7th Cir. 2000)

Vertical Restraints

Vertical restraint
A Sherman Act violation in which competitors in different levels of a distribution agree to restrain trade.

A **vertical restraint** arises when competitors in the different levels of distribution agree to restrain trade (such as a manufacturer and a supplier agreeing to restrain trade). A few of the common forms of vertical restraints include (1) resale price maintenance agreements and (2) nonprice vertical restraints. Vertical restraints typically receive rule of reason analysis, as discussed below.

Resale price maintenance agreement
An agreement in which persons at one level of a distribution (such as a manufacturer) enter into an agreement with a party at another level of a distribution (such as a retailer) to adhere to a price schedule.

RESALE PRICE MAINTENANCE AGREEMENTS. Resale price maintenance agreements are agreements in which persons at one level of a distribution (such as a manufacturer) enter into an agreement with a party at another level of a distribution (such as a retailer) to adhere to a price schedule. Such agreements can take the following forms:

1. Setting a *minimum resale price* below which a customer will resell the goods or services supplied; or
2. Setting a *maximum resale price* above which sales cannot occur.

The Supreme Court has held that under either form resale price maintenance agreements should be reviewed under the rule of reason.

Example: Watch Incorporated manufactures expensive watches. It establishes a minimum price (price floor) of $2,000 for which the watches must be sold by retailers to consumers. This minimum resale price would be reviewed under the rule of reason.

Example: Watch Incorporated manufactures inexpensive watches for sale to consumers. It establishes a maximum resale price of $30 that retailers can charge to consumers. This maximum resale price restraint would be reviewed under the rule of reason.

Nonprice vertical restraints
Vertical restrictions on trade that are not price related, such as territorial restrictions or exclusive dealing contracts.

Territorial restriction
A nonprice vertical restraint whereby competitors in distinct levels of a distribution agree to restrain trade.

NONPRICE VERTICAL RESTRAINTS. **Nonprice vertical restraints** are vertical restrictions on trade that are not price related. Common nonprice vertical restraints include (1) territorial restrictions or (2) exclusive dealing contract. Nonprice vertical restraints are reviewed under the rule of reason.

A **territorial restriction** involves a party at one level of a distribution chain (often a manufacturer) creating a territorial restriction for its dealers or suppliers as to where the products may be sold or distributed. The manufacturer often attempts to insulate a supplier or distributor from cannibalization from other dealers and suppliers of the manufacturer. Territorial restrictions may also take the form of customer restraints, where there is a prohibition from selling to a particular category of customers.

Example: Multiflex, Inc., a manufacturer of hydraulic hoses for use in oil field drilling equipment, presented evidence that Samuel Moore & Co., a long-established maker of similar hoses and who controlled at least an 80 percent share of the U.S. market, conspired with three distributors to exclude Multiflex from the market. The court held Moore's actions were an unreasonable nonprice restraint of trade. *Multiflex, Inc. v. Samuel Moore & Co.*, 709 F.2d 980 (5th Cir. 1983)

Exclusive dealing contract
An agreement where a seller agrees to sell all of its product to a particular buyer or where a buyer agrees to purchase all of its goods from a particular seller.

Exclusive dealing contracts between manufacturers and retailers are common and are generally lawful. In an **exclusive dealing contract**, a buyer is required to purchase products or services for a period of time *exclusively* from one supplier, and not from the supplier's competitors. Alternatively, exclusive dealing contracts arise when the seller agrees to sell products or services for a period of time *exclusively* to one buyer.

Example: Yagoozon Inc.® resells children's toys and related products on the internet and through a brick-and-mortar store. SCS is a competitor in the same online market as Yagoozon. Kids Fly Safe® is the wholesaler of a product called CARES Child Aviation Restraint System, the only belt and buckle airplane safety harness for children approved by the Federal Aviation Administration. When Yagoozon attempted to place an order for CARES, Kids Fly Safe refused to process the order and claimed that it had an exclusive dealing contract with SCS. Yagoozon filed suit against Kids Fly Safe and SCS, alleging that the two companies violated the Sherman Act. The court applied the rule of reason and dismissed Yagoozon's claim on the basis that it was a simple refusal to deal not protected by antitrust laws. *Yagoozon, Inc. v. Kids Fly Safe*, 2014 U.S. Dist. LEXIS 92283 (D.R.I. 2014)

Many exclusive dealing contracts are beneficial because they encourage marketing support for the manufacturer's brand. By becoming an expert in one manufacturer's products, the dealer can specialize in promoting that manufacturer's brand and may offer special services or amenities such as specially trained salespeople, larger inventory of products on hand for those products, or faster warranty service.

Sherman Act Section 1 — Which Test to Apply

Horizontal Restraints		Vertical Restraints	
Type	*Test Applied*	*Type*	*Test Applied*
Price fixing	*Per se* violation	Resale price maintenance agreements	Rule of reason
Horizontal market divisions	*Per se* violation	Nonprice vertical restraints	Rule of reason
Trade associations	Rule of reason		
Group boycotts	Typically, *per se* violation		

Monopolies (Section 2 of the Sherman Act)

Section 2 of the Sherman Act prohibits any person from monopolizing trade or combining or conspiring to monopolize trade. Both acts of monopolization and attempts to monopolize are violations of Section 2 of the Sherman Act. A **monopoly** is a company or group of companies having control over the production or distribution of a product or service. Monopolies have the ability to dictate prices and practices in the market they control.

Monopoly
A company or group of companies having control over the production or distribution of a product or service.

The Sherman Act contains no definition of the conduct declared unlawful as monopolization. However, the Supreme Court has defined monopolization as involving two required elements:

1. The possession of monopoly power in the relevant market; and
2. The *willful* acquisition or maintenance of that power as distinguished from growth or development because of a superior product, business acumen, or historic accident.[6]

6. *United States v. Grinnell Corp.*, 384 U.S. 563 (1966).

Monopoly Power

Monopoly power The power to control prices or exclude competition.

Monopoly power is the power to control prices or exclude competition. The existence of monopoly power may be inferred from the predominant share of the market. There is no definitive ruling on what market share constitutes monopoly power. The Supreme Court and federal circuit courts have provided some guidance and hold generally that market share in the relevant market at or above 70 percent is sufficient to establish monopoly power; market share in the relevant market at or below 50 percent is not sufficient to establish monopoly power.[7] Ranges between 50 percent and 70 percent are examined on a case-by-case analysis to make a determination about monopoly power.

Relevant Market

Monopoly power must exist in the relevant product market for there to be liability under Section 2 of the Sherman Act. Defining the relevant market plays a crucial role in determining whether monopolization exists. The relevant market includes both a relevant product market and a relevant geographic market.

The relevant product market includes products that have reasonable interchangeability with the defendant's products or services. Therefore, the relevant market is defined with regard to demand substitution (that is, which products are acceptable substitutes or alternatives for a buyer).

The relevant geographic market includes the geographic area in which the product or service is produced or sold. Where products are sold nationwide (such as through the internet), the relevant geographic market is the United States. If a company produces and sells products locally, the relevant geographic market would be the local area.

> **Example:** Southeast Alaska was the geographic market used to assess the effects of pulp mills' activities restraining and monopolizing the area's timber industry. Southeast Alaska formed a natural area for economic competition, was distant from other states, and was subject to transportation barriers. *Reid Brothers Logging Co. v. Ketchikan Pulp Co.*, 699 F.2d 1292 (9th Cir. 1983)

Willful Act of Monopolizing

As noted by the Supreme Court in *Standard Oil Co. of New Jersey v. United States*,[8] the Sherman Act does not include any direct prohibition against a monopoly as long as the rewards of becoming or maintaining a monopoly were obtained through pro-competitive means. It is the willful act of monopolizing that violates antitrust laws. To determine if an act is willful, the court can look to the intent of the parties who conducted the transition to determine the intent and purpose of the transaction.

Willful acts of monopolizing can be inferred from anticompetitive conduct. Actions that violate Section 1 of the Sherman Act (price fixing, group boycotts, resale price maintenance, and so on) constitute willful acts of monopolization and will violate Section 2 of the Sherman Act.

---

7. See, e.g., *Southeast Mo. Hosp. v. C.R. Bard, Inc.*, 2008 U.S. Dist. LEXIS 4480 (E.D. Mo., 2008).
8. 15 U.S.C. § 13(a).

Example: Kraft Foods Group®, one of the largest food and beverage companies in North America, requires a significant amount of wheat for its food products. To save on transportation costs, Kraft buys most of its wheat from the local Toledo wheat market as well as through the wheat futures market, allowing Kraft to buy wheat at a predetermined price in the future. After the price of wheat in the Toledo market increased, Kraft acquired an enormous, long position in wheat future contracts ($90 million), causing the cash wheat price in the Toledo market to drop. It was alleged that Kraft never intended to use the futures market wheat to meet its wheat demands for products. Kraft then acquired wheat in the cash market at more favorable prices. The district court held that Kraft's wheat futures scheme was driven by willful anticompetitive conduct to control prices. *Ploss v. Kraft Foods Group, Inc.*, 197 F. Supp. 3d 1037 (N.D. Ill. 2016)

ATTEMPTED MONOPOLIZATION UNDER SECTION 2. A company that has not achieved monopoly power may still violate Section 2 if it has committed an act attempting to monopolize. Attempted monopolization requires the party to:

1. Engage in anticompetitive conduct;
2. With a specific intent to monopolize; and
3. Have a dangerous probability of success in obtaining the monopoly power.

Dangerous probability can arise when a company possesses some market power such that there is a likelihood that the company will obtain a monopoly through its conduct.

The Clayton Antitrust Act

The **Clayton Antitrust Act** (Clayton Act), including the Robinson-Patman Act (discussed later in this chapter), prohibits discriminatory pricing and related practices. The Clayton Act was needed to address the specific anticompetitive practices that the Sherman Act did not address, and which resulted from businesses adapting to the Sherman Act. Unlike the Sherman Act, the Clayton Act specifically identifies practices or transactions that violate the Act. Among the significant provisions in the Clayton Act are the following sections:

Clayton Antitrust Act Legislation passed by Congress to address specific anticompetitive practices that were not addressed by the Sherman Act.

1. Section 2 (Price Discrimination);
2. Section 3 (Exclusionary Practices);
3. Section 7 (Mergers); and
4. Section 8 (Interlocking Directorates).

Section 2: Price Discrimination (Robinson-Patman Act)

Section 2 of the Clayton Act, as amended by the **Robinson-Patman Act**, prohibits price discrimination as well as other related practices. Antitrust laws do not dictate what prices a business can charge. They forbid a business from discriminating on those

Robinson-Patman Act Act amending Section 2 of the Clayton Act that prohibits price discrimination.

prices in certain circumstances. Under Section 2(a), it is unlawful for a seller to discriminate in price between different customers without a valid, justified reason for the cost. Section 2(a) provides in pertinent part:

> It shall be unlawful for any person engaged in commerce . . . , either directly or indirectly, to discriminate in price between different purchases of commodities of like grade and quality, where either or any of the purchases involved in such discrimination are in commerce . . . , where the effect of such discrimination may be substantially to lessen competition or tend to create a monopoly in any line of commerce, or to injure, destroy, or prevent competition with any person who either grants or knowingly receives the benefit of such discrimination, or with customers of either of them.[9]

The Act applies *only to the sale of goods*. The sale of services, real estate, securities, leases, or gifts are not covered under the Act. Sales that involve both goods and services (mixed sales) are controlled based on the dominant nature of the transaction (typically based on the value of the goods or service). To prove a violation of the Robinson-Patman Act, a plaintiff must prove the following:

1. The goods were sold through interstate commerce (goods must be sold across state lines);
2. The goods must be of "like grade and quality";
3. The goods must be sold to two or more different purchasers at approximately the same time; and
4. The effect of the discrimination must be to substantially lessen competition, to tend to create a monopoly in any line of commerce, or to injure the party who is discriminated against or injure the customer.

Indirect price discrimination Price discrimination that is not readily apparent from the purchase price of the good.

Indirect price discrimination also violates the Act. Indirect price discrimination is price discrimination that is not readily apparent from the purchase price of the good. This includes providing more favorable credit terms, advertising allowances, discounts, rebates, shipping charges, and so on.

There are several statutory justifiable defenses to liability under the Robinson-Patman Act:

1. *Cost justification*. Where it is less costly to sell to one buyer than another, a price difference is permitted. Cost justifications include differences due to manufacturing, selling or delivering a product as well as providing quantity discounts.

Example: A manufacturer provides bulk shipping discounts for retailers who purchase larger quantities of the goods.

2. *Changing market conditions*. Changing conditions affecting the market for or the marketability of the goods, such as actual or imminent deterioration of perishable goods, obsolescence of seasonal goods, or going out of business sales, are justifiable reasons for price differences.

---

9. Codified at 15 U.S.C. § 13(a).

Example: A grocery store that reduces the price of pre-cooked Cornish game hens (an item it must throw away each night if not sold) for each hour closer to closing time.

3. *Meeting price of competition.* A seller can reduce the price to a customer to meet the price of a competitor.

Example: A customer acquires a television in an electronics store for $1,500. A few minutes later another customer acquires the same television for $1,450 because that customer requested the store to match the price of the television that was offered at a competing store.

Management Application How Businesses May Violate the Robinson-Patman Act

Businesses should be aware that some practices increase the risk of violating the Robinson-Patman Act. These practices include:

1. Selling goods for *below cost* when the company charges higher prices in different localities;
2. Having price differences for identical goods that cannot be justified by reasons of cost saving or matching a competitor's prices; or
3. Promotional allowances that are not practically available to all customers on equal terms.

Section 3: Exclusionary Practices

Section 3 of the Clayton Act prohibits exclusionary practices in the sale or lease of goods. **Exclusionary practices** are agreements, arrangements, or conditions that have the effect of preventing a purchaser from using a competitor's product. Such conduct is unlawful where the effect is to substantially lessen competition or to tend to create a monopoly. Exclusionary practices include exclusive dealing contracts and tying arrangement.

Exclusionary practices Agreements, arrangements, or conditions that have the effect of preventing a purchaser from using a competitor's product.

Like the Sherman Act prohibition, the Clayton Act prohibits **exclusive dealing contracts;** however, exclusive dealing contracts are common and are generally lawful. In an exclusive dealing contract, a buyer is required to purchase products for a period of time *exclusively* from one supplier, and not from the supplier's competitors or the seller may agree to sell products for a period of time *exclusively* to one buyer. If the exclusive dealing relates to services, it does not violate the Clayton Act but it violate the Sherman Act. If the exclusive dealing contract has the effect of substantially lessening competition or has a tendency to create a monopoly, the contract violates Section 3 of the Clayton Act. The law requires that such violation must qualitatively and substantially harm competition.

Tying arrangement An agreement between a seller and a buyer whereby the seller conditions the sale of one product on the buyer's agreement to purchase another product.

A **tying arrangement** under the Clayton Act is an agreement between a seller and a buyer whereby the seller conditions the sale of one product on the buyer's agreement to purchase another product. This separate product or service is referred to as the *tied product*.

The Sherman Act also forbids tying arrangements. Section 3 of the Clayton Act has been limited to only tied goods. Where an act involves services, goods, and/or real property, the action is brought as a Sherman Act violation.

Tying arrangements are reviewed under the rule of reason test. They raise antitrust concerns to the extent that they are used to maintain or increase the seller's preexisting market power or impair competition in the tied product's relevant market.

> **Example:** If a popular coffee machine manufacturer also produced its own line of coffee pods and required a subscription purchase of its coffee pods to purchase the coffee machine, a tying arrangement arises. This arrangement could raise antitrust concerns because it forces customers who use the coffee machine to also buy the tied product.

Section 7: Mergers

While many mergers can benefit both competition and consumers by providing economies of scale and allowing businesses to operate more efficiently, some mergers can negatively affect market dynamics and harm competition. Section 7 of the Clayton Act prohibits mergers and acquisitions of all forms (mergers, consolidations, asset purchases, joint ventures, and so on) that may substantially lessen competition or tend to create a monopoly. Specifically, the Act makes it unlawful for or any "person engaged in commerce . . . to acquire, directly or indirectly, the whole or any part of the stock . . . or assets of any person engaged in commerce, where . . . the effect of such acquisition may be substantially to lessen competition, or to tend to create a monopoly."

To determine whether a merger is unlawful in violation of Section 7 of the Clayton Act, the government typically follows a two-step process: (1) defining the relevant market, and (2) assessing whether the merger or acquisition is likely to substantially lessen competition or create a monopoly in that market.

RELEVANT MARKET. As under the Sherman Act, defining the relevant market is crucial in assessing whether a merger is anticompetitive. The relevant market includes both the relevant product (or service) market and a relevant geographic market.

The relevant product market includes products or services that are reasonably interchangeable with those offered by the merging parties. The definition hinges on demand substitution (that is, identifying which products are acceptable substitutes from the perspective of consumers).

The relevant geographic market encompasses the area where consumers are likely to purchase the goods or services in question. This area could be local, regional, or national depending on the nature of the market. For example, if products are sold nationwide through the internet, the relevant geographic market is the United States. In contrast, if a company operates in a localized area, the relevant geographic market would be that specific area.

However, certain markets, particularly in digital or technology sectors, may not fit traditional market definitions. In these cases, the agencies may define narrower or broader markets depending on the specific competitive concerns, such as the impact on innovation or data control.

REASONABLE PROBABILITY OF SUBSTANTIALLY LESSENING COMPETITION. Once the relevant market has been defined, the next step is to determine whether the merger or acquisition will create a reasonable probability of substantially lessening competition or the likelihood of creating a monopoly. Mergers or acquisitions that are likely to have these effects are often enjoined by courts.

Competition incentivizes businesses to offer lower prices, improve wages and working conditions, enhance quality and resiliency, innovate, and expand choice, among many other benefits. In determining whether the merger will substantially lessen competition, the following factors are considered:

- **Competitive Impact on Prices.** One key factor is whether the merged company would have the power to raise prices without losing customers. If an increase in price would cause a sufficient number of customers to switch to products or services sold by other companies, the merger may not adversely affect the marketplace.
- **Market concentration.** Another important factor is the level of market concentration, which is determined by calculating the percentage of market share held by competitors in the relevant market. Markets with only a few companies controlling a large percentage of market share are considered concentrated, and concentrated markets pose a larger threat of lessening competition.
- **Innovation and Future Competition.** The impact of the merger on innovation is also considered. The FTC and DOJ assess whether the merger would stifle future innovation or prevent new competitors from entering the market. This is especially relevant in industries where technological advancement is crucial.
- **Labor Markets.** The effect of the merger on labor markets is another consideration. The agencies examine whether the merged entity could depress wages, reduce job mobility, or otherwise harm workers.

Market concentration Measures the extent to which a relevant market is controlled by a small number of competitors.

Example: If a large retailer holding a dominant position in a market were to acquire a smaller, but quickly growing, competitor in the same market, the acquisition could raise antitrust concerns under Section 7 of the Clayton Act, if it would substantially lessen competition in the market. Additionally, if the merger would reduce innovation, limit future competition, or negatively impact labor markets, these factors would also weigh against the merger.

PREMERGER NOTIFICATION. The Hart-Scott-Rodino Antitrust Improvements Act (HSR Act) requires certain companies (based on the value of the transaction and in some cases the size of the parties exceeding certain thresholds) to notify the Federal Trade Commission and the Justice Department in advance of a proposed merger. This premerger notification process allows the antitrust agencies time to examine the likely effects of the proposed merger before it takes place, helping to prevent the challenges of unwinding an anticompetitive merger once it has already been completed.

Under the HSR Act, the government has 30 days (15 days for all cash transactions) to decide whether to issue a request for additional information, which extends the review process by another 30 days (or 10 days for all cash transactions). The government can challenge a merger at any time after the premerger notification, even after the transaction has closed. However, the risk of a challenge is highest during the premerger notification period.

For more information on HSR Act notifications, see https://www.ftc.gov/enforcement/premerger-notification-program.

DEFENSES TO SECTION 7 ACTIONS. There are two primary defenses to a Section 7 Clayton Act violation: (1) failing company doctrine and (2) small company doctrine. Courts have narrowly applied the failing company doctrine defense to situations where the resources of the company are so depleted and the prospect of rehabilitation so remote that the company would likely disappear but for being "rescued" by the merger. Courts have considered a company failing when bankruptcy is highly probable or imminent.

The second defense, the small company doctrine, applies to companies where a premerger notification is not required. Courts have permitted these two smaller companies to merge if such a merger allows the merged company to better compete with larger market competitors.

Horizontal merger A merger between two or more companies that are competing in the same market.

Vertical merger A merger between competitors in different levels of distribution (such as a manufacturer and a supplier).

TYPES OF MERGERS. There are two common types of mergers: (1) horizontal mergers and (2) vertical mergers. A **horizontal merger** is a merger between two or more companies that are competing in the same market. Horizontal mergers pose significant antitrust concerns due to the market consolidation that they pose. **Vertical mergers** are mergers between competitors in different levels of distribution (such as a manufacturer and a supplier). Vertical mergers often pose antitrust concerns when the merged company could substantially limit its competitors' access to components or channels of distribution.

Section 8: Interlocking Directorates

Interlocking directorate An unlawful action under the Clayton Act whereby a person serves as a director or officer of two or more competing corporations at the same time.

Section 8 of the Clayton Act prohibits, under certain circumstances, interlocking directorates. An **interlocking directorate** is where a person serves as a director or officer of two or more competing corporations at the same time. The FTC establishes transaction thresholds for interlocking directorates. For 2024, no person may serve as a director or officer where either corporation has capital, surplus, or undivided profits of more than $48,559,000 or competitive sales of at least $4,855,900 or more.[10] The FTC revises the thresholds annually, based on the change in gross national product.

The prohibition on interlocking directorates does not apply to directors or officers between parents and wholly owned or controlled subsidiaries. Further, the interlocking director or officer does not have to involve the *same* individual. Thus, Section 8 can be violated when different persons from the same company sit as officers or on boards of a competing company.

Federal Trade Commission Act

Federal Trade Commission Act A federal act that is aimed at protecting consumer by targeting unfair methods of competition.

Congress passed the **Federal Trade Commission Act** in 1914 to supplement the Sherman Act and the Clayton Act. The Act created the Federal Trade Commission as an administrative agency charged with enforcing the Acts' provisions. Like the

10. Current as of the FTC threshold effective August 13, 2024.

Sherman and Clayton Acts, the FTC Act seeks to prevent unfair methods of competition and unfair or deceptive acts or practices in or affecting commerce; however, the FTC Act is broader in its application as it also prohibits from the incipiency (or beginning) combinations that could lead to anticompetitive practices that would violate the Sherman or Clayton Act. The Federal Trade Commission has exclusive power to enforce the FTC Act. The FTC is empowered to issue rules and investigate and adjudicate FTC Act violations.

Management Application
Antitrust Compliance Programs

Violations of antitrust laws will, in most cases, adversely affect the company. In some cases, the violation may lead the company to seek bankruptcy filing protection. Having a strong company compliance program is essential to avoid antitrust violations. Knowledge and an understanding of the antitrust laws and how they affect business activities, transactions, practices, and policies are essential. Businesses should adopt policies and procedures to educate and train employees on antitrust matters consistently and continually to make them effective. Strong programs will examine a company's past operations, review its present practices, and keep up to date with antitrust laws and regulations affecting the company's industry.

Using an internet search engine, identify public companies whose codes of conduct discourage discussing corporate matters with competitors.

Exemptions from Antitrust Laws

Statutes and the federal courts have created exemptions from antitrust for certain industries and organizations. They include labor unions, insurance companies, agricultural cooperatives, economic regulations mandated by a state (such as utility rates), railroads, airlines, and professional baseball. Two of these exemptions are discussed below.

Labor Unions

Labor unions are exempt from antitrust laws because the labor unions are formed with the intent to protect employees from unfair business practices. Thus, labor union activities such as organizing, collective bargaining, and boycotting and picketing are lawful and exempt from antitrust violations because the labor union actions are intended to protect employees from unfair business practices.

Professional Baseball

In 1922, the Supreme Court ruled in *Federal Baseball Club v. National League*[11] that professional baseball is exempt from antitrust laws. At the time, professional baseball was considered more of a civic organization than a business. Since the business model has changed, this exemption could very well be subject to change. In the following case, the court addressed whether this exemption also extends to *minor league* baseball players. Its holding is applicable to the Ninth Circuit teams, and other federal courts of appeal have cited it favorably in their decisions.

CASE 35.3

BASEBALL EXEMPTION FROM FEDERAL ANTITRUST LAW EXTENDS TO MINOR LEAGUE PLAYERS

MIRANDA v. SELIG

860 F.3d 1237 (2017)

United States Court of Appeals for the Ninth Circuit

Major League Baseball (MLB) is an unincorporated association consisting of 30 MLB franchises. Each franchise has about 40 baseball players on its roster who play at the major league level. As part of MLB's "farm system," each franchise also employs 150 to 250 players who compete in the minor leagues, hoping that a handful will develop into major league players. Therefore, even though minor league players train and play for minor league clubs, they are employed by an MLB club.

MLB requires all team franchises to use a standard player contract with minor league players. Any changes require approval and permission from the MLB Commissioner. The contract contains a "reserve clause," under which MLB franchises have exclusive rights to their minor league players for approximately seven years, precluding them from playing for any other team during this period. The contract also sets forth the minor league players' first-season monthly salary rate. Unlike major league players, minor league players do not belong to a labor union and therefore must negotiate on their own.

In February 2015, a class of minor league baseball players (the "Players") filed suit against Bud Selig, the former Commissioner of Baseball; the Office of the Commissioner of Baseball; and MLB's 30 franchises (collectively, the "Owners"). The Players alleged that because of the "reserve clause," most of the Players earn less than $7,500 per year and receive no salary for spring training, during which they work 50 to 60 hours per week. They also argued that MLB's hiring

11. 259 U.S. 200 (1922).

and employment policies violated federal antitrust laws by restraining horizontal competition between and among the MLB franchises and artificially and illegally depressing minor league salaries.

The Owners filed a motion to dismiss the claim, arguing that minor league baseball is part of the business of baseball exemption. The district court granted the Owners' motion to dismiss, and the Players appealed to the Ninth Circuit Court of Appeals.

Language of the Court. *In 1890, Congress passed the Sherman Act to protect trade and commerce against unlawful restraints and monopolies. Under the Sherman Act, every contract in restraint of trade or commerce among the several States is declared to be illegal. The Supreme Court first exempted the business of baseball from these federal antitrust laws almost a century ago, holding that the business of baseball does not constitute trade or commerce among the several States.*

It is undeniably true that minor league baseball falls squarely within baseball's exemption from federal antitrust laws. The Players argue that the baseball exemption does not apply to minor league baseball because precedent did not decide the issue of whether major league baseball and its constituent clubs could conspire to fix the salaries paid to minor league *players. However, MLB's farming structure belies the claim that major and minor league baseball are separate and distinct in a meaningful way for the purposes of the Sherman Act.*

Minor league baseball players are employed and paid by MLB, and MLB employs minor league players with the hope that some of them will develop into major league players. Therefore, the employment of minor league players is precisely the type of activity that falls within the antitrust exemption for the business of baseball.

Moreover, Congress has made clear its intent to maintain the baseball exemption for anything related to the employment of minor league players, the reserve clause as applied to minor league players, and the relationship between major and minor league baseball. Thus, in light of Supreme Court precedent, minor league baseball falls squarely within the nearly century-old business of baseball exemption from federal antitrust laws.

Decision. The baseball exemption to antitrust laws applies to minor league players, and thus the owners' motion to dismiss was affirmed.

Focus on Ethics

Much has changed in the "business" of baseball since 1922. As baseball is the only professional sports team not subject to antitrust regulations, do you think that it is now time to remove this exemption from antitrust laws?

Comparing and Contrasting EU and U.S. Competition Policies

As businesses become more global, they must comply with not only United States antitrust laws, but competition laws in other countries as well. Both the European Union (EU) and the United States have well-developed competition laws aimed at preventing and penalizing behavior that hurts competition.

The chart below details some of the differences between EU and U.S. competition policies.

	United States	European Union
Development of Competition Laws	Competition policy began with the Sherman Act (1890), followed by the Clayton Act (1914) and FTC Act (1914).	Post–World War II with the break-up of trusts that played a role in wartime production of weapons and supplies. The Paris Treaty (1951) was signed to avoid abuse of dominant position by firms.
Major Antitrust Legislation	Sherman Act, which was aimed at agreements or conspiracies that restrained interstate commerce. Clayton Act, which aimed at prohibiting price discrimination and establishing merger control.	Treaty of Rome, which contains provisions on anticompetitive agreements (Article 85) and abuse of dominant position (Article 86). Treaty on the Functioning of the European Union (TFEU), which forms the basis of EU competition law.
Principal Actors	Congress legislates competition law, while the DOJ and the FTC enforce the laws.	The European Parliament is consulted on legislation, while the European Court of Justice has the power to cancel or modify decisions made by the European Council. Each Member States' competition authorities may enforce the competition laws.

While there are differences, both the United States and the EU seek to advance consumer interests while protecting competition in the marketplace.

AI Feature: Prospective Merger Analysis

After reading this chapter, use an AI program to create a strategic report. You will evaluate the potential legal risks and benefits of a merger by a publicly held mid-sized technology company of your choosing that is considering merging with a larger publicly held competitor in the same marketplace.

What legal risks and benefits were identified? Propose a strategic plan to ensure compliance with antitrust laws. Provide a recommendation on whether to proceed with the merger and explain your decision.

Key Terms

- Antitrust laws, 880
- Clayton Antitrust Act, 893
- Exclusionary practices, 895
- Exclusive dealing contract, 890
- Federal Trade Commission Act, 898
- Group boycott, 889
- Horizontal market division, 888
- Horizontal merger, 898
- Horizontal restraint, 885
- Indirect price discrimination, 894
- Interlocking directorate, 898
- Market concentration, 897
- Monopoly, 891
- Monopoly power, 892
- Nonprice vertical restraints, 890
- *Per se* violation, 884
- Price-fixing agreement, 885
- Resale price maintenance agreement, 889
- Robinson-Patman Act, 893
- Rule of reason, 884
- Sherman Antitrust Act, 881
- Territorial restriction, 890
- Trade association, 888
- Tying arrangement, 896
- Vertical merger, 898
- Vertical restraint, 889

Applying the Law

35.1 Research the Law. Using an internet search engine, research the laws of your state to determine if your state has adopted its own antitrust law. What additional protections does the state law provide that federal law does not?

35.2 Research the Law. Review the Federal Trade Commission's Guide to Antitrust Laws for Mergers at *https://www.ftc.gov/tips-advice/competition-guidance/guide-antitrust-laws/mergers*. When are notifications prior to a merger required?

35.3 Standing. Stacie Somers sued Apple® alleging state and federal antitrust claims. She alleged that Apple encoded its music and iPod devices with software making its music and devices incompatible with non-Apple products and services. She alleged that Apple's practices of preventing the use of Apple music and products with non-Apple products was monopolistic. Apple defended its actions because it had used its software encoding from the beginning of its product releases and not in response to a competitor. Has Somers suffered an antitrust injury? *Somers v. Apple, Inc.*, 729 F.3d 953 (9th Cir. 2013)

35.4 Does the Sherman Act Apply? Dallas, Tarrant, and Collin Countries in Texas do not allow individual drivers to operate taxicabs. Instead, a licensed taxicab driver seeking to operate a taxicab must pay a "stand fee" to a permit holder, an entity approved by local regulators to operate a fleet of taxicabs. In exchange for the "stand fee," these drivers receive a decal that allows the drivers to operate a taxi in a particular place or places. The Association of Taxicab Operators (the "Association") was comprised of authorized taxicab drivers with decals. These drivers compete with various taxicab companies whose drivers are also holders of decals. The Defendants are subsidiaries of Irving Holdings, Inc. (Irving), which was controlled by two individuals. The Association sued the commonly owned defendants alleging they engaged in price fixing under Section 1 of the Sherman Act. Does Section 1 of the Sherman Act even apply to these defendants? Why or why not? *Ass'n of Taxicab Operators, USA v. Yellow Checker Cab Co.*, 910 F. Supp. 2d 971 (N.D. Tex. 2012)

35.5 *Per Se* or Rule of Reason. Business Electronics Corp. (BEC) and Hartwell were authorized by Sharp Electronics Corp.® (Sharp) to sell its electronic calculators in the Houston area. In response to Hartwell's complaints about BEC's prices, Sharp terminated BEC's distribution agreement. BEC sued alleging that Hartwell, the remaining dealer in the area, and Sharp conspired to terminate BEC to cut prices and that such conspiracy was illegal *per se* under Section 1 of the Sherman Act. However, because there was no further agreement on the price or price levels to be charged by the remaining dealer (Hartwell), the Supreme Court held that there was no *per se* violation. Do you agree with this holding? If the court instead applied the rule of reason, would the outcome be the same? Why or why not? *Business Electronics Corp. v. Sharp Electronics Corp.*, 485 U.S. 717 (1988)

35.6 Rule of Reason. Multiple owners and lessors (collectively, "Plaintiffs") of Mercedes-Benz® automobiles from New York, Connecticut, and New Jersey sued Mercedes-Benz and the affiliated dealerships in those three states. They alleged that the dealerships exchanged financial information, including pricing strategies and historical sales information. Mercedes-Benz U.S.A., which is the parent company of many U.S.-based dealerships, and its accountant compiled monthly and year-to-date analyses for each dealer stating the average price and gross profit realized by each dealer for each model of car sold. This information was shared with all of the dealerships, allegedly for the purpose of policing compliance with the price-fixing conspiracy. There were allegations that at the meetings dealers were lectured about the importance of not competing against each other based on price, and any dealer whose monthly reports indicated lower pricing and lower gross profit levels than the others was singled out and berated. In applying the rule of reason, is there a violation of the Sherman Act? *In re Mercedes-Benz Anti-Trust Litig.*, 157 F. Supp. 2d 355 (D.N.J. 2001)

35.7 Suggested Prices. Leegin had a policy of refusing to sell to retailers that discount its goods below suggested prices. Leegin had offered retailers incentives to become specialty stores that would support its products on a consistent basis. Leegin later discovered that PSKS had been marking down its line by 20 percent. Leegin requested that PSKS cease the discounting, but the request was refused. Per this policy, Leegin stopped selling to PSKS. In response, PSKS filed an action alleging that Leegin violated the antitrust laws by entering into vertical agreements with retailers to set minimum resale prices. Should the court use the *per se* rule or the rule of reason in deciding this case? *Leegin Creative Leather Products, Inc. v. PSKS, Inc.*, 551 U.S. 877 (2007)

35.8 Meeting Competition Defense. For approximately six years, Falls City Industries sold beer to wholesalers throughout Indiana. Vanco was the sole distributor in Vanderburgh County, Indiana, while across the state line Dawson Springs was the sole distributor in Henderson County, Kentucky. These counties are connected by several highways and are considered to be a single metropolitan area. The two distributors did not compete for sales, because of an Indiana state law that placed restrictions on the import and export of beer. After the six years, Vanco sued Falls City alleging that Falls City had discriminated in price against Vanco, by charging Vanco a higher price than it charged Dawson Springs. Does the meeting competition defense apply? Make arguments for and against such a finding. *Falls City Industries, Inc. v. Vanco Beverage, Inc.*, 460 U.S. 428 (1983)

35.9 Mergers. The Federal Trade Commission charged Procter & Gamble® with a violation of Section 7 of the Clayton Act for acquiring the assets of Clorox® Chemical. The charge alleged that Procter's acquisition of Clorox would substantially decrease competition or create a monopoly in the production and sale of household liquid bleaches. At the time of the merger, Clorox was the leading manufacturer in concentrated household bleach. P&G is a large, diversified manufacturer of household products. Does this transaction violate Section 7 of the Clayton Act? If so, why? *FTC v. Procter & Gamble Co.*, 386 U.S. 508 (1967)

35.10 Monopolies. Image Technical Services began servicing copying and micrographic equipment manufactured by Kodak®. In response, Kodak adopted policies that limited the availability of replacement parts for its equipment to make it more difficult for Image to compete with it in servicing such equipment. Image filed an action alleging that Kodak violated Section 1 of the Sherman Act when Kodak had unlawfully tied the sale of service for its machines to the sale of parts. Did Kodak violate the Sherman Act? *Eastman Kodak Co. v. Image Technical Services, Inc.*, 504 U.S. 451 (1992)

Consumer Laws and Regulations

36

The desire for safety stands against every great and noble enterprise. — Tacitus, Roman historian (55-120 A.D.)

Chapter Outline

- Introduction
- The Federal Trade Commission
- Deceptive Advertising
  - *Management Application: Excerpt of a Complaint for Damages — False Advertising*

Case 36.1: *Bowring v. Sapporo U.S.A., Inc.*
  - *Management Application: Endorsements and Sponsored Advertising*
  - *Management Application: Children's Online Privacy (COPPA)*
  - *Management Application: What Types of Emails Does CAN-SPAM Cover?*
- Labeling and Packaging
- Sales
- Legislation Aimed at Protection of Health and Safety
  - *Management Application: What Is a "Food Additive"?*
- Consumer Credit Protection

Case 36.2: *Erickson v. First Advantage Background Servs. Corp.*
  - *Management Application: What Are Credit Reporting Agencies?*
  - *Management Application: How Credit Scores Are Calculated*

Case 36.3: *Agrelo v. Affinity Mgmt. Services, LLC*
- AI Feature: False Advertising in the Fast Food Industry

Learning Objectives

After reading this chapter, you should be able to:

1. Identify when advertising is considered "deceptive."
2. Understand the importance of the Federal Trade Commission and the Federal Trade Commission Act.
3. Identify and distinguish between the various deceptive advertising techniques.
4. Describe the various federal consumer protection laws and what they aim to protect.

Introduction

Consumer transaction
A sale, lease, disposition of property (real or personal), or service to a person to be used for personal or household use.

Consumer
A person who purchases goods and/or services for personal use.

Millions of dollars of consumer transactions occur every minute. A **consumer transaction** generally refers to a sale, lease, disposition of property (real or personal), or service to a person to be used for personal or household use. A **consumer** is a person who purchases goods and/or services for personal use. Under the common law, consumers were subject to *caveat emptor* ("Let the buyer beware"). This rule meant that a consumer would assume the risk of whatever product or service she purchased. In recent years, *caveat emptor* has largely been replaced by both state and federal consumer protection laws. Additionally, the law of express and implied warranties extends protections to consumers. Today, they are afforded greater protections compared to those of the past.

Governmental consumer protection laws attempt to protect consumers from unfair trade practices, dangerous products, discriminatory or unreasonable credit requirements, and other issues that may arise during consumer transactions. This chapter explores various federal consumer protection laws. Consumers should be aware that state laws may provide additional consumer protections.

Federal Trade Commission Act
A federal act that is aimed at protecting consumers by targeting unfair methods of competition.

The Federal Trade Commission

Federal Trade Commission (FTC)
An independent agency of the U.S. government that was created for the express purpose of protecting consumers.

Congress enacted the **Federal Trade Commission Act** (FTC Act) in 1914. Section 5 of the FTC Act applies to consumer protection. It prohibits unfair methods, acts, or practices of competition that affect commerce. The FTC Act created the **Federal Trade Commission (FTC)** and provided it broad powers to issue regulations, interpret its regulations, enforce the regulations through the court system, and award monetary penalties.

Top Ten Categories of Consumer Complaints to the FTC[1]

Category	Number of Complaints	Percentages
Imposter Scams	642,137	41.9%
Online Shopping and Negative Reviews	281,504	18.4%
Prizes, Sweepstakes, and Lotteries	120,402	7.9%

1. FTC Consumer Sentinel Network, *https://public.tableau.com/app/profile/federal.trade.commission/viz/TheBigViewAllSentinelReports/TopReports* (through 2023).

Category	Number of Complaints	Percentages
Internet Services	100,758	6.6%
Health Care	85,023	5.5%
Investment Related	82,341	5.4%
Business and Job Opportunities	82,015	5.4%
Telephone and Mobile Services	74,267	4.8%
Travel, Vacations, and Timeshare Plans	42,250	2.8%
Advance Payments for Credit Services	22,030	1.4%

Deceptive Advertising

Deceptive advertising (also referred to as false advertising) under Section 5 of the FTC Act is advertising that is likely to mislead consumers acting reasonably under the circumstances due to a representation, omission, or practice. Generally, advertising is considered "deceptive" if a reasonable consumer would be misled by the advertising claim. Vague generalities and obvious exaggerations are not considered deceptive advertising. Instead, these types of advertising techniques are known as puffery. Unlike deceptive advertising, **puffery** is a legal way of promoting a product or service through hyperbole or oversized statements that cannot be objectively verified.

Deceptive advertising
Advertising that is likely to mislead consumers acting reasonably under the circumstances due to a representation, omission, or practice.

Puffery
A legal way of promoting a product or service through hyperbole or oversized statements that cannot be objectively verified.

Example: eMachines, Inc. manufactured computers and stated that its M5305 model was of "high quality" and "reliable." Further, eMachines said that its computers contained the "latest technology" with "high performance criteria" and underwent the "most stringent quality control tests." The court found that these terms were legal puffery. *Anunziato v. eMachines, Inc.*, 402 F. Supp. 2d 1133 (2005)

However, advertising will be deemed deceptive if it *appears* to be based on facts but cannot be reasonably supported by evidence.

Example: Direct Marketing Concepts, Inc.® (DMC) marketed a product known as "Coral Calcium" via infomercials. In the advertisements, DMC asserted the positive biological and medical benefits of coral-derived calcium: "I've had 1,000 people tell me how coral calcium has cured their cancer. I've witnessed people get out of wheelchairs with multiple sclerosis just by getting on the coral." DMC asserted that coral-derived calcium is superior to other sources of calcium and provided *unspecified* articles from the *Journal of the American Medical Association* and the *New England Journal of Medicine* "that calcium supplements reverse cancer."

The court also found that the advertisement's claims that coral calcium was a successful treatment for cancer were not adequately substantiated. Prior to making these claims, DMC did not receive or review any scientific substantiation for its claims. Thus, this was considered deceptive advertising. *FTC v. Direct Marketing Concepts, Inc.*, 624 F.3d 1 (1st Cir. 2010)

Advertising That Is Based on Half-Truths

Half-truth advertisement An advertisement containing true information that is missing a material fact.

There are also advertisements that contain "half-truths." A **half-truth advertisement** is a deceptive practice that omits a material fact (such as qualifying information) when making a truthful claim when the omission of that information is likely to mislead a reasonable consumer. The advertisement is therefore incomplete because while true it is missing the material fact. As a result, consumers can be misled.

> **Example:** Leatherman Tool Group® labelled and advertised its products as "Made in U.S.A." when in reality, a majority of the parts were manufactured outside the United States. Although certain parts of the products were assembled in the United States, the court found that this constituted a deceptive advertising practice because the phrase "Made in the U.S.A." is likely to mislead a consumer into thinking that there was no such foreign manufacturing. *Colgan v. Leatherman Tool Group, Inc.*, 135 Cal. App. 4th 663 (2006)

Management Application Excerpt of a Complaint for Damages—False Advertising

1. On or about [Date], defendant represented to the public, including plaintiff, by means of advertisements broadcast on television station XYZ, that "Great & Healthy Cereal," when eaten in moderate amounts, would reduce the risk of cancer in adults. A representative selection of defendant's advertisements is attached as Exhibit A.
2. Defendant's representations were untrue in that an average adult would in fact need to consume fifteen servings of defendant's cereal per day to achieve any appreciable reduction in the risk of cancer.
3. Defendant made the representations alleged herein with the intention of inducing the public to purchase defendant's cereal. . . .

Can you identify any advertising that you believe would qualify as false advertising?

The following case addresses whether Sapporo®, a popular beer distributed in the United States, misled consumers into believing a beer produced in the United States and Canada was imported from Japan.

CASE 36.1

A VISIBLE DISCLOSURE STATEMENT DOES NOT MISLEAD A REASONABLE CONSUMER

BOWRING v. SAPPORO U.S.A., INC.

234 F. Supp. 3d 386 (2017)

United States District Court for the Eastern District of New York

Sapporo is a popular beer distributed in the United States by Sapporo U.S.A., Inc. (Sapporo). Sapporo beer was originally brewed in Japan in 1877 and first imported to the United States in 1964. In 1984, Sapporo Inc. was established in the United States. Today, three varieties of Sapporo—Premium, Reserve, and Premium Light—are distributed in the United States by Sapporo. All Sapporo beer now sold in the United States is brewed in La Cross, Wisconsin, or Guelph, Ontario, Canada.

Antonia Bowring alleged that Sapporo created a misleading impression that Sapporo beer is a Japanese import, when in fact, it is produced in the United States and Canada. Bowring argues that Sapporo likely collected "millions of dollars that it would not have otherwise earned" because consumers "paid money for beer that is not what it purports to be or what they bargained for." Bowring sued on behalf of herself and a proposed class of similarly situated Sapporo consumers, asserting claims for deceptive advertising. Sapporo filed a motion to dismiss the lawsuit with the court.

Language of the Court. *Within the United States, Sapporo markets its beer using the following advertisements and slogans:*

— *A television commercial with imagery of a "Japanese landscape being traveled into American landscape," ending with the slogan "The Original Japanese Beer,"*
— *Slogans "Sapporo—the Original Japanese Beer" and "Japan's Oldest Brand";*
— *Statement on Sapporo's website that "Sapporo is the original Japanese beer"; and*
— *Image of the North Star, a "symbol of pioneers in the area of Sapporo" on labels.*

In addition, the Sapporo beers produced in Canada and sold in the United States include the word "Imported" on the front label. Each imported can or bottle also adds the following text: "Imported by Sapporo U.S.A. Inc., New York, NY" followed by "Brewed and canned [or bottled] by Sapporo Brewing Company, Guelph, Ontario, Canada." The text appears in darker contrasting font on the front label for bottles and on the side or back of canes. The labels for the beers brewed in Wisconsin do not use the word "Imported" and include the following statement on the front, back, or side of the container: "Brewed and Bottled [or Canned] by Sapporo Brewing Company, La Cross, WI for Sapporo U.S.A., New York NY" in visible, contrasting print.

Bowring alleges that independent stores and restaurants display Sapporo in the "imported beer section" and on "imported beer lists." Additionally, Bowring submitted a webpage for a liquor shop in Minneapolis, Minnesota selling six bottles of Sapporo for $8.79, along with the text: "Sapporo Draft 6pk bottles from Japan." She submits that the beer she obtained was of a lesser value than the imported Japanese beer she believed she was purchasing.

To assert a false advertising or deceptive acts or practices claim, a plaintiff must establish that the defendant engaged in consumer oriented conduct that is materially misleading, and plaintiff was injured as a result of the deceptive act or practice. To prove conduct was materially misleading, a plaintiff must demonstrate that it would mislead "a reasonable consumer acting reasonably under the circumstances." Considering each allegedly misleading statement and Sapporo's marketing as a whole, the court concludes that Sapporo's conduct would not mislead a reasonable consumer. The use of a trademarked star symbol and allusion to the company's historic roots in Japan are eclipsed by the accurate disclosure statement. The disclosure statement on Sapporo appears in contrasting, visible font, and states in clear language where the product is produced. Sapporo's use of the term "Imported" is a truthful statement, and is qualified by the visible disclosure statement specifying the beer's origin in Canada. The Court finds that Sapporo's conduct would not mislead a reasonable consumer.

Decision. The district court granted Sapporo's motion to dismiss the lawsuit.

Focus on Ethics

Is it fair that a disclosure that many consumers may not read can allow a company to avoid deceptive advertising liability?

Bait-and-Switch Advertising

Bait-and-switch advertising
A dishonest marketing tactic whereby a seller or service provider advertises an attractive product to bait a customer to come to the seller while intending to substitute a less desirable product for the customer to purchase.

Another deceptive advertising technique governed by FTC regulations is known as bait-and-switch advertising. **Bait-and-switch advertising** is a dishonest marketing tactic whereby a seller or service provider advertises an attractive product to bait a customer to come to the seller while intending to substitute a less desirable product for the customer to purchase. The switched product typically has a higher purchase price, increased profit margin for the seller, or has a less marketable characteristic than the product advertised. When this form of advertising is used, a customer may be told that the product had a limited number of units produced and is now unavailable. Bait-and-switch advertising arises when a seller:

1. Refuses to show the advertised product or service;
2. Fails to have reasonable quantities of the advertised product or service available;

3. Fails to promise to deliver the advertised product or service within a reasonable time; or
4. Discourage its employees from selling the advertised product or service.

Example: Francis telephones a local car dealership and after describing the make, model, and condition of his vehicle is quoted $4,000 as a trade-in. When he arrives at the dealership to trade in his vehicle as a down payment for a new vehicle at the dealership, he is informed that the dealership will not pay that price for his trade-in even though it meets the exact specifications he noted on the phone.

Online Deceptive Advertising

Online sales (e-commerce) account for roughly sixteen percent of total retail sales in the United States. Given the volume of transactions, the FTC governs and monitors online sales to protect consumers. While the general principles of advertising law apply online, as technology changes and new media platforms are developed, the FTC has issued guidelines to help businesses comply with the laws and to avoid deceptive advertising claims:

1. All advertisements (online and offline) must be truthful and not misleading;
2. Advertisers must be able to support the claims made in an advertisement through evidence, and advertising agencies are responsible for reviewing the information used to substantiate advertisements (they cannot rely on advertisers' assurances that they are accurate);
3. Product demonstrations must show how the product will perform under normal use;
4. The advertisement must be unlikely to cause substantial consumer injury that consumers could not reasonably avoid; and
5. Disclaimers and disclosures must be clear and conspicuous.

Example: The FTC brought a complaint against two individuals and five related companies who will pay $1.5 million for deceptively claiming that their Acai Pure supplement would cause rapid and substantial weight loss, and that their Colotox colon cleanser would prevent colon cancer. Also, despite claiming to offer a "free" trial for a nominal fee and full refunds upon request, the defendants allegedly repeatedly made unauthorized charges to consumers' bank accounts and made it all but impossible to avoid paying full price for the products, typically $39.95 to $59.95. *Federal Trade Commission v. Central Coast Nutraceuticals, Inc., et al.* Case Number 10 C 4931, United States District Court, (N.D. Ill. August 16, 2010)

DISCLAIMERS AND DISCLOSURES. The FTC guidelines require that any disclaimers or other qualifying information such as "Results May Vary" be "clear and conspicuous." A disclaimer is clear and conspicuous where the consumer can notice, read or hear, and understand the information. Generally, businesses should place any disclaimers or qualifying information as close as possible to the disclaimed or qualified claim. If that is not possible or practical, the business should place the disclaiming or qualifying information where the consumer can easily find the information.

Management Application
Endorsements and Sponsored Advertising

Today, businesses have many options to promote or endorse their products. As celebrities, athletes, and other influencers work with brands to promote or endorse products through social media and other advertising platforms, consumers can be more easily influenced by these sponsored posts. FTC guidelines provide that if there is a "material connection" between an endorser and advertiser, the connection must be clearly and conspicuously disclosed.

Some of the FTC guidelines provide that influencers must make their disclosures understandable because some consumers may not understand that a disclosure such as "#spon" means that an advertiser sponsored it.

For more information on the FTC's Endorsement Guides, see https://www.ftc.gov/news-events/topics/truth-advertising/advertisement-endorsements.

ADVERTISING TO CHILDREN. Advertising directed to children poses additional concerns because children may have greater difficulty evaluating advertising claims and understanding the nature of the information an advertiser provides. The Federal Communications Commission has also enacted regulations affecting advertising to children, including limiting the time of commercials during children's programing. The Children's Advertising Review Unit (CARU) of the Council of Better Business Bureaus (CBBB) was founded to review and evaluate advertising directed to children by monitoring broadcast cable television, radio, and children's magazines. Through CARU, the advertising industry self-regulates itself to ensure truthful, accurate, and consistent advertisements. When advertisements are found to be in violation of the regulatory guidelines, CARU seeks changes through the voluntary cooperation of advertisers.

Example: Dave & Buster's, Inc® advertised a commercial featuring a child stating that visitors needed to simply say "kids rule" and they could play video games free until 3 P.M. The commercial also featured a graphic stating "Free video games until 3 P.M." A small disclosure at the bottom of the screen noted: "Free play only valid with the same day $20 Power Card purchase or reload." This advertisement violated CARU Guidelines by making an unsubstantiated and false claim to children regarding the offer that children could play video games for free when in fact a purchase had to be made. Children's Advertising Review Unit. CARU Case Reports No. 5798, closed Jan. 5, 2015

Management Application
Children's Online Privacy (COPPA)

Congress enacted the Children's Online Privacy Protection Act (COPPA) to provide parents the power to control what information businesses can collect from children under the age of 13. The FTC enforces COPPA, and guidelines provide what businesses must do to protect children's privacy and safety online. With a few limited exceptions, the FTC provides a step-by-step plan for determining if COPPA covers a company–and what to do to comply with the Rule:

Step 1. Determine if Your Company is a Website or Online Service that Collects Personal Information from Kids Under 13.
Step 2. Post a Privacy Policy that Complies with COPPA.
Step 3. Notify Parents Directly Before Collecting Personal Information from Their Kids.
Step 4. Get Parents' Verifiable Consent Before Collecting Personal Information from Their Kids.
Step 5. Honor Parents' Ongoing Rights with Respect to Personal Information Collected from Their Kids.
Step 6. Implement Reasonable Procedures to Protect the Security of Kids' Personal Information.

EMAIL ADS AND SPAM. Most consumers have dealt with unwanted and unsolicited emails. Congress enacted the Controlling the Assault of Non-Solicited Pornography and Marketing Act (CAN-SPAM) to create a national standard to address this growing problem. The Act establishes rules for commercial emails, establishes requirements for these emails, provides recipients the right to unsubscribe, and establishes penalties for violations. The transmission of unsolicited commercial emails is permitted so long as the email is labeled as an advertisement and an opt-out mechanism is conspicuously provided. The transmission of unsolicited emails that use techniques to avoid detection, such as hiding and disguising the identities and locations of computers used to send the emails, is prohibited as a crime. The Act authorizes damages of up to $250 per email, with a cap of $2 million that could be tripled for aggravated violations. The cap does not apply to emails with false or deceptive headers.

Management Application
What Types of Emails Does CAN-SPAM Cover?

To determine whether an email is covered by the Act, the most important consideration is the "primary purpose" of the message. To determine the primary purpose of the message, the business must categorize the content of the email as either:

■ *Commercial* content, ■ *Transactional/relationship* content, or ■ Other content, which is neither commercial nor transactional.	*Commercial* content advertises or promotes a commercial product or service. *Transactional/relationship* content facilitates an already agreed-upon transaction or updates a customer about an ongoing transaction.

Type of Transaction	Exempt from CAN-SPAM	Requirements
Commercial	No	Must comply with CAN-SPAM
Transactional/relationship	Yes	May not contain false or misleading routing information

Federal Trade Commission (FTC) Enforcement

Consent decree
A settlement between the FTC and an alleged offender prior to the issuance of a formal FTC complaint.

The FTC receives millions of consumer complaints each year. Instead of prosecution of an action, most FTC advertising cases are settled through a **consent decree** between the parties. This is advantageous to the FTC, as it can save its resources for more significant cases, and for the alleged offender, who saves time, costs, and harm to the company's reputation. If the FTC accepts the consent agreement, the FTC must put the consent decree in a public record and allow interested parties to comment for a period of 60 days.

If the parties are unable to resolve the matter through a consent decree and the FTC decides that a certain advertisement is deceptive, it sends a formal complaint to the offender (the alleged seller or service provider). Once a complaint is received, the alleged offender can either (1) settle the complaint without further action by the FTC, or (2) choose to defend the claims before an administrative law judge (see Chapter 34).

FTC ORDERS AND REMEDIES. If the FTC is successful in proving that the advertisement is deceptive, the offender can face enforcement actions including the following:

Corrective advertising
New advertising intended to correct and inform the public that the company previously provided information that was misleading, false, or deceptive.

Injunction
A court order that prohibits the continued harm from continuing.

- *Cease and desist order.* This order requires the offender to stop the deceptive advertising practice. Most consent decrees include a cease-and-desist order.
- *Corrective advertising order.* The FTC may order an offender to advertise and inform the public that the prior information was misleading, false, or deceptive.
- *Disgorgement of profits.* The FTC has the power to order the disgorgement (giving up) of profits made by the advertisement.
- *Injunction.* The FTC can ask a federal district court to issue an **injunction** against the offending company.
- *Fines.* The FTC may require the offender to pay fines for FTC violations.
- *Refunds.* The offender may be required to issue refunds to repay the money or profits derived from the conduct.

False Advertising Protections Under the Lanham Act and State Law

In addition to FTC orders and remedies, false advertising claims can be protected under the Lanham Act and state law. The Lanham Act, discussed in Chapter 7 related to trademark protection, permits any person to sue another for unfair competition arising from false or misleading product descriptions. A person may file a civil suit where the advertising is (1) likely to cause confusion, or to cause mistake, or to deceive, or (2) in commercial advertising or promotion, misrepresents the nature, characteristics, qualities, or geographic origin of their or another person's goods, services, or commercial activities.

Many state consumer fraud statutes may also prohibit false, misleading, and deceptive acts or practices.

> **Example:** Texas law provides false, misleading, or deceptive acts or practices in the conduct of any trade or commerce are unlawful and are subject to action by the consumer protection division under Business and Commerce Code § 17.46.

Telemarketing Practices

Most consumers have experienced telephone solicitations (that is, telemarketing) by telemarketers trying to advertise a product or service. The **Telemarketing Sales Rule (TSR)** provides consumers a choice about whether they want to receive many telemarketing calls by establishing a national "Do Not Call" registry. The Do Not Call registry is a database maintained by the federal government, listing the telephone numbers of individuals and families who have requested that telemarketers not contact them. TSR applies to any plan, program, or campaign to sell goods or services through interstate phone calls. It also applies to for-profit telemarketers who conduct interstate solicitation of charitable contributions by phone. The following are a few provisions of the TSR:

Telemarketing Sales Rule (TSR)
A federal rule that established the National Do Not Call Registry and limits the conduct of telemarketers.

National Do Not Call Registry
A database maintained by the federal government, listing the telephone numbers of individuals and families who have requested that telemarketers not contact them.

The registry is found at https://www.donotcall.gov.

- Requires solicitors to provide their name, the name of the person or entity on whose behalf the call is being made, and either a telephone number or an address at which that person or entity may be contacted;
- Requires transmission of caller ID information;
- Prohibits solicitors from calling residences before 8:00 A.M. or after 9:00 P.M. local time; and
- Requires solicitors to honor the **National Do Not Call Registry**.

> **Example:** Dish Network, LLC® was found liable and ordered to pay $280 million for violations that included tens of millions of calls that violated the FTC's Telemarketing Sales Rule, including Do Not Call, entity-specific, and abandoned-call violations. Dish Network, LLC, FTC File No. 052 3167, Jan. 21, 2015

Labeling and Packaging

Federal laws also contain requirements for the labeling and packaging of products. Consumers have likely seen nutritional information on food packaging and restaurant menus. Typically, labels must be accurate and written to be easily understood by consumers. The Fair Packaging and Labeling Act (FPLA) directs both the FTC and the Food and Drug Administration (FDA) to issue regulations on food packaging and labeling. The Act require that all "consumer commodities" be labeled to do the following:

- Identify the commodity (such as detergent, hand soap, and so on);
- State the net quantity of the contents in terms of weight, measure, or numerical count; and
- Identify the name and place of business of the product's manufacturer, packer, or distributor.

Concept Summary What Is a "Consumer Commodity"?

Under the Fair Packaging and Labeling Act, the term "consumer commodity" includes:

1. Any food, drug, device, or cosmetic;
2. Any article, product, or commodity that is distributed for sale through retail sales for consumption by individuals either for personal or household use.[2]

The following are NOT included in the definition of a "consumer commodity":

- Meat, poultry, and tobacco;
- Economic poisons (substance used in the control of plants or animals such as a product that kills weeds) and biologics (such as vaccines, bacterins, and other products of biological origin) for animals;
- Prescription drugs;
- Alcoholic beverages; and
- Agricultural and vegetable seeds.

In addition, the FPLA authorizes additional regulations to prevent consumer deception with respect to ingredient descriptions, use of lower price labeling, characterization of package sizes, and nutritional content. The Nutritional Labeling and Education Act establishes the standard nutritional facts to be provided and regulates the use of terms (for example, "low fat," "fat free," and "fresh)."

2. 16 C.F.R. § 503.5.

Example: "Low-fat" is defined as 3 grams or less of fat per serving. "Low-calorie" is defined as 40 calories or less per serving. "Low cholesterol" is defined as 20 milligrams or less and 2 grams or less of saturated fat per serving.

Sales

Certain types of sale transactions have additional statutory protections. These include door-to-door sale transactions and telephone, mail-order, and online sales.

Cooling-Off Laws

Many states as well as the FTC have enacted what are known as **cooling-off laws**. These laws provide purchasers of goods the right to return those goods. The FTC provides that purchasers of goods sold door to door with a purchase price of $25 or more have the right to cancel their contracts, without penalty, within three business days.

Cooling-off laws Laws providing a purchaser of goods sold door to door with a purchase price of $25 or more the right to cancel their contracts within three business days without penalty.

Telephone, Internet, Mail-Order, and Online Sales

The FTC's **Mail, Internet, or Telephone Order Merchandise Rule** protects buyers who order merchandise through the mail, via the internet, or by phone. Sellers must ship the products *within the advertised time frame.* If no shipping period is specified, 30 days is considered a reasonable time.

If the seller cannot ship within the promised time, the seller must obtain the buyer's consent to a delay in shipping or refund payment to the buyer.

Mail, Internet, or Telephone Order Merchandise Rule A federal law that requires sellers who solicit buyers to order merchandise through the mail, via the internet, or by phone to ship their products within the advertised time frame.

Legislation Aimed at Protection of Health and Safety

Food safety is important; therefore, in addition to concerns with the content of information contained on a food's label and package, federal statutes also regulate the content of the products. Two important pieces of federal legislation aimed at regulating products are (1) the Federal Food, Drug, and Cosmetic Act and (2) the Consumer Product Safety Act.

The Federal Food, Drug, and Cosmetic Act

The first comprehensive federal consumer protection law was the 1906 Food and Drugs Act, which prohibited food and drugs in interstate commerce from being misbranded and adulterated. However, due to its various shortcomings that left many types of products untouched, many hazardous consumer items remained on the market. In response, in 1938, the federal **Food, Drug, and Cosmetic Act (FDCA)** was enacted. The Act, as amended, tightened the controls over drugs and food, included new

Food, Drug, and Cosmetic Act (FDCA) A federal law that protects consumers against unlawful cosmetics and medical devices.

consumer protection against unlawful cosmetics and medical devices, and enhanced the government's ability to enforce the law.

Adulterated food
Food that is unsafe for consumption.

FOOD SAFETY. The FDCA prohibits the preparation, distribution, or sale of **adulterated food.** Food is adulterated if it (1) consists in whole or in part of any filthy, putrid, or decomposed substance; (2) has been prepared, packed, or held under unsanitary conditions whereby it may have become contaminated with filth or rendered injurious to health; or (3) contains a food additive or a color additive that has not been cleared as safe for consumption. Additionally, the Act requires producers of food additives to show (within a reasonable certainty) that no harm will result from the intended use of the additive.

Management Application What Is a "Food Additive"?

The Food and Drug Administration (FDA) defines "food additive" as "any substance the intended use of which results or may reasonably be expected to result, directly or indirectly, in it becoming a component or otherwise affecting the characteristic of any food."

What food additives do you encounter in what you frequently consume?

DRUG SAFETY. The FDCA also prohibits the preparation, distribution, or sale of adulterated drugs. Under the FDCA, the FDA is responsible for ensuring that drugs and medical devices entering the marketplace are safe and effective for consumers. The FDA requires that drugs and medical devices undergo extensive testing to ensure that they are safe and effective before the product can be marketed to consumers. If the FDA determines that a drug or medical device has been mislabeled, it has the power to remove the product from the market. Additionally, the FDA can establish comprehensive procedures that pharmaceutical companies must follow prior to marketing a drug.

COSMETIC SAFETY. The FDCA defines "cosmetics" as "articles intended to be rubbed, poured, sprinkled, or sprayed on, introduced into, or otherwise applied to the human body for cleansing, beautifying, promoting attractiveness, or altering the appearance." Although the FDA is not responsible for approving cosmetic products, the FDCA allows the FDA to remove these drugs from the market if they contain unsafe ingredients or are mislabeled.

The Consumer Product Safety Act

The Consumer Product Safety Act was enacted in 1972 and established the Consumer Product Safety Commission (CPSC). The CPSC is given broad consumer safety authority, including the ability to recall and ban products.

THE ROLE OF THE CPSC. The primary responsibility of the CPSC is to protect the public from unreasonable risks of injury that could occur during the use of consumer products. Among its many responsibilities, the CPSC is responsible for:

1. Establishing and enforcing safety standards for consumer products;
2. Recalling from the marketplace products that the commission finds to be an "unreasonable risk" to consumers and arranging for their repair or replacement;
3. Conducting research on potential product hazards; and
4. Informing and educating consumers about product safety rules and recalls.

Additionally, the CPSC also enforces many other federal laws in addition to the Consumer Product Safety Act, including the Federal Hazardous Substances Act, the Child Safety and Protection Act, and the Flammable Fabrics Act.

The CPSC not only protects the public from injuries that may result from consumer products that are produced in the United States, but it also works closely with other federal agencies, such as U.S. Customs and Border Protection, to ensure that products entering the United States from foreign countries are in compliance with all applicable federal consumer protection laws.

Consumer Credit Protection

The Federal Reserve Bank of Atlanta estimates that 77 percent of U.S. households have at least one credit card. To ensure that banks, lenders, and other financial companies treat consumers fairly, Congress created the Consumer Financial Protection Bureau in 2010. The agency protects consumers from unfair, deceptive, or abusive practices in the financial marketplace. The agency has authority to enforce many consumer financial protection laws, including (1) the Truth in Lending Act, (2) the Fair Credit Reporting Act, (3) the Fair and Accurate Credit Transactions Act, and (4) the Fair Debt Collection Practices Act. These Acts are discussed below.

The Truth in Lending Act

One of the first federal consumer protection statutes enacted by Congress, the **Truth in Lending Act (TILA)** requires disclosures to consumers about the terms and costs of loans. TILA's purpose is to require uniform disclosures of terms and costs by lenders; this provides consumers the opportunity to compare lenders by the costs and credit terms provided. Consumers are also provided with the right to cancel certain credit transactions. The regulations that implemented the Act are known collectively as Regulation Z, which is intended to provide borrowers with uniform disclosure of important information. TILA applies to creditors who in the ordinary course of business extend credit or arrange for the extension of credit for goods or services to consumers (such as car loans, home loans, and retail and installment sales). TILA does not apply to transactions between two consumers or between business entities (such as corporations, partnerships, churches, unions, or fraternal organizations).

Truth in Lending Act (TILA)
Federal law protecting consumers against inaccurate and unfair credit billing and credit card practices.

DISCLOSURE REQUIREMENTS UNDER REGULATION Z. If a party is subject to **Regulation Z**, it must provide certain disclosures to comply with TILA. A lender must disclose the following terms:

Regulation Z This regulation implements TILA and requires lenders to make meaningful credit disclosures to individual borrowers for certain types of consumer loans.

- Annual percentage rate (APR) of the finance charges;
- Finance charges (including interest rate, points, other finance fees);
- Total dollar amount financed; and
- Total number and amount of payments.

These terms must be disclosed in a manner that is clear and conspicuous. Failure to comply with Regulation Z could result in civil penalties and/or fines.

EQUAL CREDIT OPPORTUNITY ACT. The Equal Credit Opportunity Act (ECOA) is an amendment of TILA that prohibits the denial of credit based on race, religion, national origin, gender, color, marital status, or age. Creditors are barred from requiring a spouse's signature, or requiring the spouse as a co-signer, on the credit application where the applicant qualifies for the creditor's creditworthiness as to the amount stated. Additionally, the Act prohibits a creditor from discriminating against an applicant based on the source of the applicant's income. This is particularly important for those who rely on public assistance programs and benefits.

> **Example:** Derek applies for credit to purchase a new vehicle. While Derek meets the creditor's standards to qualify to purchase the car, the creditor requires Derek to obtain the signature of his spouse as a co-signer. This would be a violation of the ECOA.

The Fair Credit Reporting Act

Fair Credit Reporting Act (FCRA) A federal law regulating the collection and distribution of consumers' personal information.

The **Fair Credit Reporting Act (FCRA)** protects information collected by credit reporting agencies. Consumers are protected from inaccurate or erroneous information in consumer reports. Under the Act, credit reporting agencies are required to ensure that the information they gather and distribute is accurate, relevant, and up to date as to a consumer's credit history. Consumers can verify or contest the accuracy and completeness of the report. Further, information in the credit report can only be shared with third parties for specified purposes (such as the extension of credit).

One provision of the Act requires that whenever a consumer reporting agency prepares a consumer report, it shall follow reasonable procedures to assure *maximum possible accuracy* of the information concerning the individual to whom the report relates. Courts have adopted two standards: (1) that credit reporting agencies report information that is "technically accurate"—that is, information that is not false; or (2) that credit reporting agencies report information that is both "technically accurate" and not misleading or incomplete. These standards and what is considered maximum possible accuracy are the subject of the following case.

CASE 36.2

COURTS HAVE INTERPRETED "MAXIMUM POSSIBLE ACCURACY" TO BE EITHER (1) INFORMATION THAT IS NOT FALSE OR (2) INFORMATION THAT IS BOTH NOT FALSE AND NOT MISLEADING OR INCOMPLETE

ERICKSON v. FIRST ADVANTAGE BACKGROUND SERVS. CORP.

981 F.3d 1246 (11th Cir. 2020)

United States Court of Appeals for the Eleventh Circuit

Keith Erickson applied to coach his son's Little League team and authorized a background check, including a search of sex-offender records. Despite having a clean record, the search flagged a match due to his estranged father sharing the same name. The consumer reporting agency, First Advantage, issued a report indicating a potential match and advised further review by Little League to confirm if the record belonged to Erickson.

Erickson received a notification letter and, despite efforts to clarify the error, was deeply affected by this misstep in identity. He eventually changed his family's last name and disclosed sensitive information about his father's status as a registered sex offender. Erickson sued First Advantage, alleging that the report did not meet the Fair Credit Reporting Act's ("FCRA") requirement for "maximum possible accuracy." The court ruled against him, finding the report accurate and dismissing the case. Erickson then appealed the district court's decision.

Language of the Court. *To make out a claim for a violation of [the "maximum possible accuracy" doctrine], a plaintiff must show at least two things: that a consumer report was inaccurate and that the inaccurate report caused him to suffer damages. And absent those showings—particularly the inaccurate report—the reasonableness of the reporting agency's procedures turns out not to matter. Here, the district court saw Erickson's case as doubly deficient—it concluded that the report to Little League was not "materially misleading" and that it did not damage Erickson in any event. Erickson of course disagrees.*

A report must be factually incorrect, objectively likely to mislead its intended user, or both to violate the maximal accuracy standard of the Fair Credit Reporting Act. Having defined the standard for "maximum possible accuracy," we now apply it. To begin, the Little League report was factually correct. The report stated that a registered sex offender in Pennsylvania shared Erickson's first and last name. True. And the report did not wrongfully attribute that record to Erickson. Closer to the opposite, in fact—it explained that the matching record was located using a name-only search and cautioned that the record might not be Erickson's at all.

Erickson says this is not enough. He argues that the report was "patently inaccurate": it was requested for him, it included a sex-offender record, and he is not a sex offender. But his conclusion just does not follow from his premises. The report never assigned the sex-offender record to Erickson, and again, it suggested that the record might not be connected to him. Simply put, the report was what it said it was—an alert that someone by the name of Keith Dodgson had a Pennsylvania sex-offender record.

That brings us to the second prong of the test—whether the report was misleading. And here, the only objectively reasonable interpretation of the report was one that was not misleading. A reasonable user of the report standing in the shoes of Little League—that is, a user who had hired a consumer reporting agency to search an internal database for sex-offender records, knowing that some searches would be performed only by name and knowing that further research was required before attributing any of those matched records to a particular individual—would not be misled by the report to such an extent that it would take negative action against Erickson. Little League knew that it would get what it asked for here—a search based only on first and last name. And it also knew that it could not attribute any of those matched records to an applicant without conducting further research first.

In fact, the report reminded Little League that "further review of the State Sex Offender Website" was required in order to determine if the record was Erickson's. A reasonable user would not take adverse action against Erickson based on this report because the only reasonable understanding of it was that someone with Erickson's name was a registered sex offender in Pennsylvania—not that Erickson himself was that person.

Because Erickson's claim that the report was not maximally accurate cannot go on, we need not consider the district court's independent ground for granting judgment as a matter of law—that the report did not cause Erickson harm.

Decision. The Court of Appeals affirmed the dismissal of Erickson's complaint and held that accurate reports are not actionable under the FCRA no matter how embarrassing or hurtful they may be.

Focus on Ethics

Do you think it is fair that Keith Erickson was flagged as a sex-offender due to his estranged father? Can you think of a way that the court may have been able to better remedy cases of correct information but wrong person?

Management Application
What Are Credit Reporting Agencies?

Credit reporting agencies (CRAs), also known as credit bureaus or consumer reporting agencies, are companies that gather, process, and archive information relevant to a consumer's credit and financial history. There are three major CRAs: Experian, Equifax, and TransUnion. A CRA will then sell the information to help potential lenders or employers decide whether they should grant loans or extend a line of credit or whether the potential employee is a dependable person.

Not all venders report to all three credit agencies; therefore, the information on your credit report can vary from agency to agency, resulting in different scores.

Concept Summary
Consumers' Rights Under the Fair Credit Reporting Act

Under the Fair Credit Reporting Act, consumers have a right to:

1. Access their credit reports;
2. Protected access, which limits access to their files to those who have a valid need;
3. Accurate reporting;
4. Have outdated information removed; and
5. Not have medical information in a consumer report.

The Fair and Accurate Credit Transactions Act

The **Fair and Accurate Credit Transactions Act (FACTA)** is a federal consumer rights law that amended the FCRA. Congress enacted FACTA to reduce the risk of identity theft by regulating how consumer account information is handled.

Fair and Accurate Credit Transactions Act (FACTA) A federal consumer protection law that seeks to reduce the risk of identity theft by regulating the handling of consumer account information.

FACTA added provisions that were designed to improve the accuracy of consumers' credit-related records. Among the provisions added, the Act provides consumers the right to one free credit report a year from the credit reporting agencies; further, consumers can also purchase (for a reasonable fee) a credit score along with information

Fraud alert
An alert placed on a customer's credit file requiring a business to verify the consumer's identity before it issues credit, thereby reducing identity theft.

about how their credit scores are calculated. Consumers can place **fraud alerts** in their credit files if they suspect that they have been a victim of identity theft. A fraud alert can make it harder for an identity thief to open more accounts in the consumer's name. With a fraud alert, a business must verify a consumer's identity before it issues credit. The alert stays on the report for one year, but a consumer can obtain a new one after the year is up. The Act also discourages identity theft by requiring the transaction of credit card and debit card account numbers. All persons accepting credit cards or debit cards may print no more than the last five digits of the card number and may not print the expiration date on any receipt provided to the cardholder.

Management Application How Credit Scores Are Calculated

Fair Isaac Corporation (FICO®) calculates a base credit score with a range from 300 to 850. Credit scores above 670 are considered "Good" and typically mean that a consumer will qualify for credit, though often not with the best terms. Scores above 740 are considered "Very Good" and above 800 are considered "Excellent." The score is calculated primarily through the information contained in a consumer's credit report. The FICO score is used by many lending institutions to determine if they will extend credit and the interest rate they will charge. In calculating the FICO credit score, multiple factors are taken into consideration:

- *Payment history (35%).* Timely paying bills is one of the most important factors in a consumer's FICO score.
- *Amounts owed (30%).* This factor considers the amount a consumer owes on credit accounts and the portion of the available credit the consumer is using (referred to as a credit-utilization ratio). High credit-utilization ratios can negatively impact the FICO score.
- *Length of credit history (15%).* The average age of a consumer's credit accounts is an important factor in a consumer's FICO score. A longer credit history will increase a consumer's FICO score.
- *Credit mix in use (10%).* FICO scores factor in the different types of credit accounts a consumer has, such as credit cards, retail accounts, installment loans, finance company accounts, and mortgage loans.
- *New credit (10%).* FICO scores are negatively impacted by consumers who have recently opened new accounts or had their credit checked.

The Fair Debt Collection Practices Act

When a borrower is unable to repay the debt they owe, a lender may employ a third-party collection agency to collect the debt (commonly known as debt collectors). The Fair Debt Collection Practices Act (FDCPA) prohibits third-party debt collectors (including attorneys) from using deceptive or abusive conduct in the collection of consumer debts incurred for personal, family, or household purposes, including money owed on a personal credit card account, automobile loans, medical bills, and/or mortgages. The Act applies to third-party debt collectors and not the creditor seeking to collect the debt owed to it unless the creditor misrepresents itself and the debtor believes it to be a third-party collection agency.

In the following case, the court considered whether a fine imposed by a homeowners' association was considered a "debt" under the FDCPA.

CASE 36.3

FINE IMPOSED BY HOMEOWNERS' ASSOCIATION IS A "DEBT" UNDER FDCPA

AGRELO v. AFFINITY MGMT. SERVICES, LLC

841 F.3d 944 (2016)

United States Court of Appeals for the Eleventh Circuit

Jorge Agrelo and Olga Fernandez, a married couple, owned a home in Miami, Florida. They were members of Marbella, a homeowners' association (HOA). Affinity Management Services, LLC (Affinity) was Marbella's property manager. The homeowners were bound by the HOA's bylaws, articles of incorporation, and a declaration of covenants and restrictions for Marbella Park ("governing documents"). The governing documents required HOA members to pay an annual assessment, due in monthly installments. These assessments were secured by a continuing lien held by the HOA on each property.

The governing documents also allowed Marbella to fine members for violating its declaration of covenants and restrictions. To enforce such obligations, Marbella could sue the member or foreclose on Marbella's continuing lien on the property. Marbella notified Agrelo and Fernandez that they had violated the governing documents for improperly performing unapproved construction, relocating a fence, and removing plants. The HOA gave the homeowners three weeks to correct the violations, but the homeowners took no action.

After a hearing on the violation, Marbella's board of directors fined the homeowners $100 for each day the violation went uncorrected and set the total fine at $1,000. The homeowners refused to pay the fine, maintaining that they had not violated any rule.

Over the next several months, Affinity and Marbella's attorneys sent the homeowners at least five letters on Marbella's behalf regarding the dispute. Affinity sent the homeowners nearly identical letters demanding $1,000, which Affinity characterized as a "delinquent assessment" and warned the homeowners of the consequences if they failed to pay, threatening to file and foreclose on a lien against their home, to seek a personal judgment to seize their property and garnish their wages, and to file a legal action to collect "delinquent assessments, late fees, interest, attorney's fees and other costs of collection."

After Marbella received no payment, it had its attorneys send another payment demand letter. This time the homeowners responded, again disputing the charges. The homeowners also made several requests under the Fair Debt Collection Practices Act, including three demands for proof that the attorneys were licensed to collect debts in Florida. They also challenged the amount of both the fine and the late fees, explaining that the governing documents capped the fine at $115 and the fees at $11.50.

Having received no response to their demands, the homeowners filed a complaint against Marbella, Affinity, and its attorneys, alleging that the five letters sent within a seven-month period violated the FDCPA. In defense, Marbella, Affinity and its attorneys moved for summary judgment on all claims arguing that they were not debt collectors, and the $1,000 fine was not a debt under the FDCPA. The district court granted Marbella's motion for summary judgment and the homeowners appealed.

Language of the Court. *To recover under the FDCPA, a plaintiff must show that the money being collected qualifies as a "debt." The mere obligation to pay does not constitute a "debt." Instead, a debt is "any obligation or alleged obligation of a consumer to pay money arising out of a transaction in which the money, property, insurance, or services which are the subject of the transaction are primarily for personal, family, or household purposes, whether or not such obligation has been reduced to judgment." In other words, the FDCPA applies only to payment obligations of a (1) consumer arising out of a (2) transaction in which the money, property, insurance, or services at issue are (3) primarily for personal, family, or household purposes.*

The central question is whether a contractual obligation to pay HOA assessments creates a "debt" under the FDCPA. We hold that it does. HOA assessments stem directly from the consensual home-purchase transaction. When a home buyer must contractually agree to pay homeowners' assessments in order to purchase a home, that home buyer takes on "debts" for those assessments. By agreeing to the terms of the governing documents, the homeowners acknowledged that a failure to comply with HOA requirements could result in a fine that would be deemed and treated as an individual assessment. Thus, their obligation to pay an assessment for a claimed breach of the governing documents arose out of an underlying consumer transaction.

For these reasons, we conclude that the term "debt" encompasses the homeowners' obligation to pay a fine pursuant to the governing documents.

Decision. The Court of Appeals reversed the district court's decision and held a fine is considered a debt for the purposes of the FDCPA.

Focus on Ethics

The homeowners' association fine was considered a debt under the FDCPA. Should it be so classified? That is, is it fair that those assessments be considered a debt under the FDCPA?

WHAT ACTIONS ARE PROHIBITED. The FDCPA prohibits debt collectors from using abusive, unfair, or deceptive trade practices to collect debt. Prohibited activities under the Act include, but are not limited to:

1. *Harassment.* Debt collectors may not harass or abuse the consumer. Harassment includes contacting the debtor at inconvenient or unusual times; causing a telephone to ring repeatedly or continuously with the intent to annoy, abuse, or harass; or contacting a debtor represented by an attorney.
2. *False or misleading representations.* Debt collectors cannot make false or misleading representations when collecting a debt. For example, a debt collector cannot falsely claim that the consumer has committed a crime or misrepresent the amount owed, nor pose as a police officer.
3. *Threats.* Debt collectors are prohibited from making any threats of violence or using obscene, profane, or other abusive language.
4. *Other unfair practices.* Other types of prohibited practices include a debt collector trying to collect any interest, fee, or other charge on top of the amount owed unless the contract that created the debt allows the charge or depositing a postdated check early.

AI Feature: False Advertising in the Fast Food Industry

Use an internet search engine to research prior false advertising lawsuits against fast food franchisors. There have been hundreds of lawsuits filed each year involving fast food chains, including Subway®, Taco Bell®, Burger King®, McDonalds®, and Wendy's®. Pick two such lawsuits and summarize the plaintiff's allegations and, include a graphic of the offending advertising. Then, using an AI program draft the disclaimers or conditions that you would recommend that the company should employ in future advertisements to minimize false advertising claims.

Key Terms

- Adulterated food, 920
- Bait-and-switch advertising, 912
- Consent decree, 916
- Consumer, 908
- Consumer transaction, 908
- Cooling-off laws, 919
- Corrective advertising, 916
- Deceptive advertising, 909
- Fair and Accurate Credit Transactions Act (FACTA), 925
- Fair Credit Reporting Act (FCRA), 922
- Federal Trade Commission (FTC), 908

- Federal Trade Commission Act, 908
- Food, Drug, and Cosmetic Act (FDCA), 919
- Fraud alert, 926
- Half-truth advertisement, 910
- Injunction, 916
- Mail, Internet, or Telephone Order Merchandise Rule, 919
- National Do Not Call Registry, 917
- Puffery, 909
- Regulation Z, 922
- Telemarketing Sales Rule (TSR), 917
- Truth in Lending Act, 921

Applying the Law

36.1 Research the Law. Many states and the FTC provide protection from unfair credit billing practices. Purchasers may dispute unauthorized charges, errors, and dispute alleged deliveries within a given period. Using an internet search engine, research the Fair Credit Billing Act. How does this law protect consumers? What additional protections under the act should be adopted?

36.2 Content of Advertising. A car dealership selling used automobiles advertised customers may purchase vehicles with "NO MONEY DOWN" or "NO DOWN PAYMENT" and "EASY CREDIT" for purchased vehicles. When consumers were signing the sale documentation, the dealership demanded a down payment. Moreover, the vehicles were defective in numerous respects and did not reflect those shown in the advertisement. What deceptive practices occurred with respect to the advertising? See *Garcia v. Overland Bond & Inv. Co.*, 282 Ill. App. 3d 486 (1996)

36.3 Mistaken Advertisement. A car dealership advertised a price on its website for an automobile. The potential purchaser saw that it was well priced and visited the dealership to view the vehicle. When he arrived, he inquired about the internet price. Quickly realizing the mistake, the car dealership informed the potential purchaser that there was an error in the advertisement regarding the vehicle's price. Was there a meeting of the minds as to price such that the dealership committed consumer fraud? See *Burkhart v. Wolf Motors of Naperville, Inc.*, 2016 IL App (2d) 151053 (Ill. App. Ct. 2016)

36.4 Collections. If a borrower provides a lender her cell phone number and thereafter defaults on payments to the lender, is the lender entitled to contact the borrower through the cell phone number if the borrower's cell phone number is on the National Do Not Call Registry? See *Hill v. Homeward Residential, Inc.*, 799 F.3d 544 (6th Cir. 2015)

36.5 TCPA. A customer purchased and activated 35 prepaid cell phones. She added minutes to the cell phones by buying "airtime cards" for $19.99 so that the cell phones would receive more calls. When purchasing the prepaid cell phones, the customer requested that the numbers assigned be from phone numbers in economically depressed areas. The customer believed that these people would be more likely to have defaulted on their loans or credit cards. After receiving the prepaid cell phones with those phone numbers, creditors would call the old phone numbers hoping to collect the debt owed from the previous owner of the phone number. The customer kept track of these calls with the intention of receiving treble damages under the Telephone Consumer Protection Act. Will she succeed? *Stoops v. Wells Fargo Bank, N.A.*, 197 F. Supp. 3d 782 (W.D. Pa. 2016)

36.6 Duties of Credit Reporting Agencies. Is the Fair Credit Reporting Act violated when a consumer disputes a collection record of a credit reporting agency, and the agency does not conduct a reasonable investigation? Can a reckless disregard of the act's requirements permit the assessment of punitive damages against the agency? *Dixon-Rollins v. Experian Information Solutions, Inc.*, 753 F. Supp. 2d 452 (E.D. Pa. 2010)

36.7 Fair Debt Collection Practices Act. Is a debt collection letter "deceptive" and unlawful if the letter's content can reasonably be read to have two or more different meanings, one of which is inaccurate? Is such a communication a violation of the Fair Debt Collection Act? *Gonzales v. Arrow Financial Services, LLC*, 660 F.3d 1055 (9th Cir. 2011)

36.8 Telephone Consumer Protection Act. Shyriaa Henderson received a student loan through the Federal Family Education Loan Program. Her loan obligation was assigned to USA Funds. She stopped paying on her loan after experiencing financial difficulty. Once a borrower stopped paying back their loans USA Funds no longer interacted with the borrower. It hired loan servicers such as Navient Solutions to collect on the unpaid loans. Henderson received prerecorded messages on a phone whose number she did not give to her student loan provider. Henderson alleged the debt collecting companies used skip tracers and auto dialers based on the pattern of calls. Navient did have access to reports tracking the debt collectors' performance. Though USA Funds' service agreement with Navient did not give USA Funds the ability to fire debt collectors, USA Funds could ask Navient to replace underperforming collectors and could have fired Navient if it did not comply. Henderson sued USA Funds for alleged TCPA violations related to the collection of her student loan debt. Is USA Funds vicariously liable for the violations of the act? Why or why not? *Henderson v. United Student Aid Funds, Inc.*, 918 F.3d 1068 (9th Cir. 2019)

36.9 Labeling and Packaging. According to a California statute, the average weight or measure of packages or containers shall not be less than the net weight or measure stated on the package. Several meat processors and flour millers brought a suit to stop the enforcement of the California statute pertaining to the labeling based on the weight. The millers argued that the California statute was preempted by federal laws regulating net weight labeling and sought an injunction to prevent the enforcement of those provisions. What are the requirements of the Fair Packaging and Labeling Act? Is the state law preempted? *Jones v. Rath Packing Co.*, 430 U.S. 519 (1977)

36.10 Truth in Lending Act and Regulation Z. Melvin McGowan purchased $107.86 worth of clothing from King, Inc., a retail store. He made a down payment of $3.52 and executed a retail installment contract and security agreement. King obtained this contract and disclosure statement from Tower Loan Brokers of Mississippi, a regular financer for King's installment sales. McGowan filed a suit alleging several violations of the TILA and Regulation Z for the following: (1) failure to itemize other charges; (2) failure to disclose and use the term "unpaid balance"; and (3) using a confusing rebate for payment in full. What is required for compliance with TILA and Regulation Z? Has there been a violation of TILA? What are McGowan's remedies? *McGowan v. King, Inc.*, 569 F.2d 845 (5th Cir. 1978)

Environmental Law

37

To waste, to destroy our natural resources, to skin and exhaust the land instead of using it so as to increase its usefulness, will result in undermining in the days of our children the very prosperity which we ought by right to hand down to them amplified and developed. — Theodore Roosevelt, Twenty-sixth President of the United States (1858-1919)

Chapter Outline

- Introduction
- Environmental Regulators
- Legislation

Case 37.1: *Burlington Northern and Santa Fe Railway Co. v. United States*
Case 37.2: *Michigan v. EPA*

- Hazardous Substance Laws and Regulations
- Water Pollution Laws and Regulations
- Solid Waste Disposal and Brownfield Sites
    - *Management Application: Due Diligence When Purchasing Real Property*
- State Environmental Protection Laws
- AI Feature: Comparison of a State's Environmental Statutes with CERCLA

Learning Objectives

After reading this chapter, you should be able to:

1. Discuss the roles that regulatory agencies play in implementing environmental law.
2. Discuss the purpose and importance of CERCLA.
3. Identify common hazardous substances.
4. Describe waste disposal sites and brownfields.

Introduction

There are many governmental statutes and regulations that affect some aspect of the environment and are designed to help preserve and protect the environment.

Businesses should be aware that few commercial or industrial properties are immune from being impacted by contamination. Owners of a variety of businesses such as dry-cleaning establishments, manufacturers, gas stations and the land on which these properties are located can be exposed to legal claims from adjacent property owners and individuals who suffer the adverse effects of contamination. Many businesses are required to comply with environmental laws, and the cost of compliance and the penalties for failing to comply can be quite expensive. Therefore, having a familiarity with environmental regulations and various types of contamination is important.

Environmental Protection Agency (EPA)
A federal agency that was created to protect the environment and address health concerns.

U.S. Department of Housing and Urban Development (HUD)
A cabinet department of the executive branch of the federal government supporting community development and environmental health.

U.S. Army Corps of Engineers
A federal agency responsible for the engineering, design, and construction management of selected public projects.

Environmental Regulators

The federal government has established several administrative agencies to enforce environmental laws and regulations. Several of the key environmental administrative agencies include (1) the Environmental Protection Agency, (2) the United States Department of Housing and Urban Development, and (3) the United States Army Corps of Engineers.

The **Environmental Protection Agency (EPA)** is a federal administrative agency established in 1970 to address pollution and hazardous wastes. The **U.S. Department of Housing and Urban Development (HUD)** plays a key role in protecting the environmental health and safety of the country's citizens. Every HUD-assisted project must be examined to ensure that it does not negatively impact the surrounding environment and that the site itself will not have an adverse effect on end users. The environmental mission of the **U.S. Army Corps of Engineers** includes a duty to restore degraded ecosystems, construct sustainable facilities, regulate waterways, manage natural resources, and clean up contaminated sites from past military activities. In addition, states and local governments may have their own administrative agencies to provide oversight on environmental matters.

Concept Summary
Key Federal Agencies in Environmental Law and Their Responsibilities

Agency	Responsibilities
Environmental Protection Agency	Address pollution and hazardous wastes
U.S. Department of Housing and Urban Development	Protect the environmental health and safety of the country's citizens
U.S. Army Corps of Engineers	Restore degraded ecosystems, construct sustainable facilities, regulate waterways, manage natural resources, and clean up contaminated sites from past military activities

Legislation

National Environmental Policy Act of 1969 (NEPA)

The **National Environmental Policy Act of 1969 (NEPA)** was enacted to prevent and reverse, where possible, the damage to the United States' air, water, and other ecosystems from industrial pollution. NEPA requires federal agencies to address environmental impacts for all proposals of "major federal actions that significantly affect the quality of the human environment."[1]

While the Act does not prohibit harm, it requires the advance identification and disclosure of the potential harm to inform decision makers and policy makers. The Act does not define what constitutes a "major" federal action but states that recommendations and reports on proposals qualify. Actions that are subject to a sufficient level of federal control and responsibility are typically considered major federal actions. Where a major federal action exists, an **Environmental Impact Statement (EIS)** is required. An EIS describes the environmental impacts the proposal has on the environment and provides reasonable alternatives that would avoid or minimize those adverse impacts.

> **Example:** The Department of the Navy completed an EIS to evaluate the potential environmental impacts to the air and sea space of Southern California and the Hawaiian Islands arising from Navy training and testing activities off the shores of Hawaii.

National Environmental Policy Act of 1969 (NEPA)
This law was enacted to prevent and reverse the damage to the United States' air, water, and other ecosystems from industrial pollution.

Environmental Impact Statement (EIS)
An analysis that describes the environmental impacts the proposal has on the environment and provides reasonable alternatives that would avoid or minimize those adverse impacts.

Comprehensive Environmental Response, Compensation, and Liability Act (CERCLA)

CERCLA, also known as "Superfund," authorized the EPA to clean up uncontrolled hazardous waste sites and force responsible parties to perform cleanups or reimburse the EPA for doing so. It also seeks to prevent contamination of future sites by assigning liability to parties involved in some aspect of the contamination at the site. The principal federal agency involved with its enforcement is the EPA, which coordinates its work with the Army Corps of Engineers, other affected federal land agencies, and state and local environmental agencies.

Once the EPA identifies a hazardous site, there are two different responses. The first type of response is a removal action, which is used to handle emergency oil spills or chemical releases. **Removal actions** focus on eliminating immediate risks and ensuring public safety. The second type of response is a remedial action, which handles complex sites that need long-term responses. **Remedial actions** manage releases that do not pose an urgent threat to public health or the environment and require no immediate action. Given the complexity of remedial actions, several years are often required to study the problem, develop a permanent solution, and clean up the hazardous waste.

Comprehensive Environmental Response, Compensation, and Liability Act (CERCLA)
This law authorized the EPA to clean up uncontrolled hazardous waste sites and force responsible parties to perform cleanups or reimburse the EPA for doing so.

Removal actions
Actions eliminating immediate risks of uncontrolled hazardous waste sites to ensure public safety.

Remedial actions
Long-term actions used to clean up sites that do not pose an immediate risk to public health.

CERCLA LIABILITY. Through a broad definition of "hazardous substance," liability attaches to many parties. CERCLA is a strict liability law; that is, liability can be

To learn if there is a Superfund site near where you live, see https://www.epa.gov/superfund/search-superfund-sites-where-you-live.

1. 42 U.S.C. § 4332(2)(C).

imposed upon a person for a release of hazardous substances even if that person was neither negligent nor the cause of the release. Moreover, liability may be imposed upon a party for land use operations that were lawful at the time they took place. Each party involved may be jointly and severally responsible for the entire cleanup. Prior federal decisions have held that since the waste is continuing to cause problems, the statute is not a punishment but rather a reimbursement obligation.

WHO CAN BE FOUND LIABLE? POTENTIALLY RESPONSIBLE PARTIES (PRPS). The law establishes expansive liability for many parties, including:

- *Current owners and operators of a contaminated site.* Current owners are liable even if they made no contribution to the hazardous release. Landowners who purchase a contaminated site and were aware of the condition at the time of purchase have been found liable for cleanup. This rule does not extend liability to lenders who finance the purchase of the property.
- Past owners and operators of a contaminated site at the time the pollution occurred. These parties will be held liable as well for any release of a toxic substance that occurred during their possession or control of the land.
- Arrangers, who are persons who arranged for disposal of a hazardous substance at a site.
- Transporters, who are persons who transported a hazardous substance to the site.

In the following case, the EPA attempted to argue that a seller of toxic chemicals should be held liable under CERCLA as an arranger.

CASE 37.1

KNOWLEDGE OF CONTINUING SPILLS WITHOUT TAKING INTENTIONAL STEPS TO DISPOSE OF HAZARDOUS WASTE DOES NOT RESULT IN ARRANGER LIABILITY

BURLINGTON NORTHERN AND SANTA FE RAILWAY CO. v. UNITED STATES

556 U.S. 599 (2009)

Supreme Court of the United States

In 1960, Brown & Bryant, Inc. (B&B) began operating an agricultural chemical distribution business in Arvin, California. B&B later expanded onto an adjacent parcel of land owned by Burlington Northern and Santa Fe Railway Company and Union Pacific Railroad Company ("Railroads"). B&B purchased and stored various hazardous chemicals on its site, which it purchased from Shell Oil Company ("Shell"). That seller relationship to the operator, the EPA argued, made Shell an arranger and therefore liable under CERCLA. At that time, the law was unclear as to the definition of what made someone liable as an arranger. Over time, the hazardous chemicals seeped into the groundwater, leading to significant soil and groundwater contamination. Many of these chemical spills occurred during transfer and delivery of the hazardous chemicals due to equipment failures.

In 1989, the EPA and California's Department of Toxic Substances Control ("Agencies") exercised their CERCLA authority and spent over $8 million to clean up the site. To recover their costs, the Agencies initiated a lawsuit against Shell and the Railroads. The district court held in favor of the government's finding both Shell and the Railroads were potentially responsible parties under CERCLA, holding the Railroads liable for 9 percent of the government's total response costs, and Shell liable for 6 percent. The Court of Appeals for the Ninth Circuit held that Shell as an arranger had responsibility for the disposal of hazardous substances and held that Shell and the Railroads were jointly and severally liable for the government's clean-up costs. Shell and the Railroads appealed to the Supreme Court of the United States.

Language of the Court. *Because CERCLA does not specifically define what it means to "arrang[e] for" disposal of a hazardous substance, the phrase should be given its ordinary meaning. In common parlance, "arrange" implies action directed to a specific purpose. Thus, under the statute's plain language, an entity may qualify as an arranger when it takes intentional steps to dispose of a hazardous substance. To qualify as an arranger, Shell must have entered into hazardous waste sales with the intent that at least a portion of the product be disposed of during the transfer process by one or more of the statute's methods. The facts found by the District Court do not support such a conclusion. The evidence shows that Shell was aware that minor, accidental spills occurred during the hazardous waste transfer to B&B's storage tanks; however, it also reveals that Shell took numerous steps to encourage its distributors to reduce the likelihood of spills. Thus, Shell's mere knowledge of continuing spills and leaks is insufficient grounds for concluding that it "arranged for" hazardous waste disposal.*

The District Court reasonably apportioned the Railroads' share of the site remediation costs at 9%. Calculating liability based on three figures—the percentage of the total area of the facility that was owned by the Railroads, the duration of B&B's business divided by the term of the Railroads' lease, and the court's determination that only two polluting chemicals spilled on the leased parcel required remediation and that those chemicals were responsible for roughly two-thirds of the remediable site contamination—the District Court ultimately determined that the Railroads were responsible for 9% of the remediation costs. The District Court's detailed findings show that the primary pollution at the site was on a portion of the facility most distant from the Railroad parcel and that the hazardous-chemical spills on the Railroad parcel contributed to no more than 10% of the total site contamination, some of which did not require remediation. Moreover, although the evidence did not allow the District Court to precisely calculate the amount of hazardous chemicals contributed by the Railroad, the evidence showed that fewer spills occurred on the Railroad parcel and that not all of them crossed to the B&B site, where most of the contamination originated, thus supporting the conclusion that the parcel contributed only two chemicals in quantities requiring remediation.

Decision. The Supreme Court reversed the decision of the Court of Appeals for the Ninth Circuit. It held that Shell was neither an arranger under CERCLA nor liable for the contamination at the Arvin facility. It concluded that the district court reasonably apportioned the railroads' share of the site remediation costs at 9 percent.

Focus on Ethics

Is it ethical for Shell to escape liability because it only sold the toxic substances to the operator of the facility?

Clean Air Act

Clean Air Act
An act intended to protect the public from different types of air pollution caused by a variety of pollution sources.

The **Clean Air Act** was intended to protect public health and welfare from different types of air pollution caused by a variety of pollution sources. The Clean Air Act's basic structure was established in 1970 and made subject to major revisions in 1977 and 1990. The EPA administers it, in coordination with state, local, and tribal governments. It addressed the shortcomings of earlier federal air pollution acts.

The effect of this law, as amended, is to greatly expand the regulatory role of the EPA, requiring comprehensive federal and state regulations for both stationary pollution sources and mobile sources. A stationary source is a fixed emitter of air pollutants from industrial sources (such as a power plant). A mobile source is a non-stationary source of air pollutants (such as from automobiles). The Act also significantly expanded federal enforcement activities. The 1990 amendments addressed acid rain, ozone depletion, and toxic air pollution. It also established a national permitting program for stationary sources of air pollution.

Once intended to address common air pollution, such as dense, visible smog, the law now requires the EPA to establish national ambient air quality standards based on the latest science and requires states to adopt enforceable plans to achieve the standards. State plans also must control emissions that drift across state lines and harm air quality in downwind states. The law calls for new stationary sources to be built with the best available technology, and allows less stringent standards for existing stationary sources. The cost of compliance is a factor considered by the EPA when deciding whether the regulation is appropriate and necessary.

In the following case, the EPA argued that the costs of complying with EPA regulations were not relevant. In *Michigan v EPA*, the Court held that the EPA was not acting reasonably. The EPA relied upon an earlier decision in *Chevron U.S.A. Inc. v. Natural Resources Defense Council, Inc.*, 467 U. S. 837 (1984). In *Chevron*, the Supreme Court held that a judge was required to adopt an agency's interpretation of an ambiguous statute, so long as the agency had a "permissible construction of the statute." The holding in *Michigan v. EPA* helped pave the way for overruling *Chevron*. The case that did so is *Loper Bright Enters. v. Raimondo*, 603 U.S. __, 144 S. Ct. 2244 (2024). That decision is discussed in Chapter 34.

CASE 37.2

EPA MUST CONSIDER COST, INCLUDING COST OF COMPLIANCE, BEFORE DECIDING IF REGULATION IS APPROPRIATE AND NECESSARY

MICHIGAN v. EPA

576 U.S. 743 (2015)

Supreme Court of the United States

The Clean Air Act establishes a series of regulatory programs to control air pollution from stationary sources (such as refineries and factories) and moving sources (such as cars and airplanes). One of these programs is the National Emissions Standards for Hazardous Air Pollutants Program. For stationary sources, the applicability of the program depends in part on how much pollution the source emits. A source that emits more than 10 tons of a single pollutant or more than 25 tons of a combination of pollutants per year is called a major source. The EPA is required to regulate all major sources under the program.

The EPA may regulate power plants under this program only if it concludes that "regulation is appropriate and necessary" after studying hazards to public health posed by power plant emissions. The EPA found regulation "appropriate" because (1) power plants' emissions of mercury and other hazardous air pollutants posed risks to human health and the environment, and (2) controls were available to reduce these emissions. It found regulation "necessary" because the imposition of the Act's other requirements did not eliminate these risks. The EPA then concluded that "costs should not be considered" when deciding whether power plants should be regulated.

The EPA issued a "Regulatory Impact Analysis" alongside its regulation. This analysis estimated that the regulation would force power plants to bear costs of $9.6 billion per year. The EPA could not fully quantify the benefits of reducing power plants' emissions of hazardous air pollutants; to the extent it could, it estimated that these benefits were worth $4 to $6 million per year. The costs to power plants were thus between 1,600 and 2,400 times as great as the quantifiable benefits from reduced emissions of hazardous air pollutants. The EPA also stated that its regulations would have ancillary benefits — including cutting power plants' emissions of particulate matter and sulfur dioxide, substances that are not covered by the hazardous air pollutants program.

Michigan, along with 23 other states, sought review of EPA's rule in the D.C. Circuit Court of Appeals, which upheld the EPA's refusal to consider costs in its decision to regulate. Michigan sought *certiorari* from the United States Supreme Court.

Language of the Court. *Federal administrative agencies are required to engage in reasoned decision making. Not only must an agency's decreed result be within the scope of its lawful authority, but the process by which it reaches that result must be logical and rational. It follows that agency action is lawful only if it rests on a consideration of the relevant factors. The EPA's decision to regulate power plants allowed the EPA to reduce power plants' emissions of hazardous air pollutants and thus to improve public health and the environment. But the decision also ultimately cost power plants, according to the EPA's own estimate, nearly $10 billion a year. The EPA refused to consider whether the costs of its decision outweighed the benefits. It gave cost no thought at all, because it considered cost irrelevant to its initial decision to regulate.*

The EPA's disregard of cost rested on its interpretation of § 7412(n)(1)(A), which directs the EPA to regulate power plants if it "finds such regulation is appropriate and necessary." The EPA accepts that it could have interpreted this provision to mean that cost is relevant to the decision to add power plants to the program, but it chose to read the statute to mean that cost makes no difference to the initial decision to regulate.

We review this interpretation under the standard set out in Chevron U.S.A. Inc. v. Natural Resources Defense Council, Inc., *467 U.S. 837 (1984).* Chevron *directs courts to accept an agency's reasonable resolution of an ambiguity in a statute that the agency administers. Even under this deferential standard, however, "agencies must operate within the bounds of reasonable interpretation." The EPA strayed far beyond those bounds when it read § 7412(n)(1) to mean that it could ignore cost when deciding whether to regulate power plants. Read naturally in the present context, the phrase "appropriate and necessary" requires at least some attention to cost. One would not say that it is even rational, never mind "appropriate," to impose billions of dollars in economic costs in return for a few dollars in health or environmental benefits.*

Decision. The Supreme Court reversed the Court of Appeals for the D.C. Circuit and held that the EPA interpreted § 7412(n)(1)(A) unreasonably when it deemed cost irrelevant to the decision to regulate power plants.

Focus on Ethics

The Court found that it was inequitable to expend costs for which little benefit would result. In your view, should health or environmental benefits be so measured? Is this a case where doing the right thing may cause disproportionate harm? Note that in 1981, the Court held that a cost benefit analysis was not needed before adoption of safety and health standards under the Occupational Safety and Health Act. Has the Court changed its position on the use of cost benefit analysis? Does this recent trend forbode changes in judicial deference to federal administrative agencies?

Hazardous Substance Laws and Regulations

Lead Paint

Lead is a highly toxic metal that was used for many years in products found in and around housing. Exposure causes such symptoms as abdominal pain, headaches, anemia, and, in severe cases, brain damage. Children, infants, and pregnant woman are more vulnerable to exposure as their growing bodies are more sensitive to the harmful effects lead exposure poses. Although banned for use in residential structures since 1978, lead-based paint is still present in millions of homes. It is often hidden under layers of new paint. Chipping or peeling lead-based paint creates a hazard.

Lead
Highly toxic metal that can accumulate in the body through repeated exposure.

Asbestos

Asbestos is a mineral fiber that occurs naturally in rock and soil. In the past, asbestos was frequently used in construction due to its versatility, heat resistance, and insulation capabilities. It was commonly found in many building materials, such as ceiling and floor tiles, as well as in different forms of insulation.

Asbestos
A mineral fiber historically used in construction that is a known carcinogen and causes various respiratory ailments.

In the 1970s, the EPA began to ban asbestos-containing materials in construction. Today, asbestos is known to be a carcinogen that causes asbestosis, mesothelioma, and lung cancer. Exposure to asbestos generally occurs when the asbestos-containing material is disturbed or damaged, which results in the release of asbestos fibers into the air. Prolonged exposure to asbestos can lead to serious illnesses and death.

Asbestos is still found in many buildings and products. It is not easy to determine if asbestos is present in property unless the materials are labeled. To reduce the risk of asbestos exposure, the EPA suggests having a property inspected by a trained and accredited asbestos professional for asbestos-containing material. An incorrectly performed inspection can be more hazardous than leaving the material undisturbed. Asbestos-containing material that is not damaged or disturbed should be left alone, as it is unlikely to pose any health risk.

When damaged asbestos-containing material is present in a structure, the owner has two remedies. The first option is encapsulation, which involves the treating of the material with a sealant that coats the material, so the asbestos fibers are not released. Another option is the removal of the asbestos-containing material. Both remedies should only be performed by a trained and accredited professional, as improper removal or repair could increase the risk of asbestos exposure.

Radon

One type of indoor air pollutant is radon. **Radon** is a naturally occurring radioactive gas that is found in nearly all soils. Radon is formed by the natural decay of radium, found within the soil. As it radiates into a building, serious health problems may result. Radon is estimated to cause thousands of deaths each year.

Radon
A naturally occurring radioactive gas found in nearly all soils that travels through cracks in the foundation of a home and causes lung cancer.

Radon penetrates buildings through cracks or holes in the foundation. Once inside, buildings trap the radon, allowing potentially lethal levels to accumulate. The areas with the highest potential radon levels are predominately found in the Midwest and some parts of the East Coast due to their geological formations that yield higher radon levels.

FIGURE 37.1: How Radon Enters a House

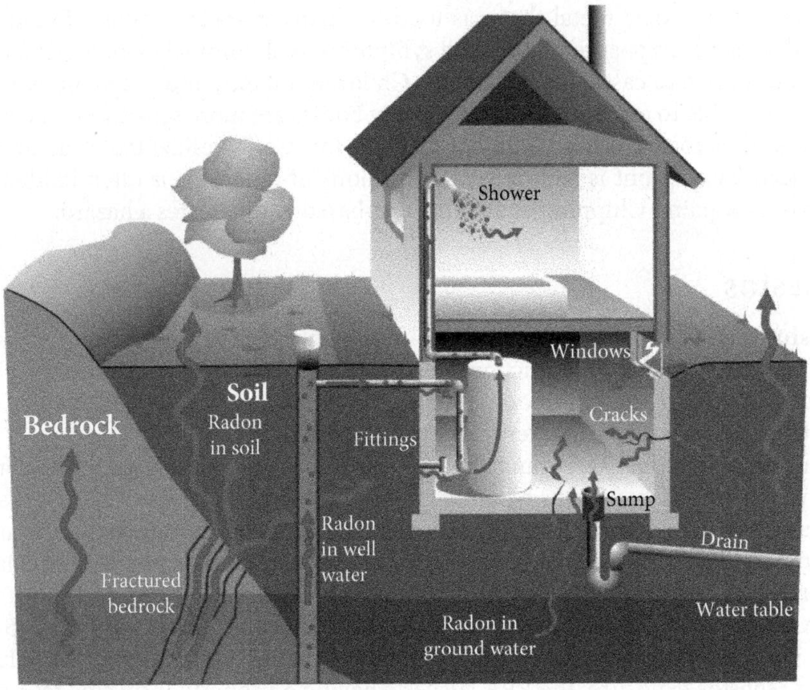

Source: U.S. Environmental Protection Agency

Radon cannot be seen or smelled, and the only way to know the level of exposure is to test for radon within the building. Exposure to radon is one of the leading causes of lung cancer and is the leading cause of lung cancer among non-smokers. The EPA suggests that a structure be tested for radon before being marketed for sale.

If the test shows a high level of radon, there are many different mitigation methods that can be used, such as installing ventilation systems and sealing cracks in the foundation. Properties can be built with radon-resistant construction techniques that are effective in preventing radon entry. When installed properly, these techniques can help reduce the indoor radon levels in homes and businesses. However, even properties built with radon-resistant techniques require periodic testing.

FIGURE 37.2: Radon Zone Map

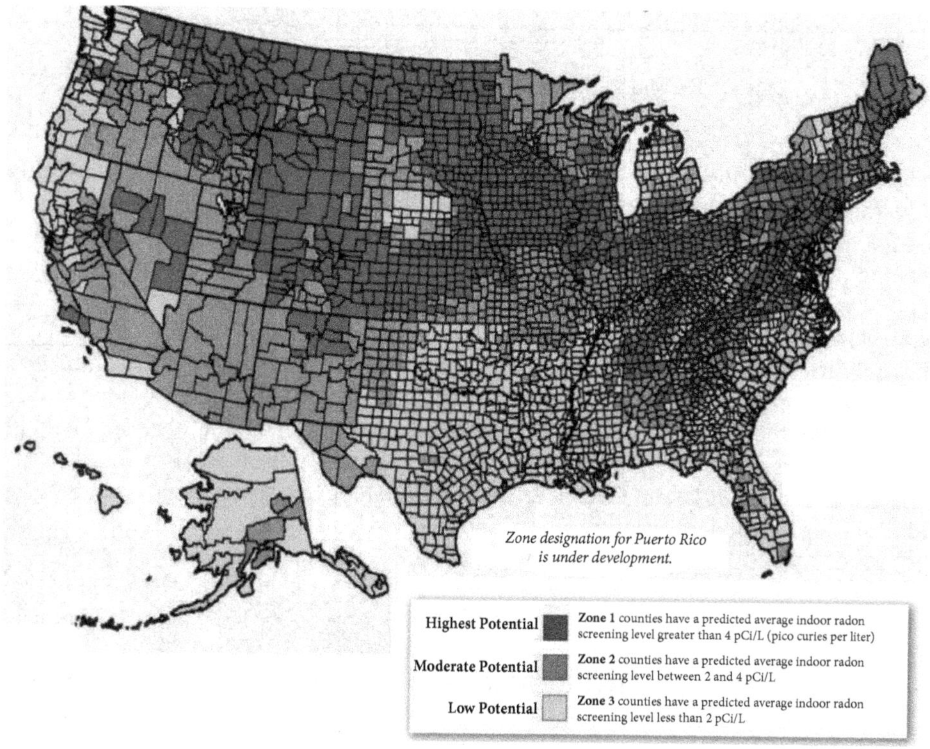

Source: U.S. Environmental Protection Agency

Concept Summary
Hazardous Substances and Their Negative Effects

Hazardous Substance	Effect
Lead	Abdominal pain, headaches, anemia, and, in severe cases, brain damage
Asbestos	Asbestosis, mesothelioma, and lung cancer
Radon	Lung cancer

Water Pollution Laws and Regulations

Groundwater

Groundwater
Water found under the earth's surface as a result of rain and melting snow.

Half of the United States' drinking water comes from groundwater. **Groundwater** is water found under the earth's surface. Most groundwater comes from rain and melting snow that is soaked into the ground. This water fills the spaces between rocks and soils and forms the water table. Groundwater's depth from the surface, quality, and chance of being polluted varies from place to place. Groundwater may become polluted naturally as water moves through underground rocks and soil picking up traces of magnesium, calcium, and chlorides. It may also be contaminated by human activities such as improper use and disposal of fertilizers, leaking underground storage tanks, improper disposal or storage of waste, and chemical spills.

Although the Clean Water Act and the Safe Drinking Water Act (discussed below) have provisions protecting groundwater quality, groundwater quality is primarily regulated at the local and state level. The local and state levels typically provide regulations that exceed federal requirements and allow for specific local conditions to be addressed.

FIGURE 37.3: Groundwater

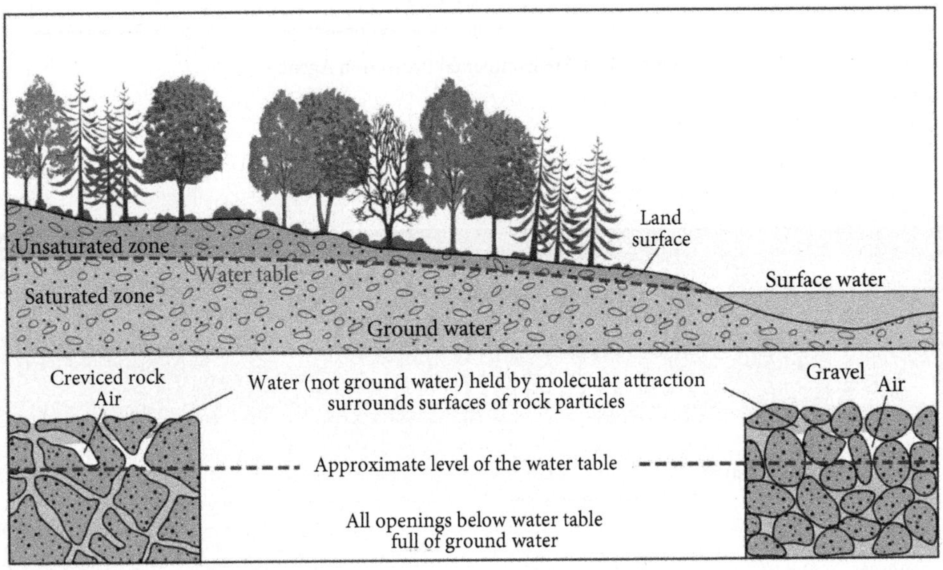

How ground water occurs in rocks.

Source: U.S. Geological Survey, Department of the Interior/USGS

The Safe Drinking Water Act

Most groundwater in the United States is safe for human use. However, contaminated groundwater has been found in every state. In an effort to provide safe drinking water to all Americans, Congress passed the **Safe Drinking Water Act (SDWA)** in 1974 and amended it in 1988 and 1996. The SDWA authorizes the EPA to set national health-based standards for drinking water to protect against naturally occurring and man-made contaminants.

Safe Drinking Water Act (SDWA) An act authorizing the EPA to set national health-based standards for drinking water found in public water systems.

The law regulates only public water systems. **Public water systems** are those that have at least 15 service connections or serve at least 25 people. **Private wells**, which serve less than 25 individuals, are not regulated by the SDWA. The law focuses not only on the treatment of water to make it safe for consumption, but also provides source water protection, funding for water system improvements, and the enforcement of standards.

Public water systems Water systems that have at least 15 service connections or serve at least 25 people.

The responsibility for making sure these public water systems provide safe drinking water is divided among the EPA, states, water systems, and the public. The EPA sets national standards for drinking water to protect against health risks. These standards each include requirements for water systems to test contaminants in the water to make sure the standard is achieved. The EPA also provides guidance, assistance, and public information about drinking water, collects drinking water data, and oversees state drinking water programs.

Private wells Wells serving less than 25 people.

Clean Water Act

The federal regulation of pollutants into the waters of the United States began in 1948. The law was significantly reorganized and expanded in 1972 at which time it became known as the **Clean Water Act (CWA)**. It has been revised and modified since. The CWA establishes the basic structure for regulating discharges of pollutants into the waters of the United States and regulates the quality standards of surface waters. The CWA also assists businesses, federal facilities, and local governments by providing them with tools to help meet environmental regulatory requirements.

Clean Water Act (CWA) A statute enacted to address water pollution in the United States.

Since its enactment, the CWA has implemented pollution control programs and made it unlawful to discharge any pollutant into navigable waters without a permit. All point sources that discharge pollution into surface water are required to obtain a discharge permit from the National Pollution Discharge Elimination System (NPDES). The EPA works closely with state agencies to implement this system. A **point source** is pollution originating from a discernible, specific discharge point. The NPDES does not require permits for a nonpoint source of pollution. **Nonpoint sources** of pollution originate from many sources. The permit requires public hearings as well as approval from the EPA and the state.

Point source A discernible, specific discharge point of pollution into surface waters.

Nonpoint source A source of pollution originating from many sources.

> **Example:** A point source would include a pipe, conduit, factory, or municipal wastewater treatment plant that is discharging pollution, while a nonpoint source of pollution would include runoff, rainfall, or snowmelt.

Concept Summary
The Clean Water Act

The primary objective of the Clean Water Act is to restore and maintain the integrity of the nation's waters. The objective translates into two fundamental goals: (1) eliminating the discharge of pollutants into the nation's waters; and (2) achieving water quality levels that are both fishable and swimmable.

The Act only applies to *navigable* waters.

When issuing a permit, the NPDES will impose restrictions and requirements on the permit holder. These limitations are based on the type of pollutant, the business industry of the discharger, the characteristics of the local watershed, and whether the discharge is from a new or existing source.

The EPA typically assesses monetary penalties to violators of the Clean Water Act. The penalties can include per day penalties or criminal penalties, including fines and imprisonment, for violators (such as corporate executives) who knowingly violate the Act.

Solid Waste Disposal and Brownfield Sites

Waste disposal site
An area of land designated for the proper disposition of discarded or discharged materials.

A **waste disposal site** is an area of land designated for the proper disposition of discarded or discharged materials. There are various types of waste disposal sites, and the classification of the site will depend on the type of waste that is being disposed.

Landfill

Landfill
A large cavity in the ground that is lined with a clay or synthetic liner to prevent any waste from leaking into the ground or water supply.

Nearly everything humans do leaves behind some type of waste. In the United States, most solid waste is disposed of in landfills. A **landfill** consists of a large cavity or depression in the ground that is lined with a clay or synthetic liner to prevent the leaking of any waste into the ground or water supply. Landfill management is important, as hazardous waste from a landfill may seep into the groundwater or release pollution into the atmosphere.

Capping
The act of laying soil and grass on top of a landfill or waste disposal site to prevent erosion and to improve aesthetics.

STRUCTURE OF A LANDFILL. Landfills must include drainage systems to remove rainwater filtering through the landfill waste. When water comes in contact with the buried waste, it transports chemicals in the waste to discharge points.

After waste is deposited in the landfill, a layer of topsoil is placed on top to compact the waste. This process of layering continues until the landfill is full, at which time it will be capped. **Capping** is the act of laying soil and grass on the top of the site to prevent erosion and to improve aesthetics.

The decomposing waste creates a natural gas called methane that can be dangerous due to its explosive tendencies. To ensure these gases are not trapped within the landfill, a ventilation pipe extends through the landfill's base to allow the gases to be collected. The collected methane gas is used as fuel to generate electricity. These sites are monitored long after the closing of the landfill, to ensure the quality of the groundwater and that the methane gas is properly handled.

FIGURE 37.4: Disposition of a Landfill

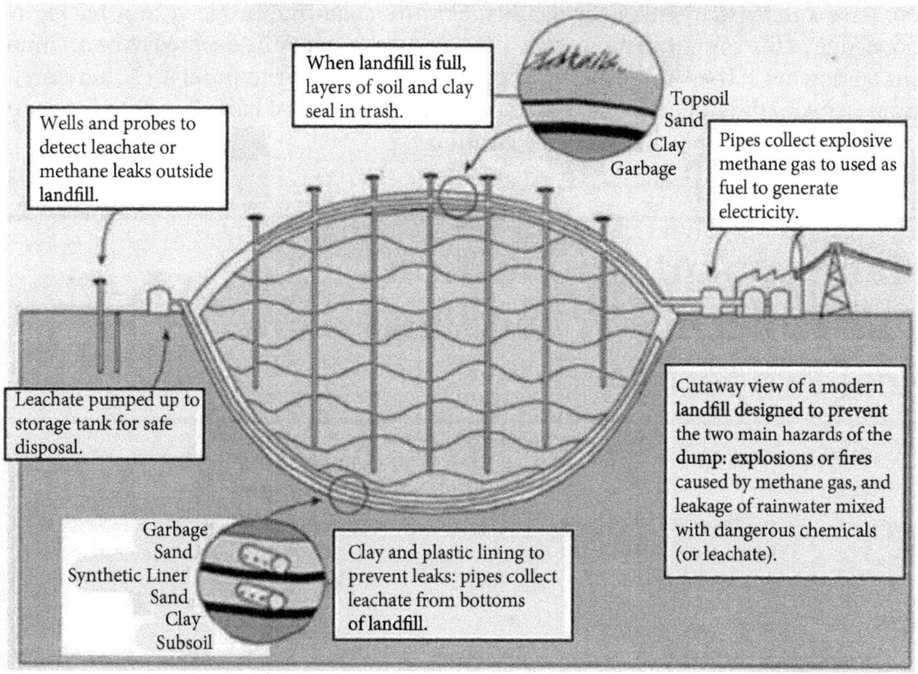

Source: U.S. Environmental Protection Agency

LOCATION OF LANDFILLS. People do not want landfills near their residence or place of business because of the potential health issues and negative effect upon property values. It is important that landfills are located, designed, and monitored in accordance with federal regulations.

Brownfields

Brownfields are abandoned, idled, or underused properties where the presence of hazardous substances, pollutants, or contaminants has impeded redevelopment of the sites. These sites include abandoned factories and other industrial facilities such as gas stations, oil storage facilities, dry cleaning establishments, and other businesses that handle or store hazardous substances. It is estimated there are as many as 450,000 brownfields throughout the United States.

Brownfields Abandoned, idled, or underused properties where the presence of hazardous substances, pollutants, or contaminants has complicated redevelopment of the sites.

To review the EPA website on brownfields sites and cleanup and reuse challenges and liabilities, see https://www.epa.gov/brownfields.

An unintended consequence of CERCLA was that developers refuse to purchase and attempt to clean brownfields for fear of taking on liability. To overcome this, an amendment to CERCLA was added to protect developers and encourage them to clean up brownfields. This provision protects a bona fide prospective purchaser, so long as they do not impede the performance of a response action or natural resource restoration.

The Small Business Liability Relief and Brownfields Revitalization Act was enacted to provide tools for the public and private sectors to support sustainable brownfields cleanup and reuse. Historically, the owner or operator of the contaminated property would be held responsible for the property's cleanup. As a result of the Act, entities may have a defense to CERCLA liability. Entities acquiring property and having no knowledge of the contamination at the time of purchase may be deemed to be an innocent landowner if they made the appropriate inquiries prior to purchase. Therefore, a purchaser who did not cause or contribute to the presence of hazardous substances or contaminates will not be liable for the cleanup.

Management Application
Due Diligence When Purchasing Real Property

As this chapter has shown, an owner or operator of a business can be exposed to liability for harm caused to property, persons, and the environment due to environmental contamination. It is imperative for prospective purchasers of businesses or commercial properties to conduct due diligence to identify the liabilities that may exist when purchasing, selling, or developing a property or businesses. An environmental consultant can assist in performing due diligence, which can include (1) reviewing state databases used to track and archive environmental contamination[2]; (2) reviewing who the prior and current owners and operators of the businesses or property were to understand the prior operations conducted on the property; (3) reviewing prior environmental reports (and, if none exist, have an environmental report prepared); (4) reviewing historical aerial photographs to reveal evidence of past operations; (5) performing site testing on the property if needed; and (6) examining the property itself for asbestos or other potentially hazardous materials. The prospective purchasers can secure warranties and indemnities from the seller that no such contamination exists and seek to obtain purchase price offsets for any cleanup costs arising from hazardous material.

What precautions would you suggest be undertaken in redeveloping properties in areas of urban renewal?

2. The State of California's State Water Resources Control Board provides a GeoTracker for sites that impact or have the potential to impact water quality in California. *https://geotracker.waterboards.ca.gov/.*

State Environmental Protection Laws

In addition to the federal acts discussed in this chapter, individuals may also have environmental protections under the common law as well as state and local environmental statutes.

Common Law Protections

Common law protections of nuisance, negligence, and strict liability (discussed in Chapters 5 and 6) can be used to protect a person's property. Under the nuisance doctrine, a person can have liability if they substantially and unreasonably interfere with the use and enjoyment of another person's property.

> **Example:** The San Francisco City Attorney's Office and nine other California cities and counties sued and were awarded a $1.1 billion judgment against several large lead paint manufacturers under a public nuisance theory. They alleged the companies marketed lead paint for indoor residential use while knowing of its dangers to children.

Businesses and individuals that fail to exercise reasonable care (such as failing to properly clean up environmental waste) may be sued under a common law negligence theory. Further, businesses that engage in hazardous activities (such as the transportation of hazardous waste) can be held strictly liable for harm caused.

State Environmental Statutes

Many states and local governments have enacted environmental statutes and ordinances to protect the environment. States can enact environmental legislation using its Tenth Amendment powers to protect the "health, safety, and welfare" of its citizens. These environmental laws may provide more stringent environmental protections than the federal law protections. States can enact legislation related to environmental issues important to the state.

> **Example:** The Michigan Department of Environment, Great Lakes, and Energy in July 2020 adopted one of the nation's most comprehensive regulations limiting PFAS (Per- and polyfluoroalkyl substances) contamination in drinking water. PFAS accumulate and stay in the human body for long periods of time and exposure can lead to adverse health outcomes. PFAS is a significant contamination problem in Michigan with thousands of residents' water supplies contaminated. Michigan's regulations limiting PFAS chemicals in drinking water exceed the current U.S. Environmental Protection Agency (EPA) guidance on the chemicals.

AI Feature: Comparison of a State's Environmental Statutes with CERCLA

Not all states have adopted comprehensive environmental statutes equivalent to federal laws, but most states have enacted some form of environmental legislation to complement federal regulations. Using an internet search engine, research the law of your home with regard to its statutes relating to environmental matters, cleanup processes, and how they are enforced. If your state has not enacted such legislation, pick a state that has done so. Then, using an AI program, compare and contrast the state's environmental laws with CERCLA.

Key Terms

- Asbestos, 941
- Brownfields, 947
- Capping, 946
- Clean Air Act, 938
- Clean Water Act (CWA), 945
- Comprehensive Environmental Response, Compensation, and Liability Act (CERCLA), 935
- Environmental Impact Statement (EIS), 935
- Environmental Protection Agency (EPA), 934
- Groundwater, 944
- Landfill, 946
- Lead, 941
- National Environmental Policy Act of 1969 (NEPA), 935
- Nonpoint source, 945
- Point source, 945
- Private wells, 945
- Public water system, 945
- Radon, 941
- Remedial action, 935
- Removal actions, 935
- Safe Drinking Water Act (SDWA), 945
- U.S. Army Corps of Engineers, 934
- U.S. Department of Housing and Urban Development (HUD), 934
- Waste disposal site, 946

Applying the Law

37.1 Research the Law. Using an internet search engine, determine the nearest brownfield site to your residence. Do you think the CERCLA Brownfields Program is sufficient to remediate the contaminated sites? Why or why not? Are there any state programs available to rehabilitate such sites for other purposes?

37.2 Research the Law. Using an internet search engine, determine which federal and state agencies have exercised jurisdiction over oil in the territorial waters of the United States. To what extent has the EPA been involved? Analyze the impacts upon the environment with respect to those you identify in your research. Is it likely that the pre-spill conditions can be restored?

37.3 Research the Law. Using an internet search engine, determine if your state mandates compliance with its regulations on improving air quality in addition to that which is required under the federal Clean Air Act. If they would otherwise be preempted by federal law, how do these state laws and regulations continue in force?

37.4 NEPA Considerations. A citizen's council sued to prevent the Forest Service from granting a permit for a ski development. Usually, the administrative decisions of a federal agency are given deference by the courts. What procedures must an agency undertake under NEPA as construed by the United States Supreme Court? What constraints are imposed upon federal agencies under NEPA? Is it permissible to support values which outweigh environmental costs? *Robertson v. Methow Valley Citizens Council*, 490 U.S. 332 (1989)

37.5 Joint and Several Liability. After years during which various companies dumped PCBs into the Fox River in Wisconsin, the EOA and a Wisconsin state agency had been working to devise and implement a remedial plan for the river. One of the companies that was designated as a potentially responsible party was NCR. After years of performing a significant amount of cleanup, it stopped. In response the regulators sued to compel NCR to complete the remediation work required under CERCLA. NCR argued that it should only be proportionately responsible under the Act. Should the court apportion liability, or could it hold NCR responsible? Should costs of remediation be relevant when considering apportionment of responsibility? *United States v. NCR Corp.*, 688 F.3d 833 (7th Cir. 2012)

37.6 Jurisdiction. Mosaic, a Florida fertilizer manufacturer engaged in phosphate mining sought to discharge dredged and fill material into protected wetlands. Its operations of manufacturing fertilizer from the mined phosphate ore generated a radioactive by-product called phosphogypsum. The Army Corps of Engineers granted the permit. The Corps concluded that it did not have jurisdiction under the Clean Water Act to deny the permit. It concluded that a denial of a permit was permitted only if the discharge itself has an unacceptable environmental impact, a conclusion it did not reach. Did the Corps act properly in protecting the environment under NEPA? *Ctr. for Biological Diversity, Manasota-88, Inc. v. United States Army Corps of Eng'rs*, 941 F.3d 1288 (11th Cir.)

37.7 Navigable Waters. The Clean Water Act makes it unlawful to discharge any pollutant into navigable waters without a permit. Would someone violate the Clean Water Act if they dumped a pollutant into a flow of water that was intermittent or lasted for a short time? Why or why not? *Rapanos v. United States*, 547 U.S. 715 (2006)

37.8 Parent Corporation Liability Under CERCLA. In 1957, Ott Chemical Co. ("Ott") began manufacturing chemicals at a Michigan plant. Its intentional and unintentional dumping of hazardous substances significantly polluted the soil and groundwater near the site. Ott was purchased by a wholly owned subsidiary of CPC International Inc.® ("CPC") and continued to pollute the surrounding area. CPC later sold Ott to Story Chemical Company, which operated the plant until it went bankrupt in 1977. The Michigan Department of Natural Resources examined the site for environmental damage and found the land surrounding the plant to be littered with waste and the surrounding soil and water saturated with noxious chemicals. The EPA planned for long-term remedial efforts; however, it required expenditures of millions of dollars. To recover damages from culpable parties, the United States sued CPC. Can a parent company be held liable for environmental contamination caused by its subsidiary? *United States v. Bestfoods*, 524 U.S. 51 (1998)

37.9 Cost Benefit. Entergy's® power plants are subject to regulation under the Clean Water Act. As a result, they must employ a variety of "best technology" standards to regulate wastewater discharge into the waters. The EPA considered the use of the "best technology available" on a case-by-case basis. In making this determination, the EPA relied upon cost benefit analysis. Riverkeeper, Inc.® sued claiming the site-specific cost benefit variance provision unlawful in maintaining national performance standards. May the EPA consider cost when determining whether a business is complying with national standards? What interests are at stake in this public policy adopted by the agency? *Entergy Corp. v. Riverkeeper, Inc.*, 556 U.S. 208 (2009)

37.10 Environmental Impact Statement. Following a record fire, the Forest Service decided to conduct salvage logging on thousands of acres of burned forest in the Umatilla National Forest without preparing an Environmental Impact Statement (EIS). Shortly after a fire, the Forest Service assessed the impacts of the fire on the watershed and developed a recovery strategy. After completing an Environmental Assessment for the project, the Forest Service issued a "Finding of No Significant Impact" and declined to prepare an EIS. Multiple environmental groups sued to enjoin the salvage, alleging that the Forest Service's decision was arbitrary and capricious. The court refused to give deference to the agency's decision not to prepare an EIS. On what grounds could a court do so? *Blue Mountains Biodiversity Project v. Blackwood*, 161 F.3d 1208 (9th Cir. 1998)

PART VII: PROPERTY

Personal Property Law and Bailments

38

Government is instituted to protect property of every sort. This being the end of government, that alone is a just government, which impartially secures to every man, whatever is his own. — James Madison, Fourth President of the United States, Property (1751-1836)

Chapter Outline

- Introduction
- Personal Property

Case 38.1: *Cooley v. Tucker*

  - *Management Application: Pause Before You Buy the Ring*
- Bailments
  - *Management Application: The Trouble with Park-and-Lock Facilities*
  - *Management Application: Special Bailment — Common Carriers, Warehouse Receipts, and Innkeepers*

Case 38.2: *Akiva v. Jurenci*

  - *Management Application: Pets and Bailment*
  - *Management Application: Excerpted Bailment Agreement*
- Lost, Mislaid, and Abandoned Property — Finders and Owners

Case 38.3: *Grande v. Jennings*

- AI Feature: Liability for Breach of Bailment

Learning Objectives

After studying this chapter, you should be able to:

1. Explain the difference between real and personal property.
2. Describe how ownership of personal property is acquired.
3. Identify the different types of bailments.
4. Explain the creation and termination of a bailment.
5. Distinguish among mislaid, lost, and abandoned property.

Introduction

Property refers to anything that can be possessed, controlled, divided, transferred, sold, and made unavailable to others. Property is categorized as real property and personal property. Within each classification, property can be further defined as either tangible or intangible. **Tangible property** interests exist in a physical form. **Intangible property** interests lack a physical form. This chapter discusses the law concerning the ownership and transfer of personal property.

Tangible property Property interests that exist in a physical form.

Intangible property Property interests lacking a physical form.

Personal Property

Personal property Property that is movable and not fixed or permanently attached to real property.

Personal property is property that is movable and not fixed or permanently attached to real property. It is sometimes referred to as chattels or goods. Generally, anything that is not real property (discussed in Chapter 39) is personal property.

Example: Both a tractor and a bond would be considered personal property; however, the tractor is tangible, while the bond is intangible.

How Is Personal Property Acquired?

Property can usually be acquired or transferred with little difficulty. This is because the transfer of property is an essential part of the U.S. economy. If acquiring or transferring property were difficult, the costs of doing business would be higher and thus hinder the economy. These barriers would be a disincentive for people to enter into transactions involving personal property. There are several ways property may be transferred: purchase; production; possession; gift; accession; by will, estate, or inheritance; and confusion.

PURCHASE. The most common way in which property is transferred is by purchase. When personal property is purchased, the title to that property is exchanged for money or another form of consideration. A bill of sale is a contract that transfers the ownership of personal property from one party to another. It serves as a receipt and provides proof of the transaction.

Example: Stefan owns a carpet cleaning business and decides to purchase a new work van from a local dealer called Victor's Vans. Stefan pays Victor $20,000 for the van. Victor then transfers title to the van to Stefan and Stefan becomes the owner of the van.

EXHIBIT 38.1: Bill of Sale

Bill of Sale

[Name] (hereinafter "Seller") on [Date] hereby sells, transfers, delivers, conveys, and assigns all rights, title, and interest in and to the following personal property: [List item(s), if they have serial, identification or registration numbers include them in the description].

The goods are sold to [Buyer] (hereinafter "Buyer") whose current address is [Address]. The goods are sold to Buyer for the sum of **[State Sales Price] ($X,XXX).** Said sum has been paid by [state how paid].

Seller acknowledges receipt of said sum from Buyer. [If the sales price is to be paid over time, then replace the preceding sentence with the following: Buyer agrees that Buyer does not acquire any right to sell, assign, or dispose of the above-listed property until it is entirely paid for; and in case of default of payment as stated above, Seller, or Seller's agents or assigned, are authorized to take possession and remove the sold property, without further demand, or notice to Buyer, whereby all rights for an action of trespass or other causes of action are waived, and to collect reasonable charges for their use.]

Buyer acknowledges receipt of delivery of the above-listed property. Buyer has inspected the property before executing this Bill of Sale and has accepted them.

Seller warrants that they are the lawful owner of the goods being sold and that the goods are sold free and clear of all liens, security agreements, encumbrances, claims, demands, and charges of every and all kind.

[If sales tax is applicable to this sale, identify which party will be responsible for its payment].

THE GOODS ARE BEING SOLD TO BUYER ON AN "AS IS" AND "WHERE IS" BASIS. EXCEPT AS SPECIFICALLY SET FORTH IN THIS AGREEMENT, SELLER MAKES NO OTHER REPRESENTATIONS OR WARRANTIES. SELLER SPECIFICALLY DISCLAIMS THE IMPLIED WARRANTIES OF MERCHANTABILITY AND FITNESS FOR PARTICULAR USE.

This Bill of Sale has been executed in duplicate originals so that Buyer and Seller have a fully executed copy.

I certify under penalty of perjury under the laws of the State of [_______] that the foregoing is true and correct.

Dated: _________

By: ___________________
[Seller]
[Seller's Address]

By: ___________________
[Buyer]
[Buyer's Address]

PRODUCTION. Another common method for acquiring ownership of personal property is production. Production is the act of taking various raw materials and using them to produce a finished product. This is best understood in the context of manufacturing, but it also applies to musicians, writers, inventors, and other similar professions.

> **Example:** A clothing manufacturer may purchase cotton, wool, synthetic fiber, thread, buttons, and other assorted items to produce pieces of clothing. The finished product is owned by the manufacturer.

POSSESSION. Possession was the first means of indicating ownership of personal property. It began with determining when a person had obtained ownership of a wild animal. In nature, a wild animal does not belong to any person; therefore, once a wild animal is captured or killed by someone, that person will have established ownership of the wild animal through its possession.

> **Example:** Jared while fly-fishing with a proper license catches an 11-inch trout. Jared will have claimed ownership of the trout through possession.

Spotlight on Ethics
Are Body Tissues and Cells Personal Property?

It has been a longstanding belief in many jurisdictions that upon death one's body does not constitute personal property of the deceased's family or loved ones. However, the medical and technological advances that have taken place in the last few decades have placed a new question before the courts; namely, what is the status of body tissues and cells that are collected during life?

Courts have been asked to interpret these questions in various factual scenarios, ranging from what happens to frozen embryos upon the divorce of a couple to the collection of stem cells and addressing the federal ban on compensating bone marrow donors. The law struggles to keep pace with the rapid evolution of these technologies. Consequently, laws are far from uniform among the states.

In the context of frozen embryos, courts generally rule in favor of the person who does not wish to have the embryos used to produce a child after the termination of the marriage. These embryos are often ordered to be destroyed because most jurisdictions conclude that no one should be forced to become a parent. In California and New York, such embryos have been destroyed, while courts in Illinois and Pennsylvania have held that the embryos belong to the woman in situations where she otherwise could not produce children. However, Arizona has taken a different approach by becoming the first state in the United States to enact a law stating that the embryos belong to the person who wishes to use them to produce a child, regardless of their ability to reproduce in the future. Those in favor of this law argue that frozen embryos are not simply tissues over which a person may claim ownership rights but are to be considered human beings entitled to their own rights.

With so much inconsistency among the states, many commentators believe that this issue is one that could come before the United States Supreme Court.

Of all our possessions, wisdom alone is immortal.— Isocrates, Greek Orator, 436-338 B.C.

Gift
A voluntary transfer of property without payment or the expectation of repayment.

Donor
Person who gives a gift to another.

Donee
Person who receives a gift from a donor.

***Inter vivos* gift**
A gift made during the donor's lifetime.

GIFT. A **gift** is a voluntary transfer of property. When title to personal property is transferred by one person (the **donor**) to another (the **donee**) without payment or the expectation of repayment, it is a gift.

Generally, persons are free to give their property to whomever they wish. As with virtually all transfers of property, the donor must possess sufficient mental capacity to understand the nature and effect of the gift for the gift to be valid. If the donor is physically or mentally incapacitated such that the required mental capacity is absent, the gift may be set aside. In addition, the donor's capacity will be an important consideration in cases where it must be decided whether the gift was the result of undue influence by the donee.

There are two different types of gifts. The first, an ***inter vivos* gift**, is a gift made during the donor's life. The second, a ***causa mortis* gift**, is made in contemplation of the donor's impending death. Both *inter vivos* and *causa mortis* gifts must meet the three requirements discussed in the section below. However, additional requirements apply only to *causa mortis* gifts. When a *causa mortis* gift is made but the donor does not die, the gift is automatically revoked by the law. This is because the donor's intent to make the gift was limited to the context of impending death. However, since the death did not occur, the donor's intent is no longer applicable. Additionally, the gift will also be revoked if the donee unexpectedly dies. Again, this is because the donor's intent was to give a gift to that particular donee. Since the donee is deceased, the donor's intent cannot be fulfilled.

***Causa mortis* gift**
A gift made in contemplation of an impending death.

Concept Summary
Inter Vivos versus *Causa Mortis* Gifts

	Timing	Requirements
Inter vivos	Made at any time during the donor's lifetime	1. Donative intent 2. Delivery of gift to donee 3. Acceptance of gift by donee
Causa mortis	Made in contemplation of the donor's impending death	1. Donative intent 2. Delivery of gift to donee 3. Acceptance of gift by donee 4. Donor dies 5. Donee survives the donor

Gift Requirements. There are three legal requirements to make a valid gift:

1. The donor's intention to make a gift;
2. The gift's delivery to the donee; and
3. The gift's acceptance by the donee.

Donative Intent. The actions or intentions of the donor must be clear, unmistakable, and unequivocal to evidence the voluntary making of a gift. In making the gift, the donor must relinquish control and all rights to the property gifted. The evidence of donative intent may be expressed in words or actions, or inferred from the surrounding circumstances, including the relationship of the parties.

Delivery. Delivery is accomplished by the unconditional transfer of property to the donee. The intention to make a gift does not constitute delivery because it is only an expression of a promise to make a gift in the future. Until delivery occurs, the promise to make a gift can be revoked.

For delivery to occur, the donor must surrender possession and control of the gift. This delivery may be either actual or constructive. Actual delivery is easily identified because the donor physically delivers the gift to the donee. **Constructive delivery** is a bit more difficult to identify because constructive delivery occurs when the donor delivers to the donee the exclusive means of obtaining possession and control of the property and relinquishes control of the property.

Constructive delivery
A method that can be used in making gifts where the donor makes a symbolic delivery of the property to the donee.

Example: A donor giving the keys to their prized convertible to their grandson would constitute constructive delivery of the gift even if the donor does not actually deliver the convertible or title to the grandson at that time.

Acceptance. Acceptance of the gift is presumed unless the donee makes the rejection clear by refusing to take physical possession of or to assert control over the property. When the donee does exercise control over the gift, the acceptance of the donee is presumed. Once the gift has been accepted, it becomes an irrevocable transfer of ownership from the donor to the donee.

The following case considers if an engagement ring is still a gift even if the marriage does not take place.

CASE 38.1

DONOR MAY BE ENTITLED TO THE RETURN OF A GIFT MADE IN CONTEMPLATION OF MARRIAGE

COOLEY v. TUCKER

200 So. 3d 474 (2016)

Court of Appeals of Mississippi

Emily Cooley and Lawrence Tucker had been dating for over two years when Tucker proposed to Cooley in December 2011. However, the relationship was a tumultuous one and Tucker's proposal occurred after numerous requests by Cooley. Tucker believed the engagement would improve their rocky relationship. At the time that Tucker proposed, he presented Cooley with a $40,000 ring. Cooley accepted the proposal, and after that she wore the ring consistently. The couple could not agree on wedding plans and a wedding date was never set. Not surprisingly, their relationship did not improve following the engagement. Tucker made numerous attempts to end the relationship, but each time he backed down due to Cooley's threats to harm herself. Eventually, in November 2014 Tucker ended the relationship via email. Tucker requested several times that Cooley return the engagement ring, but each time she refused. Tucker eventually sued to recover the ring. Both Tucker and Cooley testified before the court. Cooley asserted that the engagement ring was an *inter vivos* gift. Tucker argued that the ring was a conditional gift, with the condition being their future marriage. The court determined that the ring was a conditional gift and therefore Cooley was not entitled to keep it. Cooley appealed.

Language of the Court. *Cooley asserts that the chancery court erred in its determination that the ring was a conditional gift rather than an* inter vivos *gift. For an* inter vivos *gift to be valid, the following elements must be met: (1) a donor competent to make a gift; (2) a voluntary act of the donor with donative intent; (3) the gift must be complete with nothing else to be done; (4) there must be delivery to the donee; and (5) the gift must be irrevocable.*

However, the engagement ring is not a valid inter vivos *gift. Cooley's assertion does not meet the element that requires that the gift be completed with nothing more to be done.*

Here, the chancellor ultimately determined that "the engagement ring was a conditional gift presented in contemplation of a marriage that did not occur." It is from this determination that the chancellor awarded Tucker the ring. This conclusion is supported by Mississippi case law and by fact.

Cooley requests, in an alternative argument, that this Court create new precedents under which trial courts would determine ownership of an engagement ring following a broken engagement. We decline to do so. Existing Mississippi gift law adequately addresses cases such as this, and we will not deviate from the path set before us at this time.

Decision. The court of appeals affirmed the ruling, thereby requiring Cooley to return the ring to Tucker.

Focus on Ethics

Is it fair that Cooley must return the ring even though Tucker was the one to call off the wedding? Should it matter who cancels the engagement?

Management Application
Pause Before You Buy the Ring

Like Mississippi in the case above, other states, such as New York, Minnesota, and North Carolina, follow the conditional gift theory. These courts have found that the ring must be returned to the donor, regardless of who broke off the engagement.

In some states, such as California, Texas, and Washington, it matters who calls off the wedding. For example, California Civil Code § 1590 states: "Where either party to a contemplated marriage in this State makes a gift of money or property to the other on the basis or assumption that the marriage will take place, in the event that the donee refuses to enter into the marriage as contemplated or that it is given up by mutual consent, the donor may recover such gift."

Montana stands alone in finding that an engagement ring is an unconditional completed gift, thereby rejecting the conditional gift theory. This would allow the donee to keep the ring, regardless of who ends the engagement.

Accession

Accession
The increase in value of personal property due to an addition or improvement. Accession may occur naturally or be manufactured.

Accession occurs when the value of personal property increases due to an addition or improvement being made. An accession may either occur naturally or be manufactured. When the accession occurs naturally, it belongs to the owner. An accession that was manufactured with the owner's consent will also belong to the owner. When an improvement is made wrongfully because the owner did not give permission, generally the owner will remain in possession of title and will not be required to pay for the improvement.

When an improvement is made by honest mistake, the owner will remain in possession of the title and will not be required to pay for the improvement. However, the improver may be required to pay for any damage that occurs because of the removal of an improvement if it is easily removed. If the improvement is not easily removable, the owner will simply keep the improvements and does not have to pay the improver.

> **Example:** If Jordyn takes her car to the body shop to have the paint on her bumper touched up and the body shop mistakenly repaints the entire car, Jordyn will remain in possession of the car and will only have to pay for the work she consented to have done.

Confusion

Confusion
Confusion occurs when interchangeable goods are commingled between two or more people to the extent that one person's property cannot be distinguished from the property of another.

Confusion occurs when interchangeable goods owned by two or more people are commingled to the extent that one person's property cannot be distinguished from the property of the other(s). Interchangeable goods are often described as fungible. Each owner will own a share of the commingled goods in proportion to the amount of goods they contributed. However, if the goods are commingled wrongfully or without permission, the innocent owner will acquire title to the goods in totality.

> **Example:** When neighboring farmers decide to pool their grain into a single silo, each farmer will be entitled to take out only the amount of grain they deposited. However, the grain that they take out may be the grain of a different farmer, not their own.

Bailments

Bailment
The possession of personal property by someone who is not the true owner, without transfer of title, for a particular purpose.

Bailor
The owner of the property.

Bailee
The holder of the goods.

A **bailment** is defined as possession of personal property by someone who is not the true owner, without the transfer of title, for a particular purpose. We frequently encounter bailments in our daily life. With a bailment, title to the property is still held by the owner. When a person goes to the gym and places their belongings in a storage locker, a bailment is created. The owner of the property is known as the **bailor**. The holder of the goods — in this example, the gym — is known as the **bailee**. The bailee has a duty to return the goods to the bailor because the bailor retains title to the goods, but the bailee can possess and sometimes use the property until the item is returned to the bailor.

> **Example:** Amanda parks her car in the parking lot at the local shopping center. She is the bailor, and the parking lot operator is the bailee.

Example: An advertising firm hires a local moving and storage company to move its office furniture to a new location. The advertising firm is the bailor, and the moving and storage company is the bailee.

Example: A Virginia court found that a bailment was created between a couple and a reproductive assistance facility when the facility agreed to procure and subsequently freeze and store the couple's pre-zygote for future use. *York v. Jones*, 717 F. Supp. 421 (E.D. Va. 1989)

Creation of Bailments

Express bailment
A bailment created by contract.

While **express bailments** frequently are created by contract, such as by parking a car in a paid parking lot, most jurisdictions do not require a contract for a bailment relationship. Courts and legislatures realize that bailments often arise informally, quickly, and without much discussion between the parties regarding its creation. The law of bailment varies among the states. However, two requirements are common to all these laws:

1. *The bailee must have exclusive physical control over the personal property.* Possession of an item is insufficient to create a bailment because the bailee's ability to exercise some form of control over the object is required. Other states will recognize that possession alone can imply a bailment but do not impose any duties upon the bailee. The control element most often arises in parking lot cases.

Example: Hector paid to park his vehicle in an unenclosed lot while he attended a baseball game. After paying for parking, Hector received a "claim check" indicating his payment. He then proceeded to park and lock his car, keeping the keys, before heading to the stadium. If Hector returns from the game and finds his car has been stolen from the lot, the lot operator is not liable. Hector did not deliver control of his vehicle to the lot attendant; therefore, no bailment was created.

Example: Donald Nussbaum gave his car and his keys to the valet attendant upon his arrival at Pappagallo Restaurant. When Donald's car was subsequently stolen, the court found that Pappagallo Restaurant was liable as a bailee because Donald had delivered control of the vehicle to the valet. *Aetna Cas. and Sur. Co v. Pappagallo Restaurant*, 547 So. 2d 243 (Fla. Dist. Ct. App. 1989)

2. *The bailee must knowingly accept or intend to control or possess the item.* For a bailment to be created, the bailee must be aware of the personal property of which the bailee has taken possession. This requires that the bailee intends to possess the specific personal property in question.

Example: If an attendant receives the keys to a vehicle when a car is taken to a commercial car wash, a bailment is created because the car wash operator, as the bailee, has knowingly accepted control over the vehicle. If a laptop computer is in the trunk of the car and its presence was not mentioned to the car wash attendant, no bailment would be created as to the laptop computer.

Example: Florence Swarth parked her vehicle at Barney's Clothes, Inc., which provided a free parking lot for its customers. An attendant requested that Swarth leave her keys with him. She did so and accidentally left her wallet on the passenger seat of her car. When Swarth realized the wallet was missing, she immediately returned to her car, but the wallet was never located. She sued Barney's Clothes for the value of the wallet, but the court found that although Barney's Clothes was the bailee of the car, it was not the bailee of the wallet and thus was not liable to her. *Swarth v. Barney's Clothes, Inc.*, 242 N.Y.S.2d 922 (1963)

Situations exist where a bailee does not intend to control an item, but the law deems that bailment has occurred anyway. These situations occur when someone has lost or mislaid an item on another's property. The law imposes bailment duties on the unwitting or unwilling bailee. This is known as involuntary bailment.

Example: A passenger leaves their laptop computer in a car after exiting the vehicle. An involuntary bailment has been created when the driver discovers its presence. The vehicle operator is the involuntary bailee of the laptop computer.

Management Application The Trouble with Park-and-Lock Facilities

It can be difficult to determine if a bailment has been created, especially when it comes to the parking of vehicles. Often, bailments will be misidentified as leases or licenses. The parking of a vehicle in an enclosed lot requires the driver to take a ticket, choose a space to park, and lock the car so that it could not be moved by management would have at one time not created a bailment. This was because the management of the lot was not believed to have control of the vehicle because management lacked the ability to move it. Instead, this was believed to constitute a license. This may have also constituted a lease if a fee was paid to get past the gate. However, in some jurisdictions today this scenario would give rise to a bailment.

States such as New Jersey and Massachusetts have found that as to enclosed park-and-lock garages, the traditional elements of bailment are inadequate. Therefore, the management of the garage has a duty of reasonable care under all circumstances and must rebut a presumption of negligence. These courts have found that the requirement of taking a ticket upon entry and paying based on the time stamped on that ticket signifies that the owner does not have unrestricted control of the vehicle because they cannot leave until a payment is made. However, even if under these circumstances the court recognizes a bailment, the lot management may only be responsible for vandalism or damages to the exterior of the vehicle. The management of the parking facility may be able to successfully argue that no bailment existed for any items stolen from inside the vehicle.

Still, the law in most states is that the owner of the vehicle retains control of the vehicle by possessing the keys and bailment is not created.

Types of Bailments

There are several types of ordinary bailments. They create a standard of care owed by the bailee to the bailor. The duties of some bailees are defined by statute (such as the duties of hotel operators toward their guests). Because circumstances can create a bailment, the courts adopted three duties of care which are:

1. *Bailments that benefit only the bailor.* Situations when bailment is created without consideration or when the bailee acts gratuitously, such as the bailee taking care of the bailor's property as a favor to the bailor. The bailee owes only a slight duty of care to protect the bailed property. This standard of care excludes all liability of the bailee except for cases of gross negligence.

Example: Nigel is going on vacation and asks his neighbor Desiree to watch his dog while he is away. This is a bailment that benefits only Nigel, and Desiree owes only a slight duty of care to protect the dog.

Example: A restaurant with a coatroom attendant provides a coatroom free of charge to its customers.

2. *Bailments benefiting both the bailor and the bailee.* This is the most common type of bailment created. Some form of consideration is paid to the bailee for the bailment. The bailee owes a duty of reasonable care to protect the bailed property from harm or loss.

Example: Alex takes her vehicle to a mechanic for repairs. The mechanic, the bailee, has a reasonable duty of care to protect Alex's vehicle while repairs are being made.

3. *Bailments that benefit only the bailee.* A bailment requiring the highest duty of care. The bailee owes a duty of utmost care to protect the bailed property from harm or loss.

Example: Anton loans his pickup truck to his cousin Teri so that she can use it to move her furniture into her new apartment across town. The family member owes the duty of utmost care in protecting the pickup truck from harm or loss.

Another type of bailment is the involuntary bailment. **Involuntary bailments** arise when a bailment is imposed upon the bailee either unintentionally or without consent. These bailments can arise when property is lost and found by a finder or when property is mistakenly delivered to the wrong person. In such circumstances, the bailee owes a slight duty of care to the bailed goods. However, if the property is mislaid (that is, *intentionally* placed somewhere and forgotten), the bailee owes a duty of reasonable care to safeguard the property until it can be returned to the rightful owner.

Involuntary bailment
The law imposing bailment duties on the unwitting or unwilling bailee.

Example: Mollie's goods are accidentally delivered to her neighbor's home. The neighbor becomes an involuntary bailee and owes a slight duty of care to the package.

Concept Summary
Standards of Care

Type of Bailment	Duty Owed
Benefit to bailor only	Bailee owes a slight duty of care (liable for gross negligence)
Benefit to both bailor and bailee	Bailee required to use reasonable care (liable for ordinary negligence)
Benefit to bailee only	Bailee required to use utmost care (liable for slight negligence)

Management Application
Special Bailments — Common Carriers, Warehouse Receipts, and Innkeepers

Common Carriers

A common carrier transports goods or passengers and is licensed by state and federal regulatory agencies. They are required to carry all passengers or freight, provided there is enough space. Among the laws governing the carriage of commercial goods is Article 7 of the Uniform Commercial Code and provisions relating to bailments under state law. The document of title used in the carriage of goods is known as a bill of lading. It is a document issued by the common carrier or freight forwarder to evidence the receipt of goods for shipment. It must purport to be issued by or addressed to a bailee and to cover goods in the bailee's possession that are identified in the bill of lading. The person who enters into the contract of transportation with the carrier is the shipper while the consignee is the person to whom delivery of the goods is promised.

Unlike ordinary bailments, the common carrier is held to a standard of care of strict liability other than reasonable care in protecting the bailed goods. Liability is excused for exceptional causes of loss, such as a natural disaster.

While a common carrier may not contract away its entire liability for loss or damage to bailed goods, it may limit its liability in the bill of lading (or in a transportation agreement) where it is provided that the carrier's liability may not exceed a certain sum. Reasonable claims procedures relating to the time and manner of presenting claims and commencing litigation based on the shipment may be stated in the bill of lading.

Warehouse Receipts

A document used in the moving and storage industry is the warehouse receipt. Issued by a bailee in favor of a bailor, this document serves as a receipt for goods received from the bailor. It also acts as a document of title, which evidences the ownership of the goods it represents.

Under the Uniform Commercial Code, a warehouseman may in most situations withhold goods deposited with it from the rightful owner until the bailor's (that is, the depositor's) storage and other rightful charges have been paid. This is known as the warehouseman's lien.

Warehouse lien rights may be more restricted when a negotiable warehouse receipt is issued. It is negotiable if it states that the warehouse company will deliver the stored goods "to the bearer" of the receipt or to the "order of" a person named on the receipt.

Innkeepers

Most states have created special bailment rules for innkeepers, a term that typically includes hotels, motels, bed-and-breakfasts, bungalows, and other establishments that provide lodging to the public for compensation. Innkeepers are strictly liable for the personal property of guests during the accommodation. Strict liability is liability without fault. No matter what the intention or the level of care provided, the innkeeper will be liable for any resulting loss or harm to the bailed goods.

> **Example:** At check-in, Denise deposited her valuable jewelry at the hotel front desk. When she returned to check out, her jewelry was missing. The hotel will be responsible for the loss under strict liability.

While the underlying rule is harsh, innkeepers can avoid strict liability by placing a safe in the guest's room and making the guests aware of it. Additionally, innkeepers can limit the liability to a dollar amount if notice is provided to the guest. Many state statutes provide for a limitation of liability for bailed goods and the dollar amount to which innkeepers may limit their liability. For this reason, most guest rooms contain a safe, and on the back of most guest room doors is a limitation of liability for personal property left in the room.

> **Example:** While on vacation, Joshua visited the hotel's pool area and left his cell phone in his room in plain sight. The hotel room included a safe in the room and limited the liability for personal property to $250 in the fine print on the back of the guest room door. When Joshua returned to the room, his cell phone was missing. The hotel was not strictly liable, and the bailor must prove negligence on the hotel's part to recover damages resulting from the loss of the phone. Even if Joshua, the bailor, can prove negligence on the hotel's part, the hotel will be limited to $250 in damages because of the notice provided to Joshua as a hotel guest.

Bailment cases often appear deceptively simple but in fact present difficult issues. When courts are unable to clearly apply one of these categories to a set of facts, a standard of reasonableness under the circumstances is adopted for that case. In these cases, the bailee has the duty to exercise the degree of care of a reasonably careful owner of the personal property.

Some jurisdictions permit bailees to limit or be exempt from liability arising out of ordinary negligence under what are known as **exculpatory clauses**. For example, goods left in a storage locker might be stolen, but the bailor's damages might be limited to a refund of the storage fees instead of the value of the locker's contents. Where bailors have abandoned property or neglected to pay fees, state statutes will assist the bailee in selling or disposing of goods and permit the bailee to lawfully sell the bailed property. For example, self-storage companies can conduct public sales of stored goods for nonpayment of storage fees.

Exculpatory clause Allow bailees to limit or be exempt from liability arising out of ordinary negligence.

In the following case, the duties of a bailee to protect a dog that was left in the bailee's care for grooming are discussed.

CASE 38.2

BAILEE MUST OVERCOME A REBUTTAL PRESUMPTION OF NEGLIGENCE

AKIVA v. JURENCI

2015 Ill. App. 142977

Appellate Court of Illinois

Cathy Akiva brought her two dogs to the home and business of Susan Jurenci to have them groomed. Twenty minutes after Akiva left, Jurenci noticed one of the dogs, Lavan, had to relieve himself. Jurenci proceeded to put a leash on Lavan and take him out in front of her home. While outside, Jurenci noticed an unfamiliar man pull up to her driveway with a large dog in the back seat. When the man let the dog out of the back seat, it lunged at Lavan and began attacking him. Jurenci attempted to get the large dog off Lavan; however, Lavan sustained serious injuries. After the attack, Jurenci took Lavan to the nearby animal hospital. The veterinarian was unable to save the dog. Jurenci then called Akiva and informed her that Lavan had been attacked and killed by another dog. Akiva later sued Jurenic for negligence and breach of bailment. The trial court found in favor of Jurenci, and Akiva appealed.

Language of the Court. *A bailment is the delivery of personal property for the accomplishment of some purpose, upon a contract, express or implied, that after the purpose has been fulfilled, the property shall be returned to the bailor. The elements necessary to sustain an action for a bailment include (1) an agreement, either express or implied, to create a bailment; (2) delivery of the property in good condition; (3) acceptance of the property by the bailee; and (4) failure by the bailee to return the property or the bailee's return of the property in a damaged condition.*

With respect to bailments for mutual benefit, generally, the bailee will be liable for losses that are proximately the result of the bailee's own negligence. When a plaintiff has established a prima face case, a rebuttable presumption that the defendant acted negligently arises. The burden then shifts to the defendant who must present sufficient evidence to support a finding that the presumed fact did not exist and that defendant was free from fault. If the defendant rebuts the presumption of negligence the plaintiff must offer evidence sufficient to sustain its negligence action as if the presumption did not exist. The plaintiff must establish that the defendant failed to exercise the necessary degree of care; the question is "whether the bailee's conduct was reasonable under the circumstances."

Here, the plaintiff presented some evidence to prove the existence of a bailment for mutual benefit and Jurenci's failure to return the bailed dog presumptively establishes her negligence. Accordingly, the burden shifted to Jurenci to prove that she exercised ordinary care and the loss of Lavan occurred without negligence on her part.

Jurenci's unrebutted testimony shows that the loss of Lavan occurred when an unknown dog escaped from his owner's care, raced toward Lavan, and attacked him while he was on a leash with Jurenci. During the attack, Jurenci did everything she was expected to do to stop the attack — she naturally attempted to protect Lavan by pushing and hitting the unknown dog. Since Jurenci did not recognize the dog, she had no way of knowing whether the dog's presence exposed Lavan to a risk greater than he experienced normally in his daily life.

Decision. The Appellate Court of Illinois affirmed the trial court's ruling in favor of Jurenci finding she was not negligent in the context of the bailment.

Focus on Ethics

If you are in possession of someone else's personal property, is it fair to owe different duties of care based on the type of bailment?

Management Application Pets and Bailment

Pet owners should be cautious when leaving their pets in the care of various professionals (boarders, groomers, etc.), especially when it comes to a pedigree or designer animal that is often much more expensive than the average pet. Although the boarder is a bailee in this situation, boarders' contracts often include clauses that limit their liability to the pet owner if the pet is injured or dies. This limitation might result in the pet owner receiving compensation for their loss that is far less than the cost of the pet. If such a clause is included in the contract, these boarders can insulate themselves from liability. So long as the clause specifically addresses this limitation and the pet owner agrees to the limitation, the boarder will only be held liable up to the stated amount, regardless of how negligent his acts were. Veterinarians may also include such liability limitations in their contracts to prevent themselves from being subjected to paying the full cost of the animal.

However, courts do not favor these limitations and will often exclude the limiting clause unless it is carefully drafted. Because of this, bailees of animals typically include another clause that limits their liability to the actual cost of the animal. This ensures that even if the court voids the provision that absolves the bailee from all liability, at least the bailee will not have to pay additional damages related to emotional distress or pain and suffering.

It is important for pet owners and business owners alike to understand the risks that are involved with pet bailments as both parties have much to lose should something happen to the animal.

Does this topic change your thinking relative to the boarding of your pet?

Duration and Termination of Bailments

The duties owed in a bailment typically terminate at a fixed time or when the purpose of the bailment is accomplished. If a vehicle is being serviced for an oil change, the bailment terminates when the owner returns to pick up the vehicle. Where a bailment is set for a fixed period, the parties may mutually consent to terminate the bailment early or extend the bailment beyond the original termination date. However, if a bailment for a fixed term is terminated prematurely by one party, that party may be liable for a breach of contract action for the improper termination of a bailment. Where no fixed time for the bailment is established, either party may terminate the bailment at any time.

> **Example:** John's car breaks down and his sister Kassandra has an additional, available car. If Kassandra lends her brother the car for the weekend only, she will have created a bailment for a fixed term. When she lends John the car until whenever his vehicle is repaired, a bailment at will has been created.

Artisan Liens

Recall the discussion in Chapter 31 on liens. Bailees also can obtain a lien for their work or services through what are known as artisan's liens. When a bailee is not paid for their work in accordance with the terms of the agreement, the bailee may remain in possession of the goods until payment is received.

> **Example:** A movie director entered into an agreement with a film editor for editing services. Here the editor became the bailee and the movie director became the bailor. The director refused to pay the editor for his services, so the editor retained all the film the director had given him until the editor received payment for his services. Upon payment for the editing service, the editor was required to return all the film back to the director. *Moynihan Associates, Inc. v. Hanisch*, 201 N.W.2d 534 (Wis. 1972)

When a bailee surrenders possession of the property to the bailor, the bailee has voluntarily released their lien against the bailor's property. The bailee would only be able to sue the bailor for a breach of contract for failure to pay for the services rendered. This would occur if the bailee returned the entirety of the goods possessed pursuant to the agreement. The return of a portion of the goods will not waive the bailee's lien.

> **Example:** In the previous example, the editor returned 5,000 feet of the film to the director but retained 33,000 feet of the film when the director refused to pay. The editor's partial delivery of the property back to the director did not waive the editor's artisan lien.

Management Application
Excerpted Bailment Agreement

BAILMENT AGREEMENT

THIS BAILMENT AGREEMENT (hereinafter referred to as "Agreement") is entered into as of April 1, 2025, by and between ABC Residential Staging (hereinafter referred to as "Bailee") and Lincoln Furniture (hereinafter referred to as "Bailor"). In recognition of the mutual promises, and other good and valuable consideration, receipt of which is hereby acknowledged, Bailor agrees to deliver, and Bailee agrees to accept the bailment of certain of Bailor's property, at the cost of $500 per month for each month, or part thereof, for which the Bailed Property is in the possession of Bailee, as described hereinbelow.

1. Description of Bailed Property

Bailor shall bail to the Bailee property (hereinafter "Property") identified as: one used coffee table with scratches and two used sofas.

2. Value of Property

The declared fair market value of the Property at the time of bailment to Bailee is as follows: coffee table: $3,500; and, two sofas: $10,000 ($5,000 each).

3. Place of Delivery

The Property shall be delivered to Bailee at 123 Main Street, Los Angeles, California, on or before June 30, 2025.

4. Place of Return

The Bailee shall return the Property to Bailor's place of business at 135 Furniture Way, Costa Mesa, CA 92626 on or before September 30, 2025, with transportation paid for by Bailee. The parties may extend this period of bailment.

5. Purpose

Bailee shall use the Property only for the purpose of staging a home for sale by Bailee. Bailee's use shall comply with all laws and regulations, and with applicable requirements and instructions so long as those applicable requirements and/or instructions are provided in writing by Bailor to Bailee.

6. Title and Transfer of Property

Title to the Property furnished pursuant to this Agreement shall remain with Bailor. Bailee shall not sell, transfer, lease, mortgage, borrow against, pledge, or otherwise create a legal or equitable interest by any third party in the Property.

7. Limitation of Liability

If the Property is lost or damaged from any cause during the term of this Agreement without Bailee's fault, Bailee will not be liable for that loss or damage. If the Property is lost or damaged during the term of this Agreement and the negligence of Bailee is established, Bailee's liability under this Agreement is limited to the value of the Property declared in paragraph 2 above.

Bailor agrees to inspect its Property upon redelivery to Bailor. Any claim of damages to or loss of Bailor's Property must be reported and itemized in writing within five (5) business days of receipt of its Property following delivery.

____
[Bailor]
By: ____________________

____
[Bailee]
By: ____________________

Lost, Mislaid, and Abandoned Property — Finders and Owners

Lost Property

Lost property Property that is involuntarily left somewhere.

Lost property is property that is involuntarily left somewhere. While the old children's adage "finders keepers, losers weepers" may contain some truth, the finder of lost personal property is in a position similar to that of an involuntary bailee. As such, the finder owes a slight duty of care to the property, meaning that they must avoid gross negligence and take minimal steps to safeguard it. The finder is entitled to possession and ownership of the lost property against everybody except the true owner but must return the property if the true owner is identified. If the finder loses the property again, the original finder retains the right to possession against all subsequent finders, but the true owner is always entitled to the property's return.

> **Example:** In a famous case from eighteenth-century English law, Armory, a chimney-sweep boy, found a jewel and took it to Delamirie's jewel shop, where a jewel shop employee examined it. Learning that it had some value, the shop owner instructed his employee to retain it and offer Armory money for the jewel. Armory refused the offer and demanded the return of the jewel. The shop owner kept the jewel, and the boy sued for damages. While neither party to the lawsuit was the actual owner, the court ruled in favor of Armory and granted Armory possession of the jewel. *Armory v. Delamirie*, King's Bench 1 Strange 505 (1722)

The finder acquires title to the property subject to a claim made by the rightful owner so long as the true owner makes the claim before the finder sells or otherwise disposes of the property. In the case of lost property, the rightful owner could request a court action for **replevin**. Replevin is an action in which the court exercises its equitable powers to order the turnover of the property to the true owner. Consistent with this treatment is the rule holding that a finder who takes another's personal property with the intention of keeping it, while knowing the true owner, is liable for conversion (a subject discussed in Chapter 5).

Replevin
A procedure in which seized goods are provisionally restored to a buyer depending on a court's determination of the rights of the parties concerned.

Mislaid Property

Mislaid property is property that is intentionally placed somewhere by the true owner and then forgotten or left there. It remains the property of the owner, and the owner is entitled to its return. With mislaid property, an involuntary bailment is created and the owner of the premises where the property is mislaid is a bailee of the property. The bailee has a duty of reasonable care until the property is returned to the owner. Unlike lost property, mislaid property retains more of a relationship with its true owner.

Mislaid property
Property that is intentionally placed by the true owner and then forgotten or left there.

> **Example:** Alex found $14,200 in the dresser drawer of his hotel. Alex notified the hotel manager, who then notified the police. The officer took the money, and it was held in trust by the city. Alex sued the city and the hotel, as he believed he was entitled to ownership of the money. The court ruled that the money was mislaid property and therefore should be held in trust by the hotel until retrieved by the true owner. *Franks v. Pritchett*, 197 S.W.3d 5 (Ark. Ct. App. 2004)

Abandoned Property

Abandoned property is property the owner has intentionally relinquished all rights to control or property that was lost or mislaid, and the owner has given up attempting to locate it. Title to abandoned personal property becomes that of anyone who finds it. The title that is acquired by the finder of abandoned property is good against the whole world, even the original owner.

Abandoned property
Property the owner has intentionally relinquished all rights to control. Also refers to property that was lost or mislaid and the owner has given up attempts to locate it.

> **Example:** A vehicle deemed abandoned by the Missouri State Patrol was sold at an auction. The purchasers of the vehicle discovered the vehicle had fuel problems. The purchasers took the vehicle to a mechanic who discovered that there was over $82,000 bundled in the fuel tank. The money was given to the government. Later the purchasers sought ownership of the money. The court found the money was abandoned and therefore belonged to the purchasers of the vehicle. *In re Seizure of $82,000 More or Less*, 119 F. Supp. 2d 1013 (W.D. Mo. 2000)

Estray Statute

Some states provide for estray statutes. An **estray statute** is a statute permitting a finder of lost or mislaid property to take title to the property, against even the true owner of the property. Several steps must be undertaken:

Estray statute
A statute that permits a finder of lost or mislaid property to take title to the property, against even the true owner.

1. The finder of the property reports the property to the appropriate government agency;
2. The property is advertised as having been found; and

3. The true owner does not claim the property after a lapse of time established by the statute.

Example: Bernice went to the bank to access her safety deposit box. While in one of the safety deposit box examination rooms, Bernice found $6,325. Bernice sued the bank, believing the money belonged to her because the state's estray statute was applicable. The court determined the money was considered "lost" and found the requirements of the estray statute were met. Therefore, Bernice was deemed the owner of the $6,325. *Paset v. Old Orchard Bank & Trust Co.*, 62 Ill. App. 3d 534 (1978)

CASE 38.3

A FINDER'S RIGHTS WILL DEPEND ON THE CLASSIFICATION OF THE PROPERTY

GRANDE v. JENNINGS

278 P.3d 1287 (2012)

Court of Appeals of Arizona

When Robert Spann died in 2001, his daughter, Karen Spann Grande, took charge of his home and made repairs to it. While Grande was in possession of the home, she found hundreds of military-style ammunition cans, some of which contained gold or cash. In 2008, Grande sold the home to Sarina Jennings and Clinton McCallum.

Jennings and McCallum hired Randy Bueghly to remodel the home. An employee of Bueghly, Rafael Cuen, later discovered two ammunition cans full of cash inside the framing of a kitchen wall and two more in the framing of an upstairs bathroom. When Cuen told Bueghly about the cans, Bueghly decided not to tell Jennings and McCallum. Eventually, Cuen informed Jennings and McCallum of his finding. Jennings and McCallum called the police, who took control of the $500,000 found within the cans. Jennings and McCallum filed suit against Bueghly, claiming he had no right to the money. Bueghly counterclaimed seeking a declaration of entitlement to the money. Grande also filed a petition on behalf of Robert Spann's estate to recover the money. The cases were consolidated for purpose of trial. Grande moved for summary judgment arguing Jennings and McCallum were not entitled to the money found. The motion was granted, and Jennings and McCallum appealed.

Language of the Court. *A finder's rights depend on how a court classifies the found property. In characterizing the property, a court should consider all of the particular facts and circumstances of the case. Under the common law, "the finder of lost or abandoned property and treasure trove acquires a right to possess the property against the entire world but the rightful owner regardless of the place of finding." A finder of mislaid property, however, must turn the property over to the* *premises owner, "who has the duty to safeguard the property for the true owner." In order to abandon personal property, one must voluntarily and intentionally give up a known right. Abandonment is a "virtual throwing away [of property] without regard as to who may take over or carry on." While personal property of all kinds may be abandoned, the property must have such a character as to make it clear that it was voluntarily abandoned by the owner.*

Here, it is undisputed that Spann placed the cash in the ammunition cans and then hid those cans in the recesses of the house. He did not, however, tell his daughters where he had hidden the cans before he passed away. His daughters looked for and found many of the ammo cans, but not the last four. Here, the facts are undisputed that the estate did not intend to abandon the funds. Once Grande learned of the discovery of the last four cans, she filed a probate petition to recover the property. As a result, and as the trial court found, the funds are, as a matter of law, mislaid funds that belong to the true owner, Spann's estate.

Based on the evidence before the trial court, there were no facts from which we could begin to infer that the estate intended to relinquish any valuable items that may have been secreted within the home.

Decision. The court of appeals affirmed the trial court's ruling, finding the $500,000 was mislaid and belonged to Grande.

Focus on Ethics

Do you think the court's decision was fair? Who should have received the money and why?

Concept Summary Involuntary Bailments

Property Type	Definition	Finder's Rights	Owner's Rights	Finder's Duty of Care
Lost Property	Property that is involuntarily left somewhere	The finder is entitled to possession and ownership of the lost property against everybody except the true owner.	Entitled to the property's return.	The finder is an involuntary bailee and owes a slight duty of care to the property.

Property Type	Definition	Finder's Rights	Owner's Rights	Finder's Duty of Care
Mislaid Property	Property that is intentionally placed somewhere and then forgotten.	The finder has no rights to the property.	Entitled to the property's return.	The owner of the premises has a duty of reasonable care to the property.
Abandoned Property	Property the owner has intentionally relinquished all rights to control.	Finder acquires ownership to abandoned property.	None	Not applicable.

AI Feature: Liability for Breach of Bailment

Use an AI program to draft a memorandum analyzing liability of the following bailee. Assume that late on a Friday afternoon Kevin drove his pickup truck to Ajax Automotive, an auto repair shop, to be serviced. Kevin parked the truck where Ajax directed him to park, which was in the open-access parking lot in the strip mall where Ajax was located. No other parking was available to the shop to store the truck. Kevin gave his keys to the shop manager after discussing the needed repairs. The shop was unable to work on the truck before the close of business. However, on the following Monday, the shop manager called to tell him that the truck had been stolen. The shop manager denies providing any assurances to Kevin that the shop would safeguard his truck when at the shop. Who wins and why?

Key Terms

- Abandoned property, 971
- Accession, 960
- Bailee, 960
- Bailment, 960
- Bailor, 960
- *Causa mortis* gift, 957
- Confusion, 960
- Constructive delivery, 957
- Donee, 956
- Donor, 956
- Estray statutes, 971
- Exculpatory clauses, 965
- Express bailment, 961
- Gift, 956

- Intangible property, 954
- *Inter vivos* gift, 956
- Involuntary bailment, 963
- Lost property, 970
- Mislaid property, 971
- Personal property, 954
- Replevin, 971
- Tangible property, 954

Applying the Law

38.1 Research the Law. Using an internet search engine, research the laws of your state to determine to what types of property its estray statute applies? Additionally, to whom and for how long is notice required to be given?

38.2 Bailee's Duties. Mamie Copelin deposited some of her clothes and those of her husband with Berlin Dye Works & Laundry Co. to have their garments cleaned. Copelin realized that she had left bank books, some of her rings, and an expensive pair of her earrings in the clothes. She telephoned the cleaning business, at which time the clothes had been washed and the bank books were damaged, and some of the rings were found, but the earrings remained missing. Was the business required to search the clothes and preserve articles left in their pockets? If an employee stole the expensive earrings found in the clothes, would the business be liable for the theft? See *Copelin v. Berlin Dye Works & Laundry Co.*, 168 Cal. 715 (1914)

38.3 Gifts. Michael Gruen sued his stepmother Kemija Gruen seeking a court declaration that he was the rightful owner of a valuable painting which he alleged his father, now deceased, gave to him. He never had possession of the painting but asserted that his father made a valid gift of the title in 1963 reserving a life estate for himself. His father retained possession of the painting until he died in 1980. Kemija Gruen took possession and refused Michael's requests that she turn it over to him. Did the father make a valid *inter vivos* gift? *Gruen v. Gruen*, 68 N.Y.2d 48 (1986)

38.4 Abandoned Property and Mislaid Property. Helen Sollars purchased a home from the probate estate of Helen Valoof. Following the sale, and while performing repairs, an electrician found bundles of money hidden above the ceiling of the basement of the house. The homeowner claimed that she was the rightful owner of the money found in the house. The real estate sale agreement required the estate to remove "all personal property (including trash and debris)" that was not a part of the transaction by 5:00 p.m. on the closing date. Because of the uncertainty about who owned the money, police seized and counted it and found that it totaled about $122,000. Sollars sued for the release of the money asserting that she was the rightful owner of the money found in her house. The estate filed its own motion for the return of things seized, asserting that it did not intend to transfer any right to the money when it sold the house to plaintiff and that it remained the rightful owner of the money. Is this a case of mislaid property or one of contract interpretation? Who prevails? *Sollars v. City of Milwaukie*, 222 Ore. App. 384 (2008)

38.5 Duty of a Bailee. Timothy Mason had his car towed to a Ford® dealer's lot for warranty service. The car was not placed in an interior garage space but was locked and parked in a lighted open lot close to the dealer's building. The keys were locked in the service department office. At some time overnight, the car was broken into and damaged, and its audio and stereo equipment was stolen. The owner filed suit against the dealer to recover for the damage and theft. The dealership stated that only expensive luxury cars, police cars, and cars which could not be locked were garaged when brought in for repair work. Should negligence of the bailee be presumed in this case? *Mason v. Hartford Hoffman Ford, Inc.*, 1994 Conn. Super. LEXIS 2090 (1994)

38.6 Whose Baseball? On October 7, 2001, at PacBell Park in San Francisco, Barry Bonds hit his 73rd home run. This event was widely anticipated, and many baseball fans understood the importance of the ball. Since it would be worth a lot of money, many people who attended the game prepared for the possibility that the ball would be hit in their direction. Both plaintiff Alex Popov and defendant Patrick Hayashi came prepared to catch the baseball. Both men brought baseball gloves and positioned themselves in the arcade section of the ballpark, the general area where Barry Bonds hit the greatest number of home runs. When the ball went into the arcade, it landed in Popov's glove. While reaching for the ball, Popov lost his balance. He was tackled and thrown to the ground while in the process of attempting to catch the ball. Hayashi was standing near Popov when the ball came into the stands. Like Popov, he was also forced to the ground. While on the ground, Hayashi saw the ball, picked it up, and put it in his pocket. Who owns the ball? Make arguments for both Popov and Hayashi. *Popov v. Hayashi*, 2002 WL 31833731 (Cal. Super. Ct. 2002)

38.7 Innkeeper's Standard of Care. Marvin L. Gooden checked into a Day's Inn® in Atlanta, Georgia for a two-day stay. The motel posted a sign which disclaimed liability for guests' valuables unless they were placed in the motel's safe. Gooden temporarily left his room, leaving a paper bag containing $9,000 filled with money. Later, a hotel housekeeper entered Gooden's room to clean it. She found the bag of money and upon seeing no other personal items, assumed that Gooden had checked out. The housekeeper turned the bag over to her supervisor. The supervisor absconded with the money. Was the motel liable for the theft of the guest's bag of money? Explain the standard of care involved in this case. *Gooden v. Day's Inn*, 395 S.E.2d 876 (1990)

38.8 Accepting a Gift. Victor Fleischman was judged to be incompetent, and his son Richard began managing Victor's affairs. A year later, Richard gifted Victor's six grandchildren with checks for $10,000 drawn on Victor's account. Mickey, one of the six grandchildren and Richard's nephew, received his check. But, at his mother's request, he did not negotiate the check. The check was never cashed. Later, Mickey requested a replacement check from his uncle, but his uncle refused. He contended that Mickey did not accept the check as a gift when he did not immediately cash it. Did Mickey accept the check so that he was entitled to the funds? *Sinclair v. Fleischman*, 773 P.2d 101 (Wash. Ct. App. 1989)

38.9 Redelivery of Bailed Property. Plaintiff, Jonathan D. Morgenstern, alleged that Eastman Kodak Company® failed and neglected to develop and return his rolls of film. Morgenstern sent Kodak rolls of film for developing in prepaid processing mailers. Prepaid mailers are often used as an alternative to personally delivering the film to a local photo developer. When purchasing a mailer, customers placed the roll of film in the mailer and labeled the mailer with their return address. Kodak processed the film and delivered the prints to the post office to deliver them to the address supplied. Did Kodak breach the bailment agreement by not redelivering the film in the form of prints to Morgenstern? *Morgenstern v. Eastman Kodak Co.*, 569 F. Supp. 474 (N.D. Ohio 1983)

38.10 Finder. Jake Flax occupied a room at the Monticello Hotel, in Norfolk, Virginia. Flax left his hotel room in the morning, and when he returned to his room in the evening noticed a pear-shaped diamond brooch on the dresser. Mr. Wilder, a friend of Flax, suggested the brooch be placed in the custody of the hotel manager. Flax agreed and it was his understanding that if no one had claimed the brooch, it would be returned to him. Upon further investigation it was found that a hotel housekeeper had discovered the brooch, wrapped in tissue paper, concealed in a crevice in the margin of the bed in Flax's room and placed it on the dresser, thinking that Flax was the owner. Was the location where the brooch was found to be a significant fact? Who has standing to take ownership of the brooch? *Flax v. Monticello Realty Co.*, 39 S.E.2d 308 (Va. 1946)

Real Property and Landlord-Tenant Law

39

The first person who, having fenced off a plot of ground, took it into his head to say this is mine and found people simple enough to believe him, was the true founder of civil society. — Jean Jacques Rosseau, *Discourse on the Origins and Foundations of Inequality Among Men, Part 2 (1775)*

Chapter Outline

- Introduction
- Real Property
- Real Property Estates
- Concurrent Ownership

Case 39.1: *Perretta v. Perretta*

- Nonpossessory Interests
  - *Management Application: Excerpted Easement Agreement*
- Transfer of Ownership of Real Property
  - *Management Application: Quitclaim Deed*

Case 39.2: *Jaffer v. Hirji*

- Eminent Domain and Regulatory Takings
- Landlord-Tenant Law
  - *Management Application: Rental Rates for Commercial Properties*

Case 39.3: *Terry v. O'Brien*

- AI Feature: Draft a Conveyance of Air Rights Agreement

Learning Objectives

After studying this chapter, you should be able to:

1. Distinguish real property from personal property.
2. Describe various interests in real property.
3. Explain the nature of concurrent ownership interests.
4. Distinguish among common types of deeds.
5. Explain the rights of landlords and tenants.
6. Distinguish assignments from subleases.

Introduction

The previous chapter focused on the rights and duties associated with the ownership of personal property. This chapter will focus upon the rights and duties associated with the ownership of real property. In this chapter, we also will review both residential and commercial leases and the terminology used in lease transactions.

Real Property

Real property
The earth and all that is permanently attached and connected to it.

Real property is commonly characterized as the earth and all that is permanently attached to it (fixtures). "Land" refers to any unimproved real property. The right to own and possess land carries with it certain rights, duties, and liabilities that will be discussed in this chapter. Real estate law is governed by a complex set of rules, statutes, and regulations that govern social and economic order among individuals and businesses in society.

> **Example:** Real property includes land, buildings, landscaping, pools, mineral rights, water rights, and air rights.

LAND AND BUILDINGS. Land is the most common form of real property and includes the surface of the earth. Land may be subjected to various governmental regulations that specify the way the land may be used. Absent these regulations, landowners may use the property as they desire, so long as the use does not result in injury to others. Buildings located on land are considered real property and may also be subject to regulations concerning their use or appearance.

Air right
The right to use and develop the airspace located above the surface of the earth.

AIR RIGHTS. Air rights allow an owner to use and develop the airspace located above the surface of the earth. Most state laws recognize that within limitations the landowner owns the air rights. Absent a restriction, landowners are free to build upon land below navigable airspace as they wish. Navigable airspace is the airspace above the minimum safe altitude established by the Federal Aviation Administration. These rights allow a landowner to construct buildings and other structures so long as they comply with any other restriction imposed on the land. Air rights may also be sold separately from a landowner's surface rights. Entering into another's airspace without permission is a trespass.

SUBSURFACE RIGHTS. Like air rights, a property's subsurface rights can also be sold separately from its surface rights. The most common subsurface rights are in oil and gas. Generally, oil and gas deposits are classified as minerals, and the subsurface landowner owns the minerals. When they are below the surface, minerals are real property; once extracted they become personal property. The owner of the land may convey mineral rights to another or reserve the mineral rights for themself when they convey land to another. As with air rights, it constitutes a trespass to enter another person's subsurface area without permission.

Water rights
The rights to use water.

WATER RIGHTS. Water rights are the right to use water. Water rights, like air rights, are real property interests. Due to the varied geography of the United States, states have adopted different legal approaches to dealing with water rights. Two common law forms of ownership — riparian rights and the prior appropriation doctrine — have been adopted in the United States. The eastern states, and most of the other states, follow the riparian rights doctrine while the western states have adopted the prior appropriation doctrine. Depending on which law is employed, the rights to own, use, and allocate water differ. However, there is a modern trend in which the states will regulate water rights instead of following one of the two common law methods.

FIXTURES. A **fixture** is personal property that has become so attached to the real property that it loses its identity as personal property. Fixtures pass with the transfer of title to real property, while title to personal property remains in possession of the holder and does not transfer with the sale or conveyance of real property. In the absence of an agreement between the parties, a fixture is owned by the owner of the land upon which the structure is permanently affixed.

Fixture
Personal property that has become so attached to the real property that it loses its identity as personal property.

> **Example:** Leo and Elsa purchase lumber and supplies at a home improvement center and construct an attic bedroom. The supplies were personal property when they were transported to their home, but they became a fixture once they were installed.

The courts have developed many tests, guidelines, and rules to determine whether something is a fixture, and these tests consider all of the particular facts of a given case.

PLANT LIFE AND VEGETATION. Plant life and vegetation consist of crops, trees, bushes, and grasses that are attached or affixed to the land. They may be considered real property or personal property. Depending upon who planted them, the next harvest may belong to the land purchaser or be retained by the seller.

Real Property Estates

The subject of estates and interests entails an understanding of several concepts and a few vocabulary terms. An estate is an interest in land that has two characteristics — the right to possess the land and the length of time ownership may last.

Fee Simple

Fee simple (also known as fee simple absolute) is complete ownership of real property lasting until the end of time. A fee simple is the type of ownership most people think about when they consider someone owning real property. A holder of a fee simple absolute interest may sell, gift, or convey the interest during their lifetime. Upon the holder of the fee simple's death, the property will pass to the owner's heirs or persons stated in their will.

Fee simple
Ownership that is characterized as complete ownership lasting until the end of time.

Life Estates

One of the oldest types of a freehold estate is the life estate. A **life estate** arises where property is held for a person's lifespan. When the person whose life the life estate is measured dies, the life estate terminates and often will pass back to the grantor or to third

Life estate
An estate in which the property is held for the duration of a person's lifespan.

persons as provided for in the life estate. The person holding the life estate interest is the life tenant.

The holder of a life estate has the right to use and possess the property, but not to the extent of permanently impairing the property's value. This is known as waste. The holder of the life estate may not unreasonably use the property such that its nature, character, and improvements are lost to the holder of the future interest.

Example: "To Claire for life" is a life estate that will last for Claire's lifetime.

Concurrent Ownership

Concurrent ownership means that two or more persons own the same property at the same time. It is considered a form of joint ownership. The laws under which the real property is held determine which form of concurrent ownership is available. There are four main forms of concurrent ownership of property: (1) tenancy in common, (2) joint tenancy, (3) tenancy by the entirety, and (4) community property.

Tenancy in Common

Tenancy in common A form of co-ownership of real property in which parties may hold equal or unequal shares in the land and have separate but undivided interests in the entire property.

Tenancy in common is a form of co-ownership of real property in which persons may hold equal or unequal shares in the land and have separate but undivided interests in the entire property. An undivided interest allows a tenant in common to share in the whole of the property, not just the portion of the interest owned. A tenancy in common status is presumed unless contrary intent is expressed.

No survivorship rights exist between tenants in common. If one tenant in common dies, the other remaining tenants in common do not automatically inherit the interest of the deceased tenant in common.

Each tenant may sell, or convey by deed or will, their interest in the property. The grantee receives the same interest that the grantor owned unless the grantor conveyed to the grantee less than their full interest.

The following case expands on the premise that tenants in common are to share in the whole of the property, and not just a portion of the interest. In the following case, one of the tenants in common was living on the property and the other tenants in common believed he owed them rent for his use of the property.

CASE 39.1

PARTITION OF TENANCY IN COMMON MAY BE PREJUDICIAL

PERRETTA v. PERRETTA

143 A.D. 3d 878 (2016)

Appellate Division of the Supreme Court of New York

Louis J. Perretta, Anne-Marie Albicocco, Louis A. Perretta, Josephine Hydock, Frank Perretta Jr., and Anthony Perretta owned a four-family brownstone in the Cobble Hill neighborhood in Brooklyn as tenants in common. Anthony lived in the garden apartment on the first floor of the building with his two adult daughters. None of the other owners lived in the building, and the three remaining apartments were rented to tenants. The other owners brought a suit against Anthony, seeking partition and sale of the property to recover rent they believed they were owed for Anthony's use and occupancy. The other owners asserted that Anthony had been living on the property rent-free and had allowed the three other apartments to be rented to other tenants at below-market rates without written lease agreements. The owners moved for summary judgment on their cause of action for partition and sale. In response, Anthony moved to dismiss the cause of action to recover the unpaid rent, use, and occupancy. The trial court granted Anthony's motion to dismiss, and the other owners appealed.

Language of the Court. *"A person holding and in possession of real property as a joint tenant or tenant in common, in which he [or she] has an estate of inheritance, or for life, or for years, may maintain an action for the partition of the property, and for a sale if it appears that a partition cannot be made without great prejudice to the owners." "The right to partition is not absolute, however, and while a tenant in common has the right to maintain an action for partition, the remedy is always subject to the equities between the parties." Thus, the Supreme Court properly denied the plaintiff's motion which sought a sale of the property.*

The Supreme Court also properly granted that branch of the defendants' cross motion which was to dismiss the cause of action to recover unpaid rent, use, and occupancy. In considering a motion to dismiss for failure to state a cause of action the court should "accept the facts as alleged in the complaint as true, accord plaintiffs the benefit of every possible favorable inference, and determine only whether the facts as alleged fit within any cognizable legal theory." "A tenant in common 'has the right to take and occupy the whole of the premises and preserve them from waste or injury, so long as he or she does not interfere with the right of [the other tenant] to also occupy the premises.' " One tenant in common is generally not liable to another for use and occupancy, in the absence of an agreement or ouster. Here, the complaint failed to allege either ouster or the existence of any agreement that required the defendants to pay rent, use, and occupancy.

Decision. The appellate court affirmed the trial court's ruling granting the motion to dismiss.

Focus on Ethics

Is it fair that Anthony received a greater benefit from the use of the property than the other tenants in common? What would be the fair solution if all parties wanted to use the property in the same manner as Anthony?

Joint tenancy
A form of concurrent ownership in which two or more persons own equal shares of property, with the right of survivorship between the joint tenants.

Right of survivorship
Upon the death of one joint tenant, the surviving joint tenants automatically receive equal shares from the deceased joint tenant.

Joint Tenancy

Joint tenancy is a form of concurrent ownership in which two or more persons own equal shares of property, with the **right of survivorship** between the joint tenants. While each joint tenant owns an equal share, each joint tenant also has an equal right to possession. The biggest advantage to holding property in this manner is that upon the death of the joint tenant, the property is automatically transferred to the surviving joint tenant(s).

Because of the right of survivorship, joint tenancies are popular between spouses. The disadvantage of titling property this way arises when joint tenancy is held between unrelated parties. A joint tenant's heirs will not inherit anything if that person predeceases the other joint tenants.

Most states require express language of "joint tenants" or "joint tenants with the right of survivorship" to create a joint tenancy. These states demand clear expressions of intent to overcome the presumption of tenancy in common. In addition, states require that four characteristics of unity must be present to create a joint tenancy: (1) time, (2) title, (3) interest, and (4) possession. Where a unity is missing, the interest is held as a tenant in common.

A joint tenancy interest can be severed by conveyance, simultaneous death of the joint tenants, or by mortgaging the joint tenancy property.

Tenancy by the Entirety

Tenancy by the entirety
A form of joint tenancy limited to married couples.

Tenancy by the entirety is a form of joint tenancy limited to married couples. About half of the states allow for this form of spousal ownership. Many of the states that do not recognize tenancy by the entirety recognize community property instead.

The creation of an interest held in tenancy by the entirety is similar to the creation of joint tenancy because it requires the presence of the four unities of joint tenancy (time, title, interest, and possession) plus a fifth: unity of person. Unity of person requires that the parties be married at the time they acquire the property. In states that provide for tenancy by the entirety, most states presume that a conveyance to the spouses creates a tenancy by the entirety, unless the deed states otherwise.

In this form of title, unlike joint tenancy, the survivorship right cannot be destroyed by the acts of one spouse. Most states require that both spouses act to terminate the interest. A divorce or dissolution of marriage terminates a tenancy by the entirety interest and converts the interest into the tenancy in common with each former spouse owning a one-half interest.

Concept Summary Concurrent Estates

Type	Creation	Interest	Features	Termination
Tenancy in Common	Deed, inheritance, gift, or intestate succession.	Each co-tenant acquires the right to possession of the whole property, regardless of the actual share owned. Interest may be freely conveyed by any co-tenant.	Presumption of tenancy in common whenever there is a conveyance to two or more people.	Partitioned by mutual agreement of the co-tenants or if decided by the court.

Type	Creation	Interest	Features	Termination
Joint Tenancy	Requires: 1. Time 2. Title 3. Interest 4. Possession Cannot be created through intestate succession.	Each co-tenant acquires the right to possession of the whole property, regardless of the actual share owned. Right of survivorship prevents free conveyance of interest; surviving joint tenants automatically receive equal shares from the deceased joint tenant.	Common Law: Presumption of tenancy in common whenever there is a conveyance to two or more people. Conveyance: If a transferee receives an interest from one of the co-tenants, the transferee will be a tenant in common, while the remaining original co-tenants are still joint tenants.	Partitioned by mutual agreement of the co-tenants or if decided by the court.
Tenancy by the Entirety	Requires the four above-mentioned unities AND: 5. Unity of person	Each co-tenant acquires the right to possession of the whole property, regardless of the actual share owned. Interest may be freely conveyed by any co-tenant.	If conveyance is made to two people who are not married, the conveyance will fail as a tenancy by the entirety; in most states it will be deemed a tenancy in common.	Partitioned by mutual agreement of the co-tenants or if decided by the court.

Community Property

A minority of states have adopted community property as a form of spousal ownership. Community property origination is traceable to French and Spanish legal influences in the southern and western parts of the United States. While many variations of the community property system are found among these states, generally, absent an agreement to the contrary, assets and liabilities acquired during the marriage by the labor of either spouse are presumed to be **community property**.

Community property Property acquired during marriage that is owned equally by the spouses.

The laws in each state may differ slightly when determining how property is to be divided. The spouse could change the status of property by entering into a premarital or postnuptial agreement. Both spouses enjoy equal ownership and equal control over the community assets; therefore, neither spouse can sell or transfer community property without the consent of the other spouse. The concept of community property is that both the spouses contribute to the financial success of the marriage, and both should share equally in the results. Once property is characterized as community property, income generated from that property is also deemed community property. Assets purchased with community funds are also considered community property.

Nonpossessory Interests

Nonpossessory interests
An interest in land that constitutes less than full possession or ownership of the land.

Nonpossessory interests are valuable real property rights. A nonpossessory interest is an interest in land that constitutes less than full possession or ownership of the land. It provides some right of entry to or use of another's land. Users and owners of land often desire to use the land of another owner. Nonpossessory rights can be granted either temporarily or permanently.

> **Example:** Examples of nonpossessory rights include easements, profits, and licenses.

Easements

Easements
A right of a person to use the land of another for a specific purpose.

An **easement** gives its owner the right to use another's land for a specific purpose. When an easement exists, two parties are involved: the holder of the easement and the landowner whose use of the land is subject to the rights of the easement holder. These two parties may simultaneously make use of the same land.

Easements are common and are used for such purposes as giving a public utility the right to install and maintain utility services across property boundaries and allowing a neighbor to use a private driveway to gain access to adjacent property. Easements play a significant role in the use, development, and taxation of real property.

CLASSIFICATION OF EASEMENTS

Easement appurtenant
An easement that benefits a particular parcel of land, rather than conferring a personal benefit upon the holder of the easement.

Easements are classified as either appurtenant or in gross. An **easement appurtenant** is one that benefits a particular parcel of land, rather than conferring a personal benefit upon the holder of the easement. Easements appurtenant require the existence of at least two parcels of land. The party whose land is benefited is the dominant estate or the dominant tenement, and the party whose land is burdened by the easement is the servient estate or the servient tenement. Easements appurtenant run with the land. This means that once created the easement automatically transfers when the property is conveyed, even if the easement is not expressly mentioned in the conveyance.

> **Example:** Andre owns a home that cannot be accessed by means of the public road. His neighbor, Sami, agrees to let Andre use a driveway across her property so that Andre can access the public road. If Andre sells the property and is no longer neighbors with Sami, Andre will also no longer have an easement across Sami's property. However, the purchaser of Andre's property will retain the easement across Sami's property.

Easement in gross
An easement that benefits a person, regardless of whether that person owns any land at all.

An **easement in gross** is a personal benefit granted to someone to make limited use of another person's property. It is not tied to ownership but rather use of real property. Generally, such an easement cannot be conveyed to a third party. Subject to the terms of an easement agreement, they are often granted for specific purposes and last only for the life of the holder or until a specified event occurs. In special cases they may last in perpetuity as they are considered permanent and will continue even if the property ownership changes; an example of such an easement in gross is a public utility easement.

> **Example:** Marta obtained an easement providing her with the right to water ski on a privately owned lake. This easement is not transferable by her to another person.

While an easement appurtenant is attached to a piece of property, an easement in gross is attached to a specific individual or entity. Generally, if there is ambiguity as to the type of easement at issue, courts will hold the easement to be appurtenant in form. For this reason, an easement in gross must be clearly stated.

CREATION OF EASEMENTS. Most easements are created by grant, estoppel, necessity, implication, or prescription.

Easements by Grant. **Easements by grant** are those created by an express agreement. Most easements are easements by grant created by either a deed or another legal document. When created by grant, the easement must satisfy the requirements of the state's Statute of Frauds. Most states require that the easement be in writing, signed by the grantor, and recorded.

Easement by grant
An easement created by an express agreement.

Easements by Estoppel. Easements by estoppel arise when either through words or actions the owner of land leads another person to believe that they have an easement. It is created to prevent unfairness to the person who detrimentally relies upon the representation made by the owner of the land; however, not all states recognize an easement by estoppel.

> **Example:** Family members purchased two adjacent parcels, drilled a well on the defendant's property, and jointly installed equipment so both properties received water from the well. Relying on being able to receive water from the well, the plaintiffs built a residence on their land, which had no other source of water. A dispute arose over access to the well water, the court found it would be an injustice if the easement by estoppel were not recognized. *Mund v. English*, 684 P.2d 1248, Or. Ct. App. (1984)

Easements by Necessity. An easement by necessity is recognized when an owner conveys land to another to which there is no access except over the grantor's adjacent other property or over the land of strangers. The conveyed land is landlocked (without access). An easement for a right of way between the landlocked parcel to a public road, across the original owner's retained land, then becomes necessary. Courts grant easements because it is assumed that the parties would not have intended to render land unfit for occupancy.

The necessity must be present at the time of the original transfer and at the time the easement is asserted. Such an easement ends when the necessity for the easement ends.

Easements by Implication. Easements by implication are also known as easements implied by a prior or preexisting use. They arise where, before a unified tract of land was severed into smaller parcels, the landowner used one section of their unified tract in a way that benefited another portion of the land. For example, an original owner may continue to use an access road over severed parcels to reach a public street.

An easement by implication is permanent and continues even if the need for the easement no longer exists. Implied easements are not recorded on titles to real property. They reflect the practical use of the property.

Easements by Prescription. Easements may also be created by prescription. This is a concept equivalent to adverse possession (discussed below); that is, the easement allows someone to gain the right to use another's real property without their express permission. Prescriptive easements are available on private property but are prohibited on public land. After the statutory requirements are met, the user may continue to use the real property in a specific way. For example, a neighbor could gain prescriptive use to park a motorhome on adjacent property.

Management Application
Excerpted Easement Agreement

EASEMENT AGREEMENT

THIS AGREEMENT made and entered into this [date], by and between XYZ, a [State] [Entity type], (hereinafter referred to as "Grantor"), and ABC corporation, a [State] [Entity type] (hereinafter referred to as "Grantee").

Recitals

WHEREAS, Grantor owns certain real property, located in [city], [county], [state], legally described in the attached Exhibit A, which is incorporated into this Agreement by reference.

WHEREAS, Grantee seeks to park vehicles on Grantor's property.

WHEREAS, Grantee shall compensate Grantor for the duration of the easement stated herein as set forth in this Agreement.

In consideration of the foregoing recitals, the mutual promises and obligations contained herein, the Grantor and Grantee hereby covenant and agree as follows:

1. Grant of Easement

   This right of access allows Grantee to park vehicles in the Easement Area as long as that use does not unreasonably interfere with Grantor's use and enjoyment of the Servient Tenement.

   . . .

Profits

Profit
The right to enter another's land and take something from the land.

A **profit** (short for a *profit a prendre*) is the right to enter another's land and take something from it. These rights do not grant the profit holder the right of full possession of the land. The difference between an easement and a profit is that an easement gives the holder the right to use another's land, whereas a profit gives the holder the right to take something from the land. Easements do not allow for the removal of resources. Common examples of profits include the right to remove timber, crops, or sand and gravel.

License

A **license** is permission to enter the licensor's property. Unlike easements, licenses are often created informally. They are usually temporary and are revocable unless the parties otherwise agree. Licensees do not have possession but only a limited right to use the owner's land for a particular purpose or activity.

License
The privilege to use the land of another; usually temporary and revocable.

Concept Summary Nonpossessory Interests

Type	Description
Easement	The right to use the land of another for a specific purpose
Profit	The right to enter the land of another and take something from it
License	The privilege to use the land of another; temporary and revocable

Transfer of Ownership of Real Property

Title is the ownership of land. When title is known, the ownership of real property allows a person to transfer title of an estate from one person to another. The transfer usually takes one of several forms: sale, gift, testamentary transfer, or adverse possession.

Title
Evidence of ownership of land passed by a deed or court order.

The sale of property is the most common method of transferring real property ownership rights. After a buyer is located by the seller or their agent, a real estate sales contract is executed. Typically, this contract is required by the Statute of Frauds to be in writing. At the closing or settlement, the seller will deliver the deed to the buyer in exchange for the purchase price of the property. Failure to perform may result in a lawsuit in which the breaching party may be found liable for monetary damages or be required to perform as specified by the sales contract.

Deeds

Deeds are written instruments used to transfer real property from one person, the **grantor** (seller or donor), to another person, the **grantee** (buyer or recipient). While no deed can convey more than what a grantor possesses, the extent of the interest conveyed can vary. Such a transfer can be a fee simple interest or an estate less extensive than a fee simple, such as a life estate.

Deeds
Written instruments used to convey (transfer) real property.

Grantor
The seller or donor.

Grantee
The buyer or recipient.

TYPES OF DEEDS. State laws recognize distinct types of deeds. These deeds provide differing covenants and warranties and protection to the grantees. Among the most common types of deeds are the following:

1. General Warranty Deed
2. Special Warranty Deed
3. Quitclaim Deed

General warranty deed
A deed containing a full warranty and set of promises by the grantor to the grantee.

General Warranty Deed. A **general warranty deed** transfers the ownership of real property from the grantor to the grantee. It offers comprehensive guarantees to the property's title through six covenants (warranties) to the grantee. The six covenants are subdivided into three present and three future covenants.

The three present covenants include the following:

1. *Seisin.* Grantor conveys that they own the interest conveyed to the grantee.
2. *The right to convey.* Grantor warrants that they have the legal right and the power to convey title.
3. *Covenant against encumbrances.* The grantor promises that the property has no undisclosed encumbrance.

The three future covenants include the following:

1. *Covenant of warranty.* The grantor promises to defend and compensate the grantee for any loss resulting from all claims arising from a defect in the purported title.
2. *Covenant of quiet enjoyment.* The grantor promises the grantee's possession or enjoyment will not be disturbed by a third party's assertion of superior title.
3. *Covenant of further assurances.* The grantor promises to perform whatever acts are reasonably necessary to cure a defect in the grantee's title.

Special warranty deed
A deed containing the same warranties as a general warranty deed, but the grantor warrants that they have not caused any defects in the title during their ownership.

Special Warranty Deed. The **special warranty deed** contains the same warranties as a general warranty deed, with one major difference regarding the covenant period. In a special warranty deed, the grantor warrants that they have not caused any defects in the title during their ownership. With a general warranty deed, the grantor warrants that no one has ever caused any defects in the title.

Quitclaim deed
A deed in which the grantor coveys whatever interest, if any, the grantor has in a specific piece of property.

Quitclaim Deed. A **quitclaim deed** is a deed in which the grantor conveys whatever interest, if any, they have in a specific piece of property. In essence, the grantor states, "If I hold an interest, and I may in fact own no interest in the property, I am conveying whatever it is I do own to you." With a quitclaim deed, the grantee receives no protections and no warranties regarding title to the property.

Upon acceptance of the quitclaim deed, the grantee holds whatever interest the grantor had in the real property. If the grantor holds no interest at all, no interest passes. This is the weakest form of deed and is often used as a means of removing any ambiguities in the record of title.

Management Application
Quitclaim Deed

Prepared by: [Property Owner's Name]

QUITCLAIM DEED

On February 2, 2025, THE GRANTOR, [Property Owner's Name], an unmarried individual, enters into this agreement.

The Grantor, for and in consideration of the sum of Four Hundred Thousand Dollars ($400,000) and/or other good and valuable consideration, conveys, releases, and quitclaims to the following GRANTEE property described by this Deed:

— [Buyer's Name], an unmarried individual

The Grantor quitclaims the following described real estate, situated at the following address:

— 123 Main Street, Los Angeles, CA 90007

The property being quitclaimed has the following legal description:

— Lots 6, 7, and the North ½ of Lot 4, East 60 feet of North ½ of Lot 5, West 60 feet of Lot 2, OLD SURVEY, Los Angeles.

The property being quitclaimed has the following tax parcel number:

— 086-1-143-647

Future tax statements should be mailed to the following address:

— 456 Realist State Way, Newport Coast, CA 92507

The Grantor does hereby convey, release, and quitclaim all of the Grantor's rights, title, and interest in and to the above-described property and premises to the Grantee, and to the Grantee heirs and assigns forever, so that neither Grantor nor Grantor's heirs, legal representatives or assigns shall have, claim, or demand any right or title to the property, premises, or appurtenances, or any part thereof.

Concept Summary
Deeds

Types of Deeds	
General Warranty Deed	The grantor guarantees that they hold clear title to the property and has the right to convey. Includes six covenants and affords highest level of protection to grantee.

Types of Deeds	
Special Warranty Deed	Provides the same warranties as a general deed and also warrants the grantor has not caused any defects in title of the property; however, these warranties are only for the time period in which the grantor owned the property.
Quitclaim Deed	Grantor conveys whatever interest, if any, they have in the property.

Recording statute
A state statute providing that constructive notice is deemed to have been given to third parties by virtue of filing a document in the public domain.

RECORDING STATUTES. All states have enacted a **recording statute**. These statutes are intended to protect title by preventing fraud. Recorded deeds can be searched by either prospective purchasers or lenders to determine what type of title, if any, is owned by the prospective seller or debtor. Recording statutes are also used to establish the priority of rights between conflicting deeds on a particular property.

> **Example:** Regan purchases an unimproved lot from Geri. Regan takes title but does not record the deed. Unknown to Regan, Geri sells the same property to Karin, who is unaware that Geri has already sold the property to Regan. Karin records the deed.

All states provide that instruments affecting title to land may be recorded, including purchase contracts, leases, mortgages, deeds of trust, liens, judgments, and financing statements. A county recorder, clerk of the court, or registrar of deeds is the public official charged with operating the office in accordance with state law.

Adverse Possession

Adverse possession
A method of acquiring title by wrongfully possessing the real property of another, subject to state law requirements.

Under the doctrine of **adverse possession**, a person obtains ownership of another's real property if certain conditions are met. This doctrine rewards a trespasser with title to the property. Moreover, the adverse possessor is not liable to the original owner for the loss of title to the property. This odd concept encourages the full and beneficial use of land and can be used to help resolve disputed boundary lines between properties.

Each state has specific requirements for acquiring title by adverse possession. Adverse possession is either recognized by statute or by complying with common law requirements. One common element is that adverse possession can only occur on privately owned property; it does not apply to publicly owned property such as federally or state-owned land. In some states, the adverse possessor must pay taxes. Generally, the requirements that enable adverse possession are as follows:

1. Adverse to that of the landowner
   - □ Met when the adverse possessor takes possession without the owner's permission and in a manner that is inconsistent with the true owner's legal title to the property.
2. Actual possession
   - □ Requires that the adverse possessor use the property in a manner consistent with its nature and use based on a community standard.

3. Exclusive possession
   - ☐ Exclusive typically means that the adverse possessor cannot share possession with the legal titleholder of the property or with the general public.
4. Open, visible, and notorious
   - ☐ Requires that the adverse possessor's acts be visible and obvious enough to put a reasonable owner on notice that someone is attempting to claim the property. However, it is not necessary that the landowner be aware that the adverse possessor has taken possession of the property.
5. Continuous for the statutory period
   - ☐ The adverse possessor must continuously occupy the property without significant interruption during the statutory period. These specific state periods vary from 3 years (Arizona) to 30 years (New Jersey) and may impose longer periods for woodland properties. Some states allow the possessor to tack-on the possession time of their predecessor to satisfy the statutory period.

Each element must be present to enable an adverse possessor to acquire title by adverse possession. Whether each of them is present is a question of fact and a burden that the adverse possessor must prove.

In the following case, an intra-family dispute over ownership of a residential house developed. The occupants asserted an adverse possession claim.

CASE 39.2

ADVERSE POSSESSION STRICTLY CONSTRUED WHEN THE PARTIES HAVE A CLOSE RELATIONSHIP WITH EACH OTHER

JAFFER v. HIRJI

887 F.3D 111 (2019)

United States Court of Appeals for the Second Circuit

Mohamed Hirji originally purchased a residential house in Hartsdale, New York, in 1982. Title to the property was placed in the names of his sons Ahmed Hirji and Mustafa Hirji. According to the attorney who represented Mohamed at the purchase, Mohamed intended the property to be "a place that the family could reside in." A few years later, Ahmed and Mustafa Hirji transferred the title to their father and their brother Naushad Hirji as joint tenants with the right of survivorship. Mohamed and Defendant Naushad paid no consideration. Mohamed died and his interest in the property devolved to Defendant Naushad Hirji ("Naushad"). In 2001, Defendant Naushad deeded the property to himself and his wife, Defendant Sabira Hirji. The Defendants possessed title to the property but lived in Tanzania. Defendant Naushad testified that he never spoke to the attorney who prepared the two prior deeds. During this whole period, Defendant Naushad visited the property only once and never hired anyone to inspect it.

Ahmed Hirji and his family lived at the property for more than 20 years, maintaining it and paying taxes but not rent. When Defendant Naushad and his wife sought to evict them, Ahmed Hirji and his family claimed ownership through adverse possession. The federal district court rejected the claim. Ahmed Hirji and his family appealed to the federal court of appeals.

Language of the Court. *To establish a claim of adverse possession in New York state, one must show that the occupation of a property is (1) hostile and under claim of right; (2) actual; (3) open and notorious; (4) exclusive; and (5) continuous for the required period of 10 years. While New York courts typically presume hostility where the other elements are satisfied, this presumption does not apply where there is a close and cooperative relationship between the record owner and the person claiming title through adverse possession. In such circumstances, the party asserting the adverse possession claim must come forward with affirmative facts to establish that the use of the property was under a claim of right and adverse to the interests of the true owners.*

Ahmed Hirji pled that he conveyed the title to his brother, Defendant Naushad. In such circumstances, permission can be implied from the beginning, and adverse possession will not arise until there is a distinct assertion of a right hostile to the owner. The complaint does not contain any affirmative facts that Plaintiffs did anything that constituted "a distinct assertion of a right hostile to the Defendant owners." Accordingly, the district court appropriately granted Defendants' motion to dismiss the adverse possession claim.

Decision. The court of appeals affirmed the district court's rejection of the claim for adverse possession.

Focus on Ethics

What are the policy considerations behind requiring hostility in an adverse possession claim? What could Ahmed have done to demonstrate hostility?

Eminent Domain and Regulatory Takings

Eminent domain The government's power to seize private property for public use.

All governments in the United States have the power to take private property for public uses, a power known as **eminent domain**. The government may take property from private owners as long as the owner receives just compensation. Eminent domain and condemnation are terms often used interchangeably, but eminent domain refers to the right of the government to take property, while condemnation is the legal proceeding by which the government exercises its eminent domain power. The source of the government's eminent domain power springs from the Takings Clause of the United States Constitution.

Takings Clause (Eminent Domain Clause)

"... nor shall private property be taken for public use, without just compensation." — U.S. Constitution, Amendment V.

The Takings Clause applies to both the taking of title and depriving the owner of the possession of property.

The purpose of eminent domain is to prevent the government from forcibly taking property without paying just compensation to the private owner. Eminent domain also serves a public purpose by promoting the public interest. The public interest can be advanced by using eminent domain to secure and expand public transportation corridors, facilities, and other rights and services.

Taking of Private Property

The process of eminent domain requires that the government take private property. A taking of private property occurs where (1) the landowner is deprived of any use of the property; (2) there is a permanent physical invasion of the property; or (3) a **regulatory taking** occurs that denies the landowner all economic uses of the property.

Regulatory taking
A government regulation that deprives the owner of all economic beneficial use of the property.

Taking for Public Use or Public Purpose

Property cannot be taken by eminent domain unless it is for a **public use**. The Supreme Court's current position is that the public use requirement is met if the taking is rationally related to a conceivable public purpose. In doing so, the Supreme Court has broadly defined what is a public use. The expansiveness of the public use definition will accommodate virtually any need that addresses the advancement of the public welfare (such as increasing sales taxes). This purpose may be achieved even if it involves taking private property from one owner for the purpose of conveying it to another private owner if the public may benefit.

Public use
In the context of eminent domain, any conceivable benefit to the public welfare can be deemed a public use.

Just Compensation to the Property Owner

Just compensation is the payment of a property's fair market value at the time of the taking. If a partial taking of a property occurs, the government must pay the fair market value for the portion of the property taken. In addition, the government is responsible for paying any damages that might result in the severance and cause a reduction in the value of the land remaining in the owner's hands.

Landlord-Tenant Law

Lessor
A person who transfers the right to exclusively possess and use property for a duration of time.

Lessee
A person who acquires the right to exclusively possess and use property for a duration of time.

Lease
Contract transferring exclusive possession of a property from one party (the landlord) to another (the tenant) for a period of time (the tenancy).

Tenancy
The period of a tenant's occupancy or possession.

It is not easy to steal where the landlord is a thief.—Irish expression

Tenancy for years
A lease for a fixed period.

While landlords and tenants are sometimes referred to as **lessors** and **lessees** respectively, in this chapter we will refer to them as landlords and tenants. Before we start our study, we need to recognize where leases fit within the real estate landscape.

The landlord-tenant relationship is a blend of both contract law and real property law. It is a contract with an exchange of promises between the landlord and tenant. Some states have statutory authority governing leasing and have adopted the Uniform Residential Landlord Tenant Act (URLTA) or follow the principles in the Act. A **lease** transfers to the tenant the right to exclusively possess and use the landlord's property for a period of time. The period of a tenant's occupancy or possession is known as a **tenancy**. When the tenancy expires, the right to possession returns to the landlord, and the tenant has no interest in the property.

A residential lease is a lease for a personal purpose, such as for an apartment or house. Commercial leases are leases used by businesses and commercial purposes, such as retail, restaurants, offices, or warehouses.

Types of Tenancies

There are four types of leasehold estates:

1. Tenancy for Years
2. Periodic Tenancy
3. Tenancy at Will
4. Tenancy at Sufferance

TENANCY FOR YEARS. One of the most common types of tenancies is a tenancy for years. A **tenancy for years** is a lease for a fixed period of time. While the name of this tenancy sounds as though it necessarily lasts more than a year in duration, a tenancy for years can be for any fixed period, including weeks, months, or years. Some states limit a tenancy for years to 99 years. Leases lasting longer than 99 years may be considered fee simple estates by statute.

> **Example:** A student leasing a dormitory room for an academic year would hold a tenancy for years.

Termination. In this type of tenancy, the landlord and tenant have agreed to a fixed lease duration, and the right to possession expires at the end of the term. Neither party needs to give notice to the other of the lease's expiration. The lease terminates automatically, and the right to possession is transferred back to the landlord. Interestingly, the death of a party does not terminate a tenancy for years. The rights and duties of the deceased are transferred to the decedent's heirs or beneficiaries.

Writing Requirement. The Statute of Frauds requires that a tenancy for years covering a period of time exceeding one year must be in writing. If a lease is not in writing when one is required, a periodic tenancy (discussed below) is created.

Example: Travis enters into a lease with Rose for two years, with rent payable monthly at the rate of $750 each month. The Statute of Frauds requires this lease to be in writing to be enforceable.

Duration of Tenancy for Years Leases. So long as state law permits it, tenancies for years may have exceedingly long durations. While not an American lease, one such example is the Guinness Brewery lease. The lease was executed on December 31, 1759. It is a 9,000-year tenancy for years at an annual rent of £45.

PERIODIC TENANCY. A **periodic tenancy** is a tenancy that lasts for a fixed period of time and continues to renew for like periods of time until either the landlord or the tenant gives notice of termination. The tenancy may be year to year, month to month, week to week, or for other periods.

Periodic tenancy
A lease that lasts for a fixed period and continues to renew for like periods until terminated.

Example: A month-to-month lease beginning January 1 at the rate of $800 a month is a periodic tenancy.

Creation. Periodic tenancies are created either by express agreement between a landlord and a tenant or through implication. When parties agree to the tenancy period, they create an express periodic tenancy.

Example: Landlord and Tenant agree: "Starting June 1, on a month-to-month basis, Tenant to have the use of my guest house for the sum of $1,500 per month, due on the 10th." The landlord and tenant have created an express periodic tenancy because they agreed on the tenancy period (month-to-month tenancy).

Where a landlord and tenant agree to the terms of the lease, but the lease fails to mention its tenancy period, an implied periodic tenancy is created with the tenancy period being the frequency of the payment intervals.

Example: Landlord and Tenant agree: "Starting June 1, Tenant to rent the apartment for the sum of $1,250 per month, with payment due on the 10th." The landlord and tenant have created an implied month-to-month periodic tenancy because rent is due monthly.

In addition, a tenancy for years that violates the Statute of Frauds creates an implied periodic tenancy. The tenancy period is the frequency at which rent is collected. When the tenancy period has terminated following the expiration of a tenancy for years, and the landlord continues to receive and collect rent, an implied periodic tenancy is created.

Example: Travis enters into an *oral* lease with Rose for two years, with rent payable at the rate of $750 each month. Under the Statute of Frauds, the tenancy for years was required to be in writing to be enforceable. Instead of a tenancy for years, the lease is an implied month-to-month periodic tenancy with rent of $750 due each month.

Some leases may initially start as a tenancy for years and then provide for the lease to automatically convert to a periodic tenancy at the end of the tenancy for years.

Example: Possession of apartment 1418 to Student for one year; at the end of that period, the lease shall continue on a month-to-month basis, unless the landlord or tenant terminates this lease by notice in writing delivered to the other at least one month prior to the end of the term. In this example, the lease starts as a tenancy for years that at the end of one year would continue as a periodic tenancy until terminated by proper notice.

Continuous Renewal. Periodic tenancies do not have a fixed ending date and continuously renew until either party gives proper and timely notice. The lease is renewed with the same terms and conditions for another tenancy period (such as another month in a month-to-month tenancy). This is different from a tenancy for years, which ends upon a specific date. The key characteristic of this type of tenancy is that a periodic tenancy has a known beginning date and duration of successive periods. It does not have a fixed ending date and continues until proper and timely notice to terminate is given by either party.

Termination. To terminate a periodic tenancy, one party must give notice of termination to the other party. Except as required by statute, the notice of termination can be given either orally or in writing. This notice must be given to the other party at least as far in advance as the length of the lease period, with the exception that if the tenancy is year to year, only six months' notice is required. However, the parties can agree within the lease provisions to shorten the amount of time required to terminate the tenancy.

To review one state's practical guide for explaining the rights of tenants and landlords, see https://www.legislature.mi.gov/Publications/tenantlandlord.pdf.

Example: To terminate a month-to-month periodic tenancy, one month's notice must be provided.

Tenancy at will
A lease with no stated term and no provision for the collection of rent.

TENANCY AT WILL. A **tenancy at will** has neither a stated term nor a rent amount. It lasts only so long as both the landlord and the tenant agree to it. Either party can terminate it at any time.

Example: After graduating from college, Jerry moves back into his parents' home. Jerry's parents do not charge him rent and he is free to stay as long as he and his parents agree. Jerry has a tenancy at will.

Termination. Either party may terminate a tenancy at will at any time, although some states are now requiring that some advance notice be given to terminate a tenancy at will.

Tenancy at sufferance
A lease where the tenant remains in possession of the property after the tenancy period has terminated.

TENANCY AT SUFFERANCE. The last type of tenancy is the **tenancy at sufferance**, sometimes referred to as a holdover tenancy. This tenancy is created when a tenant remains in possession of the property after the tenancy period has terminated. The tenant stays in possession without permission and "holds over" after termination of the tenancy. A tenancy at sufferance allows the landlord to collect rental payments against the holdover tenant.

Despite the title given to the occupant, the tenant is not really a tenant at all because the occupant is holding over without the landlord's consent. There is no tenancy to terminate and notice to terminate is unnecessary. Although the lease has ended, the landlord and tenant may negotiate a new lease to permit the tenant to remain in possession; alternatively, the landlord may collect rent from the tenant, creating an implied periodic tenancy. If one of those events occurs, the tenant's status changes from one of a tenant at sufferance to a tenancy for years or a periodic tenancy depending on the terms of the lease created.

> **Example:** On January 1, Whitney leases her apartment to Sarah on a month-to-month basis. Assume Sarah gives timely notice to Whitney to terminate the periodic tenancy, with a tenancy end date of December 31 of that same year. If Sarah remains in possession after January 1 of the new year, she is a tenant at sufferance. If Sarah makes a monthly rental payment to Whitney after the beginning of the new year, and Whitney accepts it, this creates a periodic tenancy.

Concept Summary
Types of Tenancies

Type	Definition	Example	Termination
Tenancy for Years	Lasts for a fixed period.	Lease of apartment for six months.	Ends at the end of the stated tenancy period (such as at the end of the sixth month).
Periodic Tenancy	Tenancy for a fixed period that automatically continues for succeeding periods until either party gives notice of termination.	Lease of apartment on a month-to-month basis.	Ends by notice from one party to the other, given at least as far ahead as the length of the period.
Tenancy at Will	Tenancy of no fixed duration; lasts for as long as the landlord and tenant agree.	Lease of apartment for as long as either party desires.	Ends as soon as one party terminates the tenancy.
Tenancy at Sufferance	Tenant wrongfully stays in possession after the termination of a tenancy.	Tenant's lease expires on May 1, but tenant wrongfully stays in the apartment after the lease has expired.	Terminated when the landlord evicts the tenant, the tenant leaves, or a new lease is executed.

Common Lease Provisions

Leases may provide a variety of provisions, including the following: provisions limiting the use of the premises, common area maintenance, security deposits, and maintenance and repairs. Unless identified or distinguished below, the following provisions apply to both residential and commercial leases.

PREMISES. The lease will describe the premises to be rented by the tenant. The premises are the actual space or property that is to be occupied by the tenant. The tenant will have exclusive use of the premises and a right to use the common areas of the lease.

POSSESSION. Possession usually begins on the day of the commencement of the lease. A lease may provide the tenant with the right to take early possession of the property without the obligation to pay rent. This may arise when a tenant desires to complete tenant improvements before the commencement date of the lease.

RENT. The landlord has the right to collect rent, even if the amount of rent is not stated in the lease. In that situation, courts will infer that the tenant must pay a reasonable amount of rent at the end of the term.

> **Example:** If the landlord states the amount of the security deposit but fails to state an amount of rent in the landlord's preprinted lease agreement form, the courts will imply that the tenant must pay a reasonable amount of rent.

When the lease does not state the day on which rent is due, the rent obligation does not arise until the last day of the rental period. Thus, the rent is not due in advance of the rental period unless stated in the lease.

> **Example:** If a month-to-month periodic tenancy had a rental provision of $750 each month and did not provide a date on which rent was payable to the landlord, the rent would be due at the end of the month (that is, at the end of each rental period).

Management Application
Rental Rates for Commercial Properties

1. *Gross lease.* A lease in which the tenant pays a fixed amount.

   Example: A 650-square-foot space may be priced at $1.85 per square foot per month.

2. *Percentage lease.* A lease in which the tenant pays a fixed amount plus a percentage of gross sales earned by the business.

3. *Triple net lease (NNN).* A lease in which the tenant pays the landlord a fixed gross amount of rent each month and also pays for the property's operating costs (property taxes, property insurance, and property maintenance).

COMMON AREA MAINTENANCE. Many commercial leases require the tenant to pay a prorated share of the common area expenses. These expenses are known as **common area maintenance (CAM)** payments. The charges can include anything that the parties agree to, but they often include such items as the costs of common area utilities, marketing and advertising expenses, elevator expenses, landscaping expenses, building renovation costs, maintenance costs, and so on.

Common area maintenance (CAM) A pro rata share of costs a tenant is required to pay for common area expenses.

USE. The lease should provide the purpose for which the tenant intends to use the property. Tenants desire freedom of use in their tenancy and often request that their use be broadly defined as "any lawful purpose." Landlords, however, will want to specifically define the uses allowed by the tenant on the premises.

> **Example:** The agreed use of the property shall be for general office space.

DEPOSITS. Landlords often require tenants to make an advance payment to cover certain expenses or costs that may be incurred to the landlord when the tenant vacates. These advance payments are known as deposits. States often regulate the collection and use of deposits for residential leases more than they do for commercial leases. Usually there are few, if any, restrictions on a landlord's ability to collect a deposit with a commercial lease.

Security Deposits. One common type of deposit is the **security deposit**, which is an advance payment used to protect the landlord from damage caused to the property by the tenant or to compensate the landlord for lost rent if the tenant vacates before the term of the lease or fails to pay the amount owed under the lease.

State law may limit the amount of the security deposit and for what purposes the security deposit may be applied.

Security deposit A type of deposit used to protect landlords, which can cover expenses for any damage caused to the property or damages suffered because of a tenant's nonperformance of its obligations under a lease.

Prepaid Rent. Another form of deposit sometimes required at the beginning of the lease term is prepaid rent. With prepaid rent, the landlord can require the tenant to pay the first and last months' rent, several months' rent, or a combination of the two.

MAINTENANCE AND REPAIRS. Unless the lease requires a tenant to correct defects, a tenant has no general duty to correct defective conditions on the premises. However, on termination of the tenancy, the tenant must return the premises to the landlord in the same condition it was in at the commencement of the lease, except for ordinary wear and tear.

> **Example:** Assume a tenant leased space for four years and was provided new carpeting at the beginning of the lease. At the end of the four years, the law requires the tenant to return the premises in the same condition as when it was leased, except for ordinary wear and tear. If the carpet was supposed to last for seven years and had been excessively worn in those four years, the tenant will be responsible for the excessive damage to the carpet.

In essence, tenants have to protect the premises from damage so that their possession does not substantially harm the property. Tenants may also face eviction if they fail to make required repairs.

In commercial leases, it is common for a landlord to require a tenant, at the tenant's expense, to maintain and repair the premises. Commercial landlords commonly require tenants to maintain and repair the plumbing, HVAC equipment, electrical system, lighting, interior and exterior walls, ceilings, floors, windows, doors, and roof.

Waste
Destruction, harm, or injury caused to the use of real property by a person in possession of the property.

Waste. If the tenant damages the property, they are liable to the landlord for **waste**. To recover for waste, the damage must be extraordinary and beyond ordinary wear and tear. The landlord can recover from the tenant the cost to repair waste.

Notice of Repair. When a tenant discovers a defective condition that is the responsibility of the landlord to repair, the tenant must provide the landlord with notice of the condition. The tenant must allow the landlord a reasonable opportunity to make the needed repairs.

ALTERATIONS. Both residential and commercial leases will often prohibit alterations to the premises without the written consent of the landlord. This gives the landlord the ability to secure appropriate insurance, review the qualifications of the contractor, and protect itself from mechanic's liens and other remedies a contractor may seek against a landlord. Mechanic's liens are discussed in Chapter 31.

Tenant Rights and Landlord Duties

Implied warranty of habitability
An implied warranty requires landlords to provide premises that are fit, safe, and suitable for basic human habitation.

IMPLIED WARRANTY OF HABITABILITY. Historically, the common law did not imply that premises would be fit for the purposes intended. Tenants took premises "as is." Today, most states provide that residential (not commercial) leases are subject to an **implied warranty of habitability**. Generally, this duty requires landlords to provide premises that are fit, safe, and suitable for basic human habitation. States do not allow a tenant to waive the implied warranty of habitability in a lease. Generally, these are the duties imposed upon the landlord:

- The landlord must maintain safe and sanitary common areas (elevators, garages, and stairways).
- The landlord must provide basic amenities in the leased premises, including proper plumbing, running water, and lockable doors and windows.
- The landlord must fix known latent (hidden) defects or other dangers that are not easily discovered through an ordinary inspection.
- The landlord must maintain the premises so as not to violate building or fire code regulations.

Tenants' Remedies for Breach of the Implied Warranty of Habitability. The landlord's failure to maintain residential premises in a safe and sanitary condition is a material breach of the lease. The tenant may terminate the lease and abandon the premises. Alternatively, the tenant may continue the lease and sue for damages. The measure of damages will usually be a rent reduction for the difference between the fair market rental value of habitable premises and the fair market value of the premises in their current uninhabitable condition. The tenant may also cancel the lease for a condition of continuing uninhabitability. Such an implied warranty may not be waived by the tenant. In some states, a "repair and deduct" remedy for residential tenants is available. If the landlord fails to repair a material condition affecting the habitability of the premises after reasonable notice, the tenant may use a reasonable amount of rent to repair the defective condition.

Example: In California, a residential tenant may expend up to one month's rent for such repairs and may use this remedy no more than twice in a one-year period.

The following case discusses the notice requirement when determining if there is a breach of the warranty of habitability.

CASE 39.3

NOTICE TO LANDLORD REQUIRED FOR WARRANTY OF HABITABILITY TO BE BREACHED

TERRY v. O'BRIEN

134 A.3d 203 (2015)

Supreme Court of Vermont

Timothy and Penny Terry ("Terry") rented a property owned by William and Susan O'Brien ("O'Briens"). The property included a two-story house and brick building with a common wall to the rear of the house. The brick building had no fixtures and had never been inhabited. In December 2002, following foreclosure proceedings on their own home, Terry accepted landlords' offer to occupy the house rent-free for the time being. After their first year in the house, the tenants began paying rent. The parties agreed orally that Terry would pay monthly rent. In March 2005, Burlington Code Enforcement inspected the house and cited the landlords for multiple problems that required repair.

A follow-up inspection in 2006 confirmed that most of the repairs had been completed but found additional items concerning the brick building. In May 2008, Vermont Gas inspected the house's furnace and determined that it needed to be repaired or replaced because it was in extremely poor condition. In November 2008, landlords had a space heater installed on the first floor of the house, but apparently it was not enough to heat the second floor, so tenants began using space heaters on the second floor at night. During the lease, a fire started in the attic of the house, resulting in heavy fire damage to one of the bedrooms, as well as smoke and/or water damage to the other rooms. A fire investigator concluded that the fire began due to overuse of the older electrical system and the improper installation of insulation.

Terry filed a complaint alleging breach of warranty of habitability. At trial, the jury determined that the O'Briens had breached the warranty of habitability by renting an unsafe residence. The court determined that the O'Briens were not entitled to any unpaid rent due to their breach of the warranty of habitability.

The O'Briens appealed to the Supreme Court of Vermont, stating that the trial court misled the jury by instructing that notice to the landlords of the defect was not required if the defect was found to be latent.

Language of the Court. *The implied warranty of habitability covers all latent and patent defects. To bring a cause of action for breach of the implied warranty of habitability, the tenant must show that: (1) the landlord had notice of the previously unknown defect and failed, within a reasonable period of time, to repair it; and (2) the defect, affecting habitability, existed during the time for which rent was withheld. The trial court's ruling must be reversed because of our vacation of the jury's verdict in favor of tenants with respect to their statutory warranty of habitability claim. Absent their habitability claim, there is no basis for Terry to withhold rent.*

[T]o bring a cause of action for breach of the implied warranty of habitability, the tenant must first show that he or she notified the landlord of the deficiency or defect not known to the landlord and [allowed] a reasonable time for its correction. Because there is no evidence that the landlords had actual notice of a habitability defect that led to the fire, tenants' habitability claim fails.

Decision. The Supreme Court of Vermont reversed, finding that the O'Briens did not have notice of the defect and Terry could not sue under the implied warranty of habitability.

Focus on Ethics

Should tenants be required to pay landlords for uninhabitable spaces if the tenants have not given notice to the landlord that the premises is not habitable?

Application to Commercial Leases. The implied warranty of habitability does not apply to commercial leases. This trend follows from the reality that residential tenants, unlike commercial tenants, frequently do not have the skills or resources necessary to identify whether the premises are fit for use.

However, in a few states, courts are beginning to recognize an implied covenant of suitability (fitness for the purpose of the intended use) at the time the commercial tenant enters into the lease. This covenant is similar to the implied warranty of habitability found in residential leases; however, the commercial tenant can waive an implied covenant of suitability.

COVENANT OF QUIET ENJOYMENT. The landlord impliedly promises the tenant the right to use and enjoy possession of the premises without the landlord's interference. Even if this covenant is not expressly stated in the lease, it is implied in every lease. The covenant of quiet enjoyment protects the tenant from the following interferences:

1. Landlord interference with the tenant's possession of the property.

   Example: If the tenant is not in breach of the terms of the lease and the landlord changes the access codes to the premises or the locks, the landlord has breached the tenant's covenant of quiet enjoyment.

2. Any acts that substantially threaten to interfere or actually interfere with the beneficial enjoyment of the premises.

Example: A landlord who does not undertake reasonable measures to remedy substantial annoyances caused by neighboring tenants may have breached the covenant of quiet enjoyment.

Assignments and Subleases

Unless prohibited by a state statute or the lease, a tenant may assign the lease or sublet the rented premises without the landlord's consent. An assignment or sublease transfers some or all of the tenant's rights to the assignee.

ASSIGNMENTS. An **assignment** arises when a tenant, the **assignor**, transfers all of the tenant's unexpired lease to a third party, the **assignee**. The entire interest and the entire remaining duration of the lease must be transferred for an assignment. Leases usually prohibit assignments without the landlord's written consent. In such cases, if the tenant assigns their interest without the landlord's consent, the landlord may void the assignment and sue for damages. If the landlord knowingly accepts rent from the assignee, the landlord has impliedly consented to the assignment, and any right to enforce the anti-assignment covenant is waived.

Assignment
A transfer of a tenant's unexpired lease to a third party.

Assignor
A tenant that transfers all of their interests under a lease to a third party.

Assignee
A new tenant who received an assignment by an assignor.

Concept Summary
Assignment of a Lease

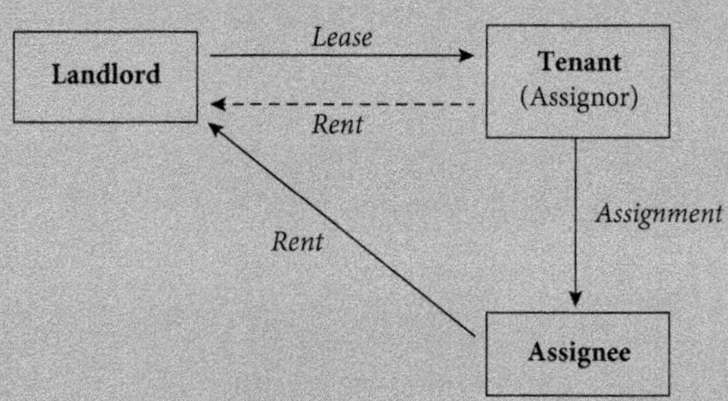

Rights and Duties. With an assignment, the assignee assumes the rights and duties of the assignor, and the landlord can enforce those duties against the assignee. However, the tenant's obligations do not end with the assignment. The tenant continues to remain liable to the landlord if the assignee defaults in any of the duties owed under the lease. This gives the landlord the ability to sue either the assignor or the assignee for any breach of a duty owed to the landlord. The landlord can release the assignor from liability and accept the assignee as having sole liability under the lease. This substitution is called a novation.

Example: A tenant and landlord enter into a 12-month lease. After two months, the tenant's employer transfers them to another state. With the landlord's permission, the tenant assigns the remaining ten months' lease to a third party, the assignee. The assignee now has the rights and duties of the tenant and owes the landlord rent; the assignee also has the benefits of the rights owed by the landlord to the tenant. If the assignee breaches a covenant in the lease, the landlord can sue to collect from either the tenant or the assignee.

Rule in Dumpor's Case. Once a landlord consents to one assignment, does the landlord waive objection to subsequent transfers? The Rule in Dumpor's Case answers this question. The English court found that the landlord's consent to one assignment destroyed the anti-assignment clause of the lease. If the landlord consented to one assignment, all other assignments were valid.

Many states have eliminated this rule or restricted its application to assignments only and not subleases. In order to avoid the application of this rule, landlords insert a lease provision stating that the landlord's consent to one assignment shall not constitute a waiver of the right to object to subsequent lease assignments.

Sublease
A transfer of a portion of the lease from a tenant to a third party (a subtenant).

SUBLEASES. A **sublease** occurs when the tenant does not transfer the entire interest in the lease to another person. Instead, only a portion of the lease is transferred. Subleases arise when the tenant transfers only a portion of the remaining term (such as three months of the remaining six-month term for years) or a portion of the property (as when the tenant leases out one of the two bedrooms that the tenant has leased from the landlord).

As with assignments, most leases contain a prohibition against subleasing without the landlord's consent. A violation of that covenant will entitle the lessor to void the sublease and/or recover damages.

Concept Summary
Sublease

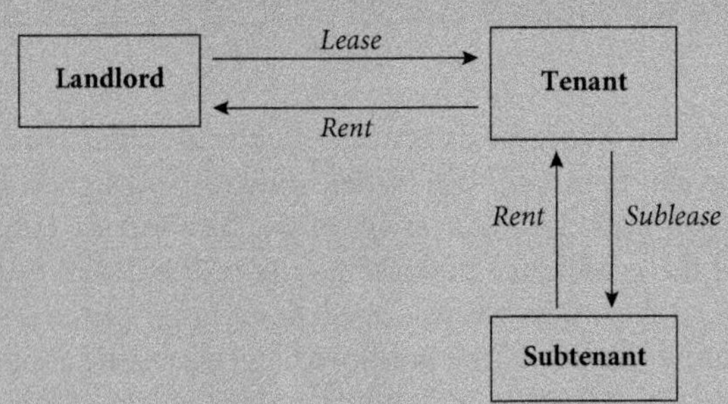

Rights and Duties. With a sublease, two leases exist. The landlord has rights only against the tenant because the landlord has a contract with the tenant but not with the subtenant. The tenant remains liable to the landlord under the terms of its lease. However, the subtenant is not liable to the landlord.

The lease between the tenant and the subtenant governs the rights of the subtenant. The subtenant is liable to the tenant, and the tenant owes rights and duties to both the landlord and the subtenant.

PROHIBITION AGAINST ASSIGNMENTS AND SUBLEASES. Landlords can prohibit an assignment or a sublease in the lease. However, courts narrowly construe this prohibition. A prohibition against an assignment does not prevent the tenant from subleasing. Similarly, a sublease prohibition does not prevent the tenant from assigning the lease.

AI Feature: Draft a Conveyance of Air Rights Agreement

Using an internet search engine, research the use of air rights by real estate developers. What real property rights are involved? How does their use create profitable commercial real estate? Identify several real estate developments throughout the country that required the purchase of air rights. What benefits are derived by those who own them and those who purchase them? Then, using an AI program, draft a conveyance of air rights agreement.

Key Terms

- Adverse possession, 990
- Air right, 978
- Assignee, 1003
- Assignment, 1003
- Assignor, 1003
- Common area maintenance (CAM), 999
- Community property, 983
- Deeds, 987
- Easement appurtenant, 984
- Easement by grant, 985
- Easement in gross, 984
- Easements, 984
- Eminent domain, 992
- Fee simple, 979
- Fixture, 979
- General warranty deed, 988
- Grantee, 987
- Grantor, 987
- Implied warranty of habitability, 1000
- Joint tenancy, 981

- Lease, 994
- Lessee, 994
- Lessor, 994
- License, 987
- Life estate, 979
- Nonpossessory interests, 984
- Periodic tenancy, 995
- Profit, 986
- Public use, 993
- Quitclaim deed, 988
- Real property, 978
- Recording statute, 990
- Regulatory takings, 993
- Right of survivorship, 981
- Security deposit, 999
- Special warranty deed, 988
- Sublease, 1004
- Tenancy, 994
- Tenancy at sufferance, 996
- Tenancy at will, 996
- Tenancy by the entirety, 982
- Tenancy for years, 994
- Tenancy in common, 980
- Title, 987
- Waste, 1000
- Water rights, 978

Applying the Law

39.1 Tenancy in Common. A bankruptcy trustee sought to sell the real property interests of the three debtors, along with the interests of their co-owners, who were not in bankruptcy. The debtors' sister, a co-owner, objected on the ground that the realty was partnership property because the partnership was not a debtor. The court reviewed the deeds, through which the co-owners acquired their interests and the partnership agreement and found that as of the filing of the petition, title to the realty was recorded in, and remained in, the names of the co-owners as tenants in common, and not in the name of the partnership. Why should the deed prevail as to the tenant in common status of the property if it were intended that the real estate remain partnership property?

Explain how this error may have occurred. What should have occurred to prevent this dispute. *Goldberg v. South East Partners Corp. (In re Sturman)*, 222 B.R. 694 (S.D.N.Y. 1998)

39.2 Tenancy by the Entirety. A bank sought to attach the bank account of Robert Olson, a married man and guarantor of a loan made by the bank. Olson's account was held with his wife as joint tenants with the right of survivorship. The bank disputed Olson's claim that the title of the account was sufficient to create a tenancy by the entirety. The bank prevailed at trial but lost on appeal. Why did the wife's property interest in the account thwart the bank's collection efforts? *Constitution Bank v. Olson*, 620 A.2d 1146 (Pa. Super. 1992)

39.3 Prenuptial Agreement. The administrator of the estate of Lucia Merlino, deceased, sued to have certain property determined to be community property and subject to probate proceedings. The surviving husband, Angelo Merlino, claimed that the property in question was his separate property. Angelo claimed that as a surviving spouse in a community property state (Washington) and the prenuptial agreement executed by the decedent made all of the community property his separate property. Was this unlimited power given to the surviving husband in the prenuptial agreement fair and enforceable? How could separate property funds become so commingled with community funds that the court would declare the entire mass to be community property? *Hamlin v. Merlino*, 272 P.2d 125 (Wash. 1954)

39.4 Easement by Necessity. For over fifty years, Chester Burnham crossed his neighbor's property by use of Ridge Road, a private road that extended from a public road to Burnham's landlocked parcel. Burnham's neighbor at the time had granted him this access out of neighborly courtesy. However, when the neighbor sold this property to Kwentus in 2008, Burnham was instructed to stop using Ridge Road and instead use a newer road. Burnham viewed this newer road as impassable and sued Kwentus, claiming an easement across Ridge Road. At trial, Burnham presented evidence that in 1937, Kwentus's property and an undivided one-third of Burnham's property was owned by Capitol Bank. At that time, Capitol Bank conveyed the one-third interest to Robert F. Young, thereby landlocking the property. When Burnham purchased the property in 1952, he began using Ridge Road across his neighbor's property, as it was his only means of accessing his property. If Burnham is the successor to Young's interest in the property, would he be able to assert an easement by necessity to cross Kwentus's property? *Burnham v. Kwentus* 174 So.3d 286 (Miss. 2015)

39.5 Easement by Prescription. Robert and Virginia Stegall did not own a private, 25-foot-wide gravel lane that bordered the northern edge of their property and that of Michael O'Dell, their adjacent neighbor, but this gravel lane was their only access to a public highway. What would the Stegall's have to prove to be entitled to have the court order the imposition of a prescriptive easement upon O'Dell's property. *O'Dell v. Stegall*, 703 S.E.2d 561 (W.V. Cir. 2009)

39.6 Profit. Clarence McKinley created twenty-four 10-acre plots from his 480 acres of land in Carbon County, Wyoming. The deeds given by McKinley to others contained language indicating that the original grantees were also granted a "privilege" to hunt and fish on the lands owned by McKinley. A substantial portion of the remaining McKinley-owned land that was subject to the "privilege" was now owned, through various conveyances, by the Seven Lakes Development Company, L.L.C. and David W. Kuhn. Two of the conveyed lots were then owned by John and Marilyn Maxson who were recreational users who asserted that they enjoyed a profit that allowed them the use of motorized vehicles while exercising their rights under the profit. Seven Lakes and Kuhn asserted that they adversely possessed the Maxson profit; is that allowable? Was the use of the motorized vehicles an unlawful expansion of use of the profit? Explain the Maxson's rights as declared by the Wyoming Supreme Court. *Seven Lakes Dev. Co., L.L.C. v. Maxson*, 144 P.3d 1239 (Wyo. 2006)

39.7 Adverse Possession. Charles Roche and the Town of Fairfield, Connecticut, owned adjacent parcels of property. Originally, the parcels had been separated by a creek and a sandspit (an extended stretch of beach material that projects out to the sea and is joined to mainland at one end). The deeds to the property referenced the Long Island Sound (which is a tidal estuary) as one of the property lines. Over time, strong storms washed away the spit, and the creek was subsumed by the Sound. The beach area increased over time as sand was deposited there. The Township erected a dike, and began using the beach, including a portion of Roche's property, for a public beach during the summer. After 18 years of use by the Township, Roche sued the township to restrain it from trespassing on property above the mean highwater mark of Roche's beach front property. Does the Town have title through adverse possession? Explain your answer. *Roche v. Town of Fairfield*, 442 A. 2d. 911 (1982).

39.8 What Is Public Use? If the government uses its eminent domain power to transfer land from one private owner to another private owner for purposes of economic development, is that considered lawful taking of private property for "public use"? *Kelo v. City of New London*, 545 U.S. 469 (2005)

39.9 Warranty of Habitability. Jorge Ruiz lived with his parents, Flaviana Cholula and Pedro Ruiz, in an apartment in New Brunswick, New Jersey, owned by Robert Kaprelian. Jorge was three years old at the beginning of this tenancy and turned four during the year. A screening program at Jorge's school revealed elevated levels of lead in his blood. As a result, the county department of health performed tests in the Kaprelian apartment and discovered lead paint in various locations accessible to Jorge.

The department ordered Kaprelian to abate the condition. Jorge suffered language and motor skills deficits and a low IQ as a result of his exposure to lead. He and his parents sued Kaprelian and another follow-on landlord for negligence and breach of the implied warranty of habitability. Does a landlord need to have actual or constructive knowledge of the presence of lead paint to be held liable for breach of this implied warranty? *Ruiz ex rel. Ruiz v. Kaprelian*, 731 A.2d 118 (N.J. App. Div. 1999)

39.10 Holdover Tenant. Mary Evans was a tenant who lived in an apartment at a resort. There was no written lease, and she lived there at will pursuant to an informal agreement with the resort's prior owner. Thereafter, J Four Realty, LLC, purchased the resort at a foreclosure sale. However, Evans was unaware of that fact and continued paying rent to the prior owner. The new owner unlawfully engaged in self-help and evicted the tenant. Was J Four Realty a landlord with respect to Evans? Was the tenancy at will with the prior owner converted to a tenancy at sufferance upon foreclosure? What advice would you give J Four Realty in this case? *Evans v. J Four Realty*, 62 A.3d 869 (N.H. 2013)

Wills, Intestacy, Probate, and Trusts

40

The life of the dead is placed in the memory of the living. — Marcus Tullius Cicero, Roman Politician (106 B.C.-43 B.C.)

Chapter Outline

- Introduction
- Wills
    - *Management Application: Property Transfers Occurring Outside of Probate*

Case 40.1: *Ferguson v. Critopoulos*
Case 40.2: *Christoffersen v. Christoffersen*

- Intestate Succession
- Probate
- Trusts
    - *Management Application: When to Use a Trust*
    - *Management Application: Reasons to Avoid Probate and Use a Trust*

Fiduciary Duties of Estate Representatives

- AI Feature: Drafting Provisions of a Will

Learning Objectives

After studying this chapter, you should be able to:

1. Describe the requirements for making a valid will.
2. Define the key terms and parties involved in the administration of wills and trusts.
3. Explain how property is distributed in intestate estates.
4. Explain the duties owed by executors and trustees to beneficiaries.

Introduction

How our property is distributed following our death is of great importance to family members, charities, friends, and even creditors. Property may be distributed voluntarily after a person's death through that person's will or trust. It may also be distributed through the laws of intestacy (which are employed when a person dies without a valid will). This chapter will discuss the ways in which a decedent's property can be conveyed.

This area of law uses unique terminology. Among those terms are the following:

- A beneficiary is the person who receives the testator's property from a will.
- A decedent is the person who has died.
- More often known now as the estate representative, an executor is an individual appointed to manage and execute the terms of a deceased person's will. There may be more than one estate representative.
- A testator (male) or testatrix (female) is a person who makes a will.
  - If the decedent dies testate, it means the person had a valid will at the time of death.
  - If a decedent dies intestate, it means the person did not have a valid will at the time of death.
- Issue are the decedent's descendants (such as children, grandchildren, great grandchildren, and so on.).
- A settlor is a person who establishes a trust. One or more trustees administer the trust.
- The process of administering the decedent's estate is known as probate.

Will
An instrument by which a mentally qualified person directs the disposition of their property following death.

Testator or Testatrix
A person who makes a will.

Omnia mors aequat. (Death levels all things.)—Latin expression

Wills

A **will** is a legal instrument by which a person (the **testator**) directs how their property will be disposed of at death. Unlike a delivered deed that transfers ownership from a grantor (seller) to a grantee (buyer), a will may be amended at any time prior to the death of the testator. A will is ineffective during the testator's lifetime. However, the property is transferred upon death; no further changes may be made to the will. Additionally, a will cannot change the characteristic of how co-owners hold property. For example, in Chapter 39, the topics of joint tenancy and other co-ownership forms of holding title were discussed. A will cannot change those characteristics.

Management Application
Property Transfers Occurring Outside of Probate

Some transfers occur outside of the laws of intestate succession. These transfers are types of non-probate transfers that are effective upon death but follow rules other than intestate-succession rules, including the following:

- A life estate held in real property
- Real property assets held in joint tenancy
- Real property assets held in trust or partnership arrangements that provide for transfers upon death

- Marital property that transfers upon the death of a spouse
- Real property assets that are subject to a buy-sell agreement
- Transfers stated in prenuptial and post-nuptial agreements

While not related to real property, other important asset transfers that occur following death outside of probate include joint tenant bank accounts, life insurance policies, annuities, and pension and retirement plan transfers to designated beneficiaries.

Types of Gifts in a Will

A devise is a gift made in a will, including real and personal property. There are several common types of devises:

- **General devise**: A gift of a specified quantity or value that can be satisfied from any property in the decedent's estate
- **Specific devise**: A gift from a decedent's estate of a particular, identifiable item or property
- **Residuary devise**: A gift of whatever remains in the decedent's estate after all other debts and devises have been paid or distributed

Protected Persons

State laws often protect certain persons against unintentional omission from wills and trusts. These people can be omitted spouses and children. Occasionally, a spouse will be omitted from a will. This may arise when, after marriage, a will was not amended to include the spouse. The **omitted spouse rule** is one that provides that an omitted spouse shall receive the same share of the estate they would have received if the decedent had died intestate. States laws vary on the treatment of an omitted spouse. For example, some states follow community property laws while others provide for a statutory share of the testator's estate as determined under state law. A spouse may have signed a waiver, such as a prenuptial or postnuptial agreement, eliminating or reducing their share of the estate.

Omitted spouse rule
A rule that permits an omitted spouse to receive the same share of the estate they would have received if the decedent had died intestate.

In the following proceeding, the stepson of the decedent petitioned to have the court declare the decedent's second wife not entitled to claim an omitted spouse share of the decedent's estate.

CASE 40.1

AN OMITTED SPOUSE WHO WAS PROVIDED FOR OUTSIDE OF THE WILL MAY NOT BE ENTITLED TO COLLECT INHERITANCE

FERGUSON v. CRITOPOULOS

163 So. 3d 330 (2014)

Supreme Court of Alabama

Dimitrios Critopoulos ("the decedent") died in 2012 without children. Additionally, his parents predeceased him, and he had no siblings. He had been married to

Dorothy Marie Hayes Critopoulos for 35 years; however, she predeceased him in 2009. Dorothy had three children from a prior marriage, one of whom became the plaintiff, Tiger Ferguson ("Ferguson") in the subject litigation. The decedent never adopted Dorothy's three children, but the decedent and the stepchildren enjoyed a parent-child relationship. The three stepchildren were named residual beneficiaries under the decedent's will. Nine months prior to his death, the decedent married Katina Critopoulos ("Katina"). At the time of his death, the decedent had a valid will; however, the will was executed prior to his second marriage to Katina and made no provision for her.

Ferguson filed a petition to probate the decedent's will. Katina filed a petition for an omitted spouse share of the decedent's estate. Ferguson filed an objection, claiming that the decedent had provided for Katina outside of the will — including checking accounts, life insurance, and retirements benefits, and was not therefore entitled to an omitted spouse share. The probate court held for Katina. Ferguson appealed.

Language of the Court. *The purpose of the probate statute is to avoid an unintentional disinheritance of the spouse of a testator who had executed a will prior to the parties' marriage. The adoption of this statute reflects the view that the intestate share of the spouse is what the decedent would have wanted the spouse to have if he had thought about the relationship of the old will to the new situation. It serves to give effect to the probable intent of the testator and protects the surviving spouse. There are two exceptions to allowing an omitted spouse an intestate share: (1) if it appears from the will that the omission of the surviving spouse was intentional or (2) if the testator provided for the surviving spouse with transfers outside the will with the intent that those transfers were in lieu of a provision in the will. If either exception exists, the surviving spouse is not entitled to a share as an omitted spouse.*

It is undisputed that the decedent executed his will in 2002 and that he married Katina in 2011. Nothing in the decedent's will indicates that the omission of Katina from the will was intentional; therefore, the first exception to the omitted-spouse share is not applicable.

As to the second exception, the decedent, during his brief marriage to Katina, changed beneficiaries on his retirement accounts and insurance policies. He was considering changing his will but did not do so. In short, he considered his old will in relation to his new marriage. He also substantially provided for Katina through inter vivos *transfers and transfers outside the will; Katina acknowledges that, if she received the intestate share, she would be receiving more than the decedent intended her to have.*

In the present case, the amount of the transfers made during the marriage, along with the testimony that the decedent considered the terms of his will, the fact that Katina was not included in the will, the fact that the decedent did not change his will, and the fact that the will ultimately benefited Dorothy's children provide reasonable proof to satisfy Tiger's burden of proving an exception to the omitted-spouse share under the facts of this case.

Decision. The Supreme Court of Alabama reversed the probate court's decision. Katina Critopoulos was not entitled to an omitted spouse's share of the probate estate.

Focus on Ethics

Is it fair for a court to determine the decedent's intent to omit a spouse because while alive the decedent provided for the omitted spouse? Why should this policy exist?

Similarly, the decedent's children may also be *unintentionally* omitted from a will. Children born or adopted after the execution of a will, or not known to be alive by the testator, are known as **pretermitted children**. Under state statutes, pretermitted children often receive the same portion of the testator's estate that they would have received if the testator had died without a will (intestate). In some states, only children born after the creation of the will are protected by pretermitted heir statutes. Other states extend protection to all children, including those who existed when the will was created. Like the omitted spouse, a frequent exception is if the pretermitted child is provided for by the decedent by transfer outside of the estate passing by the will or trust with the intention that the transfer be in lieu of a provision in the will or trust.

Pretermitted child A child who is born or adopted or not known to be alive by the testator after the execution of a will.

In contrast to these unintentional omissions is the *intentional* omission of a child. This intentional omission must appear within the decedent's will or trust. The intentional omission will result in the child having no legal right to the estate. This is because the testator's clear intent to disinherit the child is respected by the courts.

Example: A testator executes a will and states in their will, "I presently have one child, Peter Brown, who is to take nothing from my will." In this example, the disinheritance is intentional, and Peter will not inherit under the will.

Requirements for a Valid Will

Although wills can be simple documents, certain requirements must be met if a will is to be enforced. Most states recognize four requirements for an enforceable will: (1) a writing, (2) capacity, (3) the testator's signature, and (4) two or more disinterested witnesses.

WRITING REQUIREMENT. Usually, a will must be in writing in order to be enforceable. However, a few states do provide for oral wills (known as nuncupative wills). Because the circumstances of making such a will could be subject to fraud and perjury of witnesses, if a state permits the use of oral wills, it usually limits and conditions their validity. Often, oral wills are restricted to the distribution of personal property and can only be made in the case of imminent death.

The type of document used as a will (such as a letter) may be informal. However, for a document to be treated as a will, there must be a clearly expressed intention to dispose of property after death as well as compliance with other state law requirements.

> **Example:** Letters have been admitted to probate as a decedent's last will and testament.

Holographic will
A will that is entirely handwritten and signed by the testator.

Wills may be handwritten and are known as **holographic wills**. They have different requirements for validity than a properly executed and witnessed will. Generally, the material portions of the will (such as the gifts and beneficiary names) must be in the testator's own handwriting. The testator must also execute (sign) the will. Usually, no witnesses are required for holographic wills, but a few states require that they be witnessed with the same formalities as a will in regular form to be valid. Because the formalities required for a will's validity are not followed when a holographic will is at issue, they often provoke litigation among the heirs.

> **Example:** The death of Thomas Kinkade, known as "the painter of light," resulted in a will contest between Kinkade's estranged wife of 30 years and his live-in girlfriend of 18 months. The painter left two holographic wills favoring his girlfriend; his widow sued to have them set aside and a previous estate plan enforced. The dispute was settled pursuant to a confidential settlement agreement.

Electronic Wills

Wills written and stored in an electronic record are not recognized in most states. Because people can transact business electronically, many people may assume they can create an electronic will in the same manner. States have started to adopt legislation allowing for electronic wills to have legal effect. The Uniform Law Commission approved the Electronic Wills Act in 2019. The Act requires the same will formalities (writing, signatures, and witnesses) but allows for those requirements to be completed in an electronic medium. Under the Act, the will can be electronically signed and electronically validated.

In conformance with current law, the Act does not permit an audio or audio-visual recording of an individual describing the individual's testamentary wishes to constitute a will. Fourteen states, the Virgin Islands and the District of Columbia have enacted electronic wills laws.

CAPACITY. The testator must have the mental capacity to execute (sign) a will at the time of the will's execution. This element of a valid will requires that the testator possess both age capacity and mental capacity at the time of the will's execution.

Every state requires a testator to be of a certain age in order to execute a will. In most states, the testator must be at least 18 years of age. In addition to the age requirement, the testator must also have the mental capacity to execute a will. The testator must be able to understand the nature and extent of their property, name the persons to whom they wish to distribute the property, and have a general understanding of the purpose of a will. When an individual lacks the sound mind required to make a will, the resulting instrument is void.

TESTATOR'S SIGNATURE. The testator must either sign the will or direct someone else to sign the will on the testator's behalf. Where the testator is unable to sign the will, the testator may direct another person to execute the will in their conscious presence.

A will signed by a third party on behalf of the testator requires that the will be acknowledged to be valid. A will is **acknowledged** when the signature of the testator and the witnesses are notarized by a **notary public**. Wills do not have to be acknowledged, unless as required above, but an acknowledgment carries a presumption of validity.

Acknowledgment
The process of verifying the identity of the testator and witnesses of an executed will.

Notary public
A commissioned representative of a state who is charged with verifying the identity of the signer of documents.

WITNESSES. Most states require that the will be witnessed, usually by either two or three mentally competent witnesses. States may also require that the witnesses be disinterested (without a beneficial interest in the will). The witnesses sign as witnesses to the will's execution in the presence of the testator and each other.

Disinheritance and No Contest Clauses

A disinheritance clause is a provision in a will or trust clearly expressing the intention of the testator or settlor that a particular person or persons receive no property under the instrument. These are persons who would otherwise be entitled to claim a share of the testator's estate, but have not been provided for in the instrument. In contrast, a no contest clause is directed against any person who might contest the will. The clause is intended to discourage will contests by imposing a penalty of forfeiture against a beneficiary who challenges the will or trust. These are complex matters and must be carefully drafted as they are often limited by statutes or case law.

Changing a Will: Codicils

A **codicil** is a revision to a will that can modify, amend, or revoke a prior will. A codicil must be executed in the same manner as the original will in order to be valid. If the codicil amends a prior will, it must reference the will it is amending. If the codicil does not specifically state that it is revoking a prior will, the will and codicil must be read together to determine the testator's wishes. Codicils may change the testator's estate plan in a variety of ways.

Codicil
A revision to a will that can amend, modify, or revoke a prior will.

Example: A codicil may add or delete beneficiaries, change the assets to be distributed, or place conditions upon the receipt of gifts made in the will (for example, the codicil may require that a donee have attained a college degree to receive her gift).

Codicil

FIRST CODICIL TO WILL OF Kevin Fields.

I, Kevin Fields, residing in Newark, New Jersey, declare this to be the First Codicil to my Will dated September 13, 2024.

FIRST

Paragraph 5(a) on page 9 of the above-mentioned Will is hereby revoked and the following is substituted in its place: I hereby give the sum of $25,000 to my step-daughter Kristina Robinson, 1955 Monte Vista Court, Glenwood Springs, Colorado; if she should predecease me, this legacy shall become part of the residue of my estate and be disposed of in such manner set forth in such provision.

SECOND

In every other respect, I hereby confirm and republish my will dated September 13, 2024.

The foregoing First Codicil to my will dated September 13, 2024, is subscribed by on me on the 18th day of May 2026 at Newark, New Jersey.

Kevin Fields
Kevin Fields

Revoking a Will Before Death

A will can be revoked by the acts of the testator. A subsequent will or codicil can revoke a will; the testator may also intentionally physically destroy the will, or the will may be revoked by operation of law.

To revoke a will by physical destruction, the testator must intend to destroy the will, and do so. Many states do not require the will to be destroyed to be revoked. States may provide for physical destruction when a testator intends to destroy a will by tearing material portions of the will, burning the will, writing canceled or void across the will, or completely obliterating it (for example, shredding it).

> **Example:** A testator who intends to revoke their will may do so by taking the will and putting it through a document shredder.

Many states revoke or partially revoke a will by operation of law when the testator's family situation changes between the will's execution and the testator's death.

> **Example:** A divorce often revokes a will, at least as to property left to the former spouse.

Challenging the Validity of a Will

A will may be challenged only by those people who have an interest or allege an interest in the estate of the decedent. For example, an omitted heir, an heir, or anyone named as a beneficiary in a will can challenge that will's validity.

The same defenses that can be used to set aside a gift are grounds for challenging a will's validity. They are fraud, duress, mistake, and undue influence. Fraud can occur in many ways, including inducing the testator to make or change a will, committing fraud during the will's execution, and committing fraud by preventing the testator from changing or revoking a will.

Intestate Succession

"Succession" is the acquiring of title to property of a person who dies without disposing it by will. The decedent is an intestate and has died without having an effective will. The laws of intestate succession govern the disposition of property where (1) there is no will, (2) the will is invalid, or (3) property was not included in the will. When intestacy occurs, state law controls how the decedent's property is to be distributed in a process known as **intestate succession**. There are significant variations among the distribution schemes of the states.

Intestate succession The process of distributing property in the absence of a valid will.

Each state has adopted a descent and distribution statute describing who receives the decedent's property in these cases. Property that transfers by operation of law, such as property held as joint tenancy and life estate, is not included in intestate succession because it transfers automatically upon the death of the decedent. In addition, in states that provide for community property, the surviving spouse is entitled to their one-half share of community-property assets.

Distribution of Property with a Surviving Spouse

Under state law, title to the decedent's property passes immediately upon his death to the closest living heirs, subject to the payment of any nonexempt debts. Because family law and the law of inheritance is state-specific, state laws often vary when the decedent has left a spouse with children.

Usually, most descent and distribution statutes provide for the surviving spouse to inherit the whole estate or a portion of it. Often these statutes provide for the surviving spouse to inherit a different percentage of the estate depending on the number of children or grandchildren surviving the decedent.

> **Example:** A state law may provide that all the marital property of the deceased spouse passes to the surviving spouse if there are no children. If there is one child, the surviving spouse will inherit one half of the estate and if there is more than one child, the surviving spouse will inherit one-third of the estate.

Distribution of Property Without a Surviving Spouse

While the descent and distribution statute controls the distribution of property, generally, in the absence of a surviving spouse, property flows first to any living **lineal descendants** (children or issue of the children). If there are no surviving lineal descendants, the property goes to the parents of the decedent. If the parents have predeceased the decedent, the property flows to the decedent's brothers and sisters. Many states then provide that grandparents of the decedent will inherit if there are none of the above parties living. In such case, one-half of the estate will go to the paternal grandparents and the other half will go to the maternal grandparents. The descent and distribution statute will provide for further heirs to inherit.

Lineal descendants A relative in the direct line of descent of the decedent including children, grandchildren, and so on.

Escheat
A process whereby if there are no living heirs under a state's intestacy laws, the court orders that the property be distributed to the state.

At some point, when no heirs exist to receive the decedent's assets, the decedent's property **escheats**. When property escheats, the probate court will order that the property be distributed to the state. The state's descent and distribution statute dictates when property will escheat to the state.

Example: The property of a single adult who dies without children or siblings and has no surviving parents or relatives may escheat.

How Property Is Distributed in Cases of Intestacy

Usually, a will states how the decedent's estate will be distributed to their descendants. When intestate succession occurs, generally, states have adopted one of two theories of property distribution. The two most common property distribution methods are *per stirpes* and *per capita* distribution.

State laws vary in defining these two methods of distributions to grandchildren. In part, some variation exists among states because they have adopted different versions of the **Uniform Probate Code (UPC)** or made modifications to the UPC. The UPC is a uniform act governing inheritance and probate matters. It has been adopted in about one-third of the states.

Uniform Probate Code (UPC)
A uniform law governing inheritance and probate matters adopted in approximately one-third of the states.

***Per stirpes* distribution**
Form of distributing the decedent's estate in which surviving lineal descendants inherit through representation of their parents' inheritance share.

***PER STIRPES* DISTRIBUTION.** Under *per stirpes* distribution, surviving lineal descendants inherit through representation of their parents' inheritance share. The first question is to determine whether the decedent's children are living. If they are deceased, then consider whether they have living issue. Under a *per stirpes* distribution, all living lineal descendants (children, grandchildren, and so on) take the representative share that their deceased parent would have been entitled to inherit. That means the living lineal descendants split among themselves what their deceased parent would have received. If their parent is alive, they receive nothing.

Example: A, whose husband has predeceased A, had three adult children, B, C, and D. B had two children, E and F. C had one child, G. D had no children. Both B and C predecease A, but D is still alive at the time of her mother's death. When A dies, the estate is distributed *per stirpes*. In such case, D receives a one-third share of the estate, E and F each receive one-sixth of the estate, and G receives one-third of the estate.

FIGURE 40.1: *Per Stirpes* Example

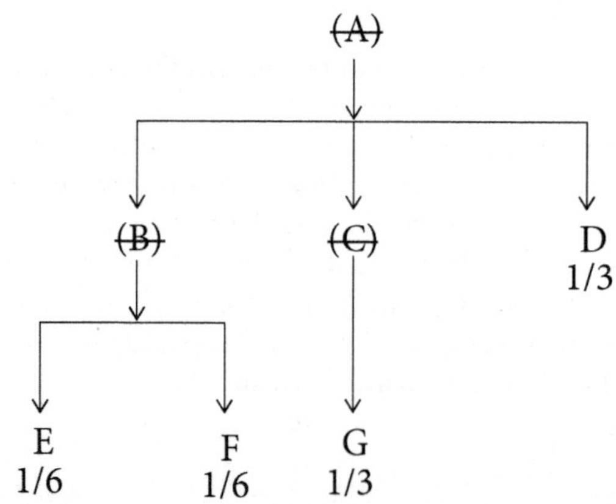

***PER CAPITA* DISTRIBUTION.** Under a ***per capita* distribution**, the living lineal descendants equally share the property of the estate. The heir's degree of relationship to the decedent does not matter. That means the children of the decedent share equally with the grandchildren, great-grandchildren, and so on. A common exception adopted in many states, and the approach the UPC takes, is that the distribution stops at the first living lineal descendant.

***Per capita* distribution**
Form of distributing the decedent's estate in which the living lineal descendants equally share the property of the estate.

> **Example:** In the example used above for *per stirpes* distribution, if A's estate were instead distributed on a per capita basis, each person would receive an equal share. In that case, E, F, G, and D would each receive a one-fourth share of the estate.

FIGURE 40.2: *Per Capita* Example

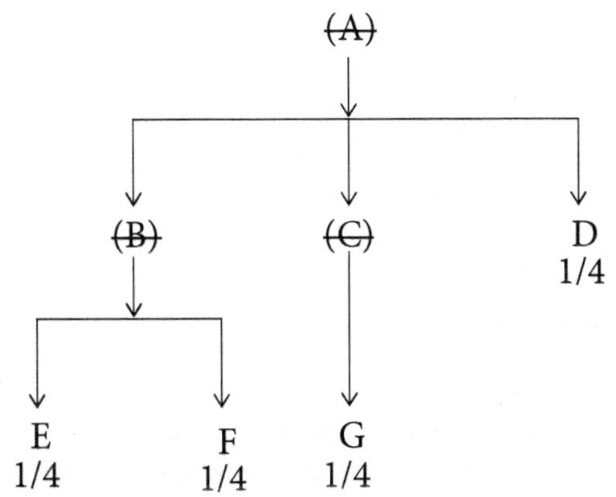

> **Example:** In the above example, if D had a living lineal descendant, the distribution under a *per capita* basis would not change. This is because many states and the UPC approach do not distribute down beyond the first living lineal descendant under a *per capita* basis.

CHILDREN. With intestate succession, questions may arise as to whether all types of children are entitled to inherit from a decedent or if any restrictions from inheritance exist. Some of the more common questions include the rights of (1) nonmarital children, (2) adopted children, and (3) posthumous children. The UPC provides uniform laws to assist in the analysis.

1. *Nonmarital children.* The decedent's marital status is irrelevant to distribution to children from their biological mother. An illegitimate child—that is, a child born outside of marriage—is eligible to take from the mother's estate. The child can also take from the biological father's estate if paternity has been established by a court proceeding or paternity is admitted by the father; otherwise, the child does not inherit from the father.
2. *Adopted children.* Children who are legally adopted inherit just as if they were biological children of the adopting parents. Once adopted, the children do not inherit from their biological parents through intestate succession. To allow

still inherit through a will provision of their biological parents.

otherwise would provide a windfall to the adopted child. However, they may still inherit through a will provision of their biological parents.

Posthumous child
A child born after the decedent's death.

3. *Posthumous child.* A **posthumous child** is a child born after the decedent's death. Such circumstances may arise from instances of postmortem *in vitro* fertilization of a widow or partner. States vary as to the inheritance rights of posthumous children. Some limit inheritance to child born within ten months of the decedent's death. This would allow for a child conceived on the day of the decedent's death to be an heir to the decedent. Other states allow children to be born years after the decedent's death and still be treated as an heir.

RELATIVES BY MARRIAGE. In most states, relatives by marriage to a decedent, other than a surviving spouse, do not receive any property through intestate succession.

> **Example:** Stepchildren (unless adopted by the decedent) do not inherit property through intestacy.

CONVICTS AND MURDERING HEIR. The UPC provides that a convict is still entitled to inherit through intestate succession. However, if the heir is convicted of murdering the decedent, the murderer does not inherit and is treated as if they had predeceased the decedent. The murderer's issue can still inherit, but some states do not provide for an inheritance to the issue of a murderer of the decedent. Note that a murderer can still inherit from parents and siblings if the murderer did not murder the person from whom they are inheriting.

SIMULTANEOUS DEATHS. While rare, sometimes both spouses die at the same time, such as can happen in accidents and natural disasters. In these cases, it is often unknown which spouse died first, and thus the laws of intestate succession cannot be applied. The UPC provides that heirs must survive for 120 hours (approximately five days) before they are entitled to inherit.

Some states have adopted the Uniform Simultaneous Death Act, which provides in such situations that each spouse is treated as if they predeceased the other. In such circumstances, each spouse's assets are distributed as if they had died without a surviving spouse.

> **Example:** A married couple is killed instantaneously in a car accident. Spouse A's assets are treated as if Spouse B had predeceased Spouse A through intestate succession. Spouse B's assets are treated as if Spouse A had predeceased Spouse B through intestate succession.

Probate

Probate
The process of collecting a decedent's property, paying the decedent's debts and taxes, and distributing the remainder of the estate.

Probate is a court process used when a person dies testate (that is, with a will). Non-probate transfers may occur and some of them are identified in the Management Application above. Transfers occurring when a decedent utilized an estate planning trust (discussed below), are administered through the trust provisions and not through court-supervised probate proceedings.

The probate court, a special state court, supervises the administration of the estate and approves the distribution of the estate's assets. In probate, the will is authenticated as the last, final, and true will of the testator.

Petition for Probate

Probate court opens with the filing of an application or petition for probate. Any person who has an interest in the estate (such as an heir) can open probate. Usually, probate is opened in the court nearest to where the decedent resided prior to death.

Appointment of Probate Representative

A representative of the estate is appointed to administer the estate. The representative is known as an **administrator** (male) or **administratrix** (female) if the decedent died intestate. If the decedent died testate, the representative appointed in the will is known as an **executor** (male) or **executrix** (female). The UPC uses the gender-neutral term, personal representative, to denote the person who administers the estate.

Administrator or administratrix
A male or female, respectively, representative of an estate if the decedent died intestate.

Executor or executrix
A male or female, respectively, representative appointed in the will.

An attorney is often retained to help with the administration of the estate, the preparation of all estate tax filings (a federal estate tax return is filed, and, in some jurisdictions, state inheritance tax filing occurs along with the payment of state inheritance taxes), and assistance in the identification of all heirs who are to receive the probate estate property.

Collection and Distribution of Estate Assets

During the probate process, the executor collects, identifies, and takes control of all of the decedent's assets. This is also known as marshalling the estate assets. Usually, a written inventory of these assets is filed with the court within a specific time from the opening of probate. The inventory is sent to all of the estate's heirs and beneficiaries. During this time, an appraisal is completed for noncash assets. In addition to collecting the assets, under the court's supervision the decedent's debts are paid. Most states require that a notice to creditors be published or served so that they may timely submit a claim for payment by the estate. Creditors then have a fixed period within which to submit their claims or be barred from recovering from the estate. The heirs are not personally liable for the payment of the decedent's debts unless they were otherwise liable for them — for example, if the heir co-signed the obligation or personally guaranteed the debt.

If the decedent died testate, the will disposes of the decedent's property existing at the time of death. **Ademption** arises when a specific item of property, also known as a specific devise, that was intended to be distributed to a beneficiary fails because the testator does not own the property at death. If the testator dies without owning the specific gift, the beneficiary receives nothing.

Ademption
When an heir receives nothing because the testator leaves a specific devise of property, and that property is no longer in the estate.

> **Example:** Shawn's will provides that his classic 1967 Ford Mustang Shelby GT500 fastback will be distributed to his niece, Ariana. If Shawn sells the classic car before his death, the property has adeemed, and his niece receives nothing from this specific gift.

If a testator's estate does not have enough assets to pay all the gifts, abatement results. **Abatement** is the proportional reduction in the distribution of an estate when the funds or assets are insufficient to pay all beneficiaries in full. Abatement may also arise when it is necessary to pay for a share owed to an omitted child, omitted spouse, or omitted domestic partner.

Abatement
The proportional reduction in the distribution of an estate when the funds or assets are insufficient to pay all beneficiaries in full.

Closing of the Probate Estate

Once the foregoing activities have occurred, the estate may be closed. The closing will require a court hearing, and the submission of a final accounting and inventory of the assets and the court's approval of the distribution of estate assets. The estate is then deemed closed and can only be reopened by order of the court.

Trusts

Trust
A legal arrangement in which one person transfers property to another to be held and used for the benefit of a third person.

A **trust** is a legal relationship in which property is transferred (by the settlor, also known as the grantor, donor, or trustor) and held and managed (by the trustee(s)) for the beneficiaries named in the trust. The settlor has control over the property in the trust during the settlor's lifetime and can amend, alter, or terminate a trust during the settlor's lifetime. The settlor of a revocable trust may serve as a trustee. A trustee may be either a person or a company (such as a bank trust department). Trusts can be created for any lawful purpose.

> **Example:** A trust can be created to financially take care of a beloved pet upon the death of the pet's owner. The trust could arrange for the cost of care and food to be funded from the trust assets.

Creation of Trusts

To create a valid trust, the following elements must be present:

1. A settlor, who creates the trust and transfers property into the trust;
2. A designated trustee, who is given *legal title* to the property. The trustee is responsible for holding and managing the property in accordance with the instructions provided by the settlor;
3. One or more beneficiaries, who receive the "benefit" of the assets in the trust;
4. Trust property that is to be placed in the trust; and
5. A valid trust purpose, which may include estate planning.

Management Application
When to Use a Trust

There are certain types of circumstances where the creation of a trust is beneficial, including:

1. *Second marriages.* A settlor may desire that upon the death of the spouse from the second marriage, remaining assets will pass to children

of the first marriage. This allows for the assets to be used by the spouse of the second marriage during the life of the settlor then transferred to the children of the settlor upon the death of the second spouse.

2. *Young couples.* A young spouse may desire that their property be set aside for the benefit of the children of that relationship.
3. *Profligate beneficiaries.* Concerns that a beneficiary may quickly dissipate an inheritance may prompt the use of a trust. A spendthrift trust can be used to protect the trust assets from being accessed or controlled directly by the beneficiary. Additionally, it can safeguard the trust assets from the actions of creditors.

Types of Trusts

While many types of trusts exist, trusts can be characterized as either *inter vivos* or testamentary. An ***inter vivos* trust** is a trust created during a trustor's life. A **testamentary trust** is a trust that takes effect upon the settlor's death. This type of trust must comply with the state laws on creating wills.

Trusts are also classified as being either revocable or irrevocable. A **revocable trust** can be changed or revoked at any time prior to the trustor's death. Revocable trusts are also known as **living trusts. Irrevocable trusts** cannot be changed or revoked during the trustor's life. The type of trust chosen can affect creditor rights to the trust assets and reduce estate taxes upon death. One of the key benefits of an irrevocable trust is asset protection. Once assets are placed in an irrevocable trust, they are no longer owned by the settlors and are thus shielded from creditors and legal judgments. By transferring assets into an irrevocable trust, the settlor removes those assets from their taxable estate, potentially reducing estate taxes. Additionally, income generated by the trust's assets is taxed at the trust's tax rate, which may be lower than the settlor's personal tax rate.

***Inter vivos* trust**
A trust created during a trustor's life.

Testamentary trust
A trust that takes effect upon the settlor's death.

Revocable trust
A trust that can be changed or revoked at any time prior to the trustor's death.

Irrevocable trust
A trust that cannot be changed or revoked during the trustor's life.

Sample Form
Cover Letter to Trustee of Irrevocable Trust

John Jones
123 Main Street
Los Angeles, CA 90007

Re: Jones Family Trust

Dear Mr. Jones:

As you are aware, you will serve as Trustee of the Jones Family Trust (the "Trust") pursuant to a trust agreement by and between Sally Settlor (the "Grantor"), and you, as Trustee (the "Trustee"). Enclosed is an initial draft of the Trust Agreement. This letter shall serve as a reminder of your duties and obligations as Trustee of the Trust. You are strongly advised to read the Trust Agreement carefully in order to fully understand your duties and obligations as Trustee.

The Trust is irrevocable, and the assets transferred to the Trust is to be managed for the benefit of Jeremy Jones (the "Beneficiary") during his lifetime and distributed to the beneficiaries named in the Trust upon the Grantor's death unless a contrary intention is expressed in the Grantor's Last Will and Testament by specific reference to the Trust.

. . .

Example: Keith Yang creates a trust and executes a deed transferring his residential home to the trust. He wishes to function as the trustee of the trust and receive the income from the trust during his lifetime. Upon his death, his children, Carson and Lenara, will have ownership of the trust property as the residential home will pass to them without having to be distributed through a probate court proceeding. This is illustrated in Figure 40.3 below.

FIGURE 40.3: Revocable Trust Example

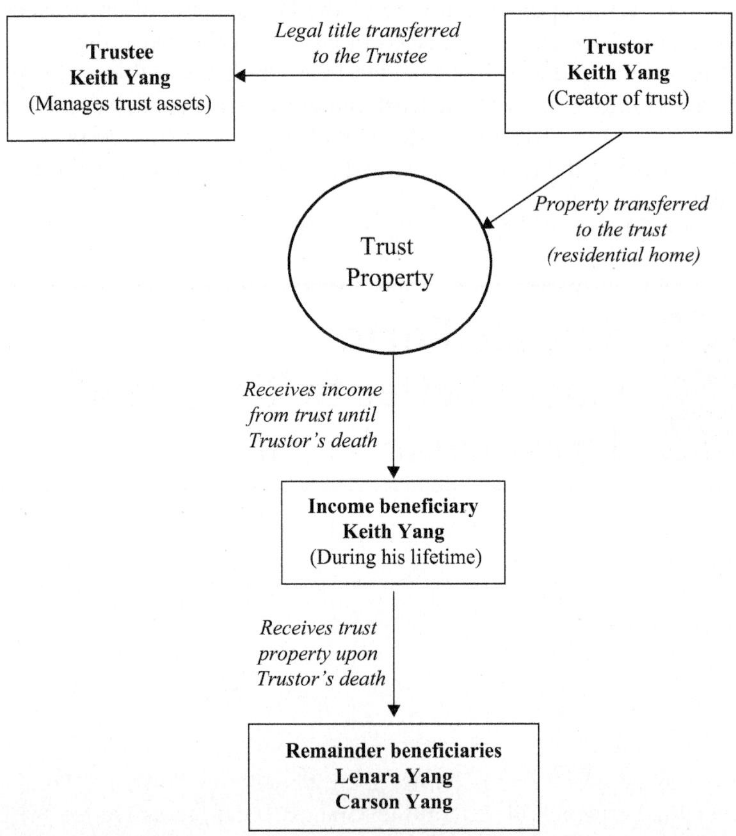

Management Application
Reasons to Avoid Probate and Use a Trust

A few of the benefits realized through the use of an estate planning trust are:

1. *Time.* The average probate length with no issues or disputes lasts about 18 months. Usually, the use of a trust bypasses the probate process. Assets can be quickly distributed to the beneficiaries.
2. *Expense Savings.* The estate of J. Paul Getty spent more than $40 million in attorneys' fees in disputes involving assets subject to probate.
3. *Tax benefits.* Trusts can be designed to reduce federal and state taxation of the trust assets.
4. *Privacy.* Courts do not supervise trusts continuously. Their jurisdiction can be invoked when needed. Unlike wills, which become public documents once they enter probate, trusts remain private. This means that the details of the trust and its assets are not disclosed to the public.

Duties of Personal Representatives and Trustees

Executors and trustees are fiduciaries. Where a trust does not name an executor or trustee, or the nominated person fails or refuses to function as an executor or trustee, the court can appoint one. Once a valid will or trust is in effect, the executor or trustee has all the enumerated powers given to the person as stated in the will or trust instrument. Usually, a state statute or case law will define the powers of an executor and will often require court consent for matters of substance, such as the sale of estate property. The personal representative must go through the court for authority, whereas a trustee can act immediately upon the creation of the trust or the settlor's death.

Notably, in the context of trust administration, the trustee manages the trust independently of the court. The trustee has implied powers used to carry out the purpose of the trust. Some of these implied powers include the power to sell trust property, incur expenses, and lease trust property. Nonetheless, whether an executor or a trustee, they owe fiduciary duties to the beneficiaries named in the will or trust. The law of fiduciary duties was reviewed in Chapter 15. Violations of these fiduciary duties are often heavily litigated. When a serious breach of them occurs, the fiduciary may be removed and replaced, as well as being held for the damages their acts and omissions caused.

DUTIES OWED TO BENEFICIARIES. For purposes of our following discussion, we shall refer to an executor or trustee as a fiduciary who owes the following duties to the beneficiaries of a will or trust they are managing:

- Duty of loyalty—acting solely in the interests of beneficiaries.
  - Note under certain circumstances a trust may permit a trustee to engage in self-dealing; nevertheless, the beneficiaries' interests must be placed ahead of their own and after full disclosure of the proposed action to the beneficiaries.

Court approval should be obtained prior to the proposed action, which is always a requirement for an executor to engage in self-dealing.

- Duty of good faith — acting honestly and with integrity.
- Duty to be impartial — not favoring one beneficiary over another.
- Duty to segregate — not to commingle estate or trust assets with their own.
- Duty not to delegate — though responsible for administering assets, this duty does not prohibit the fiduciary from relying on professional advisors in reaching a decision.
- Duty to account — provide complete and accurate information for the assets they are managing.
- Duty of care — exercising reasonable care and skill in managing assets.

Duty of loyalty
A duty requiring a trustee to administer and manage the trust for the benefit of the beneficiaries only.

Duty of Loyalty. The **duty of loyalty** requires that the fiduciary administer and manage the estate or trust for the benefit of the beneficiaries *only*. This means that the fiduciary is not allowed to engage in transactions that are considered self-dealing.

In the following case, the widow of the deceased, who was the personal administrator of her husband's estate, sought to have her personal debts paid by the estate at the expense of the estate creditors.

CASE 40.2

ESTATE ADMINISTRATORS AS FIDUCIARIES MUST AVOID SELF-DEALING

CHRISTOFFERSEN v. CHRISTOFFERSEN

928 N.W.2d 670 (2019)

Court of Appeals of Iowa

David Christoffersen ("David") owed $110,962.30 to his sister Shirley Christofferson ("Shirley") for monies borrowed and advanced on his behalf for four years before his death. When David died, Shirley sought repayment from David's estate, managed by his surviving spouse, Karen Christofferson ("Karen"). Karen had not been made aware of the debts until shortly before David's death. After David's death, Shirley sought repayment of her loans by making a claim against David's estate. Karen, as the estate administrator, did not pay Shirley's claim. However, during her estate administration, she sold a warehouse, which was part of the probate estate, and used some of the sale proceeds to repay the mortgage balance secured by the warehouse in which she had a marital property interest (known as the Chewit Properties). With the remaining balance of the sales proceeds, Karen paid two personal mortgages (one was the mortgage on the farm of David and Karen, as joint tenants with rights of survivorship and the balance on a house purchased for Karen's daughter). The unsecured claims of Shirley remained unpaid. The probate court concluded that Karen engaged in self-dealing because she improperly allocated the estate's assets by using the proceeds from the sale to pay joint personal debts owed by her and David. The probate court found that when Karen exercised her discretion to pay the personal mortgages, she enhanced her financial position relative to the general creditors of the estate. The probate court held Karen personally liable to Shirley for Shirley's claim against David's estate. Karen, as administrator of the estate, appealed that ruling.

Language of the Court. *As administrator of David's estate, Karen is a fiduciary. As such, she had a duty to act for the estate's benefit. "Self-dealing" describes a situation where a fiduciary personally profits from transactions between herself and the estate. The Iowa probate code prohibits self-dealing by a fiduciary unless the transaction is approved by court order after notice to all interested persons. Here, the alleged self-dealing involved Karen's use of proceeds remaining from the sale of the warehouse to pay off two mortgage notes signed by her and David. The probate court emphasized, "Chewit Properties was not a mortgagee on either of the additional mortgages that Karen paid. Chewit Properties was not an obligee on either note that Karen paid." The probate court further found neither note was in default, nor had lender on the warehouse mortgage, Midstates Bank, made a demand to accelerate the payment terms when Karen chose to pay the outstanding balances with the money left over from selling the warehouse. The court decided Karen's discharge of these "personal debts" ran afoul of Iowa law, which allows a fiduciary to pay an encumbrance on an asset of the estate, so long as "the making of such payment shall not increase the share of the distributee entitled to such encumbered assets." Karen, by paying off the two mortgages with the Chewit proceeds without court approval, increased her own share of the distribution at the expense of Shirley's claim. We affirm the probate court's determination of self-dealing.*

Decision. Estate administrators must refrain from self-dealing and prioritize the estate's obligations to creditors over their personal interests unless they obtain court approval.

Focus on Ethics

Does this decision imply that a court may exempt an estate representative from the duty of impartiality if the will's instructions allow for self-dealing transactions?

DUTIES SPECIFIC TO TRUSTEES. In addition to those identified above, the following fiduciary duties are applicable to trustees:

Duty to Invest. While each state has its own requirements regarding a trustee's **duty to invest**, the common law requires a trustee to function as a reasonably prudent person who is investing their own property would—trying to maximize income while still preserving the assets of the trust.

Duty to invest
A duty requiring a trustee to function as a reasonably prudent person would in investing his own property.

If the trustee breaches this duty to invest, the trustee must make good the loss.

Example: Rory is the trustee of Audra's assets which have a fair market value of $500,000. Rory invests 90 percent of that amount in ABC Corporation. Rory is at risk of violating the duty to invest, since a trustee should not invest such a substantial proportion of the trust property in one security. Doing so increases the risk of large losses resulting from market volatility.

Duty to earmark
A duty requiring the trustee to label trust property as "trust property."

Duty to Earmark. The **duty to earmark** requires the trustee to label trust property as "trust property."

> **Example:** If a trustee owns shares of stock and it is properly earmarked, the stock will be registered to "John Doe, as trustee of the XYZ Trust."

Duty to segregate
A duty prohibiting a trustee from commingling their own personal funds with the trust funds.

Duty not to delegate
A duty prohibiting a trustee from delegating decision-making powers to outside parties.

Duty to Segregate. The **duty to segregate** is closely related to the duty to earmark. While the duty to earmark requires that trust assets be labeled as such, the duty to segregate states that the trustee cannot commingle their own personal funds with the trust funds. In addition, this duty also prohibits a trustee from commingling the funds of two separate trusts, even if they have the same beneficiary.

If the trustee breaches the duty to segregate, the trustee can be removed and be held liable for any loss incurred.

Duty to account
A duty requiring that a trustee must, on a regular basis, provide the beneficiaries with a statement of any income and expenses of the trust.

Duty to Account. The **duty to account** requires that a trustee must, on a regular basis, provide the beneficiaries with a statement of any income and expenses of the trust. If the trustee fails to do this, the beneficiaries can demand an accounting by filing an action.

Duty of due care
A duty requiring a trustee to function as a reasonably prudent person dealing with their own affairs would.

Duty of Due Care. The **duty of due care** is implied in all of the duties described above. Nonetheless, there is still a general duty of due care owed, which requires the trustee to function as a reasonably prudent person dealing with their own affairs would.

AI Feature: Drafting Provisions of a Will

Using an internet search engine, research the Revised Uniform Fiduciary Access to Digital Assets Act. Using an AI program, draft provisions that you would include in your will. These should include the following provisions: nominating an estate representative and the powers you wish to bestow on that person; gifts to beneficiaries (both specific gifts and residuary gifts); access to the decedent's digital assets, and; funeral arrangements.

Key Terms

- Abatement, 1021
- Acknowledgment, 1015
- Ademption, 1021
- Administrator or administratrix, 1021
- Beneficiary, 1010
- Codicil, 1015
- Decedent, 1010
- Duty not to delegate, 1028
- Duty of due care, 1028
- Duty of loyalty, 1026
- Duty to account, 1028
- Duty to earmark, 1028
- Duty to invest, 1027
- Duty to segregate, 1028
- Escheat, 1018
- Executor or executrix (aka estate representative), 1021
- General devise, 1011
- Holographic will, 1014
- *Inter vivos* trust, 1023
- Intestate, 1010
- Intestate succession, 1017
- Irrevocable trust, 1023
- Issue, 1010
- Lineal descendants, 1017
- Notary public, 1015
- Omitted spouse rule, 1011
- *Per capita* distribution, 1019
- *Per stirpes* distribution, 1018
- Posthumous child, 1020
- Pretermitted children, 1013
- Probate, 1020
- Residual devise, 1011
- Revocable trust/living trust, 1023
- Specific devise, 1011
- Testamentary trust, 1023
- Testate, 1010
- Testator/testatrix, 1010
- Trust, 1022
- Uniform Probate Code (UPC), 1018
- Will, 1010

Applying the Law

40.1 A "Will." Gloria Waterloo belonged to a congregation of which Jack Zimmerman was the rabbi. Zimmerman and his wife, Sandie, visited Waterloo in a hospice facility. Because handwriting was difficult for Waterloo, she dictated to Sandie a document that stated in part, "After I am deceased, Jack has full instructions from me. Attached is a list of final instructions. I want to leave Jack Zimmerman a sum of $3,000,000. He has full and final guardianship of my finances and real estate properties." In the presence of the Zimmermans, Waterloo revised the one-page document, initialed each of the paragraphs, and dated and signed the document, but she dictated no list of final instructions. About an hour later, another couple from the congregation arrived to visit her. One of them read the document aloud to Waterloo and confirmed with her that it represented her wishes. The document was not witnessed. Waterloo died a month later. After her death, her heirs opposed Zimmerman's effort to have the document admitted to probate because it was incomplete because the referenced list of final instructions did not exist. As such, the document failed as a will because it did not represent Waterloo's full testamentary intent. Should the document be admitted to probate as her last will and testament? *In re Estate of Waterloo*, 250 P.3d 558 (Ariz. Ct. App. Div. 1 2012)

40.2 Intention to Make a Will. Louise R. Macool, a woman who died before she had the opportunity to definitively indicate whether the document drafted by her attorney accurately reflected her wishes as to the disposition of her estate. In 1995, Louise executed a will naming her husband as the sole beneficiary and stepchildren and others as contingent beneficiaries. She executed a codicil to her will naming two stepchildren as contingent co-executors. Her husband died. She went to her estate attorney's office who, in her presence, dictated an entire will. But the dictated will did not reflect the somewhat cryptic notes that she presented to the attorney, which notes reflected changes in contingent beneficiaries and disposition of her home. She died an hour after her meeting with the attorney without reading the new will. Were the handwritten notes a holographic will? Was the rough draft prepared by the attorney, which she had not read, her last will and testament? *In re Probate of Will & Codicil of Macool*, 3 A.3d 1258 (N.J. Super. 2010)

40.3 Pretermitted Children. Kevin Bailey's will left everything to his wife, Beth, if she survived him; otherwise, his property was to go to his "heirs at law." Beth survived him, but she encountered a challenge in administering her husband's estate. He had two children out of wedlock, Keith and Christian, and they claimed to be pretermitted children and entitled to an intestate share of their father's estate. The trial court granted summary judgment for the two sons, virtually revoking Bailey's will. The Texas Court of Appeals considered whether the will's gift to "my heirs at law" is a provision for Bailey's children preventing the application of the Texas pretermitted children statute. Does this statement constitute a mentioning of his children so that they cannot be considered pretermitted children? *Bailey v. Warren*, 319 S.W.3d 185 (Tex. App. 12th Dist. 2010)

40.4 Gifts *Causa Mortis*. Roger Hansen died intestate at age 88. During his lifetime, he made mortgage loans to his nieces and was a vendor on a land contract with his great-nephew. Hansen died before he could execute a new will providing for the forgiveness of these debts to these relatives. The personal representative, his brother, included these notes in the probate estate. The debtors moved to strike the notes from the probate estate on the grounds that Hansen forgave these debts prior to his death and that the forgiveness amounted to gifts *causa mortis*. The trial court agreed with the debtors and granted the motion to strike the notes from the inventory. On appeal, the appellate court considered whether there had been effective delivery of the gifts prior to death. If it were undisputed that Hansen intended that, upon his death, the debts owed him by his relatives would be forgiven, how should the court rule? *Meegan v. Netzer (In re Estate of Hansen)*, 810 N.W.2d 358 (Wis. Ct. App. 2012)

40.5 Trustee's Duty. Trust beneficiaries of the J.F.B. Lowrey Trust brought an action against trustee, Regions Bank, alleging breach of fiduciary duty. The beneficiaries argued that Regions failed to protect and preserve the assets of the Lowrey Trust, 20,000 acres of timberland, following Hurricane Ivan. Specifically, the trust beneficiaries alleged that Regions should have either purchased insurance on the timber or sold most of the timberland before Hurricane Ivan to diversify the investments of the trust estate. As the trustee, what arguments would you make to show there was no breach of fiduciary duty? *Regions Bank v. Lowrey*, 101 So. 3d 210 (Ala. 2012)

40.6 Ademption. Jane Kelley sued Donald Neilson, the executor of her grandmother's estate. She sought an order directing the executor to give her the proceeds from the sale of real estate that her grandmother had devised to her. But her grandmother sold the property but died before the purchase and sale transaction was completed. The executor claimed that the sale adeemed the devise. Had ademption occurred? *Kelley v. Neilson*, 745 N.E.2d 952 (Mass. 2001)

40.7 Property Distribution. Jean, whose husband has predeceased her, has two adult children, Noah and Mina. Mina has three children: Alex, Brandon, and Christine. Noah has no children. Jean prepares a will equally dividing her estate between Noah and Mina. The will does not make any provision regarding Mina's children. After the will was executed and witnessed by Jean's lawyer and Noah, Mina dies. Jean dies, after updating her will to distribute her property *per stirpes*, and her estate is now in probate. Mina's children claim the will is invalid. Based on these facts, answer the following questions:

- **a.** Is the will valid? Discuss whether the requirements of a will have been met.
- **b.** If it is, how will Jean's estate be distributed?
- **c.** Assume the will was not found to be valid. How will Jean's estate be distributed?
  - **i.** Assume the state follows *per stirpes* distribution.
  - **ii.** Assume the state follows *per capita* distribution.

40.8 Undue Influence. Charlotte F. Stafford died in 2010 and was survived by her three nephews and their children. Prior to her death, decedent served as the historian for the Town of Oxford in Chenango County. In 2001, decedent hired Vicky House to help her with some typing. During this time, decedent and House became friends and in 2004, House moved into decedent's home to take care of her. Over the years, decedent executed many wills but at issue was the will executed in August 2007. Decedent's will distributed real property to be held in trust for the benefit of the Town of Oxford and House. The new will also disinherited decedent's nephews. This will was offered for probate, and the nephews objected, arguing the will was a product of House's undue influence. Which of the requirements for a valid will are at issue, if any? Can the nephews challenge the will, and what arguments will they make? *Matter of Stafford*, 111 A.D.3d 1216 (N.Y. App. Div. 2013)

40.9 Holographic Will. During her lifetime Diana Krueger executed two wills: a holographic will, executed on January 8, 1979, and a formally attested will, drafted by an attorney, and executed on March 9, 1990. The second will ("1990 will") contained a clause expressly revoking all previous wills, including the holographic will. The 1990 will was not located after Krueger's death. One of her heirs Fred Bieber, petitioned the probate court to probate the holographic will, testified that he had made an alteration to a minor bequest in the holographic will at the testatrix's request and in her presence. Should the altered holographic will be admitted to probate? If not, how should the decedent's property be distributed? *Bieber v. Bieber (In re Estate of Krueger)*, 529 N.W.2d 151 (N.D. 1995)

40.10 Joint Tenancy. At the time of her death, Verna Chappel, the deceased, owned real estate in joint tenancy with a niece. The amount of probate claims, including a claim for plaintiff's expenses as the deceased's conservator, exceeded the amount of probate assets. The niece sold the property to a third party. Lorna Rembe, executor of the estate, sued to have the court transfer the real property the deceased held in joint tenancy with the niece to Rembe as executor for purposes of payment of claims, debts, and charges. How should the court rule? How should general creditors of the deceased be treated when this occurs? *Rembe v. Stewart*, 387 N.W.2d 313 (Iowa 1986)

Insurance

41

Justice is the insurance which we have on our lives and property. Obedience is the premium which we pay for it. — William Penn, founder of the Province of Pennsylvania (1644-1718)

Chapter Outline

- Introduction
- Why Is Insurance So Complex?
- Insurable Interest

Case 41.1: *Arthur Andersen LLP v. Federal Ins. Co.*

- Who Is the Insured?
- Insurance Agents and Brokers

Case 41.2: *United Fire & Cas. Ins. Co. v. Garvey*

- The Insurance Contract
  - *Management Application: Alleging Loss or Damage to Property— Windstorm*
- Common Types of Property Insurance
- What Will the Insurance Carrier Pay?
  - *Management Application: Underinsurance— How Much Property Insurance Is Enough?*
- Duties of the Insured
- Duties of the Insurer

Case 41.3: *Maloney Cinque, LLC v. Pacific Ins. Co.*

- *Management Application: Policy Cancellation and Non-Renewal*
- AI Feature: Research the Making of a Claim Under an Insurance Policy

Learning Objectives

After studying this chapter, you should be able to:

1. Understand the terminology used in insurance contracts.
2. Explain an insurable interest.
3. Define who can be considered an insured.
4. Describe the differences between an insurance agent and a broker.
5. Explain the process of forming an insurance contract and the key provisions of such a contract.
6. Define the common types of real and personal property insurance.
7. Describe the duties of the insured and the insurer following an insured loss.

Introduction

Life is unpredictable and can subject any of us to financial losses. Sometimes our real and personal property is damaged by a calamity such as a fire, hurricane, earthquake, flood, windstorm, or building design defect. Other times, they are damaged by the intentional acts of others or by accidents. These are frequent hazards, but insurance proceeds can mitigate some of their financial effects.

Owners of both real and personal property need property and liability insurance to protect their substantial investments. Insurance plays a significant role in stabilizing the economy and preventing widespread panic and financial ruin when large-scale catastrophes occur. Because it is so important to society, state insurance commissioners heavily regulate the insurance industry. In this chapter, we will review the requirements for an insurance contract, common insurance coverages, and the good faith duties of the parties to the insurance policy.

Insurance Terminology

Insurance
A contract that shifts the risk of loss for individuals and businesses to another in exchange for a premium payment.

Insured
The person who obtains insurance.

Insurer
The insurance company that receives payment from an insured.

Premium
The cost of insurance paid by an insured.

Policy limits
Amounts of insurance that are payable under the insurance policy.

Insurance is a contract transferring the risk of loss from one party to another in exchange for a premium payment. The party obtaining and paying for the insurance is called an **insured**. Insurance allows insureds to recover from financial losses they would otherwise suffer. The insurance company receiving payment is known as the **insurer**. The insurer assumes the risk it might have to pay the insured for a covered loss if one occurs. The payment made by the insured to the insurer is known as the **premium**. Premiums are collected from a large pool of insureds, allowing the risk of loss to be spread among many insureds. The assumption underlying the insurance concept is that not all insureds will suffer a loss at the same time. In the event of a loss covered by the insurance policy, the insurer pays the insurance proceeds to the insured.

Premiums are based upon determinations made by actuaries, who apply mathematical, economic, and statistical models to price policies so that if insured losses occur, the insurer (insurance company) will have the financial resources to pay the claims.

An insured selects the amount of insurance, called the **policy limits**, that are payable under the policy. By paying the premium to the insurer, the insured seeks to avoid a larger loss. An insurer is only required to pay a loss covered by the policy up to the amount of the policy limits. Losses in excess of the policy limits are the responsibility of the insured.

The insurance contract is known as the insurance policy and must follow all the requirements necessary to form a valid legal contract. The premiums received are invested by the insurer in the stock market, real estate holdings, and other investments to realize investment returns to pay for future claims.

Why Is Insurance So Complex?

Complex Jargon

The insurance industry loves jargon and indecipherable policy language, which can baffle even the most talented linguists. Understanding insurance coverage terminology is not always easy, because insurance carriers do not use common language in the policies. As in every other business, insurance carriers try to distinguish themselves from their competitors. Increasing coverages or reducing premiums along with coverages is common.

The complexity of insurance law is not lost upon the courts. The courts have developed insurance contract interpretation rules that favor the insured.

Regulation and Conflicting State Laws

The insurance market is heavily regulated and is the subject of legislation and enforcement at the state level. The **McCarran Ferguson Act of 1945** is a federal law that delegated regulation of the insurance industry to the states. Many policies are prepared on forms developed by the Insurance Services Office® (ISO), a nonprofit association. These policy forms, after approval by the insurance carriers, are then submitted to state agencies for review. Each state has the ability to make the insurance carriers include or exclude certain types of coverage. While many states use standard ISO forms, just as many modify the forms on a state-by-state basis.

McCarran Ferguson Act of 1945
A federal law that delegated regulation of the insurance industry to the states.

Manuscript Policies

Carriers may also develop their own forms or issue a manuscript policy, which is a policy negotiated between the insurance carrier and the policyholder. As an example, large real estate developers and owners will often persuade their insurance carriers to modify standard policy forms due to the large premiums to be paid to the carriers.

Insurable Interest

To obtain insurance on property and recover in the event of a covered loss, a person must have an insurable interest in the property. An **insurable interest** exists when an insured would sustain a financial loss if the property were lost or damaged. The insurance company will pay only those who have an insurable interest in the property. Otherwise, without an insurable interest, an insurance policy would merely be gambling on the occurrence of an event. Gambling contracts are unenforceable.

Insurable interest
A requirement that a person have a property or personal interest in the insured goods, property, or person.

Real Property

States generally agree that the following persons have insurable interests in real property:

1. Buyers and sellers (owners) of real estate.
2. Owners of non-possessory real property interests (easements) and holders of future estates (less than fee interests).
3. Persons holding a security interest (mortgage or deed of trust). Mortgage lenders require borrowers to insure the property as a condition of making the loan. The insured's failure to maintain the required insurance will trigger a default under the mortgage deed of trust.
4. Tenants who have agreed to insure the premises under the terms of the lease.

5. Owners of a common interest in real property (such as a condominium owner and their homeowners' association, both of whom have an interest in the common area).

Example: Aiden and Mia own a commercial building as tenants in common. Aiden has a two-thirds interest, and Mia has a one-third interest in the building. If a fire damages the building, Aiden and Mia each recover from the policy proceeds only up to the amount of their insurable interest (two-thirds and one-third, respectively).

When Must a Person Have an Insurable Interest

An insurable interest must exist for property insurance *at the time of the loss.* If the insured does not have an insurable interest in the property, the insured may not enforce a claim under the policy.

Example: Jamie sells his real property to a third person. After the sale, he no longer has an insurable interest in the property.

In the following case, the international accounting firm Arthur Andersen LLP sued its insurance carrier for business losses caused because of property damage to the World Trade Center and the Pentagon on September 11, 2001. In its decision, the court considered whether Arthur Andersen had an insurable interest in damaged insured property covered by the policy.

CASE 41.1

AN INSURABLE INTEREST INVOLVES A DIRECT MONETARY BENEFIT OR LOSS FROM DAMAGE TO COVERED PROPERTY

ARTHUR ANDERSEN LLP v. FEDERAL INS. CO.

3 A.3d 1279 (2010)

Appellate Division of the New Jersey Superior Court

Arthur Andersen filed a claim for business losses for $204 million in lost earnings in the three and a half months following the 9/11 terrorist attacks. Andersen's business interruption clause in its insurance policy covered losses "caused by property damage that prevented the flow of goods or services to or from the insured and necessarily interrupted the insured's business." Andersen did not own or lease any property at the World Trade Center or the Pentagon and could not identify any supplier or client whose property was damaged to support its claim. Nonetheless, Andersen filed a claim under its all-risk commercial property insurance policy for business losses that it claimed it had suffered due to the property damage to the WTC and the Pentagon, based on a comparison between expected revenue trends and actual revenue earned. Andersen sued its insurer under the policy, but the trial court granted summary judgment in favor of the insurer. Andersen appealed.

Language of the Court. *No evidence has been presented that Andersen insured or was responsible for insurance for either site or the airplane. Andersen did not own or lease any of this property. One must have an insurable interest in property to sustain recovery under a policy that insures risks for property damage. Although it is not necessary to have legal or equitable title to have an insurable interest in the property, it is clear that the interest in the property must have some value. The party that seeks to recover would also bear the burden of proving that value.*

A test to determine an insurable interest in real property is whether the insured has such right or interest, that he will either benefit by its preservation or suffer a direct loss from its destruction. Here, Andersen did not derive a direct benefit, like rental income, from the existence of the WTC and Pentagon. Additionally, Andersen did not suffer a direct loss from the damage done to those buildings on 9/11. Here, Andersen is unable to identify any relationship it had with either the WTC or the Pentagon that had an ascertainable value and provided a basis for benefit or loss.

Andersen argues that insurable interest means "any economic interest in the continued existence of the property" and exists "if the loss of the property may cause the insured an economic loss." This expansive interpretation fails because it conflicts with established caselaw and undermines the policy underlying the requirement for insurable interest.

Andersen's theory would permit an insured to allege an insurable interest in a class of property so broad as to be impossible to define and certainly not susceptible to a predictable level of risk. Just as an insurable interest cannot be viewed so narrowly as to create a windfall for the insurer, allowing it to retain the premiums without providing anything in return, the interest cannot be read as broadly as Andersen argues, allowing the insured to reap a windfall recovery for a loss so clearly unanticipated in the calculation of the premium. Such an application would undermine the very purpose of an "insurable interest" requirement, reducing an insurance contract to a "pure gamble," and we reject it as a matter of law.

Decision. The court affirmed judgment in favor of the insurer, finding Andersen had no insurable interest.

Focus on Ethics

Was it ethical for the CPA firm to assert that it had an insurable interest in either building?

Who Is the Insured?

Most policies contain a specific definition of who qualifies as an insured under the policy. These parties may include the "named insured" and "additional insureds." The **named insured** is the policy owner and is usually the party purchasing the insurance. This person has the power to cancel, modify, or renew the policy.

Named insured
In the event of a covered loss, the person or business receiving payment from the insurance company.

Additional insured
A party unrelated to the named insured who receives the benefits of the insurance policy without having to pay the premium that the named insured pays.

An **additional insured** is a third person who receives the benefits of being insured under the insurance policy without having to pay the premium. Often landlords, mortgage lenders, commercial equipment lessors, owners, and general contractors require that they be named as additional insureds to provide insurance coverage for their benefit. In this situation, the insurance company owes the additional insureds the same duties to defend and indemnify that the insurer owes the named insured. The named insured pays the additional premium cost; however, the cost is often minimal.

> **Example:** Realty, Inc. owns land and is a named insured under its own insurance policies for the land. Festival, Inc., wants to hold a summer festival over several weekends using Realty, Inc.'s land. Tens of thousands of people are anticipated at the festival which will have music, food, and alcohol. Realty, Inc. will require Festival, Inc., to obtain insurance coverage for the event and will require Realty, Inc. to be added as an additional insured under the insurance policy covering the festival events. This provides Realty, Inc. with insurance coverage specific to the event without having to pay for its own insurance policy.

Insurance Agents and Brokers

The insurance marketplace and prior claims history dictate the availability of particular coverages and the pricing of those policies. Because insurance coverages and products are constantly changing, it is prudent for a party to stay informed with respect to available coverage and policy pricing.

In most cases, a person does not purchase insurance directly from an insurer. Insurance is sold primarily through agents and brokers. Agents sell insurance for only one insurance carrier. Although **insurance agents** advise consumers on the insurance policies that best suit their needs, the insurance agent is an agent of the insurance company, not of the applicant.

Insurance agents
Agents sell insurance for only one insurance carrier and are agents for the insurance company.

Insurance broker
A broker is an agent to the insured and can place insurance with multiple insurance carriers.

An **insurance broker** can place insurance with multiple insurance carriers. In most states, the broker is the agent of the insured regarding matters connected with the application for insurance. Agents and brokers have fiduciary duties of good faith and reasonable care in handling insurance-related matters. Mistakes do occur during the application and claim management process, and the distinction between an agent and a broker can have significant consequences for the insured.

Fiduciary Duties

INSURANCE AGENTS. The agent owes a fiduciary duty to act in the best interest of the insurance company. Because the insurance agent works for the insurance company, the insurance company is liable for acts they commit. If an agent acts negligently toward a person in the process of securing the insurance policy, those acts are attributable to the insurance company.

> **Example:** If Property Insurance Company sells policies only through employed agents, and one of them negligently fails to list a co-insured on the application (such as a co-tenant), the insurer would be liable to the non-named person if they were harmed because of an insured loss.

INSURANCE BROKERS. Insurance brokers owe a fiduciary duty to act in the best interests of the insured regarding matters related to the application for insurance. Because of this fiduciary relationship, misrepresentations made by the broker are deemed to be misrepresentations of the applicant.

> **Example:** When the insured advises its broker of certain information and the broker provides contrary information to the insurer, the insurance company can later cancel the policy because of the broker's misrepresentations.

In the following case, the insurer brought an action against the insured seeking a declaration that it did not have a duty to indemnify under the property insurance policy.

CASE 41.2

AN AGENCY RELATIONSHIP MAY REFLECT THE OWNER'S PROPERTY INTEREST

UNITED FIRE & CAS. INS. CO. v. GARVEY

419 F.3d 743 (2005)

United States Court of Appeals for the Eighth Circuit

James and Beverly Garvey purchased a residential piece of property. James asked his son, Paul, to obtain insurance coverage on the property. Paul called the family's insurance agent, Dan Hebbeln, and informed him that his parents had recently purchased a residential property, and the property needed to be insured. In the past, Paul had purchased insurance on behalf of his parents and each time he did so, Paul had informed the agent he was acting on behalf of his parents. Hebbeln completed an application that Paul reviewed and signed. United Fire then issued a policy of insurance. On this policy, Paul was listed as the insured on the property. Two years later, the property was destroyed by a fire. Paul reported the loss to the Hebbeln and the insurance company, United Fire, was notified. United Fire denied the claim on the basis that Paul, as the listed insured, lacked an insurable interest.

United Fire filed an action for declaratory relief to establish that it had no duty to indemnify Paul or his parents for the loss of their property. United Fire moved for summary judgment. The district court found in favor of United Fire and held that there was no duty to indemnify. Paul Garvey appealed, arguing that he was acting as an agent on behalf of his parents. On appeal, the decision in favor of the insurer was reversed. Then, United Fire appealed that decision.

Language of the Court. *United Fire argued that under Missouri law an agent cannot obtain insurance on behalf of an undisclosed principal. Paul argued the district court was incorrect when they concluded that Paul's parents were undisclosed principals. On appeal, the jury found that Paul disclosed to Hebbeln he was acting as an agent for his parents at the time he obtained the insurance and that Hebbeln was acting as an agent for United Fire when he completed the application and submitted it to United Fire.*

Under Missouri law, an insurance broker is one who, on behalf of the insured, shops around for insurance among multiple insurance companies. In such instances, the broker is acting as the agent of the insured. Conversely, "[a] person delegated to solicit insurance for a particular company, and to refrain from soliciting insurance for any other company, is an agent [of the insurer], and not a broker." Absent special conditions or circumstances suggesting otherwise, the presumption is a broker is the agent of the insured, and any mistakes made by the broker are attributable to the insured. However, the acts of one procuring insurance as the agent of the insurer are imputable to the insurer. The facts of a particular situation dictates whether an "independent broker" is an agent for the insurer or the insured.

As Hebbeln testified, the agreement imposed an affirmative duty on him to solicit the coverage on behalf of United Fire if it was available. Based on this evidence, a jury could reasonably conclude Hebbeln was precluded from shopping the coverage to other insurers, and was not acting as a broker.

Paul does not claim an insurable interest in the property. Rather, the evidence viewed in the light most favorable to the verdict, shows he was acting as agent for his parents when he obtained the insurance. By virtue of this agency relationship, the Garveys' interests in the property are reflected in the policy.

Decision. The court of appeals reversed, holding that the Garveys had an insurable interest and United Fire had a duty to indemnify them for the fire loss.

Focus on Ethics

Would the outcome have been different if Paul Garvey had no familial ties to James and Beverly Garvey? How can an insurance company protect itself from third parties claiming to have a principal/agent relationship to circumvent the insurable interest requirement?

The Insurance Contract

An insurance policy is a contract, and the basic contract law principles discussed earlier in the text apply to it. As noted, because of the state regulation of insurance, each state may have unique requirements or may vary the general provisions discussed below.

Application

The process of entering into an insurance contract begins with the application. The completed application of the insured becomes part of the policy. Subject to certain exceptions, the applicant is liable for his misrepresentations in the application.

> **Example:** If the property owner was aware that leaking plumbing existed at the time they applied for property insurance, the insurer could seek to deny a later claim for water damage to the building, especially if the insurer would not have extended insurance to the insured had it known all the material facts regarding the property.

Effective Date

The effective date of a policy is the date on which coverage begins. The insurer may wish to conduct a visual inspection of the property before it issues a policy, and the effective date may occur well after the application is submitted. The general rule is that the insurer has no liability to the insured until the policy is issued. Because it sometimes takes time to issue the policy, an insurance agent (usually not by a broker) may provide a binder to obtain coverage from the date of the application. A **binder** is a form of temporary insurance contract that provides coverage subject to the same terms and conditions as the insurance policy the carrier will eventually issue.

Binder
Temporary insurance lasting until a policy is issued.

Insurance Contract

The insurance contract, also known as an insurance policy, sets forth the covered losses and exclusions from coverage under the policy. Most insurance carriers provide insurance coverage using standardized insurance contract forms. States may require the use of standardized forms and can mandate that certain covered losses be included and can limit the extent to which an insurer may attempt to reduce coverage.

Concept Summary
Important Policy Clauses

Choice of law	Policies can identify the state law to be applied in interpreting the policy. As insurance is regulated by the states, the insurer will attempt to select the law of a state that is most favorable to its interests.
Co-insurance	Co-insurance clauses encourage applicants to insure their properties for amounts close to their full value by penalizing insureds in the event of a loss if they fail to purchase insurance at least equal to a specified percentage of property value (usually 80 percent). If the face value of the policy is less than the required percentage, the insurer pays only a proportionate amount of the loss. The balance is paid by the insured.

> **Example:** Acme Manufacturing owns a plant valued at $2 million and has a $1.5 million fire insurance policy. If the insurance policy required that 80 percent of the property value be covered by insurance, and Acme suffered $1 million in property damage, Acme's insurance recovery would be $937,500.

Deductible clause	The policy will often state the amount the insured is required to pay before the insurance policy benefits become payable. **Example:** If a building owner has a $1 million fire insurance policy with a $10,000 deductible, and the structure suffers severe damage caused by a fire, the insured must pay the first $10,000 in damages.
Subrogation	Subrogation is the insurer's right to pursue a third party that caused the insured loss. Once an insurer pays the insured's liability, the insurer takes over the legal rights the insured may have had against third parties who caused the damages. The insured cannot pursue a claim for damages against the wrongdoer. Subrogation prevents the insured from double recovery. Without subrogation, the insured could recover from the insurer and then sue and recover against the third party who caused the damage, thereby receiving a windfall. With subrogation, the insurer has the right to recover against the third party. **Example:** If a contractor's liability insurance pays for property damage caused to a project owner, the insurer obtains the right to recover this sum from other responsible parties, such as negligent subcontractors who caused the harm.
Statute of limitations	The statute of limitations, as applied to insurance contracts, requires that an insured seek to enforce an insurance claim within a certain period after the covered loss occurs.

Covered Losses

Covered loss
An event or occurrence that triggers the duty of the insurance carrier to investigate and potentially pay an insurance claim.

The insurance contract identifies which losses are covered under the policy. A **covered loss**, also known as an insured loss, is the unforeseen, unanticipated destruction, diminution, or loss of something of value triggering the duty of the insurance carrier to investigate and potentially pay an insurance claim.

A covered loss is caused by a peril. Examples of perils to real property include fire, explosion, soil movement or failure, lightning, hail, water damage from floods, faulty plumbing, smoke damage, earthquakes, and windstorms. A single peril may cause more than one type of real property loss.

> **Example:** A broken water pipe may damage flooring and create conditions favorable to the growth of mold. The sudden occurrence of the broken pipe will be a covered peril, and the resulting mold may or may not be a covered peril under the policy.

Insureds should carefully review their policies to confirm that they have the property coverage needed. If a covered loss is not stated or reasonably inferable from the policy terminology, a loss may be uninsured.

SEPARATE FORMS OF PROPERTY INSURANCE. Four forms of insurance policy protections exist: basic (or named risk), broad, special (or all risk), and earthquake.

1. *Basic.* Under this coverage, the insurer indemnifies the insured only for losses specifically listed in the policy, such as fire, flood, or design liability. Anything not specifically named in the policy is not covered. Many mortgage lenders require that, as a condition to obtaining and not defaulting on the loan, borrowers secure basic insurance.
2. *Broad.* A broad policy includes all the items covered under a basic policy, as well as glass breakage; damage caused by falling objects; damage from the weight of snow, ice, or sleet; water damage; and additional collapse coverage.
3. *Special.* Under this coverage, the insurer indemnifies the insured from losses from any perils except those specifically excluded. The insurer bears the burden of proving that the loss was caused by an excluded peril. Virtually any physical loss to the insured property is potentially covered by an all-risk property policy.
4. *Earthquake.* Special or all-risk insurance does not provide coverage for earthquake damage. Most lenders do not require earthquake coverage, even if the property is located in an earthquake prone area.

Management Application Alleging Loss or Damage to Property — Windstorm

Excerpted below is a charging allegation from a lawsuit filed by an insured against an insurer to recover under an insurance policy covering loss from windstorm:

On or about December 31, 2025, while the policy was in full force and effect, the dwelling herein described and the furniture and the furnishings in it were damaged by windstorm as follows: the wind uprooted trees causing them to fall on the house and to tear holes in its roof and garage; the wind ripped tiles from the roof, tore doors from their hinges, and broke windows on both the first and second floors; the interior of the house, as well as the furniture in and furnishings of the house were damaged by force of both wind and rain entering through the openings in the roof and sides of the house caused by the wind and fallen trees and from rain water seeping into other parts of the house once it had entered. As a result, the plaintiff was damaged in a sum in excess of $450,000.

Exclusions

Under the law of most states, an insurer is free to select the type of risk it will assume and is liable only for the loss it defines within the terms of the policy. An insurer has the right to limit the coverage it issues, so long as the exclusion (limitation of coverage) is plainly stated. The insurer bears the burden of drafting clear exclusionary language comprehensible to the average person.

When an insured has a non-covered loss, it is likely because an exclusion was stated in the policy. Some of the most common exclusions found in policies include the following:

- *Earth movement.* Policies typically define earth movement as including earthquakes; landslides; mudslides or mudflows; land subsidence; sinkholes; and the sinking, rising, or shifting of earth.
- *Deterioration, latent defect* (a hidden defect not discoverable through reasonable inspection), or *wear and tear.* These exclusions are intended to remove coverage for any covered event that is not sudden or accidental (such as lack of maintenance claims).
- *Water damage, whether caused by floods, subsurface water, waves, sewer backups, sprays, or otherwise.* Mold is commonly excluded, or coverage is limited to a small sum.
- *Pollution, war, terrorism, and intentional acts.*
- *Vacant buildings.* Often excluded because of the higher risk of vandalism.

Interpretation of Ambiguities

If an exclusion appears ambiguous, courts will choose the interpretation most favorable to the insured, because the insurer drafted the exclusion causing the ambiguity. If the ambiguity is found in a special form insurance policy, the insurer has the burden of showing that the loss is within an exclusion.

Prohibited Conduct by Insured

State laws prohibit insurance carriers from providing coverage for intentional wrongdoing by the insured. An insurance company is liable to defend and indemnify its insured from the insured's acts of negligence but not from the insured's willful and intentional acts. Thus, if a building owner negligently maintained the electrical system in a building, the structural damage resulting from a fire would be covered. The building owner's intentional damage-causing acts (such as arson) would not be covered by insurance.

Common Types of Property Insurance

An insurance policy does not cover every conceivable type of risk. Instead, insurance policies are purchased according to the nature of the risk involved. Several common types of insurance relevant to real property are described in the sections below.

Commercial general liability policy
Policy covering bodily injury, property damage, and personal injury liability arising from the operations of a business.

Business Insurance

COMMERCIAL GENERAL LIABILITY INSURANCE. A commercial general liability policy is one of the most common liability protection insurance policies issued to business organizations. This insurance covers bodily injury, property damage, and personal injury liability arising from the operations of the business. While coverage excludes intentional conduct, liability arising out of gross negligence or recklessness is a covered peril for the insured.

Representations and warranties insurance policy
A policy used to guarantee the representations made by sellers in contracts.

SELLER'S WARRANTIES POLICIES. A **representations and warranties insurance policy** provides insurance to guarantee the representations made by sellers in contracts. It extends to any resulting financial loss if representations and warranties made by the seller in the purchase agreement are untrue. The policy can be obtained in conjunction with a general liability policy.

ERRORS AND OMISSIONS POLICIES. Also known as professional liability insurance, errors and omissions insurance provides coverage to claims arising out of any act or omission or "personal injury" caused by a failure to render "professional services." Such claims often result from failures to perform work, mistakes, or negligence.

Errors and omissions policy Provides coverage to claims arising out of any act or omission or "personal injury" caused by a failure to render "professional services."

Insurance Related to Personal and Real Property

FIRE INSURANCE POLICY. A **fire insurance policy** protects real and personal property against damages resulting from a fire and certain other perils (often lightning, smoke, and water damage). Liability insurance protection is not covered in standard fire insurance policies. It is one of the lowest levels of insurance protection a homeowner can secure.

Fire insurance policy Insurance that protects real and personal property against damages resulting from a fire and certain other perils like lightening, smoke, and water damage.

VEHICLE INSURANCE. A **vehicle insurance policy** protects cars, trucks, motorcycles, and other road vehicles. The main purpose of such a policy is to provide financial protection against either physical damage to the vehicle or bodily injury from traffic collisions and any liability that stems from such collisions. There are also vehicle insurance policies that offer additional financial protection for things like theft or vandalism of the vehicle.

In the United States, the regulations for vehicle insurance will vary depending on the state. However, each state does have its own mandatory minimum coverage requirement.

Vehicle insurance policy An insurance policy which protects cars, trucks, motorcycles, and other vehicles.

HOMEOWNER'S INSURANCE. A **homeowner's insurance policy** is considered a comprehensive insurance policy providing coverage for damage to the home and the homeowner's personal property, protections against personal liability, some legal claims by third parties (including damages caused by household members and family pets), and a limited amount of medical expenses incurred by guests injured on the property. It does not cover business or professional activities (such as activities related to a home office or home day-care services).

Homeowner's insurance policy A comprehensive insurance policy providing coverage for damage to the home and homeowner's personal property.

Covered perils usually include those contained in a fire policy, as well as coverage for winds or hail, explosions, riots, civil commotions, aircraft incidents, vehicles causing damage, smoke, volcanic eruption, vandalism, theft, and falling objects. In contrast to fire insurance policies, homeowner's insurance policies cover personal liability. This coverage provides protection against claims by third parties injured on the insured's property (such as a slip and fall) and third parties injured by the insured away from the home (for example, by a defamatory statement).

Homeowner's insurance policies typically exclude losses caused by lack of property maintenance and repair. Common exclusions include, but are not limited to:

- Structural defects whether known or unknown
- Known or hidden defects in the plumbing, heating, and electrical systems
- Known or unknown soil conditions or draining problems
- Concealment or misrepresentation of any known defects in the residential property (including soil movement and defective appliances)

CONDOMINIUM POLICIES. The condominium policy insures the personal property inside the condominium unit. Condominiums present unique problems because of the potential for shared insurance responsibility with homeowners' associations over common walls and common areas, as well as shared responsibilities for maintenance and repair. The conditions, covenants, and restrictions (CCRs) on a condominium development may divide the responsibility for maintaining insurance between the homeowners' association and the individual unit owners. Often, the condominium association will insure the building walls, roof, and floors, while the condominium owner is responsible for insuring the personal property inside the unit.

RENTER'S INSURANCE. Tenants who are leasing can purchase renter's insurance to protect from any loss or damage to their personal property. A homeowner's insurance policy does not cover the personal property of tenants residing on the premises in the event of a peril to the property. Renter's insurance is affordable and significantly cheaper than a homeowner's insurance policy. Landlords should require tenants to secure renter's insurance and name the landlord as an additional insured under the policy to ensure that the tenants have insurance to protect their personal property. Without such insurance, a tenant could sue a landlord for damage caused to the tenant's personal property.

FLOOD. Flood insurance provides insurance for property damage caused by a flood. In response to the rising cost of taxpayer-funded relief for flood victims, the federal government administers the National Flood Insurance Program (NFIP). The NFIP makes flood insurance available to properties at a reasonable cost. Policies are issued by private insurers participating in the program. The Federal Emergency Management Agency (FEMA) establishes standard flood insurance policies.

Flood insurance policy Insurance for property damage caused by a flood.

Review the website for FEMA at https://www.fema.gov.

EARTHQUAKE INSURANCE. Earthquake insurance protects against property damage caused by an earthquake and earth movements. Recall that standard commercial general liability policies exclude earth movement and earthquakes from coverage. Earthquakes have caused billions of dollars in damage to residential property. As a result, many insurers have severely restricted or refused to write new policies.

Earthquake insurance policy Insurance that protects against property damage caused by an earthquake and earth movements.

TITLE INSURANCE. Title insurance protects owners of real property against any defects in title, liens, or other encumbrances not disclosed in a title insurance policy at the close of a real estate transaction. Owners seek title insurance to ensure that clear and accurate title to the property is transferred. A title insurance policy reimburses costs incurred to defend a title case and pays for the costs involved in clearing the title, up to the policy limit.

Title insurance policy Insurance which protects owners of real property against any defects in title, liens, or other encumbrances not disclosed in a title insurance policy at the close of a real estate transaction.

> **Example:** If a buyer purchased a piece of real property and secured title insurance to it and the title to the property did not disclose unpaid taxes on the property, title insurance would pay for any costs associated with paying the unpaid taxes on the property.

BUILDER'S RISK INSURANCE. Builder's risk policies indemnify for loss of, or damage to, a building under construction. They are normally written for a specific dollar amount and apply only during construction. Most often, a contractor will be required to obtain insurance to indemnify the owner and any construction lender from damages arising from the contractor's work on the project.

Builder's risk policies Insurance used to indemnify for loss of, or damage to, a building under construction.

Example: While building a home, a welder accidentally ignited a fire that consumed the almost completed home. Builder's risk insurance funds the rebuilding of the residence.

TERRORISM INSURANCE. Property owners may purchase **terrorism insurance**, which protects against damages caused by terrorist activities. Prior to September 11, 2001, insurers often provided terrorism coverage free of charge in all-risk insurance policies. Most terrorism insurance policies cover damaged or destroyed property (such as buildings, equipment, furnishings, and inventory). Exclusions from coverage typically include nuclear, biological, chemical, and radiological attacks.

Terrorism insurance Insurance which protects against damages caused by terrorist activities.

UMBRELLA POLICY. An **umbrella policy** is a liability insurance policy that offers limits of liability protection in addition to the primary policy. Often, commercial general liability policies and homeowner's policies limit coverage to a certain sum. Property owners seeking additional insurance protection can secure an umbrella policy to increase their liability coverage beyond the coverage from the commercial general liability policies and homeowner's policies. In addition, umbrella policies are broader and can cover risks excluded from underlying policies.

Umbrella policy Liability insurance coverage that covers damages more than the basic liability policy covering real or personal property.

Example: A homeowner's insurance policy may exclude recovery for the insured's liability under defamation. An umbrella policy will often include coverage for defamation; therefore, the insured would be covered for defamation under its umbrella policy.

Umbrella policies are so called because they provide additional coverage to all policies underneath them (such as a homeowner's and auto insurance policies). Umbrella insurance often is less costly to purchase than commercial general liability policies and homeowner's policies, making it an affordable method of increasing insurance limits. It often provides broader coverage than primary coverage.

Example: If a homeowner had a homeowner's policy with a limit of $500,000 and then purchased an umbrella policy for $1 million of coverage, the homeowner would have insurance coverage up to $1.5 million.

Other Notable Types of Insurance

Discussed above are various types of property insurance; however, it is also important to insure more than just property. Individuals can benefit from the following types of insurance:

- *Disability insurance.* Disability insurance provides the beneficiary with protection from the possibility that a disability will prevent the worker from being able to perform the core functions of their occupation. Disabilities include both physical and non-physical disabilities. Additionally, a person can obtain short-term or long-term disability insurance.

- *Life insurance*. Life insurance allows named beneficiary to be paid a certain sum of money from the insurer upon the death of the policyholder in exchange for the policyholder's payment of a premium. Depending on the terms of the policy, payment to the beneficiary may be triggered upon terminal or critical illness of the policyholder rather than death. Life insurance is typically categorized as term or whole life.
  - *Term*. Term life insurance only lasts for a set period of time and as a result is significantly cheaper. If the death (or illness) arises outside of the specified term, the beneficiary will not receive a payment from the insurer.
  - Permanent Life. Permanent life insurance provides the policyholder with lifetime coverage. Therefore, the policy never lapses and so long as the policyholder pays the required premium, the beneficiary will receive payment from the insurer.
- *Health insurance*. Health insurance will assist in the payment of either all or part of medical expenses that are incurred by the policyholder or a person covered under the policy. The majority of U.S. citizens have private health insurance that is purchased through a private company, while the rest receive assistance from public programs such as Medicaid or Medicare.
  - The following link is to a helpful tool for comparing health insurance policies: https://finder.healthcare.gov/.
- *Automotive insurance*. In a contract between the policyholder and the insurance company, the policyholder's financial loss stemming from an accident or theft is limited. The majority of states require their citizens to carry basic personal auto insurance; however, this is often insufficient to cover all the personal injury and property damages that result from an accident.
  - Additionally, basic personal auto insurance will not cover accidents or thefts that occur when the vehicle is being used for commercial purposes.
  - Therefore, commercial automotive insurance should be purchased by those whose occupation requires them to use the vehicle for more than simply commuting to their job, such as pizza delivery persons and drivers employed by ride-sharing services.
  - Some states provide comparison tools for their citizens to compare types of insurance based on their age, vehicle type, mileage, and other information. The following link is to such a tool provided by the State of California. *http://www.insurance.ca.gov/01-consumers/105-type/9-compare-prem/index.cfm*.

What Will the Insurance Carrier Pay?

Insurance carriers use several methods to calculate the amount they will pay the insureds in the event of a covered peril. The insurance contract between the insurer and the insured will establish the method to be used. Typically, the insurer pays either the actual cash value or the replacement cost value. An insured, by paying a higher premium, can obtain a replacement cost value or guaranteed replacement cost coverage policies, as discussed below.

Actual Cash Value

The actual cash value is the insurer's standard method of reimbursement and is the most favorable reimbursement method for the insurer. The actual cash value of a piece of property is determined by subtracting the item's depreciation from its replacement cost.

Depreciation is calculated by establishing the useful life of an item and determining what percentage of that life remains. This method of calculating depreciation measures the replacement life percentage against the current replacement cost, not the original purchase price or cost. Actual cash value is equivalent to the value one should receive in the marketplace for the covered property.

Depreciation
The gradual loss in value of property due to its deterioration and obsolescence.

Example: If a garage were damaged by lightning, the carrier would consult industry guidelines on useful life and replacement cost. If a homeowner's garage had a 40-year useful life, had been in place for 20 years, and would cost $15,000 to replace today, the insured would be paid a maximum of $7,500.

Replacement Cost

Under a replacement cost value policy, the insurer will pay the amount required to replace the damaged property, in today's marketplace, with comparable material and quality, up to the amount of the policy. If the cost to replace a covered loss on the property exceeds the policy limit, the insurer is only obligated to pay the policy limit (that is, the owner may not be able to actually replace the property through insurance proceeds alone). Unlike actual cash value, depreciation is not deducted from the value of the damaged property. Insureds prefer replacement cost value to actual cash value.

Extended Replacement Cost

Extended replacement cost coverage will pay for the replacement costs up to a specified percentage above the policy limit. Insurance carriers typically agree to pay 20 or 30 percent above the policy limit under extended replacement cost policies.

Example: If a home destroyed by a fire had extended replacement cost value coverage of $500,000, the insurer would typically agree to pay benefits in the sum of either $600,000 or $650,000. If the cost to replace the home exceeded these amounts, it would be the insured's responsibility to pay for the difference.

Guaranteed Replacement Cost

Guaranteed replacement cost coverage is the best policy for an insured. It provides that the insurer will pay the full cost of repairing or replacing the damaged or destroyed structure, regardless of policy limits. The insurer bears the risk of securing insurance at an amount close to the actual replacement cost of the structure.

Example: If the cost to replace the home was $800,000 and the guaranteed replacement cost policy was issued for $700,000, the insurer would pay the $100,000 to cover the cost of replacing the structure.

Management Application Underinsurance — How Much Property Insurance Is Enough?

It is estimated that two out of every three homes in the United States are underinsured. Underinsurance occurs when the insurance policy is insufficient to cover the costs of rebuilding a property after a peril. To keep policy premiums at a minimum, many insureds buy only the minimum mandated coverage required by statute or their mortgage lender. In addition, insureds fail to update their insurance policy limits over time or fail to increase coverage when additions and improvements are made to the property.

The cost to rebuild a commercial property may exceed the policy limit, leaving the insured to fund the balance of the costs of repair. An insured is still responsible for paying its mortgage after a peril, even if the insurance proceeds are not sufficient to rebuild the property. In those situations, many property owners are forced to file for bankruptcy. It is prudent for the insured to check annually the amount and type of insurance on the property.

Using an internet search engine, determine the cost of construction for a part of a home such as a replacement kitchen.

Duties of the Insured

Both the insurer and the insured have certain duties in an insurance contract. Both parties must perform the obligations imposed under the insurance contract. In addition, each party owes certain duties to the other party. An insured owes to the insurer the duties to notify and cooperate and to mitigate.

Duty to Notify

Insurance policies require that the insured provide notice of a claim for a covered loss as soon as practicable. In most cases, this means that notice must be given to the insurer within a reasonable time after a loss. Failure to give notice within a reasonable time after the loss may result in a denial of coverage.

Duty to Cooperate

An insured also has the duty to cooperate in the investigation, settlement, or defense of the claim or lawsuit. Many property policies impose a duty on the insured to submit to an examination under oath to obtain information relevant to the claim's investigation.

Voluntary payments clause If an insured fixes a problem or damage and then notifies the insurer and seeks coverage, the insurer can deny coverage.

Under the **voluntary payments clause**, an insured cannot fix a problem or damage attributable to the insured and then notify the insurer of the claim or lawsuit. Generally, this means when an insured settles a claim without informing or obtaining the consent of the insurance company, the expense of settling the claim falls entirely on the insured. Repairing damage before giving notice to the insurance carrier may result in the denial of coverage.

Duty to Mitigate

The insured also has a duty to mitigate. The duty to mitigate requires the insured to take steps to avoid incurring expenses or other unnecessary costs. Failure to mitigate may result in coverage reduction and, in some instances, a denial of coverage.

> **Example:** If an insured's home suffers water damage due to a broken water pipe, the insured has a duty to mitigate by turning off the water supply to a home.

Duties of the Insurer

As discussed, the insurer and the insured owe duties to each other. The insurer has the duty of good faith and fair dealing, the duty to indemnify, potentially the duty to defend, and the duty to settle claims.

Duty of Good Faith and Fair Dealing

Duty of good faith and fair dealing
An implied promise that neither party will do anything to injure the other party's right to receive the rights of the agreement.

Courts and legislatures have imposed on insurance companies the duty of good faith and fair dealing with their insureds. The duty of good faith and fair dealing is an implied promise (covenant) in every contract that neither party will do anything to injure the other party's right to receive the rights of the agreement. All states recognize this covenant in insurance policies and the insured may sue the insurer for damages in the event of a breach.

Reservation of rights
An insurance carrier's notification to an insured that coverage for a claim may not exist under the policy.

INSURER'S RESPONSE TO A CLAIM. Insurers can respond to a notice of claim in several ways. They may unconditionally accept the demand, require additional information, deny coverage, or agree to provide a defense to the insured under a reservation of rights as to indemnity coverage. With a **reservation of rights**, the insurer agrees to defend the insured by hiring a lawyer and paying defense costs, but it reserves the right to withdraw that defense and decline coverage if all or some of the claim involves damages or injuries falling outside of the policy coverage. State laws require a carrier to issue timely, clear, and specific reservation of rights letters.

INSURER'S RIGHT TO INVESTIGATE. Some jurisdictions hold that an insurer has the right to investigate the insured's claim. Where the duty to investigate is imposed on the insurer, most courts hold that the insurer must consider all reasonably ascertainable facts before denying coverage.

Insurer's Duty to Indemnify

Duty to indemnify
A contractual duty to pay for any loss or damage suffered by another.

The **duty to indemnify** means the insurer has a duty to pay covered claims up to the limits of the policy. If the claim or damage is not covered under the policy or is excluded from it, the insurer can decline to indemnify the insured. Moreover, the insured's recovery is limited to reimbursement for losses suffered.

In the following case, the insureds filed suit against an insurer for breach of contract when the insurer failed to timely pay the damages associated with a claim.

CASE 41.3

INSURER'S FAILURE TO TIMELY PAY A CLAIM MAY RESULT IN A BREACH OF CONTRACT

MALONEY CINQUE, LLC V. PACIFIC INS. CO.

89 So. 3d 12 (2012)

Louisiana Court of Appeal

Maloney Cinque, LLC ("Maloney") owned several truck stops in the New Orleans area. These businesses included fuel pumps, convenience stores, and video poker casinos. Two of their properties, Big Easy and Mardi Gras, were damaged as a result of Hurricane Katrina. Damage to the properties was caused by wind and flood. It is undisputed that the flood waters reached a minimum of four feet at both locations. Maloney brought suit against Pacific Ins. Co. ("Pacific"), arguing that although the amounts due were paid under the policy, the amounts were not paid timely as required by law. Louisiana state law requires all insurers to pay the amount of any claim due within 30 days after receipt of satisfactory proof of loss. The parties disagreed as to when the satisfactory proof of loss was provided. Maloney argued that satisfactory proof of loss was provided to Pacific on December 13 and 18, 2005, for both locations. Pacific contended that it did not have satisfactory proof of loss until April 17, 2006, and that its payments on May 9 and 10, 2006, were timely. The disagreement arose from the parties' dispute as to the amount of loss that existed. The trial court found that satisfactory proof of loss was provided on December 13 and 16, 2006, and thus Pacific's payments were untimely. The trial court subjected these late payments to penalty and awarded Maloney $2,386,354.50. Pacific appealed.

Language of the Court. *At issue is whether Pacific made timely payments under the insurance contract and under applicable state law. Here, a timeline taken from reports and internal communications was used to determine the timing for payments. Pacific argued that it could not pay any claims earlier than April 17, 2006, the date when it had sufficient information to do so. Maloney argued it gave Pacific satisfactory proofs of loss on December 13 and 18, 2005, when it had given estimates to Pacific. The court disagreed with both Maloney and Pacific.*

Courts have determined a satisfactory proof of loss is one that is sufficient to fully apprise the insurer of the insured's claim. Where a reasonable disagreement between the insured and the insurer as to the amount of a loss exists, the insurer's refusal to pay is not arbitrary, capricious, or without probable cause, and failure to pay within the statutory delay does not subject the insurer to penalties.

However, if part of a claim for property damage is not disputed, the failure of the insurer to pay the undisputed portion of the claim within the statutory delay will subject the insurer to penalties on the entire claim. When such dispute arises, the insurer must unconditionally tender to the insured the undisputed portion of the insured's claim to avoid imposition of penalties.

We cannot agree with Maloney on the date that a satisfactory proof of loss was received by Pacific. We find that the 30-day period began to run no later than March

1, 2006. Pacific had, or should have had, all the information it needed to determine the plaintiffs' loss at that time. This is because on March 1, 2006, Pacific acknowledges that it prepared a "Large Loss Notice" and requested authority to post a reserve. As determined by the trial court, the final payments of $190,348 for the Mardi Gras and $415,974 for the Big Easy made by Pacific on May 9-10, 2006, were untimely.

However, Pacific failed to pay the claim in a timely manner; it failed to timely pay even the undisputed amount of the claim. This failure exposes Pacific to statutory penalties in an amount that far exceeds the penalties awarded.

Decision. The court of appeal affirmed the trial court's finding that payment on the claim was untimely and increased the penalty amounts to meet the statutory requirements.

Focus on Ethics

Was Pacific acting ethically in not timely paying Maloney's claim?

The Insurer's Duty to Defend

Under the **duty to defend**, an insurer has a duty to provide defense to its insured (such as paying an attorney to defend) when a complaint alleges facts that could, if proved, impose liability on the insured within the policy's coverage. It is estimated that over 40 percent of premiums paid are allocable to paying for the costs of litigation relating to claims and coverage disputes.

Duty to defend
A contractual duty obligating the insurer to provide the insured with a defense of claims, typically by hiring legal counsel.

The Insurer's Duty to Settle Claims

The duty to settle claims requires that, when coverage for the claim exists, the insurance company must attempt to settle the case within the policy limits. An insurer can settle solely the claims covered under the policy and withdraw its defense as to the claims for which the policy provides no protection to the insured.

Management Application
Policy Cancellation and Non-Renewal

The insurer is contractually bound to cover the risk for the period provided for in the policy. An insurer has no right to cancel a policy midterm, unless certain conditions arise, such as nonpayment of premiums, fraud, or misrepresentation by the insured. An insurer's bad faith cancellation of a policy can subject it to damages. However, the insured may cancel the insurance contract during the policy term.

Subject to state restrictions, the insurer has no obligation to continue the policy with the insured beyond the policy period. The insurer may refuse to renew policies for any reason whatsoever, or for no reason at all. Quite often, insurers will not renew a policy when the insured has presented a claim under the policy in a substantial sum.

Acting in Bad Faith

Bad faith
In the insurance context, where the insurance company acts in a blatant and unfair manner against the insured with conduct exceeding mere negligence.

An insurer acts in **bad faith** when it unjustifiably refuses to defend its insured or mishandles the claim's adjustment. When that happens, the insurer is liable to the insured for a judgment or settlement beyond the policy limits and for the cost of the insured's reasonable attorney fees in defending the case, plus any damages suffered due to the breach. Such damages could include the loss of prospective business, the cost of funds needed to pay for its defense, and mental distress to the insured. Some states permit the award of punitive damages against insurers who breach this duty.

Concept Summary Duties of the Insured and Insurer

The insured has three duties:

1. Duty to timely notify the insurer of a claim
2. Duty to cooperate with the insurer
3. Duty to mitigate the damages suffered

The insurer has three duties:

1. Duty of good faith and fair dealing with the insured
2. Duty to indemnify the insured
3. Duty to settle claims promptly and fairly

AI Feature: Research the Making of a Claim Under an Insurance Policy

Assume you are an insured under a comprehensive homeowner's policy. Use an AI program to answer the following questions:

- What information must be stated in a notice of claim to the insurer?
- What circumstances may exist under which failure to comply with the notice requirement could be excused?
- What are the obligations of the insurer following receipt of notice of claim?

- What are the obligations of the insured following the insurer's receipt of notice of claim?
- What are the meanings of the duty to defend and the duty to indemnify?
- What is meant when an insurer issues a reservation of rights under the policy? Draft language for the benefit of the insurer with regard to such a reservation.

Key Terms

- Additional insured, 1038
- Bad faith, 1054
- Binder, 1041
- Builder's risk policies, 1046
- Commercial general liability policy, 1044
- Covered loss, 1042
- Depreciation, 1049
- Duty of good faith and fair dealing, 1051
- Duty to defend, 1053
- Duty to indemnify, 1051
- Earthquake insurance policy, 1046
- Errors and omissions policy, 1045
- Fire insurance policy, 1045
- Flood insurance, 1046
- Homeowner's insurance policy, 1045
- Insurable interest, 1035
- Insurance, 1034
- Insurance agents, 1038
- Insurance broker, 1038
- Insured, 1034
- Insurer, 1034
- McCarran Ferguson Act of 1945, 1035
- Named insured, 1038
- Policy limits, 1034
- Premium, 1034
- Representations and warranties insurance policy, 1044
- Reservation of rights, 1051
- Terrorism insurance, 1047
- Title insurance, 1046
- Umbrella policy, 1047
- Vehicle insurance policy, 1045
- Voluntary payments clause, 1050

Applying the Law

41.1 Research the Law. Using an internet search engine, research whether your state has a privately financed, publicly managed entity to insure against natural disasters such as tornadoes or earthquakes. Review the flood insurance coverages available at *FEMA.gov*.

41.2 Errors and Omissions. For there to be coverage under an errors and omissions policy, the error and/or omission must have arisen from the performance of "professional service." Through a variety of lawsuits, a definition of professional service developed: "something more than mere proficiency in the performance of a task and [that] implies intellectual skill." Is this definition adequate to address the risks posed by a professional practice? What if the cause of the damage arises from acts of maintaining equipment and not the rendering of professional services? *Marx v. Hartford Accident & Indemnity Co.*, 157 N.W.2d 870 (Neb. 1968)

41.3 Existence of Property Damage. Eljer manufactured and sold defective plumbing systems that were installed in various buildings. Many of these systems developed leaks shortly after installation, resulting in property damage claims against Eljer. Liberty Mutual® Eljer's commercial general liability insurer, contended that property damage did not occur until a system leaked, resulting in physical injury to the walls, floors, or ceilings. Thus, as Liberty Mutual argued, it did not have to pay building owners whose systems had yet to leak. Eljer claimed that even if that were the case, there was physical injury once the system was installed, regardless of when the leak occurred. At what point does property damage occur—when the system leaks or when it is installed? See *Eljer Mfg., Inc. v. Liberty Mut. Ins. Co.*, 972 F.2d 805 (7th Cir. 1992). Consider the California Supreme Court decision in *Aas v. Superior Court*, 24 Cal. 4th 627 (2000), in which the court held the plaintiff homeowners could not recover from defendant builders for construction defects that had not yet manifested resulting in property damage. At what point should the law state an insurable event has occurred?

41.4 Actual Cash Value. Recall that actual cash value is the insurer's standard method of reimbursement. The actual cash value policy is a pure indemnity contract that is supposed to make the insured whole rather than put the insured in a better position than before the time of the loss. Courts have described actual cash value in different ways: (1) the replacement cost minus depreciation; (2) market value; and (3) a flexible rule that allows for any relevant factor to be considered. *Travelers Indemnity Co. v. Armstrong*, 442 N.E.2d 349, 355-356 (Ind. 1982). Are there material differences among these coverages? Which definition of actual cash value would an insured prefer? Why would an insurance carrier define its insurance coverages differently from those of its competitors?

41.5 Duties of the Insured. Raymond and Elaine Cox sued Tennessee Farmers Mutual, alleging breach of the insurance policy between them. They claimed that the insurer failed to pay for the loss of their home and its contents following an accidental fire. In response, the insurer argued that they did not timely file a proper proof of loss of the contents within the required period by the policy and that the insurer was prejudiced thereby. The company provided proof that the plaintiffs did not file their completed proof of loss until more than nine months after the fire. The carrier argued that there was no excuse for the delay in substantiating the loss. With what duty did the insureds breach under the terms of the policy? How could the tardy reporting have harmed the carrier? *Cox v. Tennessee Farmers Mutual Ins. Co.*, 297 S.W.3d 237 (Tenn. Ct. App. 2009)

41.6 Misrepresentations. Donald Vella, an international financial instruments broker, consulted his personal physician, Dr. Caccese, multiple times. He complained of chest pain, pain in his left arm, dizziness, light-headedness, and headache. However, his doctor prescribed no course of treatment and told Vella that it was nothing more than common anxiety. In October 1985, Vella completed an application for a "special occupational disability" insurance policy from Equitable and completed a medical history questionnaire. This policy provided that Equitable was to be liable should Vella be medically disabled from performing his job as a financial instruments broker. Equitable Life Assurance® approved Vella's application. Several months later, Vella's hearing became impaired due to a disorder known as "sensori-neural deficit" and the hearing specialist told him that his condition would worsen if Vella remained in a noisy environment. Since his job was in a noisy environment, Vella stopped working and filed a timely disability claim. Equitable refused to pay, alleging that Vella misrepresented his medical history. Make arguments for both sides as to whether Equitable should pay Vella's disability claim. How might a court rule? *Vella v. Equitable Life Assur. Soc'y of the United States*, 887 F.2d 388 (2d Cir. 1989)

41.7 Rescission of a Policy. On March 15, 1990, William Penn Life Insurance Co.® issued a $140,000 life insurance policy to Steven Ledley, effective February 24, 1990. During Ledley's application, Ledley failed to disclose his extensive history of thyroid problems and names of consulting physicians. A month after the issuance of the policy, Ledley died. The policy stated that the policy would be incontestable after two years. William Penn began an investigation and found that the insured had an extensive history of thyroid problems that he did not disclose. If William Penn seeks rescission of the policy, how would a court rule? *Ledley v. William Penn Life Ins. Co.*, 651 A.2d 92 (N.J. 1995)

41.8 Duty to Defend. Beatrice Crocker, a resident of Redwood Springs Nursing Home, sued the owner Emeritus Corporation and Richard Morris, a nursing home employee. Crocker sought compensation for injuries suffered when she was hit by a door opened by Morris. As an employee, Morris was an additional insured under the commercial general liability policy issued by National Union Fire Insurance of Pittsburg, PA®. National Union defended Emeritus, the named insured, but did not defend Morris even though the claims against him were covered by the policy. The insurer successfully defended the nursing home but did not inform the employee that he was an insured or offer a defense to the employee, even though the claims against him were covered by the policy and the insurer knew he was a named defendant who had been served. Additionally, Morris did not request a defense from either National Union or Emeritus. At trial, the court entered a $1 million default judgment against Morris. Crocker sued National Union to collect the judgment, asserting she was a third-party beneficiary to the policy. National Union argued that Crocker could not collect under the policy. What arguments would you make for both National Union and Crocker? How might a court rule? *National Union Fire Ins. Co. of Pittsburg, PA v. Crocker*, 246 S.W.3d 603 (Tex. 2008)

41.9 Insurable Interest. On November 9, 1994, Hector Valdez purchased automobile insurance through his local insurance agent on a vehicle. A few months later, Valdez sold and transferred the title of the vehicle to his adult son, Rene. Valdez did not notify Colonial, the insurance company, of the change in title. Rene could not take the car right away and left the vehicle with his father, Hector. Hector Valdez continued to use the car and pay the policy premiums. He renewed the insurance policy from November 9, 1995, through November 9, 1996. On January 14, 1996, the vehicle was stolen while parked outside Hector Valdez's house. Colonial refused to honor the claim despite accepting Valdez's premium payments for over a year and filed suit seeking a declaratory judgment that Valdez did not have an insurable interest in the stolen vehicle. Make an argument for coverage or not on the loss of the vehicle for both Valdez and Colonial. How should the court rule? *Valdez v. Colonial County Mut. Ins. Co.*, 994 S.W.2d 910 (Tex. App.–Austin 1999).

41.10 Bad Faith. William Miller sued his insurer, Allstate Insurance Company®, for bad faith for failing to inform him of a settlement offer in a case in which he was a defendant. His policy had a bodily injury liability limit of only $25,000. However, the plaintiff's damages greatly exceeded that sum. What is the duty of an insurer to act in good faith and fair dealing toward its insured in this situation? *Allstate Insurance Co. v. Miller*, 212 P.3d 318 (Nev. 2009)

Liabilities of Accountants and Other Licensed Professionals

42

The young man knows the rules, but the old man knows the exceptions. — Oliver Wendell Holmes, Jr., United States Supreme Court Associate Justice (1841-1935)

Chapter Outline

- Introduction
- General Standard of Care of Accountants
  - *Management Application: The Use of the LLP Structure*
- Duties Owed to Third Parties

Case 42.1: *1650 Broadway Assoc., Inc. v. Sturm*

- Liability for Securities Law Violations
- Tax Return Preparer Liability

Case 42.2: *United States v. Stinson*

- Confidentiality and Privilege
- Occupational Licensing in General
  - *Management Application: Codes of Professional Practice*
  - *Management Application: Regulation by FINRA*
- AI Feature: Draft a Law Permitting Paralegals to Practice Law in a Limited Capacity

Learning Objectives

After studying this chapter, you should be able to:

1. Explain the theories of liability that can be asserted against an accountant.
2. State an accountant's duties in conducting an audit.
3. Describe how an accountant or other professional may violate federal securities laws.
4. Discuss the duties of a tax preparer under the Internal Revenue Code.

Introduction

Occupations are enormously broad in scope; however, there are fields of activity whose regulation is of keen interest to state and local governments. States and municipalities enact regulatory schemes to improve the practice of a recognized professional activity and to safeguard the public from improper professional practices. Most often, the resulting laws and regulations require licensing of individuals who are engaged in specific occupations. We begin our discussion with the profession of accounting. We then highlight the subject of occupational licensing of other professionals, along with their duties of care and exposure to liability for falling below those standards.

General Standard of Care of Accountants

An accountant is a person who performs many services, including the preparation of financial statements, bookkeeping, and the preparation of tax returns. In contrast, a certified public accountant is one who has met state licensing requirements. The states uniformly require CPAs to successfully complete educational coursework, pass a rigorous examination, and have a number of years of auditing experience. Often, a non-licensed practitioner is referred to as a public accountant.

See the AICPA licensing requirements at https://us.aicpa.org/becomeacpa/licensure/requirements.

CPAs may be liable to clients and third parties based on breach of contract, negligence, fraud, or for violating federal and state securities laws. While federal securities laws were reviewed in Chapter 25, we also will review them in this chapter as they apply to accountant liability.

Roles Within the Accounting Profession

- *Bookkeeper*—An individual whose job entails the keeping of records of a business's financial affairs.
- *Accountant*—A practitioner of accounting who performs audits and analyses of financial statements.
- *Certified Public Accountant (CPA)*—An accountant who through education, audit hours practice, and passage of a competitive exam is licensed by a state to practice accountancy.
- *Chief Financial Officer (CFO)*—A senior manager whose responsibilities are for the planning and execution of the financial activities of a company.
- *Director of Finance*—A professional who possesses a broad knowledge of accounting, business, and financial principles and who seeks to direct a company toward long-term profitability.

Liability for Breach of Contract

While not applying solely to accountants, the relationship between a professional and a client is a personal service contract. The accountant must comply with the law when rendering these services—namely, the obligation to perform the scope of work with due care (that is, non-negligently) and comply with professional standards of practice.

Damages for breach of contract vary depending upon the nature and severity of the breach. Generally, damages will be limited to compensatory damages, which place the non-breaching party in a position as if the contract were fully performed (these damages were discussed in Chapter 14). Punitive damages, or those intended to punish the wrongdoer, are rare in accountant-client contract disputes and occur in cases involving egregious violations of the accountant's duty to a client. Most often these circumstances would arise from hidden conflicts of interest or a breach of fiduciary duty.

Liability for Professional Negligence

In addition to liability for breach of contract, an accountant may be liable for negligence. To prevail in this claim, the plaintiff must prove:

- A duty of care was owed to the plaintiff;
- The accountant breached that duty of care;
- The plaintiff suffered damages as a result; and
- The damages suffered were proximately caused by the accountant.

An accountant owes a duty of care commensurate with that of the average member of the accounting profession as well as any duties imposed by standards of conduct established by codes of professional ethics.

An accountant, like other licensed professionals, has a duty to exercise reasonable care and diligence. The accountant should have the judgment, competence, and knowledge possessed by an ordinarily prudent accountant in similar circumstances. Liability of an accountant to the client for negligence can arise from circumstances such as the following:

- Giving incorrect advice on an accounting or tax question;
- Failing to detect that an internal accounting fraud has been committed when it should have been detected; and
- Failing to keep accurate financial books and records.

However, the circumstances may involve gross negligence, which will arise in situations such as the following:

- Serious deviations from GAAP standards;
- Embezzlement of the client's funds; and
- Violation of federal and state securities laws.

Standard of Care of Accountants

There are two standards of professional conduct (that is, duty) with which CPAs must comply. Failure to adhere to them may result in a claim of professional negligence (accounting malpractice).

GAAP
A common set of accounting principles, standards, and procedures that companies must follow when compiling their financial statements.

IFRS
A set of accounting standards developed by an independent, nonprofit organization known as the International Accounting Standards Board.

See discussion of GAAP at https://fasab.gov, and of the IFRS at https://www.ifrs.org.

GAAS
A common set of standards evaluating the quality of audits performed.

Audit
A formal and independent examination of the accounting and financial records of a business to verify compliance with GAAP.

Auditor's opinion
Opinion of an auditor verifying whether the company's financial statements fairly and appropriately represent the company's financial condition.

Unqualified opinion
An auditor's opinion that the company's financial statements fairly represent the company's financial condition and are in conformity with GAAP.

- *Generally accepted accounting principles (GAAP)*
  - ☐ A set of rules, principles, standards, and procedures detailing how business accounting entries and reporting are to be made. Under rules established by the Securities and Exchange Commission, public companies must follow **GAAP** when accountants prepare their financial standards. While GAAP-compliant financial statements are not required for non–publicly traded companies, they are favored by financial institutions. Their purpose is to ensure a company's financial statements are complete, consistent, and comparable.
  - ☐ The framework under which accountants are to produce financial statements follows a hierarchy of rules. Foremost are statements issued by the Financial Accounting Standards Board and the Accounting Research Bulletins and Accounting Principles Board of the American Institute of Certified Public Accountants (a professional organization).
  - ☐ GAAP applies to the accounting and financial reporting of U.S. companies.
  - ☐ The international alternative to GAAP is the International Financial Reporting Standards (**IFRS**), set by the International Accounting Standards Board (IASB). The SEC has removed the requirement for non-U.S. companies whose securities were registered on U.S. stock exchanges to reconcile their financial reports with GAAP if their accounting already complied with IFRS. As global business increases and as foreign businesses increase their activities within the United States, it is expected that the IFRS standards will apply more often than GAAP.
- *Generally accepted auditing standards (GAAS)*
  - ☐ **GAAS** are auditing standards that measure the quality of an **audit** that is conducted upon company's financial records. An audit is the verification of the books and records of a business. When conducting an audit, the auditor reviews and reports on whether a company's financial records follow GAAP. Auditors review the financial data and procedures of the company to ensure compliance with GAAP. Sampling of inventory to verify the accuracy of this asset is conducted, as well as verification with third parties as to contracts, receivables, and obligations. Following the audit, the auditor issues an opinion letter stating whether the financial statements fairly present the business's financial condition. The SEC requires that the financial statements of public companies be examined by external, independent auditors. GAAS is intended to ensure the accuracy, consistency, and verifiability of auditors' actions and reports. The Auditing Standards Board (ASB) of the American Institute of Certified Public Accountants (AICPA) created GAAS.

AUDITOR'S OPINION. The opinion letter issued by the auditor upon completion of the audit (a systematic inspection of the records of a business) can be one of four types:

- *Unqualified opinion.* An **unqualified opinion** is the most common type of report. It is an independent opinion that in the auditor's judgment the company's financial statements are fairly and appropriately presented, without any identified exceptions, and in compliance with generally accepted accounting principles (GAAP). The investing public, financial institutions, and government regulators may accept the financial statements as being free of material misstatements.

- *Qualified opinion.* A **qualified opinion** states that the financial statements are fairly and appropriately presented except for, or subject to, a departure from GAAP, a change in accounting procedures, or a material uncertainty over an issue. Sometimes, a qualified opinion is rendered because a particular industry may recognize revenues in a manner inconsistent with the requirements of GAAP. In most cases, a qualified opinion is acceptable to most financial institutions.
- *Disclaimer of opinion.* In a **disclaimer of opinion**, the auditors state that they lacked sufficient information to issue an opinion. The reasons may include that the auditors did not have complete access to the company's information so they could not render an opinion, or they received less than satisfactory explanations to their questions.
- *Adverse opinion.* In an **adverse opinion**, the accountants determine that the company's financial statements do not fairly represent the company's financial condition. This may arise from material misstatements or irregularities in the accounting practices such that the investing public, financial institutions, and regulators should not trust the financial statements.

Qualified opinion
An auditor's opinion that the company's financial statements fairly and appropriately represent the company's financial condition, except for some issue, process, or transaction that prevents them from issuing an unqualified opinion.

Disclaimer of opinion
An auditor's opinion in which the auditor states they were unable to reach a conclusion about the compliance of the financial statements with GAAP.

Adverse opinion
An auditor's opinion that the financial statements do not fairly represent the financial condition of the company.

Fraud

There is no general duty of an accountant to discover fraud. An accountant is not required to discover every impropriety, embezzlement, or fraud within the company's financial records. But if the lack of discovery is attributable to the accountant's breach of an express or implied contract or negligence, the accountant may be held liable for the damages suffered.

For a client to recover because of fraud, the client must prove that the accountant or other professional:

1. Made a misrepresentation of material fact;
2. With knowledge that it was false or made with a reckless disregard for the truth;
3. With the intent that it should be relied upon; and
4. The misrepresentation was justifiably relied upon by the client to their detriment.

Liability may arise from **actual fraud** or **constructive fraud**, depending on the wrongdoer's intent.

Actual fraud
Making a false material misrepresentation, concealing or preventing the plaintiff from discovering the truth, or remaining silent in the face of a duty to speak.

ACTUAL FRAUD. There is actual fraud when an accountant or other professional (1) intentionally makes a misrepresentation of a material fact for the purpose of misleading the client, and (2) the client is injured because they justifiably relied on such a misrepresentation. A fact is material if a reasonable person would find that it is important in deciding whether to act. It also includes remaining silent in the face of a duty to speak.

Constructive fraud
Acts, omissions, and concealment involving breach of a legal duty, trust, or confidence resulting in damages.

CONSTRUCTIVE FRAUD. In the absence of an intentional misrepresentation of a material fact, there may still be constructive fraud if the client can show that the accountant or other professional acted with a reckless disregard for the truth or was grossly negligent in making the misrepresentation.

Management Application
The Use of the LLP Structure

Recall from Chapter 20 that professional service firms, including accounting firms, can be formed as a professional corporation (PC), a limited liability company (LLC), or a limited liability partnership (LLP). The latter is designed for use by organizations whose owners are licensed professionals. One of the important benefits of an LLC or an LLP as compared to a PC is that each partner (that is, owner) has the right to manage the business. A disadvantage of the LLP is that income of the practice is recognized by each partner on their personal tax returns regardless of whether the partner received a distribution.

The risk of liability for professional negligence of a partner may be addressed by professional liability insurance. An additional layer of protection may be afforded by the organizational structure as well. Limited liability partnerships are composed only of limited partners who enjoy limited liability for the debts or wrongdoings of other partners in the partnership. No partner is personally liable directly or indirectly for the debts, obligations, and liabilities of the LLP. As a result, each partner is not liable for the acts and omissions (that is, professional negligence) of another partner. Each limited partner remains liable for their own intentional or negligent acts within the scope of their practice.

Duties Owed to Third Parties

***Ultramares* doctrine**
This doctrine provides that an accountant or other professional is liable only to those who are in privity or near privity of contract with the accountant.

There are three competing views when considering to whom liability of accountants to third parties may extend. The traditional rule is based upon the *Ultramares* case,[1] decided in 1931. Under this view, an accountant is liable for negligence only to a client or third party with whom they were in contract (that is, in privity of contract).

Since its development, the *Ultramares* doctrine has been slightly modified to include third parties who are not technically in privity of contract but still have a close relationship with the accountant. The third party's close relationship with the accountant is deemed sufficient to satisfy the privity of contract requirement. This is commonly referred to as the "near privity rule" and has been adopted by only a minority of states. Near privity exists when:

1. The accountant knew that their work product was to be used for a particular purpose;
2. A known party or parties were intended to be able to rely on the accountant's work product; and
3. Some conduct on the part of the accountant evidences they understood the third party's reliance on the accountant's work product.

1. *Ultramares Corp. v. Touche, Niven & Co.*, 255 N.Y. 170 (N.Y. Ct. App. 1931).

THE RESTATEMENT RULE. Due to heavy criticism of the *Ultramares* doctrine, most courts have adopted a rule that is derived from the Restatement (Third) of Torts. This rule provides that the liability of accountants and other professionals extends to third parties, in addition to their clients, so long as the third party is a foreseeable or known user of the client's financial statements. The Restatement Rule states that liability will be extended to those to whom the accountant intends to supply the information or to those whom the accountant knows will be supplied the information by the client. Additionally, the accountant will also be liable to anyone who the accountant intends to influence or knows that the client intends to influence by supplying that information.

Restatement (Third) of Torts Rule
The liability of accountants and other professionals extends to third parties, in addition to their clients, so long as the third party is a foreseeable or known user of the client's financial statements.

Example: Fields and Company, an accounting firm, was employed to audit Acme Company's financial statements. Acme told the firm that the audited financial statements were required by its bank in connection with its lending requirements. The bank is a primary beneficiary and may recover damages caused by the firm's negligence.

REASONABLY FORESEEABLE USERS. A minority of states have adopted a broader approach that is consistent with ordinary principles of negligence. Under this view, the accountant is liable to all reasonably foreseeable third parties, which includes members of the class of persons whose reliance on the financial statements the accountant may reasonably anticipate. This view is also heavily criticized for creating too much liability for accountants due to its broad application.

Reasonably foreseeable users
An accountant is liable to all reasonably foreseeable third parties, including members of the class of persons whose reliance on the financial statements the accountant may reasonably anticipate.

Example: Fields and Company, an accounting firm, was engaged to audit Acme Company's financial statements. The firm is not informed of the intended use of these statements; however, the firm knows that they are usually distributed to those making credit decisions with respect to Acme. If the statements are negligently prepared, and a third party who relied upon those statements extends credit to Acme, the third party is a foreseeable third party.

Concept Summary
Theories of Liability

Rule	Summary	Who Uses This Rule?
Ultramares Doctrine	An accountant or other professional is liable only to those who are in privity or near privity of contract with the accountant.	This rule has been adopted by only a minority of the states.
Restatement Rule	Liability will be extended to those to whom the accountant intends to supply the information or to those who the accountant knows will be supplied the information by the client.	This rule has been adopted by a majority of states.

Rule	Summary	Who Uses This Rule?
Reasonably Foreseeable Users Rule	Accountants are liable to all reasonably foreseeable third-party users of the accountant's information.	This minority view has been adopted by a few states. This rule has been criticized for being applied too broadly and creating too much liability for accountants.

The following decision addresses the liability of accountants in cases of alleged financial improprieties within closely held businesses. The issue for the appellate court was whether accountants who provide "compilation services" are shielded from liability if they fail to disclose financial improprieties of which they become aware during their services.

CASE 42.1

AN ACCOUNTANT MUST PERFORM ALL SERVICES TO THE STANDARD OF A REASONABLE ACCOUNTANT, WHICH INCLUDES THE DUTY TO REPORT ANY APPARENT FRAUD

1650 BROADWAY ASSOCIATES, INC. v. STURM

228 A.D.3d 1 (2024)

Supreme Court of New York, Appellate Division

The iconic Stardust Diner, a family business, is owned by 1650 Broadway Associates, Inc. The Diner was originally owned by Irving Sturm and plaintiff Ellen Sturm (who, along with the two trust plaintiffs, together owned 89 percent), and their son, Kenneth Sturm (who owned the remaining 11 percent). Defendant Getzel, Schiff & Pesce, LLP is a public accounting firm that performed certain accounting services for plaintiffs, the Diner, and Kenneth. It provided these services through a series of year-after-year engagement letters. Under the terms of these letters, defendant agreed to provide "compilation services" and to prepare the local, state, and federal tax returns for the clients. The defendant's managing partner had annual meetings with Ellen at her home, during which the partner provided her only with a broad summary of the Diner's finances but never disclosed any details about the Diner's accounting, books, and records.

When Ellen stepped back from active operations of the Diner, Kenneth began looting the Diner. In particular, he gave himself large salary increases and, most damaging, he began to take unauthorized loans from the Diner. Over the course of several years, these loans amounted to some $12 million. Also, Kenneth obtained a $2.5 million line of credit from Citibank. Kenneth forged Ellen's signature on loan documents that made Ellen the personal guarantor on the loans. The books and records of the Diner reflected the loans. They also reflected certain "reductions" in the amounts of the loans. The records purporting to show the reductions were manufactured after the fact by Kenneth.

In 2019, Ellen hired new personal accountants who uncovered the loans to Kenneth. Apparently, in addition to taking the money for himself, Kenneth also used the "loan" proceeds to finance various other business ventures. The plaintiffs alleged that the defendant was the accountant to these other businesses.

The plaintiffs pled claims for accounting malpractice and aiding and abetting fraud against the accounting firm. The defendant moved to dismiss the case on the grounds that it did not breach professional accounting standards or aid Kenneth's fraud. Plaintiffs appealed the grant of the defendant's motion.

Language of the Court. *This is an action for accounting malpractice and fraud where the question on appeal is whether an accountant hired to perform "compilation services" is shielded from liability for the alleged improper activities of an officer of the company.*

Defendant primarily argues that the malpractice and fraud claims are refuted by the fact that the accounting firm was hired to prepare tax returns and other financial statements that documented the loans at issue, and thus that investigating and reporting Kenneth's alleged fraud were beyond its duties. Plaintiffs' claims, however, are not that defendant was hired to discover Kenneth's wrongdoing, but rather that information obtained by defendant during its business interactions with Kenneth and information used by defendant in order to prepare tax returns and financial statements put defendant on notice about the impropriety of Kenneth's loans to himself such that defendant had a duty to inform plaintiffs of the questionable payments. The law is very clear that an agreement to perform unaudited services does not shield an accountant from liability because an accountant must perform all services in accordance with the standard of a reasonable accountant under similar circumstances, which includes reporting fraud that is or should be apparent.

One who aids and abets a breach of a fiduciary duty is liable for that breach as well, even if they had no independent fiduciary obligation to the allegedly injured party if the alleged aider and abettor rendered "substantial assistance" to the fiduciary in the course of effecting the alleged breaches of duty. In this case, it is alleged not only that the accountant had knowledge of Kenneth's alleged improper transactions but that it participated in the alleged breaches.

Alternatively, Defendant argues that the claims of accounting malpractice and the claims of aiding and abetting fraud are refuted by the fact that the allegedly improper loans were included in the tax returns and financial statements, which plaintiff Ellen had a duty to review. However, while Plaintiffs' own negligence in monitoring Kenneth's activities in managing the Diner may have been a factor in enabling Kenneth to continue his alleged fraudulent scheme for several years, the pleadings and documentary evidence submitted do not show that such negligence was the sole proximate cause of the Diner's loss. It has not been established that such negligence impeded defendant's duties to reveal to plaintiffs what it knew about Kenneth's alleged improper conduct regarding the loans.

Decision. The order dismissing the lawsuit against the accounting firm was reversed.

Focus on Ethics

What do you think of the defendant's argument that the plaintiff's own negligence in monitoring financial records should excuse the accounting firm from their duty to reveal improper conduct? What arguments can be made for and against this position?

Liability for Securities Law Violations

Federal securities laws have two basic objectives: (1) to ensure that investors receive financial and other material information concerning securities being offered for public sale; and (2) to prevent deceit, fraud, or misrepresentations in the sale of these securities. There is an emphasis on disclosure to give investors the ability to make informed and intelligent decisions. The securities laws are more expansively treated in Chapter 25. Accountants and other professionals must comply with the federal and state securities laws.

The Securities Act of 1933 (the 1933 Act)

The 1933 Act regulates the *initial* offering of securities by requiring a registration statement to be filed with SEC prior to sale or an offer to sell. It applies only to the *initial issuance* of securities, and not to subsequent ones. For the re-sale or re-issuance of securities, the 1934 Act—which is discussed below—applies. The 1933 Act has two objectives, both of which relate to the initial offering of securities. These two objectives are (1) disclosure of all material information to potential investors, and (2) preventing fraud.

REGISTRATION UNDER THE 1933 ACT. The 1933 Act requires registration for any offer or sale of securities to the public unless a specific exemption applies. An issuer does this by filing a registration statement, which is a complete disclosure to the SEC of all material information with respect to a particular issuance. The registration statement includes the prospectus, which provides details about an investment offering and must be provided to each potential investor.

Section 11 of the 1933 Act
Imposes civil liability on accountants and other professionals for making misstatements or omissions of material facts in a registration statement or failing to find the same.

LIABILITY UNDER SECTION 11 OF THE 1933 ACT. Under **Section 11 of the 1933 Act,** accountants are liable civilly and criminally for misstatements and omissions of material facts in a registration statement. An accountant can face liability if they prepare a financial statement that is included in the registration materials and the financial statement "contain[s] an untrue statement of a material fact or omit[s] to state a material fact required to be stated therein or necessary to make the statements therein not misleading."[2] Section 11 of the 1933 Act relates only to *newly issued* securities.

Professionals such as accountants are required to exercise due diligence in preparing the financial statements included in the registration statements. Under Section 11, a purchaser or investor of a security need to prove only that they suffered an economic loss on the security. Generally, the plaintiff does *not need* to prove that they relied on the materially false statement or misleading omission.

To defend a claim arising under Section 11, the accountant must show that either:

- They exercised due diligence in their preparation of the financial statements, or
- They had reasonable grounds to believe and did believe at the time the registration statement became effective, that the statements therein were true and that there was no omission of a material fact that would make them misleading.[3]

The **due diligence defense** must show that they followed generally accepted standards and did not commit negligence or fraud during their investigation and preparation of the financial statements. Accountants must detect warning signs that suggest accounting errors or misrepresentations. Directors, officers, and others can also be found liable.[4]

Due diligence defense
Accountants may avoid liability if after reasonable investigation they had reasonable grounds to believe that statements made in the registration statement were true and there was no omission of a material fact that would make the statements misleading.

LIABILITY UNDER SECTION 12 OF THE 1933 ACT. Under **Section 12(1)** of the 1933 Act, civil liability may be imposed upon the professional if the purchaser of securities can prove one of the following events occurred:

- The required registration was not made;
- A registered security was sold, but the prospectus either was not delivered or was not current; or
- An offer to sell securities was made prior to a required registration.

Violation of this provision imposes strict liability for damages upon those who erred.

Section 12(2) of the 1933 Act creates liability of a seller of a security to *its direct purchaser* where the disclosure requirements of the Act have not been complied with (that is, there has been a misstatement or omission of a material fact by written or oral communication) at the time of the purchase. Only the immediate purchaser (that is, the first purchaser) has standing to sue. As a defense, the accountant can prove that either:

Sections 12(1) and (2) of the 1933 Act
Provisions that create liability for any person who offers or sells a security through a prospectus or an oral communication containing a material misstatement or omission, provided that the purchaser did not know about the misstatement or omission.

- They did not know and had no reason to know of the misstatement or omission; or
- The purchaser's loss was caused by something other than the misstatement or omission.[5]

2. 15 U.S.C. § 77k(a).
3. *Id.*
4. *Id.*
5. 15 U.S.C. § 77l.

Section 17(a) of the 1933 Act
Provision of the 1933 Act prohibiting schemes to defraud and recognizing liability for misrepresentations and omissions in securities offerings.

LIABILITY UNDER SECTION 17 OF THE 1933 ACT. Section 17(a) of the 1933 Act serves as a general anti-fraud provision and imposes liability on a seller for fraud, material misrepresentations, and omissions in securities sales. However, unlike other provisions of the 1933 Act, Section 17(a) does not generally allow for a private remedy for the purchaser of securities. Rather, the SEC imposes civil and criminal sanctions on those who willfully violate any of the provisions of the 1933 Act.

The Securities Act of 1934 (the 1934 Act)

Under Section 10(b), Rule 10b-5, and Section 18 of the 1934 Act, an accountant or other professional may be held liable for fraud. While the scope of these provisions is broad, a plaintiff has a higher burden of proof under these provisions because they require a showing of fraud or reckless conduct on the part of the defendant in the lawsuit. The plaintiff must show that they relied on a misleading statement and that it affected the price of the security. Mere negligent conduct on the part of the professional is not actionable.

The extent of the liability of the professional, including the accountant, is limited to only the purchasers and sellers of the securities under these provisions.

Rule 10(b)
Provision of the 1934 Act prohibiting manipulative and deceptive practices in connection with the purchase or sale of a security.

Rule 10b-5
A regulation enacted by the SEC targeting securities fraud through use of the mails, interstate commerce, or a national securities exchange.

LIABILITY UNDER RULE 10B-5 OF THE 1934 ACT. As was addressed in Chapter 25, Section 10(b) of the 1934 Act and SEC Rule 10b-5 serve as anti-fraud provisions. Under Rule 10b-5, it is unlawful for any person in connection with the purchase or sale of any security to use the mails, interstate commerce, or a national securities exchange to:

- Employ any device or scheme with the intent to defraud;
- Make any untrue statement of a material fact or omit a material fact that would be necessary to make a statement not misleading; or
- Engage in any act or business practice that would deceive or defraud an investor.[6]

To succeed in bringing a securities fraud claim under the 1934 Act, a plaintiff must show that the defendant-wrongdoer had scienter. The term "scienter" is defined as having the intent to deceive, manipulate, or defraud another.

Under Sections 10(b) and 18 of the 1934 Act, an accountant or other professional may be liable for fraud in the resale of securities (that is, following their initial issuance).

Section 18(a) of the 1934 Act
A provision of the 1934 Act imposing civil liability on a person who has made false or misleading statements in any document filed with the SEC.

LIABILITY UNDER SECTION 18 OF THE 1934 ACT. Liability under Section 18 of the 1934 Act relates to defendants' false or misleading SEC filings (though not known to be such by a plaintiff), which affected the price of the security and with the plaintiff 's reliance. To be successful, the purchaser or seller must prove:

- The price of the security was affected by the false or misleading statement; or
- The purchaser or seller relied on the false or misleading statement in making its buy or sell decision and was unaware of the inaccuracies within the statement.[7]

6. 15 U.S.C. § 78j(b).
7. 15 U.S.C. § 17r(a).

DEFENSES TO SECTION 18. In defending a Section 18 claim, an accountant may either:

- *Invoke the **good faith defense**.* To demonstrate good faith, an accountant must show that the plaintiff lacked knowledge of the false or misleading information or that they knew the information was false or misleading and acted anyway. Additionally, the accountant must show they acted without the intent to deceive, defraud, or manipulate the market for the security; or
- *Plead a statute of limitations defense.* The purchaser or seller of the security must bring a Section 18 lawsuit "within one year after the discovery of the facts constituting the cause of action and within three years after such cause of action accrued."[8]

Good faith defense
A defense an accountant may assert if they acted in good faith in preparing the financial statement.

Related Federal Securities Laws

In addition to the 1933 Act and 1934 Act, liability may also be imposed under the Private Securities Litigation Reform Act of 1995, the Foreign Corrupt Practices Act of 1977 (FCPA), the Dodd-Frank Wall Street Reform and Consumer Protection Act of 2010, and the Sarbanes-Oxley Act of 2002 (SOX). The FCPA is discussed in Chapter 43 and amends the 1934 Act to prevent bribes to foreign government officials.

PRIVATE SECURITIES LITIGATION REFORM ACT OF 1995. This Act amended the 1933 and 1934 Acts. Among its provisions are the following:

- Prohibition of solicitation or acceptance of referral fees from an attorney by brokers, dealers, and associated persons for obtaining the representation of a customer;
- Provision of a statute of limitations for private causes of action; and
- The safe harbor rules for forward-looking statements (such as a projection of revenues, income, and earnings).

The Private Securities Litigation Reform Act of 1995 offers protections to corporations that make such an announcement. Under this so-called safe harbor, a corporation is not liable if the statement is:

- Identified and accompanied by meaningful cautionary language;
- Immaterial; or
- One that the plaintiff failed to prove was made with actual knowledge that it was false or misleading.

Example: In 2010, IBM established a "2015 Roadmap" strategy to double its earnings per share (EPS) to $20 within five years. In 2014, IBM planned to sell its microelectronics unit, and when it made the announcement, IBM's stock dropped more than 17 percent from a former high price of $197.77 per share. Nonetheless, from 2010 to 2014, IBM consistently stated that its long-lived assets were tested for

8. 15 U.S.C. § 17r(c).

impairment, that there were no material impairments of non-financial assets, and that IBM was on track to reach its goal of $20 EPS.

When a union trust fund sued as a stockholder for violation of the Act, the federal court held that IBM's statement that it was "on track to reach its goal of $20 EPS" was protected under the safe harbor of PSLRA because the plaintiffs failed to explain how IBM lacked a reasonable basis when making such a statement and failed to show that such a statement was false or misleading. If anything, the court stated, it is reasonable to assume that IBM was protected because it could be argued that selling its microelectronics unit was part of the 2015 Roadmap to get to a $20 EPS. *Int'l Ass'n of Heat & Frost Insulators & Asbestos Workers Local #6 Pension Fund v. IBM*, 205 F. Supp. 3d 527 (S.D.N.Y. 2016)

Of special interest to the accounting profession are the Act's provisions with respect to audit requirements. Audits should provide reasonable assurance of detecting illegal acts that have a direct and material effect upon financial statements. The audit must be designed to identify material related-party transactions and include an evaluation as to whether there is a substantial doubt about the issuer's ability to continue as a going concern. Accountants must report illegal acts to the appropriate level of management and the board of directors or the SEC, depending upon the circumstances.[7]

Sarbanes-Oxley Act of 2002
Enacted by Congress to establish standards of best practices in response to a series of corporate and accounting scandals.

SARBANES-OXLEY ACT OF 2002 (SOX). Numerous accounting scandals involving some of the world's largest accounting firms and corporations led to the enactment of comprehensive legislation commonly referred to as SOX. SOX applies to companies subject to federal securities laws. The Act regulates public accounting firms through the Public Company Accounting Oversight Board (PCAOB). The PCAOB establishes rules to regulate the profession, and violations of the board's rules are deemed to be violations of the 1934 Act. Some of the SOX requirements include the following:

- A public accounting firm must register with the board. The PCAOB annually inspects firms that audit more than 100 public companies. All other public accounting firms are inspected at least once every 3 years.
- The Act prohibits an accounting firm that audits a public company from providing the following non-audit services to the client:
  - Bookkeeping services;
  - Financial information systems;
  - Appraisal or valuation services;
  - Internal audit services;
  - Management functions;
  - Human resources services;
  - Broker, dealer, or investment services;
  - Investment banking services;
  - Legal services; or
  - Any other services as are determined by the oversight board.
- Each audit must be assigned to an audit partner who supervises the audit and approves the final audit report. A second audit partner must approve the work of the first. The auditors must retain all audit work papers and supporting documentation for a period of seven years.

PCAOB
Accounting oversight board for public accounting firms required by SOX.

Under SOX, the PCAOB does the following:

- Registers public accounting firms;
- Establishes standards to be used in audit reports;
- Inspects and investigates the work of accounting firms; and
- Conducts disciplinary proceedings for violations and imposes appropriate sanctions.

The Act requires that a public company maintain an independent audit committee that is responsible for appointing, compensating, and overseeing the work of the public accounting firm chosen by the issuer. Each member of the audit committee is required to be an independent member of the issuer's board of directors, which means an audit committee member cannot be affiliated with the issuer.

With respect to internal controls, SOX requires that annual reports include:

- A statement of management's responsibility for establishing and maintaining adequate internal control and procedures for financial reporting; and
- Management's own assessment of the effectiveness of these control measures.

Once the registered auditor issues the audit report for a public client, that auditor must attest to, and report on, the assessment made by management in the internal control report. It is the auditor's responsibility to determine whether the entity's transaction records are fair and accurate as well as provide reasonable assurance that the financial statements are prepared in accordance with GAAP principles.

Joint and several liability is imposed only for a knowing violation of the securities laws. Otherwise, liability is proportionate to the defendant's percentage of responsibility for the total damages.[9]

> **Example:** In the WorldCom securities litigation, the federal district court held that most, if not all, the directors who were sued were subject only to proportionate liability under Section 11. They did not have actual knowledge of the accounting malfeasance occurring. *In re WorldCom, Inc. Sec. Litig.*, 2005 U.S. Dist. LEXIS 1805 (S.D.N.Y. 2005)

Tax Return Preparer Liability

A **tax return preparer** is one who is hired to prepare a substantial portion of any tax return, amended return, or a claim for a tax refund. Liability of tax return preparers is based on the Internal Revenue Code (IRC).

Tax return preparer One who is hired to prepare a substantial portion of any tax return, amended return, or a claim for a tax refund.

Under the IRC, tax return preparers should generally have a reasonable basis for taking a tax position. A preparer may generally rely in good faith without verification on information given by the taxpayer, so long as the preparer does not ignore the implications of information given to the preparer. For example, a preparer can

9. 15 U.S.C. § 78u-4(f).

estimate the amount of deductions so long as they are reasonable under the circumstances. However, some deductions are not allowed without receipts or records to prove their existence, such as expenses for traveling or meals. As a guideline, tax return preparers should exercise diligence in preparing and filing any returns or documents with the Internal Revenue Service (IRS).

Penalties

Under the IRC, any willful attempt to evade federal tax liability, including for that of another person, is subject to criminal penalties, injunctive relief, as well as imprisonment. Any person who willfully aids or assists in preparing a materially false or fraudulent return is guilty of a felony.

Other provisions of the IRC impose liabilities on CPAs. For example, a CPA who fails to provide the taxpayer with a copy of the tax return could be subject to liability. Another provision subjects a preparer to penalties for using or disclosing information other than for return preparation in the amount of $250 up to a maximum of $10,000 per disclosure.

The following case involves a tax return preparer who acted fraudulently in the preparation of returns on behalf of his clients.

CASE 42.2

A TAX RETURN PREPARER MAY BE PERMANENTLY ENJOINED FROM FILING TAX RETURNS AND ANY GAINS MAY BE DISGORGED

UNITED STATES v. STINSON

239 F. Supp. 3d 1299 (2017)

United States District Court for the Middle District of Florida

Jason Stinson began his tax preparation career with LBS Tax Services. Over time, Stinson began his own tax preparation business and expanded his business to multiple stores. Stinson personally prepared tax returns, but eventually he left the tax return preparations to his employees. Stinson was the sole owner of his tax preparation business, Nation Tax. Stinson's tax stores targeted "under privileged, undereducated poor people and earned income credit claims." Stinson described his clients as "unsophisticated" customers who needed assistance with their tax returns. Stinson's business marketed and advertised heavily, targeting low-income taxpayers with little understanding of tax laws. Stinson advertised that Nation Tax could secure large tax refunds for its clients. Clients did not have to pay a fee upfront for each tax return; instead, the fee would be deducted from the taxpayer customer's refund amount. Therefore, a larger refund was better for the client and for Stinson. Stinson often charged more than $600 per return, sometimes as much as $999, often without informing the taxpayer of the fee amount. The goal was to get the maximum refund to make the customer happy and deduct a larger fee.

The government claimed Stinson repeatedly engaged in the following fraudulent practices: (1) falsifying deductions on Form 1040 Schedule A to reduce a customer's taxable income by reporting personal expenses as business expenses and falsifying unreimbursed employee expenses and charitable contributions; (2) falsifying Form 1040 Schedule C deductions by fabricating businesses and reporting profits or losses from a false business or inflating profits and losses from an actual business; (3) claiming false education credits; (4) falsifying a customer's earned income tax credit; (5) failing to conduct proper due diligence; and (6) failing to disclose fees and provide customers complete copies of their tax returns.

Language of the Court. *The Tax Reform Act of 1976 reflects a congressional intent to prevent abuses by tax preparers in the reporting of client's income tax liabilities. To issue an injunction, the following three prerequisites must be met: (1) the defendant must be a tax preparer; (2) the conduct complained of must fall within one of the four areas of proscribed conduct; and (3) the court must find that an injunction is appropriate to prevent the recurrence of the proscribed conduct.*

The court determined that Stinson is a tax preparer by the virtue of his ownership and operation of tax preparation stores and his employment of individuals to assist in tax preparation. A tax preparer violates the Internal Revenue laws where (1) the return contains an understatement of liability; (2) the understatement is "due to a position for which there was not a realistic possibility of being sustained on its merits"; and (3) the preparer knew or reasonably should have known that the position was either frivolous or not disclosed. The court found that Stinson had both negligently and willfully prepared tax returns with false and improper claims that wrongfully reduced the taxpayer's liability. The pattern of improper claims on tax returns prepared at Stinson's stores is beyond mere mistakes and the exact same abusive claims were repeated among the taxpayer customers. The court found that Stinson engaged in other fraudulent conduct because the goal of his business model was to take advantage of low-income taxpayers. Stinson lured customers with the promise of maximum refunds. Many of his customers received large refunds, [from] which he was able to deduct a higher fee. Stinson's customers trusted him to prepare their taxes correctly because they did not know how to prepare their taxes. Stinson took advantage of his customers' lack of tax law knowledge and their deference to his expertise.

If a court finds that a tax preparer is continually or repeatedly engaged in the fraudulent conduct, the court may enjoin that person from acting as an income tax return preparer. The court may consider the following factors to determine whether a defendant is likely to violate the law again: (1) the gravity of the harm caused by the offense; (2) the extent of the defendant's participation; (3) the defendant's degree of scienter; (4) the isolated or recurrent nature of the infraction; (5) the defendant's recognition (or non-recognition) of his own culpability; and (6) the likelihood that defendant's occupation would place him in a position where future violations could be anticipated.

Under traditional equitable principles, the Government seeking a permanent injunction must demonstrate (1) it has suffered an irreparable injury; (2) remedies available at law, such as monetary damages, are inadequate to compensate for that injury; (3) considering the balance of hardships between the Government and

Stinson, a remedy in equity is warranted; and (4) the public interest would not be disserved by a permanent injunction. Based on these factors, the court determined that Stinson's conduct interferes with the proper administration of the internal revenue laws and that an injunction is appropriate and necessary to prevent future harm.

The court has also determined that disgorgement is an available remedy in this case. Disgorgement in the amount of a defendant's gains constitutes a fair and equitable remedy. The Government's disgorgement amount represents a reasonable approximation of Stinson's unjust enrichment. The court will order disgorgement in the amount of $949,952.47.

Decision. The federal court held Stinson's repeated willful filings of fraudulent tax returns warranted permanent injunctive relief, and that disgorgement of his share of the refunds was appropriate.

Focus on Ethics

Do you think it is fair that the government was able to permanently bar Stinson from preparing tax returns? Why did Stinson target poor and unsophisticated persons needing assistance with the preparation of their tax returns?

Occupational Licensing in General

See the NCSL Database on Licensed Occupations at https://www.ncsl.org/research/labor-and-employment/occupational-licensing-statute-database.aspx.

Frequently, when considering who is a "professional," we most often think of those persons who have the necessary knowledge and skill to engage in a specific professional activity. Most often the person will hold a state-issued license to practice that profession. They acquired their knowledge through advanced education and training. We are familiar with many of them, including certified public accountants, physicians, nurses, dentists, pharmacists, and attorneys. There are many additional careers that require state licensure; and there are many that do not require a college degree.

Licensing standards serve to define the minimal standard of care for licensees in those fields. Aligned with these standards are the risk that a professional's actions were negligently performed. Additionally, licensing standards provide the minimal thresholds of education and experience a licensee must possess. When harm has occurred, they assist a court in applying a minimal duty or standard of care owed to the plaintiff. A court then assesses if the harm suffered was within the foreseeable risk to the plaintiff and determines if the defendant exercised appropriate care.

Example: Licensing standards for childcare and eldercare facilities are widely adopted by the states. Failure to comply with a state's requirements may not only result in the revocation of the license to operate the facility but also establish the basis for a negligence claim against the operator.

State laws and regulations recognize specific professional standards of care. These laws and regulations are intended to identify the duty of care in these occupations because absent a duty of care, an action for professional negligence will fail. Usually, the plaintiff cannot establish a *prima facie* case of professional negligence without expert testimony. The expert establishing the standard of care must practice in the same field and must be able to testify as to the standard of care in the location where the alleged negligence occurred. Some states have eliminated the duty of care as measured under local conditions and require compliance with national and specialty standards of care. Only in cases where a lack of care is so apparent that merely common knowledge and experience are needed to comprehend that professional negligence has occurred that expert testimony is not required.

Management Application Codes of Professional Practice

Ethical codes serve as the guiding principles by which members of the profession are to abide. Frequently, they are also part of the regulatory schemes to which they must respond. The ethical codes guiding the practice of accountants are discussed in detail below.

Other professionals are also guided by ethical codes. For example, attorneys must adhere to state-specific codes of professional responsibility or the ABA Model Rules of Professional Conduct if adopted by the state in which the attorney practices. Additionally, stockbrokers may be liable to their clients because of the rules of the Financial Industry Regulatory Authority (FINRA). Using these ethical codes to guide the conduct of professionals enhances respect for the profession, maintains public trust in members of the profession, and demonstrates honesty and fairness in dealings with others.

See AICPA Code of Professional Conduct at *https://us.aicpa.org/research/standards/codeofconduct*

See ABA Code of Professional Conduct at *https://www.americanbar.org/groups/professional_responsibility/publications/model_rules_of_professional_conduct/*

See AMA Code of Medical Ethics at *https://code-medical-ethics.ama-assn.org See FINRA's Rules at https://www.finra.org/rules-guidance*

See NASW Code of Ethics at *https://www.socialworkers.org/About/Ethics/Code-of-Ethics/Code-of-Ethics-English#*

Management Application
Regulation by FINRA

The oversight of professionals working in securities and investment firms is also conducted by FINRA. FINRA can discipline brokers who violate FINRA rules, as well as federal securities laws. FINRA aids investors in seeking disciplinary action against these professionals by providing three separate procedures.

The first option is settlement, which allows the firm or broker to settle with FINRA directly through the filing of a Letter of Acceptance and a Waiver and Consent.

The next option requires the filing of a formal complaint against the broker. The complaint is filed with FINRA's Office of Hearing Officers. Then, the case is assigned to a professional hearing officer. The case is presented before the professional hearing officer and two industry panelists. The purpose of FINRA's formal complaint process is to resolve the issue in a fair and expeditious manner.

Finally, the investor may file an arbitration claim or request mediation through FINRA in instances where the investor has a dispute involving the business practices of the investment firm or a specific broker. To file a claim for arbitration or mediation through FINRA, the alleged act must have occurred within the past six years. This is different from the filing of a complaint against the firm or broker. In instances where the investor believes that the firm or broker engaged in fraudulent activities, the investor should file a formal complaint as described in the paragraph above.

Using an internet search engine, review recent formal disciplinary proceedings against a regulated securities firm. What alleged fraudulent offerings were involved, and what did the firm allegedly do that was in violation of the securities laws?

Confidentiality and Privilege

Under professional rules of conduct, professionals owe a duty of confidentiality to their clients. This includes keeping confidential all information obtained within the scope and course of representation, as well as keeping confidential all privileged communications.

Attorney-Client Privilege

Attorney's communications with their clients are protected by law. For an attorney to be able to represent his client in the most effective manner possible, the client needs to feel comfortable disclosing all pertinent facts to the attorney. This privilege provides assurances to the client that the attorney will not disclose these communications. The attorney-client privilege extends to all employees of the attorney.

Therefore, neither the attorney nor law firm employees can be compelled to testify as to the communications between the attorney and client. Although the privilege prevents disclosure by the attorney and the employees, the privilege is ultimately held by the client; therefore, the only way the privilege can be waived is if the client consents.

The SEC has attempted to work around the attorney-client privilege by creating rules under SOX that require the attorney to disclose whether a client has violated a securities law. However, disclosing this information still constitutes a breach of the attorney-client privilege, thereby posing a potential ethical dilemma for attorneys, particularly those in states that have adopted attorney-client privilege laws that attempt to zealously protect the client's confidences.

Accountant-Client Privilege

WORK PAPERS. For accountants, work papers are confidential records used while performing an engagement. These work papers are deemed to be the accountant's property and are prepared by accountants. Moreover, these work papers serve as the best evidence of the accountant's representation and efforts in the event of a lawsuit by a client.

The AICPA Code of Professional Conduct states that an accountant may be liable for malpractice if a third party is given unauthorized access to these work papers. The AICPA Code requires a member not to disclose any confidential information except with the specific consent of the client.

The AICPA Code does not prohibit an accountant from disclosing confidential client information in the following circumstances:

- In compliance with a validly issued and enforceable court order;
- In the proper discharge of their professional obligations under the AICPA Code;
- In a review of the accountant's professional practice by the AICPA or state CPA board; or
- During an investigative or disciplinary proceeding.

Example: The Supreme Court has held that when an individual surrenders their business records to the possession of a third party (such as an accountant), and the government subpoenas the third party to produce the records, the individual has no expectation of privacy in the records and the Fifth Amendment does not bar their production. *Couch v. United States*, 409 U.S. 322 (1973)

Although communication between lawyers and clients is privileged, there is no common law equivalent with respect to accountants and their clients. However, some states do in fact provide an accountant-client communications privilege. In these states, disclosure of anything contained in the work papers is not allowed except in limited circumstances depending upon the jurisdiction. If there is a privilege, it is construed narrowly. This means that the privilege can be lost if any part of the privileged communication is voluntarily submitted.

AI Feature: Draft a Law Permitting Paralegals to Practice Law in a Limited Capacity

Several states are attempting to relax their attorney licensing laws because it is argued that underserved communities lack a sufficient number of competent attorneys to render legal services to them. Alternatively, they seek to empower trained paralegals to prepare legal documents for routine matters, which would help address that need. What arguments can you make to support such a change? Use an internet search engine to research this topic. Then, use an AI program to draft a proposed law allowing such a legal practice in your home state. Ensure that you address requirements for the legal education of the candidate for paralegal licensure, whether the paralegal must be a graduate of an American Bar Association approved paralegal program, the requirements for professional liability insurance, the degree of direct supervision of the paralegal by a licensed attorney, and the scope of the services that could be rendered to the public.

Key Terms

- Actual fraud, 1063
- Adverse opinion, 1063
- Audit, 1062
- Auditor's opinion, 1062
- Constructive fraud, 1063
- Disclaimer of opinion, 1063
- Due diligence defense, 1069
- GAAP, 1062
- GAAS, 1062
- Good faith defense, 1071
- IFRS, 1062
- PCAOB, 1072
- Qualified opinion, 1063
- Reasonably foreseeable users rule, 1065
- Restatement (Third) of Torts Rule, 1065
- Rule 10(b), 1070
- Rule 10b-5, 1070
- Sarbanes-Oxley Act of 2002, 1072
- Section 11 of the 1933 Act, 1068
- Section 17(a) of the 1933 Act, 1070
- Section 18(a) of the 1934 Act, 1070
- Sections 12(1) and (2) of the 1933 Act, 1069
- Tax return preparer, 1073
- *Ultramares* doctrine, 1064
- Unqualified opinion, 1062

Applying the Law

42.1 Research the Law. In the United States accountants comply with Generally Accepted Accounting Principles (GAAP) when performing accounting services. GAAP represents a common set of accounting principles and standards that companies follow when compiling financial statements. How is GAAP enforced even though it is not a law?

42.2 Research the Law. Using an internet search engine, review differences between the Generally Accepted Accounting Principles (GAAP) and the International Financial Reporting Standards (IFRS). Summarize your findings.

42.3 Research the Law. Using an internet search engine, research the legal troubles of CPAs or other professionals, such as attorneys, who have mismanaged the investments of or embezzled from celebrity or sports-figure clients. How were the misdeeds discovered? To what degree did the victims receive restitution of their funds? What recommendations would you propose to members of professional sports leagues relative to the vetting of their financial advisors?

42.4 Professional Negligence. John Tekman participated with his brother, Nick, and his father, Ali, in several real estate investments involving the development and operation of motels and hotels during the 1990s. John took a 25 percent share in one enterprise, T & C, LLC, which was co-owned by Nick, Ali, and Ali's wife, Nuriye. At various times between 2002 and 2010, John's relatives and business partners diverted T & C's profits to themselves and used T & C's assets as collateral for other commercial endeavors to which John was not a party. His parents and siblings authorized the use of T & C's assets as a guarantee for an $11 million loan for the construction of a separate hotel project. John's signature was forged on the relevant documentation, and he received no financial interest in the new enterprise. John sued the family accountant, Herb Berkowitz, who provided a variety of accounting services to both T & C and to John personally. John alleged that Berkowitz breached his duty of care by failing to notify John of bookkeeping irregularities when Berkowitz knew that T & C assets were being used for purposes in which John was not a party. What duties does the accountant have towards John Tekman? Was Berkowitz a fiduciary to Tekman? *Tekman v. Berkowitz*, 639 F. App'x 801 (3d Cir. 2016)

42.5 Auditor's Failure to Detect Fraud. ChinaCast was an educational services company in the People's Republic of China whose common stock was traded on a national securities exchange. In 2012, ChinaCast publicly disclosed that, unbeknownst to its investors, and without consent from its board of directors, certain rogue employees, led by ChinaCast's former chairperson and CEO, Ron Chan, had engaged in fraudulent activities such as misappropriating proceeds from a stock offering, misrepresenting ChinaCast's ownership interests, and pledging substantial portions of the Company's term deposits to cover debts owed to third parties. As a result of this disclosure, ChinaCast's stock price plummeted.

A group of investors sued ChinaCast's former officers and outside auditor, Deloitte®, alleging that they violated provisions of the 1934 Act and committed common law fraud by issuing and approving false statements in ChinaCast's public filings with the SEC.

The investors argued that had Deloitte complied with basic accounting principles, it would have discovered the "red flags" symptomatic of fraud. Deloitte failed to detect the pledging of the assets and the irregularity in cash inflows and outflows, and also failed to supervise the local Chinese auditor of the company.

What theories of relief should be pursued against Deloitte? *Special Situations Fund III, QQ, L.P. v. Deloitte Touche Tohmatsu CPA, Ltd.*, 33 F. Supp. 3d 401 (S.D.N.Y. 2014)

42.6 The Restatement Rule. Max Mitchell was a certified public accountant and president of Max Mitchell and Company. Mitchell negotiated a loan from First Florida Bank on behalf of his client, C.M. Systems. He told the bank vice president that he was a certified public accountant and delivered audited financial statements prepared by his firm. The statement indicated the client had total assets exceeding $3 million and total liabilities of around $1.2 million. Mitchell also stated that his client did not have any other debt to a bank. After the bank extended a line of credit for $500,000, it was discovered that the audit report of the client's operating results substantially overstated assets and net income, as well as understated liabilities. It was also discovered the client owed money to several banks and that several material changes occurred in the client's balance sheet after the audit but prior to the loan approval. What arguments can be made for and against the finding of the accountant's liability to First Florida Bank? *First Florida Bank, N.A. v. Max Mitchell & Co.*, 558 So. 2d 9 (Fla. 1990)

42.7 Liability to Third Parties. The accounting firm Logan, Throop & Company prepared a financial statement for World Interactive Networks, Inc. (WIN), a non-publicly traded company. The statement misrepresented the value of assets, claiming they were worth the significantly higher amount of $145 million when they in fact were worth $30 million. Logan stated the financial statements complied with GAAP when they did not. A second accounting firm, BDO Seidman, LLP, issued audited financial statements in which they had also misrepresented the value of WIN's assets, claiming that they were worth more than $121 million, when they were worth less than $7 million. Seidman also misrepresented WIN's shareholder equity as $88 million, when the company was worthless. Struthers Industries, a publicly traded corporation, agreed to a reverse merger, whereby WIN would sell its assets to Struthers in return for Struthers stock. During this proposed merger, Seidman prepared a financial statement with the same false asset values and misrepresentations about complying with GAAP. The SEC had informed Struthers that the statements did not comply with GAAP, and Seidman did not inform those who owned or later bought WIN or Struthers stock about the SEC's rejection of Seidman's accounting. When WIN and Struthers filed for bankruptcy, those who relied on Seidman's and Logan's financial statements lost their investments. Both accounting firms were sued, with plaintiffs alleging causes of action for negligence and intentional misrepresentation. Should the firms be held liable to the investors for their losses? *Murphy v. BDO Seidman*, 113 Cal. App. 4th 687 (2003)

42.8 Liability Under Rule 10b-5. Ernst & Ernst was an accounting firm that prepared filings with the SEC annual reports and responses to financial questionnaires for First Securities Company of Chicago (First Securities). Some customers of First Securities invested in fraudulent securities sold by Leston B. Nay, the president of the firm and owner of most of its stock. Nay induced the investors to invest funds in "escrow" accounts that he said would yield a high rate of return. No such escrow accounts were reflected in the books and records of First Securities, nor were they included in the filings with the SEC. The investors sued Ernst & Ernst alleging that they had "aided and abetted" Nay's violations by failing to conduct proper audits. In the absence of any allegation of scienter on the part of the accounting firm, should the firm be held liable for the investors' losses? *Ernst & Ernst v. Hochelder*, 425 U.S. 185 (1976)

42.9 Tax Preparer Liability. Archie and Theodore Pugh prepared several tax returns using a "claim of right" doctrine to apply a deduction on federal income tax returns. The "claim of right" was a discredited tax evasion scheme, which falsely asserted that neither an individual nor their income is subject to federal income tax. The Pughs did not sign the income tax returns they prepared, instead reporting that they were "self-prepared." Did the tax preparers have a reasonable basis for the deductions claimed? Was it appropriate for the government to enjoin them from acting as federal tax return preparers? *United States v. Pugh*, 717 F. Supp. 2d 271 (E.D.N.Y. 2010)

42.10 Research the Law. Using an internet search engine, review the occupational licensing boards of your home state and compare them to another state's requirements for such a license. Research what initiatives states are advancing to make it easier for ex-offenders to get occupational licenses. Do these state laws establish standards of care for a licensee to follow?

International Business Transactions

43

Commerce with all nations, alliance with none, should be our motto. —Thomas Jefferson, Third President of the United States (1743-1826)

Chapter Outline

- Introduction
- Transacting Business with Foreign Governments

Case 43.1: *Chettri v. Nepal Rastra Bank*

- The International Sales Contract

Case 43.2: *Nucap Indus., Inc. v. Robert Bosch LLC*

- Transacting Business Abroad
  - *Management Application: International Franchising*
- Trade Regulations
- International Dispute Resolution

Case 43.3: *Ministry of Defense and Support for the Armed Forces of the Islamic Republic of Iran v. Cubic Defense Systems, Inc.*

- Consequences of Unethical Business Practices: The FCPA and the UK Bribery Act 2010
- AI Feature: Analyzing Subsidies as Unfair Trade

Learning Objectives

After studying this chapter, you should be able to:

1. Explain when a foreign government cannot assert sovereign immunity.
2. Describe the different ways of doing business internationally.
3. Recommend provisions to include in an international business contract.
4. Explain the international protections of intellectual property.
5. Describe the dispute resolution process involving parties from different countries.

Introduction

In the competitive global markets in which businesses operate, it is incumbent upon a manager to understand the implications of competing internationally. This chapter will review the sources of the laws that apply to international transactions, the important provisions to include in an international contract, protection of intellectual property, and pursuing different forms of dispute resolution. Finally, we address the consequences of commercial bribery in an international context.

Transacting Business with Foreign Governments

Before addressing commercial transactions between businesses, we note that governments also engage in these transactions. Resolving disputes with nations is different from resolving them with civil commercial contracts.

The Doctrine of Sovereign Immunity

Sovereign immunity Governments cannot be sued without their consent.

Foreign Sovereign Immunities Act (FSIA) U.S. law that states the circumstances in which foreign states are immune from suit and execution upon their assets.

Sovereign immunity is an internationally recognized concept that an independent state enjoys protection from having cases brought against its government in foreign courts. Courts of another nation will not involve themselves in the internal affairs of that foreign state.

Generally, a foreign state is immune to suits brought in American courts. The **Foreign Sovereign Immunities Act (FSIA)** has codified this rule. Additionally, the Act specifies those conditions in which a claim may be pursued against a foreign nation in a U.S. court. The FSIA[1] defines a "foreign state" as including not only the government of the state but also political subdivisions or instrumentalities of the nation state. An instrumentality includes any business entity that is at least 51 percent owned by the government.

The doctrine of sovereign immunity is a jurisdictional defense against a lawsuit against a foreign government. The FSIA states that a foreign nation will be immune from a lawsuit unless:

1. The foreign state has either explicitly or implicitly waived its sovereign immunity;
2. The foreign state has engaged in commercial activity within the United States, or the commercial activity, although outside the United States, has "a direct and substantial effect on the United States";
3. The foreign state has committed a tort in the United States; or
4. The foreign state has performed an international taking in violation of international law.

1. 28 U.S.C. § 1603.

Since the term "commercial activity" has been broadly defined by the Act, courts must determine what constitutes a commercial as opposed to a governmental act.

CASE 43.1

A GOVERNMENT'S ROUTINE LAW ENFORCEMENT ACTION DOES NOT CONSTITUTE COMMERCIAL ACTIVITY

CHETTRI v. NEPAL RASTRA BANK

834 F.3d 50 (2016)

United States Court of Appeals for the Second Circuit

Tarala International (Tarala) was a Colorado corporation that supplied clothing and military equipment to Nepal. Tarala's director, Wu, coordinated the procurement and delivery of those international transactions in Nepal. Wu acted as Tarala's agent in connection with contracts with Nepal.

Rastra Bank was Nepal's financial agent. Rastra Bank, on Nepal's behalf, and was authorized to open and operate accounts and issue letters of credit. The Department of Revenue Investigation is a department of the Nepalese government. Between 2006 and 2008, Nepal placed several orders with Tarala, which were financed through letters of credit. In July 2008, Tarala wired $1 million to Wu to pay for the transportation and delivery of the goods in Nepal. Bangladesh Bank (Wu's personal bank) informed Rastra Bank (Nepal's bank) that it was freezing the funds due to irregularities in the documents presented. Tarala provided evidence attesting to the funds' legitimacy, but Bangladesh Bank refused to unfreeze the funds. As a result, Tarala filed a complaint against Rastra Bank and the Nepalese government, as well as the Department of Revenue, in the U.S. district court. After a default judgment was entered against Rastra Bank and the Nepalese government, the district court reversed the judgment and dismissed the complaint for lack of subject matter and personal jurisdiction. Tarala appealed, arguing the district court did have subject matter and personal jurisdiction over the claim because it was commercial in nature.

Language of the Court. *The FSIA "provides the sole basis for obtaining jurisdiction over a foreign state in federal court." The Act renders a foreign state "presumptively immune from the jurisdiction of United States courts."*

None of the three grounds for invoking the commercial activity exception applies here. With respect to the first ground, this action is not "based upon a commercial activity carried on in the United States." The "threshold step" in assessing the applicability of the commercial activity exception is always to "identify the act of the foreign sovereign State that serves as the basis for plaintiffs' claims." Tarala and Wu cite as a commercial activity Nepal's entering into a contract with Colorado-based Tarala to supply goods and equipment. This lawsuit, however, is based not upon that contract but upon the Department and Rastra Bank's freezing of Wu's account in Nepal.

The term "'based upon' calls for something more than a mere connection with, or relation to, commercial activity." For a cause of action to be "based upon" a commercial activity and thereby fit within the FSIA exception, there must exist a "degree of closeness between the commercial activity and the gravamen of the plaintiff's complaint." This degree of closeness must be "considerably greater than common law causation requirements."

Tarala and Wu contend that Tarala wired the $1 million to Wu so that Wu could facilitate the delivery of equipment under the contracts with Nepal. Rastra Bank and the Department argue that insufficient evidence supports this contention. The dispute is beside the point, however, because, even if commercial activities had led to the conduct that eventually injured Tarala and Wu, this would not alone render such activities the basis of their suit. Tarala and Wu are not alleging breach of contract in this action. At the time Rastra Bank and the Department froze Wu's account, Rastra Bank had already paid in full the letters of credit in satisfaction of the contracts between Nepal and Tarala. This action is based upon Bangladesh Bank's allegedly tortious freezing, not the contract, and therefore the "commercial activity" exception does not apply.

Decision. The court of appeals affirmed the district court's finding that the court did not have subject matter or personal jurisdiction over the claim because none of the exceptions to the FSIA were applicable.

Focus on Ethics

Explain why the "commercial activity" exception to the FSIA exists. Does it encourage or discourage entering into commercial transactions with other countries?

Abstention

There are three doctrines that affect litigation with a foreign sovereign.

Comity
A concept of legal reciprocity whereby one nation will recognize and give effect to the laws and judicial determinations of a foreign country.

COMITY. Comity is a judicially created doctrine based upon the desire for courts to extend courtesy and reciprocity to courts in other countries. Comity permits the courts in one country to recognize the laws and court decrees of another country or defer hearing a case if it is more appropriate to have the case tried in the courts of another country.

Example: In a dispute over the interpretation of a license agreement between Turner Entertainment Company and a German firm, lawsuits were filed in the United States and in Germany. The U.S. courts stayed (suspended) the U.S. litigation pending a resolution of the German proceedings. When the German courts rendered a judgment in favor of the German firm, the federal district court judicially recognized it under comity. *Turner Entertainment Co. v. DeGeto Film GmbH*, 25 F.3d 1512 (11th Cir. 1994)

THE ACT OF STATE DOCTRINE. The **act of state doctrine** provides that every sovereign state must respect the independence of every other sovereign state, and the courts of one nation will not sit in judgment of another government's acts within its own territory.

Act of state doctrine
A doctrine providing that every sovereign state is bound to respect the independence of every other sovereign state.

The act of state doctrine will be used as a defense by a country who has been brought before a foreign court by a party that believes the country violated a law. For the act of state doctrine to be applicable, there must be (1) an act of the state, and (2) the act must have been done within the territory of that state.

POLITICAL QUESTION. Under the Supreme Court's decision in *Marbury v. Madison*,[2] a court will dismiss a lawsuit when the question before the court is political in substance. U.S. courts will carefully consider if there is a constitutional basis to exercise jurisdiction in the matter before the court.

Political question
Federal courts will dismiss a case if they find it presents an issue that is primarily political in nature.

Treaties and Conventions

Under the Supremacy Clause, a treaty is afforded the same recognition as a federal law. A **treaty** is a legally binding agreement between or among nations that is given legal recognition. It addresses issues affecting only those parties. A **convention** is a legally binding treaty created to address matters of common interest regarding a regional or global concern. In the United States, a convention, though signed by the government, is not binding unless it is self-executing or unless Congress makes it binding upon the United States. A self-executing treaty or convention is one that automatically comes into effect. It is one that is outside the exclusive law-making powers of Congress. An example of a self-executing treaty is the Montreal Convention that establishes the rights of airlines and their passengers for personal injuries or damages to baggage or cargo. Like treaties, conventions must be respected by businesses in their global operations.

Treaty
An agreement between two or more nations to address an issue affecting those parties.

Convention
A treaty addressing an issue of regional or global concern.

Example: The United States has entered into many tax treaties with other countries. These treaties specific the rate, if any, that a foreign person will be taxed for income generated within the United States.

Codified Law

International transactional law, though now present in treaties, statutes, and court decisions, was derived from centuries of deference to the law merchant and maritime law, which were the long-standing customs and practices of ancient bankers, traders, and ship owners. As these practices became widely adopted, so did the number of courts that accepted these practices as controlling law.

---

2. 5 U.S. 137 (1803).

The International Sales Contract

The uncertainty regarding jurisdiction and applicable law are among the most important considerations of the parties given the immense burden that litigating in a foreign court or under foreign law can place on a party. In this section, we significant issues of doing so.

Forum Selection Clause

Common rules for determining which court will have jurisdiction over the subject matter or parties to an international dispute do not exist. It is up to the parties to decide where a dispute will be resolved. Judicial hostility to private parties' attempts to control jurisdiction over their international disputes has recently been eased. In Chapter 3, the **forum selection clause** was introduced. Its provision will control the location of the dispute resolution.

Forum selection clause A contract provision by which the parties have agreed to the jurisdiction in which a claim may be arbitrated or litigated.

In the United States, forum selection clauses are presumptively enforceable, unless a party to the contract makes a strong showing of any of the following:

- The inclusion of the clause in the agreement was the product of fraud or overreaching;
- The party wishing to repudiate the clause would effectively be deprived of their day in court if the clause is enforced; or
- The enforcement of the clause would go against a strong public policy of the forum in which the suit is brought.

Example: Zapata, a Houston-based American corporation, contracted with a German company, Unterweser, to move an oil rig, known as the Chaparral, from Louisiana to just off the coast of Italy. The contract the parties executed contained a clause stating: "Any dispute arising must be heard before the London Court of Justice." During transportation, the rig was damaged and was towed to Tampa, Florida. Zapata filed a suit against Unterweser in Tampa, seeking $3.5 million in damages. Unterweser requested the district court to enforce the forum selection clause that was contained in the towing contract. Ultimately, the Supreme Court found the clause enforceable. The Court stated that a forum selection clause could be unenforceable where it contravenes strong public policy or where the forum is seriously inconvenient. *Bremen v. Zapata Off-Shore Co.*, 407 U.S. 1 (1972)

Other reasons not to enforce forum selection clauses that courts have recognized since the issuance of the *Zapata* decision include the following: the parties were of unequal bargaining power; legal counsel had not been consulted prior to contract execution; the clause was written in a foreign language; the clause would violate federal law; or the circumstances existing in the forum have changed (such as where the country is in a state of rebellion).

Sample Form
Forum Selection Clause

Forum. Any dispute, claim, demand, cause of action, or legal proceeding (collectively "dispute") that may relate to or arise from this Agreement shall be governed by the laws of the State of New York, without regard to conflict of law provisions. You further agree to exclusive personal jurisdiction and venue in the state and federal courts of the United States located in the City of New York, New York.

Choice of Law Clause

An important provision of an international sales contract is the choice of law provision. A **choice of law clause** states the country whose law will apply in interpreting or enforcing a contract. These clauses are enforced if there is a reasonable relationship between the law chosen and the transaction.

Choice of law clause
An agreement of the parties to a contract identifying the law of the country or jurisdiction that will apply to interpret or enforce an agreement.

Example: When the *Costa Concordia* cruise ship capsized off the Italian coast, many deaths and injuries resulted. All the claims had to be resolved according to the passenger cruise line contract, which stated: "All claims, controversies, disputes, suits and matters of any kind whatsoever arising out of, concerned with or incident to any voyage that does not depart from, return to, or visit a U.S. port . . . shall be instituted only in the courts of Genoa, Italy, to the exclusion of the courts of any other country, state or nation. Italian law shall apply to any such proceedings." The decedents' families and the injured parties had to pursue their claims in the courts of Genoa under Italian law, where the potential recoveries would be considerably less than could be obtained in other jurisdictions.

The Application of the CISG

The sales contract is the basis for recording the parties' intentions to a purchase and sale agreement. It establishes the duties and obligations of each, including future obligations such as those arising under extended warranty provisions. While cultural and societal differences influence negotiation of terms of an international business transaction, the parties will often select the Convention for the International Sales of Goods (CISG), discussed in Chapter 26, as a means of controlling their agreement. You will recall that it is applicable if the contract involves the commercial sale of goods, the parties to the contract have places of business in different countries, and those locations are within countries that have adopted (ratified) the CISG. Generally, the CISG addresses the formation of a contract and the rights and duties of the seller and buyer. It does not provide rules for consideration, genuineness of assent, contract validity, and competency of the parties. Those rules are left to the national laws of the forum. The intent of the convention is to keep the parties in contract. It allows the use of extraneous evidence to interpret a contract that the parol evidence rule, discussed in Chapter 13, would bar. Additionally, firm offers, discussed in Chapter 26, are valid even if they are not in writing. The CISG also provides that acceptance is effective when it reaches the offeror (or email inbox) and not upon dispatch.

Article 6 of the CISG permits an opt-out of the CISG if it is stated in clear and unequivocal language. Under the CISG, there is no requirement for a reasonable connection between the law chosen and the transaction. Thus, the parties will have discretion to choose the law applicable to their contract.

In the following decision, the court had to determine whether Nucap agreed to the transfer of Nucap's intellectual property to Bosch, which was stated in Bosch's purchase orders. Nucap argued that these non-negotiated terms were so surprising that it could not have assented to them. The CISG allows the subjective intent of one party, such as Nucap, to be considered with regards to contract formation. Bosch argued that Illinois law applied and that Nucap's subjective intent was irrelevant.

CASE 43.2

PARTIES MUST EXPLICITLY OPT OUT OF THE CISG

NUCAP INDUS., INC. v. ROBERT BOSCH LLC

273 F. Supp. 3d 986 (2017)

United States District Court for the Northern District of Illinois

Nucap, a Canadian corporation, sued Bosch, a corporation with its primary place of business in Illinois, over a contractual dispute. Bosch, engaged in selling aftermarket brake pads, had entered into an agreement with Nucap to purchase Nucap's brake components. Bosch asserted that its purchase orders allowed it to use Nucap's proprietary drawings. Nucap claimed Bosch misused those drawings after the relationship's collapse; it sued for trade secret misappropriation and tortious interference with contract and prospective economic advantage. In response, Bosch sought damages from Nucap. The issue before the court was to determine whether the contract between Nucap and Bosch was governed by the CISG or Illinois contract law.

Language of the Court. *Both sides agree that the U.N. Convention on Contracts for the International Sale of Goods ("the CISG") applies to some degree. They differ over whether they have opted out of the CISG and selected Illinois law as the source of the decisional rules governing contract formation under their purchase orders terms and conditions.*

Bosch maintains that the purchase orders allow it to opt out of the CISG in favor of Illinois law. Article Six of the CISG allows "the parties to exclude the application of this Convention or, subject to Article 12, derogate from or vary the effect of any of its provisions." Bosch's position is straightforward: there were over 8,000 separate offers and acceptances incorporating its purchase orders by reference, when its purchase orders began including a link to a web page it alleges included a link to them. But the CISG makes the question of whether Bosch "knew or could not have been aware" of Nucap's subjective intent regarding the purchase orders material. . . . Given the significant effective transfer of intellectual property wrought by the purchase orders, a reasonable jury could find that Bosch "knew or could not have been unaware" that Nucap would wish to negotiate the new terms had higher-level Nucap personnel been aware of it.

The Supremacy Clause makes the CISG the law of Illinois on formation here, and the CISG therefore governs the parties' battle over what terms were incorporated into Bosch and Nucap's purchase orders.

Decision. The court found that the CISG applied to the formation of the contract. Further, the subjective beliefs about their intentions would be admitted into evidence to show that Nucap did not intend to transfer its intellectual property to Bosch. The cross-motions for summary judgement were denied.

Focus on Ethics

Are there ethical concerns in binding parties to a source of decisional law to which they have not explicitly agreed?

Force Majeure Clause

The risk of an act occurring that makes the contract impossible to perform is a concern in every transaction, and this concern is greatly amplified in international transactions. Therefore, *force majeure* clauses should be included in all contracts concerning international transactions. A ***force majeure* clause**, discussed in Chapter 14, is a contractual provision mitigating risks by excusing a party from performing when specified unforeseeable events occur.

***Force majeure* clause** A contractual provision mitigating risks by excusing a party from performing when specified unforeseeable events occur.

If the controlling law of the transaction is the CISG, Article 79 sets forth the terms under which a party will not be liable for its failure to perform:

1. The nonperformance of the obligation was due to an impediment beyond control;
2. At the time the contract was formed the impediment was not reasonably foreseeable;
3. The impediment was unavoidable and could not be overcome; and
4. The other party was given notice of the impediment and the effect it would have on the contract.

Performance will only be excused if the impediment results in performance becoming impossible; otherwise, the obligation to perform will simply be suspended until the impediment no longer exists.

Transacting Business Abroad

International business law includes many subjects. Those that will be discussed in this chapter include international trade and foreign direct investments, as well as international licensing and protection of intellectual property.

Trade

Trade is the import or export of goods and services across national borders. Exporting is the most common form of international business, as it is relatively uncomplicated. Companies that do not have the money or the desire to expand their operations overseas may instead choose to simply export their goods to foreign markets. This is evidenced by the fact that small and medium-sized businesses account for over 98 percent of the number of U.S. exporters. Importing is the entry of goods into the territory of a country or the receipt of services from a foreign provider.

Review the website of the U.S. Trade Representative at *https://ustr.gov*

Direct exporting Sale of goods or services abroad without the use of intermediaries.

Indirect exporting Sale of goods or services abroad with the use of intermediaries.

Direct exporting is the type of sale of goods in which one party assumes most of the export functions: manufacturing, marking, licensing, shipping, and collecting payment. This poses considerable risk when compared to **indirect exporting**, in which specialized intermediaries outside of the principal handle specific functions, including marketing in the foreign country. This is most often done by smaller and mid-sized companies that lack expertise in all that is required for an international sales transaction.

Foreign Direct Investments

The most common way that U.S. companies or firms invest abroad is through an agreement called a joint venture. As was discussed in Chapter 21, a joint venture is a relationship between two or more businesses for profit. This allows a U.S. company to partner with another party in a foreign country. The U.S. company will be a partial owner of the company, with the balance owned by a foreign party, whether the government or a company.

Countries have restrictions limiting the ownership interest of the U.S. companies. Generally, foreign countries will require most of the ownership interest to be held by the local owners.

> **Example:** In Vietnam, the Vietnamese partner is required to hold title to the land. This is required by the Vietnamese government so that it may expropriate the property in a way that makes it more difficult for the foreign partner to institute an action against the country.

Subsidiary The corporation over which the parent company has control.

SUBSIDIARIES. If a U.S. company wishes to expand into a foreign market while exercising more control than would be possible through a licensing or joint venture agreement, the company can establish a wholly owned **subsidiary**. In addition to lowering transaction costs, a subsidiary may also allow a U.S. company to gain brand recognition aboard and forgo import tariffs. In this situation, the parent company will be in the United States and retain ownership of the facility and assets of the subsidiary. Further, the U.S. company will remain in control of the business decisions of the subsidiary. However, with this control comes liability, as the U.S. parent company will be solely liable for the acts and omissions of the subsidiary.

FOREIGN BRANCH. A foreign branch is a business presence by the investor in a foreign country. It may be a branch office or a complete stand-alone entity.

Licensing

U.S. companies may operate manufacturing facilities in a foreign country because of lower operational costs or to be closer to the purchaser. For example, BMW®, Honda®, Sony®, and other companies have established manufacturing plants in the United States. They may also enter into licensing agreements. As was discussed in Chapter 7, the holder of intellectual property (patents, copyrights, and trademarks) grants a license in that property to another party under specified terms and for a term. The royalty payment may be based on a fixed amount per unit, or a percentage of the profits generated from the goods sold.

Review the World Intellectual Property Organization (WIPO) website for protection of intellectual property at https://www.wipo.int/portal/en/index.html.

It is important that a company's intellectual property be protected. Under European law, a consolidated multinational patent application is available and "validated" in each member state. In other locales, separate applications must be made in each country in which the protection is sought. Local, experienced IP legal counsel must be retained to ensure the protection is obtained.

Management Application International Franchising

Franchising is one of the most popular means of licensing, and it is a rapidly expanding form of doing business abroad. However, there are still many factors a business should take into consideration before entering into a franchising agreement in a foreign country.

- Cultural conflicts can diminish the value of international franchising contracts. For that reason, foreign legal counsel should be retained to assist in the task of franchising abroad.
- It is important to first make sure that the company is ready for international franchising. Although there may be an urge to get into international franchising, often there is a likelihood that the urge to do so is premature.
- The company should be sure to organize potential markets into a schedule that sets realistic priorities. For example, a U.S. company may find Canada or the United Kingdom to be the most immediate markets given the cultural and legal similarities with the United States.
- Even after all logistical considerations have been made, the company should still implement a small-scale roll-out to be sure there is an actual demand within the foreign market.
- Establishing and maintaining foreign marketing will be essential in the success of an international franchise. A company should bear in mind that its domestic marketing efforts will likely not be successful abroad and that each foreign country will require its own marketing campaign.

Using an internet search engine, identify several U.S. companies with franchise operations in a country of your choice. Explain what percentage of their worldwide sales are contributed by those foreign operations.

Trade Regulations

Each country enacts trade policies to advance its own interests. These may include tariffs, quotas, or complex regulations that restrict how foreign companies may conduct business. Known as **trade barriers**, these policies are an impediment to trade in goods and services.

Trade barrier
Any barrier in the transacting of goods and services between countries.

Tariffs

Tariffs
Taxes levied on imported goods.

Tariffs are taxes imposed on imported goods. They may also be referred to as import duties. Tariffs are commonly instituted by the country of importation as a means of protecting the country's industries from foreign competition.

Tariffs are perceived to be less restrictive than other common types of trade barriers, so long as the tariff rate is reasonable. As a result, the foreign competitor can take them into account when producing goods for export.

Export and Import Quotas

Export quota
A limit on the amount of goods that may be exported to other countries in a specified period.

Import quota
A limit on the quantity of goods that may be imported in a specified period.

A limit on the amount of goods that may be imported or exported is known as a quota. **Export quotas** restrict the quantity of goods that may be exported to other countries in a specified period, permitting the subject matter of the quota to be available to the local population. **Import quotas** limit the quantity of goods that may be imported in a specified period. An import quota may result in higher prices for consumers. Additionally, other countries might impose tariffs on the country instituting the import quota as a retaliatory response.

How Trade Barriers Are Minimized

World Trade Organization (WTO)
An international organization comprised of member nations who agree to abide by certain terms.

Most Favored Nation (MFN) status
A country that has achieved this status has been granted the most favorable trading terms available by another country.

National treatment
Requires non-discrimination in respect to imported and domestic goods once the goods have cleared customs and tariffs have been collected.

Eliminating trade barriers often has a substantial impact on the global economy. Trade barriers are eliminated through treaties, agreements, and the initiatives of international organizations.

THE WORLD TRADE ORGANIZATION (WTO). The **World Trade Organization (WTO)** is an intergovernmental system that was created in 1995 to regulate aspects of international trade between member countries. The WTO primarily deals with the regulation of trade. It assists in dispute resolution between member countries (not individual companies) to enforce WTO agreements that have been ratified by the governments of those countries. A general goal of the WTO is to eliminate the use of quotas by member countries. As a result, tariffs are the preferred method of instituting a trade barrier. To minimize trade barriers, the WTO requires the member countries to grant each other **the Most Favored Nation (MFN) status**. Here one country is agreeing to grant items imported from the other country the most favorable treatment or the lowest tariff rates it gives to like products imported from its other MFN partners. The WTO also requires **national treatment**, which requires non-discrimination between imported and domestic goods once the goods have been imported into a country. WTO members are prohibited from treating the imported foreign goods less favorably than domestic goods by means of internal taxes, charges, laws, and regulations.

Additionally, the WTO sets forth how the disputes between member countries are to be resolved. By adopting the WTO rules member countries have agreed to resolve disputes through their Dispute Settlement Understanding if they believe another member state has violated trade rules. A private firm or industry may appeal to its government for assistance in resolving an issue, but there is no private right of action under the WTO.

For more information regarding the activities of the WTO, see https://www.wto.org.

U.S. Customs and Border Protection and What It Does

In addition to the WTO, the United States, along with most other countries, has its own agencies dealing with various trade issues and to regulate the flow of imports and exports. In the United States, this agency is known as U.S. Customs and Border Protection (CBP). From a trade perspective, CBP seeks to increase the United States' economic competitiveness by enforcing trade laws. These trade laws seek to limit the presence of counterfeit, unsafe, or fraudulently admitted goods within U.S. borders.

CBP establishes Priority Trade Issues (PTIs) that constantly change to match the current market climate. PTIs are issues that represent high-risk areas that can cause significant revenue loss and harm to the U.S. economy or threaten the health and safety of citizens. CBP's current PTIs include:

- Antidumping and countervailing duties
- Import safety
- Intellectual property rights
- Revenue
- Textiles/wearing apparel
- Trade agreements

To address these PTIs and enforce both domestic and international trade laws, CBP has the authority to institute several enforcement mechanisms against those who violate these laws. When the goods are found to be in violation of an intellectual property right, CBP may either exclude from entry, detain, and/or seize the violative goods. Additionally, CBP can institute what is known as an exclusion order, which will prevent any future importation attempts by the foreign entity. Lastly, CBP has the power to institute a penalty or criminal fine on those foreign entities.

TRADE AGREEMENTS. While there are several regional free trade agreements, two of them are significant.

The European Union (EU). The creation of the European Union (EU) in 1957 has had a substantial impact on trade relations by creating a common market among what are now 27 European member states. A common market seeks to promote free competition within it. Additionally, the members agree to impose a common tariff on goods imported from countries outside the EU. The law of the E.U. Community operates alongside the laws of the member states. In some cases, the EU preempts the national law of a member state. The member states agree to a common set of laws applied throughout the EU member nations. It is notable that despite that the U.S. is the EU's largest trade and investment partner, they have not agreed to a free trade agreement between themselves.

The United States-Mexico-Canada Agreement (USMCA). The United States, along with Canada and Mexico, originally entered into their own regional trade agreement to create the North American Free Trade Agreement (NAFTA). In addition to eliminating the tariffs among these countries over time, it created a competitive advantage for them as well. Because the three countries impose tariffs on goods imported from other countries, it is more cost effective for them to trade with each other. This agreement has been replaced by the USMCA, which addresses issues that have arisen since the inception of NAFTA.

International Dispute Resolution

The difference in legal systems is due to differences in the role of legislatures in enacting laws, the role and powers of the courts and their judges in applying the law, and their legal procedures. There are also differences between the civil and common law legal systems. While both systems rely upon statutes as a primary source for the law, in civil law countries the legal codes are more comprehensive and are what the court will draw upon to decide a case. They are not bound by prior court precedents. A common law system relies heavily upon prior case precedents, and the role of the court is to apply them to the facts under the *stare decisis* principle, discussed in Chapters 1 and 3. In each system, lengthy legal proceedings can deter quick resolutions to disputes.

Businesspersons want an expedited dispute resolution process. Alternatives to litigation have become commonplace in the international business context. Accordingly, arbitration clauses are frequently included in international business transaction contracts.

United Nations Convention on the Recognition and Enforcement of Foreign Arbitral Awards Also known as the New York Convention. It was created to assist in the recognition and enforcement of arbitration clauses and arbitral awards internationally.

The **United Nations Convention on the Recognition and Enforcement of Foreign Arbitral Awards,** otherwise referred to as the *New York Convention,* was created to assist in the recognition and enforcement of arbitration clauses and arbitral awards internationally. The New York Convention has been implemented by over 150 nations, including the United States.

Under the New York Convention, a court will require the parties to arbitrate their claims if the following requirements are met:

1. The parties have agreed in writing to arbitrate the matter;
2. The arbitration will occur in a nation that is a signatory of the convention;
3. The agreement contemplates a commercial legal relationship; and
4. The parties to the agreement are of different signatory nations.

The New York Convention also favors recognizing foreign arbitration awards and sets forth only certain exceptions to their enforcement:

1. The agreement was invalid under the law in which the agreement was made;
2. The party against which enforcement is sought was not provided proper notice;
3. The award contemplated matters beyond the scope of which the parties agreed to arbitrate;

4. The award exemplifies an abuse of discretion by the arbiter; or
5. To enforce the award would violate the public policy of the country in which the award is sought.

The following case considers what is required to find an arbitration award violative of a country's public policy.

CASE 43.3

GROUNDS FOR REFUSING TO ACCEPT AN ARBITRATION AWARD ARE CONSTRUED NARROWLY

MINISTRY OF DEFENSE AND SUPPORT FOR THE ARMED FORCES OF THE ISLAMIC REPUBLIC OF IRAN v. CUBIC DEFENSE SYSTEMS, INC.

665 F.3d 1091 (2011)

United States Court of Appeals for the Ninth Circuit

In 1977, Cubic Defense Systems, Inc. (Cubic), a United States corporation, entered into a contract with the Ministry of Defense and Support for the Armed Forces of the Islamic Republic of Iran (Ministry) for the sale and subsequent servicing of an air combat maneuvering range for use by Iran's military. As a result of the Iranian revolution, the contracts were not performed. In 1979, the parties agreed to discontinue the contracts, and that Cubic would try to resell the equipment, with a later settlement of the accounts. In 1981, Cubic sold a modified version of the equipment to Canada. In 1982, the Ministry filed breach of contract claims against Cubic with the Iran-United States Claims Tribunal at Hague. In 1987, the tribunal issued an order stating that it had no jurisdiction to hear the matter. In 1991, the Ministry filed a request for arbitration with the International Court of Arbitration of the International Chamber of Commerce (ICC). The ICC awarded the Ministry $2,808,519 in damages and an additional $60,000 in arbitration costs. After Cubic failed to pay the award, the Ministry filed a petition in the federal district court in June 1998 to confirm the ICC's award under the New York Convention. The district court entered judgment in favor of the Ministry. Cubic appealed the confirmation of the arbitration award against it.

Language of the Court. *Cubic argues that the district court erred by confirming the ICC's award because confirmation is contrary to the public policy of the United States. Confirmation of foreign arbitration awards falls under the New York Convention, and federal law implementing the Convention provides that the court shall confirm the award unless it finds one of the grounds for refusal or deferral of recognition or enforcement of the award specified in the said Convention. The seven grounds for refusing to confirm an award are set out in Article V of the Convention. These defenses are construed narrowly, and the party opposing recognition or enforcement bears the burden of establishing that a defense applies.*

Cubic argues that confirmation of the ICC's award "is contrary to a fundamental public policy of the United States against trade and financial transactions with the

Islamic Republic of Iran." It applies only when confirmation or enforcement of a foreign arbitration award would "violate the forum state's most basic notions of morality and justice." As evidence of this policy, Cubic points to the sanctions the United States has imposed on Iran. Cubic argues the sanctions prohibit Cubic from paying the ICC's award unless the Treasury Department's Office of Foreign Assets Control issues a specific license. Additionally, Cubic argues that even if sanctions do not specifically prohibit the award, confirmation of the ICC's award is repugnant to the public policy of the United States.

We are not persuaded by Cubic's argument, which gives too little weight to this country's strong public policy in support of the recognition of foreign arbitration awards, and too much weight to the regulatory restrictions governing payment of the ICC's award. For the reasons that follow, we conclude that the Ministry, and the United States as amicus curiae, have the better argument.

This Court simply cannot conclude that to confirm a validly obtained, foreign arbitral award in favor of the Iranian Government would violate the United States' "most basic notions of morality and justice."

Decision. The court of appeals upheld the district court's decision to enforce the arbitration award in favor of the Ministry.

Focus on Ethics

Where should courts draw the line in determining whether something is "contrary to a fundamental public policy of the United States"? Does this phrase give rise to inconsistent holdings?

Consequences of Unethical Business Practices: The FCPA and the UK Bribery Act 2010

Foreign Corrupt Practices Act

The Foreign Corrupt Practices Act (FCPA) of 1977 prohibits the bribery of foreign officials to obtain or retain business. The Act makes it a crime to corruptly give a foreign official anything of value for the purpose of (1) influencing any act or decision of such foreign official in his official capacity; (2) inducing such foreign official to do or omit to do any act in violation of the lawful duty of such official; (3) securing any improper advantage; or (4) inducing such foreign official to use his influence with a foreign government or instrumentality thereof to affect or influence any act or decision of such government. The FCPA further requires that each of these benefits serve a particular purpose, such as assisting the giver in obtaining, retaining, or directing business.

The FCPA applies to all U.S. companies, their directors, officers, shareholders, employees, and agents regardless of where they are geographically located at the time of the bribe. Violation of the FCPA will result in the turning over of any unlawful gains resulting from the bribery as well as substantial civil penalties and possibly imprisonment. The reach of the FCPA is intended to be applied broadly to bribery of foreign officials.

Review the Department of Justice FCPA Resource Guide at https://www.justice.gov/criminal-fraud/fcpa-resource-guide.

Example: Dr. Chi Ping Patrick Ho was convicted of violating the FCPA because he allegedly paid bribes on behalf of a Chinese company to the leaders of Chad and Uganda in exchange for commercial advantages. Finding that he acted on behalf of a nonprofit arm of the Chinese company that was incorporated in Virginia, maintained offices there, and used offices in New York City, the federal appellate court held that such activities were of a domestic (U.S.) business concern and subject to the FCPA. *United States v. Chi Ping Patrick Ho*, 984 F.3d 191 (2d Cir. 2020)

The UK Bribery Act 2010

The UK Bribery Act 2010 is widely considered the toughest anti-corruption law in the world. The four main offenses under the Act are (1) the offering, promising, or giving of an advantage (bribing another); (2) the requesting or accepting of an advantage; (3) the act of bribing a foreign public official; and (4) the failure of a commercial organization to prevent bribery. Violation of the Act may result in a maximum sentence of ten years in prison along with an unlimited fine and the possibility of the confiscation of property and the disqualification of directors of the corporation. The Act has extraterritorial reach that can extend to UK companies operating abroad *and* foreign companies with a presence in the UK, and UK citizens or foreign citizens ordinarily resident in the UK outside of the UK. The Serious Fraud Office prosecutes violations.

Example: Rolls-Royce PLC agreed to pay a total sum of £671 million ($800 million) to the UK government, the U.S. Department of Justice, and Brazilian authorities in connection with violating the UK Bribery Act when its intermediary companies in China, India, Thailand, Angola, Kazakhstan, and Indonesia either bribed or corrupted foreign officials.

AI Feature: Analyzing Subsidies as Unfair Trade

Use an internet search engine to define a subsidy. How does a tariff compare to a subsidy? What is the WTO Agreement on Subsidies and Countervailing Measures? What types of subsidies are banned under all conditions? Public policies are central to the discussion. For example, should fledgling industries be protected from international competition until they are profitable? Alternatively, are inefficient businesses given an unfair distribution of public funds? Use an AI program to state your position on the continuing use of subsidies. Discuss when subsidies become an unfair trade practice.

Key Terms

- Act of state doctrine, 1087
- Choice of law clause, 1089
- Comity, 1086
- Convention, 1087
- Direct exporting, 1092
- Export quota, 1094
- *Force majeure* clause, 1091
- Foreign Sovereign Immunities Act (FSIA), 1084
- Forum selection clause, 1088
- Import quota, 1094
- Indirect exporting, 1092
- Most Favored Nation (MFN) status, 1094
- National treatment, 1094
- Political question, 1087
- Sovereign immunity, 1084
- Subsidiary, 1092
- Tariffs, 1094
- Trade barrier, 1094
- Treaty, 1087
- United Nations Convention on the Recognition and Enforcement of Foreign Arbitral Awards, 1096
- World Trade Organization (WTO), 1094

Applying the Law

43.1 Research the Law. Using an internet search engine, identify recent prosecutions of alleged violations of the Foreign Corrupt Practices Act (FCPA). Are there any common characteristics to these incidents? How often are securities law violations alleged as well?

43.2 Research the Law. Using an internet search engine, research how patents are protected under international law. What are the shortcomings of the Paris Convention? Summarize the key provisions of the Patent Cooperation Treaty and the WIPO.

43.3 Waiving Sovereign Immunity. A dispute arose out of a sale and resale of oil royalties owed to the Republic of the Congo by a subsidiary of an Italian oil conglomerate. There were several written agreements whereby the Republic sold some of the royalties to Gulf Resources. Later, the parties amended the purchase agreement wherein there was a waiver of sovereign immunity. How clear does the waiver need to be, and how should the court rule? *Gulf Resources America, Inc. v. Republic of Congo*, 370 F.3d 65 (D.C. Cir. 2004)

43.4 Commercial Activity? The first clause of the commercial activities exception of the Foreign Sovereign Immunities Act provides that United States courts have subject matter jurisdiction over claims that are "based on a commercial activity carried on in the United States by the foreign state." Under this clause, is a tort claim for personal injuries suffered in connection with travel outside of the United States "based upon" a commercial activity in such a way that would waive the immunity of a foreign state? Why or why not? *OBB Personenverkehr AG v. Sachs*, 737 F.3d 584 (9th Cir. 2015)

43.5 Act of State Doctrine. An American manufacturer of electric golf carts brought an antitrust action against a Polish manufacturer, its wholly owned importer, and their distributors. The defendants filed a motion to dismiss, stating that under the act of state doctrine the court did not have jurisdiction. The Polish manufacturer argued that it had acted within its own territory and that it was synonymous to Poland because it was operating in a controlled economy. Does the act of state doctrine preclude the court from exercising jurisdiction over the Polish manufacturer? Explain your reasoning. *Outboard Marine Corp. v. Pezetel*, 461 F. Supp. 384 (D. Del. 1978)

43.6 International Organizations. In 1945, Congress passed the International Organizations Immunities Act (IOIA), which grants international organizations the "same immunity from suit . . . as is enjoyed by foreign governments." International Finance Corporation (IFC) is an IOIA international organization based in Washington, D.C., that provides loans for projects that are unable to receive private capital. IFC entered into a loan agreement with Coastal Gujarat Power Limited, a company based in India. IFC financed the construction of a coal-fired power plant in Gujarat with the provision that the company may not cause damage to the surrounding communities and that the IFC retained supervisory authority and could revoke financial support for the project. Budha Ismail Jam and other Indian fishermen and farmers sued the IFC, claiming that pollution from the plant harmed the surrounding air, land, and water. Should international organizations be immune from suits, like foreign governments? Make arguments for both sides. *Jam v. International Finance Corp.*, 139 S. Ct. 759 (2019)

43.7 When Is It a Bribe? American Rice, Inc. (ARI) exports rice to foreign countries, including Haiti. The Rice Corporation of Haiti is a wholly owned subsidiary of ARI. As a part of Haiti's import procedure, custom officials assess duties based on the quantity and value of rice imported into the country. Haiti requires businesses that deliver rice to remit an advance deposit against the sales tax, based on the value of that rice. Kay was charged with violating the FCPA, by allegedly bribing Haitian customs officials to accept false bills and documentation that intentionally understated the quantity of rice shipped to Haiti and reducing the customs duties and sales taxes. Are payments for the purpose of reducing a corporation's customs and duties and taxes within the Foreign Corrupt Practices Act? *United States v. Kay*, 359 F.3d 738 (5th Cir. 2004)

43.8 What Law Applies? Topp Paper Company (Topp) purchased label-making equipment and a printer from ETI Converting Equipment (ETI). Topp was a Florida limited liability company and ETI was a Canadian company. Topp experienced various issues with the printer. Each time they occurred, Topp's manager sent either a letter or an email to ETI explaining the issue and stating that the printer failed to work often. Despite ETI's assistance in addressing these issues, after 21 months of use Topp sent ETI a letter requesting to return the machine and receive a full refund of the purchase price. ETI refused to accept the return of the machine or to refund Topp's purchase price. Topp sued ETI under various Florida and Canadian laws, as well as under the CISG. Does the CISG apply to this case? What are the arguments supporting a fundamental (that is, a material) breach of contract? *Topp Paper Co. v. ETI Converting Equip.*, 2013 U.S. Dist. LEXIS 193161 S.D. Fla. (2013)

43.9 Forum Selection Clause. Garware Polyester and Intermax Trading entered into an agreement that contained a forum selection clause. The clauses stated that "the courts at Bombay alone will have jurisdiction to try out suits in respect of any claim or dispute arising out of or under this agreement." Will the forum selection clause apply to non-contract claims as well? *Garware Polyester, Ltd. v. Intermax Trading Corp.*, 2001 U.S. Dist. LEXIS 13877 (S.D.N.Y. 2001)

43.10 Arbitration. Alberto-Culver Co. executed a contract to purchase three businesses owned by Fritz Scherk, a German citizen. In the contract, Scherk warranted that he had the sole ownership of the trademarks for these businesses. The contract contained a clause that disputes arising under the contract should be referred to arbitration before the International Chamber of Commerce in Paris, France, and the laws of the state of Illinois should govern. Is such a clause enforceable? What was the rationale of the Supreme Court's decision in *Scherk v. Alberto-Culver*, 417 U.S. 506 (1974)

Glossary

#

706 agencies A state agency that contracts with EEOC to assist in the investigation of employment discrimination claims.

A

Abandoned property Property the owner has intentionally relinquished all rights to control. Also refers to property that was lost or mislaid and the owner has given up attempts to locate it.

Abatement The proportional reduction in the distribution of an estate when the funds or assets are insufficient to pay all beneficiaries in full.

Absolute privilege A person making a statement has the absolute right to make the statement without fear of liability for defamation.

Abuse of process Using the legal process against another in an improper, unjustified manner or to achieve a result for which it was not intended to be used.

Acceleration clause A clause in the instrument that allows the payee to demand full payment upon the occurrence of a certain event.

Acceptance The offeree's manifestation of assent to the terms of the offer, made in a manner requested or required by the offer.

Accession The increase in value of personal property due to an addition or improvement. Accession may occur naturally or be manufactured.

Accessory An individual who assists in the commission of the crime but does not directly participate in the criminal act with the principal actor.

Accessory after the fact A person who aids the principal after the commission of the crime.

Accessory before the fact A person who assists the principal in the preparation of the crime; often referred to as an accomplice.

Accord A subsequent agreement between parties to resolve a disputed debt.

Account overdrafts The act of a bank paying a check despite insufficient funds in the drawer's account.

Accredited investor A natural person with a net worth exceeding $1 million (excluding principal residence) and with annual income of $200,000 for two years for single individuals or $300,000 for two years for joint filers.

Acknowledgment The process of verifying the identity of the testator and witnesses of an executed will.

Act of State Doctrine A doctrine providing that every sovereign state is bound to respect the independence of every other sovereign state.

Actual cause The plaintiff's injury would not have occurred "but for" the defendant's tortious conduct.

Actual delivery Refers to the physical delivery of the gift from donor to donee.

Actual fraud Making a false material misrepresentation, concealing or preventing the plaintiff from discovering the truth, or remaining silent in the face of a duty to speak.

Actual malice The defendant made the statement with actual knowledge of its falsity or with reckless disregard as to its truth or falsity.

Actus reus A voluntary action prohibited by law. The act is defined as a crime.

Additional insured A party unrelated to the named insured who receives the benefits of the insurance policy without having to pay the premium that the named insured pays.

Ademption When an heir receives nothing because the testator leaves a specific device of property and that property is no longer in the estate.

Adequate protection The relief or compensation given by a court to a secured creditor whose collateral is decreasing in value because the collateral continues to be used by the debtor or is sold during the bankruptcy case.

Adjudged mentally incompetent A person who has been declared incompetent by a court and cannot make valid contracts.

Administrative agencies Agencies created by federal, state, and local governments to enforce regulatory statutes.

Administrative law The body of law that regulates the operation and procedures of government agencies.

Administrative law judge An appointed person who presides over hearings and adjudicates issues of administrative law.

Administrative Procedures Act (APA) Enacted by Congress to govern the procedures that administrative agencies must follow to propose and establish regulations.

Administrative search A search of a business of individual's premises that is conducted by an administrative agency.

Administrative subpoena A subpoena issued by an administrative agency that allows the agency to compel the attendance of persons or production of documents or to allow a search of the business or individual's premises.

Administrator or administratrix A male or female, respectively, representative of an estate if the decedent died intestate.

Adulterated food Food that is unsafe for consumption.

Adversary proceeding A lawsuit arising in or related to a bankruptcy case that is commenced by filing a complaint.

Adverse opinion An auditor's opinion that the financial statements do not fairly represent the financial condition of the company.

Adverse possession A method of acquiring title by wrongfully possessing the real property of another, subject to state law requirements.

Affirmative action Public policies that consider an individual's protected characteristic in employment, public contracting, and other public programs.

Affirmative defense (criminal) A legal defense that negates or reduces liability, even if the allegations against the defendant are true.

Affirmative defense (employment) A legal rule that limits or excuses a defendant's liability because of superseding facts or a strong public policy favoring the defendant.

After acquired evidence Evidence provided by an employer after terminating or taking other adverse employment action against an employee used as evidence to justify the employer's decision and possibly reduce its back-pay liability.

Age discrimination Employment discrimination against persons age 40 or older. The ADEA does not protect workers under the age of 40, although some states have laws that protect younger workers from age discrimination.

Age Discrimination in Employment Act (ADEA) Federal act applying to employers with 20 or more workers that are engaged in interstate commerce. Prohibits employment discrimination against persons aged 40 and older.

Agency A type of law concerned with principal-agent relationship, in which one person has legal authority to act for another.

Agency by operation of law Agency implied in law without a reference to any agreement between a principal and agent.

Agency by ratification When a principal knowingly approves an agent's actions after the fact and in doing so creates or expands the agency relationship.

Agency coupled with an interest Agency irrevocable by the principal that is created for the benefit of the agent.

Agent A person who may act for another, a principal, in dealings with third parties.

Air rights The right to use and develop the airspace located above the surface of the earth.

Alien LLC An LLC operating in a different country from the country in which it was organized.

Allocation scheme Also known as horizontal market divisions. Refers to a restraint of trade where competitors agree to divide the market in which they will engage.

Alter ego theory Permits piercing of the corporate veil when there is a unity between the corporation and another corporation or with that of the shareholder(s) such that the corporation's separateness has ceased and holding only the corporation liable would be unjust.

Altered checks A check that has been changed from the way the customer has written it.

Alternative dispute resolution A nonjudicial process that seeks to resolve disputes between parties, typically through mediation and arbitration.

Americans with Disabilities Act (ADA) Federal law imposing obligations upon employers and providers of public transportation, telecommunications, and public accommodations to accommodate individuals with disabilities.

Americans with Disabilities Act Amendments Act (ADAAA) Federal law amending the American with Disabilities Act of 1990 by expanding the definition of disability, requiring that the definition be broadly construed, and requiring commonsense, non-technical assessments in applying provisions of the ADA.

Annual meeting The meeting of a company's stockholders held each year to elect the company's directors, vote on specific corporate matters, and ratify certain actions of directors and officers.

Answer The pleading that a defendant files admitting or denying the allegations made in the plaintiff 's complaint.

Anti-Counterfeiting Trade Agreement An agreement designed to limit international trademark and copyright infringement.

Anti-Cybersquatting Consumer Protection Act Federal law designed to prevent cybersquatting.

Anticipatory breach Informing the other party to a contract that a party will not be able to perform the contract when performance is due.

Antitrust laws Laws enacted by Congress that regulate economic competition in the United States.

Apparent agency Agency arising from the words or conduct of a principal.

Apparent authority An agent's power to act on behalf of the principal, which arises if a third party reasonably infers authority from the principal's conduct.

Appellant Party seeking to reverse the trial court decision.

Appellate court Courts that have the authority to hear appeals from lower courts.

Appellee Party responding to the appellant's appeal.

Appraisal To give an estimate of the current market value.

Appraisal right The right of a dissenting shareholder in a merger transaction not have their shares appraised and be paid the fair value of those shares by the corporation.

Appropriation for one's own commercial use or benefit The unauthorized use of a person's name, photograph, likeness, voice, or endorsement for financial gain.

Arbitrary and capricious test A test applied by a court when reviewing informal adjudications and rulemaking in which orders and regulations are overturned if there is a clear error in judgment.

Arbitration A legal proceeding in which disputes are resolved by a neutral third party appointed by the parties to make a binding and final determination.

Arraignment A proceeding in front of a judge in which the defendant is informed of the charges issued against them.
Arson The willful act of setting fire to a building, car, or property.
Articles of incorporation The basic governing document of a corporation filed in the state where the corporation desires to be registered.
Articles of organization Legal document filed in the state where the limited liability company will organize.
Artisan's lien A lien for the unpaid and materials that have been furnished by a creditor to improve or repair personal property of the debtor.
Asbestos A mineral fiber historically used in construction that is a known carcinogen and causes various respiratory ailments.
Assault An act that leads another person to believe he or she is about to suffer imminent bodily harm or offensive contact.
Asset purchase A transaction in which a corporation acquires all or substantially all the assets of another business entity.
Assignee (contracts) The party to whom contract rights have been transferred from the assignor.
Assignee (landlord-tenant) A new tenant who received an assignment by an assignor.
Assignment (contracts) A transfer of the rights arising under a contract to a third person.
Assignment (landlord-tenant) A tenant that transfers all of their interests under a lease to a third party.
Assignor (contracts) The party who transfers their contract rights to a third person (assignee).
Assignor (landlord-tenant) A tenant that transfers all of their interests under a lease to a third party.
Associational discrimination Discrimination or retaliation against employees based on their association with members of classes protected under Title VII.
Associational retaliation A cause of action for third-party retaliation against persons who did not themselves engage in a protected activity.
Assume An agreement to continue performing duties under a contract or lease.
Assume an existing mortgage When a purchaser agrees to become personally liable for an existing mortgage obligation in a real estate purchase.
Assumption of risk Where a plaintiff has knowingly and voluntarily faced a dangerous or harmful situation, assumption of risk absolves the defendant from all liability.
Attorney in fact The agent appointed by the principal through a power of attorney.
Audit A formal and independent examination of the accounting and financial records of a business to verify compliance with GAAP.
Auditor's opinion Opinion of an auditor verifying whether the company's financial statements fairly and appropriately represent the company's financial condition.
Authority The legal right to bind another.
Authorized shares The maximum number of shares that a corporation may legally sell under its articles of incorporation.
Authorship The maker, originator, or creator of the expression contained by a work.
Automatic stay The suspension of legal proceedings against a debtor.

B

Bad faith In the insurance context, where the insurance company acts in a blatant and unfair manner against the insured with conduct exceeding mere negligence.
Bailee The holder of the goods.
Bailment The possession of personal property by someone who is not the true owner, without transfer of title, for a particular purpose.
Bailor The owner of the property.
Bait-and-switch advertising A dishonest marketing tactic whereby a seller or service provider advertises an attractive product to bait a customer to come to the seller while intending to substitute a less desirable product for the customer to purchase.
Banker's acceptance A type of sight draft that is commonly used in international transactions and requires the buyer's bank to pay the amount owed.
Bankruptcy discharge A court order that relieves a debtor from the obligation to pay for certain debts included in the bankruptcy proceeding.
Bankruptcy estate All legal or equitable interest of the debtor in property at the time of bankruptcy filing.
Bankruptcy plan A debtor's detailed description of how the debtor proposes to pay the creditor's claims over a period of time.
Bankruptcy trustee A legal representative of the bankruptcy estate before the bankruptcy court.
Bargain in good faith Duty of the parties to negotiate at reasonable times with the intent to reach an agreement on matters relating to wages, hours, and other terms and conditions of employment.
Battery A tort that arises through the intentional, unprivileged, and unwanted contact of another person.
Bearer instrument An instrument that is made payable to whomever is in physical possession and presents it for payment when it is due.
Beneficiary The lender identified in a deed of trust.
Beneficiary (letter of credit) The seller in a letter of credit transaction.

Beneficiary (wills) A person who receives the testator's property from a will.
Bequest A gift of personal property.
Berne Convention An international agreement on the enforcement of copyright protections.
Beyond a reasonable doubt To convict a defendant, the prosecution must establish the essential elements as to the criminal defendant's guilt to each juror without reasonable doubt.
Bilateral contract A contract where both the offeror and offeree exchange promises.
Bill of lading A document indicating receipt of goods by a carrier and the contract for the transportation of those goods.
Bill of Rights The first ten amendments to the U.S. Constitution.
Binder Temporary insurance lasting until a policy is issued.
Blank indorsement An endorsement that does not specify the indorsee.
Blank qualified indorsement An indorsement that produces bearer instruments that are negotiated by delivery and do not require indorsement.
Blue laws (Sunday closing laws) Laws prohibiting certain activities, on a Sunday, for religious or secular reasons.
Blue Sky laws State laws and regulations intended to protect securities investors from fraud.
Bona fide occupational qualification (BFOQ) Necessary quality or attribute that employers may consider in the selection, retention, promotion, and termination of employees.
Bond A long-term debt instrument in which the issuing company promises to pay the holders a specified amount of interest for a specified length of time and to repay the principal amount of the loan at maturity.
Bootstrapping An entrepreneur leveraging personal financial resources or financing through personal relationships to fund the business.
Breach A failure to fully perform a contract.
Break-up fee Liquidated damages payment by the target corporation (seller) to the acquiring corporation (buyer) if the target withdraws from a transaction.
Bribery The offering of anything of value to a recipient to obtain a personal benefit.
Brief Written legal argument summarizing the facts, relevant law, and the basis for seeking a reversal of the trial court decision.
Brownfields Abandoned, idled, or underused properties where the presence of hazardous substances, pollutants, or contaminants has complicated redevelopment of the sites.
Builder's risk policies Insurance used to indemnify for loss of, or damage to, a building under construction.
Burden of proof (civil) The duty of a party to prove the truth of their assertions.
Burden of proof (criminal) In criminal law, the prosecution has the duty to prove each element of the crime.
Bureau of Immigration and Customs Enforcement (ICE) Federal investigation and enforcement agency within the Department of Homeland Security that enforces federal statutes relating to national security and public safety, including immigration enforcement, visa fraud, and counterterrorism.
Burglary The act of entering the building of another with the intent to commit a felony while inside.
Business crimes Nonviolent crime typically committed by individuals or organizations for financial gain.
Business judgment rule A rule protecting directors and officers from liability for honest mistakes of judgment or bad business decisions so long as they comply with the process of remaining informed.
Business necessity A requirement that bears a substantial relationship to job performance.
Business plan A document describing the goals for a business and the strategy to achieve them.
Business trusts A form of business organization managed by appointed trustees who hold title to the business's property for the benefit of one or more beneficiaries.
Buyer in the ordinary course of business A person that buys goods in good faith, without knowledge that the sale violates the rights of another person in the goods, and in the ordinary course from a person, other than a pawnbroker, in the business of selling goods of that kind.
Buyout The purchase by the partnership of a partner's partnership interest after the partner dissociates (withdraws) from the partnership.
Bylaws The rules governing a corporation's internal management and structure.

C

Capacity A legally recognized level of mental ability to understand the nature of an agreement.
Capping The act of laying soil and grass on top of a landfill or waste disposal site to prevent erosion and to improve aesthetics.
Cashier's check A type of check in which the financial institution will be both the drawer and the drawee thereby reducing the payee's risk of nonpayment.
***Causa mortis* gifts** A gift made in contemplation of an impending death.
Central America-Dominican Republic-United States Free Trade agreement (CAFTA-DR) A free trade agreement between the United States and Costa Rica, El Salvador, Guatemala, Honduras, Nicaragua, and the Dominican Republic, seeking to improve market access and reduce tariffs of the member nations.

Certificate of deposit (CD) A type of note that contains a fixed maturity date and a specified interest rate and includes terms restricting the use of the deposited funds until the maturity date.

Certificate of interest A document evidencing an ownership interest in an LLC.

Certificate of limited partnership A document that must be filed with a public official that forms a limited partnership under the state statute.

Certified check Type of check by which the bank certifies that the customer has the necessary funds in the customer's account to make the payment stated on the check and also verifies the signature is genuine.

Chain of distribution All manufacturers, assemblers, distributors, wholesalers, retailers, and lessors involved in the sale or use of a product.

Chain-style franchise A type of franchise in which the franchisee conducts business under the franchisor's trade name.

Challenge for cause During *voir dire* an attorney can request that the court dismiss a potential juror for a particular reason, usually bias against their client.

Chapter 7 bankruptcy A type of bankruptcy that results in the debtor receiving a fresh start in exchange for distributing all the debtor's nonexempt assets to the bankruptcy trustee to be liquidated and the proceeds distributed to creditors.

Chapter 11 bankruptcy A type of bankruptcy that results in the reorganization or restructuring of the debtor's finances.

Chapter 13 bankruptcy A type of bankruptcy that results in the adjustment of the individual's debts and is not available to businesses.

Charging order A court order granted to a judgment creditor to attach distributions made from a business organization such as a partnership to a member, partner, or owner of the organization.

Check A type of draft drawn by a financial institution as an order to pay.

Checks and balances The system of shared power under which each branch of government can ensure that no one branch controls the others.

Choice of law clause An agreement of the parties to a contract identifying the law of the country that will apply to interpret or enforce an agreement.

Circuit courts The alternative name for the United States courts of appeals. They are the intermediate appellate courts in the federal system.

Civil law A system of law that deals with the private relations between persons of a community.

Claim A debtor's assertion of a right to payment from the debtor or its property.

Class action A lawsuit in which individuals with the same or similar claims are grouped together into a single action against the same defendant.

Clayton Antitrust Act Legislation passed by Congress to address specific anticompetitive practices that were not addressed by the Sherman Act.

Clean Air Act An act intended to protect the public from different types of air pollution caused by a variety of pollution sources.

Clean Water Act A statute enacted to address water pollution in the United States.

Close corporation A corporation which does not exceed a statutorily defined number of shareholders and is not a public corporation.

Code of Conduct A written set of guidelines describing the company's core values and the manner in which the company expects its managers, employees, suppliers, and customers to act.

Codicil A revision to a will that can amend, modify, or revoke a prior will.

Collateral The personal property, tangible or intangible, used to secure the transaction.

Collecting bank The bank handling an item for collection except the payor bank.

Collective bargaining agreement (CBA) A negotiated agreement between a labor union and an employer.

Color Lightness or darkness of skin pigmentation.

Color discrimination Discrimination based on skin color, complexion, shade, or tone, which may occur between persons of different races or between persons of the same race or ethnicity.

Comity A concept of legal reciprocity whereby one nation will recognize and give effect to the laws and judicial determinations of a foreign country.

Commerce Clause An enumerated power under the Constitution that grants Congress the authority to regulate commerce.

Commercial general liability policy Policy covering bodily injury, property damage, and personal injury liability arising from the operations of a business.

Commercial impracticability A legal concept making performance of the contract impracticable due to circumstances that were not foreseen by either party during the formation of the contract.

Common area maintenance (CAM) A pro rata share of costs a tenant is required to pay for common area expenses. Frequently found in commercial leases.

Common carrier A commercial enterprise providing transportation of persons or goods for a fee.

Common carrier (commercial law) A person company that transports goods or passengers on regular routes at set rates.

Common law Law created and developed primarily by courts.

Common stock A type of equity ownership allowing shareholders to participate in management control of a corporation.
Community property Property acquired during marriage that is owned equally by the spouses.
Comparative negligence Doctrine that apportions damages based on the plaintiff's and defendant's respective degrees of fault.
Compensatory damages (contracts) The sum of money awarded sufficient to compensate the plaintiff for the loss or harmed incurred.
Compensatory damages (torts) Damages awarded to compensate for the actual loss or harm suffered, such as for personal property loss or pain and suffering.
Competitive market analysis (CMA) An analysis used to estimate the sale price by adjusting the price paid for comparable properties.
Complaint The pleading the plaintiff files with the court, which sets forth alleged facts, breaches of duty, and the relief sought against the defendant(s).
Comprehensive Environmental Response, Compensation, and Liability Act (CERCLA) This law authorized the EPA to clean up uncontrolled hazardous waste sites and force responsible parties to perform cleanups or reimburse the EPA for doing so.
Concerted Protected Activities Right of a worker to address work-related issues with an employer, government agency, or the media.
Concurrent conditions Conditions that are to be performed at the same time.
Concurrent jurisdiction When both the federal and state courts have authority over a particular dispute.
Condition A fact, the occurrence or nonoccurrence of which creates or extinguishes a duty on the part of the promisor.
Condition precedent A condition that requires the occurrence or nonoccurrence of an act or event that must occur before the promisor's duty of performance arises.
Condition subsequent A condition referring to a future event, upon the happening of which the obligation of the party ceases.
Confirmation Bankruptcy court approval of a plan of reorganization under Chapter 11.
Confirming bank A bank in the seller's jurisdiction which handles the letter of credit transaction.
Confusion Confusion occurs when interchangeable goods are commingled between two or more people to the extent that one person's property cannot be distinguished from the property of another.
Consent decree A settlement between the FTC and an alleged offender prior to the issuance of a formal FTC complaint.
Consequential damages Foreseeable damages that flow indirectly from a breach of contract.
Consequentialism A doctrine that the morality of an action is judged solely by its consequences.
Consideration The bargained-for exchange of legal value.
Consolidated Omnibus Budget Reconciliation Act (COBRA) Federal law providing some employees with the ability to continue health insurance coverage for a limited time after leaving employment.
Consolidation The combination of two or more corporations to create a new legal entity, with neither of the original corporations surviving.
Conspiracy Conspiracy is the combination of two or more persons, by concerted action, to accomplish criminal or unlawful purpose, or some purpose not in itself criminal or unlawful, by criminal or unlawful means. The statute may require at least one of those in agreement to have acted in furtherance of the crime.
Construction loan A loan which provides the financing to pay for the cost of developing and constructing an improvement on real property.
Constructive delivery A method that can be used in making gifts where the donor makes a symbolic delivery of the property to the donee.
Constructive discharge Employee resigns from his or her job because of intolerable, extraordinary, and egregious workplace conditions.
Constructive fraud Acts, omissions, and concealment involving breach of a legal duty, trust, or confidence resulting in damages.
Constructive trust A court order transferring property held in the name of the debtor to the creditor.
Consumer A person who purchases goods and/or services for personal use.
Consumer transactions A sale, lease, disposition of property (real or personal), or service to a person to be used for personal or household use.
Content-neutral laws Laws that do not discriminate based on the substance of the speech.
Contract A legally enforceable agreement.
Contracts of adhesion Contracts that leave the weaker party with no choice but to adhere to the terms of the contract.
Contribution Rule that permits a defendant to sue other parties for only a portion of the plaintiff's damages. Typically applies when the defendant is partially at fault and desires other parties to assume their share of the damages.
Contributory negligence Where a plaintiff's negligent conduct contributes to their harm, contributory negligence prevents the plaintiff from recovering damages.
Convention A treaty addressing an issue of regional or global concern.
Conventional loan A loan made by an institutional lender that is neither guaranteed nor insured by the federal government.
Conversion The act of intentionally taking or retaining possession of another's personal property.

Cooling-off laws Laws providing a purchaser of goods sold door-to-door with a purchase price of $25 or more the right to cancel their contracts within three business days without penalty.
Cooperatives An association organized to provide an economic service or benefit to its members.
Copyright A protected intellectual property interest that is granted to original works of authorship that are fixed in a tangible medium of expression.
Copyright infringement The unauthorized reproduction of a copyrighted work.
Core values The fundamental beliefs of a person or organization that dictate behavior and can help people understand the difference between right and wrong.
Corporate governance The system of rules, practices, and processes by which a corporation is directed and controlled.
Corporate Social Responsibility (CSR) Corporations should act ethically and be accountable to their communities for their actions.
Corporation A legal entity created by operation of law that is a separate entity from its owners.
Corporation by estoppel A legal doctrine requiring a creditor that has dealt with the business as a corporation to look to only the assets of the business and not its owners for satisfaction of the obligations owed to it.
Corrective advertising New advertising intended to correct and inform the public that the company previously provided information that was misleading, false, or deceptive.
Cost approach A method of appraisal that values the cost of the land plus the current cost to construct the property less accrued depreciation.
Counteroffer A rejection of the original offer and the simultaneous making of a new offer by the offeree to the offeror.
Course and scope of employment A term relating to the time, place, or circumstances under which an injury was sustained during the performance of one's job duties.
Course of performance The series of conduct under a contract in which the contract involves repeated occasions for performance and opportunities for objection.
Course of prior dealing Describes prior conduct between the parties to a contract that establishes a common basis for their understanding.
Covenant An unconditional promise to render some performance to another.
Covered loss An event or occurrence that triggers the duty of the insurance carrier to investigate and potentially pay an insurance claim.
Cramdown A bankruptcy rule allowing the court to confirm a plan of reorganization over the objections of a class of creditors, subject to certain restrictions.
Creditor The person or institution to whom money is owed.
Creditor beneficiary A person who is owed the performance of a contract.
Creditor's committee Members appointed by a U.S. Trustee in a Chapter 11 bankruptcy proceeding who are to represent the interests of the unsecured creditors.
Cross-complaint A legal claim made by the defendant against the plaintiff or other persons seeking legal relief against them.
Cross-examination The examination of a witness by an opposing party to check or discredit the witness's testimony, knowledge, or credibility.
Crowdfunding A cooperative activity in which people network and pool funds and other resources to assist a cause via the internet.
Crown jewel A target corporation's most valuable asset that, if sold, will make the target much less attractive to a hostile bidder.
Cumulative stock A type of preferred stock, where any unpaid dividends will accumulate for years of nonpayment.
Cumulative voting A voting procedure that gives each voting shareholder a number of votes equal to the number of voting shares it holds multiplied by the number of directors up for election to the board of directors.
Cybercrime Criminal activity conducted with the use of the internet.
Cybersquatting When a party registers a domain for an established trademark with the intent of profiting from that mark.

D

Damages A sum of money claimed or awarded in compensation for a loss or an injury.
***De facto* corporation** An improperly formed corporation that is given the temporary status of a corporation.
De minimis cost for accommodation Insubstantial expense to the employer to provide a religious accommodation to an applicant or employee.
Debenture A long-term, unsecured debt instrument backed by the general credit of the borrower.
Debt security An investment in a corporation creating a debtor-creditor relationship when the corporation borrows money from an investor. Debt securities may be in the form of a debenture, bond, or note.
Debtor The person or institution that owes a sum of money.
Debtor (financing real property) A person who executes (signs) a note or contract and is primarily liable for repayment.
Debtor in possession The debtor in a Chapter 11 case that retains possession of their property and enjoys the same rights and powers, as well as obligations, of a trustee in bankruptcy.

Decedent A person who dies.
Deceptive advertising Advertising that is likely to mislead consumers acting reasonably under the circumstances due to a representation, omission, or practice.
Deed of trust A three-party instrument financing arrangement that involves a beneficiary, a trustor, and a trustee.
Deeds Written instruments used to convey (transfer) real property.
Defamation A factually false statement communicated to a third person regarding a person or business that causes injury to reputation or character.
Default A debtor's failure to fulfill an obligation to pay the creditor.
Default judgment When the court enters judgment in favor of the plaintiff, after the defendant was properly served but failed to answer the complaint.
Defect in packaging A defect arising when a product has been placed in packaging that lacks protection from tampering.
Defend Trade Secrets Act The federal law that establishes a federal cause of action for trade secret protection.
Defendant The party who has been served with a complaint and must respond to the complaint.
Deficiency judgment A money judgment obtained by the creditor against the borrower when the foreclosure sale does not satisfy the entire debt.
Defined benefit pension plan Type of retirement plan in which a participant is guaranteed a certain payout or monthly stipend at retirement.
Defined contribution plan Type of retirement plan that provides a payout at retirement that will vary among participants based on the amount of money each contributed (or that was contributed by employers on employees' behalf, as through matching programs) and the performance of the investments made with these contributions.
Delegatee The party to whom contract duties have been transferred from the delegator.
Delegation A transfer of the contractual duties arising under a contract to a third person.
Delegation doctrine A principle providing an administrative agency only those legislative, executive, and judicial powers delegated to it.
Delegator The party who transfers their contract duties to a third person (delegatee).
Delivery The unconditional transfer of property to the donee.
Demonstrative devise A general gift from a decedent's estate that is to be paid from a specific source.
Deposition When one party to an action formally interviews either a party or nonparty who is under oath, and the answers are transcribed for the record.
Depository bank The bank that receives the check for payment.
Depreciation The gradual loss in value of property due to its deterioration and obsolescence.
Derivative action A claim brought by a shareholder on behalf of the corporation against the corporation's management or board of directors.
Design defect A defect resulting from a faulty design that stems across the entire product line.
Destination contract A sales contract that allows the buyer to mitigate risk by having title pass to the buyer only when the goods are tendered at destination.
Destruction of identified goods Excusal from performance when goods that were identified when the contract was formed are destroyed as a result of unexpected events.
Devise Gift of real property under a will.
Digital Millennium Copyright Act (DMCA) A congressional act enacted to enhance the protections granted to copyright owners by imposing civil and criminal penalties for online copyright infringement.
Direct examination The first examination of a witness on a matter that is related to the trial.
Direct exporting Sale of goods or services abroad without the use of intermediaries.
Disability A recognized physical or mental impairment that substantially limits one or more of the major life activities of the affected individual.
Disability discrimination The less favorable treatment by a covered employer or entity of an applicant or employee because the person has a history of a disability or is believed to have a physical or mental impairment expected to last six months or longer.
Disaffirmance The act of rejecting or avoiding a contract by reason of the infancy doctrine.
Discharge A release of a debtor from personal liability for certain debts. A discharge prevents creditors owed those debts from taking any action against the debtor to collect them.
Discharged by performance Contract is fully executed as both parties have fully performed their contractual promises to the other party.
Disclaimer of opinion An auditor's opinion in which the auditor states they were unable to reach a conclusion about the compliance of the financial statements with GAAP.
Discovery Pretrial process for obtaining information relating to a dispute.
Disparagement False statements of fact that are made about the products, services, character, or ownership rights of another's business.

Disparate impact Discrimination that occurs when a neutral selection standard, unjustified by a business necessity, disqualifies particular races or group at a significantly higher rate than it does other races or groups.
Disparate treatment Discrimination that occurs when an individual is intentionally treated less favorably than another because of his or her race, color, sex, religion, national origin, age, or disability.
Dissociation The severance of the relationship between a partner and the partnership.
Dissolution The formal disbanding of a partnership through either the acts of the partners, operation of law, or a judicial decree.
Distribution A transfer of money or other partnership property from the partnership to a partner in the partner's capacity as a partner.
Distributional interest The member's ownership interest in the LLC allowing the member the right to receive distributions from the LLC.
Distributorship franchise A type of franchise in which a manufacturer (the franchisor) licenses the ability to sell its products to a distributor (the franchisee).
Diversity of citizenship jurisdiction A case in which the amount in controversy exceeds $75,000 and all parties to the litigation are citizens of different states, or a citizen of a state and a citizen or a subject of a foreign country.
Dividend A sum of money paid regularly by a company to its shareholders out of its profits.
Divisible contract A contract in which the performance of the contract can be divided into equal portion.
Document of title A writing authorizing the holder to receive the goods it covers.
Documentary transaction A sales transaction in which receipt of a document gives buyer legal title to the goods accounted for in the sales contract.
Domain name The internet address of a website.
Domestic LLC An LLC operating in the state where it was organized.
Donee Person who receives a gift from a donor.
Donee beneficiary The recipient of a contractual performance agreed to by two other parties, usually in the form of a gift.
Donor Person who gives a gift to another.
Dormant Commerce Clause In the absence of congressional regulation, states are prohibited from passing legislation that discriminates against or creates an undue burden on interstate commerce.
Double jeopardy The government is prohibited from prosecuting a defendant twice for substantially the same crime.
Draft An instrument between three parties that acts as an unconditional, written order in which the drawer orders the drawee to pay the payee.
Drawee of the draft The party required to pay the money as stated in the draft. May also be called the acceptor of the draft.
Drawer of the draft The party who writes the order for a draft.
Due diligence The process of identifying risks posed by a potential transaction.
Due diligence defense Defense used by accountants to avoid liability if after reasonable investigation they had reasonable grounds to believe that the statements made in the registration statement were true and there was no omission of a material fact that would make the statements misleading.
Duress (contracts) A defense asserted to the enforcement of a contract because a party was subjected to unlawful pressure or coercion to enter into the contract.
Duress (criminal law) A defense available to a defendant when they commit a criminal act under a threat of coercion, and that the action was reasonable given the threat.
Duty not to delegate A duty prohibiting a trustee from delegating decision-making powers to outside parties.
Duty of care A fiduciary duty requiring a director or officer of a corporation to be fully and adequately informed and act with care when performing duties for the corporation.
Duty of cooperation The act of suspending performance under a contract while avoiding liability when the other party fails to cooperate.
Duty of due care A duty requiring a trustee to act as a reasonably prudent person dealing with their own affairs would.
Duty of good faith and fair dealing An implied promise that neither party will do anything to injure the other party's right to receive the rights of the agreement.
Duty of loyalty (agency) A fiduciary duty that requires an agent to act solely for the benefit of the principal.
Duty of loyalty (corporations) A fiduciary duty requiring directors and officers to subordinate personal interests to their obligation of loyalty to the corporation.
Duty of loyalty (trusts) A duty requiring a trustee to administer and manage the trust for the benefit of the beneficiaries only.
Duty of reasonable care The duty to render services as others in the same occupation would render under the same circumstances.
Duty to account The agent has a duty to render a complete and proper account of all property and funds received and paid on behalf of the principal.
Duty to account (trusts) A duty requiring that a trustee must, on a regular basis, provide the beneficiaries with a statement of any income and expenses of the trust.

Duty to compensate The duty to pay the agreed-on value for the agent's services.
Duty to cooperate The duty to cooperate with agent during the course of the agent's services.
Duty to defend A contractual duty obligating the insurer to provide the insured with a defense of claims typically by hiring legal counsel.
Duty to earmark A duty requiring a trustee to label trust property as "trust property."
Duty to indemnify A contractual duty to pay for any loss or damages suffered by another.
Duty to inform the principal The agent has a duty to inform principal of information principal should know.
Duty to invest A duty requiring a trustee to act as a reasonably prudent person would in investing his own property.
Duty to obey instructions The agent has a duty to follow lawful instructions provided by the principal.
Duty to reimburse and indemnify The duty to reimburse agent for funds disbursed at the request of the principal and to indemnify agent against liabilities incurred by agent in the ordinary course of performing duties on behalf of the principal.
Duty to respect contractual terms The duty to honor the agreed-on terms of the agent's services.
Duty to segregate A duty prohibiting a trustee from commingling their own personal funds with the trust funds.

E

Earthquake insurance Insurance that protects against property damage caused by an earthquake and earth movements.
Easement appurtenant An easement that benefits a particular parcel of land, rather than conferring a personal benefit upon the holder of the easement.
Easement in gross An easement that benefits a person, regardless of whether that person owns any land at all.
Easements A right of a person to use the land of another for a specific purpose.
Easements by grant An easement created by an express agreement
Economic Espionage Act Federal law that criminalizes trade secret theft that benefits a foreign government, business, or agent.
Economic strikers Workers who strike to obtain an economic concession from the employer, such as better pay, benefits, or working conditions.
Electronic Communications Privacy Act (ECPA) Federal act enacted to prohibit the interception, recording, or disclosure of wire, oral, and electronic communications, including email and voicemail.
Electronic funds transfer (EFT) A transfer of funds where the money is electronically transferred from one bank account to another by means of a computer-based system.
Emancipation The right of a minor to be freed from parental control.
Embezzlement The fraudulent appropriation of property by a party entrusted with its care.
Eminent domain The government's power to seize private property for public use.
Employee Person who acts under a contract in the service of another, the employer, who can control and direct the means and methods of how the work is to be performed.
Employee benefit plan An ERISA-qualified plan other than salary (such as health insurance or pension) granted by an employer to its employees.
Employee Polygraph Protection Act of 1988 (EPPA) A federal law generally preventing employers from requiring lie detector tests from applicants or employees.
Employee Retirement Income Security Act (ERISA) Federal law setting minimum standards for protection of private employee-benefit plan participants and beneficiaries. Law requires disclosure and reporting of information and sets standards of conduct, duties and obligations for plan fiduciaries, and remedies.
Employer-employee relationship A relationship formed when an employer retains another while controlling the means and methods of how the work is performed.
Employment at-will A common law doctrine that states either party may terminate an employment relationship at any time for any reason, absent an agreement to the contrary.
Employment discrimination An employer's unlawful distinction between two individuals relative to a term or condition of employment because they belong to different protected groups.
Enabling legislation A governmental statute creating an administrative agency and delegating powers to it.
Entrapment A defense available to the defendant if it is proved that the defendant was induced by the government to commit a crime that the defendant was not predisposed to commit.
Entrepreneur A person who initiates and operates a new business.
Entrustment rule A UCC rule by which a merchant has the power to transfer all rights to a buyer in the ordinary course of business so long as the goods entrusted to the merchant are the kind in which the merchant deals.
Environmental Impact Statement (EIS) An analysis that describes the environmental impacts the proposal has on the environment and provides reasonable alternatives that would avoid or minimize those adverse impacts.
Environmental Protection Agency (EPA) A federal agency that was created to protect the environment and address health concerns.

Equal Access to Justice Act Act that protects individuals and businesses from harassment by federal administrative agencies.
Equal dignity rule If a contract must be in writing to be enforceable, the appointment of an agent with regard to that agreement must also be in writing.
Equal Pay Act of 1963 A federal law prohibiting wage differentials based on gender for positions requiring equal skill, effort, and responsibility and that are performed under similar working conditions.
Equal Protection Clause The Clause contained in the Fourteenth Amendment that prohibits the state from unfairly discriminating.
Equality of redemption The right of a borrower to redeem (retain) the mortgaged property before a foreclosure sale occurs.
Equitable relief Court orders providing nonmonetary relief, such as injunctions.
Equitable remedies Actions ordered by a court to resolve a breach or dispute.
Equity The value of a debtor's interest in property after liens and other creditor interests are considered.
Equity security An investment representing an ownership right in the corporation in the form of common stock or preferred stock.
Errors and omissions policy Provides coverage to claims arising out of any act or omission or "personal injury" caused by a failure to render "professional services."
Escheat A process whereby if there are no living heirs under a state's intestacy laws, the court orders that the property be distributed to the state.
Essential functions of a job The functions that an individual must be able to perform unaided or with the assistance of a reasonable accommodation.
Establishment Clause Under the First Amendment, the government is prohibited from establishing, advancing, or promoting a state-sponsored religion.
Estate Money and property owned by a particular person, especially at death.
Estray statutes A statute that permits a finder of lost or mislaid property to take title to the property, against even the true owner.
Ethical fundamentalism Persons look to outside sources to decide what action is ethical or unethical.
Ethical relativism Individuals may decide what is ethical based on their own feelings of right and wrong.
Ethics The values and principles guiding one's actions and decisions.
Exclusionary practices Agreements, arrangements, or conditions that have the effect of preventing a purchaser from using a competitor's product.
Exclusionary rule The rule that bars evidence being used against a criminal defendant if it was acquired in violation of a constitutional requirement, such as under the Fourth Amendment.
Exclusive dealing contracts An agreement where a seller agrees to sell all of its product to a particular buyer or where a buyer agrees to purchase all of its goods from a particular seller.
Exclusive jurisdiction When one court system has the only authority to hear a particular dispute.
Exclusive remedy Unless an employer intentionally injures an employee or is grossly negligent, the employee's legal relief is limited by statute or regulation to the benefits payable under workers' compensation.
Exculpatory clause A contract clause that releases one (or both) of the parties to a contract from liability.
Exculpatory clause (bailment) Allow bailees to limit or be exempt from liability arising out of ordinary negligence.
Executed contract A contract that has been fully performed by both parties.
Executive agencies Agencies that exist within the cabinet departments of the executive branch.
Executive branch The branch of government that enforces the laws, with the assistance of various administrative agencies.
Executive order Directives by President or a state governor to promote or prohibit policy decisions.
Executor or executrix (aka estate representative) A male or female, respectively, representative appointed in the will.
Executory contract A contract in which one or more parties have obligations to perform.
Executory contract or lease Agreements that have duties remaining to be performed.
Exempt employee Employees exempt from minimum wage and overtime pay provisions, or from the child labor provisions of the FLSA.
Exemption from registration Securities transactions not requiring registrations with a regulatory body such as the SEC or state agency.
Exemptions Property owned by individual debtors that the Bankruptcy Code or state law permits the debtor to keep from unsecured creditors.
Exhausting administrative remedies A litigant is precluded from seeking a remedy in the court until the agency's own procedures are concluded.
Expectation damages Also known as compensatory damages. These damages are recoverable from a breach of contract that protects the injured party's interests in what was expected.
Export quotas A limit on the amount of goods that may be exported to other countries in a specified period.
Export restrictions Imposed by a government to limit the number of goods of a specific type of industry may be exported to other countries.
Express agency Agency occurs when principal and an agent expressly agree to enter into an agency relationship.
Express authority An agent's power to act on behalf of the principal, explicitly granted by an agreement.

Express bailment A bailment created by contract.
Express contract A contract clearly stated in written or spoken words or partly oral and partly written.
Express warranty A promise made by a seller as to the quality or condition of the product offered for sale, upon which a buyer relies when purchasing the product.
Express warranty (commercial law) A seller/lessor asserts that the goods being sold or leased meet certain standards related to the good's description, quality, condition, or performance.
Extended replacement cost coverage Pays for the replacement costs up to a specified percentage above the policy limit.
Extension clause A clause in the instrument that allows the maker or drawer to extend the instruments date of maturity to a time in the future.
Extortion The use of force or threat of force to obtain something of value from another or provoke action.

F

Fair and Accurate Credit Transaction Act (FACTA) A federal consumer protections law that seeks to reduce the risk of identity theft by regulating the handling of consumer account information.
Fair Credit Reporting Act (FCRA) A federal law regulating the collection and distribution of consumer's personal information.
Fair Labor Standards Act (FLSA) Federal law applicable to employees engaged in interstate commerce of employed by an enterprise engaged in interstate commerce. Sets minimum wages and overtime and regulates youth employment.
Fair use An exception to copyright infringement that allows for certain uses of the work, without the consent of the rights holder.
False imprisonment The intentional confinement or restraint of another person without legal authority, justification, or consent.
False light Liability which may arise from the public publication of information portraying the plaintiff in a false or misleading light. The information is highly offensive or embarrassing and is published with reckless disregard.
Family and Medical Leave Act (FMLA) A federal act requiring covered employers to provide eligible employees job protections for unpaid leave due to the serious health conditions of the employee or a family member or to care for a new child.
Famous mark Trademarks that have acquired special protections due to their widespread recognition.
Federal question jurisdiction A case arising under the Constitution, treaties, or federal statutes and regulations.
Federal Trade Commission An independent agency of the U.S. government that was created for the express purpose of protecting consumers.
Federal Trade Commission Act A federal act that is aimed at protecting consumer by targeting unfair methods of competition.
Federalism The balance of power shared between the federal government and state governments.
Fee simple Ownership that is characterized as complete ownership lasting until the end of time.
Fiduciary duty A standard of care imposed by law based on a relationship of trust and confidence between parties.
Final order A decision by an administrative law judge (ALJ) not appealed by any party or a decision reached on appeal to the board, commission, or court hearing the appeal.
Fire insurance policy Insurance that protects real and personal property against damages resulting from a fire and certain other perils like lightening, smoke, and water damage.
Firm offer An offer by a merchant that gives assurances on a signed writing and is therefore irrevocable.
First mortgage The mortgage that is recorded first in time.
First Sale Doctrine The concept that copyright protection on a work expires once it has been sold or distributed.
Fixture Personal property that has become so attached to the real property that it loses its identity as personal property.
Floating lien A legal claim to a set of assets that are subject to change over time.
Flood insurance Insurance for property damage caused by a flood.
Food, Drug, and Cosmetic Act (FDCA) A federal law that protects consumers against unlawful cosmetics and medical devices.
Forbearance Refraining from an act that one has a legal right to perform.
***Force majeure* clause** A contractual provision mitigating risks by excusing a party from performing when specified unforeseeable events occur.
Foreclosure A procedure following a default, in which property serving as security for the loan is sold with proceeds applied to retire the debt.
Foreign branch A business presence by the investor in the foreign country.
Foreign LLC An LLC operating in a different state from the state in which it was organized.
Foreign Sovereign Immunities Act (FSIA) U.S. law that states the circumstances in which foreign states are immune from suit and execution upon their assets.
Forged checks A check in which the drawer's signature is forged or unauthorized.
Forgery The fraudulent creation or alteration of any written document of apparent legal status with the intent to defraud.
Form 8-K Form used to file as necessary by a reporting company with the SEC to publicly disclose certain material events.
Form 10-K A report filed annually by a reporting company with the SEC to publicly disclose significant business and financial information about the company during the most recently ended fiscal year.

Form 10-Q A report filed quarterly by a reporting company with the SEC to publicly disclose financial information, including audit financial statements, about the company.
Formal contract A contract requiring a special format or method of creation to be enforceable.
Forum selection clause A contract provision by which the parties have agreed to the jurisdiction in which a claim may be arbitrated or litigated.
Four-fifths rule An EEOC guideline that holds that a selection rate for any race, sex, or ethnic group that is less than four-fifths the selection rate of the most frequently selected group will generally be regarded as evidence of adverse impact.
Fourth Amendment Relative to employment, this Amendment protects a person's "reasonable expectation of privacy," including the right to be free from unreasonable searches and seizures by the government.
Franchise A business arrangement in which the owner of intellectual property (the franchisor) grants a license to another (the franchisee) to use the franchisor's tradename and trademarks in the distribution and sale of goods or services.
Franchise agreement A legal document that establishes the terms and conditions of the relationship between the franchisor and the franchisee.
Franchise Disclosure Document (FDD) A uniform disclosure document that requires franchisors to make disclosures of 23 specific items to prospective franchises. States may require the franchisor register the FDD with a state department prior to offering a franchise for sale.
Franchisee A party granted a franchise and license to use the intellectual property of a franchisor.
Franchisor A party who grants a franchise and license to use the intellectual property of a franchisor.
Fraud (contracts) An intentional false representation of a material fact to another person upon which reasonable reliance is placed to that party's detriment.
Fraud (torts) An intentional misstatement or omission of material fact upon which another party reasonably relies to their detriment.
Fraud alert An alert placed on a customer's credit fille requiring a business to verify the consumer's identity before it issues credit thereby reducing identity theft.
Fraudulent misrepresentation False representation of a material fact to another person upon which reasonable reliance is placed, to that other party's detriment.
Fraudulent transfer A transfer made by the debtor with the intent to hinder, delay, or defraud a creditor.
Free Exercise Clause Under the First Amendment, American citizens are protected from government interference with the exercise of their religion.
Freedom of Information Act (FOIA) A act that provides the public with the right to request and access most records in the possession of a federal administrative agency.
Frolic and Detour An employee's frolic is conduct that is not within the course and scope of employment and relieves the employer of vicarious liability. An employee's detour is a minor departure from acting in the course and scope of employment and does not relieve the employer of vicarious liability.
FTC Franchise Rule A rule published by the FTC to facilitate informed decisions and prevent deception in the sale of franchises.
Full Faith and Credit Clause State courts must respect the judgments of courts from other states.
Full warranty A warranty guaranteeing that a defective product is to be replaced or repaired free of charge during the duration of the warranty.
Fully disclosed principal A principal whose existence and identity are known to the third party.
Fundamental rights Court recognition of individual freedoms so essential to liberty that government may not intrude on them.
Fungible goods Goods whose individuals units are alike such that they are regarded as commercially interchangeable.
Future goods Goods that are not in existence at the time the contract is formed.

G

Gap-filling rule A legal practice in which a default term is inserted when a gap has been left in a contract.
Garnishment A court order allowing a creditor to collect on a debt by seizing the debtor's wages or funds held by a third party.
General devise A gift of a specified quantity or value that can be satisfied from any property in the decedent's estate.
General duty OSHA requirement that each employer must furnish a place of employment free from recognized hazards that are causing or likely to cause death or serious physical harm.
General intent The intent to commit the criminal act.
General lien All liens of a debtor's real or personal property within a jurisdiction.
General partnership An unincorporated business association of two or more persons who engage in a business for profit.
General purpose clause A clause within the articles of incorporation permitting the corporation to engage in any lawful activity.
General warranty deed A deed containing a full warranty and set of promises by the grantor to the grantee.
Generally Accepted Accounting Principles (GAAP) A common set of accounting principles, standards, and procedures that companies must follow when compiling their financial statements.

Generally Accepted Auditing Standards (GAAS) A common set of standards evaluating the quality of audits performed.
Genetic Information Nondiscrimination Act (GINA) A federal law that prohibits discrimination against applicants or employees because of genetic information.
Gift A voluntary transfer of property without payment or the expectation of repayment.
Good faith defense Defense an accountant may assert if they acted in good faith in preparing the financial statement.
Good faith provision A general presumption that the parties to a contract will deal with each other honestly, fairly, and in good faith, so as not to destroy the right of the other party or parties to receive the benefits of the contract.
Good-faith purchaser A purchaser who did not have prior notice of the claims of another having valid title to the goods.
Goods Property that is both "tangible" and "movable" when identified in a contract.
Government in the Sunshine Act Act that enhances the transparency of decision making of administrative agencies by requiring most federal agencies to announce their meetings in the Federal Register at least seven days in advance and be open to public observations.
Grand jury A panel of individuals assigned the duty of investigating and issuing criminal charges (indictments).
Grantee The buyer or recipient.
Grantor The seller or donor.
Greenmail A defensive technique in which the target corporation repurchases its stock at a premium price from a hostile bidder threatening to take control of the company.
Groundwater Water found under the earth's surface as a result of rain and melting snow.
Group boycott An agreement whereby two or more competitors in a market refuse to conduct business with another person or company.
Guaranteed replacement cost coverage An insurance which pays the full cost of repairing or replacing the damaged or destroyed structure, regardless of policy limits.
Guaranty The relationship between the guarantor, the principal debtor, and the creditor in which the creditor may seek payment from the guarantor only after attempting to collect from the debtor.

H

Half-truth advertisement An advertisement containing true information that is missing a material fact.
Harassment Persistent, frequent, or severe, offensive, and unwanted behavior in the workplace and arises because of treating individuals unfavorably due to their protected classification. Many forms include intimidation, bullying, stalking, abusive comments, actions or gestures, or hazing.
Health Insurance Portability and Accountability Act (HIPAA) Federal law that provides protections from disclosures of personal health information.
Holder A person in possession of a negotiable instrument that is payable to either the bearer or the identified person that is in possession of the instrument.
Holder in due course A person who possesses the negotiable instruments free and clear of most of the claims and defenses that could have been brought against the transferor.
Holographic wills A will that is entirely handwritten and signed by the testator.
Homeowner's insurance policy A comprehensive insurance policy providing coverage for damage to the home and homeowner's personal property.
Homestead exemption An exemption preventing the forced sale of a home to pay creditors if the home does not have a certain level of equity
Horizontal market division A restraint of trade where competitors agree to divide the market in which they will engage.
Horizontal merger A merger between two or more companies that are competing in the same market.
Horizontal restraint A Sherman Act violation in which competitors in the same market agree to restrain trade.
Hostile takeover An acquisition or merger accomplished without the approval of the board of directors of the target corporation.
Hostile work environment Workplace activity that is offensive, intimidating, or oppressive. Usually involves pattern of exposure that is intentional, severe, or pervasive; affects the individual regarding the terms, conditions, or privileges of employment; and constitutes conduct that would offend a reasonable person. Management must have either known about the conduct, or should have known, and did nothing to stop it.
Hypothecate To pledge real property as security without giving up possession to guarantee the repayment of the loan.

I

Identification Time when specific goods are recognized as the subject matter of the contract.
Illusory promise A promise in which one or more of the parties has not bound itself to do anything.
Immigration Reform and Control Act (IRCA) Federal law prohibiting discrimination against applicants and employees based upon their citizenships or national origin.

Immunity from prosecution Exemption in full or in part from legal punishment.
Immutable characteristics Unalterable physical traits, including skin color, hair texture, or certain facial features associated with persons of a particular race, color, sex, or national origin, even though not all members of that group necessarily share the trait.
Impairment Condition substantially limiting a person in the performance of one or more life activities as compared to an average person in the general population.
Impasse The stage of not reaching an agreement, where both parties believe further negotiations would be fruitless.
Implied agency Agency occurs when a principal and agent create an agency inferred from the parties' conduct and without express agreement.
Implied authority An agent's power to act on behalf of the principal, without express agreement.
Implied warranty A warranty not expressly provided for in the sale or lease contract but which is instead implied by law given the circumstances of the transaction.
Implied warranty of fitness for a particular purpose A warranty implied by law that consumer products are fit for a specific purpose.
Implied warranty of fitness for a particular purpose (sales and lease contracts) A warranty not expressly provided for in a sales or lease contract that assures the goods will meet the specific needs of the buyer or lessee.
Implied warranty of fitness for human consumption A warranty not expressly provided for that applies to food that is sold for immediate human consumption.
Implied warranty of habitability An implied warranty requires landlords to provide premises that are fit, safe, and suitable for basic human habitation.
Implied warranty of merchantability A warranty implied by law that consumer products reasonably conform to an ordinary buyer's expectations.
Implied warranty of merchantability (sales and lease contracts) A warranty not expressly provided for in the sales or lease contract that assures the goods are at least of average quality, properly packaged and labeled, and fit for the ordinary purposes they are intended to serve.
Implied-in-fact contract A contract manifested by conduct rather than words.
Implied-in-law contract A contract created to avoid unjust enrichment of one party at the expense of the other.
Import quotas A limit on the amount of goods that a country will allow to be imported into its markets in a specified period of time.
In pari delicto Parties will be denied quasi-contractual relief because they are mutually or equally at fault in violating a statute governing their contract.
***In rem* jurisdiction** Refers to the court's jurisdiction over a piece of property or "thing."
Inadequate warning A defect in which the business fails to instruct the consumer in the effective use of the product or fails to warn of the dangers involved in the ordinary use or misuse of a product.
Incidental damages Damages amounting to the seller's commercially reasonable expenses that were incurred in stopping the delivery, transportation, or caring for the goods after buyer's breach or the buyer's expenses reasonably incurred in searching for and obtaining substitute goods.
Incidental third-party beneficiary A nonparty to contract who is not identified in the contract. This person might derive a benefit if the contract is performed but the parties to the contract did not intend to benefit that person directly.
Incorporation The formation of a legal corporation.
Incorporation doctrine The process by which provisions of the Bill of Rights are made applicable to the states through the Due Process Clause of the Fourteenth Amendment.
Incorporator An individual who signs and files with the Secretary of State the articles of incorporation.
Indemnity A rule that permits an innocent defendant to sue other parties for the total amount of damages sought by plaintiff.
Independent contractor Nonemployee worker exercising independent judgment in the manner and means of performing work for a principal.
Independent regulatory agencies Federal agencies with broad powers created by Congress whose officers serve fixed term and can only be removed for just cause.
Indictment Formal criminal charges issued by a grand jury.
Indirect exporting Sale of goods or services abroad with the use of intermediaries.
Indirect price discrimination Price discrimination that is not readily apparent from the purchase price of the good.
Individual with a disability who is qualified A person with a disability who meets the legitimate level of skills, experience, education, or other requirements for a position and who can perform the essential functions of the job, with or without reasonable accommodation.
Indorsement A signature on the instrument to transfer ownership of the instrument.
Informal contract (simple contract) A contract not requiring a special form or method of creation to be enforceable.
Information A list of formal charges against the defendant and the factual basis for them. Begins a criminal proceeding.
Inherently distinct Marks that bear no obvious connection to the good or service, such that the association is unique.
Inheritance Distribution of property to heirs.

Initial order Decision of the administrative law judge (ALJ) that has not yet been appealed.
Injunction A court order that prohibits the continued harm from continuing.
Innocent misrepresentation Known as non-fraudulent misrepresentation. Misrepresentation made unknowingly or without an intent to defraud.
Inside director A person on the board of directors who is also an officer of the corporation.
Insider Anyone who has access to or receives material, non-public information about a company due to their position or relationship with the company.
Insider trading The purchase or sale of securities by individuals who have access to material, non-public information that provides an unfair advantage to those traders.
Inspection rights A right owed to shareholders allowing them to inspect a corporation's books and records for a proper purpose.
Installment contract A single contract that authorizes multiple deliveries to be accepted and paid for separately.
Installment land sale contract A contract for the purchase of real property in which the seller provides financing to the buyer and retains title to the property until the final payment is received.
Insurable interest (commercial law) A legal stake in the value of an item that allows a party to purchase insurance to mitigate loss in the event the item is damaged or destroyed.
Insurable interest (insurance) A requirement that a person have a property or personal interest in the insured goods, property, or person.
Insurance A contract that shifts the risk of loss for individuals and businesses to another in exchange for a premium payment.
Insurance agents Agents sell insurance for only one insurance carrier and are agents for the insurance company.
Insurance broker A broker is an agent to the insured and can place insurance with multiple insurance carriers.
Insured The person who obtains insurance.
Insurer The insurance company that receives payment from an insured.
Intangible property Property interests lacking a physical form.
Intellectual property The general term for the fields of trademarks, trade secrets, copyrights, and patents.
Intentional infliction of emotional distress Viewed by a reasonable person, the intentional, extreme, and outrageous conduct of another person certain or substantially certain to cause emotional distress to the victim.
Intentional torts Torts that are committed through the tortfeasor's deliberate effort.
Intentions Refers to donative intent. Must be clear, unmistakable, and unequivocal to evidence the voluntary making of a gift.
***Inter vivos* gift** A gift made during the donor's lifetime.
***Inter vivos* trust** A trust created during a trustor's life.
Interference with contractual relations Tortious conduct involving actions that intentionally and inexcusably interfere with the contractual benefits of another person.
Interlocking directorate An unlawful action under the Clayton Act whereby a person serves as a director or officer of two or more competing corporations at the same time.
Intermediary bank A bank to which the check is transferred during the collection process that is not the payor or depository bank.
International business law The law that governs extraterritorial transactions between foreign countries and businesses located in foreign countries.
International Financing Reporting Standards (IFRS) A set of accounting standards developed by an independent, nonprofit organization known as the International Accounting Standards Board.
International law A body of rules that has been established through customs and treaties.
International organizations Organizations comprised of member nations to an established treaty.
Interpretive rules Rules that explain existing statutory language but are not legally binding on the public or the court system.
Interrogatories Written questions submitted by one party to an opposing party.
Intestate When a decedent dies without a valid will.
Intestate succession The process of distributing property in the absence of a valid will.
Involuntary bailment The law imposing bailment duties on the unwitting or unwilling bailee.
Involuntary petition A petition filed by creditors of a debtor that alleges the debtor is not paying its debts as they become due.
Irrevocable trust A trust that cannot be changed or revoked during the trustor's life.
Issue The decedent's descendants (such as children, grandchildren, great-grandchildren, etc.)
Issued shares Authorized shares that have been sold by the corporation.
Issuer An individual or business offering the securities for sale to the public.
Issuer or issuing bank The buyer's bank in a letter of credit transaction.

J

Job related The specific skills, education, and training needed to perform a task.
JOBS Act A federal law passed to encourage funding of U.S. small businesses by easing compliance with securities regulation requirements.
Joint and several liability (partnerships) A doctrine under which a plaintiff may sue and collect a judgment from all the partners collectively or the partners individually.

Joint and several liability (torts) Liability imposed upon each defendant for the payment of the entire obligation owed to the plaintiff.
Joint stock company An association within a business enterprise with transferable shares of stock, except that the shareholders are liable for the debts of the business.
Joint tenancy A form of concurrent ownership in which two or more persons own equal shares of property, with the right of survivorship between the joint tenants.
Joint venture A joint undertaking in which two or more persons or businesses associate together as co-owners of an enterprise to share profits and losses for a transaction or series of transactions.
Joint venture (international business) A commercial relationship between two or more businesses for profit.
Joint will A will created by two or more testators.
Judgment The final ruling of the court from which an appeal may be taken.
Judicial branch The branch of government that interprets and applies the laws, rules, and regulations created by the legislative and executive branches.
Judicial lien A lien obtained by judgment allowing the creditor to collect on a debt.
Judiciary system The system of courts that interpret and apply the laws and provide a forum for dispute resolution.
Jurisdiction The authority of a court or agency to make a legal determination regarding a person or the property of another person.
Justification A defense that negates criminal liability because the defendant's actions were justified.

K

Kantian ethics Rules of behavior apply universally to everyone. People are not to be treated as a means to an end but as an end in themselves.
Kickback A general term for a benefit received from a party who assisted in the execution of a bribery scheme.

L

Labor union Organization or association of individuals formed for the purpose of negotiating with employers on behalf of employees regarding rates of pay, wages, hours of employment, or other conditions of employment.
Labor-Management Reporting and Disclosure Act Known as the Taft-Hartley Act. This act was enacted to restrict the activities and power of unions.
Laches The prejudice suffered by a defendant from plaintiff 's delay in filing a breach of contract case.
Landfill A large cavity in the ground that is lined with clay or synthetic liner to prevent any waste from leaking into the ground or water supply.
Lanham Act Federal law that governs trademarks.
Larceny The unlawful taking of the property of another with the intent to permanently deprive the owner of the property.
Law A set of enforceable rules governing the conduct of persons in society.
Lead Highly toxic metal that can accumulate in the body through repeated exposure.
Lean startup plan A non-comprehensive business plan that focuses only on a few key elements.
Lease Contract transferring exclusive possession of a property from one party (the landlord) to another (the tenant) for a period of time (the tenancy).
Lease agreement The bargain between a lessor and lessee with respect to the lease of goods.
Legal duty A requirement not to interfere with the legal rights of another.
Legal right The ability to have an individual interest respected by others and enforced through a legal procedure.
Legislative branch The branch of government that enacts the laws that govern the rights and responsibilities of citizens.
Legitimate business reason A business requirement that justifies treating one or more applicants or employees differently from others.
Lessee (commercial law) The party who acquires the right to the temporary possession and use of goods under a lease agreement.
Lessee (landlord-tenant) A person who acquires the right to exclusively possess and use property for a duration of time.
Lessor (commercial law) The party who acquires the right to the temporary possession and use of goods under a lease agreement.
Lessor (landlord-tenant) A person who transfers the right to exclusively possess and use property for a duration of time.
Letter of credit A document in which a promise is made by the issuer to honor the drafts or documents that are presented for payment.
Letter of intent A document setting forth anticipated terms in the beginning stages of a transaction that commonly is not legally binding upon the parties.
Libel A form of defamation through use of written false statements.
License (intellectual property) Legal permission to use a party's intellectual property.
License (real property) The privilege to use the land of another; usually temporary and revocable.
Licensing agreement A legal contract between two parties where one party grants the other the right to produce and sell goods, apply a brand name or trademark, or use patented technology owned by the licensor.
Lien A legal instrument by which property acts as a security for the repayment of a debt.

Life estate An estate in which the property is held for the duration of a person's lifespan.

Limited liability A type of liability in which the owners of a corporation will not be subject to personal liability for the debts of the corporation.

Limited liability company (LLC) A hybrid form of business organization combining the liability shield of a corporation with the federal tax treatment of a partnership.

Limited liability limited partnership (LLLP) A partnership that fully shields the partners from any liability and is characteristically like a corporation.

Limited liability partnership (LLP) A partnership in which all the partners are limited partners and no partner is personally liable for the debts, obligations, or liabilities of the partnership.

Limited partnership A partnership consisting of one or more general partners and one or more limited partners whose liability is limited to the amount of their investment.

Limited purpose clause A clause within the articles of incorporation that states the specific purposes and activities that a corporation may pursue.

Limited warranty A warranty limiting the scope of the warranty in some manner.

Lineal descendants A relative in the direct line of descent of the decedent including children, grandchildren, and so on.

Liquidated damages A contract provision whereby the parties agree at the time of entering into the contract what the amount of damages will be in the event of a breach of contract.

Litigation The process of resolving a dispute through the court system.

Local administrative agencies Administrative agencies that administer and enforce local regulatory law and may work in coordination with a federal or state agency.

Lock-up option A defensive mechanism giving a white knight the right to purchase the target corporation's crown jewel if the hostile bidder acquires a certain percentage of the target's stock.

Lockout When an employer refuses to allow employees to return to work without a signed contract.

Long arm statute State statutes that enable state courts to exercise personal jurisdiction over nonresidents, within the bounds of the Constitution.

Lost property Property that is involuntarily left somewhere.

M

Madrid Protocol An agreement among nations to provide for international trademark protection and registration.

Magnuson-Moss Warranty Act A federal statute that governs warranties on consumer products and prohibits sellers or lessors who make express warranties from disclaiming or modifying the implied warranties of merchantability and fitness for a particular purpose.

Mail and wire fraud The use of mail service or the telecommunications networks to commit fraud.

Mail, Internet, or Telephone Order Merchandise Rule A federal law that requires sellers who solicit buyers to order merchandise through the mail, via the internet, or by phone to ship their products within the advertised time frame.

Mailbox rule The offeree's acceptance was effective upon mailing the offeree's acceptance.

Main purpose rule An exception to the Statute of Frauds allowing for an oral guarantee to be enforceable if the main purpose of a transaction is to provide a benefit to the guarantor.

Major life activity An expansive definition used in disability cases for the variety of tasks important in most people's daily lives.

Maker The person who borrows money and enters into the promissory note.

Malicious prosecution A tort in which the defendant is alleged to have used the legal system as a means of harassing a person, group of people, or entity.

Malum in se Conduct constituting an inherent evil or wrong.

Malum prohibitum Conduct constituting an unlawful act by statute and not inherently evil conduct.

Manager-managed Members empower one or more manager to manage the LLC.

Manufacturing arrangement A type of franchise agreement whereby the franchisor provides the franchisee the formula or ingredients needed to make a particular product.

Manufacturing defect A defect in which a product departs from its intended design during the manufacturing process.

Market concentration Measures the extent to which a relevant market is controlled by a small number of competitors.

Market value The price agreed upon by a willing buyer and seller.

Material breach A breach of contract whereby the party renders inferior performance of their duties and fails to substantially perform the contract terms.

Material fact A fact that is important to the contract's subject matter.

Maximizing profits The traditional view of corporate social responsibility that the business should strive to maximize profits for a business's shareholders.

McCarran Ferguson Act of 1945 A federal law that delegated regulation of the insurance industry to the states.

Means test A test to determine if the debtor has adequate disposable income to pay debts in existence prior to the petition by using income derived after the filing of the petition.

Mechanic's lien A lien recorded on the title to real property by a contractor, subcontractor, or material supplier for unpaid sums owed under a construction-related contract.

Median income test A test to determine whether the debtor's familial income is above the median family income for a family of that size residing in the debtor's state.

Mediation A form of alternative dispute resolution in which a neutral third party assists the parties in a dispute to reach a settlement.

Medicare National health insurance program in the United States for people who are 65 or older and certain younger people with disabilities.

Member An owner of a LLC.

Member-managed An LLC managed by all members.

Memorandum The requirement under the Statute of Frauds that there must be evidence of a writing stating the essential terms of the contract.

Mens rea The mental state required to be convicted of a crime.

Merger An acquisition in which two companies combine into one legal entity.

Minor A person who is under the age of majority.

Minor breach A nonmaterial breach of contract by which complete performance is not rendered. The breaching party has substantially performed and the breaching party's performance deviates only slightly from the contract.

Mirror image rule An offer must be accepted without modifications by the offeree.

Misappropriation of trade secrets A legal action in tort law that accuses a party of illegally acquiring a trade secret.

Misappropriation theory An SEC rule that imposes liability on outsiders who trade on material, non-public information that was gained by a breach of a duty of trust or confidence owed to the person who is the source of the information.

Mislaid property Property that is intentionally placed by the true owner and then forgotten or left there.

Mission statement A formal summary of the aims and values of a company, organization, or individual.

Mistake An error arising when the parties to a contract differ on their beliefs about the subject matter, value, or other aspect of the contract.

Mistake of fact A defense that undermines the intent element of the crime because the defendant claims they made a reasonable mistake as to the facts of the situation.

Mixed motive evidence An employer's evidence showing that the same adverse decision would have been made against an employee even in the absence of the impermissible motivating factor.

Mixed sales A sale that involves both the provision of a service and a good in the same transaction.

Money laundering A series of financial transactions used by criminal organizations to conceal the origin of money derived from criminal activity.

Monopoly A company or group of companies having control over the production or distribution of a product or service.

Monopoly power The power to control prices or exclude competition.

Moral Minimum A business should pursue profits while avoiding intentional harm.

Mortgage A real estate security instrument. Borrower retains title but gives a lien interest and note to the lender. Also known as hypothecation.

Mortgagee The lender or creditor in a mortgage agreement.

Mortgagor The owner-borrower in a mortgage agreement.

Most Favored Nation status A country that has achieved this status has been granted the most favorable trading terms available by another country.

Motion for a new trial A request by a party, after a judgment is entered in a case, that the judge vacate that judgment and order a new trial because of legal errors or problems with the evidence.

Motion for judgment notwithstanding the verdict The trial judge may overrule the decision of a jury and set aside or amend the jury verdict.

Motion for judgment on the pleadings A request for the court to decide the case based upon the complaint and answer.

Motion for summary judgment A motion for judgment on any claim or issue will be granted where there is no genuine dispute of material fact. The court may consider evidence beyond that contained in the pleadings.

Motion to dismiss When a party makes a formal request to dismiss a case based upon the pleadings.

Mutual mistake When both parties are mistaken about the same fact regarding the contract.

Mutual wills or reciprocal wills Where two or more testators execute separate wills and leave their property to each other on the condition that the surviving person, on their death, leaves the remaining property as agreed upon by the testators.

N

Named insured In the event of a covered loss, the person or business receiving payment from the insurance company.

National Do Not Call Registry A database maintained by the federal government, listing the telephone number of individuals and families who have requested that telemarketers not contact them.

National Environmental Policy Act of 1969 (NEPA) This law was enacted to prevent and reverse the damage to the United States' air, water, and other ecosystems from industrial pollution.

National Labor Relations Act (NLRA) Also known as the Wagner Act. A 1935 federal law recognizing and protecting the rights of workers to organize and collectively bargain with employers. Requires employers to bargain with the exclusive representative of the workers.

National Labor Relations Board (NLRB) An independent U.S. administrative agency that conducts labor union elections, investigates, and decides if an unfair labor practice has occurred.

National law A law that applies to a particular country.

National origin discrimination Treating applicants or employees unfavorably because they are from a particular country or part of the world, exhibit a certain ethnicity or accent, or appear to be of certain ethnicity even if they are not.

National treatment Requires nondiscrimination in respect to imported and domestic goods once the goods have cleared customs and tariffs have been collected.

Necessary and Proper Clause Congress has the authority to enact laws deemed necessary and proper for carrying out its enumerated powers.

Negligence Torts that are committed through the tortfeasor's deliberate effort.

Negotiable instrument A signed document stating that a specified sum is payable to an identified person on either a predetermined date or on demand.

Negotiation A type of transfer of the possession of a negotiable instrument to a person who becomes the holder.

Nominal damages Damages awarded when there are no actual damages or losses from a breach of contract.

Non-cumulative stock A type of preferred stock, where any unpaid dividends will accumulate for years of nonpayment.

Nonconforming goods Goods that do not meet the specifications of the contract.

Nonexempt Employee Worker entitled to the minimum wage and/or overtime pay protections of the FLSA.

Nonpoint source A source of pollution originating from many sources.

Nonpossessory interests An interest in land that constitutes less than full possession or ownership of the land.

Nonprice vertical restraint Vertical restrictions on trade that are not price related such as territorial restrictions or exclusive dealing contracts.

Norris-LaGuardia Act Also known as the Anti-Injunction Act; this federal act barred courts from issuing injunctions against union strike activities, unless such strikes might result in dangerous or coercive conditions. Act made yellow-dog contracts illegal.

North American Free Trade Agreement (NAFTA) Trade agreement enacted to create a free trade zone for Mexico, Canada, and the United States.

Notary public A commissioned representative of a state who is charged with verifying the identity of the signor of documents.

Note A debt security with a short-term maturity.

O

Objective theory of contracts Determining a party's intention to enter into a contract or the meaning of a term by what a reasonable person in the position of the other party would conclude from the first party's objective manifestations (displays of intent).

Obtaining goods by false pretenses The unlawful act of making a false statement with the intent to defraud and obtain title to another's personal property.

Occupational Safety and Health Act (OSH) Legislation that set national standard for workplace safety. Designed to protect workers from danger but not intended to eliminate all dangers from the workplace.

Occupational Safety and Health Administration (OSHA) The federal agency tasked with administering the OSH Act.

Offer An expression of intent to enter into a binding and enforceable contract that may be oral, written, or arising from a party's conduct.

Omitted spouse rule A rule that permits an omitted spouse to receive the same share of the estate they would have received if the decedent had died intestate.

On-call time Time during which employees are not required to remain on the employer's premises but are required to be available to work and thus cannot use their time for their own purposes.

Operating agreement A contract governing the LLC's affairs and setting forth the rights and duties of the members.

Opinion and statements of value States made by the seller or lessor regarding the presumed value of the goods or an opinion or recommendation related to the goods do not create an express warranty.

Option contract A contract in which the offeree pays consideration to the offeror in exchange for an irrevocable promise to keep the offer open for a stated period.

Order for relief A court order subjecting the debtor to the control of the bankruptcy court.

Order instrument An instrument that is made payable to either the order of an identified person or to an identified person or order.

Ordinance A law created by a town or city council, county board, or other form of municipal government.

Organizational culture Shared beliefs and values established by the organization's leaders shaping the behaviors of employees and agents.
Organized crime Organizations with an identified hierarchy used to engage in a variety of criminal activity.
Originality A copyright requirement that a work be independently created and be at least minimally creative.
Output contract An output contract is an agreement in which a producer agrees to sell its entire production to the buyer, who, in turn, agrees to purchase the entire output.
Outside director A person on the board of directors who does not hold a management position within the corporation.
Outstanding shares Shares held by shareholders.
Overtime Subject to certain industry specific exemptions, the hourly rate of one and one-half times their normal pay rate due to nonexempt employees for each hour of work beyond 40 in a workweek.

P

Parent corporation The corporation owning or controlling the majority of the outstanding voting stock or other equity in another corporation.
Parol evidence Evidence of prior or contemporaneous agreement to modify, explain, or supplement the contract at issue.
Parol evidence rule A contract rule prohibiting prior or contemporaneous promises, agreements, or understandings if they would vary, add to, or conflict with the terms of a written contract.
Part performance exception An exception to the Statute of Frauds. This allows oral real estate contracts to be enforceable if any two of the following three elements are met: (1) the purchase price has been fully or partially paid, (2) the party has received possession of the property, and (3) valuable improvements have been made to the property.
Partial performance When a party is only able to execute part of his or her performance under the contract.
Partially disclosed principal A principal whose existence is known to the third party, but whose identity is not known.
Partnership A voluntary unincorporated association of two or more persons to conduct as co-owners a business for profit.
Partnership agreement (articles of partnership) A writing setting forth the rights and duties of the partners with respect to partnership business.
Partnership at will A partnership of no fixed duration that may be dissolved at any time without liability.
Partnership capital The equity or undistributed balance allocated to the partners.
Partnership for a term A partnership that has a limited duration.
Partnership property Assets used for a partnership purpose, including capital contributions by partners and acquisitions of property made by the partnership.
Pass-through entity An entity that does not pay income taxes because the entity's income and losses pass through to the owners of the entity, who then pay income taxes on their personal income tax returns.
Past consideration Unenforceable consideration based on past activities.
Patent A protected intellectual property interest establishing that the holder has the sole authority to produce, use, sell, license, or distribute their invention.
Patent infringement When a party makes, sells, imports, or otherwise distributes a patented product without authorization.
Payee A person who receives payment under a note or negotiable instrument.
Payee of the draft The party who receives the money from the draft.
Payor bank The bank of the drawee.
Penal code A written collection of criminal offenses recognized in a particular jurisdiction.
Pension plan Agreement by which salary and other contributions are deferred from taxation until retirement, when they will provide participants with income when they are no longer earning a regular income from employment.
***Per capita* distribution** Form of distributing the decedent's estate in which the living lineal descendants equally share the property of the estate.
***Per se* violation** Actions that are presumed unreasonable restraints of trade and therefore unlawful under the Sherman Act.
***Per stirpes* distribution** Form of distributing the decedent's estate in which surviving lineal descendants inherit through representation of their parents' inheritance share.
Peremptory challenge During voir dire an attorney can automatically dismiss a potential juror with no reason required. These are limited in number.
Perfect tender rule A common law principle requiring that the seller deliver goods in perfect conformity with the description in the contract.
Perfection Process of ensuring that a security interest is protected against the claims of another creditor seeking to obtain payment on a debt from the same collateral.
Perfection through filing Process of perfecting a security interest by following the necessary steps when filing a financing statement.
Periodic tenancy A lease that lasts for a fixed period and continues to renew for like periods until terminated.

Personal (*in personam*) jurisdiction Personal jurisdiction exists when the court has power over the person(s) participating in the action.
Personal appearance discrimination Unfavorable treatment due to a person's outward appearance, irrespective of sex, with regard to bodily condition or characteristics, manner or style of dress, or manner or style of personal grooming, including hairstyle and facial hair. Not protected under federal law, but subject to a few state laws and municipal ordinances.
Personal defense A defense from payment liability against all holders, but not including HDCs.
Personal property Property that is movable and not fixed or permanently attached to real property.
Persuasive authority A source of law which carries some authoritative weight but does not bind a court.
Physical or mental impairment Any disorder, condition, disfigurement, or anatomical loss that affects a major body system or mental or psychological state.
Picketing Group protest assembling outside a place of work to dissuade others from doing business with the target of their efforts.
Piercing the corporate veil A legal doctrine in which a shareholder can be held personally liable for a corporation's debts and obligations.
Plaintiff The party who files a lawsuit.
Pleadings The documents required by the court to commence the judicial process. They serve to outline the factual and legal issues, identify the parties, and provide notice to the defendant parties that litigation has started.
Point source A discernible, specific discharge point of pollution into surface waters.
Poison pill A defensive strategy built into the target corporation's articles of incorporation, bylaws, contracts, or leases that makes the target less attractive.
Police power The power of the states to regulate the health, safety, morals, and general welfare of the public.
Policy limits Amounts of insurance that are payable under the policy.
Political speech Speech that comments on or about political subject matter.
Portal-to-Portal Act Federal law specifying the types of work-related time spent that are compensable. Generally, such time includes all activity of benefit to the employer. Time for travel to and from the workplace is not compensable.
Possession The first means of indicating ownership of personal property.
Postdated checks A check in which a future date is put on the check rather than the date the check is written.
Posthumous child A child born after the decedent's death.
Power of attorney A writing executed by principal authorizing an agent to act on behalf of the principal.
Precedent The rule of law established by a court decision that can be used to decide future similar cases.
Predatory lending A term used to describe illegal and abusive lending practices.
Preemption A legal doctrine providing that federal law will prevail in the event of conflict with state laws or local ordinances on the same subject.
Preemptive rights In an option, security, or merger agreement, rights granted to an investor to maintain their percentage ownership by buying a proportionate number of shares of any future issue of that security.
Preexisting duty A duty that someone is already obligated to perform.
Preference or preferential debt repayment A debt payment made to a creditor in the ninety days prior to when a debtor files bankruptcy (or within one year, if the creditor was an insider) that gives the creditor more than the creditor would receive in a Chapter 7 case.
Preferential transfer A wrongful transfer of the debtor's property benefitting one or more creditor allowing them to receive more than they would have otherwise received in a Chapter 7 liquidation.
Preferred stock A type of equity ownership entitling shareholders to certain preferences in rights over common stockholders.
Premium The cost of insurance paid by an insured.
Presentment The act of presenting the documents of the transaction to the appropriate bank to receive the money due under the negotiable instrument.
Presentment warranties Warranties regarding payment and acceptance made to the person who pays or accepts an instrument in good faith.
Pretermitted child A child who is born or adopted or not known to be alive by the testator after the execution of a will.
Pretext An excuse created to conceal the facts.
Preventive risk management program A company-enacted program designed to ensure product quality, safety, reliability, and environmental compatibility over the product's life cycle.
Price-fixing agreement An agreement between two or more competitors to fix prices or price levels, or terms and conditions of sale for goods and services.
Primary liability When a party is absolutely required to pay the instrument.
Principal A person who authorizes another, an agent, to act on behalf of the principal.
Principal-agent relationship A relationship formed when a party is retained and given authority to act on behalf of and bind a principal.
Principal-independent contractor relationship A contractual relationship in which a person provides services or a product arising from the performance of the contract.

Priority A statutory ranking of unsecured claims that determines the order in which they will be paid, if not enough money is available to pay all of them in full.
Privacy The desire or right to be left alone or the right to restrict public access to personal information, history, and affairs.
Privacy Act Act that protects individual privacy in records maintained by the federal government.
Private equity capital Investments in a private corporation made by a private equity firm for a fixed period.
Private Securities Litigation Reform Act of 1995 Offers a safe harbor, where a corporation is not liable if statement is: (1) identified and accompanied by meaningful cautionary language; (2) is immaterial; or (3) the plaintiff failed to prove that it was made with actual knowledge that it was false or misleading.
Private wells Wells serving less than 25 people.
Privileged Information that is protected from discovery as provided by statute or legal precedent.
Privileges and Immunities Clause This Clause prevents states from unfairly discriminating against citizens of another state.
Privity The common law rule that in order to have a legal interest in a contract, one must be party to the contract.
Probate The process of collecting a decedent's property, paying the decedent's debts and taxes, and distributing the remainder of the estate.
Procedural due process Laws that burden life, liberty, or property must provide notice, a meaningful hearing, and an impartial decision maker.
Procedural law The part of the law that enforces legal rights or provides a remedy for an injured party.
Procedural unconscionability The disadvantage suffered by a weaker party at the time of entering into the contract.
Product misuse A defense to a products liability claim allowed when a consumer does not use a product as it was intended to be used and such misuse was not reasonably foreseeable.
Production The act of taking various raw materials and using them to produce a finished product.
Products liability Liability imposed by law regardless of fault upon a manufacturer, assembler, distributor, retailer, and others within the stream of commerce for harm caused by a defective product.
Profit The right to enter another's land and take something from the land.
Promisee A party to a contract who directs that a benefit be conferred to another person (the third-party beneficiary).
Promisor A party to a contract who agrees to confer performance to another person (the third-party beneficiary).
Promissory estoppel A doctrine used to prevent unjust enrichment where a party makes a promise and the promisee reasonably, detrimentally, and foreseeably relies on the promise to their detriment.
Promissory note A two-party instrument that includes an unconditional written promise made by one party (maker or borrower) to another party (payee of lender).
Promissory note (financing real property) An executed (signed) instrument acknowledging a debt and promising to pay a creditor.
Promoter A person who arranges for the structure and financing of the corporation and procure personnel, equipment, and leases.
Proof of claim A written statement and verified documentation filed by a creditor that describes the reasons why the debtor owes the creditor money.
Prospectus A legal document providing investors with information and assessment of risk factor relating to the offering of a security for sale.
Provisional application An application that allows a party to establish an earlier filing date, and allows "patent pending" to be placed on a product.
Provisional director A temporary director appointed to break a board deadlock, who has the same duties and obligations as other directors.
Proximate cause The defendant's tortious conduct was a substantial factor in causing the plaintiff 's injury and it was foreseeable that the conduct would result in a risk of unreasonable harm to the plaintiff.
Proxy A power of attorney allowing a specified person to vote the shares owned by a shareholder in a particular manner at a shareholders' meeting.
Proxy solicitation A request that a corporate shareholder authorize another person to cast the shareholder's vote at a corporate meeting.
Public disclosure of private facts Publication of information that would be highly offensive to a reasonable person and not of legitimate public interest.
Public domain The term for all works that no longer have copyright protection.
Public law A system of law that governs an individual's personal rights and obligations in relation to the government.
Public use In the context of eminent domain, any conceivable benefit to the public welfare can be deemed a public use.
Public water system Water systems that have at least 15 service connections or serve at least 25 people.
Puffery A legal way of promoting a product or service through hyperbole or oversized statements that cannot be objectively verified.
Punitive damages Damages beyond those necessary to compensate for losses suffered awarded to an injured party for intentional or egregious conduct, assessed with the intention of punishing the wrongdoer or setting an example.
Purchase Transfer of personal property by which title is exchanged for money or another form of consideration.

Purchase money mortgage A mortgage financing the purchase of a one-to-four-unit residential property.
Purchase-money security interest (PMSI) A security interest in a consumer good that is automatically perfected from the moment the good is purchased on credit.

Q

Qualified indorsement An indorsement on a negotiable instrument that disclaims or limits liability when an indorser does not want to be liable on the instrument.
Qualified opinion An auditor's opinion that the company's financial statements fairly and appropriately represent the company's financial condition, except for some issue, process, or transaction that prevents them from issuing an unqualified opinion.
Qualified privilege A person making a statement may have the right to make the statement without fear of liability for defamation.
Quasi-contract Also known as an implied-in-law contract. It is created to avoid unjust enrichment of one party at the expense of the other.
***Quid pro quo* sexual harassment** Unlawful conduct in which the harasser uses submission to or rejection of sexual requests as a basis for employment decisions, such as hiring, firing, compensation, and promotion. The Latin phrase translates as "this for that."
Quitclaim deed A deed in which the grantor coveys whatever interest, if any, the grantor has in a specific piece of property.
Quorum The minimum number of members of a board who must be present to validly transact business.

R

Race A term not defined in Title VII, but usually interpreted, in the context of discrimination, in terms of ancestry or the physical or cultural characteristics associated with a certain race.
Racial discrimination Unequal treatment in the workplace based on the race or perceived racial characteristics of a person.
Racial harassment Unwelcome conduct that unreasonably interferes with an individual's work performance or creates an intimidating, hostile, or offensive work environment.
Radon A naturally occurring radioactive gas found in nearly all soils that travels through cracks in the foundation of a home and causes lung cancer.
Ratification The acceptance or confirmation of a contract once the minor has reached the age of majority.
Rawls's social justice theory As rational, equal, and free persons we begin from an original position of equality and ignorance. Such ignorance motivates us to choose to act fairly.
Reaffirmation agreement An agreement in which the debtor agrees to pay a dischargeable debt to a creditor after the discharge in bankruptcy.
Real property The earth and all that is permanently attached and connected to it.
Reasonable accommodation Modification or adjustment to a job or work environment enabling a qualified applicant or employee with recognized disability to pursue employment or perform the essential job functions.
Reasonable Factor Other than Age (RFOA) Employers may take an adverse action against an applicant or employee over age 40 if the basis of the decision is reasonable and other than one based upon the person's age.
Reasonably Foreseeable Users Rule An accountant is liable to all reasonably foreseeable third parties, including members of the class of persons whose reliance on the financial statements the accountant may reasonably anticipate.
Receiver A person appointed by the court or the parties to preserve or manage assets in a receivership.
Receivership A legal proceeding whereby a third party is assigned to preserve or manage assets.
Receiving stolen property The unlawful receipt of property with the knowledge that the property is stolen.
Recission The cancellation of a contract.
Recognized hazard Condition or practice known to be hazardous by the employer's industry in general or by the specific employer.
Record date The cut-off date used to determine which shareholders are entitled to vote.
Recording statute A state statute providing that constructive notice is deemed to have been given to third parties by virtue of filing a document in the public domain.
Reformation Judicial correction of a change to an existing document to express the parties' true intentions at the time of formation of the contract.
Registered agent An individual empowered to accept service of process and other documents on behalf of the corporation.
Registered office The official address of a registered corporation and location where the registered agent receives service of process and other documents on behalf of the corporation.
Registration The act of filing the appropriate documentation with the SEC for any offer or sale of securities to the public unless a specific exemption applies.
Registration statement A complete disclosure to the SEC and potential investors of all material information that relates to the securities being issued.
Regulation Specific guidelines for conducting and enforcing policies established by laws.

Regulation Z This regulation implements TILA and requires lenders to make meaningful credit disclosures to individual borrowers for certain types of consumer loans.
Regulatory Flexibility Act An act created by Congress which requires the cost of proposed regulation to be measured and requires the agency to consider regulation that may be less burdensome.
Regulatory statutes Another term for administrative laws.
Regulatory taking A government regulation that deprives the owner of all economic beneficial use of the property.
Rejection The termination of an offer by words or conduct.
Relativism Individuals may decide what is ethical based on their own beliefs about right and wrong.
Religious discrimination An employer's failure to ensure that the conditions of employment allow for an applicant's or worker's sincerely held religious, ethical, or moral beliefs and practices, unless doing so creates undue hardship.
Remedial action Long-term actions used to clean up sites that do not pose an immediate risk to public health.
Remedy The relief the plaintiff seeks to cure the injury caused by the defendant, usually monetary damages.
Removal action Actions eliminating immediate risks of uncontrolled hazardous waste sites to ensure public safety.
Replevin A procedure in which seized goods are provisionally restored to a buyer depending on a court's determination of the rights of the parties concerned.
Reply The plaintiff 's response to the cross-complaint.
Repossession A remedy in the event of a default which allows the secured party to take possession of the collateral.
Representations and warranties insurance policy A policy used to guarantee the representations made by sellers in contracts.
Republic of Korea-United States Free Trade Agreement (KORUS-FTA) A trade agreement between the United States and South Korea which seek to remove 95 percent of the nations' tariffs related to consumer and industrial goods.
Request for admission A written request from one party to the opposing party, but the questions can only request the party to admit or deny the genuineness of a writing or truth of an assertion of fact.
Request for an accounting Debtor's right to ask the creditor to provide an accounting of any unpaid obligations that are secured by the collateral.
Request for the production of documents Within pretrial discovery a party may request documents relevant to the dispute.
Requirements contract A contract in which one party agrees to supply as much of a good or service as is required by the other party, and in exchange the other party expressly or implicitly promises that it will obtain its goods or services exclusively from the first party.
Resale price maintenance agreements An agreement in which persons at one level of a distribution (such as a manufacturer) enters into an agreement with a party at another level of a distribution (such as a retailer) to adhere to a price schedule.
Reservation of rights An insurance carrier's notification to an insured that coverage for a claim may not exist under the policy.
Residuary devise A gift of whatever remains in the decedent's estate after all other debts and devises have been paid or distributed.
Respondeat superior Legal rule or doctrine holding an employer liable for the tortious acts and omissions of its employees or agents while they are acting with the scope of the employer's authority.
Restatement A treatise by legal scholars addressing uncertainties as to the state of the law and indicating the common trend in understanding or the legal interpretation of an issue.
Restatement (Second) of Torts, § 205A One who invades the right to privacy of another is subject to liability for the resulting harm to the interest of the other. The right to privacy is invaded by the unreasonable intrusion upon seclusion of another.
Restatement (Third) of Torts Rule The liability of accountants and other professionals extends to third parties, in addition to their clients, so long as the third party is a foreseeable or known user of the client's financial statements.
Restitution A remedy restoring to the plaintiff a benefit wrongfully gained from the defendant's misconduct.
Restrictive indorsement Negotiable instruments that possess instructions and conditions regarding the payment of funds.
Retaliation Adverse action taken against an applicant or employee by an employer because the person alleged, participated in, or pursued a claim of employment discrimination or other violation of the law.
Reverse break-up fee Liquidated damages payment paid to the target (seller) corporation if the acquiring corporation (buyer) withdraws from a transaction.
Reverse discrimination Discrimination practiced against those in the majority in favor of members of a minority or historically disadvantaged group.
Reverse engineering The process in which a competitor dissembles, recreates, or otherwise works to discover the trade secret.
Reverse piercing The reverse of "piercing the corporate veil." That is, allowing a creditor to access the corporation's assets to satisfy the debts of a controlling alter ego.
Revised Uniform Partnership Act (RUPA) A revised model act that codifies partnership law. Most states have adopted the RUPA in whole or in part.
Revocable trust or living trust A trust that can be changed or revoked at any time prior to the trustor's death.
Revocation The act of withdrawing an offer.
Right of assurances The right to demand adequate assurance of the performance of obligations under a contract when there are reasonable grounds to believe the party will not perform.

Right of contribution The right of repayment by co-guarantors when one guarantor/surety pays in excess of their proportionate share of the liability.
Right of redemption Right of debtor to free the collateral from the security interest upon fulfilling all obligations and paying any reasonable expenses.
Right of reimbursement The right to be repaid by the debtor for all costs and expenses incurred during the guaranty upon repayment of the debt by the guarantor/surety.
Right of subrogation The rights the creditor has against the debtor become the legal right of the guarantor/surety upon repayment of the debt by the guarantor/surety.
Right of survivorship Upon the death of one joint tenant, the surviving joint tenants automatically receive equal shares from the deceased joint tenant.
Right to cure Provision of the UCC that allows the seller or lessor to cure nonconforming goods in limited circumstances.
Right-to-sue letter Notice issued by the EEOC or 706 agency to a complainant at the time it dismisses the charge(s) of discrimination filed by a claimant against an employer. Starts 90-days statute of limitations to file a federal employment discrimination lawsuit.
Rights in the collateral Debtor possess a current or future ownership interest in or the right to take possession of the collateral.
Risk of loss A term used to identify which party will bear the risk if the goods are damaged between the sale's completion and the delivery of the goods.
Robbery The unlawful taking of the property of another by force or threat of force.
Robinson-Patman Act Act amending Section 2 of the Clayton Act that prohibits price discrimination.
Royalty A set fee paid by one party to another. The fee is typically set at a fixed price per unit sold, or as a percentage of revenues.
Rule 10(b) of the 1934 Act Provision of the 1934 Act prohibiting manipulative and deceptive practices in connection with the purchase or sale of a security.
Rule 10b-5 of the 1934 Act A regulation enacted by the SEC targeting securities fraud through use of the amils, interstate commerce, or a national securities exchange.
Rule of reason An antitrust law test used to determine if an agreement constitutes an unreasonable restraint of trade.
Rule of strict compliance A doctrine that entitled a bank to reject documents that do not strictly comply with the terms of a letter of credit.
Rulemaking The process whereby administrative agencies implement, interpret, and prescribe law and policy.

S

S-corporation A corporation that avoids double taxation by election and compliance with requirements under the Internal Revenue Code.
Safe Drinking Water Act (SDWA) An act authorizing the EPA to set national health-based standards for drinking water found in public water systems.
Sale (UCC) A transfer of title to goods for consideration or price.
Sarbanes-Oxley Act of 2002 Enacted by Congress to establish standards of best practices in response to a series of corporate and accounting scandals.
Satisfaction The performance of an accord.
Scienter Knowledge that a representation was false or the representation was made without sufficient knowledge of the truth in a fraudulent misrepresentation.
Scienter (securities) Having the intent to deceive or defraud another.
Second mortgage The mortgage recorded next in time after a first mortgage is recorded.
Secondary liability Liability that applies to a drawer or indorser only when the person responsible for the payment denies the holder the payment.
Secondary meaning A mark that has acquired a connection with a specific product in the minds of consumers.
Section 1 of the Sherman Act Prohibits restraints of trade. This section requires two or more persons to act.
Section 2 of the Clayton Act Prohibits price discrimination and other related practices. This prohibits a business from discriminating in price between different customers without a valid cost justified.
Section 2 of the Sherman Act Discusses monopolization. This section states: "Every person who shall monopolize, or attempt to monopolize, or combine or conspire with any person or persons, shall be deemed guilty of a felony."
Section 3 of the Clayton Act Prohibits exclusionary practices.
Section 7 of the Clayton Act Prohibits anticompetitive mergers and acquisitions of all forms.
Section 8 of the Clayton Act Prohibits, under certain circumstances, interlocking directorates.
Section 10(b) of the 1934 Act Provision of the 1934 Act prohibiting manipulative and deceptive practices in connection with the purchase or sale of a security.

Section 11 of the 1933 Act Imposes civil liability on accountants and other professionals for making misstatements or missions of material facts in a registration statement or failing to find the same.

Section 12(1) and 12(2) of the 1933 Act These provisions create liability for any person who offers or sells a security through a prospectus or an oral communication containing a material misstatement or omission, provided that the purchaser did not know about the misstatement or omission.

Section 17(a) of the 1933 Act Provision of the 1933 Act prohibiting schemes to defraud and recognizing liability for misrepresentations and omissions in securities offerings.

Section 18 of the 1934 Act Liability relates to defendants' false or misleading SEC filings, which affected the price of the security and with the plaintiff 's reliance.

Section 18(a) of the 1934 Act Provision of the 1934 Act imposing civil liability on a person who has made false or misleading statements in any document filed with the SEC.

Section 1981 Federal law protecting individuals from intentional racial or national origin discrimination in employment and housing.

Section 1985 A federal law protecting individuals from racial and gender-based discrimination in employment and from interference with contractual, property, and other rights. Often involves conspiracies to harm or injure others based on race or gender.

Secured claim A claim secured by a valid lien on the debtor's real or personal property.

Secured creditor A creditor holding a claim against the debtor who has the right to take and hold or sell certain property in partial or complete satisfaction of the creditor's claim.

Secured debt Debt backed by a mortgage, pledge of collateral, or other lien.

Secured party The person in whose favor the security interest is created.

Secured transactions Transaction where the payment has been secured by the debtor's personal property.

Securities Act of 1933 Federal law mandating disclosure of important financial information to enable investors to make informed decisions about whether to purchase a company's securities.

Securities and Exchange Commission (SEC) A federal, independent regulatory agency that administers and enforces federal securities laws.

Securities Exchange Act of 1934 Federal law governing the secondary trading of securities in the United States.

Security A broadly defined term encompassing a breadth of investments, including stocks and bonds.

Security agreement A document providing a lender with a security interest in a specified asset of the debtor that has been pledged as a collateral.

Security deposit A type of deposit used to protect landlords which can cover expenses for any damage caused to the property or damages suffered because of a tenant's nonperformance of its obligations under a lease.

Self-defense A justification defense in which the defendant claims to have acted to protect themself from bodily harm or death and that they therefore should be found not guilty.

Self-tender offer A target corporation's offer to redeem (buy back) its own stock from its current shareholders at a premium.

Separation of powers The division of legislative, executive, and judicial power between three co-equal branches of government.

Serious health condition Illness, injury, impairment, or physical or mental condition requiring hospitalization or continuing treatment by a health-care provider.

Service of process Where the summons and complaint are served on the defendant, usually by a private process server or a sheriff.

Share exchange A transaction in which some or all of the shares of one corporation are exchanged for some or all of the shares of another corporation.

Shareholder An owner of shares in a company who has limited and indirect participation in the company's management.

Sherman Antitrust Act This Act prohibits contracts, combinations, and conspiracies in restraint of trade, and monopolization, attempted monopolization, and combinations and conspiracies to monopolize.

Shipment contract A sales contract that allows or obligates the seller to ship the goods by carrier, allows the seller to mitigate risk by passing title to the buyer at the time and place of shipment.

Short-form merger A merger in which a subsidiary merges into a parent that already owns most of the subsidiary's shares.

Short-swing profit A profit resulting from the purchase and sale (or sale and purchase) of the issuer's stock by a statutory insider within a six-month period. Under Section 16(b), the profits are recoverable by the corporation.

Sight draft A draft that is payable on sight.

Signature Any symbol adopted or executed by a party with the intent to authenticate a writing.

Signature liability Contractual liability imputed to the singer of an instrument.

Slander A form of defamation through use of spoken false statements.

Slander per se Statements that are so inherently defamatory on their face that damage to the plaintiff 's reputation is presumed.

Sliding scale standard The test courts use to determine when it is appropriate to exercise personal jurisdiction over online businesses.

Small business loan A loan that is guaranteed by the Small Business Administration in the event of the borrower's default.

Social Security A social insurance program consisting of retirement, disability, and survivor's benefits.

Sole proprietorship An unincorporated business entity owned and operated by one individual with no distinction between the business and the owner.
Solicitation Request that a corporate shareholder authorize another person to cast the shareholder's vote at a corporate meeting.
Sovereign immunity Doctrine which provides governments cannot be sued without their consent.
Special indorsement An indorsement that contains the signature of the indorser and specifies the person to whom the instrument will be made payable.
Special meeting A stockholder meeting that can be called to order at any time by the board of directors, shareholders of at least 10 to 20 percent of the shares, or anyone authorized to do so in the articles of incorporation.
Special Purpose Acquisition Company (SPAC) A publicly traded investment company formed by experienced investors which will arrange for the SPAC to acquire operating companies.
Special qualified indorsement An indorsement that creates order instruments that are negotiated by indorsement and delivery.
Special warranty deed A deed containing the same warranties as a general warranty deed, but the grantor warrants that they have not caused any defects in the title during their ownership.
Specific devise A gift from a decedent's estate of a particular, identifiable item or property.
Specific duty OSHA requirement imposed upon an employer relating to a specific safety problem or hazard.
Specific gift A gift of a specific item of property in a will. See also, specific devise.
Specific intent The intent to commit the criminal act and cause a specific result.
Specific lien A lien granted only with respect to a particular asset.
Specific performance Court order requiring a party to perform a specific act required by a lawful contract.
Stakeholder theory Another view of Corporate Social Responsibility. Provides that businesses must consider the effects the decision will have upon the stakeholders and should provide the stakeholders the opportunity to participate in managing those decisions.
Stakeholders Those who are immediately affected by the decisions that a business makes.
Stale checks A check that is presented to the customer-depositor bank six months after it is date.
Standard of proof The minimum amount of evidence required to prove the assertion.
Standing A legal requirement that a party must have a sufficient stake in the outcome of the controversy to seek relief from a court.
Stare decisis Latin for "to stand by the decision." A legal principle that requires a court to apply prior appellate case holdings as precedent binding upon the court once certain facts have been established.
State action Action by or on behalf of a governmental body that violates the civil rights or legal interests of a person.
State administrative agencies Administrative agencies that administer and enforce state regulatory law.
Statement of policy Public statements by an administrative agency that announce its methods and behaviors regarding a particular topic that the agency intends to follow in the future.
Statute of Frauds A rule of contract law requiring certain contracts to be in writing to be enforceable.
Statute of limitations (civil) A specified time within which a lawsuit must be filed.
Statute of limitations (criminal) A specified period within which a criminal charge can be prosecuted against an accused.
Statute of repose A limit on the length of time that can elapse from the date of the first sale of the defective product to the filing of a products liability lawsuit.
Statutes Laws created by the legislative branch to promote or prohibit conduct.
Statutory insider A director, officer, or any person who beneficially owns more than 10 percent of the stock of a corporation that is publicly held or registered with the SEC.
Statutory law A system of laws comprised of laws and ordinances enacted by federal, state, and local legislatures and governing bodies.
Statutory redemption period The right of a borrower to redeem (retain) the mortgaged property after a foreclosure sale occurs within a time period established by state law.
Stock option A benefit giving the holder the opportunity to buy company stock at a discounted or fixed price.
Stock purchase The acquisition of all or a controlling interest in the target corporation's outstanding stock from the target's shareholders.
Stock subscription An agreement entered into by a corporation and a subscriber for the purchase of the corporation's shares.
Stock warrant A right to acquire stock from a corporation at a set price and during a specified period.
Stop payments The act of a bank customer ordering the bank to not pay a particular check.
Strict foreclosure The creditor's acquisition of the debtor's interest without requiring a sale of disposition.
Strict liability Torts which result in liability to the defendant without finding the defendant was at fault.
Strikes A refusal to work organized by a group of employees as a form of protest in attempt to gain concessions from their employer.
Subagents An individual to whom the agent delegates as his agent with the principal's authorization.
Subject matter jurisdiction The authority of a court to hear a type of dispute.
Sublease A transfer of a portion of the lease from a tenant to a third party (a subtenant).
Subpoena A court order requiring an individual to appear as part of a legal proceeding, usually to give evidence in the form of testimony.
Subsidiary The corporation over which the parent company has control.

Subsidiary (international business) A company organized by the investor under the laws of the foreign nation but owned and controlled by the parent corporation.
Substantial evidence test An agency's decision is supported by such relevant evidence as a reasonable person would find adequate to support the conclusions reached.
Substantive due process Requires that a law be fair and reasonable, and have an adequate justification.
Substantive law The part of the law that defines legal rights.
Substantive rules A legally binding rule issued by an administrative agency.
Substantive unconscionability Refers to the fairness of the contract terms such as an unjustified allocation of risks or costs or a great disparity in the contract price from fair market value.
Successor liability Debts of the predecessor business entity that are attributable to the successor business entity.
Summons The court's written notice that a lawsuit has been filed against a defendant and that orders the defendant to respond to the complaint in a timely manner.
Supplemental jurisdiction A federal court may hear a claim against a party over whom it would not have subject matter jurisdiction if the claim against that party is substantially related to the federal claim.
Supremacy Clause Provision of the Constitution establishing the Constitution and federal laws, treaties, and regulations as the supreme law of the land.
Surety A person who guarantees to perform the obligations of another.
Suretyship The relationship between the surety, the principal debtor, and the creditor in which the creditor may seek payment from the surety at the maturity of the debt.
Surviving corporation Following a merger, either the target or acquiring corporation survives. The other corporation is dissolved.
Symbolic speech Speech that is nonverbal but expresses an idea to an observer.
Syndicate A group of persons joining to finance a project or underwrite risks of others for a price.

T

Taft-Hartley Act Known as the Labor Management Reporting and Disclosure Act. This act was enacted to restrict the activities and power of unions.
Takeover Obtaining controlling interest in a target corporation.
Taking subject to the mortgage When a purchaser buys real estate aware of a mortgage and makes payments on the mortgage but does not agree to become personally liable to repay the mortgage debt.
Tangible property Property interests that exist in a physical form.
Target corporation An acquired corporation is legally absorbed into another corporation and ceases to exist.
Tariffs Taxes levied on imported goods.
Tax return preparer One who is hired to prepare a substantial portion of any tax return, amended return, or a claim for a tax refund.
Taxing and Spending Clause Congress has the authority to tax and spend for the general welfare.
Telemarking Sales Rule (TSR) A federal rule that established the National Do Not Call Registry and limits the conduct of telemarketers.
Tenancy The period of a tenant's occupancy or possession.
Tenancy at sufferance A lease where the tenant remains in possession of the property after the tenancy period has terminated.
Tenancy at will A lease with no stated term and no provision for the collection of rent.
Tenancy by the entirety A form of joint tenancy limited to married couples.
Tenancy for years A lease for a fixed period.
Tenancy in common A form of co-ownership of real property in which parties may hold equal or unequal shares in the land and have separate but undivided interests in the entire property.
Tender of delivery Refers to an offer of goods by a seller to a buyer by putting or holding them at the disposition of the buyer and giving the buyer notification reasonably necessary for taking delivery.
Tender offer A public, open offer or invitation by a prospective acquirer to all shareholders of a publicly held corporation to sell their shares at a specified price during a specified time.
Termination statement Creditor-issued document confirming that the debt or obligation of the debtor has been repaid. Releases its security interest in the collateral.
Territorial restriction A nonprice vertical restraint whereby competitors in distinct levels of a distribution agree to restraint trade.
Terrorism insurance Insurance which protects against damages caused by terrorist activities.
Testamentary trust A trust that takes effect upon the settlor's death.
Testate When a decedent dies with a valid will at the time of death.
Testator or testatrix A person who makes a will.
Third-party beneficiary A party identified in the contract who receives a benefit of the contract, but is not one of the contracting parties.

Time draft A draft that is payable at a specified future date.
Time, place, and manner Laws that restrict speech based only on the time, location, or method of speaking.
Tippee A person who receives non-public information and trades on that information.
Tipper A person who gives non-public information to someone else to trade on.
Title Evidence of ownership of property pass by an instrument or court order.
Title insurance Insurance which protects owners of real property against any defects in title, liens, or other encumbrances not disclosed in a title insurance policy at the close of a real estate transaction.
Title VII Section of the Civil Rights Act of 1964 that pertains to discrimination in employment based upon race, color, national origin, sex, and religion. This federal law prohibits most workplace discrimination and harassment. It covers employers, state and local government, and educational institutions with 15 or more employees.
Tort A civil wrong, whether intentional or accidental, for which a claim for damages may be sought.
Tortfeasor A person who commits a tort.
Tortious intent Tortfeasor desired or believed the consequences of their act were likely to occur.
Trade acceptance A type of sight draft that is created when credit for the sale of goods is extended to the buyer from the seller.
Trade association Where member firms and individuals who also happen to be competitors can come together and exchange price or other sensitive business data.
Trade barrier Any barrier in the transacting of goods and services between countries.
Trade secret Information that has either actual or potential independent economic value by virtue of not being generally known, has values to others who cannot legitimately obtain the information, and is subject to reasonable efforts to maintain its secret.
Trademarks Symbols and designs that organizations use to mark their products.
Trademark dilution The unauthorized use of a famous mark that tends to dilute the value of the mark.
Trademark infringement Unauthorized use of a trademark that is likely to lead to consumer confusion.
Traditional business plan A business plan that is comprehensive, highly detailed, and often requested by lenders and investors.
Transferred intent The defendant's intent will be transferred when the defendant intended to commit a tort against one party, but the tort caused harm to another party. Intent is also transferred when the defendant intends to commit one tort against a party but actually commits a different tort against that party.
Traveler's check Type of check that is a prepaid, fixed amount that acts as cash for use when traveling in foreign countries.
Treasury stock Shares the corporation has issued and then repurchased that have no voting rights and are not entitled to dividends.
Treaty A formal agreement between two or more countries.
Trespass to personal property When a person intentionally takes, harms, or interferes with the personal property of another.
Trespass to real property The act of entering or remaining the land of another, or causing someone or something else to enter or remain on the land of another.
TRIPS Agreement An agreement among WTO members to enforce agreed-upon standards for all intellectual property.
Trust A legal arrangement in which one person transfers property to another to be held and used for the benefit of a third person.
Trustee The party to a deed of trust who holds (legal) title until the underlying obligation is paid in full.
Trustee's sale A type of non-judicial foreclosure proceeding where the lender waives the right to seek a deficiency judgment against the borrower.
Trustor The property owner or party to a deed of trust.
Truth-in-Lending Act (consumer protection) Federal law protecting consumers against inaccurate and unfair credit billing and credit card practices.
Tying arrangement An agreement between a seller and buyer whereby the seller conditions the sale of one product on the buyer's agreement to purchase another product.

U

Ultra vires Actions by a corporation that exceed the scope of the powers provided in the articles of incorporation.
***Ultramares* doctrine** This doctrine provides that an accountant or other professional is liable only to those who are in privity or near privity of contract with the accountant.
Umbrella policy Liability insurance coverage that covers damages more than the basic liability policy covering real or personal property.
Unauthorized aliens Persons who enter the United States without a visa or who overstay the period permitted by a visa.
Unauthorized signature A signature on a negotiable instrument signed by an agent without the authority of the principal or that is forged.
Unclean hands A legal doctrine allowing a defendant to defeat a plaintiff's claim for equitable relief because the plaintiff was involved in some wrongdoing in the underlying dispute.
Unconscionability Contracts set aside because terms are extremely unjust or one-sided.
Unconscionable contract A contract with terms that are so unfair and grossly one-sided so as to threaten important public policies or social norms.

Underinsurance An insufficient insurance policy.
Underwriter A person who purchases securities from the issuer with the intention of distributing them, directly or indirectly participates in an underwriting, or sells securities on behalf of a control person.
Undisclosed principal A principal whose existence or identity is unknown to the third party.
Undue hardship (disability) The determination that accommodation of a person's disability would be too difficult or expensive to provide, considering the employer's size, financial resources, and the needs of the business.
Undue hardship (religious discrimination) Circumstance excusing an employer from accommodating an employee's religious practices because it involves more than a minimal burden (cost or otherwise) on the employer's business.
Undue influence A defense asserted to the enforcement of a contract arising from the misuse of a fiduciary relationship.
Unenforceable contract A contract that will not be enforced by the courts but may be voluntarily performed by the parties.
Unfair labor practice Conduct and practices by either employers or unions determined under the NLRA or by the NLRB to be unlawful.
Unfair labor practice strikers Workers who strike to protest conduct and practices by either employers or unions determined to be unlawful.
Uniform Commercial Code (UCC) A uniform set of laws that are related to the sale of goods.
Uniform Customs and Practice for Documentary Credits (UCP 600) A uniform law that governs letter of credit transactions.
Uniform law A model law created by an organization for the state to either adopt or reject. Once a state adopts the law, it then becomes a part of the state's statutory law.
Uniform Probate Code (UPC) A uniform law governing inheritance and probate matters adopted in approximately one-third of the states.
Uniform Trade Secrets Act A model act adopted by the majority of states that sets out trade secret protections.
Unilateral contract A contract where the offeree must perform an act to create a contract.
Unilateral mistake When only one party is mistaken about a fact regarding the contract.
United Nations Convention on Contract for the International Sale of Goods (CISC) A treaty created to govern international sales contracts between firms or individuals located in different countries.
United Nations Convention on the Recognition and Enforcement of Foreign Arbitral Awards Also known as the New York Convention. It was created to assist in the recognition and enforcement of arbitration clauses and arbitral awards internationally.
U.S. Army Corps of Engineers A federal agency responsible for the engineering, design, and construction management of selected public projects.
U.S. Department of Housing and Urban Development (HUD) A cabinet department of the executive branch of the federal government supporting community development and environmental health.
U.S. trustee A federal government official who handles and supervises administrative tasks within a bankruptcy case.
Universal defense A defense from payment liability against all holders, including HDCs.
Unqualified opinion An auditor's opinion that the company's financial statements fairly represent the company's financial condition and are in conformity with GAAP.
Unreasonable intrusion into seclusion An invasion of privacy claim where one who intentionally intrudes, physically or otherwise, upon the solitude or seclusion of another or his private affairs or concerns, if the intrusion would be highly offensive to a reasonable person.
Unsecured claim A claim in which no property or asset serves as collateral or security for the debt.
Usage of trade Any practice or method of dealing that is so regularly observed in the industry that parties can reasonably expect it will be observed in their transaction.
Usury The interest in excess of the maximum interest rate permissible by law.
Utilitarianism Ethical theory endorsing actions producing the greatest good to society.

V

Valid contract (enforceable contract) A contract that is legally enforceable.
Value A broad term including anything that is given as consideration under contract law.
Vehicle insurance policy An insurance policy which protects cars, trucks, motorcycles, and other vehicles.
Venture capital A type of private equity investment made by a venture capital fund that is often invested in startup companies.
Venture capitalist An investor who invests in businesses in exchange for ownership or significant control.
Venue A legal requirement that the court most connected to the event in dispute, if it also has jurisdiction, must decide the dispute.
Vertical merger A merger between competitors in different levels of distribution (such as a manufacturer and a supplier).
Vertical restraints A Sherman Act violation in which competitors in different levels of a distribution agree to restrain trade.
Vesting When a third-party beneficiary is entitled to enforce a contract.
Vicarious liability Indirect liability that is imposed by operation of law to a principal for the conduct of an agent.
Virtue-based ethics Decisions involve consideration of the moral character of individuals; how character traits can contribute to, or impair, a good life.

Void contract A contract having no validity. It cannot be enforced by either party.
Void title Title in which the purchaser acquires no ownership interest, usually because the goods were stolen.
Voidable contract A contract that may be affirmed or rejected by one of the parties.
Voidable title Title in which the purchaser may receive good title to the goods so long as the purchaser did not have notice that valid title belonged to another party.
Voir dire The examination of potential jurors by the court and attorneys for the parties.
Voluntary payments clause If an insured fixed a problem or damage and then notifies the insurer and seeks coverage, the insurer can deny coverage.
Voluntary petition A petition filled by the insolvent debtor.

W

Warehouse receipt A document evidencing title to goods stored with another.
Warranty against infringements A special warranty that states that a seller or lessor who is a merchant that regularly sells or leases the type of goods provided for in the transaction warrants that the goods are not subject to any third-party copyright, trademark, or patent.
Warranty liability Liability that arises when a transferor breaches an implied warranty that was made in the negotiation of the instrument.
Warranty of good title A special warranty that states the seller of a good warrants that they have valid title to the goods being sold and therefore the transfer of title is rightful.
Warranty of no security interests A special warranty in which the seller of the goods will automatically warrant the goods being sold are free of any third-party security interest, lien, or other encumbrances of which the buyer is unaware.
Waste Destruction, harm, or injury caused to the use of real property by a person in possession of the property.
Water disposal site An area of land designated for the proper disposition of discarded or discharged materials.
Water rights The rights to use water.
Welfare plans (Welfare benefit plan) ERISA-covered plans that do not involve salary deferral and retirement plans, such as medical, dental, and disability insurance plans.
Well-known seasoned issuer (WKSI) A firm that meets certain thresholds and can file a registration statement with the SEC the day they announce a new offering.
Whistleblowing Protection from loss of employment involving an exception to the right of an employer to terminate an at-will employee.
White knight A corporation that promises to leave the target corporation and/or its management intact if it acquires the target corporation.
Will An instrument by which a mentally qualified person directs the disposition of their property following death.
Wire transfers A type of EFT between one bank or financial institutional and another where no physical transfer of money takes place.
Worker Adjustment and Retraining Notification (WARN) Act Federal law that prohibits employers from ordering a plant closing or mass layoff until 60 days after the employer has served written notice of such an order. Violations require employers to pay back pay and benefits for that period, attorneys' fees, and civil penalties to local agencies.
Workers' compensation A no-fault system of laws and regulations that often provides the only means for an injured worker to recover compensation for medical expenses and lost wages arising from work-related injuries.
World Trade Organization (WTO) An international organization comprised of member nations who agree to abide by certain terms.
Writ of attachment A prejudgment court order to seize a property interest of a debtor.
Writ of certiorari The order of the Supreme Court granting a case an appellate review.
Writ of execution The order of the Supreme Court granting a case an appellate review before the Court.
Wrongful discharge Termination of employment involving an exception to the employer's right to terminate an at-will employee.
Wrongful dissociation The withdrawal of a member from an LLC when not permitted by the operating agreement or applicable law.

Table of Cases

Principal cases and landmark cases are indicated by italics.

M

Index

B

J

N

U

Y